THE AMERICAN PEOPLE

By

DAVID BURNER, State University of New York at Stony Brook, with
EUGENE D. GENOVESE, University of Rochester and
FORREST McDONALD, University of Alabama

Library of Congress Catalog No. 79-92756

ISBN Order No. 09603726-0-1

Printed in the United States of America by **Revisionary Press,** St. James, New York 11780
a division of Revisionary Corp.

First printing . . . . March 1980

Second printing . . . . May 1980

Third printing . . . . . January 1981

In this third printing a new debate has been added after chapter VII. To accommodate students using the previous printings, we have left this addition unpaginated so page references will be the same for all students.

Special acknowledgements: for indispensable assistance to Alan January, on the chapters from 1815 to 1860, and to James Moore, on twentieth-century diplomatic history. Many thanks to to Steve Stalmack, Leon Glaser, Elayne Morga, Tom West, Jim Mooney, Diane Hamilton, Bob Marcus, Hugh Cleland, Jon Wakelyn, Mel Rosenthal, Grania Bolton, John J. Girolamo, Dick Glaser, Bob Mistretta, Rose Dunne, Ginny Volter, Robert Burner, Robert Fenyo, Jane Gover, Iris Molotsky, David Schmitz, Carmen Weyant, Deborah DiFrancesco, Bill Mullen, Joane Cheney, Gene Genovese, and to Forrest McDonald who wrote chapters one and two.

To Sandy

"The business lunch took place [in New York City] at the Plaza, an excellent first-class hotel of the old type. I like those vast and handsome hotels which are not at all in modern style but which have acquired a past through their richness and substantiality. There are living pasts and dead pasts. Some pasts are the liveliest instigators of the present and the best springboards into the future . . . . "

Le Corbusier

Table of Contents

Preface

Textbooks have beguiled generations of students into the comfortable illusion that a single history book can summarize the nation's past. As historians know, it is in fact impossible to resurrect the past exactly. In the reconstruction of events we rely on written records, along with some art objects and physical remains. Yet accounts of few occurrences have been written down. Many documents, moreover, are lost, and the historian can never be certain of having seen every manuscript; or the sources may be too voluminous to read exhaustively. A document carries the point of view, or bias, of the person who wrote it and the time in which it was written. To these documents the historian brings his or her own bias.

For these reasons I have asked two eminent historians, the radical Eugene D. Genovese and the conservative Forrest McDonald, to debate the great issues of the American past. Their differences go beyond ideology, and in setting forth distinctive viewpoints these two men may help to crystallize your own thinking. This series of debates, spread throughout the book, will provide material for class discussion and demonstrate that there is no fixed truth about the past, which makes it all the more rewarding as an intellectual study. Students in any classroom deserve a challenge; and instructors can employ these verbal interchanges in any format they deem suitable. Another feature of the book is an account of a dramatic historical event at the beginning of each chapter.

The debates will provide theoretical content. But I want the reader to recognize that narrative itself is an analytical act. Historians are sometimes ashamed to emphasize the drama of history, as though it were automatically to be equated with vapid popularization. Yet the introductory courses in the other social sciences, so popular and so simple, often fall into easy manipulation of abstract definitions, axioms, dicta, isolated from the facts that might clarify or test them. As fine historians like Samuel Eliot Morison and Allan Nevins have repeatedly demonstrated, a complex readable story is far more sophisticated for its embracing concrete and sometimes contradictory details. This textbook, in this sense, offers three different interpretations of the American past: Genovese's, McDonald's, and Burner's. There are important areas of agreement as well as of argument in the three accounts. There is but one past; there are many ways to illuminate that past. We hope this volume will introduce you to the genuine excitement historians have found in casting their own light on the history of the United States.

David Burner
Stony Brook, New York
January 1980

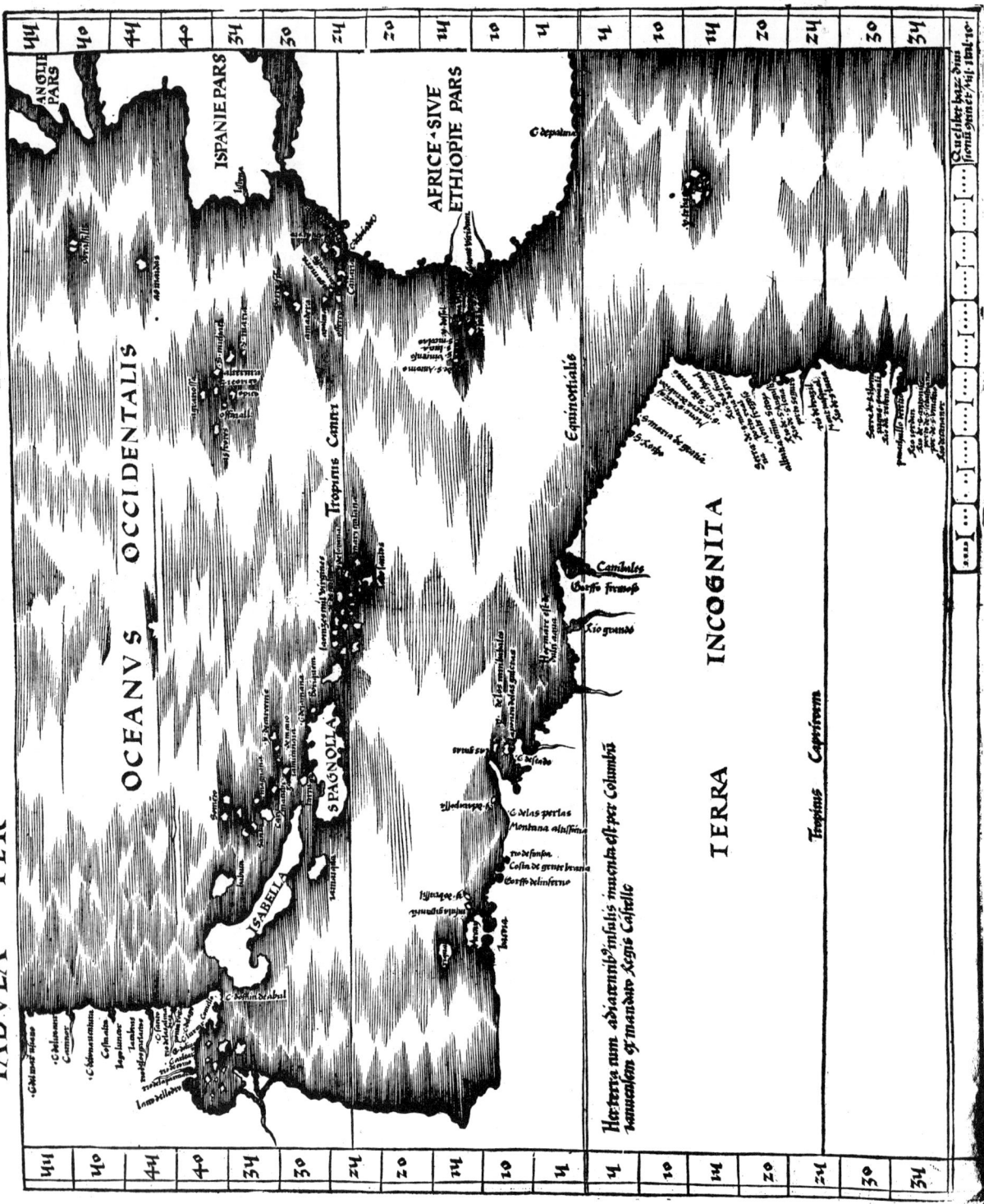

Map: *Tabula Terre Nove 1507-1513.* (N. Phelps Stokes Collection. Prints Division. The New York Public Library. Astor, Lenox and Tilden Foundations.)

Chapter I
Europe and America

Christopher Columbus

Son of a Genoese weaver, Columbus was an extraordinary weaver of dreams. The belief in riches and perfection beyond the sunset was strongest in the cultures of the landlocked Mediterranean; for the only sea route leading outward—going both everywhere and nowhere—was west through the Straits of Gibraltar and beyond the Canary Islands. America was a concept in the mind of Europe, and the writings of Columbus reveal the vividness and extravagance of the idea. It represented the possibility of wealth, freedom, and happiness, the concept of the noble savage, and the beckoning mystery of the wild frontier—elements that later went into the "American dream." The new Western Hemisphere was also primitive and frightening—full of cannibals by Columbus' testimony. This tender land was an uncharted region on which Europe could stamp its own ambivalent character and conflicting desires.

Columbus was a great mariner, and an atrocious geographer. Both qualities helped him to sell his enterprise to the monarchs of Spain. He sharply underestimated the circumference of the globe, placing Asia about 2,400 miles from the Canaries of the eastern Atlantic—the actual distance is more than 10,000 miles, most of it vast oceans. Possessed of the intellectual certainty of the self-taught (he had first learned to read as a young man), convinced of the mystical significance of his name (after St. Christopher, who carried the Infant Jesus across the waters), persuaded that the Bible supported his geographical notions and made likely his discovery of lost Christians, Columbus was an effective salesman for his grandiose project. Besieging King Ferdinand of Aragon and Queen Isabel of Castile for more years than they besieged the Alhambra, he finally got his ships, his crews, his promises of riches, and his striking title "Admiral of the Ocean Sea."

Columbus' four voyages, a story endlessly told, blaze forth with symbols of a world's transformation. He first weighed anchor on August 2, 1492, the very day upon which the last Jews who refused to convert to Catholicism had to leave Spain—most of them bound for the more tolerant countries of Islam. "After having turned out all the Jews from all your kingdoms," Columbus records in his first diary entry, "your highness gave orders to me that with a sufficient fleet I should go." The great explorer even gave assurances that he would exclude Jews from any land he discovered. The idea of a new world as a haven for persecuted people would have astonished Columbus. He envisioned himself the messenger of the "new heaven and new earth" of the Biblical Apocalypse—in which Jerusalem is recaptured and the Jews converted—but never admitted he had discovered a new world. Columbus died convinced that he had found the Eastern Indies.

On one voyage a tremendous waterspout threatened Columbus' ship. He calmed the waters by reading aloud the account in the Gospel According to St. John of the storm on the Sea of Galilee, tracing a cross in the sky and a circle around the fleet with his sword. On the same journey, marooned and starving in Jamaica, he terrified the local Indians into supplying his crew with food by threatening the divine gesture of removing the light from the moon—his up-to-date almanac correctly predicted a total eclipse of the moon. At once a modern man of science, a medieval sailor, and a mystic, he pursued his amazing destiny.

The results of Columbus' voyages hold equally great ironies. The new world which Columbus never knew he had discovered contained wealth beyond his dreams of the riches of the Indies, and offered an opportunity for the expansion of Christianity far greater than his mystical vision. America would fuel the economy of Europe and offer a haven for millions whose lives his discovery disrupted. There were other legacies as well. Columbus brought back Indian captives, initiating the Atlantic slave trade that would forcibly disrupt the lives of further millions, and these first transatlantic slaves brought with them their own revenge, carrying in their bloodstreams the bacillus of syphilis—previously unknown to Europe. It was Columbus, too, who began the colonization of the new world, introducing on the island of Hispaniola an imperialist regime and its attendant result: genocide. Columbus Day is not considered a holiday among native Americans.

The World Stage

At the time of the discovery of America, Europe was in a state of unending warfare, Europeans fighting Europeans as well as Africans and Asians. Europeans contended for control of one square mile and another of their subcontinent. Emperors, kings, princes, and dukes laid claims to empires, kingdoms, principalities, and fiefs; and wars in defense of rival claims never ceased. To be sure, the various contestants had, by the beginning of the fifteenth century, so regularized their patterns of territorial control, allegiance, and conflict inside Europe that most of the modern nation-states had begun to attain recognizable forms. Moreover, the religious life of the whole was at least minimally presided over by a single Pope. By and large, however, the unity of Christendom rested upon the hostility and contempt with which Europeans viewed all other racial, religious, and cultural groups.

The hostility was justified but the contempt was not, for Christendom, being one of the least unified, was also one of the most primitive and least potent of the world's great cultures. Indeed, for some centuries its very home territory had been shrinking rather than expanding.

In the twelfth century, the great cultures had arrived at a temporary stalemate. Islam, the most dynamic and aggressive culture on the planet for four centuries, had temporarily spent its force after subduing the Iberian peninsula in Europe, all of North Africa, and Asia Minor as far as northern India. During most of the twelfth century Islamic culture lacked political unity. However, the territory dominated by Islamic civilization did not diminish appreciably, and the Moslems retained a commanding superiority over the Europeans in science, technology, warfare, and general learning. To the east, the Hindu culture continued to dominate the Indian subcontinent, as it had for a thousand years; but the culture had long since passed its zenith and it, too, was torn by revolution and by warfare among scores of satraps, great and small. In the Orient, the Sung dynasty dominated a vast area and Chinese culture basked in its golden age; but in the 1120's the Sungs lost half their territory through war and rebellion, and before the end of the twelfth century central Asia had spawned a new Mongol Empire that would be the terror of the thirteenth.

Europe, on the other hand, so successfully gathered energy during the twelfth century that the ascendence of the West might soon have begun, but for the rise of the Mongols. The

French and British in northwest Europe, the Germans in the center, the Swedes and Danes in the north, and the Slavs in the east made enormous strides toward national unity, and the strength they gained in the doing was of incalculable magnitude. The component parts of Europe grew stronger for the obvious reason that a large territorial state is likely to be more powerful than a small one. But Europe as a whole also gained strength, for a rather less obvious reason: enormous amounts of human resources, formerly required to defend hundreds and even thousands of small frontiers, were no longer needed for this purpose, and could be diverted to other ends.

Moreover, Christendom's new-found energy was invested in enterprises that yielded even more vitality. Some of this energy went into the Crusades, a series of wars against Islamic territory along the eastern Mediterranean and particularly in the ancient Christian Holy Land. The Crusades had no lasting military or territorial consequences, but they opened up large-scale trade with the East, thereby accelerating Europe's economic development and further strengthening its civilization. Finally, despite a continuous succession of wars inside Europe, Christendom grew more tightly knit during the twelfth century, for the zeal of the Crusades spilled over into attacks on the aliens in Christendom's midst: barbarians, heathens, and heretics. These were systematically, albeit indiscriminately, Christianized or butchered.

But the thirteenth century belonged to the Mongol hordes. In the space of forty years these terrible warriors swept over three continents, totally subjugating China and pressing the other three major civilizations into small, remote portions of their home regions. By 1241 they had overrun all of Russia, subdued and ravaged Slavic eastern Europe, and penetrated into the heart of the Germanic lands. There the onslaught against Europe stopped, for the interior mountains of Europe were not suitable to their style of mounted warfare. Then the Mongols swung south to wreak equal devastation upon Islamic territory. Western India fell, and then the Near East, and westward the Mongols swept until 1260, when Islamic forces finally arrested their expansion just short of Egypt. Thenceforth, the Mongols consolidated their holdings and expanded no more: they held on for a century and then, as abruptly as they had risen, they retreated and declined into impotence.

The Mongol occupation stimulated Europe's economic development, and did so in ways that would have vast consequences. When the Mongols arrived, the wealthiest and most advanced centers in Europe were the great city-states of northern Italy; Venice and Genoa in particular had reaped large profits by supplying and transporting the armies of the Crusades, and then established themselves as the principal entrepots for the importation of spices and other commodities from the Far East. During the Mongol occupation trade from the East came overland across Asia to the Byzantine Empire, the easternmost portion of the Christian world, and then by sea to Venice and Genoa. To exploit this trade the Italians, using Portuguese and Italian Jews as intermediaries, borrowed extensively from the technological and scientific storehouse of the Moslems. In this way they learned to use the lateen rigging, which enabled vessels to sail toward the wind, and acquired a knowledge of mathematics, astronomy, and navigation that was far superior to any then current in Europe. Furthermore, late in the thirteenth century a Venetian, Marco Polo, spent twenty years in the Far East, mostly in the service of the Mongol khan; when he returned he wrote a journal describing his travels. Polo's journal gave Europeans their first direct information about the geography and civilization of the Orient, quickened their curiosity, and incidentally introduced them to a host of Chinese technological and scientific advances—including a truly revolutionary invention, gunpowder. Through such borrowings, and by their own ingenious improvements upon what they borrowed, the Italians started Europe along the way

to the technological superiority that would, in time, make Europeans masters of the world.

But Europe's hour was yet to come: for at the beginning of the fourteenth century, just as the menace of the Mongols was abating, the Moslems rose again, this time under the most terrible group of all, the Ottoman Turks. Before this wave of Islamic fury had spent its force, the Moslems would dominate a land mass extending ten thousand miles, from West Africa to Indonesia, and, through their advanced seamanship, would dominate the entire Indian Ocean as well.

This expansion had drastic effects on economic conditions in Europe. Eastern commodities could no longer be carried overland to Constantinople; they now went by water to the Red Sea or the Persian Gulf, and thence overland, through a series of what were in effect toll stations, to Mediterranean ports in Africa and Asia Minor. The price of spices rose greatly, with severe consequences to Europe. Spices were a necessity, not a luxury: to the end of the seventeenth century Europe suffered from a chronic shortage of winter feed for cattle, and the spices were needed as preservatives for the huge amount of livestock slaughtered every autumn. Moreover, the population of Europe began to increase rapidly at this time, which meant that Oriental spices were becoming scarcer and dearer as the demand was becoming greater. By 1453, when Constantinople fell to the Moslems, old trade patterns with the East had been thoroughly disrupted, and Europe's strength was at its lowest ebb in centuries.

Portugal's Crusade By Sea

African Art (Trustees of the British Museum.)

The time was therefore ripe for a new approach to the twin problems of coping with the Moslems and trading with the East; and it was Portugal that found the way. The people of that tiny kingdom, free for three centuries from Moslem domination but struggling for survival in a rocky and barren land, had turned to the sea, first as fishermen, then as traders. As seagoing traders whose home base was in the southwestern corner of Europe, and on the Atlantic, not the Mediterranean, they understandably thought of an indirect way to obtain the spices that Europe sorely needed. In western Africa below the Sahara, gold and ivory could be acquired in abundance, and these could be used to buy spices. Overland, the black kingdoms that ruled western Africa and controlled these resources could be reached only through Moslem intermediaries, but by sea, as one searched for a route around Africa to the East, it was entirely feasible to bypass the Moslems, establish trade relations with the blacks, and simultaneously edge toward the Orient.

There was no doubt that direct regular trade could be established with the black kingdoms, if they could be reached by sea, for black Africa had evolved a culture quite comparable to Europe's own. In the area drained by the Senegal and Niger rivers, the rulers of Ghana, Mali, and Songhay had successfully established imperial domains; and in a vast territory extending from the Gulf of Guinea to the savannahs on the edge of the Sahara, and from the Atlantic Ocean deep into the interior, subsidiary kingdoms had been established. Those black kingdoms which had been converted to or influenced by Islam had developed written languages; and all of them possessed most of the other attributes that Europeans regarded as the marks of civilization, including agriculture, metal tools, political organization, professional armies, social stratification, cities, creative arts, and—most important—regularized international and intercultural trade.

The man who directed Portugal's efforts to take advantage of all this was Prince Henry the Navigator. Henry began his explorations in 1415. He retired from the court and from politics, accepted a sinecure as governor of the southernmost province of Portugal, and began building a strange settlement there, on Cape St. Vincent. For the next forty years he gathered sailors, astronomers, map makers, instrument makers, and ship builders from all over Europe (although most were Italians), and subsidized expeditions to explore the west coast of Africa, seeking a route to India. The grand and audacious Portuguese undertaking was interrupted by Henry's death, but in 1497 Vasco da Gama made his celebrated voyage to India with a four-vessel fleet, returning two years later with a cargo of pepper and cinnamon. Within twenty more years Henry's grand dream was fulfilled, for Portugal had established a maritime empire that extended the full breadth of the Indian Ocean.

Meanwhile other Europeans, inspired by the Portuguese, sought to share in the glory and profit of war and trade in the East. None reckoned that they could overtake Portugal in the race around Africa, but several thought they might find an alternate course. It was reasonably well known that the earth was round, and widely assumed that the earth was about half its actual size; and America was not known to exist. It therefore followed that if a sailor could be found who had

African Art. Figures like this one were sometimes given to tribal girls when they came of age. It is decorated with cowry shells from the Indian Ocean, which were used as currency in many parts of Africa. (National Museet, Copenhagen.)

the necessary courage and skill, the Orient might easily be reached by sailing due west from Europe. The most persistent of those who so reasoned was Christopher Columbus: a native of Genoa who had several years experience on Genoese and Portuguese ships.

The Spanish Empire

The immediate consequence of Columbus' first voyage was a flurry of efforts by other Europeans to capitalize on his discovery. The Portuguese did little, for they were convinced that Columbus had not reached oriental islands, as he claimed and believed. Other European monarchs, however, including the kings of England and France backed voyages based upon Columbus' mistaken belief that he found the Indies, or a passage to them. Thus, for example, Henry VII of England sponsored voyages by the Italians John and Sebastian Cabot in 1497 and 1498. Sailing from Bristol, the Cabots explored the American coast from Labrador to Chesapeake Bay and discovered vast areas teeming with fish; but they found neither spices nor a passage to India, and Henry's England profited little from these and two follow-up expeditions by other Bristol adventurers. French and Venetian efforts were likewise unprofitable, and both kingdoms had pressing preoccupations, and so they, like England, soon abandoned the search. Hence, by process of elimination, Spain gained a virtual monopoly on exploration and discovery in the New World.

The greatest of discoverers sailing under the Spanish flag was, of course, Columbus himself. Columbus made four voyages in all (1492-93, 1493-96, 1498-1500, and 1502-04). He discovered most of the major islands of the Caribbean, Trinidad, the northern coast of South America, and the Central American mainland from Honduras to Panama, and planted colonies in several of these places. In nonmaritime activities, however, he proved inept. He so neglected and mismanaged the colonies that he had to be removed as governor; and when he died in 1506 he was still convinced that what he had explored was part of Asia.

The man who did most to correct that impression was another Italian in the service of Spain, Amerigo Vespucci—and it was after him that the new world was named. Vespucci made four voyages to America between 1497 and 1505 and wrote a series of descriptive letters to friends in Florence. When these were published in 1507 they added greatly to European knowledge and understanding of the shape and size of the New World. Henceforth all Europe knew America for what it was, a new continent and a barrier between Europe and Asia.

Nothing of any particular value had yet been found in America, and so the problem now became one of finding a strait through a landmass whose size was unknown. The search for a passage was stimulated by a chance discovery made in 1513. Vasco Nuñez de Balboa, a Spanish adventurer led a band of followers in search of gold in Central America, crossed the Isthmus of Darien, and sighted the Pacific. Spain promptly planted a colony in the vicinity, and explorers, encouraged to learn that the two oceans were separated only by an extremely narrow strip of land, renewed their search for a passage. Because the coasts of Central America and Mexico had been fairly thoroughly cruised, the most promising route seemed to be to the south, and in 1519 Ferdinand Magellan, a Portuguese sailing under Spanish auspices, set out on his monumental voyage. This voyage, completed in 1522 by Sebastian del Cano, a Spanish navigator who succeeded to command after Magellan was killed in the Philippines, had several significant effects. One was that, as the first circumnavigation of the globe, it added enormously to Europe's store of knowledge about the world. Another was that it demonstrated once and for all time that it was not feasible for Spain to try to compete with Portugal in the East by sailing west. The route was simply too difficult; and besides, by the time Magellan's vessels reached the Indian Ocean the Portuguese had already established the bases that gave them dominance of the entire area. Other nationals, much later, would resume the search for a northwest passage to the Pacific, but from the time of Magellan's voyages, Spain had to be content with exploiting what it could in America.

The various Spanish settlements had proved reasonably prosperous, establishing in some places economies based on cattle raising with Spanish labor and in others, on sugar planting with Indian slave labor. But raising cattle and sugar was scarcely the kind of activity that quickened the imagination or filled the treasuries of the Spanish monarchs. Far more exciting were rumors and information of highly civilized kingdoms in the interiors of Mexico, Central America, and northwestern South America, and of their fantastic stores of gold and silver. The stories were in fact true, and an expedition set out in 1519 to find, conquer, plunder, and Christianize these kingdoms.

The expedition was commanded by Hernando Cortes, a thirty-two-year-old soldier and adventurer. In a matter of months Cortes had penetrated the heart of the Aztec Empire and slain the emperor Montezuma, though it took two years to

Christopher Columbus Landing in the New World Greeted by Indians with Gifts (Library of Congress.)

complete the systematic looting and destruction of the Aztec capital (now Mexico City) and the total subjugation of the five million Aztec people. In the next few years Cortes' lieutenants brutally conquered the Mayan territories of Central America. And in 1532 an obscure adventurer, Francisco Pizarro, led a tiny band into Peru, seized and executed the Inca, Atahualpa, and on behalf of the King of Spain placed himself at the head of an empire of about six or eight million souls. In each instance the Spaniards effected their conquests with relative ease, partly because of their superior weapons, cunning, and courage, and partly because their victims were sedentary and highly civilized subject peoples, accustomed to total obedience; mastery over them required little more than the defeat of their existing masters. In each instance, too, the conquerors reaped fantastic wealth in gold and silver.

By 1550 all the major centers of settled population in tropical America were under Spanish control, and Spain had imposed over the entire area a highly centralized imperial system. The Roman Catholic Church, through its missionary orders, vigorously pursued the spiritual conquest of the Indians and obtained a considerable measure of power in its own right, more or less independent of the lawyers who ran the imperial administration for the king. Socially the empire had a fairly rigid caste system. At the top were the native Spaniards who held most of the political and religious offices; next came the Creoles, or pureblood Spaniards born in America, who held the larger landholdings or *encomiendas;* next were a few *mestizos,* persons of mixed Indian and Spanish blood, who at first were landholders, large and small, and who ultimately became the most numerous element in the population; at the bottom were the pure Indians. In the Spanish island plantations there was a still lower group, the black slaves.

For all its faults, and for all the follies of the Spanish kings, the Spanish Empire thus organized survived for more than two and a half centuries, and for much of the time made Spain the foremost power in the world.

The Spanish kings were never able to find anything better to do with the treasure of the New World than to spend it on crusades and conquest in the Old. In 1516 King Ferdinand was succeeded by his grandson Charles. Through a complex system of intermarriages, Charles had also inherited the Netherlands, Belgium, the Burgundian lands of France, several kingdoms in central Europe, including the Dukedom of Austria, and the territories of the crowns of Castille and Aragon (Spain, Naples, and the Americas). In 1519 he became, as well, emperor of the Holy Roman Empire, a coalition of roughly 240 kingdoms and principalities in central Europe that included all but 6 of the Germanic states. Charles opted to live in and devote his greatest attention to central Europe. Upon his accession, much of Spain erupted in disorganized rebellion.

Almost simultaneously, the centrifugal forces in the Holy Roman Empire, which for a long time had been threatening to rupture the unity of the Germanic States, received a tremendous new impetus from the teachings of the priest Martin Luther. Luther preached the radical doctrine that Christian salvation was obtainable only by faith, which made the priestly offices of the Roman Catholic Church unnecessary. He was condemned in 1521 by a grand council presided over by Charles, but was protected and sponsored for political reasons by various Saxon princes, and soon much of Germany was in revolt and most of it was breaking with Rome. Before long, the Protestant Reformation took a new and even more explosive form through the doctrines of John Calvin; by midcentury Calvinism had swept Switzerland, much of France, the Netherlands, and Scotland. Meanwhile Henry VIII of England had led his kingdom in a break with Rome. And, as if all this were not enough, Spain was at war with France for more than half of Charles' forty-year reign. Thus, while Christendom was vastly expanding abroad it was disintegrating at home.

England: The Sceptered Isle

Great Britain was left as the only prospective competitor for the spoils of the Spanish Empire, and thereby hangs the tale of the origins of Anglo-Saxon America. England had an overseas tradi-

tion: its inhabitants were tolerably secure in their homeland but, as a result of the various dynastic struggles that had taken place over the centuries, they were also accustomed to thinking that portions of France and various other parts of the European mainland belonged to them. This prepared the English, both institutionally and psychologically, for widespread popular participation in the business of foreign expansion.

Before Britain could embark upon such ventures, however, its own house had to be put into order, and its economic resources had to be mobilized to cope with the devastating inflation that was sweeping Europe. Both of these monumental achievements were accomplished under the Tudor monarchs, who ruled from 1485 until 1603.

When Henry VII, the first Tudor king, ascended the throne in 1485, the royal treasury had been depleted by a long civil war (the War of the Roses), and the throne itself was extremely insecure, a number of ruthless and powerful noble families supporting the claims of various pretenders. In the circumstances, Henry might have been expected to secure his position in the traditional way, by allying himself with various groups of nobles and playing them off one against the other. Instead, he courted the support of the commoners by raising a considerable number of "new men" to power and launched a direct attack on the nobles who would not support him. As the principal instrument for this attack he created, with the consent of Parliament, the Court of the Star Chamber, through which persons could be seized, tried without a jury, and punished by fines so heavy as to be confiscatory. In these early days the Star Chamber was looked upon, and functioned, as a bulwark protecting the common people against the tyranny of the nobles. By its means Henry weakened and divided the nobility, strengthened the Commons, and won the respect of the populace.

To solve his other problem, the replenishment of the royal treasury, Henry took a series of important steps. One was to manage his fiscal affairs efficiently and frugally. Another was to make most of his wars economically successful undertakings. He chose his wars carefully, acting only when he was likely not only to win, but also to reap profit from plunder of from ransoming captives. By the time he died in 1509 his dynasty was firmly secured, and the royal treasury was the richest in all Christendom.

His son and successor, Henry VIII, began his reign by performing the remarkable feat of dissipating the royal treasury in little more than a decade. By the early 1520's, as a result of his own extravagance and overambitious meddling in Continental politics and wars, the treasury was bare. Henry VIII now adopted his father's policy of working carefully with the Commons; this marked

a pivotal point in English history, for it made the principle of government by consent an essential feature in Henry's whole scheme of government. The policy soon served him well. In the meantime, however, the treasury was still depleted, and the problem grew rapidly more acute when the first great influx of American gold and silver into Europe accelerated the existing tendency toward inflation.

Just at this time, a number of circumstances coalesced to induce Henry to take another radical step. Of the six children borne by his wife Catherine of Aragon, only one daughter survived and Catherine was unable to have more; and so the succession of the Tudor dynasty rested on a slender reed. In addition, Henry happened to fall passionately in love with Anne Boleyn, who was quite willing to marry the king but firmly refused to become his mistress. Henry turned to the Pope with a request for an annulment, which might readily have been granted but for the fact that the Pope was virtually a prisoner of King Charles of Spain, who happened to be Catherine of Aragon's nephew. The request was refused, and in 1529 Henry called Parliament into a historic session that lasted seven years. Before it was dissolved, the English Church had severed all connections with Rome.

That opened the way for a solution to Henry's financial problems, and if he had not seen the solution in advance, his advisors were quick to point it out once the break with Rome was made. In a word, Henry confiscated the property of the church monasteries, which brought him nearly a sixth of all the land in England. Over the years Henry sold most of the land, mainly to the landholding classes on all levels, including many city merchants. A number of the new owners quickly resold their lands to smaller holders, somewhat broadening the landholding class. Henry's break with the church further stimulated the modernization, specialization, and commercialization of the English economy.

The break also precipitated drastic rearrangement of England's foreign relations. It gained for England the zealous enmity of its traditional ally, Spain, an enmity that was intensified with the accession of Philip II to the Spanish throne in 1556; for Philip was fanatically dedicated to using all the wealth and power of the Spanish Empire to suppress Protestantism. Meanwhile, the Calvinist Reformation swept through Scotland, separating that kingdom from its traditional ally, Catholic France.

Accordingly, when Queen Elizabeth, Henry VIII's daughter by Anne Boleyn, ascended the

Sir Walter Raleigh. (Library of Congress.)

throne in 1558—after a turbulent and bloody eleven-year interval in which her half-brother Edward and her half-sister Mary each occupied the throne for just over five years—England's internal order and external relations had been fundamentally rearranged.

In matters international vigorous action was imperative. Prices were spiraling rapidly and there were no more monasteries to confiscate. The obvious solution was for England to obtain a share of Spain's gold and silver through direct trade with Spanish colonies, and for Elizabeth to augment her treasury either by taxing or licensing this trade or by going into secret partnership with the English traders.

For a considerable period such undertakings were entrusted to private enterprise. The first outsider to exploit this market was the Englishman John Hawkins. The two Old World commodities most in demand in Spanish America were cloth and slaves, the first being a product of England and the other being easily obtainable in Portuguese West Africa. In 1562 Hawkins acquired 300 black slaves and sailed with them to Hispaniola, where he sold them at a handsome profit after paying official customs duties and license fees; he received payment in sugar and hides, which he sold for further profit in Europe. On his second venture the queen and several members of her Privy Council were Hawkins' secret partners, and he again made a whopping profit, this time mainly in silver. Subsequent ventures were handicapped by a Spanish crackdown, however, and by 1569 trade was thoroughly closed to outsiders. Within another four years, more or less open conflict between the Catholic and Protestant countries had begun, the rebellious Netherlanders having allied themselves with England. For the next thirty years, British and Dutch ships engaged in smuggling to Spanish America and in systematic plunder of Spanish shipping.

The greatest of the English captains in these enterprises was Sir Francis Drake, kinsman of Hawkins. Drake conducted a brilliant and profitable privateering raid in 1573, and launched his most spectacular venture four years later. With secret authorization (and an investment) from the queen he crossed the Atlantic, passed through the Strait of Magellan, plundered Spanish shipping off South America, captured a shipload of Peruvian silver, explored the Pacific coast of North America, crossed to the East Indies, concluded a treaty with a sultan who was at war with the Portuguese, bought several tons of cloves, and sailed home by the Portuguese route around Africa, returning with considerable glory and incredible treasure.

Meanwhile, Elizabeth was encouraging English maritime development in other areas. She encouraged Martin Frobisher and John Davis, who explored North America searching for a northwest passage, and supported Humphrey Gilbert and his half-brother Walter Raleigh in schemes to colonize North America. When Drake came home from his spectacular circumnavigation in 1581, the queen knighted him on his own quarterdeck and rejected all attempts by Spain to recover the stolen booty.

Open war with Spain soon followed. Spain under Philip II had had more than enough of Elizabethan "sea dogs," and, what was more important, was committed to the re-Catholization of England and Scotland. Naval warfare began in 1584. Elizabeth sent troops to aid Holland in its rebellion, and Drake was sent with more than twenty men-of-war and a royal commission to attack the Spanish position in America. In the ensuing twelvemonth Drake wreaked considerable devastation in the West Indies and sacked Santo Domingo. In 1587 he conducted an audacious raid which sank the Spanish fleet in its home harbor at Cadiz.

Philip II of Spain ordered the construction of an "Invincible Armada" of 132 vessels carrying 3165 cannon. The British hurriedly prepared for defense by constructing a more numerous though less heavily armed fleet, and one far better suited to fighting in rough seas. The Spanish were handicapped by being required to move in accordance with orders from Madrid. The free men of England were bold, swashbuckling, cocky, and infinitely more flexible. In a dramatic showdown (July 21-29, 1588) the British outmaneuvered the Spanish in the English Channel and thoroughly defeated the great Armada. Most of the Spanish vessels that escaped fled north hoping to return home by circling the British Isles, only to be destroyed by a storm off the Hebrides.

And so, at the time of Elizabeth's death in 1603, the English people—a scant three million souls, but proud, progressive, prosperous, and free—had gathered the momentum and energy that would propel them temporarily into virtual domination of the world.

During the reign of the first English king of the Stuart dynasty, James I (1603-1625), the kingdom was plagued by a religious and constitutional controversy in which the opposition to the king grew steadily and rapidly more extreme, and in which many Englishmen decided to ignore or violate the law in pursuit of their own interests. During this controversy, and partly as a result of it, colonies were planted and firmly established in Virginia and at Plymouth. During the reign of James's son and successor, Charles I (1625-1649), the constitutional and religious controversy became so extreme that it degenerated into a civil war which ended with the execution of the king and the establishment of a republican Commonwealth. During this controversy, and as an integral part of it, the colonies of Massachusetts Bay, Rhode Island, Connecticut, New Haven, and Maryland were planted and firmly established. And during the years of the Commonwealth (1649-1660) the mother country went in one direction while the colonies, almost totally ignored and isolated, went in other directions.

Mercantile and maritime adventurers fairly ached to continue the war with Spain, and toward that end developed an alternative approach: the establishment of colonies in North America, territory which James recognized as belonging to the Spanish Crown. The adventurers saw the planting of colonies as having two possible advantages. In the first place, colonization could conceivably turn out to be profitable in its own right, as many publicists and promoters had been urging for more than twenty years. And, in the second place, there was the more interesting possibility that the establishment of American colonies might goad Spain into retaliatory attacks, thus reigniting the war and reopening opportunity for plunder.

Most of the arguments advanced for colonization by the earlier publicists and promoters proved to be ill founded. Colonies were supposed to enrich the investors and the kingdom in general by producing precious metals, wine, and naval stores; but only the last of these ever materialized. It was also believed that colonization would furnish an outlet for a grievous social problem that concerned many Englishmen, namely overpopulation. As it turned out, England was far from overpopulated. It only seemed to have this problem; for London, during the late Elizabethan and early Stuart years, was teeming with the poor and the unemployed. Finally, there was the missionary argument: every colonizing company in every country in Europe asserted that spreading the Christian Gospel was among its leading motives.

Native Americans and the Settlement of Virginia

The North American Indians proved to be sparsely settled and difficult to convert; and besides, few Englishmen ever took the Christianizing task very seriously, for missionary zeal was simply not in them. Instead, Anglo-Americans generally viewed the Indian as one of the unpleasant natural conditions to be overcome in America, along with cold winters, insects, and hungry bears. As the English Separatist leader William Bradford put it, the Indians were "only savage and brutish men, little otherwise than the wild beasts."

The matter of relations with the Indians would, of course, become much more involved. In addition to killing them, the whites would also learn from them and trade with them. East of the Mississippi there were four broad Indian cultures, comprising about forty groups, each of which had numerous individual tribes that often joined in military confederations. The least developed were the eastern Algonkians, who occupied the Atlantic coast from Labrador to Albemarle Sound. Farmers and hunters, the Algonkians taught the whites how to grow maize, squash, beans, and pumpkins, became the first Indians to engage in fur trade with Europeans, allied themselves with Europeans against other Europeans and against other Indians, and were all but wiped out in a series of wars that began in 1622 and continued intermittently until 1763. Deep in the interior on the western Great Lakes a northern and western Algonkian culture shared many of the traits and, eventually, the fate of their eastern relatives. Between the two Algonkian cultures, the Iroquois Indians dominated the area between the Great Lakes and the central Appalachians. There were three distinct subgroups of Iroquois: the Hurons, located north of the Lakes, who early allied themselves with the French and who dominated the fur trade by acting as middlemen between the western Algonkians and the whites; the "Five Nations," occupying the Mohawk Valley, militarily so powerful that they were able to repel the Anglo-Americans for more than a century and a half; and a conglomerate of related tribes, including the Cherokee, Tuscarora, Moneton, and Monacan tribes, which dominated the central and southern Appalachian mountains, but were not quite as shrewd as the Hurons nor quite as formidable as the Five Nations. Finally, there was the Muskogean culture, less powerful than the Iroquois but otherwise more advanced, which occupied the lowlands of southeastern North

America. The Muskogean tribes were agriculturally and politically sophisticated, and were able to teach the whites in the one area and learn from them in the other; they came closer than any other Indians to accommodating themselves to the European invaders.

England's mercantile and maritime adventurers were eager to participate in speculative American enterprises; and in 1606, when two groups of investors, one in London and one in Plymouth, formed joint-stock companies and petitioned the king for charters of incorporation for the purpose of colonizing North America, these men supported the London group. Both companies were chartered, the Plymouth Company for operations in the northern part of the continent, the London Company for operations in the south; but full control of each of the plantations was given to councils named by the king.

In May of 1607 the London Company landed three ships, carrying 105 men, and planted a settlement called Jamestown. The site was swampy, mosquito-infested, and otherwise poorly suited for human habitation. The settlers made countless blunders in trying to learn to live there, but they did remain, and were soon reinforced by about 200 more immigrants. The colony was governed by an unwieldy and bickering council, which meant in practice that it was not governed at all; and most of the settlers took to wandering into the interior to hunt for game or search for gold, leaving no one to do the work of building the settlement and making it self-sufficient. Two-thirds of the colonists died in the first year. As a result, one of the settlers, twenty-seven-year-old John Smith, was elevated to the presidency of the local council. He took charge, drove and led the men to do the necessary work, and ensured the permanence of the settlement.

A faction arose headed by Sir Edwin Sandys, author of the charter of 1609 and one of the most influential leaders of Parliament in the constitutional and religious opposition to King James. Sandys was in many ways the archetype of two and a half centuries of Virginians to come: a fierce defender of religious freedom and champion of legislative supremacy, an implacable enemy of absolutism and mercantile adventurers alike, and capable of joining in a scheme, perfectly consistent with his principles, that might enrich himself and save the company from possible bankruptcy through a monopoly of the sale of tobacco. He recruited support from like-minded souls among the small shareholders in the company, and in 1618 succeeded in overthrowing the old management.

The Sandys group immediately instituted a series of new policies, deriving from philanthropic, religious, and ideological motives as well as from the desire for regular profit, and aimed at transforming the company into a legitimate and permanent colonization enterprise. To attract more investors, more settlers, and more servants, the company liberalized its landholding and land granting rules, providing an elaborate system of bonuses and requiring the payment to the company of moderate annual rents. Furthermore, at its own expense the company undertook to send to Virginia a variety of craftsmen and a number of female settlers, who would make the colony's economy more self-sufficient and its life more

tolerable. Finally, the company relaxed its governing rules, provided that settlers continue to be governed by English law and have the rights of Englishmen, and gave settlers a voice in the management by allowing planters to elect representatives to an assembly which would have an advisory power in company affairs. The first assembly, the House of Burgesses, met in 1619.

For the next six years new settlers poured into Virginia. One group was lost. A body of English Separatists, resident in Holland, boarded their ship, the *Mayflower,* and set sail. These pilgrims took the worst possible route across the Atlantic, and after a long passage they arrived near Cape Cod, about 500 miles north of their destination. They decided to stay where they had landed, drew up a compact of government, and established an independent settlement. They barely survived. At that, they were better off than those who made it to Virginia, for the mortality rate there was extremely high: more than 5000 emigrants had made the voyage, yet in 1624 the total population numbered only 1275. Disease was partly responsible; but far more significant both for the settlers and for the company was the outbreak of a disastrous Indian war in 1622. The Powhatan tribes of the Algonkian group, alarmed by the great influx of white settlers, gathered into a confederation of more than 30 villages and murdered more than 340 whites on a single night. Sporadic war, marked by barbarous atrocities on both sides, continued for two years, and the settlers were hard put to survive.

The New England Puritans

Puritans, who wished to "purify" the Church of England, were a fairly numerous and potentially dangerous segment of the British population. Charles I had a plan for them. In fine, the plan was to induce them to leave, by maintaining a policy of continuous though mild persecution on the one hand, and by offering them generous, even lavish, grants for settlement in America on the other. One such grant went to a group of Puritans for settlements in the Leeward Islands of the West Indies, and another went to the Massachusetts Bay Company. For good measure, Charles granted a charter to George Calvert, Lord Baltimore, for the establishment of a colony north and east of Virginia, where Roman Catholics would be permitted to settle. And in each of these grants local self-government was expressly or implicitly permitted. The policy was effective; between 1629 and 1642 there was a mass exodus to America.

Of the new settlements on the North American mainland, the most important by far was that established by the Massachusetts Bay Company. This company, organized in 1628 by a group of well-to-do English Puritans, received its charter from the king. The company elected as its governor John Winthrop of Groton Manor, a solid country squire, and voted to transfer its government to Massachusetts, since the charter did not require the company to maintain headquarters in England. Within the year Winthrop and a dozen or so other members of the company had set sail for America, and a thousand men, women, and children had gone with them. By the end of 1630 six settlements had been planted in Boston and its environs.

The organization of government and society in Massachusetts reflected traditional values of Englishmen, as well as the reaction of Puritans to the policies of the Stuart kings. In one sense, Massachusetts was a theocratic state: the government enacted into law the biblical injunctions against drunkenness, adultery, murder, theft, and violations of the Sabbath, and otherwise attempted to regulate the religion and morality of the people. These Puritans, convinced that any society failing to honor God by punishing those who violated His commandments would be subject to divine punishment, felt an acute responsibility for the behavior of their fellow men. On the other hand, in their acceptance of the doctrine of the two separate and distinct kingdoms, the Massachusetts Puritans refused to allow their ministers to have any part in government, even in the government of the church. Government of the church was the domain of the members of the congregation; and since the town and the congregation were essentially two aspects of the same thing, government of the town was also the domain of the members of the local church.

The Massachusetts Bay Company, like other English business corporations of the time, was governed by its voting members, or " freemen." At first the only members were the stockholders,

For their breakfast, that it was not so well ordered, the flour not so fine as it might, nor so well boiled or stirred, at all times that it was so, it was my sin of neglect, and want of that care that ought to have been in one that the Lord had intrusted with such a work. Concerning their beef, that was allowed them, as they affirm, which, I confess, had been my duty to have seen they had it, and continued to have had it, because it was my husband's command; but truly I must confess, to my shame. I cannot remember that ever they had it, nor that ever it was taken from them. And that they had not so good or so much provision in my husband's absence as presence, I conceive it was because he would call sometimes for butter or cheese, when I conceived there was no need of it; yet, forasmuch as the scholars did otherways apprehend, I desire to see the evil that was in the carriage of that as well as in the other, and to take shame to myself for it. And that they sent down for more, when they had not enough, and the maid should answer, if they had not, they should not, I must confess, that I have denied them cheese, when they sent for it, and it have been in the house; for which I shall humbly beg pardon of them, and own the shame, and confess my sin. And for such provoking words, which my servents have given, I cannot own them, but am sorry any such should be given in my house. And for bad fish, that they had it brought to table, I am sorry there was that cause of offence given them. I acknowledge my sin in it. And for their mackerel, brought to them with their guts in them, and goat's dung in their hasty pudding, it's uterly unknown to me; but I am much ashamed it should be in the family, and not prevented by myself or servants, and I humbly acknowledge my negligence in it. And that they made their beds at any time, were my straits never so great, I am sorry they were ever put to it. For the Moor his lying in Sam. Hough's sheet and pillowbier, it hath a truth in it: he did so one time, and it gave Sam. Hough just cause of offence; and that it was not prevented by my care and watchfulness, I desire [to] take the shame and sorrow for it. And that they eat the Moor's crusts, and the swine and they had share and share alike, and the Moor to have beer, and they denied it, and if they had not enough, for my maid to answer, they should not, I am an utter stranger to these things, and know not the least footsteps for them so to charge me; and if my servants were guilty of such miscarriages, had the boarders complained of it unto myself, I should have thought it my sin, if I had not sharply reproved my servants, and endeavored reform. And for bread made of heated, sour meal, although I know of but once that if was so, since I kept house, yet John Wilson affirms it was twice: and I am truly sorry, that any of it was spent amongst them. For beer and bread, that it was denied them by me betwixt meals, truly I do not remember, that ever I did deny it unto them; John Wilson will affirm, that, generally, the bread and beer was free for the boarders to go unto. And that money was demanded of them for washing the linen, it's true it was propounded to them, but never imposed upon them. And for their pudding being given the last day of the week without butter or suet, and that I said, it was miln of Manchester in Old England, it's true that I did say so, and am sorry, they had any cause of offence given them by having it so. And for their wanting beer, betwixt brewings, a week or half a week together, I am sorry that it was so at any time, and should tremble to have it so, were it in my hands to do again.

An Early Harvard Riot (1639)

College students have long complained about the quality of food in university dining rooms. If this very first American instance of an incipient food riot is typical, they have good reason for their complaint. Mistress Eaton, the cook and author of this letter, was wife of Harvard's first headmaster, Nathaniel Eaton. Both lost their jobs when students protested the severe discipline that Mr. Eaton dispensed and the atrocious food that his wife served.

but in 1631 the company admitted to membership more than a hundred adult male settlers. Subsequently all members of Puritan congregations were admitted as freemen of the company, and since the government of the company and the colony were the same thing, membership in the church made a man part of the government of the colony. The charter provided that company members gather as a "General Court" four times a year, and that between times the management be conducted by a governor, deputy governor, and council of eighteen "assistants," all elected annually. As the colony expanded, legislation by the entire body of freemen became unwieldy, and after 1634 they elected annually representatives from each settlement. This general structure of government, including the principle that representation was based upon place (settlement or town) instead of population, formed the archetype for most subsequent governments established in America. It was, in fact, not drastically different from the traditional and constitutional form of government in England, except that the "upper house" and the executive authority were elective rather than hereditary.

There was a flaw in the system. It was a government of, by, and for orthodox Puritans, and a sizable minority of the Puritans who poured into the colony during the 1630's were of rather different persuasions. Almost all shared John Calvin's belief that God in His omnipotence had preordained the entire history of the world, including whether each individual was to be saved or doomed. Most also shared a set of corollary beliefs. It might be assumed from Calvin's premise that a man need not make any effort to be moral and good, since nothing he did could alter his predestined fate. Not so; orthodox ministers in Massachusetts observed that religious "conversion," a personal experience by which God let a man know he was saved, often came to those who tried to lead godly lives; and such conversion could relieve the predestinarian of his greatest discomfort in life, that of agonizing over whether he had been destined for heaven or for hell. Not all Puritans reasoned the same way from these premises however, and what proved to be more disruptive, not all agreed even on the principle of cooperation between congregations. Those who shared none of the Puritans' values—for example Thomas Morton, a delightful adventurer who had directed a settlement of squatters since 1624, and whose followers enjoyed drinking freely and dancing around maypoles—were disapproved by almost everyone, and were thus easy to eject from the area. Those who were merely lethargic in their faith were also easy to manage. Those who shared Puritan values but disputed Congregationalist orthodoxy, however, were a good deal more troublesome.

In 1631 Roger Williams, a saintlike man of great personal gifts, and Separatist persuasion arrived in Massachusetts. He began immediately to point out to all and sundry the numerous defects he saw in the Massachusetts scheme of things, condemned the religious requirements for suffrage, and enunciated such seditious doctrines as the proposition that no government should have authority over religious matters. Such was Williams' charm that he became minister of the congregation in Salem despite his erratic views; but when large numbers began to share those views the government found it necessary to banish him, lest the foundation for all authority in Massachusetts be undermined. He went to the head of Narragansett Bay, established a settlement of his followers and called it Providence, created an atmosphere in which governmental authority did not extend to religious matters, and for almost half a century presided as the spiritual head of what became the colony of Rhode Island and Providence Plantations.

The Rhode Island part of this colony was the product of the subversive teachings of a woman, Anne Hutchinson. Mrs. Hutchinson was a clever and persuasive amateur theologian who took to the practice of calling informal gatherings on Sundays, after her minister had preached, to discuss the subjects of his sermons. She was soon criticizing and then sermonizing on her own, and few could counter the hair-splitting logic of her reasoning. She agreed with the accepted premise that God granted salvation with regard only to His own designs, not those of humans, but she concluded from this that good behavior was no evidence of salvation. If the grace of the Holy Spirit was in a person it was in that person, and if not, not. Accordingly, it made no difference how a person behaved. Such thinking was subversive not only of state-enforced morality, but of state-enforced order as well; and when a large segment of the population of Boston embraced her doctrines, she had become even more dangerous than Williams had been. After a government investigation she, too, was banished; and like Williams she established a settlement of her followers on Narragansett Bay.

Other parts of New England were settled simply out of an urge to have more room to move around in, both physically and politically. In 1635 a group settled along the Connecticut River. The Reverend Thomas Hooker of Newton (Cambridge) led his flock west also, to establish Hartford. In 1639 these new towns, choosing to place themselves outside the jurisdiction of Massachusetts, drew up an agreement called the Fundamental Orders.

They established their own government, which differed from the one in Massachusetts in a single important feature: suffrage was not confined to church members.

Virginia vs New England

The Civil War in England between the Royalists and Puritans (1642-47) and the resulting Puritan Commonwealth orphaned the colonies. And despite certain minor entanglements, they remained orphaned until the Stuart Restoration in 1660. In the interim they hardened institutionally and socially.

From the very beginning there was a fundamental difference between the settlers in New England and those in Virginia, deriving from their notions of what they were doing in America in the first place. The New Englanders (Rhode Islanders, always, excepted) had a strong sense of group identity and a concomitant tendency toward communal enterprise; their attitude was based upon a shared devotion to God, and a shared conception of God. The Virginians, by and large, had been prompted to move to America by a spirit of personal adventure, and they had a tendency toward individual enterprise; to the extent that they had any common loyalty, it was to the king and his bishops. Natural conditions strongly reinforced the initial tendencies of both groups of settlers. In New England the sharply contoured and heavily forested terrain, intersected by few navigable streams, made movement difficult and thereby encouraged the planting of compact group settlements. In Virginia the broad, flat terrain, intersected by swamps and tidal creeks, and the abundance of navigable waterways, made movement easy and thus encouraged settlers to spread out and act on their own.

The experience of isolation which resulted from the English Civil War drove the two groups of colonies into remarkably different, and yet remarkably similar, courses of development. In New England, the Puritan magistrates formally dissolved their connections with the Crown even before their counterparts in England had done so. Moreover, during this period New Englanders began choosing sides, separating saints from sinners. In 1643, partly because of a need to regularize Indian relations after a successful earlier encounter with hostile Indians (the Pequot War, 1637-38), various of the colonies borrowed a

tactic from the Indians and formed the New England Confederation, for mutual defense and general cooperation. Rhode Island was excluded, on the ground that it was a sinkhole of depravity and heresy. Then the member colonies of the confederation, gaining security in their identity through their isolation from England and from the sense of being surrounded by enemies—not only the Rhode Islanders and the squatters, but also hostile Indians, belligerent French trading posts to the north, and prosperous and militarily strong Dutch trading settlements on the Connecticut, the Hudson, and the Delaware—instituted an aggressive policy of dealing with their neighbors. The New England Puritans were scarcely as successful in these ventures as were those in Old England, but as a part of their expansionism they took to the sea, ventured into occasional trading activities with the West Indies, and thus laid the foundations for New England's future emergence as a maritime center of some consequence.

In Virginia the colonial government likewise separated itself from England, but for the opposite reason: Virginia proclaimed its loyalty to Charles I, and when the Parliamentarians won the Civil War Virginia declared its loyalty to the Stuart heir-in-exile, Charles II. The Commonwealth government in 1652 sent four commissioners, two of them Virginians, a fleet, and 600 troops to bring the colony into line, and though the royal governor, Sir William Berkeley, wanted to resist, he was overruled by the council and assembly. The commissioners made few requirements except the election of Puritan governors, and during the remaining years before the restoration of Charles II, Virginia virtually governed itself without interference from the Commonwealth and the Protectorate.

Maryland had a more difficult time. A group of Puritans, driven out of Virginia in 1648, was given refuge in Maryland, and the following year, at the instigation of Lord Baltimore, who from conviction as well as policy was an advocate of religious toleration, the General Assembly enacted a measure establishing complete freedom of worship for all Trinitarian Christians.

The most important thing that happened in both New England and Virginia was the response to the peculiar nature of economic life in America. It has been observed that during the Great Migration New England prospered by supplying capital goods to the newcomers. When the Civil War broke out in England the flow of Puritan immigrants stopped, but by the time the war was over in 1647 it had become clear that the population of the colonies was somehow increasing as fast as ever. In New England the increase derived from an extremely high birth rate and a low mortality rate; in Virginia it sprang from a new immigration, first in trickles and then in waves, of fugitives from the Puritanical nightmare that was unfolding in England. In both places the population increase served to accentuate local peculiarities. The New Englanders were indoctrinated from birth in the virtues of the New England Puritan way. A few of the Virginia immigrants were displaced Cavalier gentry, and a much larger number pretended to be. The fact that so many were bogus accentuated the Cavalier flavor of the colony, for the pretenders were all the more committed to affecting the posture of Cavalier gentry.

The Colonies vs. London

Charles II, his ministers, and Parliament, building on principles established by the Navigation Act of 1651, enacted a broad program designed to stimulate England's economic growth and to transform the scattered American settlements and East Indian trading posts into a world empire. The primary aim of the program was to make England and its overseas colonies a vast, closed trading area, as self-sufficient as possible, protected by an enlarged navy, and serviced by an expanded merchant fleet. Theoretically, each part of the empire would specialize in supplying the products and services for which it was best suited, and thereby contribute to the well-being of all the parts and to the strength of the whole. The colonies would produce goods that England could not produce economically—especially lumber, naval stores, and such other raw materials as fish, tobacco, sugar, indigo, cotton, and foodstuffs—and would be discouraged from competing with the manufacturing activities of the mother country. These colonial products would be sent only to England, but would have a monopoly on the English market. Insofar as was feasible, the colonies would buy their finished goods from England, even if the goods were originally produced in continental Europe. Finally, all products would be subject to customs duties and would be carried only in English or colonial ships.

Two major acts laid the legal foundations of the system: the Navigation Act of 1660 and the Staple Act of 1663. The Navigation Act restricted all colonial trade to vessels owned and manned primarily by Englishmen or English colonists, and required that certain enumerated articles produced in the colonies—tobacco, sugar, indigo, ginger, and dyewoods—be shipped only to England or to another English colony. The Staple Act required that most goods imported into the colonies, whether they originated in England or in foreign parts, must be shipped from an English port. The Staple Act aimed to benefit the Crown by increasing the customs revenues on exports from England; to help English exporters by giving them a monopoly of the colonial market (even as the Navigation Act gave colonial producers a monopoly of the English market); and to protect the colonists by confining their trade to shipping lanes that could be patrolled and protected by the English navy.

For all the laxity of its enforcement, the new commercial system was an immediate success. English commerce boomed and the merchant fleet became the largest and most profitable the nation had yet known. This was not surprising. Simply by virtue of establishing the system England took exclusive possession of a thriving ready-made business: a large and growing colonial trade which for two decades had, despite the Navigation Act of 1651 and the war against Holland in 1652-54, been as profitable to the Dutch as to the English.

The colonies also prospered under this new system. The West Indies, booming with the rapid expansion of sugar production, welcomed the naval protection afforded by the new system, for the Caribbean was teeming with pirates. The tobacco colonies, Virginia and Maryland, paid perhaps a bit more for freight than they had before, and tobacco prices continued to decline, but the establishment of a great central marketing system in England facilitated an enormous increase in production that in the long run more than compensated: by 1672 the two colonies were exporting seventeen million pounds of tobacco a year. The New England colonies, being free to elect their own governors, were also free to ignore the Acts of Trade when it was to their advantage to do so. Thus they profited from trade with the enclosed imperial market as well as from the protection of the English navy, and otherwise did as they pleased. Consequently, the merchant fleet of New England, built by a burgeoning new local industry, grew even faster than that of Old England. Another Restoration policy, the resumption of discrimination against Dissenters also promoted New England's prosperity. The migration of Dissenters was temporarily resumed, and in the decade of the 1660's the population of New England increased from about 33,000 to about 52,000.

Partly in response to a widespread Indian uprising, various colonies and colonists took actions which began to corrode the English Empire. Events in the colonies were to have vast consequences: even as the English at home were moving, however painfully, toward the eighteenth-century system of loyal opposition, those in America were becoming set in the way of the seventeenth century, that of disloyal opposition.

As was to be expected, the Massachusetts Bay Colony led the way. From the outset of the Restoration Massachusetts was troublesome. It secretly harbored two of the men condemned to death for the execution of Charles I; it ignored the Navigation Acts when it so pleased; and it clearly violated its charter by retaining on its statute books a number of laws, particularly those concerning religion, contrary to the laws of England. Very early, Charles sent orders commanding Massachusetts to make its laws conform to those of England. The colony did temporarily stop persecuting the Quakers and did modify its laws concerning suffrage, but neither action was taken in response to the king's orders: these the colonial assembly flatly ignored. And so, when the mission to seize the New Netherlands (New York) was dispatched in 1664, Charles sent four commissioners along to investigate the New England governments.

The commissioners encountered no difficulty in Plymouth, Connecticut, or Rhode Island, but when they arrived in Boston in May of 1665 they met with a reception that was at once icy and audacious. The Massachusetts magistrates referred the commissioners to the charter of 1629, refused to submit to investigation, and publicly forbade the citizens to offer any testimony. The commissioners returned to England, and three of them recommended to the king that Massachusetts' charter be revoked. Such open defiance might have provoked not only a revocation of the charter, but armed suppression as well, except for one thing: the confrontation came just at the time England was suffering from a triple disaster of plague, fire, and naval defeat. For the next six years Massachusetts, together with the other colonies, was largely ignored, and was able to take advantage of the situation.

Massachusetts seized a commercial opportunity afforded by London's distress. The price of tobacco fell in 1667 to an all-time low of about half a penny per pound. Under normal circumstances, about half the tobacco shipped to London was reexported to the Continent through Holland, and though the English market had vanished the European market continued to exist. So the merchants of New England capitalized on the situation: ignoring the Acts of Trade, they carried tobacco directly from Virginia to Holland, and from 1667 to 1672 reaped considerable profits for themselves and improved Virginia tobacco prices in the bargain.

By these and other means Virginia, the most Royalist of all colonies, and New England, the least, soon became equally disenchanted with the government in London. And in the late summer of

Numerals, wrought iron; made by original Dutch settlers, New Castle, Delaware, 1687. *(Index of American Design.)*

1675, both colonies were subjected to difficulties that would have strained any loyalties.

The difficulties in both places resulted from the renewal of Indian hostilities, and the ultimate wellspring of the trouble was, as it had been since 1670, the ambitions of France's King Louis XIV. Since the 1630's the Indians had gradually and peacefully retreated to the interior rather than face the devastating fire of English muskets. But in the late 1660's the French adopted a broad strategy of encircling the English colonies with settlements along the St. Lawrence, the Great Lakes, and the Mississippi, and forged alliances with the Indians between their own settlements and those of the English. The five Iroquois nations, who occupied what is now New York State, were traditional enemies of the French and their Indian allies. Hence the new French policy forced the Iroquois back. They, in turn, exerted pressure upon the Old Algonkian tribes of New England and the Susquehannocks of what is now Pennsylvania, with the result that in the 1670's the Algonkians engaged in warfare against the whites to the east and the Susquehannocks in hostilities toward the whites to the south.

In New England the fighting was known as King Philip's War. Philip's tribe, already hemmed in between rival governments and land speculators in Rhode Island and Massachusetts, was pressed to the point of desperation by the Iroquois drive; and just at that time the Massachusetts government ordered the Indians to disarm. They responded in the only way they could, by attacking the white settlements. The "war" was complicated by the fact that the Indians did not fight according to the rules of formal territorial warfare, European-style: a contest in which the only combatants and subjects of attack were uniformed armies, and in which both sides campaigned until one or the other surrendered. The Indians fought only intermittently, and regarded all whites, women and children included, as fair prey. There was considerable barbarism on both sides. But the whites had the advantage of superior arms and superior organization, which was even more important. The New England Confederation mobilized about a thousand men and conducted a ruthless, systematic, relentless campaign, and by 1676 the Indians had been thoroughly defeated. King Philip's War cost the white settlers about a sixth of their adult males, the total destruction of a dozen towns and some damage to at least half their towns, and almost half a million dollars. During the entire campaign, no help was sent from England.

Instead of help, even as the smoke was clearing a special agent of King Charles II arrived in Boston: Edward Randolph, come to convey new royal instructions and to investigate the enforcement of the Navigation Acts. After a less than cordial reception and a cursory investigation, Randolph submitted two reports to the Crown; he charged Massachusetts with refusing to comply with the Navigation Act, executing English subjects for their religious faith, denying appeals to king's Privy Council, and refusing to take the oath of allegiance.

In Virginia, disloyal opposition took an even more extreme form. Bands of Susquehannock Indians, fleeing the Iroquois, crossed the Potomac in the summer of 1675. Relations between the outland Indians and the Virginia planters deteriorated until a planter was killed over a fur transaction, several Indians (including five Susquehannock chiefs under a flag of truce) were killed in retaliation, and the whole Potomac frontier erupted in raids and counterraids. The royal governor of Virginia, William Berkeley, sought to stop the outbreak, but he did so from premises and with policies that were certain to alienate the frontiersmen. Berkeley was accused, perhaps with some justice, of not wanting to antagonize the Indians because he had investments in fur trade with them. But the most important element governing his policy was his staunch, even pigheaded, royalism. He had been royal governor from 1642 to 1652, had suffered humiliation and exile under the Commonwealth, and had been restored with the Stuarts in 1660; thereafter, would not yield an inch of the royal prerogative. Indeed Charles, in his gratitude for such loyalty, rashly proclaimed Virginia as one of his kingdoms, coequal with England, Scotland, and Wales.

As part of the restored royal prerogative, according to Berkeley, Indians became subjects of the king, on an equal footing with whites, and were therefore entitled to the protection of royal justice. Thus no warfare upon the Indians was to be tolerated, despite the Indian attacks—which Berkeley regarded, in fact, as minor frontier incidents.

Berkeley met the crisis by raising funds to rebuild the frontier forts and to pay and equip a band of mounted rangers, and by prohibiting fur trade by any but a handful of traders whom he himself licensed. The new tax was ill calculated to please the frontiersmen, and the new trade regulations flew in the face of the ambitions of a number of frontier fur traders, land seekers, and border barons.

The malcontents soon raised a leader who was willing to defy the governor. Nathaniel Bacon, the governor's nephew, recent settler in Henrico

County in the interior of Virginia, artful demagogue, unscrupulous Cavalier adventurer and lawyer who had been trained at the Inns of Court in London, totally disagreed with his uncle. He held that the Indians were not subjects of the Crown, that they were outside the law and could be attacked by any Englishman so disposed. In May of 1676, without a commission from the governor, Bacon marched at the head of an expedition that descended upon the Roanoke River to destroy a Susquehannock village. He was promptly accused of treason, but was pardoned by the governor when he acknowledged his offense.

Meanwhile Bacon, along with a goodly number of other radicals, was elected to the House of Burgesses. These "Baconites" proceeded to push through the Burgesses a series of enactments, collectively known as "Bacon's laws," which reversed most of Berkeley's Restoration policies by liberalizing voting, tax, and religious regulations. Bacon himself had little or nothing to do with this development, however. Instead, he took up his military career again. He raised an army of 500 men, marched on the colonial capital at Jamestown, forced Berkeley to sign his commission as a militia captain, and set about looking for more Indians to kill.

And now the tobacco planters demonstrated what recent royal and parliamentary policies had accomplished: the planters professed no allegiance at all to Parliament, and their loyalty to the Crown had become only formal, devoid of any personal, felt commitment. When Governor Berkeley again declared Bacon a rebel, the planters swore their allegiance to the rebel. When the final military confrontation came in 1676, they held to their oath, enabling Bacon to drive Berkeley's forces out of Jamestown and burn the village to the ground. Order was restored in the ensuing months, largely as a result of Bacon's fortuitous death in October.

The Dominion of New England

Late in 1686 James II began to establish the Dominion of New England: New Hampshire, Massachusetts, Plymouth, Connecticut, Rhode Island, New York, and the Jerseys were all to be governed by one governor and his council, without the interference of representative assemblies. As governor of the dominion James appointed Sir Edmund Andros, the former governor of New York.

The reorganization was not as myopic as it might appear. For one thing, the new system made a great deal of sense from an administrative point of view; for the first (and only) time in the history of the English empire in America, England had a system that was, at least on paper, as efficient as those of France and Spain. More important, Andros' administration was in many respects both shrewd and enlightened. He left most of the existing laws in force, he respected the established churches and school, and for the most part he left the towns in control of their own local affairs—and, after all, the town and congregation constituted the primary unit of government in New England. Furthermore, he governed with a strong hand; for example, he offered the merchants of his dominion the protection of the Royal Navy if they cooperated with him and threatened them with its great destructive power if they refused.

Finally, Andros tempered each of his unpopular measures skillfully. Thus, for example, while he antagonized the merchants of Boston, Newport and New York by insisting on enforcement of the Navigation Acts, he also reversed his earlier policy and stopped offering pirates haven in these principal ports; this meant, in effect, that he may have reduced the merchants' profits but that he reduced their risks as well. Again, Andros provoked considerable grumbling by declaring that the Massachusetts Bay government had proceeded illegally in granting land for town settlements, on the ground that the towns were corporations and that Massachusetts Bay, as a corporation, had no authority to create subordinate corporations. The grumbling was aggravated when he ordered all landholders, present and prospective, to obtain land titles from the governor and pay quitrents as well. But in practice virtually everyone was confirmed in his title to the land he already possessed, the rents proved to be nominal and were not collected, and it turned out to be far easier to obtain land from the new governor than it had been from the Puritan government. Andros also levied taxes without legislative approval, but the taxes were no larger than they had been when duly elected representatives levied them. Andros further encroached upon the principle of local self-government by ordering that town meetings be held no more than once a year and that control of the militia be vested in the governor; but the towns customarily met officially only once a year anyway (they met once a week as congregations, and that Andros did not change), and as it happened Andros never had occasion to call out the militia.

In short, Andros' innovations directly challenged the professed principles of the New Englanders, but altered the daily lives of most of them precious little; and this at a time when there was already a significant discrepancy between principle and practice in New England. He might very well have gotten away with it.

It is uncertain whether this experiment in enlightened despotism would have worked in America; it was never put to the full test, because it failed in England: not for an excess of despotism, but for a want of enlightenment. James's undoing came in 1688, and it came because James alienated his strongest supporters by attempting to go too far, too fast, in his efforts to restore Roman Catholicism. The Tories—who were mainly Anglican bishops and rich, powerful country gentry—were wedded to the Church of England, in at least some instances because they thought that full restoration of the Roman Church might include restoration of its lands, which happened now to belong to the Troy gentry. Indeed, to deprive Tories of their lands was to deprive them of everything.

Even then, James might have prevailed but for a sudden change in the prospects for the succession. James was in his fifties and his only children were two daughters, Mary and Anne, both by his first wife and both devoutly Protestant; his second wife, an Italian princess and a Catholic, had borne him no children. Most Englishmen, however much they despised the king, therefore thought it better to wait out the Papist storm as they had the Puritan, on the theory that little permanent harm could be done before James died and the Crown passed to a Protestant. But in June of 1688 the queen had a son, thus opening the possibility of a permanent Catholic succession. It seemed to be now or never for English Protestantism; and so seven prominent Englishmen, representing both Tories and Whigs as well as the Anglican clergy, and supported by a vast conspiracy, invited William of Orange of Holland and husband of James's daughter Mary, to rescue England from Catholic tyranny. William accepted and on November 5 landed with a force of about 14,000 at Torbay, in southwestern England. General John Churchill and Colonel Percy Kirke led a carefully planned desertion of great numbers of royal troops, and much of the remainder of James's army refused to obey their Catholic commanders. Even at this hour the revolution might have been stopped, had Louis XIV of France properly judged what was happening, for he could have spared abundant troops for James's defense. But Louis sent his armies to help out in a religious war that had broken out in Germany and Austria. James was left defenseless, and in December he fled to the continent. Eight weeks later William and Mary became joint sovereigns of England.

The reverberations were felt in America. Governor Andros was in Maine when he got news of William's landing, and he returned to Boston to prevent an anti-Royalist reaction. But he had neither army nor police, and rioting broke out in response not to James's deposition but to rumors of a Popish Plot. The mob was directed and its hysteria was fanned by a manifesto from the pen of the Reverend Cotton Mather, a famed theologian and an expert on witches. Andros fled to the local fort, but before the end of the day he and the other royal officials surrendered and were jailed. A Puritan oligarchy governed the colony for two months, until a new General Court could be elected. In July Andros was ordered to return to England.

As soon as the news of Boston's uprising reached New York that colony too was swept with a great fear of a Popish Plot, and three of its counties, those populated mainly by Congregationalist Puritans, threw out the royal officials and elected their own. In the city, Jacob Leisler, a successful German trader, led a group that ousted Andros' deputy governor and established a provisional government. At first Leisler had little support outside the city, but soon French-inspired Indian raids in the upper part of the colony lent gruesome substance to the rumors of a Papist-Indian campaign to massacre Protestants; Leisler offered firmness, discipline, order, and military strength, and became in fact governor of the entire colony.

British North America after 1688

Swift as these hysteria-inspired events in America were, they lagged behind the pace set in England. By the time Leisler had made his first moves in New York, the English at home had gone through the tortuous legal processes to legitimatize the reign of William and Mary and establish the succession, had commissioned and published a philosophical/legal justification for their "Glorious Revolution," and had become involved in a war with France.

Of these three events the war had the most subtle, and probably the most important, effect upon life in England as well as in the colonies. England was at war with France for nineteen of the next twenty-four years; indeed, though there then followed a peace of twenty-six years the two countries were subsequently at war again for forty-five of the ensuing seventy-five years. Thus continuously beset with hostilities from abroad, the English developed the habit of not fighting one another for internal dominance: permanent internal harmony was bought at the price of vitually permanent external war. In short, the English learned that if man must kill, it is preferable to kill outsiders than to kill one's own kind; and by abiding to that discovery with but one lapse, the English were able to dominate the earth for many, many years.

As for America, the new policy of perpetual war with France had its strongest effects upon those who lived in closest proximity with the French, namely the New Englanders. For three quarters of a century after the Glorious Revolution French colonists, with their Indian allies, formed a northern and western ring around New England, posing a continuous threat to soul and scalp. In terms of temperament, religion, conscience, and interest, the Yankees were the least likely members of the English empire, and the empire's least comfortable and least compliant habitants; but in terms of survival they needed the empire the most.

Equally ironic, the philosophic rationalization for revolution in England appealed most in America to those who had rebelled the least. The philosopher of the English revolution was John Locke, erstwhile secretary to Anthony Ashley Cooper, Earl of Shaftesbury. At the behest of various Whigs, former friends of his former patron, Locke published in 1689 and 1690 several celebrated essays, notably his *Second Treatise on Civil Government* and *An Essay concerning Human Understanding*. Locke postulated the notion that man is born a cipher, innocent, and capable of either good or evil, depending upon his experience with other humans. Locke reasoned that man had once lived in a state of nature, in accordance with the laws of nature (or of God), which endowed man with inalienable rights to life, personal freedom, and the property that he accumulated through honest labor. But in the natural state the strong tended to prey upon the weak, and so men formed themselves into societies

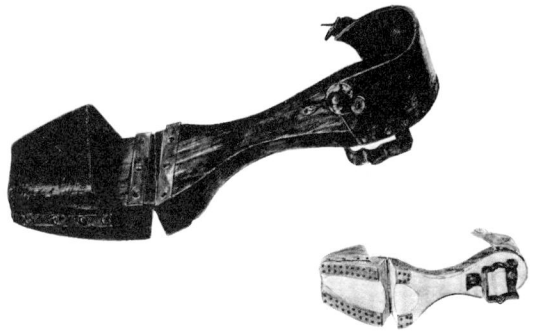

Clog, ash sole, leather toe and heel piece. *(Index of American Design.)*

and created governments. Governments existed by virtue of voluntary agreements, or contracts, between the governed and governors, and their function was to protect the individual's natural rights to life, liberty, and property. The government of James II, founded upon such a contract, had been legitimate until the king broke the contract by depriving people of their natural rights, and thus in effect declaring war upon his subjects. The people therefore had no recourse but to overthrow James's government and to establish a new contract with a new sovereign who seemed more likely to abide by his agreements, namely William of Orange.

As for legitimatization of the Glorious Revolution, a Convention Parliament proclaimed early in 1689 what a formal Parliament enacted and William and Mary approved later the same year, the Declaration of Rights. The Declaration and subsequent Bill of Rights established, for all time, limits upon the English monarchy and judiciary. The Crown could no longer make or suspend laws, levy taxes, or maintain standing armies without the consent of Parliament, and Parliament was guaranteed frequent meetings, free elections, and free debate. Some ecclesiastical courts were eliminated and others had their powers reduced, and in all courts every person was guaranteed trial by jury and protected from excessive bails and forfeiture of estates before conviction.

Equally important was a series of steps taken to regularize, modernize, and render more flexible the system of public finance, which had previously occasioned such destructive conflict between the Crown and Parliament. Henceforth Parliament did not merely grant monies, it controlled their expediture as well. To that end, it began to make specific appropriations for specific purposes, and to require estimates and accounts of expenditures—two entirely new practices—and thus to lay the foundations for modern fiscal budgets.

Finally, as a part of the process of putting things in order, Crown and Parliament attempted to regularize affairs in America.

For all their protestations of loyalty to William III and to his wars for Protestantism, the colonists had taken advantage of England's military preoccupations to profit from illegal trade. It had been possible to do so largely because enforcement of the earlier Navigation Acts had depended more upon private morality, supplemented by generous rewards to informers, than upon efficient administrative machinery; and the new Navigation Act of 1696 sought to change that order of things. For one thing, colonial governors were now held responsible, on penalty of forfeiture of office, for violations of the law. More important, regular customs officers were now appointed for each colony, whereas previously there had been only a few officers who had moved about from one colony to another. The new officers were authorized to obtain "writs of assistance" from local courts, permitting them to enter buildings in random searches for smuggled goods—a far more potent device than mere search warrants, which had to specify the particular items searched for. Moreover, trials for violations of the law were to be held in admiralty courts, where proceedings were not encumbered by juries.

But two conditions continued to impair the effectiveness of the system. One difficulty was geographical: physical circumstances in English America were simply not condusive to efficient supervision of trade. Effective customs operations require concentration of shipping, and in much of America such concentration was not feasible.

Tobacco, for example, which was by far the most valuable product of the mainland colonies, was normally loaded on ships directly at the plantations along the rivers of Virginia and Maryland and on Chesapeake Bay. Thus, short of placing customs officers on every plantation or stationing armed ships at every river and inlet, it was virtually impossible to prevent masters of local, New England, or foreign vessels from carrying tobacco anywhere they pleased.

The other difficulty was institutional. England had, as yet, no tradition of civil service, royal or parliamentary, in the colonies or at home. Posts were filled through influence, bribery, or other corrupt means more commonly than through regard for honest and efficient administration. Furthermore, colonial service attracted the least savory of a generally unsavory lot, not only because life in the colonies was far from desirable to most courtiers, but also because the legitimate rewards for lègitimate service there were small. In all the colonies except Virginia and Barbados the governor was dependent upon the local assembly for his salary, and the customs officers were paid out of fees and fines, not the royal treasury. Accordingly, most of those who filled imperial positions were quite amenable to bribes, offered in exchange for looking the other way when colonials proposed to trade outside the rules established by the Navigation Acts.

By and large, the imperial commercial system worked when it was to the mutual advantage of the colonies and the mother country to abide by it; which is to say, it worked for about three-quarters of the trade affected by the Navigation Acts. Otherwise it was generally ignored, except at those times the Royal Navy was not engaged in war and had nothing better to do than police the seas against pirates and smugglers.

Suggested Readings

Any study of the voyages of discovery can begin with Samuel Eliot Morison's superb works: *The European Discovery of America: The Northern Voyages, A.D. 500-1600* (1971) and *The European Discovery of America: The Southern Voyages, A.D. 1492-1616* (1974). Morison examines in impressive detail, and from an extraordinary number of previously unpublished sources, the personalities and the routes followed by the great navigators who explored the continents. Volume I documents the coastal discoveries north of Cape Fear; volume II traces the voyages of Columbus, Magellan, Drake, Vespucci, Sebastian Cabot, and many lesser figures. Both works have been abridged into a single volume: *The Great Explorers: The European Discovery of America* (1978). In his examination of how white Americans perceived the Indian *(The White Man's Indian: Images of the American Indian from Columbus to the Present,* 1978), Robert Berkhofer, Jr., continues his practice of applying to the study of history analytical devices developed in anthropology and the behavioral sciences. Elizabeth A.H. John, in *Storms Brewed in*

Other Men's Worlds: The Confrontation of Indians, Spanish, and French in the Southwest, 1540-1795 (1975), tells the shockingly neglected story of the settlement of the Southwest. The early history of blacks in America is brilliantly analyzed in David Brion Davis, *The Problem of Slavery in Western Culture,* (1966) and Winthrop Jordan, *White Over Black* (1968). Two books concentrate on the dominant English influence: Peter Laslett, *The World We Have Lost* (1965) tells of the highly stratified world of preindustrial England, and Michael Walzer, *The Revolution of the Saints* (1965), depicts English Calvinism transformd by the American wilderness, emphasizing this as a model for radical politics. See the bibliography following Chapter II for additional sources.

Gallow's Hill, Salem, where the witches were hanged.

THE STRAINS OF EMPIRE

Chapter II
The Strains of Empire

The Witches of Salem

The Devil in 1692 assaulted the seaport town of Salem, Massachusetts, with an unparalleled fury. This little village of a few hundred people was invaded by over one hundred witches and wizards, men and women who had leagued with the Devil to make mischief, to drive little children mad, to sicken and kill livestock and people. One witch, it seemed, had killed fourteen members of a single family. The jails of nearby Boston bulged with over a hundred prisoners awaiting trial—including a four-year-old child bound for nine months in heavy iron chains. Twenty-seven people eventually came to trial: the court hanged nineteen as witches. One man, Giles Cory, suffered *peine forte et dure:* because he refused to enter a plea, heavy weights were laid on his body until he was pressed to death.

The trouble began with a craze for the occult that had swept across Massachusetts toward the end of 1691. "Conjuration with sieves and keys, and peas, and nails, and horseshoes" at first seemed harmless activities with which to pass the New England winter. But these games turned serious when grim-visaged adults tried to discover what was causing their children's "fits" and "distempers." Salem Village's minister, Samuel Parris, was the first father to react. His nine-year-old daughter, Betty, and her eleven-year-old cousin, Abigail Williams, had fallen into "odd postures" and "foolish, ridiculous speeches." The concerned father called in a local doctor who, diagnosing no physical malady, raised suspicions of the "Evil Hand"—witchcraft.

This was a reasonable supposition. Everyone knew about witchcraft. Just as those who were saved covenanted together to form a church, so too some of those who were damned convenanted with the Devil. They "wrote in his book," joining his legions for the thrill of conjurations, midnight frolics, obscure or perhaps obscene rituals, and the power to harm their neighbors. Waves of witchcraft had swept across Europe for the past two centuries as the Reformation had inspired a direct struggle between Christ and the Devil. The Bible ordered that one should not "suffer a witch to live," and faithful to this stern injunction, tens of thousands, mostly women but many men as well, had been burned or hanged to purge the world of the Evil One's followers.

Before 1692, the Devil had paid small attention to New England, except through the incursions of his New World minions, the Indians. A handful of cases, a few hangings, no burnings—such was the entire history of New England witchcraft before Betty and Abigail's malady started to spread to a larger group of seven or eight teen-aged girls in Salem Village. Under intense questioning, and responding to this attention with yet further manifestations of demonical possession, the girls named three women as the source of their sufferings. They were likely candidates. Sarah Good, daughter of a well-to-do innkeeper who had steadily tumbled down the social ladder, was in 1692 a surly, pipe-smoking beggar whose "muttering and scolding" seemed to cause cows to die. Sarah Osborne's name swirled in contention and scandal: her battle with her own sons for control of her first husband's estate; her dubious liaison with the Irish indentured servant who became her second husband. And Tituba, the slave woman who had introduced Betty and Abigail to the practices of Voodoo she had learned in the West Indies, readily and noisily told the audience of townspeople and "possessed" teen agers at the pre-trial examination what they wanted to hear. For three days, she regaled them with stories of her comportings with the Devil—and with witches Good and Osborne, of midnight sabbaths and rides through the air with Satan whom she described as "a thing all over hairy, all the face hairy, and a long nose." She had seen the Devil's "book" and although she could not read, she had counted nine names in it. Nine names! There were more witches: soon the girls, shrieking, contorting, sobbing hysterically, dredged up more names. Not all were outcasts like Good, Osborne, and Tituba; not all were from Salem. The jails groaned, the gallows trap sprang, and the rope tightened. The girls's madness, for the better part of a year, infected a whole society until the hysteria, as mysteriously as it rose, subsided. Reason returned; probing questions were asked; the jailed sent home and pardoned.

Why did it happen? The girls's part in it is easiest to explain. The life of young girls in Massachusetts Bay was dull in the best of times. In the winter it must have been torturous. Puritans did not consider children "innocent." If unbaptized at death, they went to Hell (although to its "easiest room"). They were "willful" little creatures whose animal spirits had to be "broken," "beaten down." They had to be taught piety, responsibility, and habits of work. "I am not fond," wrote Cotton Mather, foremost Puritan and one of the ministers who finally stopped the witchcraft trials, "of proposing *Play* to [children], as a Reward of any diligent Application to learn what is good; lest they should think *Diversion* to be a better and nobler Thing than *Diligence*." Mather, like other Puritan parents, preferred to "awe them with the *Eye* of God upon them . . . . *Heaven* and *Hell* I sett before them, as the Consequences of their Behaviour here." While young men, taught to pray and work, could at least look forward to the adventure of choosing careers, girls could do little more than wonder "what trade their sweethearts should be of." But marriage was a serious business and not for the very young. When the little girls, dabbling in magic with Tituba, began to act out, it is hardly surprising that their slightly older friends and relatives would join the only excitement mid-winter had to offer. (Most teen-aged girls—including most of the afflicted ones—did not live at home where parents might spoil them, but were sent to relatives' or neighbors' houses to learn their adult roles and to be evenly disciplined.) Once the adults began to fuss over their fits, how could the young resist pursuing their adventure and showing their power over the adult community, particularly over the married women who laid on endless chores and discipline. After all, even these antics would have been relatively harmless had not the adults panicked. It is their role, not the children's, that cries out for explanation. Two generations later, when children in Northhampton behaved the same way, their minister, Jonathan Edwards, read the cues differently and made their contortions, sobbing, and fits the start of a great religious revival.

What was happening in Salem and in Massachusetts Bay in 1692 that turned mischief to madness? The 1690's was an era of turmoil. The Colony had lost its charter in 1684. Then in 1689, the Glorious Revolution in England had, in effect, left the colony without any government at all until some new determination was made. When the outbreak started, Sir William Phips, newly appointed governor, was on his way to the colony with the new charter. Until he arrived nothing could be done except to pack the jails awaiting his appointment of a legitimate court. Meanwhile, the witchcraft epidemic had fed upon Salem's local conflicts as people from different political and clerical factions hurled accusations back and forth. For Salem was an unusually angry place. Town and countryside were sharply diverging. Conservative back country farmers smarted under the growth of commercial capitalism and its accompanying secular style. Sons coming of age found difficulty establishing themselves as land became increasingly scarce. The values of Puritanism itself seemed more and more in question as ministers bemoaned the "declension" from the high ideals of the colony's founders three generations before.

Witchcraft would have seemed a plausible explanation of the tensions that gripped Salem; nearly every adult must have felt at least partially seduced by the abounding worldliness, wealth, rationalism—a changing world crowding in on what had been for two generations a largely static culture. Men and women engaged year after year in lawsuits—of which Salem had an amazing number—over boundaries and legacies must have experienced great uneasiness in confronting the founder's ideals of unity in church and community. Like the witches, they were at war with their neighbors, disrupting the church and government, bursting the old molds, and experimenting with the unknown. Were they too possessed? Had they lost the old faith? How much easier it must have been to blame everything on the literal bewitchment of one's enemies rather than one's own bewitchment with the new and perhaps dubious values and goals that were transforming Puritans into Yankees.

The New England Colonies

New England experienced much the same kind and magnitude of economic growth, political maturation, and internal pressure that was common among the other colonies, but for none of the same immediate reasons. New England had a population explosion and an attendant land boom, though it received almost no immigrants. It had a long period of prosperity and economic expansion, though it produced almost nothing in the way of a staple product. It matured politically, though it evolved little that resembled political parties. And it developed strong internal tensions, though its population remained ethnically homogeneous.

In view of the coolness, and even downright hostility, of the New Englanders toward would-be immigrants into their territory, the growth of the area's population was astounding. Yankee families were normally very large, and survival rates were high.

The growth was all the more remarkable in view of the fact that, as a condition of survival, the Yankees found it necessary to buy large quantities of manufactured goods from England, but could not produce staples in enough quantity to be sold in the parent country. Despite the myth of hardy and ingenious Yankee farmers and craftsmen who spun their own cloth and fashioned their own tools, New England was almost entirely dependent upon England for clothing or at least for the material from which clothing could be made, for almost all tools beyond the most primitive, for muskets and other firearms, and for clocks, compasses, and a host of other instruments. Furthermore, the New Englanders drank enormous quantities of tea and used considerable quantities of spices, which could be legally obtained only through the East India Company in London; and despite periodically recurring waves of puritanical hostility toward the consumption of luxuries, the Yankees sought and bought the finer things of life when they were able. Accordingly, New England's balance of trade with Great Britain was invariably unfavorable.

And yet the years from about 1715 to 1755 were ones of great prosperity, for the unfavorable balance of trade with England was more than compensated for through trade. Contrary to a long-lived myth, however, New England's commercial success was not based upon hauling freight or upon the slave trade, for the colonial Yankees were never more than marginally engaged in either of these maritime activities. Rather, New England developed an economic system that was complex, sophisticated, and eminently functional. The key to the system was the great sugar plantations of the West Indies, which, though extremely profitable, were by no means self-sufficient, for it was uneconomical to waste the labor of slaves on growing food when food could be bought so cheaply. Furthermore, the sugar islands were generally deficient in timber suitable for providing the bare necessity of wood products, even including staves for making containers in which to ship their sugar.

New Englanders made a business of producing for and supplying this market and, in the doing, not only made enough profit to pay their balances in England, but to provide gainful employment for their entire population as well. This market involved three broad categories of product: those derived from farming, fishing, and lumbering. New England farmers produced fruit, beef, pork, butter, and cheese for the West Indian market, and many also raised cattle, horses, and chickens for live export. During the seventeenth century the farmers generally supplied the forest products as well, but as the eighteenth century wore on the lumber business became increasingly specialized. As to fishing, this activity expanded enormously and became highly commercialized after 1715. By the 1730's as many as 150 new fishing vessels were being built annually, and the number of persons employed in the fisheries was more than 5000. Whaling developed as an additional specialty in some places, notably Nantucket, and there it was even more valuable than fishing.

But complications soon developed. The first was the specialization and commercialization of the lumber business. In the early days, when settlements were concentrated along the seacoast and immediately to the interior from Boston and the other ports, farmers produced marketable timber from the trees they felled to clear their lands for the plow. But timber is a bulky commodity and the only practical way to transport it is by river; and south of Salem the New England coast was almost entirely devoid of streams that extended as much as five miles into the interior. New settlers in towns beyond that distance developed the practice of burning the trees they felled and making the ashes into potash and pearlash; this could easily be carried to port towns and sold there, for the merchants found a ready market for these products in England. But the change also meant that the supply of lumber from Massachusetts and Connecticut dwindled almost to the disappearing point, just at the time the demand for lumber products in the West Indies was expanding rapidly. To supply this expanding market, a commercialized lumber industry was developed after about 1720 in New Hampshire and the Province of Maine, where there were magnificent stands of white pine and where the river systems afforded convenient transportation.

The development of a specialized lumber industry, in conjunction with the growth of the fishing fleet, also created a new problem for the merchants of New England. The merchants secured their provisions for the West Indies from the local farmers by selling them goods imported from England, but the owners of fishing fleets and lumber camps and their employees consumed precious little of such commodities. The fishermen and lumber workers did, however, consume one thing abundantly, and that was rum. Accordingly, New England merchants developed the practice of selling their goods in the West Indies partly for cash or bills of exchange drawn on London, with which remittances were made in England, and partly for molasses, which was brought home and manufactured into rum, which was then used for buying more lumber and fish.

Payment of a duty on molasses imposed by the British government in 1733 would have been detrimental to New York and Pennsylvania and ruinous to New England. Accordingly, the merchants in those places did what American businessmen would do ever after when the law ran counter to the profitable conduct of business: they simply ignored the law. It was easy enough to do so, for Britain's machinery for collecting customs and preventing smuggling in America was as yet primitive, and customs officials were almost invariably amenable to bribery. Therefore, the passage of the Sugar Act of 1733 in no way altered the course or pace of New England's economic growth, except to make the entire economy rest upon illegal foundations.

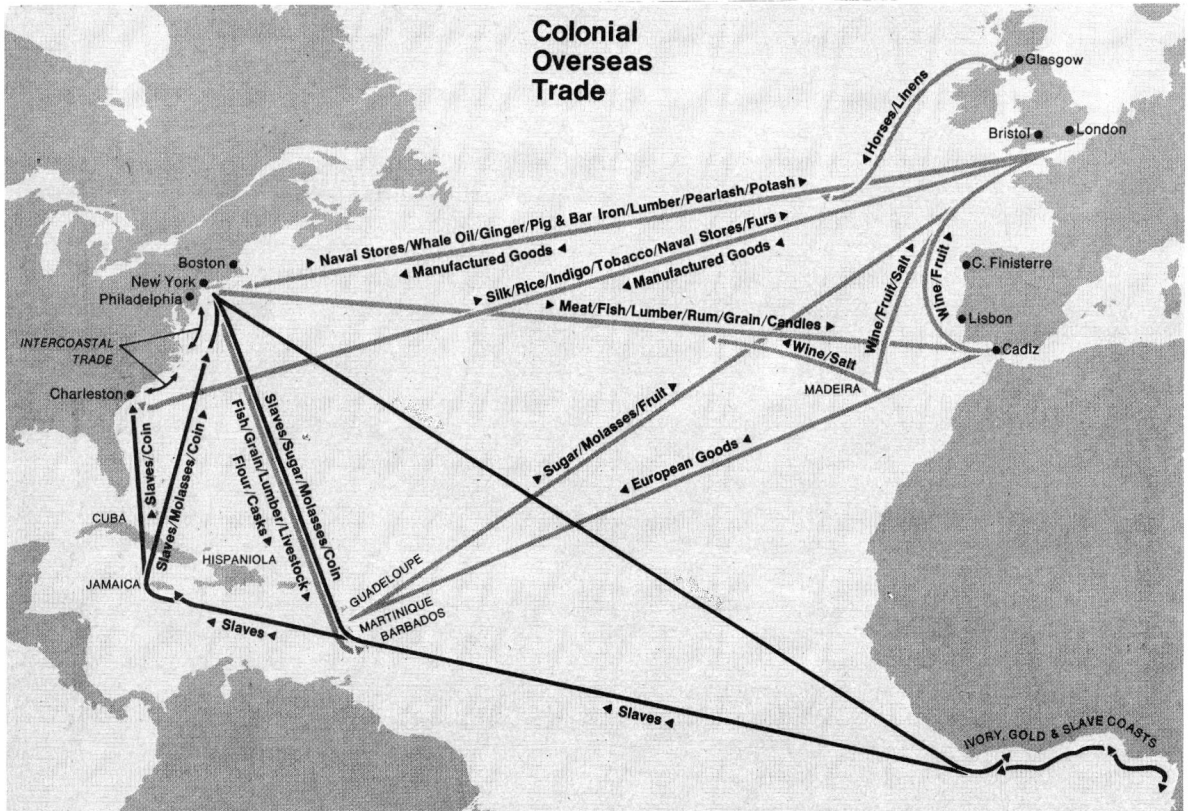

Colonial Overseas Trade

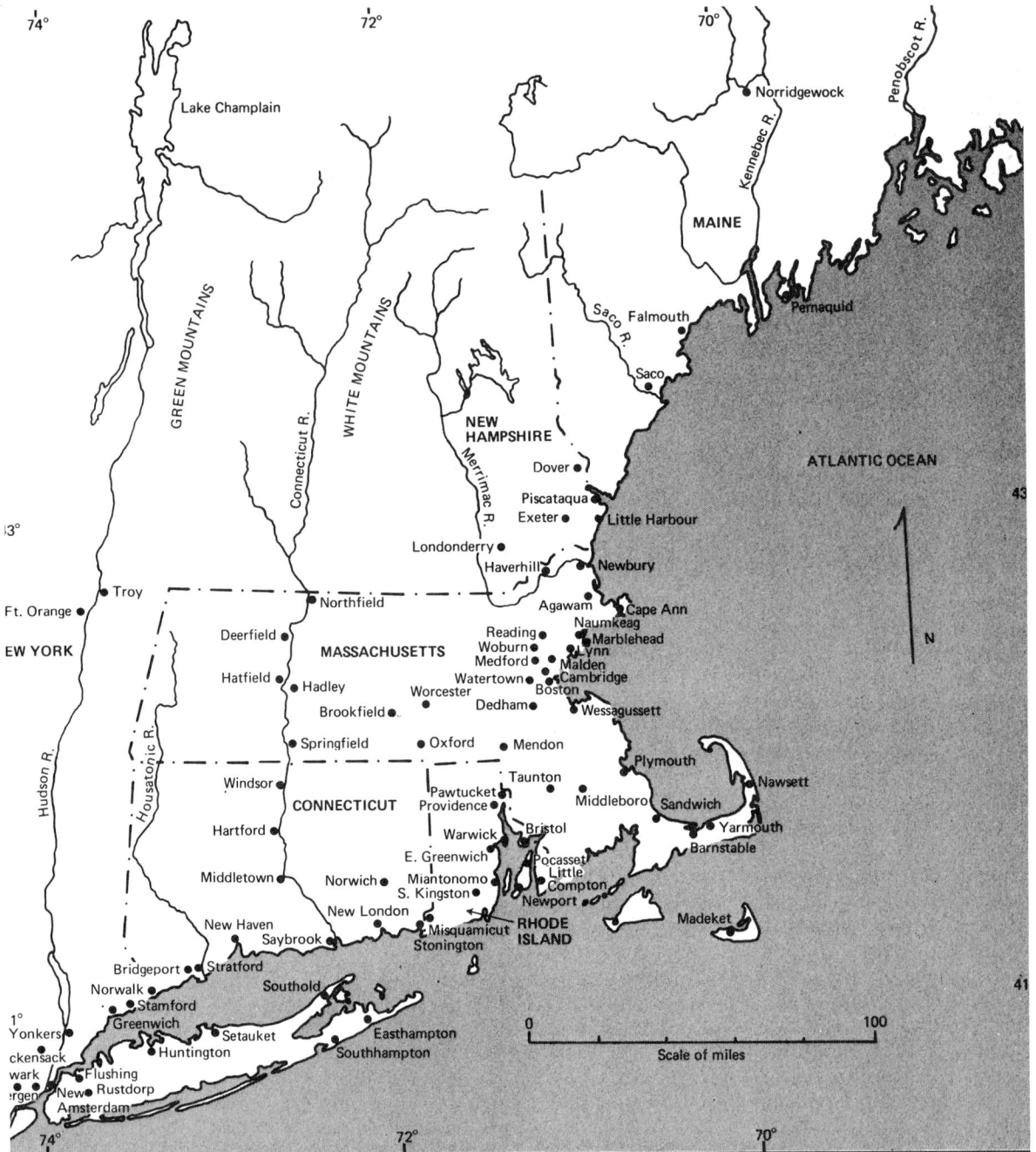

The New England Colonies

The Great Awakening and the Enlightenment

Two other developments that began in the late 1730's profoundly disrupted affairs in New England and, indeed, in the other American colonies and in Europe as well: a new outburst of moral and religious enthusiasm and a new succession of wars.

The new enthusiasm for religion and moral reform appeared almost simultaneously in continental Europe, Great Britain, and the colonies. In the 1730's, a fervent new religious movement—called Pietism on the Continent, Wesleyanism in England, and the Great Awakening in America—began to infect the ministry and to spread rapidly among parishioners everywhere. The message of the new religion was essentially the same, whatever its form: that the way to salvation did not lie in faithful performance of sacraments and rituals as the Catholics and Anglicans had always maintained, nor in "preparation for grace" by a life of good works as the Calvinists had long professed, but simply in opening one's heart to God through prayer. If one purified one's self through such a simple but total act of faith in God's goodness and mercy, God would, in His own time, cause the faithful to undergo the unspeakably profound experience of personal conversion and salvation.

Any such doctrine is potentially dangerous to any established social order, for it implicitly vests in the individual alone the capacity to judge the moral rectitude of his own behavior, to the exclusion of society and its norms. The activistic Pietism of Anglo-America was a religion of commitment, and was disruptive. It emphasized lay participation, rejected leadership by any but fellow converts, advocated the separation of converts from others and their formation into small groups, and aimed at the immediate reform and the final transformation of all of man's ways. The ultimate goal was contrary to any existing social order, and indeed contrary to the nature of man: the establishment of the Kingdom of Heaven on earth.

Various French, German, and Dutch ministers were associated with the movement, and John and Charles Wesley were the most important figures involved in England, but the most influential of all, as far as America was concerned, was George Whitefield. This restless, charismatic English preacher received some training at Oxford, persuaded the Bishop of Oxford to ordain him before he was of canonical age, and preached his first sermon. He raved and exhorted, sang and shouted, wept and thundered, and in this maiden performance, it was said, drove fifteen people stark, raving mad.

Whitefield made his first evangelical tour to America in 1738, preaching under the open air and converting hundreds in Georgia, and returned two years later to conduct a great "revival" in New England. The New England tour was the greatest triumph of Whitefield's career, though he made several successful trips to America during the next thirty years. In 1740 the populace was ready for him, if only out of restlessness and boredom: for success and prosperity, if they last long enough, breed boredom and an itch for change. New England had in fact been ready for and primed by a brief religious revival conducted five years earlier by Jonathan Edwards in Northampton, Massachusetts. Edwards had had the right message, and but for lack of Whitefield's personal magnetism and style might have set the region aflame himself. Moreover, the Congregationalist clergy of New England was, at first, also energetic in support of the crusade by Whitefield and his followers and imitators, in the understandable if mistaken belief that a new outburst of religious zeal would reinvigorate and thereby preserve a church that had lately lost much of its following.

So Whitefield infused New England, and indeed almost all the British colonies, with an enthusiasm for religious piety that matched any ever seen in America, even in the days of the Pilgrim Fathers. But the impact of the Great Awakening was not quite what was expected by the ministry that welcomed him. The number of active participants in church affairs doubled, trebled, quadrupled, and for the first time in years attracted the enthusiasm of the young: but the effect of such activity was to divide the church everywhere.

The revival movement was particularly strong in two areas: southern New England and the Scotch-Irish frontier. In Connecticut, for example, the entire community became divided into fiercely hostile camps of "Old Lights," or defenders of the existing order, and "New Lights," who embraced the new Congregationalism.

The energies of revivalism were directed equally against sin and reason, and by the early 1750's both were beginning a counterattack. Sin—or at least political corruption, high living, and gambling—flourished throughout Christendom in the fifties and sixties, the most dynamic form in America being avarice for land. As to intellect, there began in Europe around mid-century a movement known variously as rationalism, the Enlightenment, and the Age of Reason, and some of its influence reached American shores. Rationalism was essentially a fashion, however, confined to the upper classes, and one whose appeal, in the intensity and number of its devotees, ran rather behind that of clothing styles, sexual experimentation, and devil worship.

Moreover, rationalism had the wrong message for Anglo-Americans. It insisted that men think with deductive logic from abstract principles to particular actualities—a way of thinking that would, in time, help bring about some of the most profound discoveries of science—but Englishmen, and especially those in America, habitually thought the other way around. That is, they thought historically, deriving generalizations from tradition and testing them against observation and experience, and trusting no generalizations otherwise derived. And so, except for picking up some of the language (Americans talked, as Europeans did, of "the laws of nature" and of the problem of discovering those laws and bringing man-made laws into harmony with them), rationalism was far less influential in America than the antirationalism of the Great Awakening. Neither became a prime intellectual force in America. Most American intellectuals ignored both and went about their business as empiricists, more concerned with fact than with theory.

Empiricism, in its turn, produced early and important scientific studies in America. Late in the seventeenth and early in the eighteenth century the New Englanders Thomas Brattle and Thomas Robie had made a number of astronomical observations that proved useful to Newton and other Europeans, and John Banister, Cotton Mather, and Paul Dudley contributed papers on American flora and fauna that were published by the Royal Society in London. Mathematical observations of note came from John Winthrop IV, Ezra Stiles, and David Rittenhouse. Perhaps the crowning

American scientific achievements were Benjamin Franklin's experiments in electricity and his demonstration of the electrical nature of lightning.

Probably more important than these scientific discoveries were the mediums through which scientific knowledge was introduced and spread. On the more advanced level, the mediums were philosophical and scientific societies (the most important being the American Philosophical Society, established in Philadelphia in 1743) and colleges. Most colleges founded during the colonial period were founded by religious groups: Harvard (1636) and Yale (1701) were Congregationalist, as was Dartmouth, which in 1769 became a college after having been established much earlier as an Indian missionary school. William and Mary (1693) and King's College (1754, later renamed Columbia) were founded by Anglicans. Rhode Island College (1764, later Brown) was Baptist, Queen's College (1766, later Rutgers) was Dutch Reformed, and the College of New Jersey (1746, later Princeton) was Presbyterian. The only nonsectarian college founded in the colonial period, in fact, was Franklin's Academy, established in 1751, which became the University of Pennsylvania in 1791.

On the popular level, scientific and other information was spread mainly through newspapers. Elementary schools, established most zealously by Congregationalists and Presbyterians, accounted for a much higher literacy rate in America than in Europe: ninety percent or more in New England, fifty to sixty percent in Virginia, and midway between these figures among the Scotch-Irish. Before 1704 there was little for ordinary Americans to read except the Bible (which they did read, avidly), but in that year the first newspaper, the *Boston News-Letter*, was established. It was followed two decades later by *The New-England Courant*, published by James Franklin and his teen-aged brother Benjamin. But in 1725 there were still only five newspapers in the British mainland colonies. Then, along with the rapid expansion of commerce and land settlement, came a proliferation of newspapers: by 1765 there were twenty-five. Most were timorous, reluctant to face the possibility of libel suits brought by officials (despite the celebrated John Peter Zenger case of 1735, in which a New York jury held that truth was an adequate defense against a charge of libel), and the four-page weeklies were usually filled with advertisements, notices of arrivals and departures of ships, and reprints of news that had appeared months earlier in European journals. But as time went by the colonial newspapers printed more and more articles, written by their readers, in which the nature of man, society, and government was endlessly explored, and so it was largely through the newspapers that Americans formed their opinions of themselves and their world.

The Middle Colonies

Charles II had created Pennsylvania with a proprietary grant to William Penn in 1681. At first blush the intimate friendship between the dissolute Charles and the devout Penn seems highly improbable. It derived in part from the earlier friendship between Charles and Penn's father; indeed, Charles owed Penn £16,000 for services rendered by the father, an admiral, and the grant was made to pay off that debt. The friendship also derived from the fact that Penn, despite the peculiarity of his religious views, was as delightful a companion as any courtier in the kingdom: he was witty, high spirited, and an excellent swordsman. Finally, his religious convictions were actually an advantage, not a handicap, in his relationship with the king. True, he was a Quaker, and the Quakers, as the extreme individualist fringe of the Puritan movement, were almost universally despised. Wildly eccentric, governed only by their own "Inner Light," the early Quakers heard voices, appeared naked in church, preached and practiced brotherly love to the extent of refusing to take oaths or participate in war, thrived on persecution to the extent of deliberately seeking martyrdom.

Penn had earlier joined other Quakers in the purchase of the proprietary rights to New Jersey, but the inhabitants of eastern New Jersey were Congregationalist Puritans who dearly hated the Quakers, and the land in western New Jersey was poor; and so Penn sought and obtained from the king the land across the Delaware River, between the colonies of New York and Maryland. The charter required that Penn enforce the Navigation Acts, permit appeals from Pennsylvania courts to the king, submit all Pennsylvania laws to the king for approval, and provide an Anglican minister upon request from twenty colonists. In addition in an ambiguous clause the king reserved the power to impose taxes "by act of Parliament." In all other respects Penn was left free to govern his colony as he pleased.

Penn provided, in an elaborate Frame of Government (May 1682), that the governorship of the colony would be held by the proprietor or his deputy, and that legislative power would be vested in a council and an assembly, both elected by the freeholders of the colony. He proposed to earn an income from his colony by collecting quitrents from the settlers, and to attract the settlers by advertising widely the good land, free government and religious liberty available in the colony. The campaign was an immediate success: Quakers flocked to Pennsylvania from England, Holland, Germany, Wales, and Ireland. Many non-Quakers went as well, for in the wake of the reestablishment of Stuart absolutism, a new wave of refugees poured out of England; and a group of German Mennonites, driven from their homes by the Continental religious wars, also emigrated to Pennsylvania.

The Middle Colonies, of which Pennsylvania was the largest and most important, were heterogeneous from the outset: at the end of the seventeenth century Dutchmen, Quakers, New Englanders, Scots, Welshmen, Swedes, and Finns far outnumbered Church-of-England Englishmen in New York, Pennsylvania, New Jersey, and Delaware. More important, the area in general and Philadelphia in particular became the principal landing place for most of the hundreds of thousands of immigrants who moved to British America in the eighteenth century. Each successive wave of immigrants sought land for settlement in the immediate vicinity, until all the cheaply available land in the middle colonies was taken up and it became necessary to push toward the interior and toward the back country of the South. Consequently the middle colonies were stamped indelibly as America's melting pot of diverse ethnic groups.

From the outset William Penn had encouraged immigration into his colony by providing a liberal land system and a considerable measure of political and religious freedom, and that general policy was modified only gradually. Originally, Penn granted 200 acres of land to every head of a family who settled in the colony, with a bonus of 50 more acres for each servant the settler brought, and charged nothing but a modest annual quitrent. Settlers could also buy a 5000-acre tract for a cash sum of £100 and a small quitrent. As to government, the colony operated under a liberal Charter of Privileges, established by Penn in 1701 and providing for a great deal of local participation.

German immigrants managed to preserve their language and culture. Many, if not most, came as indentured servants, paying for their passage by binding themselves to serve as laborers for five to ten (normally seven) years before becoming freemen and ordinary settlers. Then, migrating to the back country, they settled in a broad area extending twenty to a hundred miles west of the Delaware River. They picked the choicest lands, especially those in the limestone valleys, cleared their farms slowly but thoroughly, and built solid buildings upon them. Because of the care with which they proceeded, by the time they were able to produce for market they were able to bring in regular and bountiful harvests. Their principal crop, as long as they remained in the middle colonies, was wheat, and thus wheat became the sec-

ESTIMATED POPULATION OF AMERICAN COLONIES:
1630 TO 1750

	1630	1650	1670	1690	1730	1750
White						
New England	1,796	22,452	51,521	86,011	211,233	349,029
Middle Colonies	340	3,786	6,664	32,369	135,298	275,723
Southern Colonies	2,450	22,530	49,215	75,263	191,893	309,588
Black						
New England	0	380	375	950	6,118	10,982
Middle Colonies	10	515	790	2,472	11,683	20,736
Southern Colonies	50	705	3,370	13,307	73,220	204,702
Total White	4,586	48,768	107,400	193,643	538,424	934,340
Total Black	60	1,600	4,535	16,729	91,021	236,420

ond great staple (or third, if New England fish be counted as such) to be produced in British North America.

The Germans continued to arrive at a steady rate, about 2000 a year, from 1717 until about 1750. By the 1730's they were beginning to overflow the middle colonies, though they continued to arrive in Philadelphia. Thenceforth, they proceeded to the Pennsylvania back country and headed south, settling the Cumberland Valley in Pennsylvania and Maryland and much of the Shenandoah Valley of Virginia before their momentum was exhausted.

By and large, wherever they went the Germans kept to themselves, retaining their own ways and making no effort to become involved in the political or social life of the colonies they inhabited. Indeed, they tended to cluster in groups that had little to do even with one another, for they represented a wide variety of religious sects—Dutch Reformed Mennonite, Dunker, Moravian Brethren, Schwenkfelder, and even Roman Catholic—and established their communities accordingly.

Considerably more numerous and far more disruptive were the Ulster Scots. The total number of Scotch-Irish immigrants was around 250,000. The first wave headed for New England, where the Ulstermen understandably but mistakenly thought that they would be welcome. The Yankees were strong Calvinists, and so were the Ulstermen, but the congregation-based church polity of New England and the presbytery of the Scotch-Irish were incompatible. Besides, the New Englanders were exclusive almost by instinct, welcoming no foreigners. What was more, Boston and its vicinity had no excess land and no shortage of labor; the inhabitants feared that immigrants would become just so many paupers to feed from the resources of their stingy land; and New Englanders generally regarded the Ulstermen as illiterate, slovenly, and filthy. Thus a few thousand immigrants of the first wave landed in Boston and, with difficulty, founded settlements around Worcester and along the Merrimack Valley of New Hampshire, but subsequent boatloads were greeted at the docks by irate mobs who refused to let them land.

The remainder of the first wave of Ulstermen and the overwhelming majority of those in the subsequent waves headed for Philadelphia, along with the Germans. The Scotch-Irish also followed the same routes to the interior, but there the resemblance between them and the Germans ends. For reasons of preference as well as circumstance, the two groups of immigrants did not mix. The pattern of settlement, all the way down through the Virginia valley, was that the German first-comers farmed staples on the rich bottom lands and the Ulstermen who came later raised cattle and corn on the hillsides and poorer lands. Moreover, whereas almost all the Germans could be expected to be industrious, frugal, orderly, and peaceful, many of the Scotch-Irish tended to work by fits and starts, to drink prodigiously, to be reckless, quick-tempered, impetuous, and likely to pick up stakes and move for no apparent reason. Having a zeal for education deriving from their Presbyterianism and the ferocity with which they embraced it, the Scotch-Irish founded schools and colleges on a scale that no other group of Americans ever approached. They loved freedom, by which they meant the right to be left alone to be themselves, and were quick to fight for it. They were in constant friction with the Indians, and had no compunctions about slaughtering them or involving colonial authorities in wars with them. They became avid politicians, skillful and disputatious, and regularly demanded a voice in the law-making process when the law affected their way of life, but they totally disregarded the law when it did not suit them. By the late 1730's Ulstermen were filling the Shenandoah Valley of Virginia; by the late 1740's they were spilling out over the Piedmont Plateau of southern Virginia and central North Carolina; and a decade later they were invading the uplands of South Carolina.

In the context of an enormous population growth—from around 75,000 in 1715 to 400,000 by the 1750's—the economic and political life of the middle colonies developed rapidly. The economy grew even faster than the population and, as had been the way in New England and the tobacco colonies, proceeded along two lines: development of small-scale production of tools and other equipment for the expanding population, and development of production for trade in international markets.

In one important respect, which would long distinguish them from the colonies to the north and south, the middle colonies differed in the business of supplying newcomers. Elsewhere, by far the biggest portion of the business was land-jobbing, but in the four middle colonies, for different reasons in each, the population at large could not participate in this lucrative enterprise. In New York the governors and assemblies continued the policy, originated by the Dutch, of granting land only in huge tracts—and only to themselves and their friends and relations. The great "manor lords" who received the grants were interested in leasing the lands but not in selling them. In Pennsylvania and Delaware the land belonged original-

80° 78° 76° 74°

Lake Ontario

La Barre

Ft. Stanwix

Ft. Edward

Ft. Oswego

N

Ft. Niagara

Onondaga

Ft. Williams

Mohawk R.

Ft. Clinton

Ft. Herkimer

Schenectady

Troy

Ft. Orange

Lake Erie

NEW YORK

MASS

42°

42°

Genesee R.

CONN

Esopus

Allegheny R.

Poughkeepsie

New Paltz

Hudson R.

Newburgh

PENNSYLVANIA

Peekskill

Delaware R.

Tappan

Huntington

Hackensack

Hoboken

New York

Ft. Augusta

Newark

Ft. Granville

Easton

Elizabethtown

Flushing

Bethlehem

Perth Amboy

New Utrecht

New Brunswick

North Wales

Princeton

40°

Ft. Duquesne

Ft. Harris

Susquehanna R.

Ephrata

Germantown

Trenton

Wrightstown

Burlington

Ft. Ligonier

Haverford

Philadelphia

Chester

Camden

40°

Ft. Loudoun

Wilmington

New Castle

NEW JERSEY

Ft. Cumberland

Ft. Frederick

MARYLAND

Salem

Martinsburg

Frederick

Winchester

Baltimore

Potomac R.

Providence

DELAWARE

ATLANTIC OCEAN

Strasburg

Shenandoah R.

Hamburg

Zwaanendael

VIRGINIA

1000

0

Scale of miles

Fredericksburg

St. Mary's

38°

38°

Staunton

Charlottesville

80° 78° 76° 74°

The Middle Colonies

ly to the Penn family as proprietors, and all proceeds from sales and rentals went to them. In New Jersey, too, the land belonged to small groups of proprietors, and though the system of land disposition was always complex the profits from land sales went to these small groups.

In other ways, however, the business of supplying newcomers was even more important in the middle colonies than it was elsewhere. For one thing, the supply of craftsmen, the abundance of raw materials, and the insatiable market combined to breed a thriving industry in farm implements, other hardware, clocks, locks, guns, flints, glass, stoneware, paper, nails, and woodwork. For another, the port of Philadelphia burgeoned: by the mid-1730's several hundred vessels were entering and clearing the port every year. At first most of these vessels belonged to others, but then Philadelphians began to acquire their own ships, and with this development came another, the establishment of a shipbuilding industry and such ancillary activities as importing and processing naval stores and manufacturing ropes, anchors, and sails.

Also by the 1730's, Philadelphia (and, to a lesser extent, New York) had begun to emerge as a major export and import center. Some of the exports were beef and pork which, along with the livestock, were produced mainly by the Scotch-Irish. These products found ready markets on the sugar plantations of the West Indies. More important, however, were wheat and flour, produced by the industrious Germans and the scores of mills that sprung up along the Delaware and Schuylkill rivers. Under the Navigation Acts colonial wheat and flour were not confined to the English market. Thus some went to the West Indies and much to the Continent, where Philadelphia merchants could acquire bills of exchange and goods for trade in England. This made Philadelphia a principal importing center for English manufactures in North America.

By mid-century, Philadelphia was fast becoming America's richest and largest city. Indeed, in another decade or two it would be the second largest city and second busiest port in the entire English-speaking world. New York port also thrived, though it developed much more slowly. Because of the colony's restrictive immigration and land policies, New York lacked Philadelphia's

business of transporting and supplying newcomers, and it also had a smaller productive base for its international trade. New York did have the Iroquois Indians in its interior, and they trapped some furs themselves and also served as middlemen between the Albany traders and many of the western Indians, who trapped furs in enormous quantities and were eager to sell them. The fur trade was lucrative, and thus for a time New York's prosperity matched that of Philadelphia, despite the slower growth of its population.

Politically, too, Pennsylvania matured more rapidly than the other middle colonies. The tide of immigration had made the Quakers a minority in the colony, albeit a wealthy and powerful one, and Quakers had lost favor with the proprietors when the sons of William Penn left the Society of Friends for the Church of England. To promote and protect their interests in the face of these reversals, the Quakers gathered allies and formed a political faction called variously the Quaker party and the Anti-Proprietary party. Because of their wealth and influence they were normally able to control the elections to the Assembly from Philadelphia and its environs and, through an alliance with the pacifist sects among the Germans in surrounding counties, were usually able to dominate the Assembly. Arrayed against them in the Proprietary party were the long-time representatives of the Penns, James Logan and his friends, together with the Scotch-Irish (who were probably America's least pacifistic people), most frontiersmen, and a considerable number of the non-pacific Germans.

In sharp contrast to the popularly based politics of Pennsylvania, politics in New York were aristocratic. This is not to say that the colony lacked numerous and vociferous lower elements, fighting one another as well as their "betters" and clamoring for a voice in government: but the lower orders largely canceled one another out in antipathies between Scotch-Irish and New Englanders and older Yorkers, between Presbyterians and Congregationalists and Dutch Calvinists, between tenant farmers and squatters and the plain folk of the city. Moreover, such of these inhabitants as could vote were normally easy for the landed aristocrats to manage, for they voted orally, in public and were thus amenable to bribery and pressure when mere deference failed to secure their vote.

The Southern Colonies

In time, more Scotch-Irish settled in the Southern colonies than anywhere else, but their impact there was considerably less than that of

another, involuntary immigrant group, the blacks. Negro slavery had existed in the colonies of Spain and Portugal since the early sixteenth century, and for an even longer time in Africa, but it was not until the eighteenth century that it became entrenched on a large scale in British North America.

Through most of the seventeenth century slavery was not of major significance on the American mainland. There was a perpetual shortage of labor in the colonies, but as long as the farm unit remained small and was worked by the owner alongside his family and such indentured servants as he could afford, servants who spoke English were preferred to others. Accordingly, the black population in the English colonies grew very slowly: the first blacks in the English colonies had arrived in Virginia in 1619, but in 1641 there were only about 250 in the colony, and as late as 1680 there were still no more than 3000 in Virginia and there were less than 7000 in all the mainland colonies combined.

But then, in the 1680's and the following decades a series of developments combined to establish slavery firmly, though still on a modest scale, in the tobacco-growing colonies of Virginia and Maryland. One was a change in the laws of both colonies that finally made it legal and even easy to buy land in large tracts. Another was that, despite a rapid increase in production, tobacco prices remained fairly high from about 1684 to about 1703. In these circumstances small farm units began to be replaced by sizable plantations, where workers could be employed efficiently in gangs, and on which the intimate relationship between master and servant, and with it the need for the English language, was dissolved. At just this time, the Royal Africa Company and other groups of English merchants were beginning to dominate the African slave trade and were looking for markets. Moreover, competition between slave traders of several nations temporarily reduced the profits of supplying blacks for West Indian sugar plantations, so the English were willing to sell slaves in Virginia and Maryland at bargain prices.

And thus, using colonial law (mainly as enacted in the 1660's) rather than English law as their legal justification, Virginia and Maryland imported thousands of African slaves and laid the foundation for the plantation system of Southern agriculture. By 1710 there were well over 30,000 slaves in the two colonies, whose total population was about 120,000. Most of the blacks came from west Africa, a settled area in which agriculture, mining, and handicraft were well established, and they adapted easily to work on American farms and plantations. They soon lost their native languages and many other aspects of their original culture, taking readily to European ways, and had it not

been for their legal enslavement, they might have merged into the polyglot colonial society along with the Germans, the Ulstermen, and other non-English groups. Slavery, however, made a crucial difference, and the blacks, no matter how talented and capable as individuals, were denied any opportunity for social advancement.

Few whites protested the use of slaves. Quaker meetings in and around Philadelphia regularly denounced slavery, but many Quakers themselves acquired slaves. A pamphlet denouncing slavery, Samuel Sewall's *The Selling of Joseph*, was published in Boston in 1701, but the renowned Massachusetts minister and theologian Cotton Mather expressed a more common attitude when he piously informed a group of blacks that slavery was "what God will have to be the thing appointed for you."

Even so, the expansion of slavery in the tobacco colonies slowed and almost stopped early in the eighteenth century, and was not renewed until the mid-1730's. One reason was that tobacco started on another long cycle of depressed prices, with the result that the spread of tobacco plantations was temporarily arrested.

But while slavery was waning, or at least not expanding, in the tobacco colonies, it was rapidly spreading in another quarter, on the rice plantations of South Carolina (and, a little later, of Georgia). Slavery was a cardinal part of life in South Carolina almost as soon as the colony passed beyond its primitive frontier stage, for many of the early settlers were immigrants from Barbados, where slavery had long been firmly established, and they brought their slaves with them. Of the roughly 3900 inhabitants of the colony in 1690, about 1500 were slaves. Then, in the early decades of the eighteenth century the South Carolinians began large-scale rice cultivation in the coastal swamps, and with a phenomenal increase in rice production, slavery increased apace. South Carolina exported 394,000 pounds of rice in 1700, 1,600,000 pounds in 1710, 6,400,000 in 1720, 18,700,000 in 1730, and 43,000,000 in 1740; in the same years the number of slaves in the colony were 2,400, 4,100, 12,000, 20,000, and 30,000. From 1720 onward, slaves outnumbered whites about two to one. Slavery in South Carolina had different effects on slave and master than it had in the tobacco colonies. To the extent that any enslavement can be called humane, slavery in the tobacco colonies was far more nearly humane than it was in South Carolina, in the same sense that life in one prison can be more nearly tolerable than in another. Planters in Virginia and Maryland, having developed slavery only after their in-

Ft. Cumberland
Ft. Frederick
Martinsburg
Baltimore
Frederick
Providence
Winchester
MARYLAND
DELAWARE
Zwaanendael
Strasburg
Hamburg
Fredericksburg
St. Mary's
Staunton
Charlottesville
VIRGINIA
Richmond
Williamsburg
Henrico
Jamestown
Ft. Chiswell
Ft. Christanna
Norfolk
Halifax
NORTH CAROLINA
Ft. Dobbs
Ft. Tuscaroras
Bath
Cross Creek
New Berne
Wilmington
Brunswick
SOUTH CAROLINA
Georgetown
Ft. Augusta
Ft. Moore
Ft. Edisto
N
Charles Town
Beaufort
GEORGIA
Port Royal
Savannah
Ft. King George
New Inverness
Frederica
0
150
Scale of miles

THE SOUTHERN COLONIES

stitutions had become pretty well established, and having retained their pretentions to being seventeenth-century gentlemen with some sense of noblesse oblige, never became quite as callous about their human chattel as did the South Carolinians, whose very origins on the sugar plantations of the West Indies inured them to feelings on the subject.

These attitudes were reinforced by differences in the physical conditions of life on the two kinds of plantation. On a tobacco plantation the atmosphere was generally healthy and the labor to be done, though fussy and tedious, was not hard, much of it within the capacity of women and children; all of which meant that it was both possible and profitable for a plantation owner to encourage breeding and some semblance of family life among his slaves. Furthermore, since tobacco was a commodity that fluctuated in price, often falling below the margin of profit, it was not economical to buy everything the slaves required for their sustenance. Accordingly, slaves were trained as craftsmen, grew much of their own food, and otherwise formed a more or less self-sufficient community. Overall, the system was not drastically different from the village-and-manor land system that prevailed in most of England and continental Europe, except for two important facts of slave life. One was that the European peasant's prospects for bettering his lot were merely almost hopeless, while those of most black American slaves were absolutely so. The other fact was that black men could not act as the head of the household or as its protector, and so the family unit normally derived its identity from the woman. This had a devastating effect upon black men.

Relative to the slaves on rice plantations, those in Virginia and Maryland lived in a veritable paradise. No gentle village-and-manor system developed in South Carolina; rice plantations, like sugar plantations, were extremely profitable but not self-sufficient, all energies being devoted to cultivating the cash crop. Moreover, rice was grown in the coastal swamps, where the climate was insufferably hot and humid and the air teemed with malaria and other disease. The work was back breaking, possible only for strong young adult males, and even these normally died from overwork and disease within five to seven years. For the few slaves, mainly women and children, who lived in or near the master's house and worked as menial servants, life was tolerable and could even be pleasant, but for the field hands it was a living hell. Consequently, whereas insurrection and flights for freedom were rare in the tobacco colonies, they were extremely common in South

Carolina. Many a Carolina slave escaped from his master and found refuge among the Creek and Seminole Indians to the south, despite a law permitting any white to shoot on sight a slave who left his plantation without a written pass from his owner. Isolated uprisings were not uncommon, and in 1739 slaves on several plantations rose in what was known as the Cato Rebellion, which was not put down until twenty-one whites and forty-four blacks had been killed and scores more of both races had been wounded.

The two other Southern colonies resembled neither South Carolina nor the tobacco colonies. North Carolina, politically separate from South Carolina since 1691, rapidly became even more separate socially and economically. Plantation slavery was extremely slow to take root in North Carolina, for the colony was covered with thick pine forests, was too dry to permit rice cultivation, and lacked the access to the sea that was necessary to the growth of tobacco plantations. Thus, until well into the century North Carolina's principal products were the naval stores that could be extracted from the pines: tar, pitch, rosin, turpentine, and masts and spars. After 1705, the production of all these commodities was subsidized by the British government.

As to Georgia, the last British colony to be established in America, development was extremely slow until the 1760's. James Oglethorpe, a Tory member of Parliament, received a royal charter to plant the colony in 1732. He conceived of it as a refuge for paupers and insolvent debtors, and as a laboratory for experiments in social and religious reform; but for the first twenty years of its existence the colony served mainly as a buffer between South Carolina and the hostile Indians to the immediate south and the Spanish colony further south in Florida. Thereafter, Georgia began to develop on a more permanent basis, largely through the establishment of a rice plantation system much like that of South Carolina.

In the early 1730's there began a boom in Virginia of unprecedented magnitude and duration, and before the boom had run its course the entire area from Pennsylvania to South Carolina had been transformed.

Actually there were two complementary booms taking place at the same time, running parallel courses, and sometimes vitally interacting; but they were different nonetheless. The first boom was in tobacco. Tobacco prices snapped back from the catastrophic levels that had long prevailed, and despite a great increase in production that soon followed, prices remained high enough to make tobacco planting profitable for most of the next twenty-nine years. The plantation system spread rapidly, and slavery spread with it: as a result of an enormous volume of importations as well as through natural increase, the number of slaves in Virginia doubled to 60,000 in 1740, passed 100,000 in 1750, and reached 140,000 in 1760.

Along the way, the effect of the second boom, that in land, intersected the first. The Penn family raised the prices and rents on Pennsylvania lands in the 1730's, driving Scotch-Irish and German immigrants to the west and south. The immigrants continued to arrive in droves, and as they poured down the great valley of Virginia into the South, North Carolina and Virginia promised freedom of worship for Presbyterians, and Virginia and Maryland liberalized their land policies. These policies stimulated an enormous boom in land sales, and Virginia in particular moved to capitalize on it. Planters and other influential inhabitants of the old tidewater settlements began to realize that there was as much money to be made from selling land as from selling tobacco, and perhaps a great deal more. The members of the House of Burgesses, in collaboration with the governor and his council, began to grant large blocks of interior lands to themselves: sometimes for nominal sums, sometimes for nothing, sometimes in exchange for their services in attracting new settlers to the colony.

In mid-century the Southern colonies, like the middle colonies, were thriving, and their growth and prosperity were largely a function of the arrival, on a grand scale, of newcomers of non-English stock. For a variety of reasons, however, the immigrants (or rather the white immigrants) had much less of an effect on the social and political life of the South.

The socio-political system that was evolved in Virginia translated conservative ideals into effective practice. That is, the system was designed to insure the primacy of a plantation gentry of English stock and of the middling sort, who were fending against the lower orders of men—slaves, Scotch-Irish and German backwoodsmen, and small farmers—on the one hand and a small group of extremely wealthy planters, large-scale speculators, great landowners, and royal officials on the other. Underlying the system was an attitude of deference on the part of the lowly, black or white, that was instilled from birth, tempered by the planters' generosity, and, in the rare instances when someone forgot his place, preserved by such severe punishments as branding with hot irons and public lashing with a cat-o'-nine-tails. To be sure, the newly arrived Scotch-Irish were unlikely to be kept in line even by such extreme means as these, but fortunately for the internal peace of Virginia they were, until the 1760's, separated from eastern Virginia by the Blue Ridge Mountains.

The social preeminence of what Virginians chose to style their gentry was reinforced by the rules governing the game of politics. Institutionalized power was concentrated into three overlapping organizations: the vestrymen (lay administrators) of the local parishes of the established Church of England, the justices of the peace who constituted the county courts, and the popular branch or lower house of the colonial legislative assembly, the House of Burgesses. The electorate, those who chose the rulers on all levels, consisted of free white adult males, members of the Church of England, who owned at least twenty-five acres of improved land and a house (or fifty acres of unimproved land, or a town lot) in the county in which they voted or stood for office. Most everyone who was not a tenant or a slave could vote, which is to say, choose the best from among those of their betters who stood for public office. In these circumstances—under which every voter was given to understand that all candidates would protect the electorate from the avaricious and ambitious hands of wealthy men and would-be tyrants—the voters invariably opted for members of the middling planter "class."

America in 1750

By the middle of the eighteenth century there were thirteen contiguous British colonies on the North American mainland, extending from Massachusetts' province of Maine to James Oglethorpe's Georgia, and containing well over a million inhabitants. Rhode Island and Connecticut were corporate colonies, existing by virtue of charters that vested the power of government in the body of freemen. William Penn's Pennsylvania and Delaware, and Calvert's Maryland were proprietary colonies, whose administration had fallen to the heirs of the original proprietors. The proprietors had the original title to all the land, and nominally the power of government, though as a result of various charters and agreements they actually served as or appointed only the executive branch; the legislative power resided in the inhabitants. In 1752, when Oglethorpe's proprietorship was terminated, Georgia became a royal colony, like the seven other. In the royal colonies the executive branch, consisting of a governor and a council that sometimes also functioned as an upper house of the legislature, was appointed by the king, as were some of the colonial judges.

The empire was held together by both formal and informal ties. Formally and legally the Board of Trade, a fifteen-member agency of the Crown, exercised general supervisory power over the entire overseas empire. It appointed most royal officials for the colonies and reviewed all legislation passed by the colonial assemblies; of about 8500 colonial laws passed in the entire period prior to 1776, all were at least nominally reviewed and 469 were disallowed. In addition, the board had established vice-admiralty courts in five mainland colonies, with jurisdiction over the acts of Parliament and the various orders concerning trade, other maritime activity, and the conservation of timber for the Royal Navy. Appeals from these courts went to the High Court of Admiralty in London until 1748, after which time the Admiralty court shared jurisdiction with the Board of Trade. Appeals from colonial courts on all other matters went to the king's Privy Council, some of whose members also sat on the Board of Trade; all told, something like 1500 court decisions were appealed prior to 1776. This jerry-built structure, cumbersome enough in theory, was doubly so in practice, for officials were generally slipshod, inefficient, and negligent in executing their duties. That left the royal governors as the principal instruments of the royal will in the colonies, but since the governors normally received their salaries from the local legislatures they were prone to identify themselves less with the Crown than with the richer and more powerful colonials.

The informal adhesives of the empire were somewhat stronger than the formal. The colonies and the mother country had common enemies, France and Spain, and that alone was enough to hold the empire together. Moreover, they were also bound by ties of economic interest: Britain and the colonies alike profited from the maintenance of a vast, enclosed common market, and when colonials wanted or needed to trade outside the empire, lax law enforcement usually made it possible to do so. Beyond such tangible considerations were common language, customs, constitutional and legal institutions, and above all pride in a heritage of freedom, of sharing the celebrated "rights of Englishmen."

Even so, Americans were well on their way to becoming a new breed of man. A number of their characteristics were so striking as to impress almost every European who encountered and commented upon them. Most British Americans, for example, were energetic or at least busy; or rather, enough of them were that way to give the impression that busyness was a central attribute of the American life style. Having vast quantities of good unoccupied land at their disposal and having accepted population explosion as a social norm, they had become eager and avaricious landjobbers: the fever for land speculation, for seizing the main chance and growing wealthy through big land deals, reached epidemic proportions in British America. For somewhat related reasons, Americans tended to be ambitious, optimistic, presumptuous, and—compared to Europeans and despite having developed their own form of social deference—egalitarian. Europeans were inclined to view them as bumpkins for those reasons and because all but a very few lacked the finer social graces; but they were in fact quite cosmopolitan, for their daily existence and their very survival depended upon keeping abreast of events all over the Atlantic world. So, at least, they believed. And, having a higher literacy rate than perhaps any nation of Europe, they read newspapers and exchanged letters with almost astonishing avidity.

Their fear of being isolated from the "real world" of Europe led them to slavish imitation of the fads and styles in clothing, architecture, and entertainment emanating from London, and led them to extreme or exaggerated attitudes and utterances. The same fear, the opposite side of the coin from their aggressive self-confidence, set up tensions within them that demanded release in one form or another. They drank coffee and tea incessantly, but the most common form of release, among the men, was alcohol: American men consumed prodigious quantities of wine and rum, and many of them drank whiskey, gin, and beer as well. As to the women, those of Nantucket Island in Massachusetts were addicted to opium, and it is entirely possible that opium and other drugs were in common use among women elsewhere, for most American women lived in nearly continuous pain, thanks to prolific childbearing without medical care. It is also entirely likely that the black slaves knew (as their masters apparently did not) the anesthetizing joy of smoking hemp, for Africans had cultivated and used marijuana and hashish for ten centuries and more, and hemp was fairly widely grown in the South, for use in rope making.

But the most important generalization applicable to these early Americans is that they defied generalization, for heterogeneity, pluralism, was their very essence. Americans were pluralistic in other than their ethnic and religious backgrounds. For example, multiple forms of social stratification existed in the colonies. Each local community—the town in New England, the manor in New York, the county or parish elsewhere—had its own hierarchy, which sometimes did and sometimes did not correspond to the gradations of power and status in the colony as a whole. The most common determinants of social rank were wealth, occupation, and ethnic stock, but the most important determinant involved connections and sponsors, especially among officials or families of high station in England.

An equally vital dimension of American society was its division along lines that later came to be called Hamiltonian and Jeffersonian, though the divisions were well rooted before either of these Founding Fathers was born. This was a division between town dwellers and country dwellers, between merchants and farmers, between international and outport merchants, between planters who were entirely dependent on commerce and those whose plantation units were largely self-

sufficient as well as commercial. Most importantly, this was a difference in attitude between those who accepted the expansive and corrupt commercialism of the eighteenth century and those who rejected it. This line of division cut across all others and defies precise definition by place and group.

One general observation about colonial economic life should be made. There was in America an abundance of natural wealth and an accompanying chronic shortage of labor and money. Together, these conditions had crucial and enduring social consequences in three areas. One was the institution of chattel slavery or, more specifically, black slavery. A second was the so-called "work ethos," the belief among white Americans that work was the justification for a man's existence, the route to salvation, and the source of all legitimate wealth and status. A third was the ideal of the all-purpose man. This institution and these attitudes were perhaps as important in shaping future American life as the body of legal and constitutional institutions that the colonists inherited from England.

Women and the Family

Colonists brought to America their conceptions about the proper relationship between man and woman. According to the Puritan leader John Winthrop, a woman's husband "is her lord, and she is subject to him, yet in a way of liberty, not of bondage: and a true wife accounts her subjection her honor and freedom." To the Puritans, this logic did not seem peculiar or anomalous. They could reconcile the apparent opposites of total subjugation and complete freedom, for their religion, particularly the doctrine of predestination, taught that man stood in a similar relationship to God. English common law also placed the woman in a subordinate role, denying a wife any separate legal identity from her husband. Under the common law, married couples could not enter into a contract with each other, for such an action presupposed the wife's distinct identity.

If free white women in colonial America held a subordinate status in the common law, female indentured servants and slaves were doubly oppressed. Indentured women were seldom allowed to marry until their servitude was fulfilled, and most masters reserved the right to lengthen the period of service if the woman became pregnant. Pregnancy supposedly reduced her capacity to work, but in most cases the extension far exceeded

the time missed due to childbirth. A poem of the early eighteenth century contains the story of a fictitious indentured servant who, after recalling her happier days and more attractive appearance in England, laments her fate in the New World:

> In weeding Corn or feeding Swine,
> I spend my melancholy Time,
> Kidnap'd and Fool'd, I thither fled,
> And to my cost already find,
> Worse Plagues than those I left behind.

Slave women lacked even the minimal rights and promise of eventual freedom which masters accorded to indentured females. Slaveholders frequently encouraged slaves to have children, who then became the property of the master. Most colonies forbade interracial fornication, but enough black women bore mulatto children to make the status of these offspring a pressing legal question. Unlike in most Latin American countries, where masters frequently acknowledged their progeny and mulatoes became a free class, in English America a slave mother's status determined that of her children.

Although the English legal tradition assigned women an inferior place, New World practice apparently raised their status considerably. Wills reveal that wives did own property, and women occasionally assumed legal responsibility in certain kinds of businesses. Colonial records show that couples occasionally contracted with each other, both before or after marriage, regarding the future disposition of their property. Such a procedure diverged from contemporary English law.

In fact, in their daily lives, married white women probably felt a good measure of equality and self-esteem because their work was every bit as vital to their families' solvency and survival as their husbands'. The colonial wife did not simply make life comfortable for her family, she made it possible. Widowers and widows rapidly remarried, less to have company in old age than to continue the essential division of labor upon which both depended. The woman made clothes, soap, candles, cloth; she milked cows and tended the garden; in busy seasons she worked beside her husband in the fields. Unlike her twentieth-century counterpart, the colonial woman was not primarily a consumer; she was a producer. And few women clamored for equality. If a remote court told her she was unequal, her daily experience contradicted the law.

In fact, the "liberated" woman of the day was not the one who worked equally alongside her husband, but the one who could enjoy the more pampered life of the colonial aristocrat. The woman without calluses on her hands and without the swollen legs from a lifetime of standing and bending was the envy of most of her sex. Colonial women viewed farm work and its laborious duties, not their husbands or the courts, as their most constant oppressors. Although their economic importance brought a sense of self-esteem perhaps absent in the lives of modern housewives, many women would have welcomed an escape from the drudgery of economic equality.

In a land where labor was scarce, children also contributed to the economic viability of the family. Unlike their modern counterparts, they were generally an asset to family income rather than a drain on it. Colonial Americans had no concept of "adolescence," and they expected children to dress and act like little adults after the age of seven or eight. But if familial responsibilities came early, the opportunities of a wilderness society also provoked tensions within the family, frequently pulling children away from home.

The apparent disruption of family life in the New World was a frequent source of complaint and worry. The president of King's College, Samuel Johnson, bemoaned that

it is obvious that our youth are apace running headlong into all sorts of debauchery and uncontrolled indulgences, which I doubt not is . . . chiefly owing to the fond indulgence of their parents.

Shortly after founding, every colony passed laws demanding obedience from children; the potential punishment for disobedience in Massachusetts and Connecticut was nothing less than death. Records do not reveal that any court ever resorted to such extreme punishment. In fact, by permitting a child to present a case in court, such laws guarded against parental abuse at the same time that they sought to curb recalcitrant children. Colonial law reflected the belief that the community, acting through the courts, had an interest in maintaining order within individual families.

In response to fears that the family no longer furnished proper guidance, a few communities also assumed the burden of providing formal education. A famous Massachusetts statute of 1642, which anticipated the nineteenth-century idea of institutionalized education for all members of society, sought to counteract the drift toward social disintegration. And as society became more secular, so did education; the inculcation of civic virtue and good citizenship took priority over religious instruction. History became important in a child's studies because, as Benjamin Franklin once explained,

history will . . . give occasion to expatiate on the advantage of civil orders and constitutions; how men and their properties are protected by joining in societies and establishing government . . . Thus may the first principles of sound politics be fixed in the minds of youth.

Despite the first efforts at institutionalized education, most young people learned pedagogical and vocational skills within their families. If a son did not want to learn his father's trade, then he might be apprenticed into another family in order to study under the direction of the master. Whatever young colonials failed to absorb from elders had to be learned on their own. Colonial newspapers and almanacs (such as Ben Franklin's *Poor Richard's Almanac*) served as early home study guides.

Colonial Americans did found several institutions of higher education during the colonial period. The Founders of Harvard (1636) were primarily interested in training ministers for the Puritan settlements, but the curriculum followed the traditional liberal arts pattern of European universities. Subsequent colleges such as Yale

(1701) and Princeton (1746) adopted programs resembling Harvard's; William and Mary (1693) in Virginia was begun under the auspices of an Anglican minister. As increasing numbers of graduates from these schools went into professions other that the ministry; the need for "practical" training grew more apparent. Some of the colleges established in the late colonial period, such as Pennsylvania (1755) and Columbia (1754), introduced courses in agriculture, navigation, and astronomy, in addition to retaining traditional liberal arts subjects found in European universities. Higher education was available to a much wider socioeconomic spectrum in America than in England, and colonial innovations in college curriculum answered the needs of a more egalitarian society.

For most American young people schooling probably seemed less important and certainly less interesting than courtship and marriage. Particularly in the cities, customs changed rapidly, disturbing the older generation, shocking rural visitors, and even surprising foreign observers. A young man described a party he went to in Quaker Philadelphia: "Seven sleighs with two ladies and two men in each, preceded by fiddlers on horseback," rode to a public house where "we danced, sung, and romped and ate and drank, and kicked away care from morning till night, and finished our frolic in two or three sideboxes at the play." In 1755 a British traveler in Virginia reported that "dancing is the chief diversion here," and another was shocked at the widespread dancing of "jigs." Claiming that the dance was borrowed from the slaves, the proper Englishman found it "without method or regularity: a gentleman and lady stand up, and dance about the room, one of them retiring, the other pursuing,

then perhaps meeting, in an irregular fantastical manner." Serenading under the window of a favored lady also came into vogue during the late colonial period. Usually the gentlemen first lubricated their throats at a local tavern, yet women reportedly considered the midnight visitation and inevitable disharmony a high compliment.

Like folk songs everywhere, those of colonial America often revolved around courtship, unrequited love affairs, or tragic lovers. American ballads came largely from Britain; "Greensleeves" was one of the most popular and graceful tunes, and it provided the melody for about eighty different sets of lyrics. The first popular folk song known to be indigenous to the colonies in both words and music also treats a tragic couple, but with considerably less lyricism. Compare the poetic beauty of the English "Greensleeves" ("Alas, my love / You do me wrong / To cast me off / Discourteously . . .") with the coarser expression of the native song "Springfield Mountain":

> On Springfield Mountain there did dwell
> A lovelie youth I knowed him well. . . .
> He had scarce mowed half round the field
> When a poison serpent bit at his heel. . . .
> They took him home to Mollie dear,
> Which made him feel so verie queer. . . .
> Now Mollie had two ruby lips
> With which the poison she did sip. . . .
> She also had a rotten tooth
> And so the poison killed them both.

The song, describing a true incident in Massachusetts in 1761, spoke with American directness about a distinctly American tragedy.

The French and Indian War

British Americans became increasingly embroiled in conflict with neighboring French settlers and Indians, and in 1756 the Great War for Empire, or the French and Indian War as it was known in America, began a seven-year run on three continents. When it ended, and as a direct result of it, Britain more than doubled the territorial extent of an overseas domain it had been building for a century and a half. And then, as an indirect result of the same war, it lost almost all of its old empire in a decade and a half.

Though they had claimed and occupied the region for more than a hundred years, the French had by no means settled it. There were only about 55,000 French settlers in North America, the overwhelming majority in the Maritime Provinces and along the St. Lawrence River and the remainder distributed in widely scattered trading posts on the Great Lakes and the Ohio and Mississippi rivers. Quebec and Montreal were the only towns of consequence on the St. Lawrence, and New Orleans the only town of importance on the Mississippi.

As buffers between their own settlements and those of the aggressive, coast-bound British Americans, the French had long depended upon the friendly but subject Indians. The sudden establishment of favorable relations between the British Americans and the Indians upset all balances and jeopardized the entire French position in North America, for the greedy and land-hungry British Americans outnumbered the French Americans by almost thirty to one.

The new governor of Virginia, Robert Dinwiddie, had instructions to promote the interests of the Ohio Company, but to do so without antagonizing the French. Accordingly he dispatched a seven-man mission, which included a twenty-one-year-old Virginian named George Washington, to urge the French to respect British rights in the area. The mission was politely received and, with equal politeness, informed that the construction of Fort Duquesne would begin at Pittsburgh in the spring. Upon being told of the French intention, Governor Dinwiddie rashly rushed a work force to the area with instructions to build a British fort on the spot. To protect the workers young Washington followed a little later, quite unaware that the work force had been expelled by the French almost immediately upon its arrival. In May of 1754 Washington was encamped at Great Meadows on the Monongahela, when he learned of the existence of a small French force a few miles ahead. He ordered a precipitous night march and attacked the French, capturing 21 and killing 10. Then he pushed on until he learned that the French were about to attack him in force. He retreated and hastily threw up a stockade, imaginatively called Fort Necessity. In June his force of 150 was reinforced by 200 more men, and on July 3 he was attacked by 500 French and 400 Indians. After a nine-day siege Washington surrendered, and the French and Indian War had begun.

It took European statesmen two years to complete the necessary formalities of choosing up sides (France and Austria, later joined by Spain, against Great Britain and Prussia) and reaching a state of official hostility. In the interim, French and English Americans were busily engaged in killing one another, or at least in discussing plans for enlisting the aid of various tribes and accomplishing their bloody tasks with maximum efficiency. Even before Washington's abortive expedition, the Board of Trade had ordered a conference of colonial officials, and even as Washington was blundering in the wilderness a congress was in session in Albany, New York, attended by delegates from all colonies north of the Potomac, save New Jersey and Delaware. The Pennsylvania

delegation, led by Benjamin Franklin (who had long since abandoned his native Boston to go into newspaper printing in Philadelphia), proposed that the British Americans adopt a broad "plan of union." The plan called for the appointment of a president-general for the British colonies to be chosen and supported by the Crown, and a grand council, representing the several colonies in proportion to their contributions to the colonial treasury. This agency was to have general legislative and taxing powers for the purpose of defense and Indian relations. The delegates approved the plan, with modifications, but the colonies and the Board of Trade rejected it; so the first effort to establish an American union was stillborn.

It remained obvious, however, that unless the British were willing to forfeit their newfound opportunities, some sort of plan would have to be devised for coping with the French in America. Accordingly, though most eminent Londoners were preoccupied with the gaming tables, court intrigues, and other pressing pursuits, someone in the capital did come up with a vague plan of action. Official British policy was to engage in what, at a later day, would be called limited warfare. One British army, manned primarily by colonial militiamen, would march up from Virginia and capture Fort Duquesne. Another and similar force, to be gathered in New England and New York, would seize Crown Point on Lake Ticonderoga and Fort Niagara. General Edward Braddock, a fat and debauched "professional" soldier who had never led troops in battle, was put in charge of the campaign. Braddock had no great acumen as a military strategist, but he did have sufficient perception to remark, on the night before he sailed for America, "We are sent like lambs to the altar."

Braddock's campaign of 1755 set the pattern for the first two years of the war. He arrived in Virginia early in 1755, made various appointments and delegated responsibility for raising troops for the multiple attack, and chose Washington as his aide-de-camp. In June he started over the mountains with a force of 2500 men. By the morning of July 8 he had pushed to within ten miles of Fort Duquesne. By the evening of July 9 he had met the enemy and been destroyed: there were 900 British casualties of the battle, including General Braddock himself. The planned expedition on Fort Niagara, directed by Governor William Shirley of Massachusetts, got as far as Oswego, half the distance, before being humiliatingly defeated. The campaign to take Crown Point, led by William Johnson, brought great accolades to the British commander but not a single victory to the British troops. By the middle of 1756 the French had taken the offensive, and throughout 1757 French forces won victory after victory. A new expedition, commanded by General John Forbes and composed of 6000 men, began in the fall of 1758 to cut its way through the forests of western Pennsylvania toward the forks of the Ohio. The French defenders of Fort Duquesne, deserted by their Indian allies as Forbes's army drew near, blew up their stronghold and fled to Canada in November of 1759. Forbes immediately began to reconstruct the defenses, rechristened Fort Pitt, and settlers began to pour into the area, despite British orders to the contrary. A second expedition, commanded by William Johnson, directed a force of 3500 Americans, 2500 British regulars, and 1000 Indians against Fort Niagara, with the aim of cutting Montreal and Quebec off from the Great Lakes region. The expedition marched in the spring of 1759 and achieved total victory. A third expedition, commanded by Sir Jeffrey Amherst, was directed to move north from New York City, clear the French posts on Lake Champlain, bypass Montreal, and lay seige to Quebec from the southwest. A fourth expedition, commanded by General James Wolfe, was ordered to move with a combined army and naval force up the St. Lawrence and attack Quebec from the other side. Amherst's expedition took both Ticonderoga and Crown Point, but was so slow in the doing that it was forced to stop on Lake Champlain for the winter of 1759-60. That left Wolfe to attack Quebec alone, and Quebec was protected by a high rock cliff that made it the most formidable natural fortress in America. The French commander at Quebec, Louis Joseph Montcalm, remained inside the fortress, confident that Amherst's proposed attack from the southwest, from which quarter Quebec was vulnerable by way of the undefended Plains of Abraham, could not materialize. It was a momentous occasion for the future of North America.

Suggested Readings

Paul Boyer and Stephen Nissenbaum attribute the witchcraft hysteria in Salem to a rift in the social structure ultimately traceable to an emergent mercantile capitalism. See *Salem Possessed: The Social Origins of Witchcraft* (1974) and three volumes almost devoid of interpretation, *The Salem Witchcraft Papers: Verbatim Transcripts of the Legal Documents of the Salem Witch-craft Outbreak of 1692* (1977). *People of Paradox* is Michael Kammen's venture onto the perilous ground of national character; he finds the hallmark of American society to be contradictions ("biformities") and tensions within colonial life that contributed to the formation of a peculiar American style that reconciled a European sense of order with a New World thirst for freedom. New England continues to inspire excellent scholarship; the works of Kenneth Lockridge *(A New England Town: The First Hundred Years,* 1970), John Demos *(A Little Commonwealth: Family Life in Plymouth Colony. Dedham, Massachusetts, 1636-1736,* 1970), Sumner Chilton Powell, *Puritan Village,* 1966), Robert Middlekauff, *(The Mathers: Three Generations of Puritan Intellectuals,* 1971), and Sacvan Bercovitch *(The American Jeremiad,* 1978), add to the traditional work of Perry Miller. See Miller's brief *Errand Into the Wilderness* (1956) for a distillation of parts of *The New England Mind: From Colony to Province* (1953). Richard Hofstadter's *America at 1750* (1971) is a social history of the thirteen colonies; the late author's famous lucid, crisp style has the effect of freezing a moment in history for close scrutiny and ready understanding.

The Death of Wolfe

Chapter III
An Independent Spirit

The Plains of Abraham

At 2 a.m. on September 13, 1759, the English major General James Wolfe ordered two lanterns raised to the maintop shrouds of his flagship, the *Sutherland*, anchored on the St. Lawrence River. It was the signal to attack the French fortress of Quebec, which lay on the heights 175 feet above the dark river.

The attack had been long delayed. Wolfe and his army of redcoats, Scottish highlanders, and American rangers had arrived before the French stronghold the previous June and had fought a score of skirmishes with the French-Canadian militia, their Indian allies, and the crack French regulars of the Guyenne, Royal Roussillon, Bearn, La Reine, and La Sarre regiments. By now time was running short. The brief Canadian summer was nearly spent, and the bitter northern winter would soon descend. The British naval commander, faced with the prospect of being trapped by ice, was threatening to sail back home with his fleet. It was now or never.

Wolfe and his men were confident. They were fewer than the French, but what they lacked in numbers they made up in morale and experience. As they prepared to cross the river at the lantern's signal, the men of Wolfe's command felt that they were destined for glory. Wolfe himself had some premonition of what was about to happen to him. In the boat taking him to the French side he recited Gray's "Elegy in a Country Churchyard." It contained the line "The paths of glory lead but to the grave."

As the small boats carrying the British troops edged along the darkened north bank of the St. Lawrence a French sentry shouted: "what regiment?" A highland officer responded in fluent French: "the Queen's." The boats were allowed to pass. Soon after, they touched the bank close to where Wolfe some days before had spied a zig-zag path up the steep cliff that separated the river from the plain stretching before Quebec city. Twenty-four volunteers leaped out and, grabbing trees and bushes, pulled themselves up the plateau. Hundreds more followed.

The invaders spied a small French encampment. They immediately attacked, captured two of the French soldiers, and put the rest to flight. Hearing the triumphant shouts of his men above, Wolfe and his remaining force disembarked and scaled the cliff by way of the path to join the advance party. As morning broke with clouds and threatening rain, 3,500 British troops drew themselves up in battle order on the Plains of Abraham a mile west of Quebec, the center of French power in America.

In the walled city itself, news of the British move provoked great alarm. For many weeks the *Quebecois* had endured bombardment from the British fleet and army. Much of the city was in ruins, although it was packed with refugees from the outlying countryside who jammed into every remaining dwelling and spilled over into the town's hospitals, convents, and public buildings. Worse than the physical devastation and discomfort was the political confusion in the city. The military commander was Louis de Montcalm, a forty-four-year-old veteran of France's wars who had been pulled from retirement to command His Majesty's troops in distant Canada. The civilian leader was Pierre de Rigaud, the Marquis de

Vaudreuil, a Canadian-born son of a previous governor of Canada. The two men did not get along, and their lack of rapport would hurt France in the hours ahead.

As news spread of the British success in scaling the heights, the French and Canadians poured out of the town to assemble on the plain outside the walls. Montcalm asked the city commander to send him big guns from the palace battery, but was given only three on the plea that the rest were needed to defend the town itself. Montcalm might have waited for troops from Vaudreuil, but the governor too held back, fearing, apparently, to be part of any defeat while at the same time reserving the right to arrive in time to claim credit for any victory. As his men formed ranks, Montcalm rode back and forth along his lines brandishing his sword and urging his troops to show their mettle for France and for the King.

At 10 a.m. the French, with the white-clad regulars in the center and the Canadians at either end, started forward against the double-ranked British, firing and shouting as they advanced. The redcoats and highlanders advanced a few yards and then stopped. When the two lines were within forty paces the British commander ordered his men to fire. Two precise volleys rang out like single shots, and then a ragged clatter followed as the men reloaded and fired at will. When the smoke lifted, it was clear that the battle was over. As far as the eye could see, the field was covered with French dead and wounded. The French troops still on their feet had stopped short and were milling around in a confused mob. The British officers now gave the order to charge. The cheering redcoats ran forward with their bayonets poised. The highlanders dashed ahead yelling in Gaelic and brandishing their broadswords. Leading the charge of the Louisburg Grenadiers was Wolfe himself. At that moment of triumph the British general was struck in the chest by a French bullet and was carried to the rear. A few minutes later he died.

By now the French were fleeing pell-mell to the safety of Quebec's walls. Borne along with the human tide was Montcalm, still mounted. Close to the walls a British shot hit him in the thigh and passed along it to lodge in his stomach. The French commander was escorted through the city gate by three soldiers and brought to the military surgeon. But nothing could be done, and he died the next day.

Meanwhile the timid Vaudreuil, despite the urging of his senior officer, refused to move his large remaining force against the exhausted British. When reinforcements arrived under the Chevalier de Levis several days later, it was too late: Montcalm's successor at Quebec had already surrendered the city to Brigadier General James Murray.

Nonetheless, fighting continued for some time before French Canada was completely subdued. In early spring 1760 the French tried to retake Quebec from the British, but were beaten where Wolfe had fallen. That summer British troops from three directions descended on Montreal, the last remaining French strong point in Canada. On September 8 Vaudreuil surrendered all of French Canada to the British.

The great war between France and Britain went on officially for three-and-a-half more years before the negotiators at Paris signed a peace treaty in 1763. In reality, it had ended on the cloudy battlefield before Quebec, where both brave commanders surrendered their lives.

Imperial Reform

News of Wolfe's victory deeply affected the North American public. The young hero had given his life to save Protestant America from the "oppression" of Catholic France and his sacrifice took on epic proportions. Grateful for the victory and moved by the young general's death, thousands of King George's subjects sang the words to Gray's "Elegy" in taverns all over the thirteen colonies.

The French and Indian War as a whole was an invigorating experience for Americans. They had fought well in a score of battles from Canada to the Caribbean. After 1763 they would exhibit a new confidence and a new pride in what they, mere provincials before, could accomplish.

Part of this new spirit grew out of the elimination of France as a major power in North America. For a century New France and then Louisiana had threatened Americans. Representing absolutism, clericalism, and militarism, French America had hung like a sword over Anglo-America and forced the colonists to acknowledge dependence on the British army and navy for their protection. That dependence, in turn, had placed a limit on the colonies' political maturity and independence of action.

The Treaty of Paris of 1763 changed all this. Britain retained Canada and was granted Florida. The French also surrendered their claims to the whole of America east of the Mississippi, except New Orleans. After 1763 only a weak Spain remained as a rival to Great Britain on the North American continent.

The British were aware of the change in the colonial temperament. During the negotiations at Paris the Duke of Bedford spoke for returning Canada to France to prevent Americans from growing too mighty and asserting their independence. Bedford's views were overruled, but in later years there would be those who believed that the conquest of New France was a mistake. Writing during the fierce debate between America and Britain that preceded independence, the loyalist governor of Massachusetts, Thomas Hutchinson, noted: "Before the peace of 1763 I thought nothing so much to be desired as the cession of Canada. I am now convinced that if it had remained to the French none of the spirit of opposition to the Mother Country would have yet appeared and I think the effects of it worse than all we had to fear from the French or Indians."

Undoubtedly, the new American self-confidence would influence the postwar relations of the colonies to the mother country. But the war had created other imperial strains. Though victorious, Britain emerged with a national debt of £140 million. By contrast, Americans were almost debt-free. During the war, they had refused to tax themselves to any significant extent. Indeed, they had profited in the war by selling goods to the British military and naval forces, and often inferior goods at that. Now that the war fought on their behalf had been won they were left almost unburdened.

By the war's end it had begun to look as if Britain would have to maintain a permanent and expensive military force in America. France was down but not out. Unreconciled to Britain's triumph the French were reported to be rebuilding their navy in preparation for further war. More immediately, the Indian tribes in the West were becoming a problem. During the war American settlers and Indian-traders had flooded into the trans-Appalachian region in the wake of British victories over the French. The newcomers were often unscrupulous. Many plied the Indians with rum and then "bought" their lands for a few cheap goods and rifles and powder. It seemed that these difficulties would become worse once the Americans poured across the mountains in force after 1763. Troops clearly would be needed in the West to hold down the tribes and assure a rational policy of Western development.

Even before the British could formally announce their Western policy the Indian frontier exploded. Indian discontent took the form of the first pan-Indian movement led by two leaders who envisioned an Indian society free of the white man's coercion and corruption. One of these men was a visionary and seer who assured his fellow redmen that if they rejected the white man's ways, they would regain their former strength and former lands. The other, the Ottawa chief, Pontiac, led his warriors in May 1763 against the British fort at Detroit and came within an inch of taking it. Pontiac's attack commenced a massive Indian uprising all along the Northern frontier; by June only three major British military posts remained.

But the English quickly struck back. Two columns went to the relief of the surviving posts. One, led by Colonel Henry Bouquet, forced Pontiac to accept a truce. Soon after, Pontiac's chief allies made peace with the English, and before long Pontiac himself "smoked the calumet" with the white men.

The war had forced the British government to focus attention on American affairs as never before and the experience had been an eye-opener. As British officials saw it, the Americans had behaved badly. They had refused to support the war financially, although their own defense was at stake. They had profited from illegal trade with the enemy and made the war more costly in men and money. For half a century a policy of "salutary neglect" had governed the relations of colonies and mother country; now, it was argued, this would have to be replaced by a tighter, more rational, and financially sounder system.

The chief advocate of this view was George Grenville, Chancellor of the Exchequer and King George III's chief minister following the retirement of William Pitt, the great wartime leader. Grenville was a man of limited vision who treated the empire as if it were a business concern. As a contemporary noted, Grenville judged "a national saving of two inches of candle . . . a greater triumph than all Pitt's victories."

Grenville first took aim at policy toward the West and the Indians. The Proclamation of 1763 set the limit of white settlement at the crest of the Appalachians. All colonists west of that line must "forthwith . . . remove themselves." British military authorities would now be in charge of all Indian territory west of the mountains; all traders in Indian territory would have to be licensed, and they could trade only at designated points under British military supervision.

The Proclamation was soon followed by a flurry of measures designed to raise revenue in America. The intention of the Revenue Act of 1764 was, by eliminating illegal trade, to increase the deplorably low receipts of the British customs service in America. The law added a dozen items to the list of "enumerated" American articles that must go first to Britain to be taxed before they could be sent elsewhere. The law also established a new set of taxes for goods imported into the colonies and set up new admiralty courts with power to enforce their collection with the aid of general search warrants called "writs of assistance." The most important change affected the trade between the mainland colonies and the West Indies. For many years, despite a prohibitively high tax on foreign-produced molasses, American merchants had relied on the French and Dutch Caribbean islands for this product, which was the chief raw material in the making of rum. Molasses was cheaper in the French and Dutch possessions than in the English islands, and the Molasses Act of 1733 imposing a six-pence-a-gallon duty on the foreign product had become a dead letter. Now the British determined to collect the money by reducing the tax to half its previous level, so that smuggling would no longer be profitable.

A second measure of 1764, the Currency Act, struck at the practice of issuing legal tender paper money; the colonials believed this to be an indispensable medium of exchange in a chronically coin-poor community. British merchants had long complained, however, that the colonial legal-tender laws had enabled American debtors, especially the Southern planters, to scale down the sums they owed. The right to issue legal tenders had already been forbidden the New England colonies. Now, the prohibition would be extended to the middle and Southern colonies as well.

Americans did not take these new measures lightly. The Proclamation threatened the ambitions of land speculators, Indian traders, and would-be settlers in the West alike. For the moment, however, the reaction was comparatively mild. Americans interested in Western development simply ignored British policy and went ahead with their own plans. As George Washington wrote a fellow land speculator: "any person who . . . neglects the present opportunity of hunting out good Lands and in some measure marking and distinguishing them for his own . . . will never regain it." Reaction to the Revenue and Currency Acts was more vigorous. In 1761 a Boston town meeting had listened to James Otis' impassioned attack on writs of assistance as violating God's "natural law" (and hence illegal), and condemned the Sugar Act as taxation without representation. Now that the Revenue Act had resurrected these search warrants, a group of Boston merchants, joined by the city's artisans, resolved to boycott several items imported from Britain. By the end of 1764 a limited boycott of British goods had spread to several other colonies.

The Stamp Act Crisis

Trouble was brewing for the Grenville program. But few people could have anticipated the full extent of American hostility to British policy. Then came the Stamp Act—the first attempt to impose an internal tax on Americans for the support of the empire.

Grenville must have realized the danger in the new policy, for when he asked for a tax that would

John Singleton Copley, Head of a Negro *(The Detroit Institute of Arts)*

apply directly to transactions in America rather than to overseas trade, he promised to consider other means of raising revenue in the colonies if Americans objected. But he gave the colonial legislatures little time to respond and when their agents in London tried to induce Grenville to withdraw the Stamp Act proposal he refused.

In February 1765 the stubborn Chancellor of the Exchequer introduced the fatal measure to a poorly attended session of the House of Commons. The debate, though brief, was significant as an expression of the different views of the colonies that were then current among Englishmen. Speaking for Grenville, Charles ("Champagne Charlie") Townshend expressed a widespread attitude of condescension toward Americans that would poison relations between the two peoples. Townshend called Americans "children planted by our care." They had been "nourished up" by British "indulgence" and protected by British arms. Would "they grudge to contribute their mite" to relieve the British people from "the heavy burdens" they suffered?

Townshend's remarks offended Colonel Isaac Barré, an officer who had fought under Wolfe and who represented the minority of upper class Englishmen who recognized the need to relax the bonds of empire. Townshend was seriously mistaken, Barré declared. The Americans had not been planted by British care, but rather by British oppression which had driven so many refugees to the New World. Nor were they nurtured by British indulgence. Rather they "grew by your . . . neglect of 'em." Indeed, these "sons of liberty" had suffered under greedy British officials for many years. Nor had they been protected by British arms; they had nobly fought for themselves.

Americans would cheer Barré's words, and "patriot" organizations would soon adopt "Sons of Liberty" as their name. But Parliament was unmoved. On March 22, 1765, it passed the Stamp Act, taxing newspapers, almanacs, pamphlets, legal documents, insurance policies, dice, playing cards, and other items. These taxes would be paid in the form of a stamp, purchasable from collectors to be chosen from among Americans residing in the colonies, and placed on the documents specified. Grenville expected the law to raise £60,000 of the £300,000 needed to maintain the British military establishment in North America.

News of the Stamp Act's passage reached America in mid-April. Consternation was immediate and almost universal. By this "single stroke," wrote the conservative jurist William Smith of New York, Britain had "lost . . . the affection of all her colonies." In the Virginia House of Burgesses at Williamsburg the young lawyer Patrick Henry denounced George III as a tyrant and implied that like all tyrants he must be overthrown. Although some conservatives reproached Henry for his rash remarks, the delegates at Williamsburg adopted resolutions attacking the Act and declaring that the right to tax rested in the people themselves or their chosen representatives. Soon almost all the other colonies had adopted similar resolutions. When the Massachusetts General Court proposed that representatives of all the colonies meet in New York in October to consider joint action against the detested measure, only New Hampshire declined.

Violence

By the time the Stamp Act Congress assembled, Americans had resorted to more than words to express their indignation. In Boston the newly formed Sons of Liberty hanged in effigy the man who was to be the new tax commissioner, Andrew Oliver, brother-in-law of Lieutenant Governor Andrew Hutchinson. Later a mob tore down a house that Oliver had allegedly built to serve as his tax office. They next marched on Oliver's home and broke all the windows. The following day a delegation of respectable citizens called on Oliver and asked him to resign his tax commission. Although he had not yet received either official confirmation of his appointment or his stamps, the terrified Oliver agreed to write to England declining his commission.

Oliver's resignation, however, did not end the violence. The Boston Sons of Liberty next attacked the house of William Story, deputy register of the admiralty court, smashed down the doors, and burned Story's public and private papers. Another contingent sacked the home of the comptroller of customs, carried away his records, and pillaged his wine cellar. The mob's final target was Hutchinson's own home. They battered down the walls, burned the furniture, destroyed the library, tore windows and doors from their frames, and cut down the trees in the Hutchinson yard. They also stole £900 in cash, and walked off with the family silver.

The mob's fury appalled even such committed Boston patriots as John Adams and Josiah Quincy. The Boston town meeting condemned the rioting, and the authorities issued a warrant for the arrest of the Sons of Liberty leader, Ebenezer McIntosh.

Meanwhile, the violence spread to other towns and other colonies. In Newport, Rhode Island, a mob burned and sacked the homes of "Tory" defenders of British power and forced the Stamp Act collector to resign. Connecticut patriots conducted a mock trial of stamp distributors. New York Sons of Liberty vented their fury on the house of the British military commander. In the words of one observer of the attack, "The Beds they cut open, and threw the Feathers abroad, broke all the Glasses, China, Tables, Chairs, Desks, Trucks, Chests." They then started a fire, threw all the remaining furnishings into it, "drank or destroyed all the Liquor," and left the major's garden in ruins. In Charleston, capital of South Carolina, a mob attacked the house of the prominent merchant Henry Laurens, whom they suspected of being the future stamp collector. Only Laurens' bold denials kept the irate patriots from doing harm to him and his property. And so it went from colony to colony. Everywhere Tories were intimidated, and collectors forced to surrender their commissions. When the stamps finally arrived, there was no one to sell them or to see that they were affixed to the designated documents.

In early October 1765, twenty-seven delegates from nine colonies convened in New York to consider united action against the detested law. This Stamp Act Congress was relatively conservative, but its Declaration of Rights and Grievances effectively summed up most of the colonists' complaints. Taxation, the Declaration asserted, could be imposed only by the people's consent, "given personally, or by their representatives." Moreover, trial by jury, ignored by the new admiralty courts, was an inherent right of Englishmen. The Stamp Act, the Congress concluded, as well as the other recent measures restricting America commerce, must be repealed.

Far more effective than the words of the Stamp Act Congress were the actions of businessmen in the major American port cities. Two hundred New York merchants agreed to make all new orders for British goods contingent on repeal of the Stamp Act. They were joined by the traders of Philadelphia, Boston, Salem, and other ports. Meanwhile, November 1, the date when the Act was supposed to take effect, rolled around. For a while business was disrupted, since very little could be done legally without the stamps. Slowly it resumed without them. The law was dead.

The British government could not ignore the American response to the Stamp Act. Some Englishmen were outraged at American defiance. Dr. Samuel Johnson, the famous English writer and lexicographer, called the opponents of the Act "incendiaries" and "fractious demagogues." But others, particularly merchants who found their American business dwindling, sympathized with the Americans and bombarded Parliament with petitions to repeal the measure. In Manchester, Leeds, Nottingham, and other English industrial towns thousands of workingmen lost their jobs as the workshops and mills dependent on the American market slowed and then stopped.

The man who had to face the uproar was no longer Grenville, but the Marquis of Rockingham, who had succeeded as Prime Minister in July 1765. Rockingham's group drew its support largely from the merchants and manufacturers and was particularly sensitive to their plight. Leading the battle for repeal in Parliament was William Pitt, the great wartime prime minister. Pitt eloquently defended the colonists' rights. "The Americans," he declared, "are the sons, not the bastards of England." The Stamp Act must "be REPEALED ABSOLUTELY, TOTALLY, IMMEDIATELY . . . ." In March 1766 Parliament complied. But at the same time, to satisfy its more conservative members, it passed the so-called Declaratory Act, asserting the power to make laws binding the American colonies "in all cases whatsoever."

Few Americans took note of the Declaratory Act amidst general rejoicing at the end of the detested stamp tax. Merchants immediately abandoned their nonimportation agreements and placed large orders with British suppliers. Several towns voted to erect statues to Pitt. The ordinary people greeted the news with special exuberance, ringing church bells, placing lighted candles in their windows, and firing off guns. The Boston Sons of Liberty built "a magnificent pyramid, illuminated with 280 Lamps," on Boston Common. Crowning the pile was a box of fireworks which went off at dusk producing a magnificent effect.

At times the celebrators displayed a spirit of arrogance and self-congratulation that disconcerted more sober folk. In the words of a crude popular song, written for the great occasion:

In spite of each parasite, each cringing slave,
Each cautious dastard, each oppressive knave,
Each gibing ass, that reptile of an hour,
The supercilious pimp of abject slaves in
    power.
We are met to celebrate in festive mirth,
The day that gave our freedom second birth.
That tell us, British Grenville never more
Shall dare usurp unjust, illegal power,
Or threaten America's free sons with chains,
While the least spark of ancient fire remains.

Blunder Again

American rejoicing did not last long. In 1765 Parliament had passed the Quartering Act requiring the colonies to provide the king's troops with barracks and furnish them with "candles, firing, bedding, cooking utensils, salt and vinegar, and five pints of small beer or cider, or a gill of rum per man, per diem." For a year or two the colonies complied. Then, in 1767, the New York assembly, believing the colony overburdened, refused. In retaliation, Parliament suspended all acts of the New York provincial legislature until it voted money for the army.

Many British leaders still wanted colonials to pay a larger share of colonial administrative and military costs, and parliamentary maneuvering over reduction of England's own land tax helped force the American issue. In early 1767, Charles Townshend, chancellor of the exchequer in yet another ministry, unveiled his program. Capitalizing on the frequent distinction between "internal" and "external" taxation, Townshend taxed a wide range of colonial imports including glass, paper, lead, and tea. These duties, he argued, would raise badly needed funds and also impress Parliament's authority to tax upon the disruptive provincials. He further proposed creation of a new American customs service as well as a crackdown on New York's continually defiant assembly. After Parliament enacted all these potentially explosive measures, the ministry indicated its determination to enforce the trade laws. It appointed several unpopular officials to the new customs board and established the body's headquarters in Boston, the center of opposition to stricter commercial regulation.

Once again, legal defiance was only a part of Britain's colonial problem. In some areas, enforcement of commercial regulations broke down almost completely. A Boston ship's captain, Daniel Malcom, drew a pistol on two revenue agents searching for illegal wine in his basement. Returning with the sheriff and a search warrant, the agents discovered the captain's house surrounded by a crowd of his friends, and the harried sheriff avoided a direct confrontation only by stalling for time until the search warrant expired. After the disgusted officials departed, Captain Malcom treated his protectors to buckets of smuggled wine. Such cases were not infrequent. Investigating past enforcement, Townshend's customs board discovered only six seizures and one smuggling conviction in all of New England during two-and-one-half years. (Mobs rescued three of the seized ships, and colonial juries ac-

quitted two other defendants.) Initially the new customs officials fared little better, enforcing restrictions only enough to enrage colonial merchants. The same Captain Malcom brought an entire load of illegal wine into Boston on small boats during the night and then boldly sailed his empty ship into port the next day. The vessel's water line clearly revealed his subterfuge, but enraged customs officers could find no Bostonian who would testify against him. Malcom's friend and fellow smuggler, John Hancock, was less fortunate; the customs board seized his ship *Liberty* in 1768. But the violent popular reaction forced most of the board's members to flee the city.

Colonialists, objecting to Britain's attempt to rule through its control of provincial legislatures, saw authority quickly being shifted across the Atlantic to London. Western land speculators and would-be settlers saw the promise of profits and of new homes in the fertile trans-Appalachian region fading. Yeoman farmers who cherished the relatively egalitarian social and economic system of America worried that the tightening reins of empire would bring a return to feudal privilege and the development of a more aristocratic society. There was also a growing fear in Puritan New England among laymen and Congregational clergymen that the new bonds of imperial control implied Anglican bishops for America and an attack on other Protestant churches.

Predictably, a great outcry greeted the Townshend Duties. This time, though, leading merchants and lawyers, kept dissent under control. In each colony, the Sons of Liberty and the merchants adopted strict non-importation agreements. In South Carolina, the legislature resolved that until the colonies were restored to their former freedom by repeal of the Townshend Duties the people of the colony would encourage and promote the use of American manufactures and refuse to import any of the manufactures of Great Britain. South Carolinians, it promised, would practice the "utmost economy in our persons, houses, and furniture, particularly that we will give no mourning, or gloves, or scarves at funerals."

By early 1769 non-importation was in force in every colony. True, many Americans were either still pro-British or so lukewarm toward the patriot cause that they were unwilling to deprive themselves of British goods to promote it. Still, the boycott was effective. And it brought American leaders together to an even greater extent than the Stamp Act crisis. It was at this time that the

General Court of Massachusetts initiated a practice of "circular letters" among the various colonial legislatures laying out British misdeeds and suggesting united continental action to counter them.

The Townshend Duties also encouraged a great deal of pamphleteering designed to create the basis for a new imperial relationship. The most effective and eloquent of these statements were John Dickinson's Letters from a Farmer in Pennsylvania (1768). Posing as a simple Pennsylvania yeoman, Dickinson cautioned against violence and expressed an affection for "mother Britain" that foreshadowed his later refusal to sign the Declaration of Independence. But on the question of British taxation he was adamant. "Let these words be indelibly impressed on our minds," he concluded—"that we cannot be free without being secure in our property—that we cannot be secure in our property if without our consent others may as by right take it away—that taxes imposed on us by Parliament do thus take it away."

In June 1768 a British customs official was locked into the cabin of John Hancock's sloop *Liberty* while the crew unloaded untaxed madeira wine. When customs officials promptly seized the vessel, patriots attacked and forced them to flee to the British garrison at Castle William. Royal officials reacted angrily at this latest instance of mob defiance. They ordered the governor of Massachusetts to demand that the General Court either rescind its circular letter attacking British policy or face dissolution. Instead, the legislature asked that Governor Bernard be recalled. Bernard in turn called on British authorities for troops to restore order in unruly Boston and prevent a repetition of the *Liberty* incident. The new British Prime Minister, Lord Frederick North, ordered two regiments of redcoats from Ireland to the rebellious Massachusetts capital.

Meanwhile, despite the tough line they were taking, North and his colleagues were having second thoughts about the Townshend Duties. Widely evaded, they brought in virtually no revenue. Particularly galling was the smuggling of untaxed Dutch tea into the colonies. And non-importation agreements were reducing annual exports to America from £2.4 million in 1768 to £1.6 million in 1769. The British government was in a quandary: repealing the duties would end non-importation, but it would also be the second time the British government had backed down.

In the end, the North ministry yielded to American pressure, but in a grudging and half-hearted way that only highlighted British weakness without calling forth American gratitude. In 1770 Parliament rescinded the taxes on glass, paper, and painters' colors; it also reduced the tea tax from twelve to three pence a pound, but did not repeal it. At the same time, the Quartering Act was allowed to expire.

This partial repeal ended the boycott. It did little to end resentment of Britain, however—as one American merchant remarked about the repeal: "Doing things by Halves of all others [was] the worst Method." Moreover, many fundamental disagreements with Britain persisted. The whole question of the constitutional relationship between mother country and colonies was still unsettled. What body, colonists asked, was the ultimate source of authority in America, the colonial legislatures or Parliament? By now some colonists were advocating an American relationship with Great Britain resembling that of the later British dominions within the British Commonwealth: the King of England would also be King of Massachusetts, New York, Virginia, and so forth, but each American colony would be autonomous in all its domestic affairs. Few, if any, as yet endorsed complete independence. Americans remained proud of their British heritage and of their rights as "free-born Britons," and even the most ardent patriots still insisted that they merely wished to preserve these rights from the arrogant usurpers who had gathered around the King.

The Boston Massacre

In the months following repeal of the Townshend Duties, resentment toward Britain remained particularly strong in Boston. Aside from the long-standing grievances the Boston townspeople shared with other communities, there was the question of the recently arrived troops. Americans had no illusions about the conduct of professional soldiers. Even when, as in the late war with France, they had come to protect the civilian population from an enemy, they had been an affliction. How much worse would they be now, when they were coming to overawe and intimidate the Americans. In the opinion of the patriot governor of Connecticut, Jonathan Trumbull, ''the Mischief, Rapine & Villainy commonly prevalent among Troops, who are kept up in idleness, are such as will be intolerable in the Colonies, and has a tendency to destroy the Morals of the people, and raise a Distrust of the good intentions of the Governors in the better sort, and stir up Strife and Contention among the whole.''

Before the British regiments arrived, the Boston town meeting called upon the people of the city to arm themselves, and demanded that the governor call a meeting of the General Court which he had dissolved in June. When Bernard refused, the patriot leaders called an assembly of the colony's towns as a substitute for the General Court. This ''convention'' helped to acquaint the citizens of Massachusetts' smaller communities with the views of the radical leaders of the capital, and it demonstrated that the Adamses, John Hancock, and the rest spoke for a large part of the colony's yeomanry, not just for the merchants and artisans of the metropolis.

The day the convention adjourned, the British troops dispatched by North arrived in Boston harbor, protected by guns of British men-of-war. While the city's dubious citizens looked on, the soldiers debarked at the Long Wharf and marched up King Street to the music of drums and fifes. It was a moving sight, even for the most ardent patriots. The men's red tunics, criss-crossed by white straps and topped by black three-cornered hats, were far more colorful than modern uniforms. Towering over the regular troops were the grenadiers, chosen for their height, a feature emphasized by their tall, mitre-shaped bearskin caps. The grenadier officers wore crimson sashes and carried swords at their sides.

Boston's pleasure at the bright display soon faded, however, and the troops found it no pleasure to be quartered on a hostile populace. While their officers had no difficulty finding good lodgings with wealthy Tories, the troops were refused barracks by the city council, and had to be scattered around the town at whatever empty buildings, generally workshops and warehouses, the British commander could rent.

Before long, the patriots' worst fears were realized. The bored troops turned for solace to Boston's cheap rum and loose women. To get money for their dissipations, many engaged in petty theft. Inevitably they got into fights, especially with sailors in the local taverns. When winter came many soldiers deserted, and although the citizens of the Massachusetts countryside had little reason to love the ''lobsterbacks,'' they also refused to help the military authorities return them

to duty. The colonists saw the redcoats as an army of occupation.

This tense situation came to a head in March 1770. On Friday, March 2, a civilian ropemaker, William Green, asked a soldier passing by, Patrick Walker of the Twenty-ninth Regiment, if he wanted work. Such part-time jobs were permitted to off-duty soldiers, and Walker said yes. Green responded: ''Then go clean my s--thouse.'' Walker retorted in kind and left, threatening to come back with some friends. Soon afterward he appeared with forty of his mates, led by a tall, black regimental drummer. The soldiers, armed with clubs, sailed into Green and his friends, who defended themselves with sticks. When other civilians joined in, the soldiers retreated.

All that weekend, rumors circulated that the soldiers intended revenge. And so they did. On the night of Monday the 5th, bands both of soldiers and of citizens roved the icy streets of Boston looking for trouble. It came at Private White's sentry post adjacent to the Custom House, when a wigmaker's apprentice baited White until the sentry hit him with the butt of his gun. When the apprentice fled, a British sergeant pursued him, brandishing his musket.

News of the fight spread quickly, and a half-dozen young men descended on the sentry post screaming ''Lousy rascal! Lobster son of a bitch!'' and other insults. Soon the swelling crowd pelted White with snowballs and jagged chunks of ice, crying ''Kill him, kill him, knock him down.'' Finally Captain Thomas Preston, officer of the day, decided he must save White even at the risk of a serious confrontation. With six grenadiers he marched on the beleaguered sentry post and surrounded White. But with angry civilians pressing on him from every direction, Preston now found that he could not return to the safety of the barracks. He tried to persuade the crowd to disperse, but they responded by daring the soldiers to shoot. At this point someone struck one of the redcoats with a club, knocking him off his feet. The soldier fired, forcing the crowd back. Now another British soldier fired, this time hitting Sam Gray in the head. A third pulled the trigger of his musket and hit Crispus Attucus, a black man, in the chest. By the time the shooting stopped, three Bostonians lay dead and three others were mortally wounded.

The whole city might then and there have erupted in a bloody rebellion. Fortunately, Lieutenant Governor Hutchinson intervened, and by promising a quick investigation and punishment of the guilty parties, prevented a blow-up. That morning, Preston and his men were arrested and confined to jail pending trial. The trial itself was conducted with propriety and fairness. Captain Preston hired as counsel two prominent Boston patriots, John Adams and Josiah Quincy, who took the case out of a combined concern for the colony's and their own good names. Fortunately for the defendants, most patriots wished to avoid any suspicion that the Massachusetts courts would not give the accused a fair trial.

In the end, Preston and his men were acquitted. Adams demolished the charge that Preston had given the order to fire. He and Quincy appealed for fairness. "The eyes of all are upon you," Quincy told the jurors. It is "of high importance to your country, that nothing should appear on this trial to impeach our justice or stain our humanity." The two defense lawyers called witnesses who demonstrated that the soldiers had been taunted and abused beyond bearing. The verdict: not guilty of murder for all enlisted men who were convicted of manslaughter but punished lightly. Massachusetts justice had been vindicated.

The Boston Massacre and the trial served as a safety valve to release pent-up pressure in Boston and the colonies as a whole. It was followed by a period of relative calm in British-American relations. During these months the non-importation agreements totally collapsed, despite the attempts of more radical patriots to continue them until tea too was exempted from duty. Actually, little had happened to settle fundamental differences, but for a time both Americans and Englishmen chose to believe that the other side had come to a more reasonable position.

The Gaspée Affair

Then, in June 1772, came the *Gaspée* affair. Rhode Island, one of the two self-governing colonies (along with Connecticut), had long been notorious for ignoring imperial trade laws. For years, its many coves and inlets had sheltered smugglers, who defied the customs authorities with impunity. To stop the traffic, the British authorities finally dispatched the ship *Gaspée* to Narragansett Bay. Tricky tides ran the ship onto a sandbar near Providence. That night a band of Rhode Island Sons of Liberty boarded the stranded *Gaspée*, overwhelmed its captain and crew, and burned the vessel to the waterline.

The British were outraged. Civilians had attacked one of the King's naval vessels in performance of its lawful duties. British authorities immediately appointed a commission of inquiry, with power to send suspects to England for trial. The commission, however —stymied by the refusal of anyone to testify against the culprits, many of them substantial citizens of the colony—adjourned without fulfilling its mission.

The *Gaspée* affair had important consequences. British officials concluded that the patriots would stop at nothing to get their way, and resolved to take a harder line. To the patriots themselves, the authorities' intention to drag men off to England to stand trial for crimes committed in America seemed ominous. It violated one of the most elementary "rights of Englishmen," and they determined to prevent it from taking place.

The instrument of this newly revived patriotic spirit was the committees of correspondence, consisting of men in each colony who dedicated themselves to sending and receiving communications of mutual concern. Before long, these men began to form a network of responsible patriot leaders who would remain at the forefront of the struggle against Britain for the next decade.

The Boston Tea Party

The *Gaspée* affair was followed by another brief period of relative calm. Then came a blow that shook the foundations of the empire. When the reverberations ended, the old empire was dead and America was independent.

The shock came from an unexpected source. In 1773 the East Indian Company was on the verge of financial collapse. Since the seventeenth century the company had exploited India and run it as its private corporate enterprise. Many Company officials had become rich through bribery and special privileges, but the Company itself had suffered. One of its few remaining assets, seventeen million pounds of tea held in its London warehouses, remained unsold because of the American boycott, and also because heavy taxes made it too expensive in Britain itself. Why not, Lord North asked, drastically reduce the English tax? With only three pence per pound to be paid on arrival in America, the tea would become so cheap that it would undersell smuggled Dutch tea. Presto! The tea would sell widely and the East India Company would be saved from ruin. This plan received legislative form in the Tea Act of 1773.

What North did not foresee was that Americans would see this scheme as an insulting bribe. To make matters worse, he consigned the East India Company tea exclusively to Tory merchants who favored British policies and obeyed the trade laws. To American eyes this seemed the final straw. The British government was clearly determined to destroy economically those whom it disliked. If tea, why not wine, spices, and other goods, until all those who resisted British oppression had been forced into bankruptcy?

A wiser leader would have foreseen the consequences of the Tea Act. But North, though witty and energetic, was a hard-liner on America who had supported the Stamp Act and opposed its repeal, and had endorsed the Townshend Duties. Such a man could not have anticipated what would now take place.

News of the new British affront enraged Americans. In New York City, most of the merchants resolved that the tea would not be sold, and local Tories feared mob violence when the tea was nonetheless put on sale. The patriot citizens of Philadelphia met and adopted resolutions declaring that since "the duty imposed by Parliament upon tea landed in America is a tax on the Americans, or levying contributions on them without their consent, it is the duty of every American to

---

I met an old friend of my father, Mr. Hugh Blair Grigsby, the Historian of the Virginia Convention of 1776. He introduced me to Ex-President John Tyler, as the great-grandson of Patrick Henry. Mr. Tyler asked me if I was the son of Colonel Wm. Spotswood Fontaine, of King William; and on my saying yes, he invited me to call at his room, as he wished to tell me something about Colonel Henry, which, perhaps, I had never heard. I accompanied Mr. Tyler to the house where he was staying.

On reaching his room, he said that his father had given him the following account of Colonel Henry's address delivered in March, 1775, in which he said: "Give me liberty, or give me death."

There were, said Mr. Tyler, many in the Convention who opposed the resolution of Mr. Henry to organize the militia and put the colony into a posture of defense; these gentlemen by some were unjustly called submissionists.

Mr. Henry was holding a paper-cutter in his right hand; and when he came to that part of his speech in which he said, "I know not what course others may take," he cast a glance at these gentlemen, and bending his head forward, and with stooping shoulders, and with submissive expression of countenance, he crossed his wrists, as if to be bound; then suddenly straightening up, a bold, resolute purpose of soul flashed over his countenance and then, struggling as if trying to burst his bonds, his voice swelled out in boldes,, vibrant tone; "Give me Liberty!" Then wrenching his hands apart, and raising aloft his hand with the clenched paper-cutter, he exclaimed: "Or give me death!" And aimed at his breast, as with a dagger, and dropped to his seat.

The effect, continued Mr. Tyler, was electrial. There was more in the tones and the action than in the words. The house was still as death. The members felt as if they had witnessed a real tragedy of the noblest days of the Roman Republic.

Then the members started from their seats. "The cry 'to arms' seemed to quiver on every lip and gleam in every eye."

Liberty or Death

The diary of William Winstan Fontaine, a mid-nineteenth-century Virginian, contains this second-hand account, dated February 19, 1859, of a firsthand observation of Patrick Henry's famous remark in the Virginia House of Burgesses in 1775.

oppose this attempt.'' Along the Delaware River, ship pilots learned that anyone who helped guide tea-carrying vessels into port would be tarred and feathered. In Charleston, patriot pressure also frightened off would-be tea importers.

Boston, as usual, responded more violently than any other town. Governor Hutchinson warned the British authorities soon after the Tea Act passed that ''at and near Boston the people seem regardless of all consequences. To enforce the Act appears beyond all comparison more difficult than I ever before imagined.'' If Hutchinson had allowed himself to be guided by this perception, disaster might have been avoided. But, though American-born, he was blinded by his Tory prejudices, and when three tea-carrying cargo ships arrived in Boston harbor he determined that they must unload, come what may.

Hutchinson had accurately judged his fellow Bostonians. On the evening of December 16, 1773, at a signal from Sam Adams, a band of men disguised as Mohawk Indians rushed down Milk Street to Griffin's Wharf. Three companies of these ''Indians'' rowed out to the anchored tea ships, boarded them, split open the tea chests, and dumped their contents into the waters of the harbor. Their mission accomplished, the men quickly and quietly dispersed.

The Boston Tea Party had ear-splitting consequences. The British saw it as an outrage far beyond any other yet committed and they determined not to let it go unpunished. In Parliament William Pitt and the eloquent Irish member Edmund Burke warned that punitive measures would lead to revolt. Burke urged the government to let Americans tax themselves, and not worry about whether they were legally required to obey Parliament. But the Burkes and the Pitts were a minority. Most politically influential Englishmen believed, as one expressed it, ''that the town of Boston ought to be knocked about their ears and destroyed.''

Determined to prevent ''the haughty American Republicans'' from ending all parliamentary control, North introduced the Boston Port Bill. Until Massachusetts had paid for the tea destroyed, Boston Harbor would be closed to shipping by a naval force, and troops withdrawn from the town to Castle William following the Boston Massacre would once more be brought into the city.

Fury in Boston itself was predictable, but the indignation of patriots was continental in scope. Messages of sympathy for Boston's plight poured in from every colony. In Virginia, George Washington urged his fellow patriots to support the Bostonians. We must not ''suffer ourselves to be sacrificed by piece meals,'' he wrote. The Virginia House of Burgesses, determined to express its pro-Boston views, convened in the Raleigh Tavern in Williamsburg after the Tory governor refused to let it sit at the capitol, and there it called for a continental congress to meet to consider united action. Similar calls for such a congress came from New York, Providence, and Philadelphia.

Everywhere Americans recognized that a final crisis had been reached, and in North Carolina patriot groups began to arm and drill in preparation for combat

Worse was yet to come. Not content with closing the port of Boston, Parliament in 1774 enacted a series of measures known collectively as the coercive or Intolerable Acts. The first of these, the Administration of Justice Act, declared that if any royal official was sued, for carrying out his official duties, he could have his trial transferred out of unfriendly Massachusetts to Britain, where he would face a more favorable jury. The Massachusetts Government Act struck a severe blow at self-government by taking away from the provincial legislature many of its powers of appointment and giving them to the royal governor. Hence-forth juries were to be summoned by sheriffs rather than elected by the town meetings, and the town meetings themselves could be called only by the governor, who would also dictate their agendas.

Another measure passed in 1774, the Quebec Act, was not intended as punishment, but so offended the colonists that it is often included among the Intolerable Acts. This law established a permanent government for the conquered province of Canada that provided few of the rights the English colonists enjoyed. It also extended toleration to the predominant religion of Quebec's inhabitants, Roman Catholicism. Most objectionable of all, the law extended the boundaries of Quebec south to the Ohio River into a region claimed by Virginia, Connecticut, and Massachusetts.

The First Continental Congress assembled in Carpenter's Hall, Philadelphia, early in September 1774. Twelve colonies were represented at Philadelphia—Georgia patriots had tried to pass a resolution to send a delegation, but had been dissuaded by the popular royal governor. Of the fifty-six delegates, twenty-two were lawyers, most of the others either planters or merchants. Almost all had been prominent in the affairs of their individual colonies, and many had belonged to the committees of correspondence.

The delegates did not all agree on the best course. Some held it sufficient to petition the King informing him of wrongs done the colonists and asking that he intervene. The Massachusetts delegates, led by John and Sam Adams, along with Christopher Gadsden of South Carolina, Charles Thomson of Pennsylvania, and Patrick Henry and Richard Henry Lee of Virginia, favored retaliatory measures such as a new non-importation agreement and a blunt refusal to pay for the tea dumped at Boston.

The delegates quickly demonstrated an emerging sense of continental unity and shared nationality. Patrick Henry, in a sample of his famous oratory, sounded the new note. "The distinctions between Virginians, Pennsylvanians, New Yorkers, and New Englanders," he declared, "are no more. I am not a Virginian, but an American." All imperial government, he continued, was at an end. "All Distinctions are thrown down. All America is thrown into one mass." Henry was exaggerating, but it is clear that the Congress would help to create a new feeling that Americans all shared a common and distinctive destiny.

The radicals achieved their ends at Philadelphia. In the midst of the debates and deliberations the delegates received a set of resolutions adopted by a convention recently held in Suffolk County, Massachusetts. These declared that Americans should not obey any of the Coercive Acts, attacked the Quebec Act as dangerous to Protestantism and American liberties, and demanded that all imports from Britain and all exports to it cease, pending repeal of the offensive measures. Over the strong objections of conservatives, the Congress endorsed the "Suffolk Resolves."

When it came to passing resolutions of their own, the delegates clashed sharply. On one side was Joseph Galloway of Pennsylvania and his supporters, who proposed a "Plan of Union" that would reconstruct imperial relationships by establishing an overall government for the colonies with a president-general appointed by the King. This official would exercise authority over a grand council of continental scope selected by the various colonial assemblies. Together the president-general and the grand council would constitute an "inferior branch" of the British Parliament. Radicals in the Congress, correctly perceiving this as a scheme to freeze into law the colonies' political subordination to Britain, defeated it.

The radicals' own plan—which was the one adopted—denounced the Coercive Acts as cruel and unconstitutional and condemned the various revenue measures Parliament had passed since 1763, the maintaining of a British standing army in America, and the dissolution of colonial assemblies by British authorities. The Congress also adopted a stringent set of regulations virtually cutting off all commercial relations with Britain until American grievances had been redressed. A final resolution called for a second Congress to meet on May 10, 1775, if by that time Britain still refused to yield.

Toward Lexington

The work of the Congress pleased many colonists. Following adjournment the Pennsylvania Assembly gave the delegates a dinner at the City Tavern, where their work was toasted and praised. In every part of the American community congratulations ensued for the Congress's efforts. Tories, on the other hand, were dismayed and depressed by what had transpired in Philadelphia. Governor William Franklin of New Jersey, Benjamin Franklin's Tory son, noted that the Congress had left Britain "no other alternative than either to consent to what must appear humiliating in the eyes of all Europe, or to compel obedience to her laws by a military force." A Massachusetts Tory insisted that the men at Philadelpia had made the "breach with the parent state a thousand times more irreparable than it was before." A New York loyalist charged that the Congress had *"erected itself into the supreme legislature of North America."*

In England itself, high officials were thunderstruck by American defiance. British merchants once more became a voice for conciliation. So did Pitt and Burke. But the North government refused to budge.

In Boston, events moved toward a showdown. For months the army commander there, General Thomas Gage, had been reinforcing the British garrison so that by the end of 1774 there were eleven battalions of redcoats, some four thousand men, in the city and at Castle William. Patriots took countermeasures by arming themselves and drilling. Outside the city, bands of militia calling themselves "minutemen" patrolled the countryside and made it dangerous for British troops to leave the city even on official business. Before long, Gage began to feel as though he were under siege and began to fortify Boston Neck against the time that he might actually be attacked. Elsewhere in New England armed patriot militia seized British military supplies and arms. To English officials and American Tories, the patriots' insistence that they were still loyal to the King by now seemed rank hypocrisy. For their part, patriots began calling the redcoats "debauched Weavers' 'prentices,' and fops who would not, and indeed could not, fight." Those who had fought beside the British in the French and Indian War claimed that "lobsterbacks" would be no match for hardy American yeomen in a straight fight. Why the British scarcely knew how to shoot a gun!

Within Boston, relations between patriots and British authorities had once reached the flash point early in 1775. First, there was a brawl between butchers and redcoats at the public market. The anniversary of the Boston Massacre in March became a second occasion for friction when some British officers heckled the patriot leader Joseph Warren as he was delivering a commemorative oration.

At about this time spies for the British informed Gage that the minutemen were collecting arms and ammunition at Concord, a few miles outside of Boston. In addition, the Massachusetts legislature, in defiance of Gage's orders, was holding meetings at Concord. Why not, Gage thought, capture the arms and, perhaps, also seize some of the rebellious patriot leaders?

On the evening of April 18, 1775, a force of seven hundred redcoats set out for Concord. Patriots in the city quickly learned of the move and dispatched Paul Revere, a patriot silversmith, and William Dawes, to alert the minutemen and the patriot leaders that the British were coming. Although Revere was captured and Dawes turned back, another rider conveyed the news to the patriots at Concord in time. When the British reached nearby Lexington after marching most of the night, they discovered seventy armed minutemen lined up on the town commons shivering in the early morning chill. The British commanding

Lantern of pierced tin called a "Paul Revere"; probably made in New England; eighteenth to nineteenth century. *(Index of American Design.)*

officer, Major John Pitcairn, immediately rode toward them shouting: "Ye villains, ye rebels, disperse! Lay down your arms!" At the same time the British light infantry began to run foward to intercept the Americans, who retreated to a stone wall at the edge of the field. At the wall the minutemen stopped and fired off a ragged volley, wounding one redcoat and Major Pitcairn's horse. The British replied more effectively, killing ten of the Americans and wounding nine others.

No one had told the redcoats to fire; confronted by the detested Americans, they had lost their self-control. The situation was similar to that of the Boston Massacre, and it is possible that the incident, had it occurred earlier, could have been dealt with by the courts as before. But April 1775 was not March 1770. Feeling between the two sides had deteriorated to the point where nothing could restrain the Americans. As the British reassembled to move on Concord, the Massachusetts countryside rose in fury. By the time the redcoats had arrived at their destination, a large force of armed and angry farmers had collected to intercept them. When the Americans began to advance on their enemy, the British tried to withdraw. At this point the minutemen fired, killing and wounding several of the redcoats.

Now began a long, dismal, and bloody retreat from Concord all the way back to the safety of Boston. As they plodded back, the British were subject to a withering barrage from behind hedges, trees, houses, and stone walls. A British lieutenant, seeking to explain the debacle, reported that his men were attacked "from all sides but mostly from the rear, where people had hid themselves in houses till we had passed, and then fired." At Lexington the original British force picked up reinforcements that had come out from Boston to join them. After a short wait to rest the exhausted Concord contingent, the combined force resumed the retreat to Boston. Once again, they came under devastating fire. Choked by dust, their heavy woolen uniforms sweat-drenched, the British troops suffered agonies. Many were hit. Occasionally detachments broke off from the main body to charge a knot of Americans or even to loot the houses along the road. Despite their contempt for amateur soldiers the British had to admit that their fire was often deadly. Clearly the Americans had learned much of guerrilla fighting from the Indians and were able to put it to good use.

The British arrived back in Charlestown in the evening and counted their losses. Of the eighteen hundred men who had been sent to Concord, some seventy-three had been killed and two hundred wounded. Only by the sheerest good luck had the Americans been prevented from cutting off the whole force and capturing it. Although complete disaster had been avoided, the Americans had won a great victory against the finest troops of Europe.

Concord and Lexington marked the beginning of the Revolution. After April 19, 1775, there was no turning back. Not all Americans wanted independence or even believed that a new fundamental relationship with Britain was essential. In the ensuing months thousands of native-born Americans would become "loyalists" (or "Tories"), fierce partisans of the King. Loyalism would prove especially strong among certain classes of Americans. Natives like Thomas Hutchinson who had close ties to the British government were natural loyalists. Anglican ministers who recognized the King as head of the Church of England also tended to take the British side, as did many Anglican laymen, especially in New England, where they formed an unpopular minority.

Generally speaking, people of conservative temperament who naturally preferred the familiar to the unknown were also to be found on the loyalist side. This does not mean that loyalists were invariably rich with a large property stake in society. Besides loyalist merchants, officials, and planters, there were also loyalist mechanics, farmers, and small shopkeepers. In the western Carolinas, where small farmers known as "regulators" had rebelled against low-country domination in the 1760's and early 1770's, there was a good deal of loyalist sentiment. Angry at the seaboard Carolina gentry for denying them representation in the colonial assemblies and for crushing their rebellion by force of arms, some of the western farmers chose the King's side after 1775, if only because the low-country Carolina planters and merchants chose the opposite one. There were even slave loyalists. In Virginia, especially, the royal governor would appeal to the slaves to help the Crown against its enemies among the planters, and many Virginia bondsmen would respond.

Like the loyalists, patriots or "rebels" came in different shapes and sizes. If many Anglican clergymen chose the King, almost all Congregational and many other dissenting ministers chose Congress. In the major port towns—Boston, Newport, New York, Philadelphia, and Charleston—the artisans, apprentices, and laborers were strongly patriotic. But so were the merchants, especially those who felt threatened by the trade regulations that had been piled on top of the existing navigation acts since 1763. The landed gentry of New York split. Families such as the Delanceys took the King's side; the Schuylers and the Livingstons, equally wealthy and aristocratic, plumped from Congress. In Virginia and the Carolinas, the patriot leaders were almost all Anglican gentlemen, many of them owners of large estates and scores of black slaves. Indeed, men such as George Washington, Henry Laurens, and Robert Morris were among the wealthiest Americans of their day.

"Bunker Hill" and the Drift Toward Independence

Despite the continuing Tory dissent, the response of most Americans to the events in Massachusetts was prompt and vigorous. In Massachusetts the Provincial Congress, as the illegal colonial legislature was called, authorized the raising of troops and appealed to the other colonies for aid. Before long, several thousand militia from Rhode Island, Connecticut, and New Hampshire, along with contingents of Stockbridge and Mohawk Indians, were pouring into the colony and assembling in a ring around Boston where Gage's troops were ensconced. The American general in charge was Artemas Ward; his subordinates included the talented Nathanael Greene and Israel Putnam.

In some ways the besiegers of Boston were in worse shape than the besieged. The men lived without sufficient tents and amidst filth. Unused to the standards of hygiene necessary where men lived together in masses, they refused to take precautions. Before long, disease invaded the American camp. The British in Boston, on the other hand, seemed to be living off the fat of the land, well housed and well supplied with food and necessities. At the end of May 1775, Gage was joined by three other high-ranking British officers, Sir William Howe, Sir Henry Clinton, and John Burgoyne. Howe took over command from Gage, who remained as civilian governor of the colony.

Sooner or later, in any event, Howe would have had to attack the Americans ringing the city, but they forced his hand by fortifying Breed's Hill, across the Charles from Boston and within cannon range of the city. On June 17 the British navy began to bombard the American positions. Confident that the untried amateur soldiers under Colonel William Prescott's command could not stand up against redcoats in a regular battle, Howe and his fellow officers decided to make a direct attack on the entrenched Americans. Soon troops of the grenadiers and light infantry, encumbered with packs containing three days' rations, were being ferried across the Charles to Charlestown peninsula. As the British troops landed on the beach,

the Americans waited silently. When the redcoats prepared to charge, however, Prescott gave the order to fire. There was a great crash and a cloud of smoke; scores of Welsh Fusiliers fell. In seconds the light infantry regiment was fleeing in panic, leaving behind their wounded, their dead, and most of their equipment. Meanwhile the tall grenadiers were advancing on the Americans atop Breed's Hill in well-dressed lines. When the redcoats were within twenty yards of the American position a volley rang out, knocking down scores. The grenadiers, unlike the Welsh, continued to advance, their bayonets fixed. The Americans, now almost within spitting range, continued to fire away. Finally grenadiers too broke ranks and fled.

Howe was not finished, however. Once more he ordered his men against the American position. Once more they were mowed down and retreated. Again Howe ordered his men to attack, this time without their heavy packs. By now the Americans were low in ammunition. Many, moreover, assumed the battle was over and, disobeying their officers, had begun to leave for home. Despite heavy casualties, this time the redcoats drove the Americans off the hill and took possession of the Charlestown peninsula.

The British had won, but at what a price! Over a thousand redcoat casualties, with at least 226 of them killed. Almost fifty percent of the British troops engaged were either dead or wounded. As Howe commented: "A dear bought victory, another such would have ruined us."

The battle, misnamed "Bunker Hill," was of vast symbolic importance. To Americans, it was a great moral triumph. Combined with Lexington and Concord, it had demonstrated that American militia could stand up to the best the British could throw against them. In reality, though, the Americans, with fifteen thousand men encamped around Boston, should have done much better. Far too many had been insubordinate; some had even shown cowardice. The Americans' staff work and supply services had been poor. Finally, American success had been as much due to British errors in using a frontal assault as to their own

A PLAN of

THE TOWN OF BOSTON,

with

the INTRENCHMENTS &c.

OF

HIS MAJESTYS FORCES in 1775:

from the Observations of

LIEU.T PAGE

of His MAJESTY'S Corps of Engineers;

and from the Plans of other GENTLEMEN.

Engraved & Printed for W.m FADEN, Charing-Cross,
as the Act directs 1.st Octo.r 1777.

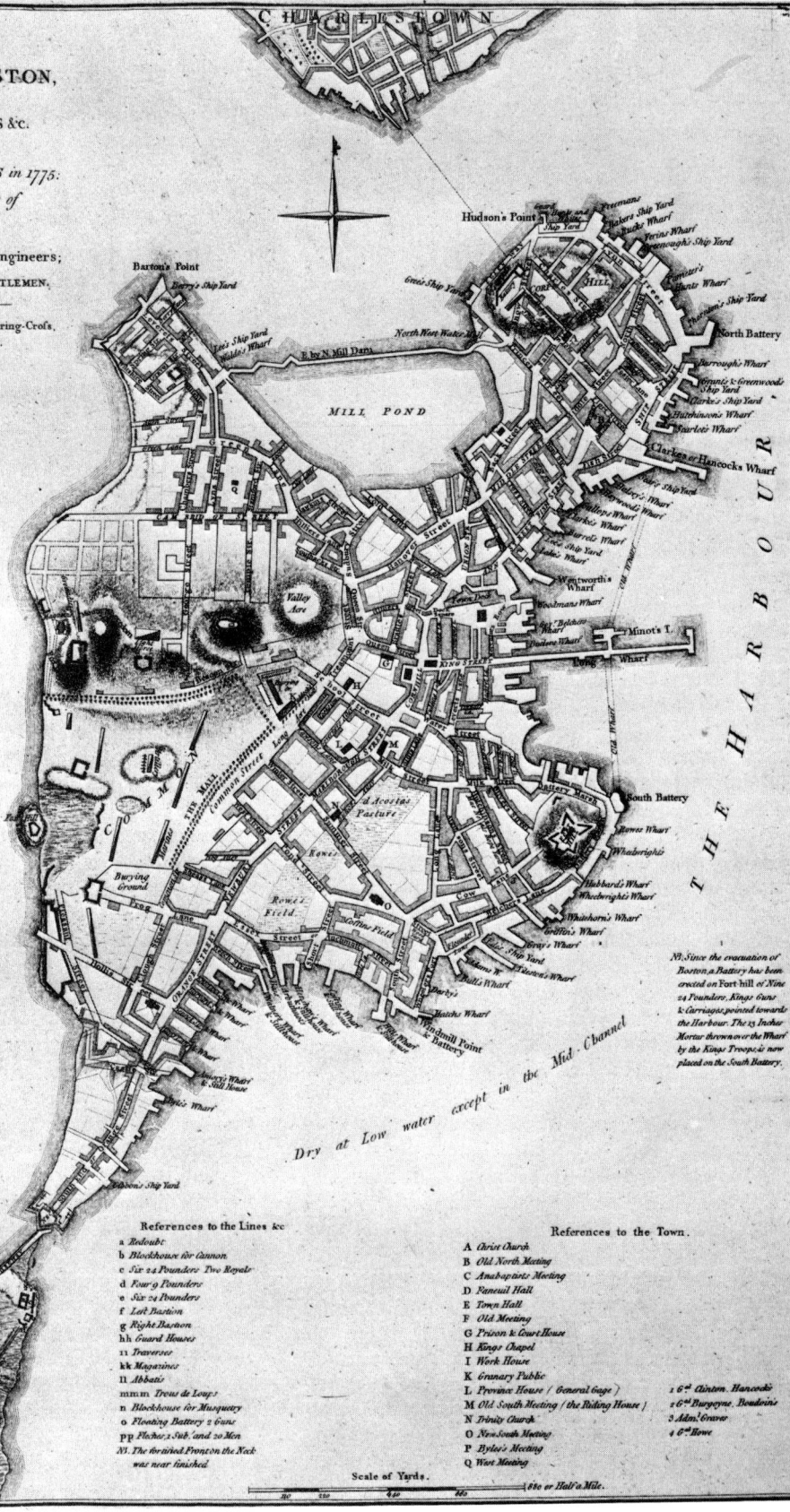

CHARLESTOWN

MILL POND

THE HARBOUR

MILL DAM
E. by N. Mill Dam

Barton's Point
Hudson's Point
North Battery
Long Wharf
South Battery

Valley Acre
Common Street
KING STREET
THE MALL

Old Acacia's Pasture
Fox Hill
Burying Ground

all this Part is dry at Low Water

Dry at Low water except in the Mid Channel

N.B. Since the evacuation of
Boston a Battery has been
erected on Fort hill of Nine
24 Pounders, Kings Guns
& Carriages pointed towards
the Harbour. The 13 Inches
Mortar thrown over the Wharf
by the Kings Troops is now
placed on the South Battery.

References to the Lines &c

a Redoubt
b Blockhouse for Cannon
c Six 24 Pounders Two Royals
d Four 9 Pounders
e Six 24 Pounders
f Left Bastion
g Right Bastion
hh Guard Houses
ii Traverses
kk Magazines
ll Abbatis
mmm Trous de Loups
n Blockhouse for Musquetry
o Floating Battery 2 Guns
pp Flesches 1 Sub. and 20 Men
N.B. The fortified Front on the Neck
was near finished

References to the Town.

A Christ Church
B Old North Meeting
C Anabaptists Meeting
D Faneuil Hall
E Town Hall
F Old Meeting
G Prison & Court House
H Kings Chapel
I Work House
K Granary Public
L Province House (General Gage)
M Old South Meeting (the Riding House)
N Trinity Church
O New South Meeting
P Byles's Meeting
Q West Meeting

1 Ge.l Clinton, Hancock's
2 Ge.l Burgoyne, Bowdoin's
3 Adm.l Graves
4 Ge.l Howe

Scale of Yards.

680 or Half a Mile.

brilliance. Still, they had reason to be proud and to look forward to the future with some hope.

Meanwhile, the Second Continental Congress had assembled in Philadelphia, as scheduled, in early May. Among its first acts was the choice of an overall commander for the Continental army who would take charge of the troops around Boston. Following the advice of John Adams, it appointed George Washington, of Virginia on June 15, just days before Bunker Hill. It also voted to raise six companies of riflemen from the middle colonies and the South to join the New Englanders at Boston and decided to issue $2-million in bills of credit to support the accelerating rebellion.

Despite the outbreak of hostilities, Congress resisted a final political break with Britain. There were those at Philadelphia who favored a bold declaration of American independence. John Adams urged his fellow delegates to accept the advice of Massachusetts and endorse the formation of new constitutions for each colony to break the tie with England. These independent states, he believed, would ally themselves in a continental league that would be equivalent to an independent nation. But even this oblique road to independence did not please most of the delegates, who still hoped for British conciliation. Adams' proposals were ignored.

General Washington arrived in the Boston area after Bunker Hill to find the largely New England army a distinct disappointment. The Yankees, he complained, were "an exceedingly nasty and dirty people." Besides, they seemed excessively concerned with money. Other observers found the troops enterprising, though highly individualistic, and unwilling to submit to discipline or even call their officers by official titles—captain, colonel, major, or whatever. The new commander in chief had his work cut out for him in seeking to turn this ragged collection of farmers and mechanics into an army and to combine it smoothly with the regiments of Virginians, Marylanders, and Pennsylvanians who began to arrive at Cambridge.

In these months of 1775, and virtually all through the war, one of the General's chief problems was simply to keep his force intact. Few Americans considered military service a full-time occupation. Farm boys were willing to enlist for a few months, especially in the winter or after the crops had been planted. But when needed at home, or when confronted with long stretches of idleness, they grew restless. Some simply deserted. Others waited until their term of enlistment had ended and, regardless of the military situation, went home. As Governor Trumbull of Connecticut expressed it, "The pulse of a New England

man beats high for liberty. His engagement in the service he thinks purely voluntary; therefore, in his estimation when the time of enlistment is out, he thinks himself not holden without further engagement."

While the commander in chief was trying to construct a Continental army out of fifteen thousand individualists encamped outside Boston, the war was not marking time elsewhere. In May a force of Massachusetts men and Vermonters under Ethan Allen and Benedict Arnold had attacked and captured the small British garrison at Fort Ticonderoga on Lake Champlain. The Americans acquired valuable military suppplies, including one hundred cannons. In August the captured British post became the jumping-off point for an attack on Canada led by General Philip Schuyler of New York and the British-born Richard Montgomery. On November 13, 1775, Montgomery captured Montreal. Meanwhile, Arnold, with one thousand volunteers from Washington's force, set out across Maine heading toward Quebec City. He reached the British fortress in November and was joined by Montgomery and his men. The combined little army attacked the city in a howling snowstorm. In the battle Montgomery was killed and Arnold wounded. A hundred Americans were killed and four hundred captured. With his pitiful remnant Arnold continued to besiege the town all through the winter. In the spring he gave up the siege and returned home.

During these early months of the Revolution the fighting was not confined to the North. In Virginia the royal governor, the Earl of Dunmore, had gathered the colony's loyalists together at Norfolk, formed them into a small army, and set them to destroying patriot-owned plantations. In November, Dunmore issued a proclamation establishing martial law and calling on all citizens to support the King. He also offered freedom to all slaves who would desert their patriot masters and join his forces. This, however, proved to be a mistake. Dunmore's little army did attract some runaway slaves, but it did the loyalist-British cause little good. White Virginians feared nothing more than a rising of armed slaves. Dunmore's proclamation, by raising the specter of slave insurrection, pushed many of the undecided into the patriot camp. Fortunately for the patriot cause, when Dunmore sallied out of Norfolk with his mixed band of loyalists and blacks, he was defeated. Soon after, he loaded his blacks and loyalists aboard ships and abandoned Norfolk to the Americans. In February 1776 he returned and set fire to the city.

While Americans and Englishmen were killing one another in the fields and forests of North America, efforts were being made to bring the two sides together. In July 1775 Congress adopted the Olive Branch Petition announcing continued American attachment to the King and asking him to desist from further hostile acts until some scheme of reconciliation had been arranged. It also adopted a "Declaration of the Causes and Necessities of Taking Up Arms." This document rejected independence, but pronounced American determination not to accept slavery, no matter what the cost. Several weeks later, Congress rejected Lord North's proposals of February, by which the British government offered to avoid repetition to forgo parliamentary taxes on any colony that would agree to tax itself for defense and to pay its own expenses.

Congress adjourned in August 1775, but reconvened in mid-September with a full representation from all thirteen colonies. In early November, members learned that the King had rejected the Olive Branch Petition and declared the colonies in open rebellion. On December 6 Congress responded to the King's declaration by disavowing American allegiance to Parliament, but acknowledging continued allegiance to George III.

While these proposals and counter-proposals flew back and forth across the Atlantic, Americans were moving rapidly toward practical self-government. Besides establishing a Continental army, Congress also appointed commissioners to deal with the Indian tribes and set up a Post Office Department. In October 1775 it organized a navy. Most momentous of all, in November it appointed a five-man Committee of Secret Correspondence to negotiate with potential allies abroad. In December the Committee made contact with a French agent, who informed them that France would aid the colonists against the British. Soon after, the French Foreign Minister, Comte de Vergennes, consulted his Spanish counterpart regarding joint action to aid the Americans. When the Spanish gave their approval, Vergennes ordered a large amount of munitions to be sent to the Americans through a "front" company, Hortalez et Companie. Congress responded to these French moves in April 1776 by opening American ports to the commerce of all nations except Britain.

Common Sense and the Declaration of Independence

By this time very little but the continued tie to the King was left of the strong connective tissue that had bound the empire together. And even the King did not appear so benevolent and wise to some Americans any longer. One firebrand patriot, the young poet Philip Freneau, declared:

From the scoundrel, Lord North, who would
    bind us in chains,
From a dunce of a king who was born without
    brains. . . .
From an island that bullies, and hectors, and
    swears,
I send up to heaven my wishes and prayers
That we, disunited, may freemen be still,
And Britain go on—to be damned, if she will.

The final wrench to the remaining ties of empire came with the publication of *Common Sense,* a hundred-page pamphlet composed by a recently arrived Englishman, Thomas Paine. Written with extraordinary passion and eloquence, *Common*

Sense denounced the institution of hereditary kingship. "For all men being originally equals, no *one* by *birth* could have a right to set up his own family in perpetual preference to all others forever," Paine declared. George was a "royal brute," not the generous father of his people, and Americans had no reason to continue to obey him or remain his subjects.

The pamphlet had an electrifying effect. Perhaps a million Americans read it as it passed from hand to hand, and were profoundly affected by its message. Washington noted that it was "working a powerful change in the minds of men." After reading it, he himself ceased to toast the King, as he had done till now through thick and thin.

By sweeping away the last illusions about George III, *Common Sense* helped precipitate independence. On April 12, 1776, the North Carolina Convention authorized the colony's delegates in Congress to vote for independence. The Virginia legislature followed soon after. On June 7 Richard Henry Lee, responding to the House of

*Common Sense
by Tom Paine*

Paine's rabble-rousing pamphlets circulated by the tens of thousands and galvanized sentiment against England.

Burgesses' resolution, offered the following motion in Congress: that "these United Colonies are, and of a right ought to be, free and independent states, and that all political connection between them and the state of British is, and ought to be, totally dissolved."

Congress responded by appointing to frame a statement of independence a five-man committee consisting of Thomas Jefferson, John Adams, Benjamin Franklin, Roger Sherman, and Robert Livingston. Jefferson was made chairman. At 33 the tall Virginian was one of the youngest members of Congress. But he was also a man of great charm and eloquence, with a reputation as a scholar. Still, if anyone had then realized how important the document would be, the choice of chief author would undoubtedly have fallen on either of two better-known members, Adams or Franklin.

Jefferson's Declaration of Independence was one of the most eloquent and moving endorsements of human freedom and equality ever composed. Drawing on the ideas of the seventeenth-century English Whigs who had overthrown James II and helped establish England's constitutional monarchy and on the writings of contemporary Scotsmen, the document announced that fundamental human rights took precedence over the legal obligations owed to rulers. "All men" were "created equal" and were "endowed by their Creator with certain unalienable Rights," the Declaration stated. Among these rights were those "to Life, Liberty, and the pursuit of Happiness." Governments were not established for the sake of rulers; they existed only to "secure rights." But when a government became "destructive of these ends," it was "the Right of the People to alter or abolish it" and establish a new one that would respect them.

The rest of the Declaration was a detailed—and not altogether fair—indictment of the British government for general attitudes and specific acts designed to establish "an absolute Tyranny" over America. Here Jefferson marshaled virtually every American grievance, both immediate and of long standing, against Britain and defended the actions of the colonists during the years since 1763. All pointed toward one inescapable end: "these United Colonies are, and of Right ought to be, Free and Independent States." "With firm reliance on the Protection of Divine Providence," the Declaration concluded, "we mutually pledge to each other our Lives, our Fortunes and our sacred Honor.''

Adams and Franklin suggested a number of changes, primarily stylistic. Congress as a body, when it received the draft, struck out several phrases and clauses. On July 4, 1776 all fifty-five members present, except John Dickinson, signed it.

In the next few days the Declaration was read to large gatherings of Americans throughout the self-proclaimed independent country. In Philadelphia John Nixon, head of the city guard, read the document to a large audience in the State House yard. When he finished, the crowd cheered. In New York, the officers of the Continental army, after hearing the Declaration read, all "went to a Publick House to testify to . . . their joy at the happy news of independence.'' Bostonians celebrated by removing the plaque bearing the King's coat of arms from the State House wall and burning it.

The United States dates its independence as a nation from July 4, 1776. But as many contemporaries knew, there was a long distance between signing a document and winning actual freedom on the battlefield. But now there could be no turning back. Victory would mean that the efforts at Philadelphia had not been in vain. Defeat might well mean the surrender of lives, fortunes, and sacred honor. The die was cast.

Windsor chair, reputed to be the sort used by Thomas Jefferson while he wrote the Declaration of Independence; probably made in New England; mid-eighteenth century. *(Index of American Design.)*

Suggested Readings

The relationship between ideas and culture in these eventful years is dealt with in two important books: Henry May, *The Enlightenment in America* (1976) and Henry Steele Commager, *The Empire of Reason: How Europe Imagined and America Realized the Enlightenment* (1977). Edmund S. and Helen M. Morgan's thesis is defined in the title of their book, *The Stamp Act Crisis: Prologue to Revolution* (1953); Pauline Maier examines the next critical phase of the move toward rebellion in *From Resistance to Revolution: Colonial Radicals and the Development of American Opposition to Britain, 1765-1766* (1972). Virginia receives an excellent study by Edmund S. Morgan in *American Slavery, American Freedom: The Ordeal of Colonial Virginia* (1975). Bernard Bailyn's *Origins of American Politics* (1968) is another book of great importance.

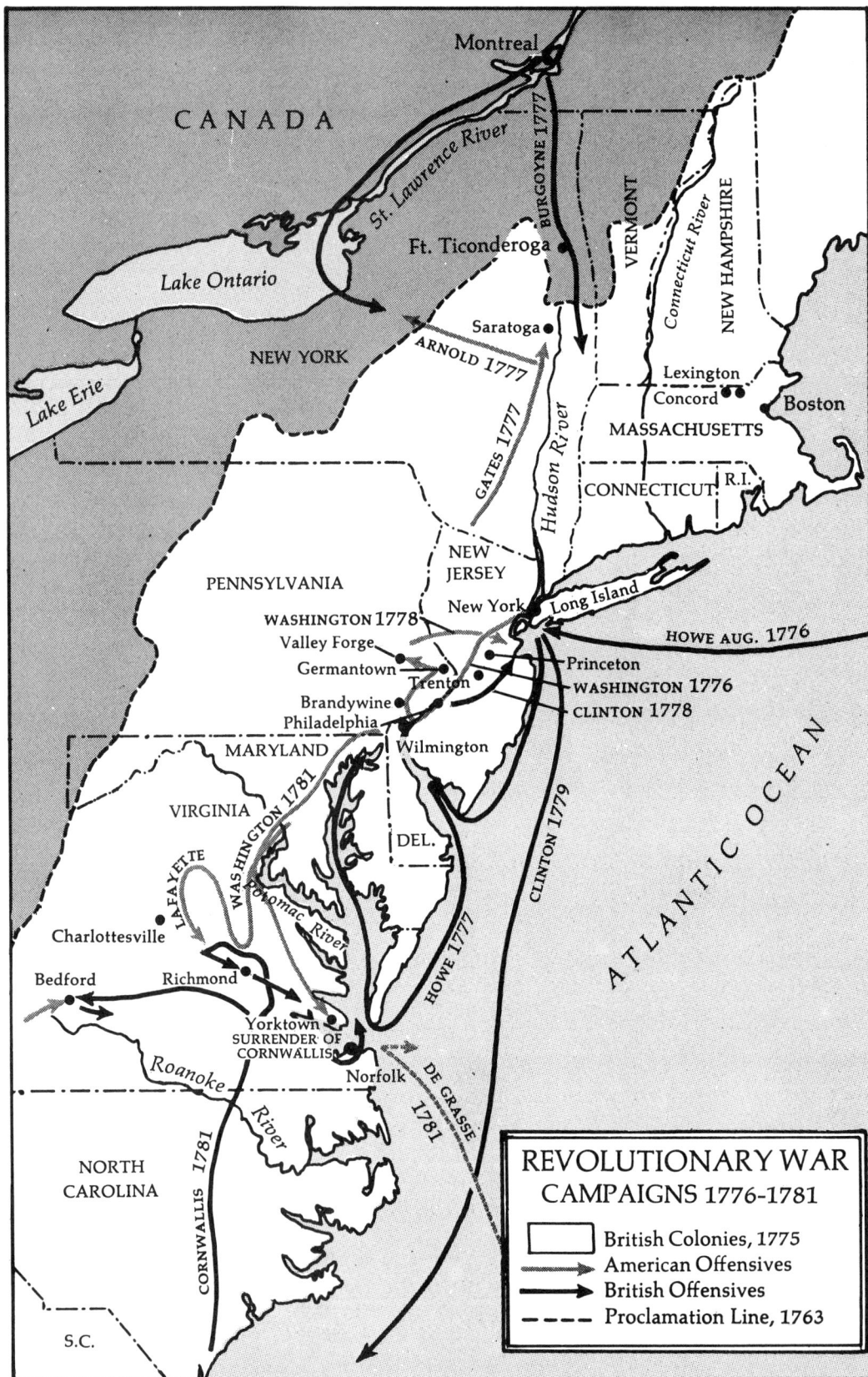

REVOLUTIONARY WAR
CAMPAIGNS 1776-1781

☐	British Colonies, 1775
→	American Offensives
→	British Offensives
- - -	Proclamation Line, 1763

Montreal

CANADA

St. Lawrence River

Lake Ontario

Lake Erie

NEW YORK

Ft. Ticonderoga

BURGOYNE 1777

VERMONT

Connecticut River

NEW HAMPSHIRE

Saratoga

ARNOLD 1777

GATES 1777

Hudson River

Lexington
Concord

Boston

MASSACHUSETTS

CONNECTICUT

R.I.

PENNSYLVANIA

NEW JERSEY

New York

Long Island

HOWE AUG. 1776

WASHINGTON 1778

Valley Forge

Germantown

Brandywine

Philadelphia

Trenton

Princeton

WASHINGTON 1776

CLINTON 1778

Wilmington

MARYLAND

CLINTON 1779

VIRGINIA

WASHINGTON 1781

DEL.

LAFAYETTE

Potomac River

ATLANTIC OCEAN

Charlottesville

Bedford

Richmond

HOWE 1777

Yorktown
SURRENDER OF
CORNWALLIS

Norfolk

DE GRASSE
1781

Roanoke
River

NORTH
CAROLINA

CORNWALLIS 1781

S.C.

Chapter IV
Revolution and Independence
1776—1787

Victory at Saratoga

Of all the generals sent by Great Britain to subdue the American rebels, the one the colonials most enjoyed hating was "Gentleman Johnny" Burgoyne. To a generation bred on tales of English decadence, corruption, and arrogance, he was the ideal enemy to defeat in the critical battle of the Revolutionary War. "Sir Jack Brag" (as one song called him) was rumored to have told the King that "with one regiment he could march triumphantly through all the American colonies."

Burgoyne initiated his campaign in 1777 with an infuriating proclamation denouncing "the present unnatural Rebellion" as "the compleatest System of Tyranny that ever God, in his Displeasure, suffered, for a Time, to be exercised over a froword and stubborn Generation"; he threatened the rebels with "the Indian forces under my direction—and they amount to thousands."

Burgoyne offered rich possibilities for parody in his pomposity. But the campaign that he directed was no joke. Colonial leaders had long worried about the English "becoming masters of the Hudson River" which would "divide our strength, and enfeeble every effort for our common preservation and security." As originally planned, one army of British, Hessian, and Indian troops would march down from Montreal, while a second came from the west through the Mohawk Valley, and a third up the Hudson from New York City, all to converge on Albany. Along a line from New York to Montreal they would create a chain of forts to cut off New England—the presumed source of rebellion.

The campaign began with a signal British victory—the capture of Fort Ticonderoga, key to the lake route to Albany, on July 6, 1777. King George III, on receiving the news, is said to have shouted, "I have beat them! I have beat the Americans." Alexander Hamilton was a better prophet than the King: "I am in hope," he wrote, "that Burgoigne's success will precipitate him into measures that will prove his ruin. The enterprising spirit he has credit for, I suspect may easily be fanned by his vanity into rashness."

Burgoyne immediately blundered. Deciding that he now had ample time to move his army a mere seventy miles to Albany, he set out through the woods rather than following Lake George. Hauling fifty-two cannon, his enormous wardrobe and wine cellar, and a female entourage through forests cluttered by thousands of trees that the Americans had felled, Burgoyne covered twenty-three miles in twenty-four days and became lost in the woods while the patriots gathered strength. Then, at Oriskany and Fort Stanwix in the Mohawk Valley, in tough hand-to-hand fighting, they soundly defeated the British army advancing from the west. Meanwhile the murder and scalping of Jane McCrea by Indian allies of Burgoyne had set the citizens of the upper Hudson Valley into a fury at the British.

"Miss McCrea," wrote patriot commander Horatio Gates in an angry letter to Burgoyne, "a young lady lovely to the sight, of virtuous character and amiable disposition, engaged to be married to an officer in your Army, was with other women and children taken out of a house near Fort Edward, carried into the woods, and there scalped and mangled in a most shocking manner . . . The miserable fate of Miss McCrea was particularly aggravated by her being dressed to receive her promised husband, but met her murderer employed by you."

Burgoyne, fearing mass desertion by his Indian allies, refused to execute her murderer and thereby aroused the entire region: for one of the few times in the war, militiamen and volunteers came and stayed to fight. When Burgoyne sent out a force to gather supplies in Vermont, two thousand minute-men from Vermont, New Hampshire, and Massachusetts threw the British back with heavy losses.

Short of troops, hungry for supplies, and facing a large and capable continental army well supported by local militia, Burgoyne was now in serious trouble. Nonetheless, as Hamilton had predicted, his vanity drove him to fight. Crossing the Hudson he stood at Saratoga facing Gates's army, which held a commanding position behind powerful fortifications built at the direction of a Polish engineer, Thaddeus Kosciusko. On September 19, Burgoyne threw his troops into action against Gates at Freeman's Farm. The battle sapped British strength while Gates easily reinforced his army. With supplies running low, Burgoyne had to decide whether to fight again or retreat. Of course he fought and on October 7, in the second battle of Saratoga, again suffered heavy losses. His position completely untenable—only the women in his company, whom the chivalrous Americans would not shoot, could get water from the nearby river—Burgoyne surrendered. A popular topical verse said it all:

> Burgoyne, alas! unknowing future fates,
> Could force his way through woods,
> but not through GATES.

The Course of Battle

Britain initially tried to repress the rebellion by overwhelming force, but guerrilla tactics confounded their efforts. From 1778 to 1780 stalemate ensued despite, or perhaps because of, the alliance between the colonists and the French resulting from Gates's victory at Saratoga. British generals could not defeat Washington's army or control the countryside, particularly in New England. On the other hand, the Americans were unable to dislodge the redcoats from major seaport cities or to prevent England's slow recapture of the southern states.

Only days after Congress proclaimed independence on July 4, 1776, in Philadelphia, a huge British fleet—a "forest of masts"—sailed into New York City harbor: 32,000 soldiers with 11,000 sailors manning thirty major ships of the line and dozens of transports. Its commander, General William Howe, anticipated victory so firmly that he carried with him a surrender document. Against this armada, the largest Britain had yet amassed, General George Washington corraled about 19,000 skilled marksmen who lacked military discipline as their officers lacked military judgment. Washington unwisely divided his makeshift army, sending about half of his troops to Long Island while the rest stayed on Manhattan. English ships slipped around both islands to block retreat, while Howe's soldiers attacked Brooklyn Heights. Realizing his mistake, Washington skillfully retreated across both islands into New Jersey, although his army was now demoralized and in disarray.

Wishing to negotiate with the Americans, not destroy them, Howe failed to pursue them quickly. Washington used this pause to regroup his armies, and on Christmas Day returned to the attack. After a polished military maneuver across the frozen Delaware River, his army surprised a camp of Hessian mercenaries at an outpost in Trenton and took nearly two thousand of them prisoner. Both generals now took up winter quarters, Howe in New York City, Washington in the hills of western New Jersey. Britain had fumbled a chance to end the war quickly.

Rather than move northward, Howe decided early in 1777 to attack Philadelphia. As his invasion force sailed for the headwaters of Chesapeake Bay, Washington and his troops scurried overland to meet the British, but could not prevent them from occupying the city. Washington retreated once more, this time to Valley Forge, one of the few iron foundries still in patriot hands.

The "revolting colonials," Lord North thought, "cannot last long." The King's ministers expected their armies gradually to wear down colonial resistance by occupying major coastal cities and luring the southern states away from the supposedly more radical northern ones. Meanwhile, the British fleet's blockade of the coastline would deprive the Americans of both income and supplies from trade. Confident that their own regular forces would suffice, the British virtually ignored the half-million American loyalists scattered throughout the nation.

This overall strategy, however, proved to be seriously flawed. One major difficulty for the British was space—the sheer vastness of the country. The redcoats fought at the end of long lines of supply; small, slow-moving wooden frigates could not maintain large land armies. American guerrillas could, and frequently did, attack and then escape easily across rivers or into forests. His Majesty's generals could find no way to strike some final, decisive blow that would crush the rebellion once and for all. Nor were the British ruthless enough to destroy American morale. Fighting to bring the rebels back into the empire, English generals did not scorch the earth or brutalize the population. Lord Dunmore, the last royal governor of Virginia, did offer freedom to black slaves if they fled or fought the Americans, but most remained with their masters. As British strategy failed to divide the states or to quell the rebellion, Parliament grew increasingly restless with the war.

American strategy played upon British weakness. Patriot forces often retreated into wilderness to strain England's supply lines and, eventually, wear down English resolve to continue the war. And yet, as matters stood, the new nation found even this passive strategy difficult to execute. Most men shunned enlistment in the Continental Army, especially as patriotic fervor subsided after 1776. Farming required the most work precisely at those times most favorable for eighteenth-century warfare, spring and early fall. With the habit of nationalism not yet firmly established, state governors maintained tight control over their local militias. Many Americans, fearful of military authority and centralized power, refused to pay taxes to support Washington's troops, and so the regular army lacked not only soldiers but also arms and equipment. The national government, too, lacked adequate revenues, so the Continental Congress paid expenses by printing millions and millions of paper dollars. This flood of currency drove up prices mercilessly. Congress could not act without unanimous consent from all thirteen states, a rule that allowed the smaller states to intrigue for large gains as the price of their consent. And the government conducted the war through cumbersome committees. In sum, a serious lack of manpower and money, compounded by defects in organization, hampered America's effort to survive.

Saratoga changed all that almost overnight. The American Revolution became a world war, and even the mighty British could not hope to defeat the world. "If old England is not by this lesson taught humility," wrote Gates savoring his victory, "then she is an obstinate old slut, bent upon her ruin." Gates's victory had brought a powerful ally into the American cause and transformed the war. As early as 1775, the Continental Congress had sent agents to France. Some, like Silas Deane and Arthur Lee, had arranged a trickle of loans and shipments of military supplies. (The small Dutch island of St. Eustatius in the Caribbean served as a transit point: French ships unloaded munitions there, and Americans picked them up.) Late in 1776, Congress sent Benjamin Franklin to Paris to negotiate an alliance. But King Louis XVI hesitated. His government was nearly bankrupt; his Spanish allies feared that the American example might encourage revolution among their own colonies; American armies seemed weak. It seemed enough to have the secret trade in military hardware supporting the patriot armies, accomplishing French objectives by tying Britain down in a protracted war. However much Franklin's republican wit and easy charm captivated courtiers at Versailles, diplomatic grace could not, by itself, gloss over hard realities. For two years, Franklin moved through France, winning many friends for the new nation and establishing his own formidable reputation. But for the time being the King avoided any overt alliance.

Nonetheless, European nations, particularly France and Spain, did see opportunities of their own in the conflict. King Louis yearned for revenge against an old enemy, while Spanish courtiers in Madrid feared the mushrooming British empire in the New World. After the battle of Saratoga opponents of the war in Britain convinced Parliament to open peace negotiations, and by early spring 1778 a delegation under the Earl of Carlisle was on its way to the colonies with an offer of limited autonomy within the British empire. It was fears that the Americans might accept such terms that finally prompted Louis XVI and his foreign minister to offer Congress a formal alliance. The patriots, skeptical of British promises and determined upon full independence, ratified the bargain on May 4, 1778, only weeks before the Carlisle commissioners arrived in Philadelphia.

The middle years of the war, from 1778 to 1780, were a dark and drifting time. Both sides reduced the scale and intensity of the fighting in North America as colonial skirmishes simply became part of an international war. Now forced to defend as well their possessions in India and the Caribbean, the British withdrew some of their fleet from North American waters. The new commander in chief in America, General Henry Clinton, lacked enough troops to try another grand assault on rebel forces, but he launched a mopping-up action in the South. Relatively small British armies attacked Georgia and then the Carolinas, a slow northward drive that took two years. Local militia harassed their march, but many Southerners were loyalists. By 1780 the redcoats were approaching Virginia. Precisely because their opponents were now so spread out, the Americans could not repeat another victory like that at Saratoga. Instead, Washington camped outside New York City, avoiding the risk of committing his army to a secondary front.

Old problems continued to plague the revolutionary forces. Local and state loyalties deprived the country of strong national unity; now more than ever it was state militias that took up the major burden of the fighting. Unwisely assuming that France would pay its bills, Congress printed more and more paper money, popularly called "continentals." By 1780 few merchants or farmers would accept "continentals" in payment for supplies. Washington had to resort to impressment—forced sales on credit—to provision his troops. By then the war had reached a stalemate. The prospect of an indeterminate war weakening both Britain and the United States benefited only the French and their allies. Some Americans worried that Louis XVI had intentionally schemed for just such an impasse.

Then the tide of battle turned in the American South. A sophisticated field commander, General Nathanael Greene, harassed British troops in the Carolina piedmont with guerrilla tactics and well-chosen field maneuvers. By midsummer 1781 the redcoats, now mostly loyalists unskilled at warfare, had retreated to the tidewater cities, principally Charleston and Savannah. The main body of English soldiers, then under Lord Charles Cornwallis, fought its way into southern Virginia, there to be supplied from the sea. Washington immediately concentrated all his available forces, moving his own army south into Virginia, where he joined with troops from local militia units. At the same time, French Admiral Francois Joseph Paul de Grasse turned northward from the Caribbean with a large fleet and some 3,000 soldiers. Both commanders aimed at trapping Cornwallis, one attacking him overland while the other cut off the

Frederick Kemmelmeyer, The American Star. (Metropolitan Museum of Art.)

sea route for resupply or retreat. The British naval commander, Admiral Rodney, slowed de Grasse with a small force, but the bulk of the British fleet stayed in the West Indies to defend English islands there. At the entrance to Chesapeake Bay, the French scattered Rodney's ships, then landed their troops along the York River. Washington arrived soon after, surrounding Cornwallis with an army twice the size of the British force. With escape impossible, Cornwallis surrendered at Yorktown on October 17, 1781.

Diplomacy Wins Independence

The defeat at Yorktown was by no means a military disaster for the British, since they still held America's major seaports. But what Yorktown did accomplish was to dramatize how slender were the possibilities for eventual British victory against the combination of American armies and guerrillas and French power. Another vital consideration was that an end to the fighting in North America would free badly needed fleets and armies to fight in the West Indies and India. Early in 1782, Parliament forced Prime Minister North out of office and demanded negotiations with the United States. Although George III disagreed, most of his subjects thought that a generous peace might conciliate the former colonists, and even draw them back into the British orbit.

The Americans, too, were ready to end the war. The Continental Congress was near collapse, and the war was creating a growing localism that might destroy national unity forever. The victory at Yorktown, however welcome, was more lucky circumstance than a triumph of superior military power or skill. Chances for a large territorial settlement and the prospect of better relations with Britain, a dangerous adversary for any nation so exposed to attack from the sea, understandably attracted many Americans. In fact, the Congress authorized its negotiating team, headed by Benjamin Franklin, to accept almost any treaty that included independence and a withdrawal of British troops. With their mutual interests so aligned, the two enemies seemed likely to conclude a quick agreement.

Yet, negotiations dragged on for nearly two years. The Franco-American alliance of 1778 bound the United States not to make a separate peace. In turn, Louis XVI and his minister Vergennes, in order to gain Spanish support, had promised ministers in Madrid much British territory as booty, especially strategic Gibraltar. Moreover, the Spanish wanted to confine the United States to the area east of the Appalachian Mountains. Although Spain could expect few concessions from England, it could still hold up a British-American settlement indefinitely. In short, America now had more to lose from its friends than from its enemies.

At last, Franklin broke the diplomatic log-jam by violating the terms of the alliance with France and opening separate negotiations with English agents. (The French, themselves weakened by a long and costly conflict, were not much upset, for Franklin in effect rescued them from an embarrassingly democratic ally.) Once started, talks progressed steadily. The series of treaties that ended the war, collectively known as the Treaty of Paris, was signed on September 3, 1783. England granted independence and promised to withdraw all of its troops from the colonies. The new nation acquired a huge dowry of land: from the Atlantic seacoast to the Mississippi River. Its boundaries in the north with Canada remained vague, however, and redcoats still occupied forts south of the Great Lakes. The Gulf coast was ceded to Spain, although both Americans and Englishmen were guaranteed navigation rights on the Mississippi. Britain successfully demanded that "no unlawful impediment" block the collection of prewar debts owned by Americans to British merchants. The treaties also pledged the United States to make restitution to loyalists who had suffered financially during the Revolution. Neither side would compromise on the complex question of fishing rights along the Atlantic coast, so the treaty ignored the issue altogether. British merchants did succeed in closing the Americans out of imperial commerce, a serious loss for the young nation. Despite these concessions and the lack of adequate enforcement procedures, the Americans had benefited handsomely from European rivalries. War and diplomacy created a new nation with boundaries generous enough to insure future growth and prosperity.

The Revolution at Home

The excitement of warfare obscured important changes within American society. The long struggle for independence accelerated forces and trends already apparent in the colonies before it began. The Revolution strengthened the possibilities of rearranging relationships among classes. Certainly there was, as one historian later wrote, "a struggle not only for home rule, but also over who should rule at home." The colonial elite aimed at preserving much of the old order so beneficial to them. Laborers, artisans, and small farmers often challenged, sometimes successfully, traditional prerogatives. Yet revolution in America involved no wholesale redistribution of property or wealth, no long-term change in the control of government. The War for Independence stopped short of creating an egalitarian society; it is doubtful that most patriot leaders really wanted one. Most people simply yearned for the restoration of harmony and for economic advancement. The colonists, now citizens, wanted to build, not destroy.

Eight years of warfare not only profited many individuals but also pushed the overall economy upward. An immense amount of money in circulation raised the prices of nearly everything. The Continental Congress and state governments spent nearly $200 million in hard money, followed by many more millions in currency. British soldiers and purchasing agents poured another $50 million into the economy. All this money created an extraordinary demand for commodities and, of course, persistent inflation. Few Americans suffered, however. War stimulated production, almost ending unemployment. The need for uniforms and arms, for example, produced vivid growth in the textile and iron industries. Merchants' inventories and farmers' crops grew in value. Bankers lent at high rates of interest to importers and privateers—goods brought through the British blockade commanded enormous profits. State and local governments often imposed price and wage controls, a device used since the Middle Ages to control inflation. Congress regulated monopolies and prevented exports of crucial raw materials. National credit institutions and common monetary problems more and more integrated local economies into a broad national market.

Despite sometimes rigorous local efforts at regulation, the pressures of wartime inflation produced extensive black markets. Shopkeepers and small farmers preferred to deal with Englishmen and private citizens who spent silver and gold coin. An indignant Pennsylvanian angrily refused to sell his grain to one of Washington's agents, saying, "Your money's not worth a damn continental." The phrase caught on. Throughout most of the war, America itself prospered while its government and army suffered penury and hardship. This paradox so angered Washington that he proposed hanging all profiteers.

Major changes occurred in the pattern of land ownership. Probably a quarter of the population was loyal to the British crown, either openly or secretly. (An older patriotism, self-interest, and fear of the mob all combined to give force to loyalist sentiment.) By 1778 all thirteen states had confiscated the property of those who "took refuge with the British tyrant." Some 100,000 already had left the country, most for Canada or England, and their estates were sold to raise money for the patriot cause. The confiscated lands were usually bought up by rich speculators or other large landowners, not by tenants and small farmers, who rarely had enough money to buy in places already settled. Instead, they and their children looked westward to those areas in or beyond the mountains. Even before the war ended, thousands had moved into Tennessee and Kentucky, northern New England and northern New York. This was one important reason why there was no major attack against property—so much was available elsewhere. Colonial elites fattened themselves on loyalist estates, while smaller farmers expanded toward the frontier.

The Revolution affected most social institutions, creating uncertain blends of old and new. Those who used the rhetoric of liberty, for example, stumbled against the reality of human bondage. Soon a voluble antislavery movement emerged. In most northern colonies, where blacks labored as field hands or household servants, patriot leaders struck decisively at the "peculiar institution." Slavery was outlawed in Massachusetts and Vermont, while New York and Pennsylvania adopted plans for gradual emancipation. Congress prohibited slavery in the territories west of the Old Northwest, that is, north of the Ohio River. But along that part of the Eastern seaboard south of the Mason-Dixon line, antislavery proposals foundered. Leaders there, mostly plantation owners like Washington and Jefferson, granted the immorality and nonrepublican nature of slavery, but accepted it as a "necessary evil."

Revolution effected profound changes in another colonial institution: religion. Patriots hounded Anglican ministers—most of whom, almost by the nature of their position, were strong loyalists—from their pulpits. Most states "disestablished" churches, ending the special privileges or civil functions of particular sects. Only Massachusetts and Connecticut still collected taxes to fund a state church; the other states viewed competing religions as equal in the eyes of the law. Tolerance did not extend to atheists, however, and most state legislatures established a religious test (aimed against Jews and Catholics) for holding public office. Blasphemy remained a crime punishable by imprisonment.

Documents like Thomas Jefferson's *Statute for Religious Liberty in Virginia,* finally enacted in 1786, granted tolerance for the free practice of religion, not a guarantee of rights for nonbelievers. If restrictive by twentieth-century standards, the Statute was for its time a model, and was proclaimed to the rest of the world as a showpiece of America's new freedom.

Historians have argued fiercely about whether or not American society became more open, more fostering of upward mobility, during the Revolutionary era. Certainly some older marks of privilege did disappear. Primogeniture and entail—feudal legal devices which prevented the breakup of large family estates by requiring their owners to will all lands intact to their eldest male heir—were outlawed. Citizens abandoned titles like "Esquire" or "Colonel" or "Your Excellency, " and instead addressed each other simply as "Mr." or "Mrs." Class distinctions based on dress waned; Franklin, for example, insisted upon wearing a simple republican black coat when he appeared in the gaily outfitted courts of Europe. The emigration of thousands and thousands of loyalists left many local political offices vacant and created new opportunities.

Despite outward changes in form, America remained firmly under the control of an elite class, although that group occasionally shifted in membership. Revolutionary ardor hardly touched the traditional "politics of deference" south of Pennsylvania: local plantation owners there never relinquished control over tidewater society and local government. These wealthy country gentlemen had little trouble beating back challeges to their power from small farmers in the highlands. In Philadelphia, New York, and Boston, long occupied by the British, a lawyer-merchant-landowner coalition dominated the cities after the war, much as it had before. The rich held disproportionate power in the Continental Congress. Robert Morris, for example, a merchant-speculator who served in the early 1780's as the nation's chief treasury official, possessed an $8 million fortune—then a huge sum.

And yet, however much an elite still controlled American life, the revolutionary years did hold out at least the prospect, if not the reality, of equal opportunity. Class barriers still protected an aristocracy from the commoners, but nowhere else in the world were those barriers so liable to be leapfrogged.

The dominant American ideology stressed the concept of liberty as defined in the writings of John Locke. Emphasizing private, individual rights, Americans feared all government as necessarily threatening liberty by depriving citizens of freedom. Presumably, majority rule would make government less dangerous. Yet Americans also recognized the right of minorities to live without fear of tyranny. Property owners, especially, worried that a quest for independence might turn into a quest for economic equality or an attack upon the privileges of wealth.

These fears were nowhere fully realized, although the war did change the balance of political power in some areas. Leaders and citizens enthusiastically applied Jefferson's declaration that "governments derive their just powers from the consent of the governed" to give stronger emphasis to the popular election of public officials. Many states liberalized voting qualifications, usually by substituting a taxpaying for property requirement. Reapportioned legislatures welcomed representatives from backcountry areas; the "middling ranks" of society—small farmers, local businessmen and artisans—came to occupy office more frequently; and bills of rights prefaced many new state constitutions. Everywhere governors lost power: elected assemblies gained control of patronage and tax matters, while governors in every state but Rhode Island lost the veto. Legislators stood for election each year. In Pennsylvania, a new constitution abolished altogether the legislature's upper house, traditionally the bastion of the wealthy.

Some less democratic practices lingered, to be sure. High political office still required the ownership of large amounts of land. (Massachusetts even increased the prerevolutionary property qualification for voting and holding office.) Upper chambers of most state legislatures could block the demands of the majority, and unfairly apportioned assemblies mocked the popular will in South Carolina, Virginia, and Georgia. (In the last-named state, for example, the piedmont contained three-fourths of the population yet received only one-fourth of the seats in the assembly, which was still rigidly dominated by tidewater plantation owners.) Nonetheless, all branches of government were elected, lower houses had most of the power, and state officials proved extremely susceptible to public opinion.

No less pervasive changes affected popular attitudes toward government. Many people never before interested in politics now demanded a voice in decision-making. Even before the Revolution, street protests and intercolonial organizations were beginning to bring together working-class people, laborers, and tenant farmers for common action. Boycotts had involved women in the vortex of debate over taxation: Should tea be served? Should British linens be purchased? "Whether we like it or not," one Boston woman told her friend, "we have to decide how to fight for our rights, too!" Public meetings, often flamboyant exchanges among artisans and sailors as much as reasoned dialogue among intellectuals, brought people unaccustomed to political activity into prominence.

Although the exigencies of war temporarily blunted a confrontation between common people and upper classes, liberating winds of change whipped through the United States in 1783. More and more ready for power, more and more knowledgeable in its use, patriots were fashioning a new nation, new in purpose and potential.

The Articles of Confederation

The same Second Continental Congress that had convened in May 1775 managed the domestic and foreign affairs of the United States for many months following the battles at Concord and Lexington. During this wrenching and momentous period Congress operated effectively as a government. It raised an army and appointed its commander in chief, negotiated with the enemy, authorized a navy, and sent agents and commissioners to France, Spain, Prussia, Austria, and Tuscany. It issued millions of dollars of paper money. Most important of all, Congress, meeting within the red brick walls of the Pennsylvania State House, had declared that "these United Colonies are, and of Right ought to be, Free and Independent States."

But however effective as a provisional government, the Second Continental Congress could not be a permanent instrument for managing the affairs of a free and independent nation. In June 1776, almost simultaneously with the resolution which led to the Declaration of Independence, Richard Henry Lee proposed a permanent new government to represent all the states. In July, John Dickinson of Pennsylvania, chairman of the committee appointed to draw up the plan of government, submitted his proposals. The Dickinson scheme contained several controversial features. The new Congress was to have broad powers, including the right to establish state boundaries and to dispose of unoccupied western lands. Each state would have one vote, regardless of its population and the number of representatives it actually sent to Congress.

The Dickinson proposals came under immediate attack when debated in open Congress. The large and influential state of Virginia, which claimed much of the trans-Appalachian West, opposed granting the new government sweeping powers over western lands. Many of Virginia's most prominent leaders had for years anticipated selling western lands to the farmers whom they expected to pour over the mountains when peace returned. On the other hand, delegates from states such as Maryland and Pennsylvania, owning no western lands, wanted the United States as a whole to acquire Virginia's claims. Only in this way, they insisted, could Americans from all parts of the new nation benefit from these millions of fertile acres. The delegates also fought over the voting provision: large states wanted voting by population size but the small states—and delegates who feared above all a strong central government—supported the Dickinson proposal; by their reasoning, this one-state, one-vote scheme meant that the new government was a league of sovereign states, while representation by population suggested that the power of the new government flowed directly from the American people, bypassing the states. Finally, the Dickinson document failed to reserve specific powers to the states, which alarmed some Congressmen.

For almost a year-and-a-half, amidst the smoke and flames of war, Congress debated the issues. Opponents of the original proposal succeeded in affixing to it a provision that Congress could exercise only those powers specifically delegated to it by the states. Another change was a victory for

John Singleton Copley, Midshipman Augustus Brine, *1782.* (Metropolitan Museum of Art.)

REVOLUTION AND INDEPENDENCE

Virginia. Under strong pressure from that land-rich state, the delegates at Philadelphia agreed to drop the provision that Congress would control the new nation's western lands. With these modifications accepted, Congress in November 1777 adopted the Articles of Confederation and sent the new frame of national government to the states for ratification.

Twelve states swiftly ratified the Articles. Maryland, however, held out for the original western-lands proviso and refused to ratify until it was restored. Fortunately, a number of prominent Virginians, including Thomas Jefferson, had a grander vision of the West than merely as a mammoth, overgrown Virginia. The great interior valley of North America, they believed, should be carved into new, self-governing states, rather than remain colonies of the seaboard. For the "good of the whole" they were willing to surrender their own state's claims. Under their influence, Virginia ceded its western lands to Congress. In 1781 the United States had its first constitution.

Artillery, both land-based and aboard vessels in the harbor, boomed out a salute to the new government. On the evening of ratification Philadelphia's citizens enjoyed an opulent "collation" presided over by Congress' chief executive officer and a brilliant display of fireworks. The *Pennsylvania Packet,* a Philadelphia newspaper, rhapsodized over the momentous event: "Thus has the union, begun by necessity, been indissolubly cemented. Thus America, like a well con-structed arch . . . is growing up in war into greatness and consequence among the nations."

Unfortunately, the *Packet's* editor spoke too soon. From the very first, the Articles proved inadequate as a basis for dealing with the difficulties of a new nation. The agreement ratified in 1781 pledged all the states to "a firm league of friendship" with one another, and committed them to mutual support against attack. It gave to Congress sole power over foreign affairs and over the issues of war and peace. Congress would also deal with the Indians, and the states agreed to surrender to one another all escaped criminals and to give "full faith and credit" to court orders, sentences, and other judicial decisions of other states.

These provisions were all essential to effective national governance—essential but not enough. For the Confederation amounted to a league of virtually independent sovereign states, not a modern nation. The new government lacked many vital powers: Congress could not tax; nor could it regulate trade and commerce either among the states or between the United States and other countries; any attempt to change or modify the Articles required a unanimous vote of all the state legislatures. Under this instrument of government however weak, Americans did succeed in bringing the war to a successful conclusion. But the Confederation's authority would soon prove too feeble to garner the fruits of victory and manage demobilization successfully.

The "Critical Period"

Yorktown in October 1781 was the war's last important clash of arms. Soon afterward the Lord North ministry in Britain fell, and peace negotiations began in Paris. British and American representatives signed the peace treaty at the end of November 1782. The following April, Congress ratified the treaty. The war was over; the United States was an independent nation.

During the months following Yorktown, the strains of nationhood, no longer obscured by military events, became painfully apparent. By early 1783 discontent plagued the army stationed at Newburgh, New York. Officers protested Congress' failure to establish a promised pension system for discharged veterans. In early March a group of officers at Newburgh threatened that if Congress did not abide by its pledge, the army would defy the government. Washington, however, soothed the hotheads who were threatening a military coup. When Congress found the means to provide the officers with five years of full pay in lieu of the pensions, the near-revolt was over.

The rank-and-file soldiers still had not received their pay, however. Congress simply could not raise the money. Some politicians wanted the individual states to make good the back pay, but that would have kept the men in service for many months, a discontented standing army with nothing to do. In the end, Congress discharged most of the troops without meeting their just demands. Most of them rushed back to civilian life with little fuss, but several hundred marched to Philadelphia protesting their shabby treatment. The legislators did not respond bravely. Unable to meet the soldiers' demands and terrified by the angry troops, they fled first to Princeton, then to Annapolis, and finally came to rest in New York, which remained the national capital for several years.

Patriots despaired over the pitiful state of the national government. Congress could pay neither its troops nor its creditors. The war had been financed by a combination of loans, paper money and, in the case of several states, some taxes. The paper money had seriously depreciated; in 1781 it was finally repudiated, ridding Congress of a very large debt. But other sizable obligations remained: Congress had borrowed directly of its own citizens, issuing IOU's in exchange for supplies, food, services, and cash. It had also borrowed from Dutch bankers. By the end of the war, all these debts went into arrears. The states had similar problems. Massachusetts and a few others imposed high taxes to pay their debts; most, however, were content to default like the Confederation government. These unpaid public debts cast a pall over the nation in the years after the war. Patriotic Americans deeply regretted seeing their nation become a common bankrupt. How could such a country not be an object of scorn in the eyes of the whole world?

Saint Acacius, *bulto,* painted wood; made in New Mexico, eighteenth century. *Index of American Design.*

Foreign and Domestic Economic Problems

The national government was powerless in foreign affairs, which offended both those whose specific interests were hurt and others who merely grieved for the state of their country. Spain controlled both Florida and the lower reaches of the Mississippi, including the all-important port of New Orleans. By the end of the Revolution 50,000 American farmers lived on the "western waters" in Kentucky and Tennessee, and many more American husbandmen were eagerly awaiting the opportunity to cross the mountains to the fertile lands of the Mississippi Valley. If these people were not to remain subsistence farmers, they would need outlets for their wheat, pork, beef, corn, and forest products. The route over the mountains was too difficult for the shipping of bulky products, but the great river that flowed to the Gulf of Mexico was a cheap and safe natural highway. Raft-like flatboats could be constructed of local lumber and loaded with barrels of pickled beef, pork, and grain to float with the current to

New Orleans. There the rafts could be broken up and sold for lumber, and the barrels reloaded on ocean-going vessels to be carried to the Atlantic coast ports, the Caribbean islands, or Europe. The farmer could then buy some horses and return to Kentucky with some cash in his pocket and manufactured goods in his saddlebags.

Control of New Orleans, then, gave Spain a vital lever of manipulation in dealing with the United States. Though lately, with France the new nation's ally against the British, conservative Spain had little use for the Americans. If nothing else, their successful fight for independence set a "bad" example for Spain's own colonies. In 1784 the Spanish government announced that it was closing the Mississippi to American commerce. Now, only Spanish subjects could use the river and the port of New Orleans. All others would be arrested.

Westerners threatened to raise ten thousand troops to march on New Orleans. Some listened to

British agents who promised protection if they would reunite with Great Britain. Washington, seriously worried at the prospect of national dismemberment, reported after a long journey through the frontier that "the western settlers . . . stand as it were upon a pivot. The touch of a feather would turn them any way."

America's diplomatic weakness was soon confirmed. Negotiations between Spain and America over the "right of deposit" at New Orleans began in 1785. Dour, tight-lipped John Jay, Congress' Secretary for Foreign Affairs, proved no match for the suave and charming Don Diego de Gardoqui, Spain's negotiator. But ultimately it was American weakness that hurt. The Spanish emissary knew that the powerless Americans were in no position to threaten Spain, and refused to grant the major American demand, the right of deposit, although he was willing to make minor boundary adjustments along the West Florida border and allow some American trade within the Spanish empire. Congress refused to accept the treaty, and it died. New Orleans remained a tight cork bottling up the mouth of the Mississippi.

Problems with England were even more difficult than those with Spain. The British had no reason to wish the Americans well. The "rebels" had gotten the independence they wanted, and they could jolly well accept all the drawbacks that the condition entailed. In 1783, Lord Sheffield, a prominent member of Parliament, published a pamphlet urging the British government to deny the Americans the trading rights within the empire that they had enjoyed before 1776. The "American states," Sheffield noted, could not "act as a nation," and so were "not to be feared as such by us." The pamphlet struck a receptive chord. In July 1783 the English Privy Council issued an order that closed the British West Indies to most American commerce.

This order struck a blow against farmers of the Northern states, who had long sent their surplus provisions to Jamaica, Barbados, and the other British islands. It also hurt the New England fishing industry, which had supplied the sugar plantations with dried cod and mackerel, and the merchants of New York, Philadelphia, Salem and Boston who had carried these goods. The shipping industry employed hundreds of seamen, and thousands more in such related occupations as shipbuilding and sail and rope-making. The British Caribbean planters connived at the smuggling of needed products, but this scarcely made up for the damage to American interests.

The Americans were in no position to retaliate. True, the British needed the American market for their manufactured goods. In the immediate postwar period, in fact, British goods flooded the United States, causing severe distress among American artisans and manufacturers who could not compete with the cheaper English commodities. Paying for imports from Britain also drained gold and silver coin from the nation. Had Congress been able to impose a tariff on British imports, it might have stemmed the inward flow of English manufactured goods, encouraged native production, and dealt with British exclusion of American agricultural products from the West Indies. Several states, urged on by mass meetings of artisans and craftsmen, did impose duties on foreign goods, but then the British found ways of sending their product through adjacent states that had no such taxes. Efforts to erect trade barriers between states created bad feeling among neighbors. Merchants of New London, Connecticut, boycotted New York; New Jersey taxed the New York lighthouse at Sandy Hook. One observer noted that, but for some good luck and an unusual instance of congressional intervention, "bloodshed would very quickly [have been] the consequence."

Nor were trade problems the only sore points between Britain and America. Under the peace treaty ending the war, the British had granted the United States all the territory south of the Great Lakes and north of the Spanish possessions—all the way to the Mississippi River—and had promised to give up their military posts in the Northwest "with all convenient speed." For many months, however, they refused to remove the garrisons. The British did not wish to abandon their Indian allies to the hostile Americans and were reluctant to surrender the rich fur trade. They justified their delay by citing two provisions of the peace treaty: the promise that the Americans would do nothing to prevent British creditors from collecting millions of pounds in prewar debts, and the assurance that Congress would try to get the states to compensate loyalists for their wartime losses. Neither of these promises had yet been fulfilled.

The Confederation tried to achieve a settlement of these issues. John Adams, the American minister to England, threatened, pleaded, and cajoled, in an effort to persuade the British to relent on trade and meet their obligations under the peace treaty. But he soon found that he was beating his head against a stone wall, for most British officials presumed the weakness of the United States and dug in their heels.

One final confrontation seemed the most humiliating of all. For many years the deys and pashas of the Barbary Coast states of North Africa,

Dress, imported brocaded silk, made in Boston. *Index of American Design.*

Algiers, Tunis, Tripoli, and Morocco, had preyed on European commerce. Most European nations either paid blackmail to these corsairs or provided naval protection for their own commerce. So long as the Americans were dependents of Great Britain, the British Navy and treasury covered them as well as Englishmen. Naturally, after independence this protection ceased. In 1785 the New England ship *Maria* was captured by Algerians, who stole its merchandise, stripped the crew of all their clothes and possessions, and then sold them into North African slavery. American merchants demanded that Congress respond to such ruthless attacks. But without a navy or the means to create one, the Confederation government could do nothing to overawe the Barbary pirates. Congress did manage to raise $80,000 to buy exemption from the deys, but this was so little that only the Moroccan leader would conclude a treaty.

Creditors of the new government, whether original holders of Congress' securities or speculators in them, saw little hope of ever being paid. Farmers who had supplied commodities to the West Indies and southern Europe, merchants who had traded with these regions, and all those in the port towns who had relied on this trade for a living saw their economic horizon lowering. Equally aggrieved were craftsmen and artisans in the towns who had found their businesses and jobs wiped out by the deluge of cheap British goods.

Debtors, too, found times hard and sought to offset the difficulties they encountered. One favorite scheme of debtor groups to counteract the postwar deflation was state-issued paper money. Once it had been said that only farmers favored such paper-money schemes, but in Maryland indebted planters supported them, in Pennsylvania and South Carolina merchants endorsed them. Planters and merchants were not only often in debt themselves, but many felt that the lack of a circulating medium made all business hard to conduct and contributed to the depressed state of the economy. Where state paper-money issues were kept under control, even the richer and more conservative had few objections.

In a number of states, however, paper money became in effect a way of confiscating a part of creditors' property. In North Carolina, Georgia, and New Jersey the paper-money issues authorized by the state legislatures quickly depreciated, yet creditors were forced to take it at face value. The most notorious case, however, occurred in Rhode Island. In 1786 that maverick little state issued 100,000 pounds of paper money. These notes were legal tender, so if any creditor refused to accept them the bills could be deposited with a judge and the debt legally canceled. Many Rhode Island merchants closed their doors rather than accept the notes. Creditors fled the state to escape debtors anxious to pay them in depreciated paper. To social and economic conservatives this situation seemed just another example of the anarchy that was inevitable when there was no strong central body to restrain abuses.

Daily Life

It would be a mistake to paint too dark a picture of the so-called "Critical Period," the years between Yorktown and the meeting of the Constitu-

tional Convention at Philadelphia during the summer of 1787. Most ordinary Americans went about their daily affairs without too much thought to the problems that beset their nation. The vast majority of the 2.8 million Americans of 1780—say, eighty percent—were farmers or members of farm families. The people who worked the soil were by no means all alike. Some 600,000, virtually all living south of Pennsylvania, were black slaves. Another considerable group was made up of white tenants or indentured white servants. A few thousand, also mostly in the South—though some were to be found in the Hudson Valley and a few other spots as well—were owners of great estates worked either by slaves, tenants, or servants. In between was the largest group of all—perhaps sixty percent of all husbandmen—free farmers who owned their own land.

Among such varied groups there was inevitably a wide range of habits, customs, and conditions. Slaves who worked in the fields wore rough cotton trousers, shirts, or dresses. They went barefoot in summer and put on crude leather shoes in winter. Their workday was long, typically from dawn to dusk. They ate corn in various forms—hominy, corn bread, roasting ears—and consumed some pork, fish, and poultry, as well as vegetables raised in their own small gardens. Some slaves were skilled craftsmen or house servants who dressed better, ate better, and had more freedom of movement and more privacy than field hands. But this privileged group was a small minority of the total, perhaps ten percent.

The day-to-day lot of indentured servants was not much better than that of slaves. But there were several crucial differences between them and black bondsmen. They were not subject to race prejudice and after a prescribed number of years—usually from four to seven—they were free and could, with luck and enterprise, rise on the social scale. A number did. Several signers of the Declaration of Independence, for example, were former indentured servants. We think of indentured servitude as primarily a colonial institution, but many such servants continued to come well after independence and even into the nineteenth century.

White tenant farmers were better off than either slaves or white servants. Aside from their personal freedom, many enjoyed full citizenship rights and could vote. Their actual lot depended a great deal on special circumstances. Yeoman farmers who owned their hundred to two hundred acres of land outright were the backbone of the country. They were especially numerous in New England, Pennsylvania, New Jersey, and the back-country and mountain areas of the southern states. Those who lived close to cities or connected to them by good roads or navigable rivers produced crops not only for themselves and their families but also for dis-

tant markets in the West Indies, the Mediterranean, and Newfoundland. These farmers were by no means rich; the trade provided the means to buy a few luxuries and goods they could not themselves produce. Farmers distant from markets had to make do with what they and their wives and children alone could make. This dependence accounts for the extra-ordinary range of household manufactures common in this period. The farmer or his wife spun cotton, linen, or wool yarn and wove it into cloth. They made shoes and clothing of skins and leather. They produced candles, beer, cheese, preserves, and pickled meats. They built their own houses with the help of neighbors and perhaps a local skilled carpenter. They worked hard and long. Fortunately, families were generally large, and children helped. Their labors created modest comfort and a rough abundance of food, clothing, and shelter even among the subsistence farmers. By comparison with that of a European peasant, the lot of an American farming family was enviable.

Figurehead, "The Quaker"; Boston. *Index of American Design.*

Broadax, wrought iron, oak handle. *Index of American Design.*

A few men got rich cultivating the soil: the growers of tobacco in Maryland and Virginia, the planters who raised rice and the dye indigo in South Carolina and Georgia, the Hudson Valley landlords who grew grain and raised livestock.

The traveler in Confederation America encountered many large mansions through the Hudson Valley, along the streams and inlets of the Chesapeake region, and in the Carolina and Georgia sea islands and coastal lowlands. Most of those built since the 1740's were of brick with plaster trim, designed in the gracious Georgian style with evenly spaced windows and classical cornices and moldings over windows and doors. With large ballrooms, imported English furniture, and many bedrooms, these structures attested to growing affluence and sophistication.

Maritime merchants of the port cities constituted another wealthy class. In Boston the average merchant left £1000 in real estate and personal property to his heirs. A few were fabulously rich. Sharing in the late-colonial prosperity in about equal measure were lawyers and doctors, especially those who practiced in the larger communities. Instead of country homes the urban rich had large townhouses surrounded by gardens. They too ate elaborate meals, dressed in silk and fine broad-cloth, wore wigs or powdered their hair, and traveled by coach or on horseback.

Far more numerous in the towns were the shopkeepers, innkeepers, clerks, seamen, laborers, and artisans. Few of the day-laborers earned more than two shillings a day. This was sufficient to keep a young man in modest comfort, but it was not enough to marry on and raise a family. Porters, pick-and-shovel workers, and the like could marry only if their wives worked as seamstresses, laundresses, or servants of some sort.

Skilled craftsmen, on the other hand, had little trouble earning a good living. Carpenters, blacksmiths, shipwrights, tailors, cordwainers, barrelmakers, masons, printers, and other artisans often owned their own shops and so were small businessmen.

The typical urban artisan family ate well. Daily clothing was often of leather or coarse wool, but each member had a good outfit for Sunday. The father often owned his own small house. The family ate off pewter, rather than silver. Some craftsmen became fairly prosperous. The tailor Ephraim Copeland had a house and land worth £226, a silver pocket watch, silver buckles for his shoes, two gold rings, six silver spoons, and furniture and household goods worth £75.

It is difficult to generalize about the day-to-day quality of life for so large and varied a group of people. Farmers were closely tied to the rhythms of the day, the week, the season. Work expanded to fill the daylight hours in spring, summer, and fall with their plowing, cultivating, and harvesting. Sunday was a day of rest, not only in Congregational New England, but also in the middle states and the South, where there were many Baptists, Methodists, and Presbyterians, as well as more easy-going Episcopalians. For the Sabbath each member of a family reserved one suit of clothes of good wool or corduroy which lasted often through a person's lifetime and was handed down to children.

Church-going and religious observance were more than quests for solace in an uncertain world, or traditional observances imposed by community pressure. They were also social events. Young people dressed up not only for God and the minister; they also dressed for one another. The church was one of the few meeting places for young men and women. Many a courtship began in church under the watchful eyes of parents and older brothers and sisters.

Many older Americans also derived pleasure from church attendance. They enjoyed the minis-

ters' sermons although these often droned on for two hours or more at a stretch. They enjoyed meeting neighbors and liked to sing hymns. Members of the new evangelical sects, such as the Baptists, Methodists, and "new light" Presbyterians, found church attendance a deeply moving emotional experience and did not confine their religious participation to the weekly meeting. Beginning in the 1780's, great revivals swept the back-country, especially in the South. Many of these were held in churches; others, however, took place at temporary encampments in open places where hundreds of pious people came for several days, well provided with provisions, to listen to eloquent preachers exhort sinners to repent their evil ways, turn to God, and find everlasting salvation. More sedate people despised these camp meetings; they sneered at the "ranting" preachers and expressed horror at the shrieks, jerks, and groans of the listeners caught up in the emotions of the event. Critics also claimed that these camp meetings were opportunities for the nubile young to indulge their awakening sexual appetites. But however unseemly or disreputable, the camp meeting provided an important emotional release for rural Americans whose lives otherwise were largely bound up in a round of toil.

The ten percent or so of Americans who dwelt in substantial towns or cities enjoyed more varied lives. Cities brought people together on a daily basis. They also offered far greater opportunities for amusement and play. During the war some Americans deplored frivolity as wasteful of money and energy, and at odds with the sobriety needed in a time of national crisis. Congress officially condemned balls and entertainments in the interests of economy. A while later it condemned plays put on by officers and men of the Continental Army stationed in Philadelphia as "disagreeable to the sober inhabitants" of the Quaker city. A number of moralists condemned the growing "licentiousness"—gambling, cockfighting, and wenching—that developed whenever large numbers of young men congregated together in barracks and military encampments.

The moralism of the early wartime years did not last, however. As the conflict dragged on, standards relaxed. To relieve the tedium of sacrifice and offset the general gloom, urban Americans sought out amusement and pleasure. In British-occupied New York, officers of the military and naval forces opened the "theater Royal" and sold hundreds of tickets for benefit performances to succor "the Widows and orphans of those who have lost their lives in his majesty's service." Patriots, too, organized theatricals. These, despite congressional disapproval, were popular with officers of the Continental Army and attracted many well-dressed ladies and gentlemen.

Dowry chest, Pennsylvania German; inscribed with name of first owner, Jacob Rickert, dated 1782. *Index of American Design.*

A popular urban pastime in these years was the street celebration or pageant. During and after the war the anniversary of the signing of the Declaration of Independence became a general occasion for bonfires, fireworks, and noisy parades. In Philadelphia, news of the treaty of peace set off a surge of revelry so boisterous that prudent citizens feared for the safety of their property. The celebration in New York when Washington came to the city for his inauguration as first President of the United States exceeded anything previously seen. The barge that brought the General across New York harbor from New Jersey was surrounded by large and small vessels of every sort full of cheering New Yorkers. Debarking at Murray's wharf, where he was greeted by Governor Clinton and other officials and escorted to the house where he was to stay, he made his way through streets lined with cheering citizens. At night the city was illuminated with bonfires, and happy celebrants crowded the city's thoroughfares and coffeehouses.

Then, as today, Americans were susceptible to fads and crazes. A peculiar one of the Confederation period concerned balloons, the first of which, inflated with hot air, had recently been launched in France. The idea of men finally freeing themselves from the force of gravity seized on the public's imagination. By midsummer 1784 it was said that nothing attracted attention unless it had the word "balloon" attached to it. Fashionable people wore "balloon" ornaments and a farmer hawking his vegetables in town sold them as "fine balloon string beans." Perhaps the fad was no more explicable than other popular fancies, but it would not be an exaggeration to say that release from earthly limits had a special appeal to newly independent Americans.

Progress Under the Confederation

Obviously, not all Americans found the Critical Period to be a time of distress. Indeed, some had reason to see it as one of progress. If businessmen engaged in the Caribbean and Mediterranean trades were hurt, others trading with France, northern Europe, and non-European parts of the world made clear gains. With the break from England, American merchants ceased to be bound by Parliament's navigation acts and began direct trade with parts of Europe from which they had been virtually excluded. Soon American vessels were showing up regularly in the harbors of Sweden, Holland, and Denmark, and even faraway Russia.

Even more interesting was the new trade with the Far East. In 1784 Robert Morris and some partners fitted out the 360-ton *Empress of China* with a cargo containing the root ginseng, which the Chinese believed to increase sexual potency. The vessel sailed for Canton around the Cape of Good Hope. It returned to New York the following year with its hold stuffed with tea, silk, chinaware, cotton cloth, and other goods that earned a profit for the promoters of almost $40,000. In a few years American ships were rounding Cape Horn, scudding up the Pacific coast to the region north of California, picking up the beautiful otter skins of the Pacific Northwest, and sailing on across the Pacific to Canton. On one such voyage in 1792, Captain Robert Gray discovered the mighty Columbia River. These voyages provided a much-needed outlet for American commodities, and at the same time created a taste for Chinese furniture, housewares, and textile patterns, as well as intense interest in Chinese civilization.

Congress showed itself surprisingly capable of dealing with at least one major problem: the settling of the West. The peace treaty of 1783 had left the United States with a princely landed domain. Between the Appalachians and the Mississippi, stretching from Canada in the North to the Spanish possessions in the South, lay enough unoccupied real estate to provide every free American family of 1775 with a tract of 750 acres, over a

Rufus Hathawan, Lady With Her Pets. (Metropolitan Museum of Art.)

square mile of land. A dense level forest of hard-woods and pines, interrupted by occasional clearings and a few rolling hills, the region remained formidable. Mosquitoes and biting flies swarmed everywhere in summer. Winters were bitter. The Indians of the region, especially the Shawnee, Wyandot, Iroquois, and Miami in the north, and the Cherokee, Choctaw, and Chickasaw to the south, claimed millions of acres as their hunting grounds; most stood ready to resist any white settlers who would come to occupy their lands. Isolated settlements of French farmers and merchants were still scattered through the region, at Vincennes in present-day Indiana and at Kaskaskia, now within the state of Illinois.

In addition to the human and physical deterrents to settlement, there were the legal ones. Virginia, with the broadest claims, had ceded its lands to the Confederation government. But other states continued to claim substantial portions of the West, a number of them awarding some of this land to their war veterans. Bit by bit, the states gave up their claims in favor of the nation, retaining in most cases only small parcels. For many years, however, state and federal claims overlapped, creating a situation that would discourage settlers and cause later trouble.

As Congress deliberated over policy for the public domain, it faced several basic questions: how should the new region be governed? Some Americans, especially Easterners who feared their own political eclipse, wanted it to remain secondary to the older states, with new settlers denied full representation in Congress. Others, more liberal in outlook, hoped to see equal sovereign states carved out of the region. On the issue of selling the land, supporters in the older states saw the public domain as a source of federal revenue. One obvious maneuver was to sell the land at high prices—to get immediate returns, large wholesale parcels could be sold to land speculators, who in turn could profit by retail sales to settlers. Pioneer farmers, often themselves settlers, urged to the contrary that cheap land be available for all Americans, and felt less concern for the Confederation government's need for money. Still another disagreement arose between those who favored the New England mode of settlement, in which after survey, the land would be settled in small, tight-knit communities, and those who preferred the Southern system, in which an individual could buy a land warrant to a certain number of acres and then simply stake out settlers' land. The first system would be slow but orderly; the second promised to work faster, but would be likely to lead to overlapping claims and confusion.

All of these conflicting views of various interest groups came to be reflected in Congress. Two measures of the Confederation government laid down its basic policy towards the West and the public domain. The Land Ordinance of 1785 provided first for a careful survey of the land and then its division into six-mile-square townships. Each township, in turn, would be divided into thirty-six "sections," each of one square mile, or 640 acres. Half the township might be sold as a unit; the other half would be offered on the market only in single sections. Actual sales at auction to the highest bidder started with a minimum price of a dollar an acre. Congress reserved four sections of each 36-section township for later use and kept one to sell for revenue to maintain local schools.

The Land Ordinance did not please everyone. It provided in effect for slow, orderly settlement, and its minimum price and prescribed plot size meant that a pioneer farmer needed at least $640 to acquire a farm—in those days, a hefty sum indeed. At the same time, it favored the establishment of family farms over speculation, however imperfectly. Congress soon violated its own principles, however, by also selling almost two million acres of land to a group of speculators organized under the name of the Ohio Company, granting them an option on an additonal five million—all for well under a dollar an acre.

Before long, Congress also reached a decision on the political organization of part of the trans-Appalachian area—the region bounded by Pennsylvania on the east, the Great Lakes to the north, the Mississippi on the west, and on the south the Ohio River. The Northwest Ordinance of 1787 was a milestone in the progress of Americans across the continent. Borrowing from a earlier plan proposed by Jefferson, the Ordinance laid out the process by which the Northwest might eventually become a group of self-governing states, equal in all respects to the original thirteen. Eventually the area would be carved into between three and five territories, governed initially by officials appointed by Congress. When a territory acquired a population of five thousand adult males, it would be allowed to elect an assembly and could send a non-voting delegate to Congress. With a population of sixty thousand free inhabitants, the territory became eligible to apply for admission as a fully equal, self-governing state. The final section of the Ordinance of 1787 reflected the most liberal and democratic spirit of the Revolutionary era. All residents of a territory would enjoy complete freedom of worship, full representation in the territorial assembly in proportion to their numbers, trial by jury, and other fundamental protections to both persons and property. In a provision that would later take on great significance, slavery was forbidden in the whole of the vast region.

There remained an important Western problem that the Confederation government could not solve: what to do with the Indians. In 1784 Congress sent five commissioners to meet with the tribes of the Northwest in an effort to open the eastern portion of the region to white settlement. At Fort Stanwix the commissioners forced the Iroquois to surrender their claims for a few trinkets.

Next, they coerced the Chippewa, Ottawa, Wyandot, Shawnee, and Delaware into giving up most of their Ohio lands. The resentful tribesmen, however, quickly repudiated these agreements and were soon trading blows with the frontiersmen now pouring into the Ohio country in advance of survey. The government sought to pacify the irate Indians by promising them additional gifts, while at the same time it strengthened the army garrisons in the West. These moves did little good. By the end of the Confederation period, the Northwest was a tinderbox ready for the first spark to set off a conflagration.

Suggested Readings

Garry Wills, *Inventing America: Jefferson's Declaration of Independence* (1978) is a readable and engaging study of the intellectual background of America's first national document. Gordon Wood's *The Creation of the American Republic, 1776-1787* (1969) explores the relationship between ideology and social and political reality. Forrest McDonald argues to restore the Founding Fathers to their original stature as men who placed a secure Republic before personal interest: *We the People: The Economic Origins of the Constitution* (1958) and *E Pluribus Unum: The Formation of the American Republic, 1776-1789* (rev., 1979). Jackson Turner Main stresses the importance of class and sectional differences in *The Social Structure of Revolutionary America* (1965) and subsequent studies. Another book by Bernard Bailyn emphasizes the importance of intellectual history: *The Ideological Origins of the American Revolution* (1967).

Chapter V
The Revolutionary Era

I. Forrest McDonald: The Conservatives' Revolution

Revolutions, we customarily think, are born amidst the poor and oppressed. The crowds call for bread; their leaders demand the release of political prisoners whose bodies are broken with torture. In the American Revolution the colonists were indeed reacting in anger. The King, wrote Thomas Jefferson in the Declaration of Independence, had "sent hither swarms of officers to harass our people, and eat out their substance . . . . He has plundered our seas, ravaged our coasts, burnt our towns, and destroyed the lives of our people." But the colonists were prosperous, enjoying security and self-government. They were conservatives, and their revolution was not for the sake of winning a bearable life against a brutal monarch but aimed at preserving a life of abundance. The English were threatening both of the significant achievements of the colonial period: not only each colony's individual identity, but also what they had accomplished in common. Their struggle for independence was the culmination of the entire colonial experience.

From the beginning, the English colonies in America were different from those of other European countries. The French and the Spanish were Catholic, the English Protestant. The French and the Spanish were rigidly controlled by their home governments, the English largely self-governing. The French and Spanish, for the most part, went to America in pursuit of adventure and the possibility of quick wealth; the English, by and large, went to America seeking permanent homes. Most importantly, the English colonists took with them different cultural baggage from that of other Europeans—different values, habits, customs, social and legal institutions. Indeed, one of the main reasons they went in the first place was to preserve their accustomed and preferred ways of life, which had become impossible to do in the Old World during the turbulent, bloody, and intolerant seventeenth century.

Those facts are crucial to an understanding of the colonies which became the United States of America, and so is one other. British North America was a land of abundance: its climate was mild, its soil rich, its woods teeming with game, and, above all, its land area was both diverse and enormous. These features of the physical environment made it possible for like-minded people to live and prosper together and to separate themselves from those who were different. In other words, British America provided ideal conditions for people who left their Old World homes to avoid changing their Old World ways.

The interplay of cultural predisposition with natural environment made the British Americans simultaneously a plural culture and a single one. During the course of the century and half between the earliest settlements and the Revolution, they developed a number of regional subcultures, different from one another and yet sharing certain institutions and attitudes which, in turn, made them like one another and different from all other peoples. Both the differences and the similarities mattered.

Each group of Americans was firmly set in its ways, and anyone who sought to force them to change did so at his mortal peril. The policies of the British government after 1763 threatened, or increasingly seemed to threaten, the ways of life of each of the American subcultures. In this sense, the American Revolution was a plural act of cultural conservatism:

Yankee traders equally with Virginia planters, New York manor lords equally with southern frontiersmen, were willing to see the British Empire dismembered rather than deviate from their accustomed norms.

The Revolution was also a common act. The Americans shared many attributes, including language, pride in the English heritage of liberty (felt even among those who were not of English extraction), and prejudice against England's traditional enemies and rivals. But the most important, and for present purposes the most relevant, were three: the colonies' systems of government and law, their systems of social order, and their economic and ideological orientation.

The form of government in every American colony generally followed a colonial image of the government of England prior to the Glorious Revolution of 1688. Every colony had a "mixed" government, including a governor who represented the monarchical principle and corresponded to the English Crown; a governor's council or upper house of the legislature, which represented the aristocratic principle and corresponded to the House of Lords; and an elected legislature or lower house, which represented the democratic principle and corresponded to the House of Commons. In the colonies and in the mother country, the power to levy taxes belonged solely to the elected branches of government. Local government in America, as in England, reflected different local historical experience and accordingly varied from place to place. The law, in this diffuse scheme of things, was not something that could be changed at the whim of government, nor was it a fixed code of the sort that prevailed on the European continent. Rather, it was "common law," a traditional body of "rights of Englishmen" and principles of natural justice which had evolved in the courts over the course of many centuries. Any legislative act that ran counter to the common law was a dangerous, unconstitutional innovation, and was therefore not binding.

The colonists' understanding of their own governments and of that in the mother country bore little relation to the way the British government actually functioned during the eighteenth century. Since the Glorious Revolution the three traditional branches had in effect merged, so that sovereignty, the supreme law-making power, now resided in a single body known as Crown in Parliament. Moreover, the British government had adopted what would come to be called the doctrine of positive law: that the law was whatever Crown in Parliament enacted, no matter what the common law or legal tradition had to say.

The British acted on the basis of that view of the constitution and laws when they attempted to tax the colonies and declared their right to legislate for the colonies "in all cases whatsoever." To the Americans that was a new and unconstitutional effort to exercise unlawful authority, one they were entirely justified in resisting. In other words, from the American point of view it was the British who were attempting to make radical changes and the Americans who were seeking to conserve traditional ways.

As for the social order, though the possibility of upward social and economic mobility was far greater in America than in any part of Europe, the gates to wealth and power had been steadily closing for a generation by the time of the Revolution. Society as well as government was dominated almost everywhere in America by a relative handful of large landholding families.

These oligarchs embraced the Revolution in much the spirit of the English feudal barons who had forced King John to sign the Magna Charta. Intent on preserving their privileges against the intrusions of outside authority, they might declaim loudly in favor of popular rights, but they were by no means eager to share their power with the lower orders of their own societies. Indeed, the aristocrats of South Carolina and New York, when the showdown over independence came, were reluctant to go all the way lest popular forces at home undermine their positions. The squires of Massachusetts and the planters of Virginia, by contrast, had no such reservations, for they were easily able to suppress the Baptists and other lower-class dissenters who tried to take advantage of political changes to improve their own standing.

Finally, and in some ways most importantly, there were the economic and ideological dimensions of the Revolution, which for most Americans amounted to nearly the same thing. The Americans had absorbed the ideology of Viscount Bolingbroke. England had once been an agrarian paradise, thanks to a balanced constitution and to relationships based upon ownership of the land, honest labor in the earth, craftsmanship in the cities, and small scale fair trade between individuals. The gentry was supreme, but all people had the security of knowing their place, and honor, manly virtue, and public spirit governed their conduct. Then came the Financial Revolution, corrupting the entire society by making money the measure of all things. With this corruption came standing armies, monopolies, and wicked "money men," undermining and alienating the landowner, the farmer, and the laborer.

Another way of describing what had happened was that Britain had given birth to a modern, dynamic, expanding economy that would improve the well-being of all its inhabitants. But Americans learned to believe only the worst, and to fear that, soon or late, the British would attempt to impose their sinister system upon the colonies. As the imperial crisis deepened in the 1760s and 1770s, that fear grew into a widespread conviction that just such a thing was happening, and then into something approaching a paranoid delusion. Finally the Americans saw no way of preserving their own agrarian paradise except to declare their independence. In this sense, the American Revolution was a conservative crusade against the forces of modernism.

To return to the point where we began: the American Revolution was culturally, politically, socially, and economically a conservative movement. But there was a supreme irony, or series of ironies, in the Americans' successful defense of their established ways. The American people emerged from the conflict with their regional subcultures more or less intact, but in each of the other three areas the Revolutionary War and its immediate aftermath bred unexpected changes. Politically, the new states found themselves unable to deal with their problems, and soon they found it necessary to create a central government with far greater powers than any that Parliament had dared try to exercise. Socially, though the semifeudal legal system that supported the local oligarchies remained in existence, a new instability arose from the departure of some aristocratic Loyalists, the rise of new-rich operators, and a general relaxation of social restraints. Perhaps most ironically, financing the war created an enormous public debt—which meant that, for the first time, Americans had the means for bringing about their own version of the Financial Revolution.

In sum, the revolution did not end with independence. Rather, it had only just begun.

II.   Eugene D. Genovese: The Radicals' Revolution

Was the American Revolution "culturally, politically, socially, and economically a conservative movement" that somehow produced unintended radical results? Professor McDonald and conservatives generally would have it so. Yet, where in the world have conservatives reacted with anything short of hostility to slogans like "All men are created equal"—the very slogans under which Americans took up arms? Where else, outside the

European far Left, was the direct participation of the lower classes in political action, let alone insurrection, viewed as other than a threat to civilization? Where else did a national movement fight for power in such a way as to bring about, virtually uncontested, a republican government, surely the most radical political experiment since Cromwell's "interregnum" after the execution of Charles I?

In creating a popular government that inspired revolutionaries—and appalled conservatives—across the world and in laying the foundations of a modern, capitalist, national economy, the Revolution accomplished its own acknowledged purposes. Only in one sense may the Revolution be considered "conservative": it preserved, indeed strengthened, the prevalent system of property. But, as a review of colonial development will show, that system of property—in which owners had nearly perfect freedom to use and dispose of real and personal property—represented the furthest point of social and radical transformation so far achieved.

The fledgling American republic threw down the gauntlet to monarchical Europe. For in breaking with the theory and practice of established hierarchy it challenged not merely the ruling classes of European societies, but all historically evolved notions of rank and privilege. To be sure, the "glorious" English revolution of 1688 set a precedent in insisting on monarchical dependence on the will of the propertied—"the King in Parliament"—but the portentous implications of the English solution took a century or more to be recognized. If the British philosophers Locke and Bolingbroke had provided an intellectual rationale for the new constitutional monarchy, political practice retained its share of pre-modern norms and values. Bourgeois ideologies in England were tempered by the power of great noble families, by limitations on free enterprise survived from the Middle Ages, and by the established church. The American Revolution broke sharply even with these European norms.

Creating a large republic shorn of kings, nobles, and established church constituted a radical act of the first order. Contemporary political theory assumed that only an Athenian city-state or a pocket territory like the Netherlands could exist without a monarch. No wonder, then, that conservatives feared and hated the new regime in America. That American act of national self-creation inherently and inescapably raised the question of who would rule—how much power would the lower classes be able to assert against the pretension of the "rich and well-born"? The revolutionary action of popular groups, urban and rural, played a big part in the Revolution and provided the strongest guarantee that the new nation would in fact be a democratic republic, not a liberal monarchy. But the American Revolution cannot best be understood as primarily the work of the lower classes, despite their enormous contribution.

The social radicalism of the Revolution lay not in some supposed triumph of the lower classes but in the explicit national triumph of middling men of property. The social and political genius of the revolutionary settlement lay especially in the strengthening of individual property holding—the extension of the free individual (and yet anomalously including slave property)—at precisely the moment at which commercial capital and its attendant differentiations of wealth were beginning to make themselves felt.

From the outset colonial society had treated property holding as an absolute right of the individual, but society developed many mechanisms for delimiting excessive individualism. Families, churches, and towns rested upon ranked distinctions between generations, sexes, masters and servants. Each individual became responsible for the proper execution of his or her appointed role, developing a set of norms that required the subordination of most persons to the interests of the whole. This attempt to guarantee cohesion found expression in fathers' control of property, especially in family farms, well past the maturity of their sons and hence in fathers' control of the labor of their grown sons; in parents' ability to dispatch their children to serve in other households while they received the children of others as servants in their own; in naming patterns, as sons and daughters received the names of same-sex parents or grandparents; in church control of the radical voice of individual conscience (e.g., the cases of Anne Hutchinson and Roger Williams); in communities' ability to insure the voluntary assumption of the role of constable; in community restrictions on economic freedom; in the power of masters over servants, which ran a gamut from the apprenticeship of middle-class children to indentured service to slavery; and in other comparable forms of social control.

By the decades immediately before the Revolution, economic and population growth and the increasing differentiation of wealth were straining these conventional patterns. As early as the Salem witch trials, commercial growth and inter-community rivalries were finding expression in sexual, generational, and religious tensions. The half-way covenant registered, in effect, the process by which the sway of the churches over the community was being dissolved. Increasingly, formal practices substituted for more organic bonds. By the middle of the eighteenth century the naming patterns of girls revealed a new sense of the daughter as one reared to leave, rather than to extend, her family of origin. Increasingly, fathers could not guarantee the succession of their own sons in their public offices. Just before the Revolution communities discovered that in order to have a constable at all they would have to pay. As younger sons and new settlers occupied western lands, they posed new challenges to the domination of the older towns and settlements. But the very changes that strained the older patterns of social control—and the elite that had presided over them—offered new opportunities for wealth to older settlers. Planters and merchants, in particular, were well positioned to profit marvelously from the dangerous and enticing fruits of commercial expansion.

The social challenge of the Revolution, therefore, must be understood as the forging of a revised but consensual social order. With the family, the church, and the small town no longer fully able to control the development of society, the fathers of families, the elders of churches, and the political leaders required institutions to replace the decaying customs that would simultaneously strengthen their authority and permit them to increase their wealth. Yet their traditions of autonomy and local control left them violently opposed to harnessing this burgeoning wealth to the glories of the English state.

Bourgeois property was not the only kind of property in America. Its antithesis, property in man, held sway in the South, where a class of powerful slaveholders was slowly forging a very different kind of society than that of New England and the Middle Colonies. True, slavery existed throughout the thirteen colonies, but only in the South did it dominate the economy and polity. At the time few reflected on the long-term conflict inherent in the coexistence of these two property systems and of the societies they were molding, although many commented on the contradiction between the principles of the Declaration of Independence and the existence of slavery. For the South, victory in the Revolutionary War meant something special: A class of slaveholders who, alone among slaveholders of the New World, had firmly established their own power at home. The significance of this would not, however, burst upon American consciousness for some time to come.

Meanwhile, northerners and southerners could coalesce against the common enemy. Taxation has always provoked disagreement between rulers and ruled. Nobles and peasants, as well as propertied free men and women, have taken up arms to protest its excesses. The radical thrust of the American Revolution lay in the refusal of Americans to be taxed without their own consent according to their own definition of who and what they were.

Their struggle with the Crown perfected their working-out of a collective identity, leading them to insist upon their own self-definition as a people. They accordingly found themselves to be "Americans"—to possess a discrete national identity that owed nothing to the unifying presence of a monarch and was, rather, a collective self-definition. Their unity arose from their social compact; it followed from that compact that they must allow the equality of all parties to it.

The equality of all men enshrined in the Declaration of Independence was not total, nor was it intended to be. But the reservations did not lie in the notion of equality, against which conservatives have always railed. The founders of our nation in fact said what they meant and meant what they said: in fundamental human and political respects, all men are created equal. The exclusion of women, children, blacks in general and slaves in particular, servants, and the insane was not understood to qualify the principle of equality but to qualify the definition of "men." For only free men, according to prevailing wisdom, were full members of the polity and therefore necessarily equal. Even among the formally free men, moreover, sharp differences of fortune and influence obtained and had social consequences. The ideology of the Revolution nonetheless proclaimed, and the Constitution institutionalized the ideal of formal equality among those recognized as free men.

There was genius in the solution—that genius of "common" sense all too frequently revealed as radical. But there was much possibility for misunderstanding as well. The principle—and for many decades the practice—invited men of very different interests and socioeconomic standing to make common cause in the governance of their new nation, even as it left them a free hand to rule their dependents at home. By thus removing women, children, and slaves to a separate and private sphere the revolutionary solution invited disparate men to see their freedom and manhood reflected in the flattering mirror of equality and to gloss over, if not to deny, the class differences that might have divided them.

The ideal of rational and equal politics simultaneously laid the foundations for the Victorian cult of true womanhood—that elevated women to a pedestal instead of giving them power—and the proslavery argument that would take clearer shape as the new nation faced more complicated problems. As antislavery, abolitionist, and feminist aspirations would demonstrate, however, the radical promise of the American Revolution was not lost even on those whose exclusion from the theory of equality made its early practice possible. And as those excluded pressed their claims, they would do so in the language of natural rights to full membership in the nation. And in time those who had a strong stake in the exclusion of women and blacks from the definition of "man" had to erect increasingly more esoteric and preposterous reasons to justify themselves, whereas others increasingly came to insist that "man" meant humanity and that such exclusions were morally intolerable.

The Revolution thus proved a compromise settlement between the apparent political "moderation" of solid bourgeois propertyholders and the vibrant radicalism of the lower classes. The settlement shook the world by its profoundly radical assertion of human equality, even as it sought to find new ways to obscure its own message and to justify class distinctions and social injustice.

Chapter VI
These United States
1787—1800

The Whiskey Rebellion

The United States in 1794 was a young and insecure nation. Although the federal government now possessed augmented powers under the new Constitution and enhanced prestige by having the national hero, George Washington, as its President, it was nonetheless a most fragile polity beset by enormous pressures. One was ideological: no one was certain what to expect from a "republic." History told of dangers from mob rule, and the contemporary French Revolution was to many a frightening drama. Moreover, renewed war between France and England pointed up American weakness. The British Navy disrupted American trade, impressed American sailors, and seized American cargoes. At the same time, the French interfered boldly in American affairs, encouraging the organization of pro-French democratic societies and commissioning privateers from American ports to prey on shipping. Finally, internal strains further tested the new government. As in any nation, different regions, political subdivision, and ethnic groups had their own interests, and looming over all were the diverging concerns of the rich and the poor, the agrarians and the developing commercial elites, the varying class and economic groups making up a sprawling land.

The new government's great initiative to unite this variegated republic was Secretary of the Treasury Alexander Hamilton's financial plan, which sought to use the federal government and the national debt to give the developing commercial clases a direct fiscal stake in the success of the new government. One cornerstone of that policy was an excise tax on alcoholic beverages to provide revenues to fund the national debt and to finance the government—including, many feared, its military capacity.

In Western Pennsylvania, the excise had a particularly bad reputation. Whiskey was the area's cash crop, often its currency. Readily transportable and salable, it stored so much better than the grain from whence it came. It gurgled and jostled in jugs and barrels swaying across the mountains on the backs of mules to slake the thirst of Easterners with coins in their pockets. Nor was it simply a question of economics. Westerners, even when they hungered for the word of God, continued to thirst for the "old Monongahela rye." The evangelical religion so strong in Western Pennsylvania had not yet come out against the drinking cup. A local historian writes of the back country habits:

The use of whiskey was universal. The quality was good, the taste pleasant, its effect agreeable. Storekeepers kept liquor on their counters and sold it in their stores, and the women customers used it as well as the men. Farmers kept barrels of it in their cellars. . . . It was good for fevers, it was good for a decline, it was good for ague [malaria], it was good for snake-bites. There was nothing named in the materia medica but old whiskey possessed some of its curative powers. . . . It made one warm in winter and cool in summer. It was used at all gatherings. Bottles of it were set out on the table at christenings and wakes. . . . Ministers drank it. . . . Rev. Father McGirr's drink was whiskey-punch, of which it is said he could drink with any of his day without giving scandal.

Westerners objected, as one petition phrased it, to "a duty for drinking our grain more than eating it." They objected as well to the appointment of excisemen with their right of entering private property and inspecting stills. And they especially objected to the trying of cases against those who refused to pay the exciseman's levy in federal court—which meant expensive and disruptive jaunts across the mountains to Philadelphia. Moreover, the West, cut off from the Mississippi trade by the Spanish, and from most trade other than in alcohol by the expense of carrying goods over the mountains, was desperately short of currency. The drain of excise payments was a burden on the region's economy. Pennsylvanians had to wonder why the government in Philadelphia (then the nation's capital) could not open the Mississippi to them rather than spending its time and effort on collecting this hugely unpopular tax.

The backcountry was not strong on being governed in any case. These western farmers, particularly the Scotch-Irish Presbyterians, had little faith in anyone's governance but their own. They were soon passing resolutions not merely calling for an end to the tax, but overtly threatening excisemen and even those who cooperated with them by paying the tax. Soon barns began to be fired, gristmills damaged, excisemen attacked. "Tom the Tinker's men," it was claimed, were everywhere "mending" stills. This became the local expression for shooting holes in stills whose owners paid the tax.

The West was not united on the issue, however. It rapidly became a battle between the small whiskey producers and the large ones, as the more prosperous distillers began to realize that this specie-draining tax would eventually drive the small producers out of business, leaving the more substantial men with a lucrative monopoly. Men of large property feared as well that this excise rebellion could ignite into a war against property. In 1794 this almost came true, as the backwoods farmers marched on Pittsburgh, threatening to burn this symbol of the advance of commercial capitalism to the ground. Only adroit maneuverings by several Pittsburgh leaders persuaded the farmers that they ran too large a risk of retribution if they fired the city.

Something had to be done about the sporadic rioting in the West. A finding that the courts had been obstructed in carrying out the excise law provided the federal government with grounds for intervention. Hamilton, eager for a show of force to establish the precedent of federal military power, led the administration in a vast overreaction. Washington himself for a time directed a larger force than he had ever at one time commanded during the Revolution. Disorganized militia, about thirteen thousand strong, slogged through endless mud during a rainy November in search of a rebellion they never found, aiming not to scare off a few rioters but to find conspirators indictable for high treason—making war on the United States. Hamilton marched with the army from start to finish but was not away from his desk overly long; the army remained in the West about three weeks before arresting a few men and marching back to Philadelphia for heroes' welcomes. A grand jury in 1795 indicted over thirty men for treason. Of these but two were convicted. Both were mentally incompetent, and Washington pardoned both.

Despite the air of comedy hovering over the rebellion—a sense that it might have resulted from a bit too much of the spirits at issue—the episode possesses considerable importance for the political and constitutional development of the United States. The rebellion, and Washington's linking it with the Democratic societies, completed the transformation of his administration into a Federalist regime. The last Democrat in the cabinet, Edmund Randolph, who had succeeded Jefferson as Secretary of State, was forced out as a direct result of the insurrection. Never again, except in moments of wartime emergency and then as a deliberate departure from the norm, would any President strive for a non-partisan rather than a party government. The disorganized frenzies of the backcountry and the calculated overraction of the Washington administration had achieved successes for both sides in the quarrel. The precedent of national power that Hamilton and Washington considered necessary for the future success of the American experiment was firmly established: without firing a shot, they had won something they had succeeded in defining as a war. What the farmers failed to achieve by rioting they got from the political activity that followed: in 1802 the new Jeffersonian government repealed the hated excise tax. Americans remained by all accounts the hardest drinking people in the world for two more generations until a new wave of evangelism from the West brought fundamental changes in American values, and millions of Americans forgot the "old Monongahela rye" and pointed at the depredations of "Demon rum."

The Drive Toward the Constitution

The move to convert the Confederation government into a more effective political instrument began when the war ended. In 1783 nationalists devised a scheme to grant Congress the right to collect duties on imported liquors, sugar, tea, coffee, cocoa, molasses, and pepper; each state would collect the duties at its own ports and then remit them to the Confederation treasury. This plan was submitted as an amendment to the Articles, and so required a unanimous vote of all the states. New York, however, refused to accept it, leaving Congress as bankrupt as ever.

Meanwhile, as Congress declined to little more than a sleepy debating society, the conduct of national affairs passed into the hands of men of vision who thought, as Alexander Hamilton of New York put it, "continentally." In early 1785, commissioners from Virginia and Maryland met at Washington's home, Mount Vernon, to discuss common problems concerning navigation of the Potomac River which separated the two states. So successful was this meeeting that it led to calls by both state legislatures for a larger conference on commercial cooperation to meet at Annapolis the following year. Only twelve delegates from five states turned up at Annapolis, however, and so consideration of the planned agenda was postponed. Instead the delegates, led by Hamilton, drew up a proposal for a new convention, to meet at Philadelphia in May 1787, to discuss every issue necessary "to render the constitution of the Federal Government adequate to the exigencies of the Union." Congress received this proposal and cautiously endorsed it.

By the time of the Philadelphia meeting, all doubts moderate Americans may have entertained about the need for a stronger central government had been shattered by the farmers of western Massachusetts. One state that took its wartime debt seriously, Massachusetts had imposed heavy taxation on its citizens to meet this obligation. At the same time, farm prices declined. Efforts to relieve the farmers' distress by issues of paper money were defeated by creditor groups who refused to be fobbed off with "rag money." In the

Berkshire hills of western Massachusetts, where few farmers had ready cash, many lost their land for non-payment of debts or taxes.

The farmers' wrath soon focused on the courts, where judges were busily ordering forced sales of land to pay taxes and reimburse creditors. In August 1786, fifteen hundred farmers of Hampshire County prevented the meeting of its Court of Common Pleas. A few weeks later, at Worcester, a hundred men armed with swords, muskets, and clubs blocked the judge from entering the courthouse. The wave of insurgency quickly spread throughout the western part of the state, and the rebels acquired a leader in Daniel Shays, a former captain in the Continental Army. Although Shays condoned the attacks against the courts, he did seek to restrain his followers from committing personal violence against judges and the militia.

Eventually Governor James Bowdoin, urged on by the more conservative citizens of the state's commercial center, sent a force of 4,400 men against the rebels. At Springfield, Shays and his men attacked the state troops, but when the trained soldiers fired, they broke ranks and fled in panic. A few days later, Shays and his small remaining force were taken prisoner. Disorders continued for some weeks thereafter, but by the spring of 1787 Shays's Rebellion was over. Shays and several other rebel leaders were sentenced to death, but a reaction set in against this harshness. The governor met defeat when he ran for reelection, and his successor pardoned the condemned Shaysites. Taxes were reduced soon after.

Yet the uprising alarmed many Americans. Washington spoke for those who had fought and sacrificed for their independence only to see their dream turn into a nightmare. "I am mortified beyond expression," he wrote a friend, "that in the moment of our independence we should by our conduct render ourselves ridiculous and contemptible in the eyes of all Europe." Henry Lee of Virginia declared: "We are all in dire apprehension that a beginning of anarchy with all its calamitys has approached, and have no means to stop the dreadful work."

The Constitutional Convention

All eyes now turned to Philadelphia and the coming conference. With its forty thousand inhabitants, the city was the largest in the United

States. During the postwar period, it had suffered like other ports from the decline of foreign trade. Nonetheless, it remained a bustling, neat, tree-lined community that reflected the original orderly plan of its founder, William Penn, and the sobriety as well as the prosperity of its Quaker elite.

The delegates who gathered in 1787 in Independence Hall comprised a mixed lot. Several men of great intellectual force and ability were either prominent national leaders or would soon become so. Others, men with modest abilities and little social vision, scarcely contributed at all to the deliberations and disappeared from history after their brief prominence. At the top, in a unique position, sat the presiding officer, George Washington. Still in his glory as the commander in chief of the Continental forces that had defeated the British and made independence possible, Washington enjoyed enormous prestige throughout the nation. His opening appeal, to "raise a standard to which the wise and the honest can repair," set the tone for the solemn deliberations that followed. Nearly as eminent was Benjamin Franklin, fresh from his triumphs as minister to France and chief negotiator of the peace treaty. Though now aged and infirm, Franklin could still inspire confidence and rally support. Both men favored a stronger central government.

As matters turned out, however, a short and lively Virginian, James Madison, proved more important at the convention that either of these two commanding figures. A close friend of Jefferson, a man of wide reading and deep reflection, Madison would contribute more to the substance of the Constitution than any other individual. A few of the more able men present at Philadelphia during the spring and summer of 1787—Robert Yates of New York, Luther Martin of Maryland, and George Mason of Virginia, for example—remained defenders of local power against expanded federal authority. Most of the delegates, however, were strong nationalists who wished and expected to remake the federal government into an effective instrument of the national will. Perhaps the convention's most extreme nationalist was New York's Alexander Hamilton, who had scant use for the states at all and preferred to see them reduced to little more than administrative units.

All through the humid heat of the Pennsylvania summer the fifty-five delegates argued, negotiated, maneuvered, and deliberated. Nearly all lawyers and educated men, they drew on their knowledge of history, especially the experience of the ancient Roman Republic, for insight. They also culled ideas from the political thinkers of modern times, most notably Montesquieu, Harrington, and Blackstone. But ultimately their own common sense, their experience of government, and the interests of their states and their sections guided their decisions. Historians once argued that most

of the delegates were either public creditors or representatives of commercial interests, and that the chief consideration determining their actions was their desire to protect their own interests and those of fellow businessmen. Surely the commercial, international, and financial experiences of the Confederation period held great importance as they met daily in the same structure where so much of their nation's brief history had been enacted. But public creditors and merchants had not been the only Americans who had deplored what they saw around them between 1781 and 1787. Almost all occupational groups in all parts of the country had reason for discontent during the Critical Period. Above all, most of the delegates conceived of themselves as patriots whose task it was to do away with the humiliations that had grown out of the feeble government under the Articles of Confederation.

THE SIGNERS

CONNECTICUT

Sam^d Huntington
Sam¹ Huntington

Roger Sherman
Roger Sherman

Wm Williams
Wm Williams

Oliver Wolcott
Oliver Wolcott

DELAWARE

Tho M:Kean
Tho M:Kean

Geo Read
Geo Read

Caesar Rodney
Caesar Rodney

GEORGIA

Button Gwinnett
Button Gwinnett

Lyman Hall
Lyman Hall

Geo Walton
Geo Walton

MARYLAND

Charles Carroll of Carrollton

Samuel Chase

Wm Paca

Thos Stone

MASSACHUSETTS

John Adams

Saml Adams

Elbridge Gerry

John Hancock

Robt Treat Paine

NEW HAMPSHIRE

Josiah Bartlett

Matthew Thornton

Wm Whipple

NEW JERSEY

Abra Clark

John Hart

Fra.^s Hopkinson

Richd Stockton

Jno Witherspoon

NEW YORK

Wm Floyd

Fran.^s Lewis

Phil. Livingston

Lewis Morris

NORTH CAROLINA

Joseph Hewes

Wm Hooper

John Penn

PENNSYLVANIA

Geo Clymer

Benj.^a Franklin

Robt Morris

John Morton

Geo. Ross

Benjamin Rush

Ja.^s Smith

Geo. Taylor

James Wilson

RHODE ISLAND

William Ellery

Step Hopkins

SOUTH CAROLINA

Thos Heyward Junr

Thomas Lynch Junr

Arthur Middleton

Edward Rutledge

VIRGINIA

Carter Braxton

Benj.^a Harrison

Th Jefferson

Francis Lightfoot Lee

Richard Henry Lee

Thos Nelson jr.

George Wythe

Independence Hall, once called Pennsylvania State House, was completed around 1756. In 1781 its Liberty Bell was rehung in a clock steeple that replaced the first tower.

The new government must be strong without being oppressive. This need for balance between liberty and order would be a constant concern as the deliberations progressed. How could a national government be effective in dealing with other governments and with its own citizens without becoming despotic?

The labors at Philadelphia represent a series of compromises. Debate opened with Edmund Randolph of Virginia presenting to the convention a proposal by his friend Madison. Dubbed the Virginia Plan, it proposed a new national legislature that would represent the people directly rather than, as in the Confederation Congress, the states. The new body would have two houses. Members of the upper house would be selected by the lower; the lower house would be chosen directly by the vote of the people of each state, and in it state representatives would be in proportion to either population or wealth. In both houses representatives would vote as individuals, not as members of separate state delegations. In addition, the new congress could define the powers of the federal government and overrule the states, appoint a national executive, and choose judges for a new national judiciary.

The Virginia Plan came under immediate attack. Many delegates believed it veered too far towards nationalism, practically obliterating the states as governing units except in relation to minor local issues. It also smacked of favoritism: the largest and richest states such as Virginia, Massachusetts, and Pennsylvania, would have many more delegates in the new congress than the smaller and poorer states such as New Hampshire, Georgia, and Rhode Island. Many delegates also worried about the explicit grant of large, though vague, powers to the national government. What would be left for the states?

Opponents of the Virginia Plan countered with a scheme submitted by William Paterson of New Jersey. The New Jersey Plan granted to a new, single-chamber legislative body powers expanded over those of the Articles of Confederation. Congress would regulate foreign and interstate commerce, levy tariffs on imports, and raise various internal taxes. It also would choose the executive and judicial branches. But all those powers not specified would remain with the states. Congress, as in the Articles, would represent the states—all equally—and members would vote by whole state delegations. Thus the government would remain a league of states as before, though presumably a more effective one.

For many weeks, debate swirled around these two proposals. Attacks on the Paterson proposal pointed out the injustice of allowing, say, a few thousand New Jerseyites to equal the voice of many more Virginians. The small-state people retorted that under the Virginia Plan the three largest states together could virtually outvote all the others. Another question loomed: who were to be counted as "population" under such a scheme as that proposed by Randolph? Should slaves, who could not vote, be considered the equals of freemen for purposes of representation? If they were, each vote cast in the South, where there were many slaves, would count significantly more than a vote in the North, where there were few.

Eventually, a set of compromises was hammered out. The major compromise, sometimes referred to as the Connecticut Plan, established a two-house national legislature. In the lower, the House of Representatives, the people would be directly represented in proportion to population. In the upper, the Senate, each state would have two members regardless of population, although each Senator could vote as he wished. A later arrangement determined that slaves would each be treated, in effect, as three-fifths of a person for the purpose of calculating representation in the House of Representatives. Other provisions of the new Constitution dealt with further issues raised by the debate between the large and the small states. Congress was given broad powers over foreign and interstate commerce, permitted to levy taxes directly on citizens, and awarded the sole right to coin money and regulate its value. But it could not be the judge of how far its powers extended.

The resolution of several large-state-versus-small-state problems did not end the clash of opinion among the delegates. The question of balance between strong government and private freedom had to be addressed. The delegates tackled this issue in several ways. Borrowing from the French political philosopher Montesquieu, they adopted a system of "checks and balances." Alongside Congress they set two other equal branches of government, the executive and the judicial, to be selected separately from Congress. The President, or executive, could be chosen by a group of "electors" in each state, the electors being in turn selected by any method deemed best by each given state legislature; the judicial branch, headed by a Supreme Court, would be selected by the President with the approval of the Senate. To insure their independence from political pressure, judges would serve for life and could not have their salaries reduced. The President, too, would be independent of Congress. His term of office would last for four years regardless of what Congress thought of him, and he could be reelected.

To maintain a balance among the three branches, and so avert the possibility of any one of them achieving tyrannical control, each branch was em-

The Constitutional Convention. (Library of Congress.)

powered to check the others. The President held the power of veto over laws enacted by Congress, although this veto could be overridden by a two-thirds vote in both houses. He would choose all federal judges, ambassadors, and high officials of executive departments, including what would later come to be called his "cabinet." But most of these appointments had to be confirmed by a two-thirds vote of the Senate. The Supreme Court also exerted a braking influence. Not only would it deal with violations of federal laws and suits between citizens of different states, but it held the power to decide whether a measure passed in Congress and signed by the President was "constitutional," or in accord with the Constitution. This responsibility, though not made explicit in the Constitution, was assumed by the delegates at Philadelphia and was soon accepted in practice.

Congress itself had a built-in brake. The delegates at Philadelphia expected the House of Representatives to be the more popularly responsive, something akin to the lower houses of the state legislatures. Members of the Senate, however, under the original terms of the Constitution were to be elected by the state legislatures rather than directly by the people of each state. The upper house would accordingly, the delegates believed, tend to be above public whims. Since any measure would have to pass both chambers to become law, the Senate could check the House. Likewise, any effort by the Senate to pass an unpopular measure could be stopped by the House. As a means (it was hoped) of assuring protection against excessive taxation, it was provided that all money bills would have to start out in the House.

By September the new Constitution had assumed its essential form. At times the debate had grown as heated as the weather, and to quiet tempers Franklin had proposed that a chaplain open each session with a prayer for divine guidance. At least three delegates objected so strenuously to what the majority had wrought that they left Philadelphia in disgust. Many of those who stayed were not much happier. A substantial number continued to object that the Constitution conferred too much power on the federal government; at least one delegate, Alexander Hamilton, believed it created too weak a government for America's needs.

Despite such differences, the Convention finished its work in September 1787. Soon after, Gouverneur Morris of Pennsylvania wrote a preamble to the document. On September 17, with only three members abstaining, the delegates affixed their signatures to their great work and commended it to Congress and to the people.

Ratification

On September 20, 1787, the document composed at Philadelphia was placed before Congress sitting in New York. A few members protested, but the majority agreed to transmit it to the states for ratification or rejection through special state conventions. For over a year, national political discussion would revolve about whether to accept the new frame of government or continue with the Articles.

Not every American, in truth, cared deeply about the issue. As in every generation, most people, even most qualified voters, felt more concern about their day-to-day lives than about matters so remote as the shape of the central government. Yet many thoughtful citizens had followed the recent course of events and, although the deliberations at Philadelphia had been private, had tried to learn what the delegates were saying and doing.

By early 1788, ratification had been carried either unanimously or by overwhelming majorities in five states. Not until the debate commenced in Massachusetts did serious opposition develop. In that state, resistance arose among the "popular" leaders because of their feeling that the new frame of government offered insufficient protection from tyranny. What these men wanted was a "bill of rights" that would impose specific restraints on federal power in the area of personal freedom. Eventually that state's popular leaders gave the Constitution their support and the convention ratified it, but the ratification contained the proviso that amendments be added to the document to protect the individual citizen's rights against encroachment by the federal government.

In March 1788 the federalists received their first setback when feisty Rhode Island rejected the Constitution. As the state where the debtor-creditor battle of the Critical Period had been the most blatant, Rhode Island represented the one clear case of a division along economic lines. The merchants and professional men, smelling certain defeat, boycotted the referendum, giving the anti-federalists a margin of ten to one. But federalist victories by large majorities soon followed in Maryland and South Carolina.

On June 21, New Hampshire became the ninth state to ratify and, by the terms of its own ratification provision, the new Constitution was now technically in effect for the nine states that had accepted it. Unfortunately, two very important states, New York and Virginia, had not yet acted. Without them, the new union would be like the limbs of a tree lacking a trunk. The federalists would have to win the two big states, or their work would be for naught. The anti-federalists in Virginia were led by the formidable Patrick Henry, James Monroe, and George Mason. Favoring the Constitution were James Madison, Edmund Randolph, and above all, George Washington. The expectation that the state's most revered statesman would be the first President of the Republic made the federalists difficult to stop. In the end Virginia ratified, but like Massachusetts requested a bill of rights.

Now the struggle shifted to New York. The inclusion of that state, with its great port and strategic mid-continental location, was essential if the union was to work. But for a while it seemed as if New York would refuse to enter the new union. The convention that assembled in Poughkeepsie was under the thumb of the state's violently anti-federalist governor, George Clinton. Arrayed against Clinton and his supporters, however, were John Jay, the Confederation Secretary of Foreign Affairs, and the strong-willed Hamilton. Soon the two New York federalists, joined by James Madison, were engaged in a war of words with their anti-Constitution opponents. Day afer day the *Independent Gazeteer* carried the short, pithy articles in which the three men, writing under the common name "Publius," explained the virtues and necessity of the new Constitution. Dealing both with immediate concerns and in universal political values, these eighty-five pieces—in later years, published under the collective title *The Federalist Papers*—constitute a classic commentary on the nature and purposes of government. Publius' articles helped change the minds of the Poughkeepsie delegates. Equally important was pressure from New York City, where merchants and artisans threatened that if New York State did not join the Union, New York City would. On July 25, 1788, after an impassioned personal address to the delegates by Hamilton, the state ratified the new frame of government.

To all intents and purposes, the battle was over.

Rhode Island and North Carolina were still outside the new Union, but they did not seem essential. After setting up electoral procedures, the old Congress then quietly passed out of existence. When the body of electors—called the "electoral college"—assembled, every presidential vote cast went for Washington, with John Adams of Massachusetts receiving the Vice-Presidency. On April 14, 1789, Washington received formal notice of his election and departed his beloved Mount Vernon to take up the duties of President in the nation's temporary capital, New York. There, on April 30, he was sworn into office and delivered his first inaugural address.

The next few months were busy ones. In the fall, Congress debated and then passed ten amendments to the Constitution, known collectively as the Bill of Rights, which were then quickly ratified by the prescribed three-fourths of the states. The first eight amendments placed certain fundamental restraints on the power of the federal government over ordinary citizens. Congress could not limit free speech, interfere with religion, keep the people from bearing arms, require the quartering of troops in private homes, or allow homes to be searched by federal authorities without search warrants. Persons accused of crimes could not be made to testify against themselves, nor could the federal government deny the citizen trial by jury nor deprive them of life, liberty, or property "without due process of law." Finally, the central government could not impose excessive bail or "cruel and unusual punishments." Amendments nine and ten ordained that the rights included in the earlier list did not preclude others, and that those powers not expressly given to the federal government or expressly denied the states should belong solely to the states.

Never before had any single document enumerated so clearly and emphatically the rights of private citizens. The Bill of Rights became, accordingly, a landmark in the history of human liberty. But we must make one qualification: the Bill applied to the federal government only. It was recognized that most of the states had similar provisions in their own constitutions. But what if a state chose to violate fundamental human rights; would a citizen have any official or agency to turn to? Not until the Civil War era would this issue be clarified.

By early 1790, the federal government under the Constitution was fully operative. How well would it perform? Would it be able to deal with the problems it had been formed to solve? What shape would the proposed solutions take?

The Hamiltonian Program

The first Congress under the new Constitution assembled in New York City on March 4, 1789. Federal Hall, the former city hall, was still being remodeled and the new Senators and Representatives took their seats amidst the carpenters' noise and flying sawdust. The confusion and disorder caused little harm, however. Only eight Senators and thirteen Representatives had slashed their way through the muddy roads of spring to take their oaths of office that opening day.

Friends of the Constitution composed most of Congress. Many of the members, in fact, had been present at Philadelphia during the momentous summer of 1787 to write the new frame of government, and the majority hoped to carry out the purposes of the nationalists: to make the United States a going concern and create respect for the republic among the older nations of the world.

Congress' first deliberations bore a near-farcical character. For three weeks its members debated the proper title of address for the President. Vice President John Adams insisted that without some such title as "His Elective Highness" or "His Excellency," the President might be mistaken for the head of a volunteer fire company or leader of a cricket club. His opponents believed any such title would be unrepublican, ill-suited to the new nation. In their eyes the pudgy Vice President's serious concern appeared ridiculous, and they took to calling him "His rotundity." Washington himself settled the momentous issue. Though protective of his dignity on all occasions, he preferred to avoid "monarchical" trappings. True, he traveled through the streets in a gilded coach and held formal receptions for visitors and guests called "levees." He also insisted on reading his annual message to Congress personally and, like the English King, he asked for a formal congressional response. But he would not accept a title of any sort, and remained "Mr. President."

Other business took up the crowded opening months of the new administration. In November 1789 North Carolina officially ratified the Constitution and entered the Union. Reluctant Rhode Island joined at last in 1790. Meanwhile, Congress had set up three major executive departments, State, War, and Treasury, and appointed a Postmaster General. At the same time it passed the Federal Judiciary Act (1789), specifying that the Supreme Court was to consist of a chief justice with five associates. This measure also established a system of inferior federal courts and created the office of Attorney General as the government's chief law officer.

One of the new government's most pressing concerns, of course, was that of providing itself with revenues. Congress passed the nation's first tariff, setting low duties on a host of imported goods. To ward off foreign competition, the measure set slightly higher rates on several commodities produced in the country; but, on the whole, the legislators were simply interested in raising money. Soon after, Congress passed the Tonnage Act, taxing American ships a few pennies a ton and foreign-built and -owned vessels at a much higher rate.

Congress now had the means to pay the army and official salaries, and to begin to meet its debts. But those debts were still troublesome. By 1789 they amounted to about $52 million—$40 million owed to Americans, and $12 million due foreigners. In addition to these obligations of the federal government, there were also the still-unpaid state debts, amounting to about $25 million.

Few people questioned that the foreign debt must be paid in full. Otherwise, the United States would not earn the respect of foreign powers or be able to borrow abroad again. But what about the domestic debt? Speculators had bought Continental IOU's for a song from those who had actually given the wartime Congress money or supplies to fight the British. Should these speculators alone benefit by the improved credit of the national government, or should the original holders also get something? And what about the state debts? Many Southern states had already paid off these obligations while many Northern states had not. If the government were to "assume" or take over, these obligations, it would benefit the residents of the middle states and New England at the expense of those south of Pennsylvania.

Congress turned over the problem of how to handle the debt as well as other pending financial questions to Alexander Hamilton, Washington's Secretary of the Treasury. A young man of 35, Hamilton was a former aide-de-camp to Washington who had married into the prominent Schuyler family of New York. Able, handsome, and well-connected, he had risen high in New York political life after his army service despite his West Indies origin and his illegitimate birth.

Hamilton was a nationalist, lacking the emotional attachment to the local community of men like Jefferson and Madison. He had so little

Mt. Vernon, Virginia: George Washington's Home

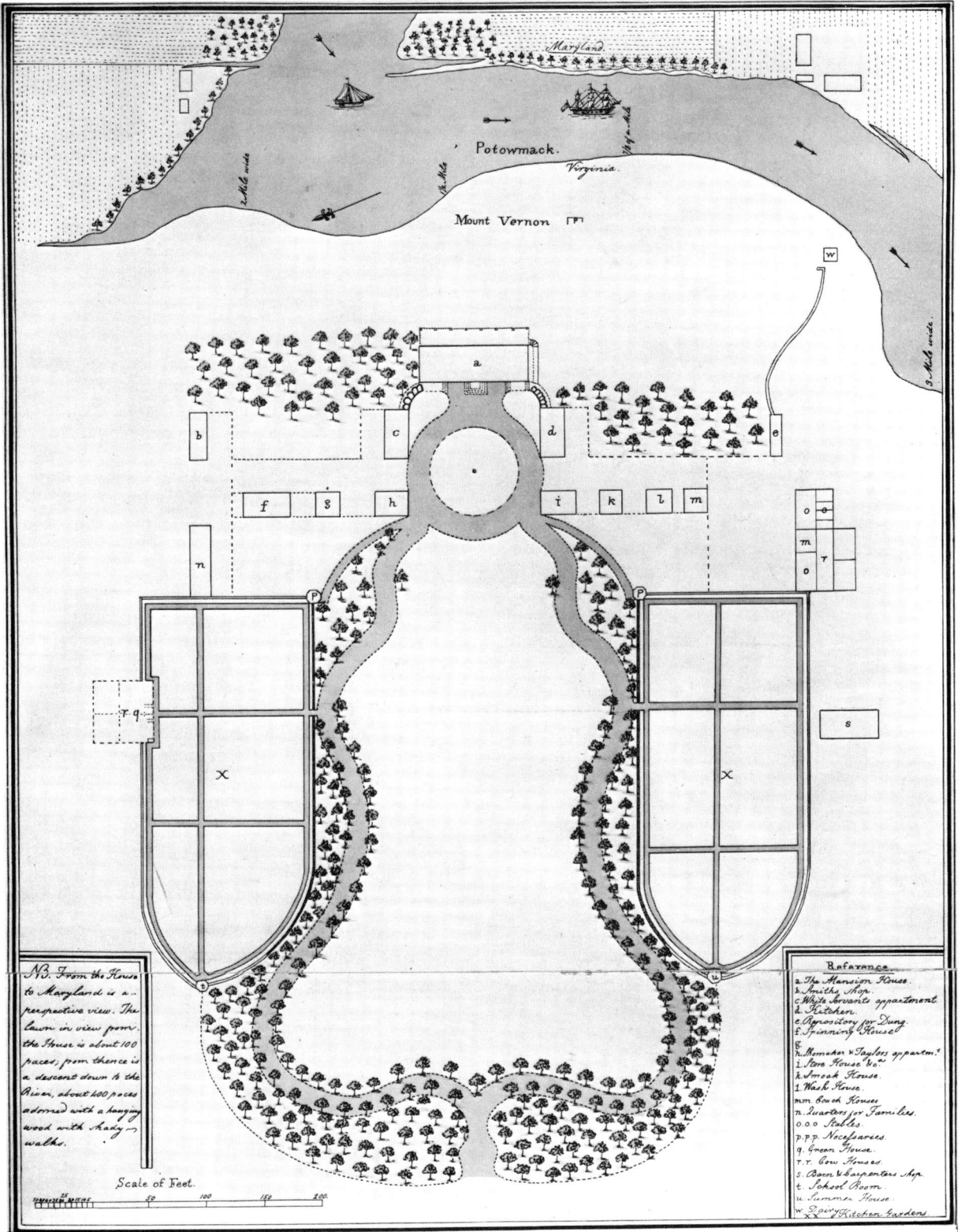

Maryland

Potowmack.

Virginia.

Mount Vernon

Scale of Feet.

50   100   150   200.

Reference
a. The Mansion House.
b. Smiths Shop.
c. White Servants appartment.
d. Kitchen.
e. Repository for Dung.
f. Spinning House
g.
h. Shoemaker & Taylors appartm.t
i. Store House &c.a
k. Smoak House.
l. Wash House.
mm. Coach Houses.
n. Quarters for Families.
o.o.o. Stables.
p.p.p. Necessaries.
q. Green House.
r.r. Cow Houses.
s. Barn & Carpenters shp.
t. School Room.
u. Summer House.
w. Dairy
xx. Kitchen Gardens

respect for the states that he had proposed their virtual elimination at the Constitutional Convention. He prized commerce, trade, and manufacturing, and believed that the United States could not afford to remain an agricultural nation, producing raw materials for Europe. Britain, rapidly becoming the industrial workshop of the world, must be America's example, he claimed. This required a vigorous central government commanding its citizens' loyalty. Finally, the New Yorker was skeptical of human nature. Men of the Enlightenment, such as Jefferson, tended to believe that human beings were inherently more good than evil, and that social and political evil existed largely because of evil institutions. Freed of these, mankind would flourish. Hamilton, on the other hand, believed that people tended to be "ambitious, vindictive and rapacious." A nation had to restrain its people lest liberty descend to license. The new government had to marshal both material interests and public affections.

Congress' problem was Hamilton's opportunity. The new Secretary of the Treasury seized the occasion to advance some of his fondest political and economic hopes. In three great *Reports* he embedded his solution to several immediate problems in his larger plans for American society. The *Report Relative to Public Credit* boldly proposed that the debt be paid in full and that the federal government even assume the still unpaid state debts.

Hamilton asserted in this *Report* that the public debt would prove a "public blessing." His *Report on a National Bank* early in 1791 explained why. Inadequate currency and banking facilities blocked the nation's economic development. Hamilton proposed to remedy these defects by a new federally chartered banking corporation, drawing its capital both from the Treasury and from private investors. The new "Bank of the United States," governed by both privately elected directors and ones chosen by the government, would serve both public and private needs. It would stimulate commerce and manufactures by lending money to private businessmen. The bank would as well hold the government's deposits, pay its bills, and accept its receipts. Most important of all, the new institution would issue the paper money of the nation, backed principally by the new funded debt rather than by gold and silver. Gold-poor America would thereby convert the national debt into a powerful engine for mobilizing its economy.

Later that same year Hamilton issued the last of the major *Reports,* on manufactures. The Secretary acknowledged that agriculture was the most important single economic activity. But he saw no conflict between agriculture and industry.

The two complemented one another; both together would benefit the nation. Noting the beginnings of the factory system in Britain, he observed that the new system of manufacture employed every class of people in productive labor, even women and children. America with its magnificent resources was potentially a great industrial nation, but to compete with other nations would require government aid. To protect "infant industries" until they could compete successfully, the government must place high tariffs on foreign manufactures. It should also offer premiums for the production of needed goods and new inventions. Above all, the proposed Bank must loan capital to entrepreneurs.

These three great *Reports* together outlined an economic revolution. Through the positive use of the national government, the country might be transformed: bustling cities, humming factories, and busy arteries of communication and transport would erupt from the quiet American landscape of prosperous farms and brooding forests.

This program, so bold in its projections, had to arouse fierce opposition. To those who envisioned an America of small farms and the simple, uncomplicated social relations of an agrarian society, Hamilton's vision was a nightmare. Many also feared the expansion of federal powers his program required. Especially fearful were the Virginia leaders—James Madison, now a leading member of the House of Representatives, and Thomas Jefferson, Washington's Secretary of State.

Jefferson deplored the industrial-urban society that Hamilton eagerly anticipated. Having witnessed industrialism firsthand in Europe, Jefferson was convinced that "the mobs of great cities" were sores on the social body, and that when people "get piled up one upon another as in Europe, they shall become corrupt as in Europe." Farmers, he insisted, were God's "Chosen People, if ever he had a chosen people," and they alone could be relied on to support the common good. The Virginia leaders also believed that Hamilton and his supporters wanted to create a plutocracy, a government of the rich. In December 1790 the Virginia legislature asserted that the funding act would "erect and concentrate and perpetuate a large money interest."

Hamilton's opponents also feared the powerful national government his plans would require. Jefferson thought that government should consist of "a few plain duties to be performed by a few servants." The Hamiltonians, said Jefferson and his followers, would create an all-powerful centralized government that would become the source of graft and curruption.

This confrontation of Hamiltonians and Jeffersonians emerged as the country's first major political division. Hamilton's friends submitted bills to Congress to implement the recommendations of his *Reports*. The bill to fund the public debt aroused Madison, who quickly became the leader of the forces arrayed against Hamilton. Madison spoke as a Southerner, aware that four-fifths of the unpaid securities and state debts were Northern. Yet he pitched his attack on a high plane. He did not oppose funding as such, he declared; rather, he feared that Hamilton's scheme unduly benefited speculators. Under Hamilton's plan these people would receive the full face value of their holdings, while original possessors would get nothing. Even now, Madison and his supporters asserted, advance news that the government would assume the state debts had been leaked by people in high places, and speculators were traveling through the South buying up securities from gullible farmers.

For many weeks the funding bill remained blocked. The particular sticking point was assumption. But then one morning in July, Jefferson bumped into Hamilton on the steps of the President's house. The Secretary of the Treasury told the Secretary of State that the deadlock in Congress was endangering the Union. Could Jefferson do anything to help? The next day the two cabinet officers met with Madison, and a deal was arranged. The national capital would be moved from New York to Philadelphia. Then, in ten years, it would be permanently located in the South between Virginia and Maryland. In return, Madison and his friends would cease to oppose assumption. The following month the funding measure passed Congress.

Next on the agenda was a national bank. The bill would charter a Bank of the United States for twenty years with a capital of $10 million, one-fifth to be subscribed by the federal government and the remainder by private investors. The Bank could issue banknotes that the government would accept in payment of taxes. Philadelphia was to be the Bank's home office, but it might establish branches in other cities.

Over the opposition of Madison, Congress passed the bill chartering the first Bank of the United States and sent it to the President for his signature. Washington was stumped. His fellow Virginian, Madison, had raised doubts in his mind as to whether the Constitution allowed Congress to charter such a bank. Might this not be an unwarranted extension of federal powers? To ease his mind, the President asked for the opinions of his Cabinet. Both Jefferson and Attorney General Edmund Randolph replied that by no stretch of its meaning did the Constitution authorize a federally chartered bank. Hamilton took the opposite view. In a masterly application of what came to be called the principle of "broad construction" of the Constitution, he argued that since a bank was necessary to the collecting of taxes, the regulating of trade, and other functions explicitly conferred on Congress in that great document, its constitutionality was "implied," if not precisely specified. Convinced by Hamilton's logic, Washington signed the bill into law. On July 4, 1791, the stock of the Bank was put up for sale. In a few hours the whole $8 million reserved to private investors was sold out and hundreds of eager capitalists had to be turned down.

The third of Hamilton's major *Reports* was not enacted into law in his own day. It stood, however, as an eloquent defense of a high tariff that would become an inspiration to later generations of "protectionists." Meanwhile, other items of Hamiltonian legislation also became law. In 1791 Congress passed the Whiskey Tax, imposing an excise on distilled liquors to help pay interest on the funded debt. In 1792 it passed the Coinage Act, establishing the dollar as the United States currency unit, dividing it into dimes and cents and making it equivalent to a specified amount of gold or silver.

Foreign Affairs

As Congress and the American people debated the Hamiltonian program, two distinct and conflicting positions began to emerge. On the one side were those led by Jefferson and his chief congressional lieutenant, Madison. These men favored state over national power, agriculture over industry, trade, and banking. They believed that limited government and "strict construction" of the Constitution were best for the nation and the American people. They claimed to have faith in the people and to distrust the rich and powerful. Many were Southerners, although in the end the

Jeffersonian party would also win support among the farmers of the middle and New England states and the artisans of the towns. Increasingly this group took on the name Republican, a label they adopted to contrast their more egalitarian political views with the supposedly more "monarchical" ones of their opponents.

On the other side were Hamilton and his followers, including John Adams and, increasingly, President Washington himself. Calling themselves Federalists, these people favored an ever-stronger federal government, if necessary at the expense of the states. They believed that America's future lay in industry, not in agriculture alone. Generally speaking, they accepted "republicanism" as best suited to the American "genius," but they did not trust majority rule as much as did their opponents, and they hoped to attract the support of the rich and the powerful to the new national government by making their interests coincide with those of the government. The Federalists could count on strong support within the major commercial towns, including such Southern ports as Charleston. As defenders of order and stability they could also count on those people who were by temperament conservative. One group that often favored the Federalist position was the defenders of the established Congregational church in New England. On the other side were to be found the Baptists, Methodists, and other dissenting groups which tended to be Republican.

The division of the country into these two opposing political camps did not come all at once. The Founding Fathers, including the authors of the Constitution, had not envisioned political parties. In fact, in the 1780's and 90's the term "party" was an epithet that conveyed the same sense as the term "clique" today. As late as 1797, when Washington stepped down from the Presidency, the Father of his Country asked his fellow citizens in his Farewell Address to avoid "the spirit of party" that would "distract the public councils and enfeeble the public administration." Ideally, the nation's early leaders believed, the public should choose the best, most public-spirited men for office. They did not envisage organized political groups with permanent officers, newspapers, campaign workers, and party treasuries, and they made no provision for them in the Constitution. It took almost a decade before the division that had appeared during the first session of Congress was accepted as a legitimate part of the American political system.

Foreign problems solidified the domestic political divisions and helped turn factions into true political parties. No sooner had the new government under the Constitution begun its work in New York than Europe erupted into one of the most colossal political convulsions of modern times. In France, our ally in the war for independence, the American struggle for liberty had struck a deep chord. "Enlightened" men and women recognized a larger significance in the event, and it strengthened their resolve to wrest power from the Bourbon monarchy, custodians of the "old regime" of privilege and inequality that for centuries had shackled the French people.

In August 1788 the French king, faced with a severe financial crisis partly induced by France's recent aid to America, called into session the Estates General to vote him more money. He expected the clergy, nobility, and middle class to give him the taxes he needed, and then adjourn. But instead the Estates were quickly taken over by groups of reformers. In a matter of a few months these men had converted the Estates General into a revolutionary body that began to sweep away the entire old regime and convert the nation into a constitutional monarchy based on respect for human rights and on wide popular political participation. On July 14, 1789, a Paris mob attacked the Bastille, the prison that had become a notorious symbol of oppression, tore down the walls, and freed the prisoners.

Americans' early response to the electrifying events in France was almost universally favorable. When the Marquis de Lafayette, who helped lead the early stages of the Revolution, sent Washington the key to the Bastille, the President hung the key prominently in the presidential mansion. He later wrote Gouverneur Morris that he hoped the disorders in France would "terminate very much in favor of the rights of man." If such a reserved and inherently conservative man as Washington could applaud the French uprising, the followers of Jefferson were certain to be still more enthusiastic. Many Republicans, in imitation of French egalitarianism, adopted the title "Citizen" or "Citizeness" in place of "Mister" or "Miss." Others began to abandon knee breeches and adopt the long trousers worn by the Paris artisans and French reformers. Republicans considered the French Revolution the beginning of a new age. As Jefferson wrote, "the liberty of the whole earth" depended on the contest in France.

This initial consensus among Americans, however, disintegrated when the Revolution took on a more radical tone. Increasingly the French radical leaders, called Jacobins, denounced the church and organized religion. In 1791 the King fled Paris with his family, but was caught and thrown into prison. By this time many enemies of the Revolution, including a large part of the French clergy and nobility, had either been driven from the country or hustled off to jail. Soon after, the Revolutionary leaders began a reign of terror against all opponents of their policies, even the moderate reformers. In 1793 a revolutionary tribunal pronounced the death sentence on Louis XVI, and the sentence was promptly carried out. In October his queen, Marie Antoinette, was also sent to the guillotine.

While the excesses of the French revolutionaries shocked many Americans, if the Revolution had been contained within France its effects on the United States would have been limited. But the radical French leaders proclaimed a crusade against conservative regimes elsewhere in Europe in the name of "liberty, equality, fraternity." Before long, France was at war with Austria, England, Prussia, and Spain.

Surrounded as it was with enemies, France sought aid from its ally, the United States. Under the Treaty of 1778 the Americans were bound to protect France's West Indies colonies against any enemy. With England certain to use her powerful fleet to blockade and, if possible, take these possessions, the United States now faced the serious prospect of war with Great Britain.

Many Americans would have welcomed such a war. Britain still limited American commerce with her own West Indies possessions. She still occupied the Western garrisons on American soil. She still stirred up the Indians of the Northwest to discourage American settlement west of the mountains. Now that Britain was locked in combat with revolutionary France, she seemed the special enemy of liberty and freedom. To make matters worse, in 1793 the British began to seize American vessels engaged in trade with the French West Indies and to throw their crews into foul dungeons.

Among the followers of Hamilton, however, France represented all that was chaotic, disorderly, irreligious. That country, exclaimed Fisher Ames, was "an open hell, still ringing with agonies and blasphemies, still smoking with sufferings and crimes." Britain, on the other hand, was seen as a bulwark of sanity and moderation, and her victory in the struggle thought to be essential for world order.

Meanwhile, the French Republic had dispatched Citizen Edmond Genet to the United States to do what he could to make trouble for Great Britain. Arriving in Charleston early in 1793, Genet immediately set to work recruiting Americans in his nation's cause. Even before presenting his formal credentials to Washington and Secretary of State Jefferson in Philadelphia, he had commissioned Americans as privateers to prey on British commerce, and opened negotiations with several American frontier leaders to attack Spanish Florida and Louisiana. Despite these high-handed actions, American friends of France cheered Genet as he made a triumphal procession to the Capitol.

By this time, however, Washington, supported by Hamilton and Jefferson, had decided to proclaim American neutrality. Genet learned of this seeming repudiation of the 1778 treaty but, convinced by his recent experience that Americans were fervent French partisans, he determined to ignore it. In short order he became the rallying point of the "Gallomen," as the friends of the French republic were called, and the chief villain of the "Anglomen," the label attached to England's supporters. During the spring the two groups clashed so violently in the streets of the nation's capital that, according to John Adams, only the arrival of the dread yellow fever "saved the United States from a fatal revolution of government."

Though at first a hero of the Jeffersonians, Genet finally offended even the friends of the French Republic. Despite protests from the British minister against the French envoy's activities, Genet expanded American privateering expeditions against British commerce. So outrageous were his actions that Jefferson wrote Madison that the French minister would "sink the Republican interest" if the Republicans did not "abandon him." Finally, after Genet threatened to appeal to the American people over the head of Washington, the administration decided it had had enough. By this time the Jacobins were in power. Genet, who did not belong to this group, most certainly would have been beheaded had he been forced to return to France. The administration, accordingly, allowed him to stay in the United States, but refused to deal with him any further.

Settlement With Great Britain

While Americans rioted in the streets for or against Genet, the United States was moving toward a settlement of sorts with Great Britain.

Early in 1794 Washington sent Chief Justice John Jay to England as special envoy. Jay, a staunch Federalist, knew that it would be difficult to get an agreement with Great Britain that would be popular. He was right.

The British wined and dined the American emissary. He in turn bowed to the Queen and kissed her hand, an act that outraged ardent Republicans. The British did not want war with the United States, but neither did they want to adopt any policy that promised to weaken their war effort against France. In the end, they drove a hard bargain. In the agreement that Jay carried back from London, the British promised finally to surrender the military posts they had illegally occupied since 1783. Other disagreements, including disputes over the pre-Revolutionary debts owed Englishmen, a boundary dispute with Canada in the Northwest, and the recent British ship seizures, were referred to British-American arbitration commissions. Left unsettled, however, were such long-standing American complaints as the Indian incitements in the West and restrictive British trade practices in her West Indies colonies. On the question of British right to limit neutral trade in wartime, Jay retreated from the original American principle and agreed that the British could seize French or other enemy property if found aboard American ships.

Jay returned to the United States to find his fellow Americans in no mood to swallow this ungenerous agreement. Just recently General Anthony Wayne had smashed the Indians at the Battle of Fallen Timbers in northwestern Ohio. Soon after, "mad Anthony" forced the tribes to sign the Treaty of Greenville surrendering all of Ohio and a large part of Indiana to the white man. This victory ended the Indian menace on the Northwest frontier despite the recent British efforts to stir them up.

As a result of the government's bold action against the whiskey rebels, most Americans gained confidence in the strength of their new government and felt even less inclined than before to give way to Britain. When John Jay arrived back in the United States, he was greeted everywhere with outrage. Wherever he went, the hapless envoy was attacked for selling out American interests. One ardent Republican, unable to contain his feelings, inscribed on his fence: "Damn John Jay! damn every one that won't damn John Jay!! damn every one that won't put lights in his windows and sit up all night damning John Jay!!!" It seems unlikely that this overwrought advice was followed, but Jay himself ruefully remarked that he could have traveled across the nation by the light of his burning effigies.

Hamilton and other Federalists nonetheless marshaled their forces and wrote articles supporting the agreement as the best that could be obtained. Most important of all, Washington put his prestige behind the treaty, although for his efforts he earned the contempt of the Republicans. Jefferson himself even remarked: "Curse on his virtues; they have undone the country." But the President's support did the trick. In June 1795 the Senate by a close vote confirmed the treaty.

Whatever its inadequacies, the Jay Treaty settled most of the disputes with Britain left over from the Confederation period. But difficulties with Spain remained. Then, in 1795, the Spanish government and the United States signed the Pinckney Treaty. This agreement granted Americans rights of free navigation on the Mississippi, restraints on the Florida Indians, and the "right of deposit" for their goods in New Orleans for a period of three years. Although the three-year provision implied possible trouble for the future, the Pinckney Treaty was greeted with great enthusiasm and was ratified unanimously by the Senate.

John Adams' Presidency

In 1796 the nation faced its first disputed presidential election campaign. By this time American voters had become strongly polarized into two distinct parties. As yet, little of the machinery of party politics or campaigns had appeared, but throughout the nation people had begun to call themselves either Federalists or Republicans and their opponents by stronger and ruder names.

No group cheered more loudly for its own side and denounced its opponents more vituperatively than the editors of the newly emerged party press. Benjamin Franklin Bache's Philadelphia *Aurora* regularly lambasted the President in scurrilous terms. John Fenno's Federalist *Gazette of the United States* declared that the Republicans were encouraging the country's youth "to imbibe the poison of atheism and disaffection." The most violent Federalist of all was the transplanted Englishman William Cobbett—in his eyes all Republicans were "cut-throats who walk in rags and sleep amidst filth and vermin."

In this charged atmosphere the common decencies broke down. Within Washington's Cabinet Jefferson, the arch-Republican, had ceased to talk to Hamilton, the arch-Federalist. In 1793 Jefferson resigned as Secretary of State and returned to his Virginia estates. Hamilton, too, left official life and went back to the practice of law in New York. Neither man, however, abandoned politics. From Monticello, his handsome classical mansion on a hill overlooking the Blue Ridge Mountains, Jefferson continued to advise by letter his friends and political allies in Philadelphia and around the nation. Hamilton also remained active politically and, indeed, would exert great influence behind the scenes in the administration that followed Washington's.

Washington, no doubt, could have held the Presidency for life had he so desired. But he was weary of politics and anxious to return to Mount Vernon; he looked forward, he said, to sitting down to dinner alone with his wife, Martha. He refused to accept a third term and, with the help of Jay and Hamilton he prepared a final address to his fellow citizens.

Contrary to popular belief, Washington's Farewell Address devoted more attention to domestic than foreign matters. The retiring President deplored the state of political conflict that had arisen and warned Americans against disunity, whether sectional or political. He also warned the nation to be wary of "entangling alliances." He did not advocate isolation of the United States from international affairs. Rather, the country must be guided by its own interests and not become too closely tied to those of others.

As the "Father of His Country" prepared to return to Virginia, the political pot came to a rapid boil. As yet there was no convention scheme of nominating party candidates. Instead, both Federalist and Republican leaders merely agreed among themselves on who should run.

The choice of the Federalists was Vice-President John Adams. Less extreme than the "high Federalists" such as Hamilton, he was, nevertheless, peppery-tempered and opinionated, as well as learned and public-spirited. Adams had been in the forefront of America's struggle for nationhood ever since the 1770's. Now he considered France the chief impediment to America's freedom. The Republicans turned to their acknowledged chief, Jefferson. Tall, loose-jointed, red-haired, the former Secretary of State was as anti-British and pro-French as ever. Britain, he believed, was determined to enslave the United States economically and under Hamilton's auspices, he felt, had come to dominate the American government.

The campaign lasted into 1797. Although in many states adult male citizens could vote for presidential electors, it was these electors themselves who chose the President and Vice-President. Not until the members of the electoral college actually cast their ballots in January were the results known. During this time the intrigues, the maneuverings, the libels and attacks were almost endless. The Republican press assailed Adams as a monarchist who, if elected, would enslave the American people. The Federalist press, in turn, accused Jefferson of being a lackey of the French. Besides, as governor of Virginia during the Revolution, he had fled his capital in a "cowardly" escape from the British.

A particularly unpleasant incident of the campaign was the airing of a personal scandal involving Hamilton. In 1791, the Secretary of the Treasury had begun a liason with Maria Reynolds, the estranged wife of James Reynolds, an unscrupulous speculator and political fixer. Soon after his meetings with Mrs. Reynolds her husband appeared on the scene, claimed that his heart was "Burst with Greef," and demanded money to repair it. Over the next few months the Secretary gave Reynolds a thousand dollars to shut him up.

But Reynolds could not, or would not, be quiet. In 1792 he told all to a group of Republican Congressmen, including James Monroe, and, in addition, he claimed that Hamilton had made money by swindling the government. Shocked and dismayed, the congressmen confronted the Secretary with their information. Hamilton confessed to the romance, but denied any financial wrongdoing. The congressmen seemed satisfied, and pledged to keep the Reynolds matter to themselves.

They did not. As political feelings became ever hotter, Monroe told Jefferson about it. In 1796 the story then leaked to John Beckley, a man who played the same role in the Republican Party as the chairman of a national political committee does today. Beckley had the story published as a pamphlet in time to provide juicy reading for the voters.

Meanwhile, the new French minister in the United States, Citizen Adet, angry at the Federalist administration for coming to terms with the British, joined the fracas. In November 1796 he published in the American newspapers a set of proclamations announcing that France would suspend diplomatic relations with the United States and clamp down hard on neutral shipping. The blame for this new policy, he declared, would have to be laid at the door of the Federalists' pro-

President John Adams. (Library of Congress.)

British policies. Besides having to cope with Adet's indiscreet interference in American affairs, the Federalists were wracked by internal dissension. Hamilton did not like Adams, whom he considered, rightly, a stubborn man not easily manipulated.

In the end, all the attacks, intrigues, scandals, and dissensions could not stop the voters and electors from keeping the Federalists in power. But the results were close. When the electors' ballots were counted, Adams had seventy-one votes to Jefferson's sixty-eight, with Thomas Pinckney—a stooge of Hamilton—coming in third. Under the existing provisions of the Constitution, John Adams was declared the second President of the United States, and Jefferson the Vice President.

The new Chief Executive faced a host of problems, especially in foreign relations. The United States by now had become a major international trader, its ships calling in virtually every port in the world. The reason for this growth was the great European war. As the British Royal Navy swept French and Spanish vessels off the high seas, France and her allies depended increasingly on the most important maritime neutral, the United States, to carry goods to and from their colonies. By 1796 American merchants were bringing in millions of dollars' worth of molasses, rum, sugar, and other products from French and Spanish possessions in the New World, landing them at New York, Baltimore, Charleston, or Philadelphia and then sending them, marked as American exports, to France, Spain, or some other part of continental Europe. They were also pouring into the French and Spanish colonies European goods that England's enemies feared to carry on their own vessels.

This wartime trade rained dollars, pounds, doubloons, and gilders on American merchants. Great mansions arose in Salem, Boston, Newburyport, Charleston, and the other centers of foreign trade. Every harbor along the Atlantic coast was dotted with the white sails and black hulls of the brigs, sloops, bargues, and full-rigged ships engaged in world trade, while on the shore the streets were crowded with clerks, stevedores, porters, teamsters, and jack-tars hurrying about their business of moving the world's goods and making money.

The British looked on aghast. America's good fortune clearly came at their expense. Not only were the Americans helping their enemies evade the British blockade of Europe and of French and Spanish America, but they were also taking over business formerly handled by British merchants. To top things off, the exploding American merchant marine was absorbing many of Britain's best seamen. Hundreds of experienced British merchant seamen preferred the high wages and clean ships of the Americans to their own, and were deserting. At Norfolk, Virginia, the entire crew of a British merchant vessel quit in a body and signed on a departing American ship. Even sailors from the Royal Navy were escaping its harsh discipline to join the American merchant fleet. The Yankees, in a word, were profiting marvelously by England's troubles.

For a while after the Jay Treaty, the British left American ships and seamen alone. But then, in 1796, when marine manpower shortages began to hurt, they resorted to impressment. Whenever a British man-of-war stopped an American merchant vessel to inspect her cargo for goods going to France, a British naval officer lined the men up on deck. Back and forth he went along the line, asking each to speak up and identify himself. Often anyone with an English, Irish, or Scottish accent was assumed to be a British subject and removed to serve in the Royal Navy.

Nor were the French any better. In the eyes of the French Directory, as the ruling body in France was called between 1795 and 1799, Adams' victory was an unfriendly act on the part of the American people. In 1797 the French government ordered that every impressed United States citizen captured aboard a British vessel be hanged, and if any single item of British make was found aboard an American ship the vessel was to be confiscated. At the same time the French gave the United States Minister his walking papers, in effect cutting off diplomatic relations.

The American government reacted vigorously to the French challenge. Knowing that the United States was ill prepared to go to war, Adams decided to negotiate and appointed three commissioners, Elbridge Gerry, Charles Cotesworth Pinckney, and John Marshall, to go to Paris to seek a settlement. At the same time, however, the administration asked Congress for money to build naval vessels and expand the army. The Republicans fought the administration's request for defense funds. Representative Albert Gallatin of Pennsylvania declared that paying the public debt would be "a much more effective way of securing the respect of foreign nations than by building a Navy." Feelings between the two parties grew so bitter that one hot-tempered Republican, an Irish-born Congressman from Vermont, Matthew Lyon, spat in the eye of his Federalist colleague, Roger Griswold of Connecticut. Lyon barely survived a move to expel him.

In October 1797 the three American emissaries, full of high hopes, arrived in Paris prepared to negotiate with the French foreign minister,

Tallyrand. They soon found that this was not an easy matter. Over several weeks they were forced to talk to three French officials whom they later identified as X, Y, and Z. The Americans, these gentlemen informed Marshall, Gerry, and Pinckney, would have to apologize for some recent anti-French statements of President Adams; they would have to promise a loan to France and, moreover, privately pay money to Tallyrand and members of the Directory. The American envoys were not naive about how diplomacy was conducted in Europe, but they refused to pay bribes before the French agreed to a settlement, and broke off the talks. Soon after, they reported back to Adams on what had transpired during their mission.

In 1798 the American government published the entire "X, Y, Z" correspondence. Whatever the worldly American emissaries felt, the American people were shocked by the French government's seeming contempt for the United States. Overnight all but the most ardent Republicans became anti-French. Wherever Americans gathered in public places—in theaters, taverns, concert halls—they sang patriotic songs and demanded to hear "Yankee Doodle" and the "President's March." Any attempt by die-hard Republicans to respond to this with the French revolutionary anthem, "The Marseillaise," was drowned out by hisses and groans. Adams, hitherto not especially popular, was cheered in Philadelphia.

Congress now acted with dispatch. Early in 1798 it appropriated money for forty naval vessels, and for trebling the size of the army. It also ended commercial contacts with France, ordered the suspension of the Franco-American treaty of 1778, and created the Navy Department. Shortly thereafter, a full-scale though undeclared naval war broke out on the Atlantic, with American frigates and French vessels exchanging broadside volleys and French privateers attacking United States merchant vessels within sight of the American coast.

Had Adams and the Federalists confined their anger to the French, they might have retained their popularity. But they did not. Instead, they seized the opportunity to use the new anti-French feeling against their political opponents. The Republicans, they said, were allies of the detested Directory and in the event of war would betray their own nation.

In this atmosphere of intense political excitement, few Federalists found it possible to regard their opponents' views as legitimate expressions of dissent. Perhaps we should not be too harsh in judging them. As yet, few Americans fully accepted the legitimacy of a party system. The government's opponents were difficult to distinguish from enemies of the nation as a whole. There was at the time no well-developed notion of a "loyal opposition." Still another fact must be kept in mind: the French Revolution went far beyond America's own Revolution in attacking traditional social institutions and social relations. To conservative Americans, it appeared to threaten chaos, anarchy, and atheism, and it seemed necessary to stop it by whatever means.

In this mood a Federalist-dominated Congress passed four measures, called collectively the Alien and Sedition Acts of 1798, designed to curb the anti-administration opposition and prevent internal subversion. The Naturalization Act extended the period of residence required for United States citizenship from five to fourteen years. The Alien Act gave the President the power to deport any alien suspected of "treasonable or secret" intentions. The Alien Enemies Act gave him the power in time of war to arrest or banish from the country any citizen of an enemy power.

These first three measures were all aimed at foreigners. The last, the Sedition Act, was aimed at native Americans, and especially at opponents of the administration. Under its terms any resident of the United States who sought to prevent the execution of federal law, who tried to prevent a federal official from performing his duties, or who attempted to start any riot, "insurrection," or "unlawful assembly," could be fined or imprisoned. Anyone convicted of publishing "any false, scandalous and malicious writing" against Congress, the President, or the government could be fined or sentenced to prison for two years.

Using his powers under the Alien and Sedition Acts, Secretary of State Timothy Pickering began a series of prosecutions of Republican newspaper editors and political leaders. The owners of four leading Republican newspapers were indicted and three Republican editors were convicted of violating the Sedition Act. Pickering also charged "Spitting Lyon," the excitable Congressman from Vermont, with libel against President Adams. Lyon was convicted, fined a thousand dollars, and hustled off to jail for four months. Faced with the possibility of a hot reception when they arrived, many foreigners called off plans to leave for America.

The prosecutions under the Sedition Act damaged Adams badly. Many fair-minded Americans considered them violations of the freedom of speech and press guaranteed by the Bill of Rights. Others saw them as totally unwarranted. The country, they said, was not in mortal danger; Congressman Lyon and the convicted editors were victims of political persecution. Before long, opponents of the measures and the prosecutions were holding meetings throughout the middle states, the South, and the West and sending petitions of protest to Congress. Great rolls of paper containing thousands of names were soon deposited on the desks of the House and Senate clerks.

Few Americans were as disturbed by the Federalist repressions as the leaders of the Republican Party, Jefferson and Madison. Both regarded the Alien and Sedition Acts not only as a blow to freedom, but also as examples of the excessive power of the federal government over the states. To help reverse the erosion of local power and prevent repression of dissent, they secretly drafted two sets of resolutions which friends steered through the Virginia and Kentucky legislatures.

The Kentucky Resolutions, written by Jefferson, and those of Virginia, composed by Madison, stated that the federal government was a compact of states for certain limited purposes. Under the Constitution the national government did not possess the sort of powers it was seeking to exercise under the Alien and Sedition Acts. Such measures were, accordingly, "altogether void and of no force." The two Republican leaders then attacked the Sedition Act as contrary to the Bill of Rights.

In later years Americans would remember the Resolutions primarily as statements of states' rights in opposition to federal power, but in their own day they seemed manifestoes of freedom. Yet, though followed by a new wave of meetings and petitions from around the country, they accomplished little. The Federalists were too well entrenched in Congress, and a committee of the House rejected them. The Alien and Sedition Acts, the committee majority declared, were both wise and constitutional. When Albert Gallatin and other Republicans attacked the committee report,

they were drowned out by loud talking, laughter, hissing, and coughing.

Despite his loss of popularity, Adams and his party were still in firm control, and the President could have gotten Congress to declare war on France. Hamilton and the "high Federalists" were in a warlike mood and deplored any attempt to negotiate differences with the French. Adams, however, was unwilling to accept Hamilton's lead. By now the President had learned that he had blundered badly in keeping Washington's Cabinet intact. His closest advisers, he had discovered, had scant respect for him and instead looked to Hamilton for advice and guidance. In 1799, without consulting the Cabinet, Adams announced that he intended to send another mission to France to resume negotiations of outstanding French-American differences.

When the American delegation arrived in Paris, they encountered a new situation. The leader of France was now First Consul Napoleon Bonaparte. His brilliant generalship had reversed sagging French military fortunes. Now, flushed with new victories, the French were reluctant to grant the Americans the indemnities they wanted for "spoliations" of their commerce. But Napoleon was not entirely unreasonable. He agreed to end the naval war and attacks on American commerce; he also agreed to release the United States from its obligations to France under the Treaty of 1778. The American envoys were disappointed, but, seeing no possibility of better terms, accepted this "half a loaf." Many Federalists called this Convention of 1800 a cowardly surrender. The President disagreed—the negotiations, he believed, were "the most disinterested, the most determined, and the most successful" of his whole career. Adams no doubt exaggerated, but his defiance of the extremists of his own party was a courageous and constructive act.

The Election of 1800

The political campaign of 1800 was one of the most momentous in the nation's history and a landmark in the evolution of modern political democracy. For the first time power passed peaceably and constitutionally from one political party to another. Not that the process was marked by sweetness and light—far from it. The Republicans attacked the President once again as pro-

British, as a monarchist and a spendthrift who had burdened the country with enormous debts.

If anything, the Federalists were still more vituperative. Jefferson, the Federalist press charged, was an atheist who placed scientific reason above the teachings of the Bible. Elect him President and religion would be destroyed, and infidelity flourish. Besides, the man was a "voluptuary" who had, it was alleged, fathered mulatto children by his female slaves. If the American people elevated such a man to the nation's highest office, it could expect "the just vengeance of heaven." The nation would suffer every calamity: "dwellings in flames, hoary hairs bathed in blood, female chastity violated, children writhing on the pike and halberd."

Federalist prospects were seriously undermined by the split that had developed within the party. By this time, Adams had concluded that he must get rid of Hamilton's influence within his official family, and in 1800 he fired Secretary of State Pickering and Secretary of War James McHenry. Hamilton considered this a declaration of war. By now Washington was dead and the New Yorker no longer felt obliged to preserve the party. Before long he was scheming with other high Federalists to replace Adams with Charles Cotesworth Pinckney of South Carolina, one of the three emissaries to France in the X, Y, Z affair. In the event, Adams remained the party's candidate, but was left in a greatly weakened position.

One item in the Republican indictment of their opponents was the extravagent cost of the new national capital being constructed on the Potomac River. Actually, by the time the government moved from Philadelphia, the "Federal City" was still more a plan than a reality. True, the District of Columbia plan drawn up by a Frenchman, Ma-

jor Pierre L'Enfant was magnificent in its broad streets, malls, plazas, and circles; but it was unrealistic, and a more modest plan had to be adopted. The government began construction of the President's house in 1792 and shortly thereafter, the Capitol began to rise. The third building to appear was a tavern.

The first government officials arrived from Philadelphia in June 1800. On November 1, President Adams and his family moved into the President's house. The new city was little more than a paper community. Besides the Capitol, the tavern, and the building that would later be called the White House, it consisted of some boarding houses, a few huts for construction workers, and not much else. Streets had been laid out, but these muddy or dusty tracks were lined, not with residences or stores, but with virgin forest. Even the President's new home was only half-completed. The First Lady, Abigail Adams, found the plastering unfinished and, in the absence of a proper laundry room, hung the family wash in the East Room. Gouverneur Morris summed it all up: nothing was lacking in the new Federal City, he observed, except "houses, cellars, kitchens, well informed men, amiable women, and other little trifles of this kind."

Meanwhile, the presidential contest reached a climax. Under the existing provisions of the Constitution, the electors in 1800 did not vote

Settler's wagon; length, over 14 feet; wagon bed, 10½ feet; wheel diameters, 42 inches and 33½ inches; about 1800. *(Index of American Design.)*

separately for President and Vice President. Each elector cast two ballots, and the person with the highest vote total was declared President; the runner-up, Vice President. The Republican caucus in Congress had designated Jefferson and Aaron Burr as the party's presidential and vice-presidential candidates respectively, but in the actual voting all the Republican electors voted for both equally. When the votes were counted, therefore, Jefferson and Burr were tied for first place. This situation threw the choice of President into the House of Representatives, where the states would vote as single units and a majority of states was needed to elect anyone.

The nation now faced a peculiar political situation. The Federalists did not control enough states to reelect President Adams, but they could deny the Presidency to anyone else. It was not likely that they would block a choice, since that would paralyze the nation, but, in effect, they were capable of excluding Jefferson and substituting Burr.

From the Federalist point of view, Burr seemed preferable to Jefferson. Unlike the "Sage of Monticello," the New Yorker was an aristocrat, a friend of banks and Hamiltonian funding, and a believer in a strong executive. True, he also had the reputation of being corrupt, ambitious, cynical, and unscrupulous, but under the circumstances that appeared to the good: he could be counted on to make whatever arrangements with the Federalists they desired without worrying too much about principles. The choice of Burr would also be sure to upset and confound the enemy party.

The Federalist leaders nonetheless recoiled from this choice. Hamilton despised Burr, who, he felt, would "employ the rogues of all parties to overrule the good men of all parties." Jefferson, on the other hand, though "tinctured with fanaticism nor even mindful of truth," had some "pretension to character." Hamilton advised voting for the Virginian if he would give the Federalists guarantees that he would uphold the Federalist fiscal system, remove no Federalist from office except those of Cabinet rank, maintain the Army and Navy intact, and maintain the principles of neutrality in foreign affairs established by the two Federalist presidents. Burr was meanwhile refusing to treat directly with the Federalists, since that would have so outraged his fellow Republicans that they would have denied him all support and so deadlocked the election entirely.

In the end, Jefferson gave the Federalists some indirect assurances and certain key Federalist Congressmen changed their votes. After thirty-five ballots Delaware switched to Jefferson, and he was declared elected. The nation could now resume as a going political concern.

Jefferson would call his victory the "revolution of 1800." The apprehensive Federalists would not have disagreed. They had not only lost the Presidency; they had also been swept from power in Congress. What would follow the advent of the "Jacobins," no man could tell. There was still hope, however—the judiciary might still be saved; and to this end, hours before leaving office, President Adams appointed a flock of Federalists to new judgeships and other legal posts created by the Judiciary Act of 1801. These "midnight judges," it was felt, might be able to stop the Republicans from totally upsetting the economic and political arrangements of the country.

Still, from the Federalist viewpoint, the future looked ominous. Would the whole structure so painfully created in the previous twelve years be destroyed? Despite the Agreement with France, could the United States avoid becoming a French satellite? Most important of all, could a republic experience a governmental turnover of such magnitude and still maintain basic stability and continuity? Only time—and Thomas Jefferson—would tell.

Suggested Readings

In *Securing the Revolution: Ideology in American Politics, 1789-1815* (1972), Richard Buel, Jr., studies the efforts of revolutionary leaders to consolidate their achievements after the adoption of the Constitution. James Thomas Flexner has abridged his four-volume biography into one: *Washington: The Indispensable Man* (1974). Forrest McDonald's *Alexander Hamilton* (1979) is an admiring and penetrating work. American legal history has been enhanced by Morton J. Horwitz's *The Transformation of American Law, 1780-1860* (1977); he traces the evolution of law from a frozen state in the eighteenth century to a dynamic one in the nineteenth. Alexander DeConde is standard on *The Quasi-War: Politics and Diplomacy of the Undeclared War with France, 1797-1801* (1966). Leonard D. White's *The Federalists* (1948) stresses the administrative achievements of the new government.

Captain Clark and his men shooting bears.

131

INDEPENDENCE CONFIRMED

Chapter VII
Independence Confirmed
1801—1815

The Lewis and Clark Expedition

The mind of Thomas Jefferson was bountiful of projects and dreams, some of which actually brought new worlds into existence. He wrote eloquently of independence, religious liberty, the education of a free people—as had other men; but Jefferson's words inspired a new nation, a bill of rights, a system of education. The expedition of Meriwether Lewis and William Clark in 1804-1806 exploring the Missouri River, the Rocky Mountains, and the Columbus River basin was a bold Jeffersonian vision become a great historical event.

Jefferson's vision of the West was even grander and more complex than Columbus' had been. Like the great Genoese, he saw the westward passage as a way to the riches of the East. Commerce might flow "possibly with single portage, from the Western ocean . . . to the Atlantic." In addition to this ancient dream, there was the prospect of more immediate riches: the "great supplies of furs and peltry" that were then flowing only into English, not American coffers. Then, too, much of the West could become a vast, peaceful garden not only for whites but for Indians weaned from their hunting ways by the advance of trade which would "place within their reach those things which will contribute more to their domestic comfort than the possession of extensive, but uncultivated wilds." Finally, the more rugged West of the great rivers and mountains would exhibit treasures of natural history. Mammoths, Jefferson suspected, might still roam the lands farther West. Perhaps the llama ranged this far north. For years, Jefferson had encouraged all who would listen to explore the great West for science, for country, for riches. As President, he could do more than exhort: he proposed to Congress that

an intelligent officer with ten or twelve chosen men, fit for the enterprize and willing to understand it, taken from our posts, where they may be spared without inconvenience, might explore the whole line, even to the Western ocean, have conferences with the natives on the subject of commercial intercourse, get admission among them for our traders as others are admitted, agree on convenient deposits for an interchange of articles, and return with the information acquired in the course of two summers.

Except for slightly underestimating the number of men who would be needed (thirty to fifty in various stages of the expedition), and with no idea that an Indian woman, her infant son, and a giant Newfoundland dog named Scammon would go along as well, Jefferson got exactly the expedition and the results he had envisioned. The expedition extended his Indian diplomacy, his commercial policies, and his diplomatic goals while furiously gathering together every piece of information about geography, plants, animals, and minerals that could be gained by observation or collection of specimens and fossils. Seven different men kept diaries; the two leaders spent every moment when they were not exploring, negotiating, or being ill, taking detailed field notes and reworking them into coherent accounts, complete with drawings, maps, and lexicons for Thomas Jefferson and the world.

Meriwether Lewis and William Clark were—like Jefferson—amateurs. Though soldiers, neither had been a professional military man, Lewis being on leave from the army to serve as Jefferson's secretary and Clark having resigned some time before. Nor were they professional scientists or explorers: once Jefferson appointed them, they had to scramble for a rapid education in geography and mapmaking, celestial navigation, mineralogy, and medicine to keep an expedition alive for two years. Lewis sought the counsel of America's most distinguished physician, Dr. Benjamin Rush of Philadelphia, who supplied him with a little information and a large supply of "Rush's Thunderbolts," his famous, violently purgative pills which Lewis and Clark used for all ailments.

The expedition went from St. Louis to the mouth of the Columbia River and back, through incredibly difficult country, with elementary equipment. The first leg, up the Missouri with a stop to winter over in a Mandan Indian village, was brutally hard work, poling, pulling, and portaging a string of boats up a huge river whose powerful current undermined banks at each bend, creating mudslides and sending vast jams of tree trunks cascading downriver to knock over the expedition's boats. Leg two, over the mountaintops through high barren badlands, was the hardest part of all. The trip down the Columbia River system was least eventful. They eventually realized that they had gone the long way around and correctly diagnosed the shortest and fastest route home through the mountains.

On the return trip they proved that there was no route, even with portages, where small boats could be carried over the Continental divide and relaunched on the Western rivers. Rather, there was a set of mountains and valleys between, requiring a substantial transshipment. The way west would not be direct or easy: the three-century-old hope of finding a "Northwest Passage" had to be forgotten.

The expedition met and studied dozens of Indian tribes, arranging trade agreements, asserting American influence, presenting gifts, recording manners and customs, seeking geographical information. Lewis and Clark identified 300 new plant and animal species of subspecies, collecting bones, fossils, and seeds. The homely names they gave the new species—since neither man knew Latin—have not survived in the naturalist literature; but creatures like *Salmo clarkii*, the beautiful cutthroat trout named for Clark, and *Asyndesmus lesis*, Lewis' woodpecker, attest to a more learned fraternity's appreciation of their works. The *Notebooks* and *Journals* of the expedition have been fundamental sources for naturalists, geographers, anthropologists, and historians.

The rigors of the journey produced much illness and hardship, yet only one man lost his life—from a ruptured appendix that in those days would have killed him even had he been in Philadelphia. The only serious injury was one sustained by Lewis himself, when one of his own men accidentally shot him in the backside. (Lewis made few mistakes, but going hunting for food with a one-eyed sergeant was certainly one of them.) There were only one or two small scrapes with Indians, although it took firm diplomacy and carefully manned swivel guns (small portable cannons) to prevent a few rough encounters from becoming dangerous. Clark's slave, York, the one black on the expedition, was the wonder of dozens of Indian tribes. The Indians would actually pay to touch his hair or run their fingers over his skin to see if the dark color would come off. One of the interpreters—a Frenchman named Charbonneau who had been hired in St. Louis because he knew the Sioux dialects—persuaded Lewis to allow him to take his Indian wife, Sacajawea, and their two-month-old baby on the roughest part of the trip from the upper Missouri over the mountains to the Pacific. Apparently, her knowledge of the Shoshonean dialects, which none of the other interpreters (including her husband) commanded, persuaded the captain to agree. When they finally made contact with the mountain Indians, the first party of braves they met had as its chief her brother, whom she had not seen since she had been forcibly abducted from his hunting party as a small child. No novelist could have gotten away with such an unlikely plot.

Jefferson had proposed the expedition to Congress before Talleyrand offered to sell the United States the Louisiana Territory, planning to grasp the trade of the West with stations on territory both unknown and unowned. By the time the expedition set out from St. Louis, Louisiana was American territory. But the Oregon country beyond the Great Divide was not. It belonged perhaps to Great Britain or maybe to Spain. Yet Lewis, once back at St. Louis, wrote of "possessions" west of the mountains, and Jefferson himself by January 1807 was referring to "our country, from the Missisipi [sic] to the Pacific." We next see Jefferson supporting John Jacob Astor's efforts to create an American fur empire that would crowd the British out of the market. In the ensuing race for the strategic mouth of the Columbia River, Astor moved his men across the trail that Lewis and Clark had blazed, while the English pushed southwest from Canada. In July 1811, when the great English explorer and entrepreneur David Thompson pushed his way to the Columbia and canoed to its mouth, he beheld the American flag flying from the parapets of four-month-old Fort Astoria. Lewis and Clark's expedition would, in the end, make Jefferson's largest vision—a continental United States—the future.

National Archives.

INDEPENDENCE CONFIRMED

Jefferson's Inauguration

Jefferson took the oath of office as third President of the United States at noon on a blustery March day. The President-elect had come to Washington the previous November and had spent the winter at Conrad and McMunn's boarding-house, where for $15 a week he dined and roomed unpretentiously. The inauguration ceremonies were brief and austere, as befitted a party that made a point of republican simplicity. Jefferson walked to the still-uncompleted Capitol. In the crowded Senate chamber, he swore to defend the Constitution and faithfully discharge the duties of his office. Then, almost inaudibly, he delivered his inaugural address.

Jefferson's address expressed the philosophy of the men who had fought the Federalists for over a decade. It confirmed the Republicans' dedication to freedom of religion and the press. It endorsed the encouragement of agriculture, and of commerce as its handmaid. The federal government, the new President declared, must conduct its affairs economically and attempt to pay off its debts. The state governments, he said, were "the surest bulwarks against antirepublican tendencies." But besides making these predictable Republican pronouncements, Jefferson sought to calm the fears of moderate Federalists. The nation, he declared, must avoid "entangling alliances" that is, the Republicans would accept the recent termination of the 1778 French alliance. They would also avoid extreme partisanship. Now that the great contest of 1800 was over, all Americans "will, of course, arrange themselves under the will of the law, and unite in common efforts for the common good." Minority rights would be protected, and no one would be persecuted: "We are all Republicans, we are all Federalists . . . . Let us, then, with courage and confidence pursue our own Federal and Republican principles, our attachment to union and representative government."

So softly did the fresh-minted Chief Executive speak that few in the crowded room could hear what he said. Fortunately, printed copies of the speech were available, and ushers distributed these to the assembled dignitaries. That evening, the President returned to Conrad and McMunn's to dine as usual. When he entered the dining room, a lady among the paying guests offered him a chair. Jefferson declined the offer and went to his usual place at the foot of the table, far from the warming fire. A new, simpler age of American politics had begun.

The United States in 1801

As the third President took up the duties of his office, the nation was beginning a new century. In many ways it had not changed since the "shot heard 'round the world" at Lexington Common, on April 19, 1775. In the twenty-five years since the opening gun of the Revolution, America's population had grown from about 2.5 million to 5.3 million; but in many respects these were, in background and outlook, the same people as before. The new nation's white population remained overwhelmingly British in origin and Protestant in religion. Germans were found in eastern Pennsylvania, the Shenandoah Valley, and along the Mohawk River in New York. The Hudson Valley contained many Hollanders, and the guttural sound of Dutch could still be heard in Albany. Scattered here and there, primarily in the towns, were small enclaves of Huguenot French and Jews, as well as a handful of Irish Catholics. The largest non-British group by far was the blacks, who numbered over a million, almost all south of Pennsylvania and almost all slaves. But the Revolution and difficulties of postwar readjustment had discouraged both immigration and the slave trade. As a consequence, the vast majority of the slaves, and those of non British origin, were native-born Americans.

Americans were a young people. Chilren were everywhere in the America of 1801. Half the population was under seventeen years old. Households were large; almost one-fourth of all families had seven or more persons living under one roof. This placed a heavy burden on families, and especially on women, who spent many of their best, most vigorous years bearing and rearing children.

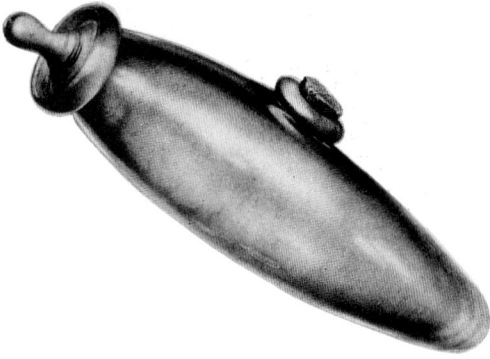

Nursing bottle, hand-blown; first half of nineteenth century. *(Index of American Design.)*

The United States in 1801 was a nation of farms and villages. Only 300,000 Americans lived in communities of even 2,500 people—fewer than seven percent of the total. Perhaps only a dozen places in the whole country truly deserved the label of "city." Of these, the largest, the most cosmopolitan, and most gracious was Philadelphia, with almost 70,000 inhabitants. Penn's town was also the most modern in the nation. Most American city-dwellers drew their water from wells or cisterns or bought it from vendors. They relied on hogs to consume the garbage dumped on the street. They were forced to tramp streets usually ankle-deep in either dust or mud, depending on the season. Not so Philadelphians: the city of Brotherly Love, after the cholera and yellow fever epidemics of the 1790's, drew on piped water from the Schuylkill River; its streets were paved with cobblestones and were regularly cleaned.

Boston, New York, Baltimore, and Charleston were the country's other substantial cities—all of them overgrown provincial towns. Boston, with 25,000 inhabitants, had fallen behind New York and Baltimore in population since colonial days. Nevertheless, it remained the commercial, financial, and intellectual capital of New England. With its narrow streets and crowded wharves, it had not much changed since the 1770's. The city government was still the same as in the seventeenth century: its affairs were in the hands of "selectmen" chosen at town meeting. Although Boston's elite was no longer composed of dour Puritan gentlemen, the Federalist merchants, ministers, and lawyers who now formed the town's upper crust retained much of the old Puritan selfconfidence and respect for learning.

The Boston brahmin George Cabot was expressing the unshakable conviction of his class when he declared that his native city possessed "more wisdom and virtues than any other part of the world."

Two hundred miles to the south of "Beantown" was New York, on Manhattan Island. The Revolution had been hard on the city, and as late as 1790 much of it still bore the marks of the great fire of 1776. In 1801 the city was still partly Dutch. Many houses were set gable-end to the street, as in Amsterdam, and were faced with the characteristically Dutch yellow brick. Even more than Boston and Philadelphia, New York thrived on commerce; most of its 60,000 inhabitants were crowded into the southeastern corner of the island, adjacent to the docks and warehouses.

Baltimore was a comparatively new city which had not acquired official municipal status until 1797. The outlet for much of the Chesapeake tobacco crop, it also tapped the flour, wheat, and privisions of the Pennsylvania back-country through the Susquehanna River. The city's aggressive merchants had pioneered a lucrative trade to Bremen, Germany, and had attracted in return a substantial number of German artisans.

The nation's fifth city, Charleston, the capital of South Carolina, was in some ways the most colorful of all. It was both a major port and a summer resort where rice planters from the malaria-ridden coastal lowlands went during the "fever season" to protect their health. Built in brick and stone after the Revolution, the city was ruled by a planter-merchant elite who gave lip service to republican principles but cultivated the aristocratic arts of good living, polite letters, fine manners, and elegant hospitality. Most inconsistant of all for these avowed republicans, they could not live without slaves. Of the eighteen thousand people who packed the little port, six thousand were blacks; they helped keep its streets clean, its markets stocked, and its wharves busy.

Any observer of Charleston between 1790 and 1800 would have noticed a particularly promising development: a new crop, cotton, was being loaded aboard ships in the harbor by black stevedores. With the invention of the cotton gin by the Connecticut yankee Eli Whitney, green-seed cotton had become a profitable crop in the interior of the Carolinas and Georgia. The South's one major Atlantic port was feeling the invigorating economic effects of the thousands of bales it shipped to Liverpool and Glasgow to feed the new textile factories of Great Britain.

All the nation's cities were coastal communities; only overseas trade employed enough people to create cities. The one potential exception in view was the as yet small town of Pittsburgh, in western Pennsylvania—a river town, situated where the Allegheny and Monongahela rivers join to form the great Ohio. With about two thousand inhabitants in 1800, it had become a supplier of manufactured goods to the burgeoning West, producing iron, glass, textiles, and vessels for the river trade. As early as 1800 an English visitor reported that the town was covered with a pall of smoke from the numerous coal fires that fueled the iron foundries and glassworks. By 1810 one expert estimated Pittsburgh's trade at a million dollars a year.

The great majority of Americans, however, were not urban people in any sense. Rather, they depended for their livelihood in some fashion on the soil. A few thousand belonged to the great landed families found, especially, in the coastal regions of the Chesapeake and the Carolina-Georgia area, or in the Hudson Valley of New York. Many were either the tenants or slaves of such families. The overwhelming majority of the nation's million-odd blacks in 1800 were slaves cultivating rice, tobacco, and corn, and now cotton as well. A majority of white male Americans owned the ground they tilled.

A typical American yeoman and his family worked hard for what they had. In the better-settled regions, the daily and yearly rounds were hard enough. Animals had to be watered; their stables cleaned. Plowing in the spring, weeding and cultivating in the summer, and harvesting in fall all required heavy labor. The women cooked, cleaned, spun, made preserves, and took care of flocks of young children.

In newer regions, the life of the husbandman and his family was still harder. Clearing new land required backbreaking labor girdling trees, clearing underbrush, and breaking virgin sod. The pioneer farmer of Vermont, western New York, or the newly opened Ohio or Alabama country was lucky if he could add more than four or five usable acres to his farm a year. Even then it took many years before the frontier farmer's land was fully cleared of stumps and he could plow a straight furrow. Meanwhile, his family lived in a primitive one-room log house with a sleeping attic above.

Despite the hard work, the yeoman family enjoyed a rough abundance. Techniques of planting and harvesting had not advanced much beyond medieval practices. American plows in 1800 were heavy wooden contraptions pulled by oxen or mules. Most farmers still used the scythe to harvest grain and threshed it with a hand flail made of two sticks joined by a leather thong. But since the soil was rich and abundant, the American farm family ate well and produced more

than it consumed. Travelers through the nation's rural regions predictably remarked on signs of prosperity. One Englishman reported of the Connecticut countryside during Jefferson's Presidency that it "had the appearance of wealth, numerous broods of poultry straying about, with sheep and cattle grazing in great numbers in the fields." Travelers who accepted the hospitality of local yeomen, rather than brave the fare of notoriously bad country inns, reported on the abundance of everything served. Breakfast tables were loaded down with boiled fish, beefsteak, ham sausages, hotbreads, and cheese. Many Europeans, however, complained at how badly these foods were prepared, and even American physicians warned that their countrymen's diets contained too many greasy foods. But virtually no one denied the plenty of the American country table.

With so many Americans living on farms, it is not surprising that the country's manners were often rude. Compared to today, the typical farm family was an isolated social unit. Except in southern New England, where the imprint of the old "town" system of colonial days still remained, the typical rural American lived in a house widely separated by fields and virgin forest from his nearest neighbor. Poor roads, widespread il-

Chicken, reputedly carved by slave of Jean Laffite; first quarter of nineteenth century. *(Index of American Design.)*

literacy, and high postal rates cut rural people off from the more genteel manners and tastes of the towns and cities. When rural Americans did get together with neighbors and friends, it was often to engage in rough-and-tumble sports that did not draw the line at overt brutality. Wrestling included kicking, biting, punching, and, worst of all, eye-gouging. "I saw more than one man, who wanted an eye," noted an Easterner as he crossed the border into Kentucky. And those willing to be brutal to fellow human beings could hardly be expected to draw the line there. Country people, especially on the frontier, "baited" bulls and bears—that is, set large dogs to attack them while rooting for either attacker or defender—or they bet on the outcome of cockfights.

Heavy drinking also marked the early Republic, especially its rural parts. Whether at taverns or religious camp meetings, at dances and "hoe-downs" or in the home, Americans consumed vast quantities of whiskey, rum, and brandy. Women drank punch or "toddies" made of these. Opium was mixed with whiskey to quiet, if not cure, the ills of infants. As a contemporary ditty went:

Hail Columbia, happy land,
If you ain't drunk, I'll be damned.

People were not all alike in the country districts, of course. Foreign travelers often noted that the New Englanders, especially, were more mannerly and "steady" than Westerners and Southerners. But in every section there were sober, well-bred, well-informed men and women who read books and newspapers, displayed elegant manners, enjoyed themselves sedately playing cricket or attending sewing and husking bees. Nevertheless, the average American bore the rude marks of a rural isolation that would not disappear until the advent of good roads, telephones, and the family automobile in our own century.

The Republicans in Power

This, then, was the crude but vital nation that Jefferson led as he began his eight years as President. The new Chief Executive was one of the most cultivated men of his day, although he affected informality in manners and dress to an extent that shocked strait-laced contemporaries. Senator William Plumer of New Hampshire, calling at the presidential mansion, mistook him for a servant. Other visitors, noting his carelessly tied long red hair, his less-than-immaculate linen, his toeless carpet slippers, and his tall, loose-jointed frame, felt that he lacked the dignity required of his office. Yet he read French, Italian, Latin, and Greek; played the violin skillfully; corresponded with many of the outstanding thinkers of Europe; was an imaginative and creative architect and inventor; and was an amateur scientist of considerable talent and range.

This Renaissance man was also a vigorous and effective leader. He shunned the trappings of high office. In place of the formal receptions of the Washington-Adams era, he substituted information gatherings where scholars, scientists, and interesting men of affairs exchanged ideas over madeira and nuts. He dropped his predecessors' practice of appearing before Congress to present his State of the Union message, and substituted written statements. He also sought to pare what he considered the bloated size of government under the Federalists. Jefferson and his Treasury Secretary, Albert Gallatin, opposed any rise in the federal debt and they managed to cut military spending to a third of what it had been under the Federalists. The President also closed the American legations in Holland and Prussia. The new administration could not abolish the Bank of the United States before its charter expired in 1811, but under Gallatin the government sold off its Bank stock at a profit and ceased to play any further banking role.

Jefferson also sought to undo or eliminate other Federalist measures and practices. He naturally allowed the Sedition Act to lapse; there would be nor more criminal persecutions for attacking the government. He also sought to weed out of the federal bureaucracy those Federalists who had taken too partisan a part in the political battles preceding 1801. Most of these were officeholders who could be removed by the President at will; but at least one, Supreme Court Justice Chase, had life tenure and could be gotten rid of only by impeachment. In 1805 a Republican House of Representatives did impeach Chase on charges of high crimes and misdemeanors, but the Senate failed to convict.

Far more significant in its consequences was the Jefferson administration's attempt to undo the effects of the 1801 Judiciary Act. Under that measure, just before leaving office, Adams had appointed a flock of Federalist judges and law officials with lifetime tenure; his purpose had clearly been to retain Federalist control in at least one

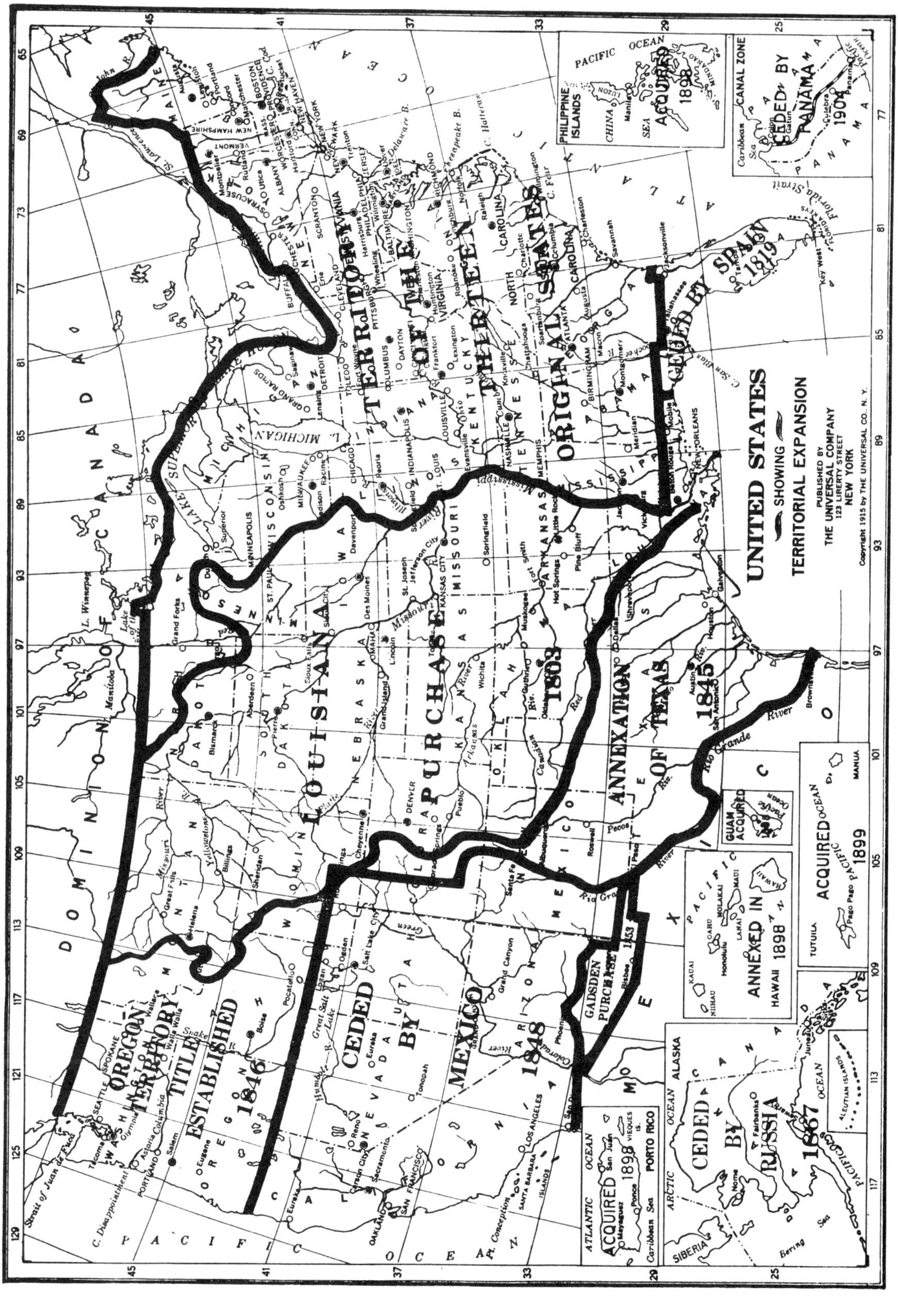
UNITED STATES
SHOWING
TERRITORIAL EXPANSION
PUBLISHED BY
THE UNIVERSAL COMPANY
123 LIBERTY STREET
NEW YORK
Copyright 1915 by THE UNIVERSAL CO., N. Y.
TERRITORY OF THE ORIGINAL THIRTEEN STATES
LOUISIANA PURCHASE 1803
CEDED BY SPAIN 1819
ANNEXATION OF TEXAS 1845
OREGON TERRITORY TITLE ESTABLISHED 1846
CEDED BY MEXICO 1848
GADSDEN PURCHASE 1853
CEDED BY RUSSIA 1867
ANNEXED IN 1898 HAWAII
ACQUIRED 1898 PORTO RICO
ACQUIRED 1898 PHILIPPINE ISLANDS
GUAM ACQUIRED
ACQUIRED 1899 TUTUILA
CEDED BY PANAMA 1904 CANAL ZONE
DOMINION OF CANADA
PACIFIC OCEAN
ATLANTIC OCEAN

Jefferson's serpentine wall at the University of Virginia; he planned the architecture and grounds of the university and of his nearby home, Monticello.

brach of government and, as the Republicans saw it, prevent the new administration from carrying out the will of the people. Hoping to frustrate this goal, Secretary of State Madison refused to deliver several newly appointed officials their commissions. One of these, William Marbury, sued the Secretary, charging that his action was illegal under the Judiciary Act of 1789. By the provisions of that measure, Marbury's lawyers argued, the Supreme Court could compel a federal official to issue a commission whether he wished to or not.

In 1803 the case came before the United States Supreme Court, Chief Justice John Marshall presiding. Marshall was a Virginian, but one who shared few views with either Jefferson or Madison. He was a Federalist, and deplored the Republican preference for a weak national government. If the Republican-dominated executive refused to govern, the Federalist-dominated judicial branch would. In its decision in the case of *Marbury v. Madison,* the Marshall court declared the portion of the 1789 Judiciary Act that formed the basis for Marbury's suit unconstitutional. Although the Supreme Court's right thus to strike down an act of Congress on the grounds of unconstitutionality had been asserted long before, this landmark in American constitutional practice was the first actual instance of its doing so.

The year 1803 was momentous for the nation for other reasons than Marshall's precedent-making decision. It was also the year that the United States acquired the province of Louisiana from France and thereby almost doubled its size. Louisiana was a gigantic wedge of territory stretching from the Gulf of Mexico in the South to somewhere in the present-day Dakotas in the North, and from the Mississippi in the East to the Rocky Mountains in the West. Its exact boun-

daries were unclear, its vastness and strategic value unquestioned.

Spain had owned the province until ceding it to France in 1801. Tentative reports of the transfer alarmed Jefferson. The President looked forward to an "empire for liberty" consisting of American farmlands stretching over much of North America. So long as weak Spain controlled the sparsely settled province, he could afford to wait until it dropped into the American lap. But if powerful France now possessed it, who knew if the United States would ever be able to make it part of a greater America? Besides, Louisiana included the all-important port of New Orleans. Whoever controlled this port controlled the trade and commercial outlet for much of the western United States. Hoping to prevent final consummation of the French-Spanish arrangement, or at least to acquire some port on the Gulf coast, Jefferson dispatched Robert R. Livingston to Paris.

Meanwhile, the French were beginning to lose interest in the territory. For a time Napoleon had hoped to fit Louisiana into a great French colonial empire that would also include the valuable Caribbean sugar island of Hispaniola. To achieve his ends, he first had to recapture the western part of Hispaniola from the blacks who in the 1790's had risen up against their French masters there and established the Republic of Haiti. Napoleon sent an army of thirty thousand men, headed by his brother-in-law, to subdue the Haitians under their brilliant leader Toussaint l'Ouverture. The task proved to be impossible. Eventually the French captured l'Ouverture by treachery, but not before their army had been virtually wiped out by a combination of enemy action and tropical disease. Napoleon decided that his entire dream of a restored French empire in the New World had been a fantasy.

It was this new situation that Livingston confronted when he arrived in Paris. France no longer cared much about Louisiana; and, with the prospect of a renewed war in Europe imminent, Napoleon was certain that he could not keep it from falling into British hands. On the American side, the situation had also changed. In October 1802 Spain, still in legal possession of New Orleans, decided to withdraw the right of deposit granted to Americans by the Pinckney Treaty of 1795. Once more, the whole American interior was bottled up and this time, so it seemed, France was behind it.

Jefferson now dispatched James Monroe to France with new orders. He should try to get New Orleans from the French, or at least part of the Gulf Coast panhandle of West Florida from

Spain, to give the United States a southern trade outlet. Two days after Monroe joined Livingston in the French capital, they learned a prodigious piece of news: Napoleon would not only sell New Orleans; he would sell all of Louisiana! The price: 60 million francs, plus up to 20 million francs additional to settle all American claims against France for the "spoliations" of the 1790's. The offer flabbergasted the envoys. They were not authorized to negotiate such an arrangment, but it was far too good to turn down, and they eagerly accepted. In short order, the signed document was on its way to Washington for Congress and the President to confirm.

It may seem surprising that any American should have questioned such an extraordinary bargain, but question it many did. One prominent Federalist denounced the purchase as "a miserable calamitous business"—the new nation would now be so gigantic that it would fall apart. Other Federalists deplored the fact that the United States had promised to grant citizenship to all the French and Spanish inhabitants of Louisiana. Even Jefferson worried that by buying Louisiana he had exceeded the authority of the federal government under the Constitution, and for a while he supported a constitutional amendment authorizing the purchase. In the end, however, neither side's scruples or reservations could compete with the reality of the most successful land deal in history. On October 20, 1803, the Senate confirmed the treaty, and two months later the United States took formal possession of the province. For a total of $15 million the United States had acquired a region almost equal in area to the whole of western Europe.

Lewis and Clark did immensely valuable work on their expedition to the new territory. They had established friendly relations with many Indian tribes. They brought news of valuable beaver streams and of many fur-bearing animals. They had discovered several usable passes through the Rockies, which they recorded on a map published in 1814. Jefferson followed up their success with several other expeditions to the West, the most successful being that led by Lieutenant Zebulon Pike. Pike explored the Colorado country, where he gave his name to a high peak of the Rockies west of present-day Denver, and crossed over into Spanish-held New Mexico. His report, published long before that of Lewis and Clark, made him famous and helped to open up the Rocky Mountains to fur trappers.

The vast new domain acquired from France was not an unmixed blessing. To the west and the north it touched Spanish and British territory, but exactly where nobody really knew. The Spaniards, especially, suspected American claims and feared Yankee designs on their possessions in New Mexico and Texas. Years before, they had secretly entered into a financial arrangement with James Wilkinson, a Kentucky adventurer, to act as their spy and agent in the American camp. Wilkinson remained in their pay while rising to brigadier general in the United States Army and to the post of military commander of the new Louisiana Territory. In this strategic position he advised his employers how to thwart American plans. At one point he even suggested that they arrest Lewis and Clark.

Meanwhile, another prominent American, Vice-President Aaron Burr, began to fish in the same troubled western waters. Burr was a complex man. Witty, charming, and intelligent, he was also ambitious and devious; son of a Presbyterian minister and a theology student as a youth, he became a notorious womanizer. John Quincy Adams, the future President, noted of Burr that with his "ambition of military fame, ambition of conquest over female virtue was the duplicate ruling passion of his life." In 1804 he had destroyed whatever shreds of reputation he still retained by killing Alexander Hamilton in a duel at Weehawken, New Jersey. The duel was the culmination of long-standing and bitter differences between the two men, including Hamilton's role in Jefferson's victory over Burr in the 1800 elections. Public outrage over the death of Hamilton forced Burr out of public life shortly afterward.

A year later, Burr was deeply involved in a scheme with Wilkinson to detach Louisiana from the United States, join it together with Texas and other parts of Spanish Mexico, and create a new nation, with themselves presumably as its leaders. Unfortunately for Burr, Wilkinson decided in the end that it was more profitable to stay in Spain's employ than to continue with this chancy venture, and he betrayed Burr. In November 1806 he wrote to Jefferson, warning that Burr intended to detach the West from the United States. At the same time he asked the Spanish Viceroy in Mexico to send him $200,000 in appreciation of his refusal to join Burr in dismembering New Spain.

Jefferson ordered Burr's arrest. Burr quickly set out for Pensacola in Spanish Florida, probably intending to escape to Europe. But he was captured and brought to Richmond, Virginia, where he was tried for treason, with Wilkinson serving as an important witness against him. The prosecution produced much damaging evidence against Burr. But the former Vice-President had the support of the presiding judge, Chief Justice Marshall; when the jury returned the verdict of "not proved," Marshall changed it to "not guilty."

The government, however, refused to drop the matter—soon after, it obtained Burr's indictment on another treason charge. This time Marshall granted him bail pending trial and rather than face another legal battle, he fled to Europe. Burr remained abroad for four years, and then returned to live a scandalous life in New York City. In his seventies he fathered two illegitimate children, and at the age of eighty was sued for divorce on the grounds of adultery.

France and England—Again

In early 1802 England and France ended their long, exhausting war. It now looked as if the American people would be spared the ordeal they had faced ever since war between the world's two most powerful nations had erupted in 1793. No longer would American commerce be the defenseless prey both of the Royal Navy and of French revenue cutters and port officials. Unfortunately, peace lasted all of fourteen months. By May 1803 Britain was once more at war with France. She was shortly joined by Austria, Russia, and Sweden, while Spain allied itself to imperial France. And, once again, America found itself caught between the British hammer and the French anvil.

The Royal Navy immediately resumed its practice of impressing seamen aboard American vessels regardless of their nationality. Outside almost every American harbor, British ships waited for American merchant vessels, stopped them, sent a lieutenant aboard, and chose those men they considered likely crewmen. By 1805, such British seizures on the high seas became virtually an everyday occurrence.

Britain's primary purpose in these actions was not to injure American commerce, but to hurt the French economy and frustrate the French war effort. Napoleon, however, could play the same game, and did. To match the British blockade of the French-held continent of Europe, he issued in 1806 the Berlin Decree, ordering the seizure of any vessel carrying British goods. The following year he directed French privateers to stop all ships, including neutral ones, suspected of carrying enemy cargo. The Berlin Decree set off a round of British countermeasures, followed by still further French retaliation. It began to seem that no American ship would be able to leave port or approach European shores without facing certain confiscation.

Surprisingly, the American response to these indignities and harassments was mixed. They infuriated those Americans who put patriotism before all else. Since Britain was violating American sovereign rights even more flagrantly than France, patriots tended to be more anti-British than anti-French. Continuing problems with the Indian tribes in the Northwest further aggravated anti-British feeling.

Not all Americans, however, agreed that strong measures were called for. Especially in the Atlantic ports, many citizens were willing to accept this harassment. For despite it, American commerce was flourishing in a war-stricken world. So pressing was the need for shipping space that ocean freight rates reached sky-high levels. True, insurance costs were also high and there was always the risk of confiscation, but profits too were unprecedented. Between 1803 and 1807 American exports, much of them in tropical goods from the French and Spanish New World colonies, leaped from $56 million to $108 million, and the American merchant marine grew from 950,000 tons to almost 1,300,000. Why not, asked the merchants of Boston, Salem, Providence, New York, Philadelphia, and other ports, accept the situation?

Still, even the most materialistic citizens could forget their immediate interests in the heat of anger at some indignity committed by the British or French. One such occasion took place in the early summer of 1807.

On June 22, the U.S.S. *Chesapeake,* a brand-new Navy frigate commanded by Commodore James Barron, left Norfolk, Virginia, for a Mediterranean shakedown cruise. Aboard were several deserters from the Royal Navy. When the *Chesapeake* was only a few miles at sea, it was overtaken by H.M.S. *Leopard,* part of the British squadron patrolling off Hampton Roads. The British captain ordered Barron to heave to and allow a naval party to board to look for deserters. This was the first time the British had attempted impressment off an American man-of-war, and Barron refused. Unfortunately, the *Chesapeake's* guns were not yet mounted, and the ship could not defend itself. After repeated murderous broadsides from the *Leopard,* Barron struck his colors; the British removed four deserters and departed. The *Chesapeake* limped back to port with three dead, eighteen wounded, and a tale certain to raise the hackles of every American patriot.

The American public screamed for war against "perfidious Albion." "The country," Jefferson noted, "had never been in such a state of excitement since the battle of Lexington." But the President, although he could undoubtedly have obtained a declaration of war from Congress, wished to avoid armed conflict. He was not a pacifist, but he deplored war and the expensive armies and navies it required; armies and navies and big treasury budgets were Federalist, not Republican, playthings. And besides, the United States, he believed, still had some powerful unused weapons short of war at its disposal. Diplomatic pressure was one such, and Jefferson immediately dispatched a message to Britain demanding disavowal of the attack, reparations for lives lost and damage inflicted, the recall of the British admiral responsible for the *Leopard's* action, and an end to the impressment policy. He also ordered all British ships out of United States territorial waters and stepped up preparations for defense in case the British forced the nation's hand.

The British response to American diplomatic demands was unsatisfactory. The Foreign Secretary, George Canning, attacked Jefferson for his retaliatory acts and quibbled about reparations for American losses. He also defended the British admiral responsible for the *Leopard's* attack, although he agreed to remove him.

Jefferson now invoked his last peaceable weapon. American trade, the President believed, was essential to both of the major belligerents. Both needed American wheat, provisions, and lumber, and the French relied on the United States to carry their Caribbean products. During the imperial crisis before 1775, Americans had forced Britain to back down by boycotting British goods. In all likelihood, he felt, they would once more yield to commercial pressure if it were applied firm and remorselessly. In any case, it should be tried before more drastic measures were invoked.

Under the President's prodding, Congress passed the Embargo Act of 1807. The law forbade the clearance of any American ship for foreign ports. Coastal vessels would have to post bond to ensure that they did not turn east and cross the open sea to Europe, or south to the West Indies. Only ships with special permits were to be ex-empted from the export embargo, a provision that would cover those engaged in public business.

The Embargo Act was popular in the South and the West. But to the trading centers of the Northeast it seemed a disaster. Almost overnight the glittering trade bubble that had lasted since 1793 burst. Ships rode at anchor, their sails furled, while worms riddled their wooden hulls. Once-busy waterfront streets stood emptied of their milling crowds of seamen, teamsters, tavern-keepers, and stevedores. One traveler to New York described it as looking like a town ravaged by pestilence.

New Yorkers and New Englanders did what they could to evade the new law. Coastal traders, once out of sight of land, often crossed the Atlantic. Jefferson had given the state governors the right to issue special permits for specific reasons. Now the merchants prevailed on the governors to grant permits for almost any excuse. Many New England merchants faced with ruin chose more legal and constructive alternatives, however: during this period many transferred large amounts of capital from overseas trade into domestic manufactures.

Overall, the embargo did not seem to have much effect. It hurt British workingmen and French colonists, but the ruling classes in both Britain and France were scarcely affected. British manufacturers, meanwhile, could continue to send over their goods in their own vessels to compete with American products in America.

So loud became the domestic outcry against the Embargo Act that Congress was at last forced to act. In 1809 it replaced the unpopular law with the Non-Intercourse Act, permitting exports to every nation except England and France. These two offenders could now neither buy from the United States nor sell to her. If either of the two powers, however, reversed its hostile policies toward the United States, this country would resume trade with it.

James Madison Takes Over

The man who had now to administer the new law was the fourth President, James Madison. Few American Chief Executives could claim as distinguished a career. No one had been so effective in fostering and shaping the federal Constitution. After the inauguration of the national government, it had been Madison who had led the forces against Hamilton and, in alliance with his good friend Thomas Jefferson, had helped to create the Republican Party. In 1801, Jefferson selected him as his Secretary of State and he had served with distinction in that office.

To many Republicans Madison seemed Jefferson's natural successor—but not to all. Opposed to him was a group of militant Republicans called the "Tertium Quids," who considered both Jefferson and Madison to be too strongly imbued with Federalist principles. Leading voice of the Quids was John Randolph, an eloquent defender of lost causes and an irresponsible verbal brawler. The

Quids tried to deny Madison the nomination, but with Jefferson's support the party caucus in Congress endorsed him. The Federalists were now clearly the minority party, and Madison easily defeated their candidate, Charles Cotesworth Pinckney of "X, Y, Z" fame.

Physically, the new President was not a commanding figure. Small and wizened, he spoke in a barely audible voice and often seemed bored. Fortunately, the First Lady, the former Dolly Todd, helped to offset her husband's dour demeanor. Buxom, pink-cheeked, and charming, Mrs. Madison was a vivacious hostess whose parties and receptions seemed to the social set a vast improvement over the widowed Jefferson's bachelor dinners. Washington was still a city of magnificent distances; the presidential mansion was still not completed. But at least the capital now had a lively social focus it had lacked before.

The new Non-Intercourse Act created difficulties for Madison. Ships leaving American ports were not supposed to touch at French or British ports, but it quickly became clear that there was no way of guaranteeing they would obey the law. The British, in particular, laughed at it; it promised to cause them little harm, and they could see little reason to settle the pending *Chesapeake* claims or satisfy American commercial demands.

Not every Englishman took a hard line against the United States. The British minister in Washington, David Erskine, believed in the desirability of placating the Americans. Contrary to instructions, he told Madison that the British intended to modify their harsh policy toward American trade. On this basis, the President issued a proclamation reopening trade with Great Britain while retaining the restrictions on France. Soon after, Foreign Secretary Canning learned of his minister's indiscretion and disavowed it. The President thereupon reimposed the Non-Intercourse arrangement on Britain.

Dissatisfaction with the Non-Intercourse Act goaded Congress into trying a new tack against the belligerents. In May 1810 it passed Macon's Bill No. 2. This measure was surely one of the most devious in American history: it allowed the President to reopen trade immediately with both Britain and France. In the event either of the two warring powers modified its trade policies toward the United States before March 1811, the President might reimpose the trade prohibition upon the other. In effect, the United States was offering to ally itself economically against whichever nation was the slower in according it its commercial rights.

During the next two years the nation edged ever closer to war. The 1810 elections sent a group of young men to Congress mostly from the West and South, who were unwilling to temporize. These "War Hawks," were led by Henry Clay of Kentucky, a young Congressman with a rare eloquence and an unusual power to charm voters and fellow politicians alike. Although this was his first term in the House of Representatives, the magnetic Clay was elected Speaker. He quickly placed young men who thought as he did in key House posts. Peter Porter of western New York became chairman of the Foreign Relations Committee, where he had the support of such fellow War Hawks as John C. Calhoun of South Carolina, Felix Grundy of Tennessee, and Joseph Desha of Kentucky.

The War Hawks felt keenly the British-inflicted indignities, a feeling unmodified by New England and Northeastern concern for profitable transatlantic commerce. England's "aggression, and her injuries and insults to us" were, proclaimed Clay, "atrocious"—far more so than those of France. Besides, British assaults on American shipping were responsible for low crop prices in the West since they interfered with sales of these crops abroad. Many Westerners, moreover, blamed the British for recent Indian troubles; the uprising of the Shawnee chief Tecumseh and his brother, "the Prophet," could be laid at the door of British agents. Although General William Henry Harrison had beaten off Tecumseh's braves at Tippecanoe, British Indian policy rankled.

Still another situation influenced the War Hawks: for years the United States had disputed with Spain the boundary of West Florida. That narrow province stretched westward along the Gulf coast from the main Florida peninsula, cutting off much of the American Southwest from a sea connection. Spain, now an ally of England, held the province loosely. If war broke out, it could certainly be wrenched easily from her feeble hands.

Nonetheless, while the War Hawks and their supporters naturally thought of attacking and taking the exposed colonies of both Spain and England in the event of war, conquest was not their chief purpose. Rather, they were nationalists and patriots of the Revolution's memory who hated British arrogance and yearned to avenge the humiliations Britain had inflicted. For twenty years, they argued, Britain had refused to treat the United States as a sovereign nation. The effort to preserve peace at any price was in effect making America once more a British colony. "What are we not to lose by peace?'' Clay asked rhetorically. His answer: "commerce, character, a nation's best treasure, honor!''

Madison was soon adopting a tougher policy toward England. In 1811 he appointed James Monroe Secretary of State and asked Congress to vote money to build up the Army and Navy. He also initiated a more vigorous policy of retaliation. In the spring of that year, the U.S.S. *President* encountered the British sloop-of-war *Little Belt*. Although the results were actually inconclusive—the powerful *President* gave the *Little Belt* a drubbing, but failed to sink the weaker British vessel— most americans considered the results ample revenge for the *Chesapeake* attack of four years before.

Despite his new resolve, however, the President found it hard to take the final step. For months in early 1812 the prospect of war hung fire while both the Chief Executive and Congress dithered. The Republicans had by now come to assume that war was inevitable, but when it came to voting money to prepare for it, their fear of extravagance

got in the way of their common sense. Little had been done to authorize the building of new ships, and appropriations for the army remained inadequate. How the country intended to defend its commerce, and pursue an aggressive policy toward Florida and Canada, nobody made clear.

In the end, war came by mistake. Early in 1812, the British finally decided to modify their commercial policies. On June 23 the British government announced that the notorious Orders in Council that had so offended the United States would be lifted. It was too late. Before the news arrived, Madison had finally lost patience and asked for a declaration of war. On June 4, the House voted in favor of it by 79 to 49, followed two weeks later by the Senate, 19 to 13. The vote had ominous implications—clearly the country was not united. If the way congressmen voted is taken as indicative, southern New England, as well as much of New York, New Jersey, and Maryland, opposed the war. It remained to be seen whether they would continue to resist once the fighting had begun.

The War of 1812

By almost any measure, the War of 1812 was mismanaged. Congress had declared war, but had done little to prepare for it. One of the government's chief problems was the financing of such an expensive enterprise. Unready for heavy taxes, Americans expected to pay for the war through borrowing. Yet in 1811 the Republicans had refused to recharter the Bank of the United States, and it had died.

Nor was this all. Physically, the country presented a logistical nightmare. To move troops and supplies over such enormous distances would be next to impossible. Roads were few and poor. The steamboat had been introduced on the Hudson in 1807, but steamboat travel on the Mississippi and the Great Lakes was in its infancy in 1812. The armed forces were unready. Only seven thousand men were immediately available for service, and most of these were scattered in small posts on the frontier. The various state militias were a potential pool of manpower, but most militiamen were poorly trained and led. The best of the state forces were those of New England, but the Yankee governors refused to allow them to be called into federal service unless their own states were threatened with invasion. Nor was the Navy ready: it consisted of seven effective, seaworthy frigates and an equal number of smaller ships. Against these the British could muster over a hundred frigates and another hundred still-larger

ships-of-the-line. Worst of all, perhaps, the country was disunited. To many Federalists the war was a mistake. It was "Mr. Madison's war," a Republican venture, not a national one. Particularly in New England, the home of High Federalism, the war also seemed likely to produce a commercial disaster. Inevitably, Yankees said, it would be their commerce that would be swept off the seas by the Royal Navy.

Strong leadership might have overcome many of these difficulties, but Madison was a better philosopher and congressional manager than a war leader. Almost all the high military officers were elderly gentlemen who had not commanded troops against a trained European army since the Revolution.

Despite all these weaknesses, the Americans began the fighting with an invasion of Canada led by General William Hull commanding two thousand regulars. But, launched from Detroit, far to the west of Canada's chief population centers, the invasion was seriously misconceived. Even if it had succeeded, it would not have destroyed British power in North America; it required extended supply lines, and to protect these long lines the Americans had to control Lake Erie. But without a naval force on the lake they could not do so. Nevertheless, the campaign at first seemed to be succeeding. Hull crossed the Detroit River into Canada unopposed. He immediately issued a

The Taking of the City of Washington in America.

proclamation that if the Canadian militia remained at home they had nothing to fear from the Americans. In a matter of days half of them had deserted the British and returned to their farms.

The British now expected an immediate attack on Fort Malden, which was garrisoned by only a few hundred regulars, some Indians, and the remaining militia. But Hull dithered and delayed. Before long he had become "the object of . . . jest and ridicule" among the British troops. By the time he mounted his guns against the British, the American garrison at Michilimackinac to his east had surrendered. Hull was certain that his supply lines were now endangered, and withdrew across the river into Michigan and locked himself up in Detroit. On August 17 he surrendered without a fight to the British commander.

Prospects of taking Canada now appeared bleak. If the American invasion prong in the West, where the people were enthusiastic supporters of the war, had failed, what could be expected in the hostile East? The answer was, very little.

In New York State, a part of the American milita crossed the Niagara to attack the British-Canadian forces. They scored some early successes, but then were pinned down. They could have been rescued and the operation saved, but the remaining New York militia refused to cross the Niagara. Without reinforcements, nine hundred Americans were captured.

The third prong of the American invasion was no more successful than the first two. This attack, aimed at Montreal, was at least strategically sound. That city was the heart of British power in North America, and its capture would have been a disaster to England. Unfortunately, the Americans delayed their operations, giving the British many months to prepare. By the time the militia force moved northward against a well-entrenched enemy, the fall was far advanced. The ill-equipped American troops slogged their way through mud and drenching cold rain, sleeping without tents on the soggy ground with dripping blankets. When the American troops reached the Canadian border, many refused to cross. After fighting a few skirmishes, their commander ordered a retreat to Plattsburg, New York. There the militia made camp amidst mud, snow; many contracted pneumonia. "The very woods," an army suregon reported, "[rang] with coughing and groaning." Shortly afterwards the invasion force dispersed. Eighteen-twelve had ended with Canada still firmly in British hands and American morale in the cellar.

Despite these three strikes, the Americans were down, not out. The naval side of the war was going better. Although the British far outmanned and outgunned the Americans at sea, they were also stretched thin, and suffered from overconfidence. The Americans, they were certain, could not match the royal Navy in battle or do serious damage to their merchant shipping. They were wrong. Many American merchant captains had secured "letters of marque" commissioning their vessels as privateers. Over the next two-and-a-half years, these ships attacked British commerce in the West Indies, off the east coast of the United States, and even in the waters around the British Isles. While many privateers were captured, others took rich prizes costing British merchants millions of dollars.

The success of the small American navy, though less significant in material terms, was important for national morale. The American frigates proved to be remarkably effective in single-ship combat. In August 1812 the U.S.S. *Constitution* sighted the British frigate *Guerriere* in the mid-North Atlantic. The *Guerriere* was a slightly smaller vessel with a lighter broadside; part of her crew moreover, consisted of impressed Americans who had to be allowed to go below rather than fight their own countrymen. The British captain tried evasive maneuvers, but Hull was able to bring his ship within fifty yards of the enemy. For two hours he poured deadly broadsides into the British ship, leaving it a wreck. The *Guerriere* struck her colors. Both sides had fought well and bravely, but the performance of the inexperienced Americans was exceptional. As Hull reported, "From the smallest boy on the Ship to the oldest seamen not a look of fear was seen. They all went into action, giving three cheers, and requesting to be laid close alongside the enemy." American sailors had fought with greater spirit and élan than American infantry.

The *Constitution* victory was only the first of several such single-ship combats that helped redeem the honor of American arms. Several weeks later the *United States*, under Stephen Decatur, encountered the H.S.S. *Macedonian* and in a bloody battle sank her with a loss of one hundred British killed and wounded to Decatur's twelve. Still another such triumph came at the end of the year, when the *Constitution* closed on H.M.S. *Java* and in a two-hour engagement leveled her masts, killed her captain, and inflicted over a hundred casualties.

Deeply chagrined by their losses, the British began to reinforce their American squadron by drawing off vessels needed elsewhere. Slowly but steadily, the British Navy began to improve its performance. Bit by bit its blockade of the American Atlantic coast became tighter and more effective, confirming all the fears of Northeasterners that war would destroy American commerce. Worse still, the Americans soon lost control of their own coasts and shortly would be unable to repel British troop landings when they came.

On land, another major attack on Canada came in 1813. In April, 8,500 Americans gathered at the eastern end of Lake Ontario under the command of the hapless Henry Dearborn. On April 25, 1,700 men of this force sailed off to attack the Canadians at the western end of the lake and two days later arrived before York (now Toronto). The town was defended by only 800 men and some unreliable Indians, but the British had prepared a surprise in the form of a giant underground mine jammed with high explosives. Unfortunately for the defenders, the mine went off at the wrong time, killing as many British troops as Americans. Dismayed and outnumbered, the British commander now withdrew hastily, leaving behind his personal papers and baggage, including a musical snuff box that delighted the Americans who "liberated" it. The Americans occupied the town for four days and then departed for the mouth of the Niagara to attack Fort George. By this time the aging Dearborn was too exhausted to lead the expedition, and he turned his command over to the vigorous Winfield Scott. Soon to join the expedition was an equally aggressive young naval officer, Oliver Hazard Perry.

The American force was transported across Lake Ontario, and successfully completed a difficult amphibious landing before Fort George. The Americans, led by Scott and Perry, scrambled ashore with their heavy equipment and secured a foothold while still more men came ashore. Supported by the guns of the American flotilla, the invasion force drove off the British counterattack. The British commander now withdrew from Fort George and retreated to Beaver Dams. Scott was all for pursuing the enemy and destroying his army completely, but was overruled by his superior in the Niagara theater of operations. When the Americans were finally allowed to set off after the defeated British, Scott remained behind. The results were disastrous. The British commander surprised the Americans in their sleep, captured their leaders, and drove them back to Beaver Dams.

The British had now regained the initiative, and advanced on the American base with their small force of Indians and redcoats. Some distance from the objective the Indian auxiliaries encountered a large group of Americans under Lieutenant Colonel Charles Boerstler, and attacked. Boerstler held the Indians off until a party of British regulars approached under a flag of truce. Lieutenant James Fitzgibbon, the young British officer in charge, told the American commander that he was being closely followed by the main British army of fifteen hundred regulars and seven hundred Indians. The Americans, Fitzgibbon argued, could not possibly withstand the attack of this force, and in all likelihood the British would not then be able to restrain the bloodthirsty red men; the American commander should surrender now and save his men from massacre. Boerstler accepted the lieutenant's advice, laid down his arms, and waited for the main British party to arrive. It never did. Boerstler had surrendered his unit of five hundred men to a force only half its size.

The American setback on the Niagara frontier was matched by a major defeat before Montreal. Advancing on the Canadian city, the Americans, under the overall command of General James Wilkinson of Burr Conspiracy fame, ran into stiff opposition and abandoned the invasion. Soon afterward, the British captured Fort Niagara. They also took Buffalo and burned the city to the ground.

Two victories lightened the overall gloom of 1813 for the Americans. In September, Captain Perry and a small, locally built fleet encountered a British flotilla at Put-in-Bay on Lake Erie and defeated it after a bloody three-hour battle. Americans were greatly cheered at Perry's dispatch to General Harrison: "We have met the enemy and they are ours." Lake Erie was now in American hands, and the British were forced to abandon Detroit. A month later, Harrison overtook a retreating party of British and Indians and at the Battle of the Thames in Canada defeated them decisively. The chieftain Tecumseh was one of those who fell on the British side. Soon afterward, Tecumseh's federation of tribes collapsed and most of Britain's Indian allies deserted her cause.

On the domestic front, the high seas, and along the Atlantic coast, 1814 would prove a difficult year. By now the British navy had established a clear superiority in the Atlantic and in American coastal waters. The Royal Navy could with impunity sail up Chesapeake Bay, attack merchant ships, and bombard strategic towns and military positions.

Amplifying British successes were American disunity and the Madison Administration's blunders. Hard-pressed New England was a hotbed of disloyalty. Yankees had not wanted war and felt little inducement to support it now that it was proving so expensive. Hoping to rescue something from the calamity, they became the chief suppliers of commodities to the British army in Canada. Madison sought to cut off this dangerous trade and induced Congress to pass an embargo bill in December 1813 restricting all exports from the United States. The effects were disastrous. American exports plummeted and prices increased sharply. The Treasury found that it could not borrow the money it needed to finance military operations, and was forced to the edge of bankruptcy. In April 1814 Congress repealed this measure.

Meanwhile the gloomy military situation promised to get worse. In the spring of 1814, Napoleon's empire collapsed and the conqueror of Europe went into exile on the island of Elba. Until then, the British had been conducting a series of holding operations in America on both land and sea. Now, with France out of the war, all the vast resources of the Royal Navy and the seasoned veterans of the European fighting would be free to teach the pesky Americans a lesson.

In early May, the first detachments of British troops began to arrive in Quebec from Europe. Their mission, as expressed in orders to the British commandant in Canada, Sir George Prevost, would be to secure Canada's safety by driving out the Americans and recovering the American Northwest. Recognizing the danger if the British were allowed to gain too great a superiority, Winfield Scott attacked first. At Chippewa and Lundy's Lane, American regular troops fought effectively and gallantly against the best the British had to offer. The campaign ended in a draw, but Scott and Brown had frustrated British goals in the Northwest.

The British soon resumed the offensive. In late summer they set out for Plattsburgh, New York, near Lake Champlain. The British plan was once again, as during the Revolution, to split the United States in two along the line of Lake Champlain and the Hudson Valley. By September Prevost's army, the largest yet seen in America, was at Plattsburg's gates. There, however, the American commander was the scrappy John Wool. Though outnumbered almost three to one, Wool put up such a fight along the approaches to Plattsburg that Prevost paused and called on Captain George Downie, in command of the British fleet on the lake, to come to his aid: together the navy and army would pound the Americans into submission and advance on New York City to complete their mission.

It was not to be. Standing between Prevost and the fulfilment of his grand scheme was the United States naval squadron commanded by Captain Thomas Macdonough. Macdonough's little fleet consisted of four moderate-sized vessels and ten tiny gunboats, but in firepower it just about matched Downie's squadon. Downie attacked the Americans. His first shot hit the deck of Macdonough's flagship, the *Saratoga*, and destroyed the coop of the sailors' champion gamecock. The bird was unhurt and immediately flew to a gun carriage where, its feathers ruffled, it crowed defiance at the enemy. The men laughed and cheered; it seemed a good omen.

For over two hours the opposing fleets poured solid and grapeshot into one another. Scores of men on both sides were either killed or wounded, and the decks of the vessels became slippery with blood. Macdonough himself was knocked unconscious three times. At last the British surrendered. Macdonough brought the defeated British officers aboard the *Saratoga*, complimented them on their bravery, and refused to accept their swords. Shortly afterward he dispatched a message to the Secretary of the Navy that "the Almighty has been pleased to grant us a signal victory on Lake Champlain."

And a signal victory it was. When Prevost learned of Macdonough's triumph, he felt he could not continue; with the enemy in command on the water, his flanks were exposed. Instead of resuming the assault, he marched his men back to Canada. Another invasion threat was over.

Meanwhile, a second British invasion prong was meeting with greater success. On August 19, 1814, Sir George Cockburn landed with four thousand men between Baltimore and Washington, and set out for the nation's capital. A hastily organized defense force of militia, sailors, and a few regulars sought to stop the British at Bladensburg, but the inexperienced Americans could not hold against seasoned veterans and many fell into British hands. Later that afternoon, after learning of the defeat, Madison and his Cabinet left the city to avoid capture. His wife, the resourceful Dolly, had already removed the sterling silver and other movable valuables from the presidential mansion. At 8 p.m. the British entered the city. The next morning they set about systematically destroying all captured arms and burning the public buildings, including the President's house, the Capitol, the Treasury, and the War Office. The following day they left the smoldering capital, having avenged the burning of York.

The capture and destruction of the capital humiliated Americans. Madison fired Secretary of War John Armstrong, who had been in charge of Washington's defenses, and took over the War Department himself.

In early September 1814, the British arrived by land and by sea and moved on Baltimore. They broke through the Americans' first line of defense and drew to within a mile-and-a-half of the city. At this point the British commander decided to call on the British flotilla offshore to bombard the city, to help soften it up for his final assault. All through the day and night of September 13 the British fired rockets, big guns, and mortars at Forts McHenry and Covington, but could not silence them. Watching the attack was a Baltimore lawyer, Francis Scott Key, who was deeply moved by the defenders' stout resistance and wrote a poem, "The Star-Spangled Banner," commemorating the event. The British failure to reduce the harbor defenses discouraged further action, and they withdrew. The city was safe.

Baltimore's escape was, of course, a welcome event, but it could not wipe out the memory of Washington's capture and the general ineptness of the American war effort. In the wake of the Chesapeake invasions a wave of defeatism swept across the nation.

The fall and winter of 1814-15 was also a time of political crisis. Massachusetts elected representatives to meet with delegates from other New England states at Hartford, Connecticut, to consider defense problems and to discuss the possibility of revising the federal Constitution. Behind this action were the profound disgust of New Englanders with the war and their feeling that their section was suffering unduly in the conflict. At Hartford the militants intended to consider either seceding from the war or seceding from the Union itself, but by the time the convention met in December they were outnumbered. New Hampshire and Vermont refused to send delegations at all; and the delegates from Connecticut and Rhode Island proved to be more moderate than anyone expected. Rather than calling for dissolution of the Union, the convention passed a series of resolutions calling for amendment of the Constitution to reduce the power of the West and the South, and to require that declarations of war, non-intercourse acts, and admission of new states to the Union all receive a two-thirds vote of Congress to be adopted. The resolutions in the end amounted to little more than a protest, and the administration could heave a sigh of relief.

The Hartford Convention was the low point of the war. Thereafter the sun brightened. Before another year had passed, the country would pass from gloom and despair into an era of bright promise and exuberant optimism.

As early as November 1813 the British and American governments, partly at the urging of the Russian Czar, had agreed to meet to discuss peace terms. Neither government was happy about the war both had sought to avoid; now, even while fighting continued, they began to arrange for its end. Negotiations conducted at Ghent in Belgium, moved slowly. The British hoped that before long their armies would occupy large stretches of the United States and they could use this territory as leverage for extracting favorable terms. Perhaps they might even get their long-held wish to create an Indian state in the Northwest, cutting the Americans off from the interior of the continent. For their part, the American negotiators, Henry Clay, John Quincy Adams, and Albert Gallatin, rejected any scheme to slice up their country and insisted on the abandonment of the impressment of American sailors as a British policy.

At first, neither side would budge. During the last half of 1814 the British began to realize that, though they could win victories, they could not count on totally defeating the stubborn Americans. Then, too, Britain and Russia began to clash at the Congress of Vienna called to sort out the complex affairs of Europe after Napoleon's defeat. Under the circumstances, war with the United States now seemed an unimportant sideshow that should be ended as soon as possible. The Americans, too, were anxious to bring matters to a conclusion, and abandoned their demand for an explicit elimination of impressment.

On Christmas eve 1814, the commissioners at Ghent finally signed a peace treaty. This agreement merely restored the situation as it had existed before the war. Commissioners from both nations would meet to settle the dispute over the boundary between the United States and Canada, a dispute that had resulted from imperfections in the geographical knowledge available in 1783.

New Orleans

Yet the war went on. News of the Treaty of Ghent did not reach the United States for many weeks, and by that time hundreds of men had died in unnecessary battles. The greatest of these was the Battle of New Orleans, which created a na-

tional hero, helped destroy the Federalist Party, and restored the nation's battered self-respect.

The hero was General Andrew Jackson of Tennessee, a roughhewn, self-made planter, lawyer, and soldier. Born in South Carolina, Jackson had gone to Tennessee when that state was still the western district of North Carolina. He had risen in Tennessee politics and had served his adopted state in Congress and as a judge. In 1813-14 he led the Tennessee militia against the Creek Indians in Mississippi Territory following the massacre of 250 whites at Fort Mims. At Horseshoe Bend, Jackson surprised the Creeks and killed 900 in a fierce battle. For his services the government made him a major general in the army and commander of the Seventh Military District with headquarters at Mobile.

While at Mobile, Jackson learned that the British, as part of their final push to crush the Americans, intended to attack New Orleans with another army of European veterans. Though weak with fatigue and dysentery, "Old Hickory" (as he was affectionately called) hurried to the city to prepare its defenses. In short order, a flood of directives—to obstruct the roads and bayous leading to the city, to build fortifications, and to strengthen the existing ones—flowed from his headquarters. Militia and volunteers from Kentucky, Tennessee, and Mississippi made up the core of Jackson's army, and he recruited additional troops from among the creoles (people of French or Spanish origin) and black freemen of New Orleans. He also agreed to accept the services of a group of river pirates led by Jean Lafitte, a colorful rogue in trouble with the governor of Louisiana.

On the morning of December 23, 1814, redcoats newly arrived from the West Indies began to disembark fifteen miles southeast of New Orleans, after a cold trip across Lake Borgne in open boats. Jackson quickly learned of the landings. A more cautious general might have waited to see if this was the main attack or a mere feint. But Jackson immediately turned to his officers and declared: "Gentlemen, the British are below; we must fight them tonight!"

With two thousand men he advanced on the British force of some sixteen hundred which was waiting for further reinforcements before advancing against the city. Jackson achieved complete surprise and gave the redcoats a serious drubbing. The British line held, however, and Jackson withdrew to a line between the river and a swamp athwart the British advance.

Here, just as the commissioners were signing the peace treaty at Ghent, Jackson and his men prepared to face the British assault behind breastworks of cotton bales and earth. Both sides were being reinforced. The British were also getting a new commander: Sir Edward Pakenham, brother-in-law of the Duke of Wellington and an experienced officer of the Peninsular War.

Pakenham moved his army to within a few hundred yards of Jackson's force in preparation for a morning assault. All night long, American raiders made sorties against the British, doing little harm, but keeping the redcoats from getting any sleep. The next morning, with the battlefield enveloped in ground fog, the British advanced on Jackson's men hidden behind their breastworks. For a while they made headway against the rifles and artillery to their front, but when the U.S.S. *Louisiana* began to fire on their flank from the river, it proved more than flesh and blood could bear, and the advance stopped dead.

For the next three days the two armies confronted one another across a field strewn with dead and dying. On the morning of December 31, the British attacked again and the battle became an artillery duel, with Lafitte's pirates doing especially effective work with their big guns. For almost five hours the cannon boomed, until the discouraged British ceased their attack. Once more both sides brought up reinforcements. When Pakenham was ready to resume the attempt to reach New Orleans, he had close to ten thousand men, far more than Jackson.

On the morning of January 8, 1815, Pakenham asked his veterans for the last time to brave the American rifles and big guns. Once more, the attack failed. As the redcoats trudged across the gound in front of the American position, their ranks were shredded by grapeshot and rifle balls. Some reached the American lines, but then a counterattack threw them back. Many British officers were hit, and Pakenham himself died on the field.

Before expiring, the British general ordered a subordinate, General John Lambert, to throw in reserves for a final push, but seeing the hopelessness of the situation, Lambert refused. Instead, he ordered his men to fall back to Lake Borgne. The battle was over.

The victory was truly amazing. Over two thousand British troops had died or been wounded, against American casualties of twenty-one! Soon after the smoke cleared, Jackson and his jubilant staff passed along the lines of cheering troops to the stirring strains of "Hail Columbia" played by the army band. Even if it had all been a mistake, it was a glorious moment for the young nation.

The Battle of New Orleans became a kind of national redemption. A mismanaged war that had humiliated Americans now became a matter of great national pride. Overnight new confidence suffused the nation. Americans had taken on the greatest power in the world, and in the end had defeated the best it could throw at them. No longer would the nations of Europe treat the

United States with the contempt they had formerly shown. The country had finally and unquestionably confirmed the formal independence achieved in 1783.

The war had momentous political consequences. The Federalists had bet on the wrong horse—England—and when she lost, they lost too. If not for New Orleans and the exhilaration that made a mismanaged national enterprise seem a triumph, Federalist opposition to the war might have been rewarded with public favor, but Jackson's victory placed the stigma of "traitor" on every Federalist who had praised England and attacked the administration. In the presidential contest of 1816, the Republican James Monroe overwhelmed the Federalist candidate, Rufus King of New York, carrying every state in the Union except Massachusetts, Connecticut, and Delaware. Thereafter, although they continued to muster some support in a few isolated pockets, the Federalists were to all intents and purposes dead as a party.

Meanwhile, however, a strange thing happened: the Republicans became Federalists! In his annual message in 1815, Madison asked Congress to pass a protective tariff, charter a second Bank of the United States, and appropriate funds for the construction of roads and canals. Led by Clay, Calhoun, and other converts to nationalism, Congress obliged. In 1816 it passed a tariff affording at least modest protection to American industry, and established the Second Bank of the United States with an even larger capitalization than the First. In the end, Madison vetoed a bill for "internal improvements" on the grounds of dubious constitutionality; but his immediate successors would not prove so scrupulous and thereafter federal subsidies would help the nation overcome its vast distances.

Finally, there was Andrew Jackson. New Orleans had created America's first genuine folk hero since George Washington. Congress struck a gold medal in Jackson's honor and confirmed his rank as major general with the munificent salary of $2,400 a year. Before long, a biographer was busy writing a life of the General for an eager public. Another man might have been content with the plaudits of his fellow citizens and easy life at the Hermitage, Jackson's gracious estate near Nashville. But not Old Hickory. Before many months had passed, Americans would hear from him again.

Suggested Readings

On Lewis and Clark read the geographer John Logan Allen, *Passage Through the Garden: Lewis and Clark and the Image of the American Northwest* (1968). Forrest McDonald's *The Presidency of Thomas Jefferson* (1976) complements Fawn M. Brodie's *Thomas Jefferson: An Intimate History* (1974). Also important on politics are Noble E. Cunningham, Jr., *The Process of Government under Jefferson* (1978) and Marshall Smelser, *The Democratic Republic, 1801-1815* (1968). James M. Banner goes *To the Hartford Convention: The Federalists and the Origins of Party Politics in Massachusetts, 1789-1815* (1970). Reginald Horsman fights *The War of 1812* (1969). Gore Vidal's *Burr: A Novel* (1973) brilliantly presents the controversial Aaron as a gentleman and portrays the vulgarities and hypocrisies of the society that surrounded him.

Young America

I. Forrest McDonald : A Hamiltonian Revolution

The most striking achievements of the United States during its first four decades as a nation were that both the country and its form of government survived. Under the circumstances, these were by no means trivial feats. The western world — Europe and the Americas — was almost continuously at war throughout the period, and most nations were conquered at least once during the long conflict. And of the score and more of new nations which came into existence in that "Age of Democratic Revolutions," the United States alone produced a stable constitutional government.

In establishing the Constitution, the Founding Fathers had to overcome both practical and theoretical barriers. The practical obstacles were mainly that the political loyalties of most Americans, nurtured by long colonial experience, were directed toward individual states rather than toward an abstract United States; and that most Americans believed their tangible economic interests would best be served by the governments closest and most familiar to them. (After all, it was out of fear of centralized power, and especially of centralized taxing power, that the United States came into being in the first place.)

The theoretical barriers proved to be even more formidable, though few thought they would be at first. When the Americans declared their independence from the Kingdom of Great Britain, they committed themselves to adopting a republican form of government — meaning one in which there are no hereditary kings or nobles and all power is derived from "the public," broadly or narrowly defined. The public was in fact defined fairly narrowly, for only white adult property-owning males had full political or legal rights; and yet most patriot leaders were convinced by 1787 that the country's political arrangements were far too democratic. Power was excessively decentralized. Neither the Confederation Congress nor the state governments had any real executive arms, and authority was concentrated in the branches of government most directly chosen by the people, the state legislatures.

But any attempt to establish an adequately strong national government on republican principles ran counter to well-established political theory. It was almost universally agreed that republics could succeed only in small territories, and the United States was an enormous country, bigger than any in Europe except Russia. It was assumed that republics could work only if there were a high level of virtue in the people, but the Founding Fathers believed that the people were woefully lacking in virtue. And it was thought that republics could last only if property were fairly equally distributed, whereas the Founders knew that inequality of wealth naturally develops in any free society. The American experiment in republicanism thus seemed doomed at the outset.

Yet the framers of the Constitution devised a system that overcame all these obstacles and, in the doing, laid the foundations for a new theory of free government. Assuming that men are motivated by selfish drives — especially ambition and avarice, the love of power and the love of property — they erected a governmental structure in which all men would be free to pursue power and profit for themselves, and yet the result would be the promotion of the public good. Economically the public good would be served because of a principle — self-interest — that had been pointed out by the Scottish philosopher and economist Adam Smith in his classic work, *The Wealth of Nations*, published in 1776: "It is not from the benevolence of the butcher, the brewer or the baker that we expect our dinner, but from their regard of their own interest." As for governmental power, the American solution to avoiding its dangers while providing enough of it was to keep it diffuse. That is, power under the Constitution would be distributed by the federal system: in which national, state, and local governments would all be supreme in their own spheres. Moreover, at each level it would be distributed among various branches, chosen by different groups, exercising different functions, holding office for different periods, and exercising checks on one another. In such a cumbersome scheme of things, the efforts of individuals and groups to gain power and further their own interest would energize the system, and yet it was unlikely that any person or group could gain enough power to threaten the liberties of the whole. The size and diversity of the United States, in this system, became advantageous rather than disadvantageous, for they increased the difficulty of the formation of combinations of dangerous groups and interests.

Though the constitutional system rested upon private self-interest, the Framers did not contemplate the emergence of capitalism. It is true that they regarded the right to property as sacred, and indeed thought that the main purpose of the creation of governments was to protect that right. But that is not the same thing as endorsing capitalism, which is an economic system in which property is put to work in the creation of more property. Instead, most Americans thought of property rights in terms of the right to *enjoy* property rather than to *employ* it. Moreover, in keeping with patterns of thought inherited from a feudal past, most Americans believed that the total quantity of property was more or less fixed and thus that the *creation* of property was a theoretical impossibility.

It was the policies of Alexander Hamilton that provided the institutional machinery for the development of capitalism. As the first Secretary of the Treasury, Hamilton proposed (and Congress enacted) a series of measures which transformed the Revolutionary War debt from a crushing burden into an enormous pool of liquid capital. New government bonds amounting in value to perhaps a quarter as much as that of all the farm land in this nation of farmers, constituted both the country's money supply and the capital for a huge expansion of commercial, banking, and manufacturing activity. Two subsequent developments complemented Hamilton's financial system. One was that American merchants and shippers reaped enormous profits from the neutral carrying trade during the French Revolutionary and Napoleonic wars. The other was that a group of judges and lawyers, working through court decisions rather than through legislative enactments, quietly brought about a thorough transformation of American law, making it biased in favor of developmental capitalism rather than—as before—in favor of agrarianism.

These changes were scarcely welcomed by most Americans, even though a great increase in national wealth was the result. For generations, Americans had been conditioned to believe that bonds, stocks, and bank notes were not only fictitious wealth but also evil instruments by which monarchists, aristocrats, and monied men corrupted and oppressed the people. Besides, slaveowning Southern planters were especially fearful of the creation of a dynamic system of capitalism, for they perceived such a system as a threat to their inherited wealth, status, and power. Planters formed the backbone of the resistance to Hamilton's program from the beginning, and it was two slaveowners, Jefferson and Madison, who organized the Republican Party in opposition to Hamilton. In 1800, the Republicans succeeded in ousting the Federalists from power.

Jefferson later referred to his election and the triumph of his party as "the Revolution of 1800"; and in one sense it was truly revolutionary. The Republicans established fiscal policies whereby the public debts would ultimately be paid off, and with the expiration of the debts the whole Hamiltonian system would collapse as well. They abolished most domestic taxes, reduced the army and the navy to shadow forces, and repealed a great deal of restrictive and oppressive legislation. To do all that was to defy precedent. It was not in the nature of government to pay debts, abolish taxes, restrict the power to coerce, or reduce its authority; rather, the tendency had always been the other way around.

But the Hamiltonian way was the way of the future. Even so, the Jeffersonians might have succeeded but for the twists of the Anglo-French wars and their unrealistic attitude toward those wars. The Jeffersonians despised all things British, and in no small measure their opposition to Hamilton was based upon the fear that his policies were designed to recast America in a British mold. When the French Revolution broke out in 1789, they cheered; when France and Britain went to war in 1793, they sided with France. That was understandable. But then the French Revolution — following the course that violent revolutions almost invariably follow — led to anarchy and bloodshed and ultimately to a military dictatorship and far more bloodshed. By 1800, and for a decade and a half thereafter, Britain stood almost alone as a bulwark of freedom against Napoleonic tyranny. In those circumstances both principle and self-interest required that the United States assume at least a moderately pro-British stance, but the Jeffersonians could never bring themselves to do so.

The results were nightmarish and almost catastrophic. To be sure, the Jeffersonians had one great diplomatic triumph, the purchase of Louisiana, but that was a matter of pure luck, and their luck soon ran out. Throughout Jefferson's second term as president and Madison's first, the United States was buffeted between Britain and France. In dealing directly with those two powers, Jefferson and Madison committed a succession of diplomatic blunders which virtually ensured war with Britain. Meanwhile, they adopted policies, most notably the embargo, which led to repression and disunion at home. They continued to emasculate the national government, partly by refusing to create an army and a navy.

The War of 1812 was not a disaster for the United States, but only because the British chose not to give America the drubbing which, in British eyes, it so richly deserved. Despite that choice, the American record during the war was sorry enough. Public finance was chaotic and business fell into ruin; nearly a third of the country was disloyal to the point of aiding the enemy and flirting with secession from the Union; and, except for a handful of naval battles and one land battle which was fought after the war was officially over, the American military performance was nothing less than a disgrace.

The lesson taught by the war was a hard one for the Jeffersonian Republicans: it was that it is folly to think that a nation can survive without a viable national government, without a sound system of finance, and without strong capabilities for self-defense. Having learned that lesson, the Republicans were prepared at war's end to re-enact the whole Hamiltonian system, and then some. Once that was done, the Jeffersonians had all but conceded that their counter-revolution had been a failure.

In addition to these political, legal, and economic developments, two technological innovations made during these years, the cotton gin and the steamboat, would have profound effects upon America's future. Between them, the gin and the steamboat stimulated and facilitated the spread of the population over the interior, an enormous expansion of Southern agriculture, and a growth of New England textile manufacturing. By these means, and by virtue of making the various parts of the country physically interconnected and economically interdependent, technology contributed to the development of nationalism and capitalism. But it also contributed to contrary tendencies. The steamboat helped scatter Americans over a vast expanse of territory and thus promoted regionalism, and it and its successor the railroad set off intense regional rivalries for control of transportation facilities. The cotton gin accentuated regional differences by revitalizing slavery. By 1790 slavery in the United States had become unprofitable except on rice plantations, which were confined to the coastal swamps of South Carolina and Georgia, and it seemed reasonable to believe that the institution would disappear in a generation or two. Every Northern state had at least begun the process of emancipation, and antislavery sentiment was strong in the tobacco-growing regions of the upper South, where two-thirds of the slaves were held. But the expansion of cotton culture that was made possible by the gin changed everything. Thenceforth, it would be futile to hope that slavery could be ended by voluntary and peaceful means.

In sum, at the end of the Second War for American Independence, the United States seemed to be becoming one nation; but in actuality, as events were soon to prove, it was on its way toward becoming two.

Eugene D. Genovese: A Clash of Cultures

America's epoch-making victory over Great Britain stunned the trans-Atlantic world, firing European revolutionaries with vast and unprecedented hopes for overthrowing the aristocratic old regimes and chilling those supporters of the old regimes who had the wit to understand that much more had happened than some settling of local accounts. For in truth, the North American colonies had done what Napoleon Bonaparte would later prophesy that the Chinese would someday do. China, he said, was a sleeping giant: Let her sleep, for when she awakes, she will shake the world. Edmund Burke, in his own way, had warned Parliament that Britain could not hope to keep North America asleep forever and would be wise to wake her slowly and safely. But, as usual, the "realists" and "practical men" prevailed. Obviously, Great Britain could put down a rebellion in some backward, undeveloped, half-savage country. Obviously, the honor, prestige, and credibility of Great Britain's world empire required that these insolent Americans be put back in their place. Obviously.

The American Revolution disposed of monarchy, although, actually, it had followed the example of the Mother Country itself, which had not only established Cromwell's dictatorial republic during the 1640's but had, for good measure, executed a king in the bargain. The question remained, Could a republic survive over so vast a territory, in the face of so many regional and local loyalties, and without adequate model, precedent, experience? And even if so, could a democratic, rather than a dictatorial or authoritarian, republic survive at all? That it did required rough measure against all forms of parochialism. The wonder is that the rough measures, against which the adherents of the Articles of Confederation were to rail so, proved so mild when evaluated by the European standards of 1789, 1793-1794, 1848, 1871, 1917.

Suffice it to say that a new country, not to mention a revolutionary republic of unprecedented historical proportions, that aspired to world power almost as soon as it tumbled from the imperial womb needed a government that could rule at home and, even then, influence events abroad. The Articles of Confederation may have pleased those who, however democratic and noble in spirit, had no such grand aspirations; it could not long please those who dared to struggle for — and dared to win — a new world of freedom and the realization of human potential.

American politics from the Revolution to the emergence of the slavery question during the Mexican War was marked by rhetorical excesses suggestive of the harshest class struggle and by practical moderation and considerable ease in the resolution of conflict. Thus, some historians, especially those of an economic-determinist persuasion or left-liberal politics, have treated the Constitution itself as the product of a counter-revolution of big property against the people, although no one has yet explained how this counter-revolutionary Constitution became a beacon of hope to revolutionaries all over the world or how a tough and well-armed people, fresh from victory in a heroic war against the world's mightiest power, surrendered to domestic reaction without firing a shot.

The bitter battles between the followers of Jefferson and those of Hamilton, who regularly accused each other of anarchism, monarchism, atheism, High Churchism, blasphemy, and corruption, not to mention treason, culminated in the election of Jefferson, which Americans, who love to dramatize themselves, have styled the "revolution of 1800." The defeated Federalists quietly surrendered power to Jefferson, whom they had just been calling—quite sincerely—a liar, a hypocrite, an atheist, an anarchist, and a Jacobin. Presumably, the great propertied classes for whom the Federalists spoke had miraculously concluded that having an anarchistic, atheistic, Jacobinnical hypocrite as chief of state might just be good for business.

And in truth it was not at all bad. The elaborate economic program advanced by Hamilton and promulgated during the Washington and Adams administrations had a double aspect. First, it rationalized national finances and established international credit; that is, it projected the new national government into economic affairs in such a way as to facilitate the growth of an integrated national economy capable of performing in an expanding world market. The second aspect, however, proved less admirable.

Hamilton firmly believed that the country ought to be run by the best people, who, as you have no doubt already guessed, turned out to be the very rich. Since the country lacked a class of very rich large enough and powerful enough to insure its own rule, Hamilton, good conservative that he was, set out to establish one by the manipulation of government policy. Hence, the mechanics of the Federalists' policy deliberately favored the speculators and encouraged the rapid transfer of wealth from the lower and middle classes to the already rich. Not surprisingly, the great mass of small propertyholders, who were rallying to Jefferson, were not amused. They even thought they spied an element of corruption, although in Hamilton's defense it is hard to see how anything sanctioned by bourgeois law can—by definition—legitimately be deemed corrupt.

Poor Hamilton had neither world enough nor time. His grand scheme could not be consolidated without a long period in power, and his opponents increasingly had the votes. (It was not for nothing that Hamilton and his fellow conservatives had no use for democracy and swallowed it choking on every bit.) What was more important, those hostile voters had guns. Reason therefore prevailed, as it generally does when well armed. The election of 1800 was no revolution. But power did pass from one party to another without bloodshed, policies were overturned, and the people did firmly decide that American development was to follow a more rather than less democratic path. Those were not trivial matters.

When in power the Jeffersonians and their heirs proceeded to destroy what they regarded as the corrupt features of state policy. They reduced the role of the Federal government to a safe minimum and, in particular, drastically reduced the national debt, which Hamilton had counted on to guarantee ownership of the state by the moneyed classes. This reform, impressive so far as it went, left untouched the structure of a funded national debt. If, in short, Hamilton's program had been thoroughly and frankly bourgeois, Jefferson's was no less thoroughly if a good deal less frankly so. Indeed, one could argue that the bourgeois program of the Jeffersonian party was more up-to-date in its preference for laissez faire than Hamilton's neo-mercantilism had been.

This American consensus on private property—on capitalism—as a social foundation did not go unchallenged by rural and urban lower classes, and the ensuing struggles constitute a vital part of our national history. But they played a minor role in antebellum America and will have to be passed over here. The immediate challenge lay elsewhere.

It is not enough to speak of a consensus in defense of private property, for the private property in question was of a specific kind—bourgeois property. That is, it was legally sanctioned as absolute in the sense developed by British liberal thought from Locke to Adam Smith; and it was specifically in the process of being integrated into a national market. But such property, in both theory and practical interest, is inseparable from the right of property in one's own person and the denial of property in man (slavery). If each man has the rights to the fruits of his labor, then a species of property like slavery in which one person has an absolute right to the property of another is a contradiction. At issue is not merely theoretical disquisition or even material interests; at issue is the ideological consensus itself.

From this point of view, there was less a single consensus rooted in property than three separate ones, which formed the political and ideological basis of the Jeffersonian coalition: a consensus on slave property in the South; a consensus on bourgeois property in the North; and a national consensus, both wishful and fallacious, that somehow these two forms of property, and the societies to which they gave rise, could coexist in a single republic, mediated by a democratic politics.

Jefferson, the agrarian democrat, lived to see his dream of a planter-farmer coalition to guarantee national harmony begin to turn into a nightmare. He read well enough the struggle over the Missouri question, which he termed "a firebell in the night." One wonders how well he, and many of his contemporaries, read the other story—that of their own relationship to America's economic miracle. For much more was at issue than the Jeffersonian acceptance of so much Hamiltonianism. In direct ways the Jeffersonian party and its successors greatly facilitated the development of American capitalism notwithstanding much anticapitalist rhetoric. The Louisiana Purchase alone contributed enormously. But the Jeffersonian commitment to low land prices and rapid Western settlement which culminated in the radical Jacksonians' demand for free homesteads, contributed enormously, too.

By undermining Hamilton's pro-business policy, which rested in no small part on the artificial creation of a large national debt—i.e., the Jeffersonians instituted cheap government—the Jeffersonians had little need to use land sales to service the debt and could afford to follow a more democratic course. The burden of their policy, in this and other respects, favored the rapid settlement of the West on a freehold basis, creating a class of potentially successful farmers oriented toward commodity production. Those farmers generated a vast market for textiles, agricultural implements and machinery, and a widening array of industrial goods; and they set up an irresistible pressure for canals, roads, railroads, and marketing facilities. American capitalism owed much to the creation of this home market, the greatest in world history, which itself arose on the basis of a democratic freehold and would have been unthinkable without a democratic politics.

The war of 1812 no doubt did teach many Jeffersonian Republicans much about the exigencies of national economy and national defense. Patriotic Americans had to reflect on the need for greater political coordination, not to say centralization. Indeed, the war had proven "sorry enough" and a "disgrace" to the United States, which clearly got beaten. (And so, the silly boast that the United States had never lost a war — fed to generations of Americans until the disaster in Vietnam — was always a lie.) But if in fact the Jeffersonian Republicans had simply represented the forces of an agrarian counter-revolution, their about face on so many questions of law and economic development would have made little sense and probably could not have been effected. Rather, they represented a complex coalition of genuinely counter-revolutionary slaveholders with various strata of bourgeois propertyholders, including capitalist farmers. The slaveholders themselves, except those of the class-conscious South Carolina low country, who were always precocious in such matters, had by no means arrived at a definitely hostile stance toward the emergent political order: They were still wavering. Other Jeffersonian Republicans, while opposing Hamiltonian policies nonetheless shared much of the basic Hamiltonian commitment to capitalist development. Had they not, they would have drawn different conclusions from the debacle of 1812-1814, or at least have shown much more resistance to the growing centralization of national power.

These policies could not handle the emerging slavery question. For however much slavery aided America's early capitalist development, it increasingly was proving itself an obstacle to the fulfillment of an apparent national destiny. At its heart, the slave system shaped a deeply reactionary ruling class with a world view radically different from that coming to dominate the business civilization of the North. The economy, notwithstanding slumps and reverses, boomed, while the politicians temporized and the threat of secession and war gained momentum. Before long, the business classes of the North would face a struggle to the knife with intransigent slaveholders, who would prove the most formidable class enemy yet to confront American capitalism.

Chapter VIII
Nationalism & Sectionalism
1816—1828

The Westward Movement

For almost 200 years American society had developed in the corridor between the Atlantic Ocean and the Appalachian Mountains. A series of mountain ranges, powerful Indian tribes, and conflict among European powers for the great, unsettled western lands discouraged most Americans from pushing into the West. Even those who crossed some of the eastern mountains found the inviting valleys angling south through Pennsylvania, Virginia, and the Carolinas far more tempting than scaling the next ridges toward an uncertain domicile in the western plains. Then, after about 1795, with the Revolution won, the Indian tribes dispersed, the European grasp on the West weakened, and the price of good land back east mounting, a vast folk migration began; only briefly interrupted by wars and depressions, it relentlessly populated the continent. The land seemed suddenly and permanently to have tilted, shaking its human burden westward in a long rough tumble toward the Pacific.

Settlers traveled by wagon, flatboat, horse, even on foot. The road west was often scarcely a road at all, but a slightly widened trail full of ruts and stumps so that for a passenger in the unsprung wagons "the pain of riding exceeded the fatigue of walking." No wonder Americans of the early nineteenth century were so hungry for improved transportation, for turnpikes, canals, and finally railroads. A modern American, in a land of motels, fast-food stands, and gas stations, cannot easily envision the world that the early traveler encountered west of the Appalachians. Try to imagine an environment that was often nothing but forest: tall hardwood trees in all directions, a dark, sinister, and gloomy wildwood. No wonder settlers gloated over the mighty conflagrations that followed a boisterous log-rolling, when perhaps hundreds of trees, felled after back-breaking labor, vanished into smoke, fire, and ash.

Yet the farmers preferred the forests to the prairies, endless meadows of tall grass sweeping across Northern Indiana and Illinois. Americans, much as they might curse the trees they had to girdle, cut, and burn, hard as they might work to let in sunshine so that crops could grow, believed that hardwood forests indicated fertile soil. The prairies (actually richer soil where thick grass strangled most other vegetation) evoked, as one traveler noted, "a certain indescribable sensation of loneliness." Amidst utter desolation, not a solitary tree intercepted the vision or broke the monotony. But rich as prairie soil was, settlers discovered that to farm this land meant first to break the thick, endless sod. In the early part of the century, when plows were still small and primitive, it was murderous labor.

The work that men and women did in the early West is also difficult for us to imagine. With implements no more sophisticated than an axe and chisel, the average settler—in addition to his back-breaking agricultural labors—would make "gates, carts, barrows, plow frames, ox yokes, wooden shovels, hay forks, troughs, benches, woodhorses, tool handles, stirring paddles, rakes, mortars, flails, cradles for mowing, swingling knives, flax brakes, and many other articles." More talented woodworkers frequently made their own wagons and furniture as well. And of course everyone, borrowing muscle from neighbors to raise the logs, built his own house.

Women worked equally hard—or harder, raising vegetables and herbs, manufacturing soap, butter, and other household articles, and carrying out every step of the making of clothing, from spinning to sewing. This labor, combined with housekeeping tasks and especially bearing children, took a heavy toll. Women often appeared old at thirty, and men widowed two and three times were common.

Homes in the West were far from comfortable or healthy. Clouds of flies and mosquitoes, drafty cabins, primitive sanitation, and mounds of animal waste around most cabins were probably more hazardous to life than the better-known dangers of hostile Indians or prairie fires. While many New Englanders traveled west singing—

Come all ye Yankee farmers who wish to change your lot,
Who've spunk enough to travel beyond your native spot,
And leave behind the village where Ma and Pa do stay,
Come follow me and settle in Michigania.
—others who had been there chanted:

Don't go to Michigan, that land of ills;
The word means ague [malaria], fever, and chills.

Davy Crockett of West Tennessee passed into legend long before he died: "I'm fresh from the backwoods," he is said to have boasted, "half alligator, a little touched with the snapping turtle; can wade the Mississippi, leap the Ohio, ride upon a streak of lightning . . . hug a bear too close for comfort and eat any man opposed by Jackson."

It has often been remarked that the pioneers were natural optimists. Surviving the journey west and the pioneer phase meant independence and wealth as nineteenth-century Americans understood it: the ownership of productive agricultural land. Cheap and fertile, however many trees stood on it and however difficult the journey, the land was worth a bout of ague and a generation of struggle. The true pioneer stage passed rapidly; mills, towns, canals, newspapers, churches, cloth imported from the East, hardware, glass, even pianos eased and elevated the crude life of the frontier, and families rapidly moved from the backwoods to the front pews.

The return of peace on the frontier after the War of 1812, and rising prices worldwide for agricultural products, set off an unprecedented westward migration. Freed at last of foreign entanglements, the continent lay before Americans, wrote Henry Adams, "like an uncovered ore bed." In 1810 only one American in seven lived west of the Appalachians; in 1820 it was one in four. Before the fever subsided, five new states had entered the Union—Indiana (1816), Mississippi (1817), Illinois (1818), Alabama (1819), Missouri (1821)—making the West a new force to be reckoned with in national affairs.

One observer in 1830, however, caught the flavor of the raw, young West in politics, as it would emerge when Andrew Jackson occupied the Presidency:

I have just witnessed a strange thing—a Kentucky election—and am disposed to give you an account of it. An election in Kentucky lasts three days, and during that period whisky and apple toddy flow through our cities and villages like the Euphrates through ancient Babylon. I must do Lexington the justice to say that matters were conducted here with tolerable propriety; but in Frankfort, a place which I had the curiosity to visit on the last day of the election, Jacksonism and drunkenness stalked triumphant—"an unclean pair of lubberly giants." A number of runners, each with a whisky bottle poking its long neck from his pocket, were busily employed bribing voters, and each party kept half a dozen bullies under pay, genuine specimens of Kentucky alligatorism, to flog every poor fellow who should attempt to vote illegally. A half a hundred of mortar would scarcely fill up the chinks of the skulls that were broken on that occasion. I barely escaped myself.

Post-war Nationalism

With the end of the War of 1812, Americans turned their attention not only westward but also to pressing national problems.

After many years of political bickering, a strange interlude of one-party politics followed the war. The Hartford Convention of 1814-15 finished the Federalists as a national party; in 1816 only Massachusetts, Connecticut, and Delaware supported the Federalist candidate for President. The decline of Federalism was curiously accompanied, however, by the shift of Jeffersonian Republicans toward Hamiltonian programs that had begun with the Louisiana Purchase. The War of 1812 had renewed a feeling of common interest at the same time it had exposed glaring national weaknesses, and a consensus developed in favor of national action to remedy these problems. For a time, nearly all voters called themselves Jeffersonian Republicans, and politics became a contest of personalities. To a people brought up with an eighteenth-century view of political parties as self-serving, divisive instruments, this actually seemed a healthy development. The "demon of party," a newspaper editor noted in 1817, had been exorcised for good.

President Madison, his strict constructionism much tempered by his recent flight from Washington, recommended a broad nationalistic program in 1815. Congress responded by rechartering a national bank, voting funds for internal improvements, and enacting a protective tariff.

The war had demonstrated the need for a national bank. When the charter of the first Bank of the United States had expired in 1811, the state banks went wild. Their number increased from eighty-eight to over two hundred, all issuing huge numbers of banknotes, most of them unsecured by specie (gold or silver). The mass of confusing, depreciated paper money worried businessmen and made counterfeiters smile. The lack of a national currency made capital transfers difficult. Then wartime borrowing overwhelmed this shaky system. By the summer of 1814 every bank outside of New England had suspended specie payments. The nation's credit had practically vanished.

To make matters worse, the Federal government after the war, to accommodate western settlers, offered for sale vast tracts of public land. Auctions at the district land offices attracted eager crowds, including squatters hoping to buy the lots they already occupied and speculators seeking choice tracts for resale at inflated prices. The government's terms were extraordinarily generous: the minimum purchase was 160 acres and the purchaser had four years to buy. In spite of efforts by speculators to stifle competitive bidding, prices at the sales frequently soared well above the minimum $2 an acre (reduced to $1.25 in 1820). Fertile bottom land near Huntsville, Alabama, brought $70 to $78 an acre in the spring of 1818. Total annual sales of public land rose from less than $3 million in 1815 to over $13 million in 1818. Much of this land was purchased with credit supplied by the steadily increasing number of state banks. "Wherever there is a 'church, a blacksmith's shop and a tavern' seems a proper site for one of them," wrote Hezekian Niles in 1816.

To remedy this situation Congress, in 1816, chartered a second Bank of the United States, with headquarters at Philadelphia. It was capitalized at $35 million, of which the government put up $7 million.

The new Bank of the United States not only made little effort at first to check the growth of the state banks, but itself proved a major source of credit expansion. Its first president, William Jones, was a good politician but a poor banker, exchanging stock in the Bank for IOU's instead of specie. Supervision over Bank branches was notoriously lax. Those in the South and West greatly overexpanded their credits and note issues. The officers of the Baltimore branch engaged in outright embezzlement. By 1818 the Bank had loaned out over $41 million. Some of this was invested in canals, turnpikes, and farm improvements; much more, however, went for speculative ventures in urban real estate, cotton futures, and western land. Indebtedness mounted, but as long as prices and rents increased, farmers and speculators could hope to meet their obligations.

Suddenly the boom collapsed. With the return of good harvests abroad in the fall of 1818, demand for American grain fell sharply. At the same time, British manufacturers finally reduced their imports of American cotton: prices for the South's great staple dropped by over one-half in 1819. Planters and farmers who had borrowed heavily to expand production could not repay their loans.

This sudden reversal left the Bank of the United States in desperate straits. Its liabilities exceeded its specie reserves by a ratio of ten to one—double the limit allowed by law. Bank president Jones resigned in disgrace. The Bank then instituted a drastic contraction, which forced the state banks to call in their loans and notes. A wave of bank failures followed, especially in the South and West; money disappeared and credit dried up, spreading economic distress throughout the country. Speculators who had purchased public land were stuck with it. Agricultural prices sank so low that many farmers resorted to barter. Merchants sold their stock at high losses or declared bankruptcy. In Philadelphia County alone, over 1,800 people went to prison for debt during 1819. Thousands were thrown out of work: in Pittsburgh, thirty percent of the population went back to the country. Americans for the first time confronted a nationwide depression—the "panic of 1819."

The economic crisis provoked a heated debate over both the causes of the depression and appropriate measures of relief. Stephen Girard, a Philadelphia capitalist, blamed the state banks, "who with their fictitious capital have acted imprudently." The state banks, anxious to conceal their own shortcomings, criticized the national Bank. Many, including President James Monroe, lamented the postwar spirit of extravagance and speculation, and called for a return to spartan ways. Advocates of a protective tariff pointed to our dependence on European trade, and urged Americans to produce more of their own manufactured goods. Congress rejected a higher tariff and a bill to abolish federal imprisonment for debt, but did agree in 1821 to extend additional time to persons who had purchased public lands on credit. Meaningful debtor relief came mainly from the states; several passed "stay" laws delaying foreclosure for debt. Various cities set up soup kitchens, and churches collected funds for the relief of paupers.

Out of the confused debate on the depression, the Bank of the United States emerged as the chief scapegoat. Charges of fraud and mismanagement filled the air. The Bank was damned for creating easy credit, and then for trying to check it. Critics likened it to a monster, foreclosing everything in its path: "I know towns, yea, cities," charged Senator Thomas Hart Benton of Missouri,

where this bank already appears as an engrossing proprietor. All the flourishing cities of the West are mortgaged to this money power . . . They are in the jaws of a monster! A lump of butter in the mouth of a dog! One gulp, one swallow, and all is gone!

Many of these accusations were unfair. Fraud and mismanagement there had been, but the Bank was not responsible for fluctuations in the world market. If it had been too lax in dealing with the state banks, so had politicians and the public. These considerations, however, made little impression on a people mired in debt and depression. The economy recovered in the early 1820's, but by this time the reputation of the Bank among certain constituencies had deteriorated beyond repair.

During the War of 1812, the nation's transportation network had proved no more adequate to wartime demands than its banking system. With coastal shipping choked off by the British blockade and canals still in their infancy, the burden fell almost entirely on the roads. In a few places in the East turnpikes had been built, but they deteriorated quickly under heavy use. Most roads were hardly more than broad country paths through the forest, filled with ruts and stumps, impassable in wet weather. In one case, it took a wagon drawn by four horses seventy-five days to travel from Massachusetts to South Carolina. Such delays produced serious food shortages in some cities.

Poor roads had severely hampered the American military effort. General William Henry Harrison reported in 1812 that his advance on Detroit could not begin "until the frost shall become so severe as to enable us to use the rivers and the margins of . . . Lake [Erie] for the transportation of the baggage and artillery upon the ice. To get them forward through a swampy wilderness of near two hundred miles in wagons or on pack horses . . . is absolutely impossible." Harrison estimated that overland hauls required "two wagons with forage [for the horses] for each one that it loaded with provisions and other articles."

In his annual message Madison called for a system of roads and canals "executed under national authority." He recommended a constitutional amendment to eliminate continuing doubts over the federal government's authority to finance such projects. Representative John C. Calhoun of South Carolina, then a vigorous young nationalist, brushed aside constitutional objections. Sheer size and poor communication, he warned the House—in words that would later haunt him—exposed the country to that "greatest of all calamities," disunion. "Let us, then, bind the Republic together with a perfect system of roads and canals. Let us conquer space." To finance this program, Calhoun proposed to set aside, as a fund for internal improvements, the government's share of the profits from the new Bank of the United States. In 1817 Congress narrowly approved Calhoun's Bonus Bill, only to have Madison veto it on constitutional grounds. The states and private enterprise would, in the end, have to finance most internal improvements.

American manufacturers found their most severe trial not during wartime but with the return of peace. Before 1807 Americans imported most manufactured goods from Europe, but Jefferson's embargo and the war had stimulated the growth of domestic industries. In New England and the Carolinas, mills were spinning and weaving cotton; a new iron industry flourished at Pittsburgh; Kentuckians began making local hemp into bagging. British manufacturers moved quickly in 1816 to crush these new rivals. They dumped vast quantities of goods on the American market at cut-rate prices, in order, a spokesman explained, "to stifle in the cradle those rising manufacturers in the United States, which war had forced into existence, contrary to the natural course of things." In order to protect these "infant" industries, President Madison proposed increased tariff duties (taxes) on competing imports. Congress was receptive, since nearly every section of the country had an interest to be protected. Southerners, who had the least to gain, supported higher duties on political and patriotic grounds. Within a few years, however, when a series of threatening events caused many Southerners to reexamine their jubilant nationalism, the tide turned.

To preside over this superficially placid era, voters in 1816 elected James Monroe as President. Like his Virginia predecessors, he had spent his life serving his country. At age eighteen he was wounded in the Revolutionary War. He later served as Minister to France, Governor of Virginia, Minister to England, and Secretary of State (from 1813 to 1815 he frequently doubled as Secretary of War). Monroe was sixty years old when he became President. Dignified in appearance, cautious in manner, he provided a link with the heroic past. At a time when most men wore trousers, he still dressed in old-fashioned knee breeches and long silk stockings. On ceremonial occasions he wore a faded Revolutionary uniform—a fitting costume for the last Revolutionary veteran in the White House.

As President, Monroe sought to create "a union of parties in support of our republican govern-

ment." His choice of cabinet members reflected this goal: he tried to pick Republicans from every section of the country. The Secretary of State, John Quincy Adams, was a New Englander. Georgian William H. Crawford stayed on in the Treasury Department. Unable to find a Westerner for Secretary of War, he finally picked young John C. Calhoun of South Carolina for the post. William Wirt, a Baltimore lawyer, became Attorney General. Restrained by their loyalty to the President, these political rivals served Monroe well. He also worked hard to gain the confidence of prominent Federalists. Harrison Gray Otis was deeply touched when the "Old Sachem" not only invited him to the White House for dinner, but "drank a glass wine with me to make friends."

In order to demonstrate his desire for national unity, Monroe set out shortly after his election on a tour of the northern and eastern states. Paying his own traveling costs, he followed the seaboard north to Portland, Maine, then headed westward, going as far as Detroit—a three-and-one-half month journey by carriage and steamboat. It was a triumphal procession. Everywhere crowds gathered to honor this "last of the Revolutionary farmers." The high point came at Boston, where over forty thousand turned out to welcome the President. At a public dinner, local Federalists and Republicans sat down together for the first time in years. Monroe's visit, a staunch Federalist editor reported, had established an "Era of Good Feeling." Newspapers throughout the country soon picked up the phrase. For a time, despite bickering on the state and local levels, it seemed appropriate. Overall during this period, aside from the economic crisis of 1819, the country was peaceful and prosperous. In 1820 Monroe was reelected without opposition; only one negative vote in the electoral college prevented his election from being, like Washington's, unanimous. By the end of Monroe's second term, however, acrimonious political differences were beginning to divide the nation along sectional lines.

The Marshall Court

During the years 1819-24, the Supreme Court, in a series of important cases decided under Chief Justice John Marshall, contributed both to the rising nationalism of the era and to the freedom of corporations from state control.

In *Dartmouth College v. Woodward* (1819) the Court ruled that Article I, Section 10, of the Con-

stitution—"no state shall pass any law impairing the obligation of contracts"—protected charters of incorporation from legislative interference. Dartmouth College had been granted a charter in 1769 by King George III. In 1816 the New Hampshire legislature, in an effort to make the college more democratic, tried to replace the self-governing trustees with a board appointed by the governor. The trustees retained Daniel Webster to fight their case. Webster's theatrics ("It is . . . a small college," he plaintively told the Justices, "and yet there are those who love it") proved effective. Dartmouth's charter, wrote Marshall, was a contractual relationship between the Crown and the College. The state of New Hampshire was a continuation of the Crown; the obligations of contract remained unchanged. So long as the trustees did abuse their powers, the state could not interfere without violating the contract clause. Coming at a time when private corporations were rapidly gaining favor in transportation, finance, and manufacturing, this defense of contracts made it more difficult for the states to control corporate activity.

In *McCulloch v. Maryland* (1819) the Court confirmed the broad construction of the Constitution that Alexander Hamilton had defended thirty years before during arguments over the first Bank of the United States. This case dealt with assaults on the second Bank, which through careless management and its favoritism to big business had aroused bitter opposition. Several states, Maryland among them, had placed high taxes on the Bank's branches within their borders. The cashier of the Baltimore branch, James McCulloch, refused to pay the tax and Maryland brought suit. In his opinion, Marshall upheld the constitutionality of the Bank. The creation of such an institution, he admitted, was not among the powers enumerated in the Constitution. But Congress also possessed "incidental or implied powers." He found full authority in Congress' power of the purse for the chartering of a national bank. "Let the end be legitimate," wrote Marshall, "let it be within the scope of the Constitution, and all means which are appropriate, which are plainly adapted to that end, which are not prohibited, but consist [ent] with the letter and spirit of the Constitution, are constitutional." Maryland's tax, which attempted to destroy a lawful agency of the federal government, was therefore unconstitutional: "the power to tax . . . is the power to destroy." States' rights advocates angrily denounced this opinion in favor of an "elastic" construction of the Constitution (and especially of its "necessary and proper" clause). Coming at the same time as the Missouri Controversy, this decision especially alarmed Southerners.

Marshall's opinion, two years later in *Cohens v. Virginia* further distressed states' rights advocates. At issue here was the right of a state to limit appeals to the United States Supreme Court from its own courts. The Cohens had been convicted of selling lottery tickets under a Virginia law that prohibited appeals from such a conviction. Asserting that the case involved a "federal question," they turned to the Supreme Court for relief. Counsel for Virginia denied the Court's right of judicial review, citing state sovereignty. The Chief Justice disagreed. He maintained that Virginia had surrendered some of her sovereignty when she joined the Union. The right of the Supreme Court to review cases involving "federal questions" was absolutely essential if the operation of the Constitution was to be uniform throughout the country. Otherwise, the federal government would be prostrate "at the feet of every state in the Union." With this opinion Marshall solidly fixed the Supreme Court as the final arbiter of all constitutional questions.

Gibbons v. Ogden (1824) was Marshall's last great decision, giving force to the clauses of the Constitution which had empowered Congress "to regulate commerce with foreign nations, and among the several states." Early in the nineteenth century a number of states began awarding monopolies to the operators of the new steamboats. In 1808 New York gave Robert Fulton and Robert Livingston an exclusive right to operate steamboats on the state's waters. It also awarded Aaron Ogden an exclusive franchise to run steamboats on the Hudson River between New York and New Jersey. When Thomas Gibbons began a rival service on this route (the captain of his boat was a young man named Cornelius Vanderbilt), Ogden brought suit to restrain his competitor. When the New York courts upheld the monopoly, Gibbons appealed to the Supreme Court.

Once again Marshall championed federal supremacy. A narrow construction of the Constitution, he declared at the outset, "would cripple the government, and render it unequal to the objects for which it is declared to be instituted, and to which the powers given, as fairly understood, render it competent." New York's law was unconstitutional because it conflicted with a 1793 act of Congress regulating the coastwise trade. Congress' power to regulate commerce, "like all others vested in Congress, is complete in itself, may be exercised to its utmost extent, and acknowledges no limitations, other than those prescribed in the Constitution." For once the public sided with Marshall. New Yorkers, who detested the steamboat monopolies, hailed the Chief Justice's decision. "Yesterday," a newspaper reported, "the steamboat *United States*, Capt. Bunker, from New Haven, entered New York in triumph, with streamers flying, and a large company of passengers exulting in the decision . . . against the New York monopoly. She fired a salute which was loudly returned by huzzas from the wharves." In a few years steamboat navigation spread to lakes and rivers throughout the country. Marshall, however, could not prevent the removal of the Cherokee Indians from Georgia and ducked a case involving the rights of free Negroes. Yet his nationalism ultimately helped to free the slaves. For over thirty years Marshall had argued that the United States was a consolidated nation rather than merely a compact of sovereign states. In 1861, when Abraham Lincoln called for troops, thousands of young men took up arms to defend the Union Marshalls' decisions had done so much to define.

Sectionalism

By 1820 the exuberant nationalism of the postwar years had begun to wear thin. As the memory of war faded and the Republican Party, lacking the discipline of electoral competition, declined as a national organization, the various sections of the country began looking to their own interests. The depression of 1819-22 produced sharp disagreement over the proper role of the federal government in the economy, and the appearance of antislavery sentiment in the North put the South on the defensive. These traditional differences between the older sections were complicated further by the emergence of a new region, the West, as a section with its own special concerns.

Tariff policy soon revealed the changing interests of different parts of the nation. Southerners quickly regretted their support for the Tariff of 1816. The South produced mostly cotton and tobacco for export, obtaining manufactured goods and even food from the North and West. Protective tariffs not only raised the prices Southern planters paid for Northern products, but threatened European retaliation in the form of high duties on Southern exports. The disastrous decline in cotton prices after 1819, which cut the planters' purchasing power, further increased the oppressiveness of the tariff.

In 1820 Southerners in Congress barely defeated a bid to raise import duties again. Four years later they were overwhelmed. Representatives from the manufacturing, grain, and wool states pushed through a bill increasing duties on a wide variety of items. Flushed with victory, protectionists held a grand convention at Harrisburg, Pennsylvania, to map out a campaign for still higher duties. In the 1828 session of Congress Northern protectionists resorted to "logrolling." They persuaded congressmen representing Missouri lead miners, Kentucky hemp raisers, Vermont wool growers, and Louisiana sugar planters to support higher rates on manufactured articles in exchange for protective duties on their own constituents' products. To save themselves, Southerners hit upon the scheme of making the tariff obnoxious to New England manufacturers by increasing the price the New Englanders would have to pay for raw materials. Southern Congressmen would vote with Northern producers to raise the duties on raw materials like wool, flax, and molasses, expecting manufacturing interests to vote with the South against the whole bill. Unfortunately for the South, this stratagem was a bit too clever. New England manufacturers, preferring the higher duties on raw materials to no protection at all, accepted the whole bill, saddling the South with the highest tariff rates between the Revolution and the Civil War.

Angry Southerners damned this "Tariff of Abominations" and threatened to boycott goods from the tariff states. Some began dressing in clothes of homespun rather than Northern broadcloth. Immediately after the tariff bill passed, the South Carolina delegation in Congress met at the home of Senator Robert Y. Hayne to begin plotting resistance. In the fall of 1828 Vice-President John C. Calhoun, bending to the changing opinion in his native state, set to work writing his famous *Exposition and Protest* developing the doctrine of nullification as a defense against the tariff.

Sectional jealousies thwarted plans for a national system of internal improvements. New England, with the country's best-developed road system, had no taste for injuring Boston by building roads connecting rival ports with the Western country. New York and Pennsylvania longed for the national government to construct such routes until, forced to spend large sums on their own roads and canals, their enthusiasm for a national system also waned. Southern support for federal improvements faded even more rapidly.

Such expenditures, increasing the need for revenue, would justify the hated tariff, and federal internal improvements implied a broad construction of the Constitution which could as easily allow the federal government to interfere with slavery.

Only the West consistently demanded a federal system of internal improvements. A shortage of capital and a vast expanse of territory made that section perpetually hungry for government assistance. Several times Congress responded by appropriating funds for Western roads, but a series of presidential vetoes blocked these appropriations, forcing state governments and private corporations in the Northwest to join in financing an extensive network of turnpikes and canals.

The older sections also differed from the West on public land policy. Land sales were a major source of federal revenues and the seaboard states, seeking maximum profits from the national domain, favored high prices. Northern manufacturers also hoped that such prices would discourage their workingmen from going West. Carolina planters feared that their worn-out cotton lands could not compete with the virgin soil of the Southwest.

The West, naturally, hungered for cheap land. Spokesmen like Thomas Hart Benton argued that low prices would encourage "a race of virtuous and independent farmers, the true supporters of their country." These noble freeholders would carry America and its democracy across the continent. On this issue, sectional rivalries worked in the Westerners' favor: the South usually voted for cheap land to gain Western support for its own special interests. In 1820 Congress reduced the minimum purchasable tract from 160 to 80 acres and the minimum price from $2 to $1.25 an acre. An act of 1830 gave special rights to the "squatter" who occupied public land he did not own; he could now purchase "his" tract prior to public sale at the minimum price, regardless of its market value. The potential for control over westward expansion, which federal ownership of Western land made possible, almost vanished. Yet the way West was not without impediments: in the slavery issue, the older sections found a powerful and dangerous ground for debating the nature of the West.

The Revival of Slavery

Slavery had always threatened the most serious divisions of all, yet the ugly sentiments that arose in the debates over the Missouri Controversy in 1819-21 surprised most Americans, who had long assumed that slavery was a dying institution. In the North the ideology of the American Revolution had given new respectability to the antislavery movement. Beginning with Pennsylvania in 1780, the Northern states had provided for the gradual abolition of slavery. In 1787 Congress decided that neither slavery nor involuntary servitude should exist in the vast region of the Northwest Territory. Even in the South, humanitarian sentiments weakened the institution. Virginia and North Carolina passed laws easing the way for slaveholders to free their human property. A Southern President, Thomas Jefferson, urged Congress in 1806 to withdraw American citizens "from all further participation in those violations of human rights which have been so long continued upon the unoffending inhabitants of Africa." Congress responded by prohibiting the African slave trade after 1807.

The South's depressed economy in the years after the American Revolution reinforced the ideological objections to slavery. Soil exhaustion and a glutted world market took its toll on Virginia's and Maryland's tobacco industry. Many planters switched to wheat, a crop that required fewer slaves to cultivate. Indigo, an important slave-grown crop in upland South Carolina and Georgia, ceased to be profitable when Britain withdrew her bounty to producers during the Revolution. Prices for slaves generally declined, and the wartime ban on slave imports continued in most states.

Planters anxiously experimented with new crops, especially cotton. Samuel Crompton's spinning-mule, James Hargreave's spinning-jenny, and Richard Arkwright's spinning-frame and water-frame, as well as other innovations in manufacturing, had dramatically lowered the cost of spinning and weaving cotton fiber into cloth, stimulating a worldwide demand for cotton goods. The appetites of English manufacturers for raw cotton became insatiable. As early as 1786 planters in lowland South Carolina and Georgia began to experiment with growing the silky, long-fibered sea-island cotton. It proved much superior to the short-staple upland variety that had been produced in small quantities for many years. When the cotton bolls were passed between two close-set rollers, the smooth black seeds of the sea-island variety popped right out; the same roller gin crushed the sticky green seeds of the upland variety, making it unmarketable. Unfortunately, sea-island cotton would grow only in the warm, humid lowlands of the coast. Large-scale cotton cultivation awaited a successful process to remove the seeds from upland cotton.

It was a Connecticut Yankee who came to the South's rescue. In 1793 young Eli Whitney, fresh out of Yale and unemployed, came South to work as a tutor. On the way he stopped to see his friend Phineas Miller, the overseer at "Mulberry Grove" near Savannah, the plantation of Catherine Greene, widow of General Nathanael Greene. At her suggestion he turned to inventing a machine to clean upland cotton of its seed. In just six months he had perfected his "absurdly simple contrivance." The cotton was fed into a hopper. A toothed roller caught the fibers of the cotton boll and pulled them through a slotted iron guard, its slits wide enough to admit the teeth and the cotton fibers caught on them, but too narrow to let the seeds through. A revolving brush then swept the cotton from the roller's teeth. One man could operate a small gin; larger ones could operate by horse or water power. Whitney and his friend quickly formed a partnership to manufacture their gins. "It makes the labor fifty times less," the inventor observed proudly, "without throwing any class of people out of business."

Whitney's statement hid a cruel irony. The agricultural depression, by throwing slaves out of work, *might* ultimately have ended slavery. The cotton gin fastened slavery on the South. Rival manufacturers and local artisans quickly copied Whitney's design. Cotton cultivation spread rapidly through upland South Carolina and Georgia. By 1820 the United States was producing 335,000 bales of cotton (a bale weighed about 500 pounds), as opposed to 10,000 bales in 1793. The opening of the rich "Black Belt" of Alabama and Mississippi after the War of 1812 pushed the crop above one million bales by 1835. The cotton boom

BY
HEWLETT & BRIGHT.
SALE OF
VALUABLE
SLAVES,
(On account of departure)

The Owner of the following named and valuable Slaves, being on the eve of departure for Europe, will cause the same to be offered for sale, at the NEW EXCHANGE, corner of St. Louis and Chartres streets, on *Saturday*, May 16, at Twelve o'Clock, *viz.*

1. SARAH, a mulatress, aged 45 years, a good cook and accustomed to house work in general, is an excellent and faithful nurse for sick persons, and in every respect a first rate character.

2. DENNIS, her son, a mulatto, aged 24 years, a first rate cook and steward for a vessel, having been in that capacity for many years on board one of the Mobile packets; is strictly honest, temperate, and a first rate subject.

3. CHOLE, a mulatress, aged 36 years, she is, without exception, one of the most competent servants in the country, a first rate washer and ironer, does up lace, a good cook, and for a bachelor who wishes a house-keeper she would be invaluable; she is also a good ladies' maid, having travelled to the North in that capacity.

4. FANNY, her daughter, a mulatress, aged 16 years, speaks French and English, is a superior hair-dresser, (pupil of Guillac,) a good seamstress and ladies' maid; a first rate character.

5. DANDRIDGE, a mulatoo, aged 26 years, a first rate dining-room servant, a good painter and rough carpenter, and has but few equals for honesty and sobriety.

6. NANCY, his wife, aged about 24 years, a confidential house servant, good seamstress, mantuamaker and tailoress, a good cook, washer and ironer, etc.

7. MARY ANN, her child, a creole, aged 7 years, speaks French and English, is smart, active and intelligent.

8. FANNY or FRANCES, a mulatress, aged 22 years, is a first rate washer and ironer, good cook and house servant, and has an excellent character.

9. EMMA, an orphan, aged 10 or 11 years, speaks French and English, has been in the country 7 years, has been accustomed to waiting on table, sewing etc.; is intelligent and active.

10. FRANK, a mulatto, aged about 32 years speaks French and English, is a first rate hostler and coachman, understands perfectly well the management of horses, and is, in every respect, a first rate character, with the exception that he will occasionally drink, though not an habitual drunkard.

All the above named Slaves are acclimated and excellent subjects; they were purchased by their present vendor many years ago, and will, therefore, be severally warranted against all vices and maladies prescribed by law, save and except FRANK, who is fully guaranteed in every other respect but the one above mentioned.

TERMS—One-half Cash, and the other half in notes at Six months, drawn and endorsed to the satisfaction of the Vendor, with special mortgage on the Slaves until final payment. The Acts of Sale to be passed before WILLIAM BOSWELL, Notary Public, at the expense of the Purchaser.

New-Orleans, May 13, 1835.

PRINTED BY BENJAMIN LEVY.

created an unprecedented demand for slaves. In 1803 South Carolina reopened its foreign slave trade. Before the federal ban went into effect in 1808, nearly forty thousand African forced immigrants had entered Charleston. A thriving trade developed between the older seaboard states like Virginia, which had a surplus of black labor, and the slave-hungry states in the Southwest. Between 1790 and 1820 the slave population of the South more than doubled, from 657,000 to more than 1,509,000. Such a massive growth had to have political repercussions.

The Missouri Controversy

Saturday, February 13, 1819, was a dull day in Washington. The Senate did not meet and the House was occupied with a proposal to reduce the number of officers in the Army. Late in the day the Representatives took up a routine bill for Missouri statehood. Without warning, James Tallmadge, Jr., of New York, offered an amendment to prohibit the further introduction of slavery into Missouri and gradually to emancipate slave children born there. An "interesting and pretty wide debate" on Tallmadge's amendment began at once. For the next two-and-a-half years the question of slavery in Missouri—which Thomas Jefferson likened to "a fire bell in the night"—convulsed Congress.

Prior to 1819 new states had entered the Union without much controversy over slavery. The Northwest Ordinance had prohibited slavery in the territory north of the Ohio River. Most of the area south of the Ohio had been ceded to the federal government by North Carolina and Georgia, with the stipulation that slavery should be permitted. After 1820 new free and slave states were added in equal numbers: Louisiana, Mississippi, and Alabama balanced Ohio, Indiana, and Illinois. In 1819 there were eleven slave and eleven free states.

The admission of Missouri threatened to upset this delicate balance. New Englanders had watched with dismay the march of settlement westward; some hoped to preserve their section's influence by checking the expansion of slavery into new territory. Federalists had long attributed the triumph of the Republican party to "slave representation," charging that the Constitution's "three-fifths" clause gave the slave states a disproportionate influence in national politics. Advocates of the tariff and internal improvements looked increasingly on slaveholders as the opponents of their special interests. Humanitarian opposition to slavery was also stirring throughout the North. If the growth of slavery was to be halted, said a New Hampshire Congressman, it was necessary "to fight the first battle at the water's edge."

Federalist leaders such as Senator Rufus King of New York aimed at reinvigorating their party with an appeal against slavery expansion. They allied with a faction of Northern Republicans under Governor De Witt Clinton of New York, who resented the Southern leadership of the party. Antislavery activists like former Chief Justice John Jay added their support. For a time Congressional politics took on a distinct sectional alignment, pitting North against South as morality, politics, and self-interest intersected after Tallmadge introduced his amendment.

The House passed Tallmadge's amendment during 1819, but the Senate rejected it. Congress adjourned without reaching an agreement, and Missouri remained a territory. A year later, when a bill for Missouri statehood was again introduced in the House, Congressman John W. Taylor of New York offered an amendment excluding slavery from the new state.

The bill, with Taylor's amendment, easily passed the House, where the North had a sizable majority. But once again the Senate said no. Restrictionists branded slavery a "monstrous institution" and accused slaveholders of seeking to turn the country west of the Mississippi into a market for human flesh. Southerners talked openly of disunion if the amendment passed. Missourians threatened to organize a state government without waiting for congressional approval.

At this point a compromise emerged. Massachusetts had agreed to the creation of a new state, Maine, out of her Northern counties, provided Congress acted by March 4, 1820. The free states hoped to admit Maine before the deadline. The Senate decided to tie the admission of Maine and Missouri together. It added to the Maine statehood bill then before Congress a section admitting Missouri without restrictions on slavery. In order to make this bill more acceptable to the Northern-dominated House, Senator Jesse B. Thomas of Illinois offered his famous amendment proibiting slavery "forever" in the rest of the Louisiana Purchase territory north of latitude 36°30′ (the Southern boundary of Missouri). In this form the Maine-Missouri bill went to the House, where, after bitter wrangling, Speaker Henry Clay secured its passage on March 2. On the key question of excluding slavery in Missouri the vote was extremely close—the motion lost by 90 to 87, with four Northern Congressmen absent.

In the summer of 1820 a convention met at St. Louis and drew up a constitution for Missouri. As expected, this document sanctioned slavery. It also required the legislature to pass laws "to prevent free Negroes and mulattoes from coming to, and settling in, this state." In November 1820, when the Missouri constitution went before Congress for approval, Northerners voiced objections to this clause. They pointed out that the United States Constitution stated that "the citizens of each state shall be entitled to all privileges and immunities of citizens in the several states." Free Negroes were recognized as citizens in several Northern states. This clause would prevent them from settling or even traveling in Missouri. This complicated issue of Negro citizenship precipitated another lengthy debate over Missouri's admission to the Union.

Missourians were understandably upset over this latest setback. Whatever the constitutionality of the exclusion clause, they pointed out that several states—North and South—had similar laws. Once again Henry Clay arranged a compromise. He proposed a resolution admitting Missouri on an equal footing with the original states, upon the "Fundamental condition" that the ob-

The House of Representatives, 1821. (Library of Congress.)

jectionable clause should never be construed to authorize the passage of any law denying to the citizens of any state the privileges and immunities to which they were entitled under the Constitution. Congress agreed to this empty resolution in February 1821. Missouri made the meaningless promise and officially entered the Union. The state legislature later violated the agreement by enacting laws in 1825 and in 1847 that barred free Negroes from entering the state.

The protracted Missouri controversy had important repercussions for the South. It helped change many slaveholders from apologists into ardent defenders of slavery. Nor was its impact on the slaves themselves negligible. In the summer of 1822 the white South was shaken by the discovery of an alleged conspiracy led by Denmark Vesey, a free black carpenter who had closely followed the Missouri debates. Supposedly he recruited hundreds of slaves in Charleston, South Carolina, to rise up at midnight, kill the whites, and fire the city. A slave revealed the plot to authorities only a few days before the uprising, and a special court sentenced thirty-five of the conspirators to death. The executions were a public spectacle: at a mass hanging on July 26 several of the condemned twisted in an "agony of strangulation," owing to "some bad arrangement in preparing the ropes—some of which were too long, others not properly adjusted so as to choke effectually the sufferers to death, but so as to give them the power of utterance, whilst their feet could touch the ground . . . "Afterwards, the bodies were left dangling for hours as an example to other blacks.

Slaves and slaveholders everywhere trembled. The court report noted Vesey's careful reading of the Missouri debates. The involvement of so many trusted family servants was especially disturbing to whites. South Carolina Governor Thomas Bennett had often left his family in the care of Rolla, his beloved personal slave. Yet Rolla turned out to be an archconspirator.

Southern lawmakers moved at once to prevent a repetition of the Vesey Conspiracy. They tightened their slave codes and outlawed the distribution of antislavery propaganda. All further discussion of slavery in the United States Congress was firmly resisted. The South Carolina legislature forbade the entry of free blacks into the state. Free black seamen who violated the law were jailed until their ships left port. When the British government protested these detentions and a federal judge ruled the law unconstitutional, the South Carolina Senate defiantly replied that "the duty of the state to guard against insubordination or insurrection" was "paramount to all *laws*, all *treaties*, all *constitutions*. It arises from the supreme and permanent law of nature, the law of self-preservation; and will never by this state be renounced, compromised, controlled or participated with any power whatever." Neighboring states quickly passed similar statutes. Henceforth, the South bristled at every criticism of its "peculiar institution."

Criticism of slavery virtually ceased in the South and proslavery theorists, who had at first labeled slavery a "necessary evil," began in the 1830's to defend it as a "positive good." Blacks, they contended, were too degraded to prosper as freedmen, and the South would be abandoned without black labor to work the cotton fields and rice swamps. Protected by benevolent masters from the burdens of sickness, unemployment, and old age, the slaves were better off than industrial workers in the North or in Europe.

The dramatic events of 1819-22 frightened politicians all over the country. Viewing the growing intransigence of the South on slavery as well as the hardening antislavery feeling in the North, most politicians resolved to mute the slavery issue in the future. For a time they succeeded, in part because the division of the Louisiana Purchase territory into slave and free soil removed the question of slavery expansion from the national political arena for twenty-five years. Beginning in 1846, with the acquisition of new territory, the furious struggle over slavery revived. Just as John Quincy Adams had predicted, the Missouri Controversy turned out to be "a mere preamble—a title-page to a great tragic volume."

The Monroe administration had attempted to drift with the apparently calm current of nationalism that followed the return of peace in 1815. Monroe's every gesture, from the diverse cabinet he selected to the fading Revolutionary War uniform he wore for ceremonial occasions, aimed at continuing the easy flow that an age of peace, an "Era of Good Feeling" seemed to permit. But instead of overcoming the divisiveness of party competition, Monroe found himself presiding over the breakup of the old Republican party. By the 1824 election, four candidates would take the field. Sectional interests tore apart the facade of national unity and the Missouri debates raised the question of the very survival of the Union.

Basically, the then-prevailing belief that political parties were incompatible with a republican government was incorrect. What was needed was not a national political harmony but a legitimate opposition that could offer structured alternatives, an orderly process for change and development that would allow the open expression of all the passions and uncertainties that the rapid alteration of American life called forth. And the belief in a national interest upon which all could agree, a plan of development that would command overall consensus, was also a dream—a dream from the Monroe administration that would make that of its successor, John Quincy Adams, a political nightmare. Needed was the process of logrolling, "pork-barreling" compromise that would give American politics in the nineteenth-and twentieth-century something of a bad name. The Monroe Administration, in domestic politics at least, was a noble failure. In foreign affairs, however, it achieved remarkable success.

John Quincy Adams and American Continentalism

For the United States, the most fortunate part of the Louisiana Purchase was that no one knew its exact boundaries. When Robert Livingston, one of the American negotiators, pressed the French minister Talleyrand on this point, he replied: "I can give you no direction; you have made a noble bargain for yourselves, and I suppose you will make the most of it." John Quincy Adams, President Monroe's Secretary of State, did just that. In important boundary treaties Adams expanded America's frontiers to continental dimensions.

Few men have been better equipped to guide American diplomacy than John Quincy Adams. In 1778, at age eleven, he accompanied his father, John Adams, to France. By the time he was thirty he had served as American minister to the Netherlands and to Prussia. Then, in 1801, Massachusetts elected him to the United States Senate as a Federalist. To the distress of his party, however, Adams proceeded to side frequently with the rival Jeffersonians. When he voted for the hated Embargo, the Federalist-dominated state legislature evicted the "scoundrel" from his seat. Under President Madison he acted as American minister to Russia and to England, and helped negotiate the Treaty of Ghent. In 1817 Monroe named him Secretary of State.

Adams took great pride in his country's military and diplomatic victories during these years. He firmly believed that both Providence and the law of nature had intended "our proper dominion to be the continent of North America." It was our national mission to expand westward to the Pacific and north and south as well. Adams developed a strong dislike for European colonialism, with its commercial monopolies and its pretentious claims to "fragments of territory . . . fifteen hundred miles beyond sea, worthless and burdensome to their owners. . . ."As Secretary of State, Adams deliberately sought to assist Providence in creating an "American Continental Empire."

Adams first had to settle quarrels with England. Controversy lingered over both the northwest boundary and the American right to fish the rich banks of Newfoundland and Labrador. The treaty of 1783 had described the boundary line as running from the northwesternmost point of the Lake of the Woods due west to the Mississippi River—an impossible line, since the Mississippi actually rose 150 miles south of the Lake of the Woods. The Louisiana Purchase had compounded the error by creating a northern boundary running all the way to the Rocky Mountains. Britain had repeatedly sought to set the boundary far enough south to gain access for itself to the Mississippi.

Trouble was brewing as well in the Pacific Northwest. Captain Robert Gray had first claimed the Oregon country for the United States in 1792, when he discovered the Columbia River. The explorations of Lewis and Clark had fired American interest in the area; John Jacob Astor's company established a fur-trading post there in 1811. Unfortunately, the United States, Great Britain, Spain, and Russia each had claims in this region. During the War of 1812 British forces had seized Astor's post, which they renamed Fort George. Britain retained this fort until 1818, when Lord Castlereagh, the Foreign Secretary, ordered it returned to the United States.

Castlereagh intended this conciliatory gesture as a first step in an Anglo-American reconciliation. Britain was absorbed by events in Europe and dared not risk a further quarrel with the United States. Moreover, the War of 1812 had shown clearly Canada's dangerously exposed position—only American military blundering had saved it. Canada had become a "hostage" for Anglo-American peace. Castlereagh next invited the United States to send commissioners to London for the purpose of settling all the differences between the two countries. At these negotiations the American envoys, acting under Adams' instructions, secured important gains for the United

States. The Treaty of 1818—which one expert has called the most important treaty in the history of Canadian-American relations—granted Americans permanent rights to fish the coasts of Newfoundland and Labrador. On the northwest boundary the United States refused to budge, and Britain agreed to draw it at 49° north latitude (approximately the line of 1783) as far as the Rocky Mountains. Adams' stubbornness had saved for the United States a strip of land containing the rich Mesabi iron range of Northern Michigan and Minnesota. West of the Rockies, however, neither side would yield its claim. As a stopgap, they agreed to joint occupation of the Oregon country, a compromise that lasted until the 1840's.

Adams inherited an even more complicated set of problems with Spain. The Spanish government had never accepted the American claim that West Florida was part of the Louisiana Purchase, nor had the border between Louisiana and Texas ever been determined, although the United States asserted a dubious claim to the Rio Grande as the dividing line. Beyond Texas, the western boundary of the Louisiana Purchase remained undefined. Spain still hoped to salvage part of this vast area, and to retain its claim to the Oregon country.

The biggest dispute concerned East Florida (the present state of Florida). The United States had tried for years to acquire this strategic area, which stood out on the map like a pistol, pointing at New Orleans, the vital outlet for the Mississippi River. Spain steadfastly refused to part with Florida; yet Spanish authorities there were too weak either to curb the repeated raids by Florida Indians into Georgia and Alabama or to return fugitive slaves. Spain's grasp on the peninsula steadily loosened after the War of 1812. The Napoleonic conflict in Europe and revolutions in Spanish America had exhausted its strength. Privateers and pirates sailed forth from Amelia Island (near Jacksonville) to prey on passing ships. When President Monroe ordered American forces to occupy Amelia Island, Spain in 1817 decided to offer Florida to the United States in return for a favorable boundary west of the Mississippi and an American pledge not to recognize the revolted provinces of Spanish America.

The two sides were still far apart in negotiations at Washington when General Jackson took matters into his own hands. "Old Hickory" had been sent to the Florida frontier with orders to adopt all "necessary measures" to halt Indian raids into American territory. Jackson, interpreting his orders broadly, advanced into Florida in 1818 with three thousand soldiers, routed the Indians, and seized the towns of St. Marks and Pensacola. For good measure, he tried and executed two British subjects who had been inciting the Indians. Jackson's actions embarrassed the Monroe administration; several cabinet members urged the President to disavow the General and to restore the occupied areas to Spain at once. But Adams defended Jackson's conduct on grounds of necessity and urged that the occupation of the towns continue until Spain sent a force sufficient to pacify the Indians. Monroe agreed, and Spain received an ultimatum: either place a force in Florida adequate to maintain order or cede it to the United States.

These bold strokes moved the negotiations off dead center. After weeks of hard bargaining the two sides reached agreement. By the terms of the treaty of 1819, Spain ceded Florida to the United States. Each side renounced all damage claims against the other, and the United States agreed to assume the claims of its citizens against Spain to a total of $5 million. Nothing was said about the recognition of the rebellious Spanish colonies. In return for fixing the Texas boundary at the Sabine River, Adams secured a magnificent transcontinental settlement from Spain, including title to all Spanish territory north of latitude 42° between the Continental Divide and the Pacific Ocean. Adams reckoned that the four nay votes on the treaty in the Senate included two Clay men, one enemy of Jackson, and one suffering from "some maggot in his brain." With this treaty Adams had at last achieved his "Continental Empire," and a place in history as America's foremost Secretary of State.

The Monroe Doctrine

The boldest assertion of American nationalism in this period came from President James Monroe. His annual message in December 1823 laid down two important principles: (1) that "the American continents, by the free and independent condition which they have assumed and maintain, are henceforth not to be considered as subjects for future colonization by any European power"; (2) that the United States would consider any attempt by the European powers "to extend their political system to any portion of this hemisphere as dangerous to our peace and safety." In later years these two maxims, known as "non-colonization" and "non-interference," came to be called together the Monroe doctrine. No other presidential statement, with the possible exception of Washington's Farewell Address, has won such universal acceptance from the American people. On the hundredth anniversary of Monroe's message, Mary Baker Eddy spoke for millions when she said: "I believe in the Monroe Doctrine, in our Constitution, and in the laws of God."

The principles expounded by Monroe in 1823 were not original. Americans had long believed in the sanctity of the two hemispheres. From the first they had sought refuge in the New World in order to escape the Old. Out of the Revolutionary experience inevitably flowed the belief that the nations of the New World, particularly the United States, should isolate themselves from the alliances, the quarrels, and the colonizing schemes of the European powers. Washington gave this idea its classic expression in his Farewell Address, and Jefferson echoed it in his warning against subordinating our affairs to Europe. Monroe and his Secretary of State John Quincy Adams, faced with specific challenges, shaped these broad beliefs into an official statement.

The Secretary of State had for years sought an excuse to forbid further European colonization in the Western Hemisphere. Russia unexpectedly gave him the opportunity. Russian explorers had long before laid claim to the northwest coast of America. By 1812 the Russian-American Company had extended its trading operations southward within only a few miles of San Francisco. Suddenly, in 1821, Czar Alexander I issued an imperial decree conferring upon this company exclusive trading rights down to 51° north latitude and forbidding all foreign vessels to come near the coast. The American government responded vigorously. In July 1823 Adams flatly told the Russian minister at Washington that the United States would assert the principle "that the American continents are no longer subjects for *any* new European colonial establishments." Here was the genesis of the Monroe Doctrine; the President inserted almost these very words into his annual message six months later.

Non-interference attacked a more fundamental European threat to American interests. In 1815 at the Congress of Vienna, the victors over Napoleon—Russia, Prussia, Austria, and England—joined in a Quadruple Alliance to crush the spirit of revolution forever. They restored the Bourbon dynasty to the French throne and agreed to meet again whenever liberalism threatened European

"repose and prosperity." In the summer of 1823, the statesmen of the Alliance (from which Britain had now withdrawn) began to talk of sending French troops to assist Spain in recovering her lost American colonies.

Spain's colonies had been struggling for independence since 1808. When Spain tried to regain her American provinces by force, full-scale war broke out. For six years, beginning in 1814, the revolutionists, led by Simon Bolivar and José San Martin, liberated one colony after another. The United States sympathized with these heroic struggles and granted belligerent status to the revolted colonies, enabling them to buy supplies in this country. But Monroe, and especially Adams, hesitated to recognize the new revolutionary governments until Britain did. The British government twice refused American invitations to do this jointly. Finally, the United States decided to go it alone, extending formal recognition in 1822 to Mexico, Colombia, Chile, Peru, and the Provinces of Rio de la Plata (Argentina). Having taken this bold step, the Monroe Administration was naturally alarmed at the prospect of intervention by the Quadruple Alliance.

Great Britain shared this concern, for the Spanish-American revolts had opened a whole continent to British trade. When rumors of possible intervention by the Continental powers reached George Canning, its Foreign Secretary, in 1823, he decided to seek American cooperation in opposing such a scheme. Canning proposed a treaty or exchange of notes between the two countries expressing joint opposition to any attempt to restore Spain's lost colonies by force; he still refused, however, to agree to immediate British recognition of the former colonies.

Monroe almost accepted Canning's offer. Former Presidents Jefferson and Madison both advised acceptance, as did all the cabinet—except the Secretary of State. "It would be more candid as well as more dignified," Adams argued, "to avow our principles explicitly . . . , than to come in as a cock-boat in the wake of the British man-of-war." At this point in 1823 Monroe drafted the famous declaration in his annual message opposing further intervention by the European powers in the Western Hamisphere. At Adams' insistence, Monroe inserted a statement disavowing American interference "in the wars of the European powers in matters relating to themselves." Here was a vigorous reaffirmation of the two hemispheres principle.

Americans cheered the President's message. The young republic's challenge to the "crowned conspirators" of Europe, boasted one newspaper editor, would be read with "a revolting stare of astonishment.'' Latin Americans at first applauded Monroe's words. But when some of the new states applied to the United States for treaties of alliance or guarantees of assistance against European intervention, the United States government turned them down flat. Adams publicly admitted that it was the power of the British navy that had enabled the United States to throw down its audacious challenge to the Quadruple Alliance.

Europe scoffed at the message, labeling it "blustering," "haughty," "arrogant." It had little effect on the actions of the Continental powers. Russia—a major object of the non-colonization clause—had already decided to limit its territorial claims in North America to the area north of latitude 54°40'. Late in 1823, Canning, tired of waiting for American agreement on a joint statement, had served an ultimatum on France. In reply, the French assured Canning that they had no intention of using force against the former Spanish colonies. By the time Monroe issued his

warning, the immediate danger of interference had already vanished. During the next twenty years Britain and France both violated the Doctrine with impunity. Not until the late nineteenth century, when the United States had become a major power, did the Old World respect the New.

Yet Monroe's message should not be dismissed too lightly. Against an Old World order founded on the doctrine of absolutism, Monroe opposed a new one, founded, at least on the surface, on the right of peoples to determine their own destiny. Only later, by a series of corollaries, did Monroe's successors turn his Doctrine into an instrument for American interference in Latin American affairs. "From a candid but commendable United States gesture against European interference," a Mexican diplomat observed bitterly, "the Doctrine was turned into a ruthless axiom utilized by Washington administrations to suit the interests of . . . *Yankee Imperialism.*' ''

The Election of 1824

From 1796 to 1816, presidential candidates had been nominated by meetings of the congressional members of each of the two parties. In 1820, when President Monroe ran unopposed, the Republicans did not even bother with a caucus nomination. By 1824 that party, lacking an organized opposition, had dissolved into a series of warring factions. President Monroe wisely declined to pick his successor from among the several Republicans battling for the nomination.

The "Old Republicans," so-called because of their devotion to states' rights and economy, pushed William H. Crawford of Georgia as their candidate for President. Crawford is an obscure figure today, but to his contemporaries he was a "plain *giant* of a man." Like many young men of his day, he had parlayed a successful law practice into a distinguished career. He married a wealthy heiress, spent a few years in the state legislature, and then went to Washington as a Senator. Crawford later served as minister to France and Secretary of War, and had, since 1816, been Secretary of the Treasury. He used this last post to pack government offices with his supporters. In 1823, however, just when his position seemed impregnable, a series of strokes left him paralyzed and speechless. As if this were not enough, medical "experts" bled him twenty-three times

within three weeks. Crawford never fully recovered, but his partisans continued to put his name forward. In February 1824 they called a caucus of congressional Republicans, and with only one-third of the eligible members present, nominated Crawford for the Presidency. The other candidates promptly repudiated the caucus as undemocratic, and accused Crawford of trying "to ride into power on 'King Caucus.'" The nomination ruined any chances Crawford may have had.

As an alternative to the congressional caucus, the other candidates accepted nominations from state legislatures and public meetings. A Tennessee newspaper likened the process to a horse race, with each state entering its own "nag." Several New England states endorsed John Quincy Adams, Monroe's capable Secretary of State. South Carolina had supported John C. Calhoun, but he dropped out when Pennsylvania Republicans failed to nominate him. The young Carolinian accepted the vice-presidential spot instead.

Two candidates received strong support in the West. One of these, Henry Clay, had been charting a course toward the White House for a decade. Born in Virginia, he migrated to Kentucky and became a highly successful criminal lawyer—so successful, according to legend, that no person who hired Clay to defend him was ever hanged. After a stint in the state legislature he went on to Congress, a perfect environment then for a man with his quick mind, engaging personality, and fondness for drinking and gambling. In 1811 his colleagues made him Speaker of the House. After the war Clay became a vigorous advocate of internal improvements, a national bank, and a protective tariff. He hoped that this program, which he called the "American System," would, by creating a strong nation free from dependence on Europe, win support in every part of the country. Clay had not anticipated rising sectional jealousies: "I will be opposed," he wrote gloomily before the election, "because I think that the interests of all parts of the Union should be taken care of. . . ."

Clay's rival for the Western vote was Andrew Jackson, a late-comer to the race. Jackson's victories over the Creek Indians at Horseshoe Bend and the British at New Orleans had made him a national hero. His arrogant conduct during the Seminole campaign in 1818 only increased his popularity. In spite of brief terms in both houses of Congress, Old Hickory was not associated in the public mind with the grimy politics of Washington; he was a "plain farmer," his backers claimed, fresh from the people. In the uncertain political atmosphere of the time, his lack of experience in public affairs probably worked to his advantage; he was all things to all men. The public and politicians alike appreciated these qualities, and Jackson's popularity mushroomed in the early twenties. While the other candidates discussed the tariff or internal improvements, the Jackson people, observed John Quincy Adams resentfully, had only to shout "8th of January [the Battle of Horseshoe Bend] and the Battle of New Orleans" to win votes.

When the ballots were counted in November, the Old Hero had received by far the largest popular count—43 percent against 31 percent for Adams, his closest rival. But none of the candidates had a clear majority in the electoral college; there were 99 votes for Jackson, 84 for Adams, 41 for Crawford, and 37 for Clay. Thus, as the Constitution provides, the House of Representatives was required to select the chief executive from among the three men with the largest number of electoral votes. Each state would cast one ballot, determined by majority vote of its delegation.

All eyes were now on Clay, whose fourth-place finish had eliminated him from the contest. His position as Speaker gave him enormous influence in the House, and the managers and friends of the three candidates besieged him with arguments and deals. Clay weighed their words—and his own political fortunes—carefully before making up his mind. He easily eliminated Crawford; the Georgian was physically unfit to assume the burden of the Presidency. He was inclined to dismiss Jackson as a "military chieftain" with no qualifications "for the various, difficult, and complicated duties of the chief magistracy." And the Hero was a dangerous rival for the Western vote; in terms of future political advantage it seemed best to exclude him from the contest. This left John Quincy Adams. The two men had quarreled bitterly in the past, but Adams was unquestionably qualified for the Presidency, and he alone shared Clay's faith in a strong national government. After consulting with friends, Clay threw all his support behind the Secretary of State. By a bare majority, John Quincy Adams was elected President.

At first Jackson took the news of his defeat gracefully. Then came the bombshell: three days after the election Adams announced his intention to appoint Clay as Secretary of State. The cry of "corrupt bargain" went up at once. "So you see," wrote Jackson bitterly, "the *Judas* of the West has closed the contract and will receive the thirty pieces of silver." Had there been a deal? No evidence, then or later, has ever clarified the matter one way or the other. Adams insisted that the Kentuckian was the best man for the job. Clay presumably could have made the same deal with any of the candidates. Politically, however, the appointment was extremely unwise. It drove the Jacksonians and the Calhoun men into immediate opposition, and put the new administration on the defensive. Jackson, heretofore a reluctant candidate, set out for Tennessee in full cry: "The people have been cheated," he charged. ". . . The corruptions and intrigues at Washington [have] defeated the will of the people." The campaign of 1828 was underway before John Quincy Adams settled into the White House.

The Second President Adams

John Quincy Adams, a biographer once remarked with monumental understatement, "was not among America's more lovable figures." By his own description, he was reserved, stubborn, and independent. "It is a question," an observer wondered, "whether he ever laughed in his life."

An English diplomat termed him "a bull-dog among spaniels at the Ghent peace conference." When he was Secretary of State, these personal qualities served Adams well; once he was in the White House, they quickly proved his undoing.

Instead of seeking to overcome his liabilities by building a political machine in the federal bureaucracy and developing a popular program, Adams did precisely the reverse. In the interest of conciliation, he appointed political opponents to his cabinet and retained outspoken critics in government offices instead of making room for his own backers. Above all, he scorned public opinion. The great object of government, Adams believed, was to improve the condition of mankind. It was the President's duty to give direction to the national government, and the people's to follow. Even when proposing a popular measure, he made no effort to dramatize it: instead of a straightforward statement urging Congress to pass a federal bankruptcy law, Adams recommended "the amelioration in some form or modification of the diversified and often oppressive codes relating to insolvency." In 1828 the Jacksonians revived a popular campaign slogan: "John Quincy Adams who can write/ and Andrew Jackson who can fight."

Adams spelled out a nationalistic program for the country. Now that America's independence had been secured and her borders enlarged, he would strengthen the country internally with a nationally planned and financed system of roads and canals, a national university, a naval academy, government-supported astronomical observatories and expeditions to map the country, and a department of the interior to regulate the use of natural resources. He expected to finance this program by selling public lands.

Unfortunately for Adams, it was not the right time for a nationalist in the White House, par-ticularly one lacking the political skill to rally support. Westerners wanted free public land, not sales at high prices to raise revenue. Southerners increasingly feared that a powerful federal government would interfere with slavery. The Old Republicans accused the President of trying to revive the Federalist policies of his father. "The cub," John Randolph remarked, "is a greater bear than the old one." The Jacksonian press demolished Adams' proposals: his reference to astronomical observatories as "light-houses of the skies" became a national joke. The Congress rejected every one of the President's recommendations.

At every turn, Adams' sense of integrity and his belief in national authority landed him in trouble. In 1825 he refused to enforce a fraudulent treaty dispossessing the Creek Indians of their tribal lands in Georgia. Governor George Troup of Georgia, anxious to open these rich cotton lands to settlement, sent surveyors into the Indian country anyway. A confrontation between the United States and Georgia threatened. In the end a new treaty averted a clash: the Creeks agreed to cede all their lands and move West. Adams' stand had been honorable, but unpopular. Southerners condemned his challenge to state sovereignty; Westerners objected to his defense of the Indians.

The failure of John Quincy Adams' domestic program had profound consequences for the country. A vast system of roads and canals, coming at a time when the forces of sectionalism were gaining strength, might have tied the nation together and prevented the disintegration of the Union. Instead, as Adams predicted, "the clanking chain of the slave" was riveted "into perpetuity" and "the invaluable inheritance of the public lands" was wasted "in boundless bribery to the West."

The Panama Congress

Adams' chief initiative in foreign policy proved equally unsuccessful. In 1824, Simon Bolivar, the "Liberator" of Spanish America, proposed a conference to be held in Panama. He hoped to tie the former Spanish colonies into a confederation to protect the hemisphere against Europe's Quadruple Alliance. Mexico and Colombia, rebuffed in earlier efforts to obtain individual treaties of alliance with the United States, added the Republic of the North to the list of participants.

All hoped to "Pan-Americanize" the Monroe Doctrine by bringing the North Americans into a hemispheric alliance. Their invitations reached Washington early in 1825, just as John Quincy Adams was entering the White House.

Secretary of State Henry Clay welcomed the idea of an inter-American conference. He had ardently supported the cause of Latin American independence. Clay envisioned an "American System" of republics, led by the United States, standing firm against the despotism of the Old World. Adams himself, as Monroe's Secretary of State, had rejected all proposals for collective security with the Latin American republics. At Clay's urging, however, he asked Congress to confirm the appointment of two delegates to the Panama meeting. Now was the time, he decided, to extend "the most cordial feelings of fraternal friendship" to our sister republics. In doing this, Adams hoped to advance fundamental American principles of commercial reciprocity, neutral rights, freedom of the seas, and non-colonization throughout the hemisphere.

Adams' request met unexpected opposition in Congress. The emerging Democrats—led by Vice-President Calhoun and supporters of Andrew Jackson—vigorously attacked the administration. They accused Adams and Clay of seeking to bind the United States to a hemispheric alliance, in plain violation of President Washington's warning against foreign entanglements. Opposition Senators bombarded the President with questions and requests for additional documents. The debates soon turned ugly. At one point John Randolph of Roanoke insinuated that Clay had procured the American invitation to further his own interests: "This Panama mission is a Kentucky cuckoo's egg, laid in a Spanish-American nest," he told the Senate. The hot-tempered Clay immediately challenged the Virginian to a duel. Americans were soon treated to the spectacle of the Secretary of State defending the administration's honor with a gun (no one was hurt).

Southerners had a deeper objection to the Panama meeting. Delegates from Haiti were expected at the conference, and the question of recognizing the black republic might arise. Recognition of Haiti, warned a Georgia Senator, would "strengthen and invigorate" the determination of these black revolutionaries, whose hands still reeked "in the blood" of their murdered masters, "to spread the doctrines of insurrection" to America.

Adams stubbornly defended his proposal. Times and circumstances, he argued, had changed since Washington's day; the United States had trebled its territory, population, and wealth; it was time to broaden our horizons. After months of debate and delay, Congress finally approved the President's choice of delegates and appropriated funds for the mission. Adams had scored a major triumph—the only one of his Presidency.

It proved to be an empty victory, however. One of the American delegates died on his way to the conference; the other arrived too late. The meeting itself was a fiasco. Only four Latin American nations sent representatives. They signed a treaty of mutual defense and alliance, and quickly adjourned from fever-ridden Panama City, planning to meet again in Mexico early in 1827. By that time, however, Bolivar had lost interest in the idea of a hemispheric confederation, and the Congress never reconvened.

The Panama Congress benefited no one, except perhaps Great Britain. The British government, anxious to deflate Latin American enthusiasm for the Monroe Doctrine, sent an observer to Panama. In the absence of any American spokesman, the British agent had no trouble sowing distrust of the United States among the delegates. At home, the issue of Haiti reopened the bitter sectional controversy that had flared in the debates over the Missouri Compromise; Southerners once again envisioned threats of the federal government moving against their "peculiar institution." Adams' proposal gave his political enemies their first opportunity to attack the President and his Secretary of State. Once again John Quincy Adams was ahead of his time; the American people in 1826 were looking West, not South. Not for another fifty years would Americans take an interest in the concept of Pan-Americanism.

His administration a failure in both domestic and foreign affairs, Adams gave up all hope of reelection. His subsequent career, however, was unique among American presidents: he served several terms in the House of Representatives, where he was a model of integrity and defended the right of petition—challenged by representatives from the South—with an eloquence that he had rarely shown when President.

Suggested Readings

The classic work on the United States of this day is Alexis de Tocqueville's *Democracy in America* (1832). Although a French nobleman, Tocqueville is prepared to view the growth of popular institutions sympathetically. He defined a clash between free and strong individuality, which he believed was nurtured in a civilization of class distinctions, and a democratic tendency to submerge individuality within mass public opinion; he found that special conditions in this country made for a reconciliation of liberty and democracy. The heart of Bray Hammond's *Banks and Politics in America from the Revolution to the Civil War* (1957) is his section on the Jacksonian assault on the Second Bank of the United States. He argues for the importance of the Bank and Biddle as necessary for controlling credit and dismisses Jackson as irresponsible. The *History of the Westward Movement* (1978) by Frederick W. Merk is encyclopedic; Ray Allen Billington's *Westward Expansion* (rev. 1974) is more readable.

Thomas Sully's Portrait of Andrew Jackson.

Chapter IX
Jacksonian America
1824—1840

Andrew Jackson's Inaugural

Washington, D.C., was a cheerless place in the winter of 1828-29 after Jackson's presidential victory. Even the victors were gloomy: Rachel, the President's wife, had just died, and with their leader in mourning, Democrats avoided too boisterous a display of pleasure over their triumph. The weather was dreadful as well: "snow storm after snow storm—the river frozen up, and the poor suffering the extremity of cold and hunger," wrote Margaret Bayard Smith, a resident who has left us the most vivid account of Washington in the winter of Jackson's inauguration.

One Washingtonian suggested in a letter to the local newspaper that the inaugural ball "be made a means of producing a fund for the relief of the poor [by] dispensing with the usual decorations and expensive accompaniments of such a fete." This suggestion was ignored, although in response to cases of people freezing to death, Congress did authorize giving fifty cords of wood to the poor.

Jackson decreed a sober and dignified inauguration: he would have no military parades, no pre-inaugural festivities. Like Jefferson, he would walk to the Capitol to take the oath, then proceed to the White House on horseback. Margaret Smith approved Jackson's "avoidance of all parade—it is *true* greatness, which needs not the aid of ornament and pomp," but wished that "the good old gentleman might indulge himself with a carriage." Nevertheless, thousands of people of every class and from every section of the country flooded into the Capitol to witness the inauguration of the "people's President."

The sun finally shone on March 4th, and tens of thousands of citizens gathered for the oath-taking. The spectacle reflected the fondest hope's of ardent Democrats. People "without distinction of rank" stood "silent, orderly and tranquil" to glimpse Jackson—who could be picked out from the crowd around him because he alone wore no hat—a servant of the sovereign people:

"There, there, that is he," exclaimed different voices. "Which?" asked others. "He with the white head," was the reply. "Ah," exclaimed others, "there is the old man and his gray hair, there is the old veteran, there is Jackson."

Jackson, in a low voice that only a handful of the massed thousands could have heard, delivered his inaugural address, which John Quincy Adams described as "short, written with some eloquence, and remarkable chiefly for a significant threat of reform." Then, in a scramble of people that reminded contemporary ladies and gentlemen of the mobs of the French Revolution, but which to a modern observer would seem reasonably orderly, farmers, politicians, women, children, carts, wagons, horses, and carriages followed the silver-haired hero down Pennsylvania Avenue to the White House. Once there they jammed inside hoping to pump the President's hand and share his offering of ice cream, cake, lemonade, and orange punch which had been intended only for the "eligible" social elite of Washington.

It was a physical impossibility—like entertaining a regiment in one's living room with no officers, no marshals, not even signs saying "entrance" and "exit." Ladies fainted from the press; in the grab for refreshments glasses and china broke, people's clothing ripped, fights broke out; strong men had to cordon off the frail President to prevent injury by exuberant well-wishers. Jackson escaped by a back door, and some practical person suggested exiting by the windows. Alert servants began carrying tubs of punch onto the lawn to thin the crowd inside the house. The event passed off with nothing worse than mudprints on the furniture (anything to catch a glimpse of Old Hickory) and broken plates and cups. It was not a party one would want to repeat, but neither was it the first scene of a social revolution.

Clearly the product of happenstance, of poor planning, the White House party spoke as much of the American populace's instinctive good-natured sense of order as it did of their new sense that the White House and the President belonged at last to them. While several aristocratically inclined observers saw the reign of "King Mob" in the inauguration, the *Washington National Intelligencer* commented editorially on the general good order of the crowds:

What particularly gratifies us, and does credit to the character of our people, is, that, amidst all the excitement and bustle of the occasion, the whole day and night of the Inauguration passed off without the slightest interruption of the public peace and order, that we have heard of. At the mansion of the President, the Sovereign People were a little uproarious, but it was in any thing but a malicious spirit.

A new, but not a revolutionary, political age had begun.

The Election of 1828

The election of 1828 was a landmark in American politics. For the first time in nearly twenty years two vigorous parties contested for the Presidency. Responding to this stimulus, the voters turned out in unprecedented numbers to elect Andrew Jackson President of the United States.

When the House of Representatives chose John Quincy Adams over Jackson in 1824, it had ignited a new era of partisan politics. During the next four years the elements of a second party system began to form. The followers of Adams and Clay and their nationalistic policies began to call themselves National Republicans; their opponents kept the name Democratic Republicans (soon shortened to Democrats).

This new two-party system rested, in part, upon long-term developments: the gradual removal of suffrage restrictions, the move in most states toward popular election of public officials and presidential electors (rather than election by state legislatures); and the growing acceptance of the legitimacy of party organizations. In addition to these legal and constitutional trends, the election of 1824 produced in Andrew Jackson the type of charismatic figure who could capture the public's imagination and infuse new glamour into national politics. Shortly after his defeat in 1824, Jackson began his second crusade for the Presidency. In alliance with a highly skilled political manager, Senator Martin Van Buren of New York, he created a new political party.

The Democratic Party fed off the Adams administration's unpopularity. At its core were the original Jackson men, those who had supported him in 1824. These included voters in every part of the country except New England, and opportunistic politicians eager to profit from this enthusiasm for the "Old Hero." They were joined after the election by the followers of John C. Calhoun, whose path to the White House had been short-circuited by the Adams-Clay alliance. Between 1826 and 1828, Van Buren brought the Southern "Old Republicans," who had formerly supported Crawford, into the party as well. United in their opposition to Adams' and Clay's nationalism, the new coalition worked in Congress to block the administration's programs.

While the Jacksonians maneuvered in Congress, they also began to build the necessary organization to boost "Old Hickory" into the White House. Because most states had adopted the system of statewide tickets of presidential electors that gave all the state's electoral votes to the winner in the popular vote (the system still in use today), there was a need for state party machinery that could mobilize voters throughout each state. Van Buren organized the Democratic Party from the top down, with central committees in Washington and Nashville. The committees worked closely with influential state leaders, who in turn organized "Hickory Clubs" at the local level. A string of pro-Jackson newspapers miraculously appeared across the country. Jackson remained at home in Tennessee, posing as the innocent victim of a "corrupt bargain." Yet he personally supervised every detail of the campaign. In order to hold together his fragile coalition, he avoided taking a stand on the issues. When asked for his position on the tariff, Jackson replied ambiguously that he favored a "middle and just course." After Van Buren quoted Jackson's tariff stand at a New York rally, one man in the audience cheered the remark and than asked his neighbor: "On which side of the tariff question was it?" Meantime, Adams steadfastly refused to electioneer in his own behalf. Too late, his friends tried to erect an organization similar to the Democrats'.

In 1828, as in 1824, more was made of personalities than of issues. The campaign itself was unbelievably dirty. No charge seemed too base. Jackson was portrayed as the son of a prostitute, a frontier ruffian, and a gambler. A "coffin handbill" charged the General with the cold-blooded murder of six militiamen during the Creek Campaign of 1814. A rhymester wrote:

All six militia men were shot;
And O! it seems to me
A dreadful deed—a bloody act
of needless cruelty.

Indignant Jacksonians replied that the six were deserters who had been executed after a proper court-martial.

Not even Jackson's wife, Rachel, was spared. The two had met while Rachel was separated from her first husband. In 1791, believing that her husband had obtained a divorce, she married Jackson. Not until some time later did the couple learn that the divorce had not become final. The earlier marriage was formally dissolved in September 1793, after which Rachel and Andrew recited their wedding vows a second time. Rumors of this technical adultery circulated for years. During the campaign a Cincinnati newspaper published the story. "Ought a convicted adultress and her paramour husband to be placed in the highest offices of this free and christian land?" fumed the editor. When his beloved Rachel, sick and shamed by the ugly publicity, died suddenly in December 1828, Jackson blamed his political opponents. "May God Almighty forgive her murderers," he cried at her funeral, "as I know she forgave them. I never can."

The Jacksonians countered with some mudslinging of their own. President Adams was accused of having, while Minister to Russia, procured an American girl for Czar Alexander I. Adams' wife was reported to have had premarital relations with her husband. Stories of the President's "aristocratic" receptions at the White House and his use of public funds to buy "gambling devices" (actually a chess set and a billiard table) circulated widely. The puritanical Adams was so offended by

these stories that he refused to attend his successor's inauguration.

Jackson's victory in November was a triumph for the Democrats and their fresh style of political appeal. The new techniques and the Old Hero struck deep chords in the American public. Over three times as many voters turned out as in 1824. The General received fifty-six percent of the popular vote, a margin unequaled in any other presidential election during the nineteenth century. He swept the South and West, a reflection of his sectional appeal, his own status as a slaveholder, and his supposed affinity for the Jeffersonian doctrine of limited national authority. Adams carried his native New England, Delaware, and New Jersey, and shared New York and Maryland with his rival. Exuberant Jacksonians hailed the election results as a revolution, a triumph of "democracy" over "aristocracy." The following January, after burying his wife, a broken-hearted Andrew Jackson set out for Washington.

The "Rise" of the Common Man

For years history books uncritically accepted the idea that popular democracy arrived with Jackson's election. They pictured him as the champion of frontier democracy, fearlessly battling the forces of privilege, corruption, and oppression. During his Presidency the common man won the right to vote and took politics out of the hands of the elite. Socially and economically, too, the Jacksonian Era supposedly saw the emergence of an unprecedented equality. With Jackson's election, wrote one historian, "a new day dawned in American history. The democratic philosophy of Thomas Jefferson became a reality."

Recent studies have substantially modified this view. Historians now realize that the common man had been rising politically for decades. Even in colonial times, the franchise was surprisingly open in some places. The Revolutionary ideology and the fierce political contests of the Jeffersonian Era had opened still wider the door to popular participation in politics. When the new states in the West joined the Union, they adopted constitutions that gave the vote to all adult white males and made most public offices elective. The older states, concerned about the loss of population to the West, generally followed their example. By Jackson's time there were only two states, Delaware and South Carolina, in which the legislature made the choice of presidential electors rather

than the people. The most notable political innovation of the Jackson period, the national convention, was invented not by the Democrats, but by the Antimasonic Party, a short-lived anti-Jackson party opposing the fraternal order of Freemasonry (Jackson was a Mason). The Jacksonians recognized the potential of this broader electorate and developed new techniques to arouse the voters, many of whom had not bothered previously to go to the polls.

Although foreigners like Alexis de Tocqueville considered Jacksonian America remarkably egalitarian, modern historians have painted a less glowing picture. Two million blacks were held as slaves—pieces of property like their owners' livestock and farm implements. For most women, free blacks, Irish-Catholic immigrants, and many others, social and economic equality were mere catchwords. Such important economic developments as the rise of the factory system and the transportation revolution, were not affected much at all by Jackson's Presidency. The most careful studies of social mobility in the era indicate an increasingly less egalitarian society, with urban elites growing in wealth while industrialism and mass immigration created new lower classes.

And yet people at the time sincerely believed that Jackson's eminence was linked to the "rise of the common man." In part, this stemmed from his extraordinary popularity as a military hero and his forceful personality. More important, he was a man with whom millions of Americans—for diverse and often conflicting reasons—could readily identify. To some, he epitomized the egalitarian spirit of America: he was a child of the frontier, self-made, independent, and democratic. They gloried in his success and hoped to follow in his footsteps. To others, yearning for a return to a simpler agrarian society, Jackson, with "his chivalric character, his lofty integrity, and his ardent patriotism," seemed to embody the ideals of a bygone era. As a big loser in the Panic of 1819, he appealed to hard-pressed debtors in the West and South. As an advocate of laissez-faire economics, he attracted support from budding entrepreneurs and Eastern workingmen alike. In a time of stress and change, the sources of Jackson's support were as complex as the man himself.

Jackson had been born in the Waxhaws, a wooded frontier area on the North and South Carolina border, in 1767. He lost both brothers and his widowed mother during the Revolution, in which young Andrew served briefly as a horseman. For a time he seemed destined to be "the most roaring, rollicking, game-cocking, horse-racing, card-playing, mischievous fellow" in the neighborhood until, fired with ambition, he began reading law. In 1788, after completing his studies, he moved to Tennessee to take a position as public prosecutor.

This developing country was the ideal place for an eager young attorney. He speculated avidly in land, slaves, and horses. As a public prosecutor, he usually sided with the creditors, executing numerous writs against debtors. In 1796 he was elected to Congress from Tennessee. Albert Gallatin remembered him as "a tall, lanky, uncouth-looking personage . . . [hair] down his back tied with an eel skin. . . . manners of a rough backwoodsman." After three years in Washington he returned to Tennessee, where he served as a superior court judge, once again siding with the land barons. He acquired a fine plantation, the "Hermitage," near Nashville, and many slaves. Although success had polished his rough edges, Jackson never lost his "roaring, rollicking" character; he was wounded three times in duels.

During the War of 1812 Jackson, already an experienced Indian fighter, led a victorious campaign against the Creeks in Alabama. When the theater of war shifted South in 1814, the desperate politicians at Washington called Jackson to save New Orleans. His famous victory over "the conquerors of Europe" electrified the country. He was America's savior, its greatest hero since George Washington. His rough handling of the Florida Indians and their British allies in 1818 was wildly popular in rural America.

Jackson lost heavily in the Panic of 1819. In its wake a group of his wealthy friends, alarmed by the growing demand for debtor-relief in Tennessee, decided to use Jackson's immense popularity to protect their assets. They began touting him as the "people's candidate" for President—a strange title for a man who had recently brought suit against 129 persons who owed him money. Nevertheless, his candidacy caught fire. Once again, what people believed about Jackson was more important than the facts. And no one understood this better than Jackson as he campaigned for the presidency in 1828.

As President, Jackson generally endorsed and supported the democratic trends of the day. He had a Westerner's inherent distrust of entrenched status and big government. As a self-made man himself, he believed in equality of opportunity and refused to dismiss men on account of low birth or poor education. He had great faith in the average man's intuitive judgment and good sense. More than any President before him, Jackson regarded himself as a man of the people, familiar with their problems and sympathetic to their aspirations.

Jackson began at once to put his principles into practice. Arriving in Washington, he found the government offices filled with entrenched bureaucrats, many of them supporters of the men who had slandered his beloved Rachel. As an astute politician, Jackson recognized the value of rewarding one's partisans with government jobs. He agreed with his New York lieutenant, William Marcy, that "to the victors belong the spoils." Moreover, Jackson firmly believed that no man had "any more intrinsic right to official station than another." Men who held office too long were "apt to acquire a habit of looking with indifference upon the public interests, and of tolerating conduct from which an unpracticed man would revolt." In his first annual message, he therefore recommended that appointments be limited to four years. Congress balked, but Jackson "rotated" officeholders anyway, insisting that: "The duties of all public officers are, or at least admit of being made, so plain and simple that men of intelligence may readily qualify themselves for their performance." In eight years Jackson replaced about twenty percent of the government's employees, sometimes with due cause. Jefferson had removed roughly the same proportion. But it was the Jacksonians, with their spirited defense of the common man, who fixed the spoils system and rotation in office firmly upon American politics.

Van Buren vs. Calhoun

The coalition that elected Andrew Jackson in 1828 was too broad and diverse to be stable. Immediately after the election a struggle broke out between two of its key figures, Martin Van Buren and John C. Calhoun. The clash between these two intensely ambitious men was inevitable. Usually dressed in black, Calhoun, with his great eyes glowing, looked as though his face were consumed by inner-fires. Having already suffered one setback in his quest for the White House, he accepted another term as Vice-President in 1828 with the firm expectation of succeeding Jackson as President.

Calhoun met his match in Martin Van Buren. This shrewd New Yorker was one of America's first professional politicians. Starting as a lawyer in his hometown of Kinderhook, Van Buren climbed the political ladder rung by rung: county surrogate, state senator, state attorney general, U.S. Senator. He fashioned a powerful political machine in New York, known as the "Albany Regency," which dispensed patronage, subsidized friendly newspapers, ran campaigns, and set the party line. Van Buren usually worked behind the scenes, wheeling and dealing, trying to mold a consensus toward his own ends. Whenever possible, he avoided controversial commitments. He had managed "to be on circuit" in 1820 when a meeting was called at Albany to endorse the prohibition of slavery in Missouri; he was accompanying "a friend on a visit to the Congressional Cemetery" during a key vote on the tariff in 1827. Enemies considered Van Buren devious, opportunistic, hypocritical; admirers nicknamed him the "Red Fox" and the "Little Magician."

In 1824 Van Buren had led William H. Crawford's unsuccessful presidential campaign. Having been burned once, he determined to pick a winner in 1828. He helped to bring the Old Republicans into the Jackson camp and worked tirelessly for the General's election. To assure New York's pivotal vote, Van Buren resigned his Senate seat to run for governor of New York, thus adding his popular name to the Jackson ticket.

Jackson rewarded Van Buren's efforts by making him Secretary of State. Otherwise, the new Cabinet was undistinguished. Jackson had no intention of calling on it for advice or of allowing powerful figures like Calhoun to undermine his own power. Instead, he relied on an informal circle of political cronies, who came to be called the "Kitchen Cabinet." Besides old Tennessee friends like Major William B. Lewis, who actually roomed at the White House, this group included several newspaper editors and, before long, Van Buren, who took up horsemanship in order to accompany the President on his morning rides.

Calhoun fretted over these signs of Van Buren's growing influence. The Vice-President had hoped to control the Cabinet appointments, and especially to make a South Carolinian Secretary of War. To his dismay, Jackson had appointed another old Tennessee friend, John H. Eaton, to that position. Calhoun was humiliated. To reassert his power, he decided to force Eaton from the Cabinet. An opportunity soon appeared. The Secretary of War had recently married the notorious Peggy O'Neale Timberlake, a Washington tavern-keeper's daughter with a dubious reputation. Eaton had lived with her while she was married to John Timberlake, a Navy officer, and even "pulled wires to send Timberlake to sea." After his death—supposedly by suicide—Eaton married Peggy with Jackson's blessing. Washington society hummed with scandal. An English diplomat described one of Mrs. Eaton's antagonists in the "Ladies' War" as having "worn the enamel off of her teeth by the slander of her tongue." The other Cabinet wives, led by the aristocratic Florida Bonneau Calhoun, refused to receive Peggy socially. All Washington was soon afflicted by this "Eaton malaria," a drawing-room disease.

The President, recalling the slander heaped on his own wife, was sympathetic to the Eatons. "I tell you," roared the old general, "I had rather have live vermin on my back than the tongue of one of these Washington women on my reputation." Jackson had a tendency to personalize issues, to make them death struggles with a hated foe. Calhoun, he announced, was trying "to weaken me . . . and open the way to his preferment on my ruin." He summoned a special Cabinet meeting to examine the evidence, then pronounced Peggy "chaste as a virgin," and demanded that she be treated with respect. When most of the Cabinet refused, further meetings were suspended. Only Van Buren, long a widower, accepted Mrs. Eaton as a respectable lady.

This petty struggle dragged on into 1831. Finally, to break the deadlock, Van Buren and Eaton offered their resignations. This calculated gesture gave Jackson a chance to reorganize his Cabinet. He asked the other Secretaries to resign and replaced them with Jackson loyalists. As a reward, Jackson nominated the faithful Van Buren to be minister to England. But in December, when Congress reconvened, Calhoun plotted revenge. A tie vote in the Senate allowed him, as Vice-President, to cast the deciding vote, and he gleefully spiked Van Buren's nomination. "It will kill him dead, sir, kill him dead," Calhoun gloated. "He will never kick, sir, never kick." But others agreed with Missouri Senator Thomas Hart Benton, who replied, "You have broken a minister, and elected a Vice-President."

Benton was right. The breach between Jackson and Calhoun widened steadily. The President had suspected for some time that it was Calhoun who had urged Monroe's Cabinet in 1818 to censure Jackson's Florida raid. During the Peggy Eaton controversy Calhoun's old enemy, William H. Crawford, provided proof. Hastily, the Vice-President published a pamphlet defending his stand and disclosing the feuds within the Administration. When Jackson saw it, his well-known temper flared: "They have cut their own throats," he said of Calhoun and his allies. Van Buren's triumph was complete. He would be Jackson's successor.

Jackson and States' Rights

The struggle between Van Buren and Calhoun threatened to tear apart the Democratic Party. The Little Magician had worked for years to build a North-South political alliance stressing laissez-faire, states' rights principles. His version of these principles, however, differed markedly from Calhoun's. Where Calhoun sought confrontation, Van Buren longed for compromise. He sought particularly to avoid conflicts over the slavery issue, fearing the rise of an antislavery party in the North, and to find a compromise on the tariff, since Pennsylvania Democrats longed for protection while Southern party voters demanded free trade.

Calhoun, on the other hand, wanted to confront the North with Southern demands on slavery and the tariff. The South Carolinian, increasingly the champion of Southern rights, believed that only a party dominated by Southerners could protect the South. During Jackson's first term, he and his followers worked in Congress to create a South-West alliance based on cheap land for the West and a low tariff for the South.

This political maneuvering soon provoked a great national debate on the nature of the federal Union. Late in 1829 Senator Samuel A. Foote of Connecticut proposed a resolution of inquiry into limiting the sale of public lands. Senator Thomas Hart Benton of Missouri promptly denounced Foote's resolution as a plot by Eastern manufacturers to prevent their workers from migrating to the West. Robert Y. Hayne, a debonair young senator from South Carolina, supported Benton by speaking vigorously in favor of a cheap land policy. Continued large revenues from land sales, he warned, would be used to finance internal improvements; they would be "a fund for corruption—fatal to the sovereignty and independence of the states. . . ."

Daniel Webster of Massachusetts rose to answer both Benton and Hayne. The New Englander was one of the great orators and constitutional lawyers of the day. He defended his own section against charges of unfriendliness to the West and heaped scorn upon Hayne's fear of a consolidated government. Deliberately goading Hayne, Webster equated the South Carolinian's appeals to state sovereignty with disunion. Hayne, with Calhoun's coaching, rose to the challenge in January 1830. He vigorously defended the right of a state to nullify a federal law that violated "the sovereignty and independence of the states." New Englanders, he reminded Webster pointedly, "were not unwilling to adopt" this same doctrine at Hartford in 1814, "when they believed themselves to be the victims of unconstitutional legislation."

The next day, before a packed gallery, Webster answered Hayne. Combining patriotism and common sense, he denounced the doctrine of nullification as "delusion and folly." The people, Webster contended, and not the states, had formed the Constitution. They, and not the individual states, were sovereign. If each of the states could defy the laws of Congress at will, the Union would be a mere "rope of sand." He compared the Union to "a copious fountain of national, social, and personal happiness," and urged the individual states and sections to subordinate their selfish interests to the common good. He closed with a moving appeal, later memorized by successive generations of schoolchildren: "Liberty *and* Union, now and forever, one and inseparable!"

Webster had voiced the feelings of a rising generation of Americans who, like him, believed that "while the Union lasts we have high, exciting, gratifying prospects spread out before us—for us and our children." It remained to be seen whether

Andrew Jackson shared this vision. The President's answer came a few weeks later, at a Jefferson Day dinner. The exponents of nullification planned to use the celebration to advertise their views. Jackson, forewarned of their intentions, had prepared his toast in advance. When his turn came the President, glaring at Calhoun, raised his glass and declared: "Our Federal Union—it must be preserved." The boisterous crowd stood in deathly silence. With the diminutive Van Buren standing on a chair so as not to miss a moment of his triumph, Calhoun, his hand trembling so "that a little of the amber fluid trickled down the side" of his glass, replied: "The Union—next to our liberties the most dear." But there was no mistaking the President's words; despite his sympathy for states' rights, he would not countenance nullification. Calhoun was further discredited. Most

Southerners and Westerners scurried back to the Jackson-Van Buren banner.

Jackson tried to keep a balance between assertion of the powers of the federal government and defense of the doctrine of states' rights. In 1830, anxious to reassure the strict constructionists in the party, he vetoed a bill providing federal aid for the construction of a turnpike from Maysville to Lexington, Kentucky. This road lay entirely within a single state, and Jackson doubted the constitutionality of funding projects of a "purely local character." Well-publicized vetoes like this were the exception, however; at other times Jackson gave his approval to substantial amounts of federal aid for building roads and canals. During his Presidency, appropriations for this purpose averaged over $1.3 million annually—nearly double that under Adams.

Georgia and Indian Removal

In one instance, Jackson actually encouraged a state in defying federal authority. As an ex-Indian fighter and experienced Western politician, Jackson gave Indian removal a high priority. Since Jefferson's time the government had been forcing the Indian tribes to sell their lands and migrate westward. In 1830 the President urged Congress to set apart "an ample district west of the Mississippi" for their permanent use. Here the "aborigines" might learn "the arts of civilization" and form "an interesting commonwealth, destined to perpetuate the race and to attest the humanity and justice of this government." Humanists like Senator Theodore Frelinghuysen of New Jersey courageously defended the Indians' right of "immemorial possession, as the original tenants of the soil," but the Indian Removal Act passed anyway. In the following years many Indian nations, recognizing the futility of resistance, signed over their lands and moved west, often with prodding from the U.S. Army.

Although disunited and demoralized by defeat, not all Indians peacefully acquiesced to the march westward. In Illinois portions of the Sac and Fox tribes, led by Chief Black Hawk, refused to leave their rich ancestral lands. Black Hawk initially hoped that, if his people remained peaceful, they would be permitted to keep their farming communities and live alongside the incoming whites. But incessant military pressure and hunger finally forced Black Hawk into war. It was a one-sided

fight. In the final battle of the Black Hawk War, the Bad Axe Massacre (1832), United States troops and militiamen killed all but 150 of the original thousand Indian men, women, and children. In the South, the Seminole War (1835-38) was even bloodier. Many Seminole tribesmen, led by Chief Osceola, refused to leave Florida. Accompanied by runaway blacks, they retreated into the swamps. Jackson sent troops, but the Indians conducted a skillful guerrilla war in the impenetrable Everglades. It took several years and $14 million to subdue Osceola's warriors.

Americans had traditionally invoked the white man's "superior" civilization to justify dispossessing the wandering "savages" of their ancestral lands. In the case of the Cherokees, Choctaws, and Chickasaws, even this shabby rationalization collapsed. They were all settled peoples, skilled in the ways of agriculture. In spite of this, the government bribed, intimidated, and lied to force the Choctaws and Chickasaws of Mississippi and Alabama to move to the Indian Country (the present state of Oklahoma). Even these tactics failed to move the Cherokees of Georgia. They adopted a written constitution and declared themselves an independent nation. In response the Georgia legislature, ignoring federal treaties recognizing Cherokee nationhood, extended state jurisdiction over them and prepared to seize their lands. Hiring William Wirt, the former U.S. Attorney General, to represent them, the Cherokees appealed to the Supreme Court for an injunction restraining Georgia from carrying out this seizure. Chief Justice Marshall, in an 1831 decision, *Cherokee Nation v. Georgia,* ruled that the Cherokees were a "domestic dependent nation" possessing unquestioned right to their lands. A year later, in *Worcester v. Georgia,* the Court held that the Cherokee nation was a distinct political community, within which "the laws of Georgia can have no force." The United States, it implied, was duty-bound to exclude intruders from the Indian lands.

Both Jackson and Georgia ignored the Court's ruling. Informed of the *Worcester* opinion, Jackson reputedly said: "John Marshall has made his decision, now let him enforce it." Georgia continued to harass the Cherokees. In 1835 a corrupt faction was bribed into signing a treaty, and General Winfield Scott began the Indians' systematic removal. As usual, the government failed to make adequate preparations for the trip westward; over four thousand of the fifteen thousand Cherokees who made the move perished along "the Trail of Tears." The Choctaws had been forced out of Mississippi in the dead of winter, "thinly clad and without moccasins." In 1838 the government forcefully removed the Pottawattomies from Indiana. They began the trek west "under a blazing noonday sun, amidst clouds of dust, marching in a line, surrounded by soldiers who were hurrying their steps. Next came the baggage wagons, in which numerous invalids, children, and women, too weak to walk, were crammed." Dozens died along this "Trail of Death." The resettlement of these farming Indians west of the Mississippi River created bitter resentment among the Plains tribes who hunted there. The government was soon forced to send troops to the West to separate the warring tribes.

The Nullification Crisis

As President, Jackson moved cautiously on the tariff question. It was a sectional and political hot potato, dangerous alike to national and to party unity. During his first term he recommended only modest reductions in the 1828 "Tariff of Abominations." He was content in 1832 to let his old rival John Quincy Adams, now a congressman from Massachusetts, take the initiative in shaping a revised tariff bill. The new act retained the principle of protection, but reduced duties to the general level of the tariff of 1824. Jackson signed it enthusiastically, telling Southerners that it removed "all their grievances." But in South Carolina news of these modest reductions came too late—the Palmetto State was on the verge of rebellion.

South Carolina's case against the Union had been building for years. It had once been a rich and prosperous state. The mucky swamps of its low country region were ideally suited for growing rice. After the invention of Whitney's gin, the Carolina upcountry became a major center for cotton cultivation; for a time the little state produced half the nation's crop. Flushed with prosperity, Carolinians shared fully in the nationalistic fervor of the early Republic. Native sons like Pinckney, Calhoun, and Cheves served ably in the nation's councils.

Abruptly, in 1819 the state's economic fortunes slid into decline. Falling world prices for cotton, coupled with the increased competition from the newer states to the southwest which produced cotton more cheaply, wrecked the South Carolina cotton-planters' economy. Their worn-out soils could not compete with those in the fertile Black Belt of Alabama and Mississippi. Facing ruin, they migrated westward by the thousands.

Those who remained increasingly focused their frustration and anger on the protective tariff. As producers of staples for export, Carolinians had always favored free trade. Only the necessities of national defense had prompted men like Calhoun to accept the tariff of 1816. When Congress began raising duties to protective levels, they objected vigorously. The planters, who depended on the domestic market for most consumer goods, would have to buy them at propped-up prices. Foreign governments, Carolinians warned, might retaliate by imposing high tariffs on American exports, such as cotton. In 1830 Congressman George McDuffie of South Carolina charged that higher prices ultimately cost the Southern planter the equivalent of forty out of every one hundred bales of cotton produced. Although the eccentric McDuffie and others exaggerated the tariff's pernicious effect on their economy, there is no question but that protective duties did contribute to hard times in South Carolina.

The state's opposition to the tariff mounted after the passage of the 1828 "Tariff of Abominations." Opponents began to advocate nullification of the federal tariff laws. Vice-President John C. Calhoun, bending to the winds of opinion at home, justified this position in his *Exposition and Protest* published anonymously in 1828. By now the cadaverous South Carolinian fitted the British traveler Harriet Martineau's description of him: "Mr. Calhoun, the cast-iron man, who looks as if he had never been born and never could be extinguished. . . . His mind has long since, "she wrote in 1835, "lost all power of communicating with any other. I know of no man who lives in such utter intellectual solitude." According to Calhoun, the states were independent and sovereign powers prior to the formation of the Constitution. They had created the federal government and endowed it with strictly limited powers. Under the Constitution, Congress might tax for purposes of raising revenue, but not to protect domestic industry. The Tariff of 1828 was therefore "unconstitutional, unequal, and oppressive." It made Southerners "the serfs of the system—out of whose labor is raised, not only the money paid into the Treasury, but the funds out of which are drawn the rich rewards of the manufacturer and his associates in interest."

Calhoun realized that the North, with its superior population, would invoke the principle of majority rule to justify protection. He claimed to have discovered a constitutional remedy for this in the "right" of a state to "interpose" its original sovereignty against "the despotism of the many." In Calhoun's view, this was one of the unspecified powers reserved to the states by the Tenth Amendment. Thus a state could call a state convention and nullify any act of Congress that exceeded the authority granted by the Consititution.

In 1828 Calhoun's remedy seemed too drastic for the many Carolinians who still turned hopefully to Jackson. In the meantime, the nullifiers worked to strengthen their cause. They were aided by a growing climate of racial fear in South Carolina, a state where black slaves outnumbered whites by a ratio of eight to one in some areas. The decade that began with Denmark Vesey's revolt (1822) and ended with Nat Turner's rebellion in Virginia (1831) left white Carolinians fearful for their property and their very lives. They blamed these unsettling events on the small but noisy antislavery movement. The bitter Missouri Controversy and the Panama debates had awakened slaveholders everywhere to the potential threat which the federal government posed to their peculiar institution. Consequently, even those whites who had not suffered by the fall in cotton prices embraced "the nullifiers" crusade in search of constitutional protection against the growing abolitionist movement.

By 1832 nullifiers like George McDuffie were spoiling for a fight. "South Carolina," he told Congress in a typical speech,

is oppressed (a thump). A tyrant majority sucks her life blood from her (a dreadful thump). Yes sir (a pause), yes, sir, a tyrant (a thump) majority unappeasable (horrid scream), has persecuted and persecutes us (a stamp on the floor). We appeal to them (low and quick), but we appeal in vain (loud and quick). We turn to our brethren of the North (low, with a shaking of the head), and pray them to protect us (a thump), but we t-u-r-n in v-a-i-n (prolonged, and a thump). They heap coals of fire on our heads (with immense rapidity)—they give us burden on burden; they tax us more and more (very rapid, slam-bang, slam—a hideous noise). We turn to our brethren of the South (slow with a solemn, thoughtful air). We work with them; we fight with them; we vote with them; we petition with them (common voice and manner); but the tyrant majority has no ears, no eyes, no form (quick), deaf (long pause), sightless (pause), inexorable (slow, slow). Despairing (a thump), we resort to the rights (a pause) which God (a pause) and nature has given us (thump, thump, thump). . . .

Once the news of Congress' failure to enact significant tariff relief reached South Carolina, events moved rapidly. Calhoun openly endorsed nullification and resigned as Vice President to accept a seat in the Senate. In October, after a hard-fought contest, the nullification party elected an overwhelming majority to the state legislature. The governor immediately called the legislature into session, whereupon it authorized a state convention and a special election of delegates. On November 19, 1832, 136 nullifiers and 26 Unionists met at the state capital, Columbia. The convention passed an Ordinance of Nullification declaring the Tariffs of 1828 and 1832 unconstitutional, and null and void in South Carolina. The collection of duties by the federal government after February 1, 1833, was forbidden, unless Congress lowered the tariff to twelve percent. Any attempt by Washington to coerce the state, warned the Ordinance, would be "inconsistent with the longer continuance of South Carolina in the Union." The legislature, at its regular session in December, took steps to implement the Ordinance and appropriated money to buy arms and raise an army.

The nullifiers soon discovered that they had painted themselves into a corner. At home, a determined band of Unionists prepared to resist their fellow Carolinians by force: both sides were soon drilling volunteers in cities and towns across the state. Neighboring slave states sympathized with South Carolina, but condemned her "reckless precipitancy." President Jackson appeared determined to uphold national authority. He reinforced federal installations in Charleston harbor and ordered General Winfield Scott to take charge of military preparations. His famous Nullification Proclamation of December 10, 1832, repudiated nullification in no uncertain terms. American nationhood, Jackson asserted, had existed before the states; the federal Constitution only made more perfect a preexisting Union. Under these circumstances, "to say that any state may at pleasure secede from the Union is to say that the United States is not a nation." The power of nullification was *"incompatible with the existence of the Union, contradicted expressly by the letter of the Constitution, unauthorized by its spirit, inconsistent with every principle on which it was founded, and destructive of the great object for which it was formed."* Disunion by armed force, Jackson concluded, was *"treason,"* in the face of which he, as President, could not "avoid the performance of his duty."

At the same time that he brandished the stick, Jackson held out a carrot to the nullifiers. He urged Congress to lower the tariff, limiting protection to articles essential to the nation's defense. In order to avoid a premature clash of arms, he re-moved federal troops from the Charleston Citadel to the forts in the harbor. He secured a "Force Bill" from Congress early in 1833, authorizing the collection of import duties from ships offshore and reaffirming his power to call up the state militias and to use the Army and Navy. Old Hickory had completely outmaneuvered the Carolina radicals. As the "Fatal First" approached, they prudently decided to delay enforcing nullification until Congress completed its deliberations on the tariff. Early in March 1833, Congress passed the Compromise Tariff, which provided that rates on protected articles would be lowered in gradual stages to a twenty-percent level in mid-1842. Even though the new rates were nearly double what the nullification ordinance had demanded, Carolinians accepted the compromise figure with relief. The convention promptly rescinded the Ordinance of Nullification, then, as a symbolic gesture, declared the "Force Bill" null and void.

South Carolina had won the battle but lost the war. The passage of the Compromise Tariff was a signal triumph for nationalism and majority rule. Nullification as a principle had been thoroughly discredited. In the process, Carolinians had learned an unforgettable lesson: successful resistance to Northern "tyranny" demanded the cooperation of the other slave states.

The Bank War

Andrew Jackson brought with him to the White House a Westerner's instinctive dislike of monopolies and entrenched privilege, and a vague distrust of banks and paper money. Beyond this, however, he had few ideas about economics; political needs shaped his tariff and internal-improvement policies. But in his very first message to Congress he had sharply criticized the Bank of the United States for its alleged failure to establish "a uniform and sound currency." He urged the lawmakers to consider carefully "the constitutionality and expediency" of renewing the Bank's charter when it expired in 1836.

After a shaky start the second Bank of the United States had prospered, especially under its third President, Nicholas Biddle. Born into a wealthy Philadelphia family, Biddle displayed a precocious versatility from the start. After graduating from Princeton at the age of fifteen, he traveled widely, served in the diplomatic crops, and wrote the classic account of the Lewis and Clark expedition. Impressed with his knowledge of banking, President Monroe appointed him a director of the Bank in 1819; four years later, at age thirty-seven, he became its President. The choice was a good one. Biddle understood banking and the function of the Bank in the American economy at a time when few others did. Under his direction it proved to be a valuable institution. The Bank marketed government securities and performed other Treasury operations. Its loans stimulated business and facilitated the swift exchange of agricultural staples. By maintaining specie payments (gold and silver coin) on its own notes, the Bank provided a currency that was sound and portable. At the same time it helped to keep the state banks from issuing reckless amounts of paper currency by periodically presenting their notes for redemption in specie. Though responsible to private stockholders, Bid-

Nicholas Biddle.

Bank was a "hydra of corruption—dangerous to our liberties by its corrupting influence everywhere." It was time, he decided, to strip the "Monster" of its malign power. Whatever his motives, Jackson once engaged in the contest, quickly personalized the dispute into another death struggle between himself and a hated foe.

For a time Biddle tried to placate Jackson, but to no avail. He then turned to the President's enemies for support. He extended generous loans to Clay, Webster, and other influential politicians and newspaper editors. In 1832 he reluctantly acquiesced in their plan to seek a recharter well in advance of the expiration date. It was an election year, and the Bank's friends reasoned that Jackson would think twice before vetoing a recharter bill. If he did, it would be a good issue in the presidential campaign.

The bill renewing the Bank's charter cleared Congress in July 1832, with nearly a third of the Democratic representatives voting in favor of passage. Jackson was enraged. "The Bank," he told Martin Van Buren, "is trying to kill me, *but I will kill it!*" He sent the bill back to Congress with a blistering veto message in which he denounced the Bank as "not only unnecessary, but dangerous to the government and country." It enjoyed a virtual "monopoly of foreign and domestic exchange"; it threatened the rights of the states and the liberties of the people; it discriminated against the West. Refusing to be guided by the opinion of the Supreme Court in the *McCulloch* case, Jackson declared the Bank unconstitutional: "The opinion of the judges has no more authority over Congress than the opinion of Congress has over the judges, and on that point the President is independent of both." The veto message dwelt at length on the fact that one-fourth of the Bank's stock was held by foreigners, and on the need for a *"purely American"* institution. He closed with an impassioned attack on the renewal bill as an attempt by "the rich and powerful" to "bend the acts of government to their selfish purposes" and pledged to resist "the advancement of the few at the expense of the many."

dle's chief concern prior to 1832 seemed always to be the welfare of the country as a whole. He liked to boast that the Bank was "the balance wheel of the banking system."

Biddle's very success proved his undoing. "Cheap money" advocates, mainly state bankers and speculators, objected to the Bank because it restrained the state banks from issuing banknotes as freely as they wished. "Hard money" men, who believed that specie was the only safe currency, condemned all note-issuing banks as instruments of speculation and stock-jobbing. Their banknotes, wrote one critic, formed "the foundation of *artificial* inequality of wealth, and, thereby, of *artificial* inequality of power." New York bankers chafed at the restraints imposed by a Philadelphia institution. Some men sincerely questioned the constitutionality or the wisdom of making an essentially private bank the depository of the public funds. Many still blamed the Bank for the Panic of 1819.

The source of Jackson's hostility to the Bank remains obscure. He did not act in response to popular demand or on behalf of state banks. In spite of his well-known suspicion of banks and paper money, Old Hickory kept his own money in the Bank's Washington and Nashville branches for years. Most likely, his antagonism stemmed from jealousy of the uncontrolled political power of the Bank. He readily believed the reports that some of the branches had worked against his election in 1828, and reached the conclusion that the

The veto message was superb propaganda but poor economics. A developing country like the United States needed a stable currency to encourage foreign investment, not wildcat banking to drive it away. The Bank was not strictly a monopoly. In 1830 it made about one-fifth of the nation's bank loans and had barely one-third of the total bank deposits and specie reserves held by American banks, a dominant but far from monopoly position. In his message Jackson completely ignored the important services the Bank provided and offered no effective substitute for it.

At first, Jackson's enemies rejoiced over the message. Biddle compared the President to "a chained panther biting the bars of his cage" and called the veto "a manifesto of anarchy." But in November 1832 the people vindicated Old Hickory. Jackson, with Van Buren as his running mate, overwhelmed the National Republican candidate, Henry Clay, by a margin of five to one in the electoral college. It was a "Waterloo defeat," crowed a Jackson newspaper.

Jackson took his decisive victory as a mandate to destroy the Bank even before its charter expired. As soon as the Nullification Crisis passed, he determined to remove the government deposits from the bank and place them in selected state banks. By law, it was the Secretary of the Treasury who had to give the actual order for removing them. When he refused, Jackson "promoted" him to the State Department and named a new Treasury Secretary. He, too, refused to do Jackson's bidding, citing the "irresponsible" policies of the state banks. The President then replaced him with Roger B. Taney, formerly the Attorney General. The faithful Taney continued drawing on the government's balance in the Bank to meet current expenses, but he began depositing the incoming receipts in certain state banks. These banks were supposedly chosen for their fiscal soundness, but political considerations were not overlooked. Prior to 1836 over seventy-five percent of the officers in these banks were Democrats. The administration's critics nicknamed them the "pet banks."

As the government's deposits dwindled, Biddle began calling in loans and curtailing note issues. In the beginning this contraction was thoroughly justifiable, since the federal deposits had served as the basis of much of the Bank's credit. But Biddle soon succumbed to baser motives. He continued the contraction into the winter and spring of 1834, in the hope of producing a short recession that would force a recharter of the Bank. "Nothing but the evidence of suffering," he reasoned, would "produce any effect in Congress." As interest rates climbed and credit dried up, the business community begged for relief. All over the country the pro-Bank forces organized meetings and flooded Congress with petitions. A Cincinnati man tried a more direct approach: "Damn your—soul," he wrote Jackson, "remove them deposits back again, and recharter the bank or you will certainly be shot in less than two weeks and that by myself!!!"

Old Hickory refused to budge. Told of rumors that a mob threatened to "lay siege to the Capitol until the deposits were restored," he promised to hang the ringleaders "as high as Haman." When a delegation of businessmen visited him seeking relief, he replied coldly: "Go to Nicholas Biddle. . . . Biddle has all the money!" In the end Jackson had his way. Biddle was forced to let up, and the economy quickly recovered. The chief result of the so-called "Biddle depression" was a marked decrease in the Bank's popularity. In 1836, when the old federal charter expired, the Bank received a new one from the state of Pennsylvania. In 1841, after a series of financial reverses, it closed its doors forever. Biddle died three years later, a broken man.

The demise of the Bank placed the country on the horns of a cruel dilemma. Jackson had destroyed the Bank in the name of sound money and "those habits of economy and simplicity which are so congenial to the character of republicans." But, in so doing, he removed the most effective restraint on "the stock-jobbers, brokers, and gamblers" he professed to despise. Aided by the government deposits, the "pets" flooded the country with paper banknotes. An orgy of speculation and inflation followed. Belatedly, between 1834 and 1836, Jackson took a series of hard-money steps designed to drive papermoney from circulation. He directed the deposit banks not to issue or receive notes worth less than $10. Land officers were instructed not to take small bills in payment for public lands.

He secured a law preventing deposit banks from issuing bills valued at under $20. Finally, in 1836, Jackson issued the Specie Circular, which prohibited the purchase of public lands in anything but coin. He acted too late. In 1837 a "mountain of debt and bad currency" helped to plunge the country into its worst depression to date.

The Whigs

By the end of Andrew Jackson's second term in 1837, the Democratic Party had changed significantly. Gone was the diverse political coalition that had elected the Old Hero in 1828; it was replaced by a smaller but more homogeneous organization with a fairly definite body of ideas. The accent was on laissez-faire and equality of opportunity. Government, the Jacksonians believed, should restrict its intervention in the economy to eliminating special privilege and monopoly, leaving a fair field for individual competition. Like Adam Smith, whose *Wealth of Nations* (1776) many of them had read, they believed that the power of the marketplace would best regulate the economy and distribute wealth equitably. In order to prevent a few rich men from using the government for special advantage, the Jacksonians also advocated universal political freedom (at least for white men) and majority rule. Although recognizing the supremacy of the Union, Jacksonians were respectful of states' rights, holding that the area of federal authority should be held within narrow bounds.

The party in the late 1830's was much influenced by the "Locofocos," a powerful Democratic splinter group in New York. These dissidents—who took their name from a type of friction match they had used to light candles when rival, conservative Democrats tried to disrupt their meeting by turning off the gas lights—opposed monopoly in any form. They denounced banks and corporations, demanding a return to hard money and unlimited liability for stockholders. They advocated free trade, labor unions, free public education, and abolition of imprisonment for debt. In short, they were neo-Jeffersonians, championing the "equal rights and privileges of the great body of the people." Although conservative Democrats rejected many of the more radical Locofoco demands, they had a keen appreciation of the political power of the masses and never missed a chance to portray the party as the defender of the common man against the forces of wealth and privilege.

The decisions of the Supreme Court in the late thirties reflected Democratic thinking. During his two terms, Jackson appointed seven associate justices. And when Chief Justice John Marshall died in 1835, he named Roger B. Taney to succeed him. Under Taney's leadership the Court shifted direction: it showed a less rigid respect for private property rights as against the rights of popular majorities, and more regard for states' rights.

In the Charles River Bridge case of 1837 the Court again took up the question posed in the Dartmouth College case of whether a state could alter an agreement with a private corporation. The Massachusetts legislature had incorporated the Charles River Bridge Company to operate a toll bridge under a long-term contract. Later it authorized another corporation to erect a toll-free bridge over the Charles River at a point nearby. The first company sought an injunction, contending that the second charter constituted a breach of

contract. Taney sided with Massachusetts. The great object of government, he declared, was "to promote the happinesss and prosperity of the community." In a collision between the rights of private property and those of the community, the rights of the people came first. The Court could not consent, he said, to take away from the states "any portion of that power over their own internal police and improvement, which is so necessary to their well being and prosperity." Although conservatives denounced the decision as a blow to business and the sanctity of contract, the decision was really a liberating one. The young American economy would have been greatly handicapped if established companies had been able to maintain monopolies and choke off competition. Taney's opinion opened the way for a host of new developments in industry and transportation.

Two years later, in *Bank of Augusta v. Earle*, the Court enlarged state powers again. Here Taney rejected the claim of a Georgia bank that under the federal Constitution a corporation, like a citizen, could automatically enter another state and engage in business there. In the absence of positive legislation, a company might do business in another state, said Taney, although that state had the power to exclude foreign corporations if it wished. In the wake of this decision, many states enacted regulatory laws for outside corporations. On the whole, they proved to be socially beneficial, since there was as yet virtually no federal regulation of interstate commerce.

The Democratic appeals for strict economy, no government favors, sound money, and equal rights struck a responsive chord among the electorate. By the late thirties there was some truth in Jackson's claim that his party represented the "farmers, mechanics, and laborers." It especially attracted the economically powerless and the less privileged: those who resented the privileges that established bankers and tariff-protected businessmen seemed to enjoy; people who had been affected adversely by changing patterns of transportation and trade; ordinary people who had been hurt by currency fluctuations and unstable commodity prices. Others supported the Democrats for special reasons. Many Southern planters looked to them to protect slavery and Southern rights from government interference. Businessmen engaged in international trade favored Jackson's call for a lower tariff. The Democratic Party early recognized and encouraged the aspirations of immigrants, particularly Irish Catholics, who flocked to the Democracy. Opponents of evangelical Protestantism, with its righteous moralizing and aggressive crusading, found the rough-and-tumble egalitarianism of the Democrats refreshing. The party attracted free-thinkers and intellectuals. Many Democratic voters just plain liked Jackson.

Jackson's political success and his policies produced growing opposition. Initially, Old Hickory's opponents lacked cohesion, and political alliances were unsettled. The Anti-Masonic Party, a group emphasizing enmity toward the fraternal Order of Free Masons, gained strong support in New England, New York, and Pennsylvania after 1826. Originally a grass-roots protest movement against the supposedly despotic political and economic power of Masonry, it soon turned into a general protest against inequality and immorality. As a religious and democratic movement of great power, it attracted ambitious young politicians—William Seward, Thaddeus Stevens, Horace Greeley, and Millard Fillmore—who welded it into an effective political party. Because Andrew Jackson was a Mason, and because his party was in power, these leaders made the Democrats the chief target of attack. In 1831 the Anti-Masons held the first national nominating convention at Baltimore, choosing William Wirt as their presidential candidate. He won just seven electoral votes in 1832, splitting the anti-Jackson vote with Henry Clay, the National Republican candidate. After that election, leaders of these two groups began organizing an alternative political force to the Democrats.

They were joined by a motley assortment of former Jacksonians. After the Cabinet reshuffle of 1831, two Calhounites, John Branch of North Carolina and John M. Berrien of Georgia, went home to lead movements against the administration. Jackson's firm rebuke to nullification drove many Southern states' righters into opposition. The Bank War caused conservatives everywhere to desert the President. The selection of Martin Van Buren as Jackson's successor aroused anti-Jackson sentiment in the South and West. Even John C. Calhoun cooperated for a time with nationalists like Clay and Webster in opposing administration measures in Congress. In 1834 James Watson Webb of the New York *Courier and Enquirer* gave this anti-Jackson coalition a name. He called its members "Whigs," after the opponents of the Stuart monarchy in seventeenth-century England, in order to identify them as opponents of the tyrannical "King Andrew."

Use of the name "Whig" by opponents of Jackson and Jacksonianism became widespread in 1834, but the actual formation of a Whig Party varied in time from state to state. It was organized first in the New England and Mid-Atlantic states, later in the West and South. The lack of an effective national organization and the conflicting views of the coalitionists hindered the Whigs in 1836. Unable to agree on a common platform or a single presidential candidate, they adopted the strategy of running strong regional candidates in the hope of throwing the election into the House of Representatives. In the South, the Whigs' choice was Hugh Lawson White, a Tennessean, who, like many southern Jacksonians, distrusted Van Buren on the tariff and slavery. In the East, they ran Daniel Webster. The candidate in the West was General William Henry Harrison of Ohio, a former Governor of Indiana Territory and the hero of the Battle of Tippecanoe. Between them the three Whigs piled up 124 electoral votes, but Van Buren, with Jackson's prestige behind him, had 170, enough to win the election.

During the next four years the Whigs slowly gathered strength and developed a more coherent political philosophy. As the Panic of 1837 worsened, people throughout the country flocked to the new banner, convinced that Van Buren's hard-money policies were somehow responsible for their woes. The Whigs' ambitious economic nationalism attracted new adherents in the South, even while it drove Calhoun and the extreme states' righters back to the Democrats.

The Whigs believed that one of the chief functions of government was to promote, actively and positively, the national economy. They advocated protection for industry, internal improvements at federal expense, and a national banking system. As they saw it, a wise government working alongside capital and labor, would harmonize the interests of every class and section. As their taunts at "King Andrew" indicated, the Whigs also believed in a strong congressional voice in government and respect for the opinions of the Supreme Court.

Whig social philosophy was conservative and middle-class. Although accepting the necessity for change, Whigs generally approved the existing social order. They had an abiding respect for private property, free enterprise, and social deference. There was a strong strain of evangelical Protestantism in Whiggery, which gave rise to a fondness for moral and humanitarian reform. According to one historian many Whigs still hoped "to Christianize America through politics." They frequently criticized Jackson's Indian policy and, in the North at least, showed a certain sympathy for the plight of the blacks. At the same time, they exhibited a strong dislike for most immigrants and for Catholics.

The Whigs attracted a substantial following among all classes of society. Many Northern merchants, bankers, and industrialists found the Whig philosophy appealing; so did large cotton, tobacco, and sugar planters and their urban business associates in the South. Farmers anxious for internal improvements often voted Whig. The party was popular among Protestants and native Americans concerned about the influx of immigrants, particularly Irish and German Catholics. Workingmen in industries hurt by foreign imports or fearful of immigrant competition for jobs supported the Whig ticket. With broad support throughout the country, the Whigs looked forward eagerly to the election of 1840.

Boom and Bust Again

On March 4, 1837, Andrew Jackson turned over the reins of government to Martin Van Buren. As the Old Hero left the Capitol, the crowds cheered him lustily. For once, remarked Thomas Hart Benton, "the rising was eclipsed by the setting sun." In his inaugural message, Van Buren painted a glowing picture of a "great, happy, and flourishing" country. But even as he spoke, the dark clouds of depression were gathering once again on the horizon.

Since the early 1820's the American economy had experienced sustained economic growth. Demand for American agricultural products seemed insatiable: exports of cotton alone increased from 92 million pounds in 1818 to 300 million pounds in 1830. In order to move these bulky products to market, immense sums were expended on transportation projects of all kinds. Turnpike and bridge construction continued in most parts of the country, and steamboat building became an important industry. The success of the Erie Canal sparked a wave of canal-building that did not peak until the late thirties, although more than three thousand miles of railroad were completed in the same period. And the construction boom went far beyond internal improvements: the rapid settlement of the West and the growth of urban areas created a great demand for new homes, barns, stores, and public buildings. Manufacturing industries, particulary cotton textiles, iron and machinery, also grew rapidly.

By the middle thirties the economy showed definite signs of overheating, as healthy growth gave way to feverish speculation. Investors, mainly English, bought enormous quantities of stock in state-owned canal companies and other public works of increasingly doubtful utility and profitability. With labor and materials in short supply, these new construction projects merely drove up wages and prices. Sales of public land—mainly to speculators—rose from only $2,300,000 in 1830 to a record high of almost $25,000,000 in 1836. With speculators snapping up everything in sight, urban land values also soared. A New Yorker told of a farm near Brooklyn that had gone begging at $20,000 in 1831, but was sold in 1835 for $102,000. When Chicago was incorporated in 1833, optimists were already buying and selling lots twenty miles from the Lake. All over the West and South, farmers and planters plunged heavily into debt for land and slaves, sometimes borrowing at rates as high as thirty percent.

The Jackson Administration's monetary policies contributed to this orgy of what contemporaries called "overbanking and overtrading." The demise of the Bank of the United States removed an important check on state banks and their number rose from 330 in 1830 to 788 in 1837. Often they were purely speculative ventures, deliberately located "out where the wildcats howled" in order to discourage note redemption. Lax state laws permitted these "wildcat banks" to issue banknotes without maintaining adequate specie reserves to back them up. The note circulation of state banks soared from $61 million in 1830 to $149 million in 1837. The shifting of government deposits to the "pet" banks and the decision in 1836 to distribute the surplus federal revenue to the states merely stimulated an already unhealthy inflation. The series of hard-money steps that the Jackson Administration finally decided to take culminating in the Specie Circular of 1836 came too late.

In 1837 the boom collapsed. The President's order requiring all payments for public lands in gold or silver led banks in the West to draw heavily on Eastern banks for coin. In the midst of this specie drain a recession in Britain depressed cotton prices and caused English investors to call in their loans. On May 10 New York banks suspended specie payments and other banks followed suit. Prices fell and credit tightened: for speculators the only question, an observer wrote, "was as to the means of escape, and nearest and best route to Texas." Numerous commercial houses and banks failed. In 1838 the economy revived briefly, owing to another infusion of state borrowing for internal improvements, but the revival could not be maintained. Fewer and fewer improvements paid their way: the credit of the states was exhausted: the confidence of foreign investors had evaporated: most improvement projects were halted. The long upswing in the economy was temporarily over. It was "national pay day," a contemporary wrote. "The nation has been drawing on the future, and the future dishonors the draft."

The depression of 1839-43 was one of the severest in American history. Prices fell by as much as one-half in some places; real-estate values and stocks declined even more drastically. The collapse of prices triggered a tidal wave of bankruptcies. Under the federal Bankruptcy Act of 1841, some 28,000 debtors freed themselves of nearly a half-billion dollars of debt. Rural areas were hardest hit by the depression, but they at least were self-sustaining. In the cities unemployment caused widespread distress. Mobs in New York sacked the flour stores in 1837 and similar violence occurred elsewhere. Once again municipalities and charitable agencies set up soup kitchens and unemployment offices. Casting about for a more permanent solution to urban unemployment, Horace Greeley advised the unemployed to "go to the Great West, anything rather than remain here." Apparently few could afford to take his advice, for public land sales had plunged by 1842 to less than six percent of their 1836 peak. With land sales and tariff receipts declining, the federal government, which had been out of debt since 1835 (for the first and only time in its history), began running a new deficit. The states, which had contracted nearly $200 million of debts, were especially hard-pressed. By 1842 eight of them had defaulted, and three had even repudiated part of their debt, thereby ruining American credit with European investors for years to come.

The widespread distress placed President Van Buren in a dilemma. His party was bitterly divided between pro-bank, paper-money conservatives who wanted the federal government to maintain some active role in managing the economy and radicals who clung resolutely to a hard-money policy and a belief in negative government. For once the "Little Magician" could not wriggle out of a commitment; after careful consideration he decided to stick with Jackson's policies. He refused to repeal the Specie Circular. Calling Congress into special session, he blamed the depression on "excessive issues of bank paper" and "reckless speculation." In order to relieve the growing strain on the federal Treasury, he asked Congress to authorize the borrowing of $10 million for current expenses and to suspend the distribution of the now non-existent surplus. He also urged the lawmakers to grant extra time to importers who had defaulted on their customs bonds. And he specifically recommended passage of a law permitting the federal government to keep its receipts in its own Treasury vaults, thus divorcing it from all connection with the nation's banks. Beyond this Van Buren refused to go. It was not the place of government, he insisted, to relieve economic distress. The framers of the Constitution had "wisely judged that the less government interfered with private pursuits the better for the general prosperity." Government assistance to one class would mean using "the property of some for the benefit of others," and he preferred "to leave every citizen and every interest to reap under its

Roller skates; mid-nineteenth century. *(Index of American Design.)*

benign protection the rewards of virtue, industry, and prudence.'' Many of the states, ignoring Van Buren's strictures, made at least some effort to relieve hunger and unemployment.

In spite of Whig protests against "leaving the people to shift for themselves," most of Van Buren's program became law in 1837. The President's opponents concentrated their fire on the Independent Treasury Bill, which required collectors of customs, postmasters, and other government receivers to hold their receipts until ordered to pay them out or to transfer them. It also directed the Secretary of the Treasury to withdraw the government's deposits from the "pet" banks and to place them in special subtreasuries. Whigs charged that the bill would curtail loans and credit, thereby stifling recovery. Van Buren's supporters countered that it would keep the government independent and the currency safe, as well as checking unwise banknote expansion. A coalition of Whigs and conservative Democrats blocked the scheme until 1840, when it finally passed Congress. Administration Democrats hailed the Independent Treasury as a second Declaration of Independence. The Whigs accepted defeat gracefully; the depression hung like an albatross around the Democratic neck, and they were after bigger game now.

The Election of 1840

In 1840 the second national party system came of age. Whigs and Democrats contested the election in almost every state. Picking a military hero as their candidate, the Whigs proceeded to beat the Democrats at their own game.

The Democratic Party in 1840 faced a political prospect as bleak as the national economy. The convention had little choice but to renominate Van Buren; however, it dropped Vice-President Richard M. Johnson, whose private life—he had fathered two daughters by a mulatto mistress—powerfully offended the sensibilities of Southerners. Unable to agree on a substitute, they left the choice to the voters. In their platform the Democrats endorsed the Independent Treasury and condemned federally sponsored internal improvements, a national bank, and protective tariffs.

The early front-runner for the Whig nomination was Henry Clay. The veteran Senator from Kentucky had been the chief spokesman for Whiggery and master of the anti-Jackson forces in Congress. The new breed of professional politicians in the Whig Party, however, had a different strategy in mind. Men like Thurlow Weed of New York wanted a candidate with "availability"—someone inoffensive who could appeal to a broad spectrum of the electorate. Clay was too closely identified with the Bank of the United States, and had too many enemies. The Whigs especially wanted a military hero. When their convention met, it passed over Clay and chose William Henry Harrison. In an attempt to balance the ticket geographically, the Whigs selected John Tyler of Virginia, a states' rights strict constructionist, as Harrison's running mate. Because there were divergent views within the party on national issues, the Whigs, in the interests of preserving their unity, adjourned without drafting a platform.

Born on a Virginia plantation in 1773, the son of a signer of the Declaration of Independence, Harrison began his career in the Old Northwest, first as an army officer, then as governor of Indiana Territory. His rout of Tecumseh's outnumbered Indians at Tippecanoe in 1811 made him a national hero. As commander in the Northwest during the War of 1812, he won the important Battle of the Thames, finally driving the British and their Indian allies off American soil. After the war, Harrison divided his time between his farm at North Bend, Ohio, and brief service as a United States Senator and then as minister to Colombia. Thereafter, however, his career languished and he was serving as a county clerk in 1836 when the Whigs tapped him as one of their presidential candidates. His strong showing at the polls—he got over half the Whig vote—kept him in the public eye until 1840.

At first, the Democrats professed joy at the Whigs' decision to run "Granny" Harrison (he was sixty-seven) instead of Clay. But when a Democratic newspaper, sneering at Harrison's presumed lack of sophistication, suggested that he would be content with a barrel of hard cider, a log cabin, and a pension of $2000 a year, the Whigs seized on the remark. Mounting an elaborate campaign, they prepared to cast Harrison in Jackson's image and to portray the Whigs as the friends of the people.

For the next several months the country was treated to a massive barrage of propaganda. In

Library of Congress

their songs and speeches Whig orators glorified Harrison as a plain, virtuous farmer whose cabin door (he actually owned three thousand acres and lived in a substantial farmhouse) was always open to strangers. "Matty" Van Buren, by contrast, was pictured as a bloated aristocrat, squandering the public funds on lavish White House entertainments in the midst of a depression. According to one Whig song:

Old Tip he wears a homespun coat,
He has no ruffled shirt-wirt-wirt.
But Mat he has the golden plate,
And he's a little squirt-wirt-wirt.

The Whigs held monster parades and rallies, with floats, flags, bands, and endless replicas of log cabins. They paraded fake Indians, to remind the voters of Harrison's record as an Indian fighter and in the War of 1812. Another such reminder was their catchy campaign slogan, "Tippecanoe and Tyler Too!" Barrels of cider were everywhere, with sweet cider for the drys and hard cider for the wets. The E.C. Booz Company of Philadelphia packaged its Old Cabin whiskey in cabin-shaped bottles, thus giving rise to the word "booze." Wealthy Whigs dressed in homespun and boasted of their humble upbringing. They distributed a campaign newspaper, the *Log Cabin*, and countless songbooks in the first musical campaign of American history.

Farewell, dear Van,
You're not our man;
To guide the ship,
We'll try old Tip!

Or,

Who never did a noble deed?
Who of the people took no heed?
Who is the worst of tyrant's breed?
Van Buren!

The Democrats tried to counter hard cider with hard money, pointing to the newly established Independent Treasury. No one listened. "We could meet the Whigs on the field of argument and beat them without effort," a Democrat lamented. "But when they lay down the weapons of argument and attack us with musical notes, what can we do?" Attracted by the ballyhoo and angry over the depression, nearly eighty percent of the eligible voters went to the polls. Harrison won a clear-cut victory, carrying nineteen out of twenty-six states and fifty-three percent of the two-party vote. Nearly unnoticed in the hullabaloo was the Liberty Party, whose meager 6,225 votes represented the first stirrings of antislavery politics in the North.

The election of 1840 established a new pattern in American politics. For the first time a President had been saddled with responsibility for hard times and turned out of office. The carnival atmosphere of the campaign inaugurated a tradition of "shouting and hurrahing" which has persisted in American presidential elections down to the present. The public had clearly adopted politics as its favorite spectator sport, and the presidential campaign as its most important national ritual. For the rest of the nineteenth century Americans in extra-ordinary numbers—usually about eighty percent of the electorate—would cheer for their party and vote for its presidential candidate.

Suggested Readings

The Jacksonian Era has inspired broad historical debate. Edward Pessen's *Jacksonian America* (rev. 1978) is a sharp critique of the traditional egalitarian view of the Old Hero. Pessen finds little to admire in Jackson and writes of a rigidly stratified society with slight opportunity for mobility. Marvin Meyers's *The Jacksonian Persuasion* (1957) examines certain American ideas and attitudes that attended Jacksonian politics, such as the conviction that the nation, having begun as a virtuous republic, needed a politics of renovation that would recover something of that lost republican austerity. Robert V. Remini's *Andrew Jackson* (1966) and subsequent works emphasize the man's administrative skill and the importance of his military campaigns and dealings with the Indians. Michael Paul Rogin's *Fathers and Children: Andrew Jackson and the Subjugation of the American Indian* (1975) is intriguing and debatable psychohistory.

Chapter X
American Democratic Capitalism

I. Forrest McDonald: A Beacon for the World

The United States did not merely survive, it thrived. In 1790 its land area had been about 888,000 square miles; in 1840, thanks to the acquisition of Louisiana and Florida, its territory had been doubled, and its people were casting a hungry eye toward California, Oregon and Texas. Its population had grown even faster, quadrupling from less than 4 million to more than 17 million. Its economic growth was greater yet, its annual exports increasing nearly sevenfold, from $20 million to $132 million.

This phenomenal growth was attended by a pair of institutional developments, capitalism and democracy, which made the young American Republic into a beacon light for the world. As for capitalism, the transition was largely a matter of casting off restraints which had shackled economic endeavors from time immemorial. Ancient Christianity had taught the palpable nonsense that the love of money is the root of all evil, and for many dreary centuries a government-ridden and priest-ridden Western civilization was paralyzed and impoverished because the profit motive was discouraged, hampered, or flatly prohibited by law and by institutional inflexibility. The American commitment to capitalism was based upon an understanding that the desire for private profit could in fact be the wellspring of great public good. The principle was as simple as it was profound: that the free interchange of goods for private profit can better serve the material needs of society than can government planning, community spirit, prayer, or love of mankind. Into the bargain, Americans embraced a new and broadened concept of human freedom: that every man is free to sell his time, his talents, and his labor as he alone sees fit, and in exchange takes his chances on survival. In other words, capitalism coupled opportunity with ability and coupled freedom with responsibility.

The American commitment to democracy was likewise based upon the proposition that people could and should be responsible for their own fate, and on the concomitant proposition that if restraints upon individual responsibility were removed, society as a whole would benefit. The growth of political democracy was not total, of course, any more than the commitment to capitalism was, for women and slaves continued to be deprived of the privilege of voting. Even so, government in America came far more nearly under popular control than it had been earlier. In 1790 every state but Pennsylvania restricted the vote to owners of substantial amounts of land; by 1840 twenty-three of the twenty-six states had abolished such requirements and allowed almost all white male adults to vote. In 1790 only the wealthy or well-to-do were allowed to hold elective public offices; by 1840 such restrictions had virtually disappeared. In 1790 the voters had only an indirect voice in choosing many public officials; by 1840 most officials were chosen directly by the voters.

Democratization was, however, a mixed blessing, for it involved some political changes that were not entirely compatible either with the nation's cultural values or with its Constitution. The framers of the Constitution had distrusted democracy as much as they distrusted monarchy, for the rights of minorities under majority rule could be as unsafe as popular rights were under one-man rule. Accordingly, they devised a mixed system of government in which the direct expression of the will of the majority was all but impossible. As popular participation in politics expanded, political leaders sought means of overcoming these constitutional barriers, and the mechanism they evolved was the political party—another thing not provided for in the Constitution.

Party development went through two distinct phases. In the first, the Republican Party of Thomas Jefferson and James Madison was organized to combat the programs and policies of the Hamiltonian and Washingtonian Federalists. The Republicans won, reshaped national programs and policies according to their own ideological principles, and succeeded so well that they became for practical purposes the only party. When that happened, a second party system developed, that of the Jacksonian Democrats and the oppositionist Whigs. The new party system—the one Americans have had ever since—differed radically from the original, for it was not organized around principles and policies, but around power and personalities.

As reconstituted during the Jacksonian age, American political parties came to exist solely for the purpose of winning elections and dividing the spoils of victory. It is true that the parties had "images" which supposedly stood for something—the Whigs being for a national bank, protective tariffs, internal improvements, and other nationalist measures associated with the Hamiltonian tradition; the Jacksonian Democrats being for states rights, low tariffs, strict construction of the Constitution, and other positions associated with the Jeffersonian tradition. Nevertheless, both parties, in Jackson's time and ever after, could and did accommodate members with the full range of political positions. What the parties did was carry out a sort of ritual substitute for war: neither party represents much in the way of ideology or govermental policies, but each represents itself as the essence of goodness, according to the prejudices of the time, and represents the other as the essence of evil. Every two years (and especially every four, during presidential campaigns), Americans vest all their hostilities and fears and hopes and dreams in the party and candidates of their choice, regarding their own as representing the forces of light and the other the forces of darkness, and do battle in the manner of a holy crusade. This mock warfare has little or nothing to do with what candidates actually propose to favor or oppose once they get in office.

The system performed an immensely valuable social function, for it provided ordinary Americans with a sense of participation in public affairs, elevated their national consciousness, and relieved tensions and animosities based upon economic, social, ethnic, or sectional differences. But it also contained some grave weaknesses. First, it kept genuine substantive issues forever out of focus, and thereby prevented Americans from perceiving accurately, and from effectively acting upon, their fundamental problems through government. Second, the triumph of the Jeffersonian and Jacksonian party systems, taken together, had another profound long-term effect: to equate American democracy with local government and with deep distrust of the national government. Third, and perhaps most importantly, the party system made capitalism and democracy into uncomfortable bedfellows if it did not indeed make them into incompatible opposites. On the one hand, Americans were committed to the proposition that if each man sought by any legitimate means to grow as wealthy as he could, the society as a whole would be enriched. On the other, the Jefferson-Jackson tradition, derived as it was from the English Bolingbrokean tradition, castigated winners in the pursuit of wealth as enemies of the people and tended to view economic activity as a "zero sum game" in which, as in poker, if one man wins another must necessarily lose.

These were especially portentous developments, for the people of the United States remained a diverse people, and the question, whether the emphasis would be upon "united" or upon "states," remained unanswered. The outcome of the political contest between Hamilton and Jefferson, and then of that between Biddle and Jackson, had in effect been a draw. That is, in the absence of a dominant national authority individual states and sections were left to establish their own rules of economic and social behavior. If the pursuit of wealth be conceived of as a social game (or games) with rules, it is obvious that those who favored the way of Hamilton and Biddle were best equipped for playing under one set of rules, the Jeffersonians and Jacksonians under quite another. The former, which were primarily (though not exclusively) suited to the North, favored commerce, finance, hard work, and living by the exercise of one's wits. The latter, which were primarily suited to the South, favored land speculation, slavery, and living by the exercise of force—or more properly, by exercising political skills and the capacity to command. Each tended to be contemptuous of the other, and neither could compete successfully by the rules of the other.

And underlying the tendency to adopt different sets of economic rules were persistent and profound socio-cultural differences. New Englanders and their kinsmen and descendants in the upper Middle West, like their English forebears, continued to live in accordance with an Americanized version of the Puritan ethos. They believed in the virtues of hard work, industry, thrift, and the accumulation—but not the enjoyment—of the things of this world. They continued to believe that success, as measured by money, was evidence of divine grace. And the millenarian religious streak in their character continued strong, which is to say they still dreamed of the perfect community and, seeing imperfection, were impelled either to destroy the evil or to remove themselves from it.

The Southerners, meanwhile, continued to follow the life patterns of their Celtic ancestors as adapted in America. The vast majority of white Southerners owned no slaves, did a little farming, and raised large numbers of animals as a "cash crop." The minority slaveowners lived well or moderately so on the yields of their plantations. What the two major elements of white society held in common was a disdain for work. To be sure, they had no prejudice against work if they could get slaves or animals to do it for them, but they were averse to doing it themselves. The herdsmen simply let their animals roam the woods—anybody's woods, for the open range system that prevailed throughout the South prevented landowners from fencing anything but growing crops—and rounded them up for slaughter from time to time. Planters simply exploited the labor of the slaves—though even the slaves did not usually work especially hard, and their material standards of living were higher than those of most agricultural workers in Europe, Asia, or Africa. Southerners, like Yankees, sought the material things of this world, but for use and enjoyment, not for Yankee-style accumulation. As opposed to the Yankee's work ethic, they preferred a leisure ethic; they were generally indolent unless roused to war (which they loved) or to some other form of violent amusement. Even their religion—the doctrine of Arminianism, which contrasted sharply with the Yankees' millenarianism—offered a lazy man's way to heaven. Arminianism, embraced by Southerners after the Second Great Awakening (1801-06), taught that eternal salvation involved only confessing and repenting one's sins and accepting Jesus Christ as one's savior.

The Yankees could and did claim that their work ethic was the way to progress, toward perfection in this life. The Southerners could and did claim that their leisure ethic was the way to civilized comfort in this life and to eternal bliss in the next life. The Southerners were somehow unable to engage in sustained effort, to be governed, to listen to the voice of reason, or to change their ways. The Yankees were somehow unable to refrain from meddling in other peoples' affairs. All told, it was a dangerous mixture of people to attempt to house under one national roof.

Not all Americans were either Yankees or Southerners, of course. Those in the middle tier of states from New York and Pennsylvania westward avoided the two extremes, as did most people in the West, northern or southern. Together, people in those areas constituted nearly half the total population. As long as they remained neutral between the extremes, the United States could remain a house divided yet not divided against itself, and the nation could continue to thrive and grow. If the middle should embrace either side, and if enough loud and shrill voices began to cry that the house must be all one or all the other, the vibrant young republic would be torn asunder.

In 1840, however, such a sinister prospect seemed remote.

II. Eugene D. Genovese: The Romance and the Reality

Many commentators at home and abroad predicted a brilliant future for the newly launched American republic. After all, its tough, free, enterprising people, its extraordinary resources, the sheer size of its open spaces—or of spaces that would be open enough once the Indians were disposed of—gave reason to hope for the best. Yet, a country so short of capital and labor would surely take several centuries to develop into a significant power. Hence, few if any of those optimistic commentators predicted, or probably even dreamed, that within fifty years the American economy would have advanced to the point from which it could take off into a sustained growth that would carry it to world power by the end of the nineteenth century. Accordingly, let us now praise famous capitalists.

Capitalism—freedom of capital and formal freedom of labor in the marketplace—performed wonders and, in so doing, made possible a more democratic polity than the world had ever seen. And vice versa: The growth of democracy had much to do with the promotion of capitalist enterprise. Alas, there were one or two discordant notes. Most notably, the economic miracle arose on the strength of an export crop that solved the central problem of the industrial take-off. The export crop paid for the industrial commodities and technology America needed to get started, and it created the conditions necessary for attracting foreign capital and labor. The export crop was cotton. It was produced by hundreds of thousands, then millions, of laborers who did not have the right to sell their labor-power in the marketplace, let alone to aspire to become entrepreneurs; in fact, to all intents and purposes they had no rights at all. These laborers were black. They or their forebears were part of the massive forced migration from Africa—part of the millions who had been shipped into the plantation colonies by a rapacious European capitalism. And they were slaves. Their vision of that Romance of American Free Enterprise so dear to the hearts of conservatives and liberals alike somehow did not get written.

Caveats aside, even those which warn of enormities, the rapidity of American economic development rested on the magnificent reconciliation of freedom and democracy—of individual liberties and majority rule—which has been the glory of our country since the promulgation of our Constitution and which continues to sustain its reputation even during this period of visible decadence.

Even the most optimistic—or alarmed—observers must have gasped at the economic performance. In 1790, indeed as late as 1820, the United States was largely an agrarian backwater. By 1870, to the astonishment of the world, it had surpassed all countries except the United Kingdom in manufacturing output. Roughly, the United Kingdom accounted for 32% of the total; the United States for 23%, or an amount equal to the combined effort of Germany and France; and with the rest of the world taking the hindmost of a bit more than 11%. By the time of the Civil War the foundations for an industrial take-off had firmly been laid in the economy; were staunchly supported by the political and legal system; and had engaged the full imagination and enthusiasm of an evolving national consciousness.

What did the slave plantations and cotton production contribute? Most obviously, the export of cotton gave the country the credit with which to pay for needed imports. And by specializing in cotton, the southern plantations created a huge demand for supplies (food, clothing, implements), which stimulated western migration to the food-growing Northwest and industrial production in the Northeast. An impressive meat-packing industry arose in Cincinnati, and before long the Northwest had a far-flung warehousing and shipping network and was demanding a national transportation system. Since the South itself, like most plantation societies, did not develop its own financial and commercial facilities at a comparable rate, northern bankers, insurance agents, factors, and assorted middlemen did a splendid business. They thereby syphoned off much of the profit of the cotton trade and in effect transferred a substantial portion of the multiplier effect of cotton investment to the free states. And European capital flowed into the country.

National economic development, however fruitful and indeed dramatic, ran a jagged course through grim financial crises, the ultimate burdens of which fell, as usual, primarily upon farmers, laborers, and others of small means. National politics, which began placidly enough, ran no less jagged a course toward what proved to be a fratricidal war of monumental proportions. At first blush, it is difficult for a historian of any political or philosophical tendency to resist the balanced judgment that credits the new party system with having mediated national quarrels and enmities. Strictly speaking, that is precisely what it did and what its most responsible architects intended it to do.

Conservatives, as well as those liberals who pose as conservatives whenever the Republicans win a presidential election, have periodically argued, especially since the 1950s, that mass participation in political decision-making ("Jacksonian democracy") undermined such institutions as the respectable churches, the bench and bar, Harvard and Yale, which might have brought reason and moderation to political disputes and of course set a higher moral tone for the great unwashed to emulate. In the hands of serious conservatives with a decent contempt for cant, this professorial twaddle emerges as the proposition, which is at least worthy of debate, that the country would have been much better off if the bankers, industrialists, big merchants, and planters had confirmed their control of government and sat down to a good dinner over which they could negotiate the country's future with a proper sense of profit and loss. Such men of affairs, with a lot of money at stake, could certainly be expected to suppress agitators with whatever degree of force proved necessary, to put an end to what General Jackson liked to call "clamors," and to maintain social order.

It will be understood that the principal agitators in question were people who wanted to abolish slavery, that the clamors concerned threats to civil liberties and civil rights, and that the social order to be maintained included chattel slavery. What is less easily understood is how these good bourgeois and slaveholders were supposed to compromise differences while they themselves were growing increasingly intransigent. More accurately, the slaveholders were certainly growing intransigent for good reasons to which we shall return in a later chapter, and the northern bourgeois included growing numbers of tough men from heartland industries who did not share the cotton mill owners' and eastern bankers' dependence upon the South and had no intention of seeing the West swallowed up by slaveholders. It is also not clear how these gentlemen, even if they had been inclined to do a deal, could have kept an armed mass of small farmers and small business men, as well as laborers and not to mention the slaves themselves, comfortably in line. It is less clear, that is, how wealthy propertyholders and learned clergymen and professors would have been one whit more effective as compromisers than those grubby politicians who in fact did negotiate one compromise after another.

To begin with, those politicians were not all that grubby. It was once fashionable to argue that secession and war might have been averted if the generation of Calhoun, Clay, and Webster had not passed from the scene at the beginning of the 1850s. These great statesmen, we were told, were replaced by lesser men of a "blundering generation." Yet, by 1850 Calhoun was in no mood to compromise on anything essential, and Clay and Webster did help push through one of those famous Compromises, which almost immediately collapsed. Stephen Douglas and others, in any case, had emerged as new compromisers and had enormous political talent. They failed. But there is no reason to think that their predecessors would have done better. And Lincoln, who would emerge as the greatest political leader in our history, might have averted secession and war by a last-minute compromise on the territorial question. He refused. He did not want war but he did want a genuine settlement. In truth, no genuine settlement could include the continuation of slavery except as a local institution on its way to slow extinction. That is, no compromise was possible without the surrender of all principles and of essential property interests. Had the wisest propertyholders in the nation, together with the professors whom they hire to invent high-minded rationalizations for their actions, been free to dictate terms during the antebellum period, it is by no means clear that matters would have ended much differently.

We shall return to these issues. For the moment let us note that attempts to correlate the breakdown of the sectional compact with the democratization of political and social life remain unconvincing. To the contrary, we may as well conclude that the mediating effects of democratization contributed much to the postponement of a crisis over slavery — a crises that might be seen in retrospect as having been unfolding , however slowly, since the startling debate over the Missouri question.

What the new party system did do, by giving ordinary people in Professor McDonald's carefully chosen words, a sense of participation, was to strengthen the ties of people in both North and South to their social systems, that is the one to free labor and the other to slavery. Thus, a political process, similar in form in both sections, generated a radically different social content in each.

The new party system did something else, which, whatever its mediating effects, would deeply scar American life and compromise its future: It corrupted everything. Or, more accurately, it proved to be the proper political form for a business society in which business itself was growing increasingly dishonest and irresponsible even by bourgeois standards. The America that emerged from the Jacksonian period, with its extraordinary impetus to capitalist development, quickly established itself not only as the world's most democratic bourgeois nation-state but as its most corrupt, self-satisfied, self-righteous, and dangerous. The clear-eyed in Europe and Latin America, who saw the potential of the deadly combination of enormous energy and power with a cult of unbridled opportunism, feared the worst — and with good reason.

During the "middle period" of American history, as it was once called, the United States pushed steadily westward to round our a continent and perch itself, more or less self-consciously, for the conquest of world power. It pushed southward too: It annexed Florida and carried out a long series of thinly disguised aggressions, interventions, and attempted annexations in the Caribbean and Central America. The westward march swallowed Texas and plunged into a series of dishonorable and hooligan acts that eventually resulted in the dismenberment of Mexico. Americans may not wish to dwell on their having seized half of Mexico's territory after provoking a war and having President Polk lie about it. Mexicans have longer memories.

The westward march, begun long before the appearance of those disagreeable incidents in the Southwest, has provided much of the stuff of American folklore. And, indeed, the story of the pioneers and settlers who hacked a modern nation out of a virtual wilderness deserves to rank among the wonders of human history. At its best, and even, alas, at its worst, it displayed heroism, ingenuity, vision. It also ranks as one of the peak moments in the history of modern genocide. Possibly—some would say probably and others would say certainly— the European settlers would have had to take the Indians' land by violence if they intended to win the continent for Western Civilization. Possibly, the end was written into the beginning. But along the way sober national leaders, especially among the more conservative Whigs, did advance proposals for more humane—or at least less disgusting—solutions. These included efforts, possibly misguided and certainly presumptuous, to integrate the Indians into American (this is, white) society, and proposals to settle the Indians on large tracts of land with incentives to enter the world economy and the modern era on their own. In the event, the United States of America, the most democratic, freedom-loving nation in the world, simply took that land by force, broke just about every treaty it signed, lied about its intentions and policies, cheated people who often made the terrible mistake of trusting the white man's word, and killed. Whatever the might-have-beens, the job could not have been done more savagely: the technology of mass death camps would not exist until another century had gone by.

At the heart of America's national Indian policy was a white racism that had long been poisoning the bloodstream of a great people. With the Indians the deed was done soon enough. With the blacks it would prove another matter.

Chapter XI
A Changing Nation
1820–1860

The Erie Canal

The idea of the Erie Canal caught George Washington's imagination, and by extension the country's, as early as 1783, when he toured the Mohawk Valley and envisioned "the vast inland navigation of these United States." The patriot poet Joel Barlow in his *The Vision of Columbus* (1787) has the explorer predict the building of a canal "From fair Albania" (Albany) to "the far lakes." Once opened in 1825, the Erie became an essential part of every tourist's itinerary: "The canal is in everybody's mouth," as one traveler of the 1820's rather awkwardly expressed it. The bustle and activity, the remarkable circumstances of its construction, its overwhelming success and national importance made it an eighth wonder of the world.

The Great Western Canal—one of its more formal names—was but four feet deep and forty feet wide (later deepened to 7 feet and widened to 70). Mule teams on the towpath zipped the fast passenger boats (called packets) along at the canal speed limit of four miles an hour, while freighters made but one-and-a-half to two miles per hour, and log rafts—like farm tractors on a modern highway—annoyed everyone by going far more slowly. Yet the trip for a passenger was not without its excitement. "Commending my soul to God," remarked a first-time rider boarding at Rochester, "and asking His defense from danger, I stepped on board the canalboat and was soon flying towards Utica."

Long trips by water had always been dangerous, and the idea of an over-300-mile trip in complete safety was utterly fascinating. Mock-heroic epics of the dangers of a storm at sea became a standard bit of the Erie's folklore: the ship pitching, the captain barking orders, the endless verses celebrating each maritime danger.

In a folk song that has survived to the present day, an ironic chorus pinpoints the *real* danger of a storm on the canal:

Oh, the E-ri-e was a-risin'
And the gin was a-gettin' low,
And I scarce do think we'll get a drink
'Till we get to Buffalo.

But even this story ends happily: Buffalo had not run out of gin and the crew, singing this song, got the bawds, brawls, and the inevitable night in the cooler they demanded:

Oh the girls are in the Police Gazette,
The crew are all in jail,
And I'm the only living sea cook's son
That's left to tell the tale.

And Buffalo was the "tame" end of the canal. At the other end, in Watervliet near Albany, the notorious "side-cut" area with its twenty-nine saloons in two blocks (with names like The Black Rag and The Tub of Blood), its fights, its large-scale vice, and an occasional body floating in the canal gained the district a reputation as "The Barbary Coast of the East."

The Erie traveler saw a splendid microcosm of young America along the canal. The men and women who made the canal work, "part water, part sand, part wind . . . but all canawler," were a colorful lot. The tough Irish workers who had dug the ditch now crewed the boats. The pompous captains, the fierce lockkeepers in endless battle with the crews, the floating showboats, saloons, general stores, and vice dens were famous among travelers, as were the legendary cooks: one "with a bosom like a boxcar," another who "stood six feet in her socks; her hand was like an elephant's ear, her breath would open locks."

These slow boats to Buffalo allowed remarkable freedom for travelers to see the countryside when they were not ducking under the famous low bridges. Even on the packets, one could walk the towpath alongside the boat for exercise. On the slower boats, poor travelers could step ashore and forage for their food, picking berries and hunting rabbits. And the scenes were grand: bustling ports, ingenious locks and romantic swamps, rivers and streams, and magnificent aqueducts; curious bridges of water allowed ships to pass over such picturesque obstacles. Sometimes the canal cut straight through primeval forests with no hint of man's work but the calm swath of canal and towpath. A British visitor, Mrs. Trollope, the most vinegary of travelers, complained that "From the canal nothing is seen to advantage, and very little is seen at all." But another Englishman, the great novelist Charles Dickens, after criticizing the packet's accommodations, vividly recalled: "the exquisite beauty of the opening day, when light came glancing off from everything; the gliding on at night so noiselessly, past frowning hills sullen with dark trees and sometimes angry in one red, burning spot high up, where unseen men lay crouching round a fire; the shining out of the bright stars undisturbed by any noise of wheels or steam or any other sound than the limpid rippling of the water as the boat went on; all these were pure delights."

The New Society, 1820-1860

Between 1820 and 1860 America burst its seams. The physical area almost doubled, and the population increased by over three hundred percent. Westward settlement accelerated, carrying the center of population from a point in north-central Virginia to the middle of Ohio. A total of eleven new states joined the Union. Even more significant than the country's physical growth was its rapid economic transformation: in 1820 Americans lived overwhelmingly in the countryside and worked the land; over the forty years that followed were laid the foundations of an industrial economy. A transportation revolution unified the country physically. Waves of immigrants provided the labor force for the mills and construction gangs. A series of technological breakthroughs launched a revolution in the production of all kinds of goods. On the eve of the Civil War the nation was second only to Great Britain in the value of its manufactures. These startling developments affected Americans everywhere.

Economic Developments: The Transportation Revolution

In 1808, when Secretary of the Treasury Albert Gallatin proposed his ambitious system of internal improvements at federal expense, it took a New Yorker three days to travel to Boston, ten days to reach Charleston, and nearly six weeks to journey west to St. Louis. The movement of bulky or heavy goods over long distances by land was prohibitively expensive: it cost more to drag a ton of iron overland a few miles than to bring it across the ocean. Farmers and merchants still depended mainly on waterways to move their crops and merchandise. Coastwise shipping was inexpensive but slow. Inland areas were peculiarly dependent upon river transportation. But this was strictly a one-way affair—downstream. The flatboats that floated down to New Orleans with Western produce had to be broken up for lumber, and the boatmen left to get home as best they could— often on foot. Unfortunately for the country, sectional jealousies and constitutional quibbles prevented the passage of Gallatin's and Clay's plans for internal improvements. Transportation remained haphazard and wasteful. Nonetheless, the fragmented American republic slowly linked itself up into a connected whole.

Early American roads were little more than broad, stump-filled paths through the forest. Impassable in wet weather, they were adequate only for local needs. A system of through routes, bringing together the chief commercial centers, was desperately needed. In the 1790's private corporations began building turnpikes along the most important routes of travel. These companies financed construction mainly by the sale of stock to investors, and sought profits by collecting tolls from persons using the roads. The best turnpikes had a firm stone foundation overlaid with gravel, drainage ditches to control run-off, and substantial stone or wooden bridges. The extreme difficulty of moving men and material during the War of 1812 stimulated a boom in turnpike construction. By 1825 these roads crisscrossed New England and the Mid-Atlantic states; Pennsylvania alone had about 2,400 miles of toll road. In the West and South, where private capital was scarce, state and local governments often financed the turnpikes. The greatest of them all, the National Road, was built by the federal government. Begun in 1811, it ultimately stretched from Cumberland, Maryland, to Vandalia, Illinois. Travelers on this great western highway encountered an endless stream of people on foot, on horseback, in stagecoaches, in "one-horse (immigrant) wagons," and driving lumbering teamster wagons.

Few of these turnpikes ever showed a profit to their owners. Maintenance proved a constant drain. The public devoted considerable ingenuity to outwitting toll collectors: short roads popularly known as "shunpikes" frequently circled around the toll gates. Most important, the turnpikes, although popular with travelers, failed to provide economical long-distance freight transportation. Even where tolls were low, it was not profitable for heavy wagons with six and eight-horse teams to make long hauls over them. As a result, many of the turnpike companies had failed even before the emergence of competition from canals and railroads.

Samuel Coleman, Storm King on the Hudson, *1866* (National Collection of Fine Arts, Smithsonian Institution.)

The steamboat provided the first economical inland transportation for both freight and people. Men had been experimenting worldwide for years with the application of steam power to water transportation, but it remained for Robert Fulton, a young American engineer, to perfect a design. His misnamed *Clermont,* equipped with an English-built engine and paddle wheels, averaged five miles an hour on its first voyage up New York's Hudson River in 1807. Spectators on shore watched in astonishment as the *Clermont* overtook the sluggish sailing vessels and "passed them as if they had been at anchor." Fulton and his partner, Robert R. Livingston, tried to keep exclusive control over their invention, but steam navigation was too important to be monopolized. By the time the Supreme Court, in *Gibbons v. Ogden* (1824), formally annulled the Fulton-Livingston monopoly in New York, steamboats had been introduced on every major river in the country.

The years from 1820 to 1860 marked the golden age of steamboating. On Eastern rivers, harbors, and bays, steamboats served primarily as passenger vessels. They were designed for speed and comfort, with razor bows, long narrow hulls, giant paddle wheels amidships, and elegantly furnished cabins. Even larger boats plied the Great Lakes, carrying thousands of immigrants west to Detroit and Chicago. But it was in the fertile valley of the Mississippi that steamboats had their greatest impact. Ingenious shipbuilders quickly adapted them to navigate the Western rivers even during periods of low water. Hulls were made broad and shallow, engines and cabins placed on deck, and paddle wheels moved to the stern. Although Western rivermen exaggerated when they boasted that all they needed for successful navigation was a heavy dew, some of their boats could operate in water as shallow as thirty inches. These floating rafts at last made it economical to ship the bulky exports of the interior to market. Receipts of produce at New Orleans leaped from $12 million in 1820-21 to a peak of $197 million in 1850-51. There larger ships took on the grain and cotton for destinations on the East Coast or in Europe. On their return upstream the steamboats carried consumer goods formerly hauled overland at enormous cost. More than anything else, these ungainly boats brought the Middle West firmly into the national economy.

Knowing the success of the early English canals, landlocked Americans had talked for years of linking the nation's patchwork of navigable rivers and lakes with artificial waterways. A major obstacle was the inability of private capital to supply the large sums—$25,000 a mile or more—necessary for canal construction. By 1816 only about a hundred miles of canals had been constructed in the United States, most less than two miles long. None had returned a profit to their owners.

The construction of the Erie Canal changed all this. Pushed through the New York legislature in 1817 by Governor De Witt Clinton's powerful political machine, it was "the most decisive single event in the history of American transportation." Beginning at Albany, on the Hudson, the canal wound 363 miles through the Mohawk River Valley to Buffalo, on Lake Erie. Along the way eighty-three locks lifted the boats up and down the 650-foot elevation, and eighteen stone aqueducts carried the canal over rivers and streams.

The Erie Canal was an immediate success. Before its opening, the cost of hauling grain across the Appalachian foothills to New York City was three times the market value of wheat, six times that of corn, ten times that of oats. Overnight these stifling transportation costs disappeared, as horses pulled hundred-ton barges loaded with freight along "Clinton's Big Ditch" at rates as low as a cent a ton-mile. At the canal's Albany terminus steamboats took over for the swift and economical trip down the Hudson to New York City (and, of course, from New York back up to Albany). By 1825, when the Erie was completed, toll revenues already exceeded a half-million dollars a year. Soon the canal's entire $7-million cost had been recovered, and state officials ordered the canal widened to accommodate the increased traffic. Towns all along the route prospered, none more than New York, which became the transportation gateway to the West and the nation's largest port.

The success of the Erie touched off a nationwide boom in canal-building. Several Eastern states, jealous of New York's position, tried to tap the Western market with canals of their own. Pennsylvania's "Main Line" system over the Allegheny Mountains required a portage railroad—a stairstep of inclined planes by which cable cars carried the canal boats up one side of the highest ridges and down the other. In the West, Ohio and Indiana raced to link the waters of Lake Erie and the Ohio River. Indiana's contribution, the Wabash and Erie Canal, was over 450 miles long. By 1840, when the boom collapsed, the American people had constructed over 3300 miles of canals, at a total cost of $125 million. State governments provided most of this huge capitalization, selling bonds against anticipated revenues. Few states or bondholders, however, recovered even a fraction of their investment. Many of the canals were poorly planned and constructed; maintenance costs were high; ice or low water closed them at certain seasons. Nevertheless, these costly ditches greatly stimulated the economy. They offered the first economical means of transferring the bulky products of the West directly eastward.

The difficulties encountered with turnpikes and canals spurred the determined search for a cheap, fast, dependable, and profitable means of overland transportation. Americans took an early interest in another English development, the railroad. Construction of a few small tramways began in the United States during the 1820's, and in 1828 the first major railroad, the Baltimore and Ohio, was chartered. Many early railroads ran only short distances, being designed to serve mainly as feeders into nearby rivers and canals, but major Eastern cities like Boston and Baltimore, which had inadequate water connections, promoted longer lines. Merchants of Charleston, South Carolina, anxious to divert upcountry cotton shipments to their wharves, built a railroad to Hamburg on the lower Savannah River. When completed in 1833, it extended 136 miles and was the longest railroad in the world. In these years ingenious American inventors made a number of important technical improvements in the design of locomotives and roadbeds. By 1840 the nation's total railway mileage equaled that of canals, and many lines were competing successfully with canal companies for business.

As with other forms of transportation, railway construction was encouraged by public funding. Between 1830 and 1843 the national government lowered tariff duties on railroad iron. State legislatures—once again taking the lead in such public assistance—granted tax incentives, required newly chartered banks to invest in railroad stock, extended large grants, and sometimes operated lines directly. It is true that outright state ownership of railroads was never as extensive as it was of canals, and the depletion of treasuries by unsuccessful waterway projects impeded the financing of new projects. Still, added to the foreign capital which American railroads attracted, government help provided strong impetus to private companies. Railroad-building boomed. Almost 9,000 miles of track was laid in the 1840's and 22,000 more in the next decade. On the eve of the Civil War railroads overshadowed all other forms of transportation in the country.

Economic Developments: Immigration

The transportation revolution, by making the movement of goods vastly easier and cheaper, opened up a vast new potential market for manufactured products. But where were the workers to produce these goods? From colonial times, labor had been in short supply in America. The easy availability of cheap land offered not only farm employment but farm ownership to attract the growing population. In 1800 only ten percent of the labor force were "employees," that is, persons who sold their labor. The rest of the white working force were farmers, self-employed artisans and mechanics, and independent tradesmen.

Early manufacturers experimented with various ways of overcoming this acute labor scarcity. One was the "domestic" or "putting-out" system: entrepreneurs furnished raw materials to people who worked in their own homes, making cloth, shoes, and wearing apparel; the entrepreneurs then collected and marketed the finished product. In a predominantly agricultural country, where most people lived in rural areas, this system, though cumbersome, allowed manufacturers to tap a tremendous pool of part-time labor, especially women and children. Other businessmen tried to centralize production, hiring whole families whom they housed in tenements adjacent to their mills. But as factories grew larger, requiring a labor force of hundreds, even thousands, factory owners turned increasingly to the Waltham system.

This system was the brainchild of Francis Cabot Lowell, an early textile manufacturer. Anxious to recruit young women from New England farms to work in his mill at Waltham, Massachusetts, Lowell built dormitories nearby to house them. In order to counteract the widespread reputation of mills as places of loose morals, he placed these dormitories in charge of respectable widows who maintained rigid rules of conduct. The factory girls typically had to be in their rooms by 10 p.m., to attend church regularly, and to save part of their earnings. A few mills sponsored evening classes and libraries for their workers.

Lowell's plan was an immediate success. Young women welcomed the chance to get away from the farm for a few years and to earn a little money of their own. In the 1820's and 1830's they flocked by the thousands to New England mill towns like

Lowell, Chicopee, and Manchester. Visitors to the textile factories usually praised the Waltham system. After a tour in 1834, Davy Crockett described Lowell's "mile of gals" as "well-dressed, lively, and genteel" in appearance and happy in their work. Insiders, however, were not so generous in their praise. They criticized the long hours, low wages, and overcrowded dormitories. The occasional strikes and walkouts that occurred would seem to indicate at least some measure of discontent. Faced with labor dissatisfaction and a shrinking supply of farm girls, manufacturers turned in the forties to a new, more docile source of labor: the immigrant.

Nothing in the country's experience had prepared for the mass immigration that took place in the early nineteenth century. Previously immigrants had come in trickles. After 1815, especially beginning in the mid-1840's, they came in seemingly endless waves, fleeing from economic distress or political turmoil in their homelands. Between 1815 and 1860 4,777,000 immigrants entered the country—more than the entire population of the United States in 1790. The largest number, over 2,000,000 came from Ireland, many to work on the construction of the Erie Canal. Germany ranked second as a country of origin, with a million-and-a-half. Another three-quarters-of-a-million arrived from England, Scotland, and Wales; most of the remainder hailed from Switzerland and Scandinavia.

These new immigrants had little in common with those who had come before the War of 1812. Most of the earlier arrivals had been literate, often skilled, fired with hope. The postwar immigrants, on the other hand, were frequently illiterate, unskilled, without resources. Lacking the know-how and money to undertake farming on the frontier,

and anxious to remain near their fellow countrymen, few of the newcomers ventured far from the ports of arrival. Crowded into cities, they formed an enormous pool of unskilled labor, ripe for exploitation. Immigrants—mainly Irish—were employed in vast numbers in canal and railroad-building, often under incredibly harsh conditions; others found work in the Pennsylvania coal fields and Illinois lead mines. During the 1840's immigrants rapidly began to replace native farmers' daughters in New England textile and shoe factories. The paternalistic spirit of Lowell disappeared quickly under the impact of increasing numbers of foreign-born laborers. "I regard people just as I regard my machinery," a manufacturer explained in 1855:

So long as they can do my work for what I choose to pay them, I keep them, getting out of them all I can. What they do or how they fare outside my wall I don't know, nor do I consider it my business to know. They must look out for themselves as I do for myself. When my machines get old and useless, I reject them and get new, and these people are part of my machinery.

Cruel as this attitude was, neither the factory system nor the great canal and railroad projects of the period could have come into existence so quickly without this exploitation of foreign labor. Between 1830 and 1850, immigrants supplied nearly half the increase in the non-slave working force. Nevertheless, America paid a high price for this economic acceleration. Mass immigration augmented the labor force, but exploitation brought problems of poverty, disease, and crime that severely strained the nation's social fabric.

Economic Developments: Industrialization

Improved transportation unified the national economy; mass immigration provided the necessary labor force. Only one additional ingredient was yet required for the American economy to "take off"—a native technology capable of sustaining mass production. Here again, America was at first heavily dependent on Britain. When Robert Fulton designed his *Clermont,* he had the engine made in England, for no one in America could produce such a complex piece of machinery.

Americans started with a number of advantages in their struggle for independence from European technology. American craftsmen had always shown a certain "Yankee ingenuity," a self-reliance and versatility compelled by America's isolation from Europe and the peculiar needs of the frontier. An absence of traditional class barriers and guild regulations encouraged experimentation. Unwittingly, Britain forced Americans to become economically independent by restricting

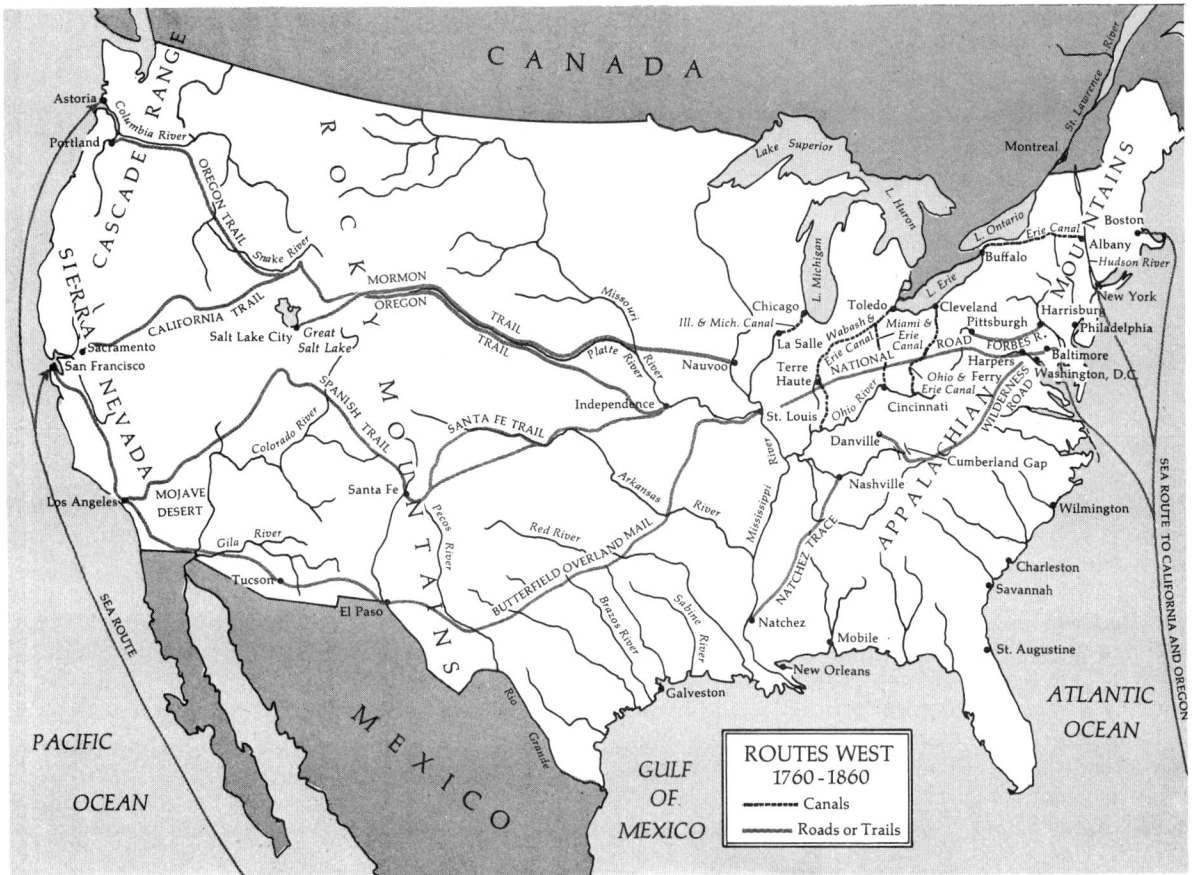

Map labels (selected, as shown):

CANADA

ROCKY MOUNTAINS · CASCADE RANGE · SIERRA NEVADA · APPALACHIAN MOUNTAINS

Astoria · Portland · Columbia River · Snake River · OREGON TRAIL · CALIFORNIA TRAIL · Sacramento · San Francisco · Salt Lake City · Great Salt Lake · MORMON · OREGON TRAIL · MOJAVE DESERT · Los Angeles · Santa Fe · SPANISH TRAIL · SANTA FE TRAIL · Colorado River · Gila River · Tucson · El Paso · Rio Grande · Pecos River · Red River · Brazos River · Sabine River · BUTTERFIELD OVERLAND MAIL · Galveston

Lake Superior · L. Michigan · L. Huron · L. Ontario · L. Erie · Montreal · St. Lawrence River · Erie Canal · Boston · Albany · Buffalo · Hudson River · New York · Chicago · Toledo · Cleveland · Pittsburgh · Harrisburg · Philadelphia · Ill. & Mich. Canal · Wabash & Erie Canal · Miami & Erie Canal · NATIONAL ROAD · FORBES R. · Harpers Ferry · Baltimore · Washington, D.C. · La Salle · Terre Haute · Nauvoo · Ohio & Erie Canal · WILDERNESS ROAD · St. Louis · Cincinnati · Danville · Cumberland Gap · Wilmington · Nashville · NATCHEZ TRACE · Charleston · Savannah · Natchez · Mobile · St. Augustine · New Orleans · Missouri River · Platte River · Arkansas River · Mississippi River · Ohio River · Independence · TRAIL

PACIFIC OCEAN · SEA ROUTE · MEXICO · GULF OF MEXICO · ATLANTIC OCEAN · SEA ROUTE TO CALIFORNIA AND OREGON

ROUTES WEST
1760-1860
--------- Canals
━━━━━━ Roads or Trails

the export of textile machinery and even the emigration of skilled mechanics. Finally, a chronic shortage of labor compelled Americans to invent labor-saving machinery. Many humble inventors became respected, successful men.

This stimulating atmosphere resulted in a host of new inventions during the first half of the nineteenth century. Besides the automated grist mill, Oliver Evans pioneered in the design of the high-pressure steam engine, a distinct improvement over the British engines of Newcomen and Watt. Norbert Rillieux, a free black, invented a multiple-effect evaporator to process the sugar cane grown in his native Louisiana. The endless fields and limited supply of agricultural labor stimulated significant improvements in farm machinery. Before Cyrus McCormick invented his reaper in 1831 a man with a sickle could cut approximately one acre of wheat in a day; with a reaper he could harvest ten to twelve. In 1837 John Deere perfected a steel plow capable of turning the tough prairie sod of Iowa and Illinois. By 1860 American technology was going full blast. In that year the U.S. Patent Office issued 4,589 new patents, a thirty fold increase over 1820.

While new inventions transformed basic industries and with them much of American life, other ingenious tinkerers sought to increase the creature comforts: the steam radiator for home heating; an immensely important ice making machine; condensed milk and concentrated coffee (which came in a cube, light and with sugar) both invented by Gail Borden in the 1850's; the paper window shade; hundreds of different kinds of new stoves and lamps; thousands of household gadgets. The rising interest in domesticity—the ideal of a comfortable home and health for all classes of society—is well reflected in this motley parade of inventions. The rise of the common man and the growing pressure to bind married women more closely to the home were both tied to the industrial revolution.

Along with new inventions came a specifically American development: mass production employing interchangeable parts. This concept had originated in Europe, but an American, Eli Whitney, first applied it successfully. His unsuccessful fight to get a legal monopoly on his cotton gin had impoverished the inventor. Anxious to recoup his fortunes, Whitney hit upon the idea of

Asher Durand, Dover Plain, *Dutchess County, New York, 1848.* (National Collection of Fine Arts, Smithsonian Institution.)

producing muskets in quantity by using machines to turn out the component parts, thus permitting uniform design and rapid assembly. "In short," Whitney wrote federal officials in 1798, "the tools which I contemplate are similar to an engraving on copper plate from which may be taken a great number of impressions exactly alike."

This was a bold proposal at a time when gunsmiths still made muskets one at a time, filing and fitting the individual pieces to mate them into a working mechanism. The government, then fearful of war with France, and highly respectful of Whitney's talents, accepted his audacious offer to manufacture ten thousand muskets in twenty-eight months. Not surprisingly, Whitney badly underestimated the difficulties of "tooling up" for this kind of operation; he was several years late in delivering the promised muskets. Gradually, however, his "uniformity system" gained acceptance and was applied in dozens of industries. Americans proved adept at designing and building the lathes, borers, and calipers necessary for the precision manufacture of parts for clocks, watches, and sewing machines.

On the eve of the Civil War, industrialization was far advanced in the United States. A modern transportation network had been laid down. A sufficient labor force had been assembled. The factory system had largely displaced household manufacture. Several industries—textiles, carpets, shoes, paper—were thoroughly mechanized. The American economy had begun to assume its now familiar shape.

The Land and the People: The Northeast

Between 1820 and 1860 manufacturing grew rapidly in the New England and Mid-Atlantic states. Both sections boasted readily available capital, labor, and superior transportation. Turnpikes, rivers, the Erie Canal, and safe harbors provided good access to raw materials and markets. Commerce and agriculture, particularly dairy and truck farming, remained important in the region, but some places —southern New England, the Hudson and Delaware river valleys—began to resemble the most industrialized areas of Great Britain in their economy and social structure.

The conditions of labor changed fundamentally after 1820, as most independent craftsmen, many men, women, and children from farms, and, finally, masses of immigrants became wage-earners. With the widespread adoption of steam power in the 1840's, factories no longer had to be located in rural areas, close to free-flowing streams, but could be placed near cities. Henceforth workers were completely divorced from the land. With the influx of immigrant labor, wages and working conditions deteriorated in many industries, creating serious poverty. Most workers had no protection against long hours, occupational hazards, illness, or unemployment. The limited attempts at unionization in this period failed in the face of periodic panics and public hostility. Not until 1842, in the famous case of *Commonwealth v. Hunt,* did the Massachusetts Supreme Court uphold the legality of trade unions. White

Southerners were often as shocked at the condition of Northern "free" labor as some Northerners were at slavery. Free labor, wrote George Fitzhugh of Virginia, "is more cruel, in leaving the laborer to take care of himself and family out of the pittance which skill or capital have allowed him to retain. When the day's labor is ended, he is free, but he is overburdened with the cares of family and household, which make his freedom an empty and delusive mockery. . . . The Negro slave is free, too, when the labors of the day are over, and free in mind as well as body; for the master provides food, raiment, house, fuel, and everything else necessary for the physical well-being of himself and family."

Under the combined impact of the transportation revolution, industrialization, and immigration, cities grew more rapidly in this period than at any other time in American history, before or since. In 1820 only 6.1 percent of the population lived in urban areas (that is, places of 2,500 or more inhabitants); by 1860 close to twenty percent of the people were city dwellers. On the eve of the Civil War there were fifteen cities (nine of them in the Northeast) with populations in excess of fifty thousand. Philadelphia exceeded 500,000 and New York had passed 1,000,000.

The cities, however, were hopelessly ill-equipped to deal with these numbers of people. Municipal water and sewage systems were in their infancy. Pigs roamed the streets in every city, the only effective street cleaners. Housing was always in short supply. Many people lived in tiny apartments, often with whole families —and perhaps a few boarders—occupying the same room. The poorest lived in unfinished cellars. In 1849 a Boston doctor found "one cellar. . . .occupied nightly as a sleeping-apartment for thirty-nine persons. In another, the tide had risen so high that it was necessary to approach the bedside of a patient by means of a plank which was laid from one stool to another; while the dead body of an infant was actually sailing about the room in its coffin."

Filth, overcrowding, and poverty produced unique problems. Cholera epidemics in 1832 and 1849 killed thousands. Fires were an everyday occurrence, sometimes leveling whole sections of cities. Crime, ranging from prostitution to burglary and murder, flourished everywhere, even on Broadway, where according to one contemporary, "whores and blackguards made up about two-thirds of the throng." Realizing that they could no longer cope with these problems on an individual basis, the business and middle classes created institutions, such as police forces, to deal with them.

Slowly, grudgingly, but inevitably, municipal debts were run up to finance water and sewer systems, street lights, schools, and parks.

Cities alternately repelled and fascinated Americans. Moralists condemned them as "sinful" and "wicked." Native Protestants expressed alarm at the rapid growth of ethnic ghettos, where immigrants retained their old customs, languages, and Catholic religion. Many people fretted over the glaring contrasts of wealth and poverty they saw everywhere.

Still, people came to the cities in ever-increasing numbers—to visit, to work, to seek their fortunes. For those who could establish some roots and find steady employment, urban life, with its shops, newspapers, amusements, and parks, had many fascinations. New York's Crystal Palace Exposition of 1853, a visitor observed, reflected on a smaller scale the essential characteristics of the city as a whole: "What a wilderness of objects! Statues and statuettes, silks and satins, china and glass, furniture of all descriptions, and for all uses. What bright colors! What never ending glitter! What crowds of people!"

The Land and the People: The Northwest

Between 1820 and 1860 the American economy showed a growing regional specialization. The Northeast concentrated on manufacturing. The South continued to cultivate staple crops for export. The third great section, the Northwest, turned increasingly to commercial agriculture. The growth of industry, and the resulting rise of cities, created a steadily expanding market for farm products, both in the Northeast and in Europe. The upper Mississippi and Ohio valleys, with their fertile soil and vast tracts of public land, were in an ideal position to meet this demand, especially after canals and railroads made it possible to ship large quantities of meat and grain directly eastward. The Northwest became the nation's breadbasket, supplying food for Northern cities and Southern plantations.

With every decade the centers of production for wheat, corn, cattle, hogs, and sheep shifted westward, as hordes of settlers opened the prairies to cultivation. Many of these newcomers had abandoned the thin soils of New England for places like Indiana and Michigan, where wheat yields were several times greater per acre. Small

farmers from the upper South flocked into the southern counties of Ohio, Illinois, and Indiana, giving that region a distinctively Southern character. Sizable numbers of English, German, and Scandinavian immigrants migrated west, fanning out through the rich farmlands of Iowa, Illinois, Minnesota, and Wisconsin. On the eve of the Civil War the population of the Northwest, which had numbered less than one million in 1820, exceeded nine million.

Farms in the Northwest tended to be small—about 200 acres on the average. Most farmers owned their own land, relying on their families, on hired help, and,—increasingly—on machines for labor. Wheat, always in demand, was the cash crop; and mechanical drills, harvesters, and threshers permitted an enormous increase in production throughout the period. In the 1840's and 1850's wheat dominated farming in the upper Mississippi Valley almost as completely as cotton dominated agriculture in the lower South. Wheat and flour became important export items in the fifties, undermining slightly the dominant position of cotton in American foreign trade.

George Caleb Bingham, Fur Traders Descending the Missouri. (Metropolitan Museum of Art.)

A CHANGING NATION

Western farmers also grew large quantities of corn and oats, but primarily as feed for livestock. The demands of Eastern cities and Southern planters assured a ready market and good prices for the beef, pork, and mutton of the prairies. Before railroads penetrated the Ohio Valley, cattle were driven overland to market; most hogs were slaughtered and packed locally. (Frequently they were "stuck" or cut in the throat, and allowed to bleed while alive—often the pioneer woman's job—then women and children took out and washed the various innards, saving the bladder to inflate and use as a football.) So much pork was processed at Cincinnati that the city became known for a time as "Porkopolis." Later, increasing numbers of livestock were shipped east by rail to city markets for slaughter.

Although the countryside contained a much larger population and gave the Northwest an agrarian character, the region's cities grew swiftly as well. Older communities like St. Louis, Cincinnati, and Louisville all expanded rapidly in this period. Even more spectacular was the progress of new cities like Milwaukee, Indianapolis, and especially Chicago. The Windy City had barely 17,000 people when Cyrus McCormick moved his reaper factory there in 1847: thirteen years later the population numbered 109,000. Yet the city remained a raw and uncomfortable place. Its mud was the subject for endless tales. Signs read "No Bottom" or "Road to China" or "Man Lost." A favorite story told of a man who saw a hat in the mud. Picking it up, he saw a man's face underneath. "Say, stranger, you're stuck in the mud! Can I give you a hand to pull you out? "Oh, no, thanks," replied the face, "I'm riding a good horse. He's got me out of the worst spots." These Western cities served principally as extensions of the rural economy, processing, shipping, and marketing agricultural products. Their mills and packinghouses led the country in 1860 in the production of lumber, flour and meal, liquor and meat. The cities were also the site of the growing farm-machinery industry.

The expansion of urban markets had a dramatic impact on sectional alignments. Between 1820 and 1860, Western farmers came increasingly to depend on Eastern cities to purchase their produce. The industrial Northeast, in turn, found a growing market for its manufactures in the Western states. A common economic bond was thus forged between the two sections, undermining the old alliance between the West and South.

The Land and the People: The South

The antebellum Southern economy was surprisingly diverse. Cotton was "King," but corn was actually the South's most widely grown crop. Many planters in Virginia and Maryland, their soil exhausted after prolonged tobacco cultivation, shifted to raising wheat or cattle. Rice grew in the swampy low country of South Carolina and Georgia. Another exotic crop, sugar, was raised in southern Louisiana. Cotton, the South's major cash crop, was cultivated throughout the lower South. The center of cotton production moved steadily westward after 1820—the inevitable result of overplanting and soil exhaustion. On the eve of the Civil War over a fourth of the 4.3 million bales grown in the United States came from beyond the Mississippi River. Southern industry was limited primarily to the processing of locally grown timber, tobacco, and grain, but a start had been made in the manufacture of cotton goods, machinery, and iron. Although mainly a rural land, a number of important cities—Baltimore, Richmond, New Orleans, St. Louis, Charleston, Mobile—dotted its navigable perimeter.

Contrary to popular belief, the South was not inhabited solely by rich planters, impoverished "white trash," and enslaved blacks. In 1860 the bulk of the South's eight million whites lived on small farms not unlike those in the North. Most farmers owned their land, cultivating it with their own hands or the help of a few slaves. With the exception of rice and sugar, these yeoman farmers raised the same crops as the planters. Many of them also grazed cattle. Outside of the older states of Virginia and Carolinas, small farmers frequently moved upward into the planter class. They had little in common with poor whites—the "crackers" or "white trash"—who eked out a meager existence in the sterile sand hills or pine barrens. These unfortunate people owed their degradation not to the competition of slave labor, but to the ravages of malaria, hookworm and pellagra.

The actual number of planters was small. The federal census of 1860—defining a planter as a person owning at least twenty slaves—counted 46,274 such persons. Most of these were "small" planters owning up to fifty slaves and five hun-

Calendar, painted wood; made by Shakers, Zoar, Ohio, 1836, *(Index of American Design.)*

dred to eight hundred acres. Typically, they were hardworking businessmen with field work to supervise, laborers to oversee, books to balance. And their wives seldom conformed to the Southern-belle stereotype. Managing a large household required energy and intelligence, as well as graceful manners. Home was more likely to be a modest frame cottage than a Tara or a Mount Vernon.

At the apex of Southern society stood the large planters. Although few in number—only 2,292 persons owned as many as a hundred slaves in 1860—these planter-aristocrats cast a giant shadow over the region. Their wealth gave them considerable social and political influence. Living in palatial mansions or elegant townhouses, surrounded by vast fields and liveried servants, they represented the ideal to which most white Southerners aspired before the Civil War.

In spite of this diversity, the South possessed a distinctive flavor overall. The great majority of

Southern whites were Anglo-Saxon and Protestant. The economy was colonial: Southerners raised staple crops for export and imported finished goods. Before the Revolution they had traded mainly with England, but in the first half of the nineteenth century Southern trade came increasingly under the control of Northerners, and particularly under the dominance of the port of New York. Above all, there was slavery, a uniquely Southern institution that exerted a powerful influence over the region. In 1860 only one white person in four had a vested interest in slavery. Those who did not sometimes sneered at the plantation "swell-hands," whose children wanted "so bad to look as if they weren't made of the same clay as the rest of God's creation." But the presence of millions of blacks gave whites of all classes something in common—a determination to keep the South a white man's country. Race consciousness helped to unify the South.

Slaves worked everywhere in the antebellum South: as common laborers, skilled craftsmen, and servants; in factories, mines, and foundries; on riverboats, wharves, and railroads; in hotels, stores, and private homes. A Charleston census of 1848 listed forty-six occupations that employed slaves. Most, of course, worked as field hands. Over half belonged to planters owning twenty or more slaves. These large units were especially common in the newer states of the lower South, where the work was harder and the conditions more brutal than in the older slave states.

On small farms the slaves usually worked alongside their masters, who directly supervised their labor. On plantations they were organized in two ways. Rice planters preferred the task system, allotting individual slaves a particular task for the day. Cotton and tobacco planters favored the gang system, dividing the slaves into work parties under the supervision of an overseer or trusted Negro driver. The plantation routine followed the seasons in a monotonous cycle. Both men and women worked in the fields, plowing and planting in the spring, weeding in the summer, harvesting in the fall. In winter and in slack times, they dug ditches, repaired fences, and sawed wood. The young and the elderly tended livestock or cared for the small children. Field hands labored from sunrise to sunset, with a rest at midday. They usually had Sunday off and received a week's vacation at Christmas. For many slaves these holidays, with their occasional feasts, dances, and visits to neighboring plantations, provided the only relief from the hardship of their daily lives.

Most slaves lived in rude cabins adjacent to the "big house." Some masters encouraged their bondsmen to marry and live as families; others left

219   A CHANGING NATION

the matter to the slaves or assigned them arbitrarily to a mate. The owner provided food, clothing, and medical care. The typical slave's ration consisted of cornmeal, fatback, and molasses; but many slaves varied this boring and unhealthful diet by raising their own vegetables or fishing. Household servants and city slaves enjoyed a somewhat easier life than field hands. In addition, many slaveholders hired out their bondsmen as servants, laborers, and mechanics, sometimes for extended periods. This practice of "hiring out" was especially common in the upper South and in the cities, where there was frequently a surplus of slaves. Many hired slaves became quasi-free men, regulating their own conduct after working hours.

Managing a plantation could be an unpleasant business, for slaves had little motivation to work hard. Although some worked willingly for kindly masters, most slaves delighted in "first-rate tricks to dodge work." Planters combined close supervision with a system of incentives—praise, additional rations, extra holidays—in an attempt to make their slaves work efficiently; but all too often they found it necessary to resort to whipping, deprivation of privileges, and other punishments to keep them in line. "The only principle that can maintain slavery," slaveholders reluctantly admitted, "Tis the principle of fear." Masters who maintained a rigid discipline had the least trouble in the long run. Those who found employing a lash distasteful—and there were many—often saw their plantation go to ruin.

Economically speaking, was it worth it to the planter? Although all the evidence is not in, the answer appears to be "yes." Investments in new plantations in the lower South consistently yielded a return upon capital sufficient to attract outside funds, an indication that a well-managed cotton plantation on good soil was at least as profitable as alternative forms of investment. Slaveholders in the less productive regions of the upper South exported their surplus slaves profitably to the Cotton Belt. For the South as a whole, however, slavery was probably less economically beneficial. It made underconsumers of four million blacks, and caused Southerners to concentrate their resources in staple agriculture at the expense of industry and transportation. In human terms, the effects of slavery were disastrous: it stifled the intellectual and creative energies of generations of black Americans and severely limited the opportunities of most white Southerners.

Slavery was more than a labor system; it was also a means of race control. The Southern states enacted elaborate slave codes touching virtually every aspect of black life. Slave marriages and divorces had no legal validity. Slaves were forbidden to leave their plantations without a pass, to be out after curfew, to congregate in groups unless a white man was present, to carry arms, or to strike a white person. They could not own property or testify in court against whites. Punishment for most crimes was left to the master, who was given immunity from prosecution should a slave die under "moderate" correction. Death was the penalty for rebellion or even plotting to rebel. To enforce these codes, the Southern states required white males to mount regular patrols, which traveled the neighborhood at night in search of arms or runaways. Members were chosen at militia muster and all members of the community—slaveholders and non-slaveholders alike—were supposed to take their turn.

In practice, humane interpretation usually tempered these repressive codes. Many masters developed a genuine affection for their slaves and showed a sense of basic responsibility for their welfare. Indulgent owners sometimes allowed them to acquire property, or taught them to read and write. Self-interest restrained all but a few owners from inflicting severe punishment on their bondsmen—the injury or loss of a prime male or fertile female was no small matter. Indeed, owners occasionally used hired labor for dangerous tasks rather than risk their valuable human property. Nevertheless, in moments of passion, masters did occasionally commit unspeakable atrocities on blacks. Charles Pettigrew, who owned many slaves, commented in his will that "it is a pity that agreeably to the nature of things, slavery and tyranny must go together." And hard-driving overseers measured a slave's worth by how many bales of cotton or bags of rice he produced.

Enslaved blacks faced the constant task of adjusting to the condition of bondage. Cases of rebellion were rare, for outright resistance was suicidal: when Nat Turner, a slave preacher, led a band of armed followers on a bloody rampage through Southampton County, Virginia, in 1831, killing sixty men, women and children, terrified whites retaliated by slaughtering at least one hundred blacks. The South was on edge for months afterward. No one knew when this black fury, like some smothered volcano, would erupt again. Individual acts of resistance, such as arson, running away, or even suicide, were not uncommon. Instead of confronting their masters directly, most blacks developed various stratagems of accommodation and subtle resistance. They became particulary adept at malingering, breaking tools, and mistreating livestock—effective ways of attacking the system.

Considering the hardships of slave life, blacks did remarkably well in preserving their identity and creating a unique culture. The black family, for example, may have been a more cohesive unit than historians and sociologists once believed. If plantation records contain instances of families being broken up, these same sources reveal many more cases in which they remained intact over several generations. And even when spouses and children were sent to other areas, black people retained a powerful sense of family. After emancipation, thousands of blacks wandered across the South in search of relatives and loved ones.

The vast treasury of folklore demonstrates the extent to which slaves retained a sense of identity. Slaves blended African and New World materials into their own culture. Black spirituals reveal the sorrows of slave life and refute the legend of contented "darkies" singing happily in the fields. As Frederick Douglass wrote, "Every tone was a testimony against slavery. . . . Slaves sing most when they are most unhappy. The songs of the slave represent the sorrows of his heart." Spirituals spoke not of freedom in the realm of heaven but of liberty on this earth. One song,

ostensibly about Biblical Samson, expressed the wish that "if I had my way, I'd tear this building down." Similarly, field hollers and work songs, rather than indicating contentment, served a definite purpose in the slaves' own society. In addition to combatting the boredom of mindless field labor, they provided the coordination and timing essential to people working under close and difficult conditions:

Massa in the great house, counting out his
    money,
Oh, shuck that corn and throw it in the barn.
Mistis in the parlor, eating bread and honey.
Oh, shuck that corn and throw it in the barn.

Religion also played a vital part in the slaves' lives. Repelled by the brand of religion their masters taught, the slaves formulated new ideas and practices in the quarters. They conducted praise meetings of their own, often in defiance of the law. Shouting, singing, and preaching, the slaves released their despair and expressed their hopes for freedom.

A Reforming Spirit

During the first half of the nineteenth century, rapid change sorely tested the American tradition of individualism and decentralized government. The age-old problems of poverty, disease, and illiteracy became more concentrated and apparent as cities grew. The transportation revolution broke down barriers of distance and isolation, uprooting established communities and existing markets. Increasing reliance on machines reduced independent craftsmen and sturdy farmers to wage-earners. Americans sought to cope with these changes in a variety of ways. A few questioned the very foundations of capitalism. Some turned to religious or social experiments designed to reform society. Most aimed at correcting specific problems. These reformers disagreed on goals and methods, but they also shared many attitudes: frustration at the disorder in society; apprehension about the loss of consensus and community; fear of declining morality. Above all, they shared a faith in the ultimate perfectibility of American society. The result was a vigorous and many-sided movement for reform, which picked up steam in the 1830's and continued down to the Civil War.

The American labor movement had its roots in the economic upheavals of the Jacksonian Era. In dozens of cities, craftsmen and artisans organized associations and sponsored strikes for better hours and wages. A few city-wide federated unions and one national federation—the National Trades' Union—formed before hostile judges and the economic cataclysm of 1837 dragged them under. Labor also entered the political arena. In the early 1830's, for example, New York City workingmen organized politically to seek improved working conditions, free public education, abolition of imprisonment for debt, and an end to chartered banks and other monopolies. Most of their demands were eminently practical; unfortunately, some of their leaders were not.

Frances Wright and Robert Dale Owen attracted a considerable following in New York. "Fanny" Wright's avowals of atheism and her intemperate attacks on organized religion caused one conservative newspaper to brand her "the great Red Harlot of Infidelity." Owen advocated birth-control measures to alleviate the miseries of the poor. Their chief remedy for society's ills, however, involved education. According to their plan, the state would become the guardian of all children. It would provide them with equal food, clothing, board, and education. Only then could they enter a highly competitive world on an equal footing. Opponents immediately denounced state guardianship as an infringement on parental rights and a covert attack on marriage. The question of endorsing it caused a permanent split in the ranks of New York workingmen.

George Henry Evans was another who believed he had the remedy for unemployment and poverty: "Let us . . . emancipate the white laborer, *by restoring his natural right to the soil.*" As early as 1834, Evans advocated free land grants to actual settlers and a limitation on the holdings of any one person. Adopting the motto "Vote yourself a farm," he tried for years to convince Eastern workingmen that their happiness and independence could be found only in agriculture. In 1862, six years after Evans' death, Congress passed the Homestead Act, providing free grants of Western land. Only then did the fallacy of Evans' scheme become apparent: workingmen did not have the capital, the knowledge, or the desire to go west and take up farming. Free Western land was no cure for the evils of industrialism.

A Reforming Spirit: Religious Movements

During the first half of the nineteenth century, America experienced a second "Great Awakening" of religious enthusiasm. Relying on the excitement of revival meetings, a wide variety of evangelical sects sought to turn the masses toward spiritual regeneration. Evangelists like Charles G. Finney rejected the harsh traditional Calvinist view of original sin and predestination and emphasized eternal salvation as within the reach of all good Christians. Their teachings generally involved a literal interpretation of the Bible and, most often, a belief in the Second Coming of Christ and the establishment of God's Kingdom on earth. To an important degree, this religious resurgence reflected distinctly American values and attitudes: its message was intensely democratic; it stressed individual free will and immediate salvation; it exuded optimism; it brought religion to the people in simple language they could understand.

Like the first Great Awakening of a century before, the new evangelicalism was more than a religious movement. For ordinary people caught up in the throes of social and economic change, it restored a sense of orderliness and coherence to their daily lives. In isolated frontier areas the churches served as socializing and civilizing agencies. Religious enthusiasm rapidly increased the membership of most Protestant denominations, with Methodists and Baptists growing the fastest. But new sects also arose. Each new prophet, interpreter, or mystic found followers willing to join him in anticipating the literal fulfillment of even the most outlandish prophecies. West New York State—often called the "burned-over district" because it was seared so many times by the fires of religious enthusiasm—was the incubator for many infant movements, but converts came from a larger field, stretching from northern New England to the Ohio and Tennessee valleys.

Some of the fervent young religious movements of the early 1800's encouraged believers to join together in exclusive communities of the faithful. The more unique or distinctive the tenets of their faith, leaders reasoned, the more necessary the intensive instruction and supervision that community living made possible. This often led to communal property-holding and cooperative economic enterprise. Many of these religious communities barely survived the death of their founders; others, such as the Shaker Society, lasted a century or more.

Ann Lee led the Shakers to America in 1774. The community received its name from one of its most distinctive practices, a sacred dance during which the members "shook" their bodies free of sin through their fingertips. "Mother Ann," as she was called, felt she had received direct revelations from God and, since she preached millennialism—that is, the imminent coming of the millennium, the period of Christ's rule on earth—she saw no need for the Shakers to have children. The members therefore practiced celibacy. After reaching a membership of some six thousand in the 1830's, the Shakers gradually died out. Their furniture and housing arrangements, which were simplicity itself, are their best-remembered achievements.

By far the most important of the religious communitarians were the Mormons. Social unrest and economic instability in the poor farming region of upstate New York produced a state of mind suscep-

Tall clock, Shaker; made by Benjamin Youngs in Watervliet, New York in 1806. *(Index of American Design.)*

Although Mormonism borrowed freely from the beliefs and practices of evangelical Protestantism, it offered a simple alternative to the confusing proliferation of Christian sects. By extending salvation to all adherents and clerical status to each adult white male, the Mormon church infused poor farmers, artisans, and mechanics with a sense of importance. By stressing the sanctity of secular accomplishments and the need for a community of "saints" (the church's official name was and is "The Church of Jesus Christ of Latter-Day Saints"), the new faith tapped the energies and talents of the unsuccessful and the neglected. In Joseph Smith, a prophet who stood at the top of the church hierarchy and received instructions or "revelations" directly from God, Mormonism provided theological truths and authoritarian leadership to those who craved practical and spiritual guidance.

After converting a small group of relatives and friends, Smith moved his flock to Ohio and then to Missouri in an attempt to establish a commonwealth of believers. In each place, however, non-believers persecuted the Mormons and drove them from their lands without compensation. In 1839 Smith led his followers to Illinois. After securing political authority from state officials, Smith founded a city, called Nauvoo, which became a self-sufficient religious community. The success of Nauvoo, which grew to fifteen thousand inhabitants by 1844, as well as its voting power in state elections, attracted the envy and hostility of outsiders. Smith's increasingly eccentric behavior (he declared himself a candidate for President in 1844) also produced unfavorable publicity. When a disgruntled Mormon confirmed that Smith and other members of the church's elite practiced polygamy, state officials arrested Smith and his brother. Soon after their confinement at Carthage, a mob of disbanded militia murdered them both.

When the harassment and violence continued, Brigham Young, Smith's successor as president of the church, led the Mormons on the long difficult exodus from Illinois to uninhabited Mexican territory beyond the Rocky Mountains. Under Young's stern but effective leadership, the Mormons established a thriving agricultural community near Great Salt Lake. Believers recall a miracle that saved that first band: after a desperate winter, the Mormons had planted a small crop and irrigated it by hand, a back-breaking task. Then, just as harvest time approached, a hoard of locusts swept down upon the fields. Near despair as they watched the insects devouring the only food available for the next winter, the Mormons suddenly heard the calls of

tible to intense religious emotions. "Enthusiastic" sects—Adventists, Universalists, Oneida Perfectionists, and Spiritualists—all flourished here. And Mormonism, drawing on the fundamentals of these unorthodox religions of the heart, strikingly elaborated this new theology of free will, direct revelation, universal salvation, the expectation of Christ's imminent return, and the establishment of a millennial Kingdom. In 1830, at the age of twenty-five, Joseph Smith of Palmyra, New York, published the *Book of Mormon*. He had transcribed it, he claimed, from gold plates that had lain undisturbed in a nearby hillside for more than a thousand years. The angel Moroni had directed him to the spot where the plates were buried. Using two magic "seeing stones" fixed in silver bows, Smith translated the ancient script into a readable text. The finished book was a curious mixture of Old Testament theology, popular history, and contemporary social beliefs.

hundreds of seagulls. The mysterious visitors, a thousand miles away from any ocean, ate the locusts and saved the community. This "miracle" gave fresh impetus to their vision of a new Zion, and Mormons zealously dedicated themselves to God's glory. By 1877, the year of Young's death, the commonwealth numbered some 350 settlements with a total population of 140,000.

Organized like a medieval kingdom, the church collected an annual tithe (tax), either in goods, labor, or money, from each individual and channeled this surplus into projects that benefited all. By banning or discouraging the use of tea, coffee, tobacco, liquor, fashionable clothing, and elegant furniture, the church curtailed wasteful spending and assured the development of an industrious community. This mixture of collectivism and private enterprise avoided the worst evils of uncontrolled capitalism and prevented Utah from becoming dependent on imports from the industrial East.

Although the Mormons wished to be self-sufficient and independent, they also considered themselves Americans and asked for Utah's admission to the Union. Congress, however, balked at the Mormon practice of polygamy. In actual fact, only a small percentage of the community participated in this patriarchal institution; but most of the American public thought that Brigham Young's twenty-seven wives and fifty-six children were typical, and they considered polygamy to be a form of "Oriental" debauchery. (To be sure, Mark Twain, who visited the territory's capital, Salt Lake City, in 1861, took a more kindly view of plural marriage. After observing the "poor, ungainly, and pathetically homely" Mormon women, he declared that a man who married one of them had performed "an act of Christian charity"; anyone who married "sixty of them" deserved the nation's tribute.) In 1890 the church formally renounced polygamy, signaling a Mormon retreat from the attempt to establish a society operating in entire accordance with religious principles and communal ideals. Mormonism was shortly reduced to a religion of the spirit that did not interfere conspicuously with the American way of life. Congress admitted Utah to the Union in 1896.

Not content with establishing an earthly paradise, some Americans eagerly embraced the New Testament prophecy of Christ's Second Coming—and, more particularly, looked to its fulfillment in their own time. The foremost exponent of millennialism was William Miller, a hardworking farmer in upstate New York who became caught up in a revival shortly after the War of 1812 and spent the rest of his life pondering religious questions. A literal interpretation of the Bible led him to a graphic belief in the Second Coming (or Advent), which he calculated would occur in about 1843. Aided by the widespread economic distress of the late eighteen-thirties, Miller made crowds of converts throughout New England with his vivid sermons depicting the glory of the Advent, the joy of those who would be saved, the suffering of the unrepentant. In a single year he gave 627 hour-and-a-half lectures before eager audiences, often of a thousand or more. Ministerial disciples with a knack for publicity spread Miller's views over an even wider area.

Miller hesitated to give his frantic followers a definite date, promising only that deliverance would come soon, in God's appointed time. As 1843—the Last Year—passed, March of 1844 came to be accepted as the crucial month. (A little girl told her mother, "I want to die this summer—I don't want to live next year and *be burnt up*.") Finally, when nothing happened, a weary and discouraged Miller frankly admitted his mistake, explaining that he had done his best. But his lieutenants were not yet ready to quit. They chose October 22, 1844, as the new "Advent Day" and talked Miller into accepting it. Excitement mounted higher than before as extensive preparations were made to enter God's Kingdom. The faithful made themselves white "ascension robes" and neglected nearly all secular business. Voting in the fall elections was very light in some districts. Crowds blocked the streets near Boston's Millennial Tabernacle, forcing the mayor to close the building.

On the night of October 21, Millerites gathered on hilltops to meet the new world together. No provisions were made for eating or sleeping, and many suffered as the night and the next day and then another night passed; in some places severe thunderstorms added to their misery. Some claimed to have seen a jeweled crown in the sky. In western New York, an earthquake intensified the sense of expectation. A few Adventists committed suicide—one man leaped over Niagara Falls. This day of the "Great Delusion" effectively ended the Adventist movement, although isolated Adventist sects continued to flourish.

Adventism was only one manifestation of the desire among many Americans to break down all barriers between this world and the next. Various forms of spiritualism, or attempts to contact the spirit world, also attracted widespread interest during the Second Great Awakening. Mesmerism, electro-biology, clairvoyance, phrenology, magnetism—each had its following. In 1848 a series of occurrences at the home of John Fox, a New York farmer, set off a mania of spiritualist excitement. Wherever Fox's two young daughters, Maggie and Katie, appeared, mysterious rapping sounds were heard. Eventually the girls and their mother worked out a system of communication with the presumably otherworldly source of the rappings. Soon the neighbors flocked in to observe these conversations with the spirit world. With an older sister acting as manager, the Fox girls began holding exhibitions—at the insistence of the spirits, of course—and quickly developed into professional fee-charging mediums.

With the wide publicity given the Fox sisters, mediums rapidly appeared all over the country, and spiritualist circles developed in nearly every town and village. These mediums refined their techniques as they went along; the Foxes' managing sister, for instance, discovered that total darkness could produce many more manifestations of the spirits' presence. Table-moving, spirit-writing, and cold, ghostly hands soon supplemented the mystic rappings, and within a few years all the now-familiar paraphernalia of spiritualism were in use. The spiritualist excitement, though dismissed by many, filled for thousands of people a real need to become more comfortable with the mysteries of death and immortality. A number of intellectuals saw in spiritualism a replacement for traditional Christianity—a proof of the existence of a supernatural world for a scientific age which could not accept revelation resting only on faith. Even when the Fox sisters some years later admitted that their whole career had been a great fraud (the rappings had from the first been produced by moving the joints of their toes), many spiritualists remained undeterred.

John Wesley had led within the Church of England a revival movement in the eighteenth century that produced a separate denomination, the Methodist church. Methodists believed in free will. In its early days especially, Methodism had a strong element of emotional revivalism; but it also preached a rigorous piety and a morality of self-discipline, industry, thrift, and good works. Methodism was powerfully attractive in Great Britain to the working classes and to the poor, and in this country to people on the frontier, and it is said that in both nations it had something to do with the bringing of an ordered moral life to previously disordered sections of society. While the Methodist church did have an organization, in its first period it did not stress the role of bishops or of a highly trained ministry. That made it possible for Methodism here to develop a distinctive and effective system in which preachers, many with little if any formal religious education, would travel about on the frontier, bringing a sustaining Methodism to the families and communities at which they stopped, each preacher working a "circuit" or route that covered a particular area. Francis Asbury, who had come to this country in 1771 and was influential in the beginnings of Methodism here, was an early and influential traveling preacher. The typical circuit rider went by horseback, depended on friendly settlers for food and shelter, and was very much a part of the frontier environment: Peter Cartwright could thrash a rowdy who tried to disrupt a Methodist meeting. The Methodists divided their territory into regions, each holding an annual conference that heard reports, appointed new preachers, and assigned circuits. As the frontier became heavily populated, large circuits—some had been hundreds of miles long—were replaced by smaller ones, and by about the middle of the nineteenth century these had given way to settled parishes. By that time the Methodist church had become the largest Protestant denomination in the country.

A Reforming Spirit: Secular Communitarianism

Many Americans believed that small communitarian groups, isolated from society, could develop social principles that would spread to and purify the whole nation. Dozens of experimental communities built upon a trust in human perfectibility sprouted up in the nineteenth century; their consistently short lives, however, demonstrate the difficulty of spreading communal ideas in a highly individualistic nation.

Robert Owen, the famous English socialist whose model factory town at New Lanark, Scotland, inspired so many American utopians, organized his own communal experiment at New Harmony, Indiana. Owen believed that the American West provided the unspoiled and egalitarian climate that a new social system required, and in 1825 he collected a motley group of followers whom he intended to transform into a prosperous self-governing community. By stressing cooperation and common ownership of property, Owen hoped to eliminate individual selfishness and want. But he soon discovered that it "was premature to unite a number of strangers [to operate] for their common interest, and live together as a common family." Quarrels and internal dissatisfaction finally forced Owen to abandon his misnamed experiment in communism. Such experiments, his son Robert Dale Owen later concluded, were bound to fail in a country where cheap land and high wages fostered excessive individualism and discouraged cooperative action.

An experiment of another sort was Brook Farm, a New England community that existed for a few years in the 1840's. Most of its members, such as Nathaniel Hawthorne and its founder George Ripley, were New England intellectuals; and it was influenced by transcendentalism, a moral and spiritual doctrine to which numbers of New England writers and social critics adhered. Transcendentalism was an American variant of the idealist philosophy that teaches that the world of material objects as we see them is really no more than an expression of mind or consciousness. Transcendentalists believed that since it is mind rather than the objective and physical world that is the ultimate reality, the mind can draw into itself and perfect its own powers. Transcendentalist intellectuals opposed slavery and other institutions that they perceived as getting in the way of individual and collective perfection. Brook Farm aimed at combining manual and intellectual work; this, its members hoped, would develop and enrich the inner self. Brook Farm was remembered for the high and not always practical intellectuality of its life. Residents operated a successful experimental school.

John Humphrey Noyes, whose social ideas rested on a religious creed known as perfectionism, founded a community at Oneida in upstate New York. Residents operated thriving manufacturers, but the community was better known for its sexual arrangements. Wishing to substitute cooperativeness for competitive individualism, Noyes prohibited "special love" and instead established "complex marriage," a system in which every member resident was considered married to every other of the opposite sex. Behavior was not promiscuous but strictly regulated. Women had sexual equality with the men and shared in the work; the entire community had responsibility for the children. The community had a prosperous and successful existence. Later in the century, it abandoned complex marriage in the face of attacks from moral critics.

A Reforming Spirit: Social Reform

Communities like these—there were many besides and there have been many since—were implicitly in a double relationship to society as a whole. In part they were withdrawn from that society and existed to provide for their own residents; yet they could want also to provide examples for the rest of humankind, and such communitarians as Robert Owen and the Brook Farm people spent lives of reformist activity outside the experimental communities as well. The United States during the Jacksonian era and afterwards was thick with reformers who gave themselves not to communitarian experiments but to efforts to improve society in general. Such organizations as the Bible Society, the American Tract Society, and the Home Missionary Society worked to instill religious principles in the population or portions of it; meanwhile, revivalists like Charles G. Finney preached to crowds. Other reformers worked for education, women's rights, improvement of prisons, care of the insane, temperance in drinking, total abstinence from drink, or the abolition of war. The best known of the reform movements, of course, were those opposed to slavery. Some opponents of slavery wished to colonize former slaves in Africa; some wanted to keep slavery from being permitted in the Western territory; others, the most militant, called for abolition of slavery in the South. For all its varieties and conflicts of objectives, much of the reformist activity in the United States was of a single mind in its restless morality, its conviction that the world can be improved and that we are under obligation to set ourselves to improving it.

Personal experience motivated such reformers as Angelina and Sarah Grimké and the black abolitionist Frederick Douglass. Others, especially those associated with the Bible societies and the American Tract Society, came from an upperclass, Calvinist elite. Fearing that social disorder would grow worse unless the masses were inculcated with "proper values," they took it upon themselves to serve as the moral stewards of the nation. "The gospel is the most economical police on earth," said a leader of the Home Missionary Society. The religious enthusiasm of the 1830's inspired such men as the antislavery activist Theodore Dwight Weld and the temperance advocate Neal Dow. And the prevalent belief in moral perfectionism sharpened the conviction of many reformers. The abolitionist editor William Lloyd Garrison, for example, became so obsessed with the need to maintain moral purity that he publicly burned a copy of the Constitution, thereby symbolically dissociating himself from a nation contaminated by the evil of slavery.

From colonial days Americans had exhibited a distinct fondness for alcoholic beverages. When Thomas Jefferson returned from France in 1789, he brought back over three hundred bottles of wine. Less affluent New Englanders settled for rum, which the doughty Puritans distilled from West Indian molasses. Before the advent of canals and railroads, farmers often sent their corn to market in a jug: whiskey cost less to ship over long distances and found a ready market. In many places it was safer to drink than water. An early nineteenth-century traveler in Ohio found the use of ardent spirits near universal: "A house could not be raised, a field of wheat cut down, nor could there be a log rolling, a husking, a quilting, a wedding, a sheepwashing, or a funeral without the aid of alcohol." Concerned over the antisocial effects of this excessive use of spirits, particularly its danger to the family, reformers mounted a determined attack on "Demon Rum."

The temperance crusade seemed, superficially at least, to be one of the most successful reforms. Using techniques borrowed from religious revivals and mass politics, temperance workers distributed leaflets, held "cold water parades," and organized lecture circuits of reformed drunkards who made emotional appeals for converts to sign "temperance pledges." In the late 1830's a million people belonged to temperance societies. Timothy Shay Arthur's lurid account of the evils of drink, *Ten Nights in a Bar-room, and What I Saw There (1854),* ranked just behind *Uncle Tom's Cabin* as the bestseller of the 1850's. A book of etiquette of the period instructed a lady to write as follows to a young man addicted to drinking: "Under ordinary circumstances, I would be delighted to go to the opera with you. I regret to add, however, that I have undoubted evidence that you are becoming addicted to the use of the wine-cup. With an earnest prayer for your reformation, ere it be too late, I beg you to consider our intimacy at an end."

Yet, in spite of the impressive numbers of pledges obtained, moral suasion had obvious limitations. Pledges of abstinence did not affect hard-core drinkers who did not care to sign, and the pledges represented no more than the good intentions of those who did. The fervent converts of one day could be staggering out of the taverns the next.

As growing numbers of German and Irish immigrants entered the country in the 1840's, temperance crusaders grew more fearful. Might not these foreigners, with their fondness for beer and whiskey, threaten the American values of thrift and hard work? Many women's-rights activists also joined the cause. Although drunkards were usually male, feminists argued that intoxicating beverages affected women most of all. Amelia Bloomer answered the claim that women had no business speaking out on this matter:

None of woman's business, when she is subject to poverty and degradation and made an outcast from respectable society! None of woman's business, when her starving naked babes are compelled to suffer the horrors of the winter's blast! . . . . In the name of all that is sacred, what is woman's business if this be no concern of hers?

Slowly, purely moral appeals gave way to political action. Under the leadership of Neal Dow, Maine passed America's first statewide prohibition statute—the celebrated "Maine Law"—in 1846. In the next decade over a dozen states followed Maine's lead, although not all of these measures remained on the books.

Like temperance, educational reform appealed to Americans who felt that dangerous influences and moral decay were spreading throughout the land. Horace Mann, the first Massachusetts superintendent of education and a crusader for state-financed education, warned that "the unrestrained passions of men are not only homicidal, but suicidal; and a community without a conscience would soon extinguish itself." How could individuals and society be saved? Universal education—entailing moral guidance and firm discipline—must become the responsibility of the state.

Mann and his supporters in the "Common School" movement also argued that leaving education in the hands of families, or preserving it as a luxury of the elite, threatened America's political and economic stability. Public schools would encourage social mobility and minimize class differences by providing rich and poor with a common educational background as a basis for the pursuit of future careers. The schools would also prepare Americans for the exercise of intelligent, informed citizenship. "In a republic," Mann wrote, "ignorance is a crime; and

If we do not prepare children to become good citizens—if we do not develop their capacities, if we do not enrich their minds with knowledge, imbue their hearts with the love of truth and duty, and a reverence for all things sacred and holy, then our republic must go down to destruction, as others have gone before it; and mankind must sweep through another vast cycle of sin and suffering, before the dawn of a better era. . . .

Coupled with the growing civic interest in free schools, these arguments produced results. In 1800 there were no public school systems outside New England; by 1860 every state had at least some public elementary and secondary schools, although Northern states surpassed Southern in the percentage of white children enrolled.

Public schools required a new, more practically oriented curriculum, in place of the traditional, classical one designed for an elite. The study of Greek and Latin or of classical authors would be of limited value for future generations of farmers and mechanics. McGuffey's *Reader* and Webster's *Speller*, whose short lessons simultaneously taught useful skills and proper moral habits, became standard classroom texts, and teachers added exercises in geography, United States history, and science. Gradually, the look of the classroom changed—maps, globes, and blackboards all made their appearance.

Institutions of higher education also proliferated, and similarly developed a more practical bent. New kinds of schools opened: technical schools such as Rensselaer Polytechnic Institute in New York; colleges for women; state universities in most Western states; and literally hundreds of denominational colleges. Most of the older universities modified their curricula, reducing the heavy dose of theology and the classics in favor of modern languages, "political economy," and the sciences. Several added professional programs in law, medicine, and engineering. A number of Western colleges adopted the unusual concept of student self-help through manual labor. Founded by radical reformers, these schools, such as Oberlin in Ohio (also the first to be coeducational) and Knox in Illinois, became centers of both educational experimentation and antislavery activism.

The shifting of the primary obligation for education from the family to the state paralleled the development of other state-run institutions designed to deal with the dependent and the deviant. Formerly, responsibility for them had also been left to the family or to local authorities; but as an increasing density of population intensified social problems, reformers began seeking better solutions. To the Christian cult of perfectionism these humanitarians added a growing belief in the power of environment to shape human character. The result, in the words of one historian, was "the discovery of the asylum."

Criminal reform received the most attention. At the urging of reformers, most states rewrote their colonial penal codes, abolishing imprisonment for debt and restricting the application of the death penalty to murderers. For lesser offenses, imprisonment took the place of such brutal corporal punishments as whipping, ducking, and branding. To house and rehabilitate prisoners, the states began to build modern prisons (Connecticut had formerly housed felons in an abandoned copper mine.) New York, with the construction of its new prison at Auburn (1821), inaugurated the system of individual confinement by night and group labor by day. Under the theory that isolation would promote moral reflection (in fact it often promoted suicide), Pennsylvania's new penitentiary (1829) provided for strict solitary confinement of prisoners at all times. After studying the two systems, most observers agreed with Alexis de Tocqueville that, while the Pennsylvania system made "the deepest impression on the soul of the convict," the Auburn system was "more conformable to the habits of man in society, and on this account effects a greater number of reformations." This period also saw the creation of specialized correctional facilities for juveniles, and for minor criminals such as drunks and vagrants.

Thanks to these dedicated reformers, states and municipalities also began accepting responsibility for the care of dependents and defectives. Some cities built almshouses for the poor, although most Americans continued to see poverty as a problem of individual character, to be cured by moral instruction rather than by governmental action. Several states made appropriations for schools to educate the deaf and the blind, and built asylums to care for the insane. Before 1840, victims of mental illness had been cared for privately—in locked rooms, cages, or outhouses— or else confined to jails and poorhouses. Appalled by these conditions, a frail Massachusetts schoolteacher, Dorothea Dix, undertook an investigation of the problem in her native state. Armed with the facts, she prepared a memorial to the legislature. Pledging to "tell what I have seen," she described graphically "the *present* state of insane persons confined within the Commonwealth, in *cages, closets, cellars, stalls, pens! chained, naked, beaten with rods, and lashed into obedience!*" Shocked by her descriptions, the lawmakers voted funds in 1843 to enlarge the state hospital for the insane. During the next decade Miss Dix traveled over thirty thousand miles in behalf of her cause. As a result, nearly every state made some provision for the care and treatment of the indigent insane.

The career of Dorothea Dix illustrates nicely the general plight of women in mid-nineteenth century America. Although intelligent, educated, and an expert in her field, she was obliged, in the interests of maintaining a "womanly dignity," to work mainly behind the scenes, rarely speaking in public herself. The only professions open to upper-class woman at that time were those of teacher, missionary, or writer; women of other classes worked in factories and at such jobs as laundresses, seamstresses, and servants.

Women were expected to concentrate upon housekeeping and child-rearing, leaving public affairs to men. With more and more men working in offices and factories, women were enshrined as guardians of the home. Woman, wrote one (male) observer, "cannot too studiously shun the gaze of the multitude. The strife and tumults of the senate-house and the platform are too much even for her eye to rest upon, much more for her voice to mingle in. Her chastity is her tower of strength, her modesty and gentleness are her charm, and her ability to meet the high claims of her family and dependents, the noblest power she can exhibit to the admiration of the world." Public opinion and economic circumstance were effectively reinforced by the law. Females were regarded as perpetual minors: married women had no rights over their property or children; they could not sue in their own name; they could not even sign contracts.

Gradually, women began to rebel against these restrictions. Lucy Stone, an antislavery and women's-rights activist who retained her maiden name after marriage, refused to pay taxes because she was not represented in the government. Scores of "radical" women rejected long skirts in favor of the less-constricting "Bloomer" costume. Susan B. Anthony helped a woman kidnap her child from her husband's custody. A group of women in New York—objecting to the double standard that required middle-class women to abstain from sex before marriage while not requiring the same of men—started a society to reform the city's prostitutes. Such activities, although offen-sive to most Americans, effectively dramatized women's problems.

The predominantly middle-class women who took up feminist causes had begun by becoming involved in other social reforms. As women extended their interests outside the home, met together, assumed leadership, and became adept at public speaking, they soon came to realize their own low status as women. "In striving to strike *his* [the black man's] irons off, we found most surely, that *we* were manacled ourselves," wrote Abby Kelley, a women's right leader. But if the antislavery cause helped launch the women's rights movement, it also contributed to its at least temporary demise. Even many sympathetic men abandoned feminist causes when they threatened to divert or divide the antislavery crusade. Led by Lucretia Mott, Elizabeth Cady Stanton, and Susan B. Anthony, women held conventions (the first met at Seneca Falls, New York, in 1848) and brought their concerns before the public. They asked for full rights to hold property and leave bequests, for educational and economic opportunities, and for the right to vote. But despite the feminists' energy and intelligence, fundamental changes in popular attitudes, occupational choice, legal status, and political participation came slowly. The "cult of true womanhood," emphasizing women's mindlessness, frailty, and domestic dependence, remained strong among America's middle and upper classes.

Not all the reform movements of the period were positive in outlook. Inherent in the evangelical search for perfectionism and immediate salvation was a certain intolerance for opposing views and half-measures. Thoughtful temperance advocates, for example, never quite reconciled their belief in individual liberty with the adoption of coercive measures such as prohibition. Many upper-middle-class reformers, motivated by fears of social deviancy and loss of status, harbored feelings of prejudice and even hatred for those who supposedly threatened the nation's social fabric.

Bigotry and intolerance combined in the recurring outbursts of anti-Catholicism after 1830. Before then, American Catholics had been too few in number to attract much attention. Over the next thirty years, however, mass immigration swelled the Catholic population of the United States from barely two to ten percent of the national total. To many native Protestants these newcomers, with their "strange" customs and peculiar faith, posed a threat to America's Protestant heritage and democratic institutions. The Irish who built the Erie Canal received the first blasts of this an-

Dorothea Dix. (Library of Congress.)

tagonism. One woman recounted the "poor fellows, strung along the canal, stupid from drink . . . they are for the most part covered with mud, where they have rolled when drunk." Such prominent men as Lyman Beecher and Samuel F. B. Morse warned against "papal puppets" working to "inflame and divide the nation, break the bond of our union, and throw down our free institutions." Militant Protestants formed societies aimed at converting "Papists to Christianity" and stoutly resisted all suggestions of public aid to parochial schools. Zealots composed and circulated fictitious stories of convent life replete with sex orgies. Maria Monk wrote her *Awful Disclosures* (1836) of life in a Montreal nunnery where, she claimed, priests and nuns used trapdoors and secret passageways to engage in licentious practices: "I can form only a rough conjecture," she wrote, "of the number of infants born, and murdered of course. . . ." Several efforts were made to form nativist political parties, with curbs on immigration as the principal demand. This agitation culminated in outbreaks of violence in the 1830's and 1840's, during which Catholic convents and churches were burned in New York City, Boston, and Philadelphia.

The Arts

During the Age of Jackson America at last achieved cultural independence of Europe. Architects launched a Greek revival that filled the country with handsome public buildings and pretentious temple-fronted houses. A nationalistic school of nature painters won acclaim. American authors like Nathaniel Hawthorne and Edgar Allan Poe attracted international attention. The newly popular lyceums and public lectures furnished native talent with an audience. In 1860 knowledgeable Europeans would no longer ask, as one English literary wit had in 1820, "In the four quarters of the globe, who reads an American book? Or goes to an American play? Or looks at an American picture or statue?"

Speaking at Harvard in 1837, the philosopher Ralph Waldo Emerson attacked "the timid, imitative, and tame" in American creative life. It was time, he asserted, for Americans to work with their own hands and speak with their own minds.

"Whaling Scene," scrimshaw engraving on whale tooth; New Bedford, Massachusetts, nineteenth century. *(Index of American Design.)*

Responding to the challenge, American painters abandoned the formalized, classical style of the eighteenth century. Influenced by the romantic movement and nationalism, they experimented with more individualistic, democratic, emotional styles of painting. Genre painters like William Sidney Mount and George Caleb Bingham took their studios outdoors to capture revealing incidents of American life. Bingham's "Stump Speaker" and "Country Elections" are miniature essays on Jacksonian politics. Nature painters like Thomas Cole (leader of the so-called Hudson River school) tried to glorify the spectacular qualities of the American landscape.

American architects also sought to cast off their slavish devotion to eighteenth-century styles derived from Europe. Their search for a pure, simple, democratic architecture led naturally to Greek Revival. Among the best examples of this style are Benjamin Latrobe's Bank of the United States at Philadelphia and Robert Mills's Treasury Building at Washington. Later, responding to the individualistic and romantic impulses of the age, American architects branched out into a wide variety of styles. By 1850 Philadelphia had an Egyptian jail, a Greek bank, medieval cottages, and Moorish churches, while New York boasted a Jewish synagogue with a Gothic tower.

American writers and poets were also influenced by the forces of nationalism. Breaking with the neoclassical of the eighteenth century, they sought a literature that was expressive, imaginative, intuitive—one filled with "the animating spirit of democracy." To Walt Whitman, the true poet merged himself with the spirit of the times

John James Audubon, Ivory-Billed Woodpeckers. (Metropolitan Museum of Art.)

and his country's culture, incarnating its "geography and national life and rivers and lakes." His *Leaves of Grass* (1855) represented a culmination of these trends. In his poem he used free verse and slang words; he borrowed freely from music, religion, and politics for his imagery and metaphors. *Leaves of Grass* was American.

The same trend was apparent in prose. Edgar Allan Poe became the master of the short story. Each tale was "a complete, finalized moment of emotional tension." Nathaniel Hawthorne brought intensity, depth, and craftsmanship to the American novel. In works like *The Scarlet Letter* (1850) and *House of the Seven Gables* (1851) he moved from fact to symbol, probing the souls of American Puritans and Quakers. Herman Melville aspired to be a "thought-diver." His *Moby Dick* (1851) reverberated with imagery and hidden meaning. Together, these writers put American literature on the world stage.

Then, as now, the mass of Americans preferred a different sort of literature. With the development of more efficient printing techniques, inexpensive books and newspapers circulated widely. The most prolific type of fiction was the sentimental-domestic novel, written by what Hawthorne called "a damned mob of scribbling women." Filled with scenes of domestic joy and sorrow, these novels preached conventional morality and pictured church, home, and family as anchors against life's trials. Novels like Mrs. E. D. E. N. Southworth's *Retribution* and Mary Jane Holmes's *Tempest and Sunshine* were bestsellers for years.

Another form of popular culture was the humorous essay, which dated from Benjamin Franklin's Poor Richard. It gained new popularity in the 1830's with Seba Smith's *Jack Downing Papers*. Downing was a "crackerbox philosopher" who commented on current events and poked gentle fun at American foibles. Smith soon had dozens of imitators, among them James Russell Lowell's Hosea Biglow, Charles F. Browne's Artemus Ward, and Johnson Hooper's Simon Slugs. Plays, minstrel shows, lectures, and public speaking also provided entertainment and education.

The demand for cultural independence was merely one manifestation of a growing American nationalism. By 1840 Americans had survived two wars for independence; they had expanded the country's boundaries nearly to the Pacific and the Rio Grande; they had conquered fifteen hundred miles of wilderness. Pride in these achievements and a desire to combat the divisive force of sectionalism gave rise to a growing cult of patriotism. Holidays were increasingly devoted to skyrocketing oratory, parades, and patriotic enthusiasms. Monuments and statues appeared by the hundreds, and biographies of American heroes sold by the tens of thousands.

Americans anxiously sought to adopt the traditional symbols of national pride. In place of the hated British lion, they adopted a native bird, the eagle. For holidays they chose Washington's Birthday and the Fourth of July. "Uncle Sam," a creation of the War of 1812, soon displaced "Yankee Doodle" as the national prototype. Although not adopted officially as the national anthem until 1913, Francis Scott Key's "Star-Spangled Banner" gradually replaced "My Country 'Tis of Thee." No token of nationalism became more important than the American flag. Originally created in 1777, the stars and stripes remained chiefly a naval flag until 1834, when the army adopted it, too.

Along with symbols, Americans needed heroes. They turned naturally to the Revolutionary War for material. By Jackson's day each of the important figures in the War—Francis "Swamp Fox" Marion, Ethan Allen and his "Green Mountain Boys," John Paul Jones, the martyred Nathan Hale—was celebrated in song and prose. Jackson himself became an instant hero after the Battle of New Orleans. Above all other national heroes was George Washington. Even before his death Washington had almost attained the status of a deity, thanks to Mason Locke Weems. In 1800 this itinerant book salesman and evangelist published his *Life of Washington*. Although partly fabricated (the cherry tree story started here), the book fulfilled the American public's need for larger-than-life heroes. It became a bestseller, going through many editions.

Most Americans were swept up in the outpouring of nationalism. "We were taught every day and in every way," recalled one contemporary, "that ours was the freest, the happiest, and soon to be the greatest and most powerful country in the world. . . . We read it in our books and newspapers, heard it in sermons, speeches, and orations, thanked God for it, in our prayers, and devoutly believed it always." Not even the cult of patriotism, however, would forever stem the disruptive effects of the slavery question, which burst on the country again in the 1840's.

Suggested Readings

Good studies of economic development are Thomas C. Cochran's *200 Years of American Business* (1977) and George Rogers Taylor's *The Transportation Revolution, 1815-1860* (1951); the economic changes underway in the pre-Civil War Era are receiving careful attention in statistical studies published in leading historical journals. Herbert Hovenkamp, *Science and Religion in America, 1800-1860* (1978), is a useful survey of the relation of religious to scientific thought in the early republic; no synthesis was achieved. Rush Welter's *The Mind of America, 1820-1860* (1975) is a good survey of intellectual history. Two books finally tell some of the story of women in this era: Ellen Carol DuBois' *Feminism and Suffrage* (1979) and G. J. Barker-Benfield's *The Horrors of the Half-Known Life: Male Attitudes Toward Women and Sexuality in Nineteenth-Century America* (1976). In *The Discovery of the Asylum: Social Order and Disorder in the New Republic* (1971), David S. Rothman argues that people believed the "asylum"—the orphanage, the penitentiary, the poorhouse—would rehabilitate the individual and provide a model of social organization.

Chapter XII
Expansion and Division:
The 1840's

The Alamo

In nineteenth-century America, no place had a wilder reputation than Texas. Men tired of society could move to the frontier; if the frontier offered too little excitement, elbow room, danger, opportunity, they could go to Texas. Behind this reputation lay a long history. For nearly three centuries Texas had belonged to Spain, but throughout that long period, the Spanish system of colonization—missions, soldiers, conversion of Indians, entrance of white settlers—had failed. Hundreds of miles of deserts and mountains separated Texas from the other Spanish lands, and the Indians of the region—Karankawas, Comanches, Apaches—were "tough hombres" who preferred to race their swift horses across the plains than to settle with the friars. This land, which Mexico inherited with its independence, remained ungovernable.

The Alamo was an apt symbol of this history. The mission at Bexar opened in 1718; construction on the now-familiar stone building began in 1757, and it acquired its historic name soon after. Three-quarters of a century's work by the friars and the Spanish army created the largest settlement in Texas—about seventeen hundred people, living, alas, in filth, poverty, and irreligion. When the friars left in 1793 in search of more fertile fields for their work, there were only about forty converts. The mission itself was then in decay, housing a few squalid Indians and half-breeds. In 1802 Spanish troops evicted these unfortunates, and the Alamo became a fort. By that time the Spaniards needed all the forts they could man. Not only had they failed to defeat the Texas Indians, they now faced rebellion from the Mexicans and—after 1803, when the United States acquired Louisiana—new and dangerous neighbors to their east.

American adventurers found the Mexican war of independence, which dragged on for a year, irresistible. Some came to fight for liberty in a war they understood as much like their own Revolution; some looked for land, wealth, and power; others sought danger, excitement, or a chance to extend the borders of the United States. In 1812 a force of American adventurers and Mexican revolutionaries combined to conquer Bexar, winning the first Battle of the Alamo. A Texas republic was set up, which, however, shortly met its end at the hands of another army sent by the Spanish. When Mexico finally became independent in 1821, Texas was joined to the state of Coahuila, with a promise that when its population was large enough, it would become a separate Mexican state. It was this promise that led eventually to revolution.

The newly established Mexican government had no intention of repeating the Spaniards' failure in Texas. It planned to turn a profit from the territory and to end Indian power by allowing Americans to develop agricultural settlements, provided they became at least nominally Catholics and Mexican citizens. The plan worked, perhaps too well. With Americans pouring in—many of them unruly frontiersmen—and the United States government making clumsy overtures to "buy" Texas, the Mexicans could easily envision this potentially rich province slipping from their grasp. So they forbade immigration, raised tariffs, set trade restrictions, and reinforced their military presence. The situation was further complicated by internal revolution in Mexico. Antonio Lopez de Santa Anna, Mexico's most brilliant general, was in conflict with his own government. When war came in Texas it was by no means a straightforward battle for independence on the part of Americans. It began, in fact, as a demand for their rights as Mexican citizens. but once Santa Anna took control in Mexico City and then moved to garrison his northern province, the Texans of course fought to defeat his army. Independence would be an outcome of the war, not its initial objective.

The Texans, by and large, were fighters, not soldiers. Skilled marksmen, deadly with knives and fists, they loved a good scrape. The slow, boring routine of soldiering was another story. The Texans picked up an army—or several armies. But enlistments were for very short periods, often as little as sixty days, and volunteers, answerable to no one, often outnumbered the loosely disciplined regulars. Men who would risk their lives in a moment would then refuse to carry out such mundane tasks as building fortifications, gouging gun slits in the Alamo's walls, or erecting fences.

The rebels had managed to defeat Mexican detachments in several small battles and had forced the Mexicans to abandon Bexar. But then their amateur status began to tell: their general took a vacation; the men began drifting off to their farms or to the *cantinas* and *señoritas* in the town. Sam Houston, struggling to put together a military strategy and an army to carry it out, doubted that Bexar and the Alamo could be held, given the limited number of men and the difficulties of communication. He picked a man he trusted to go to Bexar and decide whether to destroy the fort and retreat or to hold it. The man was Jim Bowie, a legendary figure of the tough Southwest frontier. Houston must have known what his man would choose. Bowie, who had recently turned from land speculation, gambling, and personal fights with his famous eight-and-one-half-inch-long knife, to battling the Mexican army, encountered a discouraging situation at Bexar. It would have taken a thousand men to defend the Alamo adequately, not the 104 unpaid and discouraged soldiers he found there. But Bowie's instincts led him to an inevitable decision: "We will rather die in these ditches than give them up to the enemy."

The Alamo needed reinforcements. It got a few, powerful in legend but not in number. William Barret Travis, a militant advocate of war and independence and now a regular officer in the rag-tag Texas army, was ordered to Bexar with all the troops he could muster. He arrived with 30 men. When Bowie contracted pneumonia, it was the able Travis who took command of the beleaguered fort. Davy Crockett arrived from Tennessee with twelve men. Then as now, he was the epitomé of the American frontiersman, a living legend, the teller and subject of tall tales. Following his legend right into the West as the sun goes, by some unerring instinct he arrived (having had no previous connection with the Texas revolution) at the place that would transform his essentially comic legend into real and towering heroism. Eventually another 30-odd men arrived. And so it was that, all told, about 180 men garrisoned the old mission, when on February 23, 1836, Santa Anna's army of thousands began its siege.

With Mexican guns tightly ringing the fort, the Alamo's defenders abandoned their hopes for further reinforcements. Travis called the men together, explained why it was essential to hold the fort, and indicated their probable fate. At the conclusion of his speech, in a gesture duplicating Pizarro's centuries before, he drew a line in the dust with his sword, stepped across it, and asked who would join him and who would leave. All but one man—who got through the Mexican lines and lived to tell the tale—crossed the line. Bowie, from his sick-bed, asked to be carried across. Travis wrote his final letter, correctly predicting that "The victory will cost the enemy so dear that it will be worse for him than defeat." The next morning revealed Mexican cannon virtually under the wall. In one more day the cannonade finally blasted a sizable hole in the old mission's wall. The final assault had begun.

Santa Anna knew he would take huge losses in the assault; the Texan marksmen had already picked off hundreds of his soldiers. Some of his commanders counseled continuing to pound the walls with cannon until they could wipe out the garrison with grapeshot. But the general knew what this siege was costing him. Bowie had been right to defend the Alamo. Had the fort not held so long and so bravely, Santa Anna would have swept the Texans off the field before they could have fully mobilized.

Before dawn on March 6, the Mexicans—four thousand strong—attacked, almost catching the exhausted Americans by surprise. The first assault with scaling ladders was repulsed with dreadful carnage. A second wave was more successful, actually getting ladders onto the walls, only to have the men driven off by rifle butts, tomahawks, and Bowie knives. Then came the third assault, and there were simply not enough Texans, enough cannon, nor enough wall left any longer. Taking incredible losses—one battalion lost 670 of 800 men—the Mexican soldiers poured in. Abandoning the central plaza of the Alamo, the defenders retreated to the smaller rooms, to kill and then to die in hand-to-hand battle. Crockett and two of his men were found after the battle under a heap of seventeen dead Mexicans, indicative of the kind of fight that raged at the last. Jim Bowie, confined to a sickbed in the chapel, was one of the last to die. The first two soldiers who burst into the room he dispatched with his brace of singleshot pistols, then he was helpless, too weak to wield his famous knife. One of the few survivors, the wife of an officer, deliberately spared to spread the news of Texas' defeat, remembered seeing his body being tossed on the bayonets of a dozen soldiers when the battle ended and the wanton mutilations began. By 9 a.m. on March 6, 1836, the siege had ended with all the Alamo's defenders dead.

No question at all: Santa Anna's "victory" in this battle cost him the war. He lost sixteen hundred of his best troops, with many more wounded. He lost not only the weeks it took to besiege the fortress, but the weeks his army needed afterward to recover. The Texans, sobered and inspired, declared their independence, settled their quarrels, and gave Sam Houston a chance to build an army.

Santa Anna chased Houston and caught up with him at San Jacinto, an elbow formed by the confluence of a river and a bayou. Dramatically Houston burned his bridges behind him so that neither his army nor Santa Anna's could retreat. The Texans, shouting as their battlecry "Remember the Alamo!" destroyed the Mexican army in an afternoon. Texas was now an independent nation, the Lone Star Republic, until 1845, when it became part of the United States of America.

In 1840 the future of the young American Republic seemed rich with promise. In fifty years the population had increased by over four hundred percent, while the land area had more than doubled. Regional economic specialization and improved transportation was fostering a growing interdependence between the different sections. With two national parties competing for office in every part of the country, the political system worked to bind the country together. The vast majority of Americans remained English in speech, Protestant in religion, lower middle-class in social status, agricultural in occupation; these shared characteristics, together with the experience of two wars against England, formed for most Americans the basis of a common national loyalty. Each July 4, they gathered in every part of the country for elaborate ceremonies glorifying the American Union. A renowned French visitor, Alexis de Tocqueville, was deeply impressed by one such celebration at Albany, New York, with its dramatic reading of the Declaration of Independence and its parade of Revolutionary veterans "preserved like precious relics, and whom all the citizens honor. . . ."

And yet, even as economic interdependence and patriotism strengthened the bonds of Union, there was one issue that threatened the country with disruption: slavery. In the 1830's a militant crusade against slavery arose in the North. During the next decade the slavery question became entangled with the issue of territorial expansion, and the combination was explosive: the slavery question gradually eclipsed all others. Unable to settle the question peacefully, Americans resorted in 1861 to force of arms.

The Antislavery Crusade

The roots of the antislavery crusade in America stretched back to the eighteenth century. Confronted by the powerful forces of rationalism and revolution, many Americans had condemned chattel slavery as incompatible with the egalitarian rhetoric of the Declaration of Independence. In 1787, Congress excluded slavery from the area it organized north of the Ohio River as the Northwest Territory. That same year the delegates to the Constitutional Convention agreed to a compromise permitting (though not requiring) Congress to abolish the African slave trade in 1808. In the meantime, a number of Northern states abolished slavery within their own borders, and abolition societies multiplied even in a few Southern states.

Most Americans, although opposed to slavery, rejected the idea of its immediate eradication in the South—a course fraught with serious constitutional, economic, and social difficulties. Many favored a policy of gradual emancipation, to be followed by deportation. With the support of such influential men as Henry Clay and John Marshall, these gradualists founded the American Colonization Society in 1817. The Society worked to resettle emancipated American blacks in Africa. Although many of its members sincerely looked on the colonization of free blacks as a first step toward a general, compensated emancipation, others saw it as merely an opportunity to get rid of these unfortunate people. Free blacks themselves objected to colonization. "We are *natives* of this country," one protested; "we only ask that we be treated as well as *foreigners*." Their opposition gradually undermined the Society's efforts.

During the early 1830's a small but vocal band of activists began calling for the total and immediate abolition of slavery. To these crusaders, slavery was both a national and an individual sin; Americans could not wait for time or Divine Providence to eradicate it. For these abolitionists, gradual emancipation and colonization were dead ends. Any large-scale deportation of blacks would have raised both enormous practical obstacles and grave moral difficulties. And Southern opposition to gradual emancipation, which stiffened after the invention of the cotton gin, indicated that the opponents of slavery had little to lose by adopting a more radical stance. The victory of the British abolitionist movement in 1833 gave new hope to advocates of immediate emancipation in the United States. The President of Harvard, Edward Everett, registered the intensity of these militants' feelings when he responded to criticism of his having allowed a Negro boy to take the entrance test: "If this boy passes the examination he will be admitted; and if the white students choose to withdraw, all the income of the college will be devoted to his education."

Abolitionism was an integral part of the reform ferment of the Jackson Era. Most abolitionists drew their inspiration from revivalistic religion, with its doctrine of "perfectionism." Perfectionists argued that all people, through an act of conversion, could cleanse themselves of sin (defined as voluntary selfishness) and live in harmony

Illustrations of the American Anti-Slavery Almanac for 1840.

"Our Peculiar *Domestic* Institutions."

Northern Hospitality—*New-York nine months law.* [The Slave steps out of the Slave State, and his chains fall. A Free State, with another chain, stands ready to re-enslave him.]

Burning of McIntosh at St. Louis, in April, 1836.

Showing how slavery improves the condition of the female sex.

The Negro Pew, or "Free" Seats for black Christians.

Mayor of New-York refusing a Carman's license to a colored Man.

Servility of the Northern States in arresting and returning fugitive Slaves.

Selling a Mother from her Child.

Hunting Slaves with dogs and guns. A Slave drowned by the dogs.

"Poor things, 'they can't take care of themselves.'"

Mothers with young Children at work in the field.

A Woman chained to a Girl, and a Man in irons at work in the field.

Branding Slaves.

Cutting up a Slave in Kentucky.

Paid. Unpaid.

Library of Congress.

with divine law. When enough individuals embraced God's way, the larger society could be purged of evils such as slavery. Slaveholders had only to recognize their complicity in sin and renounce it. It was by using the techniques of moral suasion—appealing to Americans' consciences rather than employing legal coercion—that abolitionists hoped to end human bondage in America.

One person led to abolitionism by perfectionist beliefs was the young William Lloyd Garrison. He embraced a number of reform causes in the 1820's and worked with the famous Quaker abolitionist Benjamin Lundy before establishing his own antislavery newspaper, the *Liberator*, at Boston in 1831. In unequivocal, though bombastic language, Garrison preached the cause of immediate abolition with no compensation to slaveholders: "I *will be* as harsh as truth, and as uncompromising as justice. . . . I will not equivocate—I will not excuse—I will not retreat a single inch—AND I WILL BE HEARD." Obsessed with a concern for moral purity, he denounced the churches as "cages of unclean birds" because they tolerated slavery, and he burned copies of the Constitution because it recognized slavery. Northerners at first dismissed Garrison as a fanatic; only eleven persons accepted his invitation to form the New England Antislavery Society. But the Nat Turner revolt of 1831 made him a household word, as nervous slaveholders connected the "incendiary publications" of Garrison and others with the bloody events in Southampton County, Virginia. The Georgia Senate offered a $1000 reward for his arrest and conviction. Newspapers throughout the country began reprinting Garrison's fiery editorials, and the stern, ascetic Massachusetts editor soon became the very embodiment of abolition.

Abolitionism had other leaders, to be sure, and support outside of New England. Some of Garrison's contemporaries, and a few later historians, considered Theodore Dwight Weld an even more important figure. Like Garrison, Weld entered the movement because of intense religious convictions about the evils of slavery. After being converted by the famous evangelist Charles G. Finney, he devoted his life to the cause of moral reform. In 1834, while a student at Cincinnati's Lane Theological Seminary, he organized debates on the slavery question. After eighteen nights of discussion, the students endorsed immediatism (i.e., immediate abolition) and rejected colonization. When their antislavery activities aroused opposition among Lane's trustees, Weld and forty others left Lane to attend Oberlin College near Cleveland. Securing funds from two wealthy New York City reformers, Arthur and Lewis Tappan, the Lane rebels made Oberlin a center of abolitionist activity. By employing the techniques and rhetoric of the religious revival, they converted to abolitionism thousands throughout the Old Northwest and nearby areas of New York and Pennsylvania. Weld also joined with his wife, Angelina, and her sister, Sarah Grimké, to write *Slavery as It Is* (1839). This popular tract, a compilation of Southern newspaper accounts describing the cruelties of slavery, offered documentary evidence to support the abolitionists' moral outrage. "Slaves," they wrote, "are often hunted with bloodhounds and shot down like beasts, or torn in pieces by dogs . . . they are often suspended by the arms and whipped and beaten till they faint, . . . and sometimes till they die; . . . they are maimed, multilated and burned to death over slow fires. All these things, and more, and worse, we shall PROVE."

Initially, the abolitionists' demands for emancipation and an end to racial discrimination angered many people in the North, and during the mid-1830's anti-abolitionist mobs harassed and assaulted prominent abolitionists. A Boston mob dragged Garrison through the streets with a rope around his neck in 1835; two years later a hostile crowd at Alton, Illinois, killed the abolitionist editor Elijah Lovejoy. Generally it was leading citizens—lawyers, doctors, bankers, merchants—who directed these actions; for them, as for many other Americans in the Jackson Era, mob violence was a legitimate means of protecting society against "disruptive" elements, rather than itself a threat to law and order. To these "gentlemen of property and standing," abolitionists were troublemaking outsiders, audacious newcomers who bypassed traditional local elites and pitched their radical message directly to the mass of citizens by means of printed propaganda and traveling speakers.

Southern Counterattack

The rise of militant abolitionism, coupled with the Nat Turner uprising, stimulated another round of soul-searching among Southern whites. In 1831-32 the Virginia House of Delegates debated at length a plan for the gradual emancipation and deportation of all slaves. The proposal was at last defeated, and this defeat marked a turning point. Thereafter, Southerners almost universally contended that slavery was sanctioned by the Bible and the laws of nature; it provided a harmonious solution to the South's racial dilemma and offered beneficent schooling to "inferior" blacks. A scientific apologist, Dr. Josiah Nott, of Mobile, Alabama, published his *Types of Mankind* in 1854, concluding on the basis of head size that blacks were a separate and permanently inferior species fit only for slavery. Other writers contrasted the "security" which slaves enjoyed with the brutal exploitation suffered by Northern workingmen.

Southerners took more concrete steps to shore up their "peculiar institution." Legislatures enacted tougher slave codes and further curtailed the liberties of free blacks. Although black people bore the brunt of the restrictions, the repression touched whites as well. Slave-state lawmakers forbade the publication or distribution of antislavery propaganda—sometimes under penalty of death. Public pressure silenced other critics of slavery: several prominent university professors left the South. The antislavery societies that had existed throughout the region quickly disappeared. With whites moving toward at least an outward consensus on the question of slavery, dissent became rare after 1830.

Southerners also sought to stifle criticism from without. Backed by a war chest of over $30,000, abolitionists embarked in 1835 on their "great postal campaign," an attempt to send hundreds of thousands of antislavery pamphlets to all parts of the country. A mob of South Carolinians seized the materials from the Charleston post office and burned them, along with effigies of Arthur Tappan and Garrison, in a huge bonfire. Afterwards, Postmaster General Amos Kendall, with President Jackson's approval, authorized Southern postmasters to censor the mails and stop the flow of antislavery material into the South. Southern politicians urged the House of Representatives not to receive petitions demanding the abolition of slavery in the states or the District of Columbia. Traditionally, Congress had accepted such memorials and then rejected the request as "inexpedient." Following angry debate, the House now approved a modified "gag" rule; henceforth it would receive antislavery petitions but automatically table them without formal consideration.

Repressive tactics, however, though outwardly successful, rebounded against slaveholders in the long run. The censorship of mails, "gag" rules, mob attacks, and other violations of civil liberties created a reaction that broadened the antislavery movement's appeal. Sounding a note that would grow into a symphony by the 1850's, abolitionists charged that a vast "slavepower" conspiracy was threatening the liberty of Northern whites as well as Southern blacks. Slaveholders and their Northern allies, those "gentlemen of property and standing," stood ready to destroy all Americans' freedoms in order to safeguard slavery.

Antislavery Disunity

As they struggled to influence popular opinion, abolitionists promoted one broad organization: the American Antislavery Society, founded in 1833. Garrison, Weld, the Tappan brothers and the Grimké sisters all belonged to the Society, which claimed as many as thirteen hundred local chapters. Under Weld's direction, the Society's members bombarded Congress with petitions opposing slavery in the District of Columbia and urging an end to the interstate slave trade. The petition campaign attracted widespread support after Southern Congressmen obtained their "gag" rule. Former President John Quincy Adams led the battle to vindicate the historic right of petition. Year after year "Old Man Eloquent," though never an advocate of immediatism, fought to get his petitions before the House of Representatives for discussion, winning thousands to the antislavery cause in the process. In 1844, Adams finally secured repeal of the "gag" rule. American abolitionists also sought closer ties with British reformers, and in 1840 many attended the World Antislavery Convention in London.

Despite these successes, the antislavery movement faced deep internal divisions. A variety of issues splintered the movement: doctrinal conflicts among different religious denominations, personality clashes, and fundamental differences over strategy. The split over strategy and tactics involved conflicting interpretations of American society and the role of abolitionism in American life. Shocked by anti-abolition mob violence, Garrisonians concluded that American society was sick. Slavery was one of the symptoms of moral decay, but there were others—the oppression of women and the poor, militarism, expansionism. Only a total reformation of the nation's ethical values, stimulated by a radical attack upon all of America's ills, would suffice. Abolitionists, Garrison maintained, must "revolutionize the public sentiment" by an expanded campaign of moral suasion; having done this, they would accomplish the overthrow of slavery.

Garrison's opponents in the antislavery movement possessed a broader faith in the possibilities of American society and a narrower vision of reform. When they surveyed the events of the 1830's, they concluded that abolitionism had made considerable progress. Efforts to link the movement too closely with other causes, they felt, risked alienating people who had been converted by the postal campaign or angered by Southern violations of civil liberties. "Garrisonian fanaticism," they feared, only endangered the future of abolitionism.

Women's rights and the form and nature of political action were two major sources of abolitionist discord. Involvement in the antislavery movement fostered female abolitionists' demands for their own equality as women. When Garrison's New England Antislavery Society voted to accept women on equal terms with men, several important male leaders promptly resigned. At the London World Antislavery Convention of 1840, female abolitionists found themselves segregated in the gallery, prompting Garrison and other sympathetic men to join them there. The Garrisonians' active support for the women's cause angered many antislavery activists; they charged that feminism would only sidetrack the crusade against slavery.

The question of involvement in politics proved even more divisive. The "Log Cabin and Hard Cider" campaign of 1840 symbolized Americans' new fascination with mass politics, and many antislavery leaders wanted to get involved. The success of the petition drives and other quasi-political activities offered some hope that electoral politics and antislavery would be joined. Over the strident objections of Garrison, a group of abolitionists formed the Liberty Party in 1840; they selected James G. Birney, a slaveholder turned abolitionist, as their presidential candidate, and framed a platform calling for the abolition of slavery in America. Lost in the hoopla of the Whig-Democratic contest between Harrison and Van Buren, the Liberty Party attracted little attention. Birney, in London for the World Antislavery Convention, did not even campaign. But in the next presidential election Birney polled almost 65,000

votes. Although an improvement over 1840, this still represented only 32 out of every 1,000 votes cast in the North.

Garrison and his followers consistently opposed the Liberty Party experiment. Political organizations, they argued, implied acceptance of the legitimacy of the existing system, which for them was morally diseased at its root. Rejecting all types of coercive measures and retaining his faith in perfectionism, Garrison refused even to vote.

Nevertheless, abolitionists—including Garrison—were generally more than simple idealists or frustrated politicians. Most were hard-headed reformers who recognized the need for many types of nonviolent action. They tried, unsuccessfully, to organize a boycott of slave-produced products; they worked to impel churches into an antislavery stance; a few helped slaves escape Southern bondage on the celebrated "underground railroad" (more legend than reality); many courageously demanded equal rights for blacks in the North.

Whites did not fight the antislavery battle alone. By 1850 nearly a quarter-of-a-million blacks lived in the free states. These Afro-Americans, however, were free in name only. In most places they could not vote, hold office, or testify in court. They were confined to menial jobs and wretched housing. Everywhere law and public opinion combined to exclude or segregate them: in railroad coaches, schools, restaurants, theaters, churches, even cemeteries. Most Northerners, including some who condemned slavery, viewed this not as a departure from democratic principles, but as the working out of natural laws, the inevitable consequence of the Negro's racial inferiority.

The abolitionist crusade offered Northern blacks their first opportunity to play a major role in American public life. Their subscriptions kept Garrison's newspaper alive, and Boston blacks protected him from violence. David Walker, a free black who had migrated from North Carolina to Boston, electrified the country in 1831 with his *Appeal,* a pamphlet urging militant resistance to slavery. Escaped slaves like Frederick Douglass lectured and wrote of their experiences before freedom. Harriet Tubman, an escapee who made nineteen trips into slave territoy to bring out runaways, had a price of $40,000 on her head. Initially the protégés of white abolitionists, blacks gradually asserted their independence. They founded newspapers and civil-rights organizations of their own and established vigilance committees in Northern cities to protect black fugitives from slave-catchers. "Should any wretch enter my dwelling, any pale-faced spectre among ye, to execute this [fugitive slave] law on me or mine," a black abolitionist warned defiantly in 1850, "I'll seek his life, I'll shed his blood." From these activities Northern blacks gained a heightened sense of self-respect and reinforced a determination to do something for the millions of their race still in bondage.

Slavery in the Territories

In spite of some modest successes, the antislavery movement still faced an uphill fight in 1840. Abolitionist sentiment was vague, sporadic, and moralistic; the slavery interest was concentrated, practical, and testily defensive. Moral suasion had utterly failed to convert Southerners, who feared not only a loss of property but a loss of racial mastery. Most Northerners scorned the abolition movement as potentially dangerous. Since the North was also a white-supremacist society, the vast majority of whites there discriminated against free blacks and were content to leave slavery alone where it existed. Northerners may have opposed slavery in the abstract, but few favored actual emancipation—unless accompanied by colonization—for fear that the free states would be overrun with emancipated blacks. Slavery also had powerful allies among Northern businessmen dependent on the success of Southern crops.

The United States Constitution itself was a source of discouragement for abolitionists. Both sides in the slavery controversy conceded not only that the Constitution recognized slaves as property, but that the federal government could not abolish slavery in the states. This was a decision for the people of the states themselves to make. The Southern states were free to uphold a Constitution and a Union that protected slavery. After the Missouri Compromise, both Whigs and

$200 Reward.

RANAWAY from the subscriber, on the night of Thursday, the 30th of Sepember,

FIVE NEGRO SLAVES,

To-wit : one Negro man, his wife, and three children.

The man is a black negro, full height, very erect, his face a little thin. He is about forty years of age, and calls himself *Washington Reed*, and is known by the name of Washington. He is probably well dressed, possibly takes with him an ivory headed cane, and is of good address. Several of his teeth are gone.

Mary, his wife, is about thirty years of age, a bright mulatto woman, and quite stout and strong.

The oldest of the children is a boy, of the name of FIELDING, twelve years of age, a dark mulatto, with heavy eyelids. He probably wore a new cloth cap.

MATILDA, the second child, is a girl, six years of age, rather a dark mulatto, but a bright and smart looking child.

MALCOLM, the youngest, is a boy, four years old, a lighter mulatto than the last, and about equally as bright. He probably also wore a cloth cap. If examined, he will be found to have a swelling at the navel.

Washington and Mary have lived at or near St. Louis, with the subscriber, for about 15 years.

It is supposed that they are making their way to Chicago, and that a white man accompanies them, that they will travel chiefly at night, and most probably in a covered wagon.

A reward of $150 will be paid for their apprehension, so that I can get them, if taken within one hundred miles of St. Louis, and $200 if taken beyond that, and secured so that I can get them, and other reasonable additional charges, if delivered to the subscriber, or to THOMAS ALLEN, Esq., at St. Louis, Mo. The above negroes, for the last few years, have been in possession of Thomas Allen, Esq., of St. Louis.

WM. RUSSELL.

ST. LOUIS, Oct. 1, 1847.

Library of Congress.

Democrats shunned the potentially divisive slavery issue in order to preserve harmony between their respective Northern and Southern wings.

There was one area, however, where many Americans in 1840 did believe the federal government held power over slavery: the territories. The Constitution authorized the Congress to make "all needful rules and regulations" respecting the territories. For decades an informal division of territory into free and slave soil had dampened disputes over the issue. The Northwest Ordinance of 1787 had prohibited slavery north of the Ohio River. South of the Ohio, North Carolina and Georgia ceded western lands to the national government on the specific condition that slavery should be permitted in the states that would eventually be formed from these lands—Tennessee, Alabama, and Mississippi. The Missouri Compromise line of 1820 divided the vast Louisiana Purchase into slave and free soil. These arrangements covered all the existing United States territory, leaving nothing after 1820 for argument in Congress. Slavery had been "denationalized." Abolitionists were left to battle over such narrow issues as the status of slavery in the District of Columbia, where Congress had undisputed authority.

Suddenly, in the 1840's, the slavery issue revived. Congress now had to deal with slavery in the territory acquired from Mexico. On a more personal level, people who had not considered themselves implicated in the question of slavery in the Southern states could not escape their responsibility for it in the territories. After 1848, antislavery in the North found its true target in the issue. For the next fifteen years, this question dominated national politics as no issue before or since.

Manifest Destiny

In March 1841 jubilant Whigs flooded Washington, hungry for government offices. The crush of office-seekers proved too much for the elderly and infirm William Henry Harrison. A cold contracted while doing the White House grocery-shopping soon developed into pneumonia, and on April 4—just a month after the inauguration—he died. Two days later, Vice President John Tyler, summoned hastily from his Virginia plantation, took the presidential oath. Since Harrison was the first president to die in office, questions arose over Tyler's exact status. Was he actually President, or merely the Vice-President assuming the duties and responsibilities of the Presidency? Tyler insisted that he had become President in every sense of the word. His conduct in support of this claim set an important precedent.

Fifty-one years old when he entered the White House, Tyler had already had a distinguished career in Virginia politics. Lean and hawk-nosed, with a Virginian's pride and a streak of obstinacy, he had started in politics as a states' rights Democrat. Tyler and the Whigs were mismatched from the start. The new President refused to be dominated by Henry Clay and Daniel Webster, the acknowledged leaders of the party. He had no sympathy for the Whigs' economic nationalism. In September, when he vetoed Clay's bill to reestablish a national bank, the entire Harrison Cabinet resigned except Secretary of State Daniel Webster; Webster stayed on to conduct negotiations with Great Britain over various outstanding problems, especially the disputed northeastern boundary between Maine and New Brunswick. In 1842, he concluded the Webster-Ashburton Treaty, which settled the Maine boundary and other problems by compromise, setting an example for the friendly resolution of future Anglo-American problems. Shortly after the treaty was signed, Webster too resigned.

The Cabinet resignation completed the break between Tyler and the Whigs, who henceforth referred to the President as "His Accidency." Tyler was not a free agent. He appointed a new Cabinet heavy with Southern Democrats, and began searching for issues that would win him reelection. For the North he signed the Tariff of 1842, restoring protective duties to roughly the level of 1832. To soothe Southern bitterness over the tariff, Tyler offered a daring proposal—the annexation of Texas.

The broad, often fertile plains stretching west and south of the Sabine River had long been a magnet for Americans. In the 1820's, Americans such as Moses and Stephen Austin obtained Mexican land grants in Texas and began colonizing Americans there. Lured by the cheap land, several thousand settlers emigrated. Mexican law required them to become nominal Catholics as well as Mexican citizens; otherwise the colonists enjoyed considerable autonomy and retained their American character. Stephen Austin advised them to "play the turtle, head and feet within your own shell," but differences soon arose between the Texans and the Mexican government. The settlers, mainly Southerners, brought slaves with them in defiance of Mexican law. They refused to pay the high Mexican tariff on goods imported from the United States. Alarmed by these signs of independence, and by the rapid increase in the number of Americans in Texas (30,000 in 1835), the Mexican government tightened its control and prohibited further American immigration. After several armed uprisings, the Texans declared their independence in 1836. Mexico's ruthless treatment of the defenders of the Alamo—designed to intimidate the rebels—only united them behind General Sam Houston, whose ragged forces routed the Mexican army at San Jacinto, near Galveston, and captured its commander, General Santa Anna.

Americans had adopted a distinctly unneutral attitude during the Texan war of independence. Money was raised for supplies, and many volunteers—among them the famous frontiersmen Jim Bowie and Davy Crockett—swelled the ranks of the Texan army. After independence, the public on both sides of the United States border strongly favored annexation. But since Mexico refused to acknowledge Texan independence, annexation might provoke war. Politicians also feared to aggravate the rising antislavery sentiment in the North by incorporating new slave territory into the Union. President Jackson waited until his last day in office before recognizing the new Texan republic. His successor, Martin Van Buren, carefully avoided the question of annexation. Texas drifted for several years, developing ever-closer ties with Great Britain.

The movement for annexation revived dramatically in 1842. Texas President Sam Houston, facing an empty treasury and renewed hostilities with Mexico, made overtures to Washington and found an enthusiastic ally in John Tyler. Annexation was politically expedient, and, like most slaveholders, Tyler was convinced that continued expansion was vital to the slave economy and the Southern way of life. After the unsympathetic Webster resigned as Secretary of State, Tyler appointed a fellow Virginian, Abel P. Upshur, and ordered him to seek a treaty of annexation.

The move was well-timed: Americans were preoccupied with renewed dreams of continental empire. Southerners feared that Britain was working to abolish slavery in Texas. Northern commercial interests sought American control of valuable Pacific coast ports as trading centers. Americans, like most peoples, were strongly nationalistic; they arrogantly assumed a responsibility for carrying their "superior" civilization and Protestant religion to the "underdeveloped" areas of the Southwest. It was America's "manifest destiny," they argued, to overspread and civilize the continent. Secretary Upshur, confident that the Senate would approve a treaty, negotiated with Texan representatives. After Upshur's death the new Secretary of State, John C. Calhoun, completed the arrangments for annexation and submitted the treaty to the Senate.

Unfortunately for Tyler, the Senate delayed action until after the 1844 party nominating conventions, at which Texas suddenly emerged as a major political issue. Both the leading candidates, Henry Clay and Martin Van Buren, came out against annexation. The Whigs nominated Clay, but the Democrats bypassed Van Buren in favor of an avowed expansionist, James K. Polk. This political maneuvering and Calhoun's defense of annexation as a proslavery measure sealed the fate of the treaty. A combination of Whigs and disappointed Van Buren Democrats killed it. Tyler refused to surrender; he sent a message to the House of Representatives three days later proposing to annex Texas by other means.

Tyler had forced the issue of expansion to the center of American politics. Democratic politicians hoped to preserve sectional harmony within their party with a platform promising both the "re-annexation" of Texas and the "re-occupation" of Oregon all the way to 54°40'. Too late, Clay sensed the public mood and endorsed annexation "upon just and fair terms." That November, James Knox Polk won a narrow victory in the presidential election, and Tyler interpreted this as a mandate for Texas annexation. Just before he left office in March 1845, the President obtained a joint congressional resolution (which required only a majority vote in each house) admitting Texas to the Union. When Polk entered the White House, Texas annexation was a settled question.

Polk set two other objectives: the settlement of the Oregon boundary question and the acquisition of California. Formidable mountain barriers had retarded American settlement in the Pacific Northwest until the 1830's. when traders and missionaries began publicizing the area. By 1845 five thousand Americans had migrated there, settling mainly in the fertile Willamette Valley. Throughout his campaign, Polk had promised to assert American control over all the Oregon Territory, which the United States and Great Britain had occupied jointly since 1818. Once in power, however, Polk began a search for compromise with Britain, preferably at the 49th parallel. The British government at first rejected such a proposal, which would place the Columbia River wholly in American hands. Polk then called upon Congress for authority to give the required one year's notice terminating joint occupation. America, he announced, would look John Bull "straight in the eye." Congress consented. Polk served the expected notice in April 1846; on both sides of the Atlantic, people talked of war.

Neither side, however, really wanted a fight. Britain had all but abandoned the area between the Columbia River and the 49th parallel to the advancing wave of American settlers. Polk, anticipating war with Mexico at any moment, could no longer afford a quarrel with Britain. He therefore welcomed a British offer to divide Oregon at the 49th parallel. The Senate approved this arrangement, despite angry protests from Northwestern Democrats, who charged that Polk and his Southern Democratic allies, having acquired Texas, had reneged on their promise to acquire "all of Oregon or none." Their residual bitterness combined with abolitionist sentiment to hamper Polk's conduct of the Mexican War.

The Mexican War

Polk's other objective, acquiring California, was not so easily accomplished. Mexico had no intention of selling the province. The proud Latin republic had broken diplomatic relations with the United States in March 1845, in protest over the American decision to annex Texas. Worse yet, a bitter controversy had arisen over the question of just what had been annexed. Texans asserted that their republic stretched as far south as the Rio Grande; Mexico insisted that the province's boundary stopped at the Nueces River. Mexico probably had the better case. Polk nevertheless claimed all the disputed area for the United States and used the Texas boundary question to press Mexico to a settlement on California.

In July 1845, Polk ordered General Zachary Taylor, with nearly four thousand troops, to take up a position south of the Nueces. Taylor halted at Corpus Christi, where he remained for several months. At about the same time, the President issued secret orders to American naval officers in the Pacific to occupy the California ports in the event of war with Mexico. He worked actively to encourage a Texas-style revolution among American settlers. Just in case the dissatisfied Anglos needed any help, the President sent Colonel John C. Frémont and a party of heavily armed engineers on a "scientific expedition" to California.

His weapons now primed and ready, Polk sent John Slidell, a Louisiana politician, to Mexico in November 1845 to negotiate. The President, refusing to compromise on the Rio Grande boundary, offered only to assume payment of American claims against the Mexican government in return for its acquiescence. He also authorized Slidell to purchase all or part of Upper California and New Mexico. When two successive Mexican governments refused to risk public disfavor by receiving him, Slidell withdrew. "Be assured," he wrote to the Secretary of State, "that nothing is to be done with these people until they shall have been chastised." Polk had reached the same conclusion. In January 1846 he sent General Taylor's army to the Rio Grande. Taylor took up a fortified position opposite the Mexican City of Matamoros; American naval units then blockaded the mouth of the river. For several months, nothing happened.

In Washington, Polk eventually lost patience. He decided to ask Congress for a declaration of war against Mexico for failing to pay the claims due American citizens and refusing to receive Slidell. News arrived that very evening of a skirmish between Mexican and American forces on the north bank of the Rio Grande. Polk at once revised this war message. Mexico, he told Congress, had "invaded our territory and shed American blood upon American soil." Congress, not fully aware of the President's maneuvering behind the scenes, voted overwhelmingly for war. Thousands of volunteers enthusiastically answered the call.

Polk and his Cabinet agreed at the outset that the United States must acquire both New Mexico and Upper California (the present state, as distinct from Lower California, still part of Mexico) and secure the Rio Grande boundary. New Mexico and

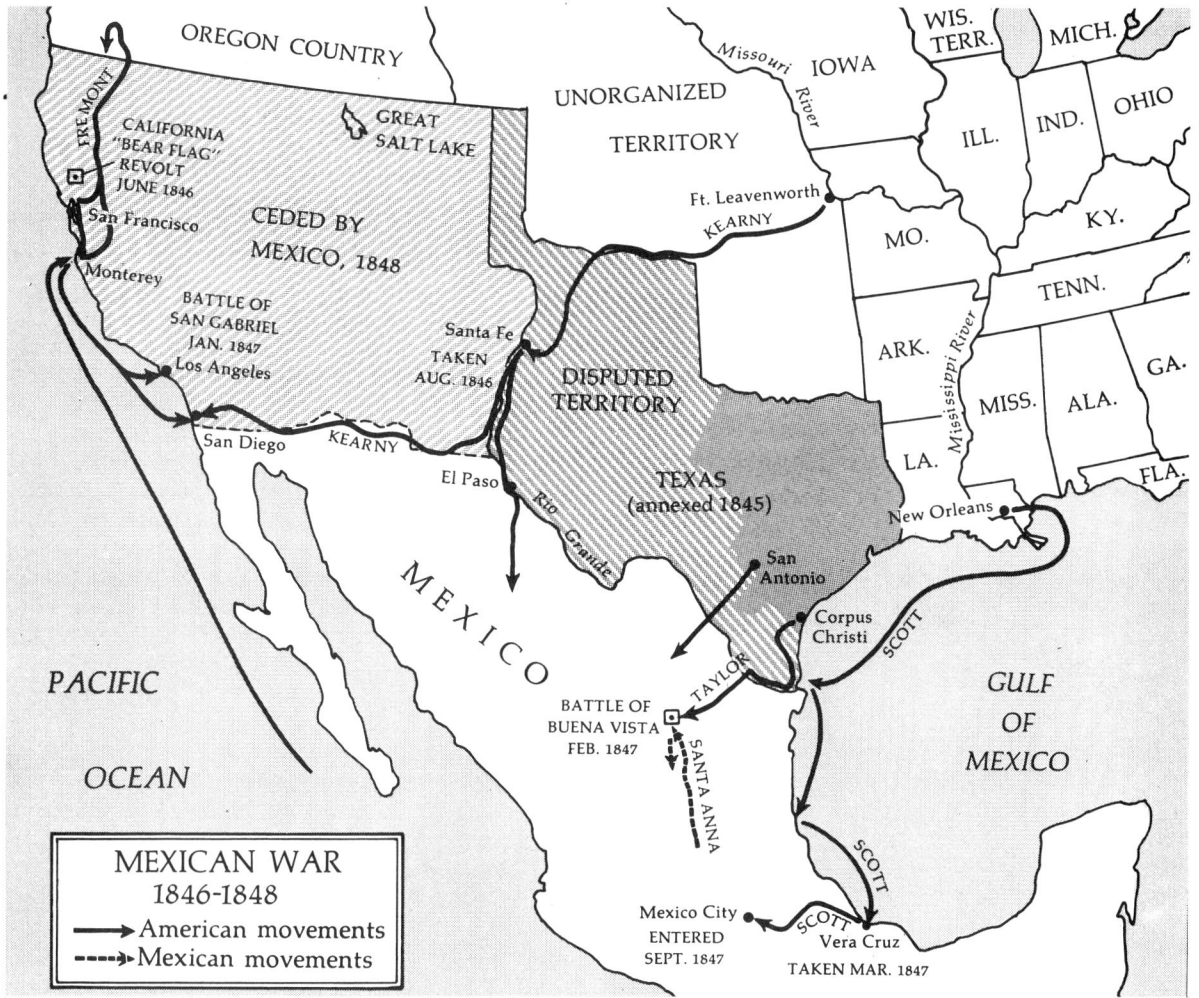

MEXICAN WAR
1846-1848
→ American movements
---→ Mexican movements

California took but six months to conquer. During the summer of 1846 Colonel Stephen W. Kearny's "Army of the West" (actually just sixteen hundred men) marched from Fort Leavenworth, Kansas, to Sante Fe, capital of New Mexico and occupied it without opposition. Kearny then proceeded with part of his force to aid the Navy in the conquest of California. A column of Missouri volunteers under Colonel A. W. Doniphan descended the Rio Grande to El Paso, marched from there into the interior, and in March 1847 occupied Chihuahua.

Polk's objectives in Mexico were unclear. Apparently he hoped that an advance into Mexico would force General Santa Anna into a quick settlement. Taylor at once pushed the Mexicans back across the Rio Grande and occupied Matamoros. The enthusiasm of the volunteers waned as the summer advanced. From a camp on the Rio Grande, one reported: "The water here unless well-qualified with brandy has a very peculiar ef-

fect on one. . . . it opens the bowels. . . . Gen. Scott came to see us the other day. He complimented Major Sumner very warmly on our improvement and especially on the extraordinary vigilance of our scouts—who, as he said, were peering at him from behind every bush as he approached the camp. To those aware of the disease prevalent here, the mistake of the General is ludicrous." Nevertheless, in September Taylor captured the Mexican stronghold of Monterrey and moved on to Saltillo and Victoria. The following February he repulsed Santa Anna at Buena Vista. "Old Rough and Ready's" victories and Doniphan's occupation of Chihuahua secured northern Mexico and California from further attack.

In the meantime, Polk had decided to bring the stubborn Santa Anna to terms with a strike at Mexico City itself. Polk, hating the Whigs even more than the Mexicans, picked General Winfield Scott to lead the campaign instead of Zachary

Caballero suit, owned by Don Antonio Franco de Coronel; southern California, mid-nineteenth century. *(Index of American Design.)*

Taylor, who was already being pushed as a Whig presidential candidate. Landing at Vera Cruz in March 1847, Scott pushed inland through the mountains, routing Santa Anna at the pass of Cerro Gordo, after a party of engineers under Captain Robert E. Lee had hacked a path through ravines and underbrush to surround the Mexicans. On September 13, Scott's army stormed the for-

tress of Chapultepec guarding Mexico City. The capital fell the next day.

Polk was by now desperate to end the fighting, and the intense domestic opposition to "Mr. Polk's War." Whig politicians—among them a young Illinois congressman named Abraham Lincoln—charged him with provoking Mexico into war as an excuse for expansion. Antislavery spokesmen like James Russell Lowell accused the President of wanting "bigger pens to cram with slaves." The American Peace Society grew in membership, and Henry David Thoreau counseled civil disobedience. Some critics of the war even longed for American defeat. As Scott's army approached Mexico City, William Lloyd Garrison thundered in the *Liberator:* "We only hope that, if blood has had to flow, that it has been that of the Americans, and that the next news we shall hear will be that General Scott and his army are in the hands of the Mexicans. . . ." (This attitude resembled that of some critics of the Vietnam War more than a century later.) At the same time, "Continental Democrats" were urging the President to take all of Mexico. Polk had previously dispatched Nicholas P. Trist to Mexico as a peace negotiator, and although in late 1847 he called Trist home, the emissary ignored Polk's order and stayed to sign the Treaty of Guadalupe Hidalgo on February 2, 1848. The United States gained the Rio Grande boundary, New Mexico, and California in return for an agreement to assume the claims of its citizens against the Mexican government, and to pay $15 million to Mexico.

The war was over. Writing in 1848, a Mexican historian observed: "To explain then in a few words the true origin of the war, it is sufficient to say that the insatiable ambition of the United States, favored by our weakness, caused it." For an apparently small price the United States had rounded out its continental domain, acquiring the present states of California, Nevada, Utah, New Mexico, and Arizona. Eventually, however, the cost would prove enormous: the problem of organizing this vast new territory reopened the explosive issue of slavery expansion, ultimately splitting in two the new transcontinental republic.

Throughout the 1840's, aggressive proponents of American expansion had generally tried to avoid any link with slavery. During the next decade expansionists, especially in the Democratic party, sought acquisition of new territory for avowedly pro-slavery purposes. The result was a distinct slowing in the pace of manifest destiny.

President Franklin Pierce sounded the call for further expansion in his 1853 inaugural address. "My administration," he boldly proclaimed, "will not be controlled by any timid forebodings

*Essay on Civil
Disobedience*
*by Henry David
Thoreau*

Thoreau was ardently
opposed to the Mex-
ican War; here he
gives his reaction to
the related problem
of slavery.

*How does it become a man to behave toward this American
government to-day? I answer, that he cannot without disgrace be
associated with it. I cannot for an instant recognize that political
organization as my government which is the slave's government
also.*

*All men recognize the right of revolution: that is, the right to
refuse allegiance to, and to resist, the government, when its tyranny or its inefficiency are great and unendurable. But almost all say
that such is not the case now. But such was the case, they think,
in the Revolution of '75. If one were to tell me that this was a bad
government because it taxed certain foreign commodities brought
to its ports, it is most probable that I should not make an ado
about it, for I can do without them.*

*When a sixth of the population of a nation which has undertaken
to be the refuge of liberty are slaves, and a whole country is unjustly overrun and conquered by a foreign army, and subjected to
military law, I think that it is not too soon for honest men to
rebel and revolutionize. What makes this duty the more urgent is
the fact that the country so overrun is not our own, but ours is
the invading army.*

*If the injustice is part of the necessary friction of the machine
of government, let it go, let it go: perchance it will wear
smooth,—certainly the machine will wear out. If the injustice has
a spring, or a pulley, or a rope, or a crank, exclusively for itself,
then perhaps you may consider whether the remedy will not be
worse than the evil; but if it is of such a nature that it requires
you to be the agent of injustice to another, then, I say, break the
law. Let your life be a counter friction to stop the machine. What
I have to do is to see, at any rate, that I do not lend myself to the
wrong which I condemn.*

of evil from expansion." True to his word, Pierce
dispatched James Gadsden of South Carolina to
Mexico with instructions to purchase additional
territory. At the very least, Gadsden was to acquire the Gila River region, which lay along the
proposed southern railroad route to the Pacific. In
addition, he might offer up to $50 million for the
northern provinces of Mexico. The Mexican
government, however, refused to sell anything
more than the Gila River region. Even this small
triumph of Gadsden's proved too much for the
Senate. Northern Senators, suspecting a Southern
plot to expand the domain of slavery, accepted the
Gadsden Treaty only after 9,000 square miles
(one-sixth of the total) had been cut from the purchase. For the first time in its history, the United
States had refused to accept land ceded to it.

Despite this setback, the hapless Pierce embarked upon a new imperialist venture. This time
the object was Spanish-owned Cuba. Southerners
had long desired to acquire Cuba, with its large
and valuable slave population. It would compensate the South for the loss of California and prevent England from prohibiting slavery on the
island. President Polk had tried without success to
purchase it from Spain. During 1853 the Pierce
administration lent support to John A. Quitman
of Mississippi and others who proposed to
"liberate" Cuba by force. When Quitman got
cold feet, Pierce instructed the American Minister
in Madrid, Pierre Soulé, to offer Spain as much as
$130 million for Cuba. Spain indignantly rejected
the American offer. Soulé then arranged a
meeting at Ostend, Belgium, in October 1854,
with the American Ministers to London and Paris,
to consider further action regarding Cuba. Their
recommendations to Washington, known as the
"Ostend Manifesto," soon found their way into
print, to the great embarrassment of the Pierce administration. Particularly damaging was the state-

Harriet Tubman.

Sojourner Truth.

Sojourner Truth, an illiterate former slave, spoke eloquently for abolitionism. Harriet Tubman, of similar background, carried her words into action by leading hundreds of brothers and sisters to freedom as a result of dangerous excursions into the South.

ment that, should Spain refuse renewed American offers to purchase Cuba, the United States would "by every law, human and Divine, be . . . justified in wresting it from Spain" if it possessed the power. Both American and European critics branded the Manifesto "a robber doctrine," "a highwayman's plea." The administration promptly repudiated the Manifesto, whereupon Soulé resigned amidst bitter recriminations. Manifest Destiny, like popular sovereignty, had suffered by its association with slavery. Renewed expansion would have to await the return of sectional peace.

The Costs of Manifest Destiny

Barely three months after the start of the Mexican War, the question of slavery in the territories erupted in Congress. During debate on a military appropriations bill in August 1846, Representative David Wilmot, a Pennsylvania Democrat, introduced an amendment that would prohibit slavery forever in any territory acquired from Mexico. On the question of adopting Wilmot's amendment, the roll call produced an ominous division—not between Whigs and Democrats, but between Northerners and Southerners. The House of Representatives passed Wilmot's Proviso; the Senate refused to accept it. Congress adjourned without further action.

With the end of the war, the question surfaced anew. Governments had to be organized in the lands acquired from Mexico, especially in California, where in 1849 the discovery of gold attracted thousands of eager settlers overnight. In the absence of a government, these "Forty-niners" frequently established vigilante organizations to maintain order.

Congress remained in deadlock. Every time a bill was introduced in Congress to organize the New Mexico and California territories, Northerners in the House voted to add Wilmot's Proviso. Southerners, who controlled the Senate, just as promptly voted to strike it out. The slavery question soon crowded out all others in Congress. Senator Thomas Hart Benton compared it to the Biblical plague of the frogs: "You could not look upon the table but there were frogs, you could not sit down at the banquet but there were frogs, you could not go to the bridal couch and lift the sheets but there were frogs!" So it was with this slavery question, "forever on the table, on the nuptial couch, everywhere!"

With each new debate, tempers rose on both sides. "We will establish a cordon of free states that shall surround you," Columbus Delano of Ohio warned Southerners, "and then we will light up the fires of liberty on every side until they melt your present chains and render all your people free." Southerners responded by threatening to break up the Union if slavery was barred from the territories. Moderates on both sides sought to break the impasse by removing the decision over slavery in New Mexico and California from Congress. President Polk recommended dividing the Western territories into slave and free soil by extending the Missouri Compromise line to the Pacific. Senator Lewis Cass of Michigan advocated "popular sovereignty"—leaving the question of slavery or non-slavery to the people of each territory. These compromises satisfied neither Northern "free soilers," who upheld the absolute authority of the federal government over slavery in the territories, nor Southern states' righters, who now denied that the federal government had

any authority to restrict slavery in the common territories.

The divisiveness of the slavery question entered into the 1848 presidential election. Both major parties turned to military men in hopes of diverting attention from slavery. The Democrats nominated Lewis Cass, a hero of the War of 1812 and an ardent expansionist. His advocacy of popular sovereignty in the territories made him especially attractive; but just to play safe, the Democrats circulated one campaign biography of Cass in the North and another in the South. The Whigs picked General Zachary Taylor, hero of the Mexican War, who had never so much as voted in an election before. The Whig convention then adjourned without adopting a platform. During the campaign Taylor was pictured in the South as a friend of slavery (he personally owned over one hundred slaves), and in the North as a friend of the Wilmot Proviso.

A third party, the Free Soil, was formed out of a coalition of three elements—the abolitionist Liberty Party, "conscience" or antislavery Whigs, and Northern Democrats alienated by Polk's pro-Southern attitude on internal improvements, the tariff, and patronage. The Free Soilers made opposition to slavery expansion their main plank. For President they chose Martin Van Buren. Although these heterogeneous elements could barely stifle their differences long enough for a campaign, theirs was the first broadly based antislavery party. In November 1848 the Free Soil Party failed to carry a single state; nevertheless, it captured an impressive ten percent of the popular vote. By cutting heavily into Democratic margins in New York, Massachusetts, and Vermont, Van Buren made possible Taylor's victory.

The Compromise of 1850

When Congress met in December 1849, the situation was critical. It took three weeks and fifty-nine ballots to elect a Speaker of the House. Californians, tired of waiting for Congress, had held a convention at Monterey and drafted a state constitution prohibiting slavery (they simply did not want to compete with black labor). Without waiting for congressional approval, California chose a governor and legislature. Only one obstacle—formal admission to statehood—remained.

In this supercharged atmosphere the new President, Zachary Taylor, decided to break the con-

gressional deadlock himself. Although an ardent defender of slavery, Taylor did not regard expansion as necessary for its protection. Like Polk, he considered California and the Southwest as unsuitable for slavery. The President therefore recommended to Congress that California and New Mexico be admitted directly to statehood, bypassing the territorial stage. The residents could then decide the slavery question for themselves, removing Congress' embarrassment. Southerners, seeing that California had already prohibited slavery and expecting New Mexico to do the same, realized that Taylor's plan was as effective as

Wilmot's provision in keeping slavery out of this area. When they protested, the old soldier took a hard line, threatening to use force if necessary to preserve the Union.

To Southerners this was the final straw: Taylor had betrayed them. California would be the first in what they feared would be a flood of new "free" states admitted to the Union. The South's precarious equality in the Senate would be lost. Northerners would make war upon slavery—an institution, Southern spokesmen insisted, "upon which is staked our property, our social organization and our peace and safety." When a call went out in October 1849 for the Southern states to send delegates to a convention at Nashville the following June to consider secession, most of these states accepted.

At this moment, with disunion threatening, an aged Senator Henry Clay offered a compromise that he hoped would settle for good the territorial crisis and other disputed issues between the sections. Clay's plan, introduced in Congress in January 1850, contained five key provisions: (1) immediate admission of free California; (2) organization of the rest of the area acquired from Mexico into two territories (Utah and New Mexico) without restriction on slavery; (3) assumption of the Texan national debt by the federal government; (4) abolition of the slave trade in the District of Columbia; (5) a tough new fugitive slave law.

The debate on Clay's compromise was the last hurrah for the generation of statesmen who had guided America's destinies since 1812. Twice before, in 1820 and 1833, stirring appeals to love of Union, flag, and Constitution had soothed sectional tensions, opening the way for compromise. During the winter and spring of 1850, Senate veterans tried to revive this tested formula. Day after day, packed galleries followed their speeches. Clay took the floor first, urging the North not to demand the principle of the Wilmot Proviso—nature would as effectively exclude slavery—and to honor the constitutional obligation to return fugitive slaves. He reminded the South of the many benefits she enjoyed in the Union. The "Great Pacificator" closed his two-day oration with an appeal to both sides to pause at the edge of the cliff, before leaping "into the yawning abyss below." Should disunion occur, Clay expressed the hope that he would not live to see it.

Clay's compromises did not go far enough to satisfy John C. Calhoun. The old Nullifier, his body wracked by tuberculosis, sat defiantly while his speech was read for him. The North, he charged, had taken advantage of tariffs and other federal favors to outstrip the South in population

and power. To restore equilibrium between the sections, he demanded not only that the North grant slaveholders equal rights in the territories but that it pass constitutional guarantees giving the South equal power in the government. The only alternative for the South was secession.

Daniel Webster spoke on March 7, displaying an eloquence reminiscent of his brilliant reply to Hayne two decades before. He pleaded with both sections to show tolerance for the sake of Union. He criticized the abolitionists' ethical absolutism and deplored the agitation over slavery in the territories. The law of nature precluded a slave economy there, he asserted, and no legislation was needed to reenact God's will. He took sharp issue with Calhoun's talk of "peaceable secession": "There can be no such thing as a peaceable secession. Peaceable secession is an utter impossibility." A thousand physical and social ties bound the sections together. Disunion, he warned the South pointedly, "must produce such a war as I will not describe, *in its twofold character*" (a hint at the prospect of slave revolts). Much to the discomfort of abolitionists, who criticized it savagely, Webster's Seventh of March speech did much to rally Northern support for compromise.

For all his skill, Clay had miscalculated. Patriotic appeals for Union could not overcome sectional bitterness in 1850. When Clay's package of compromise measures (known as the "Omnibus" bill) came to a vote in July, opponents of the individual measures ganged up to defeat it. With his bill and his health in ruins, Clay withdrew into retirement. Thirty-four-year-old Stephen A. Douglas assumed his place in steering the compromise through Congress. Only five feet four, nicknamed "the Little Giant" and "a steam engine in britches," this brash, hard-driving Senator from Illinois devised a new compromise strategy. He introduced Clay's measures separately, relying on sectional blocs and a few "swing" votes to form majorities for each. The individual bills, one Senator remarked, resembled "cats and dogs that had been tied together by their tails for months, scratching and biting, [but] being loose again, every one of them ran off to his own hole and was quiet."

Douglas' strategy worked. The North won admission of free California and a ban on the slave trade in Washington. The South had a more stringent fugitive slave law and a promise of no congressional prohibition on slavery in the New Mexico and Utah territories. The federal government assumed the Texas debt. Two events immeasurably aided Douglas' efforts that hot summer. The first was the death on July 9 of President Taylor, who had obstinately opposed any compromise plan but his own; his successor, Millard Fillmore, supported the Clay-Douglas measures. The second was the lobbying of Texas bondholders, who stood to gain handsomely if the federal government purchased their depreciated securities.

Most Americans enthusiastically welcomed the Compromise of 1850. Celebrations were held in many cities. In Washington, word went out that it was the duty of every patriot to get drunk. Before the next morning dawned, many citizens, including Senators Foote, Douglas, and Webster, had amply proved their patriotism. To most Americans, it now seemed that the slavery question had at last been settled.

Events, however, soon revealed that the Compromise settled nothing at all because of the deliberate ambiguities embedded in it. The Utah and New Mexico territories had been organized without congressional restriction on slavery. Could the people of these territories now restrict it if they chose? Or did the extreme Southern doctrine apply—no restriction before statehood? The Compromise said only that Utah and New Mexico would be admitted to statehood with or without slavery, as their constitutions prescribed "at the time of their admission." Northerners were left to believe that popular sovereignty applied, while Southerners assumed an unrestricted right to hold slaves in these territories. The critical question of slavery in the territories had merely been evaded. There had been no compromise in 1850, only an armistice. This fragile truce would survive only until the next wave of westward expansion.

Suggested Readings

Eugene D. Genovese's *Roll, Jordan, Roll: The World the Slaves Made* (1974) is a monumental literary study of slave life before the war. He discusses the slave family, the black work ethic, slave resistance, miscegenation, and slave language, all within a framework that sets off the paternalistic ideology of the Southern planter and the accommodation between master and slave; Genovese's *The World the Slaveholders Made* (1969) elaborates on the class structure of Southern society. Herbert G. Gutman, in *The Black Family in Slavery and Freedom, 1750-1925* (1976) challenges theories that speak of the disorganization of the black slave family—and the lasting effect of that disorganization on black life; instead, he argues, the black family was resilient and adaptive. It is impossible to escape the debate over a two-volume study by Robert Fogel and Stanley Engerman, *Time on the Cross* (1974). This book by two economists quantifies the Southern slave economy to conclude that slaves were productive and efficient, rarely abused, well-fed, and enjoying a variety of incentives. Excellent critiques of this idyllic existence include Paul A. David *et al., Reckoning with Slavery: A Critical Study in the Quantitative History of American Negro Slavery* (1976) and Herbert B. Gutman, *Slavery and the Numbers Game: A Critique of 'Time on the Cross'* (1978). Frederick W. Merk studies the Mexican imbroglio from the standpoint of slavery in *Slavery and the Annexation of Texas* (1972); his *Manifest Destiny and Mission in American History* (1965) is standard.

Charles W. Peale, *George Washington at Princeton*. (Pennsylvania Academy of the Fine Arts.)

John Neagle, *Pat Lyon at the Forge.* (Courtesy Museum of Fine Arts, Boston.)

William Sidney Mount, *Dancing on the Barn Floor*, 1831.

William Sidney Mount, *Farmers Nooning*, 1846. (Courtesy, Melville Collection, Suffolk Museum and Carriage House, Stony Brook, Long Island.)

J.E. Buttersworth, *Great Republic*. (The Peabody Museum of Salem.)

William Sidney Mount, *California News,* 1850. (Courtesy Melville Collection, Suffolk Museum and Carriage House, Stony Brook, Long Island.)

Washington Allston, *Moonlit Landscape*, (Courtesy Museum of Fine Arts, Boston.)

261

Albert Bierstadt, *The Rocky Mountains*, 1863. (The Metropolitan Museum of Art, Rogers Fund, 1907.)

135,000 SETS, 270,000 VOLUMES SOLD.

UNCLE TOM'S CABIN

FOR SALE HERE.

AN EDITION FOR THE MILLION, COMPLETE IN 1 Vol., PRICE 37 1-2 CENTS.

" " IN GERMAN, IN 1 Vol., PRICE 50 CENTS.

" " IN 2 Vols., CLOTH, 6 PLATES, PRICE $1.50.

SUPERB ILLUSTRATED EDITION, IN 1 Vol., WITH 153 ENGRAVINGS.

PRICES FROM $2.50 TO $5.00.

The Greatest Book of the Age.

Chapter XIII
Distant Thunder:
The 1850's

Uncle Tom's Cabin (1852)

When Harriet Beecher was fifteen-years-old (in 1826), she had already read much of her father's theological library. Mrs. Stowe later recalled with fondness her "non-resistant" childhood in Massachusetts and Cincinnati and her admiration for her "God-like" father, Lyman Beecher, later appointed president of Lane Theological Seminary. There Harriet met a young teacher, Calvin Stowe, whom she married. Stowe encouraged his wife's first writings for literary magazines, and she supported him during his long encounter with hallucinations and intellectual inertia. In 1850, Bowdoin College offered Calvin Stowe a professorship. Within a few months of Harriet's arrival in Maine she began to turn her moral attention to matters of a worldly nature. American black slavery arrested her with "an icy hand" after a chance reading of a Southern slave-dealing newspaper. Mrs. Stowe began a considerable research into the institution of chattel labor, reading Southern defenses of slavery as well as the virulent attacks on it by Theodore Weld and Frederick Douglass, himself an ex-slave.

The Fugitive Slave Law of 1850 precipitated her creative energy, and she wrote *Uncle Tom's Cabin* in serial form in 1852. Mrs. Stowe later described the novel as having been "dictated" to her from a source outside of herself. One measure of the novel's power was its generating of imitations. More than fifty novels with slavery as their essence appeared after 1852, thirty of which were intent on showing the institution as beneficial. None of these reached Mrs. Stowe's great audience: sales in book form set publishing records: 300,000 copies the first year, a million in seven years. Adapted for the stage, the story quickly became America's most popular play. By 1861, millions of Northerners had thrilled over Eliza's dramatic escape and wept for Tom's fortitude under the lash.

The book was a success in spite of its overdrawn characters and clumsy plot. Avoiding the usual abolitionist stereotypes of saintlike slaves and vicious slaveholders, Mrs. Stowe cut right to the heart of the matter: it was not fundamentally people who were evil, but the system under which they lived. Given absolute power over their slaves, few masters could resist the temptation to use it. Slavery often dragged down even "good" masters when circumstances occurred beyond their control. At its worst (Simon Legree's plantation) the "peculiar institution" brutalized everyone—black and white. Mrs. Stowe's vivid account of the plight of blacks as human beings trapped in a system of bondage was the most effective critique of slavery up to that time. Although it is difficult to measure the exact impact of *Uncle Tom's Cabin*, the Northern attitude toward slavery was never quite the same after it appeared. There was an element of truth in the remark with which President Lincoln allegedly greeted Mrs. Stowe when she visited the White House during the Civil War: "So you're the little lady who wrote the book that made the great war."

To Mrs. Stowe's nineteenth-century audience—the largest audience for any previous work of American fiction—she was not pursuing slavery with a bludgeon. Her instrument was at least as delicate as a surgeon's knife, and she operated on the national psyche, not just the system of slavery.

The slave was commercial property, and the business of slavery passed through Northern as well as Southern hands. The trade in human beings tore against the fabric of a society whose warp was the family and whose woof was Christianity and the morality it supports. She possessed a firm sense of the uneasiness that many Americans felt over the disrupting tendencies of commerce and a mobile society. Instead of making slavery a direct contrast with the "free" society of the North, she made it a grotesque extension and intensification of that world. Men "alive to nothing but trade and profit—cool, and unhesitating, and unrelenting as death and the grave roamed the American earth, building things and disrupting and destroying lives." Under slavery, men of commerce could take their avarice to its final extension: trade in human flesh. Mrs. Stowe originally subtitled her book *The Man That Was a Thing*, and correctly noted—despite the paternal ideals of some slaveholders—the entrepreneurial bent of the *system* of slavery. Northerners understood her picture of slavery because it reached the uneasiness they felt about their own society. Southerners knew this too: their many replies to *Uncle Tom's Cabin* often aimed ineffectual blows at Northern commercial society. No wonder Southerners were so unrelievedly furious.

The Fugitive Slave Law

President Fillmore had barely signed the Compromise of 1850 into law before the slavery controversy erupted anew. Ironically it was the Compromise itself that rekindled the quarrel. Among its several provisions was one designed to assist slaveholders in recovering their runaway property. This fugitive slave law had been passed in response to Southern complaints that the original law of 1793 was weak and ineffectual: it put slaveholders to great personal expense, and failed to provide for assistance from federal officers. The new law of 1850 remedied these defects, and did more. It created special commissioners to deal with fugitive-slave cases. These commissioners had only to be convinced of a fugitive slave's identity before granting the owner authority to seize the runaway and take him home. They were empowered to call on federal marshals to enforce the law, and to compensate slaveholders in cases for undue expense. Anyone who aided fugitives or obstructed their arrest was subject to fine and imprisonment. Here was a slaveholders' dream.

As might have been expected, however, the law outraged many Northerners. Especially controversial were the sections denying fugitive slaves the right to a jury trial, or even to testify in their own behalf. The legislation was a heavensent issue for the abolitionists. Unlike the complicated constitutional question of federal versus state sovereignty in the territories, here was a law with immense emotional impact. The spectacle of fugitive slaves being led southward, handcuffed and guarded, aroused considerable sympathy in the North. Cases of mistaken identity and kidnapping of free blacks shocked even normally unsympathetic Northerners.

The abolitionists played up the fugitive question for all it was worth. They described the law as "a hateful statute of kidnappers" and "a filthy enactment," and pledged resistance. The fugitive question became a rallying point for the splintered antislavery movement; it was something that political activists—Garrisonians, free-soilers, Whigs, Democrats, and blacks—could all agree on.

This spirit of opposition sparked several well-publicized acts of resistance to enforcement of the fugitive slave law. In 1851 a mob of blacks in Boston burst into a courtroom during the extradition hearing of a fugitive slave named Shadrach. While the crowd struggled with the police, two husky blacks grabbed the startled Shadrach and carried him bodily out of the building. Once in the street, a witness recalled, Shadrach "found the use of his feet, and the three went off toward Cambridge like a black squall, the crowd driving along with them and cheering as they went." Shadrach was soon spirited off to Canada. Later that same year, black and white abolitionists successfully resisted enforcement of the law at Syracuse, New York, and Christiana, Pennsylvania.

Still, such acts of resistance were the exception; in over eighty percent of the cases brought under the law, slaveholders successfully recovered their property. Nevertheless, spectacular rescues like that of Shadrach confirmed most Southerners in their conviction that the fugitive slave law could not be enforced north of the Mason-Dixon Line. As a result, relatively few slaveholders took advantage of it. This conviction was reinforced by the passage in certain Northern states of "personal liberty laws" designed to hinder recovery of fugitive slaves. Such actions gave rise to a widespread feeling among Southerners that the North had failed to fulfill an essential part of the Compromise.

The Kansas-Nebraska Act

The settlement of the Oregon boundary controversy and the acquisition of California made the United States a Pacific power. American commerce quickly expanded across the Pacific. In 1844 Caleb Cushing, the first American Minister to China, negotiated a treaty granting Americans special trade privileges in that country. A decade later, Commodore Matthew Perry gained a diplomatic and commercial toehold in Japan. Closer to home, the American government sought unsuccessfully in 1854 to annex the Hawaiian Islands, already a cultural outpost of the United States. Forward-looking Americans proclaimed the dawn of a great commercial era in the Pacific.

In order to shorten the route from Atlantic ports to the Orient and to improve communications between the two coasts, the United States began considering an interoceanic canal. An 1846 treaty with Colombia granted Americans the right to transit across the Isthmus of Panama, in return for American recognition of Colombian sovereignty there. American efforts to control the alternative canal route through Nicaragua aroused protests from Britain, which had bases of its own in the vicinity. In 1850 the two sides compromised their differences in the Clayton-Bulwer Treaty. Each party agreed not to seek exclusive control over the proposed isthmian canal or to colonize the surrounding area. In spite of this official enthusiasm, however, American capitalists showed little interest in the idea of building a canal. Travel across the isthmus remained a primitive affair until 1855, when a railroad replaced muleback and coach as the chief means of transportation.

As an alternative to a ship canal, many Americans advocated a transcontinental railroad. Asa Whitney, a New York merchant who had made a fortune in the China trade, labored throughout the 1840's to persuade Congress to finance construction of a railroad from Lake Michigan to the mouth of the Columbia River. This route, although mountainous, had the advantage of passing north of Mexican California. The Treaty of Guadalupe-Hidalgo eliminated Mexico from the picture, but a new stumbling block—sectional rivalry—soon appeared. The South favored a southern route for the railroad, running from New Orleans to California via Texas and the Gila River Valley. The North preferred either Whitney's northern route or a central route, extending from Chicago or St. Louis by way of South Pass to San Francisco. Unable to agree on one route, Congress in 1853 authorized surveys of all three.

This delay was intolerable to Stephen Douglas of Illinois, the foremost advocate of a central route. From his position as chairman of the Senate Committee on Territories, Douglas had pioneered in opening the Mississippi Valley to settlement. A Pacific railroad would help his "Great West" reach its full potential. Douglas was also motivated by political and personal considerations: his home town of Chicago, where he had heavy real estate investments, would be the probable eastern terminus of a central railroad.

One roadblock stood squarely in the way of Douglas' plans. The region west of Iowa and Missouri—known as Nebraska—was still unorganized Indian country. Until the region was established as a territory, it could not be surveyed and opened for settlement. In this respect, advocates of a southern route had a real advantage: all the area along their route had already been made into states or territories.

As Douglas analyzed the situation late in 1853, he had to find some way to induce Southerners in Congress to vote for a bill organizing Nebraska. Unfortunately for him, Southerners had no motive to support a measure that cleared the path for a rival railroad route to the Pacific. And Southerners had absolutely no reason to vote to create what would become another free territory. As part of the Louisiana Purchase, Nebraska had been made "forever" free by the Missouri Compromise of 1820. Senator David Atchison of Missouri spoke for many Southerners when he vowed that he would "sink in hell" before he handed Nebraska over to the free-soilers.

Douglas therefore decided that he would have to make a concession to the South. He offered the repeal of the Missouri Compromise line excluding slavery north of 36°30'. Douglas' territorial bill, introduced in Congress in January 1854, called for the creation of two territories—Kansas and Nebraska. It specifically repealed the Missouri Compromise restriction on slavery. In its place, Douglas substituted the principle of popular sovereignty. The people of these territories were free "to form and regulate their domestic institutions in their own way." Thus, to enlist Southern support for his railroad, Douglas held out the bait of making Kansas and Nebraska slave states by the operation of popular sovereignty.

As Douglas himself had predicted, repeal of the Missouri Compromise line raised "a hell of a storm." Most Northerners regarded the Act of 1820 as an inviolable pledge to freedom. They looked on repeal as part of a slaveholder's plot to make free territory into "a dreary region of despotism, inhabited by masters and slaves." In Congress, many Northern Democrats joined their Whig colleagues in opposition. Objections came not only from abolitionists but from moderates who had accepted the Compromise of 1850, but who now lost all confidence in the good faith of the South. Douglas and his co-conspirators, wrote Horace Greeley in the *New York Tribune,* had made "more abolitionists than Garrison . . . could have made in half a century."

Douglas vigorously defended his proposal. Slavery, he insisted, was an outmoded institution, unsuited by climate and geography to the plains of Kansas. Thus, popular sovereignty would just as effectively bar slavery as would exclusion, at the same time as it removed the moral stigma on slavery that the Missouri Compromise line implied. After three months of bitter debate, Douglas, with the support of President Franklin Pierce, carried his bill.

Passage of the Kansas-Nebraska Act had profound consequences for the country. It shattered what little remained of the uneasy truce of 1850. It turned Kansas into a battleground and fatally ruptured the Democratic Party. By using popular sovereignty to open free soil to slavery, Douglas discredited what until then had been an effective instrument for compromise. Rarely in American history had so much been risked for so little. The next year—1855—when Douglas introduced his long-awaited Pacific Railroad bill in Congress, his enemies had their revenge by killing it. At Douglas' death in 1861 his great Pacific railroad, on which he had expended so much energy and prestige, was still bottled up in Congress, a victim of the sectional conflict he had helped to revive.

"Bleeding Kansas"

With the passage of the Kansas-Nebraska Act, the slavery contest moved from the halls of Congress to the plains of Kansas. Both sections attached great importance to the decision over slavery there. By making Kansas a slave state, Southerners hoped to restore the political balance between the sections. Slavery expansion also had great symbolic importance to Southerners. By denying the South's right to expand, the North seemed to be denying Southern equality. Southerners reasoned that if they could not take their slaves into the common territories, they would no longer be the equal of Northern citizens.

For opponents of slavery, the territories were "the" battleground in the fight against slavery, since all antislavery persons—radical and moderate—agreed that this was one place where the federal government had undisputed authority to ban slavery. Anti-expansion also had a darker side. Many Northerners, especially in the Midwest, were determined to preserve the rich prairie soils for the white race. Here, said David Wilmot, "the sons of toil, of my own race and color, can live without the disgrace which association with Negro slavery brings upon free labor." These same racial prejudices applied to free blacks, who encountered widespread discrimination in the North. Such racist attitudes increasingly dominated the antislavery movement, and conditioned the public views of even sincere opponents of slavery like Abraham Lincoln. Ironically, the demand for free soil greatly broadened the antislavery movement's appeal at the same time as it diluted the purity of the movement.

From the beginning, the contest in Kansas over slavery was mainly the work of outsiders. In the North, groups like the New England Emigrant Aid Company, founded in 1854, subsidized the migration of free-state settlers to Kansas. To protect them, the Company sent new breech-loading rifles known popularly as "Beecher's Bibles," after Harriet's ministerial brother, Henry Ward Beecher, who proclaimed them a greater moral agency in Kansas than the Bible. Bands of Missouri "border ruffians" regularly crossed into neighboring Kansas to aid the proslavery cause. In March 1855, at the first election for a territorial legislature, their votes helped to give the proslavery party a majority. This assembly immediately enacted a slave code for the territory. Free-state settlers, refusing to recognize this legislature, elected one of their own. By late 1855, Kansas had two rival governments, neither of which would recognize the other's laws or participate in its elections.

Under these circumstances, orderly government was impossible. Extremists on both sides of the slavery question took advantage of the confusion to carry on a private war of their own. After proslavery men raided the free-state stronghold of Lawrence, the fanatical John Brown and seven followers (four of them his sons) retaliated by rounding up five proslavery sympathizers at Pottawatomie Creek and hacking them to death with broadswords. The typical settler, whose chief concern was land and not slavery, was caught in the middle and frequently took sides only in self-defense.

This warfare in Kansas was given extensive coverage in the press, thanks to the recently established telegraph system, which now made it possible to provide up-to-date reports of far-away events. Newspapers in both sections often slanted the news from Kansas for their own purposes. The "sack" of Lawrence, for example, was pictured in the antislavery press as an orgy of destruction and killing. In reality, it was a rather tame affair; only one person was killed, and he a proslavery man

Samuel Clemens (Mark Twain)

. . . I about made up my mind to pray, and see if I couldn't try to quit being the kind of a boy I was and be better. So I kneeled down. But the words wouldn't come. Why wouldn't they? . . .I was trying to make my mouth say I would do the right thing and the clean thing, and go and write to that nigger's owner and tell where he was; but deep down in me I knowed it was a lie, and He knowed it. You can't pray a lie—I found out.

So I was full of trouble, full as I could be; and didn't know what to do. At last I had an idea; and I says, I'll go and write the letter—and then see if I can pray. Why, it was astonishing, the way I felt as light as a feather right straight off, and my troubles all gone. So I got a piece of paper and a pencil, all glad and excited, and set down and wrote:

Miss Watson, your runaway nigger Jim is down here two mile below Pikesville, and Mr. Phelps had got him and he will give him up for the reward if you send.

I felt good and all washed clean of sin for the first time I had ever felt so in my life, and I knowed I could pray now. But I didn't do it straight off, but laid the paper down and set there thinking—thinking how good it was all this happened so, and how near I come to being lost and going to hell. And went on thinking. And got to thinking over our trip down the river; and I see Jim before me all the time: in the day and in the night-time, sometimes moonlight, sometimes storms, and we a-floating along, talking and singing and laughing. But somehow I couldn't seem to strike no places to harden me against him, but only the other kind. I'd see him standing my watch on top of his'n, 'stead of calling me, so I could go on sleeping; . . . and at last I struck the time I saved him by telling the men we had small-pox aboard, and he was so grateful, and said I was the best friend old Jim ever had in the world, and the only one he's got now; and then I happened to look around and see that paper.

It was a close place. I took it up, and held it in my hand. I was a-trembling, because I's got to decide, forever, betwixt two things, and I knowed it. I studied a minute, sort of holding my breath, and then says to myself:

"All right, then, I'll go to hell"—and tore it up.

Huckleberry Finn
by Samuel Clemens

struck on the head by a falling brick. Early in 1857 federal troops restored order to Kansas, and the free-and slave-state parties each promptly fell to quarreling among themselves. Before the year was out, a visitor to Kansas reported that "speculations run high [here], politics seldom named, *money* now seems to be the question." Nevertheless, the territory remained deeply divided, with each side retaining its own government.

The struggle in Kansas forced the slavery issue back into Congress. (This was ironic, since the intent of popular sovereignty was to get the slavery question out of Congress.) In 1856 the House of Representatives sent a fact-finding committee to Kansas. Meantime, Congress endlessly debated the Kansas question in an atmosphere of steadily rising tension. Passion spilled into violence on the floor of the Senate in the Sumner-Brooks affair. Senator Charles Sumner of Massachusetts delivered a violent antislavery speech entitled "The Crime Against Kansas." In it he made

several tasteless personal references to Senator Andrew P. Butler of South Carolina. To avenge these insults to an elderly kinsman, Butler's nephew, Representative Preston S. Brooks of South Carolina, stole up behind Sumner at his Senate desk during a recess and beat him severely over the head with a cane.

This incident shocked Northerners, who looked on "Bully" Brooks's conduct as another example of the domineering insolence of slaveholders. The injured Sumner became an instant martyr of the antislavery cause. Most Southerners, although many privately disapproved, publicly applauded Brooks's action and showered him with canes inscribed with slogans like "Use Knock-down Arguments." When Brooks resigned from Congress, his Carolina constituents reelected him. This incident, and the controversy over "Bleeding Kansas," further polarized a country already divided by the Kansas-Nebraska Act.

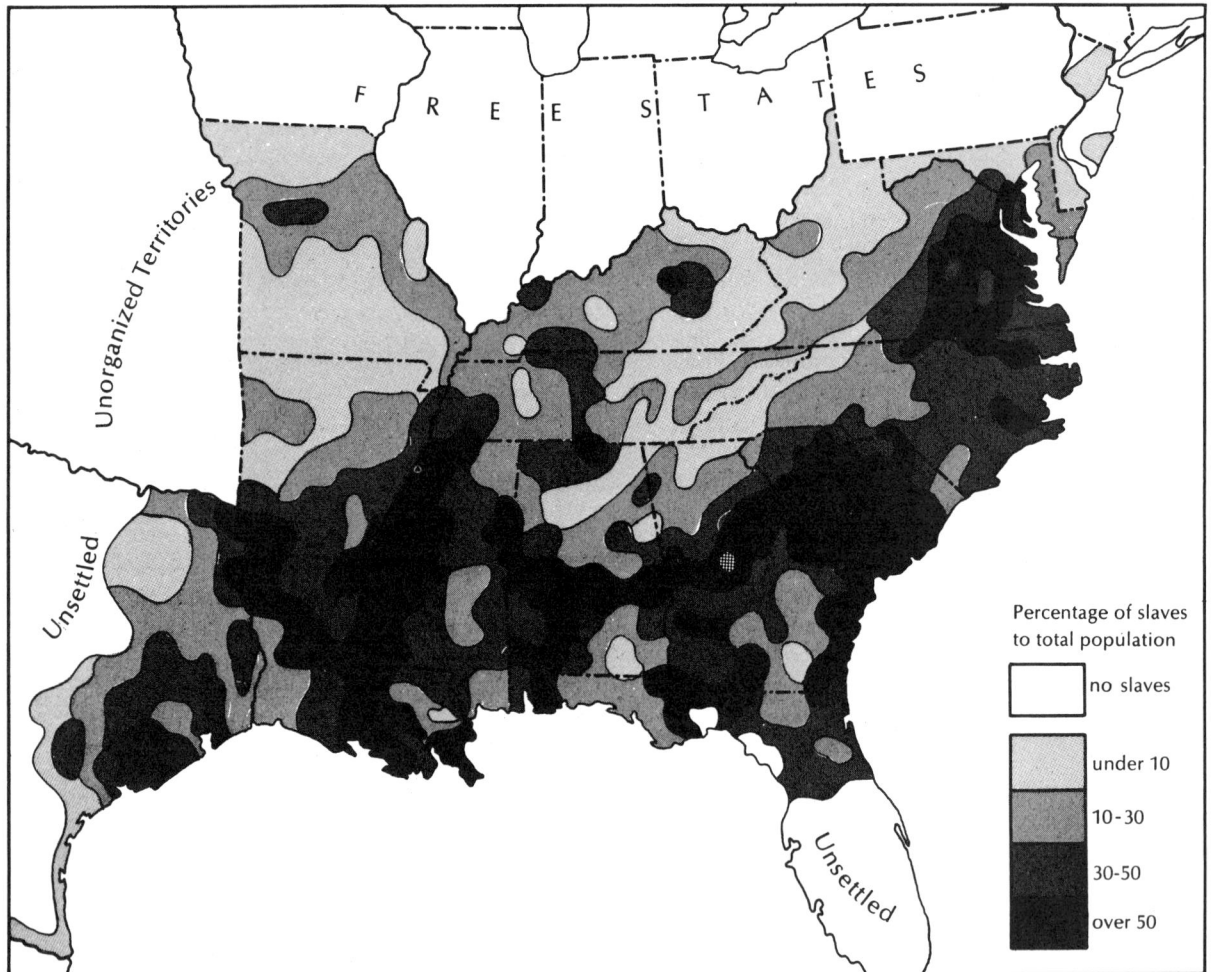

Percentage of slaves to total population

no slaves

under 10

10-30

30-50

over 50

Political Upheaval

Before 1850 the country's political system had been a strong bond of union. The two major parties, Whigs and Democrats, were both national organizations with support throughout the country. In each party strong Northern and Southern wings worked together—especially at presidential election time—in their mutual interest. The dependence of each wing on the other served to override the potentially divisive effect of issues like slavery. So intense was party loyalty that William Pitt Fessenden, a Whig stalwart, declared that he "would vote for a dog, if he was the candidate of my party." The Compromise of 1850 and the Kansas-Nebraska Act, however, drastically altered the system, destroying one party, disrupting another, and creating a third. As a result, the political system became sectionalized.

It was the Whigs who felt the strain of slavery first. They had never been as strong organizationally as the Democrats. Furthermore, the Whig Party drew its strength in the North from Yankee Protestants whose sense of moral stewardship made them especially sympathetic to the antislavery cause. The abolitionist and Free Soil movements made many converts among these "conscience" Whigs. At the 1852 Whig convention the dispute over slavery broke wide open. So intense was sectional distrust that the two sides even disagreed over the choice of a minister to lead the opening prayer. Northern Whigs refused to support President Fillmore, the favorite of Southern Whigs, because he had supported the Compromise of 1850. The Northerners backed instead General Winfield Scott, another Mexican War hero, and Scott was finally chosen after fifty-three hard-fought ballots. In retaliation, Southern Whigs rammed through a platform endorsing the Compromise, including the Fugitive Slave Law, which was so hated in New England.

Saddled with a candidate unpopular in the South and a platform unpopular in the North, the Whigs lost disastrously in 1852. Franklin Pierce of New Hampshire, the Democratic candidate, carried twenty-seven of thirty-one states—the most lopsided election victory since 1820. Surveying the ruins, antislavery Whigs began to seek a new alliance.

Not long afterward, it was the Democrats' turn to feel the divisive effects of the slavery issue. The Kansas-Nebraska Act bitterly antagonized Northern Democrats with antislavery leanings, and their frustration found expression in the "Appeal of the Independent Democrats," composed in 1854 by Charles Sumner, Salmon P. Chase, and other antislavery Democratic congressmen. The appeal invited all opponents of slavery expansion to form a common front "to rescue the country from the domination of slavery."

This rebellion among antislavery Democrats set the stage for a dramatic restructuring of Northern politics. Antislavery politicians—former Whigs, breakaway Democrats, some of the more moderate abolitionists—struggled to create the coalition called for in the appeal. The new organization came formally into existence at a convention held in Ripon, Wisconsin, in February 1854; the delegates adopted a statement of principles proclaiming their opposition to the extension of slavery in the territories. The new party officially adopted the name "Republican" a few months later.

This political transformation did not take place without complications. Another party—the "Know-Nothings"—was now in the field. The flood of Irish and German immigrants to America after 1840 had raised cries of alarm from old-stock Protestants, who feared that these predominantly Catholic immigrants would undermine republican institutions. Those "governed by a head in a foreign land," exclaimed one nativist editor, "holding no sympathy with our institutions, where Papal power prevails," and where "*no genuine liberty, either civil or religious*" exists, must not "control the American Ballot Box." The newcomers were also charged with corrupting the nation's morals; according to another nativist, they brought "grog shops like the frogs of Egypt upon us." The visit of a special papal envoy to the United States in 1853 triggered a series of riots in Cincinnati, Pittsburgh, and elsewhere. A mob in Charlestown, Massachusetts, burned a Catholic convent to the ground.

Building upon this anti-foreign and anti-Catholic prejudice, Charles B. Allen of New York formed a secret "patriotic" society, the Order of the Star-Spangled Banner, in 1849. Members, when questioned by outsiders, customarily answered, "I know nothing." For a few years the society remained an obscure local organization, but in 1854, hoping to capitalize on the breakup of the old party alignments, nativists went political and formed the American, or "Know-Nothing" party. For a short time the Know-Nothings demonstrated amazing political strength, capturing several state governorships and seventy-five seats in Congress. They were strongest in the

Northeast and the border states. The Know-Nothings soon discovered, however, that as a bisectional party, they enjoyed no more immunity from the disruptive influence of the slavery question than the other parties. After a bitter quarrel at the 1855 national convention, the party disintegrated. Most Northern Know-Nothings went into the new Republican Party, which had been actively wooing the nativists with pledges of "No Popery and Slavery."

The 1856 elections provided the first test of strength for the Republicans. Its convention resembled a revival meeting. "There is but a slight quantity of liquor consumed," a journalist reported, "very little profane swearing is heard, and everything is managed with excessive and intense propriety." The platform condemned slavery as a "relic of barbarism" and reaffirmed Congress' "right and duty" to prohibit it in the territories. For President the Republicans nominated John C. Fremont, the dashing "Pathfinder" of western exploration. The Democrats bypassed President Pierce and Stephen Douglas, who were too closely identified with the Kansas-Nebraska Act, in favor of James Buchanan of Pennsylvania. Buchanan was a veteran politician and diplomat who, happily, had been out of the country during the Kansas-Nebraska struggle. A third candidate, ex-President Millard Fillmore, was nominated by the still-existing Southern wing of the Know-Nothing Party.

The election itself was not a three-cornered affair, but rather two separate contests—one between Buchanan and Frémont in the North, the other between Buchanan and Fillmore in the South. As the only really national candidate, Buchanan benefited from the fear that a clear-cut sectional victory would split the Union. In November, "Old Buck" won, carrying all the slave states but one, plus Pennsylvania, New Jersey, Indiana, Illinois, and California. In the other eleven free states, Frémont made a clean sweep—an impressive showing for a new party. The real winner in 1856 was sectionalism: with the exception of Ohio, all eleven Frémont states were farther north than any of the twenty Buchanan states. No longer was the national political system a bond of union. Another of the cords tying the country together had snapped.

Dred Scott

After 1848 the slavery question, like some evil curse, seemed to poison everything it touched. It divided churches, shattered political parties, turned Congress into a battleground, and ruined presidential careers. Only one institution—the Supreme Court—remained unstained. Pressure had been building on the Court for a definitive judgment regarding slavery in the territories. In 1857, in the case of *Dred Scott v. Sanford,* the Court's pro-Southern majority abandoned judicial impartiality in the hope of settling this nagging question once and for all. The justices assumed that respect for the Court would insure acceptance of its decision by all sides. Rarely had American public men so misgauged the popular temper: rather than settling the slavery question, the *Dred Scott* decision propelled the country forward on the road to civil war.

The case involved a Missouri slave, Dred Scott, who had sojourned with his master for several years in Illinois and in Minnesota Territory. Upon returning to Missouri, Scott sued for his freedom, contending that he was emancipated by virtue of his residence on free soil. Chief Justice Roger B. Taney, speaking for a majority of the Supreme Court, rejected this claim on three grounds: (1) as a Negro he could not be a United States citizen, and therefore had no right to bring suit in the federal courts; (2) as a resident of Missouri the law of Illinois prohibiting slavery had no bearing on his status; (3) his sojourn in Minnesota Territory had not emancipated him because the provision of the Missouri Compromise prohibiting slavery north of 36°30' was unconstitutional. Congress, Taney declared, had no right to deprive citizens of their property—human or otherwise—in the territories without "due process of law."

On nearly every point the Chief Justice's opinion was either plainly wrong or open to serious dispute. To declare that Negroes in general, and hence even free blacks, were non-citizens who, as Taney said, had "no rights [that whites] were bound to respect," was to fly in the face of American history. Free blacks had always been recognized as citizens in at least some Northern states, and therefore did have the right to sue in the federal courts. In rejecting interstate comity, Taney ignored several earlier decisions in which

Missouri courts had recognized the claim to freedom of slaves who had sojourned in free territory. The supreme authority of Congress over the territories had previously been upheld no less than three times by the Taney Court itself. As for the phrase "due process of law," this term referred only to the means of enforcement, not to the substance of the law. Even the Southern states had provided for forfeiture of slaves as a consequence of disobedience to the law.

Taney's pronouncement declaring congressional exclusion of slavery in the territories unconstitutional provoked a storm of criticism in the North. Republicans were especially distressed, since it in effect nullified the main plank of their platform. They dismissed the decision as part of the "slavepower conspiracy." According to Horace Greeley's *New York Tribune,* it was entitled "to just so much moral weight as would be the judgment of a majority of those congregated in any Washington bar-room." The decision also embarrassed Northern Democrats such as Stephen A. Douglas. They had pinned their hopes on the doctrine of popular sovereignty. But if Congress could not exclude slavery in the territories, it followed by implication that it could not delegate the authority to do so to the people of a territory. Southerners, of course, hailed the *Dred Scott* decision as a vindication of their claim that slavery could not be excluded from the territories prior to statehood. In effect, the Supreme Court had endorsed one extremist position at the expense of the other. By striking down popular sovereignty, it had destroyed just about the last middle ground for sectional compromise.

The *Dred Scott* decision set the stage for another savage battle in Congress over Kansas. In 1857 the proslavery faction in Kansas held a convention at Lecompton, drafted a constitution recognizing slavery, and applied for statehood. Although a clear majority of the territory's residents opposed the Lecompton Constitution, President Buchanan accepted it and asked Congress to admit Kansas to statehood. The President took this fateful step out of fear that a rejection of Lecompton would antagonize Southern Democrats.

Buchanan's action outraged Stephen Douglas, who had proposed popular sovereignty as a democratic solution to the question of slavery in Kansas. Bucking the administration, he denounced the "Lecompton fraud" as a travesty on popular sovereignty and joined with Republican congressmen in opposing it. Douglas' opposition to Lecompton offended Southerners and probably ruined his presidential prospects. After a bitter struggle, Congress in 1858 sent the Lecompton Constitution back to the people of Kansas to be voted on again. This time a fair election was held, and Kansas rejected the "Lecompton fraud" by a margin of 11,300 to 1,788. Kansas remained a territory until after the Civil War had begun.

Buchanan's attempt to ram the Lecompton Constitution through Congress, coming so soon after the Kansas-Nebraska Act, proved the final blow to the Northern wing of the Democratic Party. Few Northern Democrats who supported him on Kansas survived the 1858 mid-term elections. From this point on, Southerners dominated the Democratic Party. The sectionalization of politics was complete.

The Emergence of Lincoln

While the Democrats feuded among themselves, the Republicans sought to strengthen their position. To demonstrate that they were more than a strictly nonslavery party, and to widen their appeal, they began speaking out on a broad range of issues. They sponsored legislation in Congress favoring free homesteads, government-aided internal improvements, a protective tariff, and land-grant agricultural colleges. In each case, however, Southern Democrats blocked their efforts. This opposition was consistent with Southern theories of state sovereignty, but to Northerners it smacked of simple resistance to progress. By

obstructing the dynamic economic forces then at work in the North and Midwest, the South forced these two sections to work together, thereby hastening the redirection of the Northern economy along an east-west axis.

The leading contender for the Republican nomination in 1860 was William Seward. After four years as governor of New York and twelve in the Senate, he enjoyed a national reputation. But suddenly, in 1858, a new Republican contender appeared. Throughout that summer, newspapers carried reports of a series of debates between Stephen A. Douglas and a previously little-known

Abraham Lincoln. (Library of Congress.)

Illinois lawyer and former congressman named Abraham Lincoln. The occasion was the contest for Douglas' seat in the Senate. When it was over, Lincoln had lost the election but had become a figure to be reckoned with in the Republican Party. "You are like Byron," a friend wrote, "who woke up one morning and found himself famous."

The Supreme Court's *Dred Scott* decision, which in effect denied to the people of a territory the right to exclude slavery within its boundaries, had placed Stephen Douglas in a difficult situation. The "Little Giant" was the foremost advocate of popular sovereignty. If he accepted the Court's decision, he would probably lose the election in Illinois, where free-soil sentiment was strong. But if he reaffirmed the right of settlers to decide the slavery question for themselves, he would lose the support of Southerners, which he desperately needed if he hoped to win the Democratic presidential nomination in 1860. According to legend, Lincoln took advantage of Douglas' predicament to further his own political ends. At Freeport he asked Douglas whether, in light of Taney's opinion, the people could still exclude slavery from a territory. Douglas replied yes; they could still exclude slavery merely by withholding the police regulations and local laws that slavery needed in order to exist. The Freeport formula, summed up in the phrase "unfriendly legislation," supposedly assured Douglas' reelection to the Senate, but cost him the support of Southerners in 1860. Lincoln, so the legend goes, had thus with superhuman foresight sacrificed the short-run of a Senate seat in the interests of winning the big prize in 1860.

This story, like so many pieces of Lincoln lore, is much more fiction than fact. Douglas had announced his doctrine of "unfriendly legislation" months before the Freeport debate. By the time of his confrontation with Lincoln, popular sovereignty was no longer a major issue. The real issue between the two men—and the one Lincoln strove constantly to develop—was the ultimate one of the morality of slavery. Here Lincoln and Douglas differed fundamentally.

Basically, Stephen Douglas did not regard slavery as a moral issue; he did not see it as a ques-tion of right or wrong. His attitude followed naturally from his conviction of the innate inferiority of blacks, which in his view would forever keep them from achieving equality with whites, whatever their status. Whether they were subordinated as slaves, therefore, or merely as second-class citizens, was not a matter of burning concern for him, and it certainly was not an issue worth breaking up the country. Personally, Douglas disliked slavery; but what to do about it, he felt, should remain a purely local decision. Southerners had chosen to keep it, Northerners had decided to get rid of it. In the territories Douglas would let the local residents decide by popular sovereignty. He would never try to impose an overall national policy on the slavery question.

For Lincoln, on the other hand, slavery was a profound moral wrong. This conviction stemmed from his belief in the common humanity of whites and blacks. Although political considerations and respect for constitutional guarantees to slaveholders often impelled Lincoln to compromise his egalitarian views in public, he never forgot the fine line separating white freedom from black slavery. It was because of this underlying concern for black humanity that Lincoln could never say—as Douglas could and did—that he did not care whether slavery was "voted up or voted down."

Lincoln differed from Douglas on another point: he insisted that slavery *was* a national problem, and so did require a national policy. Lincoln would not interfere with slavery where it existed; but as a moral wrong, it must not be allowed to expand. According to Lincoln, the Founding Fathers, recognizing the wrong, had placed restrictions on slavery designed to produce its eventual extinction. But Douglas and the Democrats, by refusing to recognize the moral wrong, had provided constitutional sanctions for slavery and made possible its expansion.

In 1858, Douglas narrowly won reelection to the Senate. But it was Lincoln who had sensed, and who shared, the growing moral and emotional concern over the slavery issue in the North. This would prove crucial in the election of 1860.

The Election of 1860

The repeated sectional crises during the 1850's had further eroded the position of those advocating compromise on the question of slavery in the territories. Signs of polarization on the issue became increasingly apparent as the decade drew to a close. In 1859, for example, Senator Jefferson

Davis of Mississippi introduced resolutions in Congress designed to impose upon the Democratic Party the extreme Southern position on slavery in the territories. These upheld the constitutional right of slaveholders to go into territories, and called for the creation of a federal slave code for these areas. Senate Democrats finally adopted the Davis resolutions, over the vigorous objections of Stephen Douglas. At about the same time a movement was launched in the South to revive the African slave trade. This proposal had no chance of success, even among Southerners; its main purpose, successfully achieved, was to irritate Northern sensibilities.

Southerners had no monopoly on militant positions, however. During the same period several Northern state legislatures showed their disapproval of the Fugitive Slave Act of 1850 by passing new "personal liberty" laws. Usually these prohibited slave officers from aiding federal officials in their efforts to reclaim fugitives. But in 1854 the Wisconsin supreme court carried defiance of the federal government a step further by declaring the Act of 1850 unconstitutional. Eventually the United States Supreme Court overturned this judgment, whereupon the Wisconsin legislature, taking a line from the Kentucky Resolves of 1798, declared this move to be "an act of undelegated power, void, and of no force." Both sides, it seems could play fast and loose with the Constitution when it suited their purpose. In this tense atmosphere only a spark was needed to touch off the fires of civil war. John Brown's raid at Harpers Ferry, Virginia, provided that spark.

Four months after John Brown's execution, the Democrats convened their national convention at Charleston, South Carolina. The choice of convention site was unforunate; Charleston was the hotbed of Southern radicalism. For the Democrats, 1860 was the climax of the bitter intraparty struggle between the Northerners whose spokesman was Stephen Douglas, and the dominant Southern faction. Ever since the split over Lecompton, both sides had been spoiling for a showdown over the question of slavery in the territories. Most Southern delegates came to Charleston pledged to the adoption of the Davis Resolutions. When the convention rejected their inclusion on the platform, delegates from eight Southern states walked out. The convention then adjourned for several weeks, reassembling at Baltimore on June 18, where the fight immediately resumed. This time delegates from eleven Southern states (all the future states of the Confederacy) walked out. The remaining delegates nominated Douglas for President on a platform endorsing popular sovereignty. The bolters met in another hall and nominated John Breckinridge of Kentucky for President. Their platform upheld the Davis Resolutions. The split between the Democrats was complete.

A number of factors entered into this fatal action by the Southern Democrats, which virtually assured a Republican victory in November. A few hotheads sought deliberately to split the party, precisely in order to produce the Republican victory that would, they anticipated, precipitate secession. Some delegates hoped merely to force the election into the House of Representatives. Simple emotion also played a part, to be sure: the Democrats met amidst extreme excitement, and many delegates were simply swept away by the violent speeches of "fire-eaters" like William Yancey of Alabama. They bolted without fully considering the consequences. Right up to November, many of the bolters assumed that somehow the intra-party split would be patched up.

Between the two Democratic conventions another party had met at Baltimore. This was the Constitutional Union Party, composed mainly of old Whigs from both sections and of Southern Know-Nothings. These elderly conservatives had only two things in common: a dislike for both major parties, and a general concern for the safety of the Union. For President, they nominated John Bell of Tennessee, a lifelong Whig and a large slaveholder, although not an extreme advocate of Southern rights. As their platform, the Constitutional Unionists settled for a vague pledge to uphold the Constitution and the Union.

The Republican convention convened at Chicago on May 16. The Republican strategy in 1860 was simple: to win the White House the party had only to win the same states Frémont had carried in 1856, plus just thirty-four additional electoral votes. This meant carrying Pennsylvania (27 votes) and either Illinois (11), Indiana (13), or New Jersey (7). Significantly, these were all "border" states, adjoining the South, and so their populations were overall more moderate on slavery than the Republican strongholds in the "upper" North. In addition, each of these four states had special interests of one kind or another, such as the tariff or internal improvements.

It was this consideration that largely dictated the working of the Republican platform: it treated the slavery question cautiously. The delegates reaffirmed Republican opposition to slavery expansion, but promised to leave slavery alone where it existed. Most of the platform was devoted to recognizing the special interests of the "border" states. It pledged support for a protective tariff, a Pacific railroad, and a homestead law.

This same criterion governed the choice of a candidate. The front-runner, William Seward, was considered too extreme on the slavery question, and the party's congressional and local candidates in the border states did not want to run with him. After reviewing the other contenders, the party pros settled on Abraham Lincoln as the man most "available": he resided in the important state of Illinois, was a moderate on slavery, had never been identified with nativism, and had made fewer enemies than his rivals. Lincoln also benefited from the shrewd tactics of his managers, who packed the galleries at the convention hall by distributing counterfeit tickets, and stationed men around the floor to begin noisy demonstrations on a prearranged signal.

In 1860 the national political system effectively ceased to operate. There were two campaigns that year: one in the North between Lincoln and Douglas (Bell and Breckinridge were also on the ballot, but neither had much support); the other in the South between Bell and Breckinridge (Douglas was also on the ballot in the slave states). In time-honored tradition, Lincoln, Bell, and Breckinridge stayed close to home, letting their respective supporters do the campaigning. On the real gut issue of the campaign—the possible dissolution of the Union—Lincoln and Breckinridge remained silent. Stephen Douglas was the real hero of 1860. He campaigned hard and actively throughout the country—at some risk to his personal safety in the South—in an attempt to break down the barriers between the two sections.

Despite Lincoln's victory in November, the forces of moderation might have been strong enough to gain the upper hand. Conservatives within the Republican Party hoped to rally support in the upper South around a common platform of "popular sovereignty" in the territories instead of the more radical position of "no more slave states." But a single event stuck in the craw of Southerners, the act of a madman—or a saint—John Brown's nightmare attack at Harpers Ferry.

Suggested Readings

The politics of the 1850's is increasingly well-covered, notably in Michael F. Holt, *The Political Crisis of the 1850's* (1976); David M. Potter, *The Impending Crisis: 1848-1861* (1976); Gerald W. Wolf, *The Kansas-Nebraska Bill: Party, Section, and the Coming of the Civil War* (1977); Don E. Fehrenbacher, *The Dred Scott Case* (1978); and Eric Foner, *Free Soil, Free Labor, Free Men: The Ideology of the Republican Party Before the Civil War* (1970). Holt argues that voters could not discern substantial differences between the old parties in the fifties (the "second American party system" of the Whigs and Democrats), and that as a result there was a crisis in confidence in political institutions. Other important recent studies include George B. Forgie, *Patricide in the House Divided: A Psychological Interpretation of Lincoln and His Age* (1979), Drew Gilpin Faust, *A Sacred Circle: The Dilemma of the Intellectual in the Old South, 1840-1860* (1978); and George M. Fredrickson, *The Black Image in the White Mind: The Debate on Afro-American Character and Destiny, 1817-1914* (1971). Stephen B. Oates's biography of John Brown is entitled *To Purge This Land With Blood* (1970).

Chapter XIV
Civil War

I Forrest McDonald: An Episode in Nationalism

Most of what has been written about the Civil War—and the volume is enormous—has been devoted to two aspects of the subject which, on the broad canvas of history, are of relatively small consequence. The largest part of the literature has been concerned with the fighting itself. That is understandable, for in addition to being the first "modern" war, fought with mechanized transportation and rifled weaponry, the Civil War produced a thrilling array of battles which, taken together, constituted a veritable textbook in the classical principles of warfare. And yet, when the shooting was done, the brilliance and the blunders of commanders on both sides had contributed little more that was new to the art of war than had the heroism and cowardice of the common soldiers on both sides.

The second largest amount of writing on the subject has been concerned with trying to account for the "causes" of the war. Many explanations have been offered and plausibly defended: it was the fault of an aggressive Southern slaveocracy; it was the handiwork of Yankees who sought to pervert the Constitution in their own greedy interest; it was an inevitable conflict between different civilizations and therefore nobody's fault; it was a needless war that was precipitated by a blundering generation of inept politicians; slavery caused the war, technology caused the war, sectionalism caused the war, capitalism caused the war. And yet, when all this verbal warfare is done (if it is ever done), the fact will remain that there is really nothing to explain. Warfare is a normal, not an abnormal, condition among members of the human species; it is the intervals of peace and harmony that want explanation. Besides, every western nation state had at least one internal war, and most had several, before its diverse peoples could be brought under the sway of a single government. That is part of the price of nationhood, and there is no reason to suppose that the United States should have been exempted from paying a toll that all others were required to pay.

It is therefore more meaningful to disregard such tangential matters and to view the Civil War in terms of its consequences. The consequences, in turn, can best be viewed in the perspective of an ongoing process, of which the events between Fort Sumter and Appomattox were partly outcome and partly beginning, partly arrester and partly accelerator.

Three fundamental sets of differences—cultural, social, and eco-political—underlay the sectional confrontation. Culturally, Yankees and Southerners remained worlds apart, as they had been since the arrival of the first British colonists in North America. Yankees were dedicated to work and achievement; Southerners preferred to have others do their work for them, or else to let it go undone. Yankees were realistic, Southerners romantic. Yankees were cerebral: they calculated, bargained, negotiated, put success ahead of scruple. Southerners were visceral: they dreamed, bragged, fought, put honor ahead of money. Yankees were egalitarian in regard to their own kind, contemptuous of others; Southerners were deferential toward one another as well as toward outsiders. Yankee life was oriented toward the community and the marketplace, Southern toward the family and the farm. Perhaps most importantly, eternal salvation was, to the Yankee, a community matter, whereas to the Southerner it was intensely personal.

On another scale, what was at issue was whether social relations in the United States should be fixed or free. The South was defending a way of life in which relations among people were determined by birth, by law, by custom, and by a stable social structure. The North was defending the idea that a man's status and wealth, his place and his privileges, should be determined by what he did on this earth, and not by what his ancestors had done before him. The Southern way was as old as man, and was in fact all that man had ever known. The Northern was a radical experiment, not yet a century old, but one that had already wrought astonishing changes. The Southern cause was supported by the record of history, the Northern by the promise of the future.

In the dimension of the political economy, the issues were rather more complex. As a constitutional matter, to be sure, the question was clear: it was whether the Constitution had established a political union of the American people and a national government superior to the state governments, as the North maintained, or a compact between states which retained their ultimate sovereignty, as the South insisted. But people on each side had embraced each position more than once in the past, depending upon which controlled the national government at a given moment, and people on each side had more than once flirted with both nullification and secession. What was genuinely at stake, therefore, was not the nature of the federal Union but the uses to which the powers of the federal government were to be put.

And on that fundamental question the positions of the two sections had undergone a curious repolarization during the three decades since Andrew Jackson had become President. The South had long adhered to the agrarian tradition of Bolingbroke and Jefferson. The North had forsaken that tradition to embrace the innovative financial order created by Alexander Hamilton after the manner of Sir Robert Walpole. The original purpose of the architects of the financial revolution had been to tear down institutional, legal, and local barriers to the development of a free market economy. Increasingly, however, after the mid-1830s, political representatives of the two American sections sought to use the power of government in ways quite at odds with the traditions they cherished. The South advocated a system of free trade between nations and a policy of laissez-faire at home; and in fact, through its dominance of the federal government, or more properly through its dominance of the Democratic Party, it largely succeeded in creating such a system and establishing such a policy during the 1840s and 1850s. Meanwhile, ever-larger portions of the North, and ultimately almost all of it, advocated high tariffs and active governmental interference in behalf of the promotion of economic development; and, though the North lacked the political clout until 1858 to bring such a program to pass on the federal level, it increasingly employed the power of state governments toward that end through the instrumentality of the corporation and other devices. The surge of the Republican Party to power in the House elections of 1858 and its victory in both the congressional and the presidential elections of 1860 portended the total triumph of the new Northern system of political economy. That prospect, more than the moral and emotional issue of slavery, may have been what triggered the Southern movement to secession.

Two other sets of developments, one preceding and perhaps helping to precipitate the conflict, the other taking place during the war, strongly reinforced the North's commitment to its form of political economy. The prewar development was a great burst of technological innovation: the number of patents granted by the United States government, which did not reach 1000 until 1844, reached almost 8000 by 1860. Among the more significant inventions were the telegraph, pulp paper, the passenger elevator, precision instruments, machinery for making shoes and textiles, new processes for manufacturing iron and steel, and a variety of farm implements including the steel plow and horse-drawn mowers, planters, and reapers.

Most importantly, there were improvements and new adaptations of the stream engine—in manufacturing, in steamboats, and above all in the railroad. Together, these inventions revolutionized transportation, communication, and the production of material goods. Transportation became faster than anyone had dreamed possible; communication became instantaneous; and one American, in 1860, was able to do more work than five had been able to do a century earlier.

This technological revolution—the first phase of a grander one soon to come—helped bring the Civil War about, for it went a long way toward homogenizing the previously somewhat diverse northern United States. Moreover, because the technological changes were of little influence in the South, they separated the sections even further. Nor was that all: the North's resulting technological and material superiority contributed greatly (though not, as some would argue, decisively) to the Union's ultimate victory on the field of battle.

Possibly as important, in the long range, were policies adopted by the federal government during the war. These measures, taken partly in response to Republicans' commitment to an activist system of political economy and partly as a means of conducting the war, laid out the terms under which the new technology would be exploited. There was the principle of indirect subsidy in the form of protective tariffs: the average level of taxes on foreign products was raised from about 20 percent at the beginning of the war to nearly 50 percent by 1869. There were also direct subsidies: constitutional scruples about internal improvements at federal government expense were abandoned, and a series of acts granted scores of millions of acres of the public domain to subsidize railroad corporations in the building of new lines. For good measure, another act granted vast acreage to underwrite the establishment of "land-grant colleges," which were to provide agricultural and mechanical training and provide extension services as well. There were the beginnings of a permanent federal bureaucracy: the number of nonpostal federal employees trebled during the war, and would treble again during the next decade. Finally, there was a new monetary system: the national banking acts of 1862 and 1864 provided the means for transforming a huge federal debt, incurred to help pay for the war, into a form of money. Monetization of the public debt had been done before, after the Revolution and the War of 1812, but this time there were fundamental differences. Earlier, the Bank of the United States had been the agency of monetization, and state banks had existed and grown side by side with the National Bank. This time, the instrumentality was private banking corporations, chartered by the national government, and state banks were virtually driven out of existence by federal taxes.

And so the Civil War came and went. The Union was saved, the slaves were freed, democracy reigned triumphant. A far more powerful federal government, dedicated to the active promotion of business, industry, and overall economic growth, had emerged. The United States was on its way toward becoming the freest, richest, and most powerful nation in the history of the world.

The blessings, however, were not unmixed. Though slavery was abolished, the defeat and devastation of the South left a third of the nation's people outside the free and prosperous mainstream of American life, and it remained problematical whether Southerners, white or black, would be able to rejoin the mainstream. The emergence of a new national political economy would produce enormous material benefits, but it remained to be seen whether federal activism, once started, could be stopped short of a return to mercantilism or even to serfdom. Democracy had triumphed, but the American Republic had been founded on the principle that no government, and especially a democratic one, was to be trusted. It remained to be seen whether the Founding Fathers had been wise or foolish—whether democracy would lead, as it always had before, to tyranny.

And there was one other thing. The Yankeeization of America nationalized the New England compulsion to purify all outsiders. In less than a generation, New England ministers would be calling upon the nation "to impress its institutions upon mankind," to "spread itself over the earth." For all the goodness and might of the United States, that was more than a trifle presumptuous. In the fullness of time, it might prove to be suicidal.

II   Eugene D. Genovese: Slavery and a Class System

Like original sin, war may be the normal condition of humanity. At least, until we have a genuine world peace the hypothesis cannot safely be ignored. But unlike original sin war takes place for discrete reasons, aims at discrete ends, and has discrete consequences, which cannot properly be evaluated in isolation from the circumstances that brought on the Civil War. There is nothing tangential about the problem of the "causes" of the war, for its origins have discernible relationships to its outcome. If the one sheds no light on the other, then all historians, regardless of ideology or philosophy, are wasting their time and ought to go into some other business. The war of 1861-65 was not inevitable—no historical event is—but the antagonism between North and South was intrinsic, not tangential, to our national development. Accordingly, war became increasingly likely as slave labor provided the basis of southern society and free labor of northern.

Northerners and southerners had much in common—the English language; Protestant forms of Christianity; a common Constitution that established a republican government and guaranteed an unprecedented range of individual and states' rights; a common history of struggle to conquer a continent and break the power of the mother country; and much more in attitude, experience, sentiment, culture. No wonder, then, that so many contemporaries, northern and southern, and so many historians ever since, have seen the war as a ghastly misunderstanding or a needless fratricidal bloodbath. Were the combatants not one people? Did they not constitute one nationality? Did they not share common ideals and a common vision?

Yes and no. Yes, they shared enough to impart to the war a tragic dimension; no, in essential respects they were not one people, but two. The magnitude of their differences will be forever debated, and perhaps they did share much more than they did not. But a Korean or an Indonesian or a Tanzanian might readily argue that the French and Germans, not to mention the Russians and Poles, have immeasurably more common features than different ones—race, Christianity, the culture of the Enlightenment, much more—yet they have repeatedly fought each other on a grand scale.

The question, then, concerns not the extent of the similarities but the depth of the differences. And, increasingly, the differences between northerners and southerners pit one vision of civilization and social order against another; increasingly, there emerged not only deep regional economic, political, and social differences, but differences over the very definition of morals and human values. The root of the differences was slavery, which permeated southern life and shaped southern sensibilities and southern destiny.

To say "slavery" is not enough. For it suggests a system, and all systems become mere abstractions when not analyzed with specific reference to the flesh-and-blood human beings who participate in them. Slavery as a system pit two social classes against each other. Masters confronted slaves. That they were of separate races had profound consequences for the South and for the nation as a whole. The racism inherent in the enslavement of one race to another poisoned American life from its inception and poisons it still. But it is doubtful that the slaveholders as ruling class in pursuit of fundamental economic and political objectives would have acted much differently if their slaves had been white.

It is true that the majority of whites owned no slaves; the South was nonetheless a slave society. A much smaller percentage of Americans today own capital; yet, few if any would argue that American society is therefore not capitalist. On the contrary, capitalism, like slavery and all other class-dominated systems, presupposes that the few live off the many—that the ruling class is a minority that exploits the labor of much larger numbers. The slaveholders were the leading class—the wealthy and the powerful—in society, and they were so precisely because of their ownership of slaves, that is, their ownership of the region's primary capital assets and, simultaneously, of its labor force.

Although the slaveholders faced constant and increasing challenge from the yeomanry and the middle classes, they nonetheless established their rule in southern society. In other words, they managed to get the slavery question effectively out of southern politics during the last decades before secession, after having steadily narrowed its scope in the decades previous. Thus, they reduced the direct internal threat to their property system to a minimum, although they could not eliminate the indirect threats mounted by nonslaveholders over issues that threatened to undermine their power in the long run. Much more research into the yeomen and the middle classes needs to be done, but it is becoming clear that the slaveholders' push for secession was at least partially determined by their growing fear of an anti-planter political challenge with dangerous antislavery potential. For our immediate purposes, however, the nonslaveholders were loyal enough to the slaveholders' regime: They raised no powerful antislavery movement before the war and, with significant exceptions, fought bravely for the Confederacy when the war came.

The nonslaveholders supported—or at least did not actively oppose—the slaveholders' regime for a variety of reasons besides Negrophobia, the role of which was certainly important and persistent but has been much exaggerated. The yeomen in the plantation areas were tied to the slaveholders by blood, as kinship lines crossed class lines freely in a region so recently a frontier. They suffered no direct exploitation by the slaveholders, and only the most knowledgable could glimpse the ways in which the slave system as a whole oppressed them. Their small surpluses of foodstuffs or cotton had to be sold to, or marketed through, the wealthy planters, who were ideally placed to offer friendship and needed services. In short, these and other relationships formed a complex that maximized the ties between planters and yeomen and minimized the antagonisms.

The nonslaveholders of the upcountry, however, had little direct contact with the planters, chafed under their pretensions, and fought them over a wide variety of state issues: transportation, education, banking practices. Above all, they controlled their own communities and shaped their own lives. Paradoxically, the slaveholders could give them the thing they wanted—the right to be left alone or at least to run their local affairs. Hence, for all the animosity of the upcountry yeomen toward the slaveholders, no direct challenge to slavery itself was likely. Only when war came and the Confederates tried to levy taxes, requisition supplies, and draft young men into the army did the active opposition crystallize. Several such communities defected to the Union side or declared neutrality, and many others harbored deserters and anti-Confederate guerrillas.

The achilles heel of the Confederacy, like that of the slave states before the war, was, however, the slave population itself. As a result of the work of many historians during the last decade or two, we now know a great deal about how the slaves actually lived, about how they adjusted to and resisted their enslavement, and about the culture they forged. Among the oppressed peoples of modern times none has overmatched the courage and resourcefulness of the blacks who struggled for survival in the throes of slavery. Despite laws that denied them the right to marry and have legitimate families, despite every attempt to foist upon them a religion of submission to the will of their masters, despite the whip and separation from loved ones, despite countless abuses and indignities, they created a powerful religious and family life of their own, which sustained their sense of humanity, justice, and deliverance—which kept alive their determination to be free. Without this heroic cultural struggle they could have had no significant political history.

A political history they did have—and necessarily so. For the South was not just another society that tolerated slavery on its periphery; it was a slave society. Its value system, its notion of moral as well as social order, its fundamental economic and political interests, and the sensibility of its ruling class all rested on slavery—more precisely, on the deadly consequences of the master-slave relationship. The slaveholders were very much a breed apart, with a host of contradictory qualities rooted in their special condition as outright owners of human flesh. They had their virtues, which even many of their harshest critics admired: graciousness, generosity, tolerance of human foibles, physical courage, a strong sense of personal and family honor, and more. And they had their vices, which their warmest admirers conceded: hot tempers, a frightening penchant for violence, an inability to brook contradiction on any matter that touched their honor, and a fearful habit of defining their honor to include everything and anything. These qualities, in their peculiar combination, were rooted in slavery itself—in the slaveholders' theoretically absolute mastery of other human beings. And they hardly prepared the slaveholders to understand, much less imitate, the calculating bourgeois who were coming to dominate northern society. This growing psychological gap might not have mattered much if the interests of northerners and southerners had not been diverging—if their economic and political ambitions were not getting in each other's way. Instead, those interests were clashing, and the psychological gap guaranteed that the clash would not easily be resolved short of bloodshed.

And the North? The course of northern development was by no means simply upward and onward, though it was breathtaking. Several postwar decades would be needed to position the United States for its bid for world power, but the foundations had been laid by 1860: heavy industry and railroads, unprecedented achievements in agriculture, a burgeoning world commerce, an increasingly sophisticated financial system—in short, the base and infrastructure of a modern industrial nation.

With it came problems familiar to the process of capitalist industrialization. Labor was abused and exploited, although a labor shortage kept the rate of exploitation below that of most other countries. The need to attract immigrants brought peoples with different religions, languages, habits, and political attitudes to a basically Anglo-Saxon country ill-prepared to accept them. To the resultant social problems were added those of the new and raw cities: slums, grossly inadequate health facilities, municipal corruption, and the excesses of political machines.

Where there is imperfection there will be reformers, whose benevolent attention is not always welcomed by those to be reformed. The antebellum era provided no exception: temperance, women's rights, public education, evangelical Christianity, suppression of prostitution, gambling, crime, corruption, sin. These and other moral causes and crusades often became excrutiatingly self-righteous, and they have remained easy to make fun of. At their worst they looked like candidates for H. L. Mencken's delightful definition of puritanism as "the haunting fear that someone, somewhere, may be happy."

Yet, at their best—and they were often at their best—they stood for a decent concern with human suffering and injustice, and they asserted a common duty to create a more humane and responsible society. None did so better than the abolitionist movement. As a movement, abolitionism was complex, internally rent, often confused and pompous; it was also courageous, indeed heroic, in its single-minded commitment to human freedom. It became the conscience of a nation that, for all its remarkable virtues, badly needed one, for it tolerated the greatest crime against humanity to defile the nineteenth century. And it is worth recalling that the Abolitionist movement, among its accomplishments, opened the way for the direct participation of blacks and women in northern political life.

The abolitionists waged a long, hard struggle to mobilize the country against slavery and the power of the slaveholders. They were ignored, ridiculed, and slandered. When stronger measures were needed, they were run out of town, had their meetings broken up and their printing presses smashed by well dressed mobs of respectable citizens, and were murdered by those who, ironically, viewed them as a threat to law and order. They persisted, fought back, made nuisances of themselves, scandalized respectable opinion by preferring truth and justice to good manners; and they slowly insinuated themselves into the national consciousness by emphasizing not only the moral degeneracy of slaveholding but of its threat to the civil liberties and economic opportunities of white people. Northerners proved willing enough to live with the moral degeneracy of slaveholding, especially since they were hardly partial to blacks themselves. They did not prove willing to tolerate assaults against their own civil liberties and economic opportunities.

By the 1850s the abolitionists were scoring heavily, albeit indirectly and in strange forms that sometimes made them furious. The abolitionists' ultimate victory had been forecast in the struggles over the "gag rule" and the censoring of the mails during the Jackson years, and more tellingly in the fierce resistance to the Fugitive Slave Law during the 1850s. The abolitionists could have shouted forever that slavery meant reactionary and arrogant onslaughts against the rights of whites as well as blacks. Northern opinion remained skeptical at best. It took the slaveholders themselves to demonstrate the truth of the proposition.

But why did the slaveholders do it? Why did the southern leaders, who ranked as perhaps the most politically astute in the country, jeopardize their northern support by demanding measures that threatened to drive moderates into the hands of their enemies? On these and other issues the slaves scored their revenge. Had there been no slave revolts, plots, and periodic outbursts of more limited slave violence, the slaveholders would not have had to live in constant fear of their lives. But there were and they did. The number and extent of actual revolts remained small, but even a few were enough to establish the deadly possibilities. Hence, the slaveholders required maximum vigilance: The slaves must be kept illiterate, lest they gain access to dangerous materials; and those who would disseminate dangerous materials must be suppressed, no matter what part of the United States they lived in.

Similarly, the crude and oppressive provisions of the Fugitive State Law, so offensive even to many conservative northerners, would not have been necessary if runaway slaves had not created a serious problem. And more, the issue became a point of honor. The only excuse the northerners had for refusing to return runaways was the immorality of slavery itself. But that judgment represented an assault on the morality of the white South; it could not be tolerated. Enforcement of the law, with its contempt for traditional American rules of justice, became everyone's test of everyone else's sincerity and peaceful intentions.

In the end, it was not abolitionism, pure and morally defined, that swept the North; it was "free soil, free labor, and free men." But it is hard to see how the new antislavery ideology could have taken root without decades of prior abolitionist agitation and political education. Slavery came increasingly to be identified with economic retardation, political reaction, and social disorder. The bourgeois ideology of the marketplace increasingly spread a vision of boundless expansion—of enterprise and riches, of liberty and democracy, of free land and booming manufactures, of a continent to be conquered and a wider world beyond. Few northerners outside the abolitionist ranks wanted to interfere with slavery in the South, but countless others could not tolerate the expansion of slavery into the West, where it could monopolize land that ought to go to free working farmers and bolster the political power of the country's strongest opponents of bourgeois values and practical measures.

But to be closed out of the West, to be penned in, meant more to Northerners than merely to lose important economic advantage and political power; it meant to accept a degraded status as part of a social system marked as immoral and unjust and doomed to disappear. The slaveholders, however, had long since made their peace with slavery. Indeed, for them it had become a "positive good"—the foundation of a proper social order. Better secession and if necessary war than surrender of their way of life.

Two alternative social systems—systems of class relations—had coexisted in the Union. They could coexist no longer, and neither side was prepared to give way gracefully. And the war came.

John Brown's "fort," once on grassy embankment (right) in Harpers Ferry. W. Va., has since been moved.

Chapter XV
Civil War and Reconstruction

John Brown's Raid

In the summer of 1859, the nation apparently was still capable of veering off from the collision course on which both sections seemed to be proceeding. Then John Brown, who had upset many by his highhanded activities in Kansas, suddenly shocked millions with a bold desperate stroke in western Virginia.

Brown, whom William Lloyd Garrison described as a "tall, spare, farmer-like man, with head disproportionately small, and that inflexible mouth," had gone to Harpers Ferry, about sixty miles northwest of Washington, D.C., at the confluence of the Potomac and Shenandoah rivers, in July 1859. Renting a farm near the town, he gathered an "army" of twenty-one men—sixteen white and five black, and using funds supplied by several abolitionists, accumulated 198 rifles, a load of pistols which he could not use because he had purchased the wrong firing caps for them, and 950 pikes with which to arm slaves. His plan—to seize the United States Arsenal there and to arm the slaves—was known to at least eighty people. One had actually written to the Secretary of War who had ignored the letter. On the evening of October 16, his little band set out to capture the town, the federal properties, and the arms. No slaves voluntarily joined them, and the townspeople, militia from the county, and then United States Marines led by Robert E. Lee, besieged them. Within thirty-six hours, Brown and his army were captured. Ten of them died, including two of Brown's own sons. That was all there was to the raid, a total failure and, had people accepted it as such, a demonstration of the impossiblity of starting a slave insurrection.

That was all there was to the raid, but not all there was to John Brown. "He is the gamest man I ever saw," admitted the governor of Virginia who came to question the wounded captive. Brown replied to every questioner at his interrogation and at his trial with crisp assurance borne of clarity of purpose. Then, after his conviction, his many letters breathed saintly dedication to the biblical injunction to remember them that are in bonds as bound with them. Brown never wavered, showed no fear, no vindictiveness toward his captors, no selfish purposes at all. He awed his enemies and captured the respect of much of the North for a deed that few would actually have condoned. He transparently but consistently lied about his purposes in making the raid, just as he was evasive to the point of dishonesty about his role in the Pottawatomie Massacre in 1856. (In retaliation against a proslavery group, Brown and a small band had murdered five proslavery settlers near Pottawatomie Creek, Kansas.) The man whose tiny army had accumulated rifles and pikes to distribute to slaves nonetheless asserted: "I never did intend murder, or treason, or the destruction of property, or to excite slaves to rebellion, or to make insurrection." "It was all so thin," Robert Penn Warren observed of Brown's argument before the court. "that it should not have deceived a child, but it deceived a generation." This generation, trapped between its idealism about liberty and the intractibility of the slavery issue, would forgive a great deal for the certitude obtained of John Brown. Henry Ward Beecher said it in a sermon delivered during Brown's trial: "His soul was noble; his work miserable. But a cord and a gibbet would redeem all that, and round up Brown's failure with a heroic success." "Good" wrote Brown on a newspaper copy of the sermon.

John Brown's favorite saying was that "without the shedding of blood there is no remission of sin." When his eldest son was less than ten years old, his father had kept a record of John, Jr.'s sins in an account book:

John Jr.
     For disobeying mother . . . . .8 lashes
     For unfaithfulness at work . . . . .3 lashes
     For telling a lie . . . . .8 lashes

Eventually Brown declared his son "bankrupt" and collected one-third of the debt "reckoned in strokes from a nicely-prepared blue-beech switch." Then the elder Brown removed his own shirt, handed the boy the whip and ordered him to "lay it on." "I dared not refuse to obey." John, Jr., remembered, "but at first I did not strike hard. 'Harder!' he said' 'harder, harder!' until he *received the balance of the account*." The son also remembered the "drops of blood showing on his back."

It was only years later that John, Jr., began to think that he understood this bizarre event. It was, he decided, a "practical illustration" of the Doctrine of Atonement. "I was then too obtuse to perceive how Justice could be satisfied by inflicting penalty upon the back of the innocent instead of the guilty." In 1856 on Pottawatomie Creek in Kansas, and in 1859 at Harpers Ferry, John Brown offered an entire nation a dramatic "practical illustration" of the Doctrine of Atonement which he had derived from his family heritage and from "the ponderous volumes of Jonathan Edwards' sermons which father owned." John Brown, a lifelong failure, a bankrupt, sometimes a thief, eccentric, fanatic, liar, perhaps insane, would take upon his own back the nation's giant sin, would remove the debt that a society gone morally and politically bankrupt before the debt of slavery could not discharge.

Brown's acts struck terror in the South, aroused many fears and uncertainties in the North, yet played upon the deepest chords of the Puritan conscience. Brown's Christlike behavior facing execution, which impressed even his captors, caught the imagination of millions who accepted the doctrine of atonement, voiced most eloquently in Lincoln's Second Inaugural Address.

Nonetheless, there is something peculiar, bizarre, even blasphemous in Brown's practical theology: the Son of God, not the son of Owen Brown, atones for mankind's sins. Brown actually believed that the shedding of his own blood and the blood of other innocents (for Brown appears to have felt no guilt over either the Pottawatomie Massacre or the deaths at Harpers Ferry) could save the nation. His last words, sent out to the world as he mounted the wagon that would carry him to the gallows, burn both with prophecy and with his disappointment at the realization that he is not somehow the Christ:

I John Brown am now quite *certain* that the crimes of this *guilty, land: will* never be purged *away;* but with Blood. I had *as I now think*: *vainly* flattered myself that without *very much* bloodshed; it might be done.

Yet the link of Brown and Christ was astonishingly easy for many Northerners to make. Ralph Waldo Emerson predicted that Brown "will make the gallows as glorious as the cross." Julia Ward Howe (whose husband, Samuel Gridley Howe was one of the "Secret

Six'' supplying Brown with arms and money) wrote *The Battle Hymn of the Republic.* One stanza—the one about Christ—reads:

In the beauty of the lilies Christ was born across the sea,
With a glory in his bosom that transfigures you and me,
As he died to make men holy, let us die to make men free,
While God is marching on.

But Union troops, marching to the melody sang:

John Brown's body lies a moldering in the grave.
John Brown's body lies a moldering in the grave.
John Brown's body lies a moldering in the grave.
His truth is marching on.''

Secession

Appropriately, South Carolina led the way toward secession. As soon as Lincoln's election was certain, the South Carolina legislature called for a state convention. On December 20, 1860, the convention met at Charleston and unanimously declared "that the Union now subsisting between South Carolina and other States under the name of the United States of America is hereby dissolved." Similar actions occurred in rapid succession in Alabama, Georgia, Florida, Mississippi, and Louisiana. The smooth course of these proceedings was upset only in Texas, where crusty old Governor Sam Houston, a staunch Unionist, refused to summon a special session of the legislature. The lawmakers met anyway, and called an election of delegates and a convention without Houston's authorization.

Up to this point, the secession process had moved forward with electrifying speed. In the space of forty-two days, seven states, stretching from South Carolina to Texas, had seceded from the Union. On February 4, 1861, however, the tide turned momentarily against secession when the voters of Virginia elected a majority of convention delegates opposed to immediate secession. Subsequently voters in four other Upper South states—Tennessee, North Carolina, Arkansas, and Missouri— either voted not to hold a convention or elected a Unionist majority. The three remaining slave states—Kentucky, Maryland, and Delaware —did not even call conventions. The strong personal and economic ties between states of the Upper South and the North, as well as the smaller ratio of blacks in these states' populations, account for their decisions to delay or reject secession. For the moment, the Lower South was isolated.

Nonetheless, at Montgomery, Alabama, on February 7, 1861, delegates from the seven states proceeded to adopt a provisional constitution for the Confederate States of America. It was modeled closely on the United States Constitution; however, several changes were made to safeguard state sovereignty and slavery. The Confederate constitution reserved to the states the power of amendment and even permitted them to impeach Confederate officials under certain circumstances. It guaranteed the property rights of slaveholders both in the existing states and in any future territory the Confederacy might acquire. To lead the new government the delegates chose Jefferson Davis of Mississippi as provisional President and Alexander H. Stephens of Georgia as Vice-President.

The reasons for secession were spelled out in declarations issued by the various state conventions. South Carolina's was typical. It emphasized the compact theory of the Constitution: the United States Constitution, the declaration began, was a compact between sovereign states for the purpose of establishing "a government with defined objects and powers." Like all compacts, this one bound the contracting parties to certain mutual obligations. The failure of one of the parties to perform these obligations, in whole or in part, released the other from its bond. In these circumstances the injured party was free to resume its status as a free and sovereign state.

The South Carolina Declaration went on to list what Southerners considered to be the specific violations of the compact that had justified secession: the Northern states had refused to fulfill their constitutional obligation to return fugitive slaves. They had denounced slavery as "sinful" and tolerated abolition societies "designed to disturb the peace and steal the property of the citizens of other states." They had encouraged "servile insurrection" (a reference to John Brown). At last, the Declaration continued, a sectional party "hostile to slavery" had captured control of the federal government. This party was dedicated not merely to excluding slavery from the "common territory," but to slavery's "ultimate extinction." In their own words, then, Southerners seceded out of a conviction that their slaveholding society could no longer exist safely in the Union. There was no mention of other issues, such as states' rights or the tariff. For the majority of Southern whites, independence was the goal. "If we had a government of our own," explained the secessionist Robert Barnwell Rhett, "the post office, all the avenues of intercourse, the police and the military of the southern country would be under our exclusive control."

With the benefit of hindsight, we can now see that even in their own terms, Southerners were wrong: slavery would have remained far safer in the Union than out of it. Democrats and Southerners still had a majority in both houses of Congress. Lincoln could not have acted without their approval. There were also important constitutional guarantees protecting slavery in the states where it existed and Republicans had pledged themselves not to interfere with it there. Lincoln even expressed his willingness early in 1861 to support a constitutional amendment to that effect. If the Southern states had remained in

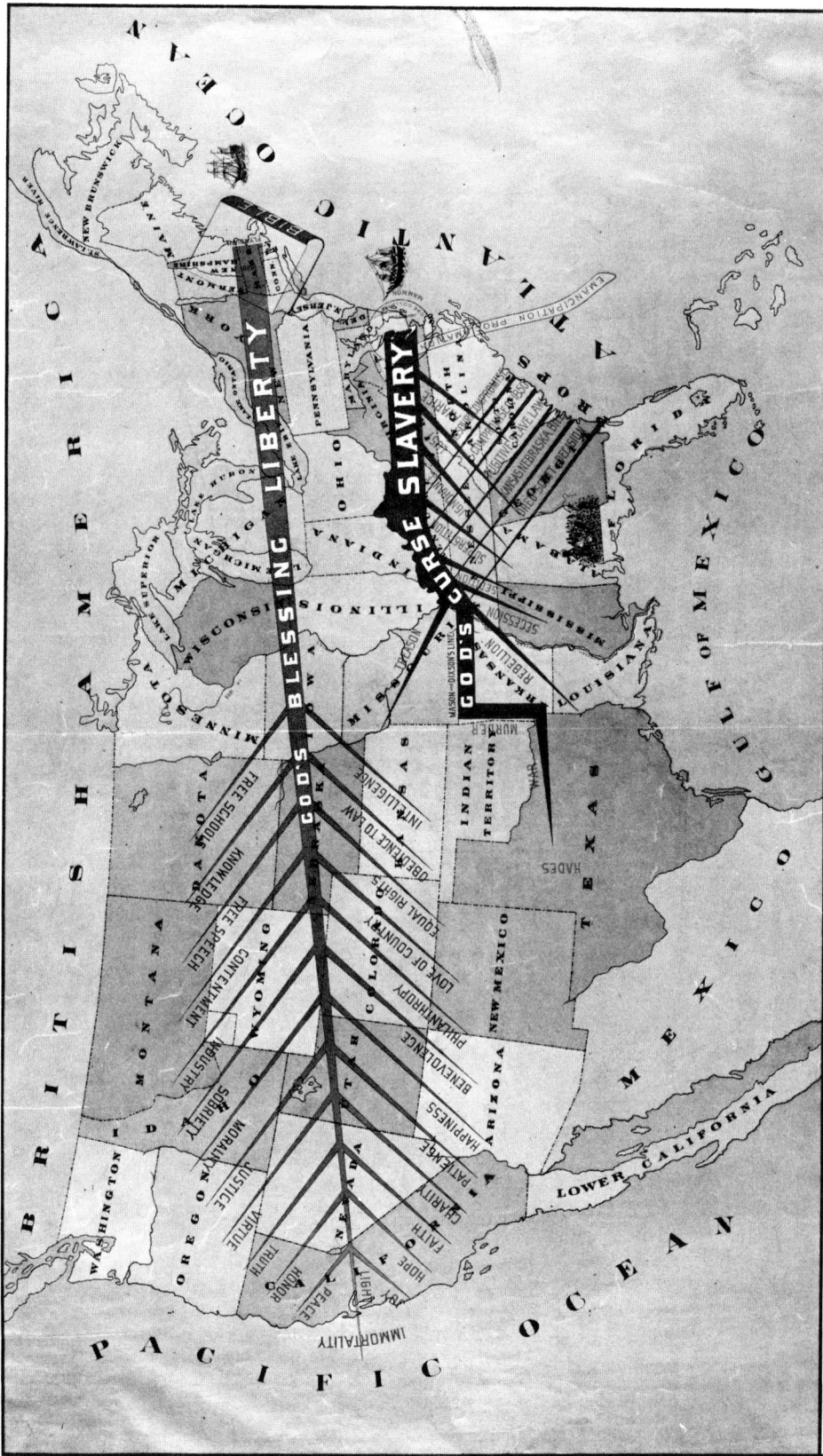

HISTORICAL GEOGRAPHY.

Entered according to act of Congress in the year 1888 by John F. Smith, in the office of the Librarian of Congress at Washington.

A Textbook Map Dated 1888

the Union, the Republicans could never have put through a constitutional amendment abolishing slavery. This could only have been done by act of war. Thus, by seceding, Southerners united a North previously divided on the question of slavery and sealed the fate of their peculiar institution.

Secession as the founders of the Confederacy viewed it was not an act of revolution but a defense of a traditional order. It was, they argued, a return to the honorable system of independent states out of which the Constitution had come, a resumption by individual states of the exercise of a sovereignty they had never surrendered to the United States. The object was to preserve a social system and to protect a form of property, the holding of slaves. Yet secessionists would not have described themselves as repudiating the modern world. Their society, so they thought, was one of freedom—for white people—and of enlightened republican government.

While Southerners of this sort would associate the case for slavery with the case for secession, claiming that both slaveholding and states' rights were old institutions strongly founded by law, the two issues were in fact quite separate. In previous years a few northern opponents of slavery had proposed that free states secede from their slaveholding sisters; and in 1860 there were sympathizers with slavery who were also supporters of the Union. Earlier in the century political and constitutional quarrels had made for debate over whether it was the Union or the states that possessed sovereignty. The argument looked back to the process of ratification, in which each state had held a convention to decide whether that state should adhere to the Constitution. Nineteenth-century champions of state sovereignty concluded from this that ratification had been by individual states, each state retaining sovereignty and the right of independence; and they believed that sovereignty belonged also to the states formed after ratification. Advocates of the authority of the federal government held that ratification had been by the American people as a whole, acting for mere convenience in separate state conventions and that the states were subordinate to the unified American people and to the Constitution. In 1860 and 1861 reasoning of that kind, in this age that took seriously such philosophical inquiries into political and constitutional questions, must have been in the minds of Unionists. Even a citizen convinced of the legal right of secession might be a Unionist out of patriotism toward the Union or a sense of its economic and strategic benefits. In appealing to secessionists to change their minds and to other Southerners to stay by the United States, Unionists could keep away from the slavery issue,

on which they could not have made converts, and instead could make use of the self-interest, the patriotism, or the constitutional arguments that might draw slaveholders to the Union.

By early winter 1861 when Lincoln was on his way to Washington, seven states of the deep South had seceded and formed themselves into the Confederate States of America, with Montgomery, Alabama, as their capital. The crisis was the greatest since the Revolution. Washington was astir with worry and excitement.

The nation's capital, tucked between the slave states of Virginia and Maryland, was a largely southern city. For decades southern politicians, or "northern men with southern principles," had dominated the political, business, and social life of the capital. The city still had hundreds of slaves in its population, although since the 1850 Compromise the slave pens and auction blocks had gone. Now, in the country's greatest crisis, the southern sympathies of Washington's citizens were visible everywhere. At the city's many bars the imbibers of "toddies" and "flips" announced that Lincoln would never be inaugurated: proud "southrons" would not allow it. At the government executive departments young clerks wore "secession cockades" much as we wear campaign buttons in presidential election years.

Unionists who found themselves in the capital during the secession winter were apprehensive. The young Henry Adams, who had come to Washington as private secretary to his father, Congressman Charles Francis Adams of Massachusetts, thought the Southerners "demented." Confident of independence, they were already cultivating the good will of their future Yankee customers. The feeling was not reciprocated. Senator Stephen Douglas, waiting for Congress to begin its session, talked darkly of the "slave power" conspiracy that had connived at defeating him for President and was now intent on breaking up the Union. Other unionists were charging that the conspirators could be found in President Buchanan's cabinet itself. Cabinet members Howell Cobb of Georgia, Jacob Thompson of Mississippi, and John B. Floyd of Virginia, they said, were providing the Confederacy with guns and ammunition from federal arsenals and threatening the weak-willed Buchanan that if he tried to move against the secessionists he would be either assassinated or impeached.

Indeed, from the unionist view it looked at first as if the seventy-year-old James Buchanan had been terrified into inaction. The Democratic President had proclaimed secession illegal and declared the Union "perpetual." But he denied that the federal government had any constitutional authority to force the return of seceded states, and he feared that any attempt at coercion would make the situation worse. The whole trouble Buchanan attributed to fanaticism on the part of abolitionists and to the menace the free-soil movement posed for the South. The President hoped for some new compromise that would still the issue of slavery as had the arrangements of 1820 and 1850.

Efforts at compromise were not wanting. The issue needing resolution was that of whether or to what extent the territories should be open to slavery. Early in 1861 the Washington Peace Convention, a gathering of statesmen under the chairmanship of former President John Tyler, looked for a solution. Congress also debated. A plan pressed by Senator John J. Crittenden of Kentucky would extend the Missouri Compromise line to the Pacific and add a constitutional amendment protecting slavery wherever it existed. But the extremists dominating politics in the cotton states would probably have turned down the plan, and the Republican party could not have abandoned its principle of "free-soil," the opposition to slavery in the territories.

While attempts at compromise were unsuccessful, neither secession nor war appeared anything like a certainty. Republican and Democratic upholders of the sovereignty of the United States perceived secession as an impulsive and irrational act that the South could decide to reverse. War, or at any rate a prolonged one, must have been almost unthinkable. While many, and perhaps almost all, Northern statesmen along with some Southerners would have agreed that secession was unconstitutional, it was not clear that the federal government had the constitutional means to prevent it by force: President Buchanan denied that the government did. Nor could supporters of the Union have any confidence that the Northern people could summon the will to march against the seceded states. For President-elect Lincoln and prospective members of his cabinet, the problem was to find a political solution to the crisis.

The Problem of the Forts

Lincoln in his inaugural address told the South that he would enforce the Fugitive Slave Law and support a constitutional amendment protecting slavery where it already existed. But he did not modify his position on free soil; and he condemned secession, pledging to "hold, occupy and possess" all Union property within the regions that had announced their secession.

By February 1861 the issue was largely symbolic, but not the less critical for that. Throughout the lower South federal forts, customs houses, and post offices had fallen into the hands of the Confederate or state authorities soon after secession. But two key posts held out, Fort Pickens at Pensacola, Florida, and Fort Sumter in Charleston harbor. For the Confederates to concede these to the United States meant accepting the intolerable presence of a "foreign" power in the new Southern nation's territory. For the Union to surrender them would be acquiescence in Southern independence. The Pickens problem was not acute, since in Florida authorities were for the moment willing to tolerate the presence of the forces of the United States. At Charleston serious trouble brewed.

As the citizens of the charming Southern port went about their business, they were aware of the drama at their doorsteps. Across the harbor they could see the stars and stripes flying defiantly over Sumter, while on confederate-held Morris Island and at the city's main fortifications uniformed men rushed here and there moving big guns, ammunition, and powder.

For weeks South Carolina officials had been negotiating with both the Washington authorities and Major Robert Anderson, the garrison commander, for evacuation of the fort. Anderson had holed up at Sumter when he concluded that his small force was inadequate to occupy all three federal strong points in the harbor, but from that grim, gray bastion he refused to depart. Soon after the new year Buchanan, his resolve stiffened by four new unionist cabinet members, dispatched the *Star of the West,* an unarmed steamer, to reinforce Anderson with men and supplies. The Charleston authorities ordered their guns to let loose at the vessel. Anderson came within an eyelash of returning the fire to protect the ship, but before he could, it turned back.

Lincoln inherited the Sumter problem from his predecessor. He sought advice from his cabinet members and other statesmen. William Seward of New York, his Secretary of State, startled him

President and Mrs. Jefferson Davis. (Library of Congress.)

CIVIL WAR AND RECONSTRUCTION

with the suggestion that the administration bring the country together by getting into a war with Europe. On April 4, 1861, the President announced the sending of a squadron for the relief of Fort Sumter.

News of Lincoln's intentions infuriated the Confederate authorities in Montgomery, who believed that the Republican President had assured them he would evacuate Sumter. Convinced that they could not avoid a clash without seeming to be weak, they reluctantly ordered that Sumter be reduced by attack before the promised reinforcement could arrive.

The hotheads at Charleston, the moral intellectual capital of "Secessia," rejoiced. Happiest of all, perhaps, was the venerable Edmund Ruffin. Now a silver-haired man of sixty-seven, Ruffin had been among the staunchest defenders of southern rights and had long advocated secession. When his own state of Virginia proved slow to take up the Northern challenge he had come to fire-eating Charleston and, despite his age, had joined the Palmetto Guard of the South Carolina infantry. When the order to attack Sumter was given early on the morning of April 12, the elderly gentleman was positioned at the great Columbiad cannon pointing at the federal fort. Later Ruffin would insist that he had fired the first shot of the war. In reality his shot was preceded by a mortar barrage. But it was to him the symbolic honor went.

The bombardment lasted for ten hours, a respectable period for the outnumbered Union force. Then Anderson, his food and gunpowder both low, sent word that he was ready to surrender. The next day the flag was lowered and the Palmetto banner of South Carolina raised.

The attack on the fort began the Civil War. In the absence of Congress, President Lincoln issued a proclamation requesting seventy-five thousand volunteers for the suppressing of "combinations too powerful to be suppressed by the ordinary course of judicial proceedings." Upon its reassembling that summer, Congress gave legality to this proclamation along with other actions that Lincoln had taken in the military emergency.

And the War Came

With the coming of war it became a matter of urgency that the President keep within the Union as many of the slave states as possible. In Delaware, Maryland, Kentucky, and Missouri the slave system was not so extensive as in the deep South and the feeling for it was less passionate. Even the states of Virginia, North Carolina, Tennessee, and Arkansas did not secede until the encounter at Sumter; after the secession of Virginia, Richmond became the capital of the Confederacy. A mob favoring the South attacked federal soldiers in Baltimore and cut the rail line between that city and Washington, and Lincoln sent troops that subdued the disorder; but Maryland stayed in the Union. In response to the President's call for volunteers Kentucky declared its neutrality. Lincoln sent rifles to Unionists in western Kentucky but otherwise used mild political persuasion toward the state that had been his birthplace as well as that of Jefferson Davis, the president of the Confederate States. Kentucky remained loyal to the old nation.

In the next four years the Confederate government would have difficulty in imposing the degree of unity it needed for prosecution of the war against the North. A few state courts aided evaders of the draft, to which the South resorted,

Civil War drum, Ninth Regiment, Vermont Volunteers, U. S. infantry, made about 1860. (*Index of American Design.*)

by issuing writs of *habeas corpus*, an order commanding officials to bring a prisoner before a court. Periodically governor Joseph Brown of Georgia recalled the militia from service outside the state. Much of the trouble of this sort was predictable for a new nation, its very legality in doubt, its citizens unused to obeying it, its institutions and lines of authority as yet unsettled and unclear. But the Confederate government was in some sense embarrassed in the very exercise of power, for its foundation was on the principle of state sovereignty, strict limitation of central government. President Davis' administration also lacked access to some definable political party that could enlist the continuing support of large numbers of political leaders throughout the South and draw the votes of a consistent portion of the electorate. The offices of attorney general, secretary of war, and secretary of state each changed hands several times. Davis had disagreements with his vice president, Alexander Stephens. Taxes and loans together did not bring in enough revenue. To support itself the government turned to "tithing in kind," collecting from farmers one-tenth of their produce in certain crops, and printed great amounts of paper money, which was not legal tender and had the effect of putting sounder kinds of money out of circulation.

More serious than the problems of governing, and contributing to them, were the weaknesses in the southern economy. Most of its railroads were short lines, the rail system consisted of eleven track gauges, and there was not enough equipment. The South in 1861 did only a fifth of the whole nation's manufacturing, and it lacked the skills and technology for quick growth. By the award of generous contracts, the Confederate and state governments gave their encouragement to industries such as textile mills and iron works, and by the end of the war Atlanta had become a considerable industrial center; in 1861 Richmond had been the only important manufacturing town. But some manufacturers had to do with makeshifts, such as lard in place of grease, and cloths soaked in linseed oil as a substitute for machine belts. The South had to import much of its arms and civilian goods, slipping a good part of them through the Union blockade.

The War Strategies

On paper the resources of the North from the beginning of the war appear to have been immensely superior to those of the South. The North had a population of 22 million, while the South consisted of 9 million. Moreover, black slaves, who furnished labor but were politically unpredictable, made up one-third of the Southern populace; and many white Southerners remained loyal to the Union. In its railroad system and its industrial plant the Confederacy was far behind the North. The South had no navy capable of challenging in any consistent way the Northern blockade of its ports. The Confederate government was new and its authority shaky. The governmental financial credit and the currency of the South were weak. On the matter of slavery the South was in moral isolation from the rest of the western world.

The South could not have won a head-on conflict with a determined North. What the Confederacy could do was to demonstrate to the federal government and the Northern people that the old Union was no longer a single, workable nation. A few decisive Southern victories might have done that; so might a successful defensive war, prohibitively expensive to the North in time, wealth, and human lives. The South could also hope for considerable sympathy on the part of governmental officials in Europe. However hostile Europeans were to slavery, there was respect for the Confederacy as a people struggling to be independent, and the self-interest of European governments could incline them to wish for the dissolution of a single, strong United States into two weaker nations.

The Civil War, like other wars, began with neither side having a clear notion of how long and costly an ordeal it would be. Deciding on a quick strike against Richmond, Lincoln sent an ill-trained army into Virginia. Following them were well-to-do Washingtonians in carriages; they expected to see some sort of entertaining clash and a Union victory. At Bull Run, or Manassas, the Union troops met up with a similarly ill-prepared Confederate army under General Thomas Jackson—"Stonewall," he would come to be known because his soldiers held firm on this day. Two armies fought with a courage beyond their experience; the fight ended with a retreat by the Union forces that became confused and turned into a rout, troops mingling with the fashionable civilian observers. The North had not gotten its fast victory; and if Southerners had any conviction just after the first battle of Manassas that Confederate independence was as good as won, they were soon disappointed. The Union settled into a strategy that involved moving against the Confederacy on several fronts. Much of the Southern effort was defensive; but the South also conducted attacks intended to crush a major Union army or to demoralize the North into acquiescence in Southern secession.

Part of the Northern strategy was to impose a naval blockade on the South. The blockade included the stopping of foreign merchant ships and the confiscation of nonmilitary goods that they were carrying to the Confederacy. In a regular war between independent countries such seizures would have been contrary to international law, and the United States faced complaints from Europe. But the South, the federal government responded in effect, was not an independent nation at war, to which citizens from neutral countries could have the right to ship nonmilitary provisions; it was instead a rebellious part of the United States, and the national government therefore had the authority to exclude commerce from Southern ports. The Southern navy could not successfully take on the Union fleet. For one day in 1862 in a battle off Hampton Roads, Virginia, the Confederate vessel *Merrimac* did much damage to Union naval forces. In a great technological innovation, the ship had been covered with iron plates, and against them Northern naval guns had little effect. The next day the North set its own ironclad *Monitor* against the *Merrimac*, rendering it harmless. Later in the war Northern commerce suffered from the raids of the Confederate raider *Alabama*, built in Britain by a private company while Charles Francis Adams, the American minister to that nation, protested to the British government for its failure to stop the construction. The Union navy finally sank the *Alabama*. After the war the United States would win compensation from Britain for losses the ship had inflicted. Confederate privateers could attack merchant ships, but were no threat to the Northern navy. While the blockade could not keep the Confederacy from the sea trade, it was effective enough to deprive Confederate society of much that it needed for smooth functioning.

While the North was pinching in the Confederacy from the sea, it was slashing away in the West. Early in the war there were campaigns in

Gone With the Wind, *1939. The Civil War and Reconstruction was the setting for perhaps the most entertaining film made in America. History, costumes, indirect social commentary, and, above all, romance, made a dazzling mixture. The South depicted in the film was not entirely the stuff of myths, as the still indicates, but Scarlett, Rhett, Ashley, and Melanie, the principal characters, were the perfect embodiments of Romance.*

Tennessee. Then came the important push, with combined naval and land forces, that won the Mississippi River for the Union: New Orleans had fallen to the North earlier. The last bastion of the Confederacy on the Mississippi was Vicksburg. On July 4, 1863—the day of the great Union victory at Gettysburg—Vicksburg surrendered. The Western war proved to Lincoln the worth of Ulysses S. Grant, who was then in command of the Union troops in the West and not yet head of all the Union's armies. And from the West was launched General William T. Sherman's campaign of 1864, which took him through Georgia and South Carolina and into North Carolina in a march that devastated the South.

But the enterprise that seemed to be the particular preoccupation of the federal government was the effort to take Richmond, the capital of the Confederacy. That had been the objective of the action that ended disastrously for the North in the first battle of Manassas. Winfield Scott, hero of the Mexican War, was the first commander of the Union armies. An early exponent of the policy of squeezing the South that was the Union strategy throughout the war, Scott had warned against going into Virginia with insufficient preparation. Federal troops attempted an advance on Richmond in 1862 from the peninsula formed by the Maes and York Rivers in Southern Virginia. The skill of Confederate General Robert E. Lee

Soldiers on the Mississippi. (National Archives.)

defeated the attempt, but General George McClellan departed with this army intact. A popular general with his troops, McClellan was a fine tactician but so methodical that Lincoln would say that he would like to borrow the army sometime if McClellan were not using it.

The big battles at Fredericksburg (December 1862) and Chancellorsville (May 1863), both Confederate victories, were part of the fighting over Virginia that engaged so much of the Union and the Confederate forces in the war. At Chancellorsville Stonewall Jackson was killed by misdirected fire from his own troops, and the South was deprived of a splendid tactician. Late in the war General Grant assumed leadership of the Union armies, but the hero of the war—even though he was enlisted in defending so dubious a moral cause as slavery—was Robert E. Lee of Virginia.

Lee had been no enthusiast for secession. Family tradition opposed it: his father "Lighthorse Harry" Lee had been a Revolutionary War hero. His wife was the great granddaughter of Martha Washington, and Lee had grown up surrounded by momentoes of George Washington, upon whom he modeled his life. Lee had received his education from the United States government at West Point and had served all his adult life in the United States Army, distinguishing himself in the Mexican War, serving for a time as the superintendent of West Point, and achieving some eminence as an army engineer. When secession came, the Lincoln administration sounded him out about taking command of the Union army. Yet Lee saw no choice but to resign his commission rather than to face the responsibility of leading troops against his native state. Lee in the end was a Virginian.

Assuming direction of the Confederacy's forces had merely been an extension of his role in Virginia. He was never a Southern nativist, only a Virginian in a bad season. Most of Lee's role as a general was in defending his home state. He had to keep the Union armies from Richmond while seeking to strike the dramatic blow that would either destroy the Union's will to fight or would bring in the European powers on the Southern side. Several times he came remarkably close, but always he lacked the manpower to follow up his victories and rout the Union army. His most daring campaign ended at Gettysburg early in July 1863 when the Union lines only barely held and his armies took losses they would never replenish. To appreciate the daring of this campaign, one need only glance at a map. Gettysburg is far from the Virginia peninsulas that Lee had to defend. It is north of the District of Columbia, north even of Baltimore, very much in the enemy's country. Lee's associate, General James Longstreet, noted the "subdued excitement" that ran through the generally calm Lee when he went over to daring attack. Like his hero, Washington, Lee had to retreat most of the time even when his instinct was to attack. He usually kept a balance between the two approaches—as Washington had—but he had no French alliance no reliable navy, and his enemy's supply line did not stretch across an ocean. Eventually his army could be worn down, and once he had an opponent willing to suffer the casualties that victory would cost, he had to lose.

The tactic of the North, particularly in the last phases of the war, was one of attack, while the blockade denied the South the resources it needed to keep its economy going. But the Confederacy was also capable, during much of the war, of waging creditable offensives. On September 17, 1862, in the Battle of Antietam in Maryland, Union troops under General George McClellan stopped an invasion by Lee. Had he undertaken one more assault, McClellan would probably have defeated the Southerners. As a result of the general's caution, Lincoln removed him from command. (Maryland was a slave state that had stayed with the Union; the South had hoped to detach the state from the North and thereby leave Washington surrounded by enemy territory, or to attack the federal capital from Maryland.) The technical Northern victory at Antietam persuaded Great Britain to put off diplomatic recognition of the Confederacy as a separate nation. That recognition would have given a tremendous lift to Southern morale and a blow to that of the North, and would have given the British grounds for strongly challenging the federal blockade, which was not following the rules that international law dictated for a war between sovereign nations. In 1864, in a region of Virginia known as the Wilderness, Grant kept his troops grinding against Lee's outnumbered army. The campaign, which was costly to the Confederacy, showed a brilliant knowledge of the use to which superior resources could be put. Grant was perhaps an even better military strategist than the great Lee. In April of 1865 Grant, having hammered South and taken Richmond, caught up with Lee's shrunken forces and at Appomattox Court House, received his opponent's surrender. That, and the surrender soon afterwards of another Confederate army to General Sherman in North Carolina, meant the end of the war.

Life in the Confederacy

During the first rush of enthusiasm following Sumter many Southerners rejoiced at the prospect of glory and independence. "I feel as tho' I could live poetry," exclaimed Mrs. Catherine Edmonston, mistress of a North Carolina plantation. But the joy was anything but universal. Among the South's white population thousands wondered whether their section had not made a colossal mistake. Even slaveholders had their doubts. One Mississippi planter anticipated the defeat of the Confederacy and saw the time "when the northern soldier would tread her cotton fields, when the slave should be made *free* and the proud Southerner stricken to the dust in his presence."

Still more skeptical were large groups of people who owned no slaves. In the mountain backbone that split the older from the newer South, Unionist sentiment existed everywhere. In the first two years of the war the inhabitants of Virginia's western counties would carry their dissent so far as to secede from "Secessia" and form the state of West Virginia. In eastern Kentucky and Tennessee and western North Carolina, many also deplored secession. Thousands of young men from the mountain region joined the Union army. This dissent was not confined to the Appalachian plateau. Wherever small farmers tilled their acres with the sole help of their families or a few hired hands, the Union found favor. In places like northern Louisiana, Alabama, and Mississippi, however, it proved more difficult for dissenters to express their preferences than in the mountain region.

At the outset, when Lincoln sought to play down the slavery issue, blacks had little reason to prefer the Union to the Confederacy. Through much of the war black Southerners continued to contribute to the Confederate effort, though no more willingly than they had to the running of private plantations. The Confederate government set impressed or hired black labor to building fortifications, cooking for troops in the field, driving wagons, and working in hospitals, and for other purposes. When in 1865 Confederate prospects sank, the Richmond government even authorized the recruitment of slaves and free blacks into the Confederate army.

In later years defenders of the Confederacy would note how loyal blacks had been to their Southern masters. When Southern white men were off fighting Yankees and blacks had a chance to revolt, they remained at their jobs providing the Confederacy with its food and manufactured goods. The picture of loyal blacks is badly flawed.

At the beginning, southern slaves went along with the flow of events. But gradually they changed. The experience of the Shepard G. Pryor family furnishes an example. In 1861 Pryor left his Georgia farm and his thirteen slaves in charge of his wife to fight in Virginia. Mrs. Pryor chose as her overseer a white man who had no control over the slaves; they simply ignored him. Eventually she made a crucial decision: she would appoint one of her slaves, Will, as overseer. The choice was fateful for the Pryors' corner of the slave system. For a while Will performed as his master and mistress wished, and he successfully managed the 1862 crop harvest. But soon Will was hiding slave runaways and in general refusing to cooperate with the slave system. The authorities finally arrested him for sheltering slave fugitives. By late 1863 the slave system was disintegrating in many parts of the South. Nowhere was there a major slave uprising, but black people were helping to pull the system apart in other ways. Whenever rumors spread of Yankee troops nearby the slaves of the neighborhood would desert the plantations in droves. Many of those who remained became disobedient and refused to work.

In general, life in the Confederacy was difficult for everybody after the early months of enthusiasm and high hopes. Confederate finance, combined with the Union blockade and the inefficiency of the Southern transportation system, produced uncontrollable inflation. Shortages and, by the last years of the war, invasion and the sense of defeat were the lot of the Southern population.

The price of flour in Richmond more than doubled in the first year of the war. Soap, made from scarce animal fat, went up a thousand percent in price. Imported coffee, selling for 12½ cents a pound before the war, went to five dollars by 1863. In late December 1863 some Richmond prices in Confederate money were: apples, $65 to $75 a barrel; onions, $30 a barrel; Irish potatoes, $6 to $9 a bushel; sugar, $3.50 a pound; and eggs, $3 a dozen. Worst of all to one young soldier stationed at the Confederate capital was the price of whiskey. "It would cost about fifty Dollars to get tight here," he wrote his family in 1863.

At times essential commodities were unavailable at any price. Shortages were more common in the cities, swollen with war refugees and soldiers, than in the countryside. In the spring of 1863, three hundred Richmond women, some brandishing revolvers and others bowie knives, attacked the city's business district demanding affordable food. The riot soon got out of hand and the women looted the jewelry and clothing stores before they were stopped. And even in the country districts food and clothing shortages provoked direct action. In 1863 fourteen women armed with "guns, pistols, knives, and tongues," attacked a mill near Thomasville, Georgia and seized a large supply of flour.

Southern white women found their lives transformed by the war. They were often fiery Confederate patriots. It has been said that young Southern belles, by favoring army volunteers and shunning young men who avoided the war, were the most effective recruiters for the Confederate army. Middle and upper class Southern women had always managed large households. As the war progressed, their administrative skills were put to running the plantations and businesses their husbands had left behind. Wives of ordinary farmers, too, took over managerial duties. The Confederate Treasury hired hundreds of women clerks. Women found jobs in the South's factories or worked in Confederate hospitals. Few of these gains lasted beyond the war, but they demonstrated what women were capable of and foreshadowed expanded opportunities in later generations.

Life in the Union

Initially the Northern economy faltered as businessmen, fearful of disruption and disorder, sought to call in debts. In many Northern cities, especially New York, Chicago, and Cincinnati, the loss of Southern customers did serious injury to the economy. Some economic historians claim that on the whole the Civil War slowed economic growth. Yet the newspapers of the day reveal that, after the middle of 1862, the Union experienced an economic boom. The draining of men into the military left shortages of labor. On some farms women filled in. The North, however, had more machines than the South with which to replace manpower; during the years from 1860-65 the McCormick Reaper Company received more orders for its harvesting machines than it could fill. The continuing influx of immigrants, almost half a million during the war years, relieved labor shortages in the cities.

Yet the Union had an inflation rate only slightly less staggering than that of the Confederacy. The policy of financing the war by a combination of heavy borrowing and paper money was a cause; so was the scarcity of labor that machines and immigrants only partially offset. And the wartime prosperity bestowed itself unevenly. While consumer prices had risen by 1865 between seventy-five and a hundred percent, the wages of skilled workers went up during the same period about sixty percent, and those of common laborers rose just under fifty percent. Meanwhile the business and professional classes crowded Broadway in New York and Michigan Avenue in Chicago and Pennsylvania Avenue in Cincinnati, buying at the fashionable shops, attending the theaters, and dining at the fancy restaurants. Some of these people were profiteers who had made a good thing out of the swelling orders from the War and Navy Departments and the flow of greenback currency. Charging the government high prices for desperately needed supplies, some profiteers also provided uniforms and shoes that disintegrated at the first heavy rain, powder that would not explode, and beef, pork, and flour that was inedible.

In the Army

Of about two million federal troops, 360,000 died. Among the more than one million who at some time served in the Confederate military, about 250,000 never came back. Only one in three of these died of battle wounds; the others succumbed to disease or accident. There were also about half a million wounded, many of them severely maimed.

The Civil War was more dangerous for participants than many that preceded and most that followed. During the 1860's infantry weapons became highly destructive while infantry tactics continued to follow older concepts. Most soldiers carried rifles rather than smooth-bore muskets. These hurled a lead ball for hundreds of yards with deadly accuracy. Yet until the very end of the war commanders on both sides frequently ordered their men to charge the enemy across open fields as if they faced the older, less accurate musket. Toward the end of the war attackers had to face

General Ulysses S. Grant (Library of Congress.)

the fast-firing breech-loaders with which more and more soldiers were being equipped.

If a man were wounded his chance for survival was not very good. Nothing was known about infectious bacteria, and military surgeons performed operations without sanitary precautions. Soldiers contracted gangrene and other deadly infections. Though anesthetics were known, doctors did not always have them on hand, and shock, followed by death, was often the consequence of major surgery. Long delays occurred in getting the casualties to medical aid stations or hospitals. Following the battle of Seven Pines in mid-1862, wounded federal soldiers were carried to the rear for shipment to the hospitals around Washington. The trains were slow to arrive, a sensitive observer noted, and the men "lay by the hundreds on either side of the railway track . . . exposed to the drenching rain . . . shivering from the cold, calling for water, food, and dressings . . . the most heart-rending spectacle. Many died from exposure, others prayed for death to release them from their anguish."

In every part of the battlefront were mosquitoes, lice, and biting flies, which helps to explain the high incidence of malaria and other diseases. Heat in the deep South and cold, particularly in the mountain areas and the upper South, afflicted the soldiers. Wool uniforms were standard year-round issue and soldiers of both armies simply shed as much as they could during the summer. If Northern troops were often over-dressed, rebels were often half naked. As the Union blockade took hold and internal transport broke down, Confederate soldiers found it difficult to get replacements for worn or torn uniforms. Many ended up wearing homemade garments sent by relatives and friends. Others relied on captured Yankee shoes and other clothes. Especially serious was the shortage of boots and shoes. In the last winter of the war the troops accompanying General J. B. Hood on his campaign through Tennessee often marched barefoot through snow and sleet. The path of Hood's army, it was said, was marked by a red trail of blood.

Few Union soldiers went hungry, but the diet of salt pork, bread, and coffee was deficient nutri-

tionally and undermined health. The Confederate soldier's standard diet consisted of bacon, corn-meal, and coffee—when he could get them. Coffee, an imported item that had run the Union blockade, went quickly; the bacon lasted longer, but it, too, was often in short supply and Southern troops supplemented their meat rations with cuts of mule, horse, racoon, and even bear. Sometimes Confederates were reduced to consuming little more than parched corn. Chewing the grains, reported one Southern soldier, was "hard work"; it made "the jaws ache and the gums so sore as to cause unendurable pain."

At the beginning of the war, North and South had relied on volunteers and militia. In time, both sides resorted to a draft. The Union conscription law permitted a drafter to find a substitute. He could also make a payment in place of service; that feature drew charges that the law favored the wealthy. In neither North nor South was conscription popular. In 1863 an antidraft riot broke out in New York City. The rioters lynched several blacks and burnt a black orphanage, and federal troops had to be called in. But volunteers continued to come in; the large bounty the Union offered was an inducement, as was the threat of the draft.

While it was not until almost the end of the war, when the South was badly in need of additional troops, that the Confederacy contemplated the recruitment of blacks, the Union was accepting them as early as 1862. Earlier Lincoln's government had held back, fearing that the presence of black soldiers would seem to indicate that the war was not only for restoration of the Union but for the abolition of slavery. The acceptance of black volunteers came at the urging of black leaders and white abolitionists. By the end of the war, blacks composed about a tenth of the army and a fourth of the navy. For most of the war, black privates got three dollars a month less than whites. Some were relegated to labor units. Some confederate commanders declared a policy of putting black prisoners into slavery or of killing them. But in combat the black soldiers won the respect of their officers and helped to discredit further the remnants of the slave system.

The War and Civil Liberties

In the extraordinary danger that the nation faced at the time of the war, free civil institutions continued to operate in the North and for the most part in the border states. Lincoln's government

did not attempt in any major and consistent way to put those institutions aside. But it was conscious that disruption or demoralization among the people in the regions loyal to the Union could bring to the Confederates the victory that they were not far from achieving.

Lincoln suspended the writ of *habeas corpus*—the power possessed by a court to have a prisoner brought before it—in cases in which an individual was suspected of illegal disruptions of the war effort. The suspension meant that the federal government could hold people for long periods without trial, for without the writ the courts could not bring the accused to trial. Despite protests, Lincoln in the autumn of 1862 issued a proclamation subjecting to martial law and to trial in military tribunals anyone who discouraged others from enlisting or committed any disloyal act. The War Department in the course of the conflict arrested at least thirteen thousand people, most of whom never came to trial.

The chief Northern political opponents of the conduct of the war were the Peace Democrats, or Copperheads as supporters of the war called them. The most prominent of the Peace Democrats was Clement Vallandigham of Ohio, who insisted that the war was strengthening the central government at the expense of civil liberties. Vallandigham called for "the Constitution as it is, the Union as it was." In 1862 he was defeated for reelection to Congress. He continued his attacks on the war and after General Ambrose Burnside arrested him in 1863, a military tribunal sentenced him to prison for its duration. The affair was an assault on the constitutional right of free speech; protest was widespread, and the situation was a political danger to the administration. To deflect the issue, Lincoln by use of his executive power banished Vallandigham to the Confederacy. But the Ohioan returned to the North and kept up his criticisms. The administration now left him alone. When Vallandigham tried to get the Supreme Court to consider his claim that the government had acted unconstitutionally, the Court in 1864 ruled in *ex parte Vallandigham* that it had no jurisdiction over the proceedings of military tribunals. In 1866, however, the Supreme Court did find the methods of the war administration to have been unconstitutional. In *ex parte Milligan* the Court held that martial law and the subjection of civilians to military trials were illegal when the civil courts were open and in full operation.

Emancipation

At the beginning of the war the federal government was careful to insist that it was fighting only to preserve the Union and not to free the slaves. The war, said a resolution adopted by Congress, was not for "overthrowing or interfering with the rights or established institutions" of the seceded states. The government wanted to convince those proslavery Southerners who were prepared to be sympathetic to the Unionist cause that the institution of slavery was not in danger. But it is reasonable to suppose that something beyond mere political strategy lay behind the caution of the President and Congress about interfering with slavery. Neither Lincoln nor most of the national legislators had been abolitionists; and however distasteful slavery may have been to much of the government, the slave system had been so firmly established, and so hedged with legal protections, that even opponents might have had doubts about the sudden military abolition of slavery. Politicians and statesmen, like the rest of humankind, are hesitant to imagine any workable society that is far different from whatever one they are accustomed to; and it took time and the events of the war to make the government see the tangible possibility of wiping out slavery at a stroke.

General John C. Frémont issued a military order freeing the slaves in Missouri, but Lincoln modified Frémont's order. He did, however, ask Congress in 1862 to grant federal funds to any state adopting a scheme of emancipation. Though Congress did not respond, it declared in the Second Confiscation Act of 1862 that wherever the Union army was in control, all slaves owned by rebels would be free. The Act was both a substantial measure and a somewhat limited one. It did not apply to slaves held by southern Unionists. But the Second Confiscation Act did something toward breaking Union politicians of their timidity about abolishing slavery, and the very existence of the Act must have provided a certain momentum toward abolition. Abolitionists meanwhile were urging a wider policy of emancipation. Such a policy, moreover, could have desirable diplomatic effects. The apparent success of the South in maintaining its independence, and the advantage that European countries might gain from a dividing of the United States, raised the danger that they might recognize the Confederacy as a sovereign nation, which would greatly weaken the Union effort. Lincoln believed that if European nations could see the war as a struggle not merely between Union and secession but between freedom and slavery, they would be less likely to recognize the slave republic. And while Lincoln had not been an abolitionist, he had been a free soiler and a moral opponent of slavery. Surely his conscience welcomed the decision toward which political considerations were pushing him.

The Union victory of Antietam gave Lincoln the opportunity to issue in September 1862 a preliminary Emancipation Proclamation, announcing that as of January 1, 1863, all slaves in those regions still in rebellion on that date would be free. Lincoln was offering to secessionists an alternative to loss of their slaves: they could voluntarily bring their communities back into the Union. The Emancipation Proclamation itself, issued on January 1, carried out the terms of the preliminary proclamation: it declared that all slaves in areas still in rebellion were "then, thenceforward, and forever free." Lincoln was drawing on the power he possessed as Commander in Chief; the Proclamation was essentially a military order, on somewhat the same principle as the instructions an officer might give his troops for the treatment of citizens and property. The Emancipation Proclamation, like the Second Confiscation Act, was of sharply limited scope; it freed no slaves immediately because it did not apply to the border states or to regions already under Union control. But it was understood at the time, as it has been understood ever since, as the great symbolic moral action of the war, a public state-ment, in however confined a form, that the war was now for freedom. After the preliminary Proclamation the military had begun seriously taking in black volunteers. It was a logical consequence of the events of the Civil War that in 1865 the nation adopted the Thirteenth Amendment outlawing slavery.

Within the war Congresses there was a variety of opinions on racial matters. At one extreme were several Democrats who were reluctant to make changes in existing institutions. At the other extreme, as the war progressed, was a small but important group of Republicans who wanted the strongest possible policy of abolition and of protection for the rights of the freed slaves; and within this faction ideas emerged for going beyond emancipation and bringing about changes in the social and economic condition of black Americans. Congress in the course of the war repealed a law prohibiting blacks from carrying the mail and a ban on testimony of black witnesses in federal court, outlawed slavery in the territories, and established a scheme for emancipation in the District of Columbia that would provide compensation to the slaveholders. Blacks were allowed in places from which they had once been excluded: the congressional visitors galley, lectures at the Smithsonian. Some states got rid of a number of discriminating laws. The country was taking some halting steps beyond emancipation and toward equality or at least a concept of justice.

Politics and Economics

The successful waging of the war required that Lincoln have as much popular support as he could get. In his campaign of 1864 for reelection he ran as a Republican but as the candidate of a coalition of Republicans and Democratic supporters of the war, which called itself the Union party. The vice-presidential candidate of the party was Andrew Johnson, a Tennessee Democrat who had remained loyal to the Union. The presidential candidate of the regular Democratic party was General McClellan. McClellan, who had been commander of the Union armies, was loyal to the war effort, and in effect he rejected his party's pronouncement that the war was a failure. By the time of the campaign and election the war had been going so successfully for the North that Lincoln's victory was assured.

While the winning of the war was the most important objective for the Republicans, they were committed also to an entire political, social and economic policy within which the emancipation of the slaves and the preservation of the Union were elements. Before the Civil War much of the antislavery movement had been connected with political forces that wanted a more vigorous national government working for the achievement of an advanced industrial and agricultural economy. Some Americans had gotten a vision of what a powerful American economy and society might be: an industrialized Northeast trading its manufactured goods for the produce of a great agricultural West. The federal government, these people believed, should stimulate Eastern manufactures through a protective tariff,

Charleston, S.C.—The South in Ruins. (Library of Congress.)

populate the agrarian West by giving government lands to settlers, and tie together the two regions by a railroad system built with federal aid. Northern politicians who thought this way could wish to exclude slavery from the territories not only because they genuinely disliked slavery on moral grounds but also because they desired that the western lands be reserved for free American farmers. And in the years before the Civil War they had clashed with the South on other political issues: the Southern cotton interest had opposed a protective tariff, wanting instead to bring manufactured goods more cheaply from Europe, and had resisted the construction of a Northern railroad from East to West, holding out of a Southern route. This is not to say that the Republican party represented a single economic and ideological point of view. The economic interests could compete with one another, and abolitionists could differ radically with politicians who wished merely to keep slavery from spreading farther westward. It is fitting that political circumstances put the Republicans in command of the war for the saving of the Union; for the Union came to mean strong central government presiding over a vast and economically progressive nation, while secession would have broken the country into weaker republics. It is fitting also that the Republicans became the champions of federally enforced emancipation.

In 1861, just before Lincoln's inauguration, Congress passed the Morrill Tariff, a protectionist measure putting duties to the levels they had been at in 1846; and later the national legislature raised duties higher. The war put a strain on the system of banking and currency. In response, Congress reformed the system in a way that agreed with the Republican concept of strong government in the service of a national economy. The National Banking Acts of 1863 and 1864 provided that, in return for investing one-third of their capital in federal bonds, private banks could issue national bank notes that would serve as paper money: these could be in amounts up to ninety percent of the market value of the securities the banks had pur-

chased from the government. The notes of state banks, which had circulated as a form of money, were unstable and injured the economy; in order to suppress them, Congress later placed a ten percent tax on the notes of all institutions that did not take part in the national bank system.

The Republican idea of supplying federal lands for settlers triumphed in the Homestead Act of 1862. A settler who filed a claim to a quarter-section of one hundred and sixty acres of federal land and lived on it for five years would get ownership of it after payment of a small fee. The Act did not work as expected. Later in the century considerable amounts of the land went to timber and mining companies that had employees put in claims for homesteads. Many more settlers got cheap lands from land companies or from the railroads than from the federal government. But at the time of the adoption of the Act, there was some expectation that it would pull labor from the East to the free lands; and in face of the labor shortage that the war was bringing about, Congress authorized immigration of contract workers from Europe and the Orient, permitting employers who paid the laborers' passage to deduct that cost from the pay. Congress made another use of federal lands. The Morrill Land Grant Act of 1862 offered lands to states that in return would finance colleges offering schooling in agriculture, engineering, and military science. It was a less dramatic measure than others of these wartime years, but a significant one: it made the national government a partner to modern technical education.

The absence of legislators from the deep South made it easier for Congress during the war to adopt a scheme for a transcontinental railway running through the middle of the country from Omaha to California; Southerners would have fought for a more Southern road. During the 1860's the national legislature granted to railroad developers thirty million acres of federal land and made them large loans. It was one of the first of many extensive projects in which the government has joined with business.

Reconstruction: Wartime Plans

President Lincoln hoped for a quick restoration of the seceded states to the Union. Once it became clear that the government was committed to getting rid of slavery, he wanted emancipation to be gradual and mostly under control of Southern state officials. He had indicated his belief that the best answer to the racial problem was for black Americans to colonize outside the United States.

Winslow Homer, A Visit from the Old Mistress, 1876. (National Gallery of Fine Arts, Smithsonian Institution.)

CIVIL WAR AND RECONSTRUCTION

The question of restoration or a more thorough-going reconstruction of the Southern states came down to this: what system of government and laws would a former Confederate state have to adopt, or how would its citizens have to go about adopting that system, before its representatives could sit again in Congress? In late 1863 Lincoln outlined a "10 percent plan" for restoration; whenever, in any seceded state, whites equal in number to one-tenth of those who had voted in 1860 took an oath of future loyalty to the Union, they could form a state government. The President recognized such governments in Louisiana, Arkansas, and Tennessee and set up Unionist governments elsewhere.

Congress would not admit representatives of these regimes into its ranks. The national legislators were looking for a plan that would more firmly insure that the new Southern governments would remain loyal. The Wade-Davis Bill of 1864 required that, before a formerly seceded state could form a government, 50 percent of the adult white males in that state would have to take an oath of loyalty to the Union. The state could then hold a constitutional convention to make a new government for itself; but voting for delegates to that convention would be limited to people who had taken an oath that they had never supported the secession. The state must outlaw slavery. The plan was not to go into effect until the war had ended. Thinking the Wade-Davis Bill too severe and an invasion of presidential responsibility for reconstruction, Lincoln vetoed it. The federal government still lacked a scheme for bringing the seceded states back into the Union.

Neither Lincoln's plan nor that of the Wade-Davis Bill provided for blacks to be given the vote. But some Republicans in Congress wished for a program of reconstruction that would grant a wide range of rights to the freedman and guarantee protection of these rights. Congressmen of this kind wanted the national government to have strong control over former confederate states, so that their legal and social systems could get thoroughly reshaped and white Southerners would not get the chance to bring back the old slavery system in a new form. Some Republicans who favored a coercive policy toward the South wanted a constitutional doctrine that by the act of secession the Confederate states had forfeited their status of statehood and reverted to the condition of territories. If they were no longer states, they were not entitled to the rights of states and could be subject to the will of the federal government. Never during the war were the more radical reconstructionists able to put through a program

of their own liking, but events were pushing the nation beyond the milder policies of Lincoln. Not long before his death, in fact, Lincoln was moving somewhat on the issue of suffrage: black Union veterans and "very intelligent" black people, he declared, must be allowed to vote.

Lincoln was not to live into a time when he might have found himself confronting the radicals, or possibly in alliance with them. At the beginning of the spring of 1865 the President and the Union public did have a few days to savor the triumph of final victory. On April 4 Lincoln went to Richmond to view the Confederate capital now evacuated by the government of Jefferson Davis. Accompanied by his son Tad and a military escort, he walked up Main Street to the Confederate executive mansion. Black men and women crowded around the presidential party and sang and shouted. When he entered the Confederate president's house and took a seat in Davis' chair, the Union troops, black and white, cheered. Later the President toured the captured city that for four bloody years had been the supreme goal of Union armies. Like many other large Southern towns Richmond was in ruins: it was blackened by a fire set accidently by the Confederate authorities before they withdrew.

Lincoln returned to Washington on April 9, the day Lee surrendered to Grant at Appomattox Court House. The news reached Washington the next day and the government declared a holiday for its employees. On the tenth throngs gathered on the streets of the capital. Navy yard workers and other celebrants dashed back and forth, accompanied by bands and men firing howitzers. The crowds eventually converged on the White House, where Lincoln was working at his desk. They interrupted him several times by their shouts for a speech until he finally made an appearance. He would deliver some appropriate remarks the following evening, he said, but for the moment he would just order the bands to play "Dixie." The Confederate anthem, he noted, was now the lawful property of the Union.

The next evening the President came to the upper window of the White House as he had promised and made some graceful remarks. "We meet this evening not in sorrow, but in gladness of heart" he began, and then went on to deliver a thoughtful address, his last, on the problems to come. If the crowd had wanted a rousing cock-crow of triumph, it was disappointed. At least one man in the audience, however, the actor John Wilkes Booth, found himself deeply moved, but to rage and anger. A Marylander from a distinguished acting family, he felt deeply for the

Store for Freedmen
Beaufort, S.C.

(National Archives.)

South and its defeat had sent him into despair.

On the evening of April 14 the President, accompanied by his wife and several friends, went to see the comedy *Our American Cousin* at Ford's Theater. The President's party arrived late but quickly settled down to enjoy the story of a shrewd comic American visiting his English relatives. During the third act the sounds of a muffled shot and a scuffle came from the President's box. Suddenly a tall figure leaped from the box to the stage and shouted *Sic semper tyrannis!* (thus ever to tyrants), the motto of Virginia. Before he could be stopped Booth escaped into the night.

They carried the unconscious President to a house nearby and placed him on a bed. While high officials and family members gathered around, the doctors examined him. The bullet had entered the rear of his head and lodged near his eye. Nothing could be done. He died at 7:22 a.m.

Andrew Johnson

Andrew Johnson came to the presidency on the death of Lincoln. A Democrat, he had received the vice-presidential nomination of the Union party, Lincoln's coalition of Republicans and war Democrats, and now was a Democratic President who had to deal with a Republican Congress. Johnson was a Southern white supremacist, willing and perhaps happy to accept emancipation and some rights for black Americans but cooperative with Southerners who wished to place strict controls over the black population. This brought him into conflict not only with the increasingly strong band of radical Republicans in Congress but with moderates as well. Courageous and stubborn but belligerent and lacking in political tact, Johnson both endured and to an extent brought on himself one of the most troubled presidential administrations in American history.

Johnson wanted an easy restoration of the seceded states. There was no clearly defined program that would instruct a rebel state in how it must go about reorganizing itself so as to be accepted back into the Union. So Johnson gave his own approval to Southern state governments, with former Confederate leaders among their officials, that had adopted "black codes" placing a number of restrictions on blacks, including requirements that they work and penalties for unemployment or the lack of a permanent residence. The black codes looked much like a system of modified slavery. Their existence, and the presence of former rebels in the new governments, suggested to Northerners that the South was about to reestablish its old institutions, that the war had won almost nothing. In 1866 it passed a bill giving to the Freedman's Bureau, which had been formed the previous year as an agency for aiding the freed slaves, the power to try by military commission anyone charged with depriving freed men of their civil rights. It also put through a civil rights bill that gave the freedmen citizenship and civil rights. Johnson vetoed both bills on constitutional grounds. Congress thereupon enacted the Civil Rights measure over his veto, passed another bill for a Freedmen's Bureau, and overrode Johnson's veto of it. The national legislature refused to seat representatives from the Southern governments the President had recognized.

Relations between Congress and the President became unworkable. Convinced finally that Johnson intended to obstruct Congress in its efforts to devise a policy of reconstruction, Republican opponents of the President got the House of Representatives in February 1868 to impeach him—to charge him with misconduct. That meant that Johnson was to go on trial before the Senate, which would decide whether to remove him from the presidency. The trial took place in the spring of 1868. The President's accusers argued that a number of his actions, and more particularly his dismissal of Edwin M. Stanton from the office of Secretary of War in violation of a statute of Congress, were outside his presidential authority and made his removal necessary. Johnson's defenders insisted that removal could be only for violation of a criminal law. The vote in the Senate was one ballot less than the two-thirds needed for conviction.

Reconstruction: The Actuality

During much of Johnson's administration and afterwards, congressional policy toward the South was under control of those Republicans, called "radicals," who aimed to use the force of the federal government for the protection of full citizenship for black Americans and the improvement of their social condition. The leaders of the radical group included the Massachusetts Senator Charles Sumner and Congressman Thaddeus Stevens of Pennsylvania. The Civil Rights law and the Freedmen's Bureau that Congress had enacted not long after the war were early attempts to do something beyond the mere grant of emancipation. But Radical Reconstruction really began with the four Reconstruction Acts passed in 1867 and 1868, under which Congress put the less cooperative regions of the South under military rule and saw to it that Southern states would respect the rights of their black citizens. The Fourteenth Amendment to the Constitution, ratified in 1868, declared that no state could deny any person "life, liberty, or property without due process of law" or "deny to any person within its jurisdiction the equal protection of the laws." Congress had required Southern states to ratify the Amendment as a prerequisite for readmission to the Union; and reconstruction governments in the South, representing black voters and others sympathetic to the cause, voted for ratification. The Fifteenth Amendment, ratified two years later, provided that a citizen's right to vote "shall not be denied or abridged . . . on account of race, color, or previous condition of servitude."

The critics of Radical Reconstruction, Northern as well as Southern, used to describe it as the work of vindictive Northern politicians who wished to crush the old South, and as a Republican scheme to turn the reconstructed states, with their black Republican voters, into bastions of the party. This view spoke of corruption in the Reconstruction regions and pictured a Southern society fallen victim to the lawlessness of former slaves who had not yet learned how to use their freedom. Until very recently this interpretation predominated. But according to an economic interpretation of the period, the motive behind Reconstruction was not vindictiveness but a determination on the part of capitalism to break the political power of the old Southern agricultural interest, which had opposed such measures as a protective tariff. Reconstruction, according to this interpretation, was an incident in the replacement of an agrarian order by a modern industrial and capitalist system. But historians have now become far more sympathetic to Radical Reconstruction. Reconstruction, many commentators on it now believe, was a wholly reasonable effort to provide black citizens with the equal rights that former secessionist Southerners clearly intended to deny them, and within the black community in the South it was a time of self-discovery and of independent economic and social progress. It should be said also of Reconstruction that it had something in common with the economic policy of the Republican party and with the party's conduct of the Civil War: it represented that commitment to strong and active central government toward which the Republicans tended, partly for reasons of ideology and partly because events pushed them that way. For the first time in our history, the federal government was lending its resources to a legal and social revolution. If Reconstruction is to be blamed for anything, it is for not being thorough enough to complete the transition from slavery to equality that it began.

The war devastated the South. The hurtling back and forth of great armies, the scorched-earth policy of Union commanders, the wearing out of equipment—all added to the exhaustion of the region. Wherever travelers went in the months following Appomattox they saw abandoned fields, twisted rails, and burnt structures. The defeat of the Confederacy had also wiped out millions of dollars of bank capital and made all Confederate money worthless. The human price was immense. For decades to come, men hobbling on one leg or with empty sleeves would be common sights throughout Dixie. In 1866 the state of Mississippi would spend a fifth of its revenues on artificial arms and legs for Confederate veterans. But most unsettling of all the changes the war had brought was the end of slavery. For generations it had been the foundation on which the entire Southern economy rested. Now that it was gone, what would take its place? As white Southerners looked about them after April 1865 they were not reassured.

Many former slaves remained on farms and plantations, but others had departed. Some had gone to the towns where life seemed more interesting than in the sleepy countryside. Others took to the road to test their new freedom. Even more went traveling to seek out lost relatives and friends separated years ago by the migration of white masters or by the domestic slave trade. The tide of wandering freedmen in the immediate postwar months attests to the strong ties of kinship among them. Eventually most would return to the land somewhere in the South.

In the economic and social adjustment to postwar conditions, black Southerners had some help from the outside. The Freedmen's Bureau, which had only a brief existence, is perhaps the first modern social agency the national government has ever set up. Critics now emphasize the paternalistic attitudes some of its officials displayed toward blacks, the prejudice of others, it failure to do more for the black community. But it did supply some relief, sought employment opportunities for people, supervised labor contracts, and was alert for violations of the freedmen's legal rights. Private groups were also at work in the South. Churches, notably the Congregational Church, sent money and agents. Churches provided schooling for children and aided in the establishment of black colleges and industrial schools.

In many areas, the first system that came in the absence of slavery consisted of wage labor. Guided and prodded by agents of the Freedmen's Bureau, blacks signed contracts to work for so much a month and were provided with cabins, often in the former plantation slave quarters, and sometimes with food. Yet work in the fields at the white man's bidding, on the white man's land, under the immediate supervision of a white overseer seemed far too much like old slavery in a new guise. Many blacks would have none of it and sabotaged the arrangement. One way was to collect wages during the planting and cultivating months and then just before the crucial harvest decamp, which left the owner with the problem of gathering in the cotton or tobacco without a work force.

The ideal system, from the point of view of the freedmen, was outright land ownership. They yearned for land. A few radicals, notably Thaddeus Stevens of Pennsylvania, advocated confiscation of some plantations and redistribution of land to the former slaves. But Northerners recoiled at the prospect of such disregard of property rights. The freedmen were not going to get the "forty acres and a mule" that rumor had told of.

The land and labor system finally devised in the postwar South was share-cropping. In this form of tenancy the black worker contributed labor and perhaps the use of some tools and a mule, and received from the landlord some land to farm. At harvest time the cropper got to keep from half to two-thirds of the crop, the remaining portion going to the landowner as rent.

The system had some advantages. Blacks now had some personal freedom; there was no overseer to supervise their work. Instead of living in the old slave quarters, moreover, each black family could reside apart on its own rented piece of land. Some blacks simply raised the slave cabin from the old quarters and removed it to their own farm. Blacks could now decide how to spend their money. And they could arrange their own family division of labor. Almost immediately, some black women abandoned field work and began to confine themselves to the roles of mothers and wives like white women.

The sharecropper system, though, was a poor substitute, for tenants had little incentive to improve the land they farmed; since they did not own it, they could not expect to be the beneficiaries. As a consequence, Southern soil fertility declined, and the region's fences, barns, and cabins deteriorated. The credit system that grew up alongside share-cropping was its worst element. Tenants usually could not wait until harvest time to buy the things they needed during the year. Storekeepers sold them cloth, tools, knick-knacks, and even food on credit, taking out a lien, a kind of mortgage, on the crop as security until harvest time in the fall. Then, when the crop was sold, the storekeeper subtracted the debt from the cropper's share. Those caught in this crop-lien process might not ever see any cash once the storekeeper and the landlord had taken their shares. Goods bought on credit were far more expensive than those bought with cash. The system also allowed many opportunities for fraud. Storekeepers, themselves under considerable economic pressure, kept the accounts and sometimes juggled the books to make sure that the sharecropper remained permanently in debt. Such a tenant remained tied to the storekeeper as a perpetual customer, unable legally to deal with any other storekeeper until the debt was discharged. Some scholars have seen this "debt peonage" as the virtual reenslavement of the South's black population. It certainly destroyed any chance that share-cropping could become a way-station to land ownership for any sizable number of former slaves. Though Congress did not renew the Freedmen's Bureau in 1869, it did for a time continue to make laws in the interest of black Americans.

The Compromise of 1877

Reconstruction remained, at least in fragments, into the 1870's. After white organizations, among them the Ku Klux Klan, had begun threatening and committing violence on black citizens for exercising their newly acquired rights, the national legislature in the early 1870's put through several Force Acts that aimed at restraining the terrorist groups. The administration of Ulysses S. Grant, elected President in 1868 as the candidate of the Republican party, broke the first Klan by the end of 1871. In 1875 Congress passed a Civil Rights Act—which in 1883 the Supreme Court would find unconstitutional—that required states to provide equality to blacks in public places and prohibited the exclusion of blacks from jury duty. For a while in the 1870's, some Southern states had Reconstruction governments that represented black as well as white voters. And in 1876 there were still a few federal soldiers in the South whose object was to defend the rights of the black community. But by 1876 American politics had been turning away from Reconstruction for some time.

In 1868 Grant, as a war hero, had won a solid victory over Democratic presidential candidate Horatio Seymour of New York. But in the years following, Democrats made politically effective attacks on Reconstruction policy, winning voters unsure of the wisdom of Radical Reconstruction or unfriendly to the rights black people were gaining. Some Republicans were also challenging the Party's Southern programs. In 1872 Democrats and a faction of Republicans put up newspaperman Horace Greeley as presidential candidate. Grant won reelection. But his administration suffered from a number of political scandals that suggested widespread corruption. In the elections of 1874 the Democratic party won control of the House of Representatives and cut into Republican strength in the Senate.

The Reconstruction governments in the South were facing both political opposition and violence from citizens who wanted whites to be in firm control of Southern society. White Democrats formed terrorist organizations, disrupted Republican gatherings, and threatened blacks. The federal government, tiring of Reconstruction, did little to stop all this.

Then, in the events that followed the presidential contest of 1876 between Republican candidate Rutherford B. Hayes of Ohio and Democrat Samuel J. Tilden of New York, the Republican party ended Reconstruction and abandoned black Southerners and their rights. After the general election, which chose the presidential electors who were to cast the actual vote for President, charges of irregularities had arisen concerning procedures in three Southern states, South Carolina, Florida, and Louisiana. There the election boards that had counted the popular presidential vote, giving it in each case to the Republicans, were under the control of Republican, Reconstruction forces; and Democrats suggested that the vote in each state had actually gone for the Democrats. Republicans challenged the legitimacy of one Democratic elector in Oregon. Unless the Republican claims could stand in each of the four states, the majority in the whole electoral college would be Democratic and Tilden would be the next President. Democrats and Republicans worked out a scheme for a commission that was to decide among the disputed electors; it was supposed to be balanced between Democratic and Republican members, with one other member who would be independent of either party in his decisions. When it came to appear that this member, a justice on the Supreme Court, was going to decide in all cases in favor of the Republicans. Democrats believed that they were about to have the election taken away from them. After the dispute had lasted for months, during which there was talk of civil war, the parties came to a solution. In return for Democrats ceasing to oppose the selection of Hayes electors, Republicans agreed that a Republican presidential administration would not only remove the remaining federal troops from the South but also give political patronage to white Southerners and be friendly to economic legislation beneficial to Southern states. Hayes, who earlier had expressed concern for the rights of black Southerners, presided over the end of a policy that by 1877 no longer had the necessary political support. But the events of 1877 did mean that the Republican effort to protect civil rights in the South in a major way had ceased.

Suggested Readings

The standard work on the era is James G. Randall and David Donald, *The Civil War and Reconstruction* (rev., 1973), although Kenneth Stampp's *The Era of Reconstruction, 1865-1877* (1964) is more thorough on those years. An important new study of the consequences of freedom for blacks is Leon F. Litwack, *Been in the Storm so Long: The Aftermath of Slavery* (1979). Two major books on the response of intellectuals to the war are George Fredrickson, *The Inner Civil War: Northern Intellectuals and the Crisis of the Union* (1965) and Daniel Aaron, *The Unwritten War: American Writers and the Civil War* (1973). Robert Manson Myers, ed., *The Children of Pride: A*

True Story of Georgia and the Civil War (1972), gives us a history in the first person: his collection of the letters of a Georgia planter's family gives us its religious sentiments and attitudes toward human property, the day-to-day demands of running a plantation, and the dissolution of a way of life. Michael Les Benedict, *The Impeachment and Trial of Andrew Johnson* (1973) is a superior analysis of the divisions and alignments within the Reconstruction Congress and its relationships with a President whom the author depicts as a villain. C. Vann Woodward's *The Burden of Southern History* (1960) is a collection of essays that takes as its theme the South's heritage as distinct from that of the rest of the nation.

Library of Congress.

Chapter XVI
The Ironies of Industrialism
1865—1910

The Centennial Exhibition

"The year of the great anniversary," 1876, had as its centerpiece the Centennial Exhibition in Philadelphia. About one in five Americans would visit the dozens of exhibition halls, the restaurants, the galleries, the train ride through the grounds, all the accoutrements of a great world's fair combined with the special importance of the nation's hundredth birthday. "Centennial mania" dominated the summer of '76. People wore centennial hats and scarves, attended centennial balls, drank centennial coffee, listened to centennial songs. Some dressed in the fashion of 1776 or contributed artifacts from the nation's history—including even a pair of George Washington's false teeth. Temperance organizations provided free ice water to all visitors, building a giant fountain in the form of a Greek temple with twenty-six spigots.

Celebrating the centennial of the Union seemed particularly important to the men and women of 1876. The Civil War was both a recent memory and a live issue in national politics, and the road to reconciliation between the North and South remained bumpy. But on opening day, May 10, 1876, over 100,000 people came to see the "greatest spectacle ever presented to the vision of the Western World." Banners, flags, and streamers festooned the usually staid city. Before a vast platform filled with dignitaries from all over the world, a 150-piece orchestra played national songs of all the countries represented at the fair. As the maestro called for the Brazilian National Hymn, Emperor Dom Pedro of Brazil—a Bourbon, a Braganza, and a Hapsburg—appeared on the platform, the first reigning monarch (at least the first white-skinned one) ever to appear on American soil. The republican crowd made him the hero of the day, wildly cheering this plainly dressed "true Yankee emperor with go-ahead American traits." Dom Pedro, whose travels had been closely attended by the press, had endeared himself to Americans with his interest in translating the "Star Spangled Banner" into Portuguese. He had also ordered the abolition of slavery in Brazil.

The arrival of President Grant signaled the orchestra to begin the "Centennial March," a piece which the Women's Centennial Committee had purchased from Richard Wagner for $5,000, followed by a commissioned cantata, Sidney Lanier's "Centennial Meditation of Columbia," and a hymn, whose words were written by John Greenleaf Whittier. The Exhibit, with its galleries, its statues (the hand and torch of the unfinished Statue of Liberty was a major attraction), its exhibits of inventions, machinery, furniture, publications (the Newspaper Pavilion had 10,000 up-to-date newspapers, each in its own pigeon hole, for visitors to read), its historical artifacts, commercial displays, concessions and spectacles was a microcosm of American achievements—gaudy, good natured, diverse and even disorganized, always hopeful, never accepting the limitations of the present. The chief symbol of the Centennial was in the great Machinery Hall. When President Grant and Dom Pedro entered it on the first day there, spread over fourteen acres, were silent machines—machines to saw logs, machines to spin cotton, machines to print newspapers—hundreds of different

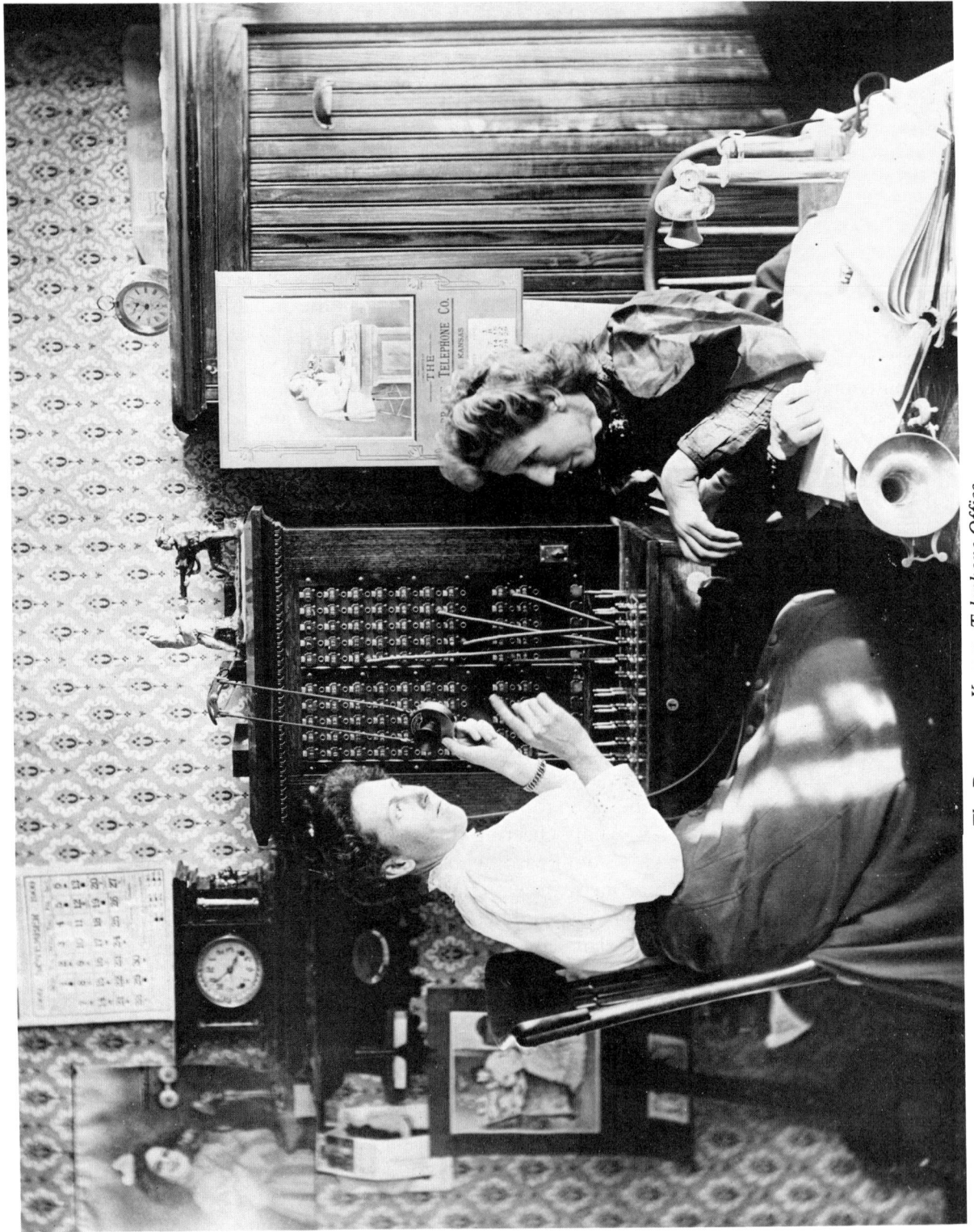

The Dorrance, Kansas, Telephone Office.
(Kansas State Historical Society, Topeka, Kansas.)

THE IRONIES OF INDUSTRIALISM

kinds waiting to drive the nation into a glorious commercial future. At the center of the hall stood the giant Corliss engine: forty feet high, 700 tons, capable of generating 2500 horsepower. The Emperor and the President each turned a lever at the bottom of the vast machine, a hiss of steam escaped, the giant beams of the engine began to rise and fall, and as this power was transmitted over thousands of shafts, belts, pulleys, and gears, all fourteen acres of machinery leapt into life at once. Foreign visitors recognized that the United States was now the world leader in machinery and invention. American commentators waxed rapsodic: "Nowhere else are the triumphs of ingenuity, the marvels of skill, and invention so displayed," affirmed the *Atlantic Monthly*. "Surely here, and not in literature, science or art, is the true evidence of man's creative powers. Here is Prometheus unbound." To author William Dean Howells, the Corliss engine held the promise of future cultural renaissance: "by and by the inspired marbles, the breathing canvases, the great literature; for the present America is voluble in the strong metals and their infinite uses."

Few would have linked the gigantic Corliss engine to the issue of rights for women, but a few determined women saw the obvious connection: that replacing brawn with steam should open the workplace to women. The Women's Centennial Committee, headed by Mrs. Elizabeth Duane Gillespie, an energetic great-granddaughter of Benjamin Franklin, organized subcommitteees in every state which raised money for a Women's Pavilion run completely by displaying only the achievements of women. The Empress Teresa, Dom Pedro's wife, opened the Pavilion on May 10, doing the honors much as her husband had done in Machinery Hall. She pulled a golden cord which started a six-horsepower steam engine that ran all the spinning frames and looms on which were displayed the work of female artisans, as well as a printing press which turned out a magazine, written, edited, printed, and published by women, *The New Century for Women*. The steam engine had posed a problem: Mrs. Gillespie had scoured the country in search of a woman who knew how to run a steam engine, finally having to import from Canada Emma Allison, "an educated and accomplished lady" who became one of the stars of the fair. Operating a steam engine, she assured countless audiences, was far less complicated than caring for a child. The Women's Pavilion was one of the great successes of the Exhibition and contributed to the activism for women's rights that marked the year of the century.

While it did not compete for the public's heart with Emma Allison or the arms and torch of the Statue of Liberty, the competition among inventions for Exhibition awards in June produced perhaps the most lasting legacy of the Centennial Exhibition. A reluctant Alexander Graham Bell, who felt that he should stay in Boston where he had examinations to grade and a speech course to finish teaching, reluctantly took the train to Philadelphia to display his recent not yet patented "invention in embryo," the "speaking telephone." On a Sunday when the exhibits were closed and sounds could, therefore, be carefully tested, the ubiquitous Dom Pedro and nearly fifty scientists trudged from exhibit to exhibit. Late in the afternoon, they lingered long over the display of one of Bell's competitors in the race to perfect the electronic transmission of sound. Bell thought they would have ceased their labors for the day if not for the personal interest of the Emperor, who had met Bell in Boston and was impressed by his work with the deaf. While at the Little Big Horn River in Wyoming on June 25, 1876, Chief Sitting Bull and 5,000 braves were destroying the army of General Custer, Dom Pedro and the other judges listened to Bell's voice over the wires from across the long gallery asking "Do you understand what I say!" then declaiming the "To be or not to be" soliloquy from *Hamlet*. "I hear, I hear!" shouted the excited Emperor who then raced across the gallery at a very un-emperor-like-gait to congratulate the inventor. The Centennial Exhibit had indeed been a total success, not only celebrating the Republic's one hundred years of difficult survival, but heralding many of the themes of its future.

The Great Surge

In the half century between the Civil War and World War I the United States became the world's largest industrial power. In 1860 America was already a rich nation relative to almost all the others, but its prosperity largely depended on the output of its bounteous fields, forests, and mines. Pre-Civil War Americans had lived well as a result of cheap food, lumber, and fuel. Many of the manufactured items they used came from abroad, paid for by cotton from the South, gold from California, and the shipping services of the efficient American merchant marine. Not that the extractive industries alone accounted for the high American standard of living. The textile industry of the Northeast, iron manufacturing in Pennsylvania and Ohio, flour mills along the Delaware and on the Chesapeake, and shipbuilding along the New England and Middle Atlantic coast also contributed to American incomes. But as of 1860, the United States was still primarily a producer of food and raw materials for its own people and for consumers elsewhere in the Atlantic world.

By 1910 the American economy had been transformed. In the fifty years between the eighth census (1860) and the twelfth (1910), the country's population soared from 31.5 million to 92.4 million, an increase of almost three times. During these same years the gross national product (GNP), representing the dollar value of all the goods and services produced each year, had leaped from about $7 billion to over $35 billion. This meant an average increase in output from $150 to about $380 for every adult and child in the nation. Other western countries also registered large gains in total and per capita GNP in these years, but none at so fast a rate.

Much of the surge in wealth production came from factories, mines, and mills. But it would be a mistake to ignore agriculture's contribution to American growth. In 1860 the total value of all farm products was about $1.5 billion. In 1919 it reached $7.5 billion. Clearly, American agriculture was highly productive and capable of meeting the expanding needs of consumers at home and

around the world. Yet as a proportion of all economic output it had declined from well over a quarter to about seventeen percent. Meanwhile, manufacturing and mining had come to dominate the American economy.

The advance of industry was spectacular in the half century following the Civil War. In 1864 the United States produced 872,000 tons of iron and steel; in 1919, over 24 million tons. Coal production exploded from about 20 million tons in 1860 to 500 million in 1910. Lumber output at 12.7 billion board feet in 1869, reached over 40 billion by 1910. In 1860 the United States produced 40 million barrels of flour; in 1910, 107 million. In 1860 some 845,000 bales of cotton were used to produce cloth in the United States. In 1910 the total amount was 4.8 million bales. Petroleum output went from half a million barrels in 1860 to 209 million in 1910.

Americans who lived through the half century of growth did not need to see figures and graphs to understand what had taken place. Everywhere the country displayed the signs of the change. Lying over the Lehigh Valley of eastern Pennsylvania, the Mahoning Valley of eastern Ohio, the Ohio Valley at Pittsburgh, layers of smog covered the steel and glass mills. Everywhere new cities and towns appeared to shelter people at the newly opened mines and mills. Not only did the new industrial economy leave its mark on the Northeastern quarter of the country; it could also be observed in the West and even the South. During the 1880's, Marcus Daly, head of the Anaconda Copper Company, turned a railroad construction camp into the major mining and copper-refining center of Butte, Montana. In northern Alabama by the 1890's the largest town was Birmingham, a community of 26,000, which twenty years earlier had been an empty cornfield. In almost any community in the country, outside the most rural and isolated portions, time was marked off by the blast of factory whistles summoning employees to work early in the morning and signaling an end to the day as darkness fell.

The Railroads

Much of the economic expansion of these years depended on the railroads, which knitted together the nation. In 1860 the network was already exten-

sive, measuring over 30,000 miles. But it did not yet constitute a complete system. There was little mileage beyond the Mississippi, and none beyond the Missouri. The South had a decent amount of track, but it was in short stretches, not tied up with major through routes and connected at only a few points with northern lines. The country had hundreds of different railroad companies and several distinct rail gauges that required unloading of freight and reloading on different boxcars. It is not surprising that in 1860 movement of freight and people was still slow, difficult, and relatively expensive. The railroads were inadequate for the development of national markets. Manufacturers and other producers of commodities could not reach out to customers across the country. Nor could they draw on distant raw materials. The cost and uncertainties of shipment were simply too great, and local firms could count on keeping their business even though they were neither cheap nor efficient. Around each local population center

there remained a ring of small producers providing goods for the neighborhood on a small scale—and often at a high price.

Many Americans were conscious of the deficiencies of the country's rail network and sought to overcome them. In the better settled parts of the country it was only a matter of time. There traffic was potentially heavy and private capital was readily forthcoming, though even in the populous Northeast railroad promoters often raised funds by promising local communities rail connections if they would lend the promoters money or provide other bonuses. In newer areas the hurdles were greater. Railroads across empty country could be justified on the ground of society's overall need, but not on the basis of immediate profit to investors. It might be highly desirable, for example, to connect California with the rest of the nation,

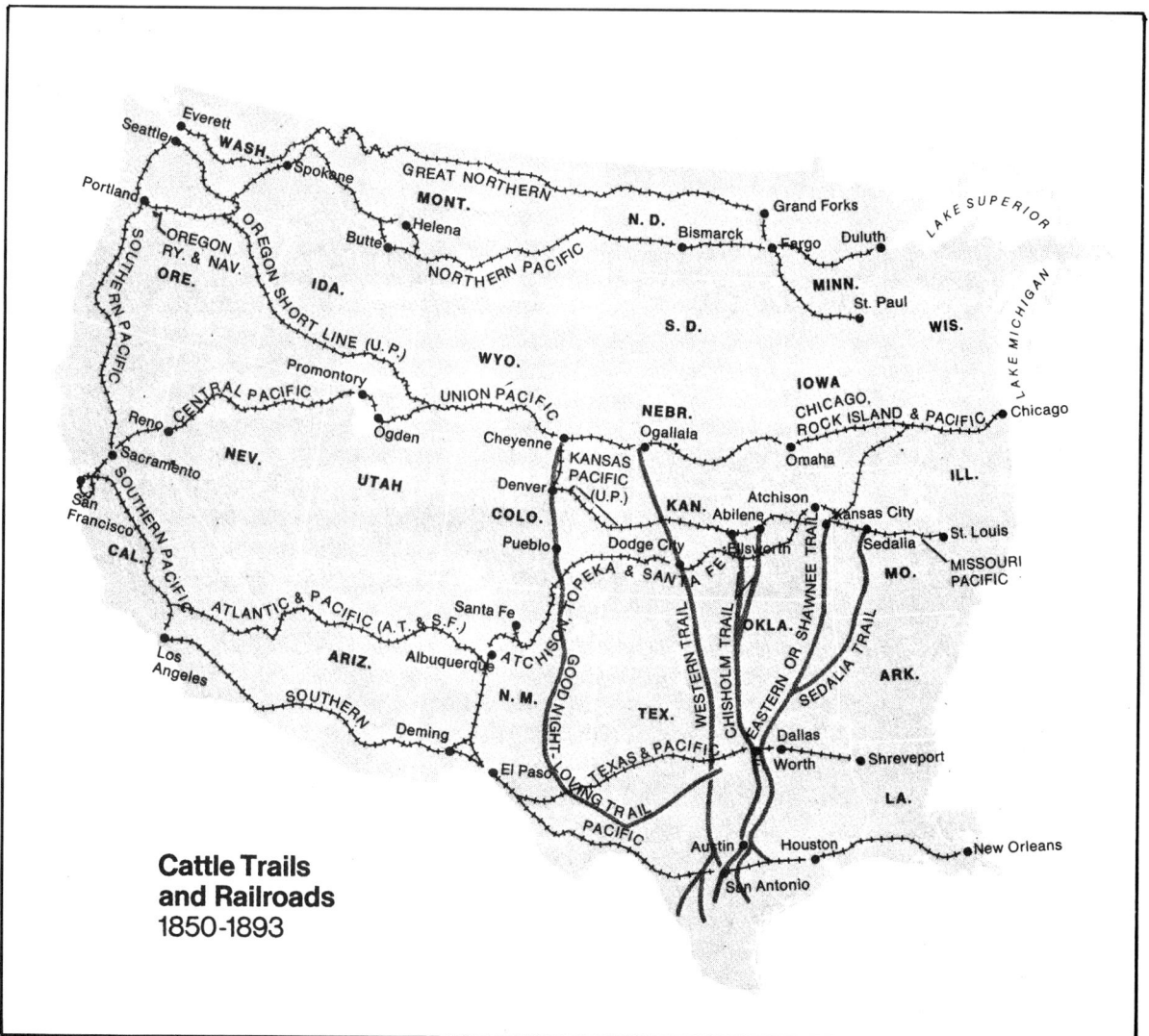

Cattle Trails and Railroads 1850-1893

Why Was Ice-Making an Important Industry? (National Archives.)

THE IRONIES OF INDUSTRIALISM

but who or what would travel the road during the years when it was being constructed? There were neither cities nor farms along most of the route to generate traffic and revenues. And then, even when the railroad was finished, how much through traffic could be expected? Eventually, no doubt, the railroad would create its own business by opening up the country. But that might take years and meanwhile what would the investors do for dividends?

It seemed clear to many Americans that if the country was to have railroads connecting the settled portions of the East with the West Coast it would have to be willing to pay for them in some fashion; private capital alone would not do the job. For a decade or more before 1860, businessmen, journalists, and politicians had debated how to finance a Pacific railroad. Following a practice of land grants that went back as far as the Land Ordinance of 1785, the federal government in 1850 had transferred several million acres of the vast public domain to promoters who promised to build a railroad connecting the Great Lakes with the Gulf of Mexico. During the years of sectional conflict preceding 1860 this policy could not be applied to a road that would tie the settled portions of the United States to the Pacific coast. Northerners and Southerners agreed on the need for such a road, but they fought furiously over whether the route should be a southern, a central, or a northern one. Not until the South left the Union was the issue settled by the Pacific Railroad bill of 1862.

The Union Pacific-Central Pacific was the first of the "transcontinentals" subsidized by federal land grants. In 1864 Congress chartered the Northern Pacific Railroad and gave it an even larger land grant but no cash loan. Another road, later to become the Atchison, Topeka, and Sante Fe, also received a land grant as did a far south route that eventually received the name the Southern Pacific. In all, Congress handed out over 131 million acres of federal land to railroad promoters, while the states gave an additional 49 million acres. The total was finally as large an area as the state of Texas.

In later years, many Americans would harshly criticize the railroad land grant policy as a colossal give-away to powerful interests which benefited a few at the expense of the many. Agrarians would claim it had deprived American farmers of vast expanses of land that might have helped preserve the family farm. Other critics would charge that the railroad promoters had made vast fortunes by seizing the common heritage of all Americans.

There can be no doubt that aggressive promoters were eager to get government land and were not always scrupulous about the methods they employed to win the favor of congressmen and legislators. It is also true that some of the promoters made large profits out of the land they received. We should remember, however, how serious were the risks of building railroads across wildernesses in advance of settlement—and for the purpose of encouraging that settlement. And in most cases the government received cheap rates for shipping its own freight over the transcontinentals, a boon that saved millions of federal dollars in the long run. It also gained by the rising value of federal land adjacent to the railroads. Finally, it is a mistake to assume that the railroads held back much land from farmers. On the contrary, they were anxious to sell it to settlers, both to raise cash and to generate traffic, and carried out large scale "colonization" operations. Each of the Pacific roads set up a department that sold land to settlers at from two to eight dollars an acre, often arranging credit and providing free transportation for prospective customers. Each also maintained a Bureau of Immigration that did advertising in Europe and the eastern United States promoting the state's lands.

Between the end of the Civil War and 1910, the country increased its railroad main trackage to 240,000 miles, eight times the 1865 total. Innumerable crossroad hamlets had their spurs connecting them to the major commercial trading and manufacturing centers of the nation and the major ports of the world. By 1910 almost every American farm was within convenient wagon distance of some railroad depot and thence connected to the world's markets. Railway roadbeds were improved, steel rails substituted for iron, and iron locomotives made larger and more efficient. In 1886 the last company shifted to the standard gauge of $4'8\frac{1}{2}''$. Thereafter freight and passengers could be sent long distances over several companies' trackage without interruption. The completion of the railroad network helped to create a national market. Now for the first time manufacturers could locate their plant almost anywhere within broad limits and be assured that they could bring in raw materials cheaply and send their finished products wherever they could find customers. Every region of the country could specialize in crops best suited to its climate and supply consumers with food at lower prices than their own neighborhoods could. These changes help to explain the rising GNP of these years.

Haying. (Library of Congress.)

THE IRONIES OF INDUSTRIALISM

Government and Agriculture

The government's role in the economy during these years was not confined to transportation. The federal government also sought to encourage agriculture in various ways.

Here, as in transportation, the Civil War served as a watershed. In 1862 Congress created the United States Department of Agriculture as a separate, non-cabinet division within the federal government. In 1889 the Commissioner of Agriculture was made a regular member of the Cabinet. By this time the department's budget had reached $1 million annually. Also in 1862, Congress passed the Morrill Land-Grant College Act, donating thirty thousand acres of federal land to each state for each senator and representative it had in Congress. This land was to be used to support at least one agricultural college in the state, although ultimately the new schools also taught engineering and a multitude of other subjects as well.

Under the Morrill Act some sixty-nine land-grant colleges were established. Where the states managed their land allotment well, choosing public lands shrewdly and selling it at a good price, the institutions were often strong ones; where the fund was mismanaged, they were weak. By the 1890's, however, there was a flock of state "agricultural and mechanical" colleges which taught animal husbandry, horticulture, agricultural chemistry, entomology, and other courses designed to train farmers in scientific techniques. In addition, many of these institutions maintained laboratories and experimental farms where their faculties sought to develop new fertilizers, new plant and animal strains, and new ways of dealing with plant and animal diseases.

This agricultural "research and development" was further encouraged by another federal measure: the Hatch Act of 1887. This law appropriated to each state $15,000 a year from public land sales for the establishment of an experiment station. By 1899 there were fifty-six such stations, in every state and territory, receiving overall more than a million dollars a year to try out new crops, new fertilizers, and new plowing, harvesting, and tillage techniques.

Federal aid was by no means the only element in agricultural progress in these years. Besides the railroads, there were also the agricultural editors whose state and regional agricultural journals encouraged farmers to be good businessmen, bold innovators, and careful cultivators. Still another group whose efforts encouraged agricultural advance were the inventors and farm equipment manufacturers, such as Cyrus McCormick and the Marsh brothers (harvesters), James Oliver (the chilled-iron plow), James Buchanan (the threshing machine), Manly Miles (the silo), and S.M. Babcock (the cream tester). Finally, there was the farmer himself. Oriented toward profits, relatively well educated, largely unsentimental about his occupation, the typical American farmer was quick to adopt new techniques and methods. Still, the federal role was of great importance in producing the miracle of productivity that characterized the nation's agriculture in the generation following the Civil War.

The extent of the miracle was immensely impressive. Between 1866 and 1900 the number of American farms increased from 2.6 million to 5.4 million, and total farm acreage between 1870 and 1900 from 493 million acres to 839 million acres. Cattle on American farms leaped from 24 million head in 1870 to 52 million in 1900. Cotton output, some 2.1 million bales in 1866, reached 11.2 million in 1898; wheat, at 152 million bushels in 1866, went to 675 million in 1898; corn production shot up from 731 million bushels in 1866 to 2.6 billion bushels in 1900. By the end of the nineteenth century, the United States was not only a dynamo of industry but also an agricultural powerhouse, producing vast amounts of grain, meat, fiber, and other farm products not only for its own growing population, but for a large part of the Atlantic world besides. Although we think of American economic growth after the Civil War as largely an industrial event, we must not forget that without the corresponding boom in agriculture the economic achievements of this period would have been far less impressive.

Industry

While new transporation facilities were creating a single national market, that market was being rapidly supplied with the products of the nation's burgeoning factories. In 1859 there were 140,000 establishments that had any claim to the label "factory." Most of these were tiny undertakings with one owner and four or five "hands." In 1914 there were 268,000 factories, many of them being large firms with scores of employees.

If any industry seems characteristic of the great economic surge following the Civil War, it is steel. Before the Civil War steel was an expensive material, produced in small amounts by hand labor and used largely for knives, razors, swords, and springs. Iron came in two forms. Cast iron could be poured into molds, but the large amounts of dissolved carbon it contained made it brittle; wrought iron, containing little carbon, was soft and ductile, and used largely for ornamental shapes, nails, and horseshoes. Neither of these forms of iron was very useful in construction where great strength and ability to take shock were vital. As a consequence Americans built their bridges, public buildings, factories, and ships of wood, brick, or stone. Even machinery in these years used much wood.

During this time two new processes appeared— the Bessemer and the open-hearth—that revolutionized the production of steel. Both removed the right amount of dissolved carbon in cast iron to create a form of steel with great strength. Unlike previous steel-making techniques the new methods used little labor for producing large quantities and brought down the price of steel. Suddenly it became possible to use steel in place of wood, brick, or inferior iron, with tremendous gains in strength, durability, costs. The first great use of the new cheap steel was in rails, where it resulted in increases in safety, durability, load-carrying capacity. Before long, the use of steel spread widely. The first steel bridges came in the 1870's. Steel soon became common for ocean-going vessels, and was the foundation for the giant passenger liners of 20,000 tons or more that plied the Atlantic by the end of the century. In the construction industry steel made possible the skyscraper, a building constructed around a light but strong metal frame that could soar many stories from the street without the thick, space-wasting walls formerly necessary for tall structures.

The steel industry's expansion in the fifty years following 1865 was phenomenal. In 1860 the United States produced 13,000 tons of steel. By 1879 American furnaces were turning out over a million tons a year. By 1910 the United States was making over 28 million tons, and was by far the largest producer of steel in the world.

No one individual can be given credit for this extraordinary transformation. If we can link any single name to the process, it is that of Andrew Carnegie.

Carnegie was not a typical business leader of this period. Historians who have looked into the social origins of late nineteenth-century businessmen have concluded that they generally came from native-born elite backgrounds and had received excellent educations for the day. Carnegie, however, was born of working class parents in Scotland and came to the United States with his family as a thirteen-year-old lad in 1848. In Pittsburgh, where the Carnegies settled, Andrew started at the bottom as a $1.20 a week helper in a textile factory. He quickly moved on to a telegraph office and then, during the Civil War, became a manager with the Pennsylvania Railroad. Wherever he worked the sprightly lad impressed his employers with his energy, intelligence and enterprise, and they consistently pushed him ahead and let him in on opportunities. Gradually, as he accumulated money, he invested it in various new enterprises including oil refining, pullman cars, and a company that built iron bridges. In 1872, Carnegie, by now thoroughly familiar with the processes of business and finance, organized the Union Mills to manufacture Bessemer steel.

Neither an inventor nor a gifted financier, Carnegie never really understood the chemistry of iron and steel. Nor did he ever engage in any of those elaborate stock deals that helped enrich speculators such as Jay Gould and James Fisk. Carnegie's chief talents in steel-making were in choosing competent subordinates who knew their jobs well and in ruthlessly cutting costs by the elimination of bottlenecks and by the running of all equipment full blast even if this meant replacing it early. While others were cutting back on costs during the depression that began in 1873, Carnegie was taking advantage of the cheapness of equipment and improving his plant. His business skill above all was that of a cost accountant who examined every expense to see whether it was needed or could be done without.

Of course Carnegie was riding the wave of economic expansion that each year created ever greater need for cheap steel. Still, he forged far ahead of all other steel producers. By the beginning of the twentieth century the Carnegie works in the Pittsburgh area were producing 700,000 tons of steel a year, more than all of Great Britain. In 1895 the Carnegie Company earned a profit of $5 million; in 1900 it took in $40 million. Since Carnegie owned by far the largest share of the firm, most of this went into his own pocket.

The production of steel is an example of a good producer's industry—that is, an industry that manufactures a product used by other businessmen rather than by the public directly. Many other fast growing industries in these years belong in the same category: coal mining, copper smelting, cement manufacture. Other great industries supplied

Bessemer Steel Being Made in Pittsburgh. (Library of Congress.)

consumers with goods or commodities. An outstanding instance was meatpacking.

Before the railroad age most Americans consumed beef and pork that they raised for themselves or, if they lived in towns, came from animals slaughtered in the immediate neighborhood. The advent of cheap fast transportation changed this arrangement. Gustavus Swift saw that the railroads offered an opportunity to center slaughtering operations in one place, preferably close to cheap corn and grass, and distribute meat nationally. Live cattle had been sent to eastern consumers from western grasslands and the corn belt for years, but live animals did not travel well. Swift's idea was to slaughter cattle in Chicago and ship the trimmed carcasses to Eastern distributors. Freight costs would be lower, the slaughtering process would be cheapened, and with vast herds disposed of in one spot, by-products such as bristle, bone, hides, and fertilizer could be used profitably. For a while the scheme worked only in the winter months, when the cold reduced spoilage. But by 1880 the refrigerator made it possible to ship beef- and hog-carcasses all year round. By 1890 the Chicago packers were shipping a million trimmed sides of beef a year.

Retailing

In the early nineteenth century when most Americans lived in villages and on farms, they bought either from traveling peddlars or from general stores those goods they did not produce for themselves. The general store, in turn, received agricultural commodities from the surrounding farmers often in exchange for other goods. A farmer's wife, for example, who wanted a bolt of cloth would pay the merchant with a few dozen eggs or several wheels of cheese if she did not have the cash. Most of the local merchant's goods, especially his tropical products and manufactured items, however, came from the merchants of the big coastal cities who imported them from the Caribbean or from England and France. To stock their shelves, country merchants treked annually to the big port towns—New York, Boston, Charleston, Philadelphia, Baltimore, or New Orleans—to visit the warehouses of the large importers and buy on credit. The general store sold almost everything: silk ribbon, needles, hammers, nails, gunpowder and lead shot, flour, tea and coffee, yarn and cloth, candy, eggs, sides of bacon, pickled fish, books, and whiskey. These items were seldom packaged. Except for patent medicines, already being packaged in colorfully labeled bottles and jars, they were placed in barrels or bins and sold by weight or volume. Generally they were carried away in the customer's own container. Prices were not necessarily uniform. Customers bargained with the storekeeper. They often received credit; they often paid in commodities.

The development of manufacturing altered this pattern in several ways. As more and more of the finished goods that consumers bought were produced in the United States, importers became less important to local retailers; they turned instead to wholesalers who bought up the output of home factories. Located in the larger inland cities as well as on the East Coast, these wholesalers dealt either in a number of items or in some "full line" such as hardware or "drygoods." In the growing cities and towns more and more general merchants began to specialize in selling specific products such as hats, shoes, or books, though general stores continued in smaller communities until the twentieth century.

During the years following the Civil War new kinds of retail outlets, the chain store, the mail-order house, and the department store, revolutionized the merchandizing of goods to consumers. Actually the department store first made its appearance in the 1840's when a few American merchants began to imitate a Paris institution, the Bon Marché, which combined a number of distinct specialty shops all under one roof. The first great American department store magnate, A. T. Stewart of New York, was followed soon after by John Wanamaker of Philadelphia. As these stores grew in size it became impossible for owners to bargain with customers over prices. Since an owner did not care to delegate the responsibility to a clerk, the one-price-only became the normal practice. First adopted by R. H. Macy's in New York, it quickly became standard for department stores and then for most other retail establishments.

The one price policy was not the only innovation of the department store magnates. Selling goods on such a large scale, the big stores could exert an enormous amount of market leverage. Rather than dealing with wholesalers, they could

The New Architecture. (Buffalo office building)

go directly to the manufacturers and so were able to bypass a whole layer of middlemen. By promising large volume orders, they could also compel manufacturers to give them good prices for their products. Another advantage of the department store was its range of services. It delivered purchases to customers and it guaranteed quality. At what later became Marshall Field, Potter Palmer, the manager, was willing to accept returns from dissatisfied customers. "Your money back if . . . " became one of the Chicago store's mottos.

Department stores soon sprouted in major cities all over the country. New York had A. T. Stewart and Macy's, the largest store in the world under one roof, as well as a flock of others. Philadelphia had Wanamaker's and Gimbel's. In Boston there was Jordan Marsh and Filene's. Chicagoans shopped at Marshall Field and Company and Carson, Price, Scott. In Columbus the big store was Lazarus; in Dallas, Neiman-Marcus; in Los Angeles, Bullock's; in Brooklyn, Abraham and Straus. Many of the department store owners were either New England Yankees or German-Jewish merchants who had begun as peddlers or small shopkeepers before the Civil War and carried their marketing skills over to the new form when it appeared.

Along with the department store came the chain store. These establishments flourished especially in the grocery and "variety" trades, of which the A & P (the Great Atlantic and Pacific Tea Company) and the Woolworth "five and ten" were the prototypes. Each store in a "chain" was expected to make a profit by itself, but all were tied together by management and accounting. Still more significant from the consumers' viewpoint was that the chains, like the department stores, could also buy cheaply from suppliers. They refused credit, selling for cash only on a one price basis. The effect was to cut prices to the consumer. This made customers happy but displeased small storekeepers who charged that the chains engaged in "unfair" competition. Appealing to traditional American sympathies, store owners also noted that the chain outlets were owned by "absentees" not like the local people who operated the small "ma and pa" store. The protests did little good. By the time of World War I the chain store had become an established feature of American economic life.

So had the mail order house. Unlike chain stores and department stores, the mail order or "catalogue house" catered largely to a rural or small-town clientele. Like the other two forms, it sought to replace the middleman, in this case by selling goods ordered from a catalog. As Aaron Montgomery Ward, the first great mail order magnate, expressed it: "Having had experience in all classes of merchandise, and traveling salesman, and a fair judge of human nature, I saw a great opening for a house to sell direct to the consumer and save them the profit of the middleman." Looking to the Grangers, a rural movement that had as one of its objectives the reform of an economic system that forced farmers to buy from middlemen, Ward advertised his firm as "The Original Granger Supply House." By the 1890's the Montgomery Ward catalog contained 24,000 items.

Ward's success owed not just to his shrewd judgment of customers and the hostility of farmers to middlemen. He, and his arch rival, the firm of R. W. Sears and A. C. Roebuck, also benefited from the transportation revolution. By the end of the century a quickening of railroad traffic had improved postal services immensely, and within a few years "rural free delivery" was bringing letters and packages to the farmer's front door, and he no longer had to go to the village post office to get his Montgomery-Ward or Sears-Roebuck winter underwear, kerosene lamp, shovel, or hat.

Money, Banking, and Finance

All the business of the nation, whether manufacturing, wholesaling, or retailing, rode on a sea of money and credit supplied either by the federal government or by the private banking system. In this era the system of money and credit was a complex structure that aroused controversy not only among businessmen and financial experts, but also among politicians and ordinary citizens. At times it became the focus of fierce and raucous political debate.

Many of the financial issues of the Gilded Age were related to the Civil War. The war had forced the Union government to issue almost a half billion dollars worth of greenbacks, paper money which the government made a legal tender for all debts. It had also sold many hundreds of millions of dollars worth of bonds. Linked to the bonds was a new banking system. Promoters of a new "national bank" had to deposit bonds with the federal Comptrollers of the Currency, who would then issue bank notes to the extent of ninety percent of the value of the bonds. These bank notes entered general circulation when the banks lent money to borrowers, and, along with the greenbacks, they became the paper money that Americans used until 1913. The system, though an improvement over the chaotic banking structure prevailing from 1836 to 1863, had many drawbacks.

One of its failings was that the supply of currency did not grow fast enough to meet the needs of the nation's expanding economy. The system also failed to establish a central bank that could come to the rescue of hardpressed financial institutions in time of panic when money went into hiding. Agrarians particularly objected to the provision of the national banking acts that forbade the federally chartered banks to lend on mortgage security. There was a parallel state banking system, and during these years it expanded primarily to fill rural needs, but it never could fully meet the farmers' demands for abundant cheap credit on the security of their lands.

The very existence of the bonds and greenbacks made for controversy. Advocates of "sound money"—especially bankers, merchants, and conservatives—wanted to see the greenbacks withdrawn from circulation. They also insisted that the bonds be repaid in gold, as they claimed the government had promised. These were the "sound" and "honest" things to do and were essential to confidence and to financial stability. "Soft money" partisans—identified immediately after the war with some manufacturers, farmers, and other groups of "producers"—were opposed to retiring the greenbacks; hard money could bring sharp deflation and loss of profits as well as compelling debtors to pay back in hard dollars more valuable than the soft dollars they had borrowed.

Some partisans of soft currency insisted that the greenback issue be actually enlarged. This scheme, called the "Ohio Idea" because its champion was the Ohio Democratic Senator George Pendleton, became a major issue between the parties shortly after 1865. In later years the idea of increasing greenbacks became the basis of a political movement to expand the country's money supply. During the 1870's and 1880's various greenback parties fought for soft money as debtor relief and for general programs of aid to wage earners.

Meanwhile, still another sound money-soft money battleground emerged when, in the mid-1870's, a group of politicians and publicists discovered that the nation's "producers," as radicals defined farmers and workers, had been deprived of relief when Congress demonetized the old silver dollar. Calling the action of Congress the "Crime of '73," they insisted that it had been a plot by bankers and other capitalists to contract the currency further for the purpose of depressing prices and raising interest rates. Then in 1879 the treasury returned to the gold standard after the eighteen year lapse brought on by the Civil War. This meant that all paper money would now have gold as its backing. Unless the nation restored silver to the money supply at the ratio of sixteen ounces of silver to one of gold, argued the soft money people, the country's growth and prosperity would be at the mercy of the bankers, especially those with international connections. Deflation would continue, laborers and farmers would be hurt, and only the plutocrats would benefit. On the anti-silver side were the "gold bugs," as their enemies called them, who believed that the international gold standard was necessary for business confidence and sound international trade. Some gold bugs went far beyond this: the gold standard was the very basis of civilization.

The struggle between the two groups see-sawed back and forth. In 1878 the silverites got Congress to pass the Bland-Allison Silver Purchase Act requiring the treasury to buy between $2 million and $4 million of silver on the open market and coin this bullion into dollars. The adding of silver to greenbacks and national banknotes, the advocates of this measure hoped, would not only give the country some needed immediate monetary relief, but make it impossible to uphold the gold standard, since the amount of currency would be too great to be redeemable in gold. But the treasury had a large enough gold reserve to treat the new silver dollars as just another kind of paper money. Any one who wished might come to the banks and get a gold dollar for a silver one in the same manner as bank notes. In 1890 came the Sherman Silver Purchase Act requiring the treasury to purchase 4½ million ounces of silver each month and to issue new paper money against it redeemable in either gold or silver. Once more the sound money forces in the administration were able to contain their opponents. There the issue rested until the Panic of 1893 produced a great monetary crisis by undermining public confidence in the treasury's reserve and sending thousands to convert their silver and paper into gold coin.

The Investment Bankers

The national and state banks had their failings, but they successfully performed daily business for the nation. In the cities the national banks handled thousands of daily transactions, making business loans, discounting commercial paper for merchants, and transferring funds from place to place. In the small towns and country communities the state banks helped local feed-and-grain merchants, advanced cash to carry farmers over until the time for selling their crops, and lent money on mortages to enable them to buy machinery or build a new barn.

Paralleling these institutions were the investment bankers, who operated on the highest levels of domestic and international finance. These businessmen did not accept deposits and make loans to merchants. Rather, they marketed securities for cities, states, counties, and even the federal government, as well as for large private corporations.

The investment bankers put much of their funds into the stock market, the institution located on Wall Street in lower Manhattan, where securities of all sorts—government and private corporation bonds and corporation stocks—were bought and sold. The New York Stock Exchange was a private body of brokers who managed their affairs like a club, but a loosely run club with scant regard for the public. During the Gilded Age buying and selling securities on the Exchange, especially trading in common stock, resembled the operations of a gambling casino, with "bull" speculators betting on a rise in stock prices and "bear" speculators betting for a fall. Few conservative investors cared to buy the "common stock" traded on Wall Street. The competition of bulls and bears made for wild fluctuation in prices and ownership seldom brought substantial dividends. Too much of the common stock was "water," issue in excess of the real productivity of the companies putting it out, and even the most profitable firm could sel-

dom pay much per share. On the other hand, the stock market provided a fair indirect investment to banks and other financial institutions with some excess funds to invest for short periods. Brokers and stock gamblers could use such money and were willing to pay good rates of interest for it. This created a "call loan" market where money could be lent on a day-to-day basis, subject to instant recall by the lender. The call loan market introduced another element of instability into the country's financial structure. Every fall when money was needed for marketing the country's crops, money left Wall Street to return to the farm areas, and the tightness in the stock market sometimes turned into a panic, as in 1873, 1884, and 1907.

Not until the very end of the nineteenth century did Wall Street become a true money market where people with capital to lend on a long-term basis made deals with those who needed capital for long periods. The enormous expansion of industry after 1865 created great need for billions in capital. Investors were willing to buy corporate bonds since these represented a debt of the firm and had to be paid, interest and principle, before any other obligation even if the firm made no profit in a given year. Useful in marketing these securities were special "investment" bankers who agreed to sell large blocks of bonds, taking a commission for their work. Slowly the public also developed an interest in common stock, especially if it was sold by one of the large investment houses like Kidder, Peabody of Boston, Kuhn, Loeb of New York, and J. P. Morgan and Company. These firms not only stood behind the issues in a general way but also often insisted on putting one of their partners on the corporation's board of directors as insurance to purchasers that the corporation's affairs would be well managed and common stock holders not be defrauded.

Mergers

An increasingly furious battle among firms for customers characterized the last decade of the century. To keep their share of a given business, manufacturers and railroad operators had to cut their prices and costs. This was fine for consumers. In the course of a price war among the

trunk railroads connecting New York to Chicago, the rate for a carload of cattle, normally costing the shipper $110, dropped to one dollar. But competition was hard on businessmen, and numbers of them sought in every way possible to reduce this brutal competition. Often firms in a particular business would arrange informal "gentlemen's agreements" assigning each company a fixed share of the market. This ended any need to cut price in pursuit of a steady business. Pools were similar arrangements but involved an actual written contract among the participants. Both were impossible to enforce. When the agreements fell through, businessmen created other devices for achieving an end to competition. One of these, the "trust," required stockholders of several firms to turn over their voting rights to trustees who thereafter ran the businesses as a unit, paying any dividends to the original shareholders. John D. Rockefeller, in his effort to reduce the competition in the refining business during the early 1880's, was the first to employ the trust scheme. When state and federal courts declared trusts illegal, ingenious businessmen turned to the "holding company." Taking advantage of a New Jersey law of 1889 allowing one corporation to hold stock in others, corporation lawyers arranged for a single large firm (a "holding company") to acquire stock in other, competing ones. The holding company executives, of course, could then decide to limit competition among the firms they controlled in any way they chose.

During the 1870's and 1880's consolidations took place on a wide scale in many consumer goods industries: leather products, salt, sugar, biscuits, starch, kerosene, rubber boots, and gloves. During the depression of the early 1890's the consolidation movement stopped. Then, after 1897 it resumed with a rush, primarily in the producers' or capital goods industries, but also in a few newer consumers' good fields, such as meat and cigarettes, that catered to city people primarily. In the eight years from 1898 through 1905 more than 3,000 important business mergers occurred in industries that included steel, machinery, tobacco, copper, and cans.

In this second wave the role of investment bankers was especially prominent. The holding company that controlled the formerly competing firms had to raise capital to buy up their stock and this meant the services of bankers. The investment bankers were also useful for reassuring stockholders of the individual companies and those with savings to invest that the new firm would be reliable. One of the classic instances of mergers in this era was the formation of the United States Steel Company in 1901.

By the early 1890's, as we have seen, Carnegie had organized a powerful steel firm that was both efficient and profitable. Meanwhile, other steel men were creating parallel firms that unlike the Carnegie Company turned out various finished steel shapes and products. When Carnegie threatened to undertake this kind of work, he frightened his competitors badly. These men turned to J. P. Morgan and asked him to organize a merger that would stop this impending war.

At first Carnegie was reluctant to join the merger, but then he yielded. Since the Homestead Strike of 1892, the "star-spangled Scotsman" had lost much of his zest for business and money-making. He had long dreamed of withdrawing from business and devoting his time to culture and his money to good causes. Here was his chance, and when Morgan offered him the equivalent of almost half a billion dollars, he agreed to the deal. Most of the money was in the form of bonds and stock in the United States Steel Company, a firm organized out of the Carnegie firm and a dozen others with a total capitalization of $1.4 billion. United States Steel at its moment of birth controlled sixty percent of the country's steel business as well as vast reserves of ore and coal, and over a thousand miles of railroad. It was the largest corporation in the world. Carnegie himself enjoyed his money to the full. But not in the usual way. He founded 3,000 public libraries and provided over 4,000 churches with organs. He founded the Carnegie Institute of Technology, built the Peace Palace at the Hague for the International Court of Arbitration, and Carnegie Hall in New York as a showcase for concerts and cultural events. He set aside $125 million for the Carnegie Foundation. When he died he had given away virtually all his Morgan money.

A Business Civilization

Though Carnegie's entrepreneurial role illustrates the ways businessmen contributed to the ever-growing productivity of the country, he was scarcely typical of most Gilded Age businessmen in his economic philosophy. Carnegie believed and acted on the conviction that "he who dies rich, dies disgraced." His attitudes towards labor, too, though not consistent, were probably more generous than those of American business as a whole. Influenced by his chief aide, Captain Billy Jones, and by his own family's politically reformist background, Carnegie sought to be a good employer. He favored good wages and even endorsed labor unions. When the workers in his Connellsville coal mines struck for higher wages in 1887, Carnegie ordered his manager, Henry Frick, to settle on their terms.

Carnegie was a maverick. Other big businessmen despised trade unionism and believed that they alone were the proper judges of labor's well being. When John Mitchell, leader of the anthracite coal strike of 1902, asked George Baer of The Philadelphia and Reading Coal Company to submit the dispute to arbitration, Baer responded: "The rights and interests of the laboring man will be protected and cared for, not by the labor agitators, but by the Christian men to whom God in His infinite wisdom has given control of the property interests of the country, and upon the successful Management of which so much depends." Many businessmen fought to retain control of wages, hours, and working conditions, and refused to share their power with anyone else, whether politicians or labor leaders. The only arrangement they recognized as legitimate was the individual bargain struck with the worker.

The attitude of employers toward unions was at bottom a matter of simple self interest. It also had to do with a more general notion about economics that much of society, and even workers themselves, shared in some measure.

That notion had as one of its components an academic doctrine, the principle of laissez-faire, that came of the teachings of the British thinkers Adam Smith, John Stuart Mill, and David Ricardo. The principle held that the way to get the greatest and cheapest possible productivity was to leave the individual employer and the individual worker to the free market. Any attempt to interfere through unions or through govermental action would distort the market and reduce total production, to the injury of laborers, employers, and consumers. At times laissez-faire thinkers invoked divine sanction for their theories. One economist believed that free markets were governed by "God's laws," and claimed that observing these laws would not only benefit individuals in this life, but prepare them "for the life that is to come."

Ideas such as these had long circulated in the United States. Laissez-faire was the basic economic doctrine of college courses and enjoyed enormous prestige among educated Americans. After about 1870 it had reinforcement from another set of principles, often called Social Darwinism, drawn from the ideas of Charles Darwin, the English naturalist, and elaborated by the English philosopher, Herbert Spencer. Just as Darwin, according to his earliest interpreters, had shown that in the biological world progress from the lowliest creature to man depended on a fierce struggle for survival, so social Darwinists argued that social progress depended on competition in daily life and in the economic arena. To interfere with this struggle in any way would result in the collapse of civilization or, at the very least, in stagnation. When one social disciple of Darwin was asked what he would do to alleviate the economic evils of the day, he replied: "Nothing! You and I can do nothing at all. It's all a matter of evolution. We can only wait for evolution. Perhaps in four or five thousand years evolution may have carried man beyond this state of things. But we can do nothing."

Social Darwinism, in fact, had scant approval, if any, from biologists in its use of theories of evolution; it was a mistaken effort to find similarities between biological events and economic events. Recent scholarship has indicated that not many businessmen took much serious account of the idea, or perceived of a sound economy as being as brutally competitive as social Darwinists would seem to insist. But social Darwinism, along with the more solid free-market doctrines that colleges had been teaching for many years, did represent the dominance in American thinking of the principle of laissez-faire. It had further support from a moral and constitutional conviction that individuals should be free to manage their property as they please and to enter into contracts of their own choosing, and that any major interference on the part of the government in relations between labor and management would violate both the employer's property rights and the right of employer and worker to make a contract.

Whatever sense this concept of free contract might make in a small-town or rural economy, in relations between a shopkeeper and an employee of virtually the same economic class, it was nonsense in an era of giant corporations and great disparities in property. There was no equality between the bargaining position of a coal miner and that of Baer's coal company over the terms of employment, no free contractual agreement between equals; the individual worker was free only to accept the employer's terms or to accept hunger in place of them. The use that conservatives and businessmen made of doctrines of laissez-faire brought other contradictions as well. Critics pointed out that businessmen actually detested

Built in the 1880's, this residence in Portland, Oregon, resembles a gingerbread house.

competition when it threatened profits. "Cut-throat" domestic competition had fueled the merger movement. Afraid to compete with foreign manufacturers, the iron producers, the textile mill owners, the woolen manufacturers, and many others who faced formidable competition from abroad fought for ever higher protective tariffs. In these years Congress often gave in to the pressures of American industrialists and raised tariffs far beyond where they had been before the Civil War. Nor were businessmen averse to direct government subsidies when they could be gotten. Railroad promoters gave no evidence of being troubled that the federal and state policy of making land grants to railroads was contrary to the teaching of laissez-faire.

Despite the inconsistencies, it would be a mistake to dismiss the laissez-faire principle as a rationalization and a sham. Many people are capable of believing two conflicting ideas simultaneously. Ideas, moreover, are not merely rationalizations. They frequently take on a life of their own and become powerful forces. In these years many Americans deeply believed in private property and economic freedom. It was assumed that society was open and allowed for movement upward of the hard-working, the sober, and the able, and that no one need settle permanently for a place in the economic cellar. The story of a boy's odyssey from poverty to riches became an influential genre in the skilled hands of Horatio Alger, a fertile writer who pounded out scores of novels with such titles as *Work and Win, Strive and Succeed, Do and Dare, Sink or Swim, Risen from the Ranks,* and *Facing the World.* Alger's typical hero is a boy of about fifteen, the age for starting life in this period. He possesses all the virtues of honesty, sobriety, willingness to work hard. Ironically, it is not these that make his fortune. The Alger hero succeeds by a stroke of good fortune such as marrying the boss' daughter or coming to the attention of a rich benefactor. But along the way the young male reader was made aware of the great possibilities open to him in America.

Many ordinary Americans had some reason to believe the success story. A common experience among Americans in the years from 1859 to the early part of the twentieth century was the accumulation of some property over an entire working life. Many rose occupationally either in level of skill or from manual to white collar status. Others saw their children move upward.

Another reason that made the nation willing to give business a considerable measure of acceptance on its own terms was the large proportion of Americans who were themselves businessmen of one sort or another. An enormous number of American family heads in this era were farm owners who raised crops for sale. In 1890 there were about 3.3 million of these out of about 13 million families in the country. Add to this another million non-farm business concerns in that same year, mostly small firms, and we have a figure that suggests that about a third of all American families of 1890 made their incomes from producing and selling commodities or services. By 1890 many farmers were becoming skeptical of "big business" views and activities, but on two points they certainly agreed: private property deserved protection from those who would attack it; and there was nothing intrinsically wrong with the profit system.

The attitudes of the Supreme Court in these years reflected and reinforced values favorable to business. The Court in a number of important decisions resisted governmental regulation of economic life.

Such views did not prevail at first. In 1873 a state was sued to have a monopoly grant to a slaughterhouse corporation declared invalid under the Fourteenth Amendment's provision for "equal protection of the law." The purpose of the Amendment, the Court declared upholding the state in the "Slaughterhouse" cases, had been to protect the Negro, not to place the federal government in the position of protecting citizens' property rights against a state legislature. In the more important case of *Munn v. Illinois* (1877) the Supreme Court upheld a law the Illinois legislature had passed to regulate the price charged by grain elevator companies for storing grain. This was one of a flood of laws passed during the 1870s by midwestern states at the behest of the farmer groups called "Grangers" and designed to regulate railroads and middlemen. Chief Justice Morrison Waite, speaking for the Court, declared that in the case of a business "clothed with a public interest," such as the one in question, it was the right of a legislature to protect that public interest. The elevator company could not claim that it was being deprived of its property "without due process of law" under the Fourteenth Amendment. Advocates of laissez-faire attacked Waite's decision as dangerous. Justice Stephen Field declared that the "doctrine announced . . . practically destroys the guarantees of the Constitution intended for the protection of private property."

Then business had its triumphs. In two cases in the mid-1880's the Court virtually deprived the states of all their rights to regulate business firms. In *Santa Clara Co. v. Southern Pacific Railroad* (1886) the Court accepted the view that corporations were legal "persons" and so, like black people, protected by the Fourteenth Amendment against being deprived of property "without due process of law." That same year, in *Wabash, St. Louis & Pacific Railroad Company v. Illinois*, it struck down an Illinois law regulating railroads on the grounds that it infringed on Congress' exclusive right to regulate interstate commerce.

Congress, under pressure from various farmer and merchant groups, rushed to fill the gap created by the *Wabash* case. The result was the Interstate Commerce Act of 1887. This measure declared illegal all rebates—portions of rates returned to the payers—that a railroad might make to its more extensive users; all customers must be charged alike for services. The law made it unlawful for railroads to engage in the practice, common at the time, of charging higher rates for short hauls than for long ones. It outlawed the forming of railroad pools. The Act required that "all charges . . . be reasonable and just." It established a five-member Interstate Commerce Commission that could examine complaints or investigate railroad practices on its own initiative. If the Commission found that a railroad had violated the Act, it could bring the violation before the federal courts and compel the railroad to comply with its ruling.

On the face of it the law seemed an effective assertion of federal power to regulate interstate transportation in the public interest. It was not. Thomas M. Cooley, the first chairman of the I.C.C., was a lawyer who deplored "hostility to railroad management," and believed "antagonism to acquired wealth" to be "dangerous." Under Cooley the I.C.C. took a generous attitude toward the railroads and allowed them more or less to charge what the traffic would bear. It even warned against freight and passenger rates that were too low. When the Commission did attempt to limit what the railroads might charge, the Supreme Court in 1897 in the Maximum Freight Rate Case, declared despite the intent of Congress that the I.C.C. had "no power to prescribe the tariff of rates which shall control in the future."

Responding to widespread public demand that the government intervene to prevent "trusts" and monopolies, Congress in 1890 passed the Sherman Antitrust Act. The measure declared that "every contract, combination in the form of trust or otherwise, or conspiracy, in restraint of trade or commerce among the several States or with foreign nations, is hereby declared to be illegal." A person who violated the Act would be committing a misdemeanor. A human being found guilty would be subject to fine or imprisonment. "Person" within the meaning contemplated by the Act referred also, and more importantly, to corpora-

tions, which by law are definable for some purposes as persons. A guilty corporation might pay a fine and receive an order for the dissolution of the illegal combination. Federal district attorneys could prosecute suspected violators and those wronged by their actions could sue for triple damages.

In the first important anti-trust case brought before it, *United States v. E.C. Knight* (1895), the Supreme Court gutted the Act. The Knight case involved purchases by the American Sugar Refining Company of several refineries in Philadelphia that when added to its existing capacity gave American Sugar control of 98 percent of all American refining. Few monopolies could have been more inclusive. Yet in a decision that dismayed even many lawyers who were partisans of business, the Court declared that sugar refining was manufacturing, not trade or commerce, and was therefore not subject to the Sherman Act. Thereupon, until Theodore Roosevelt and the progressives invoked it in the new century, the law was made inactive as a regulation of business. Meanwhile it was applied vigorously against labor unions on the grounds that strikes were devices to restrain trade. Under this interpretation the courts issued several injunctions to keep labor unions from interfering with business. In the Danbury Hatters Case (1905), the Supreme Court also decided that a labor union could not, under the Sherman Act, initiate a "secondary boycott," that is could not boycott one business to force it to put pressure on another engaged in a labor dispute.

Toward the end of the century an increasing number of state legislatures began to pass laws limiting the working hours of women and children, and of men in unhealthy or dangerous occupations. This represented a new social concern that in the new century would culminate in a mass of "progressive" social legislation. To defenders of laissez-faire, these laws seemed yet another violation of fundamental economic law; and doctrinaire champions of private property thought them an invasion of the rights of employers to control their business. In *Lockner v. New York* (1905) the Supreme Court declared unconstitutional a New York law limiting the hours at which employees in the baking industry could be kept at work. In a famous dissent Associate Justice Oliver Wendell Holmes, Jr., attacked the basis of the majority opinion. The Constitution was "not intended to embody a particular economic theory, whether of paternalism . . . or of *Laissez-faire.*"

Holmes's remarks can be a bit misleading. The Supreme Court did not base its decision—not explicitly, at any rate—on economic doctrines that claim that governmental regulation lessens the productivity of economic processes. It drew rather on the legal doctrine that the act of entering into a contract concerning the conditions of work is a fundamental right—a right that in this case, so the Court believed, the Fourteenth Amendment protected against certain kinds of interference on the part of state governments. Holmes was on strong ground, however, in warning the Court against going beyond its proper role. The real economic world—in which often no actual equality of bargaining power exists between employer and employee and poverty may force people into unhealthy occupations—can make a mockery of such philosophical and constitutional abstractions as the rights of property and the rights of free contract. The Supreme Court had to learn to allow legislatures considerable freedom to look for the real and particular facts of economic life and to make laws accordingly.

In a flock of decisions from 1904 onward the Court did allow the Sherman Act to be a weapon against combinations in restraint of trade. In 1908, in *Muller v. Oregon*, it refused to strike down an Oregon law limiting the working hours of women. Yet despite this moderate change of heart the Supreme Court would remain skeptical of the constitutionality of laws in major regulation of economic activity. Not until well into the New Deal era would it come down with some consistency on the side of public interest as expressed by Congress against the private interest of property holders and business firms.

The City

Besides transforming the incomes and political attitudes of Americans, the rapid growth of industry changed where many of them lived and worked. Between 1860 and 1910 hundreds of thousands of newcomers flocked to the urban centers of the nation. In 1860 over 25 million Americans lived in rural areas compared to 6.2 million in "urban territory," which the Census Bureau defined as communities of 2,500 or more. Urbanites represented only about 20 percent of total American population on the eve of the Civil War. In 1910, 42 million Americans out of 92 million resided in communities that were urban by the government's definition. In 1860 there were no cities of a million, and only two, New York and Philadelphia, with over half a million. By 1910, three American cities had a million people or more, and five additional ones ranked over half a million.

The northern and western Europeans from Britain, Germany, and Scandinavia who came to the United States before the 1880's often settled in rural communities. The Irish did not, but they were in some ways exceptional. The newcomers of the last two decades of the nineteenth century and the early part of the twentieth differed from their predecessors in some ways. These "new immigrants" came largely from southern and eastern Europe. Many were from Italy's depressed south or from Sicily. Others were from lands controlled by Austria, Russia, Turkey, and included thousands of slavic Poles, Croatians, Bohemians, and Serbs, as well as non-slavic Greeks and Jews.

Besides the crowds that crossed the Atlantic, there were the thousands who crossed the continental borders from Canada and Mexico. Many of the new arrivals were peasants, and we might expect them to be drawn to the land. But circumstances had changed since the 1840's and 1850's. Land prices had risen and farm prices fallen, and American agriculture was less attractive to newcomers. After 1880, more and more of the immigrants settled in cities to work as wage earners in factories.

Native Americans from the nation's farms were going to the towns and cities. Some Americans in these years sentimentalized farm life. But to young people, particularly, the farmer's lot seemed a hard one and farm life drab and cramped. When the parents of Hamlin Garland, the novelist, returned from an Iowa village to live again on a farm, their two sons were bitterly disappointed. They despised the "ugly little farmhouse" and the "filthy drudgery of the farmyard" and yearned for the "care-free companionable existence" of town. Girls and young women found the routine and labor of farm life particularly grim and the pull of towns and cities especially powerful. Writing in *Good Housekeeping* just before World War I, a journalist remarked on how many young women "were pining for neighbors, for domestic help, for pretty clothes, for schools, music, art, and the things tasted when the magazines came in."

These two human streams, one from abroad, one from the rural areas of the nation, converged on the towns, villages, and cities in record numbers in these years. There they were joined by the natural increase of the city population itself to make for an urban swell of huge proportions.

By the standards of the great European capitals, the American cities of this period were disappointing. Few places, not even Washington until the twentieth century, could boast the monuments, the boulevards, the imperial buildings of Berlin, Paris, Vienna, St. Petersburg, or London. Too many were dominated by commercial structures. Their streets were jammed with horsedrawn wagons and carriages, and with people pushing carts and wheelbarrows. Overhead the sky was often virtually blocked out by a tangle of wires for the city's telephone and telegraph messages. There were few trees or parks. The needs of commerce had won out over beauty and amenities, and almost all public land had been sold off for housing or commercial "blocks." A few cities, notably New York, Boston, Washington, San Francisco, and New Orleans, had some individuality, but virtually all the others seemed to be built on a uniform monotonous plan of right-angle streets, with dreary stores and shops and utilitarian hotels.

Worse still was the level of sanitation and housing that newcomers experienced. By the 1870's a few of the largest American cities had installed underground sewers. But many still used privies and cesspools that had to be periodically cleaned out. In 1877 Philadelphia had 82,000 of these, and Washington, D.C., was not far behind. In some cities, notably Baltimore, New Orleans, and Mobile, sewage was actually allowed to run through open gutters. And even communities with better sewage collection facilities spilled their waste in the surrounding waters. Boston Harbor was "one vast cesspool, a threat to all the towns it washed." Nor were garbage disposal arrangements much better. Port cities usually dumped their garbage at sea, hoping it would not return at the next tide. Inland communities sold local farmers organic garbage for feeding to hogs. The result was a high incidence of trichinosis among swine and also among human beings who ate undercooked pork.

During the 1860's and 1870's Louis Pasteur in France, Robert Koch in Germany, and Joseph Lister in Britain were learning about the connection between bacteria and disease, and by the next decade the discoveries were influencing the planning of sewage disposal facilities and water supplies. Even before the Civil War, New York, Philadelphia, and a number of other communities had developed decent systems of aqueducts to collect pure water from distant streams and pipe it into homes. Now, with the new knowledge at hand, the authorities began to clean up the water supply. Some cities depended on the piping of clean water. Others adopted filtration or chlorination. By 1910 over ten million city people drank filtered water; that innovation contributed to the sharp decline in death rates from typhoid fever and cholera. This change was accompanied by the appearance of sanitary bathrooms and running water, improvements that owed as much to rising living standards as to the growing awareness of infectious organisms.

All over the world, wherever and whenever cities have grown rapidly, housing for the poor has been woefully inadequate. American cities of the late nineteenth century were more successful perhaps than Third World cities of the present in solving their housing problems, but not by a great deal. Some of the urban poor crowded into shantytowns at the edges of the cities where they illegally built shacks on land they did not own. In 1870 New York City's West Side north of fifty-ninth street looked like the outskirts of San Juan or Rio today. Others took over the castoff houses of the middle class now departing for newer residential sections. These structures were cut up into small apartments that the newcomers could afford. Landlords threw up flimsy buildings for the poor in what had been spacious backyards. Few of the more substantial dwellings put up in response to the growth in the numbers of the poor were adequate in space, comfort, safety, or sanitation. Many cities relied on the row house of brick and two or three stories. Though monotonous, these were moderately spacious and possessed adequate light and air and decent sanitary facilities. Less desirable were Newark and Boston's four-story "three deckers." Many of these were wooden and fire hazards. New York's "old law" tenements were still worse. These structures were of four or five stories without hot water and proper bathrooms. After 1879 the city fathers required that all new tenements have at least one window in every room and two water closets to a floor. But the resulting "dumbbell" apartment with narrow air shafts on each side of the building was not appreciably better. In the absence of other means of disposal, air shafts became receptacles for garbage. Inadequacies in construction and in bathing and cooking facilities subjected everyone to noise, disorder, and bad smells. "How is it possible to preserve purity amid such homes, or to bring up children to be moral or decent?" asked one reformer.

Much of the congestion of New York and the nation's other large cities would have disappeared if transportation had been adequate between outlying neighborhoods and the downtowns, where the stores, shops, small factories, and wholesale establishments were located and where working people earned their livings. When men and women had to rely on their own legs or some equally inefficient means of transport they had no choice but to take nearby housing no matter how dilapidated or congested.

Before the Civil War a few of the country's largest cities had begun to develop public transportation systems. Horsedrawn omnibuses—essentially elongated carriages—running over regular routes had become common in New York, Philadelphia and Boston by 1860. These were slow. The horse-drawn streetcar, running on rails, was somewhat better and became almost universal after 1865 in the larger towns and cities. But still the system was inadequate and reformers demanded some means of "rapid transit" that would help end the congestion on city streets.

A breakthrough came in 1867 when the nation's largest city built the first "el," a steam railroad placed on high pillars above the traffic. New York's elevated system had its drawbacks. It darkened the streets below, scattered ashes on pedestrians, increased the noise level, and constituted an eyesore. But it did move people quickly. It was soon widely imitated. By the opening of the new century, Chicago, Boston, Kansas City,

and Brooklyn had all built "els." Meanwhile the horsecars had been replaced at street level by electric "trolley" cars drawing their power from overhead wires. Richmond was the first city to adopt the electric cars. By about 1900 there were 15,000 miles of electric street car line in American cities under the control of some 900 companies.

The final innovation was the subway. Following the lead of London and Budapest, Boston in 1895 began construction of an underground railway that would avoid the street level congestion of downtown. New York with an even greater congestion embarked on a still more ambitious scheme and in 1904 completed the first leg of what would become the largest subway system in the world.

The new transit systems, especially the electric street car, opened up the cities. Now, usually for a fare of five cents, a wage earner who lived several miles from the job could get to work on time. Recognizing the opportunities, builders and developers laid out streets and lots on what had been open fields and put up small houses for city people to buy. Many thousands would put the whole family to work and devote all savings to the single goal of purchasing a home. Before long many cities were surrounded by rings of streetcar suburbs housing families happy to escape the noise, dirt, congestion, and other ills of the city centers.

Crime

Cities in this era, as in others, were places where the broken as well as the successful congregated. Crime was by no means exclusively an urban affliction, of course. On the frontier, gangs like the James and the Dalton boys roamed the countryside attacking trains and stagecoaches, and made forays into town to rob banks. Communities responded to such lawlessness, at times, by the counterlawlessness of vigilantism.

Yet crimes of violence and against property were far more common in the cities than in rural areas. And they seemed to be increasing as cities grew. At the very end of the century, the *Chicago Tribune* estimated that murders and homicides nationally had increased from 1,266 in 1881 to 7,340 in 1898, or from about 25 per million people to over 107 per million. Statistics on other, lesser crimes are not available, but most contemporaries believed that all felonies had skyrocketed, a view seemingly confirmed by the startling increase of fifty percent reported for the national prison population between 1880 and 1890.

Urban crime flourished in the slums. Chicago's crime-ridden West Side in the 1890's was described as consisting of "filthy and rotten tenements, . . . dingy courts, and tumble-down sheds, . . . foul stables and dilapidated outhouses, . . . broken sewer pipes [and] . . . piles of garbage fairly alive with diseased odors . . . ." New York's slums seemed even worse. Jacob Riis, police reporter for the *New York Tribune*, described one dwelling in the notorious Five Points: "One, two, three beds are there, if the old boxes and heaps of foul straw can be called by that name; and a broken stove with crazy pipe from which the smoke leaks at every joint, a table of rough boards propped up on boxes. . . . The closeness and smell are appalling." Clearly the slums were nurseries and havens of city crime.

In the Five Points area, criminal groups such as the Whyos, the Dutch Mob, and the Molasses Gang preyed on pedestrians and householders, besides fighting one another viciously. San Francisco's Barbary Coast, with streets carrying such labels as Murderers' Corner and Deadman's Alley, was the haunt of hundreds of thieves and murderers. When in New Orleans the French Quarter gangs killed the chief of police, citizens carried out a mass lynching of Italians that had international repercussions.

In the minds of contemporaries, crime was closely associated with "vice." The term often meant prostitution. Always a profitable and widespread occupation except in tight-knit, small communities, it achieved in the Gilded Age city a particular flamboyance. In New York the Bowery, a street given over to saloons, music halls, and beer parlors, was the center of the trade. Chicago's "sporting houses" were concentrated in the area between Harrison and Polk and Clark and Dearborn streets. In New Orleans, "Storyville" in the French Quarter was a semi-official red light district, as well as the birthplace of a music ancestral to present-day jazz. These districts and their denizens were the objects of any number of crusades against vice, usually conducted by middle class, civic-minded women and ministers.

The crusaders often turned up a connection between the police and madams that protected the trade, but they accomplished little in ending it. The problem persisted because society was ambivalent about it as about so many other violations of the law. Most middle class Americans were shocked. Yet many people believed that there was no way of denying men access to sex for sale, and numbers of men, especially bachelors, saw nothing wrong with using the services of prostitutes. The willingness on the part of many men to pay for a service that was illegal created a gray area where graft and pay-offs could flourish. There were other examples of such arrangements. Laws against Sunday sports, cock fights, boxing, gambling, and drinking beyond certain specified hours opened similar opportunities for entrepreneurs to make money by bribes to police and officials. Reformers might protest and denounce, but they could do little to stop vice or prevent it from becoming a fertile source of political corruption.

City Political Machines

The beneficiary of much of this corruption was the city "machine." Machines were political organizations that paralleled the legal government of the city. At their head was a "boss." Few bosses were mayors, but they exercized much of the governmental power in the cities. Below the boss were lieutenants, "ward captains" or, to critics, "ward heelers," whose responsibilities and duties were confined to the small "ward" divisions of the city. Surrounding the ward leaders were crowds of hangers-on and underlings who served the machine at the neighborhood level. The local political clubhouse was the place where the captain and his underlings conducted their business. Most machines were affiliated with the Democrats; in Philadelphia and a few other cities they were Republican.

The successful machine actually ruled the city. The mayor and members of the city council or Board of Aldermen were members of the machine. Decisions regarding conduct of city affairs and appointments to office were actually made in the clubhouses or by the boss and merely confirmed by the legal city officials.

Many critics saw the city machines as merely sores on the body politic, instruments for bilking taxpayers, furthering criminal behavior, and lining the pockets of the boss and his followers. And they were these things. In St. Louis, Lincoln Steffens reported, "franchises worth millions were granted without one cent of cash to the city, and with provision for only the smallest future payment; several companies which refused to pay blackmail had to leave; citizens were robbed more and more boldly; pay-rolls were padded with the names of non-existent persons; work on public improvements was neglected, while money for them went to the boodlers." "Doc" Ames in Minneapolis was willing to sell exemptions from arrest to any criminal who was willing to pay the price. New York's Tweed Ring collected millions of dollars from builders and contractors who built the municipal court house at wildly inflated costs and then kicked back part of the money to boss William Marcy Tweed and his Tammany Hall henchmen.

There can be no question, then, that the machines were corrupt and expensive for citizens. But if they had been intent only on self-aggrandisement they would not have survived. Some of their victories at the polls, to be sure, were achieved or swelled by direct bribery. Five dollars was the going price for a vote in many American cities on election day; sometimes it was as little as a shot of whiskey. But city machines conferred more important boons on voters than a few dollars in early November, and it was these favors that explained their success.

Late nineteenth-century American cities were difficult places to govern. In most, authority was fragmented and action on any of the city's many problems hard to arrange. Chicago had eleven different governing bodies in 1890, each with taxing powers and its own set of officials. The city did not have the right to grant several types of franchises or even tax property directly. Anyone wanting to do business with the city had to deal with a multitude of officials, legislative bodies, and agencies. Under the circumstances it often proved impossible to get anything done. Most American cities suffered the same handicaps.

Here the machine could help. The effective boss not only controlled the Board of Aldermen, but also "owned" the county board of assessment, the local water and police commissioners, and in addition, often exerted strong influence in the state legislature where much city authority was actually lodged. To get something done, businessmen, civic leaders, and ethnic groups need only go to the boss and, if he was so inclined, or could be induced to support their request, it could be accomplished. The boss then was a kind of coordinator for a decentralized system of governing late nineteenth-century American cities. And he was more.

Newcomers to the city faced poverty, disease, congestion, unemployment, and trouble with the law. Cities had their "charity" societies, counties their "poor houses." In addition, the Chicagoan, Philadelphian, or New Yorker could turn to the minister, priest, or rabbi. Toward the end of the century, moreover, groups of middle-class philanthropists were establishing settlement houses in city slum neighborhoods to provide the urban poor with educational services, meeting halls, and places where they could get help and advice. But all these were not enough. Too often the middle class charity and settlement workers patronized the poor or imposed harsh conditions for dispensing aid. Not so the boss and the ward captain. Few were prudes, and they refused to judge the morals or customs of the local people. Many of them were Irish Catholics, yet they were tolerant of ethnic, religious, and racial differences. Gregarious glad-

---

Honest Graft and Dishonest Graft

Everybody in talkin' these days about Tammany men growin' rich on graft, but nobody thinks of drawin' the distinction between honest graft and dishonest graft. There's all the difference in the world between the two. Yes, many of our men have grown rich in politics. I have myself. I've made a big fortune out of the game, and I'm gettin' richer every day, but I've not gone in for dishonest graft—black-mailin' gamblers, saloonkeepers, disorderly people, etc.—and neither had any of the men who have made big fortunes in politics.

There's an honest graft, and I'm an example of how it works. I might sum up the whole thing by sayin': "I seen my opportunities and I took 'em."

Just let me explain by examples. My party's in power in the city, and it's goin' to undertake a lot of public improvements. Well, I'm tipped off, say, that they're going to lay out a new park at a certain place.

I see my opportunity and I take it. I go to that place and I buy up all the land I can in the neighborhood. Then the board of this or that makes its plan public, and there is a rush to get my land, which nobody cared particular for before.

Ain't it perfectly honest to charge a good price and make a profit on my investment and foresight? Of course, it is. Well, that's honest graft. . . .

Plunkitt of Tammany Hall

George Washington Plunkitt's reflections on his political experience were recorded, and perhaps embroidered upon, by the journalist William L. Riordan

---

handers, they mixed easily with the city poor and shared their ceremonies, social events, joys, and sorrows.

Among their services was the dispensing of jobs. In the absence of effective municipal civil service procedures, they could hand out jobs at will in the police and sanitation departments, in laboring occupations, even in schoolteaching. Many a poor family owed its regular income to the precinct captain's generosity toward the family breadwinner. There was also the temporary help of a Christmas turkey or some coal to a destitute family in winter. Boss Tweed, as member of the New York State legislature, got the state to con-tribute money to Catholic charities, though it violated the principle of separation of church and state. The machine, through its control of munici-pal judges and courts, also got minor violations of the law dismissed.

The city's "better element" objected to these favors as expensive, inefficient, or corrupt. The boss did not care. As Martin Lomasney of Boston's Thomas Hendricks Club remarked: "I think there's got to be in every ward a guy that any bloke can go to when he's in trouble and get help—not justice and the law, but help, no matter what he's done."

Education

City life was not all slums, smells, bad housing, and political corruption. Cities were also places where people learned and enjoyed themselves. In them talent from all over the country congregated in pursuit of training and development, audiences, and fame. In cities the newest and most interesting ideas got displayed, argued over, and exchanged. There millions of immigrants learned about American life and acquired the skills needed for a living.

Those of us used to the failings of big city schools today would be startled to discover that during the Gilded Age and early twentieth century the city public school systems were at the forefront of American education. Before the Civil War most of the Northern and Western states had created free public school systems. The South, meanwhile, had lagged behind. Then in the 1870's the South joined the free school movement while the Northern and Western states adopted laws requiring attendance at school. In 1878 there were 9½ million pupils in the country's public schools; by 1898 fifteen million attended. Growth and improvement, though present everywhere, came disproportionately to the city systems.

The typical rural school in 1890 was a small building with a single teacher and students of all ages and levels. These "little red school houses" were not the cozy institutions that a later generation would recall with nostalgia. Some were drafty and cold in winter and stifling and airless in spring. There was only a single class, and underpaid teachers might find it impossible to deal with fifteen-year-olds and children of eight simultaneously. In the crowded room discipline could be bad. Few teachers stayed for more than a year or two. Fortunately for the inmates of these rural institutions, sessions were usually rather short, seldom lasting more than a hundred days a year. And most students did not stay for even this short session. Compulsory attendance laws notwithstanding, parents often kept their children out of school for household or farm chores.

City schools were superior in every way. They enforced attendance laws. Each level of pupils had its own classrooms. Teachers were relatively well paid and well trained. The school year sometimes lasted twice as long as in the rural districts. City schools also had money for laboratories, auditoriums, indoor gyms. Many city school systems toward the end of the century adopted kindergartens, borrowing the idea from Germany. Free secondary education first appeared in the cities. Fewer than 100,000 attended public high schools in 1878; in 1898 there were over half a million, vir-

tually all of them located in large or middle-sized urban centers.

City schools of this era had their problems. By our standards the curriculum was limited, being confined to the "basics" of reading, writing, and arithmetic, with some history, geography, literature, and "civics." The public high schools included Latin and geometry, and had begun to include science, some commercial courses, and modern foreign languages. Nowhere as yet was a public school pupil exposed to the wide range of practical and "living" courses that, for good or ill, are available to students today. Pedagogy tended to be unimaginative. Much learning was still by rote memorization from a text and students who were slow might receive punishment by ridicule or even by paddling with a hickory stick.

The greatest task, and triumph, of city school systems in this era was the assimilation of foreign-born children or "second generation" offspring of recent immigrants. In many big city neighborhoods these pupils were virtually the only ones. Their teachers were almost always young women either of native stock or of assimilated immigrant backgrounds. Some of these teachers found their pupils strange and difficult to communicate with. Some disliked the religion or ethnic backgrounds of those they taught. The pupils often reciprocated those feelings. It is a wonder that the schools did remarkably well. One study shows that in 1900 the American-born children of European parents were more literate than white children of native-American parents. The schools also imbued their charges with American middle-class values, the work ethic, and knowledge of American history and institutions. There were debits as well. Learning to be Americans meant for some children learning to despise their own early culture. Aside from doing emotional damage to the children themselves, the assimilation process often caused considerable conflict between children and their families and between children who were deeply affected by their school experience and their peers who failed to accept Americanization as thoroughly.

The rapid advance of higher education in these years was by no means exclusively an urban phenomenon. Most of the state universities and the land grant colleges that contributed so much to the American achievement in scholarship and learning were located in small college communities such as Urbana, Ann Arbor, Madison, Berkeley, or Ithaca. Yet many of the leading institutions in this era were urban. Beginning with Johns Hopkins of Baltimore

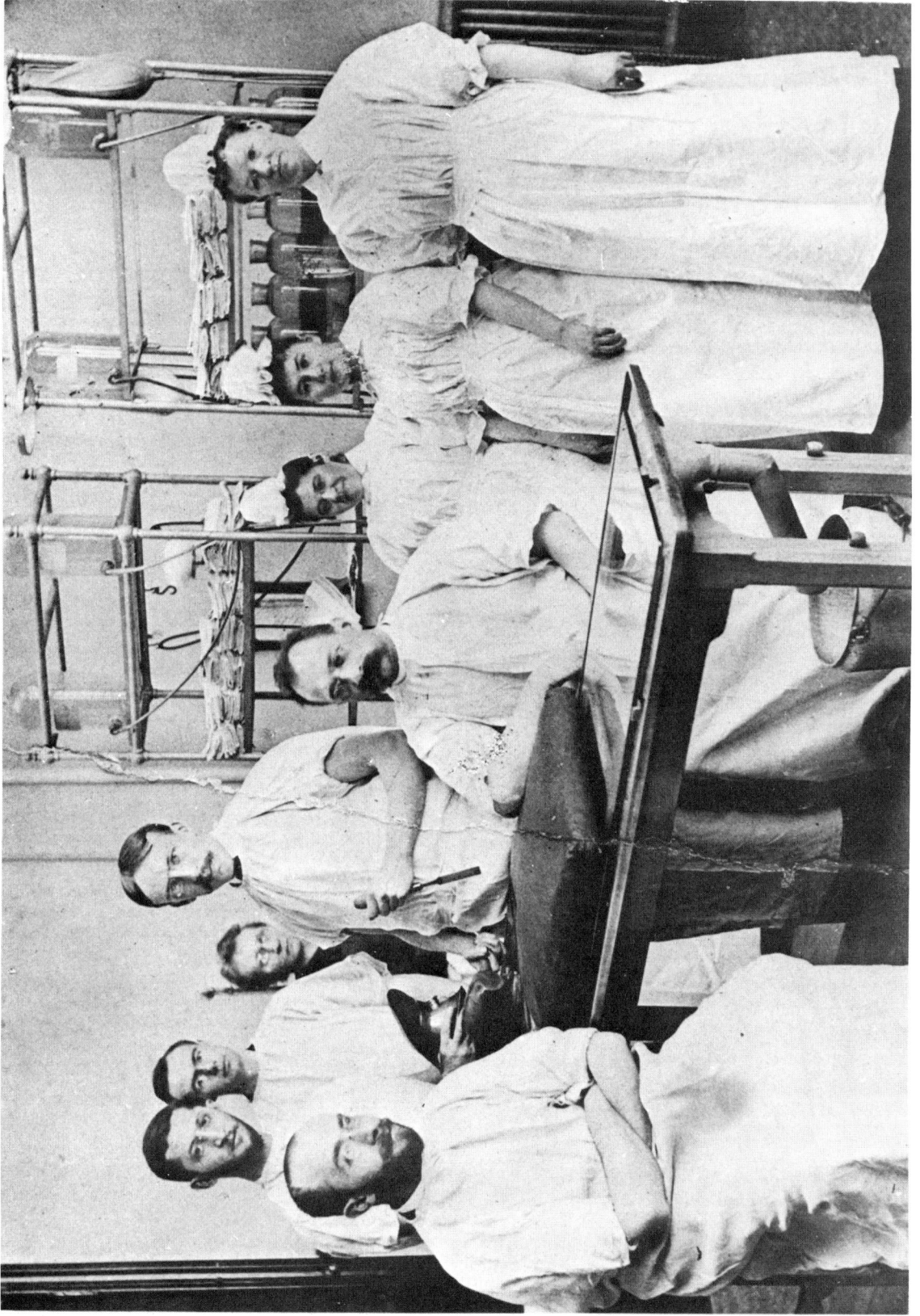

Lenox Hill Hospital, 1896.

and joined soon after by the University of Chicago, Columbia, Harvard, Yale, and other city-centered universities, the urban institutions led the movement into graduate education and research that converted the college into the university and brought American higher education to the level of Europe's best.

Amusements

Children have played games wherever they have been. But rural adults, engaged in strenuous physical activities in the open air, seemed to have relatively little need for sports. The amusements we associate with rural adults were usually meetings, dances, "socials," house-raisings, and "bees" designed to bring isolated people together. The cities made for a different attitude. Confined to monotonous work in factories or sedentary work in offices and stores, city dwellers craved recreation in the open air. As one observer noted in 1902, "the disappearance of the backwoods and the growth of large centres of population have created the demand for an artificial outlet, and . . . games are the natural successors of the youthful activities of a pioneer period."

Often the facilities did not match the craving. Open space was hard to find. City folk flocked to the parks on weekend afternoons to play baseball, or picnic or stroll. But until well into the new century there simply were not enough open spaces, and at some risk children played "tag," hide-and-seek, and stickball on the city streets.

One solution to the space problem was basketball, invented by James Naismith in 1891, which could be played indoors. Another was the bicycle. Until the 1890's bicycles had enormous front wheels and tiny rear ones, and it was difficult for anyone but trained athletes to use them. Then came the "safety" bicycle with two wheels of equal size. Bicycling soon became a virtual craze. Thousands, including many women, took it up. Frances E. Willard, the prominent temperance advocate, wrote *A Wheel Within a Wheel: How I Learned to Ride the Bicycle* to advertise the pleasures of "wheeling." Ultimately, however, city people accepted to a large extent the role of spectator.

Even here there was a difficulty. Many American cities and towns had ordinances against Sunday spectacles of any sort, whether baseball games or theatrical performances. These "blue laws" sought to keep Sundays as a day of worship and religious contemplation. Largely the work of evangelical Protestants, the sabbath laws often met resistance from Catholics and others. Toward the end of the century the strict keeping of the Sabbath began to give way. "Where is the city in which the Sabbath is not losing ground?" lamented one rock-ribbed gentleman in 1887. "To the mass of the workingmen Sunday is no more than a holiday . . . it is a day for labor meetings, for excursions, for saloons, beergardens, games and carousels."

One of the major beneficiaries of this change was baseball. Descended from several children's games, baseball in its modern form appeared during the 1840's in the New York area as a gentleman's game. A decade later it began to attract some artisans and laborers, some of them forced to play at dawn before going to work. Soon people were coming to watch as well as play, and teams charged admission to their fenced fields. During the Civil War, informal soldier teams spread interest in the sport, and that led to a proliferation of teams in the years following. In 1869 the Cincinnati Red Stockings began to hire players for paid admission exhibition games, and soon after William A. Hulbert organized the National League of Professional Baseball Clubs with teams in New York, Philadelphia, Hartford, Boston, Chicago, Louisville, Cincinnati, and St. Louis. Baseball got still greater attention from the next generation as city crowds reached out for things to keep themselves amused. By the late 1880's annual attendance at the National League games had reached eight million a year, with semi-professional groups and small town clubs pushing this figure up still further. In 1886 *Harpers Weekly* noted: "the fascination of the game has seized upon the American people, irrespective of age, sex or other condition." Interest culminated in the formation of the American League in 1899. For a while each league fought to supersede the other. But then they settled their dispute and in 1903 they joined in the first "world series."

Although baseball had by this time clearly become the "national game," city people were also paying admission to see other sports contests. Boxing, though many Americans considered it

Polo Grounds, New York City, ca. 1900. (New York Historical Society.)

brutal, attracted city crowds. During the 1880's and 1890's some Irish-Americans—Paddy Ryan, Jake Kilrain, Robert Fitzsimmons, and, above all, John L. Sullivan—dominated the heavy-weight lists. Like other sports, however, boxing was a ladder up for the talented of all races. In 1908 Jack Johnson, a black man, won the heavy-weight championship, inaugurating a long series of outstanding black boxers. In later years there would be Italian-American, Spanish-American, and Jewish-American champions as well.

During most of this period sports remained primarily a male interest. Women bicycled, played such genteel games as croquet, and practiced archery. They also became baseball enthusiasts in fair numbers. But girls were treated as fragile and generally forbidden body-contact sports or anything that seemed too strenuous. A few girls or women rebelled against these limitations; others accepted the general view that vigorous physical activity was somehow unladylike. It would take another generation before women's interest in sports came to seem perfectly normal, and until almost our own day before professional women athletes would come into their own.

While both participation in sports and observance of them had ancient precedents, and both could take place in rural as well as in urban cultures, they are strongly expressive of modern urban civilization. Sports as an activity not only serves in the absence of the daily physical routines of agriculture but also represents in some degree the modern bent for turning the process of living into rational, purposeful projects. Just as for several centuries the western world, according to some social historians, has made of work something more specific, more conscious and deliberate, more clearly timed than it once was, so in the last century we have pursued exercise and sports as specific activities, instead of merely letting exercise happen in the course of the day. Spectator sports are modern in another way. They are events that engage large numbers of strangers in similar acts of observing and judging, so that people at opposite ends of a city in the late nineteenth century had opinions of the same baseball player on the home team. This bringing together of strangers who will observe and think about the same event gives sports something in common with the plays and the musical performances that flourished in late nineteenth-century urban culture. What is happening in all these instances is the shaping of a modern urban public.

Theater and Music

Theater greatly improved in this period. Until the 1880's serious drama, outside of a few imported European classics, seldom played American theatres. They produced comic pieces or sentimental melodramas. In the eighties Bronson Howard began to write plays with believable characters and situations. James Herne's *Shore Acres* (1892) was the first American play infused with the new mood of "realism." The works of David Belasco and Charles Hoyt written between 1890 and 1910 were witty comedies rather than the broad farce of earlier decades.

Many cities established major orchestras. New York's symphony, begun in 1878, the Boston symphony, initiated in 1881, and the Chicago symphony, which dates from 1891, soon rivaled Europe's best. In 1883 a group of wealthy New Yorkers built the Metropolitan Opera House for the first resident American opera company.

But neither classical music nor the "legitimate" stage attracted the urban masses in overwhelming numbers. Music, to most Americans of the day, meant the sentimental, catchy products of Tin Pan Alley. New York's music publishing district turned out reams of sheet music to be played on the family piano while mother, father, and the children warbled out the words. Much of this music was saccharine or excessively sentimental, but some of it entered into the folk heritage of the American people. Tunes such as "After the Ball" (1892), "The Sidewalks of New York" (1894), "On the Banks of the Wabash" (1896), and "O Promise Me" (1889), are still remembered and sung today.

Meanwhile a considerably zestier brand of popular music had appeared in the "darktowns," the black ghettoes of American cities. Ragtime was syncopated, with the emphasis on the upbeat. Much of it was instrumental to be played on the piano or on wind instruments. When vocal, it was often fitted with risqué words that offended prim and proper people. Attacked by critics as "vulgar, filthy, and suggestive music," it attracted the young as well as those Americans who had had their fill of sentimental ballads. In the hands of

THE IRONIES OF INDUSTRIALISM

Scott Joplin, a black musician from Texas, it reached a level of sophistication much appreciated today. By 1914 the ragtime craze was over, but it had left its permanent mark. The "Jazz" that became nationally popular in the years after World War I had borrowed from ragtime.

Sheet music was only one form for disseminating popular music. In the cities the vaudeville performance, the stage revue, the minstrel show, and the musical comedy were display cases for popular songs.

In 1907 the impressario Florenz Ziegfeld began to present his reviews, which would feature comedians such as Burt Williams, Eddie Cantor, and Fannie Brice, along with scantily clad showgirls and a flock of tuneful songs. More widespread was vaudeville. Composed of comic skits, acro-batic acts, comedy routines, animal performances, dancing, and musical performances both serious and comic, vaudeville achieved immense popularity with city audiences between 1890 and 1920. At one time New York had thirty-seven vaudeville houses, Philadelphia thirty, and Chicago twenty-two. Hundreds of performers made excellent money touring one of the better "circuits" that took them to scores of American cities. During its heyday, according to one study, about one in seven Americans attended the vaudeville show at least once a week.

In the working-class neighborhoods and ethnic ghettoes of the great cities lived thousands who could not afford the fifty cents of a vaudeville seat or spoke no English and could not follow the skits and comedy routines. By the opening years of the

HOME WASHING MACHINE & WRINGER.

HOME WASHER

DEPOT 24 CORTLANDT ST., NEW YORK.

new century a medium had arrived that would appeal to these people, and attract millions of others as well.

Motion pictures had awaited the development of electric or arc lights, photography, flexible celluloid film, and electric motors as well as lenses. The whole complex of inventions was put together by the fertile brain of Thomas Edison, though not at first as a projected film. Edison's Kinetoscope of 1889 was a black box with a light. The viewer looked through an eye piece at a backlighted moving film strip recording a brief story, or bit of moving scenery, or some action. Edison made these peepshows in a tarpaper shack at his laboratory in New Jersey. He rented these to arcade operators, who quickly learned that the public would pay a penny or two for the novelty of seeing lifelike miniature figures moving before their eyes.

The great drawback of Edison's peepshows was that they could handle only one paying viewer at a time. By 1895, however, the projector that showed a large picture on a screen had appeared. This enabled the operator to display a film to many viewers. All he needed was an empty store where he could place some chairs and his projector. But the new, large audience also called for something more ambitious than a one- or two-minute sketch, and with more people to pay it also became commercially feasible to provide these features. Before long Edison and a dozen other enterprisers were producing full reel films running for twenty minutes or half an hour with a wide range of stories and themes. These featured chases, comic sketches, dancing, travel scenes, and even early trick photography showing fantastic happenings. Some of the early titles were "Umbrella Dance," "Venice," "A Narrow Escape on the Baltimore and Ohio Railroad," "The Ups and Downs of Army Life," and "The Kiss." The first fully realized film with a story that provided a beginning, development, and denouement, was *The Great Train Robbery* (1903), the work of one of Edison's cameramen, Edwin S. Porter.

By the opening years of the twentieth century the "movies" had become a major form of big city entertainment. To enjoy a film no one had to be literate or even understand English; since films were silent it was essential for producers to make them understandable by visual means alone. By 1905 three thousand primitive movie theaters were in operation, most charging only a nickel—hence the name "nickelodeon." Soon afterwards a few operators began to design halls exclusively for movie viewing and these became ever more elaborate. By the eve of the First World War there were 13,000 movie houses catering to from five to seven million viewers a day. Audiences belonged to all ranks of society, but much of the popularity was among the poor. As one magazine noted, "in the tenement districts" the movies had "well nigh driven other forms of entertainment from the field."

And so, by the second decade of the twentieth century, the lives of millions of Americans had been transformed by the forces of industrialization. In the year 1860 most adult Americans had worked as farmers or tillers of the soil of some kind, living in isolated farmsteads, cut off from much of the world around them. By 1910 far fewer than half were farmers. For millions in the cities life was congested, noisy, hectic, and often unhealthy. But it was also richer, more colorful, more interesting, and more aware than rural living had been. And many of the city problems, it would soon become apparent, were not intractable. By the opening years of the new century there would be those who would call the American city "the hope of democracy."

Suggested Readings

Anthony F. C. Wallace, in *Rockdale: The Growth of an American Village in the Early Industrial Revolution* (1978), analyzes, from the standpoint of a cultural anthropologist, the social and ethnic composition of a nineteenth-century community as it became industrialized, and considers the religious and moral ideology that the social and business elite fashioned for conditioning the population to the disciplines of industrialism. Alfred D. Chandler, Jr., *The Visible Hand: The Managerial Revolution in American Business* (1977), follows the development of a managerial structure in American business and the reasons for it. The work argues that it was not the "invisible hand" of unregulated economic forces but the conscious decisions of managers that has given shape to the American economy. Irwin Unger won a Pulitzer Prize for *The Greenback Era: A Social and Political History of American Finance, 1865-1879* (1964). On cities see Howard Chudacoff, *Evolution of American Urban Society* (1975) and Zane Miller, *Urbanization of America* (1973). Samuel P. Hays, *The Response to Industrialism* (1957), is a classic study. Robert W. Fogel uses a quantitative approach in *Railroads and American Economic Growth: Essays in Econometric History* (1964). Thomas Haskell's study describes a division in the American Social Science Association between older members who see a simple causation in social events and a younger generation convinced that causes are complex and hidden: *The Emergence of Professional Social Science* (1977).

The Station.—Strikers watching for " scabs," Homestead, Pa., U. S. A.
Los huelguistas en aseche por los sustitutos, en Homestead, Pa.

(Library of Congress.)

Chapter XVII
The Outsiders
1865—1900

The Homestead Strike

Homestead, Pennsylvania, in 1892 was a town of about twelve thousand inhabitants. Seven miles east of Pittsburgh on the left bank of the Monogahela River, the town was dominated by a Carnegie, Phipps plant that made steel boiler plates, structural steel, armor plate, and beams. The workforce of the plant—thirty-eight hundred people, and their families—was the town. Most of this force was unskilled labor working for wages as low as fourteen cents an hour and belonging to no union. Many were recent immigrants, predominantly Eastern European. But eight hundred of the skilled workers, many of them earning about $200 per month, belonged to the Amalgamated Association of Iron and Steel Workers. This union, with about twenty-five thousand members, was probably the strongest union in the country, just as the Carnegie Corporation, forerunner of the United States Steel Corporation, was among the most powerful and successful corporations in the nation. Since 1889 the union had worked under an agreement by which their wages would rise and fall with the market price of steel billets, although below a certain point—$25 per ton, wages would fall no further. The agreement was set to expire on June 30, 1892.

In the spring of 1892, Carnegie, who no longer actively managed the business, and his chief manager, Henry Clay Frick, agreed that they would destroy the union at Homestead and henceforth run all their plants on a non-union basis. Carnegie in 1886 had written that "The rights of the workingmen to combine and to form trades unions is no less sacred than the right of the manufacturer to enter into association and conference with his fellows. . . . My experience has been that trades unions upon the whole are beneficial both to labor and to capital." But the steel business had been changing rapidly: the number of unskilled workers as compared to skilled ones was increasing as more processes were automated, and Henry Clay Frick, Carnegie's manager since 1889, had a sinister reputation as a union-buster in the coke industry.

Frick negotiated with the union in the most cursory way while literally preparing for battle. He turned the steel plant into an armed fortress, with solid board fencing complete with gun holes and topped with barbed wire and high platforms with electric search lights. He arranged with the Pinkerton Detective Agency for three hundred armed men to guard the plant so that he could bring in non-union workers, then announced the new terms: no union, and wage reductions that averaged somewhat over twenty percent.

The workers were confident they could beat the corporation. They were not a downtrodden desperate proletariat. Rather, the Amalgamated members were the obvious leaders of the town, part of the local elite. They assumed—correctly—that the unskilled workers would follow their leadership, that the merchants and professionals of the town would be on their side, extending credit to the men and using their influence to settle the strike to their advantage. Most of all, these skilled men, proud of their abilities as rollers or heaters, or shearers, or cutters, did not believe that the plant could be run without them. In the face of national union support, other men with their skills would never become "black sheep" and work for Carnegie as strikebreakers. The pride, even arrogance of the men was expressed in a speech given by "Honest John" McLuckie, the Burgess of the town (and himself a Carnegie worker), at the first workers' meeting before the men were locked out of the plant:

It is Sunday morning, and we ought to be in church but are here to-day to see if we are going to live as white men in the future.

The workers, in short, were prepared for the kind of local labor struggle they had won in 1889 and in which other workers in the small industrial towns of the Middle West had so frequently succeeded thanks to local support, official neutrality, and the interest of management in preventing a lengthy shutdown while competitors stole their markets. They were not, however, prepared for Henry Clay Frick who was determined to do away with the union at practically any cost, and who had little to fear from his weak competitors.

The great Homestead Strike was technically not a strike but a lockout, since Frick initiated it by shutting the mill hours before the contract was scheduled to expire. The company placed ads in newspapers around the country for workers. The workers, virtually one with the local government anyhow, literally took over the town, arranging patrols to prevent the influx of strikebreakers, consulting with the saloonkeepers to prevent drunkenness, and generally securing order.

In the early hours of July 6, 1892, the news spread that two barges filled with men were being towed up the river. A huge crowd of workers and even their wives and families assembled at the landing. The Pinkertons in the barges attempted to land, a shot rang out—no one knows from where, and Homestead was at war. All that day, the workers besieged the three hundred men in the barges until at 5:00 p.m., after nine of the workers and three of the Pinkertons had been killed, the "Pinks" surrendered. The workers marched their captors to a temporary prison in a skating rink and fired the barges.

With the Pinkertons sent home, the union men resumed their control of the town, laboring strenuously to keep the peace. Meanwhile the strike spread to other Carnegie plants, and the A F of L Executive Council began picketing labor recruitment agencies in the major cities.

Despite the peace that now appeared to prevail in Homestead, the governor of Pennsylvania called out the Naitonal Guard on July 10. The strikers and town government planned a great reception with bands and speeches of welcome, but General Snowden, the Guard commander, had come to put down "revolution, treason, and anarchy." Under the protection of the troops, Frick reopened the plant with non-union men and began legal prosecutions of a number of the leaders. Frick hoped to break the strike by convincing the men that the plant could operate without them and by tying up their leadership in court battles. Frick's plans probably would have succeeded in any case, but the strategy of identifying the strikers with ambitions more sinister than union recognition and the maintenance of their pay scales received unexpected assistance. On July 23, a young Russian emigré anarchist, Alexander Berkman, burst into the corporation's office in Pittsburgh, shot and then stabbed Frick, seriously wounding him. The unions instantly dissociated themselves from this episode, but it nevertheless made it easier for the legal machinery to shift into a higher gear. In addition to charges against individuals for murder of the Pinkertons, charges of conspiracy, rioting, and treason were now lodged against the Advisory Committee directing the strike.

The legal strategy worked. The union fought almost two hundred separate charges, exhausting its resources and its leadership. Not a single worker was found guilty, but the legal tussle had their desired effect. Despite considerable support from unions across the country and strong local support, the workers simply lacked the resources for staying out indefinitely. By November, with the strike over five months old and the winter approaching, the entire town, not simply the strikers, was at the point of desperation. The union surrendered and the men began trickling back to the plant. The twelve-hour day with a twenty-four-hour stretch every other week when the shifts changed, and unusually low wage scales, soon became the norm for the steel industry. True to its promise, the Carnegie mills, and its successor the United States Steel Corporation maintained non-union plants, and led national efforts to retain the "open shop" until the C.I.O. succeeded in organizing steel in the waning years of the Great Depression of the 1930's.

(Library of Congress.)

THE OUTSIDERS

Times of rapid change are inevitably periods of social and intellectual upheaval. Even when the shifts are in a positive direction, men and women, finding their lives transformed, experience discomfort and disorientation. The familiar past seems better than the novel present, not to speak of the uncertain future, and those who live through the changes often suffer from a vague but pervasive unease. Social discontent is certain to be even greater among those who are on the losing side of change. Not all Americans benefited from the shifts that marked the years from 1865 to 1900. Large groups of citizens were hurt by the economic transformations that thrust the United States into the front rank of industrial nations; others, even when we can today demonstrate that their incomes or opportunities were in fact improved, perceived their lot at the time as worsened. Still others compared themselves to the most favored groups in society and were angered by their relative bad fortune. All these people were the "outsiders," and their struggles and plight form the subject of this chapter.

The American Wage-Earner

In 1870 relatively few Americans worked for wages. Most adults of working age, housewives aside, were still farm owners or else, in the case of the South, belonged to the new class of sharecroppers that the breakdown of slavery had created. By 1900, however, a very large proportion consisted of wage-earners rather than self-employed persons. Of the 27 million in the labor force in this latter year, about 19 million, or roughly two-thirds, were people who primarily sold their labor or skills to others for a daily or weekly wage.

How did these people fare? There is no simple answer. Prices of course were far lower a hundred years ago than today. In 1890 round steak cost about 12^c a pound, pork chops 11^c, potatoes about 1.6^c, and eggs 21^c a dozen. Rents were comparable. In 1883 it was possible to rent a small house in Belleville, Illinois, for $6 a month; in Joliet, Illinois, that same year a slightly larger house went for $5 a month. City rents were higher, but still very low compared to today.

Few wage-earners were the sole support of their families. Bachelors in this era were usually young men who lived with their families, or with some other family, and shared in their general prosperity. Many working families, then, had several wage-earners besides the male head. These were usually sons but, increasingly, daughters and sometimes even the mother of the family worked outside the home for wages. When all went well these earners, even when unskilled, could provide a family with a more-than-adequate living. The case of an Illinois coal miner during the 1880's is instructive. This man had a wife and four children, some of them grown sons. He earned $420 a year while his sons earned another $1,000 all together. All told, then, the family income was over $1,400 annually, which enabled its six members to live in a six-room house on an acre of land; eat breakfasts of steak, bacon, butter, potatoes, and coffee; and spend $100 a year on books, insurance, and extras. A Wisconsin iron-molder's family in 1888 reported an income eighty percent higher than this one as a result of the combination of higher initial wages of the family head with the earnings, similarly, of other family members.

At the other end of the scale were families where special circumstances—lack of skill, sickness, many young dependents, or some other problem—brought down living standards to a pitiful level. A Joliet, Illinois, railroad brakeman supported his wife and eight children on $360 a year in 1883. All ten people in his family were crammed into a three-room house where they ate chiefly bread and potatoes. The reporting investigator noted: "Clothes ragged, children half-dressed and dirty. . . . They all sleep in one room regardless of sex. The house is devoid of furniture, and the entire concern is as wretched as could be imagined."

Black, Woman, and Child Workers

Several classes of "Gilded Age" workers were worse off than adult males. Women were one such group. In 1880, out of 17.4 million gainful workers, women represented 2.6 million, or about one-seventh of the total. Unlike men, who normally worked their entire lives, most women

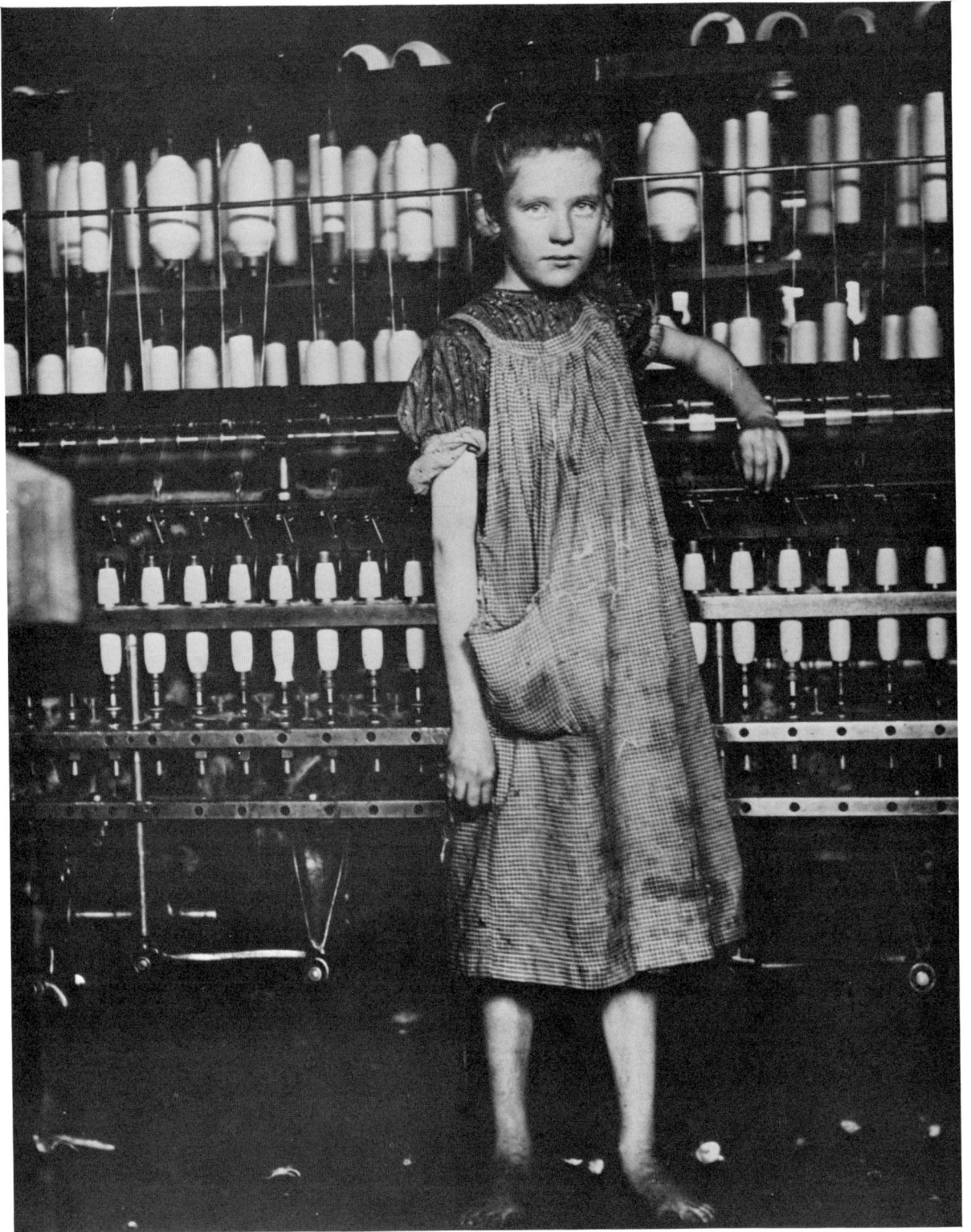

(National Archives.)

THE OUTSIDERS

worked only a few years, usually in their teens, twenties, and early thirties. Most were single women who lived with their families. In 1890, of the 3.7 million women in the labor force, only half-a-million were married.

There can be no question that women in this era were discriminated against in the job market. At the top they were virtually excluded from the learned professions. By 1900 a few hundred women had become doctors, largely owing to the efforts of such courageous pioneers as Elizabeth Blackwell, who became the first women with an M.D. degree in 1850. But there were virtually no women in the legal profession or the Protestant ministry and only a handful, including the astronomer Maria Mitchell and the anthropologist Erminnie Smith, in the natural sciences or social sciences. Although in the ultimate sense male prejudice, often shared by "womanly" women, explains much of the exclusion, in the short run it was related to the inadequate education women received. Fortunately, the situation after the Civil War was far better than it had been before. The new land grant colleges founded under the wartime Morrill Act were coeducational. In addition, various philanthropists had founded a flock of women's colleges after 1865, including Vassar, Wellesley, Smith, Barnard, Radcliffe, and Bryn Mawr. Despite these advances, the pool of young women trained in the sciences or prepared to enter professional training remained relatively small after 1865.

The picture was not all bleak, however. During the last half of the nineteenth century well-educated middle-class women found expanding opportunities in a number of newer areas. Women had been schoolteachers, of course, for centuries. But before the antebellum period it had usually been on the very lowest levels of informal "dame schools" where young children learned their ABCs. With the advent of the publicly supported "common school," women began to replace men in the better elementary school jobs. With the arrival of the public high school, largely after the Civil War, they also displaced men in the secondary schools. In 1860 about twenty-five percent of the country's public school teachers were women; by 1880, sixty percent; by 1910, eighty percent.

This is not to say that women encountered no discrimination in the educational profession. At every level of training and grade, men teachers were paid better than women. In addition, men usually occupied the supervisory jobs of principals, commissioners, and superintendents. Indeed, one reason why so many women were hired by school systems was that they were cheaper than men and placed less of a burden on taxpayers. Yet however imperfect the system, there can be no question that the development of the teaching profession was a great boon to many women.

Nursing, a new profession, was another breakthrough. Before the Civil War hospital attendants were invariably male. The work of the attendant was considered dirty, harrowing, and hard and so unsuitable for "ladies." During the Civil War, the crying need for nurses with the armed forces, as well as the example of the Englishwoman Florence Nightingale during the Crimean War of 1853-56, broke down resistance. After 1865 several major hospitals established training schools for female nurses, and gradually these raised their standards of admission and training. By the end of the century the new profession, or semi-profession, of "trained" or "registered" nurse had come into being, providing a decent occupation for hundreds of ambitious young women.

A final professional opportunity for women, one that appeared at the end of the century, was that of social worker. Until the post-Civil War period, charity of various kinds had been dispensed primarily on an informal, emergency basis by churches, benevolent societies, and local governments. Most of those who administered the dispensing of funds were volunteers, usually middle-class people, often women, who considered their efforts simply in the light of good deeds or as a matter of social responsibility. Toward the end of the century, in an attempt to deal more systematically with the disruptions of city life, various reformers established citywide charity organizations to dispense welfare on a "scientific" basis. Accompanying the charity-organization movement was the growth of a professional class of full-time charity dispensers who supposedly understood how charity could be used most effectively to rehabilitate the poor and not merely sustain them in idleness. By the end of the century a new class of professional social workers had appeared to do the job required by the new theories. Many of these were women. Much of the growth of "social work" as a profession would come in the early twentieth century, but by 1900 a new opportunity for educated, middle-class women had already appeared.

Although these gains were impressive, it was, all told, only a few score thousand women, almost all from middle-class backgrounds, who found opportunities in the new or expanded professions. Most working women had to be content with menial, low-paying, jobs.

One of the largest categories of women workers was that of "servants" or "domestics." Of the 5 million gainfully employed women workers of

1900, 1.5 million were listed as "private household workers." About a fifth of these were laundresses; the rest, "housekeepers" of one sort or other. The conditions under which these women lived and labored varied a good deal. Many, especially among the older women, were married and came into their employers' households to work for the day. They had their own homes, and generally their wages were supplements to their husbands' income. In principle, this arrangement did not work out too badly. True, wages for laundresses, maids, cooks, and other domestics, were not good—less than a dollar a day. On the other hand, the women had lives of their own after hours. The situation of the "widow-lady" who had to support herself by her wages as a servant, or even herself and young children, was far less tolerable. Equally unhappy was that of the live-in "servant girl" who was at the beck and call of her middle-class "mistress" or master for incredibly long hours and who, living in her employer's household, seldom had much privacy. No doubt there were cases where young women found kindly friends and protectors in their employers; no doubt there were cases where servant girls became loyal and cherished family retainers within middle-class families. But the circumstances of the live-in maid were inherently unenviable. Fortunately, it was seldom permanent.

Generally speaking, by the late nineteenth century domestic service was not—outside the South—a job that native-born women performed. It seemed far too menial for them. In farm regions, the "hired girl" called in to assist the farmer's wife during the busy harvest season when there were many extra hands to feed, was often the daughter of a neighbor. But she considered her job merely "helping out," and therefore without stigma. Long-term domestic service was largely confined to Irish and German women in the North and to black women in the South. Without skills, these young women had little alternative. Yet "Bridget" did not make an ideal servant from the point of view of the middle-class housewife since she often seemed ignorant of the required hygienic and culinary standards. Still, given the perennial "servant problem," there was often no choice, and middle-class women had to make do.

One of three ironies of domestic service was that in order for middle-class women to have leisure, whether for mothering, being hostesses for their husbands, or pursuing volunteer activities or in some cases, professions, they had to count on the menial labor of other women. For this was an era without the kitchen and laundry equipment that has eased the labor of the modern housewife. The only alternative, then, was a large pool of cheap female labor to serve as scullery maids, cooks, laundresses, and parlor maids. This seam in the fabric of "sisterhood" would continue to our own day.

Another large category of female workers consisted of factory "operatives." Like servant girls, most of these were young and unmarried; like their sisters in domestic service, they were underpaid, especially relative to men. The job of the factory girl seldom had anything to recommend it except a modest return that helped to supplement their family's income. The few middle-class women who had any contact with the life found it grim. Factory work was often a harsh and squalid life for young women, one that coarsened their perceptions and dulled their appreciation of what the conventional wisdom of the day considered "higher things."

In the half-century following the Civil War, the vast majority of black people remained in the South, attached to the soil. This continuity with the slave past was in part the result of natural human inertia and the ignorance of opportunities elsewhere among people held down for generations by bondage. Yet it was not the legacy of slavery alone. Racial prejudice was another potent factor in keeping blacks in their accustomed place, socially and geographically. In the South, the cotton mills that sprang up during the 1880's refused to accept black operatives; the new jobs were reserved for rural whites straight off the farms. Northern employers, too, preferred white European immigrants to native American blacks. Among white workers themselves, bigotry was pervasive, and many attempts by black workers or laborers to find jobs in industry was met by threats or violence.

This antipathy was aggravated by the willingness of white employers to use black strikebreakers when their usual labor force refused to work. Southern blacks, eager to get Northern wages, often did not understand what they were being hired to do, but however inadvertently on their part, this encouraged anti-black working-class prejudice. Few local unions would admit skilled black workers into their ranks. Among the national unions organized after the Civil War, only the ineffectual Knights of Labor actively sought out black members. When it declined in the late 1880's and 1890's, black workers found themselves without protection. The craft-oriented American Federation of Labor, which replaced the Knights, at first welcomed black members. An 1890 resolution of the AF of L declared that the

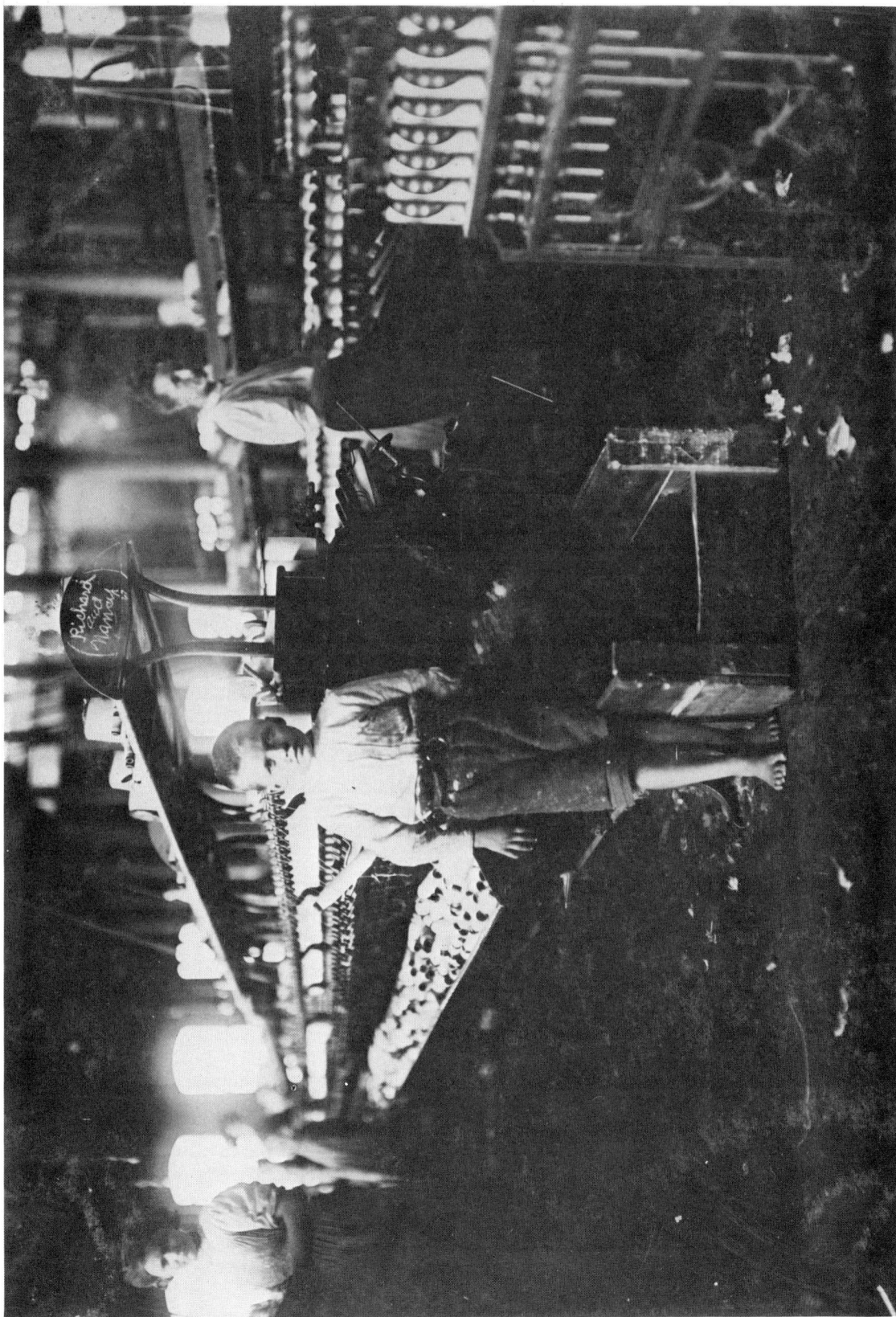

(National Archives.)

Federation looked "with disfavor upon trade unions having provisions which exclude from membership persons on account of race and color." But then Federation officials began to yield to the prejudices of the skilled workers who made up its constituent unions. Efforts to organize all-black unions proved feeble, and in the end few black workers benefited from the AF of L's ability to improve the lot of its members. Indeed, as the craft unions that made up the Federation increased their control over jobs, their anti-black bias intensified the exclusion of blacks from all but the most menial jobs in American history.

A final labor group that fell behind the white male average consisted of child workers. There were many of these: the census of 1900 showed that four out of every hundred non-agricultural jobs were held by individuals between the ages of 10 and 15, a total of about 700,000. They worked at a wide range of occupations. In the big cities many were messengers and errand boys. Others were newsboys or shoeshine boys. In the Pennsylvania coal fields, hundreds of lads labored for ten hours a day over rushing belts of coal picking out slate and stones while breathing in dangerous dust-laden air. Both boys and girls worked in city loft cigar factories rolling tobacco to make cheap "cheroots." In the Southern piedmont, young girls worked from sunup to sundown in the newly established cotton mills.

Child labor was not a new practice that had appeared abruptly in the Gilded Age. Children had worked for time out of mind on the farms of the Western world. But there child labor had been part of a family enterprise with mothers and fathers as supervisors and employers. To some extent, it continued to be part of a family enterprise in the early textile mills, especially in Rhode Island. In the new Gilded Age, however, it largely ceased to be part of a family system and, once freed of parental supervision, the practice became far more exploitative and cruel. One Southern novelist described the cotton-mill children of the Tennessee Valley early in the twentieth century:

They were children only in age . . . little, solemn pygmy people, whom poverty had canned up and compressed into concentrated extracts of humanity . . . the juices of childhood had been pressed out . . . no talking in the mill. . . . No singing—for songs came from the happy heart of childhood, though the children were there. They were flung into an arena for a long day's flight against a thing of steam and steel. . . . They were more dead than alive when, at seven o'clock, the Steam Beast uttered the last volcanic howl which said they might go home . . . in a speechless, haggard, over-worked procession.

At first, the influence of traditional farm habits stilled the outcry against child labor. But then, toward the end of the century, as the rural experience receded and new attitudes toward child nurture and extended education began to take hold, protests against the system began to grow. In the 1890's the National Consumers' League, organized by New York and Chicago women, began to demand that child labor be abolished. Educators too attacked it, arguing that it was inconsistent with an educated citizenry. Yet the practice had its defenders: besides employers anxious to keep down labor costs, there were many working-class parents who either saw nothing wrong with supplementing the family income out of child labor or believed they had no choice in the matter.

The Labor Movement

As we look at the circumstances of American wage-earners during the Gilded Age, we observe a mixed picture. The average real wages rose in this period, probably by about twenty-five percent between 1860 and 1900. Many American workers were able to advance in their jobs, and move up the economic scale. Social mobility was by no means an uncommon experience among working people of this era. Especially in larger communities, such as Boston, the advance of workers, both native-born and Jewish and North European immigrants, was remarkable. And even in a backwater community like Newburyport, Massachusetts, those workers who remained in the city for a substantial length of time usually could look forward to some property or savings at the end of a long working life.

Yet there were also many things wrong with the lot of the average American wage-earner in these years. For every male worker who stayed put and advanced in his job or accumulated some property, there were several who failed and departed to seek their fortune in some other place. One of the most remarkable qualities of working-class social life in this era was the geographical mobility of the average family head. During the six decades from 1830 to 1890, the population increase of Boston was about 387,000. In this period, however, over 3 1/3 million had at one time or another arrived in the city to live. For the vast majority of new arrivals, then, Boston was a revolving door, and we can only assume that most of those who departed had been disappointed in their economic hopes.

Job insecurity was rife in this period. Without strong unions to worry about, an employer could let any worker go for whatever reason he wished. His reasons were often frivolous or unfair: union activity, "uppityness," refusal to accept a speed-up. Even more serious were the periodic depressions of these years. In the period 1873-79, 1884-86, and 1893-97, there were severe business slumps when many thousands of men and women lost their jobs. In the last of these, as many a 4 1/2 million wage-earners were out of work—over eighteen percent of the labor force.

Poor health and safety were two other serious drawbacks of working-class life in this era. This was a period when men and women worked amid the smoke, flame, and din of furnaces and exposed machinery. Boiler explosions, mine cave-ins, train wrecks, uncontrollable fires, and other accidents were grim events in the lives of industrial workers. Thousands were maimed or killed, and of these few could count on collecting anything to compensate them or their families for loss, pain, or suffering. Where workers escaped sudden death or injury, they often fell victim to the slower processes of industrial disease. Maladies that we today would recognize as "black lung" disease or some form of industrial poisoning generally went undetected. The most serious disease of all that working people regularly contracted was the "white plague," tuberculosis, a product of crowding, overwork, and poor nutrition that afflicted thousands, especially in the big cities.

Finally, there was the matter of working hours. The workday in American mines, mills, factories, and construction sites was long throughout the half-century following the Civil War. In 1890 factory workers typically labored some sixty hours a week at their machines. Bituminous coal miners had an equally long workweek. Bakers and steel-workers averaged sixty-five hours or more. In the building trades fifty-one or fifty-two hours a week was more common, but only postal employees and other government workers, with their forty-eight-hour week, approached modern standards.

Whatever its overall achievements, the American industrial economy provided ample cause for wage-earner unrest. In the post-Civil War era this discontent would erupt in spasms of violence that shocked middle-class public opinion profoundly and injured the cause of labor.

The murder and intimidation that swept the Pennsylvania anthracite coal regions during the 1860's and 1870's is an early instance of such violence. The Pennsylvania unrest has traditionally been ascribed to a secret society called the "Molly Maguires," an outgrowth, supposedly, of the Ancient Order of Hibernians, an Irish-American benevolent society. The so-called Mollies flourished in a milieu of low wages, physical danger, and employer repression, to which they responded by violence against coal company officials and miners who threatened to reveal their secrets. The Mollies probably did not exist as an organized conspiratorial body, but there can be no doubt that violence against unfriendly mine operators was common in the east Pennsylvania coal fields, and that intimidation was used to reinforce the more conventional labor weapons of strikes and boycotts.

In 1873 Frank B. Gowen, the tough, anti-union president of the Philadelphia and Reading Railroad, an owner of coal mines, hired an agent of the Pinkerton private detective agency to infiltrate the union supporters. At enormous risk, James McParlan, passing himself off as a semi-criminal, joined the Hibernians. Over the next months McParlan gained the confidence of the members by treating liberally at the local saloons and by his happy-go-lucky demeanor and ability to tell smutty jokes.

By this time a major strike had broken out in the coal fields, a dispute marked by violence on both sides as the operators brought in vicious strike-breakers and company police and the miners attacked the "scabs." In the end, after five months of arson, murder, and threats, the miners surrendered and went back to work. With the strike over, McParlan surfaced with evidence naming union leaders who had been directly involved in the murder of company officials.

During the Molly Maguire trials that followed, McParlan was the state's chief witness, although at least one of the accused turned state's evidence and testified against his fellow workers. Some scholars believe the evidence against the accused to have been seriously flawed, but in any event twenty-four men were convicted, ten of whom were hanged and fourteen sent to jail. It was many years before the anthracite coal miners were in a position to challenge the mine owners again.

The trials of the Molly Maguires had scarcely concluded before the country experienced an eruption of violence that went far beyond the coal field

PINKERTON'S NATIONAL
DETECTIVE AGENCY.

ALLAN PINKERTON, PRINCIPAL.
Geo. H. Bangs, Gen'l Sup't.
Robert A. Pinkerton, Sup't., 66 Exchange Place, NEW YORK.
R. J. Linden, Sup't., 45 South Third Street, PHILADELPHIA.
F. Warner, Sup't., 191 & 193 Fifth Avenue, CHICAGO.
W. A. Pinkerton, "
Clarence A. Seward, Attorney and Counsel for the Agency, 29 Nassau St. New York.

We never sleep.

LIST OF FUGITIVE MOLLIE MAGUIRES,
1879.

WILLIAM LOVE.—Murderer of Thos. Gwyther, at Girardville, Pa., August 14th, 1875. Is a miner and boatman; 26 years old; 5 ft. 9 in. high; medium build; weighs about 150 lbs.; light complexion; grey eyes; yellow hair; light mustache; has a scar from burn on left side of neck under chin, and coal marks on hands; thin and sharp features; generally dresses well. Lived at Girardville, Schuylkill Co., Pa.

THOMAS HURLEY.—Murderer of Gomer Jamas, August 14th, 1875. Is a miner; 25 years old; 5 ft. 8 in. high; well built; weighs about 160 lbs.; sandy complexion and hair; small piercing eyes; smooth face; sharp features; large hands and feet; wears black hat and dark clothes; lived at Shenandoah, Schuylkill Co., Pa.

MICHAEL DOYLE.—Murderer of Thomas Sanger and Wm. Uren, September 1st, 1875. Is a miner; 25 years old; 5 ft. 5 in. high; medium built; dark complexion; black hair and eyes; full round face and head; smooth face and boyish looking generally; wears a cap. Lived at Shenandoah.

JAMES, ALIAS FRIDAY O'DONNELL.—Murderer of Sanger and Uren, is 26 years old; 5 ft. 10½ in. high; slim built; fair complexion; smooth face; dark eyes; brown hair; generally wears a cap; dresses well; is a miner and lived at Wiggan's Patch, Pa.

JAMES McALLISTER.—Murderer of Sanger and Uren, is 27 years old; 5 ft. 8 in. high; stout built; florid complexion; full broad face, somewhat freckled; light hair and moustache; wears a cap and dark clothes, lived at Wiggan's Patch, Pa.

JOHN, ALIAS HUMPTY FLYNN.—Murderer of Thomas Devine, October 11th, 1875, and Geo. K. Smith, at Audenreid, November 5th, 1863. Is 53 years old; 5 ft. 7 or 8 in high; heavy built; sandy hair and complexion; smooth face; large nose; round shouldered and almost humpbacked. Is a miner and lived at New Philadelphia, Schuylkill Co., Pa.

JERRY KANE.—Charged with conspiracy to murder. Is 38 years old; 5 ft. 7 in. high; dark complexion; short brown hair; sharp features; sunken eyes; roman nose; coal marks on face and hands; wears black slouch hat; has coarse gruff voice. Is a miner and lived at Mount Laffee, Pa.

FRANK KEENAN.—Charged with conspiracy to murder. Is 31 years old; 5 ft. 7 in. high; dark complexion; black hair, inclined to curl and parted in the middle; sharp features; slender but compactly built; wears a cap and dark clothes. Is a miner and lived at Forrestville, Pa.

WILLIAM GAVIN.—Charged with conspiracy to murder. Is 42 year old; 5 ft. 8 in. high; sandy hair and complexion; stout built; red chin whiskers; face badly pockmarked; has but one eye; large nose; formerly lived at Big Mine Run, Pa. Is a miner. Wears a cap and dark clothes.

JOHN REAGAN.—Murderer of Patrick Burns at Tuscarora, April 15th, 1870. About 5 ft. 10 or 11 in. high; 40 years old; small goatee; stoop shouldered; dark hair, cut short; coal marks on hands and face; has a swinging walk; wears shirt collar open at the neck.

THOMAS O'NEILL.—Murderer of Patrick Burns, at Tuscarora, April 15th, 1870. About 5 ft. 9 in. high; 35 years old; light hair; very florid complexion; red moustache and think red goatee; stoop shouldered; walks with a kind of a jerk; think has some shot marks on back of neck and wounded in right thigh.

PATRICK B. GALLAGHER, ALIAS PUG NOSE PAT.—Murderer of George K. Smith, at Audenreid, November 5th, 1863. About 5 ft. 8 in. high; medium built; dark complexion and hair; latter inclined to curl; turned up nose; thick lips; wears a frown on his countenance; large coal cut across the temple; from 32 to 35 years old; has been shot in the thigh.

Information may be sent to me at either of the above offices,

ALLAN PINKERTON.

outburst. In 1873 a sharp panic set off a severe depression. In an economy still marked by fierce business competition, employers found themselves forced to cut back or face bankruptcy. Their natural target was wages, and as the economy flattened out, they unilaterally imposed wage cuts on their men.

Few actions by management are as appalling to workers as wage cuts and when, in 1877, the Baltimore and Ohio Railroad announced the second ten-percent reduction for its workers in eight months, the men blew up. First at Baltimore and then at Martinsburg to the west, the men uncoupled cars from locomotives and stopped passage of trains. Egged on by railroad management, the governor of Maryland called for federal troops and himself sent in state militia to force the men to let the trains through. The militia clashed with the workers and before the week was out, the strike had spread to all parts of the B&O and to other roads coast to coast. By the time it ended it had affected fourteen states and produced a casualty list of over a hundred killed, including strikers, militia, federal troops, and bystanders. Millions of dollars in railroad property went up in smoke.

The 1877 strikes shook the confidence of the middle class in the stability of the economic system. The Philadelphia *Inquirer* charged that the railroad workers had "practically raised the standard of the Paris commune," while the president of the Pennsylvania Railroad noted that what had begun as a riot had grown into an "insurrection." Allan Pinkerton, the head of the strike-breaking detective agency, claimed that the strikes were "the direct result of the communist spirit spread through the ranks of railroad employees by communistic leaders and their teachings." In the wake of the upheavals, many states passed laws making "conspiracies" among workers to injure employers criminal offenses.

With the return of good times in 1879, relative quiet descended over the labor scene. But during the next twenty years, whenever workers were confronted with wage cuts, they protested angrily and often violently. In 1886, after a political meeting called by Chicago anarchists to protest the labor policies of the McCormick Reaper Company, someone threw a bomb at police in Haymarket Square. The explosion killed one policeman and injured seventy. The ensuing wave of anti-labor feeling swept decent men from their moorings and led to the hanging of four anarchists and the imprisoning of four others, although there was no valid proof of the direct involvement of any of the men

convicted in the crime. In 1892 violence occurred at the Carnegie steel plant at Homestead, Pennsylvania, when Henry Clay Frick, Carnegie's lieutenant, tried to break a strike by using scabs. Two years later, President Cleveland sent federal troops to put down violence in Chicago following a railroad strike in support of the Pullman Palace Car workers in the company town of Pullman, Illinois.

These events suggest that American workers invariably took their grievances into the streets. Yet that would be a misreading of the Gilded Age labor movement. For one thing, working people were as often the victims of violence as its perpetrators. Relatively few wage-earners ever fired a pistol at a company official, threw a torch through a railroad roundhouse window, or hurled a brick at a Pinkerton-hired strike-breaker. In fact, it can be argued that American workingmen were overall rather conservative, and generally accepted the capitalist institutions of their country. When confronted with a particularly blatant violation of their rights or a brutal assault on their sense of fair play, they could blow up. But normally it was difficult to get them to devote sustained effort to challenging the system of capitalism or even fighting consistently for some sort of cooperative action to advance their common well-being.

During the Gilded Age, American workingmen neither could sustain an effective labor movement nor would support radical political action in substantial numbers. Labor organizations had a way of growing in times of prosperity and declining when times were bad, precisely when they were needed most. During the years immediately following Appomattox, the National Labor Union, built around demands for an eight-hour day and a desire to establish producers' cooperatives to enable workers to escape the "wage system," flourished for a brief period. In 1872, the NLU turned to politics and supported a labor party. With the panic of 1873 and the depression that followed, however, the NLU collapsed, along with a number of other unions that had confined their work to particular trades.

With the economic revival of the late 1870's, the Knights of Labor, established in 1871, began to gain adherents in large numbers. Headed by Terence V. Powderly from 1878 to 1893, the Knights was open to almost every variety of working person. During the years of its prosperity it seldom supported strikes or "collective bargaining" for the sake of raising wages and improving working conditions. Rather, it tended to focus on political agitation for the eight-hour day, a graduated income tax, consumers' and producers' cooperatives, and, in labor disputes, the use of boycotts and arbitration.

Despite its professed principles, however, the Knights struck several railroads in the mid-1880's. Its initial success brought a wave of supporters who pushed the membership list to over 700,000. But thereafter, as a result of specific defeats in strikes as well as the wave of anti-union feeling that accompanied the Haymarket incident, the Knights precipitously declined. During the 1890's it survived as a shadow of its earlier self largely with agrarian support.

Meanwhile, the Knights had been eclipsed by the American Federation of Labor, a new federated union, founded in 1886 by Peter McGuire, Samuel Gompers, and Adolph Strasser. The last two were cigar makers who in 1879 had organized the skilled cigar workers when they ceased to be independent self-employed craftsmen following introduction of the cigar mold. As leaders of the AF of L, they elevated the techniques they had earlier learned into a set of principles that enabled the new union to weather the ups and downs of the business cycle and become the first truly successful national trade union in American labor history.

Under Gompers, the AF of L avoided politics. A former Socialist, he had found socialist ideas too windy and impractical. Capitalism, he concluded, was in America to stay, and it was essential for wage-earners to gain their benefits within the capitalist system. If nothing else, taking up with radical movements would only alienate the middle class and make trade-union advance that much more difficult. Even engaging in middle-of-the-road politics was a mistake. Better to stick to "pure and simple" trade unionism. As Strasser stated the AF of L case in a famous observation:

Our organization does not consist of idealists. . . . We have no ultimate ends. We are going on from day to day. We are fighting only for immediate objects—objects that can be realized in a few years.

However limited—or perhaps because of its very limitations—the AF of L formula worked. Skilled workers, largely of native background, swelled the ranks of AF of L affiliates. Since they could not easily be replaced, their threats to strike were often effective and they were able to maintain a privileged position as an American labor elite. By 1902 there were over a million wage-earners in unions, three quarters of them in affiliates of the Federation. Unfortunately, this meant that many millions of other American workers remained without the advantages of collective bargaining and mutual support that unions provided. Outside the union movement was the great mass of industrial workers. With the possible exception of the garment industry centered in New York, the overwhelming majority of semi-skilled factory workers were forced to deal directly with powerful employers as individuals, with results that were unimpressive at best.

Socialism

Trade unionism was not the only strategy that wage-earners employed against the system they confronted. Some, like the young Gompers himself, placed their faith in some form of Socialism.

The first Marxist Socialists in America were Germans who brought their new theories with them before the Civil War. During the 1870's the Marxist Workingmen's Party and the Social Democratic Party attracted a few foreign-born workers and a still smaller group of native Americans. In the early 1880's, the Socialists split into two wings; one rejected capitalism only, and one—the anarchists—rejected both capitalism and the state as inherently repressive institutions.

Socialists of every variety hoped to abolish private property and replace it by social control of the means of production. Only in this way could laboring people—the proletariat—be assured of the fruits of their labor, which under capitalism was expropriated by the owners of productive property, the capitalists. Capitalism, according to Marxist theory, had in its early stages been a progressive force that had increased mankind's wealth immensely. When they smashed the power of the feudal landed nobility, the capitalist class—also called the bourgeoisie—had advanced world history to a new and higher stage. But by the mid-nineteenth century capitalism had developed certain inner "contradictions" that would soon prevent further advance. With the passing years, capitalist society would be faced with ever-more-serious economic crises that capitalists would attempt to escape from through colonialism. This attempt would fail. Depressions would become deeper and longer; working people would lose whatever gains they had made; the smaller capitalists would be squeezed out and fall into the ranks of the proletariat; more and more wealth and power would be concentrated in the hands of great monopolies and corporations. In the end, the proletariat, made class-conscious and militant by its experiences, would rise up against the now-rotten system and overthrow it. Thereafter, mankind would be free of economic exploitation and injustice and would finally advance to a new stage of steady progress, equality of wealth and power, and an end to class struggle.

How the final overthrow would be brought about was a matter of contention among the different kinds of Marxists. Some believed that it could be done through peaceful means: a Socialist party in a democracy could win a majority and legislate capitalism out of existence. Others believed that only violence could oust the capitalists from the seats of power. Anarchists, especially, were violence-prone and at times seemed to elevate direct action to an end in itself, although some also advocated the "general strike," whereby all workers would simply refuse to work, as an equally effective way to bring down the capitalist system.

At no time did the Socialists ever win the support of more than a fraction of the American working class. During the nineteenth century they gained some converts among German-born and eastern European workers, but to American working people in general the ideas of class struggle, organized violence, and hatred of private property were alien. Daniel DeLeon's Socialist Labor Party, founded in the late 1870's, had fewer than fifteen hundred members in the early 1880's. At the very end of the century Eugene V. Debs, former leader of the American Railway Union, who was sent to jail for defying a federal injunction during the Pullman strike, helped organize the Socialist Party of America. In 1900 the SPA, with Debs as

its presidential candidate, won about 100,000 votes. In the next decade, after the arrival of many thousands of additional eastern European immigrants, the Socialist Party vote and membership leaped. In 1912 its growth would peak with the achievement of almost one million votes for Debs in that year's presidential election, about six percent of the total.

Despite this modest performance overall, Socialism made its mark on American life. A number of intellectuals were attracted to it, especially in the pleasant domestic version retailed by Edward Bellamy in his 1888 utopian novel, *Looking Backward.* During the 1890's writers, artists, editors, and just ordinary middle-class men and women joined Nationalist clubs dedicated to the Bellamy "principle of association," that is, to cooperation instead of competition as the basic mode of social and economic conduct. Socialism created a kind of conscience for America that reinforced the social justice and egalitarian aspects of the American democratic credo. In later years, when middle-class reformers confronted the social ills of the nation, they would be conscious of the Socialist alternative to reformism and would be spurred on, lest the Socialists profit from continuing social ills.

Unfortunately, there was also a negative side to this relationship between reform and revolution. Conservatives saw Socialism as an extreme danger and were not averse to using fears of violent uprising to stigmatize all reform, or indeed all attempts to improve the lot of wage-earners. After the Haymarket affair, conservative journalists and opinion-makers were quick to attack all labor union leaders as "agitators" and dangerous radicals, no better than the anarchists who had thrown the bomb at Haymarket Square. In later years, all those who dissented from the social and economic status quo would suffer similar attacks. These assaults would be a heavy burden for both reformers and revolutionaries.

Black Americans

Among the outsiders within American society were millions of people whose race, national origins, and cultural traditions set them apart from the native white Protestant majority. In various ways, and to varying degrees, these Americans failed to share fully in the economic,

social, and political benefits of the richest and most democratic nation on earth.

The largest single "minority" in Gilded Age America consisted of black people of African ancestry. By 1880 there were 6.6 million black Americans out of a total population of a little over

George Washington Carver. (Library of Congress.)

50 million, or somewhat over thirteen percent of the whole. Overwhelmingly, these black citizens lived in the South, with the deep South of the old Confederacy having the largest proportion. They were also mostly rural, the majority being tenant farmers, living on and working on land owned by others and experiencing more than their share of the general poverty of their region.

Not only were black Americans poor; they were also despised by their white fellow countrymen. Here and there in this period a voice was raised to defend blacks against their detractors and exploiters; a few philanthropists interested themselves in black education or the health of black citizens. But few white Americans cared to involve themselves in the apparently stale battles of the Reconstruction era. Black Americans accordingly were largely thrown back on their own limited resources in their battle for decent treatment, fair play, and a reasonable chance for economic success.

In many ways the lot of black Americans deteriorated in these years. We have already seen something of the poverty and economic stagnation that afflicted them as sharecroppers in the post-Civil War South, and how they lost the fight to retain political rights during Reconstruction. By the 1880's they had also begun to be surrounded by rising walls of legal segregation which excluded them from a wide range of public facilities, including good schools, colleges, and universities, and from decent housing in the towns and cities. Black Americans fought back as best they could against "Jim Crow," but with few allies they could accomplish little. In 1883 the Supreme Court, reviewing a suit under the 1875 Civil Rights Act brought by five black Americans, declared that the law limited only the right of states to discriminate, not the right of private individuals. Most of the modest federal protection left was eliminated when, in *Plessy v. Ferguson* (1896), the Court upheld a Louisiana law requiring segregation of blacks on the state's trains. So long as "equal" facilities were provided, they could be "separate" without violating the equal-protection clause of the Fourteenth Amendment.

Reinforcing Jim Crow was a growing regime of terror. As a means of keeping blacks in their place the less reputable elements in Southern white society turned more and more to extra-legal vigilante action. In 1882 forty-nine blacks were lynched in the South. Ten years later there were 161 victims of white mobs unwilling to await the outcome of normal legal processes. In the new century the number of lynchings declined, but, as if to make up for this, race riots increased in frequency. In 1906 a wave of rioting broke out in Atlanta that left four dead and millions of dollars' worth of property destroyed. Nor were Northern communities exempt from anti-black violence. A 1908 racial incident in Springfield, Illinois, set off several days of lynching and rioting that led to six dead and seventy injured.

As the new century opened, a new group of black leaders emerged to take over from the timid ones of the past. Over the next two generations, these men—most notably Booker T. Washington, W. E. B. DuBois, and Marcus Garvey—would help transform race relations in the United States in fundamental ways.

George Washington Carver, pictured opposite, was an agricultural chemist born of slave parents. Educated at Iowa State, he became director of agricultural research at Tuskegee Institute, Alabama. He used empirical research methods on the peanut, sweet potato, and soybean, and he strongly influenced the shift of the Southern agricultural economy from a single-crop basis to a more healthy diversified foundation.

Immigrants

Another large group that did not fit comfortably into the social environment of the Gilded Age was the foreign-born. No more than blacks did they constitute a new "problem." America had experienced great waves of immigration in the past and adjusted to the newcomers. Yet the late nineteenth-century experience was different: the "New Immigrants" of the post-1880 period came largely from the underdeveloped lands of eastern and southern Europe, regions culturally more distant from the heritage of old-stock Americans than the Ireland, Germany, and Scandinavia from which past immigrants had arrived.

Americans exaggerated the differences between the Old immigration of the Irish and Germans and the New of the Slavs, Italians, Jews, Greeks, Syrians, and Chinese. They held, for example, that the new immigrants tended to be disproportionately composed of men who came to America not to stay, but merely to make money and return home. It was true that with trans-Atlantic passage now cheaper and quicker some of the newer immigrants were indeed mere sojourners; but many others came to stay and did so. Another supposed distinction between the "old" and the "new" was in education and skills. The old Irish and Ger-

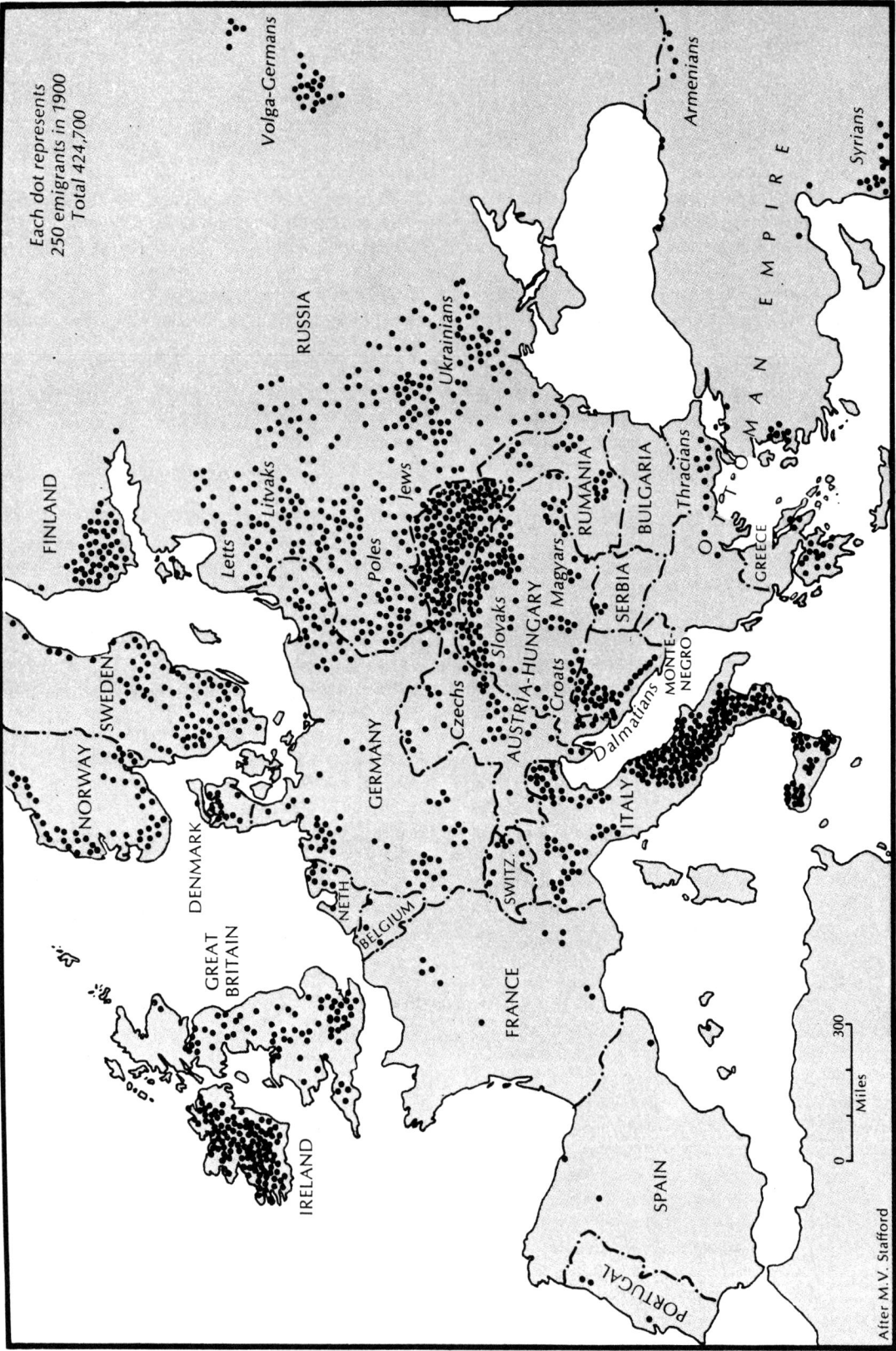

Each dot represents
250 emigrants in 1900
Total 424,700

Volga-Germans

Armenians

Syrians

OTTOMAN EMPIRE

RUSSIA

Ukrainians

FINLAND

Letts

Litvaks

Jews

Poles

Thracians

RUMANIA

BULGARIA

Magyars

SERBIA

GREECE

Czechs

Slovaks

AUSTRIA-HUNGARY

Croats

Dalmatians

MONTE-
NEGRO

NORWAY

SWEDEN

DENMARK

GERMANY

SWITZ.

ITALY

NETH.

BELGIUM

GREAT
BRITAIN

FRANCE

IRELAND

SPAIN

PORTUGAL

0   300
Miles

After M.V. Stafford

Emigration from Europe to the United States in 1900

mans, it was said, were literate, while the newest newcomers were not. Again, this was only a partial truth: Jews, northern Italians, and Bohemians, among the new immigrants, were more skilled and literate than most of those who had come before 1860.

The problem with the common native American estimate of the post-1880's newcomers, then, was that it lumped them all together and made no allowance for individual and group differences. Nevertheless, there are still valid distinctions between Gilded Age and antebellum immigrants. The latest newcomers were largely from lands where industry was backward and they knew little besides agriculture. Their countries of origin were also largely autocracies, and they had little experience with democratic government. They were poorer than most of the pre-1860 immigrants, and they were far less likely to be Protestant. Moreover, the country they came to was notably different from the one entered by their predecessors: in 1850 the United States was still overwhelmingly agricultural, and many of the new arrivals could take up land and become farmers. By the 1880's, however, most of the best land was gone and the former peasants from Poland, the Ukraine, Serbia, Greece, Romania, and the south of Italy had little choice but to work in factories and live in towns and cities.

As in the past, most of the post-1880's Europeans settled in the Northeast or Midwest; few went to the South. Wherever they put down roots, they planted their Old World customs and traditions. Most fundamental of these was religion, which for most of these newer groups was an essential part of daily life. A majority were Catholic, and by the 1880's the Catholic Church had been firmly established in the United States. Catholic Italians and Slavs, then, were not coming to a "heathen" land. Yet in the Gilded Age the American Catholic Church was largely English-speaking and Irish-dominated, and for many years the newcomers would battle with the earlier arrivals over such issues as the dominance of the Irish among the clergy and hierarchy, and the language of sermons.

The Jews, too, found that the presence of earlier-arrived coreligionists presented problems. Many of the German Jews of the antebellum period were by now thoroughly Americanized, and they had revised and modernized Jewish religious practices so that they were more closely aligned with prevailing American modes of religious practice. To the great mass of eastern European Jewish newcomers, their German-Jewish predecessors seemed scarcely Jews at all. To the

German Jews, in turn, their Polish, Russian, and Romanian brethren appeared to be outlandish folk, entirely out of tune with the modern world.

If native Catholics and Jews considered their own coreligionists alien, how much stranger did they seem in the eyes of old-stock native Protestants. During these years anti-Catholic feeling ran high in parts of Protestant America, leading to demands for immigration restrictions and for laws to prevent the Catholic Church from intruding into what the critics conceived of as secular affairs. This movement culminated in the formation of the American Protective Association in 1887; its members were pledged to work to exclude Catholics from political office, to seek to keep Catholic workers from taking jobs of Protestants, and to refuse to join Catholics in strikes. In the 1890's the group allied itself with the Republicans in the Midwest in battles over the funding of parochial schools, and its members boycotted Catholic merchants.

Anti-Semitism, an old affliction of the Christian world, also flared up in these years. In the 1870's Jews had begun to suffer social ostracism and exclusion from resort hotels and clubs. In the 1890's they encountered physical violence at the hands of ruffians and were verbally attacked by both Populists like Ignatius Donnelly and aristocrats like Henry Adams as vulgar, bad-mannered, and mercenary.

In addition to the bias that had a religious taproot, there was the hatred of immigrants that derived from economic competition. Immigrants were willing to work for less and so drove down the wages of native Americans, it was said. In these years unions were often "nativist," and in California, with its large Chinese population, white workers organized an anti-Chinese Workingmen's Party in 1877, led by an Irish-American agitator, Dennis Kearney. Hostility to immigrants also had a more generalized basis in feelings of "xenophobia," fear of things foreign. Each group had customs, practices, and qualities that affronted native Americans. One group was said to be violent, another given to drink, a third criminally inclined, a fourth dirty, a fifth stupid, a sixth immoral. And so it went: to insecure and narrow-minded folk the deluge of newcomers seemed a frightening and distasteful event.

It was inevitable that anti-immigrant feelings should take the form of efforts to exclude the newcomers. In 1882 Congress responded to strong anti-Chinese sentiment by excluding Chinese laborers from the United States for ten years. Later this was made permanent. In 1894 a group of upper-class Bostonians organized the Immigration Restriction League to limit the number of new foreign arrivals by imposing a literacy test. This, it was thought, would exclude newcomers from Slavic and Latin lands while still allowing northern Europeans to enter the country. In 1897 Congress responded to the League's pressure by imposing a literacy test on immigrants, only to have President Cleveland veto it. The League continued to agitate against free immigration, but each time Congress passed such a literacy bill it failed to receive the President's signature.

The opposition the restrictionists encountered derived from a number of sources. Immigrants themselves fought against measures to exclude their fellow countrymen. Since many urban politicians now relied on their votes, they wielded considerable power. There was also the American tradition of free immigration to reckon with: the nation had always served as a refuge for Europe's impoverished and oppressed millions, and it was not easy for Americans to abandon the credo of generations. Despite their uneasiness, many Americans believed in the endless possibilities of assimilation, the ability of American society to take the foreigner, strip him of his outlandish clothes, language, and folkways and make him

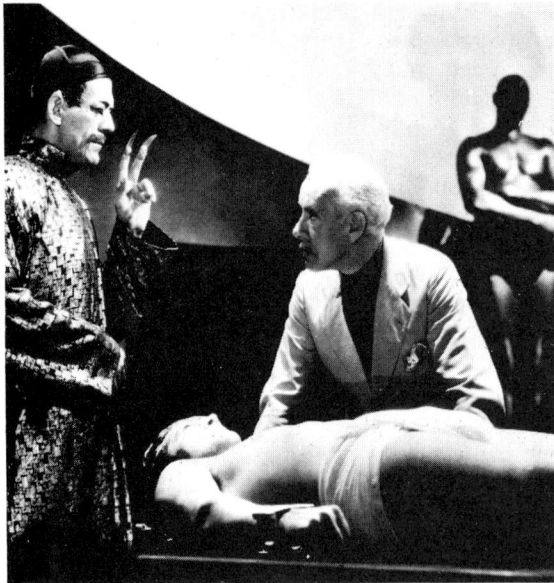

The Mask of Fu-Manchu. *In this movie Boris Karloff as the insidious Dr. Fu-Manchu is about to work his will on the drugged youth. Fu-Manchu was a comic-strip racist story, but it typifies attitudes toward Asians in a period when many movies were set in the European colonies of Asia. Equally pernicious was the treatment of blacks; they were presented as lovable idiots or loyal servants to white masters; if "natives" in Africa, they were fools, totally manipulated by whites.*

over into a "true" American. To assimilationists, whether native Americans or immigrants themselves, the hope for a successful solution of the immigration problem rested with the schools, especially the urban public schools. In these the immigrant child would study American history and traditions, and learn to read and write English; in a few years, it was assumed, he or she would be indistinguishable from the child of the Pilgrim fathers. A few native Americans went one step further in their liberalism and were willing to accept "cultural pluralism"—that is, a society that accepted differences in culture and outlook among its citizens and considered such differences valuable and enriching.

There was also an economic dimension to the anti-restriction view. If some native workers feared the foreigners' "coolie wages," others recognized that they benefited from the cheap labor pool that the immigrant represented. Immigrant workers needed native American foremen and managers, and their arrival in vast numbers thrust up literate oldstock workers into white-collar or managerial ranks. Middle-class people also relied on immigrants as servants. Most important of all, employers valued the cheap and willing labor of eastern and southern Europeans. Their well-financed campaigns against laws to limit their numbers were probably the most formidable opposition the restrictionists faced.

It would be a mistake to see immigrants solely as victims. Their lives were not constant confrontations with bigots. In the communities where they settled, they found a rich life among their fellow countrymen, pursuing the old ways, eating traditional foods, speaking their native languages, and practicing Old World customs. Native Americans of a more open turn of mind found the immigrant ghettoes of the big cities to be fascinating places. One reported of New York's Little Italy:

The sons of Italy . . . are fond of music and outdoor life; and in New York they enjoy both of these luxuries when the band plays in Mulberry Bend Park. Then they pour forth from a hundred tenements . . . and stand listening in rapt delight by the hour to the strains of "Il Trovatore." . . . Nearly all the Italian societies give festivals annually, and these have been accompanied . . . by . . . a racket of fireworks. . . . Frequently great wooden and pasteboard shrines are erected on the sidewalk and the streets are arched with lines of Chinese lanterns. In a recent Elizabeth Street fiesta great wire brackets arched the street at intervals of one hundred feet for a quarter of a mile, and huge painted candles, eight to ten feet in

Hester and Clinton Streets, New York City, ca. 1896. (New York Historical Society.)

height ... were presented by the wealthier families to the Madonna. ...

Nor were the immigrants invariably poor and downtrodden. Most no doubt started at the bottom of the economic ladder. Poles and other Slavic people manned the coal mines and the iron mills. French Canadians replaced the Yankees and Irish in the New England cotton mills. In the Southwest, Mexicans worked on the railroads as laborers. Italians pushed wheelbarrows and wielded picks and shovels in the construction industry. Jews cut and sewed in the garment industry in Chicago, New York, and Rochester. Most groups, however, had their small contingent of professionals and intellectuals who served as doctors, lawyers, priests, teachers, newspaper editors, shopkeepers, and small manufacturers.

More significant was the relative speed of upward movement. The evidence here is conflicting: some scholars believe that the advance up the economic ladder was relatively slow for immigrants; others are impressed by its swiftness. The most convincing formula holds that it varied from place to place and from group to group. Boston's Italians, for example, improved their occupational positions more slowly than the city's Jews and people of British origin. On the other hand, one scholar finds that between 1880 and 1915 among both the Italians and Jews of New York, many individuals moved upward from the working class into the self-employed category. Complicating matters further here is that occupational mobility was not the only source of striving and satisfaction to immigrants. Some, such as the Poles, found home ownership the most desirable goal and marked their success by the extent to which they could achieve it.

Nonetheless, although the picture is complex, its overall outlines are clear: immigrants did find the United States a land of opportunity, a place where they could improve their lives and those of their children. And this conclusion only stands to reason. Why else did immigrants come in such enormous numbers over so long a period unless experience demonstrated that in America things were indeed better?

Agrarian Discontent

Another group in America that perceived itself as outside the main thrust of progress consisted of the farmers. Not all farmers were restless and aggrieved in the decades following 1865, but enough of them were to create a major political force that for a time seemed likely to alter the shape of American political life.

American agriculture was as much a success story as American industry in the Gilded Age. The farmer advanced in every index of output and productivity, and helped supply the food and fiber needed by the nation's growing urban population, besides providing large surpluses for export to other industrial lands. Yet the generation following 1865 was a trying period. Northeastern farmers, even since the transportation revolution before the Civil War had opened up the fertile Middle West, had been forced to adjust to the stiff competition of the newer region. This competition continued after 1865 and pushed many people off the land in New England and the Middle Atlantic states. Many farms were simply abandoned. Others were shifted to the production of fruits, vegetables, dairy products, and other perishables, where closeness to city consumers gave an advantage. By the 1870's farmers of the Midwest were also being forced to make painful adjustments. As the wheat belt moved further west into the Plains, farmers in the "Old Northwest" found they could no longer compete. And so, along the Great Lakes and in Wisconsin they turned to dairying to supply the large Midwestern cities. Further south they shifted to corn for feeding hogs and cattle. By the 1880's the prairie lands of Illinois, Iowa, Indiana, and eastern Kansas and Nebraska were covered with fields of maize as far as the eye could see. In the barns and pens, hundreds of "porkers" grew fat from eating the previous year's crop.

During the years of adjustment, Eastern and, especially, Midwestern farmers expressed their discontent in no uncertain terms. Through the Patrons of Husbandry, popularly called the "Grange," they organized to improve their lot. The Grange analysis of the farmer's plight focused on the middlemen, those who stood between the farmers and the consumer and took such a large part of the money paid by the consumer for his food, or who charged such a high price for supplying machinery and other items the farmer himself needed. To get around these middlemen, the

Grange organized cooperative buying schemes for farmers and sought to establish farmer-run businesses that could produce what farmers needed at moderate cost. Grangers also tried to reduce middlemen's costs by imposing fixed rates on what railroads and grain elevator companies could charge for their shipping and storage services. This effort brought the Grangers into politics, and by the mid-1870's farmers' parties had been organized in eleven states, mostly in the Midwest. In at least four of these—Illinois, Wisconsin, Iowa, and Minnesota—the Grangers gained control of the state legislatures and enacted legislation authorizing the setting of railroad freight and grain elevator storage charges. It was these "Granger Laws" that the Supreme Court upheld in 1877, before it reversed itself on regulation and laissez-faire.

The Granger era lasted until about 1880. Thereafter, the return of prosperity, together with a successful readjustment to corn-hog and other specialty agriculture geared to domestic urban markets, pacified the Midwest. In the next two decades, the farmers of the prairies and the Northwest would refuse to be drawn into the battles that unsettled the political life of the nation.

The Alliances

To the farm population of the Plains and the South, the 1880's and 1890's brought deep discontent. Wheat and cotton, respectively the chief crops of these areas, depended on overseas markets far more than did the pork, beef, fruits, vegetables, and dairy products of the Northeast and Midwest. This meant that the chain of middlemen between producer and consumer was even longer for wheat and cotton than for the perishables of the Midwest and Northeast. In addition, the prices of wheat and cotton fell sharply beginning in the 1870's, dropping to about half of their initial level by the early 1890's. It is true that all other prices fell as well in the quarter-century between 1870 and the mid-1890's—railroad freight rates declined, interest rates declined, as did the price of farm machinery and of many of the manufactured goods that farm families consumed. But it is probably correct to say that the prices of the two great staples of the Plains and the deep South fell faster than those of other goods and services.

We must not imagine, however, that the Gilded Age was a period of unrelieved disaster for grain and cotton farmers. The deflation of staple prices could be offset by cutting costs and getting a larger output with the same investment. This effort to keep up with deflation explains much of the heavy investment of wheat farmers in machinery during these years, and of cotton farmers in fertilizers. By careful attention to the best practices it remained possible to make a profit growing wheat and cotton. Such constant vigilance necessarily took a heavy, psychological toll; and it is not surprising that in the South and Plains farm leaders sought to find other answers to the relentless battle against insolvency, and that they fastened on middlemen and financiers as scapegoats to explain the farmer's plight.

To be sure, there were at last some legitimate grounds for charging railroad operators, mortgage lenders, bankers, and industrialists with exploiting Plains and Deep South farmers. In both the South and the trans-Missouri West, railroad rates were higher than in the Northeast. So were credit costs, a condition that was particularly galling when the dollar was appreciating in value and so making each debt contracted in a given year harder to pay the next. Manufacturers, too, seemed to take advantage of farmers, with the farm machinery "monopoly" appearing as a particularly effective agency for gouging them.

Yet, despite these realistic elements in the farmers' plight, there were others that now seem rhetorical at best. During these years farm spokesmen developed a mythology that depicted the nation as divided into the wicked and the good. The children of light were the "producers," especially the tillers of the soil. The children of darkness were those who produced nothing, but grew fat as parasites on farmers and laborers. Most prominent were the financiers who conspired to reduce the money supply of the nation in order to raise interest rates and push up the value of the dollars they lent to others. This focus on finance had been responsible in the 1870's for the "free silver" movement which had culminated in the Bland-Allison Act of 1878 and the Sherman Silver Purchase Act of 1890.

At the end of the 1870's, various new farmers' groups began to appear, dedicated to fighting for the farmers' cause and against their enemies. In 1880 Texas farmers organized a Grand State

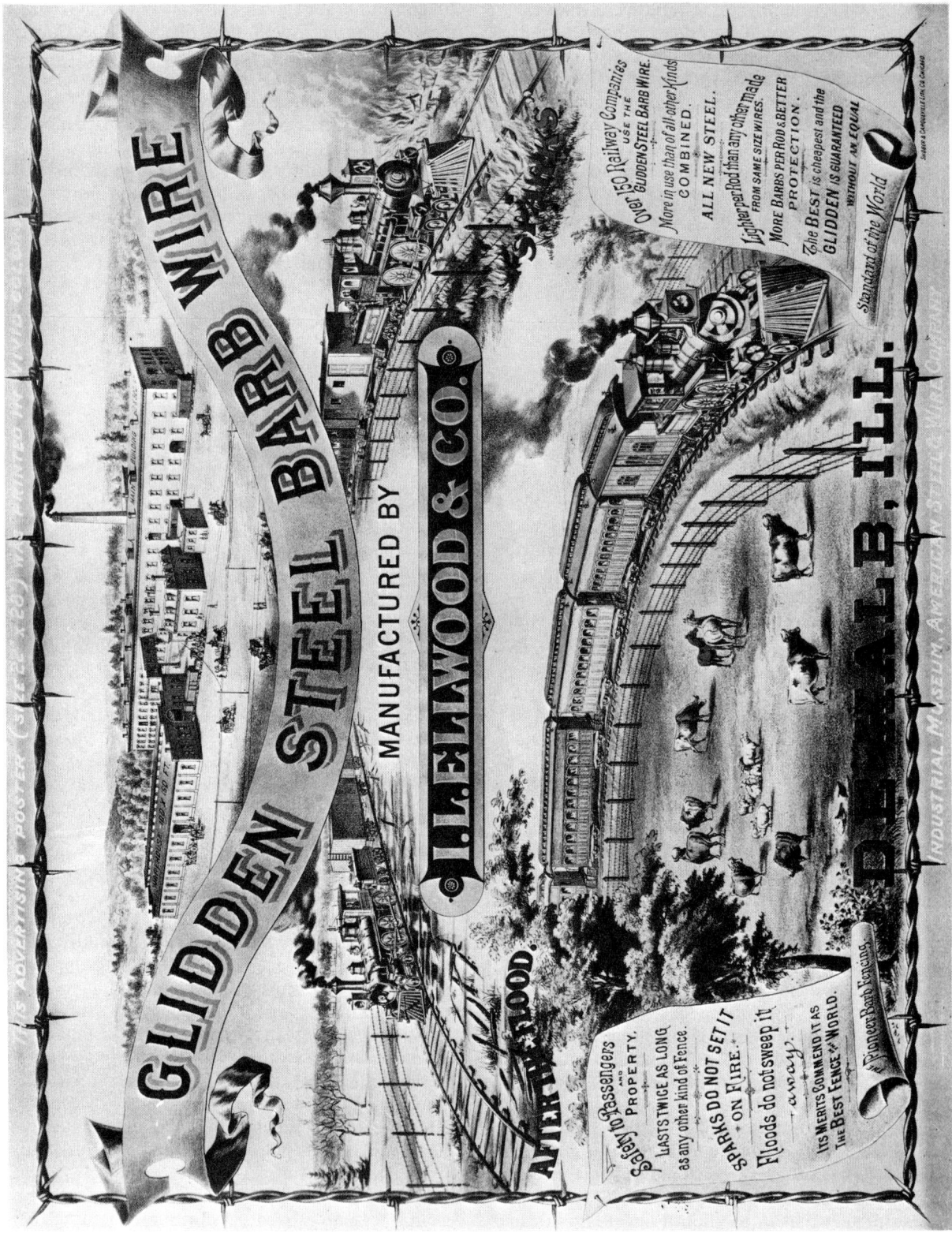

ITS ADVERTISING POSTER (SIZE, 18 x 26) WAS PRINTED IN VIVID COLOR.

GLIDDEN STEEL BARB WIRE

MANUFACTURED BY
I. L. ELLWOOD & CO.

DE KALB, ILL.

Over 150 Railway Companies use the GLIDDEN STEEL BARB WIRE.
More in use than of all other kinds COMBINED.
ALL NEW STEEL.
Lighter per Rod than any other made FROM SAME SIZE WIRES.
MORE BARBS PER ROD & BETTER PROTECTION.
The BEST is cheapest and the GLIDDEN IS GUARANTEED WITHOUT AN EQUAL.
Standard of the World

AFTER THE FLOOD.

Safety to Passengers AND PROPERTY.
LASTS TWICE AS LONG as any other kind of Fence.
SPARKS DO NOT SET IT ON FIRE.
Floods do not sweep it away.
ITS MERITS COMMEND IT AS THE BEST FENCE IN THE WORLD.
Pioneer Barb Fencing

INDUSTRIAL MUSEUM, AMERICAN STEEL & WIRE COMPANY

(Smithsonian Institution.)

Alliance to fight low prices, the evil of crop liens, and the high charges of country storekeepers. By 1886 this group had expanded its demands to include higher taxes on land held by speculators, higher railroad taxes, more paper money, and laws against commodities speculation. Over the next few years the Texans linked up with various Farmer's Clubs, Agricultural Wheels, and other groups. By 1890 the Southern Alliance, resulting from the merger of these, had membership of over a million. The all-white Southern Alliance was paralleled by the Colored Farmers' National Alliance and Cooperative Union, with a million-and-a-half members in 1890. Meanwhile, a similar development in the Northwest produced the National Farmers' Alliance, or Northwestern Alliance. On a platform demanding federal regulation of railroads and free coinage of silver, the North-west Alliance expanded rapidly in the wheat belt. By 1890 there were 130,000 Northwest Alliance members in Kansas, with Nebraska, the Dakotas, and Minnesota not far behind.

Before long, Alliance leaders moved to merge the two regional groups into one nationwide organization; this, however, proved difficult, as each group refused to abandon its own special interests and concerns. By the 1880's the Alliances also began to enter politics in their respective states, usually by associating themselves with one or the other of the two major parties. For a substantial group of farm leaders from the West and South, the mainstream parties were abysmally failing to come to grips with the plight of the rural regions and, beginning in the early 1890's, they came together to organize a new party that would express and seek to fulfill the needs of their constituents.

The Mainstream Parties

The task of any third party was made difficult in this period by the continued strength and power of both Democrats and Republicans. The two were remarkably well matched. From the 1870's onward, control of the national government seesawed back and forth between them. Between the end of the Civil War and the mid-1890's there had been more Republican than Democratic Presidents, but in at least two cases—Tilden in 1876 and Cleveland in 1892—it could be argued that the Democrat, having received more popular votes than his Republican opponent, was really the victor. Dominance in Congress, too, shifted from one party to the other. All told, there were very few years between the end of Reconstruction and 1896 when one party simultaneously controlled the Presidency and both houses of Congress.

In 1868 Ulysses S. Grant defeated his Democratic opponent, former governor Horatio Seymour of New York, on a platform endorsing Radical Reconstruction but also promising sectional peace. Grant's electoral college victory was decisive, but his popular margin was only 300,000 out of almost six million ballots cast. And in 1872 Grant badly beat the Democratic candidate, Horace Greeley. In 1880 the Republican Party pitted Congressman James A. Garfield of Ohio against former Union General Winfield Scott Hancock of Pennsylvania. Garfield won with a solid electoral college majority of 214 to 155, but his popular majority was under 10,000 votes!

Four years later the Republicans rejected Chester Arthur, who had succeeded to the presidency after Garfield was shot by a disappointed federal office-seeker after only four months in office. Though the former "spoilsman" had made a surprisingly effective and dignified President, the party regulars turned to the charismatic James G. Blaine of Maine. The Democrats chose the reform governor of New York, Grover Cleveland. The campaign was a dirty one. Blaine was accused, with good reason, of having taken bribes from a Southern railroad for his support while serving as United States Senator; Cleveland, with equally good reason, of having fathered an illegitimate child. Despite the charge of personal immorality, the honest government "mugwumps" rallied to the New Yorker. Meanwhile, Blaine inadvertently offended Catholic voters when he failed to reprove a bigoted Protestant supporter who, in his hearing, declared the Democrats the party of "rum, Romanism, and rebellion." Cleveland won, by a hair: electoral votes, 219 to 182; popular votes, 4.9 million to 4.8.

Cleveland was the first Democratic President since James Buchanan before the Civil War, and his administration was marked by controversy with Union veterans unused to a man who had not served in the Union Army. They resented deeply his vetoes of pension bills and his effort to have the War Department return to the Southern states captured Confederate battle flags. Honest government men, however, admired his principled stands on civil service, sound money, and a reduction in the protective tariff.

In 1888 Cleveland was renominated and emphasized tariff reduction during the campaign. The Republicans nominated the aloof but eloquent Benjamin Harrison of Indiana on a platform supporting pensions and the high tariff. In the end the election turned on the foolish statement of the British minister to the United States that he would like to be able to vote for Cleveland. This "Murchison letter" was published, and many Irish-Americans defected to Harrison to give him the election. But the results again were close. Cleveland actually won 100,000 more popular votes than his rival, but lost the key states of New York and Indiana and received an electoral minority.

As President, Harrison rewarded his business supporters by endorsing the McKinley tariff of 1890, pushing rates to the highest level ever. With federal revenues at an all-time high as a result of the tariff, the government ran large surpluses, and Congress sought to reduce them by enormous giveaways including the most generous pensions ever awarded Union veterans. So spendthrift was Harrison's first Congress that critics labeled it the "billion dollar Congress." In the 1890 congressional elections the Democrats won a large majority, gaining control of the House of Representatives.

The election of 1892 again pitted Cleveland against Harrison. This time a strong Democratic current was running and Cleveland, emphasizing his support for "sound money" and a moderate tariff position, defeated his former opponent by a popular vote of 5.5 million to 5.2 million and an electoral count of 277 to 145.

The relative parity of the two major parties on the national level was not matched at the local or regional level. New England tended to be strongly Republican, and areas where people of New England descent lived in northern New York and the older Midwest also voted strongly for the "Grand Old Party" (GOP). The South, on the other hand, was overwhelmingly Democratic, except in a few areas where, during the Civil War period, pro-Union sentiment had been strong. In the Midwest, the areas settled by Southerners before the Civil War—"Copperhead" or peace Democrat country —also voted for the "Democracy."

The reason for these sectional patterns is not hard to discern. In part, they were an extension of the old anti-slavery battles of the 1850's: those Americans committed to striking slavery down continued to vote for the party of Lincoln; those who had then been on the opposite side continued to vote against it. The war experience itself further

reinforced these commitments and loyalties. Republican voters remembered the Civil War, and if they did not, were quickly reminded of it by Republican politicians frantically waving the "bloody shirt." "Every unregenerate rebel . . . calls himself a Democrat," shouted Republican Senator Oliver Morton in one typical fiery speech. "Every bounty jumper, every deserter, every sneak who ran away from the draft. . . . Every man . . . who murdered Union prisoners . . . calls himself a Democrat. . . . In short, the Democratic party may be described as a common sewer . . . into which is emptied every element of treason North and South . . . which has dishonored the age." Republican politicians also went out of their way to cultivate the Union veteran vote and to woo the Union veteran organization, the Grand Army of the Republic (GAR). Former boys-in-blue were urged to "vote as you shot."

There were, to be sure, more concrete inducements for veterans to vote Republican. Whenever they could muster majorities in both branches of government, the Republicans appropriated money for disabled Union veterans and their families. The billions paid out as pensions were justified, no doubt, as expressions of a nation's gratitude to those who had served it well. But they also served to weld the Grand Old Party more firmly to the veterans of 1861-65.

If white voters remembered the antislavery battles and the Civil War, so did black ones. In the years following "redemption" in the South, many blacks were excluded from the franchise by unfriendly Southern state governments. Yet, until the 1890's, here and there pockets of Southern blacks continued to cast their ballots. In the North, black Americans voted Republican, in gratitude to the party of Lincoln for their emancipation and as protest against the party of slavery and "rebellion."

There were other bases for party support in these years besides memories of the recent historical past. The two parties differed in their attitudes toward personal life-styles and the place of government in citizens' daily affairs. Republicans tended to believe that government had a legitimate role to play in imposing moral behavior on the citizenry. Republican politicians often supported temperance laws to restrict the sale of liquor and "blue laws" to keep businesses closed on Sundays and prevent sporting events on the Sabbath. Democrats, outside the South at least, took the opposite tack: a person's private habits were no business of the government. These differences stemmed from the differing nature of Democratic and Republican voters, and in turn affected who was attracted to the two parties. Democrats—

again, outside the South—were apt to be Catholics or some member of a Protestant church group that was long on ceremony and short on concern for personal salvation. The Democracy also attracted the unchurched of all sorts. These groups resented the meddling of government in what they considered private affairs. On the other side were the people who belonged to the evangelical Protestant churches and who regarded the maintenance of piety and upright behavior as a proper goal of government.

Aside from these cultural and historical differences, the two parties tended to attract people of differing economic philosophies. The Democrats were more committed to laissez-faire than the Republicans. Democrats in this period usually supported lower tariffs, for example, and opposed government aid to railroads. Republicans, on the other hand, endorsed the protective tariff and federal subsidies to railroads. On the all-important questions of paper money and free silver, Democrats were more willing to tolerate inflation; Republicans were more apt to be "hard-money men." As these emphases suggest, the Democrats were more closely identified with the agricultural regions of the country—especially the South—and with exporters and importers; while the Republicans were more closely associated with the industrial regions of the nation and with manufacturing.

Neither party fitted the simple image of "party of the rich" or "party of the poor." Irish-Catholic wage-earners in Boston voted Democratic; but their Yankee Protestant counterparts in, say, Cleveland were apt to vote Republican. An Illinois farmer who fought with the Union was apt to vote for the GOP, while his erstwhile "Copperhead" neighbor would in all likelihood vote for the Democracy. A rich New York banker was more likely to be a Democrat than a rich Pittsburgh manufacturer.

Despite this confusion of economic identities, few eligible American voters in this era failed to exercise their franchise. Elections were exciting events, and the voters came out in droves to cast their ballots. Turnouts often reached ninety percent of those eligible. Nor were there many "independents." At least one group of upper-class well-educated gentlemen refused to pledge loyalty to either party. These "Mugwumps," as they were called, favored "honest government," civil service reform, sound money, and free trade, and were willing to use either party to achieve their goals. In the presidential election of 1884, they opposed the Republican candidate, James G. Blaine, because they believed him corrupt, and their defection may have swung the election to his Democratic opponent, Grover Cleveland. But the Mugwumps were unusual and not typical of their time.

Populism

As they contemplated the prospect of challenging the two major parties, agrarian dissidents could not have been unduly optimistic. However muddled the Democratic or Republican line on the major issues of the day, both parties were deeply entrenched in American tradition and both seemed to fit the emotional and psychological needs of the American people. Nonetheless, these farm leaders' profound dissatisfaction impelled them forward on this new course.

In 1889 Alliance leaders met at St. Louis to forge a political bond with the Knights of Labor. Adopting a platform endorsing greenbacks, free silver, confiscation of excess railroad lands, economy in government, and public ownership of "the means of communication and transportation," the meeting recommended that all farmers and laboring men support candidates who were willing to pledge themselves to these principles. The following year, the Southern Alliance and the

Colored Farmers' Alliance, at Ocala, Florida, adopted a similar platform. Labor leaders at Ocala urged the formation of a new party, but Southern white Alliance leaders, fearing to break white control over Southern politics by undermining the Democrats, refused to go along. Over the next few months resistance to a third party collapsed and at St. Louis, in February 1890, the People's Party—the Populists—was formally established. That July the first Populist convention assembled in Omaha to select candidates and a platform for the 1892 election.

The Omaha meeting was a colorful assemblage. Most American males had by now given up the Civil War era practice of wearing beards. Not so the delegates at Omaha. To one observer, it seemed that there must be some connection between political dissent and abundant facial hair (a connection also made by others in our own time). Another distinguishing characteristic of the

Populists was the number of women activists. Mary Elizabeth Lease—Mary Ellen to her friends, "Mary Yellin' " to her critics—was the most prominent of these. Eloquent, courageous, mother of four, and member of the Kansas bar, Lease had made hundreds of speeches for the agrarian cause. In one of these, supposedly, she had declared "what . . . farmers need to do is to raise less corn and more *Hell*." There were even some black delegates, four to be exact—one each from Kansas and Virginia, and two from Texas.

Amid roars of approval that impressed a reporter as having the "likeness of the enthusiastic Bastille demonstration in France," the convention adopted a platform that summed up the outlook and program of the agrarian dissenters. Written by the romantic and flamboyant Minnesota editor-politician Ignatius Donnelly, the platform preamble sounded the note of emergency that Populists felt. The nation was on "the verge of moral, political, and material ruin." Corruption, it stated, dominated "the ballot box, the legislatures, the Congress. . . ." Business was prostrate, the homes of Americans mortgaged to the hilt, labor was impoverished, and the land was "concentrating in the hands of the capitalists. . . . The fruits of the toil of millions are boldly stolen to build up colossal fortunes for a few, unprecedented in the history of mankind; and the possessors of these . . . despise the republic and endanger liberty." Turning to a favorite agrarian theme, Donnelly declared that "silver . . . has been demonetized to add to the purchasing power of gold by decreasing the value of all forms of property as well as human labor; and the supply of currency is purposely abridged to fatten usurers, bankrupt enterprise and enslave industry. . . . A vast conspiracy against mankind [had been] organized on two continents" by the money power, and "if not met and overthrown at once [would produce] terrible social convulsions, the destruction of civilization, or the establishment of an absolute despotism."

After this overwrought invocation, there were specific platform planks: free coinage of silver, a graduated income tax, government ownership of the railroads and the telephone and telegraph systems, the secret ballot, direct election of United States Senators, immigration restriction, and use of the initiative and referendum to further direct democracy. To help attract wage-earners, there were also planks attacking the Pinkertons, favoring reduced working hours, and endorsing the Knights of Labor in their current battle with Rochester clothing manufacturers. The moment the platform was adopted, "the convention broke over all restraint and went wild" in a demonstration that lasted a full twenty minutes. With the nomination of General James B. Weaver of Iowa and James G. Field of Virginia, the convention adjourned.

In the election that followed, the Populists went on to win a million popular votes out of about 17 million cast, and to garner 22 electoral votes. This was the best showing by far of any third party since the Republicans in 1856, and seemed to promise much for the future. Close analysis, however, must have suggested that something was wrong. The Weaver-Field ticket had done very well in three small Rocky Mountain states—Idaho, Nevada, and Colorado; it had also done well in the wheat states of Kansas, North Dakota, South Dakota, and Nebraska. Except for Alabama, the South largely rejected the Populists. Worst of all was the showing in the industrial Northeast and older Midwest, where the Populist vote had scarcely reached five percent of the total.

The 1892 voting pattern reveals the nature of the Populist appeal. Despite efforts to make the agrarian battle the cause of suffering mankind, Populism spoke only to limited groups. Silver miners in the Mountain States voted for Weaver because his victory promised to increase the price of silver and benefit the silver mining interests. The Plains wheat farmers, too, voted Populist because they saw direct benefits: free silver inflation and government ownership of railroads would raise their prices and reduce their costs. Southern farmers to some extent were also attracted to Weaver, but the threat that a strong Populist Party might pose to white political control through the Democracy frightened off potential Weaver supporters. Southern Populists' efforts to win black voters deserve great praise, but they probably damaged the People's Party's showing among white farmers. As for voters of the northeastern corner of the nation, it was here that the Populists revealed their chief limitations. Despite efforts to win the labor vote, wage-earners in the cities and factory towns of the Northeast failed to catch fire at the Populist vision of an America saved from the brink of ruin by government control, more direct democracy, and inflation. Indeed, inflation seemed at best a dubious advantage for wage-earners who feared that higher prices for wheat, corn, and cotton meant a higher cost of living for them. Nor did the specialty farmers of the Northeast and the cornbelt see much advantage to themselves in the Populist program. Having adjusted successfully to the urban-industrial transformation that had wrenched the nation, they could not take seriously the

Populists' vision of imminent crisis and need for drastic change.

Within months of the 1892 election, the nation's economy faltered. In early 1893 a severe panic swept the nation, ushering in five full years of depression. Hard times would alter the political perceptions of the American people and intensify the mood of political and social dissent.

To President Grover Cleveland, the cause of the severe business downturn and the economic distress seemed clear. Ever since the passage of the Sherman Silver Purchase Act (1890), he believed, business had been jittery. As the amount of silver coming into the Treasury's vaults grew larger and larger, it had become increasingly difficult to uphold the gold standard. Speculators and ordinary citizens, worried about the government's ability to redeem silver coin or paper money in gold on demand as the gold standard required, were coming to the Treasury to demand gold. With each passing month gold reserves had diminished, making speculators and citizens still more nervous. It was this uncertainty that had knocked the economy off balance. And worse would surely come. Now with the panic, scare withdrawals of Treasury gold had become a flood, and it looked as if the country would have to go off the gold standard. To "gold bugs" like Cleveland and other Eastern conservatives, such a prospect was terrifying. The fall of gold, they were certain, would mean the collapse of civilization itself.

One of Cleveland's first moves against the depression was to demand the repeal of the Silver Purchase Act. Predictably, the Populists in Congress resisted fiercely. So did many Southern and Western Democrats and a few Mountain State Republicans. By this time, Populist ideas, especially regarding finance, had deeply penetrated the Western and Southern democracy, and Democratic Congressmen from these sections were willing to break with the Eastern wing of their own party over the issue. Despite the opposition, Cleveland was able to muster enough votes to get the measure repealed; but the administration's stand widened the crack between the Northeastern and Southern and Western wings of the party into a vast gulf.

The repeal did little to help the economy. As the depression tightened its grip, imports declined, and with them government gold revenues. At the same time, continued public fears further depleted the Treasury's reserve. By December 30, 1893, it had fallen to $80 million. To save the gold standard, Cleveland began to borrow gold from the bankers in exchange for government bonds. But then, owing to continued public fears, the gold that came into the Treasury promptly flowed out again. By early 1895 the reserve was down to $45 million, and it looked as if the silverites and other inflationists would finally see realized their dream of the nation off the gold standard.

At this point, Cleveland's Secretary of the Treasury, John Carlisle of Kentucky, approached the international banking house of J. P. Morgan and Company and August Belmont, a representative of the European Rothschilds. In exchange for $62 million in federal bonds, they promised him 3 1/2 million ounces of gold. This move stemmed the withdrawals temporarily, but led to angry charges by the silverites that the government had sold the nation out to the money power. Finally, after another $100-million gold purchase in 1896 the public became convinced of the Treasury's ability to maintain the gold standard, and the threat to the reserve ended. Cleveland had saved the gold standard—but only at the cost of worsening the split within his party.

Meanwhile, with each passing day the economy sank lower and lower. In 1894 cotton dropped to an all-time low. Wheat fell to 49 cents a bushel the same year, and corn touched 21 cents in 1896. In the industrial regions, factories closed, and thousands of men were thrown out of work, many to tramp the streets, others to "ride the rails" from town to town, looking for handouts and clashing with local police. One expression of the general breakdown was a march on Washington organized by Jacob Coxey to demand that Congress appropriate $500 million in greenbacks to finance a public-works program. This, it was argued, would not only create jobs but also help restore prosperity to business and agriculture. Starting from various parts of the country, including the far West, several thousand men in "Coxey's Army" set off for the nation's capital. Many dropped out of the line of march or were detained by the authorities, who feared that the "petition in boots" represented a dangerous radicalism. In late April 1894, about four hundred soldiers of the army straggled into Washington, where, before they could present their petitions, their leaders were arrested for trespassing on the Capitol lawn.

I brag and chant of Bryan, Bryan, Bryan,
Candidate for president who sketched a silver Zion,
The one American Poet who could sing outdoors,
He brought in tides of wonder, of unprecedented splendor,
Wild roses from the plains, that made hearts tender,
All the funny circus silks
Of politics unfurled,
Barlett pears of romance that were honey at the cores,
And torchlights down the street, to the end of the world.

There were truths eternal in the gab and tittle-tattle.
There were real heads broken in the fustian and the rattle.
There were real lines drawn:
Not the silver and the gold,
But Nebraska's cry went eastward against the dour and old,
The mean and cold.

It was eighteen ninety-six, and I was just sixteen
And Altgeld ruled in Springfield, Illinois,
When there came from the sunset Nebraska's shout of joy:
In a coat like a deacon, in a black Stetson hat
He scourged the elephant plutocrats
With barbed wire from the Platte.
The scales dropped from their mighty eyes.
They saw that summer's noon
A tribe of wonders coming
To a marching time. . . .

Prairie avenger, mountain lion,
Bryan, Bryan, Bryan, Bryan,
Gigantic troubadour, speaking like a siege gun,
Smashing Plymouth Rock with his boulders from the West. . . .

Election night at midnight:
Boy Bryan's defeat.
Defeat of western silver.
Defeat of the wheat.
Victory of letterfiles
And plutocrats in miles
With dollar signs upon their coats,
Diamond watchchains on their vests
And spats on their feet.
Victory of custodians,
Plymouth Rock,
And all that inbred landlord stock.
Victory of the neat.
Defeat of the aspen groves of Colorado valleys.
The blue bells of the Rockies,
And blue bonnets of old Texas,
By the Pittsburgh alleys.
Defeat of alfalfa and the Mariposa lily.
Defeat of the Pacific and the long Mississippi.
Defeat of the young by the old and silly.
Defeat of tornadoes by the poison vats supreme.
Defeat of my boyhood, defeat of my dream.

**Bryan, Bryan, Bryan,
Bryan**
by Vachel Lindsay

The Campaign of
Eighteen Ninety-six,
as Viewed at the
Time by a Sixteen-
Year-Old, etc.

The Bryan Campaign of 1896

Given the circumstances, 1896 promised to be an exciting election year. Both parties had their silver wings, and it looked as if there would be major internal battles in each over both platforms and candidates. In March 1895, two western Democrats, Congressmen Richard Bland of Missouri and William Jennings Bryan of Nebraska had thrown down the gauntlet to the Eastern leaders by demanding the immediate adoption of free and unlimited coinage of silver. Clearly, the Democratic battle would be especially bruising and might even tear the party apart.

In June 1896, the Republicans met at St. Louis to choose their candidates. Supported by his close friend and financial backer, the industrialist Mark Hanna, Congressman William McKinley won the nomination. A rather colorless man, McKinley had long been identified with the industrialists through his protectionist principles, and his choice represented a victory for the Northeast—a victory confirmed by the convention's adoption of a high-tariff platform, with only an incidental nod to silver. In reaction, Senator Henry Teller of Colorado and a number of other Western Republicans bolted the Convention and soon afterward organized the National Silver Republicans.

The battle at Chicago, where the Democrats met in July, was far more bitter and divisive. "Silver Dick" Bland was the front-runner as the delegates gathered, but coming up fast was ex-Congressman Bryan. Young, dynamic, handsome, eloquent, Bryan was in many ways a politician's dream. Born in Illinois in 1860, he had attended a small Protestant college where he had absorbed a moralistic view of society and the oratorical rhythms of the Bible. In 1887 he moved to Lincoln, Nebraska, where he practiced law and joined the Democratic Party. In 1890 he was elected to Congress; he was reelected in 1892, and served until March 1895.

Bryan was a sincere and simple Christian who accepted the truth of the Bible and interpreted human history as a titanic struggle between good and evil. To a Nebraska Democrat at that time, this meant perceiving gold as a symbol of the dark forces and silver as one of truth and light. He sincerely believed that humanity was being oppressed by the money power and could only be saved by free and unlimited coinage of silver at sixteen to one. While in Congress he had fought for silver, and after leaving the House of Representatives had lectured on the subject on the Chautauqua circuit and issued pro-silver manifestoes as editor of the Omaha *World-Herald*. In preparation for the struggle in Chicago, he had honed and polished an address with which he aimed to electrify the convention, and thereby obtain the nomination.

Bryan achieved his goal. Battle was first joined over the platform, with the Eastern gold bugs insisting on support of the gold standard and the Western-Southern bloc demanding "the free and unlimited coinage of both gold and silver at the present legal ratio of 16 to 1, without waiting for the aid or consent of any other nation." Speakers for the West and South, including Senator Benjamin Tillman of South Carolina and Governor John Peter Altgeld of Illinois, denounced gold and Cleveland. In response, David Hill of New York declared: "I am a Democrat, but I am not a revolutionist. My mission here to-day is to unite, not to divide—to build up, not to destroy." The Western-Southern silver platform, he insisted, would destroy the party in the East.

One of the last speakers on the platform issue was the young Nebraskan, Bryan. The crowd, knowing his reputation for eloquence, was expectant; they were not disappointed. Starting with a modest disclaimer of any special insight, he announced that "the humblest citizen in all the land, when clad in the armor of a righteous cause, is stronger than all the hosts of error." Bryan went on to challenge the Eastern view that free silver would disrupt the business of the nation. Gold, he said, had already disturbed the business of the West and South. Bryan denied that he felt any sectional animus. He would not, he declared, "say . . . one word against those who live upon the Atlantic coast, but the hardy pioneers who have braved all the dangers of the wilderness . . . these people . . . are as deserving of the consideration of our party as any people in this country." After reviewing the other planks of the silver group's platform, Bryan moved on to the "paramount issue"—gold versus silver. Here his rhetoric soared. Turning the words of Secretary Carlisle against him, he proclaimed that the battle was between "the struggling masses" and "the idle holders of idle capital." The Democratic idea, he insisted, is that if you "make the masses prosperous, their prosperity will find its way up through every class which rests upon them." The "gold Democrats" claimed that the great cities were in favor of the gold standard; the silverites replied that the cities rested on the foundation of the nation's "broad and fertile prairies." "Burn down your cities and leave our farms and your cities will spring up again as if by magic; but destroy our farms and the grass will grow in the streets of every city in the country.''

Bryan now began his wind-up. Denying the need to wait until Great Britain, the great defender of gold, had been convinced that silver was acceptable, he demanded silver now. Then he launched into his defiant conclusion. If the gold bugs came into the open, the silver men would "fight them to the uttermost.''

Having behind us the producing masses of this nation and the world, supported by the commercial interests, the laboring interests, and the toilers everywhere, we will answer their demand for a gold standard by saying to them: You shall not press down upon the brow of labor this crown of thorns, you shall not crucify mankind upon a cross of gold.

A half-hour of bedlam followed the address, with Western and Southern delegates cheering and parading up and down the aisles of the Chicago colosseum. When brought to a vote, the silver platform passed overwhelmingly. The next day the delegates began to ballot for their presidential candidate. On the fifth roll call, Bryan defeated Bland and with Arthur Sewall, a Maine businessman-silverite as his running-mate, became the Democratic standard-bearer.

The Bryan nomination posed a dilemma for the Populists, who met at St. Louis shortly after the Democrats adjourned. Was Bryan—as some argued—a Populist in all but name, and would the People's Party best get its program enacted by supporting him in the fall? So-called "Fusionists" favored this course. On the other side were those Populists who opposed reducing their program to the single issue of silver. No doubt Bryan's rhetoric was populistic, but was he a real reformer? No, better to nominate a separate ticket, even at the risk of electing McKinley. These were the "middle-of-the-roaders." In the end the delegates at St. Louis "split the difference," nominating Bryan for President and choosing Thomas Watson of Georgia, rather than Sewall, for Vice-President.

One more convention was necessary before the full roster of candidates was complete. After Chicago, most disgruntled Eastern Democrats returned home determined to sit on their hands in the fall. A few, however, were too outraged at their defeat to remain simply inactive. In September these gold Democrats met in convention and chose John M. Palmer of Illinois on a National Democratic party ticket.

The campaign that now ensued was one of the most exciting ever. As we look back on the 1896 presidential contest, it is clear that the struggle was largely sectional. If Bryan had won, in all likelihood there would have been a shift of political emphasis toward the needs of the South and West. On the other hand, it is hard to believe that any major change in labor-capital relations, or any major shifts in wealth and power, would have resulted from victory. It is not even certain that Bryan as President would have succeeded in getting the nation to abandon the gold standard. Be that as it may, he and his supporters saw the campaign as a great crusade for the people, and wherever "the boy orator of the Platte" went, he urged his audiences to support the cause of the "toiling masses." In the West and South, Bryan gathered great crowds who cheered him as an evangelist, but in the East he made little headway. A sober speech before a large audience in New York's Madison Square Garden, designed to quiet Eastern fears, was a disappointment and thereafter the Nebraskan entertained little hope of winning the East. Meanwhile, McKinley conducted a dignified "front porch" campaign. Delegates would come to the McKinley home in Canton, Ohio, with prepared questions and remarks, and the Republican candidate would respond in a neighborly way.

During the campaign, money problems plagued the Bryan forces. Contributions from the silver mine-owners did not materialize, and the Democratic candidate had to make up in personal campaigning what he lacked in funds. The Republicans, on the other hand were gorged with cash, raised by Mark Hanna from among fearful industrialists and bankers. This enabled them to send out scores of speakers to follow Bryan to rebut his charges, and to mail out millions of pamphlets and broadsides warning the public that a Bryan victory meant revolution and the collapse of the dollar. At times the attacks descended to viciousness. One anti-Bryanite declared that the Democratic candidate was advocating "a doctrine that leads to anarchy" and was standing on "a platform made in hell." Other Republican critics charged that Bryan was trying "to stir up hatred, envy, and malice between Americans and foreigners, between classes, and between sections." Meanwhile, businessmen warned their employees that a Bryan triumph would result in closing their doors and mass unemployment.

There was a more positive side to the Republican campaign. McKinley was depicted as the herald of prosperity. The Republican tariff would restore good times and usher in the era of "the full dinner pail." Republican campaigners also spoke

(Library of Congress.)

for unity and an end to ethnic and class conflict in the nation.

McKinley's victory in November was decisive. With 7.1 million votes to his opponent's 6.5 million, he carried twenty-one states in the Midwest, Northeast, and West Coast, leaving Bryan twenty-six Southern, Plains, and Mountain states. And even the South was not solid for the Democratic candidate; for the first time in a generation Delaware, Maryland, West Virginia, and Kentucky went Republican. Even more significant was Bryan's failure to capture the traditionally Democratic cities. Many wage-earners, perhaps following the lead of Gompers' AF of L, refused to support free silver; the tariff apparently seemed more attractive than an inflated dollar. But beyond this, Bryan's evangelical style, his identification with the rural regions, his homespun quality, failed to captivate the urban "toiling masses." Nor did the Democratic candidate, any more than Weaver in 1892, inspire the more successful farmers of the older Midwest.

McKinley's victory was a turning point in the political history of the era. Thereafter politics became less of a balancing act, as the Republicans forged ahead of their opponents and became the normal majority party of the nation. Over the next thirty-five years the Democrats would win the Presidency only twice, and the first time largely as the result of a severe Republican split. Meanwhile,

without the cliff-hanger quality of the past to spur interest, voting percentages declined and more and more Americans stayed home on election day.

One factor that explains the anticlimax of 1896 and the years that immediately followed was prosperity. By the time of McKinley's inauguration the country was experiencing a vigorous economic revival. Prices for farm commodities and other products began to rise by 1897, bringing prosperity to farmers and businessmen and providing a lively labor market for wage-earners. During the next decade, except for a brief setback in 1907, the economy advanced rapidly, raising living standards and calming economic discontent. In 1900 the silver issue was laid to rest for thirty years by passage of the Gold Standard Act, confirming and reinforcing the American commitment to gold as the backing for the American dollar, and providing for some farm-credit needs by authorizing national banks in rural communities.

And there was one other reason why the "outsiders" ceased to raise their voices in loud protest. Within a year of McKinley's inauguration, the country was at war with Spain over Cuba. Before long, patriotism and the appeal of imperial glory had captured the imaginations of Americans, muting the dissonance of the recent past. When new protests appeared, they would come from different people and be couched in different vocabulary.

Suggested Readings

Irwin Yellowitz tells of the efforts of labor unionists in the late nineteenth century to halt or modify the mechanization of production that threatened to disrupt older ways of work: *Industrialization and the American Labor Movement, 1850-1900* (1977). Two older studies of immigration are still current: John Higham, *Strangers in the Land: Patterns of American Nativism* (1955) and Milton Gordon, *Assimilation in American Life: The Role of Race, Religion, and National Origins* (1964). Robert D. Marcus examines the structure of the Republican Party toward the end of the nineteenth century in *Grand Old Party* (1971). Lawrence Goodwyn, *Democratic Promise: The Populist Movement in America* (1976), presents a new interpretation of Populism, emphasizing the place in it of its left wing, the Southern alliance. After experimenting with cooperative marketing as a solution to the farmers' troubles, the Alliance went on to a radical politics that called for such programs as a subtreasury system to provide farmers with credit. In *One Kind of Freedom: The Economic Consequences of Emancipation* (1977), Roger L. Ransom and Richard Sutch appraise the credit and landholding systems that historians have singled out as evils of the postwar South and argue that the two bore much responsibility for the lack of progress in the region. Having no ownership or secure possession of the land they worked, poor blacks and whites had no incentive to improve it. But blacks suffered more from simple white racism than from an unfair economic system.

THE OUTWARD THRUST

Chapter XVIII
The Outward Thrust
1865—1900

The Golden Spike

"What do we want with . . . this region of savages and wild beasts, of deserts of shifting sands and whirlwinds of dust, of cactus and prairie dogs?" asked Daniel Webster in 1845. "To what use could we ever put those endless mountain ranges, impenetrable and covered to their bases with eternal snow? What could we do with the western coast three thousand miles away, rockbound, cheerless and uninviting?" When Webster made this estimate of the future value of California, the four hundred Americans who lived there knew nothing of the gold beneath their feet. To get there they had traveled for months over waterless plains and forbidding mountains, or sailed completely around the Americas, or made the dangerous crossing of the Panamanian isthmus. In 1855, the U.S. Army Engineers published in twelve detailed volumes *The Pacific Railroad Surveys of 1853-55,* which pointed out that California—its riches now well known—could be conquered before the least military assistance would arrive from the East. With the coming of the Civil War, a federally subsidized transcontinental rail connection became a political and military necessity to assure that California would remain part of the Union.

On July 1, 1862, Congress granted charters to two companies: the Union Pacific, to build westward from Omaha, and the Central Pacific, to build eastward from San Francisco across the Sierras and through Nevada. A federal subsidy, in the form of alternate sections of land along the right-of-way, and government bonds for each mile of completed track induced each company to race ahead so as to move the final meeting point as far into their competitor's territory as possible.

The race was on. The Union Pacific rolled steadily across the plains. In this flat country, nature was easy to subdue. Not so the Indians, however, seeing their land about to be permanently split by steel rails. The Union Pacific organized its crews which were swelled by ex-soldiers, in military fashion—some working, some as armed guards, with occasional aid from the United States Cavalry.

Meanwhile, the Central Pacific brutally shouldered its way up the Sierra Nevada, blasting and tunneling, indifferent to expense, winter storms, or workers' lives, hoping to reach the profitable flat plains where the government subsidy would be worth twice the cost per mile of construction. Charles Crocker, relentless boss of the construction crews, had solved the problem of where to find tens of thousands of railroad workers in labor-scarce California by hiring Chinese. An associate had at first objected because the Chinese workers "were not masons," but Crocker had lightly countered that the Chinese had built the greatest piece of masonry in the world—the Great Wall. They quickly proved their worth in breaching the great wall of the Sierra. In 1866-67, under white foremen, Crocker's work gangs within a space of twenty miles crossed the mountain summit at the famous Donner Pass. Working furiously to get tunnel headings constructed before they were locked in snowdrifts, the crews continued to work throughout the winter, gouging out the insides of hill after hill.

For the next year they labored down the east slope of the Sierra. On May 1, 1868, the Central Pacific reached Reno, Nevada, a one-month old townsite named for a Civil War general. "We arrived at Reno late in the afternoon," reported a newspaper correspondent on the first passenger train, scarcely four months later. "The noise of hammer, and plane, and saw re-echoed on all sides, and the city rises like an exhalation. It is a complete mirage on the desert, and will probably be as magnificient, and as transient." Even then Reno was a place to bet on races, and the desert before it a suitable place to test for speed.

The great "iron horse race" aroused extraordinary feats in 1868-69 as the two roads pushed ever closer. On the single day of October 27, 1868, the Union Pacific crews, after elaborate preparation of men and teams and materials, laid over seven miles of track: "the achievement of the year," boasted Oliver Ames, one of the railroad's principal owners. Not to be outdone, Crocker boasted that his men would top ten miles in a day, and legend has it that he backed up his words with a $10,000 bet. On April 27, 1869, after the Central Pacific had spent days hauling material into place and rehearsing four thousand men in their duties, an engine ran off the track, ending the day's proceedings. But the next morning at 7 a.m., railroad cars, small hand cars, horse teams, and disciplined crews began dropping rails and spikes along the prepared grade and eight Irish rail-handlers began moving rails into place. As the rails were bolted by Chinese gangs, fresh rails were hauled along the new track and the process was repeated. Maintaining a frantic pace, this collective John Henry advanced six miles before the foremen called a halt for lunch. Working more slowly through the afternoon, by seven in the evening, the crews had added ten miles and fifty-six feet of new track, a formidable day's work. The rail handlers, heroes of the day, had each lifted 125 tons of iron in that one long march.

The two lines met reluctantly, on May 10, 1869, at Promontory Point, Utah, on the northern shore of the Great Salt Lake. The meeting had in fact been scheduled for May 8, and then delayed by rain. In San Francisco and Sacramento, plans for festivities for the 8th had advanced too far to be cancelled, and those two points on the new transcontinental route were forced to celebrate the momentous event for three days. Elaborate national preparations included wiring the final spike, made of pure gold, to the Western Union telegraph system so that the blows of the hammer could be heard throughout the nation. In several cities, cannon were wired to the telegraph to detonate from the blow thousands of miles away. The man given the honor of striking the blow, to be heard "the fartherest of any mortal man"—Leland Stanford, governor of California and president of the Central Pacific—was not up to the occasion: he missed the spike. The local telegraph operator closed the circuit anyhow, so that the cannons, bells, and whistles blasted across the nation on schedule. "This is the way to India," intoned General Grenville Dodge of Union Pacific at the dedication ceremony. Governor Stanford, a practical man even if not adept with a hammer, talked more plainly of transporting "coarse, heavy and cheap products for all distances at living rates to the trade." The great hopes of a transcontinental nation and the practical aspirations of hard-headed men had come together "1,086 miles west of the Missouri River, and 690 miles east of Sacramento City." The golden spike was a fit symbol for a nation that had endured four bloody years to remain indivisible.

Filling in the Continent

Between the Civil War and the end of the nineteenth century Americans enormously increased the lands they effectively occupied. In 1865 the continental United States had already reached its present three million square miles, but vast expanses remained virtually empty of people; and nowhere beyond the compact borders did the American flag wave over detached territory. In the next thirty-five years the American community swept across the sparsely settled plains and overleaped its bounds to the west, the north, and the southeast. By the beginning of the twentieth century the United States had not only filled in its continental limits; it had expanded its land area to 3.6 million square miles by acquiring non-adjacent territory. Besides this, it had extended its influence and economic power far beyond the borders of the parochial nation that existed at the time of Appomattox.

In 1865 the frontier line, where the population dropped to under two persons per square mile, had begun to encroach on the Great Plains-Great Basin regions from both east and west. To the west of the Basin were the settled communities of California, Oregon, and the region around Puget Sound in Washington Territory. To the east of the Plains the settled area in 1870 extended a third of the way across Kansas and Nebraska and then, to the north, curved east to avoid the Dakotas completely.

The vast region between these two slowly approaching lines presented formidable problems and challenges to would-be settlers. The Plains were an enormous flat plateau rising gradually to about 5,000 feet above sea level, where it reached the edge of the Rocky Mountains. The Great Basin to the west of the Plains was a vast shallow bowl dotted with a few mountainous regions, be-

---

As I passed by Tom Sherman's bar-room,
 Tom Sherman's bar-room, quite early one morn,
I spied a young cowboy all dressed in his buckskins,
 All dressed in his buckskins, all fit for his grave.

"Then beat the drum lowly and play the fife slowly,
 Beat up the death marches as they carry me along;
Take me to the prairie and fire a volley o'er me,
 For I'm a young cowboy and dying alone."

"Once in my saddle I used to go dashing,
 Once in saddle I used to ride gay;
But I just took up drinking and then to card-playing,
 Got shot by a gambler, and dying to-day.

"Go gather around me a lot of wild cowboys,
 And tell them the story of a comrade's sad fate;
Warn them quite gently to give up wild roving,
 To give up wild roving before it's too late.

"Some one write to my gray-headed mother,
 And then to my sister, my sister so dear;
There is another far dearer than mother,
 Who would bitterly weep if she knew I were here.

"O bury beside me my knife and my shooter,
 My spurs on my heels, my rifle by my side;
Over my coffin put a bottle of brandy,
 That the cowboys may drink as they carry me along."

The Cowboy's Lament

Albert Bierstadt, Western Landscape, 1868. (National Collection of Fine Arts, Smithsonian Institution.)

THE OUTWARD THRUST

tween the eastern Rockies and the Sierra-Cascade ranges of California-Oregon-Washington. Both regions were deficient in rainfall, though the Basin was drier, approaching true desert in places. Both regions were treeless, except along stream banks or in other especially moist spots. The Plains were covered with short grass; the Basin was sprinkled with sagebrush, cacti, and creosote brushes. The Plains rivers—eastward-flowing to the Mississippi—were shallow, especially in the fall. In the Basin, the few streams had water only in the spring, when meltoff from mountain snows filled their banks. None of these had any ocean connection. They simply died out in some "sink" where the water gave out.

The weather of the Plains-Great Basin provinces can most charitably be described as interesting. The climate was of the type called "continental" by geographers. Winters were often fiercely cold, with temperatures plunging to as low as 40 degrees below zero. On the Plains, especially, the frost was accompanied by roaring blizzards that covered the land with a white layer which often drifted roof-high. Springs were frequently balmy, with the ground covered by a carpet of wildflowers brought forth by melting snow or brief rains; they were usually short, however, and were followed by brutally hot summers when temperatures climbed into the nineties and the sun beat down remorselessly from cloudless skies. Among the more disturbing characteristics of the region's climate and weather was its inconsistency:

in the arid Basin, where rainfall seldom exceeded one or two inches per year, there could be a sudden cloudburst when the average yearly allotment could descend in an hour or two. The Plains did not usually experience such deluges, but rainfall could vary sharply from year to year and decade to decade. Some periods were quite dry and drought-afflicted. These would be followed by extended periods of abundant rainfall when the grass remained green and copious for a large part of the year.

The Plains and Basin sheltered a profusion of animals. Antelope, rabbits, gophers, squirrels, wolves, and cayotes were found everywhere. Along many streams, especially at the mountain edges, were beaver with thick, soft pelts prized as raw material for felt hats. The most visible and abundant of all the Plains animals were the bison or American buffalo, the "natural cattle" of the North American grasslands.

For the native peoples of the region, the buffalo were an extraordinary asset. Fresh buffalo meat was a staple item of their diet. Dried meat, sliced thin, was carried on long trips, along with pemmican—dried meat mixed with berries, fat, and marrow and stuffed into a buffalo-gut bag. Buffalo skins served as clothing and as the walls of tents, or tepees, and was used to make containers of various kinds. Buffalo sinews became rope and bowstrings. Even buffalo droppings or "chips" were valuable: when dried, they made an excellent fuel on the treeless Plains.

The Native Peoples

Before the coming of the whites, several score thousand Indians inhabited the region, divided into many major tribes and dozens of bands.

The major tribes of the Basin included the Bannock, Shoshoni, Paiute, Ute, and Snake. Theirs was a harsh environment where agriculture would have been impossible without a highly developed social organization to promote irrigation. They lived almost entirely by food-gathering supplemented by a little hunting. In the spring they would collect edible plants in the valleys. Later they would wander to higher land where they gathered berries, nuts, seeds, and roots. They also ate lizards, mice, birds, and grasshoppers. Their use of sticks to extract roots prompted Mark Twain to give them the contemptuous name "Digger Indians."

The simplicity of the Diggers' economy was matched by other material characteristics. They lived in brush huts and even in hollowed-out depressions in the earth. The Diggers' clothing was rudimentary. The men wore breechcloths; the women, an apron of milkweed fiber. Often both wore nothing at all. They had baskets, but no pottery. They lacked any sort of domesticated animals.

The Great Basin Indians' social organization was also simple. Tribes existed as linguistic entities, but they were never joined politically. The only true social unit was the "extended family" of about twenty-five to thirty individuals. There were no chiefs, only "talkers," influential men considered wise and worthy of being consulted. Each

Native Fisherman of the Colorado River, 1907 (National Archives)

winter a group of families might gather together to take shelter in some especially warm spot. During these months they would form loose personal and group connections. But in the spring these "villages" would break up.

At the eastern fringes of the region, the Great Basin tribes merged with the more affluent, more sophisticated, and more numerous Indians of the Plains. Originally an agricultural people, the Plains Indians by about 1500 had, except in the more humid eastern parts, become overwhelmingly nomadic hunter-gatherers whose chief source of sustenance was the buffalo. About 1700 this nomadic pattern was reinforced by the arrival of horses, strays from the Spanish lands at the northern fringes of Mexico.

The Plains Indians are the classic "redmen" of American legend. Tall, bronzed, well-muscled, hawk-nosed, wearing fringed leather clothing and feathered war bonnets, living in colorfully decorated tepees, magnificent horsemen, renowned as marksmen with the bow and arrow, they have above all other American Indians entered our folk history as the worthy opponents of the cavalry or, in children's versions, the "cowboy."

There were many Plains tribes. To the north, spilling over into Canada, were the Blackfeet, a confederation of several tribes. Adjacent were the Crows. In western South Dakota and Nebraska, as well as parts of Montana and Wyoming, were the various bands of the Sioux. South of these were the Cheyenne, while on the southern Plains there were the Comanches, Kiowas, and Kiowa-Apaches.

Before about 1650 the Plains tribes hunted the buffalo on foot and killed them with bows and arrows or by driving the animals over cliffs. They traveled with the herds, and transported their possessions by the *travois*, two trailing poles pulled by a dog with a sack suspended between. During the seventeenth century, however, they began to acquire horses by trade or theft. By 1740 every Plains tribe was mounted on fast ponies. Eventually, they also got firearms from the white man.

At the opening of the nineteenth century the Plains culture, as white Americans came to know it, had fully emerged. The horse was, of course, a far better draft animal than the dog, and enabled the tribes to travel farther and faster carrying heavier loads. Food became less of a problem. A fast pony and a rifle made hunting easier and left more time for ceremony, religion, the arts, feasting, and war. The Plains Indians, as nomads, never developed as elaborate a material culture as the sedentary woodland Indians of the East or the town-dwelling farmers, the Pueblos, of the Arizona-New Mexico area, but they were far ahead of the "Diggers." The Plains tribes decorated their leather clothing with beads, quills, eagle feathers, and pictures; they recorded important occurrences and drew calendars with paint on leather. Their tepees were often large structures with abundant room for a whole family. The Plains Indians' social organization was also more complex than that of the Basin peoples. Tribes were often large and were guided by chiefs, though ruled by councils of leading men. The typical social unit—that is, of people living together on an ongoing basis—was the band of a few hundred, rather than the tribe. Within the bands there was often a multitude of male societies that resembled white men's lodges, with regalia, ceremonies, officers, and songs. The societies were also charged with the authority to police behavior.

Unlike the Indians farther west, the Plains people gave scope to the full tribe. Periodically there were gatherings of whole tribal groups where people visited, gambled, played games, raced, met in councils, and shared in religious ceremonies. Many of the Plains tribes performed a ritual called the Sun Dance, usually held in the summer. Sun Dance performers gathered near a painted pole and danced for days on end without food and water until they fell down exhausted. The purpose of the dance was to produce a trance and visions. Some tribes sought to produce trances or religious ecstasy by self-torture that included suspension from a sacred tree by skewers inserted through slits in the chest.

The white man intruded into this region and into these cultures as a disruptive conqueror. The first white forays came well before the Civil War. During the war itself, the railroads began to penetrate the area, stimulating wide bands of settlement along their rights-of-way. To protect the railroads and then the settlers, the federal government established numerous army posts that became centers of white culture and points of contact between white and red men.

Relations between the Indians and whites were complex and ambivalent. The red men both feared whites and admired them. White numbers and technology exceeded anything the Indians had, and many recognized that the force of white pressure would prove irresistible. Respect for this physical power was often combined with a desire to acquire the white man's ways. Frequently this meant only borrowing the white man's technology—as in the case of the Plains Indians' adoption of the horse and rifle. Sometimes it meant the white man's vices: ever since the colonial period, rum and brandy had been used in the Indian trade, and by the end of the nineteenth century drunkenness had become a chronic problem among many tribes. At times, however, it also meant the white man's religion and other such elements of his culture. The Georgia Cherokees are a case in point. Before they were expelled from their lands in the 1830's the 15,000 members of the Cherokee nation owned 22,000 cattle, 2,000 spinning wheels, 31 grist mills, 8 cotton gins, and 10 sawmills, and ran 18 schools where young Cherokees learned to read and write their own language in a script invented by Chief Sequoya.

White attitudes toward Indians were equally ambivalent. In general, Anglo-Saxons—unlike the French, Spanish, and other Latins—did not intermarry with Indians. Whether this was due to racism, the religious particularism of Protestants, or some other cause, is not clear. More compelling as a source of antagonism was sheer greed on the part of the whites. The red man had what the white man wanted: land—millions of acres of the finest land on earth. To the would-be Western farmer or the prospective land speculator, the red man's presence was an obstacle in the way of livelihood and profit. But even many people not directly involved in Western development asked if a few thousand "primitives" should be allowed to retain so much of America's rich resources while each year the nation's white population grew at an explosive rate. Undoubtedly there was a large element of cultural chauvinism and just plain self-serving in this, but on the other hand, by white standards, the retention of so much of the West by a few thousand hunter-gatherer nomads could only seem a criminal waste of resources.

Yet, greed and contempt were not the sole white responses to the Indians. Generally the most aggressive opponents of Indian claims were Westerners, those close to the scene of Indian-white conflict. Easterners could afford to be more generous and philosophical, and by the mid-nineteenth century many sincerely regretted the shabby way the Indians were treated. Few of these people actually wanted to surrender the great West permanently to the tribes, but they did wish to guarantee fair treatment, within broad limits. Many also hoped that the Indians could be weaned away from their traditional nomadism, "civilized," and confined to settled compact agricultural communities where they could support themselves as small farmers—like other Americans. The tragedy and hypocrisy of the Cherokee case lie in the fact that the Cherokees actually conformed to this prescription, but were swept aside anyway. Unfortunately, in this era, virtually no one respected the traditional Indian way of life or could see how it could be maintained in the face of white population pressure.

The Plains Indians Subdued

Before the Civil War, American Indian policy had at first been based on the idea of a "permanent Indian barrier" in the trans-Mississippi region into which whites would not intrude. In the late 1840's, after thousands of whites had begun to cross the Plains on their way to Oregon and California, the policy was changed to one of establishing Indian reservations, with the land between made available to settlers. Meanwhile, the California and Oregon migrants pushed through the tribal territories, altering the environment and economy of the Indians. In the Treaty of Fort Laramie, the Plains tribes, in exchange for a promised long-term federal subsidy, agreed to move to reservations.

The new arrangement did not preserve peace. White men encroached on Indian lands; Indians found the reservations too confining after their free roaming life. During the war itself General John Pope, the failed commander of the Union Army of Virginia, set about to subdue the Sioux of the northern Plains, an Indian group not yet brought under the reservation policy. After Sioux attacks on several Minnesota towns, Pope ordered his deputy, Colonel Henry Sibley, to make an example of the Sioux. "They are," he ordered, "to be treated as maniacs or wild beasts, and by no means as people with whom treaties or compromises can be made." Sibley attacked the Indians in September 1862 and captured eighteen hundred warriors, more than three hundred of whom he condemned to death. President Lincoln reprieved all but thirty-eight, to the disgust of Minnesota settlers, who believed, like many frontiersmen, that "the only good Indian was a dead Indian."

SITTING BULL WENT OUT one day, far from his lodge, in the hope of being . . . enabled to communicate with the "Great Spirit." On the second night he was seized with a strange feeling, and near morning he met the "Great Spirit," clad in a beautiful robe. His hair flowed upon his shoulders and reached almost to his feet. When Sitting Bull beheld this wonderful apparition, he fainted and lay there he knew not how long, and had a strange dream. He related his story of the trance to the author, as well as to the Indians thus:

"The Great Spirit appeared to me with a formidable band of Sioux, who have long since been dead, and they danced, inviting me to join them. Presently I was restored to my senses, and the Great Spirit talked with me. He asked me if the Indians would not be glad to see their dead ancestors and the buffalo restored to them, and to life. I assured him that they would be deeply gratified. Then the Great Spirit told me that he once came to save the white race, but that they had persecuted him; and now he had come to save and rescue the defenseless and long-persecuted Indian race. All day the Great Spirit gave me evidence of his power and instructed me.

"He said that the white men would come to take me, but as they approached the soil would become quicksand, and the men and horses would sink. He showed me how to make medicine to put on war-shirts to turn aside the bullets of the white man. He told me the Indians had suffered long enough, and that he was now coming for their deliverance. We are to occupy the earth again, which has been taken from us. Great herds of buffalo will wander about as they did long ago, and the Indian who now sleeps in death will rise again, and forever wander over the earth. There will be no reservation; no messenger from the government to say to the Indians, come back here, stay here, starve here on this spot of ground.

"The Great Spirit said that the Indians must keep dancing; that the earth was theirs at his command, and for all this privilege, they must dance the dances which are pleasing to him. He said that all the Indians who would not listen to his words, or refuse to join in the ceremonies which are pleasing to him, will be destroyed with the white race."

Sitting Bull's Trance
by Fred M. Hans

Sitting Bull describes his preparation for the famous encounter where he wiped out the forces of General George Custer at the Battle of the Little Big Horn (1876)

Other troubles soon followed. Efforts to force the Cheyenne and Arapaho into smaller land areas than those promised sparked an Indian war throughout Colorado Territory in 1861. In 1864 the Indians sued for peace, but instead were treated brutally. In late November 1864 the Colorado militia under Colonel John Chivington surrounded a friendly band of Cheyenne at Sand Creek in eastern Colorado Territory, and attacked them without provocation. The militia fired volleys at the men. Women and children who fled to nearby caves were dragged out to be knifed or shot. An Indian trader at the scene later testified: "They were scalped, the brains knocked out; the men used their knives, ripped open women, clubbed little children, knocked them in the head with their guns, beat their brains out, mutilated their body in every sense of the word." Only fifty of the red men escaped the bestial Chivington massacre.

For the next three years many of the Plains tribes went on the warpath. In 1867 President

Johnson appointed a commission which patched up a peace. During the next thirty years the military commanders at the Plains army posts had to deal frequently with hostile tribesmen who found the reservations confining and longed to return to their old ways. A few of the commanders were insensitive or cruel men; officers like General Oliver O. Howard and George Crook, however, were men of their word whom the Indians respected. But they had the thankless task of defending every renegade white man, however brutal he had been toward the Indians, and of enforcing the basically harsh reservation policy.

The result was a series of Indian depredations, raids, and pitched battles that lasted until the 1890's. At times the Indians wreaked havoc on the United States Army. In 1866 they wiped out Captain William Fetterman's detachment of eighty men on the Bozeman Trail. In 1876 General George Custer's troop of two hundred sixty-five men set out after Sitting Bull's Sioux warriors who had left their reservations in protest against the government's allowing gold prospectors to trespass on their reservation in the Black Hills. Custer encountered the Sioux at the Little Big Horn River and foolishly attacked the much larger force of Indians. He and his band were wiped out to a man. Cruelties and brutalities were committed on both sides. One scholar even maintains that between 1798 and 1898 some four thousand Indians were killed by whites, while the Indians

themselves killed some seven thousand soldiers and civilians. These figures, however, do not include the many Indians who died by starvation and disease as a result of federal policy.

In the end, it was not the army that "tamed" the Plains Indians. Rather, it was the destruction of the buffalo. So long as the tribes could hunt the great shaggy beasts, they could survive off the reservations. Once the buffalo were wiped out, the red man's dependence on the white man's largesse became almost complete.

The buffalo disappeared abruptly between 1867 and about 1883. During the building of the Union Pacific, thousands were killed to supply food to construction crews. Later, when the road was complete, sportsmen shot at the bison from the windows of Union Pacific passenger cars, killing yet more thousands. Then, in 1871, a Pennsylvania tanner discovered that buffalo skins made good leather. From then on, the animals'—and the Indians'—fate was sealed. With hides selling at two to three dollars apiece, a hunter could make a fine profit slaughtering the dumb beasts. Soon groups of hunters accompanied by wagons were swarming over the Plains, killing often fifty or more a day, skinning them, and leaving the carcasses to rot. Between 1872 and 1874 alone, some nine million animals were killed. By 1878 the southern herd was no more; by 1883 the northern one was gone. In 1903, in the place of all the millions that had once thundered across the Plains, there survived a total of thirty-four bison.

Without the buffalo the Indians were tied down to the reservation. Yet even now they were not completely "tamed." In 1890 the Teton Sioux of South Dakota, faced with hunger as a result of drought and congressional niggardliness, became restless. In this mood they fell under the spell of a prophet, Wovoka, who told them that if they performed certain dances the white men would be driven out and Indian lands restored. The "Ghost Dancers" alarmed the local whites, who called for troops. The soldiers, in turn, frightened the Indians. The upshot of all this was the massacre at Wounded Knee, when soldiers armed with Gatling guns mowed down two hundred Indians of both sexes, young and old.

Although Wounded Knee was the last actual Indian battle—at least until our own day—the Indian "problem" did not go away. In the East, groups of reformers, who deeply regretted the nation's often brutal expropriation policy, sought to change it. Through such organizations as the Indian Rights Association they worked to awaken sympathy for the Indian. A particularly effective piece of propaganda was the book *A Century of*

Branding iron, cast iron about 34 inches long; made in Arizona in 1891. (*Index of American Design.*)

THE OUTWARD THRUST

THE FAR WEST.—SHOOTING BUFFALO ON THE LINE OF THE KANSAS-PACIFIC RAILROAD.

(Library of Congress.)

Dishonor (1881), by the novelist Helen Hunt Jackson.

The basic aim of most reformers was to create an assimilated native-American population. As a first step toward this goal, they advocated dividing Indian tribal lands among individual families. Although violating Indian tradition and was eventually abandoned, this policy was enacted into law by the Dawes Severalty Act of 1887. At about the same time the reformers induced Congress to ap- propriate money for establishing schools where Indian youths could be taught the white man's ways, especially agriculture and mechanical trades.

The whole policy of assimilation was gravely misguided. All it accomplished was the destruction of tribal life and the further demoralization of the Indians. Though well-intentioned, it provided a sadly fitting conclusion to the American sweep across the continent.

The Miners' Frontier

The departure of the Indians and the buffalo opened the trans-Mississippi West to white exploitation. First on the scene were the miners and prospectors who streamed to Colorado when gold was discovered there in 1859 and then successively moved on to western Nevada, Idaho's Snake River Valley, and western Montana, when strikes were announced in those areas. Many of these men came to the Great Basin and the Plains from the

William S. Hart in a typical pose as the lone movie Westerner. Hart's films contributed to the mythology of the cowboy, but the physical details of the settings and some of the plot elements had a gritty reality. The stylized Western with its laundered and ironed cowboys dominated the form.

diggings in California, having failed to find wealth there or, having found it, lost it again. Other hopefuls departed from Missouri River towns, following in the footsteps of the California argonauts of 1849. Each of these river towns did a land-office business outfitting and supplying the gold-seekers. An observer reported of one: "The streets are full of people buying flour, bacon, groceries, with wagons and outfits, and all around the town are little camps preparing to go west."

Few who joined in these "rushes" and later ones (Leadville, 1870; Black Hills, 1874; and Coeur D'Alene, 1883) ever saw many golden flakes in their pans. Most of the unlucky drifted on to the next strike. Those who did strike it rich—and some of those who did not—stayed on and became the founding fathers of Denver, Boise, Helena, and other flourishing cities that grew up around the mining camps.

Meanwhile, for a few years in each of the mining regions, a unique form of society appeared —colorful, democratic, and often violent. The most striking feature of the mining towns was the absence of women. At first, generally, there were no women at all, and when one put in an appearance, miners would come from miles around to gape at her. Soon, contingents of "fancy women" arrived on the scene—dance-hall girls and prostitutes, to help relieve the miners of their new-gained wealth. Eventually, when and if the mining camp struck roots and became a permanent community, respectable women arrived: wives, sisters, mothers, as well as a few decent working women schoolteachers, seamstresses, and shopkeepers. The arrival of "decent" women usually marked the end of the initial, disorderly and unstructured phase of a mining town's existence.

In this early phase, the towns were cosmopolitan places where professional men and scholars rubbed elbows with roughnecks and illiterates.

The gold-seekers were of every race and nationality. Most were probably native white Americans from the Midwest and South, but there were many Europeans along with blacks, Indians, and a substantial number of Mexicans. Overall, they were an unruly bunch. The presence of easily portable wealth in the shape of gold dust or nuggets encouraged theft and gambling. "Claim-jumping," the stealing of someone else's strike, was a daily occurrence in the mining camps and a constant source of violence. And even men without families and with money in their pockets often lost their moral balance and took to heavy drink and general hellraising. At times desperadoes virtually took over whole communities, terrorizing the decent folk and killing and stealing without restraint.

Generally, it was at this point that the forces of law and order would rally and organize a "vigilance committee." The term "vigilante" is now in bad repute—it has come to suggest the repression of dissent, and we associate it today with serious restraints on freedom. In the post-Civil War mining camps, however, it was often an expression of grassroots democracy. In the absence of any formally established local government, the law-abiding people of the community simply took matters into their own hands. The vigilance committee usually drew up a constitution under which the members agreed to function until order could be restored. Then, confident of their strength, they would make examples of the worst rogues by sudden arrest, quick trial, and prompt hanging on the nearest tree. A few of these swift executions were generally enough to end the reign of violence and establish (relatively) civilized reactions once again.

Vigilante justice was in part a response to the federal government's slowness in providing government for the mining frontier. It often was many months before Congress took note of the political needs of the mining population and established a territorial government with a governor, courts, and federal law-enforcement officials. In several cases, the people of a region established a provisional regime well before Congress acted, and began to pass laws for dealing

with the normal problems of any civilized community. Eventually, the laggard Congress responded, and in a few years the Great Basin region was covered with organized territories, repeating the process of state-making that had begun back in the 1790's farther east.

The Cattleman's Frontier

The level Plains, east of the Rockies, followed a different course of development from that of the Great Basin region. The vast grasslands of the Plains were ideally suited to grazing and quickly became a stock-raiser's frontier. The process was gradual and took the form of a slow spread from south to north. The original focus of the Plains cattle industry had been west Texas where, before the Civil War, ranchers had raised thousands of cattle. The Texas longhorn was of Spanish ancestry, a hardy beast that could fend for itself on the open range without shelter or fodder. It was not a particularly good beef animal, but that made little difference: the markets for beef were too far from Texas, given the primitive transportation connections, in any case. Hides were another matter, and thousands of Texas cattle were slaughtered for the tanneries of the Northeast in the 1850's.

During the Civil War, Texas was cut off from its chief customers and the cattle, unculled, multiplied rapidly. Soon after Appomattox some ranchers conceived the idea of herding the cattle north to Sedalia, Missouri, where they could be shipped east over the Missouri Pacific railroad. Unfortunately, the farmers along the way objected to Texas cattle as disease-carriers and as a danger to standing crops, and did not allow the ranchers to pass through. But the idea of the "long drive" had been born and soon became a practical venture when directed farther west through unsettled country.

As fully developed between the end of the 1860's and 1880 the long drive became an annual overland expedition northward from Texas to the nearest east-running railroad. The drives set out when the grass was green so that the cattle could graze along the way. Each group consisted of a thousand or so head driven by "cowboys"—Mexicans, blacks, and whites—who kept the herd moving and prevented strays from wandering off, or stampedes of frightened animals. Leading the band was a cook and his "chuck wagon," carrying food and supplies, followed by the wrangler with the spare horses, both followed by the herd itself.

After the Sedalia fiasco, the drives were rerouted along the Chisholm Trail, due north to Abilene in central Kansas. There, on the Kansas Pacific railroad, an Illinois cattle dealer, Joseph McCoy, had in 1867 constructed stockyards, cattle pens, loading ramps, and a hotel. McCoy chose the hamlet of Abilene because, as he wrote, "the country was entirely unsettled, well watered, excellent grass, and nearly the entire area of country was adapted to holding cattle." Once arrived in town, the drovers sold herd to McCoy or some other dealer and departed with money in their pockets. The cattle were loaded on freight cars and sent east.

Abilene was only the first of a number of cattle towns. As the region around this small city became settled farming country, the Texas drives were deflected farther west to Ellsworth, Newton, and Dodge City. In each case the trade was much the same and the cattle towns nourished by it took on many of the same characteristics. Like the mining camps, they were at first almost all-male communities. Cowboys with money were just as wild as miners in the same lucky situation. The cattle towns also attracted rogues and outlaws, although probably never in such numbers as the mining camps. They usually had from the beginning a large stable element of businessmen and families that kept them from ever being as disorderly as the communities farther west. In fact, much of the carousing and hell-raising was tacitly sanctioned, since the city fathers who ran the local banks, hotels, saloons, and clothing and dry-goods stores recognized that they had to cater either to the ranchers' and cowboys' tastes or see their business go to competitors.

The annual long drive lasted until about 1880. During the years it prospered, about four million cattle overall were driven north from Texas to Kansas railroads for shipment east. By 1880, the fate that had overtaken Abilene also claimed the other cow towns: an ever-denser farm population increasingly interfered with the drive. In addition, new railroads through the Texas plains made it possible to ship cattle directly from the local ranches of the Texas panhandle. By this time, too, northern plains—the Dakotas, Wyoming, Montana, and Colorado—were stocked with cattle, hybrids with the hardiness of longhorns and the eating qualities of Angus and Herefords. In short order, these animals became the major source of beef for the thriving cities of the East.

For a decade and a half the Northern Plains range cattle industry flourished. Young cattle could be bought for a few dollars and put out to pasture on government land. The rancher did not have to invest in barns or other buildings. All he needed was a cabin by a streambank from which he and his hands could ride out occasionally to inspect the stock. The cattle wintered out and gained weight on the nutritious grass. Twice each year —spring and fall—the rancher and his hands conducted a "roundup," separating out the mingled herds of neighbors and branding calves with their owners' mark. When shipped to market after four or five years, a calf had increased in value by about ten times.

So long as winters were moderately mild and the range not overstocked, the system worked. But its very success became a pitfall. Attracted by dazzling profits as well as the supposed glamour of the ranchers' life, investors went into the cattle industry by the hundreds. The romance of the open range attracted Easterners such as the New York aristocrat Theodore Roosevelt, who became a rancher in 1883 in the South Dakota Badlands. It also attracted Europeans. For a while, London investors were in a dither over potential profits in Western cattle. "Drawing rooms buzzed with stories of this last of the bonanzas; staid old gentlemen, who scarcely knew the difference between a steer and a heifer, discussed it over their port and nuts." In the cattle kingdom itself, the ranchers tried to stem the flood of new cattle through various "live-stock associations," but they were unable to prevent overstocking. By the mid-eighties so many cattle were pouring into the Eastern markets that prices began to tumble.

Then disaster struck. The hard winter of 1885-86 was followed by a hot, dry summer that withered the grass. Prices of steers dropped from $30 apiece to $8. The winter of 1886-87 was a catastrophe. By November the snow on the northern Plains was so deep that cattle could not dig down to the grass. In late January the worst blizzard on record roared across the Plains from the Canadian border to Texas. This was followed by a cold snap that sent temperatures plummeting to 68 below zero. On the open plains, cattle froze upright in their tracks. Many thousands crowded into gullies and stream valleys for shelter and were buried in drifts. In the spring, the freshets from melting snow washed thousands of steer carcasses into the tributaries of the Missouri.

Over the next few years, the cattle industry painfully reorganized. Many of the more speculative enterprises, including many large cattle corporations representing Eastern and European investors, went bankrupt. Survivors came to recognize that they had to give up the idea of the open range. As one Western editor remarked: "A man who turns out a lot of cattle on a barren plain without making provisions for feeding them will not only suffer a financial loss but also the loss of the respect of the community in which he lives." Thereafter the ranchers turned to smaller and better herds on fenced land—either owned or rented —where they grew hay to provide fodder.

Some cattlemen, especially on the dryer, eastern margins of the plains, turned to raising a hardier species of animal—sheep. Others resisted the sheepmen, and for a while open warfare raged in parts of the former cattle kingdom between the ranchers and the herders. Danger came from the other direction too: equipped with barbed wire to fence off the timberless grasslands, with well-digging machinery and windmill pumps to provide drinking water for stock and human beings, and

Spur with leather toe strap; made in southern California, nineteenth century. (Index of American Design.)

with new techniques of dry farming to offset sparse rainfall, the "nesters" poured into the more humid portions of the Plains from the East. By the 1890's vast areas of the Dakotas, eastern Montana, and Colorado were covered with wheat fields. In the fall, these "bonanza farms" were crisscrossed by great harvesters pulled by six horses cutting enormous swaths through the yellow sea of grain.

By 1890, then, the Plains had finally been "conquered," and the last continental frontier had ceased to exist. The event was marked symbolically by the words of the Superintendent of the Census in an 1890 bulletin: "Up to and including 1880 the country had a frontier of settlement, but at present the unsettled areas have been so broken into by isolated bodies of settlement that there can hardly be said to be a frontier line. In the discussion of its extent, its westward movement, etc, it can not, therefore, any longer have a place in the census reports." Frederick Jackson Turner, in a paper before the American Historical Association in 1893, made this bulletin the starting point for the formulation of his famous "frontier thesis," which ascribed many of America's social and political characteristics to the presence of a western frontier for almost three centuries. Scholars have since pointed out how premature the announcement actually was: much land remained to be settled. Yet it is clear that in the eyes of many Americans by about 1890 the frontier ex-perience was at an end, and with it the expansionist phase of the nation's history. But not all felt this way. To some it seemed as if only the first chapter had ended. Now the vigorous people who had conquered the North American continent must look outward toward the larger world across the seas—there, they said, lay the country's new destiny.

The Outward Thrust: Beginnings

It would be a mistake to see American overseas expansion as a completely new development in the 1890's. In fact, it dated to before the Civil War, when American interest in the Pacific resulted in the famous visits of Admiral Matthew Perry's naval squadron to Japan in 1853-54 and the almost simultaneous effort of Southerners to compel Spain to sell Cuba to the United States. The United States acquired no territory as the result of either of these two probes and during the Civil War American foreign relations, like all other national concerns, were subordinated to the urgent goal of defeating the Confederacy and preserving the Union.

The war's end brought a resurgence of interest in the world beyond the nation's shores and borders. Secretary of State William Seward, President Andrew Johnson's chief foreign policy adviser, was an aggressive man. As Secretary of State during the Civil War, Seward had had to pursue defensive policies against European opportunists seeking to take advantage of the Union's preoccupation with the rebellion. During these war years France sent troops to Mexico and established there the regime of a puppet emperor, the Archduke Maximilian of Austria. Meanwhile, Spain tried to regain control of the Dominican Republic and made demands on several South American countries. Seward deplored these violations of the Monroe Doctrine, the policy of excluding Europeans from major influence in the Western Hemisphere, as first announced by President James Monroe in 1823. He complained, expostulated, and protested, but he was forced to bide his time.

With the war's victorious conclusion, Seward quickly began to exert pressure on the French and Spanish to desist from their aggressions. He warned the Spanish minister to Washington that if the country persisted in its course, the United States would actively support the Latin American republics feuding with Spain. The Spaniards quickly abandoned their Western Hemisphere ambitions. France was a far more powerful nation, yet behind Seward were fifty thousand Union veterans under General Philip Sheridan's Texas command; if these linked up with the forces of Maximilian's Mexican opponent, Benito Juaréz, the French puppet empire was done for. In November 1865 Seward told the French that "the presence and operations of the French army in Mexico, and its maintenance of an authority there, resting upon force and not the free will of the people of Mexico, [are a] cause of serious concern to the United States." In 1866 he demanded that the French set a time limit for ending their occupation of Mexico. By now the French Emperor, Napoleon III, was convinced that the Mexican adventure was becoming too costly and he removed his troops. Juaréz's forces quickly took over, captured Maximilian, and executed him. Thanks to the United States, the Mexican people were now once more masters in their own houses.

Having thus dealt with Europe's version of expansion, Seward was now free to turn to his own. He wanted to make America's presence felt in the Pacific, and to this end he favored acquiring the Hawaiian Island, then an independent kingdom. He also wished to buy the Virgin Islands from Denmark and to establish a major United States naval base in the Dominican Republic, recently evacuated by Spain. All of these schemes, however, fell through. The American people, if not their indefatigable Secretary of State, had had enough of such vigorously outreaching national policies and, now that the South was defeated, wished to return to private concerns. Opposition to the Danish treaty prevented the acquisition of the Virgin Islands at this time, although the United States would finally buy them in 1917.

Seward's one great expansionist success was Alaska. That vast northwest corner of North

America was then a Russian colony, having been first explored and exploited by the Tsars' agents during the eighteenth century. A beautiful land, it had at most a few thousand inhabitants, almost all either Indian or Eskimo, and few known resources except furs. The fur trade had flourished at first under the aegis of the Russian-American Company, but by 1865 the fur-bearing animals were gone and the company was in financial trouble. Not only was the region becoming a financial liability to the Tsarist regime, but it was also so far from the Russian heartland that it could not easily be defended. In case of war with Britain, especially, the Russians could see no way of retaining the colony. Better, then, to sell it to the Americans—besides the money, Alaska as an American colony would be a buffer between Russian Siberia and British Canada.

With these ends in mind, the Russian minister in Washington asked Seward if the United States was interested in buying Russian-America. The Secretary leaped at the chance: not only would this represent a major addition to American territory, but it also promised to further another Seward hope: the eventual annexation of all of Canada. Seward quickly arranged a treaty paying Russia $7.2 million for the cession and sent it to the Senate, where the support of Charles Sumner of the powerful Foreign Relations Committee produced speedy adoption. In 1867 Russia formally transferred the territory to the United States.

All this had taken place at breakneck speed, before the American public could react. But now a problem arose. Congress as a whole, not merely the favorably inclined Senate, had to appropriate the money to pay for the territory. Before the proposed appropriation came before the House of Representatives, the public had time to respond to the purchase and the response was at best mixed. A few expansionists, like Seward himself, saw the cession as another step toward the nation's eventual dominion over the entire continent. Some Americans hoped that Alaska's purchase would serve to restrain the hungry British lion. Others favored the treaty because they felt kindly toward Russia, which they believed had supported the Union during the Civil War. A still larger number of Congressmen, apparently, were willing to be convinced of the cession's advantages by generous personal "gifts" from the Russian minister. Yet the opposition was strong and angry. It seemed to some newspaper editors that the treaty was "a dark deed done in the night." Besides, what was this place for which Americans were paying millions? It was, said critics, "a barren, worthless, God-forsaken region." It consisted of "walrus-covered icebergs"; it was the land "of short rations and long twilights." The New York Herald suggested that Seward might "make both ends meet" by also buying Patagonia at the southern tip of South America. In the end, Congress did appropriate the $7.2 million, but it was a near thing.

Seward's tenure as Secretary of State ended in 1869, when Grant succeeded Johnson, and for the next decade or more the United States pursued a rather unaggressive foreign policy. During these years the nation settled its Civil War-inspired dispute with Great Britain. The Treaty of Washington in 1871 provided for an international tribunal to assess the degree of British blame for allowing the escape of the Confederate raider Alabama, and this tribunal awarded the United States $15.5 million in damages. In 1878 the United States received rights to establish a naval base at Pago Pago in the Samoan Islands in the mid-Pacific. Yet, on the whole, this was an era when few Americans paid attention to international events. Indeed, American foreign policy of the 1870's had been described as the "nadir of diplomacy." As for expansion beyond continental limits, that seemed a preposterous idea. The Chicago Tribune noted soon after the Civil War: "we already have more territory than we can people in fifty years."

Overseas Expansion

Gradually, attitudes began to change. Many separate and distinct aspects entered into the new view that emerged in the 1880's of America's role on the world stage. Some of these involved responses to economic conditions; others belonged primarily to the realm of ideas; still others seem to have been psychological in nature; some represented a merger of philosophical and psychological elements. Wherever or however derived, these elements helped create a new conviction among influential Americans by the 1890's that the time had come to abandon earlier notions regarding the outside world. The United States, they felt, was—or should be—a great world power, and like other such powers must wield its influence widely and even acquire an overseas empire.

One philosophical basis for the change in outlook lay in the doctrines of Social Darwinism. We have already noted how Darwinian ideas reinforced laissez-faire during the Gilded Age by providing a supposedly scientific rationale for a governmental hands-off policy in economic matters. And Darwinian concepts also seemed applicable to one nation's relations to others. Social Darwinists likened individual countries to distinct species. In their inevitable competition those that were superior would—and indeed, deserved to —triumph and garner for themselves power and wealth. Needless to say, most American Social Darwinists had little doubt that the United States —along with Britain, and sometimes Germany— was admirably equipped to compete in the race for power, riches, and glory. The "fitness" of the Anglo-Saxon "race," claimed John Fiske, justified its expansion "until every land on the earth's surface that is not already the seat of an old civilization shall become English in its language, in its political habits and traditions, and to a predominant extent in the blood of its people."

There was obviously a racist element in Fiske's view. The new racism held that human characteristics were largely biologically determined, that "nature" counted for far more than "nurture." Joined with this at best dubious notion was another distinctly dangerous one: that some races were inherently superior to others. "Scientific" racists at the end of the nineteenth century were proclaiming a doctrine of Nordic supremacy that, they claimed, justified excluding the new immigrants from southern and eastern Europe and also gave sanction for the United States's extension of its dominion over foreign areas where "lesser breeds without the law" still held sway.

But Social Darwinism was only one of the intellectual currents that affected American attitudes about overseas expansion from the 1880's onward. However chauvinist and racist this doctrine, it offered nonetheless an optimistic view of the nation's role. Paradoxically, there was also a gloomy attitude concerning the nation's future that contributed to the change of heart as the century drew to a close. In these years influential Americans in increasing numbers began to fear that what was to come would fall short of what had already transpired. Brooks Adams, grandson of one President and great-grandson of another, envisioned his country losing its "virility" and falling under the sway of plutocrats, rich men without vision or creativity. Other Americans deplored the decline of the martial virtues which they saw as resulting from a whole generation of

peace. In the words of the naval theorist Alfred Thayer Mahan, Americans were ceasing to be "fighting animals" and "becoming fattened cattle fit only for slaughter."

Many of the pessimists linked these "unfortunate" trends to the end of the frontier. In the mid-1880's, a perceptive British observer of America, James Bryce, predicted that when Americans had fully occupied their empty interior, "it will be a time of trial for democratic institutions." A few years later, William "Coin" Harvey, a Populist spokesman, noted that "the unexplored portions of the world . . . were escape valves for the poorer people. . . . The damming up of the stream has now come . . . and justice now stands at bay."

The most famous argument for the end of the frontier as a turning point in American history was that of Frederick Jackson Turner. Turner's remarks before the 1893 conference of the American Historical Association did more than announce the end of a phase of American development; they also implied danger ahead. The frontier, Turner declared, had encouraged individualism and democracy. On the frontier, moreover, people of widely diverse origins had blended together into a new characteristically American mixture. Now that the frontier experience was past, America had to begin a new phase. Turner, in his 1893 statement, did not say what this new phase would be like, but it did not take much imagination to see what must lie ahead: in place of democracy, privilege and hierarchy; in place of individualism, collective action to achieve group ends; in place of the melting pot, ethnic diversity. The picture was implicitly one of conflict, disorder, and social stress.

To a small group of the brightest and most sensitive young men of the period, the only way to avoid these catastrophes seemed to be a revival of the martial spirit and an aggressive expansionism. Mahan, in his influential 1890 book, *The Influence of Sea Power on American History*, argued that a nation could only achieve greatness by sea power. The United States must build a great navy if it was not to sink in world esteem. Adams declared that "Imperialism would grant a reprieve for individualism by continuing the frontier conditions that made it possible." Franklin Giddings, a sociology professor at Columbia, after noting the enormous energy of the American people, asserted that without an opportunity to employ this energy on overseas expansion it might well "discharge itself in anarchistic, socialistic, and other destructive modes that are likely to work incalculable mischief."

Adams, Mahan, and Giddings were all essentially intellectuals, but learning from them and seconding them was a group of young politicians who in the next few years would have an enormous impact on the country's political life. The most prominent of these was Theodore Roosevelt, scion of a "Knickerbocker" family long prominent in New York business, political, and charitable affairs. Ever since his childhood Roosevelt had made a fetish of the "strenuous life." During the 1880's, as we have seen, he had been attracted by the cattle frontier and had become a rancher in the Black Hills. Roosevelt had no doubt that the long peace since 1865 had made Americans fat and complacent. Whenever it appeared that there was a chance for the country to get into a fight, he became enthusiastic. In 1889, the United States clashed with Germany over Samoa, and he declared that he "should not be sorry to see a bit of a spar with Germany." In the next decade, when a crisis with Britain developed over Venezuela, he wrote his friend Henry Cabot Lodge: "I rather hope that the fight will come soon. The clamor of the peace faction had convinced me that this country needs a war." Lodge, scarcely less bellicose, was forever "finding" enemies who, if not stopped, would endanger America's vital interests. Finally, there was the young Indianan Albert Beveridge, who first came to the attention of the American public for his blatant advocacy of imperialism. In 1898, when he ran for the Senate, Beveridge brought his audiences cheering to their feet recounting how the "march of the flag" had taken the American people from the original boundaries of 1789 to the Pacific. It was now inevitable, he intoned, that the next stage must begin with the flag over "an Isthmian canal . . . over Hawaii . . . over Cuba and the southern seas. . . ."

The fears of cultural and political stagnation and decline that preoccupied these men had an economic counterpart. Especially in the depressed 1890's, many Americans feared that the end of the frontier meant an end to expanding domestic markets for the enormous output of the American economy. During these years, businessmen and business spokesmen constantly urged the government to help industry find new markets abroad. "We must have more customers," explained a cotton manufacturer, to absorb "the excessive production of our mills." Francis Thurber, president of the United States Export Association, proclaimed that the expansion of American markets "is absolutely necessary in view of our increasing productive capacity. . . . We must have a place to dump our surplus, which otherwise will constantly depress prices and compel the shutting down of our mills . . . and changing our profits to losses."

Businessmen were not alone in this concern. Farmers and their spokesmen also expressed the urgent need for overseas markets of one kind or another. "Foreign markets," announced the New York Grange, "are essential to the prosperity of the American farmer." "Any person who opposes [efforts] intended to further our commerce with Japan and the east," remarked a farm journal, "is simply turning his hands backwards on the dial of history."

Some scholars have concluded that these demands for overseas markets were in fact the primary motivating force behind the drive for empire at the century's end. Actually, very few of the business or farm groups advocated the grabbing of colonies. Francis Thurber, whose lust for overseas markets we have noted, denied that he favored "imperialism" and the problems that absorbing hordes of foreign peoples might bring. What he wanted was simply expanded trade, and he, like his colleagues, strongly supported an active role by the federal government in opening up foreign markets hitherto closed to American exports. Nevertheless, there is an obvious overlap between these trade expansionists and the outright imperialists. Both were dissatisfied with an isolationist America; both favored more use of American muscle in foreign relations; both feared the effects of the nation turning inward on itself.

Finally, in considering the attitudes and ideas that prepared the way for America's late-nineteenth-century outward thrust, there is the element of altruism, however misguided or misplaced. All nations, it is true, seek to put the best face on their aggressive actions towards other nations and peoples. It is easy to treat these professions as nothing more than rhetoric, empty words designed to assuage the national conscience or convince the gullible elsewhere in the world. Yet however self-serving the altruism, it is possible to underestimate both its persuasiveness and its sincerity.

Every nation has an image of itself that emphasizes its special claim to distinction or nobility, or both. The American self-image has been that of a "redeemer nation," one meant to be an example of freedom and opportunity for all the world. At home, this implied openness and prosperity; abroad, it involved championing the world's oppressed. In line with this outlook, all through the nineteenth century the United States government felt free to scold other nations for their mistreatment of their own people. Some of this, no doubt, was just good politics, with Congress or the President seeking support from ethnic constituents. But even where votes were not in question, the American government often depicted itself as a moral force in the world—as, for example, when in 1848 it protested the Austrian suppression of a liberal-national revolution in Hungary.

In the era of expansionism, this notion of the redeemer nation cut both ways. It set a limit to American appetites: Americans could not easily condone outright conquest, nor could they readily swallow the role of a *herrenvolk*, a super race that had the right to enslave others. Obviously, some Americans—the "Nordic supremacists," for example—could and did accept this idea, but they were never more than a tiny minority. And even when Americans exhibited a sense of racial superiority, this often produced arguments against imperialism rather than for it. Since the American tradition of expansion implied self-government for newly acquired regions, the incorporation of peoples of alien race, traditions, and language —unsuited, presumably, for American democracy —served as a deterrent to political incorporation. Such people could never be assimilated, therefore let them alone, was the reasoning.

The redeemer nation self-image nonetheless did also serve to encourage a form of expansionism, especially when clothed in the vestments of religion. Even when they deplored physical conquest, Americans were often willing to condone cultural and religious conquest. Few doubted that their combination of Protestant Christianity and material progressiveness was a boon to the world. If these could be exported, "backward" peoples might benefit immeasurably. As far back as the 1820's, societies dedicated to bringing the Protestant-Christian word to the "heathens" of Asia and Africa had been sending missionaries east and west to foreign parts. The missionaries' impact had been especially strong in the Pacific region. In Hawaii they transformed Polynesian culture utterly and for good or ill brought the islands headlong into the modern age. A far broader field for evangelization was the "Celestial Kingdom" of China, a vast society with an ancient, sophisticated, but non-Christian civilization. American missionaries first arrived in China in the 1830's. By 1851, out of a total of 150 Protestant missionaries in China, 88 were American.

The purpose of the missionaries was primarily religious: to gather souls for the Lord by converting the "heathen Chinese" to the true faith. But their work had effects far beyond this. For the missionaries brought not only the Bible but also Western ideas of democracy, the scientific method, material progress. The mission compounds took in Chinese orphans and taught them, along with the word of the Lord, Western concepts of sanitation and practical Western mechanical skills.

In purely religious terms, the missionaries' success was quite limited. No mass conversions occurred, and by the late nineteenth century there were only a few thousand "rice Christians" out of China's vast millions. But the missionaries did succeed in creating a small elite imbued with Western ideas and skills. In the process, they had also created antibodies in the form of a deep anti-Westernism that would have consequences both destructive and constructive.

Meanwhile, back home the missionary societies played an important role in directing the attention of Americans overseas. On Sundays, in thousands of Protestant churches across the United States, worshippers listened to pleas for contributions for benighted China, or Samoa, or some other exotic land. One of the best-sellers of the 1880's was the Reverend Josiah Strong's *Our Country*, a volume that advocated a Christianized world under American auspices. Strong's message was not only religious. He also pleaded for Western "civilization" and Western material progress, with an added bonus thrown in—enhanced foreign trade. "The world is to be Christianized and civilized," *Our Country* announced, but then "commerce follows the missionary. . . ." Strong's pleas did not fall on deaf ears. During the 1890's the college-based Student Volunteers for Foreign Missions adopted as its slogan "The evangelization of the world in this generation."

These, then, were the ideas and forces that during the 1880's began to erode the isolationism that had followed Seward's departure. One manifestation of the new mood was the building of a new ocean-going navy of steel vessels to replace the decrepit wooden fleet left over from the Civil War, beginning with Congress' authorization of a number of modern steel ships in 1883. The real turnabout did not come until the early nineties, following a Navy Policy Board report that recommended the building of two hundred additional warships to provide America with a wide reach, befitting her new status as a major world power. Although at first Congress indignantly rejected this ambitious program, in the next few years it appropriated funds for constructing the first American battleships with large guns and wide cruising ranges. In 1880, the United States Navy ranked twelfth in the world; by 1900, the nation's fleet made it the third-largest naval power.

The 1880's also marked the onset of "spirited diplomacy," under the auspices of Secretary of States James G. Blaine. Previously a powerful Republican Senator from Maine, Blaine had been a major figure in American political life for two decades when he became President Garfield's Secretary of State in 1881. Garfield's tragic death at the hands of an assassin within months of his inauguration ended Blaine's effort to call a conference of all the independent Western Hemisphere nations to discuss economic cooperation. But Blaine got a second chance when Benjamin Harrison succeeded Cleveland in 1889, and he once again became Secretary of State.

Blaine's "Pan-Americanism" was in some ways a refurbishing of the Monroe Doctrine. Although he himself was a jingoist (that is, a person who aggressively favored his country's interests), he recognized that the United States could not treat its special relationship with Latin America as a purely one-way street. This nation should, he believed, involve the Latin republics in their own defense in some sort of loose association with the United States. In our own day, Pan-Americanism has in fact moved increasingly in the direction of mutual defense and cooperative association in the Western Hemisphere. But a more immediate goal of Blaine was the improvement of trade relations. Although Latin America sent vast amounts of coffee, sugar, fruits, and other tropical and semitropical products to the United States, it bought most of its manufactured goods from Europe. This trade imbalance disturbed Blaine, and when

in 1889 he once more found himself heading the State Department, he worked hard to end it. As luck would have it, his Democratic predecessor had already called a second Pan-American conference, although he had not stayed long enough to preside over it; now it was Blaine who was in charge.

In seeking to wean the Latin Americans away from Europe and toward the United States as their source of manufactures, Blaine resorted to a highly organized and unorthodox approach. Before the conference got fairly down to business, he sent the Latin American delegates on a six-thousand-mile railroad journey across the country, to impress them with the might and efficiency of American industry. All this trip probably accomplished was to wear the delegates out. When the conference reconvened, Blaine proposed a customs union among all the American nations so that the goods of each could pass freely among all without the payment of tariffs. He also suggested the establishment of arbitration machinery to settle disputes among the states of the hemisphere. Neither proposal was adopted, however, and the significance of the 1889 conference consists largely in the precedent it set for the later Pan-American movement and in its marking the beginning of United States emergence from the shell of isolationism.

Hawaii

Blaine's "spirited diplomacy" was also being deployed in the Pacific area. With regard to Samoa, he negotiated with Britain and Germany an arrangement for joint three-power rule over the islands, the first true example of an offshore American political protectorate. He also pushed for the annexation of the Hawaiian Islands. This beautiful mid-Pacific chain had long attracted Americans—traders, whalers, and missionaries. The last-named had brought literacy, the Bible and a long shapeless gown designed to cover the bare skin of Hawaiian women. The sons of the missionaries had stayed and become businessmen and sugar planters. In 1875 the kingdom of Hawaii negotiated a treaty with the United States by which, in exchange for the free admission of its sugar to the American market, it agreed not to allow territorial concessions to other foreign nations.

In the next decade, Hawaii prospered as a supplier of sugar to the United States. It was also

pulled into the American political orbit, a process welcomed by the many Americans living in the islands. In 1887 Hawaii, in exchange for granting the United States the exclusive right to use Pearl Harbor as a naval station, secured an extension of the sugar agreement. By this time the American contingent had come to control about two-thirds of the islands' taxable real estate and to exert a strong influence on the policies of the Hawaiian government.

In 1890 the United States Congress removed the tariff on all imported sugar, thus ending Hawaii's advantage in the American market. The Hawaiian economy took a nose dive. Meanwhile, the Hawaiian government was becoming, at least from the standpoint of the resident Americans, increasingly capricious, arbitrary, and tyrannical in its actions. When Queen Liliuokalani succeeded her brother on the Hawaiian throne in 1891, matters became still worse. The physically formidable

Queen despised the liberal constitution that the American residents had recently imposed on her "weak-kneed" brother, and early in January 1893 she issued a royal edict abolishing it in favor of one far more autocratic. The Americans and other whites in the islands feared that their expulsion, or at least the confiscation of their property, would soon follow; and to forestall any such possibility they arranged a coup. Calling on the American minister, John L. Stevens, for support, they set up a provisional government and proclaimed it the legitimate authority in Hawaii. The Queen —unable to act because of American armed men called in by Stevens from an American vessel in Honolulu harbor—could do nothing. On January 17, 1893, Stevens extended United States recognition to the revolutionary government. Soon afterward Liliuokalani abdicated, and Stevens declared Hawaii an American protectorate.

By this time a delegation of white Hawaii residents had arrived in Washington to arrange for the islands to become part of the United States. Blaine was no longer Secretary of State, but his successor was equally enamored of expansion and supported the move. The Harrison administration submitted a treaty of annexation to the Senate.

At this point, however, the hitherto headlong process of transferring Hawaii to the United States hit a snag. Many Americans were still not ready for the acquisition of an overseas empire. The case of Samoa was at worst ambiguous; but Hawaiian annexation would be undisguised colonialism. One writer caught the public doubts in verse:

"Shall we take Hawaii in, sirs?"
    that's the question of the day.

Would the speedy annexation of that
    dusky country pay?
Would the revenues from sugar and
    from smuggled opium
Counteract the heavy burdens that
    with them are sure to come?

Fortunately for the anti-annexationists, the Senate was at the moment a lame-duck body with little time to act. Before it could approve the treaty, the Harrison administration turned over the reins of power to Grover Cleveland, now about to begin his second administration.

Cleveland was skeptical of expansion of any kind, and particularly suspicious of the course of events by which Hawaii was being dumped into American laps. In 1893 he abruptly withdrew the treaty from the Senate and appointed a special commissioner, James Blount, to go to Hawaii on a fact-finding mission. As the President told old friends, "We ought to stop, look, and think." Blount's report confirmed Cleveland's doubts: the Hawaiian revolution, the commissioner declared, had been fomented not by the native Hawaiians but by the whites, and would not have succeeded without improper American intervention. These findings decided Cleveland, and over the next few months he tried to return the Queen to her throne. Unfortunately, Liliuokalani insisted that she would cut off the heads of the revolutionaries if and when she resumed power, something Cleveland found entirely distasteful. Nor would the provisional government surrender power. In the face of this impasse, Cleveland chose to do nothing. Hawaii remained an independent nation, one governed by its white residents.

Venezuela

Meanwhile, the United States was becoming embroiled in Latin American affairs once again. For years Venezuela and Great Britain had disputed the proper location of the Venezuela-British Guiana boundary. To the British the disagreement seemed at first a minor matter; the Venezuelans, concerned with control of the mouth of the mighty Orinoco River, took it more seriously. In 1887 they suspended relations with Britain and turned to the United States for support, invoking the name of the "immortal Monroe." Early in the following decade they hired an American

publicist to write a pamphlet called "British Aggressions in Venezuela, or the Monroe Doctrine on Trial." This publication they circulated widely, paying particular care to get it into the hands of American congressmen. During this period, the United States government suggested several times that the dispute be submitted to arbitration, but the British consistently refused.

There matters stood when Cleveland returned to office. The Democratic President was not a jingoist, but he did dislike the British, and indeed, many Americans were Anglophobes who considered Great Britain arrogant and overbearing. Irish-Americans in particular despised England for its harsh politics in their ancestral homeland over many generations, and it had become a popular practice for politicians occasionally to "twist the lion's tail"—insult Britain—to win voter support. By itself this anti-British bias might have been sufficient to make the administration favor Venezuela. But besides this, the Cleveland administration was under pressure for other reasons to deal sternly with Britain. Republicans and other Americans believed that Britain's seizure of the customs house at Corinto, Nicaragua, in 1894 on the pretext that the Nicaraguans had insulted the British consul, had been handled weakly by Cleveland's Secretary of State, Walter Gresham, and they were accusing the Democratic administration of cowardice.

In mid-1895 Gresham died and was replaced by Richard Olney, a man of different temper. Gresham had been preeminently a man of peace. Olney was far more pugnacious, as his behavior in the Pullman Strike had shown. Soon after taking office he drafted a dispatch that, when transmitted to the British government by the American ambassador in London, caused a first-rate international furor. Asserting that the Monroe Doctrine was an integral part of American law, he demanded to know if Britain intended to submit the Venezuela boundary dispute to arbitration. If it did not, the United States would consider it to be in violation of the Monroe Doctrine. This semi-ultimatum to Great Britain was aggressive enough in itself, but its effect was intensified by Olney's arrogant tone. "To-day the United States is practically sovereign on this continent," Olney lectured Lord Salisbury, "and its fiat is law upon the subjects to which it confines its interposition."

The Olney note deeply offended the British, and Salisbury, when he replied after a four-month delay, lectured the Americans back: the United States was mistaken in believing that the Venezuela boundary was a Monroe Doctrine is-

sue; Olney had his history all wrong. As for arbitration, the answer was "No."

The British response made Cleveland "mad clear through," and late in 1895 he sent a warlike message to Congress, asking for funds to appoint an investigating commission to determine where the boundary should be drawn. The line so determined should then be forced on Britain, come what may. "I am fully alive to the responsibility incurred, and keenly realize all the consequences that may follow," the President ominously concluded. Swept by a sudden burst of patriotism, Congress unanimously appropriated $100,000 for the boundary commission. Meanwhile, in the country at large the war spirit soared, with Civil War veterans volunteering their services and one Irish-American group pledging 100,000 men to fight "perfidious Albion."

Fortunately, clearer heads finally prevailed. In England, too, leading politicians and molders of public opinion moved to calm things down. British policy-makers had been startled by the fury of the American reaction and recognized that then was not the time to goad the Yankees into war. Such a war would expose Canada to dangerous attack, but Britain had other reasons for not wishing to create a new enemy for itself. It was already deeply embroiled in South Africa, in a dispute that would soon lead to the Boer War. At the same time, Imperial Germany was beginning to challenge Britain internationally. To get into a war with America over a few thousand square miles of malarial jungle seemed foolish indeed.

Before many weeks had passed, the worst of the crisis was over. When the American boundary commission began its work, it found the British cooperative. Britain signed a treaty with Venezuela in early 1897 providing for an arbitration commission, as the United States had proposed. By the time the commission had handed down its decision, few Americans cared very much. The confrontation had been resolved without war.

Cuba

The Venezuelan boundary crisis represented a shift in public opinion that would have wide consequences. Although in the end Americans proved reasonable, the quick flare of anger against Britain betokened a change of attitude. Cuba would prove to be even more of an incitement.

Ever since the 1850's the "Pearl of the Antilles," one of Spain's few remaining possessions in the New World, had attracted the interest of Americans. After the Civil War a ten-year Cuban revolt (1868-78) against Spain embroiled the United States in the island's affairs.

Americans sympathized with the Cubans, whose struggle for independence seemed to parallel America's own a hundred years earlier. Various revolutionary Cuban *juntas* were allowed to operate from New York and other American cities, raising money and men for Cuban independence. At one point President Grant's Secretary of State, Hamilton Fish, even offered to guarantee Cuban debts to Spain in exchange for Cuban freedom. In 1878 the revolt was finally put down, and peace returned, temporarily, to the island. During the years of civil war, however, many sugar planters had suffered serious losses. Eager to get out, they sold their lands to Americans, who acquired some $33 million worth of property in Cuba.

Civil war erupted once again in Cuba in 1895. This time it was even more bitter than before. The rebels, anxious to involve the United States, attacked American property. When they spared it, it was often only in exchange for ransoms that were then used to finance the revolution. Both sides resorted to brutal methods. The *insurrectos* dynamited passenger trains and took civilian hostages. The Spaniards, in turn, under General Valeriano Weyler, rounded up thousands of civilians and put them in "reconcentration" camps where they could not give aid and support to the rebels. Inadequate food and medical supplies, combined with bad sanitation, soon killed off hundreds.

Americans watched the mounting barbarism in Cuba with alarm. The handful of American businessmen with investments on the island favored direct United States intervention, but their views were not typical. Most of the business community favored a hands-off policy. Ever since 1893, times had been bad. By 1897 they were beginning to improve. For the United States to become involved in a war with Spain over Cuba promised to nip recovery in the bud. In October 1897, the *Commercial and Financial Chronicle* noted that war would destroy "the trade prosperity we are all enjoying." Six months later, with the country on the verge of a war declaration, it announced that "every influence had been . . . tending strongly towards a term of decided prosperity, and . . . the Cuban disturbance, and it alone, has arrested the movement and checked enterprise."

But the business community's attitudes were not decisive. American sympathies were overwhelmingly in favor of *Cuba libre*, free Cuba. Aside from their anti-colonialist attitudes noted above, Americans also despised the Spaniards. General Weyler's actions in Cuba seemed only the latest chapter in a centuries-long Spanish record of

cruelty in the New World. "Butcher Weyler" seemed a perfect lineal descendant of Hernando Cortes and the other early conquistadores whose brutality toward the Aztecs and Incas had decimated those native peoples.

The atrocity ledgers were closely balanced between rebels and Spaniards, but the American people heard little of the *insurrectos'* misdeeds and much of Spain's. The United States daily press seemed to function in effect as the revolutionaries' propaganda department. Particularly effective were the *New York World* and the *New York Journal*, edited by Joseph Pulitzer and William Randolph Hearst respectively. In the later nineties these two papers were engaged in a great circulation war and sought to outdo one another in their constant revelations of new Spanish atrocities. Every heavyhanded Spanish move produced headlines in one paper or the other, inciting its rival to find, or invent, something equally sensational.

Hearst was perhaps the more unscrupulous of the two publishers. In 1898 he sent the famous American artist Frederic Remington to Cuba to illustrate Spanish misdeeds. When Remington arrived in Havana, he found matters much quieter than he had expected, and wired his boss that he wished to return: "There is no trouble here. There will be no war." Hearst wired back: "Please remain. You furnish the pictures and I'll furnish the war."

It would be a mistake to see American intervention in Cuba primarily as a propaganda victory for the "yellow press." Without the deeply embedded anti-Spanish attitudes, and without a decade of growing concern over the end of the nation's open spaces combined with a sense of American destiny and American superiority, the Hearst-Pulitzer press war would have meant little. Joined with this was the widespread public sense that the country had grown soft since the 1860's. The period from 1865 to 1898 was the longest stretch of peace in the nation's history. A new generation of young men had reached maturity without having experienced directly the horrors of death and mutilation of their forebears of 1861-65. By the late 1890's, many of these were almost eager for a good fight, especially in such a worthy cause as Cuban independence.

The martial spirit affected politicians as well as ordinary citizens. Congress was strongly pro-Cuban and in 1896, by a large majority, passed a concurrent resolution to recognize the Cubans as belligerents. Meanwhile, men like Theodore Roosevelt, Henry Cabot Lodge, Albert Beveridge, and others attacked Spanish policies and acts in Cuba and demanded that America take action to stop them, even at the risk of war.

Unfortunately for the jingoists, neither Cleveland nor his Republican successor, William McKinley, was an interventionist. At one point Cleveland told a group of belligerent Congressmen that if Congress declared war against Spain he would "not mobilize the army." McKinley's reluctance to take action provoked Roosevelt to exclaim that the President had the backbone of a chocolate eclair. In reality, McKinley deplored Spanish policy and hoped to end Weyler's brutal repression. If it continued, he did not see how the United States could fail to intervene directly. But he did not insist on Cuban independence, nor did he want to force Spain to move faster than it was politically possible for her leaders to do.

McKinley, however, found himself unable to control events. In June 1897 he sent Stewart Woodford, a level-headed New Yorker, to Madrid as American minister. Woodford arrived in September and transmitted McKinley's wishes to the Spanish government: the United States must have assurances that repression would stop. This country would volunteer its good offices to settle the conflict between Spain and the Cubans, but if Spain refused, America would feel free to take action directly. The Spanish government, afraid of its own jingoists, responded slowly and evasively. It promised to recall Weyler and agreed that reforms in Spanish administration would be necessary, including some degree of Cuban autonomy. But then it proved slow to act. Meanwhile the American militants, hot for war with Spain, bombarded the President with demands that he brook no delay in ousting the Spaniards from Cuba.

By the beginning of 1898, McKinley was under intense pressure to intervene. This would soon become irresistible. In January the President ordered the battleship Maine to Havana, ostensibly as a friendly "courtesy," but actually to protect American life and property. The Spanish government was not pleased with this move, but when the vessel arrived, Spanish officials received the Maine "correctly" and wined and dined the officers and crew. It looked as if the visit might help the cause of peace.

While the Maine lay at anchor at Havana, Spanish-American relations took an abrupt turn for the worse. The Spanish minister to Washington, Enrique Dupuy de Lôme, was a proud and narrow aristocrat who despised the give-and-take of American politics. He was also indiscreet. In December 1897 he had written a Spanish friend in Madrid calling McKinley "weak and a bidder for the admiration of the crowd, besides being a would-be politician." The letter was intercepted by a Cuban rebel and sent to Hearst's Journal, where on February 9, 1898, a copy was printed below the headline "Worst Insult to the United States in Its History." The Cubans themselves saw the indiscretion as a victory. "The de Lôme letter is a great thing for us," declared a member of the Cuban junta in New York. Although the Spanish government quickly recalled its minister and apologized for his mistake, Spanish-American relations had been badly damaged.

Far worse now followed. On February 15 a massive explosion sank the Maine at its berth in Havana harbor, with a loss of 260 sailors, almost its entire crew. During the next few frantic days, the President cautioned against too hasty a judgment. "I have been through one war," the former Union major remarked, " . . . and I do not want to see another." The jingo press observed no such restraint. Certain that the explosion came from outside the ship and had been set by Spanish agents, they demanded action. "The Maine Was Destroyed by Treachery," thundered the Journal. "The Whole Country Thrills with War Fever." The World declared a free Cuba "the only atonement" for the dastardly deed.

Public reaction revealed a new warlike fervor. In Buffalo and other cities, mass meetings demanded that McKinley declare war, while around the country college students began to drill in preparation for a retaliatory attack on Spain. Congress, already bellicose, on March 9 appropriated an additional $50 million for the Army and Navy. Soon after, Senator Redfield Proctor of Vermont, just back from a tour of Cuba, further inflamed public opinion by confirming charges of Spanish bestiality in the reconcentration camps. The final blow was the report of an American commission that the explosion had been caused by a land mine, and could not have been internal.

In reality, to this day, no one knows who or what sank the Maine. It is certainly hard to believe that the Spanish government, which feared American intervention, was in any way responsible. Perhaps it was a lighted cigarette tossed into the ammunition hold. But the American people had made up their minds.

McKinley was reluctant to move, yet he recognized that he had to act. A few days after he received the Maine commission report, he instructed Woodford in Madrid to demand an immediate armistice in Cuba and to insist on an end of the reconcentration-camp policy. If peace terms were not achieved by October, Spain would have to accept McKinley's arbitration of the Cuban problem. As the President awaited the Spanish reply, Congressmen and the public stormed and thundered for immediate action. One angry Republican Senator barged into the office of Rufus Day, Assistant Secretary of State, and, waving his cane about, shouted that if the President did not "do something, Congress will . . . declare war in spite of him! He'll get run over, and the party with him!"

When the Spanish reply came, it was unsatisfactory. Madrid promised to investigate the *Maine* incident and to abolish the reconcentration camps in some areas, but it refused to suspend hostilities or allow American arbitration. In addition, the tone of the response was insulting. McKinley now knew that he had no choice and turned reluctantly to composing a war message. Still, he moved slowly, allowing the public to get angry and Spain to have

second thoughts. On April 10, while Americans awaited war expectantly, the Spanish government agreed to suspend hostilities in Cuba. A few days earlier the President might have used this concession as an excuse to avoid a declaration. But now it was too late: the public wanted war. On April 11, McKinley asked Congress to be allowed to use the Army and Navy to end the conflict in Cuba. Congress responded on April 19 with a four-part statement declaring that Cuba was free, that Spain must withdraw, that American armed forces would be used to achieve these ends, and that the United States had no intention of annexing Cuba. The last section of this war document was the so-called Teller amendment, and expressed the views of many American that they would fight for Cuba's freedom, not America's gain.

The Spanish-American War

The war that followed was the briefest in American history; on July 26 the Spanish government requested peace terms. The war was also cheap in its human cost. Only 379 of the 274,000 officers and men who served in the armed forces died as a result of enemy action. The financial cost, too, was small: about $250 million.

From the beginning, the war went America's way. Fortunately Spain was a weak nation, a shadow of the great power that had once ruled half the world. By contrast, the United States was a young giant, a nation of continental proportions, and also by now the world's leading industrial power. In addition, the American Navy had been thoroughly modernized; its morale was high, and it had vigorous leadership. The Army, by comparison, was weak and decrepit. Yet even on land, American numbers and industrial potential would have to tell, and did.

Actually, most of the burden of the war was borne by the Navy. Years of rebuilding from the lows of the early 1880's now showed their value in the fleet's state of readiness. With four first-class battleships and many other vessels, it outgunned the Spanish navy by a large margin. At the top, in Washington, moreover, was the Assistant Secretary of the Navy, Theodore Roosevelt, a whirlwind of energy and intelligence who had been looking for this fight for many years. Though technically the subordinate of the Secretary, Roosevelt was by far the more forceful man and in the frequent absence of his Washington-hating

chief, often served as acting secretary. Just before the outbreak of official hostilities, in Secretary John D. Long's absence, Roosevelt telegraphed Admiral George Dewey, in charge of the American Asiatic squadron, that he was to proceed to Hong Kong and keep his vessels fully coaled for an attack on the Spanish-owned Philippines. On May 1, 1898, following the official declaration of war, Dewey steamed into Manila Bay, the harbor of the Philippine capital. Five times the American ships sailed past the Spanish vessels stationed there, hurtling salvos with each pass. In a few hours the entire Spanish fleet consisted of smoking hulks. Then Dewey quickly smashed the land-based Spanish batteries. A contemporary English writer called the battle of Manila Bay "a military execution rather than a real contest."

Meanwhile, in the main Caribbean theater of operations, matters moved more slowly. The war served as a unifying force among Americans. Volunteers flocked to the colors at McKinley's call; 223,000 men had enlisted. They came from every section, South as well as North. In fact, the South's enthusiasm for the fight put an end, many contemporaries said, to the sectional estrangement that had prevailed ever since 1860. They came from every social stratum. Many black Americans expressed their patriotism—as well as their desire to escape Southern poverty—by enlisting. At the opposite end of the social scale were volunteers like William Jennings Bryan, McKinley's 1896 Democratic rival, who enlisted as colonel of

Nebraska volunteers, and Assistant Secretary Roosevelt himself. Unable to stand by while others dashed about firing rifles, TR quit his post to lead the "Rough Riders," a cavalry regiment of Western cowboys and Eastern "swells" that he had assembled himself.

Despite the enthusiasm, the Army—small, lethargic, poorly led—was not ready. Its civilian chief was Secretary of War Russell A. Alger, a Civil War veteran but an easy-going, inefficient man. Part of the bungling that would mark military operations in Cuba was clearly Alger's fault; he would also serve as a convenient scapegoat for the nation's neglect of its army, and the inevitable military sloth of a great continental democracy.

Alger had promised the President that he could get forty thousand men to Cuba in ten days after the outbreak of war. It actually took seven weeks to get seventeen thousand men to the island. Thousands of volunteers poured into Tampa, Florida, without guns, uniforms, or other equipment, and were forced to wait in the hot spring weather to see action. The problem was logistical mismanagement: whole trainloads of equipment were backed up on sidings. The men soon got bored and restless; many contracted disease. Several months elapsed before the giant tangle could be unsnarled and troops put aboard transports for Cuba.

On June 22, the first American troops finally landed at Daiquiri near Santiago, amidst near-total confusion. At Los Guasimas there was a brief but bloody skirmish. The war's major battles took place on July 1-3. These were small operations, but relatively bloody. The terrain was hilly and wooded and the Spaniards, equipped with ac-curate Mauser rifles, were well entrenched. Fortunately, though poorly led overall by the ponderous William Shafter, the troops were recommended in the field by vigorous and spirited officers. At San Juan Hill Roosevelt found himself at the head of his dismounted Rough Riders and a collection of black troops. Always impetuous, he led them on a charge which swept the Spanish troops off the hill and opened the road to Santiago. In his later account of his experiences in Cuba, *The Rough Riders*, Roosevelt greatly magnified his role, yet there can be no doubt that his aggressiveness was an important element in the victory.

Meanwhile, the American Atlantic fleet had destroyed the Spanish fleet. The Spanish Admiral, Pascual Cervera, had sailed from the Cape Verde Islands in late April headed for the Caribbean. For a while news of his departure had created a panic along the east coast. He evaded capture and slipped into Santiago harbor on May 19, unable to go any farther owing to lack of coal. With the American troops on the verge of capturing the town, he was faced with the choice of trying to escape or surrendering without a battle. Under pressure from the provincial governor, he reluctantly steamed out of Santiago into the waiting arms of America's powerful flotilla. In a few hours the Spanish squadron was destroyed, with three hundred of its sailors dead. The Americans had not lost a ship and had suffered only two casualties. The match was a grossly uneven one, yet it too attested to the effectiveness of the new American Navy. Two weeks later, Spanish officials surrendered Santiago. The fighting was over.

Making Peace

The quick succession of victories thrilled the American people. Yet the sense of triumph was mixed with chagrin. Not only had the United States been inept in getting the troops equipped and sent, but once the fighting was over they appeared unable to get the victorious army off the unhealthful island. While citizens and Congress fumed with impatience, yellow fever and dysentery began to inflict greater damage on the Americans than had the Spaniards' Mausers. And even the Navy was not exempt from criticism. True, it had defeated Cervera, but it should have provided better support for the ground troops, the critics declared. A series of congressional investigations would exonerate the officials in charge, but alloying the joy of victory would be the feeling that the war could have been conducted more efficiently.

Nonetheless, most Americans felt carried along on a wave of exhilaration as they considered the "splendid little war." Cuba was free and the detested Spaniards had finally been removed from the Western Hemisphere, a fact fully established by General Nelson Miles' capture of Puerto Rico a few days after Santiago's surrender. In the flush of victory, Congress finally accepted Hawaiian annexation by joint resolution.

Annexation was symptomatic of the change of opinion that the war had produced. Many Americans continued to doubt the wisdom of imperialism, but others abandoned their hostility to the idea of colonies. Particularly dramatic was the shift within the business community. Skeptical of the war before it began, by mid-1898 many businessmen had come to believe that the country's commercial destiny lay in the Far East, where a vast "China market" beckoned.

Those shifts in attitude affected the peace negotiations which opened in Paris on October 1. By this time both parties had agreed to the departure of Spain from Cuba and its ceding to the United States of Puerto Rico and Guam. Still undecided was the fate of the Philippines. Soon after Dewey's naval victory, American troops had landed at Manila and, in cooperation with Filipino rebels, had begun to extend their control of the chief island of Luzon. Meanwhile, a German fleet hovered off Manila, a cause of anxiety to the American military and naval commanders, who feared that Imperial Germany, ever interested in new colonies, had designs on Spain's collapsing Far Eastern empire.

In Washington, McKinley at first was uncertain what course to take regarding the Philippines. He had not been a strong expansionist before the war, but he had, as the Spanish minister had indiscreetly charged, been a crowd-pleaser. The changing public mood now affected his own attitude. Particularly important with the President was the new-found zeal of the Protestant clergy for a fresh field of missionary endeavor. Unaware that most Filipinos were Roman Catholics—or indifferent to this fact—they hoped to uplift the "heathen" and make them into good Christians. The pious McKinley found their interest a powerful incentive to change his mind, and he instructed his commissioners to the Paris peace conference that "the United States cannot accept less than the full right to sovereignty of the island of Luzon." On October 26 he demanded all of the Philippines. "The cessation must be the whole archipelago or none."

At first Spain balked. Spain had been present in the Philippines for over three hundred years, and the Spanish government could not lightly surrender this vestige of the nation's former grandeur. No one seriously considered the feelings of the Filipinos themselves, although the Americans, by calling witnesses of the right persuasion, convinced themselves that their "little

brown brothers" desired American tutelage above all else. In the end, the Spanish negotiators capitulated and in exchange for $20 million agreed to cede the whole island chain to the United States.

But problems remained. When the treaty came before the Senate for ratification, there was unexpected opposition. Despite the opinion shift of the previous months, some Americans were still strongly opposed to colonies. Many anti-imperialists felt that the acquisition would violate American traditions. Hitherto American expansion had been into empty territory, they held, where people of the white race and Anglo-Saxon institutions could form self-governing states like the original thirteen. Was it conceivable that these Filipinos, long governed by tyrannical Spain, speaking barbaric languages, and unused to self-government, could ever become Americans? Implicit in this attitude was a fair amount of racial and cultural chauvinism: the "little brown brothers" were deemed inferior to northern Europeans. But there was also a more generous aspect. The philosopher William James argued that American rule in the Philippines would not "uplift" the Filipinos. Such a belief was "sniveling, loathsome" cant. Acquiring the islands would be a "shameless betrayal of American principles." "What could be a plainer symptom of greed, ambition, corruption and imperialism?" he asked.

Outside Congress the anti-imperialists, many of them Mugwumps who had fought against political corruption during the 1870's and 1880's, organized the Anti-Imperialist League in November 1898. The league sent out thousands of broadsides and pamphlets to influential clergymen, politicians, businessmen, and farm leaders. These bore titles like "The Hell of War and Its Penalties" and "The Cost of a National Crime" and condemned the impending treaty. In Congress itself, Senator George F. Hoar of Massachusetts and Congressman Thomas B. Reed of Maine, fought such arch-imperialists as Henry Cabot Lodge and Albert Beveridge, who believed in America's Far Eastern destiny and its mission to uplift, as well as the commercial and strategic advantages of possessing the Philippines. One telling argument for annexing the islands was the likelihood that if the United States did not take them, the Germans would.

A key figure in the Senate debate was William Jennings Bryan. Though skeptical of colonies himself, the former Democratic standard-bearer believed that it was important to end the war officially. The impending presidential election, he claimed, could serve as a referendum on the an-

nexation and if the vote went against the supporters of colonies, the decision to annex could be
reversed. This was not very clear thinking.
Americans are not equipped for national referen-
dums, and in any case once the matter was decided
there was little chance of reversal. Bryan's argument, however, probably changed the minds of a
few Democratic Senators and on February 6,
1899, the Senate ratified the peace treaty by a vote
of 57 to 27, two votes more than the necessary
two-thirds.

An American Empire

And so, as the old century ended, Americans
found themselves with an empire; their country
had now joined the great powers as a colonial nation ruling over millions of non-Europeans. It is
undoubtedly true that the new status brought
satisfaction to many citizens who gloried in their
nation's added prestige. The European powers
now clearly saw the United States in a new light,
and after 1898 more and more of them upgraded
the rank of their representatives in the United
States from "minister" to that of "ambassador."

But Americans also found themselves facing a
new set of problems and difficulties. Even as the
Senate was considering the treaty with Spain, the
Filipinos were rising in anger against the Yankees.
Welcomed at first as liberators, they now seemed
merely new conquerors no better than their
predecessors. By the spring of 1899 a full-scale
war, the so-called Philippine Insurrection, was
raging over the archipelago. This was a dirty war
reminiscent of Vietnam two generations later.
Under the leadership of Emilio Aguinaldo, the
Filipino rebels attacked American troops and, in
the manner of guerrillas everywhere, committed
barbaric atrocities against their enemy. The
Americans, with less excuse, responded in kind;
and before long, scandalous reports were reaching
the United States that American soldiers were
butchering prisoners, while at least one American
field commander had ordered his men "to kill and
burn and make a howling wilderness of Samar,"
one of the rebel strongholds. Before the insurrection was put down in mid-1902, some seventy
thousand American troops, four times the number
sent to Cuba, had been engaged in fighting the
Filipinos.

Few Americans took pride or pleasure in the acquisition of the Philippines. Eventually, after
peace, an American administration under William
Howard Taft brought civil liberties and municipal
self-government to the islands. In 1902, Congress
passed the Philippine Government Act, setting up
a Philippine legislature elected by popular vote.
The Jones Act of 1916 anounced the United
States's intention of withdrawing from the islands
as soon as a stable government was established,
and conferred self-government in domestic matters on the Filipinos. The act also provided for
free trade with the United States, a move that
brought a degree of prosperity but also subordinated the Filipino economy to American interests. Finally, in 1934, Congress made provisions for Philippine independence in the Tydings-
McDuffie Act. Passed at the behest of anti-
imperialists, as well as of beet-sugar producers
who disliked the competition of Philippine sugar
and of trade union leaders who wanted to end the
influx of Filipino workers, the measure provided
for Filipino independence after a twelve-year
"commonwealth" period during which the islands
would be governed by their own legislature and
elected governor. This was the islands' status
when the Japanese invaded in early 1942, yet the
Philippines received their independence in 1946 as
provided.

In other possessions such as Guam and Puerto
Rico, the question of self-government was less
pressing. Guam was a small island with a small
population and eventually became little more than
an American naval base. Puerto Rico was large
and more densely populated. At first, Puerto
Rican nationalism was quite weak, and most
islanders seemed content to remain in the
American orbit. But what should be their status
within that orbit? In the *Insular Cases* (1901) the
Supreme Court declared that while inhabitants of
American possessions were entitled to enjoy some
fundamental constitutional guarantees, they did
not possess all the rights of United States citizenship. The court noted, though, that Congress
could choose to confer such rights if it wished, and
in the next few years Congress did. The Foraker
Act of 1900 had already provided for a partially
elective legislature with an appointive governor. In

Governor-General Taft. (Library of Congress.)

THE OUTWARD THRUST

1917 Congress granted Puerto Ricans United States citizenship and gave them the right to elect both houses of the legislature. Puerto Rico was also to be part of the American free trade area, and its products were to enter the United States duty-free.

During the first few decades of American control, Puerto Rico became the haven for millions of dollars of American capital, invested especially in sugar. The Puerto Ricans themselves, except for a small middle class, benefited relatively little. The sugar plantations gobbled up much of the level soil, displacing many peasants and small farmers. High birthrates compounded the island's problems. By the 1920's most of its two million people were poverty-stricken cane workers and day laborers. It was in these decades that Puerto Ricans began to debate their relationship to the United States. Some favored complete independence; others demanded full statehood within the American Union. A large middle group preferred the benefits of American affiliation combined with home rule. The problems of the island were not solved by the generation of Americans who acquired it, and they remain largely unsolved to our own day.

Cuba, too, produced its customary problems for the United States. For months following the Spanish surrender, it remained under the American military. During this period Cuban finances were set in order, and American doctors and public health authorities succeeded in wiping out the yellow fever that had afflicted the island for generations.

This was the more benign side of America's Cuba policy. But there was another one as well. In 1900 the Cubans adopted a constitution modeled after that of the United States. Unfortunately, it did not guarantee full autonomy. Under American pressure the Cubans incorporated into the document four clauses pledging that: (1) they would not enter into a treaty with any foreign power that would impair Cuban independence; (2) they would not contract any public debt beyond their ability to repay; (3) they would allow the United States to establish a naval base on Cuban soil; and (4) they would permit the United States to intervene to preserve Cuban independence. These clauses, collectively known as the "Platt Amendment," established a virtual American protectorate over the island that made a mockery of *Cuba libre,* the

professed reason for the war with Spain. Not until it was abrogated in 1934 was Cuba truly independent, and even then the Yankee colossus continued to cast its economic and cultural shadow across the island.

The "Open Door" policy in China had been more English than American in origin, although it was Secretary of State John Hay who in 1899 had sent notes to the major powers requesting equal commercial opportunity there. After some Chinese had staged the "Boxer Rebellion" in 1900 to drive foreign "devils . . . into the sea," Hay sent another round of notes insisting on China's "territorial integrity," an act partly reflecting traditional Sino-American friendship. But between 1900 and World War I, Americans basically decided against imperialism. In 1917 the nation bought the Virgin Islands from Denmark for $25 million. But this was the last territorial acquisition until after World War II. Colonies were disappointing. After the first flush there appeared little glory in empire; American destiny, it seemed, did not rest on colonial possessions after all. Nor was there any need, it seemed, for a social safety valve. Prosperity returned with the advent of the new century, and so did American confidence. Finally, an empire did not seem necessary for foreign trade. Americans would invest millions of dollars abroad in the years before 1914. Some went to the Philippines, Cuba, and Puerto Rico, but even more of it would go to Canada, Mexico, and other relatively stable, independent nations that were not American colonies. Nor did the China market work out—it eventually proved an illusion, and direct government action was necessary to induce American businessmen to risk money in that decaying empire.

In the end, then, the American overseas empire proved to be a temporary aberration. This is not to say that the United Staes ever returned to a state of indifference toward the rest of the world. As the economy expanded, so did American overseas commercial interests and concerns and, in the form of "dollar diplomacy," the United States would continue to wield its power indirectly in many regions of the globe. But as an alternative to the sweep across the continent that had marked the American community's first three centuries, overseas political expansion would be abandoned. As the colonial dream died, the American people began to turn to new domestic concerns.

Suggested Readings

Two recent studies of social Darwinism are Michael Ruse, *The Darwinian Revolution: Science Red in Tooth and Claw* (1979) and Cynthia Eagle Russett, *Darwin in America: The Intellectual Response, 1865-1912* (1976). Milton Plesur's *America's Outward Thrust, 1865-1890 (1971)*, sampling newspapers, commercial journals, and other sources of public opinion, concludes it was not merely economic interests but ideology that took the United States into the expansionism of the period. Other major books on foreign affairs in the late nineteenth century include Walter LaFeber, *The New Empire: An Interpretation of American Expansion, 1865-1898* (1963), David Healy, *United States Expansionism: The Imperialist Urge in the 1890's* (1970), and Charles S. Campbell, *The Transformation of American Foreign Relations, 1865-1900* (1976).

Chapter XIX
Industrial Capitalism

I. Forrest McDonald: The Beneficent Corporation

During the last third of the nineteenth century the United States came closer to attaining a system of pure, unbridled capitalism—of free private enterprise for profit—than ever before or since. It was not that anyone planned it that way. Rather, what happened was that economic enterprise expanded so rapidly that government on all levels was unable to keep up with it. Not coincidentally, the same years constituted the most creative, as well as the most disruptive, epoch in American history, and perhaps in the history of mankind.

Underlying the economic expansion was technological change: Americans and western Europeans, having finally undergone the social, political, and economic changes that made technological innovation both advantageous and acceptable to them, made a series of scientific and technical breakthroughs that altered man's relations with his natural environment. Among the more important of the innovations were the reciprocating steam engine, with its transportation counterparts; the internal combustion engine; the airplane; the electrical inventions, including their transportation and power applications; the radio; the telephone; the refrigerator; and dynamite, nitroglycerine, and other explosives. Each of these, in some fundamental way, liberated man from his environment.

The instrument through which these inventions were developed and exploited in America was the corporation, and, given everything, it could not have been otherwise. To be sure, government might theoretically have undertaken the task, but that was never really an option; besides, though government could doubtless have mobilized the necessary capital it could not supply the necessary competence, for ineptness among public officials was endemic to America's democratic political system. The corporation, by contrast, could attract the nation's best talent, for the lure it offered was money, and among a people committed to the pursuit of wealth, money had become the standard against which virtually all achievement was measured. But the corporation did more than buy talent, and it did more than accumulate capital whereby labor and raw materials and markets could be exploited: it also *created* talent, capital, jobs, raw materials, and markets. A single example will illustrate the ways it did so. West of Lake Superior lay the Mesabi Range, which turned out to be one of the richest lodes of high-grade iron ore in the world. For hundreds of millions of years, however, that range had been just so much rock, utterly worthless to mankind, and so it remained until corporate enterprise provided the machinery, labor, transportation, and markets that transformed it into riches. For purposes of creating wealth, the American business corporation proved to be the most effective instrument since the invention of credit.

Material progress wrought by the corporation, to the turn of the century and beyond, was of nearly miraculous proportions. The most obvious achievements were in the heavy industries, where production of coal, iron, and steel increased by as much as 2000 percent. The vast, previously isolated spaces of the United States were tied together with the world's most extensive railroad system, and railroad freight (carried at steadily decreasing rates) increased from 8 billion ton-miles in 1870 to 150 billion in 1900. At the time of the Civil War the total power of all "prime movers"—animals and machines—in the United States was about 13 million horsepower, and two-thirds of it was animal power. Four decades later the total had increased tenfold and four-fifths of the power was being generated by steam engines.

The social benefits of this harnessing of capital and machinery were equally impressive. So efficient were the American transportation and marketing systems that wheat farmers in the Dakotas (which had been virtually uninhabitable in 1870) were, at the turn of the century, able to put bread on the table of peasants in Central Europe cheaper than those peasants could produce it for themselves. The number of jobs in nonfarm occupations increased by 6 million between 1870 and 1910, enabling the United States to absorb an average of 600,000 immigrants and as many more migrants from American farms annually—and provide jobs for them all, at real wages which increased 50 percent during the period. Moreover, individual freedom—of movement, of occupation, of choice, of opportunity—expanded apace.

But there were social costs as well as social benefits, and therein lay the seeds of discontent. When the corporate and technological revolutions began, Americans welcomed both in the naive assumption that they would bring material advantages without entailing any fundamental changes in their accustomed ways. They also failed to recognize that increased freedom and opportunity go hand in hand with increased insecurity. Accordingly, they were entirely unprepared for the dislocations that their phenomenal economic expansion entailed. Farmers found themselves caught up in an international market whose mysteries they could not comprehend: the success or failure of those Dakota wheat farmers turned not upon how hard they worked, or even upon the vagaries of the weather, but upon whether crops succeeded or failed in such remote and exotic places as the valleys of the Danube and the Dnepr. Urban workers, though better paid than their counterparts anywhere else in the world, were subject to unpredictable unemployment, and the economy as a whole was staggered by major depressions in the 1870s and 1890s. Material progress skipped one part of the country entirely: in the former slave states of the old South, what developed was not free capitalism but something approximating feudalism, as the plain folk of the region, white and black alike, were reduced to the peonage of the sharecropper system. In the Northeast, old patrician families found their dominant status challenged by the rise of vulgar, new-rich entrepreneurs. Similarly, local elites all over the nation—country squires and small-town merchants, bankers, manufacturers, and lawyers—suddenly found their traditional power and status undermined; for what local consumers gained from the rise of Sears Roebuck and United States Steel, the local storekeeper and ironmonger lost in proportion.

In sum, as the twentieth century dawned Americans had achieved so much control over Nature as to suffer the illusion that they had nearly become Her master; and yet, into the bargain, millions of them felt that they had lost control of their own lives, felt hopelessly entangled in a jungle of institutions of their own making. In the circumstances, they characteristically looked about for someone or something to blame. They found scapegoats in abundance, but they singled out three in particular: corporations, cities, and immigrants.

The corporation was the most obvious candidate for the role of scapegoat, and despite the benefits it brought it was regularly and publicly castigated from the late 1880s onward. In part the attacks were a sham: many a venal politician orated against big corporations and voted to pass laws hampering their legitimate and necessary operations, only for the purpose of setting them up for private bribes to wink at the law. In part, too, the attacks were a matter of trickery among business rivals. New York merchants, for example, secretly underwrote the Midwestern "Granger Laws," ostensibly the work of farmers, in an effort to use political clout to win cheaper freight rates for themselves; and that other great "agrarian crusade," the Populist movement, was financed by silver miners seeking to use government power to inflate the price of their product. But such shenanigans, bogus as they were, struck responsive chords among the American people. Corporate wealth inspired widespread resentment because, as privileged wealth, made possible by government-granted charters, it ran counter both to the work ethic and to deep-rooted popular prejudice. Moreover, corporate business was the most visible symbol of the technological revolution, and thus it was more or less inevitable that the "trusts," as they were misleadingly called, should bear the brunt of the blame when things went wrong.

But the corporation was not the only object of the anger born of frustration. A second was the city. The growth of urban areas, like the corporation, was at first welcomed and encouraged, and cities mushroomed everywhere. New York burgeoned from 1.4 million people in 1870 to 3.4 million in 1900, Chicago from 298,000 to 1.7 million, Seattle from 1107 to 80,000, Los Angeles from 5700 to 102,000, Denver from 4700 to 133,000, Birmingham from 3000 to 132,000. Yet city governments were totally unprepared for the massive influx of newcomers, even as they promoted additional industries to attract more newcomers. Public health measures were in their infancy, and public sanitation facilities were almost nonexistent. The old common law prohibition against public nuisances proved inadequate to control pollution. Ward-heeler politicians organized the newly arrived and provided trivial services in exchange for votes. Reform politicians alternated between being pests and jokes, and were ineffectual in almost everything they undertook.

It was businessmen and not government, inspired by the love of profits and not by a professed love of humanity, which provided such humane relief as urban dwellers got; and, though the cities had their slums and sweatshops and crime, the relief was in fact considerable. The construction industry performed so well that two-fifths of the urban population lived in owner-occupied dwellings by 1900, and the number was growing steadily. (But for government restrictions against monetizing mortgages, the percentage could have been even higher.) The utility companies provided streetcars, electricity and gas, and centralized water supply, which made urban transportation cheap and fast, made indoor living cleaner and more comfortable than ever before, and made life in large cities less perilous to health than it had been at any time in human history. The entertainment industry flowered, producing vaudeville, opera, and spectator sports for the multitudes. In sum, though life in the city was fast and hard, it was also exciting and filled with opportunity for the enterprising. For those reasons, nearly ten million Americans deserted their farms and small towns in search of better lives in urban areas during the three decades after the Civil War.

To be sure, three-fifths of the American people still lived in rural and small-town areas, but by 1900 city dwellers and country folk alike realized that the future belonged to the great concentrations of power—financial, commercial, industrial, intellectual, and cultural— that were the essence of the city. Having no future, the country dweller could have no self-respect, for in America (unlike the rest of the civilized world) the future was more venerated than the past. Without a future, the sturdy yeoman that Jefferson had idealized would become a hayseed, God's chosen people would become just so many hicks. Accordingly, for a full generation beginning in the 1890s, country dwellers threw themselves by the millions into efforts to stop the wheels of history. Having numbers and therefore political strength, they joined crusades to purge the cities of sin, which is to say of the orgies of pleasure they believed characterized life in the city, and their efforts resulted in laws imposing censorship, governing sexual behavior, and prohibiting the sale and use of drugs. More ominously, they elected to state legislatures and to Congress representatives pledged to besiege the economic foundations of urban growth.

The third great object of popular resentment was the new immigrant. The United States had always been a nation of immigrants—throughout its history as an independent country about a fifth of its inhabitants had been foreign born, another fifth had foreign-born parents, and another fifth had foreign-born grandparents—but Americans had somehow managed to view themselves as a nation of White Anglo-Saxon Protestants. They could do so only by counting Celts as Englishmen and by disregarding the millions of blacks, central and northern Europeans, French, and Mexicans in their midst, but they were able to sustain the illusion until the 1890s. Then it became increasingly evident that the immigrants now arriving on an unprecedented scale were in fact different from old-stock Americans. Of the three million natives of Imperial Russia who fled to America at the end of the nineteenth century and early in the twentieth, half were Polish Catholics and most of the others were Jewish; and the twelve million Italians and subjects of the Austro-Hungarian empire who came during the same years spoke three dozen languages but most owed religious allegiance to the Pope.

Barriers of prejudice were erected against the new immigrants on all sides—job discrimination, housing restrictions, quota limitations in education—but still they came, in ever increasing numbers. They did so because, for all the obstacles they faced in America, the United States provided far more freedom and far greater opportunity than they had in their old countries. And as they came, demands for their exclusion grew louder and angrier.

Given all these ingredients, the United States seemed primed for an explosion in the mid-1890s. An explosion, in fact, almost came, for the severe depression of those years was attended by an eruption of radicalism, both rural and urban. Then the frustrations were suddenly and unexpectedly swept away and a new wave of euphoria engulfed the land.

The elixir, the magic potion which brought about the transformation, was the Spanish-American War. To modern students, come of age in the post-Vietnam era, it might seem strange that any war, and especially one that was clearly imperialistic, could be an exhilarating experience. But to be mystified is to be ignorant of the American psyche. Though the war resulted in, and to some extent was fought for, territorial gain, the motive for it was by no means the same as that which was impelling European imperialism at the same time—the search for colonial sources of raw materials and outlets for manufactures. Indeed, the United States, in that sense, was more like a colonial dependency than an industrial metropolis, for it was still a net exporter of raw materials and foodstuffs and still a net importer of European manufactures. Rather, the wellspring of both the war and the new enthusiasm lay deep in the Yankee character: to Americans, the war was a crusade to rid the world of the evil of Spanish tyranny and to liberate, uplift, and Christianize subject peoples.

Thus armed with renewed confidence in the righteousness of their historic mission, and growing richer and more powerful with each passing year, Americans plunged into the twentieth century determined to remake the world.

II. Eugene D. Genovese: The Ruthless Corporation

The last third of the nineteenth century—or better, the period roughly from the Civil War to World War I—introduced something new into the world: the massive concentration of capital in a shrinking number of banks and industrial corporations; the increasing domination of society—not merely of the economy but of politics and culture as well—by those relatively few giant corporations; and the subjugation of the rest of the world, especially the colored peoples, by Great Britain, France, the United States, and a few other Western imperialist powers. Whether one looks at the United States, Japan, or Western Europe, this was the era of oligopoly, price-fixing, the brutal suppression of the labor movement, the rape of the small farmers and small businessmen, and the systematic looting of Asia, Africa, and Latin America. Naturally, the devotees of capitalism look back on it nostalgically as a Golden Era of Free Enterprise—the one thing it certainly was not.

Were Professor Burner a Marxist, or a conservative for that matter, he would have written a different book. That much is obvious. What may be less obvious is that it would have been different not only in its interpretation of issues and events but in its organization and "periodization." The period that began with the Civil War may be viewed as not having run its course until World War One, when the United States joined the rest of the bourgeois powers in falling on each other and thereby declaring the moral and political bankruptcy of capitalism and putting it on the road to extinction.

In essence, in this period the United States, like Japan and Germany and to a lesser extent Belgium, Italy, and France, entered the age of monopoly capital—of oligopoly and the increasing control of state policy by the giant corporations—and of imperialism. Together, they divided the world, or as much of it as the British had not already cornered. They plunged into a desperate scramble for world markets, other people's resources, and the glories of "world power." Until 1914, apart from the periodic shooting-down of their own rebellious workers and poor, they largely limited their penchant for slaughter to the colonial peoples, whom they killed in the millions, either directly through conquest and the suppression of resistance or indirectly through the famines and dislocation introduced by their brutal policies of economic exploitation. Since 1914 they have had less luck with the colonials and Third World peoples, although they have killed quite enough; but they have done a much better job killing each other.

During the last quarter of the nineteenth century European and American capitalism underwent a transformation that marked the end of its competitive phase. By the end of the century, after twenty years of intermittent crises marked by falling prices and profits, oligopoly dominated the landscape. The crises had in fact provided a passage through which the capitalist economy shook down, sloughed off its weakest sectors, and emerged not only transformed but strengthened. Capitalism now confronted its most dangerous enemy to date—revolutionary socialism—which it struggled to contain. In the United States the young socialist movement started well and had fair prospects until its demise during the World War One era; in Western Europe it had greater success and was put down with considerable difficulty, only to reappear in mass communist parties after World War Two. It was in the East, first in Russia and then elsewhere, that the breakthrough came. In any case, for the immediate period under consideration, global commercial and industrial integration, fueled by European finance, produced an interdependent world system within which the United States was already laying claims to leadership; yet, at that very moment the political struggles between nations and the social struggles within each nation were growing steadily sharper.

Imperialism expressed not only the economic tendencies of monopoly capitalism but also a distinct political culture. A massive export of capital accompanied the division of the world into colonies and spheres of influence. Military and naval confrontations at the well-known flashpoints (Sudan, Morocco, Persia, Cuba) provided dress rehearsals for the central struggle of World War One in the European heartland, where Germany and Great Britain played the starring roles. Pretenses aside, they were the only European nations with the wherewithal, at least potentially, to match their global ambitions. The United States, having made a bloody debut against a weak Spain in 1898, began to mount its own challenge, which the British were prepared to accommodate while they took a hard line against the Germans.

In Britain, Joseph Chamberlain stumped for a "national" policy to create a protected metropolitan-imperial economy that, he argued, carried the twin promises of economic vitality and social integration at home. To this extent, imperialism was as much "social" in its domestic applications as it was "economic" in its concern with foreign investment and the extraction of raw materials. In our own country more and more "Progressives" expected an expansionist foreign policy to realize "the promise of American life."

As the struggles among nations escalated, the collaboration between capital and labor became more vital to those who sought grand imperial solutions to longstanding social problems. Liberal and reformist movements, and in time even the great social-democratic parties, yielded to monopoly capital and smoothed the way to "national unity" under corporate leadership. In Russia especially but elsewhere as well, there were socialists who did not yield and who prepared to play for table stakes. Their time was not yet, as the world moved into a savage world war on behalf of its giant corporations. But neither was it far off.

Thus, the glories of American capitalism—the rise of giant corporations, the rapid spread of industrialization, and the plunge into colonial conquest and, more important, economic spheres of influence—represented a domestic version of what was happening in Western Europe and Japan. There were of course important differences. For one thing, American capitalism was unquestionably much more flagrant in its corruption. France, among others, had its share of scandals, but they paled in comparison with the forthright way in which the Federal government of the United States aided and abetted corporations in their wholesale looting of the public domain. Then, too, the United States had immeasurably more resources to loot.

Conservatives love to tell us about the achievements of private enterprise. They neglect to mention that a large if still unmeasured part of the capital risk was absorbed by the public, which directly and indirectly subsidized business. Conservatives also find tiresome such details as the appalling working conditions that were imposed, the brutal suppression of strikes, the periodic murder of union organizers and militants, and the unspeakable mass suffering that accompanied the periodic depressions. Nor do they find relevant the condemnation of millions of black freedmen to a renewed servitude, excruciating poverty, and wholesale humiliation and deprivation of rights. These trifles, along with the fate of the immigrants, poor farmers, and the working class generally, were ostensibly mere pimples on the posterior of corporate progress.

None of it was inevitable. Spokesmen for monopoly capitalism tell us that only the emerging big corporations could have transformed the country into a fully industrialized power between 1860 and the beginning of the new century. In fact, Germany and Japan had remarkable transformations themselves, also under monopoly capitalism but with the frank support of centralized governments. And in the 1930s Stalin's Soviet Union outdid everyone in the speed and thoroughness of its socialist industrial revolution in barely a single decade.

No matter. There had been alternative paths of development in all the capitalist countries. They were crushed by violence, fraud, intimidation, and legal manipulation of the media, schools, churches, and other institutions. The socialist movement in Germany, Italy, and France—whatever may be said about its weaknesses and errors—took hard blows both legal and illegal. In the United States an unusually powerful capitalism had an easier time, but even it faced challenge. The first great challenge was mounted during the Civil War and subsequent Reconstruction. The economic processes and government policies that led to the consolidation of business in fewer and fewer hands met stout resistance not only from workers and farmers but from small and middle businessmen. The struggles over the money supply and the tariff were too complex for summary here, especially since the coalitions shifted markedly over time. But some points are in order.

The bourgeois radicals like Thaddeus Stevens who fought a rear-guard action against monopoly capital were probably doomed before they started. Their solution could not transcend measures to maintain small business at competitive levels and, as such, could hardly do more than slow down the process of capital accumulation inherent in the rising level of technology and the international market structure. And the detrimental effects of the new phase of capitalism on small businessmen, farmers, and workers—not to mention the freedmen—did not fall at the same time. Therefore, a grand coalition against big capital proved impossible to create, and the victims went down to defeat one at a time.

It was no accident that Radical Republicans like Stevens fought so hard for Negro rights and especially for the distribution of land to the landless poor whites and black freedmen. Such a policy would have created a solid class of white and black farmers in the South who would have had to rely on their coalition with northern Republicans and who would have simultaneously been driven by their economic position into opposition to big business. Stevens sincerely believed in Negro rights, but most of his colleagues probably did not. They did not have to: They had a practical stake in the heroic struggle being waged by the freedmen in their own cause. The defeat of "Black Reconstruction" and the restoration of white conservatives to power in the South as allies of northern big business ended any hopes of checking the power of a rapidly emerging monopoly capital.

The late nineteenth century was marked by violent economic contractions and widespread misery, as well as by impressive economic achievements. The misery threw up powerful anticapitalist movements: the Populist movement, the radical wing of which advocated "cooperative" alternatives to monopoly capital and the state-centralizing tendencies of socialism; and the socialist movement, which arose after the demise of Populism but drew heavily on it in some parts of the country. These movements engaged millions of Americans and represented early efforts to find a humane alternative to capitalist development. Among other virtues, the Populists and, later, the Socialists brought those millions into direct political participation. Not since then have so many Americans practiced daily politics through genuinely democratic organizations of their own.

The rise and fall of these movements constitute a long story, for which even the best of textbooks do not seem willing to devote much space. They lost and therefore, it is assumed that they deserved to lose and that their failure was inevitable. But today, when world capitalism is crumbling, and even its strongest bastion in the United States does not look like a good bet for the long haul, it would seem wise to recover the historical record of these great movements. The questions they raised remain with us, and some of their answers look more attractive than ever. Those who would preserve freedom and democracy in an age of a worldwide transition to socialism would do well to study their experience.

(Brown Brothers.)

A CHANGING NATION

Chapter XX
A Changing Nation
1900—1930

The Triangle Shirtwaist Factory Fire

In 1900, when Joseph J. Asch began construction of his modern "fireproof" loft building at the corner of Greene Street and Washington Place in lower Manhattan, the shirtwaist had just become the vogue among American women. The ideal American woman now had to look like the "Gibson Girl," as drawn by the artist Charles Dana Gibson: stately and aloof with tousled pompadour, heavy-lidded eyes, sensuous mouth, strong chin, full bosom, and wasp waist. She wore a sheer "shirtwaist," vaguely masculine in its high collar but billowing out to accentuate the bosom, then gathered in a mass of tucks, darts, and pleats to the narrow waist above a tailored skirt. The resulting look seemed peculiarly suited to an age in which women were going to work in increasing numbers: in a shirtwaist and skirt a woman looked tall, tailored, free, yet feminine. It became that generation's uniform, shared by poor working girls—such as those who made shirtwaists in Mr. Asch's building—with the women of elite families—such as those taking their first socially conscious interest in the plight of women workers.

The Asch Building was 135 feet high on a 100′ by 100′ plot. Construction was steel frame and stone, but because the building was less than 150 feet tall its trim, window frames and floors were all made—quite legally—of wood. It had no sprinkler system. The building had several elevators, but only two staircases, plus a fire escape which ended about 20 feet above a courtyard that—soon after the building's construction—became fully enclosed by other buildings. It had never been the scene of a fire drill. Except for some doubt over whether the fire escape constituted a third staircase, the structure met all legal requirements. It had easily passed fire inspection in October 1910.

At about 4:30 on Saturday afternoon, March 25, 1911, the workday was just ending for five hundred employees—mostly young Italian and Jewish immigrant women—of the Triangle Shirtwaist Company, which occupied the top three floors of the building. Just as the cutters were hanging their patterns on the wires above the long work-tables on the eighth floor, a flash fire broke out in a bin stuffed with rags beneath one of the tables. It quickly spread to the patterns and the freshly cut pieces of thin cotton and almost instantly passed out of control. Within minutes floors, tables, and partitions were aflame, windows were popping from the pressure, and smoke and fire spread relentlessly through the building. Attempts at an orderly exit turned to panic as frightened workers discovered doors locked to keep employees hard at work, a stairwell with no exit to the roof, clawing crowds struggling to gain entrance to the elevators, masses of humanity pressed against metal doors that opened inward to the loft. Scores of women were trapped by the flames and forced to the windows. There they made a grim choice. A passerby below saw something that looked "like a bale of dark dress goods" falling from one window. "Someone's in there all right. He's trying to save the best cloth," remarked another observer. Then came the next bundle, and halfway down it seemed to open and reveal that it was no bolt of cloth, but a young girl. "Don't jump! Here they come!" men shouted on the sidewalks gesturing toward the arriving fire engines. Firemen spread life nets; the falling bodies tore them from their hands, smashing holes in the pavement. "Raise the ladders!" screamed the crowd assembling on the sidewalks. The ladders reached up six floors. Then the firemen turned on the new high pressure hose system. It reached up eighty-five feet—only to the seventh floor. "Thud—dead! Thud—dead! Thud—dead!" so began the eyewitness story by United Press reporter William Gunn Shepherd. On Washington Street he saw the trapped men and women watch those a moment before them on the sills "every inch of the way down." On Greene Street he saw them "jammed into the windows. They were burning to death in the windows. One by one the window jams broke. Down came the bodies in a shower, burning, smoking, flaming bodies, with disheveled hair trailing upward." And watching this holocaust, reporter Shepherd remembered something:

I looked upon the heap of dead bodies and I remembered these girls were the shirtwaist makers. I remembered their great strike of last year in which these same girls had demanded more sanitary conditions and more safety precautions in the shops. These dead bodies were the answer.

By a little before five o'clock the bodies had stopped falling. One hundred and forty-six people had died.

No one went to jail for the Triangle fire. The company's owners were tried for manslaughter, but the state could not prove that they knew that the loft exits were kept locked (to prevent pilfering by employees). The fire and building departments blamed each other. The International Ladies' Garment Workers Union and the cream of New York's elite combined to raise an enormous relief fund for the stricken families. The Women's Trade Union League—a remarkable organization that combined trade-union reformers like Jane Addams and members of the social elite—rented the Metropolitan Opera House for a vast memorial meeting, which almost broke up in disorder, so strong were the feelings of anger and sorrow. Finally, the funerals stirred the greatest emotion. Almost the entire East Side gathered on April 5 for a memorial parade. Amid constant rainfall, about 120,000 people marched through the arch at Washington Square and up Fifth Avenue with neither bands nor banners save a single streamer reading "We Demand Fire Protection."

As a result of the tragedy, New York City created the Bureau of Fire Prevention, ending much of the divided responsibility that had made the inspection of factory buildings so ineffective. The state created a special Factory Investigation Commission and placed it in charge of two rising young urban politicians, Robert F. Wagner, Sr., and Alfred E. Smith. In four years of legislative work, the Commission made New York the most advanced state in the protection of factory workers. Perhaps the brave young shirtwaist makers, whose strike in 1909 had turned the ILGWU from a tiny group with no treasury into a major union, and whose tragedy in 1911 had created a modern factory inspection system and close regulation of woman and child labor, had not died wholly in vain.

Progressive America

Much of what came to be known and celebrated as the "American Standard of Living," a critical tenet of the democratic credo, emerged from the economy of the first three decades of the twentieth century. New products and new means of transportation and marketing transformed the lives of millions of people—especially the middle class—in their homes, their leisure, and their work. Yet middle-class Americans, though well aware of their new comforts, did not yet take them for granted, and they showed increasing consciousness of the problems of those who still lacked the affluence they themselves enjoyed.

A vast array of new goods was the key to the modern consumer society. Refrigerator cars, innovations in canning, and the proliferation of home iceboxes (consumption of manufactured ice more than quadrupled between 1899 and 1921) enriched the previously dull and rather monotonous American diet by putting a wide variety of foods on the table, regardless of the season; these included a steady supply of fresh fruit, vegetables, and meat. Modern pasteurizing plants introduced between 1907 and 1910 made milk safe to drink, even in urban areas. Chains like the Great Atlantic and Pacific Tea Company, with over a thousand stores by 1915, offered "cash-and-carry" and lower prices through large-scale purchasing, high volume, and the elimination of credit and the middleman—incidentally helping to standardize the quality of products available on the shelves. More and more Americans bought their household goods in the new "five and ten cent" stores pioneered by F. W. Woolworth, or in the large department stores, aptly described as "palaces of consumption" by one historian. Millions of others, especially rural Americans, met their clothing and household needs through the great catalogues distributed by Sears, Roebuck and Montgomery Ward, which helped to lessen the traditional isolation and monotony of farm life. "Ready-to-wear" clothing, an industry that burgeoned in this era, made fashionable styles and good-quality fabrics available to all but the poorest Americans. In fact, foreign observers complained that in the United States it was impossible to tell a person's class from his clothing. New immigrants rushed to enter this democracy of style. "Now you won't look green," an experienced relative assures the "greenhorn" arrival being outfitted for a new life, in a famous American-

Jewish novel, Abraham Cahan's *The Rise of David Levinsky* (1917).

Standards of cleanliness and comfort also rose as the inventions and appliances of the late nineteenth century, which were at first the luxuries of the well-to-do, became the necessities of the middle class. The introduction of the porcelain bathtub and flush toilet, along with the development of the septic tank, made the private indoor bathroom increasingly common in middle-class households. Home electrification, made possible in the 1880's by the development of the central power station, had spread rapidly by the turn of the century, and generated a wide variety of new appliances to make household tasks easier. The first electric household appliance, the flatiron, made its appearance at the Chicago World's Fair in 1893. Washing machines followed making laundering easier, although housewives now developed higher standards of cleanliness, so that probably at least as much time continued to be spent in this traditional activity. Gas stoves made cooking easier, and mechanical refrigerators began to supplant the widely used icebox by about 1912. Central heating, which spread rapidly after the large-scale production of the cast-iron radiator in the 1890's made the luxurious comfort of hotels available both to individual houses and to new "skyscraper" apartments and office buildings in the cities.

Americans spent their increased leisure time in new ways too. George Eastman developed the Kodak camera, first marketed in 1888 under the slogan "You press the button, we do the rest." Its almost immediate popularity turned photography from the esoteric skill of a few who recorded only important events to a means available to everyone for capturing everyday experiences and making it memorable. The phonograph, with the new flat-disk "record," first marketed in the 1890's for $25, was by 1914 being produced at a rate of some five hundred thousand per year. Before the advent of mass-audience radio, the phonograph made a wide variety of popular and classical music, drama, and literature available to millions of Americans in their homes. So popular was it that composers like John Philip Sousa issued warnings about the dangers of "mechanical music." With the development of the motion picture in the 1890's Americans also began attending the new "nickelodeons" where, for a nickel, the audience

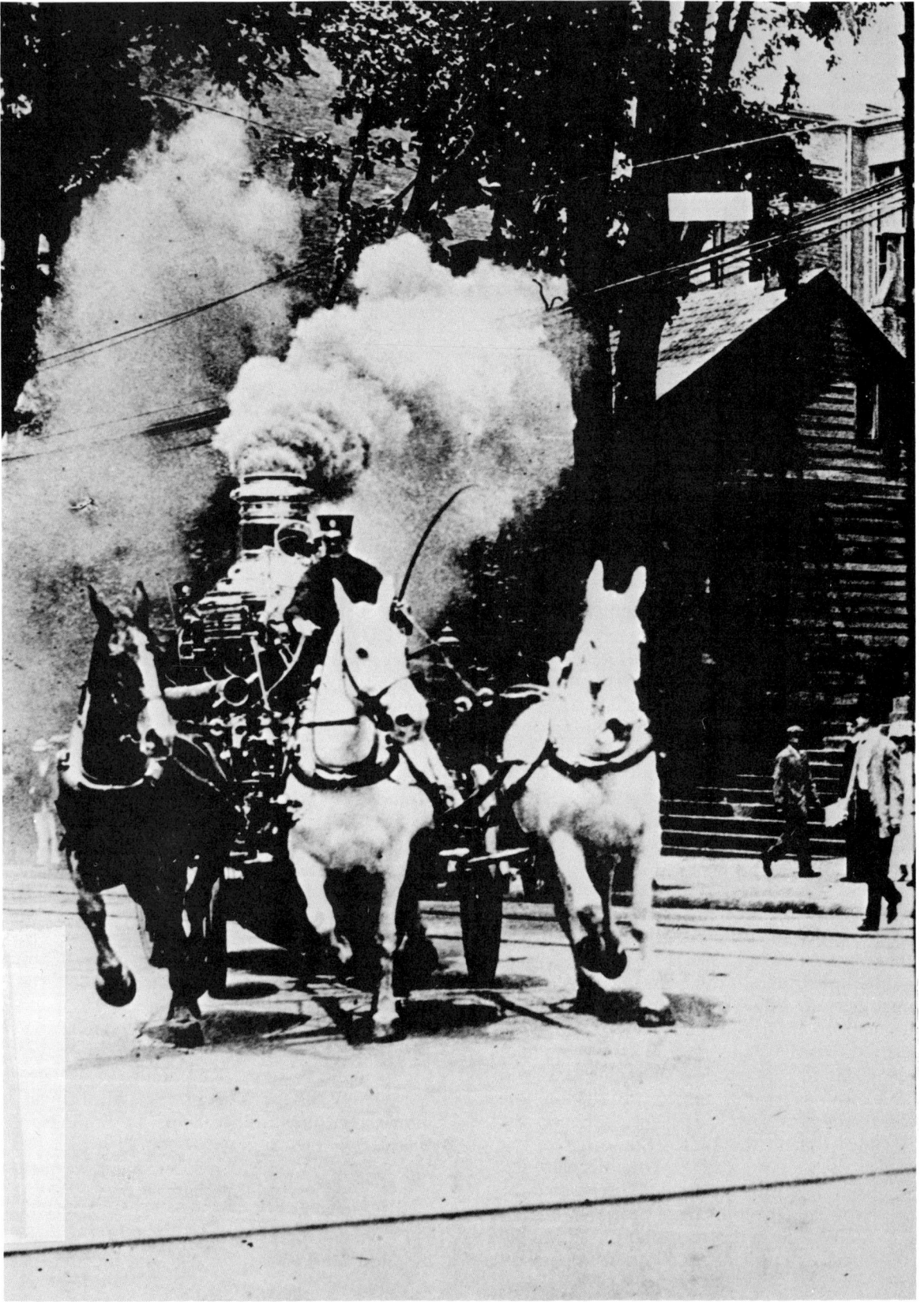

enjoyed short silent films. By 1908 there were eight thousand nickelodeons in the country. By 1920, the movies had become the most popular form of commercialized amusement, and seventeen thousand theaters around the nation showed movies to millions of viewers each week.

Economic Growth

This rising standard of living was rooted in—and, in turn fed—a healthy and growing economy rapidly eclipsing that of any other industrial nation. After the depression of the nineties, economic growth accelerated at about six percent per year. Total physical production increased about seventy-five percent in the first decade of the twentieth century. National income grew by almost 50 percent from 1897 to 1911. Per capita income increased in real dollars from $496 to $608 in this same period. The burgeoning domestic economy was buttressed by American's increasingly favorable position in world markets. After 1892 the United States continuously enjoyed favorable trade balances, with investment abroad quadrupling from about $635 million in 1897 to $2.7 billion in 1914. By 1900 industry had assumed the leading role in the economy, with the value of manufactures almost doubling, from about $13 billion in 1900 to 24.3 billion in 1914.

Even more startling was the unprecedented prosperity enjoyed by farmers. Although agriculture's share of the national product was declining relative to industry, the long era of depression that had spurred the agrarian protest movements of the eighties and nineties was now over. Between 1900 and 1920 the value of farmland and crops increased almost fourfold, and the price of farm products nearly tripled. Later, the New Deal of the 1930's would officially establish the 1909-1914 period as the "golden age of American agriculture" by using conditions then as the standards for parity between farm income and prices.

Rising public investment also contributed to increased economic growth. Between 1903 and 1913, in such areas as education, roads, playgrounds, public health, and the civil service, the combined expenditures of federal, state, and local governments almost doubled, from $1.7 billion to $3.1 billion.

These tangible signs of prosperity and progress attracted both rural Americans and European immigrants to urban areas. In 1900 there were only thirty-eight cities with more than 100,000 people; in 1920 there were sixty-eight; in 1930 over a hundred. About seventy percent of the new urban population consisted of rural migrants and of immigrants largely from "new" regions in southern and eastern Europe. In the first decade of the twentieth century alone, 8.8 million immigrants entered the country.

Declining death rates, however, were the key to more than half of the population increase. With better nutrition, sanitation, and public health facilities, as well as immigration including relatively few children, the average age of the population rose from 22.9 in 1900 to 25.3 in 1920.

Getting Around

New forms of transportation and communication sped Americans to work, took them on their vacations, and lessened their isolation from one another. The telephone was invented by Alexander Graham Bell in 1876; by 1940 fully half the people of the United States were within talking distance of each other. In cities and towns after 1890, electric street railways, or "trolleys," replaced horse-drawn cars. These enabled the middle class to move to the newer suburbs of Boston, Chicago, and elsewhere beyond the traditional "walking city." This rapid suburbanization initiated the segregation of work and living places so characteristic of American cities today. The period also encompassed the invention of the airplane and the first successful flight by the Wright brothers at Kitty Hawk, North Carolina, in 1903, although for the most part there was no significant development of commercial aviation until well after World War I.

Daredevil Flying. (National Archives.)

The Progressive era was preeminently the golden age of the railroad. The first business hotel opened in Buffalo in 1908 and business travel accounted for most passenger service, but the railroads were also successful in promoting pleasure excursions. Millions of Americans took trains romantically named the *Adirondack Express* or the *Seashore* to their spots, while mythical personalities like Phoebe Snow, who extolled the cleanliness of the Lackawanna ("my dress stays white though I ride all night, when I take the road of anthracite,") advertised the ease and comfort of passenger travel. The glossy *National Geographic,* its frequent colorful articles on the West, also helped lure American families traveling long distances for pleasure. Freight mileage grew rapidly as well, doubling and then doubling again in the two decades after 1900.

Innovation and new investment, particularly in the period from 1898 to 1906, allowed the railroads to overhaul their antiquated stock and track, improve the safety of rail travel, and build architecturally significant monuments like New York's Grand Central Station to handle the increased volume of traffic. Perhaps the most important spur to increased long-distance passenger travel was the introduction of the ornate and luxurious Pullman sleeping, dining, and parlor cars in the years after the Civil War. Pullman journeys rose from 5 million in 1900 to 25 million in 1914. In 1902 the age of luxury rail travel—symbolized by the seemingly always genial black sleeping-car porter—arrived with the inauguration of non-stop all-Pullman trains like the *Twentieth Century Limited,* traveling on a twenty-four-hour schedule between major American cities.

Even comfortable accommodations probably would not have lured the millions of rail passengers without improvements in safety and efficiency. The introduction of the Westinghouse air brake made it possible to brake simultaneously, from inside the locomotive, all the cars of increasingly longer and heavier trains. New types of more powerful steam locomotives and larger all-steel cars carried more passengers and freight at greater speed; new refrigerator and tank cars also added to the volume of freight. Accompanying the improvement in stock was the rebuilding of miles of dilapidated track and the addition of second, third, and even fourth main-line tracks and heavier rails. Hundreds of wooden trestles and bridges were replaced to support the newer, heavier locomotives. The automatic coupler made it unnecessary to have workmen standing between cars, enabling railroads to exchange cars on a national basis and slightly reducing the incredibly high accident rate as well. Although more limited, electrification of some lines in urban high-traffic areas, automatic block signals on some main lines also helped reduce the still appalling number of railroad accidents.

Around World War I, however, the railroads began slowly to decline, while the automobile and truck commenced a rise that would soon become meteoric. Borrowing from and adapting earlier German and English "horseless carriages," American bicycle-builders, mechanics, and repairmen like Henry Ford, R. E. Olds, Elwood Haynes (called "the father of the automobile in America") and Charles E. Duryea were constructing and selling workable motor-driven vehicles by the mid-1890s. By 1895 there were some three hundred automobiles on the roads, perhaps one-third of them electric, then favored for their relatively quiet and clean ride and their maneuverability. By 1905—within a single decade—the number of registered vehicles had reached 77,988. Nonetheless, the automobile remained an object of popular suspicion, the toy of the mechanically inclined and a luxury of the rich. Autos, argued Woodrow Wilson in 1906, "are a picture of arrogance of wealth [that] spreads socialistic feeling." American capital continued to shun them, and manufacturers resorted to staging races to encourage their use. This somewhat inauspicious start did not deter a new magazine, *The Horseless Age,* from prophecies of a great future for automobiles.

Within a few years American technological improvements and production advances had put the automobile within financial reach of the average citizen. Even before World War I the mechanically simple and more powerful gasoline engine had largely displaced steam and electric cars. The development of the electric self-starter in 1911—the major technological improvement in this period—ended the ordeal of cranking a car; it now became common for women to drive. More powerful four, six, and eight-cylinder engines, cord tires, steering wheels instead of tillers, and front radiators improved the appearance and performance of automobiles. Most important to increased sales, however, was their declining price. With the introduction of the Model T in 1908, the Ford Motor Company offered at $950 an awkward-looking but sturdy vehicle with simple standardized mechanical parts that almost anyone could repair. Within a few years, assembly-line production gave the Ford Motor Company a daily production capacity of 1,000 and an annual figure of almost 250,000. The base price eventually dropped to $290 and the popularity of the "horseless carriage" was assured.

Ford and his Model T became an enduring part of American folklore. For several years beginning around 1914, the nation was overwhelmed with "Ford jokes" spreading like a respiratory infection from mouth to mouth, then hawked in paperbound books: "two hundred good jokes for only fifteen cents." Not all were that good. Many stressed the car's "tinniness." A farmer who stripped the tin off his barn's roof and sent it to Ford received word that "While your car was an exceptionally bad wreck, we shall be able to complete repairs and return it by the first of the week." Others were merely reworked ethnic jokes, such as the one about the madman who took two Chinese laundrymen for a ride in his Model T and was hit by a train at a railroad crossing. The car fell apart so totally that "all they could find was a nut and two washers." There were even Ford jokes about Ford jokes: a man in a theater refused to believe that a show was over, saying "That can't be—I haven't heard a Ford joke yet."

The increasing popularity of the automobile helped stimulate a "good roads" movement. Until the turn of the century, state and local governments were the prime builders and custodians of the country's approximately 2 million miles of mainly unpaved rural roads. The bicycle craze of the 1890's and the general desire for rural improvement spurred farm, business, and citizens groups to agitate for better roads. Fuel taxes and automobile registration fees, state aid, and highway supervision did not develop fully until after World War I, but their beginnings occurred during the Progressive period.

Making Things

The automobile industry was a spectacular example of a fundamental shift occurring in the American economy. Between 1899 and 1919, as industrial output doubled, the production of machines, tools, and other "durable goods" increased at a rate nearly twice that of industries making products for direct human consumption, such as meat-packing and flour-milling. During the same years the share of manufactures in the nation's overseas trade grew from one-third to almost one-half of all exports, and the overseas demand for machines and tools grew still more rapidly.

The manufacture of automobiles illustrates the interdependence of the new industries and the new technologies. After the first experimental years, automobile production moved from garages and shops into the factory. Here new ideas and methods quickly revolutionized the manufacture of cars. Recognizing that some men got their work done more quickly than others, Frederick Taylor, an engineer and apostle of efficiency working with the Bethlehem Steel Company, pioneered in "time motion studies" of specific tasks with the aim of improving worker performance and increasing production. Breaking jobs down into their smallest components, Taylor analyzed the "best" way of completing tasks using the perfect tool for the given job. Through ground-breaking work on shoveling, he made it possible for Bethlehem to cut its work force of pig-iron shovelers from 600 to 140, and to cut the cost of handling the material in half. This new discipline of "scientific management," despite considerable opposition from fledgling labor unions, spread rapidly in American factories and shops and was a major contribution to the development of mass production after 1910.

Mass production—perhaps the key element in the eventual development of the consumer society—awaited an expanded population, technological progress, prosperous times with available capital, and, not least, the imperative demands of wartime. Henry Ford preached the gospel of "a standardized, low cost car for every adult person in America." Improving upon the production of interchangeable parts pioneered by Eli Whitney near the end of the eighteenth century, Ford developed the machinery for standardized quantity production of automobile components. Since the manufacture of cars was essentially a problem of assembly, Ford began with "stationary assembly," and one hundred assembly stations were set up. Within a few years, to speed up the process further, a conveyor belt brought the Ford chassis to the worker and moved it along at a constant speed. Parts all arrived at the appropriate moment and were assembled in proper order to complete the car. Each worker accomplished a small and specialized task, infinitely repeated. Ford described this technique as one that "lifted the hard work off the backs of men and laid it on steel and motors." When the car reached the end of the line, it was driven off on its own power. Assembly time was cut from almost

12½ hours to slightly over 1½ hours, production skyrocketed, and prices dropped. The Model T was so popular that Ford produced it for almost twenty years, offering it in any color "so long as it is black." Increased car sales spurred the growth of the petroleum industry and improvement in the processing of rubber used for tires. Mass production was particularly suited to the automobile industry, but soon standardized interchangeable parts and the assembly line spread to the production of complicated machinery and machine tools needed in rapidly mechanizing American industrial plants.

Between 1899 and 1919 bigger and better machines and, particularly, advances in electrical engineering tripled the horsepower capacity in factories and significantly increased the output per worker. The development in the 1890's of hydroelectric power and the invention of the steam turbine made possible the production of cheap and abundant electrical power. Electric motors, which had supplied only five percent of factory power in 1899, generated fifty-five percent in 1919. In just one industry, steel, each wage-earner produced 85 tons of finished steel in 1900 and 114 in 1920.

Steel manufacture expanded greatly in the Progressive era, with innovation meeting the challenge of new needs. By 1900 the open hearth furnace had replaced the older Bessemer process in more than half the steel produced resulting in a tougher less brittle product. Recognizing that steel production was basically a chemical process, manufacturers produced a variety of alloys adaptable to numerous needs. The modernizing of railroads consumed steel for heavier rails and larger cars, and wooden bridges gradually gave way to steel. Western cattlemen increasingly used wire fencing and barbed wire. Wire nails, new ships and naval vessels, and the beams and girders of modern skyscrapers also used steel.

The automobile made a major contribution to the expansion of American industry, but other new industries were significant, too. Innovations in the relatively new chemical industry raised the value of its products from $48 million in 1899 to $158 million in 1914. Americans began production of "artificial silk," later called rayon, in 1911. An electrolytic process for refining aluminum made this hard but light metal increasingly popular for kitchen utensils, automobile parts, and electrical equipment. Industrial research financed by commerical concerns ensured that manufacturing innovation would grow geometrically in the years to come.

Corporations and Capital

In 1898 there were just 82 relatively small trusts. By 1904, 318 large combinations with a total capitalization of $6 billion ran such industries as railroads, meat-packing, steel, copper, tobacco, and petroleum. The census of 1900 reported the existence of 73 huge firms capitalized at over $10 billion. A year later, Andrew Carnegie formed United States Steel, the nation's first billion dollar corporation, absorbing an incredible 158 companies. By 1909 one percent of all the industrial firms in the country were producing forty-four percent of the nation's manufactured goods.

Many of the new combinations were themselves organized by the "money trust," investment banking firms like J. P. Morgan and Company and Kuhn, Loeb and Company which emerged when heavy industry's need for credit made it look to Wall Street for guidance. Finance capital meant that a few titans virtually controlled the credit resources of the country. In fact, in both 1893 and 1907, when the nation hovered on the brink of financial collapse, it was the Morgan firm that came to the rescue. The Pujo Committee, organized to investigate banking control of industry, reported in 1913 that Morgan's actions alone could cause a major financial panic and industrial depression.

Such unprecedented power instilled fear in many Americans. Although the new way of doing business gave order to several key industries, small local competitors increasingly lost out to large national—in some cases international—companies. The small merchant or manufacturer no longer felt important; indeed, his economic survival was frequently threatened. Finance capitalists were accused of manipulating "other people's money," and making fantastic profits without producing any tangible goods or services. They lived somewhere, usually in the East, far away and unconnected to the communities and sections their actions vitally affected. Their great wealth, displayed in monumental mansions surrounded by landscaped estates, overshadowed the moderately comfortable local gentry who composed most small-town elites. There was but limited comfort in learning of the bad taste with which the rich spent their money. Middle-class readers might feel a bit less awed when they read *House Beautiful's* description of a room in a typical mansion:

Passing from the Hall you enter the Drawing-room. More money; less taste. The upholstered ceiling, the tortured walls, the bedecked and begilded furniture, the costly and trumpery ornaments wage a continual battle. All the nations of Europe are represented in this apartment and they keep up on international warfare. . . . the French furniture hurls invectives at the German draperies. . . . Count the cost—the thousands expended here—and rejoice that you *cannot* go and do likewise—

Workers

Paralleling the rise of organized capital was a similar, if less spectacular, growth of organized labor. The growing number of industrial workers, some thirty-five percent of the labor force in 1900, toiled—when there were jobs—an average of fifty-nine hours a week for wages of less than $2 a day. And many workers' real income actually declined in the period. Wives and children also entered the factories, contributing even lower wages to the precarious maintenance of their families. In 1910 some 2 million children and about one-quarter of American women held jobs, many in agriculture but also in industry. Few of these children attended school; only seven states had compulsory attendance laws in 1900. Life for America's working-class families was hard. One pioneer social worker described the lives of the working poor: "They were in poverty, but they were self-respecting; they were hard-pressed, but they were ambitious, determined, and hard-working. They were also underfed, underclothed, and miserably housed. The fear and dread of want possessed them, they worked sore, but gained nothing, they were isolated, heart-worn, and weary."

Work in the factories, mines, railroads, and mills of the nation was hazardous and insecure. The United States had the highest rate of industrial accidents in the world. In 1917 over 11,000 workers were killed, and nearly 1.4 million injured. Increasing numbers of immigrants, composing the majority of workers in many major industries like steel, contributed more than their share to these appalling statistics. Often single men willing to take manual and unskilled jobs for the most minimal compensation, they depressed wages and threatened the already low status of native American workingmen. Even skilled workingmen, the elite in many industries, began to find themselves replaced by new machinery; for others, Taylor's "scientific management" appropriated and depersonalized time-honored craft skills. Taylor himself alienated many labor leaders with his description of his prize pig-iron shoveler as a man "more or less of the type of an ox."

Although the ranks of unionized workers had been decimated in the setbacks of the 1890s, the American Federation of Labor—founded in 1886 to represent the interests of skilled workers in national trade unions—survived and expanded rapidly during the prosperous years of the Progressive era. In the seven-year period from 1897 to 1904, its membership grew from 250,000 to 1,670,000; by 1914 its affiliates had doubled to 110. Perennially led by Samuel Gompers, who preached and practiced a "partner-ship" with capital, the AFL regarded the strike and boycott as last resorts and tried to steer clear of partisan political action. While Gompers worked to free organized labor from such legal restraints as anti-union injunctions against the strike and boycott, he preferred to win higher wages, shorter hours, and safer jobs through union recognition and collective bargaining. Trade agreements cemented the joint responsibility of labor union and employer for better conditions. Such unionism was "craft, job conscious, business and wage conscious," not class conscious.

Many Socialist labor leaders argued instead that workers should develop "class consciousness," organize a labor party with candidates supporting their own interests, and fight the capitalist system. Some even opposed working for improved conditions and shorter hours because these were palliatives that perpetuated the inherently evil capitalist system. Always a minority of organized workers, Socialists were influenced by European radical ideologies or by the inadequacy of "business unionism" in dealing with the real miseries of industrial life. Although Gompers vigorously fought Socialist leadership in the

AFL—"economically, you are unsound; socially, you are wrong; industrially, you are an impossibility"—by 1912 Socialists led about one-third of AFL affiliates and controlled unions of miners and machinists. Socialist candidates won office in more than three hundred cities across the nation, including Milwaukee, Schenectady, and San Francisco. Eugene V. Debs, former president of the American Railway Union, polled over 900,000 votes as the Socialist candidate in the 1912 presidential election.

Debs and most other moderate Socialist leaders, like the New York lawyer Morris Hillquit or Milwaukee editor Victor Berger, never advocated violent revolution. Yet in 1905, after the Western Federation of Miners staged a series of bloody strikes that the AFL failed to support, they helped organize the militant Industrial Workers of the World led by "Big Bill" Haywood. Organizing migratory laborers and lumbermen, Western miners, Northeastern textile workers, and other unskilled industrial labor largely ignored by the AFL, the IWW sought one united labor organization of all trades, skill levels, and races and ethnic groups. Derisively called "Wobblies" by an American public that developed a largely unfounded fear of their power, they relied on strikes and sabotage to achieve their "One Big Union." When they took their fight for "free speech" to the streets of Spokane, Fresno, and San Diego, they were bitterly repressed, and they were opposed by moderate labor leaders for their violent tactics and their concern for the unskilled. The IWW gained few victories—although one outstanding exception was the 1912 wage increase won for 30,000 textile workers in Lawrence, Massachusetts. Even at its peak it probably never had more than 60,000 members, and after 1913 its membership declined. Vigilante action and federal prosecution during the war finished the IWW by 1920. Yet its inclusive approach, and its interest in immigrants, blacks, and the marginal and unskilled workers spawned by modern mass industry made it a forerunner of the Congress of Industrial Organizations of the 1930's.

By 1917 membership in 133 national unions reached a total of 3,104,000, representing about twenty percent of all industrial workers. Unionized women, particularly in the clothing industries, grew from 76,700 in 1910 to 386,900 in 1920. Most of the national unions were in the AFL, but the vast majority were "amalgamated" unions of workers in interrelated trades rather than pure craft unions. The four railroad brotherhoods of over 400,000 skilled workers remained independent of the AFL. Key advances in

unionization took place in mining, the building trades, and the clothing and transportation industries. Spectacular strikes like that of the United Mineworkers under John Mitchell in 1902 and the International Ladies' Garment Workers' "Uprising of the Twenty Thousand" in 1909 consolidated union power in important industries.

Few employers welcomed the advances of organized labor. Big business was inclined to see the virtues of Gompers' conservative unionism, and corporate leaders like George Perkins of the House of Morgan and Andrew Carnegie joined with him in 1900 in the National Civic Federation to promote "industrial peace." But most businessmen instead rallied under the banner of the National Association of Manufacturers, organized in 1895 to fight any and all union recognition, and of the American Anti-Boycott Association, which opposed labor's prime weapons in the courts. In an effort to discourage unionization and promote worker loyalty and efficiency, some businessmen turned to employee welfare schemes. Corporation welfare frequently meant amenities like restrooms, recreation areas, and classes in language, music, and the arts, but businesses also introduced benefit associations for the sick and injured, pension funds for the disabled and aged, and group insurance. A few organized profit-sharing plans. Company unions instituted "industrial democracy" by giving employees a voice, sometimes more apparent than real, in running the plant.

Many members of the middle class, too, feared the violence and "conspiracy" of strikes and

The Musketeers of Pig Alley, *1912. Filmed on real city streets as well as in a studio, this story of struggling slum dwellers indicates the appetite of audiences for social realism.*

boycotts and worried about the revolutionary appeal of foreign agitators. They also felt caught, and helpless, between big business and big labor. "The struggle for life," wrote the novelist William Dean Howells, "has changed from a free fight to an encounter of disciplined forces, and the free fighters that are left get ground to pieces between organized labor and organized capital."

After almost three decades of declining prices, Americans in the Progressive era experienced a puzzling inflation. In the years between 1897 and 1917 the cost of living doubled. Industries and fields produced more and more, but the worker found himself struggling to stretch his dollar to buy the same amount of goods it bought a few years earlier. Popular magazines like the *Ladies Home Journal* and the *Independent* ran articles by women asserting that the high costs of rent, food, and fuel made it necessary to have smaller families and women working outside the home. Few un-

derstood the phenomenon, but urban middle-class Americans, perhaps the hardest hit, indicted the trusts. As Woodrow Wilson put it: "The high cost of living is arranged by private understanding." Others saw the increased wages of organized labor pushing up the prices of consumer goods.

Actually, recent economic historians have argued that such inflation is normal and that the long nineteenth-century years of deflation were an "aberration": large-scale investment in "priority" industries like railroads, iron, and steel went into the increased production of goods and services, thus lowering their prices. In contrast, during the Progressive period new forms of long-term investment in both old and new industries deferred the production of consumer goods. This pushed the prices of commodities up. Whatever the cause, inflation convinced many Americans that there were important areas of their lives over which they had no control.

New Americans

New and strange—to many Americans—was the flood of immigrants who arrived in the United States during the Progressive years. Between 1900 and 1930 19,000,000 newcomers came in the largest migration in American history. In the peak year 1907 alone, over 1,285,000 people disembarked at American ports. Unlike the "old" immigration, which was mainly from northern and western Europe, especially Ireland and Germany, some eighty percent of the new arrivals were from southern and eastern Europe—mainly Russia, Italy, Austria-Hungary, the Balkans, and Poland. Between 1896 and 1915 Italy sent 3,400,000 *contadini,* over 500,000 annually, while 2,700,000 Russians, two-thirds of them Jews, settled in America. By 1914 a million Poles had come. Some immigrants were "birds of passage" who migrated to American jobs in the spring and returned home in the fall, but most stayed. Jews often brought their families with them, but the majority of Italian men came alone, sending for their families when they could.

Like most of the "old" immigrants, the "new" groups were drawn to the United States by both hardship at home and American economic opportunity. Pogroms and economic restrictions pushed Jews out of their *shtetls.* Italians, particularly in the parched south, could scarcely eke out a living on the increasingly small, barren plots. Polish

peasants also suffered overcrowding on their lands. Some emigrants had seen their countrymen returning from America "well dressed, with an overcoat, a cigar in the mouth," and others received word of successful friends and relatives. Agents of employers in search of cheap labor recruited many with the promise—the reality was often far different—of good jobs and comfortable lives. *Padrones* rounded up gangs of willing Italians to go to work on the railroads, mines, and farms. And steamship companies induced millions to undertake the arduous journey. By 1890 the Hamburg-Amerika line and others like it had networks of thousands of European and American agencies to ensure regular supplies of passengers. By 1900 two-thirds of immigrants traveled on prepaid tickets, the money remitted from the United States. All came to the "Promised Land" lured by the burgeoning industrial economy, high wage scales, and vibrant, growing cities.

Once in the United States, finding work presented new hardships. Immigrants almost universally started at the bottom of the occupational ladder as manual or unskilled workers; the "working poor" were overwhelmingly of foreign birth. By the turn of the century they formed the bulk of the labor force in each of America's basic industries. Italians worked as "diggers in the soil" in construction and railroads; Jews, although few had been tailors in Europe, flocked into the garment factories or did "sweat" piecework at home, often with their wives and children. Poles and Slavs concentrated in iron and steel. Exploiting enmities between nationalities, and even among different groups from the same countries—northern Italians hated southern, assimilationist German Jews wanted nothing to do with Orthodox eastern European Jews—employers sometimes hired a variety of ethnic groups to discourage unionization. Almost all newcomers earned shockingly low wages—8 cents an hour, 13 hours a day, six days a week, was not uncommon. At the slightest expression of discontent they were easily replaced by more recent immigrants. Their inability to understand warnings of danger shouted in an unfamiliar tongue contributed to the appalling rate of industrial accidents.

Living where they could get work, few traveled beyond the Altantic ports and major industrial cities. About two-thirds of the Jews settled in New York, Chicago, Philadelphia, and Boston. The lower East Side, "in the shadow of Brooklyn Bridge," was the largest Jewish community in the world. Italians also concentrated in the industrial Northeast, while large numbers of Poles lived in Chicago. The investigator Robert Hunter found in 1904 that thirty-five percent of the people in New York were foreign-born, and over eighty percent of foreign parentage. In thirty-three of the largest cities the immigrant population outnumbered the native-born. Most immigrants settled in dense ethnic communities, segregated in the inner cities and isolated from the mainstream of American life. As one aspiring American wrote in 1914:

I am polish man. I want to Be American citizen . . . But my friends are polish people—I must live with them—I work in the shoes—shop with polish people—I stay all the time with them—at home— in the shop—anywhere. I want to live with american people, but I do not know anybody of american . . . In this way I can live in your country many years. . . and never speak-write well english—and never be good american citizen.

The major cities were mosaics of many nationalities: New York's East Harlem had twenty-seven different groups, including blacks and Chinese while Bohemians, Germans, Italians, Irish, Jews, Syrians, and Poles all peopled Chicago's Nineteenth Ward.

Packed into tenements and decaying slums abandoned by "old" immigrants who had moved up and out of the central city, the new arrivals suffered many miseries. Boarders and relatives crowded into already inadequate quarters:

A family with two children rents an apartment of three rooms and then goes ahead and rents out the kitchen and the living room to two or three boarders. Sometimes there would be shifts, people would sleep in the daytime, and the same place would be used by somebody else at night.

Privacy, even for birth, sickness, and death, was virtually unknown. Poor sanitation and ventilation made only too common such diseases as tuberculosis—the "white plague"—diphtheria and scarlet fever. Infant and maternal mortality were high. In one tenement five of nine children died in one year. Hunger, language barriers, and the desire for an easier life lured confused and gullible young girls into prostitution. Few children attended school full time, and those who did often sat in overcrowded classrooms, read battered books, and afterward played in the streets. Working children endured back-breaking labor in factories and sweatshops, stunting their growth and robbing them of vitality forever. Family ties were strained and often broken, but many immigrant wives—notably among Italians and Jews—chose to work at home to maintain family life. Filthy streets and exorbitant street railway fares assaulted the new strangers outside their homes. The industrial cities of America seemingly gave immigrants the opportunity to live and die in squalor.

Yet immigrant experience also evoked a rich variety of social and cultural institutions to cope with the bewildering new environment. Foreign-language newspapers were found everywhere; some, like the Jewish *Daily Forward* and the Italian *Il Proletario,* spoke for labor. Others, probably most, simply expressed in a familiar language the attitudes and aspirations of their readers, informed them about community activities, and introduced them to American ways. Cafes and saloons gave a respite from toil and functioned as communications centers for the neighborhood. Mutual aid societies provided sickness and death benefits. Members of fraternal orders like the Odd Fellows, and of service organizations like the Sons of Italy and the Ancient Order of Hibernians, helped each other through hard times. Religion was important too—feast days were occasions of colorful celebration. Hebrew schools passed on Old World language, history, and customs to new generations. Although leisure time was limited, immigrant wards supported an energetic popular culture. East Harlem had "Yiddish theaters and Italian marionette shows, not to mention movie and vaudeville houses. Our secondhand book shops are as good as those of Paris. So are our music stores." In some of the smaller industrial towns, nickelodeons and libraries provided relaxation for tired workers and their families. In many places, settlement houses were neighborhood centers with men's and women's clubs, day nurseries, gyms, art, music, and language classes, meeting halls, and discussion groups.

Most Americans greeted their new countrymen with little enthusiasm and blamed many of the ills of the discordant cities on them. Some argued that cleaning up the slums and improving city services required getting rid of corrupt ward politicians, who bought the immigrant's vote for a turkey at Christmas, a little money when times were bad, or a job. Child-savers, prison reformers, and charity workers noted the high proportion of foreigners among juvenile delinquents, criminals, "paupers," and the insane. Organized labor charged the new arrivals with being "strike-breakers and scabs" who lowered wage levels and reduced living standards to their own "pigsty mode of life." Complaining that immigrants were hard to organize, labor sought laws to restrict the employment of unnaturalized aliens as factory workers.

Many progressives and conservatives alike, sought to exclude them. Despite an increasingly rigorous checklist of physical, social, and mental characteristics which officials at the new Ellis Island depot used to detain undesirables after 1898, some Americans, like the Immigration Restriction League continued to ask:

Do you want this country to be peopled by British, German, or Scandinavian stock, historically free, energetic, progressive, or by Slav, Latin, and Asiatic races, historically down-trodden, atavistic, and stagnant?

Responding with a resounding "no" to the latter alternative, they proposed literacy tests to keep the "unassimilables" out and buttressed their beliefs with the best scholarly arguments. One bigoted academic intoned:

The recent immigration from eastern and southern Europe, however, will, it seems agreed, decrease the average stature of the American. It is said that the skull will become shorter and broader. There will also be psychological changes resulting from the mixture of races. What the final man will be no one can foretell. . . .

Respected socialists and economists like Edward A. Ross and John R. Commons worried about "race suicide" and the "harmful" effects of the high immigrant birth rate. The House-Senate Dillingham Report in 1911 declared the "new immigration" to be "unassimilable," and suggested the need for a quota system. Old-stock Yankee Protestants, like the well-known poet Thomas Bailey Aldrich, shared their fears:

Wide open and unguarded stand our gates,
And through them presses a wild, motley throng—
Men from the Volga and the Tartar steppes,
Featureless faces from the Huang-Ho,
Malayan, Scythian, Teuton, Kelt and Slav,
Flying the old World's poverty and scorn;
These, bringing with them unknown gods and rites,
Those, tiger passions, here to stretch their claws,
In street and alley what strange tongues are these,
Accents of menace alien to our air,
Voices that once the Town of Babel knew!
O Liberty, white Goddess! Is it well
To leave the gates unguarded?

An alternate view came from abroad; from the British playwright Israel Zangwill, who urged Americans to regard the new immigrants as a challenge. In his 1908 play, *The Melting Pot,* Zangwill wrote:

America is God's Crucible, the great Melting Pot where all the races of Europe are melting and reforming . . . God is making the American . . . He will be the fusion of all races, the coming superman.

Making their contribution to this future, progressives in the settlement houses sought, in the words of Mary Simkhovitch, to "get the slant of the neighbors" while easing newcomers into American life with language courses and civic instruction. Randolph Bourne, a young disciple of John Dewey, celebrated their diversity and predicted a "cosmopolitan federation, national colonies of foreign cultures" in a future "Trans-National America." Considerably less appreciative of European cultures were groups like the North American Civic League for Immigrants, which was originally formed to provide help in adjusting to the new environment, but which eventually made it its chief concern to steer newcomers away from threatening radical groups. The YMCA ran perhaps the most successful Americanization programs.

The immigrants themselves responded ambivalently to efforts to Americanize them. Abraham Cahan's fictional David Levinsky gradually abandoned all the outward signs and observances of Judaism. Many Americanized second-generation children, like the hero in *The Odyssey of a Wop,* experienced excruciating embarrassment at the trappings of the Old World in their homes: "I am nervous when I bring friends to my house: the place looks so Italian." Yet others suffered from the condescension with which the Americanizers approached their cultures. As sincere as some of the Americanizers were, in the end they imposed a standard of immigrant performance that left those who did not conform extremely vulnerable to nativist attacks. In the wake of World War I, anti-foreignism surfaced again in a particularly virulent form.

A New Middle Class: Ideas for Progress

A major part of the middle class was a new creation of industrial society. The new bureaucratic, salaried middle class included clerical workers and salespeople, salaried professionals and technicians, government workers, and the like, constituting nearly two-thirds of the middle class by 1910. These were the "consumers" ravaged by inflation to whom progressives—particularly in the cities—appealed. They also included the social workers, teachers, government scientists, and public officals whose professional activities often brought them in direct touch with the problems of poverty, sickness, exploitation, and corruption which the politics of the era struggled to address.

The older middle class of independent professionals and entrepreneurs had their own grounds for uneasiness over the development of American society. Small businessmen, in particular, were often enthusiastic progressives. They worried over the large corporations controlling their supplies and goods, fretted over railroad rates, feared unions, and distrusted—with good reason—the creaky national banking system heavily controlled by private bankers often located on New York City's Wall Street. Independent professionals—lawyers, doctors, ministers—saw their independence eroding and their world changing. Ministers unable to match the styles of their rich parishioners or the expertise of secular authorities in many fields saw themsleves being replaced as social arbiters. Salaried employees gradually took over such mechanical jobs as title-searching which had enabled many a lawyer to prosper while waiting for more interesting cases. The medical profession crusaded in the Progressive era against quacks armed with bottled cures for diseases like diphtheria—as well, unfortunately, as against midwives with folk knowledge that predominantly male doctors often lacked. A sharp upgrading of medical education, the rapid spread of immunization and antiseptic surgery, and great advances in the field of public health made the Progressive era the formative years of American medicine.

The new and better-educated middle class faced the major task of squaring its inherited moral standards with the social and economic world it encountered. Its members still retained the sense of individualism and personal responsibility that had characterized nineteenth-century American religion and culture; yet they recognized the need for large-scale organization and flexible, collective action to make the increasingly complex society around them function well. Immigrants and uprooted countryfolk new to the cities had to be fitted into an increasingly interdependent society. Reformation of dubious ethical practices in politics and business awaited a detailed investigation and the careful formulation of practical alternatives. Earlier reformers had been repeatedly accused of being soft-headed, abstract, impractical. The Progressives, however, would seize intellectual weapons from the new arsenals of progressive thought, the universities. The most persuasive description of this new intellectual landscape had come from the Harvard University philosopher and psychologist William James, whose popularizing essays enjoyed wide influence.

James, elder brother of the great novelist Henry James, was first a psychologist, then a philosopher, at Harvard for thirty-five years. With a serious interest in art, a degree in medicine, travel in Europe, and even early experience on a scientific expedition to the Amazon, James had a range of interests and a flexibility of mind rare among scholars of his time. In addition, he was a man of great charm and vivacity, and good social background, all of which were clearly reflected in the urbane sparkle of both his lectures and his popular prose. He was doubtless the most widely known American intellectual since Ralph Waldo Emerson.

James's seminal work in psychology, *Principles of Psychology* (1890)—first, and probably the last, readable psychology textbook—was an extraordinarily effective critique of the determinism and pessimism that characterized social Darwinism, with its view that evolution and change were a process over which human beings had no control, and whose consequences they could only accept, whatever they were. His concept of the "stream of consciousness," which so encouraged writers of the twentieth century to probe the inner states of their characters, presented human behavior as the uniqueness and creativity of each individual's moment-by-moment experience of the world. After reading James, no student could believe in the hitherto fashionable theory of human activities as mechanically determined by natural law. Many a young man or woman, wrestling as the philosopher had with the threat that science seemed to pose to the historic American spirit of optimism, found in James new courage to view the future as indeterminate, and humanity as active and creative. In this sense, James was indeed the guiding light of the progressive era.

James in the 1880's moved from psychology to formal philosophy, and here too his ideas were important to Progressives. Along with lesser-known figures such as Chauncey Wright and Charles Sanders Peirce, as well as younger men—of whom John Dewey was by far the most important— James developed pragmatism, the first characteristically American school of philosophy. Pragmatism looked upon ideas as tools to be tested by measuring them against reality. James even spoke of the "cash value of ideas." This philosophy emphasized a process of forming hypotheses; gathering large bodies of data to test them; modifying theories according to the results; and finally discarding them for new hypotheses when the old ones ceased to fulfill expectations. Even long-accepted fundamental principles should be abandoned if they were found not to produce results. This was an intellectual declaration of independence from abstract formal "laws" as the basis of any discipline, and provided a rationale for the new social sciences, which took people away from their desks to examine, measure and question, and finally to recommend new policies, procedures, and institutions. Pragmatism helped connect the new universities to the industrial society around them although the long struggles for academic freedom in the twentieth century indicate that bringing the learned disciplines to worldly concerns exacted a price on American intellectual life.

John Dewey's development of "progressive education" was a prime example of the new ways of thinking. Dewey found in James's *Principles of Psychology,* which he experienced as "a ferment to transform old beliefs," a means of combining older philosophical traditions with the new scientific doctrines of Charles Darwin. Dewey sought to apply an active evolutionary psychology, such as James was teaching, to the process of learning itself. How could children genuinely learn rather than simply absorb? How could their education include the experience of forming and modifying hypotheses, gathering data, and applying the knowledge acquired to practical tasks?

Dewey began, of course, by experimenting. In 1896 at the University of Chicago, he and his wife, Alice Chipman Dewey, founded their Laboratory School in which students, by pursuing the activities required in agriculture, crafts, and industry under the supervision of subtle and effective teachers, discovered their need for the various kinds of knowledge that make up the subjects usually taught in schools. This approach, adroitly managed, could keep schools in touch with the rest of society and allow them to change to meet the changing demands of a world in constant flux. The progressive school, in Dewey's concept, was geared to what is new in society. Students discovered directly what it was valuable to know, just as others had once discovered such things as part of their farm chores, their encounters with nature, their dealings with other men, their search to meet social, moral, and economic needs. The school, by embodying "an embryonic community life," would produce people who create "a larger society which is worthy, lovely, and harmonious." Progressive education, which has influenced American educational practice ever since, did not meet all the goals which Dewey had charted. Nonetheless, it enabled schools to face the challenge of an urban industrial society, introducing an increasingly diverse and foreign-born school population to enduring parts of the American ethos, and motivating students to learn what they could see as relating to their future lives.

In the field of law, the pragmatic ferment was apparent in the writings of Oliver Wendell Holmes, Jr., who later served thirty years on the United States Supreme Court. Holmes, from the 1880s onward, expounded what came to be called "legal realism," interpreting the law as a practical instrument for dealing with public and private disputes rather than as a body of sacred, immutable principles passed down in awesome splendor from Roman and medieval times. The job of a lawyer, according to Holmes, was to predict as best he could what a judge would decide in a particular case and to advise his client accordingly. A knowledge of legal reasoning and precedent was valuable in the service of that utilitarian purpose rather than as an end in itself. Similarly, a judge's decisions ought to reflect the practical situation before him rather than abstract principles. The law, like everything else in man's world, changed with the changing times. The legal past was a guide to society's expectations and therefore important in making decisions, but so were the statistics, the data, the empirical information about the present that ought to be (and, Holmes claimed, actually always was) taken into consideration in deciding a case. The great "people's lawyer" of the Progressive era, Louis D. Brandeis, took this doctrine seriously in the famous case of *Muller v. Oregon* that he argued before the Supreme Court in 1908. Brandeis was here defending state laws limiting hours of labor for women, and in this defense he emphasized the sociological and economic effects on women of long working hours; he cited legal precedent only briefly. The court was persuaded in this case, although for many years such "Brandeis briefs" were more popular in law schools than before judges.

Every branch of the social sciences illustrated this same evolution from abstract principles to empirical observation. Political scientists moved from discussing constitutional issues of sovereignty to analyzing the actual workings of institutions like Congress—as in Woodrow Wilson's *Congressional Government* (1885)—or to studying the activities of pressure groups, as in Arthur F. Bentley's *The Process of Government* (1908). Economists began to collect economic statistics and to study in close detail corporations, railroads, the banking system, and the like, rather than deducing correct economic behavior from the laws of classical economics. As a result, their relationship to policy-makers became closer. Sociologists studied urban life, prostitution, labor organizations, poverty. The *Hull House Maps and Papers* (1895), a study of Chicago's Nineteenth Ward by a group of economists, socialists, and social workers connected with the activities of Jane Addams' Hull House settlement, exemplified the many fine studies of American life that provided the basis for reform.

Her book aimed "to present conditions rather than to advance theories—to bring within reach of the public exact information concerning this quarter of Chicago rather than to advise methods by which it may be improved." This striking volume, with its chapters on working conditions, schools, housing, charities, settlements, and other institutions was essentially a guidebook for Progressivism, one of the dozens of studies that aimed at reform. Such academic experts would play a large role in the Progressive era.

Theodore Roosevelt in the White House, Woodrow Wilson as governor of New Jersey and then as President, Robert M. La Follette in Wisconsin, and other Progressives would turn to academic experts for detailed studies of problems and for the drafting of legislation and programs.

The Muckrakers

A new journalism now arose to make a vast public aware of society's problems. Technological innovations in publishing—cheap high-quality paper, improvements in the printing of photographs—allowed inexpensive mass-circulation magazines to flourish, beginning in the 1890's. New currents in literature also encouraged the realistic portrayal of American society. Finally, a creative and enterprising publisher, Samuel S. McClure, assembled a stable of ambitious, college-educated journalists and gave them the time and expense money for thorough research on articles about American life. They produced a series of startling exposés in many areas.

Lincoln Steffens reported on "The Shame of the Cities"; Ida M. Tarbel revealed the questionable practices that had created the Standard Oil trust; Ray Stannard Baker investigated railroads, labor unions, racial problems; Burton J. Hendricks exposed the inner workings of the insurance companies; Samuel Hopkins Adams attacked medical frauds. All listed names and carefully described illegal or immoral activities; the absence of successful libel suits against them attested to their journalistic accuracy. Theodore Roosevelt attacked these new journalists by recalling the passage in Bunyan's *Pilgrim's Progress* about the "Man with the Muckrake, the man who could

William James. (Library of Congress.)

look no way but downward with the muckrake in his hand''; but his attack gave them the name that they accepted as a badge of honor: "to muckrake" became a common verb for the art of exposing social wrongs.

In the decade after 1902 over two thousand muckraking articles were written by journalists, professors, reformers, ministers, public officials, and the like. Muckraking dominated the magazines particularly in the period from 1902 to 1906. *McClure's* continued to be the leading journal, but important articles appeared as well in *Collier's Weekly, American Magazine, Everybody's, Cosmopolitan, Arena, Pearson's,* and many other magazines selling for between 5¢ and 15¢ a copy.

The typical article combined a careful accumulation of facts with heavy Protestant moralizing, rather than concrete suggestions for reform. The basic tactic was to induce shame. "The spirit of graft and of lawlessness," wrote Lincoln Steffens, perhaps the greatest of the muckrakers, "is the American spirit. The people are not innocent. . . . My purpose was. . . . to see if the shameful facts, spread out in all their shame, would not burn through our civic shamelessness and set fire to American pride." The tactic worked: Steffens' exposures of American cities left a trail of civic renewal in their wake as respectable citizens mobilized—for a while at least—to throw the rascals out.

Americans enjoyed their orgy of guilt and reveled in the discovery of how bad things were because they believed themselves capable of setting things right. Mr. Dooley, Peter Finley Dunne's fictional saloon-keeper, caught the spirit:

This country, while wan iv th' worst in th'
wurruld, is about as good as th' next if it
ain't a shade betther. But we're wan iv th'
gr-reatest people in th' wurruld to clean house,
an' th'way we like best to clean th' house
is to burn it down.

This appetite for learning the worst, however, was gradually sated and, with some help from the pressure exerted by advertisers, muckraking faded from American magazines after 1912. By then national politics had caught up with the issues the magazines had exposed. The muckrakers served a major purpose in focusing the diffuse uneasiness of the American public on concrete problems. The progressive crusades of the times had their goals defined and explained by the muckrakers.

Social Feminism

Women were a major part of the reform coalition. Suffrage for women had been an active movement in the late 1860's and early 1870's, and several national organizations had kept the spark alive. The National American Women Suffrage Association, founded in 1890, made little progress at first, and its leaders realized they would have to do something dramatic to get the attention of the American public. The first suffragette parade was held in New York City, and although it disturbed some New Yorkers it also attracted many new followers. Outdoor rallies and mass demonstrations became regular tactics.

The participation of women in a variety of Progressive reform movements underscored the importance of the vote. Crusades largely supported by the work of women included those to eradicate drinking and prostitution, to improve family life and child-rearing, to make education compulsory, to stamp out pornography, and to educate the young in the scientific but "proper" knowledge about sex.

Jane Addams and her friend Ellen Gates Starr borrowed the idea of settlement houses from Great Britain, opening Hull House in Chicago's run-down Nineteenth Ward in 1889. These new institutions, arising in many cities, opened new careers for women in social service, education, and policical activism. The settlements, wherein women played a far more active role than in the English model, provided nurseries and playgrounds for children, adult education for parents, and opportunities for study for visiting experts. Women and men residents entered reform politics and used their education in the settlements to develop plans for sanitary legislation, factory reform, labor legislation, and a host of municipal programs. One Christmas, the residents at Hull House were puzzled when neighborhood children refused gifts of candy, until they learned that the children were working six days a week in a candy factory. From the settlements, middle-class Americans could learn to appreciate the culture of the new immigrants and become aware of the armies

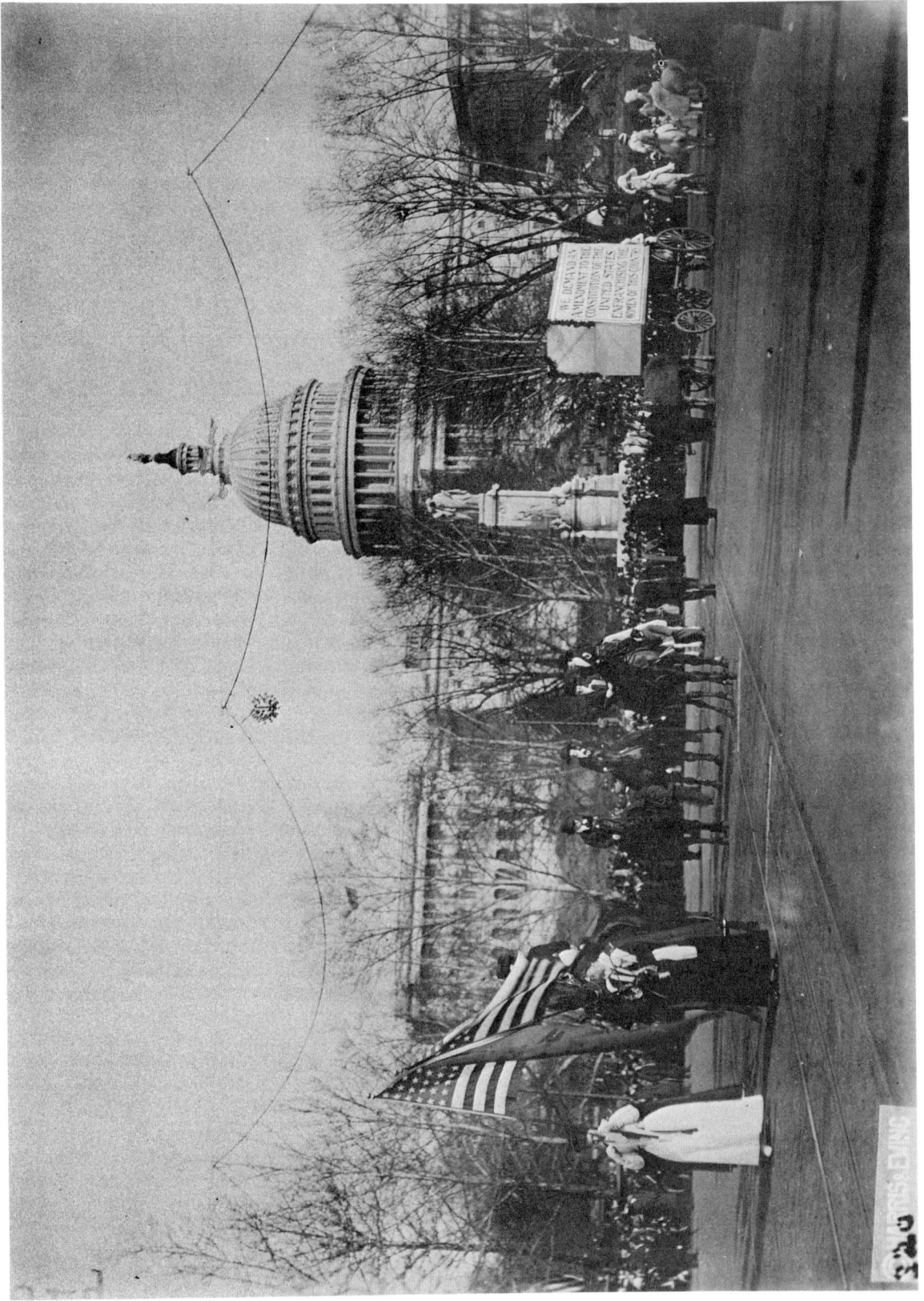

Women Marching for Suffrage. (Library of Congress.)

of working women and children that marked the age.

During this time other women's organizations were taking on social and political power. Despite the advice of ex-President Grover Cleveland, writing in *The Ladies' Home Journal,* that women should not join clubs other than those with "purposes of charity, religious enterprise, or intellectual improvement," the General Federation of Women's Clubs reached over two million members in 1910. And it lobbied for progressive causes, supporting conservation, consumer legislation, child labor laws, and other legislation benefiting children. A club campaign produced over a million letters in support of the Pure Food and Drug Bill in 1906.

The National Consumer's League—modeled after an English organization—became a powerful lobby for legislation protecting women and children. "I do not know why it is that women and children are invariably classed together," the reformer Mary Simkhovich wrote; "I suppose it came from two reasons: one because of the maternal relation; and second from their common political disabilities." Under the able leadership of Florence Kelley, the league boycotted manufacturers employing children, and pushed through the Ten Hour Law in Oregon that Louis Brandeis would defend successfully before the Supreme Court. The Women's Trade Union League paired wealthy women and reformers to aid working women in their efforts to organize unions.

Another important reform involving women was that of birth control. In 1915 Margaret Sanger had formed the National Birth Control League to work for its improvement and legalization. Although middle-class, educated people had access to birth control information, most poor people did not. Laws made it illegal to distribute birth control literature on grounds of obscenity. In 1923 Margaret Sanger set up the first birth control clinic in New York City, staffed by women volunteers and women doctors. Other clinics were soon opened in cities outside New York. Women were interested in birth control because they saw it as a way toward happier and healthier family life; they also believed it would reduce poverty and disease. Supporters of birth control understood that their message would appeal to those who advocated a strict immigration policy.

Not all women supported the birth control movement. Many feared that it would cause a split along religious lines, and some were unwilling to discuss the subject because it embarrassed them. Nevertheless, the combined work of the groups and the clinics forged one of the few links between the poor, working woman and the more affluent middle class woman.

Gradually all of these women's groups and the constituents of their reform movements coalesced around the issue of votes for women, convinced not only that it was right, but that it would improve political and social life. Women would vote out the crooks, support social welfare legislation, and generally increase the likelihood of achieving the reforms that they had been championing. That liquor interests and large corporations financed the fight against suffrage reinforced the women's sense that their movement was critical to Progressivism and that progressivism was important to them. After 1914 the General Federation of Women's Clubs came out squarely for woman suffrage, giving the cause fresh respectability.

Two women who had journeyed to England and admired the militant struggle women had waged there, Alice Paul and Lucy Burns, formed the Congressional Union to oppose President Woodrow Wilson in 1916. Starting in January 1917, Union members picketed in front of the White House for the next year and a half in behalf of a constitutional amendment requiring all states to allow women the vote. Shortly after the picketing began, the United States entered World War I. The women were faced with a difficult decision: should they stop protesting or continue to press for the vote and risk appearing unpatriotic? When they chose to continue to work for the vote, police arrested many picketers and while some newspapers were sympathetic, most were not. By the end of the year 218 women had been charged and 97 went to jail. Many of these women were prominent, and their imprisonment shocked the country. Stories circulated about physical abuse and forced feeding; these served to draw more attention to the cause and to gain further sympathy. Not all of the women's organizations agreed with these militant tactics. Carrie Chapman Catt, president in 1915 of the National American Suffrage Association, counseled moderation. She supported public education in order gradually to change public opinion. Many women worked hard in the state legislatures and finally managed to persuade President Wilson to support a constitutional amendment.

In 1920 the Nineteenth Amendment became part of the Constitution: the right of citizens of the United States to vote could never again legally "be denied or abridged by the United States or by any State on account of sex." The struggle had taken over seventy years. The effects of the political victory went far beyond politics. With the vote, women had the means to enlarge their world outside the home and the church. Yet the postwar period did not prove to be one of great change. Many women did not vote; many who did simply followed the political advice of their husbands or fathers.

The Twenties: A Social Politics

The decade of the twenties is distinguished by the attention it gave to social issues. Politics often revolved about topics like prohibition, the Klan, and the new immigrants. The twenties possessed one great "reform"—prohibition—and a "reform" organization, the Ku Klux Klan, helped to enforce it. Prohibition's history dates back to the mid-nineteenth century and before when Americans consumed huge amounts of liquor and even the ills of babies were commonly quieted, if not cured, by doses of whiskey (and opium). But particularly during the Progressive Era the "dry" organizations drew support from the eugenics movement, which favored the banning of alcohol for the improvement of the race; from women who saw their husbands spend wages in saloons or who wished to "uplift" the urban poor; and from nativists who viewed the movement as a symbolic battle against the new immigrants. Then came the war: drinking the products of German brewers became an unpatriotic use for grain that could feed the army and war-torn Europe; and the purchase of whiskey diverted money from the war effort. And so with the passage of the Eighteenth Amendment in 1919, the country went dry.

In many urban areas prohibition popularized drinking by forcing it to be secretive and therefore romantic. While the immigrant poor could make their own home brews, the young middle class—both male and female—had fun in dark speakeasies. Movies depicted drinking by the hero and his girl friend. Prohibition helped to make liquor fashionable and probably did little to ward off alcoholism. For the quality of available liquor declined as well as the quantity. Now there came mixtures called Old Stingo or Cherry Dynamite concocted often with a dash of iodine, sulphuric acid, creosote, or embalming fluid. Poisoned liquor sometimes killed those who could not afford the steady flow of Canadian Club that entered from the North sometimes on sleds drawn by dog team, or spirits brought in by Caribbean and Atlantic "rum runners."

Organized crime existed well before the twenties, but by taking over the illegal distribution of liquor the gangs flourished. Prohibition's fairest flower, Al Capone, a vicious Chicago mobster re-sponsible for hundreds of deaths, called the St. Valentine's Day Massacre, which culminated a gang war in Chicago, "bad public relations." For some immigrant Americans a life of crime was a route to higher status.

By the later 1920's many of the drys's promises to Americans had not been fulfilled. Taxes had not fallen. Prohibitionists complained of lax enforcement, but as the Great Depression cast its shadow the public was turning against the great experiment. With increased need for revenue and a desire in hard times for solace in beer, the Twenty-First Amendment embodying repeal became a reality in 1933.

The Ku Klux Klan functioned as a dry organization, but it was primarily a fraternal order of white Protestant Americans who lashed out at Negroes, Catholics, and Jews. Patterning itself on the Klan of Reconstruction days, it aimed to restore prewar values. In the South it worked to keep blacks from voting or rising socially. In the rest of the country it worked largely as a nativist group that tried to keep the new immigrants in their place.

The Klan, which at its height had a membership of at least two million, won acceptance by passing itself off as an arm of a town's Protestant churches and patriotic clubs. It also copied the established fraternal organizations, although the Klansmen—as you could tell by their shoes when they paraded in white-sheeted regalia—were largely lower in economic and social status. The Klan also thrived on a lucrative system of recruitment whereby Klan organizers received a large share of each ten dollar initiation fee.

Although the Klan rarely engaged in violence, it lobbied with Congressmen to pass immigration restriction acts. By measures adopted in 1921 and 1924, immigration was restricted to two per cent of any nationality living in the United States as of 1890. Scandal as well as success broke the Klan. There were incidents of Klan leaders molesting women and of funds stolen from national headquarters. Although the organization faltered, the prejudices it fed upon remained potent for many decades afterwards.

Urban-Rural Tension

For traditionalists from the farms and the small towns, the city stood for all that was alien to American life. Descended from many generations of Americans, they worried about the communities of "foreign" stock that formed in the cities: the Irish and the Southern and Eastern Europeans. The politics of traditionalism was typically an affair of fundamentalists, those Protestants who hold to belief in the literal meaning of Scripture. The preachers and lecturers of fundamentalism would talk about the growing power of the Catholic Church, drawing its strength from the immigrants and their offspring in the urban centers; or they would warn that the great cities were the place of skepticism and agnosticism, and of modernist Protestant theologians who refused to accept the Bible in its clear and simple sense. Hinterland moralists knew that the cities, infected with atheism and false religion, were gone also into more general decadence. New York City housed cultural enterprises like the opera and the ballet that many rural Americans thought snobbish and unmasculine. It was the home of Tammany Hall, the great political machine based in immigrant-stock votes. And New York city gave the country Alfred E. Smith, a Catholic of Irish descent who opposed prohibition and as governor of New York State signed bills legalizing Sunday baseball and professional boxing.

Finally, traditionalists identified the city and the immigrants with the vice of alcohol and the political forces working for the repeal of the Eighteenth Amendment. The Democratic presidential candidacy of Al Smith in 1928 embodied those forces, and Smith symbolized the urban culture feared by traditionalists. A feeling in the 1920's that the values of the city were winning over those of the towns and the countryside intensified the aggressiveness of spokesmen for the hinterland. What hurt the traditionalists most of all was to see the most promising young people move to the city and succumb to the temper of the metropolis.

Religious fundamentalism as a fairly definable movement is traceable to the later nineteenth century, when conservative Christians set themselves against the scientific idea of evolution and against modernist theological attempts to interpret passages in Scripture by historical scholarship. While it had its urban followers in the nineteen twenties, many of them were displaced rural people holding to their familiar institutions. In the Scopes Trail of 1925, the fundamentalist drama played itself out in the small town of Dayton, Tennessee, where a high school biology teacher had taught his students, in disobedience of state statute, that man had descended from an ape-like creature. William Jennings Bryan—hopelessly naive about religion—offered himself as a witness for the prosecution and was intellectually pounded by the great criminal lawyer, Clarence Darrow, an agnostic. In one sense, the encounter of 1925 merely pitted authority against authority—"the Bible teaches" against "Science says"—for many street-corner evolutionists, like much of American society, took science to be a giver of revelations rather than a complex method of doubt, inquiry, and tentative hypothesis.

Hostility to immigrants has had a long history in America, and had reached a high point just before our entrance into the World War, at a time when more than a million immigrants from the east and south of Europe, with their vividly foreign tongues and customs, were arriving every year. Anti-Catholicism was a major cause. Then war-time brought its violence against German Americans, while the activities of anti-war radicals evoked the old image of the immigrant revolutionist, an image that loomed large during the Red Scare of 1919. In the early twenties, labor found it convenient to blame its hard times on immigrants and their susceptibility to radical ideas, as well as their competition in the labor market. Even in business, which was interested in cheap labor, there was some distrust of immigrants as being vulnerable to labor radicalism.

Another ground of nativism was the scientific and pseudo-scientific racism that was having its vogue at this time. The social psychologist William McDougall of Harvard studied results of World War I intelligence tests, which showed lower I.Q. scores for southern Europeans and Negroes. Having little knowledge of the distortions that differences in environment make in such tests, he concluded that they demonstrated the superiority of the Anglo-Saxons over other peoples. Madison Grant's *Passing of the Great Race* went through new editions in the twenties. Drawing on Darwinian catchphrases like "struggle for existence" and "survival of the fittest," it defined the Nordic "race" as the highest product of the evolutionary process, and urged Americans of old stock to preserve the purity of the race against infusions of immigrant blood. The popular novelist Kenneth Roberts purveyed many of these notions to the middle class in a series of *Saturday Evening Post* articles collected in *Why*

The Ku Klux Klan, Beckley, West Virginia. (Library of Congress.)

Europe Leaves Home. Some of these books enjoyed a vogue in Nazi Germany during the 1930's.

The immigration law of 1921 imposed a nationality quota: 3 per cent of the number of each group in America in 1910. The 1924 legislation reduced the quota from 3 to 2 percent, and set the date for computing it back to 1890. Whatever the niceties of statistics concerning restriction, its thrust was against the cities and the recent immigrant. The Japanese were badly treated in the 1924 law; through a diplomatic bungle the Gentleman's Agreement, by which unskilled workers were barred except for those with families already here, was abrogated and Japanese immigration totally banned. It was an insult to a proud people, and an incident in a continuing history of insults to Japan that did their part to prepare the ground for World War II.

The Jazz Age

We have a way of thinking by decades, as though "the twenties," "the thirties," or "the sixties" each defines by some logic of numbers a distinct cultural situation. The nineteen-twenties are especially susceptible to this, for the decade is neatly marked off at its edges by the Great War and the Great Depression. It was a colorful time that became quickly and heavily stereotyped. Frederick Lewis Allen set one pattern in his *Only Yesterday,* published in 1931, an entertaining and intelligent book in which the author, by his own later admission, overemphasized the sensational. Allen emphasized such events as flagpole-sitting records, six-day bicycle races, and the flamboyant 103-ballot Democratic Party Convention of 1924.

Another early recollection of the period, which obliquely reinforced Allen's, was *Exile's Return,* by Malcolm Cowley, also published in 1931. Cowley, a major literary figure of the twenties and afterward, wrote sympathetically of his fellow writers; but he described them as "exiles," whose education and understanding of art taught them to pursue art in its purity rather than to know some particular land and people and culture. Their condition of exile ended, Cowley said, when the Depression awakened them to tangible economic and social facts.

The shape of the twenties has also been obscured by the Depression that followed. it. The America of the twenties has borne much blame for having no suspicion of what was going to happen in 1929. And in the grim earnestness with which they thought about social questions, some writers of Depression times looked back with scorn upon the era of the twenties because its literary life was so "artistic," so playful, so concerned with the secret recesses of the self. What critics of this kind missed was the subtle morality of the art of the twenties: moral in its honesty, painstaking craftsmanship, determination to explore, and the radical critique it made of the human condition.

Even if the twenties is simplified down to its public character, it possessed the contradictoriness that is to be expected of any period in history. Under a rhetoric of individualism, the United States was collectivizing its productive and financial institutions. An ideology of retrenchment coexisted with an expansion of bureaucracy. America talked isolationism and extended its influence abroad.

Defined by some of its most striking qualities, the "twenties" did not even open with 1920 or 1921, but was launched well before then. There had been bohemians in Greenwich Village, Chicago, and San Francisco as early as 1910. American women had begun to assert themselves, leading in the field of social work, entering a few of the professions, and demanding the vote. As early as 1914, H. L. Mencken coined the term "flapper" for a new, less inhibited type of woman. Unsettling literary influences were coming in from abroad: D. H. Lawrence in England, the decadent symbolists in France, the mystic novelists and short story writers in Russia. Experiments in poetic form were particularly notable. Some young people began to think of themselves as a new generation, and to denounce their elders as puritans. World War I sped these and other changes. Before 1914 people had read Freud and interpreted him as blaming sexual repression for neuroses, but the war made Freudians take notice also of his emphasis on man's irrationality. After the experience of the conflict, and later the Great Depression, the influential Protestant theologian Reinhold Niebuhr would begin his lifetime advocacy on the need for social reform to mitigate the effects of man's unending potentiality for evil.

The kind of attention the twenties deserves must come from a recognition of its virtues: the strengths of its economy and its many distinguished accomplishments in the arts. The 1920's introduced or continued the work of durable figures: Eugene O'Neill, Gertrude Stein, Ezra Pound, e. e. cummings, Willa Cather, Sinclair Lewis, Sherwood Anderson, Ernest Hemingway, Walter Lippmann, F. Scott Fitzgerald, John Dos Passos, Joseph Wood Krutch, Theodore Dreiser, Robert Frost, Hart Crane, Robinson Jeffers, Edna St. Vincent Millay; Vernon Parrington, John Dewey, and many others. The theater enjoyed a highly creative period, and there was active experimentation, both artistic and technical, in the young medium of the movies. In technology and in social and economic arrangements, the period was vigorous, skillful, and innovative, with its mass-produced automobiles, appliances, telephones, and radios, its silent movies and professional sporting events, its advertising and public relations, its consumer credit and expansive stock market. Technological and social life had, like the literary and artistic, a vibrant character. And while the literary intelligentsia claimed often to despise the "vulgarity" of their cultural environment, they must surely have absorbed some of their own restlessness from the restless country in which they lived, and some of their willingness to experiment and innovate from the science of the day. For technology was taking the old common-sensical world and breaking it into a thousand new spinning playing patterns. This sharing of temperament between the artistic and literary community and the society around it was one of the numberless ways in which the twenties constituted a unity.

A good way to approach the literature of the day is to describe it by its attitudes toward tradition. Despite the notable cultural heritage that the era's writers in fact possessed, it was their firm conviction that twentieth-century man was going to have to get by without contact with a past or any other sustaining context. Precursors to this notion had appeared earlier in the century. The "New History" of James Harvey Robinson and Charles A. Beard would turn away from any attempt to discover the past on its own terms, and instead would ask of it questions that could serve the present. William James's philosophical pragmatism and John Dewey's instrumentalism both denied that truth exists in some timeless frozen structure; instead, ideas were to be judged by their workability. Postwar writers celebrated the sensitive, aberrant self, living on its own resources because it lacked a past from which to receive its nurture. Some of the radical experimentation in technique and outlook suggested the notion that the universe does not press forms upon the artist but receives them, cunningly wrought, from his hand. One art form, "Dada," denied form itself, or at any rate form as men would recognize it, and

in violent gestures, deliberately absurd, mocked a civilization that proclaimed order and practiced the absurdity of war. Walter Lippmann made a less severe statement in *A Preface to Morals* (1929). A mature man must accept the "vast indifference of the universe"; his response, of course, would be a personal one: the recovery of moral insight and the substitution of a personal code for traditional authority.

Ernest Hemingway worked out for himself another king of code through which to achieve self-identity and meaning in an empty universe. His fiction exalted personal heroism, achieved in the formal grace of the bullfight or in other encounters with death; and his influential style—simple, crisp, vernacular—had a clean strength, almost ascetic, that concorded well with his message of heroism. In a later novel, *For Whom the Bell Tolls* (1940), a story of republican guerrillas during the Spanish Civil War, Hemingway would seek to relate the individual to a community of purpose and loyalty; but in his early novels, the hero is without society. F. Scott Fitzgerald, in a different but fluent and excellent style, was more curious about society—the society of the wealthy. Its glamour, vitality, and power tantalized and troubled him, and the vulnerable characters in his novels move longingly about or into it, risking destruction.

I'll Take My Stand (1930), a book of essays by twelve Southern writers, was a strong counterattack against modernity. The Agrarians, as the contributors were called, agreed with the modernists that tradition, except in bits and pieces, had ceased to exist as a guide or anchor for human life. In sharp contrast to the modernists, however, they lamented this loss and advocated the restoration of tradition. They wanted their civilization to turn back to its past by whatever means it could find and more specifically, for their own region, the South, to reaffirm its historical self. Some critics have dismissed the book as a misguided attempt to restore a past that never existed. But the idea of that past did exist in the thought and behavior of those who held it. A farm or a community can be loved, they observed, but the intangible world of credit and production cannot. And when a man loses touch with the folk, with nature, and with tradition, he loses the way to a meaningful aesthetic and religious existence. The increasing tempo of the assembly line destroys the satisfactions of daily life by making those, too, "brutal and harried."

Nonetheless, the culture of the American people in the 1920's was richer in traditions, in a sense of community, and in sustaining virtues than some of the nation's critics supposed. It possessed in the

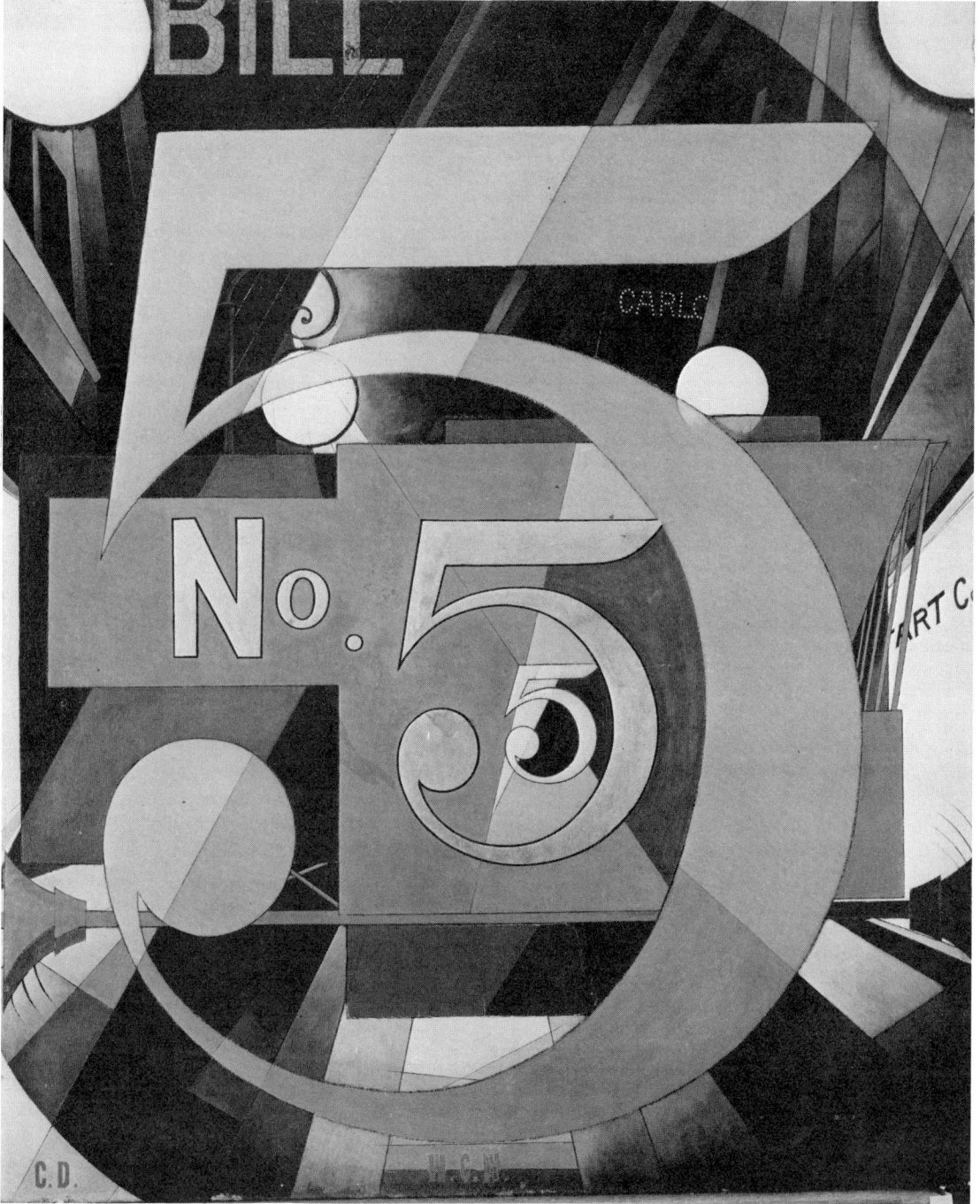

Charles Demuth, I Saw the Figure Five in Gold. (Metropolitan Museum of Art.)

novelist Sinclair Lewis an observer who satirized it stingingly—and came to reveal his love for it. As Lewis indicated in his preface to *Main Street* (1920), the town of Gopher Prairie could be found anywhere—in the Middle West, the South, or upstate New York. The story, set early in the twentieth century, is about the efforts of the mildly feminist Carol Kennicott to bring a higher culture to Gopher Prairie, or at least to survive her own boredom there. *Main Street* depicts a town still untouched by the upheaval of values that followed World War I; Carol thinks of the wives of American villagers as part of the oppressed classes of the world. Lewis' satiric treatment has echoes of the prewar muckraking era. Another of his books, *Arrowsmith*, romanticized scientific progress with a fervor out of the Progressive Era. Possessed of a phonographic as well as a photographic memory, Lewis was able to reproduce the monotonous tones and platitudinous content of everyday speech, along with the town's routinized life and drab appearance—its main street is muddy in spring and autumn, dusty in summmer, and filled with the frozen ruts of wagon wheels in winter. The same authenticity in talk and manners, and in the small feelings that make up the surface of consciousness, give strength to *Babbitt* (1922), a satirical novel about a businessman in a much larger Midwestern city, the fictional Zenith. In his perception of detail, Lewis reveals his emotional closeness to his subject; and his sympathies—no more than ambivalent in much of his important work (though quite clear in some of his very early fiction)—would become clear in later stories which openly praise the virtues of the American middle class.

Another avenue to an understanding of the American town—a term taken here to include small cities, particularly those located in rural areas and dependent in part on agrarian commerce—is advanced in a sociological work, *Middletown* (1929). This study of Muncie, Indiana, by Robert and Helen Lynd, is based on things that can be counted. The Lynds *know* the divorce rate, or can describe the way one highly typical American town divides itself into neighborhoods or holds its jobs.

Middletown was no longer a Gopher Prairie, if it had ever been one; it was closer to the Zenith of *Babbit,* and indeed hinted at what much of American society would soon become. The idea of the small town survived the reality. Suburbs, residential and industrial, metropolitan areas, and new demographic categories like neighborhood and region, created by the automobile and other forms of transportation, were replacing the older, simpler categories of town and city.

The majority of residents in Middletown did not attend church regularly. (In a "Snappy Song Service," a whistle tooted whenever a dollar bill hit the collection plate; one take totaled 105 toots.) But one vital area was the rising role of women. Of 446 girls in the three upper high school classes in 1924, eighty nine percent were planning to work after graduation. While the "revolt of youth" associated with the twenties was hardly raging in Muncie, middle-class girls were reported to be calling boys on the telephone to make dates, and in a neighboring small city there was a lawsuit over the right of a schoolgirl to wear knickers instead of a skirt to classes. The whole family structure and the dominance of the home were giving way under the influence in part of the automobile, as the ride in the country replaced the visit in the parlor. *Middletown* does not contradict the somewhat exaggerated image of the new female presented in *Only Yesterday* or the Fitzgerald novels: boyishly slender figures, shorts skirts, cropped hair, and lipstick and rouge suggesting a saucy new free-speaking woman who might smoke and drink or be inclined to think in terms of sex instead of romantic love. The rising vogue of Freudianism, along with other influences, eventually quieted the liberated female, making her ashamed to enter the world of men for fear of abandoning her femininity; but she had taken higher ground that she would not quickly relinquish.

Gopher Prairie represents the America of farms and small towns, and the Lynds' Middletown, along with Lewis' Zenith, a range of cities that were a mixture of largely provincial qualities. For a moment, the older American society came into so articulate a cultural conflict with the larger American cities of the seaboard East, and with the urban civilization creeping into the provinces, that the struggle became an important part of national politics.

The Movies

Long before television's domination of the mass media, audiences of the twenties were living vicariously through the larger-than-life images which flickered enticingly across the screens of movies theaters throughout the United States. In this decade, movies provided the populace with a common visual and emotional experience, an alternative to the genteel, middle-class values of the preceding Victorian generation. A form of entertainment once ignored by the middle classes, or at least one they considered to be fit only for lower-class consumption, the movies in the 1920's became not only respectable but also a popular art form. American culture was experiencing a rebirth throughout the period, and film was one example of this new spirit of creatively.

In addition to an artistic renaissance in Hollywood, the burgeoning film industry became big business. True to the spirit of American industry, films became a commodity valued according to their box office success. By the end of the decade at least one ornate movie house could be found in almost every American town and city. White-gloved doormen and uniformed ushers, baroque lobbies, balconied theaters—all testified to the public's total enthusiasm for the country's favorite form of entertainment.

To gain such popularity, the film-makers directed their appeal to the large middle class, and picked subject matter which would attract all classes. In particular, movies of the twenties reflected the transformation in moral values that prevailed in the years following World War I; scenes of sex, drinking, and infidelity depicted in films expressed newly indulgent attitudes. In 1919 a Cecil B. DeMille production, *Male and Female* (a master-servant romance considered very daring for the period), contributed to the erosion of social lines. DeMille, a "consummate sentimentalist," provided glimpses of sexual fantasy while at the same time remaining true to the established moral order. In later films, the director Erich von Stroheim relied on basically the same formula as DeMille. His *Greed,* for example, is close to much of DeMilles' work in its expression of a moral lesson learned by the major protagonist.

The presence of European actors and directors in Hollywood films released emotional responses in the public not generated by the standard American film of the twenties. The American interest in Europe—or, rather, the popular stereotype of Europe and Europeans—was emphatically demonstrated by the status in Hollywood of Rudolph Valentino, who embodied the romantic, sensual hero in *The Sheik.* Among other European stars whose passionate images stirred American fantasies, Greta Garbo's was legendary. During the 1920's Garbo played numerous roles as the temptress. Charlie Chaplin advocated dramatic revisions of the social structure. Chaplin became a star in 1914 playing in *Tillie's Punctured Romance* and the continued to dominate silent comedy

throughout the 1920's. At the end of the decade, however, talkies virtually ended the particular comedy tradition that wove together social consciousness and laughter.

The Great Depression caused many to join the ranks of the fifteen million unemployed, brought businesses to a standstill, and banks to the brink of disaster. It is therefore astonishing that, broke or not, sixty million Americans every week proved that for them film-going was not a luxury but rather a necessity. For Hollywood, the 1930's became a decade of sound and superstars, gangsters and gangbusters. The films at first reflected both the era's despair and its social concerns; as the Depression persisted, however, Hollywood turned to the production of escapist fare. The first "talkie," Al Jolson's *The Jazz Singer* (1927), inaugurated the era of sound, and with it a time when movies dominated American popular culture.

The classic gangster movies, such as *Little Caesar* (1930), *Public Enemy* (1931), and *Smart Money* (1931), were all propelled by the same dynamic. They emphasized the individual—the self-made man who seeks somehow to transcend his environment. The disorder of the heroes' lives reflected the turmoil and confusion of the early Depression years. *Little Caesar* (played by Edward G. Robinson), the first of a long succession of films in this genre, is the story of Rico, a man outside the law and at the same time a personification of the American dream. Rico's life follows the

Easy Street, *1917. Charlie Chaplin ingeniously subdues the bully with gas from the street lamp. Slapstick short movies were so popular that several companies profited through producing only one-and two-reel comedies.*

pattern of a nineteenth-century Horatio Alger success story. Starting his career as a "nobody," he climbs to the pinnacle of achievement in his own milieu. Once at the top, however, he dies—the only accptable ending for a man who lives outside the law. In the sordidness and frustrations of their lives, the characters depicted in these movies represented the many victims of widespread social chaos and deterioration.

Little Caesar, *1930. Edward G. Robinson, as the gangster boss, receives a calling card from a rival gang. While flaming youth was being extinguished by the deepening Depression, the suppliers of their fuel, the bootleggers, became the movie rage. Gangsters confused the categories of hero and villain: they made money on sound things like cupidity, greed, and fear—things not subject to business cycles.*

I Am A Fugitive From A Chain Gang, *1932. Paul Muni played an unjustly imprisoned man (based on a true story) in a drama that symbolized the fate of thousands caught not in legal toils but in social and economic forces they were helpless to combat. At the end, asked how he lives, Muni replies, "I steal!"*

The heroines of Depression era films—played by (among others) Constance Bennett, Tallulah Bankhead, Joan Crawford, Marlene Dietrich, Barbara Stanwyck—often reaffirmed the themes of the gangster film. Glamorous contrasts to the dreary facts of everyday life, their roles as prostitutes and mistresses seemed to show that one way out of despair and poverty was by breaking the moral—or even the criminal—code. These "fallen women," however, usually followed a downward path; lacking a pure and enduring love, they had to perish.

The films of the Depression years had a lighter side as well. The Marx brothers, W. C. Fields, and Mae West all represented versions of the anarchic character in comic guise. Their comedy routines depended upon verbal humor. W. C. Field in *The Fatal Glass of Beer* mocks the family, while in *Animal Crackers* the Marx brothers acclaim an anarchic world. Mae West jokes irreverently about sex in *I'm No Angel*. None displays much respect for the accepted social values.

When in the mid-1930's Hollywood's self-censorship virtually put an end to this cynical brand of humor, "screw-ball" comedies appeared to fill the gap. These films commented upon marriage and social classes. Perhaps none did it better than the very first of this type, Frank Capra's *It Happened One Night* (1934). Two dozen or so of these comedies appeared during the later part of the decade, with such stars as Cary Grant, Carole Lombard, Katherine Hepburn, Irene Dunne, and Clark Gable. They celebrated romatic love and marriage and offered the pursuit of pleasure as acceptable behavior

Musicals of the 1930's also presented romantic escapism and one or another version of the success story. The three most popular, *Forty Second Street, Gold Diggers of 1933,* and *Footlight Parade,* were constructed around Depression themes.

The escapist "screwball" comedies and musicals contrasted with other films of the period that emphasized social and economic problems. Labor dissension, slum conditions, and, of course, unemployment were only a few of the issues facing the country and appearing on screen. They encouraged sympathy for the working man and a commitment to the democratic system. A film such as John Ford's *The Grapes of Wrath* (1939) was notable for its touching portrayal of rural farm workers, its unquenchable optimism, and its belief in the ultimate triumph of American institutions. If the 1930's was a decade of despair, it was similarly a time of cultural awareness and commitment.

Suggested Readings

Robert Wiebe's interpretation of the Progressive Era is still the major work: *The Search for Order* (1968) makes it a response to the breakdown of the "island communities" in American society, the emergence of an industrial economy of interdependent parts. The Progressive social critics as Wiebe explains them believed that the new economy, with its technological sophistications and its capacity for change, needed to be subject to continual administration by experts, and the reform they advocated was toward giving government this role. An older study, Richard Hofstadter's *The Age of Reform* (1955), at its time of publication, represented a break with the tradition of scholarship that grouped together differing reform movements in American history as expressions of a common and virtuous democratic impulse. Hofstadter, who liked to conjecture that the opposite of received truth is indeed the fact, is still full of insights for the receptive reader. Bradley Robert Rice examines the working of the commission system, a plan that a number of American cities adopted early in the twentieth century as a means of bringing efficiency to city government. In *Progressive Cities: The Commission Government Movement in America, 1901-1920* (1977), Rice claims that the commissions did not respond sufficiently to the need for social reform and the provision of welfare services. Henry F. May, *The End of American Innocence* (1959) finds the beginnings of "modern" America in the years just before the world war. Paul A. Carter takes a fresh look at the 1920's in *Another Part of the Twenties* (1977). On feminism see the important books by Lois Banner, *Women in Modern America* (1974), and by William O'Neill, *Everyone Was Brave: The Rise and Fall of Feminism in America* (1969). Thomas Reed West's *Flesh of Steel: Literature and the Machine in American Culture* (1967) defines in the culture of modern technology an element of discipline and one of imagination.

Work at the Chicago Stockyards

Chapter XXI
The Politics of Progressivism
1900—1933

The Jungle

Upton Sinclair, whose novel *The Jungle* (1906) is remembered chiefly as an exposé of the packing houses and for its role in the passage of the Meat Inspection Act of 1906, was not the first writer to make—in Winston Churchill's description—"the great Beef Trust stink in the nostrils of the world." In 1899 the Hearst newspapers revealed the scandal of rancid adulterated "embalmed beef" supplied to the United States Army during the Spanish-American War. Muckraker Charles Edward Russell in 1904 published a series of articles attacking the meatpackers as "The Greatest Trust in the World." In 1905 the Attorney General of the United States indicted five such corporations under the Sherman Antitrust Act.

The "Beef Trust" was an obvious target. The emergence of the packinghouses and the refrigerated railroad car had rapidly transformed the sale of meat from one of the most local of industries to a nationwide enterprise. The old-time butcher who slaughtered and dressed his own meat had been a familiar figure in American life. Most butchers were, according to American folklore, rotund and ruddy, walking testimonials to the quality of the meat they sold. People talked knowingly of Butcher Watson's or Butcher Smith's chops, convinced that in watching the man carefully cutting up the animals, they had a guarantee of quality that, years later, they did not feel when they saw a label reading "Armour" or "Swift."

But exposing the meat-packing industry was not Upton Sinclair's main purpose in writing *The Jungle*. A recent convert to socialism, he had received a $500 advance from *The Appeal to Reason*, the nation's leading socialist newspaper, to write what one socialist described as "the *Uncle Tom's Cabin* of wage-slavery." Choosing to write about packing-house workers who had just lost a strike in the summer of 1904, he determined to go to Chicago, infiltrate the stockyards, and write a novel exposing their miseries.

Sinclair's socialist connections gave him access to workers' homes, and by dressing poorly and toting a dinner-pail like the workers, he could wander at will through the packing houses. He soon had the material for a tract, though not the characters for a novel. Then, one Sunday afternoon, wandering through the "Back of the Yards" neighborhood, Sinclair chanced on a wedding party in the rear of a saloon and joined the group as an observer of the festivities:

There were my characters—the bride, the groom,
the old mother and father, the boisterous cousin,
the children, the three musicians, everybody.

Leaving Chicago and returning to a miserable eight-by-ten-foot tar papered cabin in Princeton, New Jersey, with a desk, chair, and coal-burning stove, Sinclair wrote through the winter. The result was a sensation that, in the words of Churchill, reviewing it for an

English audience, "disturbed in the Old World and the New the digestions and perhaps the consciences of mankind."

The Jungle is the story of struggling immigrants destroyed by American industry. The hero, Jurgis Rudkus, goes through a series of industrial horrors which wreck his entire life and finally bring him to socialism. The book ends on an upbeat note—the socialists have shown their first strength:

There were telegrams to the national office from enthusiastic individuals in little towns which had made amazing and unprecedented increases [in the Socialist vote] in a single year: Benedict, Kansas, from 26 to 260; Henderson, Kentucky, from 19 to 111; Holland, Michigan, from 14 to 208; Cleo, Oklahoma from 0 to 104. . . .

But somehow it was not Sinclair's plea for socialism that impressed the public. What made the book a best seller, quickly translated into seventeen languages, was its graphic description of the packing houses in which Jurgis and his relations worked:

There was never the least attention paid to what was cut up for sausage; there would come all the way back from Europe old sausage that had been rejected, and that was moldy and white—it would be doused with borax and glycerine, dumped into the hoppers, and made over again for home consumption. There would be meat that had tumbled out on the floor, in the dirt and sawdust, where the workers had tramped and spit uncounted billions of consumption germs. There would be meat stored in great piles in rooms; and the water from leaky roofs would drip over it, and thousands of rats would race about on it. It was too dark in these storage places to see well, but a man could run his hand over these piles of meat and sweep off handfuls of the dried dung of rats. These rats were nuisances, and the packers would put poisoned bread out for them; they would die, and then rats, bread, and meat would go into the hoppers together. . . . . there were things that went into the sausage in comparison with which a poisoned rat was a tidbit. There was no place for the men to wash their hands before they ate their dinner, and so they made a practice of washing them in the water that was to be ladled into the sausage.

President Theodore Roosevelt quickly responded to the public outcry aroused by *The Jungle.* Reading the book and inviting Sinclair to the White House, he worked out a plan to investigate Sinclair's charges against the packers: "I would like a first-class man," Roosevelt wrote to his Secretary of Agriculture, "to be appointed to meet Sinclair, as he suggests; get the names of the witnesses, as he suggests; and then go to work in the industry, as he suggests. You must keep absolutely secret your choice of a man." Then he held off the impatient Sinclair for months ("Mr. Sinclair," he once wrote, "you *must* keep your head.") while the investigation confirmed all that Sinclair had written.

The packers had made large contributions to Roosevelt's campaign fund in 1904 and could not believe that he would go through with strict legislation. They spread rumors that he was attacking them out of spite for his failure as a Dakota cattleman in the 1880's. But Roosevelt had the goods on them and released the tamer part of his investigators' discoveries. The "Beef Trust" senators began negotiating; and the President—who did not actually want to hurt the industry or overly damage its sales of meat products abroad—compromised rather more than Sinclair liked.

Still, Roosevelt had achieved a significant piece of legislation. In his memoirs he takes full credit for the Meat Inspection Act of 1906 and makes no mention of Sinclair, whose socialism he disapproved of and whose bumptious giving of unwanted advice made Roosevelt wish that the writer would "go home and let me run the country for a while." Sinclair himself said that the passage of the act "was some satisfaction to me, but not my main interest. . . . I aimed at the public's heart and by accident hit it in the stomach."

The Progressive Era

The first years of the twentieth century have gone down in history as the "progressive era." Americans have made progress—and suffered setbacks—in all ages of their past, but in the era before World War I the sense of change took on a special prominence. Americans believed, more fully than they had before or would afterward, that they could bend the future to their moral will, that enlightened public opinion and technological change would cushion the shocks of advancing industry and spreading cities without slowing the advance of "progress." National leaders like Theodore Roosevelt and Woodrow Wilson, colorful mayors like "Golden Rule" Jones and Hazen Pingree, dynamic reformers like Robert M. La Follette and Jane Addams, social thinkers like Simon Patten, labor leaders like John A. Mitchell believed in common that the conscience of the people and the knowledge of experts could be fused into public policies that would meet society's major needs: to alleviate the suffering of the poor, safeguard the health and lives of workers, regulate commerce, protect consumers, and preserve opportunity. Some believed that progressive American values had a role to play in other nations as well.

The progressives also shared a joy in combat, a relish for debate, a high capacity for moral indignation that made public life exhilarating to literate Americans. Politics, now far more issue-oriented than had been customary in the nineteenth century, energized the middle class even when it discouraged many poorer citizens and new immigrants from voting. In some ways, the progressive movement was the culmination of a series of responses to industrialism reaching back half a century. In other ways, it marked the beginning of a twentieth-century age of reform that led to the New Deal in the 1930's and the Great Society of the 1960's. It was like earlier reform in its moralism and yearning for social justice, but different as well, being more experimental and practical, more concerned with detailed investigation, quicker to apply the findings of the social sciences to social policy, desiring efficiency in addition to the traditional goal of ending corruption. And many of the characteristic features of the modern polity had their birth: the social welfare state, the imperial presidency, the role of government in labor-management relations, consumer protection, the regulation of business and labor conditions.

Urban Progressivism

In seeking to reform the cities, the progressives trod a well-worn path. Generations of reformers before them had attacked the corruption that had become the lubricant of city government in the United States. But while earlier reformers were, as one politician put it, like "morning glories" that faded in the noonday sun when the public that supported them wearied of the battle, the progressives went beyond the goals of "good government" to create new political coalitions devoted to making urban government more efficient and serviceable. Unlike earlier reformers who concentrated primarily on reducing the cost of government by eliminating graft and bribery, the progressives had positive concrete programs that might as easily expand government as streamline it.

Reformers began to modernize America's cities in the 1890's. One of the earliest of these urban leaders was Hazen Pingree who became mayor of Detroit in 1889. He built schools and parks,

forced reductions in gas rates and streetcar fares, reformed the local tax structure, and even introduced work relief during the depression of the nineties. In Toledo, Samuel M. Jones, better known as "Golden Rule" Jones, built playgrounds and golf links, promoted municipal concerts, and established kindergartens in schools. He introduced the eight-hour day for some municipal employees and removed the police force from political influence. In Cleveland, Tom Johnson won his fight for the "three cent fare" on streetcars, passed effective public health ordinances, built recreational facilities, improved municipal garbage collection, reformed the police department, upgraded the city water works. These three men, whose example spread to cities across the country, were all successful businessmen who had turned to political reform. More than simply crusaders against the party machines, they all had a vision of government as a public business to be run efficiently by skillful and educated men and women providing services and social justice for a wide range of citizens.

Many of the younger progressives, fresh out of college or the new graduate schools, entered public life "hypnotized" by these older reformers. Tom Johnson's administration shone with bright young men who went on to fame as progressives: Newton D. Baker, later Wilson's Secretary of War; Frederic C. Howe, veteran of dozens of reform crusades and Wilson's Commissioner of Immigration; Edward W. Bemis, a leading progressive economist; and many others. Urban reform, particularly after Lincoln Steffens's "muckraking" articles began to appear, provided progressivism with its most transparent moral drama. The lines between heroes and villains—the reformers and the bosses—were clearly drawn, with far less of the confusion and compromise that surrounded state and national progressivism.

The urban progressives mobilized the middle class which had long felt shut out of power in the cities, creating allies among the churches, the settlement houses, the social workers, teachers, lawyers, doctors, and small businessmen. They usually moved away from the decentralized ward-based government that had characterized the old regimes. Instead of a council or board of aldermen, with each member controlling a little fiefdom in his neighborhood, they wanted a strong mayor supported by the middle class of the entire city. To some extent they pitted the middle-class neighborhoods on the cities' peripheries against the poorer central cities. In many smaller cities progressivism went even further, obliterating the old political structure and centralizing executive and legislative functions in a commission form of government, or even hiring a professional manager to run the city. They sought to separate governing from politics, a movement more in the direction of modernization and efficiency than towards the "democracy" of which they so glibly spoke. Indeed, in many cities fewer citizens voted after these progressive reforms than before. On the other hand, all classes in the cities received more services, and the quality of government im-proved. The progressive era, despite numerous setbacks then and later, initiated a long period in which city schools, hospitals, parks, police and fire departments, and welfare agencies—even in many cases city-owned utilities—brought vastly increased benefits to generations of urbanites.

State Progressivism

Urban progressives quickly found themselves at the state legislatures' doors demanding new laws to carry out their programs, including various forms of home rule. State franchise laws might restrict what a city could do in dealing with its utilities and streetcar lines, and laws passed in the state legislature might undo reforms achieved in the cities. In 1902, for example, the Ohio legis-lature, seeking to defeat "Golden Rule" Jones's campaign against police brutality, removed the police and the police courts of the city of Toledo from the mayor's jurisdiction.

The city reformers found allies in the state government among rural and small-town re-formers seeking to control railroad rates, reduce tariffs, improve rural life, increase farm credit, and attack "trusts," banks, and labor unions. Rural progressivism became a powerful force in the Midwest and Far West, as well as in parts of the South, and eventually even entered Eastern states like Massachusetts and New Jersey.

Despite many obvious differences in the focus of their concerns, rural and urban progressives shared important common perceptions of the cen-tral problems of American politics. The united to free the political system from control by "the in-terests." They believed that the true will of the people was being thwarted by an "invisible gov-ernment" of corrupt politicians in secret alliance with large "vested interests" such as the railroads and corporations. Big business, in this view, sup-ported corrupt politicians in order to gain unfair advantages over their competitors, to evade their just share of taxes, and to raise their prices or otherwise bilk the consumer without fear of retribution from government. Progressives hoped to defeat this nefarious combination both by changes in the political system and by close regula-tion of business.

The progressives stocked their arsenal of politi-cal reform with a number of weapons. The Australian or secret ballot dated from the 1880's in the United States (before then the parties pro-vided ballots for their voters); in the progressive era it was adopted by every state. Laws limiting the uses and amounts of money spent in cam-paigns also spread in the first decade of the new century. The direct primary gave all members of a political party the opportunity to participate in the choice of the party's candidates, and was a favor-ite among innovations designed to make politics a more open and less boss-ridden process; it soon replaced the system of local and presumably easy-to-control, conventions. The initiative, referen-dum, and recall were experiments in direct democracy. Laws could be proposed by direct petition under the initiative and passed by direct vote through the referendum. Officials could even be "recalled" before their terms expired if citizens became sufficiently dissatisfied with their perfor-mance.

The long-term effect of these structural reforms has been a subject of controversy. Some historians and political scientists believe that by loosening party organization and adding extra expenses for primary campaigns the direct primary actually weakened the democratic process and increased the importance of money in elections. The in-itiative and referendum, they point out, can serve conservative as well as progressive purposes, and they put a premium on expensive organizing and lobbying campaigns. Yet these reforms have in fact lent themselves predominantly to progressive and liberal causes. In this, as in so many other areas, the progressive movement charted the direc-tion that American society has taken in the years since.

Progressive measures to regulate business, re-form tax structures, and introduce or improve social services—what the progressives called "social justice"—all pointed in the direction that revitalized state government would move in the twentieth century. State-level progressivism as a major force began in 1900, when Robert M. La Follette became governor of Wisconsin. When his initial moderate reform package was defeated by party opponents in the legislature, La Follette, stamping, demanding, and scolding, created a majority for reform and then ruled it with an iron hand. Stubborn, humorless, and fiercely independent, La Follette became a reform "boss," ruthless in the use of patronage, absolute in his demand for loyalty, implacable in dispatching his enemies in the good cause of honest government.

La Follette pushed through a wide range of political reforms: the direct primary, anti-lobbying laws civil service acts. Determined to make state government efficient and useful as well as honest, he called on outstanding academic experts to draft legislation, man commissions, and generally improve the quality of government. And there was a lot to do in Wisconsin: La Follette's farm program included a strong railroad rate commission, sharp increases in the taxes paid by corporations and railroads, conservation and water power measures, state banking regulation, and a host of other social and economic reforms. Under his prodding, Wisconsin became the first state to pass an income tax. Theodore Roosevelt, always ready with an apt phrase, called Wisconsin "the laboratory of democracy," a worthy title so long as the La Follette tradition remained powerful.

Where Wisconsin led, other states followed. Albert Baird Cummins in Iowa, Joseph Folk in Missouri, Jeff Davis in Arkansas, Hiram Johnson in California, Hoke Smith in Georgia, Charles Evans Hughes in New York, and Woodrow Wilson in New Jersey were among the governors of the era who adopted the "Wisconsin Idea" and, in various degrees succeeded in modernizing their state governments and passing political and economic reform legislation. Revitalization of state government was one of the major achievements of the progressive era.

McKinley's Gone: Enter TR

President William McKinley's election victories in 1896 and 1900 had opened up new possibilities in national political life. The easy Republican dominance and the confusions of the Democrats had destroyed the rigid partisan mold based on issues that grew out of the Civil War and Reconstruction. A door had been opened. New publics—the concerned citizens of the cities and towns eager to tidy up American life and to assume more control of their surroundings, women active in social movements, the new professional, the increasingly self-aware immigrant groups, the new white collar class—could support a new national politics focused on the issues of industrialism, urban life, and the growing interdependence of all communities across the nation. And yet, this was not the door that William McKinley himself, who had been promoted to major at the battle of Cedar Creek in 1865, cared to walk through. Standing close behind him, however, cautiously nursing hopes for the presidential nomination in 1904, Vice-President Theodore Roosevelt, was eager to throw open wide that entrance to the twentieth century.

Then, a cloudy-minded young man, Leon Czolgosz—whose knowledge of anarchism scarcely inxtended beyond the popular information that anarchists had a habit of assassinating people like czars, kings, and presidents—pumped two bullets into McKinley. The President, shot on September 6, 1901, while attending the Pan-American Exposition at Buffalo, died on September 14. Roosevelt, informed while in Vermont, sped by special train to Buffalo where he behaved with dignity and restraint. His ambition, and the great difference in age and ideology between the two men and in what they might do impressed contemporaries. Rumors circulated of a cursing J. P. Morgan, his face a flaming red, staggering to his desk in fear of possible damage to his interests. A contemporary song stressed Roosevelt's eagerness for the White House, his aristocratic background, and his reputation as a horseman:

He jumped on his horse and pulled down
  through Maine:
He said to his horse you've got to outrun this
  train;
    [carrying McKinley's body]
Buffalo to Washington.

Now Roosevelt's in the White House drinking
  of a silver cup
McKinley's in the graveyard, he'll never
  wake up.
He's gone; he's gone.

McKinley was gone, and national progressivism had its leader.

Just under 43 years old when he took office, Theodore Roosevelt was by far the youngest President in American history. He contrasted sharply with the staid chief executives of the previous quarter century. Articulate, excitable, and energetic, with a range of interests extending far beyond politics, he and his young family —particularly his beautiful elder daughter, Alice—lent a fresh glamour and excitement to national events. Already famous as a military hero, he immediately captured a vast public, becoming their beloved "Teddy" (a name he disliked) and making them allies during the noisy campaigns he delighted to wage. A young girl in the 1870's had written in her diary of the adolescent Theodore: "He is such fun . . . the most original boy I ever knew." Throughout his life, he remained "fun" for millions of his adorers. Perhaps, too, he remained a "most original boy" throughout his life as well: "You must always remember," wrote a close friend, "that the President is about six." The ebullient man with the thick pince-nez glasses over his large nose, the face as square as his moralism, the high-pitched voice, the gleaming teeth, the vigorous gesturing style, was a cartoonist's—and the nation's—delight. A college classmate long before had wondered "whether [Roosevelt] is the real thing, or only the bundle of eccentricities he appears." The public soon discovered that he was the real thing, a skillful leader and shrewd politician, not just a colorful character.

Theodore Roosevelt was born in 1858, the first child of a public-spirited New York merchant and a Southern lady. He enjoyed a happy and comfortable childhood, despite the health problems that entered American folklore in place of the birth in a log cabin once considered essential for aspirants to the Presidency. The Roosevelts' Manhattan brownstone was scarcely a log cabin, and the young Roosevelt was hardly an instinctive democrat. Even at Harvard he chose his company carefully. Graduating twenty-first in his class of 158—a creditable showing—he wrote his sister that "only one gentleman stands ahead of me." His precocious interest in nature and love of the outdoors almost led him to a career as a scientist. Perhaps he was too much the dilettante for such a calling; young Theodore needed a career to satisfy his enthusiasms for literature, sports, society, nature, to meet his father's high ideals of public service, and to give him a limitless field in which to compete, for he clearly was one of the most competitive of men, whether in boxing, hunting, politics, or literature. Roosevelt "always thought he could do things better than anyone else," wrote his cousin Maude. The inevitable choice for this argumentative young man, impatient of the discipline of either science or business, was public life. "I intended, "he later wrote, "to be one of the governing classes." Some study of law—never completed—and the slightly unconventional act for an urban aristocrat of joining a local Republican Club, soon landed him in the New York State Assembly for a single term. Roosevelt had begun a lifelong career as a regular Republican politician who nevertheless was counted among the reformers because of his family antecedents and high moral tone.

With time out for exploring the Dakotas and for literary endeavors, Roosevelt continued what was for a man of his background a characteristic career in public service. He received appointment to various offices for which his energy and connections made him suitable: the United States Civil Service Commission (1889-95), the Board of Commissioners of the New York City Police (1895-97), and Assistant Secretary of the Navy (1897-98). Meanwhile, he was available when the Republican machine needed a reform candidate, as happens periodically to every party, however wicked their usual behavior. In 1886 he was a predictably unsuccessful Republican candidate for mayor of New York City and in 1898, after he had become famous in the war with Spain for leading the Rough Riders in their charge up San Juan Hill, and with the state party facing a scandal, he was elected governor of New York.

Roosevelt acquitted himself well as governor, just as he had in his other offices. But the broad executive responsiblity of the office brought out surprising assets beyond any that could have been predicted from his previous career. Well organized, hard-working, and with a flair for the dramatic, he was a successful and popular governor. He showed that he could battle to improve the public service without wholly alienating the professional politicians. He made modest but useful efforts to increase taxes on corporations—a key progressive design. He steered through the legislature several bills that strengthened state regulation of working conditions and hours of labor for women and children. His programs gained solid underpinning from the range of academic and legal experts whom he enlisted to investigate conditions and draft legislation. His New York State progressivism was a modest Eastern version of the "Wisconsin Idea."

Reformers put in office by machine politicians rarely serve more than one term. New York Republican boss Tom Platt, thoroughly tired of struggling with the moralistic governor that fate and scandals had forced on him, easily maneuvered Roosevelt out of the statehouse and into the Vice-Presidency, a usually trivial and to Roosevelt's mind maddeningly dull office for a "comparatively young man." McKinley's previous Vice-President, Garret A. Hobart, had died in office, and it would be but a small exaggeration to say that no one had noticed.

Roosevelt loved campaigning for the national ticket: " 'Tis Teddy alone that's runnin', he's gallopin'." But then, just before his lessons with a Supreme Court judge were to begin, he became President. And that he loved.

Odd as the course of his public life had been, as little as it had been a definable *career,* he was superbly suited for the office. He was ready to preach to a nation that wanted a new kind of secular preacher. He had advanced ideas about the needs of an industrial society, but he would couch them in terms of a vanishing morality. His zest for competition would lead him to revive disused powers of the office. He was in touch with the new generation and its new ideas, yet he was a Republican regular in an age of clear Republican majorities. Most of all, he was good copy in the greatest age of American journalism, a good speaker at the end of the great age of American oratory, a telling phrase-maker in an age of popular literacy. An old-fashioned spokesman for the issues of a confusing new era, an aristocrat embracing a democratic age, he was just what the broad American middle class wanted.

"I wish to say that it shall be my aim to continue, absolutely unbroken, the policy of President McKinley for the peace, prosperity, and the honor of our beloved country," Theodore Roosevelt promised his cabinet moments before taking the presidential oath. Roosevelt had many good reasons to avoid any sudden upsets at the beginning of his accidental administration. The McKinley administration's identification with "prosperity," after the harsh depression of the nineties, meant that any upset of business confidence would be blamed directly on the White House—which might then get a new occupant after the 1904 election. Moreover, the focus of power in Washington was clearly not in the White House, but at the other end of Pennsylvania Avenue, specifically in the United States Senate. The Senate was the keystone that joined and held together the overarching powers of business and the Republican Party. Organized under tight party discipline to a far greater extent than it had been earlier or would be later, the upper house was ruled by a small handful of powerful Republicans.

Nelson W. Aldrich of Rhode Island, John C. Spooner of Wisconsin, Orville H. Platt of Connecticut, and William B. Allison of Iowa—called "The Four" by contemporaries—ran the formal machinery of the Senate. Mark Hanna of Ohio was the administration's man in the Senate during the McKinley administration and was the party's great fund-raiser. All directly represented the major industries, frankly seeking subsidies and favors for their pet interests while standing firm against any reforms that might disturb "confidence." Their influence over the Senate, many newspapers, business opinion, and campaign funds gave them a wide range of powers that no President could directly match. They expected the weak and largely ceremonial Presidency that had evolved in the late nineteenth century. Roosevelt worried them: they could see his assertive personality, knew his active role as governor of New York, and were old enough to remember that the Presidency could be transformed into an immensely powerful office, as during the Civil War.

Roosevelt had no intention of remaining within the mold that the leadership had cast for his office. But he wisely refrained from hopeless confrontation with The Four. He saw that he would have to begin in areas remote from legislation to develop a public and to exercise the long-disused muscles of the office. In all his actions he was highly conscious of the precedents he was setting

Mechanical toy bank, "Teddy and the Bear," cast iron; made in the Stevens Foundry, Cromwell, Connecticut about 1900. *(Index of American Design.)*

and was more than willing to let an immediate result go if he could create a valuable precedent for himself and his successors.

Even his everyday routine was designed to invoke wonder and fasten attention on the White House. At his desk every morning by 8:30, he saw dozens of groups each day, not just Senators and other party dignitaries, but writers, reformers, social workers, scientists, even labor leaders. The great Spanish cellist Pablo Casals performed in the White House, as he would do again sixty years later when John F. Kennedy—of all Presidents, the most like TR—was in office. And he saw people during breakfast, lunch, and dinner and during his daily horseback ride through Rock Creek Park. Scarcely a month after moving into the White House he invited to lunch the most celebrated black leader of the era, Booker T. Washington. Southerners protested bitterly and Roosevelt, although he insisted that he would have Dr. Washington "to dine just as often as I pleased," was never pleased to do so again.

The Roosevelt Leadership

But style and glitter do not make a presidency. Five months after taking office, the new President made his first real move, on the "absolutely vital question," as he later called it, of government regulation of the large corporations. J. P. Morgan provided Roosevelt's opportunity when, late in 1901, he formed the Northern Securities Company. This $400 million combination was essentially a peace treaty which Morgan imposed on all the groups competing for rail traffic in the Northwest. The first important holding company, it brought together the Hill, Harriman, Rockefeller, and Morgan interests and inflated their holdings by one-third. It extended the Morgan rail monopoly of the Eastern lines across the country, bringing unified management and the threat of higher rates to a large part of the nation's freight. Unpopular with the public, it nevertheless seemed safe from attack, since the Supreme Court had sharply restricted the scope of the Sherman Antitrust Act in *U.S. v. E. C. Knight Co.* (1895).

Roosevelt, consulting only Attorney General Philander C. Knox, ordered him to file suit for the dissolution of the holding company and two years later the Supreme Court, reversing the Knight decision, upheld the President in *Northern Securities Co. v U.S.*

The "trustbuster" image which Roosevelt gained was more important than any particular antitrust actions he undertook. A famous cartoon of the time showed Roosevelt in his shirtsleeves scrubbing an American eagle with "Antitrust soap." Another cartoon pictured the "Sherman Anti-trust Law" as a corpse having come to life wearing boxing gloves. As a weapon with which to attack shrewd and powerful businessmen, the Sherman Act was largely inefficient, and Roosevelt did not necessarily believe in breaking up most large corporations. Rather, he wished to use the threat of antitrust action to establish the precedent of regulation and to assure the public that the Presidency stood above the demands of any one economic interest group. Roosevelt personally objected to Morgan's attempt to treat him, in effect, as "a big rival operator," yet once the regulatory power of government was accepted in principle, he was eager to negotiate a "gentlemen's agreement" to approve in advance new acquisitions to the vast Morgan empire. Running with both the hounds and the hares, Roosevelt made his point without alienating either the Senate or the business commuity.

After the Northern Securities case, Roosevelt's legislative program actually fared a little better than before. Congress agreed to the establishment of a Bureau of Corporations within the Department of Commerce and Labor then being organized to collect statistics and investigate the activities of corporations. The Elkins Act, passed with railroad support in 1903, outlawed rebates to large shippers and increased the powers of the Interstate Commerce Commission. Together these acts created an enduring American legend. A song written during his second administration presents the popular Roosevelt image:

Not long ago the railroads owned the whole
  United States,
Their rates were high to farmers, but a trust
  could get rebates,
Who stopped this crime of freight rebates
  among the railroad men?
Who fixed it so the railroads carry
  people now and then?
It's Theodore, the peaceful Theodore;
Of all the rulers great or small
He is the greatest of them all.

Alice Roosevelt, the President's Daughter. (Library of Congress.)

Roosevelt was neither for nor against large corporations as such, but sought to find moral grounds for distinguishing "good" ones which increased services and efficiency or lowered prices, from "bad" ones which limited competition and raised prices. He reached the same position on labor unions, which had also flourished in the years of trust-building and inflation after 1897. Roosevelt accounted himself one of those "who stand against socialism; against anarchic disorder," at the same time as he stood against "plutocracy." Roosevelt's opportunity to push the Presidency into labor-management relations in a way that would establish his conception of a "square deal" for all sides came in 1902, when old conflicts between the operators and the workers again erupted in the coal fields.

In 1900 the anthracite coal workers had threatened a massive strike. Anthracite was the hard coal used to heat houses and workplaces, and despite the ready availabilty of a usable but less satisfactory substitute, bituminous or soft coal, Americans perceived "misery and death" for "the great mass of the people in our large cities" once the coal cars stopped rumbling over the Pennsylvania hills. To head off this election-year threat, Mark Hanna had persuaded the operators to make concessions to the union. Two years later, however, when John Mitchell, the United Mine Worker's president, called for a new wage scale, the operators—no longer cowed by fears of William Jennings Bryan being elected President—determined to crush the union. They rejected all overtures for negotiation, refusing not only a wage increase, but any recognition, formal or informal, of the union. Given the general unpopularity of unions at that time, the operators could expect the support of most of the public.

Mitchell, only twenty-nine years old, remained moderate in his demands and restrained in his tactics, despite the rising bitterness of his men, whose gains of two years before had vanished with inflation. Told that the miners had to contend with miserable conditions, the leader of the operators, George F. Baer, insisted that the miners "don't suffer; why, they can't even speak English." On May 12, 1902, the miners began the largest strike to date in American history. Mitchell kept his men in order and saw to it that the soft-coal workers stayed in the mines digging coal to compete with anthracite and contributing part of their paychecks to the strike fund.

Roosevelt hoped at first to bring an antitrust prosecution against the six railroad corporations that owned seventy percent of the mines and controlled the movement of the coal to market, but Attorney general Knox did not consider the case strong enough. As summer dragged into fall with the price of coal soaring and the public in fear of a cold snap, first Mark Hanna and then Roosevelt made efforts to end the strike; but the operators steadily rejected all overtures toward a settlement. The New York City schools had already closed down for lack of fuel. Finally Roosevelt, "at my wits' end how to proceed," and supported even by conservative Republican leaders, took the novel step of inviting the leaders of both the operators and the union to confer with him.

It was a dramatic scene as these men who were not speaking to each other assembled and Roosevelt, in a wheelchair from a recent accident, pleaded for a settlement. Mitchell offered to accept binding arbitration, but Baer, who had shocked religious Americans a few months before with his claim that "God in his infinite wisdom" agreed with his course of action, vilified Mitchell and (in Roosevelt's careful prose) "in at least two cases assumed an attitude toward me which was one of insolence."

The famous conference was at the time considered a failure, but Roosevelt used it to turn his intervention into a success. Threatening a military seizure of the mines unless the owners agreed to arbitration, Roosevelt forced J. P. Morgan into his corner. With Morgan's aid, the men went back to work and the threat of warfare in the coal country faded. The arbitrators gave the workers a ten percent pay hike and corrected some minor abuses, but on the larger issue of recognition the union lost totally. The board passed on the cost of the settlement to the public by granting the operators a ten percent increase in prices, establishing a pattern that would be common in periods of inflation.

Nonetheless, Roosevelt had broken decisively with the older precedent of government intervening only in the interests of public order—and therefore on the side of management. Government as a third force in labor-management disputes was now an accomplished fact. Roosevelt in 1902 had at last provided a response to the middle-class fear of being "ground to pieces between organized labor and organized capital." He had made the public feel better; whether he had made the system work better—or differently—remained to be seen.

The Second Term

Roosevelt's nomination for a term "in his own right" was a foregone conclusion by early 1903, and his reelection by an increasingly admiring nation seemed inevitable. In addition to outstanding success in foreign affairs, Roosevelt had captured the leadership of the forces of reform, which accepted the achievements of his first administration, however limited, as a giant step beyond the policies of previous Presidents. At the same time, he had not alienated the business community or the Senate conservatives who, eager to continue Republican party dominance, rallied to his support in 1904 with political aid and huge campaign contributions. He had won the hearts of the people and the heads of the leaders. The Democratic opposition had nowhere to go, and in fact went no place at all. Feeling outflanked on the left by Roosevelt's initiatives, they turned away from William Jennings Bryan to nominate a colorless New York judge, Alton B. Parker. The Democrats futilely attacked Roosevelt's activism, then awkwardly switched ground and attacked him as the candidate of big business. The Republican National Committee collected over $2-million, almost three-quarters of it gifts from large corporations, and Roosevelt swept to an overwhelming victory. He won every state outside the South, achieved a margin of 2½ million in the popular vote, and carried with him a hundred-seat Republican margin in the House of Representatives. Flawless political management simply added to Roosevelt's huge personal acclaim. His one blunder came on election night when, as part of his victory statement, he announced that "under no circumstances will I be a candidate for or accept another nomination." Roosevelt, who would be only 51 years old when he left office, would have abundant cause to regret this noble pledge.

The second Roosevelt administration was quite different from the first—in some ways far more successful, in other ways less so. Roosevelt's initiatives grew far bolder, while opposition within his own party rose. As he widened the national agenda of reform, he began to strain the Republican alliance. It would be his hand-picked successor, the stately William Howard Taft, who would inherit the troubles of Roosevelt's second term. His great political opponent Woodrow Wilson would then capture Roosevelt's program and much of his public in 1912 to translate into action Roosevelt's increasingly fiery reformism.

In the months after his reelection, Roosevelt announced a bold and comprehensive set of goals. Noting that the Elkins Act of 1903 had failed to end the rebate evil, he called for the strict regulation of railroads. To do this, he would greatly increase the power of the Interstate Commerce Commission and limit court review of its actions. He proposed as well a minimum wage for railroad workers, employers' liability laws, and for the District of Columbia, a variety of reform legislation—such as child labor, factory inspection, and slum clearance—designed to make it a model of progressive legislation for the states.

The Republican Congress wanted none of this. "Congress will pass the appropriation bills and mark time," predicted Speaker Joseph G. Cannon, the plain-spoken autocrat who ruled the House of Representatives. Roosevelt quickly decided to concentrate on the railroad regulation issue, one of the two questions then exciting the Middle West and the West. The other was the tariff, a sensitive economic issue all over the country which the Republican leadership, happy with the current high rates, refused to touch. "We know from long experience," Cannon once observed, "that no matter how great an improvement the new tariff may be, it almost always results in the party in power losing the following election."

Roosevelt's strategy was to threaten the leadership with a tariff bill in order to force concessions on railroad regulation. Cannon eventually swallowed his distaste for railroad regulation and allowed the House to pass stringent bills by huge majorities. But the Senate, whose members at this time were still elected by state legislatures, was more independent and more conservative than the popularly elected House. There Aldrich used all his formidable parliamentary skills to block a strong bill. At one point he opened the bill to an unlimited number of amendments from the floor. Another time he turned it over to a Democratic Senator, the one-eyed, foul-mouthed "Pitchfork Ben" Tillman of South Carolina, whom Roosevelt particularly detested. But the President, continuing to whip up the wrath of the small shippers and farmers and rallying middle-class opinion to the cause, kept a steady pressure on the Senate. He worked—through an intermediary, to be sure—with the hated Tillman, played off against each other the radicals and the conservatives who recognized that some bill was necessary given the state of public opinion, finally accepted a few painful compromise a got a useful bill.

The Hepburn Act, as finally passed in 1906, allowed the Interstate Commerce Commission to set railroad rates on the complaint of a shipper, subject to court review. It permitted the ICC to examine the railroads' books and prescribed bookkeeping standards. The scope of the Commission was broadened to include regulation of pipelines, private-car lines, and terminal railroads. What it did not do, however, was to permit the ICC to conduct evaluations of the value of a road's physical property, a power that Robert La Follette had argued was essential to give teeth to the fixing of fair rates. The judicial review permitted under the act was broad indeed: the courts could pass not only on the procedures of the commission, but on whether the rates set were "reasonable." Nonetheless, the act did for the first time allow a governmental body actually to set rates and also for the first time opened the books of the companies. Both steps were epoch-making.

Roosevelt took another dramatic step in 1906 in response to public clamor, signing the Pure Food and Drug Act and the Meat Inspection Act. The national market in foods, drugs, and particularly meats had brought a vast increase in the availability of these products while at the same time eroding the public's confidence in its ability to determine purity and quality. No longer was this a matter of personal acquaintance with the supplier and some knowledge of the processes of production. National manufacturers like the great meat-packing firms of Armour and Swift, using new techniques to process every part of an animal, had revolutionized that industry. Similarly, new preserving processes and the introduction of artificial flavorings and colorings had made it increasingly uncertain what exactly was in the food or the medicine that one purchased. Dr. Harvey W. Wiley, longtime chief chemist for the Department of Agriculture and leader of a crusade against adulterated food, had conducted a constant and vigorous campaign for regulation. Taking advantage of the sensation created by the publication of Upton Sinclair's *The Jungle*, Roosevelt achieved a major precedent in making the federal government overseer of the consumer's health and safety. Thanks to Teddy progressive families could now enjoy their beefsteak and canned sausage with more confidence.

From his founding of the "Roosevelt Museum of Natural History" in an upstairs bookcase sometime before he reached the age of ten, Roosevelt maintained a continuous passion for nature. In his public life this translated into a concern for the conservation of natural resources. Although Roosevelt possessed both a scientific interest in the natural world around him and a romantic attachment to the preservation of wilderness and scenery, his conservation policy was expressed predominantly in practical terms.

"The fundamental idea of forestry is the perpetuation of forests by use," he wrote in recommending "selective cutting" in the national forest reserves. The government should "make the streams and rivers of the arid region useful by engineering works for water storage," he wrote in supporting what became the Newlands Act of 1902 to reclaim arid lands in the West. The goal of conservation policy was "while using the natural resources of the country for the benefit of the present generation, also to use them in such manner as to keep them unimpaired for the benefit of the children now growing up to inherit the land." Always the emphasis was on *use*, on long-term efficiency in expending the country's natural wealth. Coming after centuries of reckless exploitation of a seemingly inexhaustible treasury of land, water, plants, animals, and minerals, making conservation a national movement was TR's most decisive precedent for the new century. He established national parks, wildlife refuges, and monuments, set aside hundreds of millions of acres as national forests and nationally controlled mineral lands, and put federal land and water policy on a solid and coherent basis.

In conservation, too, Roosevelt could expect but limited support from the conservative Congress: "Uncle Joe" Cannon snapped that the government should spend "not one cent for scenery." And indeed, the legislative harvest was limited—but nonetheless important. The Newlands Act was the first major piece of legislation passed during the Roosevelt administration. It created a revolving fund out of revenue from sales of land in the arid regions to build reservoirs and irrigation projects. During Roosevelt's Presidency, thirty projects affecting three million acres were begun. Other legislation reorganized the Forestry Service under Roosevelt's close friend Gifford Pinchot—the Chief Forester, and principal architect of Roosevelt's conservation policies—and provided the administrative basis for executive action far more bold than anything Congress had envisioned.

"Is there any law that will prevent me from declaring Pelican Island a Federal Bird Reservation?" the President inquired in 1903. Told that there was not, he intoned, "Very well, then I so do declare it." In the next six years, he so declared fifty more times, establishing a substantial network of federal wildlife refuges. Congress, particularly Westerners, reacted harshly to his setting aside 150 million acres of land as national forests, imposing limits on their exploitation while his Chief Forester developed stringent regulations on their cutting which, ironically, only large corporations would be able to meet. In 1907 an amendment to the Agricultural Appropriations Act (which Roosevelt had to sign to keep the Forestry Service going) forbade the laying aside of any additional forest reserves in six Western states. Roosevelt and Pinchot hurriedly established twenty-one new forest reserves totaling 16 million acres while the bill sat on the President's desk. Only after officially proclaiming the new reserves did Roosevelt sign the appropriations bill, amidst rising howls of "executive usurpation" and complaints from the Far West that policy was retarding the region's economic development.

This battle was one of the last successes of Roosevelt's second administration. Only Teddy's indomitable good spirits and self-righteousness saved him from discouragement—for his legislative program proceeded no further. Noting the continued rise of labor, the growing attractiveness of Socialism, the genuine distrust of the wealthy obvious in the public mind, the discomfort over rising prices, and the great desire for reform, Roosevelt preached an increasingly radical message. He called for further increases in the regulatory powers of the federal government, with increasing stridency criticized big business and their favorite branch of government, the courts, and called for "industrial reform" to give the workingman a "larger share of the wealth."

Yet, as always, some of Roosevelt's actions pointed in a different direction. When a short, sharp panic struck Wall Street in 1907, his administration rushed in with tens of millions of dollars in deposits to stabilize shaky banks, and he gave informal approval to the Morgan interests when they proposed having United States Steel purchase the Tennessee Coal and Iron Company, a financially troubled competitor whose acquisition

would give the House of Morgan control of over sixty percent of U.S. iron and steel production. Unlike Standard Oil or the Santa Fe Railroad, U.S. Steel was a "good trust" in Roosevelt's mind because it had cooperated with his Bureau of Corporations.

Despite his increasingly broad denunciation of the corporations, Roosevelt in fact understood their critical role in American life. He did not want to destroy them; he wanted them to be orderly, predictable, rational, and moral. What this meant was a great secret, not so much between him and them as between him and the great community of "plain people" he liked to address. Historians will continue to argue over the true meaning of the precedents that Teddy Roosevelt so elaborately established. Were they intended to deal concretely and forcefully with the problems of managing a complex industrial society in a way fair to all, or were they designed merely to offer comforting symbolic victories, indications that someone representing the "plain people" cared and at least paid attention to their concerns.

In personal terms, Roosevelt remained by far the most popular man in American life. He had succeeeded in convincing millions both that he understood the new bustling world of giant industry, big labor, international rivalries, and mass immigration and that he retained and found applicable to this new world , the moral values of a simpler time. His hand-chosen successor, the portly William Howard Taft whom Roosevelt billed as a stout defender of "my policies," would have to be far more nimble than he looked to meet the demand for reform that Roosevelt had raised to fever pitch.

Taft

Roosevelt was the first President to choose his successor since Andrew Jackson had picked Martin Van Buren. As TR's Secretary of War, Taft had become an informal "assistant President" carrying out presidential policies close to Roosevelt's heart, particularly in supervising the construction of the Panama Canal and in completing various initiatives in foreign policy. "If only there were three of you!" he had exclaimed to Taft upon appointing him, and however comical the image of a half ton of William Howard Tafts might be—for he weighed comfortably over

300 pounds—Taft did indeed perform many functions in addition to his duties at the War Department.

Yet for all his closeness to Roosevelt and his administrative experience, Taft was in some ways a curious choice. He had, as one historian puts it, risen "to the presidency through the appointive route." A loyal Republican lawyer from a distinguished Cincinnati family, Taft became President of the Philippine Commission, and then the first Governor General of the Philippines, a role in which he achieved outstanding success in pacifying the islands and establishing limited self-government. In 1904 Roosevelt brought him into his cabinet, where he quickly became the first among equals. Clearly, he was qualified for the task of administering the federal government; but his ability to lead the Republican Party and to provide the public with the image of presidential leadership that Roosevelt had created was far more questionable. "Politics, when I am in it, makes me sick," Taft had admitted in 1906.

Taft was a lackluster campaigner. The popular songs written for the campaign of 1908 sang more loudly of Roosevelt than of the candidate:

The greatest man that ever ran the greatest
   land on earth
Is Teddy R., whose shining star is only in its
   birth
We'd like some more of Theodore, but
   Theodore has said,
That TAFT was meant for President to follow
   in his stead.

CHORUS:
Get on the raft with Taft, boys
Get in the winning boat,
The man worthwhile, with the big glad smile,
Will get the honest vote . . . .

William Jennings Bryan's energy as head of the Democratic ticket was no match for Taft's well-financed campaign, and the Ohioan rolled up a million-vote popular margin, winning the electoral college vote by 321 to 162.

At state and local levels, however, the Republicans did not fare quite so well. Taft ran ahead of the local Republican tickets. Thus, in all but a few states in which progressive Republicans dominated the party, though defeated in the presidential race, the Democrats had demonstrated renewed strength, and the progressive Republicans would be demanding that the new President continue Roosevelt's pressure against the standpatters in the House and Senate.

Taft received less credit from contemporaries for carrying out Roosevelt's policies of "political, social and industrial reform" than he deserved. His administration enforced the Sherman Act with far more vigor, even if with less drama, than had Roosevelt. Where Roosevelt in eight years brought 44 antitrust suits, Taft's Attorney General George W. Wickersham, in four years brought 65. Roosevelt had carefully avoided one of the issues dear to Western progressives: revision of the tariff; but Taft plowed into this thicket, securing an unsatisfactory—and politically disastrous—bill, the Payne-Aldrich tariff, which in fact did reduce

some rates. If the Hepburn Act of 1906 was the first measure to put some teeth into railroad regulation, then the Mann-Elkins Act of 1910, which Taft supported and helped lobby into law, was a veritable great white shark. "Bully! Bully!" Taft exclaimed to reporters—for once in a Rooseveltian mood—upon hearing that the bill had passed. Mann-Elkins enabled the Interstate Commerce Commission to initiate rate changes and to regulate telephone, telegraph, cable, and wireless companies, and placed squarely on the railroads the burden of proof that a given rate was inequitable before it could be raised. The act's practical effect was to prevent the railroads from raising rates until the government seized the lines during World War I. (Liberal historians have praised Mann-Elkins for its securing effective control of rates, whereas Albro Martin, a historian sympathetic to the railroads, has called it "a killer" for preventing an appropriate rate of reinvestment in the lines.) As a conservationist, Taft set aside forest reserves at an even more rapid rate than had his predecessor. And Taft's record on labor issues was one that he could vigorously and correctly defend during the 1912 campaign:

"We passed a mining bureau bill to discover the nature of those dreadful explosions and loss of life in mines. We passed safety appliance bills to reduce the loss of life and limbs to railroad employees. We passed an employers' liability act to make easier recovery of damages by injured employees. We have just passed through the Senate a workman's compensation act . . . requiring the railroads to insure their employees against the accidents of a dangerous employment. We passed the children's bureau bill calculated to prevent children from being employed too early in factories. We passed the white phosphorus match bill to stamp out the making of white phosphorus matches which results in dreadful diseases to those engaged in their manufacture."

And, he might have added, he appointed as chief of the new Children's Bureau a veteran labor reformer, Julia Lathrop, the first woman in American history to be appointed a bureau chief. Perhaps most important of all was his initiating the Sixteenth Amendment — the income tax. Without this levy it is hard to see how any of the welfare state measures of later years could have been financed.

Nonetheless, Taft has gone down in history as both a conservative and a failure as President. (He was more successful later as Chief Justice of the Supreme Court, from 1921 to 1930.) He carried out far too many progressive reforms to rank as a successful conservative, while his political ineptitude and his personal style made him a stranger to the progressives. Taft was genial, easygoing, and legalistic. Insofar as he was ever comfortable in politics, he was most at ease with conservatives, disliking the progressives' evangelism and ardor for change. He named none to his cabinet, and his dealings with the progresssives in Congress, even when he and they agreed, were always difficult. In the course of the Payne-Aldrich tariff debates, where he in fact sided with the progressives, he became personally closer to Aldrich, leader of the opposition. When he later stated that this unsatisfactory measure was the best tariff bill the party had ever passed, progressives were furious.

Taft's most dramatic clash with progressives, dramatic because it pitted him directly against one of Roosevelt's closest friends, was the Ballinger-Pinchot controversy. Richard A. Ballinger was Taft's new Secretary of the Interior, a Western lawyer, sympathetic to the Western view which favored "the free distribution of the available areas of the public domain to the landless settlers." Though committed to upholding federal law on conservation, soon after he took office, he began to point out to the President acts of the Roosevelt administration in withdrawing public lands that he considered illegal. Taft, referring tartly to the "transcendentalists" in Chief Forester Pinchot's office who had exceeded the law, had Ballinger return over a million acres to the public domain. Pinchot, in retaliation, picked up on and publicized the findings of an investigator in the General Land Office that Ballinger, before becoming Secretary of the Interior, had been involved in a shady land transaction which had delivered an enormous windfall in Alaskan coal lands to a Morgan-Guggenheim syndicate.

Taft bought none of this; he exonerated Ballinger, although he went out of his way to state his continuing desire that Pinchot remain as Chief Forester. Pinchot, however, was not appeased, and he began a surreptitious press war against Ballinger and the President. Then he took the further step of having a progressive senator, Jonathan P. Dolliver, read on the Senate floor a letter from Pinchot accusing Ballinger of being an enemy of conservation and admitting that confidential material appearing in the press had come directly from the Forest Service. Taft now had no choice but to fire Pinchot, and he then had to defend his action before a Joint Congressional Committee investigating the affair. As he feared, his defense of the Secretary of the Interior came across to the public as opposition to Roosevelt's policies, and therefore to conservation.

Roosevelt returned from Africa in June 1910 bearing the hides of dozens of large animals and the hopes of the thousands of progressives now in conflict with Taft. Conservationists smarting over the Ballinger-Pinchot affair, progressive editors disappointed in Taft and angered as well by his plans to raise sharply the second-class postal rates that magazines paid, Westerners disappointed with the Payne-Aldrich tariff, all looked to Roosevelt for an alternative. The ex-President—whom Taft himself still routinely referred to as "President Roosevelt"—promised amidst the pomp of his arrival (a flotilla of United States naval vessels commanded by twelve vice-commodores had steamed down New York Bay to meet the returning hunter's ship) that he would "make no comment or criticism for at least two months." But a vow of silence was surely the hardest possible promise for Roosevelt to keep. Within a week the newspapers were full of his opinions, and in less than two weeks they would note that he had conferred with both Pinchot and Senator La Follette—Taft's worst enemies.

Late that summer, Roosevelt, fearing an "ugly" party split, delivered two major speeches designed, he claimed, to provide "a common ground upon which Insurgents and Regulars can stand." If this was his real intention, he was deluding himself, for the speeches, particularly one at a gathering of Civil War veterans at Osawatomie, Kansas, had everything to horrify the "Regulars" and cheer the progressives. Calling for a "New Nationalism" that would greatly extend the powers of the federal government, particularly over the corporations, and sharply criticizing the courts which stood in the way of such a program, Roosevelt made it obvious that while his successor had been drifting toward the right, he had grown more radical. Taft complained that the speech "frightened every lawyer in the United States" and began identifying himself as a conservative.

With the Republicans in disarray, divided between Western progressives and Eastern Conservatives, between Roosevelt men and Taft loyalists, the 1910 congressional elections became a loud signal of the dangers the party would face two years later. The House of Representatives went Democratic for the first time sine 1892; state and local victories introduced to the public a new set of attractive, reform-minded Democrats such as the new governor of New Jersey, Woodrow Wilson, former president of Princeton University. Only the Western progressives did well among the Republicans, and Taft already considered them "assistant Democrats" rather than true members of his party.

The last act in this curious drama of personal and ideological division came in 1911, when Taft ordered an antitrust suit against the United States Steel Company. One prominent piece of evidence for the monopolistic character of U.S. Steel was the corporation's acquisition in 1907 of the Tennesee Coal and Iron Company, a deal that then President Roosevelt had tacitly approved and that, so Teddy recalled, he had discussed with his Secretary of War several times. Privately he excoriated Taft's "small, mean and foolish" act; publicly he attacked Taft's "archaic" attempt to break up the trusts rather than to regulate them effectively. Taft and Roosevelt would battle for the Republican nomination.

The Election of 1912

In 1912 progressive energies were approaching their height. Of the four candidates who took the field in 1912—Taft for the Republicans, Woodrow Wilson for the Democrats, Roosevelt for the newly established Progressive Party, and Eugene V. Debs for the Socialists, even the most conservative among them, President Taft, claimed large credit for progressive reforms. The four-way race itself was evidence of the power of this impulse to create and destroy political coalitions. The heightened political debates of the era, the increasing number of issues on which partisans could divide, had a pulverizing effect on the major parties. The Democrats had remained sharply split since 1896. The Western progressive democracy behind William Jennings Bryan and the conservative Eastern Democrats who had run Alton Parker for President in 1904 vied through years of sterile wrangling for the support of the Southern delegates at national conventions. Even the Socialists could barely hold together through the 1912 campaign. And the Republicans, coming apart in the ideological feud between progressive insurgents and conservative, did fracture completely in 1912, as the personal conflict between Taft and Roosevelt moved the warring factions beyond party bounds.

By 1912, Roosevelt and Taft were publicly accusing each other of broken faith, dishonesty, and hypocrisy. As Roosevelt swept through the new direct presidential primaries (he even won Taft's home state of Ohio) and Taft used his patronage to pick up the delegates in the non-primary states, the party split widened. The belligerent Roosevelt, confident that he had the support of the majority of Republicans, personally attended the national convention decked out in his Rough Rider outfit topped by a giant sombrero. But the President's men, who controlled the party machinery, awarded themselves all the many disputed delegate seats and nominated their man with ease—while Roosevelt's supporters began to plan a new party.

"One of the things that Mr. Roosevelt has not learned in all his long and useful and honorable life," Taft had commented before the convention, "is to be a good loser." Furious at his loss to these "political thugs," and convinced that it was due to corruption in the selection of delegates, Roosevelt was ready to forsake the allegiance of a lifetime and bolt the Republican party. When supporters guaranteed financial backing for a new party, the Progressive Party was born. Adopting the symbol of bull moose—an animal to which Roosevelt enjoyed comparing himself (and no sillier after all than the Republican elephant or the Democratic donkey)—the party's national convention had the flavor of a religious revival. Roosevelt offered a "confession of faith," while delegates sang "Onward Christian Soldiers" and "The Battle Hymn of the Republic." The platform endorsed a wide range of progressive reforms, including tight regulation of the trusts, unemployment insurance and old age pensions, woman suffrage, a tariff commission, and national presidential primaries. By its platform, the Progressive Party was stating the agenda for a generation of reform; by splitting the Republican Party, however, it was insuring that those reforms would come through the Democratic Party.

The Democrats, fixed in the role of the hapless and quarrelsome opposition, required a generous measure of luck to profit from their opportunity to elect a President. Only the national party rule requiring a two-thirds majority of the delegates for nomination prevented them from putting forward the hard-drinking and eccentric Bryanite Champ Clark of Missouri. After forty-six ballots interspersed with furious negotiations, the party finally managed to nominate its ideal candidate, Woodrow Wilson, a Southerner who was attractive to many different elements within the party. He was an intellectual—making him a fit match for Roosevelt. He had been a Gold Democrat in 1896—which pleased some, and had become a

Eugene Debs.

progressive by 1912—which pleased others. Most of all, he had been a Democratic executive who had carried out a progressive program in a state that was Eastern and Republican, as well as infamous for its corruption and conservatism. With his "New Idea" program, Wilson had overhauled a decadent electoral system, introduced a direct primary, established a public utilities commission, regulated women's and children's hours and conditions of labor, passed a clean-food act, and accomplished much else. And he was an eloquent, forceful speaker, matching Roosevelt in the fervor of his rhetoric. Wilson inevitably sought the highest moral tone, eager to explain—like a good professor—why he was right. His thin, intense, angular face seemed to fit his ascetic eloquence. "A Scotch-Irishman," he was fond of remarking, "*knows* that he is right." This righteousness, which could be so irritating in direct personal contact, proved capable of swaying millions in 1912 and the heady years after.

While Taft defended his record and Debs made earnest pleas for socialism, Roosevelt and Wilson each announced reasonably coherent philosophies of government for the nation's future. Roosevelt developed the theme of a "New Nationalism." Borrowing language from Herbert Croly's *The Promise of American Life* (1909), he called for a frank recognition of the need for more centralized government and closer regulation of economic life. Laissez-faire, he argued, was out of place in a complex, interrelated society. Concentrated industries were here to stay: the trusts should be regulated, not "busted." Government had to shoulder responsibility for social welfare and labor-management relations.

Wilson's response—the product of long hours of discussion with "the people's lawyer," Louis D. Brandeis, the great legal mind of the age—was the "New Freedom." Wilson demanded regulation of competition, not of corporations. Vigorous, effective antitrust activity would open the avenues of commerce to "men on the make." The rules of fair business dealing would be carefully established, and violators subjected to harsh penalties. Wilson was somewhat vague on how he would accomplish this restoration of competing small units, but this basic stance appealed to people frightened by "bigness" both in industry and in government.

While informed citizens argued over the need for big government and its potential dangers and contemplated the trade-off between the efficiency of Rooseveltian government by experts and the greater freedom and opportunity Wilson promised, it was partisan politics that largely determined the outcome. Republican voters split, the progressives going for Roosevelt and the regulars for Taft. The Democrats, however, solidly backed Wilson. He won forty-two percent of the popular vote—not a majority, but a sizable plurality: Roosevelt gained a little over a quarter of the voters, and Taft a little less than a quarter. Even the Socialist candidate won nearly a million voters: Wilson had slid between two halves of a majority party to win the Presidency. But even as a minority President, his mandate for reform was clear.

The Negro American

The Civil War officially ended slavery in the United States, but in the postwar decades of Reconstruction and the rebuilding of the "New South" slavery was replaced by other forms of economic and social bondage. Sharecropping and peonage plus the persistence of racial segregation in the form of "Jim Crow" laws, assured white Southerners of continued control over the black population. Lynchings, beatings, and other forms of violence perpetrated by white supremacist groups like the Ku Klux Klan kept blacks in "their proper place." Imposition of the poll tax and the "grandfather clause," waiving voting prerequisites if one's father or grandfather had voted in 1876, further limited black civil rights. Out of these tensions arose three major black figures who defined the ideological perceptions of American black society from 1880 to 1930.

The period from 1880 to 1915 has been characterized as the "Age" of Booker T. Washington—a period when his self-help and "accommodationist" ideology held ascendance. Black church life, business, family, and organizational activities adapted easily to Washington's philosophy, which offered a means of dealing with the extremes of discrimination and segregation which blacks faced. The life of Booker T. Washington reveals a Horatio Alger-like epic in which the black leader pulled himself from the depth of poverty and persecution in the post-Civil War South to a position of power and influence. Throughout his life, Washington exemplified what was required to be a successful American black—to wear the mask, to play the expected role. But despite Washington's image of an "Uncle Tom," recent scholarship depicts him as a man of action, a political infighter often defiant of traditional racial conventions.

Born in 1856 in Virginia, the son of a slave woman, Washington never knew the identity of his white father. At first he mined salt and coal in Malden, Virginia. Then, a stint as a houseboy in the home of a well-to-do white woman, Mrs. Lewis Ruffner, had a profound influence on the young Washington. He attended Hampton Institute in Virginia, which stressed vocational skills for its black student body. Washington arrived at Hampton footsore, dirty, and penniless; on his graduation three years later, he was endowed with a basic education and a high moral commitment. Washington taught school, becoming increasingly convinced of the necessity for teaching young black men and women practical skills and a belief in self-help and the dignity of labor.

In 1881 Washington became the founder and principal of Tuskegee Institute in Alabama. Tuskegee became his creation. He acquired the land, built buildings, raised money for books, equipment, and salaries. For fifteen years Washington worked tirelessly to establish an all black teachers' college with similar goals to those of Hampton. Graduates of Tuskegee became teachers throughout the South and Africa.

In 1895 Washington became nationally known. That year at the opening of the Cotton States and International Exposition in Atlanta, he stood before blacks and whites and enunciated his accommodationist doctrines to the cheers of his audience and the acclaim of the nation. In 1901 his autobiography, *Up From Slavery,* became a bestseller.

The climax of Booker T. Washington's career, however, is often considered the luncheon invitation to Theodore Roosevelt's White House in 1901. This incident caused dismay among Southern whites who perceived it as a plot to erode

Booker T. Washington. (Library of Congress.)

racial mores. The larger implication of the meeting was the political power it symbolized; Washington now acted as a behind-the-scenes presence in American political life, influencing both Roosevelt's and Taft's appointments and racial policies. In addition, his strong contacts with industrialists and financiers provided another avenue for blacks to benefit from powerful white philanthropic support. Disillusioned by the failure of the political process during Reconstruction, Washington conceived of black progress in economic rather than political terms. He aimed to elevate the black masses by involving them in business, trade, and especially agriculture.

Black opposition to Washington is represented by William Monroe Trotter and his militant newspaper, *The Guardian,* W. E. B. DuBois' Niagara Movement, the NAACP, and its publication, *The Crisis.* Trotter bitterly reproached Washington for obstructing black opportunity in the South, and DuBois complained that Washington "practically accepts the alleged inferiority of the Negro races." Northern whites, however, generally regarded him as a "genius" (Teddy Roosevelt) and "wonderful" (Andrew Carnegie). Few contemporaries were willing to delve behind his optimistic, conciliatory demeanor. Washington, in fact, was not adverse to applying whatever tactic necessary to stifle critics. He was a powerful backstage figure constantly seeking to strengthen the Tuskegee Machine, a network of black political and business organizations throughout the country.

The year of Washington's death, 1915, marked a significant point in American Negro history. Events in Europe, discrimination and segregation at home, and the black exodus to Northern cities set the stage for W. E. B. DuBois' challenge to the established progressive gospel of Washington. Militant rhetoric, pressing forward in legal and political channels and a commitment to an elite black leadership distinguished DuBois from Washington.

In background and personality these two leaders were worlds apart. Born in Massachusetts in 1868 into an environment dominated by the white New England middle class, DuBois' contrasted sharply with the Southern slave setting known by Washington. An exceptional student and a descendant of an old, established black family, DuBois encountered little racial discrimination. Not until his student years at Fisk University in Nashville, Tennessee, did DuBois develop any real racial identity. At this Negro institution, DuBois began to perceive the implications of the race situation and to adopt a faith in the role of black intellectuals.

In 1889 DuBois began a socially isolated life at Harvard College and Graduate School. He found satisfaction in the scholarly life and was influenced and stimulated by William James and George Santayana. DuBois earned a doctorate in history, the first American black to be awarded such a degree from Harvard. Travel and study in Europe completed his education and confirmed DuBois' view of himself as an American black with a special destiny.

Just a herd of Negroes
Driven to the field,
Plowing, planting, hoeing,
To make the cotton yield.

When the cotton's picked
And the work is done
Boss man takes the money
And we get none,

Leaves us hungry, ragged
As we were before.
Year by year goes by
And we are nothing more

Than a herd of Negroes
Driven to the field—
Plowing life away
To make the cotton yield.

Share-Croppers
by Langston Hughes

After a short period as a teacher, DuBois entered a phase of his life notable for its scholarly achievements and his evolution from an accommodationist position to one of agitation, pressure, and propaganda. A sociological survey conducted for the University of Pennsylvania, *The Philadelphia Negro,* is still noted today as a significant piece of research. It emphasizes the need for the black upper class to encourage the progress of the race. In this extensive study DuBois called for the "the mastery of the art of social organized life."

Black women responded to his call while reflecting the progressive mentality of the age. Under the mantle of both DuBois' ideology and Washington's doctrines middle-class black urban women recognized in club work a means to achieve self-help. The names of Ida Wells Barnett, Fannie Barrier Williams, and Josephine St. Pierre Ruffin are virtually unknown today, yet at the turn of the century these women were noted for their contributions. Black women joined these clubs to administer to the needs of the poor, the sick, the old. In addition, the groups promoted the idea of the black woman as an important social and moral force in the black community. In their adoption of the progressive formula of opportunity, ambition, frugality, and perseverance, these women seemed closest to Washington. Yet in their reliance upon social organization and racial pride they followed the tenets of DuBois.

At Atlanta University in 1897 DuBois supervised sociology programs and directed a series of conferences on blacks sponsored by the University. Through this program, he published a series of monographs aimed at social reform while stressing the significance of the "talented tenth." College-trained and inspired young people would become community leaders, business organizers, and members of a cultural avant-garde. DuBois presented this black man in all his variety to the white American public in 1903 in a collection of essays, *The Souls of Black Folk.* Described by the Negro poet James Weldon Johnson as having "a greater effect upon and within the Negro race in America than any other single book published in this country since *Uncle Tom's Cabin,"* the book affirms the unique black status. It includes essays on topics ranging from the Freedmen's Bureau to rural Southern schools.

In succeeding years the measured tone of *The Souls of Black Folk* receded. In subsequent literature (his biography of John Brown), in response to crisis (the Atlanta race riot of 1906), and in lectures, DuBois steadily emerged as a forceful propagandist impatient for the attainment of

black goals. The burgeoning radical stance evidenced itself in the Niagara Movement, a direct response to the tactics of Washington. Founded in 1905 at Niagara Falls, Ontario, the movement confirmed DuBois' belief in direct agitation. Twenty-nine representatives from thirteen states and the District of Columbia met to alert blacks to the injustices perpetrated by whites. The organization's "Declaration of Principles" demanded suffrage and civil rights, and called attention to Southern peonage. The movement's elite basis was an obvious organizational weakness that thwarted its founder's hopes for wide support. By 1911, the movement itself had petered out. DuBois himself, however, continued to agitate.

The principle distinction between DuBois and Washington lay in their educational theories; DuBois favored an elite, college-educated black population compared to Washington's advocacy of industrial training. On the suffrage question the leaders also disagreed: DuBois supported immediate voting rights, Washington preparation for black suffrage. Whites, of course, were attracted to Washington's gradualism and feared DuBois' predictions of black revolution if their rights were not granted.

The Niagara Movement was born in the so-called age of Booker T. Washington. In this context it was ahead of its time and was doomed to failure, but it provided the groundwork for the establishment of the National Association for the Advancement of Colored People, which contained an interracial membership. The social workers Lillian Wald and Jane Addams, and *The Nation* editor Oswald Garrison Villard, were among the prominent whites involved. The organization took a radical stance on matters of racial equality and segregation, denouncing the political and economic subordination of blacks. In association with the NAACP, DuBois edited *Crisis,* a magazine reflecting his views. The organization and the magazine increased the prestige and influence of DuBois, who emerged as the most significant black leader. Throughout the 1920's and 1930's DuBois' ideology manifested an increasingly socialist-labor orientation, a philosophical stance that many NAACP board members found difficult to accept.

As a member of the black intellectual elite, DuBois was an integral part of the cultural phenomenon known as the Harlem Renaissance. Representing in part an integration of white and black culture during the 1920's, it was both an assertion of black pride, of white fascination with Africa, and a part of the larger American cultural upheaval of the time. The Harlem Renaissance demonstrated a new awareness of blacks by whites

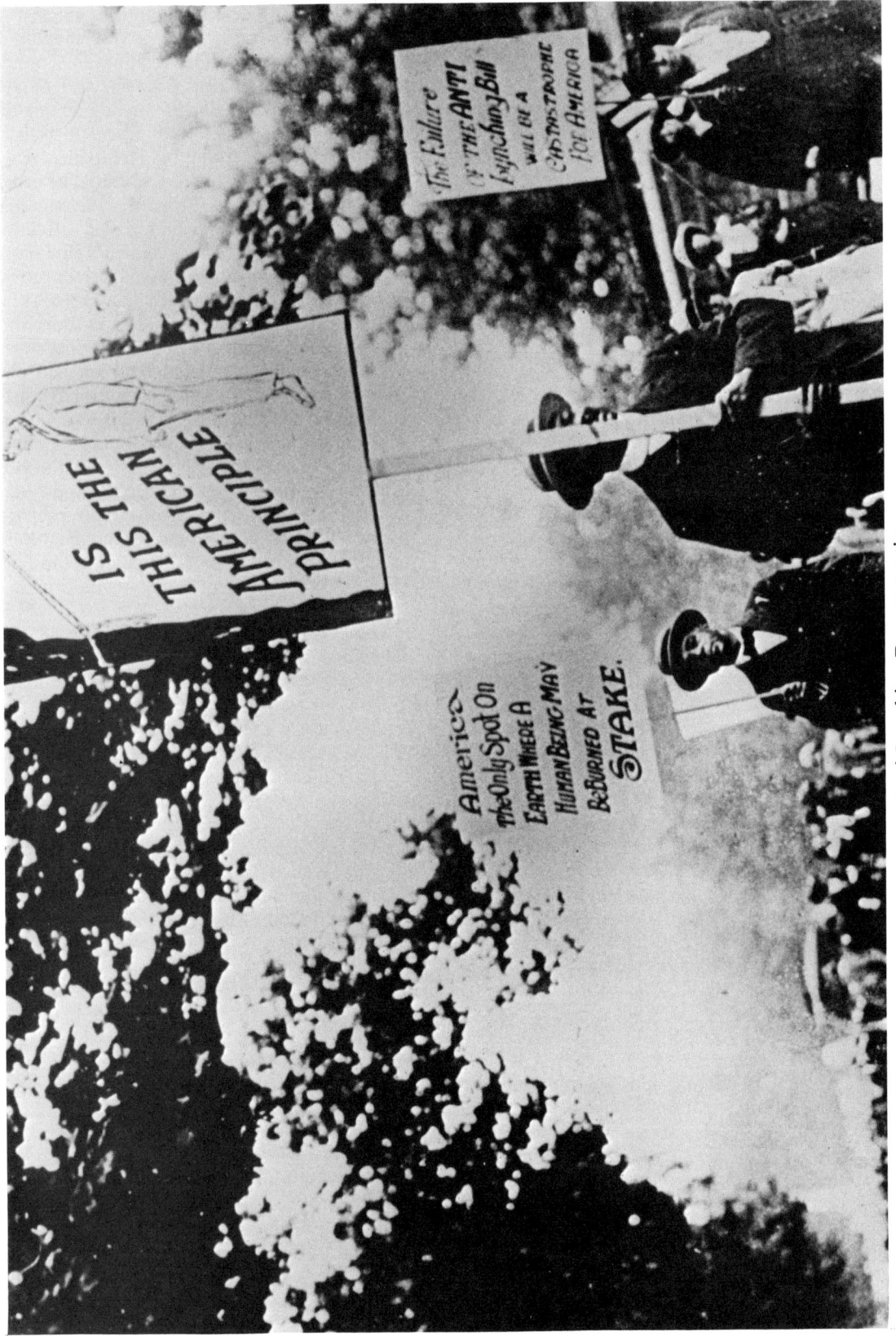

Anti-Lynching Demonstration

and an opportunity for intellectuals of both races to mingle in salons (often organized by wealthy white women), studios, and theatres. Like other blackwhite alliances, this artistic merging was tenuous and in the Great Depression the Harlem Renaissance declined. Throughout the Renaissance DuBois was a dominant figure, but other scholars, playwrights, poets, and musicians participated. Countee Cullen, James Weldon Johnson, Claude McKay, Zora Hurston, and Langston Hughes were all a part of the "New Negro Renaissance." This expression of artistic creativity also included black literary and political magazines *(Harlem, The Messenger, Fire)*, theater and art groups, and political associations. The Schomberg Library Collection in New York City became Harlem's cultural nucleus. White acknowledgement of the black as a creative artist was in itself a revolutionary concept, causing many to foresee an American society of cultural pluralism.

Pan-Africanism, a special vision of DuBois, was particularly popular after World War I. DuBois dreamed of a great free central African state to encompass a "unity of the colored races." An NAACP session in 1919 supported DuBois' grand scheme, but no grass roots support was ever apparent. DuBois' movement eventually clashed with that of Marcus Garvey, whose plan flourished through his showmanship, flash, and emotionalism.

Garvey has been described both as a "charlatan" and a "crook" and as "the greatest thing that happened to a black man." Born in Jamaica in 1887 of poor peasant parents, Garvey attended local secondary schools. A youthful experience of rejection by the white daughter of a Methodist minister taught Garvey that "there were different races, each having its own separate and distinct social life. . . ." Garvey pursued a short-lived printing career before his involvement in the Jamaican labor movement.

Before coming to the United States, Garvey's most significant achievement was the founding in Jamaica of the Universal Negro Improvement Association. Its purpose was to unite "all the Negro peoples of the world into one great body to establish a country and government absolutely their own." This interest in black uplift and fulfillment encouraged a correspondence with Booker T. Washington, which resulted in a plan to visit the United States. Unfortunately, Washington died before Garvey's departure, but the Jamaican still determined to raise funds and interest other blacks in America in his plan for the formation of a black economic community. This visit coincided with traumatic events in the American black experience: the emergence of the second

Ku Klux Klan, a continued tightening of Jim Crow laws, and a boll weevil infestation that caused Southern blacks to flock to Northern cities. But life in the urban ghettos was no better. Unemployment, bad living conditions, and economic and social discrimination usually prevailed. Garveyism appealed to these displaced, unhappy rural people as well as to the disillusioned urban worker. By 1919, Garvey's UNIA claimed thirty branches in American cities and the organization flourished until 1927.

Garvey spread his ideology through the publication of a weekly newspaper, *The Negro World.* Printed in Spanish, French, and English, the paper celebrated black heroes of the past, recalled slave rebellions, and promoted the grandeur of Africa. Emphasis on racial pride had tremendous impact on the black community which responded enthusiastically to Garvey's black nationalist ideas and racial separation.

Encouraged by Garvey toward the vision of an African homeland and inspired by the assertiveness preached by DuBois, black men and women displayed racial pride and a commitment to achievement of their constitutional rights. Whether down-trodden ghetto dwellers or depressed tenant farmers, blacks asserted their rights to protect their freedom and property from white violence. Returning soldiers and industrial workers began to see themselves as part of the American system. Southern sharecroppers and peons similarly expressed their dissatisfaction by leaving the land and streaming to Northern cities.

Envisioning a world-wide unity among blacks, Garvey in 1919 established a steamship company, the Black Star Line. Only blacks were entitled to buy shares in the company and thousands made the investment. Many blacks and whites criticized Garvey's plan as extortion, but Garvey consistently expressed his belief that "the Black Star Line will sail to Africa if it sails in seas of blood." Unfortunately for his investors, the three ships of the line eventually were lost at sea and the company went bankrupt. This failure did not deter Garvey's plans for black self-determination. The establishment of a Negro Factories Corporation, still another steamship company, and plans for the settlement of American blacks in Liberia testify to Garvey's unflagging spirit.

One of Garvey's most impressive accomplishments was the organization of three UNIA conventions. Thousands of delegates came to Harlem and drafted a Declaration of the Rights of the Negro Peoples of the World. The document planned a free Africa under an all black government, as well as a call for legal and political equality. Blacks acclaimed Garvey for providing a new image of American Negroes.

Interwoven with Garvey's spectacular successes were ignoble failures. In 1919 Garvey was questioned by New York City's Assistant District Attorney about selling unincorporated stock in the Black Star Line and was also involved in libel suits instigated by comments printed in the *New World*. His legal problems culminated in a trial that sought to prove Garvey guilty of using the mails with intent to defraud. Found guilty, Garvey lost an appeal in 1925 and was further discouraged by the refusal of the Supreme Court to review his case. He served three years of a five year sentence and was deported to Jamaica where he continued his efforts toward fulfillment of his grand scheme. In 1935 he moved to London where he died in poverty five years later.

Spanish-Speaking Immigrants

In the twentieth century Mexicans, Puerto Ricans, and Cubans have become the largest ethnic groups arriving in the United States.

Mexican-Americans, or Chicanos, have a longer history in the United States than many of the European groups that immigrated during the late nineteenth century. First as citizens of Spain and then of Mexico, Spanish-speaking people were the first Europeans to settle what is now the Southwest United States. When the Treaty of Guadalupe-Hidalgo was signed in 1848, America acquired the land of California, Arizona, New Mexico, Colorado and parts of Utah and Nevada while at the same time annexing Texas. As many of the place names in California and the southwestern states bear out, there was already a significant Mexican presence in the Southwest by the time the first Americans arrived.

Mexican immigration to the United States has been characterized by a push-pull relationship. The push of an excess labor force in Mexico has been present throughout this century, while the pull of America's job needs has fluctuated. This has led to an uneven pattern of immigration, but since 1900 Mexicans have increasingly come to the United States. Capitalist development followed American control over the Southwest and Mexicans were and still are primarily employed in agriculture, finding seasonal employment more profitable than similar work at home. This work also allowed the workers to return home to their families at off times. Coming mostly from the serf or peon class in Mexico, they worked at $1.25 a day for a ten-hour stint, attractive to the immigrant as well as profitable to the American. Mexicans worked in urban areas as well. By 1920 in El Paso, Texas, the most important port of entry for Mexican immigrants, they were employed particularly as construction workers and in the railroad yards and various unskilled jobs. Women worked in agricultural jobs and as domestics, laundresses, sales clerks, and garment workers.

From 1900 to 1917 an "open border" existed between the United States and Mexico with few restrictions to prevent the influx of Mexicans. The lure of work in America was the main attraction for Mexicans to immigrate, but social instability helped to spur some to move north. In northern Mexico, where most of the immigrants came from at this time, Pancho Villa and other revolutionary groups were operating, creating a disturbed situation both politically and economically.

In 1917 Congress passed an immigration law aimed primarily at Europeans that required a literacy test and a head tax. This temporarily slowed the movement of Mexicans northward, but the decline of European immigration and labor needs of World War I persuaded the Department of Labor to suspend the law for most Mexicans. Like Southern blacks they manned many jobs left vacant by Americans in the armed services.

With Mexico in a state of revolution during the 1920's, record numbers of legal immigrants entered the United States. And many others crossed the border undiscovered and undocumented. In response, groups such as organized labor and nativists worked for quotas on incoming Mexicans. The proposed Box bills of 1928 and 1930 were blocked by the Department of State, which was concerned with America's overall Latin American policy as well as with Mexican relations, and by southwest industrialists and agriculturalists who wanted the supply of Mexico's cheap labor to continue. In the 1930's the economic stagnation of America's economy offered few jobs for the new immigrants, and close to half a million Mexicans returned to their native land. The second World War reversed the process. In 1942 agricultural growers and the federal government established the Bracero Program in conjunction with Mexico.

Fort Stanton, New Mexico. (National Archives.)

The Mexicans agreed to send an undisclosed number of workers to the United States in return for certain wage guarantees for their workers. This program again brought a stream of workers, furthered the growth of the Chicano culture, and slowed the assimilation of Mexicans already in America. Braceros numbered 55,000 by 1947, and the federal government had appropriated $120 million for the program to subsidize agribusiness and, incidentally, to discourage unionism. In the 1950's came another round of deportation proceedings. With war needs over and Senator Joe McCarthy exploiting anti-foreign sentiment, more than two million Mexicans and Chicanos were deported. The 1960 census documented the Chicanos' impoverished condition in comparison with other Americans. Their per capita income was $968 as compared to $1044 for blacks and $2047 for whites. Over eighty percent of the Chicano population was urbanized, mostly in the Southwest. In the 1960's political awareness increased in the Chicano communities, over eighty percent of which were now urban. Lyndon Johnson's "war" on poverty brought new programs into the barrios, and in 1962 Cesar Chavez began to organize farm workers in the National Farmworkers Association. But in the 1970's almost one hundred percent of the deported aliens were Mexican and the border patrol was riddled with corruption. As relations with oil-rich Mexico became more delicate in the 1980's, it was likely that Mexican Americans would win some of the status that capitalism usually bestows on the wealthy.

Since 1917 Puerto Ricans have been citizens of the United States. In a sense, their migration to the mainland is a part of the general movement by Americans from one section of the country to another. But since the culture of Puerto Rico is substantially different from that of the mainland, their experience more closely resembles that of earlier European immigrants.

Puerto Ricans were living on the mainland when the island was still a Spanish colony. As early as the 1860's, political exiles were working from a base in New York for the independence of the island. As a result of the Spanish American War, Puerto Rico was ceded to the United States. Thus began the slow movement to the mainland. By 1910, 1,513 Puerto Ricans were living on the mainland, more than one third residing in New York City. In 1917, just before the United States entered World War I, the Jones Act granted citizenship to all Puerto Ricans. German ships were in the Atlantic and the United States was solidifying its interests in the Caribbean. After World War II, the economic boom on the mainland attracted unskilled and semiskilled workers from the island where unemployment was high and wages low. Between 1940 and 1950 the United States Puerto Rican population quadrupled to 301,000. Throughout the 1950's, recruiters from the mainland went to the island seeking workers for industries, often sweatshops and needlework. A trend developed towards settling away from New York City; communities began to grow in Pennsylvania, Illinois, New Jersey, and Connecticut. By the recession of the 1970's, prospects for jobs on the mainland became so dim that the flow of migration reversed.

Several influences have pulled Puerto Ricans to the mainland. With improved medical services at home the death rate declined and, by 1950, reached a point lower than on the mainland. The birth rate, however, continued to remain high, causing a rapid population increase in an underdeveloped economy. The economy was based on the seasonal production of sugar, tobacco, and coffee, all of which left the majority of workers unemployed for a great part of the year. Transportation has also been an important factor in migration to the mainland. Before World War II, the journey was expensive and unpleasant. After the war, commercial air travel enabled individuals to fly between the island and the mainland for relatively modest sums.

Unlike the other Spanish-speaking immigrants who have come to the United States during the twentieth century, most Cuban immigrants have come for political reasons. Few Cubans lived in the United States when the island nation, ninety miles off Florida's coast, became separate from Spain in 1898. While Cuba gained independence, the United States was to dominate Cuba politically and economically. Yet this situation did not lead to a great movement of Cubans to the mainland. For the most part, the island was able to employ the majority of its population in urban areas, mining, or the large sugar industry. Although the standard of living for most Cubans remained near the subsistence level, there was no great migration north.

After World War II the number of Cuban immigrants began to increase greatly. In the decade from 1951 to 1960 almost 79,000 Cubans came into America, mostly through Miami or New York City. An unsteady political situation impelled these Cubans to seek a new home. The corrupt Batista government was challenged during this decade and finally overthrown by Fidel Castro and his followers in 1959. What began as a trickle of Cuban refugees, mostly strong Batista supporters such as police and army officials in 1959, was by the middle of 1962 a flood. Right before the missile crisis in 1962 as many as 3,000 Cubans a week were arriving in Miami before air traffic was discontinued between the countries. Between 1961 and 1970 some 208,500 Cubans left their homeland to seek refuge in the United States. These political immigrants came largely from the upper and middle classes of Cuba. In 1977 Cubans passed Mexicans as the single largest nationality migrating to the United States.

Woodrow Wilson

In the election of Woodrow Wilson, as in that of Theodore Roosevelt, progressivism triumphed nationally. Wilson's inaugural address called for reform of the tariff and the banking and currency system, for regulation of industry, and for conservation. Under conservation Wilson included the preservation of human resources. This notion that the government was to treat human beings as resources, promoting their health and development as assets to the national economy and society, was current among progressives. Combining a scientific or technological vision of a well functioning society with a vision of human well-being, it took national progressives about as far as they were ready to go toward reform. The President and Congress, both of its Houses Democratic, would bring about important new legislation. But the progressive measures, like other programs that twentieth-century American political movements have effected, were something less than their rhetoric might suggest. They were closely fitted to the shape of existing institutions, which they attempted to make more efficient and humane.

Early in his administration Wilson, having called Congress into special session for reform of the tariff, did something that no President since John Adams had done: he appeared before Congress to present his program. The Underwood Tariff that he thereupon got through the national legislature cut rates; the same bill also imposed a federal income tax—a progressive measure formally enacted by the Sixteenth Amendment to the Constitution. Wilson kept Congress in session through the summer in order that it could achieve reform of banking and currency. The product was the Federal Reserve Act of 1913.

The Act was the most impressive domestic measure of Wilson's administration. Yet its scope indicates something of the limits of American reformist ambitions when they translated themselves into actual legislation. A major contributor to the popular sentiment for the reform had been an investigation by a congressional committee, with Representative Arsene Pujo as its chairman, of the "money trust," the forces that managed finance and credit. The investigation had found that the interests of J. P. Morgan and John D. Rockefeller controlled over $22 billion. It might therefore have led to a law that would severely restrict or regulate the nation's private financial agencies. The Federal Reserve Act did make large changes. It set up a Federal Reserve system of twelve banks that would issue currency to private banks in exchange for secured notes that those banks received from their borrowers. A Federal Reserve Board, its members appointed by the President, was to set the rediscount rate that private banks would pay in trading their notes for Federal Reserve bills. All this provided for a more flexible currency, somewhat less dependent on the price of gold than currency had been; and it established some public control over the banking system. But it was not a radical measure. It accepted and left almost completely intact the institution of private banking, and Wilson appointed to the Reserve Board bankers who were sympathetic to the banking business.

Other legislation of the Wilson years had, in its application, a similar character of both reforming and adhering to the basic character of American business institutions. The Smith-Lever Act of 1914 financed the agricultural extension services in the aid they were giving to farmers who wanted to know how to improve agricultural methods. But by working with the more prosperous farmers and by encouraging mass production on the farms, it unintentionally pointed agriculture in the direction that New Deal policies, again unwittingly, would later take it: toward consolidation into large farming businesses. The Federal Trade Commission was a regulatory agency much more powerful than Theodore Roosevelt's Bureau of Corporations, which it replaced; but Wilson's appointees to it were friendly to the wishes of business. While the Clayton Antitrust Act of 1914 contained stronger provisions for breaking up business trusts than the Sherman Antitrust Act had embodied, court decisions would weaken the

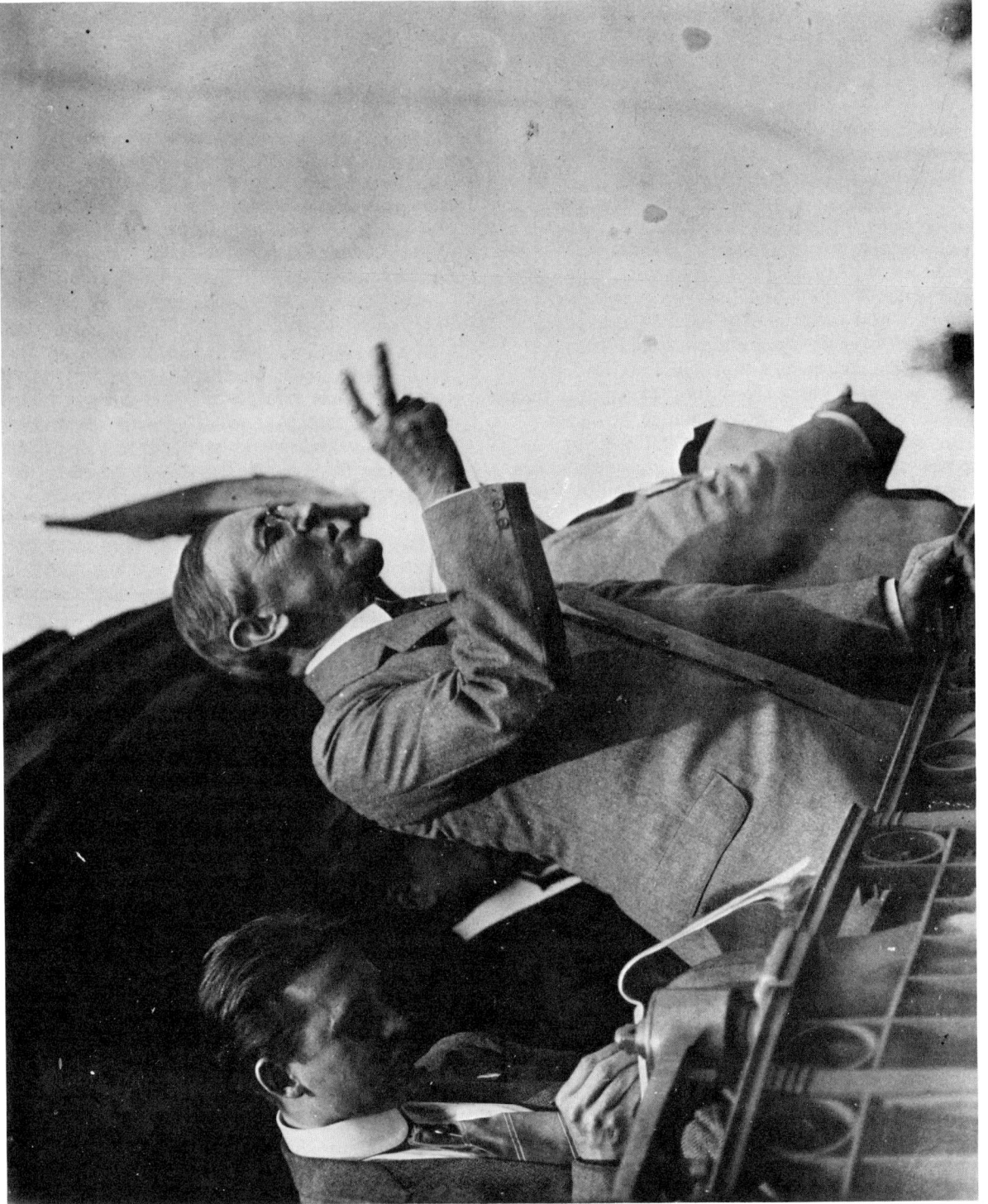

Woodrow Wilson. (Library of Congress.)

THE POLITICS OF PROGRESSIVISM

effect of the legislation. The Act also offered to labor unions some degree of exemption from the antitrust actions and injunctions that the Sherman Act had led to. Yet it did not prevent courts from issuing injunctions against strikes and boycotts.

Other reforms intended to bring direct relief to people who much needed it. The La Follette Seaman's Act required more humane conditions in the merchant marine. Two pieces of legislation signed in 1916, the Federal Farm Loan Act and the Warehouse Act, eased for farmers the problem of credit. The Keating-Owen Act outlawed child labor in enterprises engaged in interstate commerce. In 1918 the Supreme Court found the law unconstitutional. The Adamson Act of 1916 raised the salaries of railroad workers and instituted an eight-hour day.

What emerged from Roosevelt's and Wilson's progressivism, and even from the actions of President Taft's administration, was a collection of federal programs that imposed on business a degree of social responsiblity and, for that very reason, made it an active partner of government. This was not an entirely new concept. The nineteenth-century grants of federal lands to railroads for the building of lines needed by the nation as a whole had constituted a somewhat similar partnership. Presidential progressivism did, however, much expand the practice of putting business to the service of the public, adding some fairly sharp restraints on business. The humane federal laws of the later years of progressivism meant a further involvement of the government in American society and economics. But these measures did not fundamentally address the fact of economic hardship. The Wilson administration did nothing visible for black Americans; and in fact this Democratic administration, tied to a party that had the white South as one of its major bases, extended segregation in government.

Some additional measures passed Congress during Wilson's second term, particularly in the postwar years. The Esch-Cummins Transportation Act of 1920 returned to private ownership the railroads which the federal government had taken over in wartime. The Act came close to requiring government arbitration of railway labor disputes. The Merchant Marine Act of the same year instructed the wartime Shipping Board to sell its ships cheaply to American corporations and set up a loan fund for private industry. At the same time that this law benefited industry it served the public good, by imposing safety standards in a largely unregulated field. The General Leasing and Water Power Acts empowered Congress to regulate rates in the absence of state legislation.

The Democratic Party ran an Ohio governor, James Cox, for President in 1920, but the ticket is memorable not for Cox but for his vice-presidential running mate, Franklin D. Roosevelt of New York. Roosevelt, warned the Republican National Chairman, was "making friends" on the campaign trail. Nonetheless, the Republican candidate, Senator Warren Harding, rode the anti-Wilson tide and won the election by almost a two-to-one margin. The new Republican Vice President, Calvin Coolidge, observed that the election marked "the end of a period which had seemed to substitute words for things."

Demobilization and the Red Scare

None of the plans for postwar demobilization submitted to the Wilson administration was implemented. Some congressmen simply dismissed careful planning as socialistic; others, concerned over the mounting federal debt, would not appropriate the necessary funds. Just before the war ended Congress debated, with echoes of the Civil War, whether reconstruction was a presidential or a congressional responsibility. Congressmen feared that Wilson might continue to dominate them in peacetime. In fact, Wilson said that "people would go their own way." They would want a relaxation of wartime restraints and Wilson, who viewed the public as the final repository of support for his League of Nations, had no wish to alienate them.

Demobilization, when it came, was rapid. Almost immediately following the armistice the government discharged 600,000 veterans. Four million more returned to the peacetime economy during the next year; most of them reached their homes by the summer of 1919, carrying gas masks and helmets as souvenirs. At first the United States Employment Office set up a veterans' employment agency. But Congress cut back its funds, refused to pass a public works bill requested by the President, and would not even back completion of most government housing projects then under way.

But commitments to government war spending inevitably continued into peace, and no early postwar deflation occurred. Nor was there massive unemployment in 1919. Economically, the first world war lasted until 1920. The Treasury made a last major war loan and further rehabilitation loans to European nations. Demobilization itself required some spending, and dismissal pay for veterans soon found its way into circulation. Consumer savings also entered the marketplace as goods scarce in wartime became available once again.

Yet the unsettled economy contributed to postwar unrest. Many people moved from one job to another, never certain of the future. The high cost of living was a constant irritant; consumer prices almost doubled between 1914 and 1920, and rose fastest in the postwar period. It was a time not of high unemployment but of economic dislocation.

Labor-management friction intensified after the war. Labor unions, which had been granted some government protection during the hostilities, determined to maintain collective bargaining and to push the closed shop requiring union membership. Leaders of management, resolved to restore their earlier dominance, promoted the "American Plan," an ingeniously named call for the open shop. They denounced the closed shop as a restriction on liberty. Strikes ensued.

In some ways the men who managed the steel industries were the least enlightened in all management. In 1910, 30 percent of the labor force in steel worked a seven day week; 75 percent worked a twelve-hour day—and some even labored on two consecutive twelve-hour shifts every other Sunday when they changed from day to night work. The average work week for the whole industry was sixty-eight hours. During the war the industry, to avoid government intervention, agreed to pay time-and-a-half for work beyond an eight-hour day, and a severe labor shortage raised wages faster than inflation could erode the gains. Unions flourished; by the war's end almost 100,000 steel workers belonged.

The great steel strike began on September 23, 1919. Management, which refused to meet with union leaders at all, knew it held the upper hand. The national organization was unready, lacking money and adequate preparation for a venture thrust upon it by militant locals. William Z. Foster, the author of tracts in favor of revolution, was an unwise choice for leader. In the Chicago-Gary, Indiana, area U.S. Steel imported thousands of Southern Negroes to man the plants. By January the strike was dead.

In the meantime, the President's Industrial Conference convened in October in Washington, D.C. Its objects were to find ways of avoiding strikes and to suggest means for the resumption of natural economic development. Its constituents included a group intended to represent the public and named by President Wilson, labor spokesmen picked by the AFL and the Railroad brothers, and an employers' group chosen by several management associations. The Conference disagreed over the principle of unrestricted collective bargaining, the right of a union majority, local or national, to representatives of its own choosing. Steel management had rejected the principle in the current strike, insisting that the delegates for the workers at any particular factory must come from their own immediate ranks. In a moral victory for the unions, the public group at the Conference endorsed unanimously Samuel Gompers' own statement of labor's unrestricted right of union representation. Even management voted 10 to 7 against, another triumph for unionism. But the strikes—some 3,600 in all during 1919—continued.

A bituminous coal strike in November 1919 revealed clearly the divisions on labor within the Wilson administration. The President, now gravely ill, had sought accommodation in the steel walkout, but considered the coal strike "unjustifiable" and "unlawful" and warned that it could interfere with European relief programs. In any event the President now left such responsibilities to more aggressive cabinet members. Secretary of Labor William B. Wilson offered generous arbitration to the coal workers, headed by a young leader John L. Lewis. But Attorney General A. Mitchell Palmer, conscious of growing public wrath against labor, especially opposed the coal strike which threatened fuel shortages in the coming winter. Palmer, with the President's acquiescence, issued two injunctions; to enforce them, the government sent troops into coal fields and the strike ended.

The years following the first world war were a noteworthy time of innocence assaulted by experience. Having finished a war the nation thought it could handle on the simplest and purest moral terms, it discovered those terms meant little to Europe. The compound emotion of a modern war, the perfect fusion of lofty idealism with the baser feelings of chauvinism, had settled easily upon an America technologically advanced enough for total mobilization and still naive enough to believe in splendid adventures with noble goals. The war passion was orchestrated by the Committee on Public Information, which set professors from the best universities to writing propaganda. The organization and George Creel, the Denver progressive who directed it, shared in the popular enthusiasm they elicited. When the war ended and the Committee dissolved, the emotion remained and sought out new enemies on which to spend its aggression. Among them was Bolshevism.

Although World War I ended with the armistice of November 1918, many Americans remained shell-shocked until early in 1920. It has been customary to explain the domestic "Red Scare" of 1919 as an irrational reaction to the war. In an attempt to restore old values feared damaged amid wartime hysteria and the influence of European ideas, patriotic Americans lashed out at a supposedly imaginary radicalism. The radicals may have been few in number, but their deeds proved them capable of scaring most of the country. They found sustenance in the Bolshevik Revolution of 1917 and the Third Internationale, which Soviet leaders created in March 1919 as an agency of worldwide revolt.

The Socialist Party, once a thriving progressive organization under the leadership of Eugene Debs, had fallen into disrepute for its opposition to the war. Debs himself, persecuted under Wilson's harsh Sedition Act, remained silent in jail. Wartime fever had extinguished the more radical Industrial Workers of the World or "Wobblies." By 1919 many socialists had joined either the native Communist Party of America or the Communist Labor Party, composed mainly of foreign-born urban Americans. Both parties combined amounted to considerably less than one percent of the population. Their very existence, however, provided some business groups, anxious to keep labor from extending its wartime gains, with a convenient target on which to blame postwar problems.

In the winter of 1919 the city of Seattle, Washington, experienced something almost totally unfamiliar in American history, a general strike. In sympathy with striking longshoremen, the unions that ran the city—streetcar employees, clerical workers, even firemen—walked off their jobs, leaving Seattle paralyzed. A Committee of Public Safety, which sounded vaguely foreign and revolutionary, maintained essential services. But the strikers could not agree on demands, public opinion turned against them, and Mayor Ole Hanson brought marines into the city to end the strike.

After the Seattle strike Mayor Hanson's office received a package wrapped in brown paper. Since the mayor was in Colorado selling war bonds, it was put aside and some liquid leaked out, burning a wooden table. The package was a homemade bomb. A similar missive went to the home of a Southern Senator favoring more stringent immigration restriction—and blew the hands off his black maid. A New York City postal employee read about the packages and remembered putting some others aside for insufficient postage. Marked with a "Gimbel's Brothers" return address, they were found at the main post office in New York City or in transit; newspapers compiled a "bomb honor list" that included Supreme Court Justice Oliver Wendell Holmes, financier J. P. Morgan, Jr., and Attorney General A. Mitchell Palmer. Whoever mailed the packages apparently intended that they should arrive around May Day, the Communist holiday. In June a bombthrower blew himself to smithereens with his own missile on the steps of Palmer's house in Washington. After this incident Palmer, once known as a progressive, became notorious for rounding up aliens and endeavoring to deport them.

In the summer of 1919 a bloody race riot occurred in Chicago, where 600,000 blacks would move in the decade beginning in 1917. A black boy unable to swim had clung to a railroad tie that drifted into an area of Lake Michigan reserved for whites. Whites swam menacingly toward him: he moved away for a few strokes, then sank and drowned. When police refused to arrest any whites and instead took a protesting black into custody, a riot ensued killing 23 blacks and 15 whites. Riots occurred in other cities, and in the course of 1919 some 70 blacks were lynched, including at least 10 veterans. In September the whole Boston police force went out on an unprecedented strike. The mayor fired them, the President called the strike "a crime against civilization," and Governor Calvin Coolidge said that there was "no right to strike against the public safety by anybody, anywhere, anytime." In November an IWW member provoked into shooting an American Legionnaire was taken from prison by an angry mob who beat and castrated him, hanged him from a bridge, and riddled his body with bullets. In early January 1920 the New York State Assembly refused to seat five legally elected Socialists: but this action surprisingly brought protests from distinguished citizens.

The Red Scare culminated in the Palmer Raids of January 2, 1920, when Justice Department agents, striking simultaneously in dozens of cities, rounded up thousands of aliens. Held incommunicado for days in violation of their civil rights, they would have been shipped to Europe had Palmer got his way. He wrote:

I have been asked . . . to what extent deportation will check radicalism in this country. Why not ask what will become of the United States Government if these alien radicals . . . carry out the principles of the Communist Party? The whole purpose of communism appears to overthrow the decencies of private life, to usurp property . . . to disrupt the present order of life regardless of health, sex or religious rights . . . [They] include the I.W.W.'s, the most radical socialists, the misguided anarchists, the agitators who oppose the limitations of unionism, the moral perverts and the hysterical neurasthenic women who abound in communism.

The opposition of Acting Secretary of Labor Louis F. Post, a former single-tax proponent who now held technical power over deportations, prevented Palmer from acting in many cases. When nativist congressmen sought to impeach Post in the House, he reminded them of the Bill of Rights and refused to budge. At the same time that Post was refusing to effect Palmer's will, the nation was tiring of its attorney general and his repeated warnings against the Reds. By the spring of 1920 the Red Scare was on the wane, soon to be replaced by concern over a serious depression and then the pleasure-seeking mood of the 1920's. A bomb that killed dozens in Wall Street in 1920 was correctly regarded as the work of immoral anarchist cranks.

Traces of the Red Scare suffused the twenties. The newly-formed American Legion grew rapidly, preaching "one country, one language, one flag." A burgeoning new Ku Klux Klan reached a membership of some two to four million by 1924. The trial of two Italian anarchist immigrants, Bartolomeo Vanzetti and Nicola Sacco, for the robbery and murder in 1920 of a paymaster in South Braintree, Massachusetts, also revealed the Red Scare's lingering influence. While modern ballistics indicates that Sacco was probably guilty, the fishpeddler Vanzetti was probably innocent. What is memorable about the trial is its xenophobic atmosphere. The judge privately referred to the defendants as "those anarchistic bastards," and his conduct of the trial was scarcely less prejudiced. Since the accused were radicals and Italians, most people believed them guilty and the Court agreed. Before his execution in 1927 Vanzetti delivered a moving oration:

We were tried during a time that has now passed into history. . . . I am suffering because I am a radical and indeed I am a radical. I have suffered because I was an Italian, and indeed I am an Italian; I have suffered more for my family and for my beloved than for myself; but I am so convinced to be right that if you could execute me two times, and if I could be reborn two other times, I would live again to do what I have done already.

Harding, Coolidge, and Business

Warren Harding, a likeable, hardworking President, had inherited from Woodrow Wilson a disintegrating Presidency and a drifting foreign policy. He also faced a severe postwar depression, (1920-22) growing out of tight money policies and cutbacks in federal spending, that was worsening as he entered the White House. Nevertheless, Harding took over the White House with the same careful leadership he had exercised during his presidential campaign. He appointed three important progressives to his cabinet: Charles Evans Hughes to State, Henry C. Wallace to Agriculture, and Herbert Hoover to Commerce. Astute programs from these men helped him to recreate confidence among businessmen. A President's Commission on Unemployment, called by Hoover, marked the first time in United States history that the federal government had acted in a con-

siderable way to curb hard times. At the behest of both Hoover and Wallace, Congress passed a series of laws granting credit to farmers, exempting their cooperatives from anti-trust prosecution, and regulating packers and stockyards. By the end of 1922 there was a consensus that good times for business lay ahead. The Fordney-McCumber Act of that year restored high tariffs. In his first two years as President, Harding by his bland, reassuring manner had accomplished what Dwight Eisenhower would do for the country a generation later—give it a respite from factional strife and a sense that old values were still alive.

Harding's personal cronies brought his downfall. Secretary of the Interior Albert Fall accepted sizable "loans" from oilman Edward L. Doheny who sought advantages in the stock market from leasing government oil lands in Elk Hills, Califor-

Coolidge and Sons. (Library of Congress.)

nia, and Teapot Dome, Wyoming. Fall found it hard to explain how he managed to spend $170,000 renovating his New Mexico ranch on his $12,000 salary. Fall eventually went to jail, but nothing was proven against Attorney General Harry Daugherty, who was also implicated. Beginning in 1923 there were suicides and resignations among Harding appointees below the cabinet level. Charles R. Forbes, head of the newly-formed Veterans' Bureau, made off with a quarter of a million dollars and was sentenced to Leavenworth prison for two years. Liberals exaggerated the scandals: there was no vast giveaway of natural resources, no sinister Ohio gang. But there was criminal wrongdoing, and had not Harding died of heart disease in August 1923—a death hastened perhaps by his knowledge of the impending scandals—he would have had a hard time winning reelection. The new President, Calvin Coolidge, muted the effect of the scandals by appointing an independent investigating committee under the chairmanship of a Democratic senator, Thomas J. Walsh.

By the spring of 1924 the Harding scandals had faded from the public mind as swiftly as had the Red Scare of 1919. In an age that lived in the newspapers, readers grew tired of the tedious hearings on Teapot Dome and devoured intriguing stories such as that about the strange "pig-woman" and her relation to a murdered New Jersey rector and his mistress in the famous Hall-Mills case. Harding, soon forgotten by the general public, always has held historical interest because of his affairs with beautiful women, both in and out of the White House. (He suffered his first heart attack after climbing several flights of stairs to keep one of these rendezvous.) A born compromiser, Harding had tried to maintain some moderation in his ideological position; Coolidge almost always sided with big business. He encouraged Secretary of the Treasury Andrew Mellon to reduce taxes especially on the wealthy. Mellon, a wealthy industrialist from Pittsburgh, also worked to reduce both the national debt and government expenditures.

Coolidge, an odd man who slept incessantly, suffered indigestion, and enjoyed his reputation as a parsimonious Yankee, took as his motto—"Don't hurry to legislate." His ideal day, H. L. Mencken remarked, is one on which nothing whatever happens. He spent only about four hours daily on his executive duties in an effort to avoid controversy. He was clever enough, and a master of detail, but would not permit economic and social problems to intrude much on his equanimity or his moral sense. He honestly thought they would go away. They often did.

Pungently honest, he was a good symbol in an era of change: a "Puritan in Babylon."

Business was regarded with great veneration in the Coolidge era. People credited it with providing the appliances, radios, cars, electricity, and indoor plumbing that finally became commonplace in the decade. Coolidge asserted: "The man who builds a factory builds a temple . . . the man who works there, worships there." Some preachers compared Jesus Christ to a great business executive whose parables were effective advertisements. Jesus also embodied the ideal of public service, and during the 1920's a policy known as welfare capitalism had developed. Large corporations particularly began pension plans and early forms of unemployment insurance. Social critics acknowledged the importance of business by concentrating their fire on it; Sinclair Lewis' Babbitt (1925) depicted a small-town real estate salesman whose optimistic boosterism was made believable by an overlay of self-doubt. Despite the puritanism symbolized in the White House by Coolidge, American values were changing rapidly. While the President embodied the traditional idea of thrift, advertising was teaching consumers habits of installment buying. The ad copywriter was learning to pay less attention to the quality of his product and more to the common desires to be young and desirable, to be rich, to keep up with the neighbors—in short, to be envied.

The predominance of big business almost assured that its traditional opponent, organized labor, would suffer in the twenties. It did. Membership in the AFL declined sharply to a scant three million. The Railway Brotherhoods felt the sting of an unfriendly government: the Railway Labor Board approved a 12 percent reduction in the wages of railway shopmen, and Attorney General Daugherty ended the resulting strike with an injunction. Hardest hit of all were soft coal miners. Highly competitive market conditions brought union-busting and bloodshed, particularly in the Appalachian South. The Jacksonville Agreement, engineered in 1924 by John L. Lewis of the miners and Secretary Hoover, broke down after bringing a brief interlude of peace. The Supreme Court added its weight against unions in Bailey v. Drexel Furniture Company (1922), which declared unconstitutional a federal tax on products manufactured by children. The next year in Adkins v. Children's Hospital the Court decided against a District of Columbia law setting minimum wages for women.

Many farmers also fared badly in the decade. In 1920 government wartime price support ended at the same moment the European market was

Edward Hopper, *The Lighthouse at Two Lights*, 1929. (Metropolitan Museum of Art.)

shrinking. Large operators bought out small ones, and three million people left the farms between 1921 and 1928. For some people on the farms, a "depression" seemed real enough. Price levels varied immensely from one crop to another. Wheat suffered precipitous price cycles and grave problems of surplus; tobacco and dairying flourished. Cattle and hogs fluctuated. Shifts in consumption (away from breads, toward dairy products) and in international demand (away from wheat and cotton in particular) threatened special groups of farmers, as did unusual severe droughts or flooding.

In the twenties, as today, one half the farmers produced over 90 percent of the agricultural product. In an economic sense, only the 50 percent were professionals. What about the lower half? They owned small farms, sometimes of submarginal land, or were tenants or sharecroppers. Many were deficient in skills and unable to adjust to new tools or changed demands of the market, while others simply could not afford tractors. The real bottom of agriculture, and a huge one, included Southern sharecroppers, farm laborers, and particularly migratory workers. These forgotten Americans had no political power, and remained practically invisible until the thirties and, to a large extent, until the sixties.

All politically successful ideas for agriculture reform in the twenties promised one thing—higher price levels, yet without direct subsidies and without mandatory controls over production. A number of laws designed to help agriculture passed Congress in the early twenties; they provided higher tariffs, more government credit, regulation of the grain exchanges, packers, and stockyards, and the freeing of farm cooperatives from prosecution under anti-trust laws. Three other more sweeping plans dominated the policy debates in the middle and late twenties: a protected domestic market through government controlled foreign marketing; a rationalized domestic market through large marketing cooperatives; and a controlled domestic market through some form of domestic allotment. Each method was conceptually subtle and mechanically complicated. Perhaps few farmers really understood them in all their detail.

Controlled foreign marketing was most important. It gained the loyalty of most farm organizations and farm-state Congressmen; its authors were George N. Peek and Hugh S. Johnson, two farm machinery industrialists of Moline, Illinois. In the form of several, slightly divergent bills (all called McNary-Haugen after congressional sponsors), this proposal remained before Congress from the mid-twenties to 1929. Two such bills survived both houses of Congress, only to be vetoed by President Coolidge. The McNary-Haugen bills provided for a government-owned marketing corporation to purchase all surplus agricultural production in major crops at a high price level. In its original form, the plan defined this level as being that of an established "parity" price comparable to prewar levels. In compensation for losses the government might incur in selling its surpluses abroad—losses that were quite likely, since the controlled dumping of surpluses into the foreign market would tend to depress further the already low world price—the processors were to pay the government an equalization fee making up the difference between the home price and the world price. Tariffs would protect the farmer against foreign competition. The higher domestic prices would be paid by consumers because of an artificially created scarcity. The plan could only have worked in an expanding world market; in the existing, contracting one it would have forced retaliatory tariff action by foreign governments and would have added to inflation at home and surplus abroad.

Herbert Hoover offered an alternative proposal—cooperative marketing. He wished not only to leave all managerial decision to the farmers, but also to leave price determination to the free market. Yet Hoover wanted farmers to rationalize their production, and to control their marketing in behalf of both higher and more stable prices. For this purpose he advocated government aid for large marketing cooperatives—similar to trade associations in other industries—made up in each case of farmers producing a given commodity. He hoped that a given cooperative could successfully recommend annual production quotas to individual farmers, make marketing agreements with purchasers, rationalize marketing by calculated storage and by better processing, and possibly even expand markets by advertising. In 1929 Congress passed the Agricultural Marketing Act, which authorized a Federal Farm Board to implement it. The Board made loans to cooperatives; it also included two farm stabilization corporations, one for cotton and one for wheat, empowered to purchase commodities in order to stabilize wide shifts in prices. After the collapse of farm prices in 1930-31, the stabilization corporations purchased to the limits of their funds in a vain attempt to hold up wheat and cotton prices. By 1932 they were broke. But as minor price-support programs they set a precedent for supports in the New Deal, and it is hard to say how effectively they would have worked in more prosperous times.

The Democrats

The Democratic Party, badly split between its rural and urban components, went nowhere in the 1920's. At the famous 1924 Convention in New York City delegates voted for 103 ballots before turning down both the New York governor Alfred E. Smith and the ruralists' hero William Gibbs McAdoo, and finally selecting a compromise candidate, the colorless lawyer, John W. Davis. Will Rogers reported frankly on that scene: "Ah! They was Democrats today. They fought, they fit, they spit, and adjourned in a dandy wave of dissension. That's the old Democratic spirit. A whole day wasted and nothing done." Only a third party of progressives led by Senator Robert La Follette gave interest to the 1924 campaign; despite rising farm prices, La Follette won almost twenty percent of the vote, nearly as much as Davis.

Some three years later, at about noon on a showery day in South Dakota, August 2, 1927, thirty or so reporters in attendance on President Calvin Coolidge filed into the mathematics classroom of the Rapid City High School.

Coolidge was already there, and when the door was closed he told the newsmen "the line forms on the left." As they passed by, the slight man from Vermont handed each a slip of paper which read: "I do not choose to run for President in nineteen twenty-eight." The country by and large accepted the statement at face value, and Secretary of Commerce Herbert Hoover came correctly to mind as the likely Republican presidential nominee in 1928.

But the more familiar story of the 1928 campaign concerns not Hoover—who went on to become President—but governor Alfred E. Smith of New York, the unsuccessful Democratic nominee. "Al" Smith, born on New York's lower East Side, was a faithful Roman Catholic, a practicing opponent of prohibition, and a product of New York City's Tammany Hall. In the thinking of many Americans, a more threatening combination could not be imagined. Smith's presence on the ticket sparked the worst bigotry in any recent presidential campaign, especially but not exclusively in the South.

This July 4, 1924, Klan gathering in New Jersey burned an effigy of Governor Al Smith of New York. A Klan wedding and the christening of ten babies were celebrated next.

The South was encouraged to refuse Smith its traditional hospitality when he made a campaign trip there. Newspapers patronizingly reported that at the town of Biltmore, North Carolina, Smith had said to a cheering crowd: "I hope to meet yez-all personally." In his autobiography, Smith wrote that in Louisville a policeman accused him of being drunk, the whole police force was rude, and someone turned the heat too high in the auditorium where he delivered a speech. It appeared that although most of the Southern politicians had accepted Smith at the 1928 Houston convention the majority of voters would not support him.

While it was most pronounced in the South, the denominational attack on Smith was national in scope. A large contingent of ministers, including the popular Billy Sunday, fought Smith by every means available. Sunday called himself the "Ambassador of God" out "to defy the forces of hell—Al Smith and the rest of them." And in Riverside Park, New York, Dr. Ed Bywater delivered his popular sermon "To Hell with the Pope." Dr. Mordecai Ham of the First Baptist Church, the largest in Oklahoma City, made the penalty for voting Democratic clear enough: "If you vote for Al Smith, you're voting against Christ and you'll all be damned."

Such was the denominational opposition to Smith; the nationwide attack it fostered was in most cases the least fair of the campaign, for it was the most difficult to combat. Smith was accused of all the crimes of the Spanish Inquisition and the medieval popes. The fundamentalist *Fellowship Forum* caricatured Smith driving a beer truck bearing the sign "Make America 100 percent Catholic, Drunk, and Illiterate," and another cartoon, showing a buxom woman giving a cup to a reclining priest, bore the caption "The Pope Converted the Vatican into a House of Ill Fame." The flavor of the *Fellowship Forum* is caught in its advertisement for an "eye-opening" ten-cent pamphlet: "Can a Bobbed-Haired Woman Go to Heaven?"

To the America that lay west of the Hudson River, Smith projected the image of a provincial New Yorker. He was public in his Catholicism: he kept an autographed picture of the Pope in his Albany office, publicly he kissed the ring of a visiting Papal prelate, and he received words of political encouragement from the Pope himself by way of his talkative wife, who visited Rome in 1925. Smith, moreover, drank and served liquor during prohibition in the Albany Executive Mansion. When the governor appointed as his presidential campaign manager John J. Raskob, an outspoken antiprohibitionist closely identified with the Catholic church, many Americans assumed that he wished to flaunt what was most controversial about his candidacy. A telegram of acceptance to the nominating convention confirmed this feeling: Smith declared for "fundamental changes" in the provisions of national prohibition.

Religion and prohibition did not stand alone as issues in the campaign. Opponents saw them as but two of a complex of characteristics that marked the New Yorker as a personality alien to the American grain. Smith was not merely a wet; he was a "Bowery wet," and his position toward alcohol, like his faith, affronted not only the most ignorant but also Americans of genteel, middle-class tradition—offended their gentility or their morals. Over the radio, then a new and impressive contribution to presidential campaigns, Smith's voice could be heard only with difficulty, for he spoke indistinctly and insisted on dashing from one side of the microphone to the other. He employed "ain't" and "he don't," and changed "work" to "woik." His language, gestures, and physical appearance, all of which the new motion-picture newsreels conveyed, stamped him as an intruder in national politics. Even the two spittoons in Smith's Albany office seemed to speak loudly of his social origins. His eighth-grade education was insufficient, critics insisted, to equip him to face national and world problems, and Smith himself admitted that he was interested only in the "concrete" and did not read books. On one occasion, he joked with reporters about the needs of the states west of the Mississippi: "What states are west of the Mississippi?" he asked. He did not even hesitate to make a potentially abrasive public demonstration of fellowship with Tammany Hall; because it has lasted a century, he said, it must be "all right."

Herbert Clark Hoover, on the other hand, had none of Smith's disadvantages and a large career already behind him: a Quaker orphan who became a self-made millionaire working on the frontiers of five continents, the supplier of relief to Belgium and later to much of Europe and the Soviet Union. During the twenties Hoover had converted his Commerce Department into an instrument for a free-flowing international trade intended to replace the relationships of force and war; into a center of communication among manufacturers; and an ideological representative of industrial self-regulation and voluntary cooperation among businesses. Hoover was the Great Engineer and the Great Humanitarian. In an era of prosperity the nominee of the party in power would undoubtedly win by a wide margin—and he did.

With his rural background and success as a technologist, Hoover was an acceptable progressive candidate. People expected much of him: "He sweeps the horizon of every subject. Nothing escapes his view," a delegate had observed. But Hoover worried about "the exaggerated idea the people have conceived of me. . . . If some unprecedented calamity should come upon the nation, I would be sacrificed. . . ."

Hoover and the Great Depression

For many years before Herbert Hoover became President, he had been warning against the "crazy and dangerous" stock market, while President Calvin Coolidge told press conferences that stocks were underpriced. But as Hoover feared there was a great deal wrong with the American economy. While it resisted inflationary temptations and increased the real income of all classes, a larger proportion of the new wealth went into the hands of the very rich. This brought trouble when the stock market average ended its dazzling ascent and slumped downward. Once the market crashed, the array of consumer goods, no longer in demand for the average household, quickly piled up in warehouses and factories, bringing a halt in production.

What is striking about the Great Depression—which lasted until the second World War—is that we still are not precisely sure of its origins. Was it a crises in confidence as Hoover grimly assumed and as a modern school of economists argues? Was the weak banking system, another culprit singled out by Hoover, largely to blame? Did an inadequate supply of money in circulation cause the Depression? Or as John Kenneth Galbraith suggests in his witty account *The Great Crash* —a book rarely to be found in airport terminals—was the market crash itself the primary cause? In the four years from 1929 to 1933, Montgomery Ward fell from a high of 138 to 4; one mutual fund, United Founders, dropped from well over a hundred dollars a share to fifty cents. Many economists thought the Depression would end only after prices sank low enough and unemployment rose high enough; then businessmen would restart their plants. Deficit government spending—now a favored weapon—was feared because it would compete with entrepreneurs for available capital. A lot of the blame for the Depression falls on the economics establishment; the discipline was simply too ignorant to advise business or the administration on what course to take.

At first the stock market fell rather gradually. After serious collapses in late October 1929, the market staged a recovery, particularly early in 1930. Not until mid-1930 did prices fall steadily, week by week, until they sank to a low point in 1933. Employment began to drift lower in 1930 and reached serious proportions in the winter of 1930-31; by 1933 almost one-quarter of the labor force was without work.

Herbert Hoover had predicted the depression; he instructed his own brokers to liquidate his common stock portfolio in May 1929 "as possible hard times coming." He tried various measures to prevent collapse. For instance, he wrote a statement that his reluctant Secretary of the Treasury, Andrew Mellon, released, saying bonds were undervalued. But the new President feared taking

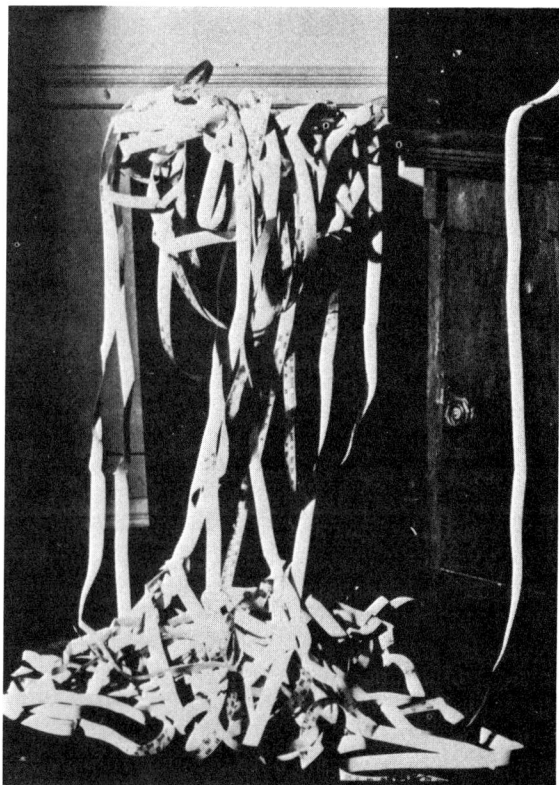

Ticker-Tape.

responsibility for pricking the bubble of speculation that would bring an end to the "New Era" of Coolidge and Harding. When the crash came, he said: "the only trouble with capitalism is capitalists—they're too damned greedy." The popular mind blamed Hoover; one refrain ran:

Mellon pulled the whistle,
Hoover rang the bell,
Wall Street gave the signal,
And the country went to hell.

Hoover was more willing and quicker than most politicians, including the Democratic Congress that met in 1931, to use the government to cushion the fall. Right after the crash he successfully urged the maintenance of high wages. He increased spending for public works at all levels of government. Above all, he concentrated on reviving the stagnant economy as a whole rather than dealing directly with unemployment, unprofitable low prices, or agricultural overproduction. Within the limits of economic solutions then entertained by leading economists Hoover moved quickly; but he refused to step outside these boundaries. And as chief executive at the outset of the Great Depression, Hoover could hardly present himself as the solution to it. This shy President, who knew the importance of confidence, could not bring himself to manufacture it. Hoover's opposition to direct federal relief programs furnishes our worst memory of him. He accused progressive senators of "playing politics at the expense of human misery" by recommending expensive relief programs, and he hinted darkly at the evils of the public dole as practiced in Great Britain. In fact, it was some of the best things in Hoover's past that stood in his way. His relief projects in the era of World War I had trained him to believe that people voluntarily contribute their money and time, that the most enormous problems of logistics and supply could be solved by a combination of good will and expert knowledge. He feared hordes of government subsidy seekers, who would indeed crawl out of the woodwork during the New Deal. He believed that more fortunate Americans would come to their neighbors' aid.

Hoover set up government agencies to encourage and coordinate private and local relief efforts. But his main anti-Depression measures were the Agricultural Marketing Act and the Reconstruction Finance Corporation. The agricultural legislation, passed in 1929, was not intended for relief. It was designed to aid farmers by encouraging cooperative marketing. It lent from a government revolving fund for purposes designated by agriculture's own representatives. Once the Depression began, the fund was used to stabilize the market, and it had the helpful effect of slowing the descent of farm prices. It was, in effect a relief agency.

The Reconstruction Finance Corporation was a grander vision adopted late in 1931 after a similar non-governmental scheme had failed. Patterned after the War Finance Corporation that made loans to industries during World War II, the RFC could loan up to $2 billion to banks and other agencies. Hoover overcame his fear of the duplication, slowness, and wastefulness of bureaucracy out of anxiety to give it full power to accomplish its objectives. He worried that business interests would wish to manipulate it. Confirming the President's worst fears, the RFC continued its existence for two decades. It was one of the government's most effective anti-depression weapons. Under Hoover, in 1932, it began to loan substantial sums to the states for relief.

Hoover had no hope of winning a second term in the Presidency. Yet he was by no means the grumbling reactionary that New Dealers portrayed. Depression had forced him to abandon a host of reforms that he planned to pass into law. One radical piece of legislation that he did achieve was a steeply graduated income tax. While many of Hoover's programs—such as the RFC—anticipated the New Deal, Roosevelt did far more than simply flesh out Hoover's plans. Mainly Hoover cleared ground for the New Deal by giving private enterprise a chance to cure the Depression, ultimately demonstrating that it was timid and unwilling. By 1932 the election of a Democrat was a foregone conclusion. In less than four years the mood of the country had changed completely. The song "Brother Can You Spare a Dime?" replaced "My God, How the Money Rolls in!"

The new governor of New York, Franklin D. Roosevelt, had beaten out his predecessor, Al Smith, for the Democratic nomination in 1932. The Brooklyn boss James McCooey said that Roosevelt could go to Europe for the campaign and still win. Instead, to demonstrate his vitality, he delivered sixty speeches on a national tour by railroad. His talks, vague in substance and dynamic in delivery, were well received by Depression audiences. One telegram to Hoover at the end of the campaign captured the voters' sentiment: "Vote for Roosevelt and make it unanimous." As the popular historian Elizabeth Stevenson put it: Hoover's "reputation was murdered publicly, noisily, and painfully—as a thing once loved." He received only 41 percent of the vote.

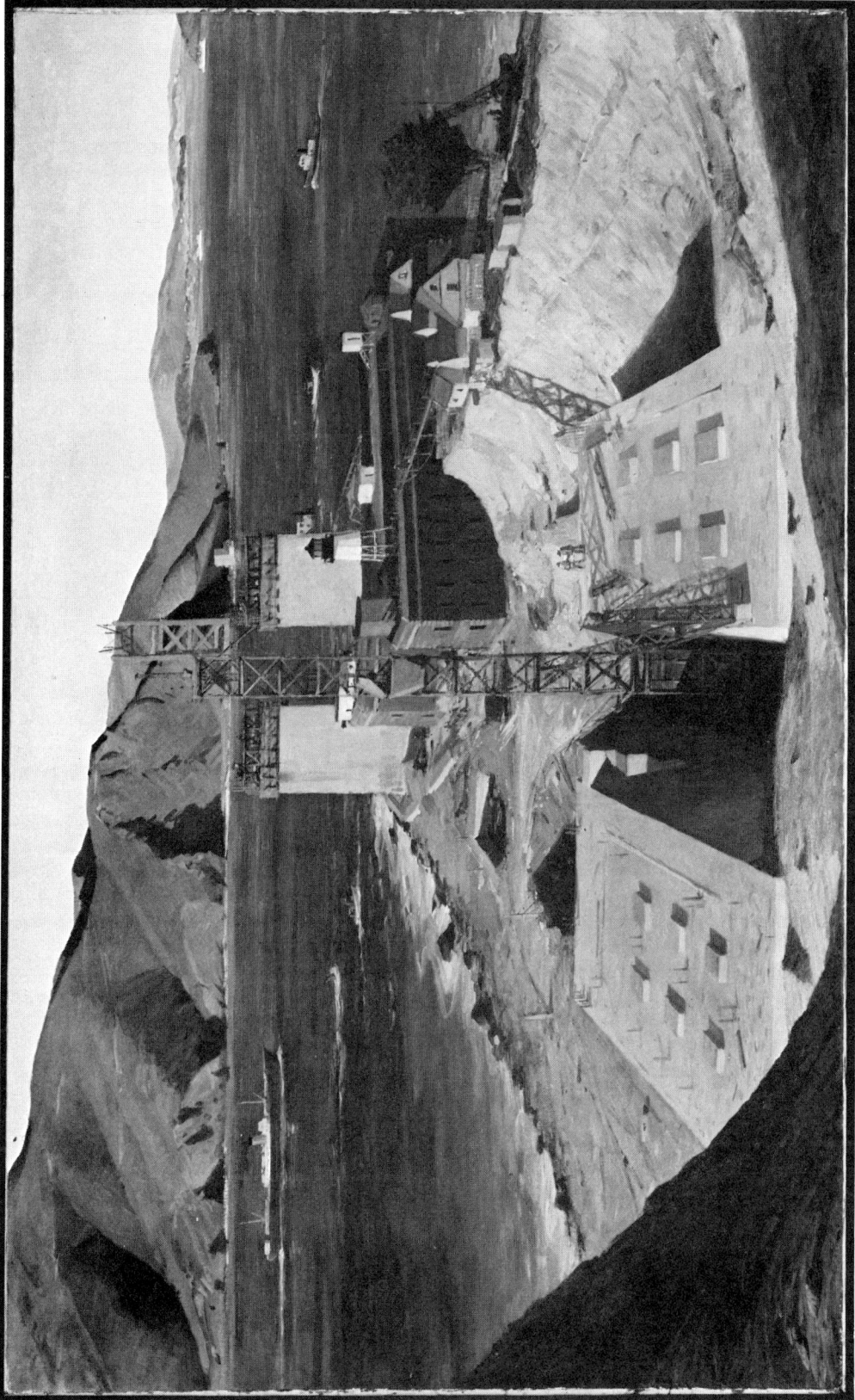

The Golden Gate Bridge, its construction authorized under Hoover, was completed during the New Deal. This photograph was taken in 1934. (Smithsonian Institution.)

Although *Time* labeled Hoover, "President Reject," he would have to labor under the burden of the depression presidency more than four months longer. His attempts to secure Roosevelt's cooperation in formulating anti-depression policies failed, partly because of FDR's evasiveness and partly because of his own dogmatism. By March 4 the country's banking system was in total collapse. One quatrain caught the nation's contempt for the outgoing President:

O 'Erbert lived over the h'ocean
O 'Erbert lived over the sea;
O 'Oo will go down to the h'ocean,
An drown 'Erbert 'Oover for me?

Suggested Readings

Gabriel Kolko, in *The Triumph of Conservatism . . . 1900-1916*, argues that much of the support for regulation of business came from big business itself, which wished for a safe and orderly existence under government regulation in place of the discomforts of uncontrolled competition. Good, straightforward political studies include George E. Mowry, *The Era of Theodore Roosevelt, 1900-1912* (1958) and Arthur S. Link, *Woodrow Wilson and the Progressive Era, 1900-1917* (1954). Stephen Thernstrom pursues *The Other Bostonians: Poverty and Progress in the American Metropolis, 1860-1970* (1973); see also Tamara K. Hareven and Randolph Langenbach, *Amoskeag: Life and Work in an American Factory-City* (1978). David Burner has written two books on the politics on the 1920's: *The Politics of Provincialism: The Democratic Party in Transition, 1918-1932* (1968) and *Herbert Hoover: A Public Life* (1979). The best general survey of the decade is still William E. Leuchtenburg, *The Perils of Prosperity, 1914-1932* (1958).

Charles A. Lindbergh (Library of Congress)

Chapter XXII
The United States and The World
1900 — 1933

Lindbergh's Trans-Atlantic Flight

At almost 8 a.m. on May 20, 1927, after a sleepless night, Charles A. Lindbergh, carrying five sandwiches, climbed into the cockpit of his small plane, which was loaded with as many extra containers of gasoline as it could carry. He left his parachute on the ground to conserve twenty pounds of fuel. The engine seemed sluggish as he slowly maneuvered down the muddy Roosevelt Field runway, and his wheels left the gound dangerously late. He managed to clear a steamroller at the end of the field and then missed some telephone wires by less than twenty feet. As he crossed Long Island Sound and Connecticut, Lindbergh's speed reached only 100 miles an hour. As the plane chased the horizon, it used more and more fuel, easing the strain on the engine and the trembling wings. It was when he left Massachusetts and headed toward Nova Scotia that Lindbergh first sensed the danger of his unique solo flight—he had never before passed over a large body of water. Below him lay the awesome span of the Atlantic. His single propeller droned on.

Suddenly, over the rugged countryside of Cape Breton Island, the weather turned bad. Cross winds, driving rain, and turbulence buffeted the tiny craft; the primitive weather forecasts had suggested nothing of this. But just as unpredictably the sky cleared, and he dipped his wings over St. John's, Newfoundland, before heading out over two thousand miles of rugged ocean. Night came on swiftly, and now Lindbergh had to fly with a compass and an altimeter, but no lights, no flares, no means of contacting human beings. There was nothing to do but fly. Fog decended along with wintry gusts, and he climbed to 10,000 feet. He became sharply aware of the cold. Using a flashlight, he saw ice forming on the wings and knew he was in an ice cloud. In his autobiography Lindbergh wrote: "They enmesh intruders. They are barbaric. . . . They toss you in inner turbulence, lash you with hailstones, poison you with freezing mist. It would be a slow death, a death one would have long minutes to struggle against . . . climbing, stalling, driving, whipping, always downward toward the sea." Fortunately, he soon emerged into clear air under a dome lighted by stars. Now he need only fight off sleep, having tossed restlessly the night before. He passed the midway point.

For diversion he drank some water that came with the sandwiches picked up at an all-night diner in Queens. The weather warmed as he met the Gulf Stream. The sun rose. He became more alert. Dense fog banks descended, then evaporated. Twenty-six hours after leaving Long Island, the young flyer sighted a land bird and knew he was approaching Ireland. He swooped down over a fishing boat, asked for directions, but received no response from the astonished crew. At last, there it was: a rocky shore and green fields. But the aviator flew on—over England, over the Channel, over France—until he saw the lights of the Eiffel Tower dead ahead. Lindbergh circled it to mark his victory and, 33½ hours after takeoff, set down at Le Bourget Field, where a mob engulfed his plane even before the propeller stopped. After a night's sleep he called his mother four thousand miles away to confirm his safe arrival.

Greeted at home by massive ticker-tape parades, he was America's last hero. "He has," orated Charles Evans Hughes at a dinner for Lindbergh in New York, "displaced everything that is petty, that is sordid, that is vulgar." "Lucky" Lindy had shown a decade that it was not rotten to the core, that it could put ethics and achievement above wealth, that modesty and courage were really the great virtues after all.

To "Slim" Lindbergh—barely more than a boy fresh from Wisconsin—air travel was almost a religion. He liked being up in the sky alone, and he seemed unacquainted with fear. Lindbergh admired other pilots who had made names for themselves, but his vision looked beyond personal fame; he saw and took delight in a future of extensive air travel. He made a natural hero, a shy individualist with a winning, modest smile—and always averse to publicity and ballyhoo. Yet Lindbergh entitled his story of flying solo across the Atlantic *We*—the aeronautical "we," the flying pronoun—for his achievement depended on a machine, his airplane *The Spirit of St. Louis*. Lindbergh symbolized an innocent, prewar era, but at the same time became an acceptable emblem of change, married to the new technology that was making over America.

Theodore Roosevelt's World Vistas

Despite his reputation for bombast, Theodore Roosevelt was a sophisticated diplomat. He pursued American interests overseas with a combination of guile and deft skill that he encapsulated in his motto, "Walk softly and carry a big stick." Only one nation, Great Britain, could impress American leaders with superior power, and Roosevelt neither provoked the British nor took advantage of their growing preoccupations with Germany.

Friendship with England freed Roosevelt for daring adventures in areas where strategic security and local weakness promised large gains with little risk. Gradually Roosevelt and the country took on a world-wide role. American influence ranged from the Far East to the Balkans; the American fleet sailed all seven seas; American merchants roamed both hemispheres.

Asia

The Philippine Islands symbolized American imperialism. William Howard Taft, the local governor-general, and his staff bought farm land from Catholic friars and redistributed it in small plots to pro-American peasants. Western schools propagandized a generation of natives. Special tariff arrangements for sugar tied the islands to mainland markets. Secular administrators discouraged both the Catholic faith of the Spanish conquistadors and the native Muslim beliefs. After a long tutelage (Roosevelt spoke once of "a century or so"), Filipinos might learn enough to rule themselves once again. Opposition to Yankee imperialism crystallized around an insurrection of mountain peoples. Roosevelt called their leader, Emilio Aguinaldo, a "Chinese halfbreed," and proclaimed that the United States must "uplift the islands or watch them sink back into barbarism." Six thousand American soldiers fought for three years, finally crushing the Filipino rebellion in 1902. The Philippine Islands taught another imperialist lesson: colonies beget troubles with other imperial powers.

Japan, aiming at dominion over East Asia, was slowly increasing its presence in the strategic, mineral rich region of Manchuria. China countered by permitting the Russian tsar to station troops in northern Manchuria. The rituals of diplomacy soon broke down into an imperialist war between Japan and Russia for control of the province. In 1904 Japanese sailors destroyed Russia's Far Eastern squadron during a surprise attack; six months later a skilled Japanese attack pushed Russian troops out of Manchuria. Then Russia's Baltic Fleet, hastily sent into the war by a desperate government in St. Petersburg, was annihilated by Admiral Togo. The Japanese, though everywhere victorious, kept secret the near-bankruptcy to which war had brought their fragile economy. In Washington, meanwhile, President Roosevelt worried that a jubilant Japan, unchecked by Russian power, might close the open door in China and threaten America's tenuous colonial empire in the Western Pacific. So he offered to mediate. Both belligerents eagerly accepted, perhaps hoping to gain more by talk than by renewed struggle.

Roosevelt cajoled the two enemies into a peace. According to the terms of the Treaty of Portsmouth, signed in that New Hampshire town on September 5, 1905, the tsar granted Japan a "paramount interest" in Southern Manchuria and Korea. Russia avoided the humiliation of an indemnity and ceded only half of Sakhalin Island, not all of it as leaders in Tokyo had wanted. Still, Japan's new protectorates upset the balance of power in East Asia. Three times Roosevelt's intermediaries reached executive understandings aimed at easing his country's rivalry with the Japanese. The Taft-Katsure Agreement of 1905 recognized Japan's power in Korea; in return, Japan foreswore "all aggressive designs whatever" on American colonies in the Pacific. In the so-called Gentlemen's Agreement of 1907-08, Japan voluntarily limited the emigration of her laborers to the American West Coast. But California continued its anti-Japanese policies, soon limiting their right to own or lease farm land. In 1908 the Root-Takahira Agreement pledged both countries to respect the Open Door in China. Roosevelt realized that words could not always restrain the obstreperous Japanese, now a first-class world power. For imperialist powers, colonies invited danger as they reflected supposed glory.

Europe

A sense of the fragility of world peace prompted Roosevelt to meddle in Europe's affairs. Arguments over colonies had brought Europe's major powers to the edge of war, but never as dangerously as during the Moroccan crisis of 1904-05. French and British leaders had already worked out an entente that eventually ripened into alliance. They settled disputes over African territory by awarding protectorates to each other, an English hegemony in Egypt, a French hegemony in Morocco. Both these colonial pretensions and the budding alliance angered Germans, resentful of nations that stood in the way of German ambitions at rightful world power. Kaiser Wilhelm flamboyantly called for an open door in Morocco, while his government demanded that France oust its foreign minister, Theophile Delcasse, the author of entente. Leaders in Paris bridled over such heavyhanded intervention in domestic affairs, but the Germans hinted that any delay might bring war. Roosevelt skillfully maneuvered the angry parties into a conference at Algeciras, a resort city in Southern Spain. American delegates urged their English and French counterparts "to stand up to the Germans." Roosevelt meanwhile played to the Kaiser with long telegrams praising his "masterly politics." Once the conference formally opened, Wilhelm followed Roosevelt's lead. The President brought about an agreement that assured French control in Morocco, but managed still to convince the Germans that they had achieved "epochmaking success."

Most Americans probably did not realize the closeness of war or the extent of their President's involvement in the Algeciras meeting. Roosevelt had contributed in a major way to European peace, which, he privately wrote, "was essential to American security and prosperity." For his peacemaking efforts in both Europe and Asia, the Nobel Committee awarded Roosevelt its Peace Prize for 1906.

The Caribbean

However much Roosevelt pursued a balance of power in Asia and Europe, closer home he worked for an American empire centered in the Caribbean Sea. Pursuit of this goal in Cuba and Puerto Rico had already angered Latin Americans. Elsewhere he would accomplish high-handed interventions that were to alienate our hemispheric neighbors for a generation.

A delicate problem in international finance roused Roosevelt to further assertiveness. Unscrupulous bondbrokers had persuaded many governments in Latin America to issue bonds whose proceeds too often financed lavish living for politicians rather than economic development for their countries. Gullible buyers of Europe snapped up the dubious issues because they promised a high rate of return. When the inevitable defaults occurred, European governments supported bondholders who clamored for restitution. More than once, Roosevelt acted to restrain European nations from military enterprises in the western hemisphere.

During the Venezuela affair of 1902-03, France, Britain, and Germany blockaded the country, demanding immediate, full payment for a defunct bond issue. Worried that the next step might be occupation, Roosevelt spoke strongly to Germany, whose leaders had talked of a "temporary possession" of territory. The President forced an arbitrated settlement. The tribunal appointed to hear the case ordered Venezuela to pay all its debtors, beginning with those from countries that had manned the blockade.

The idea of a canal across the narrow neck of Central America had long intrigued traders with China. Then the acquisition of empire in the Pacific and renewed troubles in Europe convinced military men of a need to shift the United States's fleet rapidly from ocean to ocean. The fashion of imperialism, too, sharpened American appetites during these years when white nations imposed Western cultures on peoples overseas and profited from them. Roosevelt worked doggedly for an American-owned canal. The second Hay-Pauncefote Treaty, signed with England in 1902, cleared the diplomatic path: the Senate had rejected an earlier version which did not allow the United States to arm the area.

Next Roosevelt selected a route. Engineers thought the marshy, flat plains of Nicaragua more tricky to trench than the rocky passage over the Isthmus of Panama, then part of Colombia. A

President Roosevelt Running an American Steam-Shovel at Culebra Cut, Panama Canal. (Library of Congress.)

French company had already spent some $400 million on a Panama canal; its corporate successor, the New Panama Canal Company, promised to sell its assets for $40 million. So the United States negotiated a treaty with Colombia promising a payment of $10 million, and annual rental of $250,000 for a ninety-nine year lease on a zone across its Panamanian province. But the Colombian legislature stalled, perhaps anticipating legal maneuvers to confiscate the French company's $40 million in assets. Roosevelt exploded. "These contemptible little creatures in Bogota," he wrote Secretary of State John Hay, "ought to understand how much they are imperiling their own future." Hay agreed, calling the Colombians "greedy little anthropoids."

Two agents for the New Panama Canal Company, most local citizens in the province, and America's President proceeded to manufacture a revolution. On November 2, 1903, the U.S.S. *Nashville* arrived at Colon. The next day, Colombian troops entered the port city, but railway officials there refused to transport them farther. Street protests and blunt words from the *Nashville's* commander persuaded the Colombians to withdraw. That night, revolutionary mobs roamed the streets, and local police joined them. The canal company's principal agent, Philippe Bunau-Varilla, negotiated for Panama, now independent. Just two weeks after the United States hastily recognized the new regime, Panama handed over a strip of land ten miles wide for the same $10 million fee and $250,000 yearly rental offered Colombia and became, in essence, an American protectorate. Latin Americans everywhere protested. At home anti-imperialists brewed a storm of criticism. Perhaps chastened, Roosevelt asked his attorney-general to draw up a legal draft defending his actions. Philander Knox replied, "No, Mr. President, if I were you I would not have any taint of legality about it."

Soon afterwards, Roosevelt defined a specific role for his nation. "The United States can not see any European power occupy the territory of the Latin American republic," he told Congress in early 1904, "not even if that is the only way to collect its debts." The United States would act in place of European nations on behalf of their legitimate interests, taking to itself an "international police power" to discipline "flagrant wrongdoing in the western hemisphere." The policy is known as the Roosevelt Corollary to the Monroe Doctrine. That famous Doctrine had warned Europe against expansion into the western hemisphere; Roosevelt was now indicating that the United States, by protecting the just claims of European countries, would make up for excluding them from a military presence in the hemisphere.

Roosevelt's announcement was specifically in reference to a dangerous situation in the Dominican Republic. Some Americans and Englishmen had seized local customs houses there after the government had negotiated a repayment scheme favoring French, Belgian, and Italian bondholders. Roosevelt ordered the marines into the capital of Santo Domingo, where they imposed a peace of sorts upon the feuding business community. The United States then negotiated a treaty with the local regime that handed control over customs to an American, a retired colonel who divied up tariff receipts among the little nation's creditors. Grumblings from native revolutionaries prompted Roosevelt to use the United States Navy "to keep the island in the status quo." Although financial solvency slowly returned under American administration, nationalists in the Dominican Republic plotted against the intruders. One such attempt brought American occupation of the island, from 1916 to 1924. The Roosevelt Corollary, designed to prevent European encroachment, had led to an American one instead.

Imperialism in Latin America, 1909-1917

Roosevelt set a course in foreign policy that his successors navigated for almost a decade. Japan and European powers had established their own spheres of influence in East Asia; Presidents Taft and Wilson confined themselves for the most part to territory closer to home. Neither man looked much beyond the Caribbean, which soon came completely under the domination of their country. The economic influence of the United States pervaded Cuba and Central America, where the United Fruit Company wielded more power than most governments. Critics derided "dollar diplomacy," the employment of State and Commerce Department officials for the promotion of private business. William Howard Taft once said, "I hope to substitute dollars for bullets." Yet United States marines marched through Nicaragua, Haiti, the Dominican Republic, and Mexico. Woodrow Wilson saw nothing wrong with this. "I'll teach them to elect good men," he bragged.

Humanitarians hoped to reform corrupt, poor countries, while strategists readily appreciated the need for stability in a region vital to American security.

The dictator of Nicaragua threatened during 1909 to cancel a valuable mining lease held by an American company and to permit the Japanese to build a canal across his country. Fearing both economic loss and naval threat, Taft seized upon a pretext to destroy the regime. When two Americans caught dynamiting ships in the San Juan River during a street revolution were executed, Taft broke diplomatic relations and financed a makeshift government dominated by the United States. New York City bankers regulated the country's finances. A mining company employee asked Taft in 1912 to send a "legation guard" of 2,700 marines to "keep order." The troops stayed for more than two decades. A treaty signed in 1916 granted the United States an exclusive right both to build any canal and to lease naval bases on Nicaragua's Atlantic and Pacific coasts.

Woodrow Wilson carried the game just short of annexation in Haiti. Perennial misgovernment there had declined into near chaos by 1915. In less than four years, seven presidents—some of them eventually either blown up or poisoned—had looted the public treasury. Revolution had become almost permanent. President Vilbrum Sam, who defaulted in early 1915 on some $24 million in debts owed to Americans and western Europeans, launched a vendetta against his opponents, killing 167 of them. Outraged townspeople in Port-au-Prince killed and dismembered Sam. Wilson ordered in the marines. Several thousand of them occupied the capital. Wilson's cabinet officers teased Secretary of the Navy Josephus Daniels during their meetings, "Hail, the King of Haiti!" Daniels' young assistant, Franklin D. Roosevelt, wrote a new constitution for Haiti, and said later that he had "looked after a couple little republics that our Navy is running." An American general dragooned thousands of natives into road building schemes. New York City bankers, now familiar with the techniques of financial control, once again traveled to the Caribbean. A hastily elected local government signed a treaty that gave control of foreign policy to the United States. Some Haitians revolted; marines crushed them. Haiti remained a virtual protectorate for almost twenty years.

A dictator, Porfirio Diaz, had ruled Mexico since 1876. Though Roosevelt's secretary of state, Elihu Root, rhapsodized that Diaz was a "great man to be held up for the hero worship of mankind," Mexicans rejected the advice. Nationalists objected to economic concessions that had given away oil and mining rights to British and American companies. A collection of middle class reformers, socialists, Indian nationalists, adventurers, and radical Catholics played skillfully upon Mexico's discontents, calling for land reform, national ownership of raw materials, and racial equality. Diaz retired and confusion followed. Power drifted into the hands of Francisco I. Madero, a gentle, indecisive, eccentric man unable to give direction to an emerging revolution. Demanding immediate redistribution of land, regional leaders like Emilio Zapata and Pancho Villa assembled armies south and north of the capital. Worried by this growing threat to their economic interests, foreign companies and the domestic Catholic hierarchy appealed for help to the American ambassador. He hinted of Madero's ineptness, and the country's ambitious military chief, Victoriano Huerta, understood. He organized a palace revolt, took control of the regional armies, and installed himself as lifetime president of Mexico. His agents murdered Madero and imposed a military dictatorship over most of the country.

Huerta's brutal rise occurred just before Woodrow Wilson took office on March 4, 1913. "I will not," the new chief executive said, "recognize a government of butchers." He refused to talk with Huerta's diplomats, arguing that from now on the United States would deal only with "republican governments based upon law, not irregular force." This novel policy, which judged a nation's morality, departed dramatically from past recognition procedures. These required only that a regime be in control of its territory. Wilson hoped to isolate Huerta, and persuaded the British to follow his lead. Instead, a diplomatic standoff ensued. Words could scarcely hurt Huerta, who used Yankeephobia to prop up his faltering regime.

Barely a month after Wilson assumed office, Mexican authorities arrested a group of American sailors in Tampico. The arrests were legitimate, for the men had drifted into a restricted area by mistake. But their commander, Admiral Henry T. Mayo, demanded an apology and a twenty-one gun salute to the American flag. Nine days later, Wilson delivered an ultimatum: salute the flag or face the consequences. Huerta, whose government was built on anti-Americanism, refused. So the President ordered marines to occupy Mexico's chief gulf port, Veracruz, on April 21. (As a pretext, he claimed that a German freighter carrying arms for Huerta was about to dock in the city.) Street fighting produced a large number of casualties, sixty American and over 500 Mexican. Many people in the United States, unaware that relations with their neighbor had so deteriorated, were stunned. The marines remained in Veracruz for six months.

The Tampico incident and occupation of Veracruz humiliated Huerta, disgracing him in the eyes of most nationalists and preventing any foreign help for his regime. His power disintegrated. Venustiano Carranza, who had gathered an army outside Mexico City, easily occupied the capital. Like Madero, Carranza was a middle-class reformer buffeted by the winds of revolution; like Huerta, he was a vigilante, not a legitimate ruler. So the chaos in Mexico and the deadlock with the American President continued. Then Pancho Villa, a restless adventurer from the far north, raised a rebellion against his former friend. The *villistas* added an anti-clerical element to the revolutionary brew of economic reform and extended the scope of violence. On January 11, 1916, Villa attacked a train at Santa Ysabel and slaughtered sixteen American citizens; two months later he raided the New Mexico town of Columbus, burning it to the ground and killing seventeen more Americans. He calculated that an armed intervention by the United States would destroy Carranza just as it had Huerta. Reacting as Villa had hoped, Wilson ordered General John J. Pershing across the border with 6,600 men in pursuit of the guerrilla bandit. The *villistas* eluded the army, so Wilson next called out 150,000 national guard troops to seal off the entire southwestern border. Time passed. Pershing rushed fruitlessly around Mexico's northern provinces; Carranza held on in Mexico City. Early in 1917, at the approach of war with Germany, Wilson quietly withdrew federal forces from Mexico, granted Carranza full recognition, and abandoned his efforts to instruct a nation in democracy. Preoccupied with their revolution, Mexicans withdrew into a sullen hostility toward the United States. Thus ended that interlude of imperialist good intentions. The cloak of empire fit awkwardly, too awkwardly some thought, upon American shoulders.

Neutrality 1914-1917

However tempting or vexatious for the United States, the lands around the rim of the Caribbean Sea always were less important than the international balance of power in Europe and Asia. (Indeed, the existence of just such a balance had made possible America's expansion in the early years of the twentieth century.) Intellectuals and military people, including Wilson, thought their country perfectly protected from the outbreak of war in Europe in 1914 by those "great watery moats" of the Atlantic and Pacific. No power on earth could sustain a full-scale attack across thousands of miles of water. Though strategically secure, Americans worried when trench warfare stalemated in northern France.

German predominance over continental Europe might harm American economic interests and be the basis for an attempt later at world dominion. An Anglo-French victory, on the other hand, might freeze Americans out of vast markets in their growing empires.

The American public preferred neutrality. "Our people," Wilson later said, "did not see the full meaning of the war. It looked like a natural raking out of Europe's pent-up jealousies." Orders for war goods stimulated an American economic boom. Why, then, did the United States change from a determined neutral in 1914 to a belligerent in 1917? The answer lies in considerable part in the way that the Germans had to fight the war.

Both the Central Powers—Germany, Austria-Hungary, Bulgaria, and Turkey—and the Entente or Allied nations—Britain, France, Russia until its revolution, and Italy—had planned for a quick, decisive war. Indeed, the need to keep armies mobilized one step ahead of potential enemies had accelerated after the murder of the Archduke Franz Ferdinand of Austria on June 28, 1914, into a general war by early August. A huge German army plunged through Belgium and into northern France, trying to outflank French troops and capture Paris from behind. Rather than holding fast on the Rhineland border, French generals moved their units westward. As each army tried to get beyond the other, a virtual race to the North Sea resulted. Thereafter, both sides settled into trench warfare, a tactic particularly favorable to the defense. The war stalemated: battles became a bloody attrition. On the huge plains of eastern Europe, armies found more room for maneuver, but here, too, the armies became locked together. Poorly-trained Russian troops moved ponderously against smaller but better-equipped German and Austrian armies. Neither side was gaining a victory, though the Kaiser's troops slowly advanced.

Stalemate and tactics of attrition forced each side to deny its enemy access to the products of American industry and agriculture. International law at the time sharply limited the circumstances in which a belligerent could prevent ships of neutral countries from carrying goods to the enemy. The belligerent power could legally do so only in a region of the sea in which it had established an effective blockade. The rule forbade "paper blockades," random declarations covering wide areas with no prospect of systematic enforcement and carried out only by occasional seizures of neutral merchant vessels. Even in the case of an effective blockade the belligerent had to obey the principle "free ships make free goods," the principle that a neutral ship could take to a warring country whatever goods were not of direct military use. The crew of a warship of the nation imposing the blockade could board a neutral ship. If it found armaments—which were legitimately "contraband," forbidden—it could seize or sink the merchant vessel. Otherwise it must allow the ship and cargo to proceed. Against the merchant ships of any enemy nation, of course, international law allowed a belligerent a wider liberty to act. But there, too, there was a restriction: before sinking the merchant vessel, the warship must give warning and must take on board the crew and passengers. The conditions of the world war made these rules obsolete.

Britain declared the entire North Sea a military region and mined its waters. The captains of neutral ships had to stop for sailing directions at Dover, where British officials found pretexts to keep them there: the usual device was a greatly expanded notion of what constituted "contraband." Germany retaliated by declaring its own war zone in the North Sea where its submarines or U-boats, would attack any vessel. The British thereupon armed their merchant marine and prepared it to fight. Thereby they trapped the Germans in a cruel dilemma. The fragile submarines, so small they carried a crew of only a few men, could not obey the rule that a warship must give warning to the merchant vessel and must take on its passengers: steel merchant ships could easily ram the U-boats, which in any case were not large enough to carry many passengers. Successful use of the submarine required breaking principles adopted before they had existed; otherwise the Germans would have to allow the Allies a commerce that could provide for a German defeat.

Early in 1915, when the Kaiser prepared for unrestricted submarine warfare in the North Sea,

Wilson responded with a warning, holding the Germans "strictly accountable" for the property and lives of any American citizens lost as a result. Then, on May 7, 1915, came news that a German U-boat had sunk the famous *Lusitania,* grandest ship of Britain's Cunard Lines. (A torpedo set off secondary explosions in the ship's hold, where a large amount of munitions were stored. This, not the torpedo itself, caused the vessel to sink rapidly.) Twelve hundred people drowned, 128 of them American citizens. The act outraged Americans. Protestant evangelist Billy Sunday condemned the sinking as "damnable, absolutely hellish." Some newspapers called for war. A wave of anti-German hysteria, the first of several, victimized innocent Germans living in America. Wilson protested vigorously, so vigorously that Secretary of State William Jennings Bryan, a pacifist, resigned. The Kaiser backed down, ordering his U-boat captains not to attack passenger liners in the future. Still, damage to German prestige was immense. "The torpedo which sank the *Lusitania,*" *Nation* magazine editorialized, "also sank Germany in the opinion of mankind."

The year 1916 tested American neutrality even more. Stalemated land war prompted leaders in Berlin to expand the ocean war. About fifty U-boats swarmed into the North Sea, attacking naval patrols and armed merchant ships. On March 24, 1916, an over-eager German commander torpedoed an unarmed French channel ferry, the *Sussex.* Wilson reacted with a virtual ultimatum: the United States would break diplomatic relations if Germany ever again attacked civilian ships. Though furious at Germany, Wilson was also angry with Britain. During the summer of 1916, the British Cabinet issued a blacklist of neutral firms that had traded with the Central Powers. The British announced that they would confiscate whatever goods of such firms their ships could seize. It was a blatant violation of rights. Wilson wrote to his close advisor, Colonel Edward M. House, "This blacklist business is the last straw!" The British army had already crushed a rebellion in Ireland, and many Irish-Americans were angry. Peeved with both sides and anxious about the presidential election in the fall, Wilson took up peacemaking. House traveled several times to Europe, where he hinted that if one side refused an armistice, the United States would join forces with its enemy. Both sides thereupon presented peace proposals, but they were so far apart that reconciliation was impossible. The mediation effort did sustain Wilson as "the peace candidate" during his narrow win over Republican Charles Evans Hughes. (The Democrats had used the slogan: "He kept us out of war!") But peace remained as elusive as ever; neutral rights withered more and more.

Then the German High Command decided once again that unrestricted U-boat warfare might wrest a final victory. Its war of attrition against Russia had brought the weak tsarist regime to the point of collapse. Seemingly endless carnage in the western trenches had demoralized outnumbered French troops. If Britain could be isolated, even for a short time, its allies might succumb to one last offensive. German generals realized the risk of a violent reaction from the Americans, but they calculated that their armies could end the war before the United States could rescue the Allies.

The Imperial Government announced that unrestricted submarine warfare would resume on February 1, 1917; two days later, Wilson severed diplomatic relations. A determined antiwar group in Congress blocked the President's call for arming merchant ships, but by late February a rush of events compelled most of them to accept the inevitable. German submarines sank a Cunard liner, the *Laconia,* and torpedoed three American freighters, killing several Americans. Soon after, British intelligence officers made public a startling secret. Germany's foreign minister, Arthur Zimmermann, had promised the Mexicans a chance "to reconquer lost territory in New Mexico, Texas and Arizona," if they declared war on the United States. A stunned, angry American public now eagerly followed where Wilson led. On April 2, 1917, the President asked Congress for a declaration of war. The resolution passed four days later. "The Yanks are coming!" newspapers headlined. But would they arrive in time?

The Arsenal of Democracy

Despite the years of fighting in Europe, the United States was not ready for war in 1917. No one in government had plans ready for mobilizing an American army or for converting industry to military production. Treasury officials and bankers paled at the complexities of war finance. Millions and millions of Americans opposed their country's involvement. Urban socialists, especially powerful in the Northwest and upper Midwest, thought the war a capitalist trick against the working class. Many Germans and Irish felt England the villain, and that America had chosen the wrong side. Then, too, the United States had suffered no attack: the European war did not threaten its security. If America were to become an arsenal of democracy, the nation must organize its economic power and invigorate its morale.

Raising an army proved easier than equipping one. Wilson and most members of Congress wanted a national army, not a collection of volunteer corps gathered locally as during much of the Civil War. (Theodore Roosevelt never understood this. For months he futilely importuned the President for permission to organize his own division, himself commanding, and take it to France.) A conscription law—the "draft" to most Americans—garnered nearly twenty-five million men between the ages of eighteen and forty-five into a national pool of potential soldiers. Of these, nearly three million were inducted and another two million volunteered. Yet the army had stockpiled in April 1917 only 600,000 rifles and 900 heavy guns, field weapons so crucial to trench warfare. American industrialists quickly converted their plants to munition and small arms production, but the British and French had to supply almost eighty per cent of the artillery used by American forces. Nor did Yankee ingenuity meet the challenge of the war's new weapons, the tank and the airplane. By the armistice, just 64 tanks had rolled off American production lines, and poor design and even worse management plagued aircraft output.

The Allies, though, needed money more than military know-how, and here the Americans responded hugely. War finance at first set off a bitter dispute in Congress: conservatives wanted high taxes on consumer goods, while liberals in both parties fought for large inheritance, personal income, and excess profits taxes. They compromised by charging most of the war's expenses to future generations. War Revenue Acts taxed away nearly two-thirds of large personal and corporate income. (Radicals in Congress were not appeased; they pushed for confiscation of all earnings above $100,000.) Although the richer classes probably bore a greater share of the tax burden, this extraordinary revenue brought in about $10.5 billion, about one-third of the war's total cost. The government borrowed the rest. The Treasury sold some $25 billion of "liberty bonds" directly to the public, avoiding charges of collusion or profiteering by Wall Street banks. This niagara of dollars financed the American armies, of course, but billions poured overseas to pay for armaments for the Allies and to prop up British and French currencies. (Later, repayment of these loans—the "war debts"—harshly divided the former allies.)

More than money or munitions, though, the United States contributed a special morale to the war. Yankee doughboys marched into French units on the front lines chanting, "Lafayette, we are here!" Their spirit rekindled hopes for victory long dulled by the monotonous death of trench warfare. At home, too, Americans steeled themselves for the unfamiliarity of violence with an enforced gaiety and a harsh patriotism. George M. Cohan, the Broadway star, wrote a musical about the war, composing one song, "It's a Grand old Flag!" so spirited that Congress awarded him a Medal of Honor. Another ballad, "Over There,"

cheerfully promised, "The Yanks are coming, the Yanks are coming, and the war will soon be over, over there!" But dark bigotries clouded America's thoughts, too. An unreasoning hatred of Germans and all things Germanic swept across the country, particularly in Pennsylvania and the upper Middle West where millions of German immigrants and their descendants lived. Mobs stormed German language newspapers, often closing them down permanently. Schools and universities dropped courses in any way related to the "enemy's" culture, even classes in German literature and psychiatry. Town elders changed street names: ball park vendors rechristened their frankfurters "hot dogs"; cooks spoke of "liberty cabbage," not sauerkraut. Though slow to enter the war, once involved Americans quickly became its impassioned partisans.

At War 1917-1918

The Central Powers pushed forward. In late October 1917 an Italian army disintegrated under hellish artillery fire and hand-to-hand combat near Caporetto. Almost a million Allied soldiers died or were captured. Submarine warfare mauled British shipping all that fall. Only after months of hard lessons did the Allies have enough ships and enough knowledge to convoy merchantmen safely to port. On the eastern front, meanwhile, Russia's ability to stay in the war seemed less and less likely. Battles there had wiped out most of the country's fledgling industry; only large munitions shipments from Britain and the United States kept disspirited, poorly-led Russian troops in the field. In February 1917, socialists and middle-class liberals had taken over the government of Russia from Tsar Nicholas. When the tsar called for troops to oust the usurpers, none responded; they were too disillusioned by military failures, and autocracy was no longer acceptable. Radical groups clamored for an immediate peace and sweeping economic reforms. Germans abetted the growing chaos by slipping Lenin, leader of the revolutionary Bolshevik party, back into the capital city. Once there, he orchestrated the chant, "Peace, Land and Bread," into a program for revolution. The prospect of an anti-capitalist Russia abandoning the war panicked the Allies. Wilson and Prime Minister Lloyd George pressured Russian leaders such as Alexander Kerensky to keep on fighting, regardless of public sentiment. But more and more

Russian troops—nearly one-third of them virtually unarmed—simply deserted. The eastern front would soon disintegrate.

The German High Command, now under the leadership of Erich Ludendorff, massed its troops for a decisive assault. Ludendorff's strategy was clear: attack boldly, at whatever cost, in the west and move in the east toward a total victory. If the French army could be broken and if radicals gained an upper hand in Russia before American replacements arrived, Germany could force a settlement leaving itself dominant in Europe. A guarantee to respect the British Empire might lure England into peace. The plan almost worked.

German troops overran the Baltic provinces, occupied most of the Ukraine, and attacked the suburbs of both St. Petersburg and Moscow. A mania for peace gripped the Russian people; curiously, only Lenin's radical band took up the popular plea. Already discredited and disillusioned by the war, moderates quietly gave in to a palace revolution staged by the Bolsheviks in November 1917. Lenin then capitulated to the Germans. A peace treaty signed at Brest-Litovsk, in January 1918, surrendered nearly half of European Russia to the Kaiser.

Just at this point, the Germans attacked violently all along the western front. Their dangerous offensive lasted five months. During March and April 1917, Ludendorff's most battle-ready troops stormed across Allied lines in northern France and

National Archives.

National Archives.

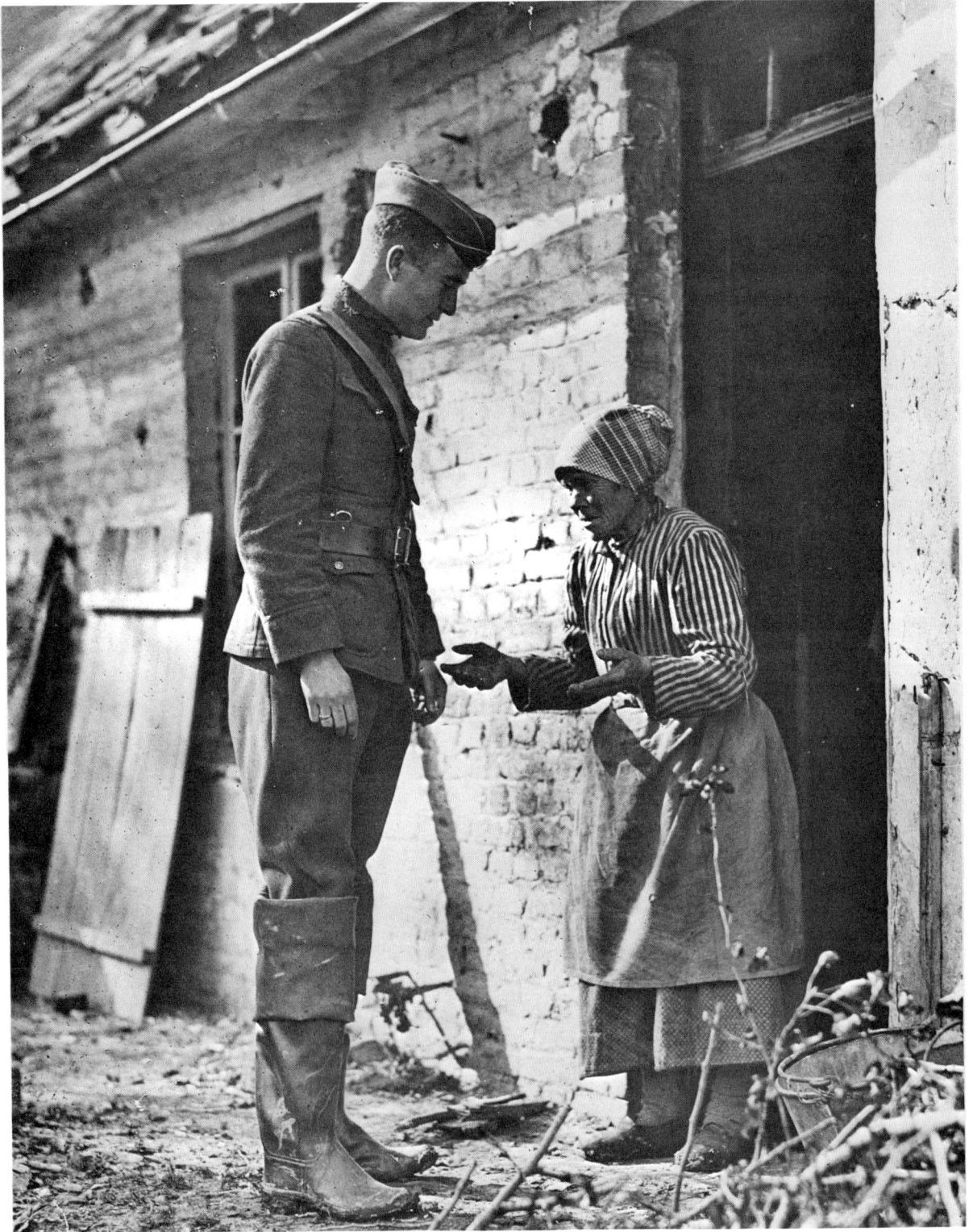

National Archives.

THE UNITED STATES AND THE WORLD

National Archives.

> I have a Rendezvous with Death
> At some disputed barricade,
> When Spring comes back with rustling shade
> And apple blossoms fill the air—
> I have a rendezvous with Death
> When Spring brings back blue days and fair.
>
> It may be he shall take my hand,
> And lead me into his dark land,
> And close my eyes and quench my breath—
> It may be I shall pass him still.
> I have a rendezvous with Death
> On some scarred slope of battered hill,
> When Spring comes round again this year
> And the first meadow flowers appear.
> God knows 'twere better to be deep
> Pillowed in silk and scented down,
>
> Where Love throbs out in blissful sleep,
> Pulse nigh to pulse, and breath to breath,
> Where hushed awakenings are dear. . . .
> But I've a rendezvous with Death
> At midnight in some flaming town,
> When Spring trips north again this year;
> And I to my pledged word am true,
> I shall not fail that rendezvous.

I Have a Rendezvous with Death
by Alan Seeger

This was John F. Kennedy's favorite poem. Seeger died in the first world war.

Belgium. British counterattacks stopped their advance, but only after Germans had penetrated some thirty miles, more ground than either side had gained since the beginning of trench warfare in 1914. This near disaster prompted the Allies to set up a unified command under French general Ferdinand Foch and accelerated the movement of American troops into the war. Britain converted a huge number of its ships into transports, and recruit camps in the United States mushroomed. Soon nearly 250,000 fresh, hastily trained American soldiers were taking to the lines every month, over two million by the fall of 1918. Meanwhile, the Germans attacked again, this time east of Paris. In just three days, the enemy reached the strategic village of Chateau-Thierry on the Marne River, only fifty miles from the capital. A French army, now well fleshed out by American divisions, blocked further advance; then the Americans by themselves pushed the Germans out of Belleau Woods, restabilizing the front. Twice again Ludendorff massed armies for an offensive down the Marne River Valley toward Paris; twice again, Franco-American armies stymied him. By mid-summer 1918, the grand German offensive was broken. With Americans streaming up to the front, the military advantage shifted permanently to the Allies. That fall, Foch launched a counterattack along a two hundred mile front, aimed at destroying German's supply lines behind the Meuse River. General John Pershing, now commander of an exclusively American army, fought on the easternmost flank, for five weeks slugging through the Argonne Forest. The Yanks finally triumphed, wiping out German armies long entrenched in the difficult terrain. Sedan fell, Pershing's forces captured the railways that had supplied German forces farther west in late October 1918. British and French troops had already destroyed German positions north of Paris, and German armies everywhere reeled back across France into Belgium. As the western front crumbled, the German High Command surrendered any hope of victory. "Open armistice negotiations as soon as possible," Ludendorff telephoned the Kaiser.

Wilson's war message to Congress, designed to rally domestic public opinion, had pledged "to make the world safe for democracy." Such generalities had little to do with secret Allied agreements that granted to Britain a dominant role in the Middle East and to France its long-coveted frontier on the Rhine. Even before the United States entered the war, Wilson had called for "a peace without victory," a peace between equals that avoided mutual hatreds and the seeds of future war. Then came the losses in Italy and the collapse of Russia. Lenin's revolution appeared to threaten the capitalist world. Partly to counter Bolshevik propaganda, partly to thwart his Allies' imperialist schemes, partly to reinvigorate western morale, Wilson presented an extremely attractive set of war aims. In a speech to Congress on January 9, 1918, he outlined his Fourteen Points, which defined a new world order of justice, peace, and prosperity: freedom of the seas, removal of trade barriers, disarmament, national self-determination in central and eastern Europe, and a new era of collective security. This last idea, institutionalized in a League of Nations, would make war forever impossible: all countries would pledge to attack any single nation guilty of aggression, and the prospect of certain defeat would deter the potential wrongdoer. Critics pointed out that such provisions actually masked an Anglo-American movement toward global domination. But Wilson's ringing rhetoric thrilled public opinion at the time on both sides of the Atlantic. A new era seemed close at hand.

As American armies turned the battle in northern France, the Allies yearned for a knockout blow. On October 3, 1918, Germany's leader, Prince Max, appealed to Wilson for an armistice—not a surrender—based upon the Fourteen Points. It was a peculiar situation: Wilson's enemies, and not his friends, had accepted his peace terms. He brought British and French statesmen into line with a threat to withdraw from the war altogether if they did not agree to an armistice. They yielded, none too gracefully, after several weeks of pressure. Allied generals then worked out details for a cease-fire that would prevent Germany from renewing hostilities. Western armies occupied both banks of the Rhine, and Germany's troops surrendered most of their military equipment. The belligerents agreed to the armistice on November 11, 1918, the Germans once again reiterating that they did so on the basis of Wilson's Fourteen Points. Guns along the western front fell silent.

The League of Nations

Woodrow Wilson's League of Nations was a grand vision. It was to be a social contract among nations, leading the peoples of the world out of a condition where armaments produced only fleeting security. America, in fulfillment of its historic mission, would be the agent of regeneration. Because America was the embodiment and champion of "liberal" values, its pursuit of its own safety and eminence was for the good of the world community it sought to renew. Or so the Wilsonians believed. Wilson's great importance for twentieth-century foreign affairs lies in his casting of the American national interest into a perfectly honest if self-deceptive rhetoric of liberal internationalism.

Postwar policy was as anti-Bolshevist as it was anti-German. Bolshevism was the enemy in Siberia where in the winter of 1919 we joined our allies in an intervention and suffered considerable casualties. In part we went to Siberia because we had the health of Russia at heart, wanting an end to the single-party rule of the Bolsheviks and a restoration of the ideals of the March 1917 Russian Revolution. The destruction of Lenin's forces would also have strengthened our position in the rest of Europe, where Wilson competed with Communist Parties for the support of democratic socialists. Finally, we could certainly not applaud Lenin's stated object of a world revolution. Rather, Wilson visualized a world system hospitable to free trade—ordered by the League and led by the United States. His central aim to establish, on the grave of German expansion, an American-inspired world system as an alternate to classic imperialism or socialist revolution. This would also best assure America's moral and material preeminence.

Wilson was probably wise to go to Paris to negotiate the Treaty of Versailles that ended the war. He displayed more knowledge and greater energy at the peace table than did any other major world leader, and he took with him a host of intellectual advisers to provide him with up-to-date analyses of problems to be solved. Yet he did not, perhaps could not, prepare the Senate and the American people for acceptance of his work, particularly for the many compromises between ideals and European national interest. Wilson lost in his attempt to scale down to reasonable size the reparations from Germany demanded by the Allies, but thought that a future American presence on the reparations commissions would insure a fairer settlement. He was ambivalent toward Germany, at once wanting just punishment yet visualizing a reformed country integrated into the league. He was perhaps most effective in resisting excessive territorial encroachments on Germany by the Allies, and setting political boundaries that conformed in the main to lines of nationality.

Wilson's role in rearranging national boundaries lost him domestic support. Italian-Americans, for example, never forgave him for acquiescing in the award of Fiume to the new state of Yugoslavia. Wilson did not support Japan's demand for a racial equality clause in the Treaty and lost face among liberals by agreeing to let that country keep the Chinese province of Shantung. A paternalistic mandate system gave to modern countries presumably backward and unwesternized territories they were to govern and prepare for eventual self-rule. In fact a means of dividing the spoils, it subjected the governing powers to various restrictions and was by no means a simple extension of imperialism. Yet, Wilson's moral rhetoric did not quite accord with the necessary compromises. On balance he achieved a reasonable treaty, and one redeemed, in his estimate, because it contained the Covenant of the League of Nations.

The vast majority of Americans favored some form of a League at the end of the war, but this support drifted away when they had to agree on a particular League. Republicans were the first to be estranged. By his October 25, 1918, appeal for a Democratic Congress, Wilson invited a partisan response on postwar policies. By failing to take senior Republicans with him to Paris, and by leaving them ignorant of his progress there, he widened the gulf. The off-term elections produced a Republican Congress. He assailed anti-League Senators, calling them "bungalow minds" whose heads were "knots tied to keep their bodies from unraveling." Wilson apparently assumed at Versailles and thereafter that it was the Senate's duty to provide a rubber stamp for such momentous presidential negotiation. Therefore, it is not surprising that the Republicans—led by a jealous Senator Henry Cabot Lodge, Chairman of the Foreign Relations Committee—insisted on modifications of the League Covenant.

Wilson's willingness to barter away advantage at Versailles in exchange for a secure League lost him the support of many fellow idealists, such as John Maynard Keynes, Walter Lippmann, Brand Whitlock, and Herbert Hoover. Unwilling to accept Wilson's argument that a League could correct inequities in the treaty, they became convinced that the President had betrayed his famous Fourteen Points, outlining the basis for a just peace. The points, it was said, were mere propaganda, issued after the new Bolshevik government had made known a series of secret agreements among the Allies. The Treaty was punitive and reactionary and no amount of dickering in a League could set it right. Liberals decided that Wilson had succumbed to the fear of Bolshevism in Europe, and even had this fear in mind as he determined boundaries along ethnic and national lines.

The League issue divided the President's own party. The immigrant vote, traditionally Democratic, became as bitterly opposed to Versailles as the most intractible isolationists. Several nationalities resented the Treaty's impact on their motherlands. The heavily Democratic Irish, attuned to the struggle for Irish independence, saw the League as an instrument for oppression at the hands of the British, who would control a sizable number of votes in the League Assembly. German-Americans easily sought revenge against Wilson for the war and the reparations settlement. Americans of Italian descent resented the disposition of Fiume. Jews disliked the eastern European territorial settlements, the failure at Versailles to create a new Jewish homeland, and the administration's treatment of Jewish radicals.

By the fall of 1919 wartime idealism had fallen victim to the continuing and fruitless League debates in and out of the Senate. By the time Senator Henry Cabot Lodge had finished his Foreign Relations Committee hearings, the public thought of the League not as an instrument for peace but largely as a vehicle for unending war. For the Republicans argued that Article X of the League Covenant—a statement guaranteeing national boundaries—would simply mean one police action after another, with the United States obliged to contribute. Wilson invited Republican Senators to the White House and tried to reason with them; he even drew up four unpublicized reservations to the Covenant, which he planned to offer if needed. All was to no avail.

Wilson had a final strategy. He would go to the people. Although weakened by influenza, he began a speaking tour in September to generate support for his League. He delivered some thirty major speeches, pointing out the economic benefits the League would bring, arguing that Article X was a moral rather than a legal commitment, and generally portraying the League as man's best hope. On September 25 he suffered a physical breakdown in Pueblo, Colorado, and shortly after that a paralyzing cerebral hemorrhage. Had

Wilson died in 1919, his dream of American participation in a League might have become a reality. As it was, secluded in the White House, he became an object of gossip and slander.

The Versailles Treaty with the League Covenant attached first came before the Senate in November 1919. The critical vote was on whether to accept entrance with reservations, which protected Senate prerogatives and such traditions as the Monroe Doctrine. Loyal Wilsonian Democrats opposed to the reservations joined isolationists to insure its defeat. In succeeding months the Senate waited for some hint that Wilson, though he detested the reservations, would compromise, as he had considered doing before his illness. A word to his partisans would have assured passage; exhausted, sick, and emotionally embittered, he remained silent. The Senate nonetheless voted again: perhaps enough members in favor of a League would finally accept compromise. Three of the first four Democrats previously in opposition voted for the Treaty. The final vote was 49 in favor and 35 against—just 7 short of the necessary two-thirds. In retrospect, perhaps, the decision was not so unfortunate as it seemed. Staying out gave us a freer hand in foreign affairs, and the nation by no means retreated into an isolationist shell.

War and the diplomacy of peace had rebuilt the arena of international affairs, but few Americans realized it. Long secure behind their ocean moats, most people ignored the pasted-over cracks in the Versailles settlement: a sullen German nation, soon the strongest in Europe, watchful for revenge; the new Soviet regime in Russia, shunned by all; economic dislocations throughout Europe. Even the victors suffered. Proud French armies patrolled the Rhine, but their generals knew they could never repeat the battles of the Great War. Too many had died, too much treasure was gone. Only a veneer of power remained, and that only if English leaders fully backed the French against "the German menace." Yet the King's ministers in London divided their attention between the European continent and a sprawling British empire, then one-third of the world's population. World war had drained Britain, too, and leaders there vacillated, never acting decisively in Europe, fearing revolt in Africa or Asia.

As in politics, stability in world trade and finance had succumbed without quite yielding a new balance. Formerly the world's largest importer of capital, the United States now became its chief supplier, shifting abruptly from debtor to creditor. An unrealistic pattern of debt and default destroyed the value of currencies. Asia and

Africa and the Americas had learned to live without European goods during years of warfare. Germany and England could regain old markets by lowering their prices, yet to do this required lower wages in the face of war-induced inflation. Each solved the dilemma differently: Germans forced wages down, so everyone worked; Englishmen kept wages high, so unemployment persisted throughout the 1920's at "an intractable tenth"—ten percent—of the labor force.

Most Americans, like most people everywhere, overlooked these fundamental and, ultimately, fatal flaws in the European settlement. But, the Senate, strong after its recent triumph over Woodrow Wilson, claimed a full and equal role in foreign policy making. Public opinion, too, hampered executive leadership. A majority of Americans believed that the force of their peaceful example, vigorously expressed, alone could resolve conflict. Living happily and securely in the western hemisphere, they shunned Europe's greedy, evil pursuits. Yet "isolationism," as newspapers and historians have dubbed this curious stance, was never escapist or inward turning. Americans looked upon the world with a certain gusto, sure that morality, like a beacon, might beckon nations to general peace. Industrialists glimpsed a more worldly vision, the call of markets and opportunity for profits beyond national borders.

Power and Peace: Diplomacy, 1921-1929

The most vexing problem for the new Republican administrations came in East Asia, where Japanese ambitions challenged both China's integrity and America's security. The Bolshevik Revolution had destroyed Russia's traditional check upon Japanese expansion, while world war had weakened the area's major colonial powers, Britain, France, and the Netherlands. Japan's alliance with England forestalled unilateral action by the United States. In this favorable diplomatic circumstance, ministers around Japan's emperor fashioned a sea-based empire in the western Pacific and dreamed of still grander glories on the mainland: dominion over the industrial heartland of East Asia, Manchuria, and the huge populations of central China.

The affable, handsome Warren Harding once told a reporter, "I don't know anything about this diplomatic stuff. You must see Mr. Hughes about that." More than most presidents, he turned foreign affairs over to his Secretary of State, the talented Charles Evans Hughes. A full-bearded, nattily-dressed man, Hughes looked like a diplomat. Well trained in law, the former Supreme Court justice and presidential candidate brought a precise, unflappable style to the conduct of postwar American foreign policy. He was a realist in a nation of moralists. "Foreign policies are not built upon abstractions," he insisted. "They are the result of practical conceptions of national interest." His greatest achievement, perhaps overly praised by contemporaries, stabilized the explosive situation in East Asia by limiting the world's major naval fleets.

Disarmament readily attracted the public imagination. In the aftermath of war, many people thought that weaponry itself created a climate for violence. Then, too, taxpayers complained about the vast burden of peacetime armaments. Japan's government spent nearly one-third of its annual budget upon its navy; strategic armaments severely hampered British leaders struggling to repay the country's large war debts; Congress blocked appropriations for the Naval Act of 1916, designed to create an American fleet that would be the largest in the world. Since the destruction of Germany's navy in 1919, why maintain such battalions of seapower?

At the Washington Naval Conference Hughes skillfully used these impulses toward disarmament to recreate a strategic balance in the Pacific. He proposed that the five great naval powers limit future building so as to preserve their battleship and carrier fleets at a constant ratio of total tonnage: Britain and the United States, 525,000 tons each; Japan, 315,000 tons; France and Italy, 175,000 tons each. At public sessions in Washington, D.C., delegates argued long over military details. Behind the scenes, diplomats and ministers in Washington, Tokyo, and London perfected the political basis for a balanced peace in East Asia.

The Washington Conference of 1921-22 produced three major treaties, each named after the number of countries participating in it. A naval agreement, the Five-Power Pact among Britain, France, Japan, and the United States promised to respect each others' insular possessions and to consult, presumably for joint action, in the event any outsiders challenged this status quo. The Nine-Power Pact, signed by all the colonial powers in East Asia except Russia and, of course, Germany, pledged each to respect the Open Door in China.

The three treaties included losses and gains for everyone. The United States won naval equality with Britain and formal recognition of the Open Door principle, but Hughes had to acquiesce in Japan's island occupation of the Carolinas, Marshalls, and Mariannas. Britain jettisoned its centuries-old naval dominance but gained security for its extensive Pacific possessions and escaped possible trouble with the United States by way of its alliance with Japan, now formally abrogated. The Japanese lost territorial prerogatives in China and remained a second-class naval power but won secure control over an island empire in the Pacific. Newspaper editors wrote that the Secretary of State had "frozen over the Pacific."

Hughes also dealt with many diplomatic questions left over from war. After the Senate rejected the Treaty of Versailles, State Department officials negotiated separate agreements with Germany, Austria, Hungary, Turkey, and Bulgaria which granted America all rights guaranteed to the other victors. More perplexing, though, was the League of Nations. At first, bureaucrats refused even to recognize its existence, widely ignoring mail from the world body. Not until the end of 1921 did Hughes begin to answer letters from the League's headquarters in Geneva, Switzerland. Two years later he sent an American delegation to an opium conference sponsored by the League. His successors broadened this policy of joining in non-political functions, and the United States had participated in fifty such gatherings by 1932. Ambassadors to Switzerland took up the role of unofficial observers at League meetings, a private conduit of information outside the view of the American public and the Senate. The World Court ruled only upon cases brought to it with the consent of both parties. The Senate approved a treaty for United States membership in 1926 with reservations so sweeping that other members refused to accept them. The issue smoldered throughout the interwar period, but no Congress ever permitted America's entry.

At the beginning of his full term as President, Calvin Coolidge appointed Frank Kellogg to replace the retiring Hughes. Kellogg deftly handled a tricky negotiation with his French counterpart, Aristide Briand. Peace factions in the United States, long discontented by their country's cautious foreign policy, persuaded an all-too-willing Briand to publish an open letter on the tenth anniversary of America's entry into World War I. The letter called for a Franco-American treaty "renouncing war" between them. Kellogg and his advisers quickly realized the proposal was a negative military alliance. After a six-month delay, Kellogg cleverly countered with an offer to all nations to join in "outlawing war forever." Some sixty-four powers ultimately signed what became known as the Kellogg-Briand Pact, which deepened the illusion of international stability.

Kellogg dealt less convincingly with perennial difficulties in Latin America, especially in Mexico and Nicaragua. Bickering over the presidency in Nicaragua descended into a fierce struggle, and Coolidge unwisely sent several thousand marines into the small country in 1926. When America's puppet seemed more intent upon looting the public treasury than in building democracy, the President dispatched Henry L. Stimson to settle the dispute. Under the Peace of Tipitapa, American troops policed a national election. Then the marines trained a local militia, a job they did so well that after they left in 1933, its chief seized power.

The Republicans navigated an even stormier course in Mexico, where social revolution continued. A new constitution in 1917 had claimed all subsoil wealth as the property of Mexico's people. This legal maneuver brought stinging rebukes from the American and British governments, whose oil companies had invested heavily in the area. Hughes worked out a compromise in 1923, confirming foreign ownership of rights acquired before 1917. Mexico might nationalize property purchased after that year, provided the government reimbursed owners. Unfortunately, Mexico's president, Plutarco Calles, and the foreign companies fought bitterly over a "fair price." The Secretary of State finally denounced Mexico as "a center of Bolshevik activity," but Coolidge backed down and sent to Mexico City Dwight Morrow, a friendly, skillful negotiator who restored a measure of amity between the two nations. Morrow's compromises postponed a clash between foreign oil and Mexican nationalism until the late 1930's, when Mexico seized all concessions with only modest compensation.

Despite such episodes of neo-colonial meddling, Coolidge and Kellogg moved generally toward greater neighborliness with Latin America. In 1924 American troops left the Dominican Republic, though Yankees supervised government finances there until 1940. The United States paid Colombia an indemnity of $25 million for its loss of Panama. Late in his term Coolidge asked J. Reuben Clark, an official in the State Department, to outline the precise limits of the Monroe

Doctrine. His brief, published in 1930 as the Clark Memorandum, argued that "the Doctrine states a case of the United States versus Europe, not of the United States versus Latin America," thereby repudiating Roosevelt's Corollary which had justified unilateral intervention in domestic matters. Yet leaders in Washington never abandoned a high commitment to American security in the Caribbean, an attitude continued to this day.

War Debts and Reparations

The United States government loaned over $7 billion to seven nations fighting Germany during World War I; post-armistice reconstruction loans to twenty countries amounted to $3.5 billion more. The debtors soon realized, however, that if they shipped gold to the United States, their own economies would collapse for lack of credit and a cover for currencies. High American tariffs blocked sales of many European goods in the United States, thereby discouraging the debtors from earning dollars. The allies also argued that the money represented America's contribution to the war effort and an unequal one at that: Americans lost dollars, but Europeans lost millions of lives and suffered frightful physical destruction. Most of the money had been spent in the United States where it stimulated industry and kept employment high. American presidents and public opinion bluntly rejected pleas for cancellation, though. Coolidge said only, "They hired the money, didn't they?" Europeans must repay what most Americans thought was both a legal and moral obligation. The debtors, in turn, carped at "Uncle Shylock."

Worried by rumors of default, Congress early in 1922 created the World War Foreign Debt Commission, headed by Secretary of the Treasury Mellon, to negotiate specific repayment schedules. This group adjusted interest rates and other technical details to each debtor's capacity to repay. Most European leaders, privately supposing they could simply collect reparations from Germany and pass them along to the United States, went along with this proposal. Overall, the Debt Commission reduced the original debt-plus-interest totals by about half. Many Americans felt flim-flammed, a sentiment which strengthened the desire to stay out of Europe's affairs.

Meanwhile, foreign officials together with private American bankers stabilized the German economy and set up a schedule of reparations which paralleled war debt payments to the United States. In 1924, Germany and its former enemies ratified the Dawes Plan. Germany pledged its profits from railroads and mines to reparations. British and American bankers promised loans to speed recovery in the Rhineland, the center of German industry. In late 1928, Germany and its creditors reorganized reparations again under the guidance of the banker-industrialist Owen D. Young. The Young Plan limited payments to the next fifty-nine years on a sliding scale determined by Germany's economic health. Still, nothing changed the underlying nature of such rickety agreements: reparations, like war debts, could be paid only if countries allowed an influx of foreign goods. The general prosperity of the 1920's temporarily hid this economic truism.

Depression Diplomacy: Hoover and the World, 1929-1933

The Depression upset delicate postwar balances of power. As international problems became more complex, the American people turned inward, preoccupied by greater worries of their own. Ironically, a new President, Herbert Hoover, dreamed of further disarmament, economic collaboration, conciliation in Latin America, even modest collective security efforts. Yet obstinate Congresses and depression—that mystery apparently so insoluble—stymied Hoover's internationalism. The times and the man were uniquely mismatched.

The international economy gave way with surprising swiftness during the first eighteen months of the 1930's. National banks in central Europe had borrowed funds from private banks in New

Herbert Hoover. (National Archives.)

York and London to relend to domestic businesses. As depression ruined sales both at home and abroad, the German and Austrian central banks discovered they could collect neither interest nor principal on many of their loans. Scared by the prospect of financial collapse, foreign investors sold property and securities. Others frantically tried to exchange paper marks for gold or "solid" currencies. These pressures forced Germany to default on all its loans, public and private, and to abandon the gold standard during the summer of 1931. Many British banks had invested heavily in high-risk, high-yield German ventures which now were worthless. Depositors rushed to withdraw their money from London banks, and soon Britain too had left the gold standard. Prime Minister J. Ramsay MacDonald decided to devalue the pound, making British goods cheaper and, in turn, stealing markets from other countries still burdened by "expensive" gold currencies.

President Hoover responded to these events with dramatic measures. In an effort to prevent a general default in Germany, which he feared might bring down several large banks in New York City, Hoover postponed for 18 months all war debts and reparations payments. This did slow the pace of collapse in central Europe, but because the Hoover Moratorium provided no new funds for banks or industry, the President's efforts eventually failed. Britain's aggressive, unorthodox use of monetary devices frightened Hoover into financial alliance with the only other major gold power, France. During talks with French premier Pierre Laval in October 1931, Hoover secured a pledge from the Bank of France to support the dollar with its own gold. In return, the President hinted that he might cancel war debts entirely if the Allies canceled German reparations. This arrangement stopped speculation against the dollar, and the Allies soon gathered at Lausanne, Switzerland. There they pared German reparations to a token $700 million. But this boon—Germany could use money earmarked for reparations to pay off private debts—had a price: the United States must write off war debts. This chain of events embarrassed both Hoover and Roosevelt, now in the midst of a presidential campaign. Both men realized the economic logic of cancellation but appreciated equally the political folly of saying so. Even after the election they shied away from decisive action, so all America's debtors except Finland defaulted during 1933.

Economic crisis also upset the delicate naval and political balance in East Asia. A group of advisers around Emperor Hirohito convinced him that Japan's future prosperity required control over the mainland. On September 18, 1931, Japanese armies in Manchuria, stationed there under an agreement with China to guard the strategic Chinese Eastern Railway, attacked along most of its length and soon routed poorly defended Chinese positions. This early triumph emboldened local commanders to begin a systematic conquest of southern Manchuria. Victory there, they hoped, would discredit moderate leaders at home and commit Japan to armed expansion in China and Southeast Asia. Aircraft bombed villages and raided China's largest city, Shanghai, early in 1932. All Manchuria fell to the invaders that spring, when a puppet ruler signed a protective alliance with Japan. Hirohito's generals next assaulted the provinces of north China. Chiang Kai-shek, the leader of the ruling Nationalist Party, could not check the Japanese advance. Russians already had skirmished with his troops along the border in 1929, and a persistent Communist rebellion led by Mao Tse-tung drained still more troops from the battle. Chiang turned to the United States and the League of Nations for help.

Peace machinery clanked slowly into motion. Faced with the first serious challenge to collective security, the League dispatched a fact-finding group under Lord Lytton for an on-the-spot investigation. While its members tramped over rough terrain and interviewed village elders, Britain's foreign secretary, Sir John Simon, labored to put together a coalition to push Japan out of Manchuria. France and Italy nervously offered token help; Simon did not even ask Germany and the Soviet Union. The issue became starkly simple: would the United States and Great Britain in defense of the Nine Power Pact and the principle of collective security risk war with Japan? Secretary of State Stimson hinted that the answer might be "yes," but Hoover overruled him. The Quaker from Iowa sensed what Americans later learned: conventional land warfare in East Asia was beyond United States power. Most citizens thought Japanese aggression regrettable but not a threat to their security. Hoover politely declined Simon's idea, taking up instead the device of nonrecognition. Stimson notified the signatories of the Nine Power Pack that the United States "can not admit the legality of conquests in violation of treaty commitments." Most other countries rallied to this Hoover-Stimson Doctrine. Late in 1932, the Lytton Commission Report found Japan guilty of aggression; the League of Nations formally condemned Hirohito and his country; Japanese delegates left Geneva. Wristslapping did not halt Japan's aggression against China. Battles continued there intermittently until 1937 when the emperor's troops unleashed a full-scale war of conquest.

Good intentions lured Hoover down another road, that of disarmament, with equally ineffective results. Early in his term, Hoover invited British Prime Minister MacDonald to Washington for wide-ranging talks which soon took on the image of an Anglo-American effort to settle the world's major problems. (Hoover even suggested that Britain might trade one or more of its colonies for war debts owed the United States.) As they sat on a log near a stream at Hoover's private retreat in the hills of northern Virginia, the two rhapsodized about peace and disarmament. They agreed on details for another naval limitations conference to be held in London during 1930. That meeting granted parity to the United States for all classes of ships, long an American objective, but isolationist senators worried that secret clauses might ally the country with England. They demanded all documents pertaining to the negotiations; Hoover refused, citing executive privilege. The Senate eventually ratified the work of the London Naval Conference, but the new treaty was far less effective than its predecessors. France and Italy did not join, and an "escalator clause" allowed building past agreed limits under certain circumstances. The signatories altogether ignored enforcement measures. The President also supported plans for a general disarmament conference which finally convened in 1932. American delegates put forward a scheme to scrap all offensive weapons and reduce armies by fifty percent. French leaders demanded security before dismantling their land forces, then the world's strongest. Japanese aggression in Asia mocked even the idea of general disarmament. The Conference dragged on for two years, delegates talking more and more about less and less. Limiting arms either on land or at sea succumbed to military complexities and national jealousies. Violence and poverty destroyed Hoover's early hopes for a diplomacy of cooperation.

Suggested Readings

William Appleman Williams argues, in *The Roots of Modern American Empire* (1969), that behind the American imperialist push at the turn of the century was the American farmer, who wanted his country to open markets abroad. Williams shows how American ideals of self-determination blended with self-interest: keeping peoples free from domination by European powers would insure the availability of their markets to American commerce; but the idea of the virtuousness of open markets made its own appeal. Still standard on the first world war are Ernest R. May, *The World War and American Isolation* (1959) and the multivolume biography of Woodrow Wilson by Arthur S. Link, *Wilson* (1947--). An excellent new study is Frank E. Vandiver, *Black Jack: The Life and Times of John J. Pershing*, 2 vols. (1977). Ralph A. Stone, in *The Irreconcilables: The Fight Against the League of Nations* (1970), investigates the reasons that motivated each of the sixteen senators who refused to ratify the Versailles Treaty. David McCullough is now standard on *The Path Between the Seas: The Creation of the Panama Canal, 1870-1914* (1977), but see also Walter LaFeber, *The Panama Canal: The Crisis in Historical Perspective* (1978).

Chapter XXIII
Progressive America

I. Forrest McDonald: A Meddlesome Government at Home and Abroad

The mood of the American people at the beginning of the twentieth century was best expressed by the great inventor and folk hero Thomas Edison. Edison believed in measuring everything against the Almighty Dollar, he believed in progress, he believed in his country; but he recognized that the creative orgy of technological change and economic growth since the Civil War had made rather a mess of things, that the time had come for the nation to consolidate its gains by restoring order upon American life.

"You see," he said, "getting down to the bottom of things, this is a pretty raw, crude civilization of ours—pretty wasteful, pretty cruel, which often comes to the same thing, doesn't it? And in a lot of respects we Americans are the rawest and crudest of all. Our production, our factory laws, our charities, our relations between capital and labor, our distribution—all wrong, out of gear. We've stumbled along for awhile trying to run a new civilization in old ways, but we've got to start to make this world over."

The key word in Edison's diagnosis and prescription was "wasteful." The nation got caught up in enthusiasm for eliminating waste, for making every aspect of life organized, orderly, rational, efficient. Government at all levels was infused with "experts," real and pretended. Business was consolidated until, in industry after industry, one or a handful of integrated companies controlled most of the production and marketing; and workers in the larger corporations were brought under systems of "welfare capitalism," or what one manager called "benevolent despotism over the human side of manufacturing." ("A happy worker is an efficient worker," said another.) The professions—not only doctors and lawyers and dentists but also historians, anthropologists, economists, and others who now took to calling themselves "social scientists"—formed national organizations, became increasingly specialized, adopted uniform standards of qualification. Charity became organized and professionalized. Preachers, teachers, and women's clubs plunged into the effort to make America less "wasteful," less "cruel." It was an age of experts and engineers, an age when the word "efficient" came to be a term of the highest praise and "special" came to have sinister overtones, an age when the delusion spread that the quality of life could be reckoned in numbers. In sum, Americans began to worship a machinomorphic god with technocrats as its high priests; they deified the machine and tried to refashion themselves and their society in its image.

That turn of events was a logical and perhaps necessary outgrowth of what had gone before, and in many respects it was beneficent. To the extent that statistics can in fact measure the quality of life, they indicate a steady and even spectacular improvement in the material standards of living for most Americans. The average worker, in 1930, put in one-sixth fewer hours (the equivalent of one day a week) than in the 1890s, but was bringing home three times as much in wages, and work was safer and more healthful. Of the roughly 30 million American families in the 1920s, only 6.6 million were still confined to the drudgery of farm life, and except in the South even life on the farms had grown easier. Most of the non-farmers enjoyed comforts and conveniences which, in earlier generations, would have been unimaginable luxuries: nearly nine-tenths had electricity and indoor plumbing, four-fifths had automobiles, two-thirds had radios, and close to half had refrigerators and phonographs. Ninety million Americans *a week* attended movies, and untold millions attended professional baseball and college football games, vaudeville shows, outdoor concerts, and other forms of public amusement. Health care improved astonishingly: the infant mortality rate declined from 162 per 1000 in 1900 to 69 in 1930, and life expectancy increased from 47 years to nearly 60 in the same period.

There were, to be sure, attendant drawbacks. Some of these were inherent in the emergence of a society based upon mass production and mass consumption. Standardization in the interests of efficiency required, by definition, a proportionate sacrifice of individual preferences, personal differences, and creativity. Mass marketing and the development of genuine mass media entailed mass advertising, which in turn gave rise to the art of "public relations"; and both advertising and public relations injected a certain vulgar, hollow sameness and phoniness into American life. (For the first time in history, millions upon millions of Americans were, again and again on a given evening, doing precisely the same thing, namely listening to the same radio program.) What was at once more subtle and more portentous, the rise of a mass psychology undermined traditional American individualism, putting hero-worship in its stead, and weakened the American tradition of self-reliance by teaching people in ever increasing numbers to rely upon the great corporations as the source of their well-being.

But it was in governmental and political responses to changing American ways that the most ominous developments took place. Government responded to the rationalization movement by establishing hosts of regulatory agencies which, though sometimes billed as anti-business, were in actuality designed to facilitate the orderly consolidation and expansion of business. In addition, governments on all levels took large strides toward rationalizing their own operations—which, in the nature of things, meant depoliticizing them and making them less democratic. Of the 150,000 or so federal officials in the 1890s, for instance, four-fifths were either elected or appointed directly by elected officials and were subject to firing after every election. Of the 600,000 federal employees in 1930, three-quarters held their jobs by virtue of civil service examinations and retained them no matter what the will of the voters.

Yet even as government was becoming less democratic, politics was becoming more so, at least ritualistically. Increased democratization of national politics, and especially of presidential politics, was perhaps inherent in the development of mass communications media, but it began because of the personality of one man. Theodore Roosevelt, president by accident, was a courageous man, a forceful leader, and a head of state who exuded the confidence the nation needed; but above all he was a consummate showman.

Roosevelt restored to the presidency a prestige it had lacked since Jefferson's time, and into the bargain transformed the office into the one truly democratic branch of the national government, the only branch representing all the people. A chief of state with whom ordinary people can identify is necessary as a living symbol of nationhood, and doubly so in a mass society; and in that respect Roosevelt made a profound contribution to the psychic health of the United States. Moreover, the values he personified were, by and large, among the more wholesome aspects of American character.

But in two important particulars he epitomized far less wholesome aspects of that character. One was the Bolingbroke-Jefferson-Jackson tradition of hostility and envy regarding commercial and financial activity, discredited during the Civil War but revived by the anti-corporate spirit of the late nineteenth century. Roosevelt was by no means opposed to the rise of gigantic corporations; indeed, his administration approved and quietly supported the greatest wave of monopolistic and oligopolistic mergers the country had yet known. But, as part of his campaign to win popular favor for a powerful and prestigious presidency, he engaged in a great deal of theatrical "trust-busting." That is to say, when he did favors for business he tended to disguise what he was doing in anti-business rhetoric. Many businesses followed his lead, sponsoring campaigns of self-vilification in support of legislation which actually worked to their advantage. This was doubly dangerous. It kept alive an absolute anti-corporate and anti-business tradition in a civilization that was increasingly dependent upon corporate business enterprise. It also failed to take into account a peculiar reality of American life: that political rhetoric, no matter how much it may be recognizable as hokum when it is first uttered, ultimately takes on a life of its own and, if repeated regularly and long enough, comes to be accepted as true. Thus in time everybody including Roosevelt himself came to believe that his "progressive" presidency had been a long campaign against "the trusts" and to regard that misconception as an almost sacred part of the American political tradition.

Roosevelt's other unfortunate contribution was a vitalization of the Yankee penchant for meddling. His corollary to the Monroe Doctrine, his Far Eastern policy, and his naval policy thrust the United States into involvement in the internal affairs of foreign peoples, wherein Americans had no business interfering, had nothing to gain, and had a great deal to lose.

Then, after the interlude of the unfortunate William Howard Taft—whose most serious flaw as president was giving the impression that the government had lost control of the tide of events, which in fact it had never controlled in the first place—came the unmitigated calamity of the presidency of Woodrow Wilson. Wilson has long been a darling of liberal intellectuals because he cast his every word and deed in eloquent pleas for the rights of a downtrodden and oppressed mankind; for liberal intellectuals, even as they emerged as a privileged special-interest class and toadied to power and wealth wherever they found it, liked to fancy themselves as the champions of the downtrodden and the oppressed. But Wilson was missing one of the characteristics of his fellow intellectuals: he had no trace of the hypocrite in him. That made him the more dangerous, for it meant that his sternly moral approach to all problems was heartfelt, that his puritanical self-righteousness actually motivated his conduct.

Like Roosevelt, Wilson contributed to the democratization and increased power of the presidency. Significantly, he was the first president to speak of the United States as a democracy, his predecessors having uniformly referred to it as a republic. His principal innovation in the presidency was likewise democratic, after a fashion: he initiated the practice, in conscious imitation of the British parliamentary model, of drawing up entire legislative programs and assuming responsibility with the voters for the legislative output of his administration. Again like Roosevelt, Wilson was an interventionist in foreign affairs—but with a fundamental difference. When Roosevelt despatched the Marines to straighten out the government of a Latin American banana republic, he did so to protect American interests or to put on a show of power for prospective rivals in Europe. When Wilson did the same thing he did so for the benefit of the unenlightened Latinos, to teach them the blessings of democracy whether they liked it or not. Roosevelt's way reflected some measure of enlightened self-interest, was inherently restrained, and had a safe and sound quality to it. Wilson's way reflected a combination of presumptuousness and naivete, was inherently unrestrained, and had in it the seeds of disaster.

Wilson's main legacy was American involvement in World War I and its attendant aftermath. That war was, on all sides, a sordid contest for power, territory, and wealth; but Wilson managed to convince himself that one side was moral and democratic (which terms he tended to use interchangeably) and that the other was evil and tyrannical. So convinced, he permitted American bankers and industrialists to support the Allies but not the Central Powers, and thus to acquire a large stake in an Allied victory. Then, when German U-Boats attacked supposedly "neutral" American shipping, he led the nation into a war to make the world safe for democracy. Somehow he forgot that the function of the United States government is to make the world safe, not for democracy, but for itself and its citizens.

It is impossible to catalog all the catastrophic consequences of World War I, for the consequences are still being felt. In short-range terms, however, several can be singled out. One was the tremendous stimulus the war gave to particularly ugly forms of ethnic, religious, and racial prejudice in the United States. Now, xenophobia—distrust of outsiders, of strangers, of people different from one's own—is natural to mankind and, within limits, not altogether undesirable. But during the war government encouraged mobs persecuted and physically assaulted not only German sympathizers but also German-Americans of unquestionable loyalty. Immediately after the war, during the great Red Scare, hatred of Germans was redirected by the Wilson administration toward radicals—communists, socialists, and anarchists—a goodly portion of whom were or seemed to be ethnically identifiable as Jews or Italians. By the early and middle twenties a new Ku Klux Klan, patterned after the Southern organization of Reconstruction times but now nationally based, had arisen and was spewing its venom upon blacks, Jews, and Catholics, and even upon WASPs who failed to comport themselves in accordance with puritanical norms.

A second immediate product of the war, less obviously inimical to a free society but, in a quiet way, more dangerous, was the emergence of the national government as an active participant in the rationalization of the economy. During the conflict the War Production Board and a number of other agencies made quick studies of segment after segment of the economy and recommended changes that would render the whole more orderly and efficient. Throughout the postwar decade those recommendations were implemented, and though the promised efficiences did materialize, business and government—which meant business and politics—became inextricably bound together. The interconnection was strengthened by the emergence of the decade's most dynamic industry, that of automobile manufacturing, whose expansion depended directly upon government expenditures of tax revenues for the building of roads. In more ways than one, the unnatural marriage of business with government would produce deformed offspring.

A third result of the war was the creation of an international power vacuum. The Austro-Hungarian empire was dismembered, leaving central and eastern Europe a polyglot of ethnic states which scarcely had a chance of survival as independent nations. Imperial Russia collapsed and the horrors of the tsars were succeeded by the even more bloody and repressive regime of the bolsheviks. Germany disintegrated, then gave birth to Nazism. France and Britain, the principal "winners," never fully recovered from either the shock or the economic devastation inflicted by the war. Only the United States emerged richer and stronger at the end of the war than at its beginning. The United States might in these circumstances have been able to furnish the leadership and the resources necessary to restore Europe's political and economic health, except for two things. One of those was that Europeans regarded the Americans as naive and unrealistic about international affairs. The other was that the Europeans were right. (Underlying the naivete and lack of realism was a peculiarity of the American character, an ingrained sentimental attachment to the underdog. Softness for the underdog equips a nation ill for playing the role of top dog.)

Finally, and most devastatingly, the war in combination with the peace settlements at Versailles led inexorably to the world economic collapse of the 1930s. The most important thing to understand about the Great Depression is that is stemmed not from the failings of laissez-faire capitalism but from the policies of governments. In brief, the causal chain was as follows. The war resulted in the destruction of tangible wealth in the amount of roughly a third of a trillion dollars—several times as much as the gross national production of the United States and every nation of Europe combined. Simultaneously, it resulted in the creation of paper wealth—in the form of bonds pledging repayment, by various governments, of debts due to their own citizens, to citizens of other countries, and to other governments, and also in the form of treaties requiring the defeated to pay reparations to the victors—in the amount of another quarter of a trillion dollars. Had governments been able and willing to behave intelligently, they would have cooperated to bring the western world's capacity to produce and its debts back into balance, which could have been managed in any number of ways. Instead, they followed deflationary policies which increased the imbalance. In the ensuing dislocations, every western nation adopted fiscal and tax policies which impaired its own economic health and aggravated the international malaise. In the United States, government policy created an excess of liquid capital and excessive money flow into capital accumulation at the expense of an adequate flow into consumer buying power. The speculative orgy of 1929 was set off by Federal Reserve policies which increased that misdirection of the flow of money. When the bubble burst the American government, like every European government, did the wrong thing at each step along the way. And thus, on the morning of March 4, 1933, when President Herbert Hoover and President-elect Franklin Roosevelt drove down Pennsylvania Avenue for the inauguration ceremony, the world's economy lay in ruins.

There had been depressions before, and the American economy had weathered them; but in one crucial respect things were different this time. Always before, government had allowed the economy to heal itself, and it had always done so. Now, given everything that had happened between the presidencies of the two Roosevelts, the American people were institutionally and psychologically unprepared to accept that remedy.

II. Eugene D. Genovese: Reform and Reaction

Much might be said about the Progressive period, when big business decided, under various pressures from within and without, that widespread political corruption and cutthroat economic competition were too expensive, not to mention a bit unseemly, and that gound rules and civilized deportment had to replace the anarchy that passed for free competition. More and more businessmen came to a grudging appreciation of the role of the government as a referee for their battles just so long as the government was certain to favor big business in general. Indeed, much of the subsequent regulation and intervention which the business press has always denounced as "socialistic" and God-knows-what else, nicely shored up those giant corporations which had gotten in trouble through their own incompetence and inefficiency—a practice that has had its most recent manifestation in the bailing out of a huge automobile corporation by a wondrous coalition of Democrats and Republicans, liberals and conservatives, regulators and free-marketeers.

In some respects the period was genuinely progressive. The worst abuses of bourgeois barbarism—child labor, illiteracy, slums, disregard for human life in a multitude of ways—came under public scrutiny and the wrath of middle-class reformers and popular movements. The struggle for women's rights, for example, assumed new proportions and culminated in a substantial victory with the acquisition of the vote. And contrary to the chatter of neanderthals, the Republic did not fall when women got the vote, nor did Motherhood disappear, nor did women start to frequent the Men's Room, nor did immorality and sin ravage a stricken nation—at least not more than they were doing anyway.

The women's movement, which was never restricted to the suffrage campaign, illustrates the wholesome qualities of the reform movements and also their limitations and less admirable qualities. It reached into many areas of capitalist society and frequently offered its own critique of the harsh, acquisitive competitiveness of capitalist social relations. Crusades for social purity, inspired and frequently led by women, attempted to extend the values of the private sphere into the public. Leaders of the social work movement sought to provide services for the urban, largely immigrant poor. They stressed "Americanization" and adaptation rather than opposition to monopoly capitalism and, in this respect, repudiated the workingclass movement while criticizing business norms. The temperance movement, which scored its great success after the war, was largely a female counter-attack against men—the primary consumers of alcohol—and the violence they perpetrated against women.

Women, working together in such organizations, as well as for educational opportunities and many other social goals, developed a sense of their collective presence in public affairs. The Women's Club movement, with its many offshoots, brought together women concerned with the fate of their country and their community. Black women, in their own religious groups and club movement, did much to provide badly needed services for the black community—schools, hospitals, welfare in various forms—and to shape the emergence of an increasingly effective black middle class. Radical women, poor women, immigrant women participated in socialist, populist, and trade-union affairs and thus identified themselves with the most radical indictments of monopoly capital. The women's movement as a whole, however, both criticized capitalist brutality as male irresponsibility and strengthened capitalist social relations by easing their impact and accepting "the system" as such.

Big business did have its wrists slapped by the progressives and their favorite politicians. Anti-trust legislation and government action reigned in some of the more flagrant and appalling of corporate abuses. For the most part, however, little changed in essentials: The power of the giant corporations over the government steadily increased in the ways that counted. Nothing so clearly demonstrated the power of big capital and the superficiality of the "New Freedom" and "New Deal" than the inability of Wilson to withstand the pressure to enter World War One and make the world safe for Wall Street.

The war and its aftermath brought an international windfall for American monopoly capital, which emerged as top dog in the struggle for the world market. Still, American capital almost squandered its advantage by a display of postwar greed and irresponsibility that was staggering even by prevalent bourgeois standards. For a decade it indulged itself in dangerous speculation, a wild credit expansion, a cult of the automobile the financial effects of which it could not control, and a breath-taking disregard for the economic experience and common sense that should have told it to expect a crash and contraction in the wake of the expansion.

Those who blame the government and the unions for depressions in general and the Great Depression in particular display a wonderful sense of humor. Allegedly, if the market were left free, then all would be well. Never in the history of capitalism has there been such a market, and the interference generated by monopolies, trusts, cartels, and oligopolies somehow escapes the attention of the defenders of "pure" capitalism. In any case, the 1920s was a period of minimum government interference against business interests, and it was not until the 1930s that the labor movement had much muscle. To the contrary, the wildly irresponsible policies of business, largely encouraged by the supine administrations of Harding and Coolidge and not effectively checked by the worried administration of Hoover, set up the country and whole capitalist world for an unprecedented economic disaster.

Such apologetics for the market miss the dynamics of the capitalist system. Periodic depressions are inherent; they purge the market of its weak and inefficient producers and correct distortions and imbalances. Thus, conservatives may have a point in arguing that government interference prolonged the Great Depression. What, as usual, they fail to discuss is the unbearable suffering of the millions of unemployed. To see them through the crisis means to interfere massively in the market. To fail to see them through means to shift the burden of the crisis from the backs of those weak and inefficient capitalists to the backs of their workers. If one takes what the conservatives offer in analysis and adds to it what they leave out, one has a splendid quick account of what capitalism is in fact all about.

It is not at all clear that the self-regulating force of the market remained compatible with prolonged prosperity much after the turn of the century. During the years before 1914 the economy was limping badly, and the recovery of 1909-14 was not especially strong. World

War One came to the rescue, much as World War Two and the Korean and Vietnam wars would do later. A strong argument can be made out for American capitalism's having entered a long-range decline at the end of the nineteenth century, notwithstanding boom periods and some extraordinary technological advances.

In retrospect, the prosperity of the 1920s looks like a short respite between catastrophes, and a remarkably flimsy one at that.

World War One did more than bail out the economy and position the United States to bid for world supremacy. It created a system of massive government regulation, which largely lay hidden during the prosperous 1920s, when big business needed a free hand, but which reemerged, greatly expanded, during the depressed 1930s, when the whole economy, including much of big business itself, needed all the help it could get.

Directly and indirectly the war changed American life, not merely the economy. Wilson's racist policies at home fed a new burst of colonial looting abroad, as the German and Turkish empires were gobbled up by victorious allies. The repudiation of American pledges to effect a generous peace in Europe created conditions of embitterment and disarray that guaranteed to make a mockery of the claim that we had fought a war to end all wars. In the wake of the Treaty of Versailles came American popular disillusionment, cynicism, and fostering a new illusion, at least among the middle class—the illusion that little mattered besides making money and that the road was wide open to those who dared.

The democracy for which Wilson had made the world safe had its finest expression at home in the combination of his racist policies with the institution of a brutal purge of socialists, anarchists, Bolsheviks, suspicious-looking foreigners, and of course anyone with the courage to call an imperialist war just that. After the war the purge continued during the "Red Scare," in which any semblance of a left opposition was crushed, civil liberties trampled on, and the labor movement terrorized.

No one need be surprised that these splendid measures to purify the country were accompanied by the prohibition of alcohol and national campaigns on behalf of God, Motherhood, and America the Beautiful. This cultural obscenity would be repeated during the 1950s, albeit without the prohibition of alcohol. On the contrary, the martini, straight up or on the rocks, with olive or twist, would replace the eagle as our national symbol—as if to prove that some progress is inevitable even within cyclical historical patterns.

Fittingly, the hero of this splendid decade, 1919-29, in which Wall Street owned both political parties outright, was the American businessman. After all, he had brought prosperity and the good life. Well, for some: Unemployment rates ran, according to shaky estimates, from 5% to 13%, and millions of Americans struggled at poverty levels. The hero was not, however, just any businessman. The Roaring Twenties had brought forth a new type who specialized in advertising, promotion, and the art of convincing people that they just have to have the latest model of the latest product—whatever it might be.

Listen to Bruce Barton, founder of one of the country's largest advertising agencies and later a Republican congressman. In 1924 he published a book, *The Man Nobody Knows: A Discovery of the Real Jesus*, which became a runaway best-seller:

He picked up twelve men from the bottom ranks of business and forged them into an organization that conquered the world. . . . Nowhere is there such a startling example of executive success as the way in which that organization was brought together.

Thus, Jesus Christ, ostensibly worshipped by a majority of Americans as Lord, Savior, and Redeemer, finally revealed Himself to a sinful humanity that craved His inspiration. He had risen on the third day after his crucifixion to sit on the right hand of God the Father, where he served as Chairman of the Board of whatever advertising firm was servicing U. S. Steel.

One dark day in 1929 those who peddled and bought this blasphemous self-adulation suffered a rough awakening.

David Blythe, *Post Office*, ca. 1862-64. (Museum of Art, Carnegie Institute.)

Thomas Eakins, *Max Schmitt in a Single Scull*, 1871. (The Metropolitan Museum of Art, Purchase 1934, Alfred N. Punnett Fund and Gift of George D. Pratt.)

Andrew Wyeth, *Northern Point,* 1950. (Courtesy Wadsworth Atheneum, Hartford.)

Museum, Mitchell, South Dakota)

Harvey Dunn, *Dakota Woman* (Friends of the Middle Border

Stane Jagodic

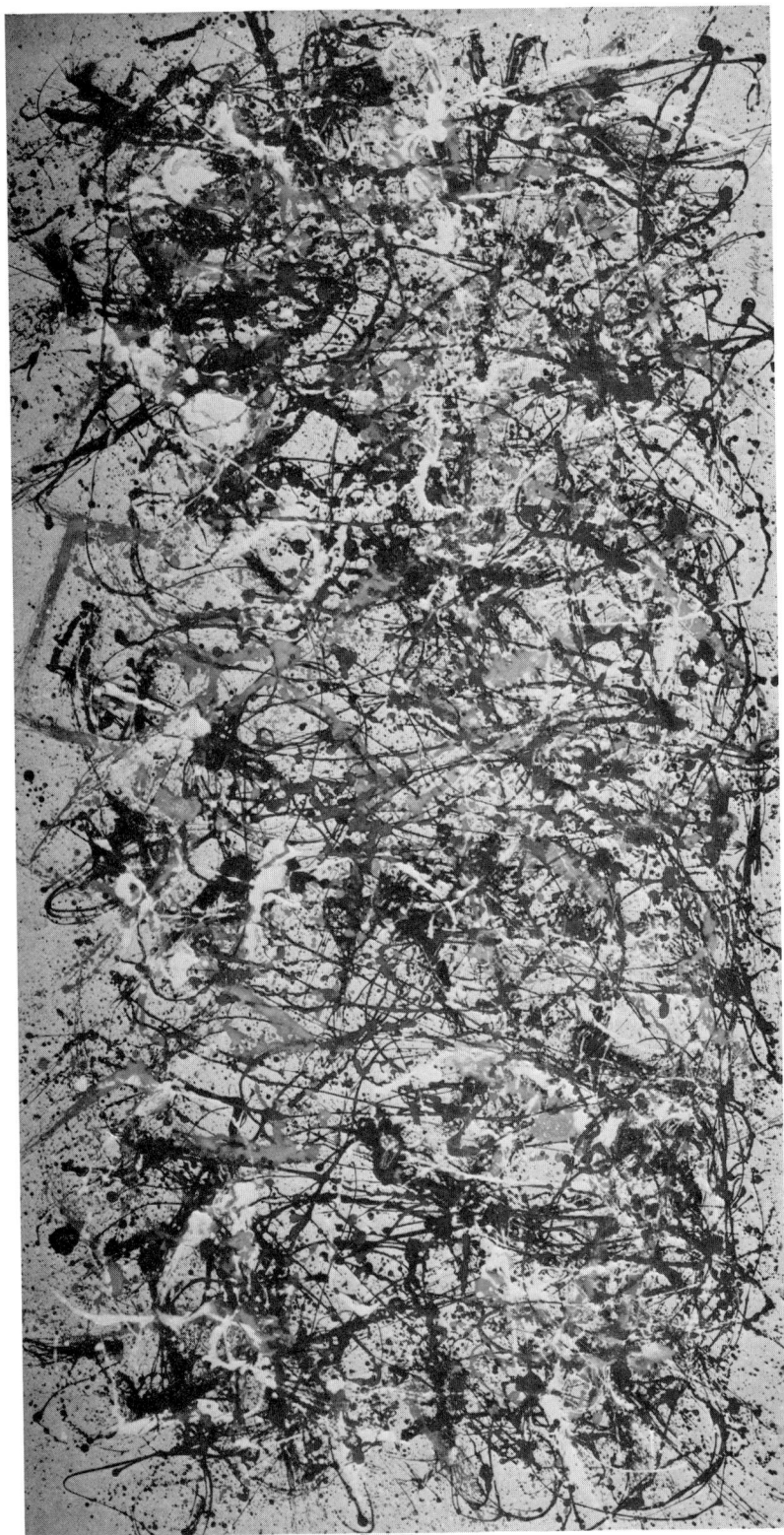

Jackson Pollock, *Autumn Rhythm.*

Jupiter and its four planet-size moons, called Galilean satellites, were photographed in early March 1979 by Voyager I and assembled into this collage. They are not to scale but are in their relative positions.

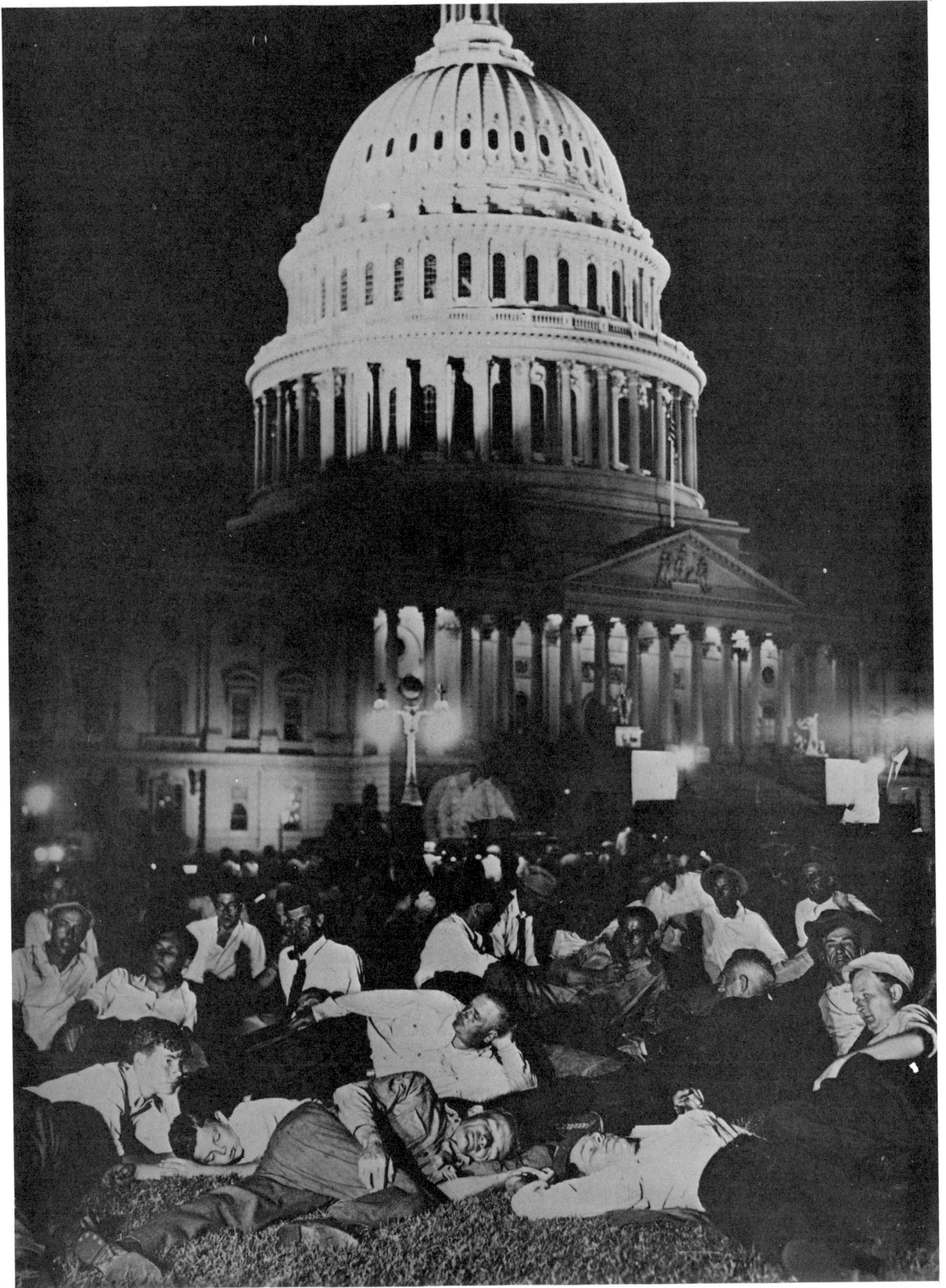

The Bonus Marchers. (Library of Congress.)

Chapter XXIV
The New Deal

The Bonus Army of 1932

In the spring of 1932 few newspaper readers paid much attention to reports that some 300 unemployed First World War veterans were traveling in Union Pacific freight cars rocking and swaying over the Rockies from Portland, Oregon, to Pocatello, Idaho. Some accompanied by their families, they were headed for Washington, D.C., to convince Congress to approve early payment of a soldier's bonus not scheduled for distribution until 1945. This "Bonus Army" picked up fresh recruits at almost every city, and finally became national news when the B & O Railroad tried to stop them in the "Battle of East Saint Louis." Local railroad union leaders averted bloodshed by moving truckloads of men, women, and children across Illinois to the Indiana border. Then each state governor hurried the band as swiftly as possible across Indiana, Pennsylvania, and Maryland until they reached the District of Columbia. There they met other veterans from every state in the Union, a total of more than 20,000 people.

President Herbert Hoover allowed the veterans to settle in abandoned buildings, and on the largest site, Anacostia Flats in Maryland, he quietly provided the District police commissioner with army food, clothing, beds, tents, and even medical supplies—characteristically keeping his humanitarian acts secret.

Like Hoover, Governor Franklin D. Roosevelt of New York disapproved early payment of the bonus, and offered his state's veterans both transportation home and guaranteed employment. While the bonus bill passed the House on June 5, 1932, two days later the Senate defeated it. Next, Hoover initiated federal loans to provide transportation home to any veteran who applied. But some 10,000 stayed on, waiting for something to happen.

On July 9 some 250 Californians arrived, led by a Navy veteran, Roy W. Robertson, who camped out with his men on the Capitol lawn. While in the service Robertson had broken his neck falling out of a hammock; he wore a leather brace supported by a tall steel column rising almost a foot above his shoulders, giving the eerie impression of a man with his head perpetually in a noose. For three days and four nights his men took turns slowly walking single file in a "Death March" vigil around the Capitol building. His head held high in the rigid brace, Robertson was a study in determination. While an angry mob of fellow veterans occupied the building's steps, Congress adjourned and its members escaped by subterranean passageways.

Army Chief of Staff General Douglas MacArthur stood ready for trouble with a sizable Regular Army force. MacArthur's opportunity came when the administration on July 28 forced the eviction of veterans from a small downtown area of government buildings scheduled for demolition. A riot ensued between a gathering of as many as 5,000 veterans and fewer than 800 police. One veteran was dead, another lay fatally wounded.

MacArthur ordered his troops to assemble at the Ellipse behind the White House. Hoover specifically directed MacArthur only to move the rioting veterans out of the business district and back to their camps. He was also repeatedly ordered not to follow the veterans across

Anacostia Flats, July 1932. (National Archives.)

the Potomac into Maryland. His staff aide, Dwight D. Eisenhower, was shocked when the Chief of Staff, resplendent in full military regalia, appeared personally to take command, although Hoover had ordered him to take instructions from the police commissioner. MacArthur—who liked to speak of himself in the third person "MacArthur, a Man of Destiny"—saw "revolution in the air." Using cavalrymen with drawn sabres and infantry with tear gas, MacArthur dispersed both veterans and spectators *en masse*. Then, ignoring the President's orders, he sent his troops across into Maryland. The whole camp became ablaze with light—setting fire to their own huts was the veterans' final symbolic act of defiance. Eisenhower recalled "a pitiful scene, those ragged, discouraged people burning their own little things." Soldiers fired the remaining empty huts. Fleeing the capital, the veterans became refugees from a government more immobile than heartless, more ignorant than cruel. Hoover, the great humanitarian who had fed the starving Belgians during World War I, received all the blame in the election—and Depression—year of 1932. The incident helped assure victory for the Democratic candidate, Franklin Roosevelt.

The Roosevelts

The Democrat who challenged Hoover in the 1932 election possessed a personality precisely suited to the times. Franklin Delano Roosevelt would speak of the nation's troubles only to express confidence that they could be banished. He did not hold himself back from the people, but seemed eager to meet each one personally. One woman, trying to express to her grandchildren in later years her feeling toward Roosevelt, remarked that if the President had come into her kitchen for morning coffee she would have been perfectly comfortable and not the least bit surprised. A young soldier, standing outside the White House at night after hearing of the President's death, said: "I felt as if I knew him. I felt as if he knew me—and I felt as if he liked me." In 1932 this personal charm contrasted sharply with the stern aloofness of the stiff, reserved, unsmiling Hoover.

Franklin Roosevelt as a boy.

Someone remarked that Roosevelt could say "my old friend" in ten languages while Hoover could say it in none. While the programs put forward in their campaign speeches differed in only a few respects, Roosevelt won the election by taking all but six states—with a margin in the popular vote of seven million—against an incumbent President himself elected overwhelmingly four years earlier.

Born in 1882 to a wealthy and aristocratic family in Dutchess County, New York, Franklin grew up as the sheltered only child of an aging, indulgent father and a domineering but intensely loving mother. His monopoly on parental affection, and the luxury and material comforts of the family estate at Hyde Park, made him secure and self-assured. At the Reverend Endicott Peabody's Groton School Roosevelt learned the values of a "better" class: patriotism, public service, and a simple and straightforward Christianity. Both at Groton and later at Harvard, he lived a life of gentility, manners, and fellowship rather than one of serious intellectual effort. While acquiring the polish of an educated man through a bit of classical learning, a brush with modern languages, and a smattering of knowledge from diverse fields, Roosevelt poured most of his energies into extra-curricular activities, managing teams at Groton and editing the Harvard *Crimson*. For him, competition always remained something of a game, not a vital struggle for wealth, recognition, or power.

Even the candidate's handicap—since 1921 his legs had been badly crippled by polio—became an asset during the 1932 campaign. Some Republicans sneered cruelly that he was just "a name and a crutch." But the optimism and courage he showed in the face of his disability did much to suggest that he was equal to combatting the Depression itself. The disability helped, moreover, to make the public forget his wealthy background.

But Roosevelt's personality would not have been enough to rouse Americans from the spiritual depression that accompanied the economic one had he not also demonstrated a capacity to act. And Roosevelt had long before cast himself in an activist mold. As the friends of his youth have recalled, he took his distant cousin Theodore as a model and planned to follow his succession of offices to the Presidency. Franklin began well by winning election to the New York state legislature and then before the First World War achieving TR's old job of Assistant Secretary of the Navy. Trying to skip over the gubernatorial level, he accepted the 1920 Democratic nomination for Vice-President in the party's losing cause, but returned to the track in 1928 when he followed Al Smith as governor of New York. In that office, Roosevelt backed important if not drastic reforms in agriculture, public utilities, welfare, and conservation, making New York one of the states most vigorous in its attempts to cope with the Depression. By 1932, he had experience in governing and a national reputation as a reformer.

While Roosevelt's programs as governor and President were never organized into a logical, coherent effort to achieve specific goals, they did at least give the impression of energetic action. Personal interests, recent meetings with advisers, and responses to emergencies comprised his "platform," within the bounds of certain general and ambiguous values. The essence of the "New Deal" was perhaps best summed up by a revealing bit of FDR's campaign wisdom: "The country needs bold, persistent experimentation. It is common sense to take a method and try it. If it fails, admit it frankly and try another. But above all, try something." Whatever else it did, this approach promised movement—and, just as important, the appearance of movement—in a country that seemed mired in despair.

Roosevelt managed repeatedly to seem bold and innovative by breaking with traditional behavior while at the same time affirming the values in which he and most of the country believed. After being nominated on the fourth ballot by the Democratic convention, he surprised and thrilled the delegates by flying through stormy weather from New York State to Chicago to accept their nomination in person. Using radio as a new political tool, Roosevelt delivered "fireside chats" to the nation, explaining his policies and plans in a conversational, easily understood manner and projecting his personality into millions of homes. During his twelve years in the White House, Roosevelt's popularity would rise and fall among various groups, but with a broad segment of the population he remained consistently—and astonishingly—their friend, the President. Almost immediately after his election he won another important ally, the press, by opening his news conferences to offhand questions and joking with reporters, rather than simply delivering answers to written questions as his predecessor had done. By mid-1934 a contemporary list of precedents broken by the new President included "swimming in the White House, driving his own car, sailing his own yacht, going to the people over the radio, naming a woman (Frances Perkins) to his cabinet and another (Ruth Bryan Owen) as an ambassador, greeting a British Prime Minister (Ramsay MacDonald) at the White House door, and talking

with a French Premier (Edouard Herriot) without an interpreter." None of these actions challenged fundamental beliefs or carried a great deal of political significance, but together they indicated a man unafraid of new things in the White House.

The First Lady also lent a special aura to the administration. Eleanor Roosevelt, as no previous President's wife, involved herself deeply in public life, establishing a personality that competed for public attention with that of her remarkable husband. Anna Eleanor was also a Roosevelt, niece of Theodore and distant cousin of Franklin. Perceiving herself as unattractive and awkward, the young Eleanor was extremely shy. Her beautiful mother called her "Granny" and made fun of her in front of visitors. She died when Eleanor was eight. Her father Elliott, though kind, soon drank himself to death. Her parents' early deaths, which left her to grow up with a grandmother and without many playmates, deepened her withdrawal. After marrying her confident and attractive cousin Franklin in 1905, Eleanor gave birth in rapid succession to six children who, in upper-class fashion, were brought up by servants. As the years passed, however, she gradually gained greater maturity and self-confidence; and she began to take a more and more active interest in her husband's career and in public affairs generally. Mrs. Roosevelt's public role became increasingly visible as Franklin proceeded from office to office.

Eleanor Roosevelt.

After the Roosevelts settled into the White House in 1933, Eleanor shocked those who expected another in the tradition of virtually invisible First Ladies. With her husband unable to walk or to travel easily, she became the President's eyes and ears. Although their relationship was no longer intimate and beginning in 1932 she developed a loving affection for a lady journalist, Eleanor had Franklin's respect and trust; he encouraged her to see people and problems first hand and report to him. The First Lady showed up in so many places that her adventures became legendary. One cartoon of the period showed coal miners deep underground looking up to say "Here comes Mrs. Roosevelt." But however influential her reports to the President may have been, Eleanor was humble about her role, commenting that "I would never presume to make recommendations." Beyond her innumerable trips and lectures, Mrs. Roosevelt produced after 1935 a newspaper column called *My Day* which purposefully remained rather chatty and trivial although it occasionally floated a political balloon, and she published several books on her life and on broad political questions.

From the first months of her husband's administration, Eleanor Roosevelt's activities provoked criticism. Her involvement in public affairs seemed improper to some, especially to those opposed to her liberal ideas and attitudes. Eleanor was a champion of black people in Washington and intervened personally when prejudice barred the black singer Marian Anderson from Constitution Hall. She also supported the American Youth Congress, which a red-hunting House committee charged was Communist-dominated. When challenged, Eleanor was quick to assert her independence and to deny any responsibility to the electorate since "I have never been elected to any office." Yet had she been in an elective post, there seems little danger that she would have been unseated. In a January 1939 Gallup poll, 68 percent of the population approved of Mrs. Roosevelt, a higher rating than her husband achieved. Repeatedly, ordinary people remarked on how neighborly she seemed, an impression seemingly confirmed in 1939 when she roasted hot dogs for the King and Queen of England.

Roosevelt himself was not a simple man; Frances Perkins, his Secretary of Labor, recalled him as "the most complicated human being I ever knew." He seldom gave fully of his love or attention to specific individuals, but his warmth embraced millions and called forth a passionate loyalty in associates. He seldom followed ideas beyond the level of general understanding, yet his appetite for new opinions and programs allowed him to put diverse ideas into operation and gave government an air of intellectuality. His special talents enabled Roosevelt to work political magic in the early thirties.

The Hundred Days

Between Roosevelt's election in November 1932 and his inauguration on March 4, 1933, the American economy slid even lower. During this "interregnum" more than a quarter of the labor force was out of work. Neither the defeated President nor the waiting President-elect could initiate major new policies, and bitterness remaining from the campaign inhibited cooperation between them. The banking system, under grave pressure since 1931, collapsed in the first months of 1933. Depositors stood in line at banks in every part of the country to demand their savings; such "runs" emptied the cash drawers of more and more weaker institutions, forcing them to close. On February 14 the governor of Michigan closed that state's banks for eight days. By Roosevelt's inauguration, state governments had closed or placed under restriction nearly all the nation's financial institutions.

The banking crisis in one sense eased Roosevelt's task. Everyone from the conservative businessman to the most liberal reformer admitted the need for drastic action; for a time all bowed to his lead almost without question. In his inaugural address the new President had proclaimed that "the only thing we have to fear is fear itself" and promised "to wage a war against the emergency." The so-called "Hundred Days" from March 4 to mid-June 1933 marked the first major campaign in that war. Roosevelt introduced the New Deal with one of the most productive bursts of law-making in American history. Congress passed nearly everything the White House requested, with no coherent opposition in sight. The only element that unified the legislation of the Hundred Days and beyond was the personality of the President. Although Roosevelt brought to Washington a "Brains Trust" of college professors including Raymond Moley, Adolf A. Berle, Jr., and Rexford G. Tugwell from Columbia, and Felix Frankfurter of Harvard Law School, none of these intellectuals put his stamp on the New Deal as a whole; nor did they collectively give order and system to the administration's programs. Roosevelt's cabinet also reflected the President's penchant for variety. Men like Secretary of the Treasury Henry Morgenthau were models of caution. At Agriculture and Interior were the progressives Henry A. Wallace and Harold C. Ickes respectively, both Republicans. And running the Department of Labor was an urban liberal, Frances Perkins, the first woman cabinet officer in United States history. Untroubled by either philosophical or personality conflicts, Roosevelt mixed diverging ideas and interests to satisfy the taste for action.

The President first attacked the banking crisis. On March 6 he dramatized his new leadership by declaring a four-day national bank holiday. On March 9, the first day of the special session of Congress called by Roosevelt, the Emergency Banking Relief Act was introduced, passed, and signed within hours, with Congressmen shouting their support before the final version was complete. The Act confirmed the President's power to do as he had already done, provided guidelines for reopening sound banks, and strengthened federal authority over the currency. These measures backed by Roosevelt's firm public insistence on the soundness of the banking system enabled about 75 percent of member banks in the Federal Reserve System to reopen within three days, and boosted stock market prices 15 percent in the next two weeks. The panic eased as people began returning their money to banks.

Despite the threats in Roosevelt's inaugural address about driving the money changers from the temples, the Banking Act, drafted in collaboration with the big banks, was a conservative piece of legislation. As would happen again and again, Roosevelt's angry speeches produced "safe" legislation well within public expectations. Other financial laws of the Hundred Days included the Economy Act—a futile effort to reduce federal expenditures and to balance the budget; the Federal Securities Act, requiring full disclosure to investors of information on new securities issues; and the second Glass-Steagall Act, creating the Federal Bank Deposit Insurance Corporation (later the familiar FDIC) to guarantee bank deposits up to a prescribed limit—at first $2500, as

well as expanding the membership and authority of the Federal Reserve System.

One of Roosevelt's favorite programs addressed the problem of unemployment among young men. The Civilian Conservation Corps (CCC) employed men aged 18 to 25 in reforestation, highway, antierosion, and national park projects under the direction of army officers. At its peak the CCC payroll contained the names of 500,000 conservation soldiers, and by 1941 it had employed a total of over 2,000,000 young men. One aging enrollee recalls:

"I was sent to Utah. I'll never forget the ride up the mountains in this battered old truck. We had an old grizzled army sergeant in charge. When we got to the area, it was just thick woods. 'Where's the camp?' I asked. The sarge waved his hands around the trees. 'This is it. Break out the axes and chop like hell if you don't want to sleep on the ground.' We chopped and built cabins and even a mess hall. For the next three years I grew up, physically and mentally and spiritually, in that beautiful country. It was one of the most rewarding experiences of my life. Before I left I was offered a job as a ranger. To this day I wonder whether I was a fool in turning it down and coming back east. A large number of the CCCs stayed on. Some own ranches today."

One of the most striking New Deal programs passed during the Hundred Days created a sweeping experiment in regional planning for the valley of the Tennessee River. During the First World War the federal government had constructed a large hydroelectric power facility and two munitions plants at Muscle Shoals, Alabama. When, after the war, the government was unable to obtain a reasonable price for these facilities from private interests, Senator George W. Norris twice shepherded through Congress, in 1928 and 1931, legislation allowing the federal government to operate the plants to provide power and fertilizer for the region's inhabitants. Republicans Coolidge and Hoover respectively vetoed these measures, on the grounds that such a project would compete with private enterprise. But Roosevelt, who visited Muscle Shoals in January 1933, saw the possibilities for a broad regional development of the valley based on the careful control and use of water resources. Congress in that year created the Tennessee Valley Authority (TVA), an independent public corporation with the authority to build dams and power plants, to produce and sell electric power and nitrogen fertilizers, and to sell explosives to the federal government.

The intent behind the TVA was larger than this. In addition to providing a "yardstick" for judging the rates charged by privately owned utilities, Roosevelt and Norris hoped to further the entire social and economic well-being of the region through erosion and flood control, land reclamation, reforestation programs, recreational development, and the encouragement of mixed industry. By 1944 nine dams on the main river and many on tributaries had greatly improved the economic outlook in six states. The TVA remains one of the most successful of all planning programs.

FDR's major prescription to ease the burdens of depression lay in two key programs initiated during the Hundred Days, one in agriculture and one in industry. Roosevelt liked to think of himself as a gentleman farmer and always expressed admiration for rural life. The Agricultural Adjustment Act, creating the Agricultural Adjustment Administration (AAA), aimed at restoring the security and the purchasing power of farmers. After an unhappy experiment in plowing under crops and killing piglets to cut surpluses and raise prices, the administration attempted to accomplish future reductions by paying subsidies to farmers for the voluntary reduction of acreage and output in certain basic commodities. The AAA would obtain funds for these subsidies from a tax on the processors of listed farm products. The Act also provided funds for refinancing farm mortgages through the Federal Land Banks. The Farm Credit Act, also of 1933, went much further, offering loans for agricultural production and marketing and allowing farm mortgages to be refinanced on longer terms at low interest. Together, these two laws did for farmers what another act of the Hundred Days—the Home Owners Refinancing Act of June 13, which created the Home Owners Loan Corporation (HOLC)—did for non-farm debtors. Within less than two years, the government had refinanced about 20 percent of all home and farm mortgages, offering both immediate relief and some hope of future security.

At the heart of Roosevelt's plans for reviving industry was the National Industrial Recovery Act (NIRA). One part of this broad legislation created the Public Works Administration (PWA) for direct public employment in the construction of roads and public buildings and a variety of other projects. The PWA under Interior Secretary Harold Ickes spent over $4 billion dollars on some 34,000 ventures.

Another section of the NIRA attempted to stimulate business activity by halting the downward spiral of prices and wages. It encouraged representatives of various industries to draw up "codes of fair competition" establishing fair wages, working conditions, and prices. Once created and approved by the President, these codes were to be exempt from anti-trust actions and enforceable by law. The National Recovery Administration (NRA), for the first year headed by the brash General Hugh Johnson, had the difficult task of policing the codes and encouraging consumers to buy only from those businesses that participated.

One small part of the NIRA also gave labor unions a long-desired legal basis. Section 7a guaranteed workingmen the right "to organize and bargain collectively through representatives of their own choosing." A National Labor Relations Board, with Senator Robert Wagner of New York at its head, was charged with assuring the right of collective bargaining. Organizers cleverly, if not entirely accurately, used this legal prop to persuade workers that the President wanted them to join a union, and an era of intensive unionization and labor-management strife got underway. Led by John L. Lewis of the mine-workers, a new type of unionism began to spread that organized industry-wide rather than by crafts. Despite conflict within the movement over this new form of organization—the older AFL had no enthusiasm for this daring strategy—by 1935 the Congress of Industrial Organization (CIO) was already overshadowing the parent organization and setting the scene for the mass unionization to come later in the decade.

After the Hundred Days

The Hundred Days brought excitement to the national government and a sense of movement to people's lives. The new administration's bright young enthusiasts evoked a style that contrasted sharply with the stodginess of the Coolidge and Hoover regimes. The new programs, especially the NRA, exhibited dynamic activity. In the name of its symbol, the blue eagle, public relations gimmickry and hoopla whipped up support for the program. Sailors lined up to form the letters

"NRA" on the deck of an aircraft carrier. A line of bathing beauties posed with their backs to the camera to reveal a blue eagle stenciled on each set of shoulders. Nearly every market, diner, and corner store sported stickers and posters.

The repeal of Prohibition also contributed to the new mood. On March 22, 1933, Congress passed the Beer-Wine Revenue Act permitting the sale of beer, ale, and wine with no more than 3.2 percent alcohol by weight. The First World War had helped pass Prohibition by providing the argument that the nation had better uses for grain than to make spirits; now the Depression helped repeal it, since the sale of alcoholic beverages was an important potential source of desperately needed tax revenues. On December 5, 1933, the Twenty-first Amendment to the Constitution achieved ratification, repealing the "Prohibition" Eighteenth Amendment. Men stood in saloons with glasses raised awaiting the new era, crowds sang "Happy Days Are Here Again" and bootleggers went out of business.

Congress continued to churn out legislation all through 1933 and 1934. Many new laws simply expanded the legislation of the Hundred Days or filled in gaps. The AAA had depended on voluntary crop reduction, but the Cotton Control and the Tobacco Control Acts of 1934 made cutbacks for these specific crops compulsory, fixing a national production limit and then providing farmers with individual allocations. The Home Owners Loan Act made it possible for the HOLC to make additional loans for home maintenance or repair. Separate laws addressed another persistent problem of the Depression by dealing with municipal, corporate, and farm bankruptcies and providing methods of reorganization.

A number of federal agencies now long familiar to Americans were the products of congressional activity in 1934. The Securities and Exchange Commission (SEC) was established to regulate the trading of securities and to prevent the manipulation of values or overspeculation. The Federal Communications Commission (FCC) was created to oversee all interstate and foreign uses of telegraph, cable, and radio. Still another law added to the New Deal alphabet soup the letters "FHA," standing for the Federal Housing Administration, which insured loans made by private lending institutions to construct or improve housing if certain standards were met. Each of these agencies has directly or indirectly affected millions of Amercians, and each remains active today.

And yet, despite this rich harvest of legislation, the Depression refused to fade away under the brilliance of Roosevelt's smile. The economy did revive somewhat, but there was little long-term recovery. Manufacturers, for instance, increased their inventories, driving up industrial production, because they expected labor costs to rise under the NIRA; this gave an appearance of rapid success for the New Deal while actually providing no sustained improvement. By the spring of 1935 when Roosevelt had been in office two years, nearly 20 percent of the labor force remained unemployed and national income had risen only slightly from the depths of 1933.

Any administration and any plan of action would have faced great difficulty in ending the Depression, but Roosevelt's policies met special problems. The hastily drafted New Deal legislation often failed to withstand legal challenge. Roosevelt's taste for a balanced budget got in the way of his desire to increase purchasing power and put people to work through spending on public works. Many programs simply did not work, and some conflicted with one another.

The NRA faced particularly substantial problems. Instead of national planning, it produced codes for separate industries written largely in isolation and usually under the influence of big corporations. Progressives worried about this

William Gropper, Detail from Mural, 1935-37. (Smithsonian Institution.)

revival of monopoly, small businessmen and workers saw their positions eroding, and consumers feared rising prices under the new codes. Company unions continued to flourish despite the NIRA's section 7a. General Johnson, for all his enthusiasm, proved to be an incompetent administrator, and was fired after a year. While the NRA virtually ended child labor and provided encouragement for labor unions and improved labor conditions, on the whole it served the interests of big business and, like the AAA, produced higher costs for consumers. As a device to create economic recovery it had clearly failed even before May 1935 when the Supreme Court in *Schechter v. U.S.* declared the legislation that had created the NRA unconstitutional. It had conferred legislative power on the executive branch.

The AAA encountered similar difficulties. Farmers did plant less acreage in order to receive federal subsidies, but they took out of production their poorest land and on their better acreage actually increased the size of their crops. Farm income rose, but marginal farmers and farm tenants were pushed off the land, and the burden of higher food prices, and of the processing taxes used to finance subsidies, fell on the consumer—including even the unemployed.

Roosevelt himself harbored conflicting ideas and notions which left his administration floating somewhere between opposite poles. Essentially a traditionalist, he never seemed quite safe to businessmen and was unable to instill the confidence that is considered to have so much to do with stimulating commercial activity. The President frightened business leaders by attacking them in a righteous tone on the one hand, and by failing to condemn all sorts of radical possibilities, on the other. In actuality, his legislation never came close to the rhetoric, for Roosevelt rejected the overthrowing of past values. Despite the TVA, he remained cautious about the federal government competing with private industry and refused to allow wages in public projects to equal those in the

private sector. Later, when private industry began to revive, Roosevelt would drop even the most successful federal programs to avoid such competition. While he alienated business by both his rhetoric and the style of the young New Deal intellectuals who trailed him into the Washington agencies, Roosevelt remained temperamentally unable to go far enough to develop possibilities of recovery which did not depend on the active cooperation of big business.

FDR's dilemma was real, not just a product of limited vision. Many of the nation's economic institutions required serious reform in order to avoid another collapse, and public bitterness toward the corporations made the political demand for reform overwhelming. Yet recovery required a renewal of business investment, while serious changes in regulations and policies could only frighten the rich. Roosevelt had begun with reforms that invited and encouraged business cooperation. The Banking Act was the bankers' act, yet it improved a desperately weak link in the chain of economic institutions. The NRA was a dramatic initiative which in fact built on the trade-association movement among big industries of the 1920's. Similarly, the selection of an old Wall Streeter, Joseph P. Kennedy, as first chairman of the Securities and Exchange Commission insured the investment community a voice in its own reform. And the AAA respected to a painful degree the dominant power of the large farmers in American agriculture.

For all this caution, conservative opposition was aroused by Roosevelt's avowed willingness to experiment, his several less conservative initiatives such as the obviously socialistic TVA, large expenditures for relief, and the labor provisions of NRA, as well as his sometimes radical rhetoric. At the same time, millions now began to demand major and immediate changes to better their lot. The Depression, affected only somewhat by all the New Deal's relief efforts, continued.

Down and Out in the Land of Opportunity

"It's the big trouble," she explained. "That's why I'm on the rails." Nearly one million youngsters like her understood the slang: depression had turned them into twentieth-century nomads riding steel rails. Millions more adults, ashamed of their past and even more anxious about the future, stared out of empty freight cars

day after day. America was on the move, as always, but for the first time it was not going anywhere. Statistics alone cannot convey to later generations how desperate many people felt during the thirties. Pictures of the poor—the farm workers Dorothea Lange or Walker Evans photographed—impart something of what poverty did to people. Hard times lashed out first at the un-skilled, those with the least resources to tide them over. Some areas suffered more than others: the southern Appalachians with its depleted mines; the Great Plains made barren by wind erosion and drought; the old Southern cotton belt with too many people on too little good land. Grayness and worry settled over the poor and the lower middle class.

Loss of employment, or the threat of it, had a startling impact on social customs. Even the familiar comforts of family sagged under economic adversity, which could undermine parental authority and yank children out of the home. The equation of home and family ceased altogether when banks foreclosed mortgages. Parents became so discouraged that between 1935 and 1940 the numbers of new babies fell below zero growth rate. Young couples postponed children until times improved, and for the same reason the number of marriages decreased by nearly one fourth. Only because of a drop in the death rate to eleven per thousand—boosting life expectancy to sixty-three years—did the population increase as much as seven percent in the course of the decade. The number of divorces dropped sharply, perhaps because legal costs, child support, and alimony were beyond the reach of most people.

The Depression burdened family life in less tangible ways. Across the country, indigent relatives moved in with more fortunate aunts or brothers or cousins. Generations crowded in on one another, grandmothers and mothers arguing over how to raise children or run the household. Youngsters were suddenly confronted with orders from many adults, not just two. Rising unemploy-ment forced women back into the home, often destroying the hopes for a more independent life that had seemed possible during the twenties. Most available jobs for men went to unskilled laborers at low wages; railroads, for example, paid only $10 a week for work on road gangs. As a result, fathers often sat at home, losing their tradi-tional authority over the family while their sons worked.

Inventive Americans discovered new ways to earn a living. During the twenties, people had avoided jury duty; now they shoved their way into court buildings eager to receive the allotted $4 per day served. An army of new-fledged salesmen went from door to door, peddling everything im-aginable, and in cities they spread out their wares along the street curbs. Arguments went on over whether permanent investment in a shoeshine kit would produce more income than hawking apples or newspapers. (The International Apple Shippers

Association, faced with a large surplus, sold its product on credit to the unemployed; some 6,000 people sold apples on New York City streets in 1930.) Sunday papers sold from door to door in apartment houses offered an income, and more and more newsboys walked the side streets. Enter-prises given up earlier as an uneconomical use of labor—vegetable and fruit pushcarts, for ex-ample—reappeared. Yet all these undertakings betrayed a surrender to hard times, an acceptance of economic stagnation, a loss of ambition.

Many tried to escape family tensions and an un-promising future. For the first time since the fron-ier had disappeared in the late nineteenth century, Americans once again bustled about in large num-bers. Attachment to place evaporated for millions. By 1940 about sixty percent of the people lived in urban areas, and rural population had declined by more than a fifth in the course of the decade. Drought and low commodity prices prodded many Midwesterners toward California or into middle-sized towns. Whole families, unable to find work or to continue paying rent or the mortgage, piled into the old car and took to the highway, bewildered bits of humanity driven from town to town by a strange force called a "depression." Migratory workers usually moved with the seasons, but some simply rushed into regions where rumor pointed to jobs. Perhaps as many as five million people became vagrants, perpetually unemployed, perpetually hounded out of towns. These hoboes "rode the rails" or gathered together in camps remote from state troopers. Woody Guthrie wrote a famous song about his own "Hard Travelin' ":

I've been doin' some hard travelin',
I thought you knowd
I've been doin some hard ramblin'
Away down the road . . . .
I've been layin in a hard rock jail,
I thought you knowd
I've been out ninety days
Way down the road.
The damed old judge, he said to me,
It's ninety days for vagrancy,
And I've been doing some hard travelin',
    Lord.

About 900,000 tramps were children. The Union Pacific Railroad reported in 1933 that freight cars had killed hundreds of these inexperienced boys and girls. For nearly a sixth of the population, depression meant permanent emigration, always leaving someplace, never really going anywhere.

Middle- and Upper-Class America in the Depression

Even in the worst depression years, most American workers had jobs. Essential skilled laborers, both farm and factory, or those in the few powerful unions, generally rode out the decade with few scars. Clerks, typists, and many white-collar workers fared less well as business activity slowed. Professionals like lawyers and doctors lost income as the earnings of their clients lagged. Schoolteaching, especially in college, was usually a stable, much-prized job despite sometimes lowered salaries. Government work became the most desirable of all: Washington, D.C. possessed the healthiest economy of any city in the nation. Although wages from these middle-income jobs declined, so too did prices. If such workers bought few luxuries, they seldom worried about the necessities.

For small businessmen lucky enough to survive until New Deal agencies ended deflation, the Roosevelt era restored a measure of stability. Though banks hoarded money, making long-term expansion almost impossible, grocers, druggists, and oil dealers, for example, could rely upon a small but stable income, low taxes, and assets slowly rising in value. After 1933, they rarely worried about paying the rent or sending the children to college. In fact, many merchants took advantage of abysmally low prices to invest in land or the stock market. And as the years passed, more and more middle-class entrepreneurs criticized New Deal "experiments." They carped that government agencies needlessly complicated business affairs; they fretted that high taxes might take away high profits, if prosperity ever returned. A few probably realized that depression had severely battered middle-class self-confidence and America's well-deserved reputation for innovation. Times were not good for the small, independent businessman, and he was losing his central role in the American economy, but then times were not bad either.

Except for the worst months at the end of 1932 and the beginning of 1933, the Depression scarcely touched the very rich, that top five percent of the population who owned three-fourths of the nation's wealth. The stock market crash had wiped out plungers more often than those with carefully diversified investments. Although dividends and rents shrank during those long, weary years, prices also declined. Ice cubes still tinkled against cut glass at cocktail parties, although now such affairs moved away from speakeasy brownstones and back into expensive apartments. Well-dressed women copied Parisian styles, wearing long scarves, low hemlines and close-fitting hats. The rich collected objects of art during the thirties. Porcelain, antique silver, paintings, French furniture, and jewelry flooded into the United States as the wealthy bought treasures from Europe's harder-pressed upper classes. Winter vacationing on the shores of the Caribbean became popular, with Miami and Havana the new watering holes for the very fashionable. More and more islands built resort hotels and legalized casino gambling; even American administrators in Puerto Rico and the Virgin Islands gave in to the universal desire to lure rich tourists from New York and Chicago. On the mainland, conspicuous consumption revived, through not the public lavishness of the twenties. General Motors reported large declines in their sales of Chevrolets, but none at all for Cadillacs. Canadian fur raisers experienced a boom when *Vogue* magazine decreed mink for the winter of 1935. Depression neither narrowed the gap between rich and poor nor permanently reduced the living standards of America's wealthy.

Although their pleasures and comforts continued almost without interruption, the very rich realized that they had lost of control over America's destiny. Perhaps this explained their irrational hatred of Franklin D. Roosevelt, "that man in the White House," who had, many thought, "betrayed his class." Tales of Roosevelt's alleged insanity, of strange laughter in the night, found a ready credence among usually skeptical wealthy businessmen; lurid jokes slandered both President and First Lady. Yet the fact was that in propping up American capitalism, the New Deal had secured the wealthy in their property. Overlooking this irony, many American millionaires piously worried about a decline in self-reliance among the working classes or ritually complained about high taxes—though in the year 1936 the tax on a $1 million income increased only $1,800, about two-tenths of one percent. Their anger was not over economic loss; they realized that the failures of business society during the Hoover years had permanently stripped them of independent power and prestige. Only a few of the enormously wealthy—men like John D. Rockefeller, Jr., for example, who replaced nine square blocks of Manhattan slums with skyscrapers without borrowing from any bank—could still exercise that unbridled power which the wealthy, as a class, had lost.

The Grapes of Wrath, 1940. The plight of tenant farmers during the Depression and Dust Bowl of the 1930's, the bitter lives of migrant agricultural workers and the dauntless strength of the American family were the themes of this film. Social criticism as a movie subject vanished until after the War, then returned not as protests against economic inequalities but as attacks on racial and ethnic prejudice.

Opponents of the New Deal

Although the Democrats picked up a total of nine seats in the House and Senate in the 1934 elections—unusual for the party-in-power in a non-presidential year—the New Deal had acquired a variety of enemies. Some, out of either principle or pigheadedness, refused from the beginning to accept Roosevelt's programs, while others who began as supporters or at least neutrals turned sour when the New Deal failed to meet their particular expectations. The crisis of the Depression led voters to entertain both cure-alls and prejudices that they would have dismissed in normal times. The New Deal retained majority support, but on all sides voices grew increasingly strident as exotic plans bloomed abundantly.

From the two established radical parties, the Communists and Socialists, came the expected attacks on an administration which they immediately recognized as trying to save capitalism. Aided by the Soviet Union, the Communist Party extended its membership and influence in the early thirties while using the militant rhetoric of Stalin's "left" period in denouncing capitalism and the New Deal. But by 1935 the new Soviet strategy of the "Popular Front"—cooperation with liberal democracies against Hitler—had virtually ended Communist criticism.

The Socialists were never as uncompromising as the pre-1935 Communists. To them Roosevelt was a decent and well-meaning man though not a strong leader, and the New Deal presented merely a conglomeration of weak measures offering no real change: Roosevelt was wasting a precious historical moment when a major reshaping of the system was possible. As Norman Thomas of the Socialist Party put it, the New Deal was like an attempt "to cure tuberculosis with cough drops," and the danger existed that halfway programs would still the voices of protest and destroy the chance for true reform.

From the right the most extreme criticism came from American Fascists. Some groups, like William Dudley Pelly's Silver Shirts, used the swastika; most lavished an ample store of hatred on Jews, blacks, Communists, foreigners, and other scapegoats while talking of saving democracy, Christianity, free enterprise, and America.

Unlike the Fascists, who desired sweeping changes to institutionalize their nativism and prejudice, political conservatives wanted little change of any kind. By the fall of 1933, after cooperating in the crisis of the Hundred Days, conservatives—who made up a substantial portion of the business community, the profesions, the press, and the Republican party—began to organize in opposition to Roosevelt. They charged the New Deal with extravagant spending, Socialist leanings, trampling on the Constitution, overtaxation, and wasteful and meddling bureaucracy. With Herbert Hoover prominent in their ranks, many conservatives increasingly charged that recovery had been about to occur when Roosevelt took office, and that a hands-off policy would have ended the Depression, whereas Roosevelt's foolish programs were prolonging hard times. The well-financed Liberty League issued anti-New Deal propaganda, attracting several prominent Democratic conservatives, including the former presidential nominees Al Smith and John W. Davis.

Beyond the predictable opposition of radicals and conservatives to the New Deal, various specific movements arose in the early thirties which, though often propounding a narrow and simplistic program, threatened the popular base of Roosevelt's government. In 1934 Upton Sinclair, author of *The Jungle* and other muckraking novels, left the Socialist party and with the help of the unemployed obtained the Democratic nomination for governor of California. In a program known as "End Poverty in California" (EPIC), Sinclair called for turning silent factories and fallow farmlands into nonprofit cooperatives which he hoped, while operating inside the capitalist system, would provide large-scale relief and convert millions to socialism. Although Sinclair at first had strong support and the implicit approval of the White House as the party nominee, California interests and state Democratic leaders soon organized to oppose him as communistic, atheistic, and un-American. Sinclair was badly defeated at the polls. Other protest movements rose to champion agricultural interests. Milo Reno, a longtime agricultural radical, supported the traditional populist solution of currency inflation, and demanded government guarantees of the farmer's production costs and a further extension of farm mortgages. His "Farm Holiday" movement proposed an agricultural strike, and his followers attracted attention by blocking highways, dumping milk on the roads, and forcibly preventing eviction sales. Such gestures at least gave farm problems national prominence.

More serious challenges to Roosevelt's leadership came from movements led by two demagogues and a country doctor. Huey P. Long, from the hard-scrabble hills of Northern Louisiana, was a formidable opponent of the New Deal. Long went from traveling salesman to lawyer to railroad commissioner to governor at age thirty-five, and finally United States senator in 1933. Possessing both intelligence and a notable lack of scruples, he taxed oil profits as governor and used the taxes (after keeping a share for himself) to provide school books, health services, and other benefits to the people of Louisiana, including poor blacks. He was no egalitarian, but blacks were part of the coalition of the poor to whom Long appealed with the slogan "Every Man a King." By 1934 he held virtually dictatorial power in Louisiana, establishing a base for national ambitions.

Though an early supporter of Roosevelt, Long quickly moved away to advance his own "Share Our Wealth" program, and denounced Roosevelt as a stooge of Wall Street. Long suggested seizing all private fortunes of over $5 million and taxing the portion of annual incomes over $1 million at 100 percent; the money collected would be redistributed to provide every American family a "homestead," a yearly income of between $2,000 and $3,000 plus pensions and government-guaranteed educational benefits. The uninhibited, brash, but clever "Kingfish," a name he appropriated from the Amos 'n' Andy radio show, gleefully gained as an associate Gerald L.K. Smith, a shouting evangelical preacher who helped build his following. By 1935 twenty thousand Share-Our-Wealth clubs claimed several million members, and Long was taking aim at the White House—actually writing a book entitled *My First Days in the White House.* His colleague Senator Carter Glass of Virginia hoped he would not make it: "I understand that in the ultimate decadence of Rome they elected a horse to the Senate. At least it was a whole horse." Some believe that Long hoped to achieve the Presidency in 1936, but more likely he sought to lay the basis for a triumph in 1940. The question became moot when, on September 8, 1935, an assassin fatally wounded Long in the marble corridors of the Louisiana state capitol, destroying both Long and his movement.

Rivaling Long in national influence during the early thirties was the "Radio Priest," Father Charles Coughlin. In his mellifluous voice he had been broadcasting a weekly religious message since 1926, but in the thirties his messages became increasingly political. At first an enthusiastic supporter of the New Deal, he came to dislike Roosevelt's financial policies and was soon searching for ever more sensational topics to hold his audience among low-income people, particularly urban Catholics in the Midwest. Coughlin not only called Roosevelt a "great betrayer" and a "liar," but eventually gave expression to anti-Semitic themes, suggestive of European Fascism. Coughlin, his audience estimated at between thirty and forty-five million listeners, seemed a major political threat.

The third challenger of the New Deal was not a demagogue like Long or Coughlin but a rather bland, white-haired, retired doctor living in California, Francis E. Townsend. Disturbed by the terrible effects of depression and unemployment on the elderly, Townsend proposed a recovery-retirement scheme whereby the government would give each person over 60 a pension on the conditions that the person not work and that he spend the entire amount within the month. The presumption was that such spending would create jobs for younger workers and stimulate economic recovery. Critics, however, quickly noted that Townsend's plan would require the expenditure of about 25 billion or half the national income to support 10 percent of the population. Yet Townsend had tapped an important new interest group in politics, the elderly, who made up an increasingly large segment of the population. Townsend Clubs singing "Onward Townsend Soldiers" and a national weekly with a circulation of over 200,000 suggested to politicians that they would do well to give some attention to the needs of older citizens.

In 1936 the remnants of Long's movement, Coughlin's National Union for Social Justice, and the Townsendites came together in the Union Party to oppose Roosevelt. Although the Union Party won only a few hundred thousand votes in the election, these protest movements reflected real dissatisfactions with the New Deal's progress in ending depression. The despair of 1932 had become hope in 1933, and for some that hope had become frustration since even at its best and most effective the New Deal could not possibly satisfy everyone's expectations. But Roosevelt was no political novice, and did not ignore the common man's hostility toward big business and his desire for social justice. By early 1935 he was moving to expand the New Deal dramatically in ways that would confound all his opponents in 1936.

The Second Hundred Days

At the beginning of 1935, Roosevelt's annual message to Congress called for new initiatives in resources policy, provision of relief, slum clearance, and some form of social legislation to protect against sickness, unemployment, and penniless old age. Yet, by the time Congress prepared to adjourn for the summer, it had passed only the Emergency Relief Appropriation Act. This important bill established the Works Progress Administration (WPA), which, universally called by its initials, became the very symbol of the New Deal. To some a giant boondoggle, to others it was a vast, imaginative use of federal dollars to provide work for the unemployed. In eight years, the WPA spent $11 billion—then a giant sum even for the federal government—employing over 8½ million people in nearly 1½ million projects, constructing and repairing roads, bridges, parks, airports and public buildings, hiring artists and writers to spread culture to even the tiniest villages, performing a bewildering array of services, some priceless when the project was well designed, some doubtless a waste. But however humanitarian, however useful in pump-priming the economy, the WPA remained essentially a relief measure and, as such, a far cry from the promised program of reform.

Then, suddenly, Roosevelt seized the initiative. A series of executive orders established several important agencies: the Resettlement Administration, to help poor farm families and to establish "greenbelt towns" for low-income city-dwellers; the Rural Electrification Administration (REA),

an extraordinary success that vastly speeded the spread of modern conveniences to farm families; the National Youth Administration (NYA) which offered jobs to young people, helping millions to survive and hundreds of thousands to complete college. The President also demanded that Congress remain in session to pass five pieces of "must" legislation as well as several other bills. Sweating in the Washington heat, congressmen prodded and driven from the White House entered upon the "second hundred days," enacting laws that have had a permanent effect on American society.

Roosevelt called for a social security system, government sponsorship of collective bargaining between employers and organized labor, the centralization of major banking operations in the Federal Reserve Board, the control of public-utility holding companies, and a new tax plan soon dubbed "Soak the Rich." In one form or another, Congress responded on all these issues and several more.

The National Labor Relations Act of 1935, long pressed by Senator Robert Wagner of New York but only now supported by FDR, radically shifted the balance of power in labor-management relations by guaranteeing labor's right to organize. The Wagner Act reestablished and even strengthened labor rights gained under the NRA and lost at the hands of the Supreme Court. The National Labor Relations Board established by the act could supervise elections among workers, certify duly elected unions as bargaining agents, and collect

Migrant Family Shack. (National Archives.)

data on management's "unfair labor practices" including refusal to bargain.

Thereafter the rise of organized labor, while still tested in bloodshed as well as court battles, proceeded without serious interruptions. The newly powerful mass unions quickly became an essential element of the New Deal coalition and a recognized if still not fully accepted part of American life.

The Social Security Act of 1935 had consequences equally far reaching. It established a vast system providing a very modest cushion for most Americans against unemployment, dependency, old age. Coverage, to be sure, was limited: domestics, agricultural workers, people working in small businesses (fewer than eight employees) were excluded, and the payroll deduction provision had a deflationary effect on the weak economy of the thirties by taking money out of circulation. Nonetheless, the act signaled a basic change in the country's direction and outlook—the United States was becoming a welfare state. Despite its strong capitalist base, it had at last joined industrial nations in providing social insurance against the worst shocks of modern economic life.

The Banking Act, the Holding Company Act, and the Wealth Tax Act were all aimed squarely at Roosevelt's opponents, and they represented his recognition of and response to the public hostility toward big business and banks reflected in the popularity of Long and Coughlin. The Banking Act opened the way for closer central control over the banking system, although as it turns out presidents have not usually controlled the Federal Reserve Board. The Holding Company Act and the Wealth Tax Act aroused some of the fiercest controversy in the summer of 1935. William Randolph Hearst, the great newspaper baron, decreed that all his editors should henceforth refer to the New Deal as the "Raw Deal" because of the wealth tax, and the public utilities invested over a million dollars on bogus telegrams to Congress opposing the Holding Company Act. Roosevelt's respectable conservative enemies could generate more hatred toward him, as well as more publicity against him, than all the demagogues whose programs Roosevelt had borrowed from and whose supporters he had recaptured.

Some historians have referred to the second hundred days as a "second New Deal" fundamentally different from the first. They see the "first New Deal" as more conservative and pro-business and the second New Deal as an anti-business coalition. But whatever elements of planning, or regulation, or counterbalancing powers, or basic safeguards for individuals Roosevelt championed and experimented with, his thinking and that of the majority of his public never went beyond the seeking of adjustments within the system of private enterprise, within the system that had produced the nation's wealth and power—as well as its Great Depression. New Deal, old deal, raw deal, square deal, most critics now agree that he continued to deal from the same deck as Theodore Roosevelt, Woodrow Wilson or, for that matter, Herbert Hoover. As the Socialist Party's veteran presidential candidate Norman Thomas remarked: "FDR said to me, 'Just look at this. I've saved their system and the U.S. Chamber of Commerce denounces me.' " Thomas went on: "I was opposed to most of the New Deal program. The NRA reminded me of Mussolini's corporate state. But TVA was a beautiful flower in a garden of weeds."

The Election of 1936

In 1936 the Democrats joyfully renominated Roosevelt at their convention in Philadelphia and promised more reform. (If the Supreme Court blocked economic regulation by the government, the platform hinted darkly, Congress and the people must seek "a clarifying amendment.") Then on the evening of June 27 the President delivered one of the great speeches of American political history to a radio audience of millions. "In the place of the palace of privilege," he told his excited listeners, "we seek to build a temple out of faith and hope and charity." Castigating "economic royalists," he grandly called the country to its mission: "There is a mysterious cycle in human events. To some generations much is given. Of others much is expected. This generation of Americans has a rendezvous with destiny."

Not all Republicans were ready to concede a Roosevelt triumph. Despite the severe drubbing of the 1934 congressional campaign, those who survived thought that the welfare politics of 1935-36—the second New Deal—had alienated conservatives in the border South and Far West. Townsend, Coughlin, and Gerald L.K. Smith all

Charles Goeller, Third Avenue, *ca. 1934.* (Smithsonian Institution.)

pumped out anti-Roosevelt propaganda to their followers in critical states like California and Michigan. The Depression continued with persistent double-digit unemployment that also heartened the Republicans. But they worried about a nominee. Hoover took himself out of the race, relieving realistic politicians. Senator William Borah of Idaho wanted the nomination, but his well-publicized attacks on big business destroyed his chances. So the GOP finally turned to Governor Alfred Landon of Kansas, a man with few enemies and one of the few Republicans still in office. Best known for fiscal caution—Landon had balanced the Kansas budget every year—the nominee and his party platform nevertheless boldly approved unemployment relief, farm subsidies, collective bargaining, and antitrust action. Landon even spoke the language of liberalism, repeatedly asserting that "industrial plutocrats" must not abuse the rights of average people. But most Republicans still denounced the style, if not the substance, of the New Deal as "socialistic" and as "unconstitutional dictatorship."

During the campaign, Roosevelt countered charges about his "radicalism" by arguing that "a true conservative corrects injustices to preserve social peace." Constantly he asked workers to compare their life in 1936 with conditions in 1933; his friendly speeches convinced voters of his personal concern for their welfare. Exasperated by FDR's popularity Landon bitterly assailed the welfare state. GOP conservatives applauded, but the average citizen was unimpressed.

A splinter coalition of the discontented, the followers of Coughlin, Townsend, and Long, also fielded a presidential candidate, William Lemke of North Dakota, under the banner of the Union Party. The third party worried Roosevelt: its blatant appeal to special groups might polarize American politics. Still almost everyone realized the popularity of the New Deal and Roosevelt's personal magnetism guaranteed a Democratic sweep. (Only the famously incorrect *Literary Digest* poll, based upon telephone subscribers in a few large cities, forecast a Landon victory. The magazine folded shortly thereafter.) But few could believe the election eve prediction of James Farley, the President's campaign manager: "Roosevelt will carry every state except Maine and Vermont."

He was exactly correct. That coalition of farmers, workers, blacks and middle-class wage earners which had voted against Hoover in 1932 now, even more strongly, validated New Deal reforms. Roosevelt won over 60 percent of the popular vote, and all the electoral college votes but eight. Only 88 Republicans remained in the House of Representatives. The election of 1936, like its counterpart in 1896, transformed national politics for a generation. It institutionalized the New Deal, cementing a coalition of Democratic voters that insured that party's dominance in the United States for many years thereafter. In only four years out of the next forty would the Republicans hold a majority in Congress.

Still, ironies dogged both the contest and the contestants. Republicans nominated a liberal who embraced the New Deal, then rejected it. Roosevelt's almost legendary victory came despite the persistence of depression, and he subsequently frittered away his overwhelming mandate.

Roosevelt and the Supreme Court

As Roosevelt's reelection appeared more and more certain, the Supreme Court struck broadly at the government's legal power to manipulate free enterprise. Early in 1936, the justices, in *United States v. Butler*, wrecked the administration's agricultural policy by declaring the AAA unconstitutional. Congress had overextended its taxing power, the Court charged, and had interfered with states' rights. Then in June, the "nine old men" vetoed a New York law which legislated minimum wages for women: the state, they said, had encroached upon the exclusive federal jurisdiction over interstate commerce (*Morehead v. New York ex rel. Tipaldo.*) The justices had apparently blocked economic regulation by any level of government. Roosevelt himself avoided any direct assault on the Court during the campaign, no doubt calculating that a great election mandate could create its own opportunity. During the last weeks of the campaign he pledged "a more equitable distribution of income" and in his second inaugural address in January 1937, sketched new vistas. "I see one third of a nation ill-housed, ill-clad, ill-nourished," he told the American people. Yet the Court now stood in the way of any great expansion of the New Deal.

Roosevelt decided to remove the obstacle that had blocked the will of President, Congress, and people. Early in 1937, he suddenly released a White House plan to "reform" the entire federal judiciary. Thirty-five additional district judges could speed decisions in lower courts. The extreme age of six Supreme Court justices—all over seventy—slowed its deliberations, the proposal argued; unless each retired, Congress should allow the President to appoint another judge to assist him. The ill-disguised purpose of the maneuver was clear: Roosevelt wanted to add to the Court liberals certain to approve New Deal reforms. Roosevelt accused the Court "of improperly setting itself up as a third House of Congress." He told Americans during a fireside chat on March 9, 1937: "We must take action to save the Constitution from the Court."

Suprisingly, the most popular President since Washington now encountered a sudden barrage of opposition. Most Republicans and many conservative Democrats condemned Roosevelt, some publicly, as a "dictator"—they feared that the "court-packing scheme" might end the separation of powers. But Roosevelt's abrupt manner on this issue also angered many liberals as well. Chief Justice Charles Evans Hughes testified during Senate hearings that the Court regularly completed some ninety percent of its docket every year. Additional justices, he charged, would slow the Court's work, for "more must discuss, more must decide." The justices who had already approved a minimum wage law, then made a series of unexpected decisions: they accepted social security benefits, then startled even labor leaders with a confirmation of the Wagner Act. A conservative justice, Willis Van Devanter, retired during the spring; Roosevelt's replacement, presumably, would tilt the Court toward a five to four liberal majority. The final blow to Roosevelt's plan came that summer when Joseph T. Robinson, floor manager for the bill in the Senate, died. Thwarted by the Court's new direction, his own clumsy tactics, and congressional independence, Roosevelt quietly admitted defeat.

The President later claimed that he had "lost a battle but won the war." Then, too, Congress had drafted the "second New Deal" more carefully, basing these reforms on the Constitution's commerce clause rather than relying on its less firmly fixed taxing power. Between 1937 and his death in 1945, Roosevelt appointed seven new justices, all liberals. For the first time since the Civil War, the judges widened the scope of government activity, particularly its right to regulate the economy. The Court also vigorously expanded those First Amendment freedoms so eloquently defended by Oliver Wendell Holmes some forty years earlier, and hastened the great judicial revolution in civil rights that led to the destruction of the system of Jim Crow in the ensuing decades. During the middle third of the twentieth century, in fact, the Court would become the most reformist branch of government.

The Waning of the New Deal

The Court fight, a sharp economic downturn, and the approach of war in Europe largely halted liberal efforts at social engineering. Congress itself grew increasingly assertive. An alliance of Southern Democrats determined to perpetuate racial segregation, and northern Republicans, equally determined to preserve business prerogatives, effectively blocked further challenges to the status quo. Shrill debate between isolationists and interventionists over America's role in world affairs more and more filled the public arena. Reform lost some of its public, and much of its urgency.

The sudden and dramatic success of labor's drive toward national organization in 1936 and 1937 both gave the New Deal a permanent institutional base and solidified opposition to it. At the very end of 1936, workers at the General Motors Fisher Body plant in Flint, Michigan, seized the factory, sitting in instead of walking out. The new "sit-in" strategy spread across the nation, achieving more success for unionization in a year than organized labor had accomplished in decades. With businessmen fearful of having their equipment damaged along with their new-found hopes of industrial recovery, and with both the federal and state governments visibly resistant to the traditional use of force to put down such disruption, industry after industry yielded to the workers' new militancy. Despite a rising tide of fury over this "lawless" tactic, the country somehow acquiesced in a rapid and major shift in power. Workers sometimes threw pop bottles or nuts and bolts, and in a few celebrated incidents heads were cracked and blood flowed; but overall it is astonishing that much of industrial America was organized in scarcely a year with so little violence or destruction of property. The workers were for the most part orderly and disciplined, the owners careful and cowed, the government calmly neutral. In 1936 before the great strikes began, scarcely four million workers belonged to unions. By the end of 1937, the figure was over seven million. The nation entered World War II with over 11 million workers organized. The workers had found a home; the New Deal had found its steady base both in funds and in votes; and many hesitant middle-class Roosevelt supporters had joined with his early opponents in fear of big labor and big government and big brother in the White House.

Depression intensified during the winter of 1937-38. Record crops glutted markets no longer controlled by the now unconstitutional AAA; prices fell, and many farmers stopped buying manufactured goods. Industry cut back output, laying off more and more workers. Business investment slackened. Roosevelt already had pared federal spending in a step toward a balanced budget. Then for several months Roosevelt wavered, doing nothing. Why return to deficit spending if it apparently had failed to restore prosperity? Inactivity, however, seemed the greater error.

Several of the President's economic advisers now urged a fresh round of relief spending. Influenced by the theories of the great British economist John Maynard Keynes, they argued that government spending could compensate a fall off in private purchasing thereby encouraging fresh private investment. Others pressed Roosevelt to reduce expenditures to calm businessmen wedded to orthodox views of government's limited role in the economy. Roosevelt compromised by calling for a $3 billion public works program. This was too small to be a major boost to the economy, but it was the right size for Congress, which passed it in just two months.

A new farm bill, the second AAA (1937), allotted acreage quotas to individual farmers; in return for planting only a part of their land, the Department of Agriculture bought up their crops at artificially high prices. These subsidies, called parity payments, aimed at boosting income to 1909-14 levels. Most farmers willingly joined the voluntary program. To reduce its own surplus holdings and to alleviate the impact of higher food prices on the poor, the government distributed food stamps to the unemployed.

Then, after a long struggle, the administration finally pushed through Congress the Fair Labor Standards Act of 1938, which set the minimum wage at twenty-five cents per hour and limited the work week to forty-four hours. The law also barred goods manufactured by child labor from interstate commerce altogether. Southerners had worried that national regulation would deprive their region of its competitive advantage which was based on low wages and long hours. Some labor leaders also had fought the measure, fearful that minimum wages might become maximum wages.

The Wagner-Steagall National Housing Act —complementing the earlier Federal Housing Administration Housing Act which guaranteed home mortgages for the middle class—sought to fill the huge demand for low income housing and to revive the long depressed construction industry. Local governments received $600 million in loans and built nearly 150,000 units over the next three years. Rentals averaged $14 a month, and only families with incomes under $700 a year could move in.

Angered that politicians in his own party had thwarted progressive hopes for regional development schemes, wider redistribution of wealth, and limited civil rights measures, Roosevelt decided to purge the Democratic Party of its conservative "old guard" in the 1938 congressional elections. During the spring and summer primaries of that year, he opposed the renomination of three senators from the South and one New York representative. The Congressman, John J. O'Conner, lost. But the Southerners lashed back at Roosevelt for his meddling, waged racist campaigns, and won their all-important primaries. Even worse from a liberal standpoint, the voters in November replaced many liberal New Dealers with conservatives. Although the Democrats still enjoyed lopsided margins in both the Senate (69 to 23) and the House (261 to 169), the new Congress curtailed spending for relief and public works even as it extended social security coverage and raised farm subsidies. Congress and the American people did not want to scuttle the New Deal, but neither did they want to extend it.

Ignoring It All

Americans did not gloom their way through ten years of depression. Economic troubles were so common and widespread that a kind of camraderie bubbled up: almost everyone was in the same boat. People took up a variety of pastimes. Parlor games changed to meet the need and the opportunity for inexpensive, readily available entertainment. Card playing, especially the new game of contract bridge, became immensely popular. After Ely Culbertson and his wife beat Sidney Lens and Oswald Jacoby in a 150-game "Battle of the Century" on radio, over twenty million people learned the Culbertson system of point count and bidding. Other inexpensive crazes—jigsaw puzzles, Monopoly, Ping Pon —helped many adults keep their minds off their problems.

For American stay-at-homes the most ubiquitous entertainment came over the air waves. The number of radio sets quadrupled during the decade to over forty million. Most households listened three or four hours each day to a wide range of programs. Dance music from New York City nightclubs or popular singers like Kate Smith filled many hours, but most popular of all was comedy; after all what was more needed? George Burns and Gracie Allen drew laughs with their routines about a dizzy but insightful housewife; Jack Benny and Mary Livingstone played off his "stinginess." Ethnic comedies like *The Goldbergs* introduced millions to the habits and cultures of the country's many minorities. One program above all fascinated Americans during the thirties: *Amos 'n' Andy.* While this series about two black men played by whites presented stereotyped racial

Dracula, 1930.

attitudes, it had the general aim of poking fun at the dilemmas of individuals caught in situations beyond their control.

The media and the times matched perfectly; radio came after the decline of vaudeville but before television. Although President Hoover's fears about "air waves chocked full with advertising chatter" had come true, the public did not much mind. Radio changed Americans in ways they perhaps did not fully realize. As it broadcast major-league baseball contests and Broadway show tunes, it did much to homogenize the nation, to create universal symbols.

Outside the home, bingo games, slot machines, pinball boards, and prize contests offered a chance to win something for (almost) nothing. A lucky bingo card, often selling for only a penny, might win a ham or a new shirt. Slot machines, then legal throughout most of the country except the East Coast—returned on the average seventy-five cents on each dollar, one of the few games which offered money rewards. Thousands danced on weekends in local "hippodromes" to the sounds of swing music—happy tunes with a quick beat—made famous by Benny Goodman. Doing the "Big Apple" or the "Lindy" under twirling specks of light reflected overhead from hundreds of little mirrors calmed worries about the next paycheck. When Rudy Vallee sang "Life is just a bowl of cherries" he was counseling his listeners not to take the Depression too seriously:

Life is just a bowl of cherries,
Don't make it serious,
Life's too mysterious.
You work, you save, you worry, so,
But you can't take your dough when you go- go- go,
So keep repeating it's the berries . . . .
The sweet things in life,
To you were just loaned,
So how can you lose what you've never owned.
Life is just a bowl of cherries,
So live and laugh at it all.

As the Depression accelerated an earlier trend toward more and more free time, the country still spent about ten percent of its national income on vacationing and recreation. Even more than the new streamlined trains with air-conditioned Pullman cars, the country's highways took people to inexpensive vacation spots such as national parks and seashores. Automobile ownership actually increased during the thirties, as low fuel cost and the appearance of inexpensive tourist camps and cabins enticed millions onto the roads. Auto trailers also began to appear in large numbers.

Enforced leisure revived the recreation movement, begun some thirty years earlier by employers anxious to provide wholesome activity for their workers. The Works Progress Administration (WPA) spent huge amounts on local parks, swimming pools, tennis courts, and beaches. States contributed as well to the nearly $1 billion lavished on new recreation areas. In New York, for example, Public Works Commissioner Robert Moses opened for public use miles of bathing beaches on Long Island and built roads and bridges to reach them. Admission to pools alone surpassed the annual attendance at all spectator sports. Hard times revolutionized sedentary habits. The public engaged in amateur sports more than they did in watching professional contests. Depression weakened the popularity of football, of necessity a costly amusement, although some institutions took advantage of cheap labor to erect enormous stadiums such as the Yale Bowl, built to hold 55,000. The most popular activities—swimming, golf, and the new game of softball—reflected a tendency away from family-oriented recreation toward individual activity.

Sports heroes embodied this trend. Big-league baseball remained an important urban sport, but superstars like George Herman "Babe" Ruth and Lou Gehrig had reached their prime in the twenties. The athlete of the decade was the black boxer Joe Louis. Son of an Alabama sharecropper, the "Brown Bomber" turned pro in 1934 and defeated the former heavyweight champion Max Baer the next year. Millions followed his career on the radio as he won bout after bout, losing only to Max Schmeling, the great German fighter. In 1937 only three years after his debut, Louis knocked out James Braddock to win the world heavyweight championship. The next year, wanting to avenge his earlier defeat, Louis again met Schmeling. Patriotic Americans, and especially blacks, hoped ardently to see him humiliate the white man who Hilter bragged had proved Nazi theories about the Aryan "master race." Their hopes were realized. Louis destroyed Schmeling in the first round.

And yet, despite the solace many drew from religion, sports, and parlor games, an unnerving sense of decline afflicted the daily life of most citizens. Americans found a strange reassurance during the Depression years in contemplating ritualized acts of crime, which some discovered to be a twisted upward path of social mobility. The ending of Prohibition and the onset of hard times halved the revenue from organized crime. Predictably enough, crimes against property increased dramatically during the thirties, as did arrests for vagrancy and drunkenness. But personal assaults declined. More surprisingly, an old American type

reappeared, the bandit or outlaw who panicked whole regions with sprees of violent revenge against society. One memoir of the Depression recalled thirty years later:

Al Capone operated a soup kitchen . . . . .He was becoming kind of a Robin Hood in that era. He would go to ball games, people would get up and cheer him. They didn't regard him as an underworld character. They thought of him as a sport.

Some outlaws, like Clyde Barrow and his moll Bonnie, were pathetic people too buffeted by depression and ignorance to understand why they compulsively, happily robbed banks and killed. John Dillinger reveled in his notoriety as J. Edgar Hoover's "Public Enemy Number One." Federal agents or state police staged elaborate ambushes of such figures, gunning down Dillinger outside a movie theater in Chicago and brutally assassinating the Barrow gang along a back road in Louisiana. Newspapers headlined the violent careers of these bandits, and the American people seemed to take a certain consolation from their tragic examples. The average man may have wor-

A shot of a human kaleidoscope from a Busby Berkeley musical of the 1930s. Berkeley's musicals usually were stories of backstage life, silly but enjoyable. He was the only movie maker successfully to commercialize surrealism by disguising it as a production number.

ried about his job, but he knew he was at least not a crook.

And Americans still dreamed of a better future. Twenty million people visited the "Century of Progress" exposition in Chicago during 1933-34 to stare at the technological gadgetry and wonder over the possibilities of science. Others clamored over a huge reconstructed Mayan temple, or watched the bubble dances of stripper Sally Rand. Five years later, an even more ambitious undertaking, the Golden Gate International Exposition in San Francisco, looked to a future of swift transportation and near-simultaneous communication. Ironically enough, this 400-acre pageant took as its theme "Recreation—Man's Gift from a Machine Age." But all these papier maché fantasies reached their height at the gigantic New York World's Fair of 1939. All told, nearly fifty million people strolled around the "Trylon and Perisphere": a 728-foot needle pyramid and a 180-foot globe which symbolized "The World of Tomorrow." Huge exhibits, sponsored by businesses and governments from all over the world, portrayed the panorama of a future built around cooperation and the rational use of the earth's resources for the benefit of all mankind. These earnest hopes were shortly dashed by the beginning of yet another war among the great powers—a war that, in one of history's profound strokes of irony, would finally bring to an end the decade-long Depression.

Suggested Readings

William Leuchtenburg's *Franklin D. Roosevelt and the New Deal, 1932-1940* (1963) is an excellent comprehensive survey. Paul Conkin's *The New Deal* (rev. 1975) is critically alive and surrounds the period with controversy. On the Depression itself the most readable study centers on the stock market crash, John Kenneth Galbraith, *The Great Crash* (rev. 1979); Robert Sobel's *The Great Bull Market* (1968) is more analytical. Donald Lisio is thorough on the Bonus Army: *The President and Protest: Hoover, Conspiracy, and the Bonus Riot* (1974). The two standard biographies of Roosevelt are Frank Freidel's (1952--) and James MacGregor Burns, *Roosevelt: The Lion and the Fox* (1956) and *Roosevelt: The Soldier of Freedom* (1970). Joseph P. Lash has written a sympathetic biography of the widely admired Eleanor Roosevelt, *Eleanor and Franklin* (1971). Thomas K. McCraw goes thoroughly into the fortunes of the Tennessee Valley Authority, one of the most important New Deal innovations: *TVA and the Power Fight, 1933-1939* (1971). Elliot A. Rosen questions the generosity of some recent historians to Herbert Hoover. In *Hoover, Roosevelt, and the Brains Trust* (1977), Rosen claims that Hoover had a commitment to individualism that his ideas of cooperation did not sufficiently modify. Rosen also argues that before Roosevelt took office he and the Brains Trust had thought out a general coherent public policy for coping with the economic crisis. Rosen's claim contradicts the familiar belief that the New Deal had no consistent ideas and made itself up from one moment to the next.

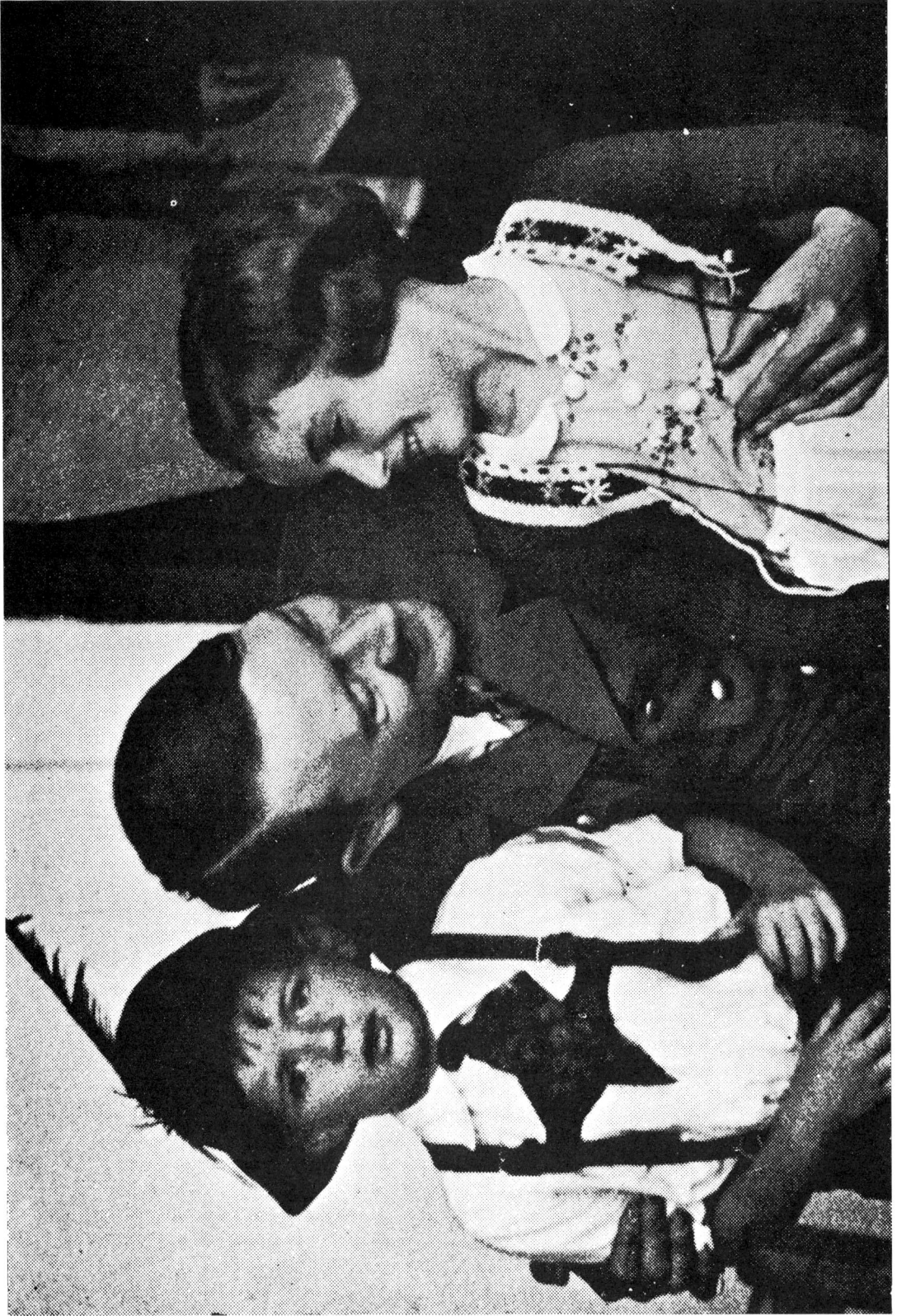

Chapter XXV
Diplomacy and War
1933—1945

Kristallnacht

On October 28, 1938, the German government suddenly rounded up about 18,000 Polish Jews living in Germany. Thousands of stormtroopers snatched children from the streets, plucked the ill out of hospitals, herded both young and old into trains and trucks. Allowed only to take the clothes on their backs and ten marks ($4), they were dumped across the Polish border to find shelter in the no-man's land between these hostile nations' frontier outposts.

The deportees, whose Polish citizenship had been threatened, suffered terrible hardship, particularly those at Zbaszym, whose plight attracted worldwide attention. One of them, Zindel Grynszpan, described his family's suffering in a letter to his seventeen-year-old son, Herschel, who had escaped from Germany to Paris. Wild with grief, the young man bought a pistol and went to the German embassy in Paris. He was sent to the office of a minor official, Ernst vom Rath—himself under investigation for suspected Jewish ancestry. Convinced he could not see the ambassador, Grynzpan shot Vom Rath.
As the German official lay dying, the German S.S. was said to teletype orders throughout Germany for a "spontaneous" pogrom. Vom Rath's death on the afternoon of November 9 was the signal; at 2 a.m. the next morning began *Kristallnacht,* the "night of broken glass." The *New York Times,* on the following day, described it as

"A wave of destruction, looting and incendiarism, unparalleled in Germany since 'The Thirty Years' War'. . . . Beginning systematically in the early morning hours in almost every town and city in the country, the wrecking, looting and burning continued all day. Huge but mostly silent crowds looked on and the police confined themselves to regulating traffic and making wholesale arrests of Jews for their own protection."

The orgy of violence continued for several days. Hundreds of synagogues were burned, thousands of shops looted or destroyed, and tens of thousands of Jews thrown into concentration camps. While the destruction continued, the German government issued a set of decrees which essentially expropriated all German Jewish property and barred Jews from virtually all but the most menial employment.

American religious and civic groups and hundreds of newspapers demanded that something be done. German propaganda minister Josef Goebbels replied coolly to worldwide protests: "if there is any country that believes it has not enough Jews, I shall gladly turn over to it all our Jews." The United States government retorted with a mild, diplomatic move of calling back its ambassador to Germany "for consultation" (a gesture less serious than a formal recall). President Roosevelt expressed his shock at a news conference, but was evasive on the question of the United States accepting more refugees. Trade with the Third Reich continued as usual.

In response to the "night of broken glass" the Netherlands, Belgium, and Great Britain admitted several thousand refugee children, inspiring a movement among clergymen to do the same in the United States. Senator Robert F. Wagner of New York and Representative Edith Nourse Rogers of Massachusetts proposed the Wagner-Rogers or Child Refugee Bill, which would have admitted up to 20,000 German children up to the age of fourteen as an addition to the next two years' regular German quota. Advocates of the bill assured a joint House-Senate Committee which held hearings that "none will come here save those who are, in the opinion of trained specialists, good material for American citizenship." They pointed out how few refugees the United States absorbed and gave assurances that there was a surplus of good homes for these children. Mrs. Calvin Coolidge and Herbert Hoover were among the people offering to sponsor these children.

The course of the hearings vividly illustrates the problems American society experienced in trying to meet the needs of Jewish refugees throughout the Hitler era. The bill had the support of the churches, of many educators, businessmen, and organized labor, and of Eleanor Roosevelt. Eddie Cantor, perhaps the most popular entertainer in the country, offered to take responsibility for finding families for all the children. Wagner, in speaking for the bill, emphasized that almost half of the refugee children would not be Jewish. His dramatic appeal concluded with the Biblical injunction, "Suffer little children to come unto me and forbid them not; for of such is the Kingdom of Heaven."

The bill, however, was in trouble from the start. The congressional hopper was crammed with sixty different anti-alien bills, including one—officially endorsed by the American Legion—to abolish all immigration to the United States for ten years. Patriotic societies opposed immigration generally. One hostile witness saw the children as the entering wedge "to break down the whole quota system." Another characterized the refugees in question as "thousands of motherless, embittered, persecuted children of undesirable foreigners." Others worried about spies among the children or talked of sinister "pressure of foreign nationalistic or racial groups." Republican Senator Robert A. Taft of Ohio echoed a common argument: "20,000 American children could profit if such nice homes were available."

The Roosevelt administration retained a tomblike official silence. The President was then struggling to pry from Congress funds to build naval bases and to expand the Army Air Corps in preparation for the country's possible involvement in another world war. His secretary had warned Eddie Cantor that "we might get more restrictive rather than more liberal immigration laws and practices from the present Congress." Despite his genuine concern over the fate of all of central and eastern European Jewry, whose future he described at this very time as "exceedingly dark," he let the Refugee Bill (and probably the refugees) die.

The United States never met Goebbels' challenge. The American public believed not only that it had enough Jews, but that it had more than enough aliens in general. Not until 1944 did American policy against the atrocities become vigorous, and by then there were pathetically few refugees to save. In December 1944, after American troops had already reached some of the death camps, a public opinion poll showed that most Americans still believed that the Nazis had killed fewer than 100,000 Jews. The American government and its allies refused or delayed too long throughout the war on numerous opportunities to save a few thousand refugees here, a few tens of thousands of refugees there. The United States admitted about 250,000 Jewish refugees in the entire era in which six million European Jews died. No American bombers destroyed the ovens at Dachau or Auschwitz, although they had the capacity to do so. A government that made military detours to preserve the art of the Japanese city of Kyoto, and the architecture of the German city of Rothenburg, never moved from its rigid strategy of trying to "prevent" a Holocaust only by defeating the Axis.

The World Economic Conference

Foreign affairs were but an afterthought on March 4, 1933, a windy, steel-gray day in Washington, D.C., as silent, anxious Americans gathered on Capitol Hill or listened on the radio to a new President. Recovery at home, the problem of unemployed workers, closed factories, bankrupt banks—it was these that preoccupied Franklin Delano Roosevelt, not distant drums in the Far East or continental Europe. "I favored as a practical policy," Roosevelt said, "the putting of first things first." Certain of his country's impregnable security, he girded up for a war against depression at home, not enemies overseas.

Yet the new leaders in Washington were not true isolationists. Roosevelt and the Democrats, long identified with Wilsonian internationalism, repeatedly glanced abroad for cures to the nation's economic ills. While Congress debated New Deal recovery measures, a debate that lasted until early summer, Roosevelt restlessly took up a proposal left over from the Hoover administration for a world economic conference.

Even since a financial panic had forced Great Britain off the gold standard in 1931, world leaders, especially in France and the United States, had groped after an international solution to the spreading economic crisis. Depression, it seemed to them, had a common origin in the collapse of world trade: as overseas markets disappeared, nations threw up high tariffs against imported goods to preserve domestic markets for their own industry. But the upward spiral of tariffs only further constricted world trade creating a vicious circle. Debtor nations, now unable to sell goods abroad, often could not pay their debts. Their creditors, principally Britain and America, tried to recall their loans, but this only forced the debtors to default. Many banks and individuals lost heavily on overseas investments during the early 1930's, drying up capital that might otherwise have contributed to domestic recovery. As early as October 1931, President Hoover and Premier Pierre Laval of France had discussed ways to loosen trade restrictions and free "frozen" capital. But the Europeans were more interested in escaping their war debts than in fashioning a cooperative recovery, and Hoover himself shied away from innovative approaches.

By the time the World Economic Conference convened in London on June 12, 1933, no coherent strategy had emerged. During an almost pleading opening address, King George V declared, "It cannot be so beyond the ability of man to end the current depression." But the delegates themselves knew that Roosevelt's experimental plans were at odds with those of the so-called Gold Bloc, those nations whose economic interests required continuation of the status quo. Conflict between these two forces soon erupted over monetary policy: the French refused to accept American plans for simultaneous devaluation and announced that they would rather "see the Conference fail than adopt radical, unsettling measures." Roosevelt, his hands considerably freed by the adjournment of Congress, fired back with a statement soon called the "Bombshell." He rejected out of hand the French demand that the United States return to a full gold standard. "The old fetishes of so-called international bankers are being replaced," he boldly challenged, "by efforts to plan national currencies." Discussions in London drifted on for a few weeks, but the gathering which could have ended the crisis of confidence only worsened it by dashing the hopes it had raised. Even Secretary of State Cordell Hull—a devout Wilsonian committed to expanding world trade by lowering tariffs—decided that "The best contribution America can make to world prosperity is its own domestic recovery."

And so, the country turned inward to seek its economic salvation—a luxury the United States thought it could afford because of an impregnable security afforded by the world's great oceans. The New Dealers did devalue the dollar by some forty percent in 1933, which attracted immense amounts of gold into the United States. And Roosevelt also negotiated reciprocal trade treaties with nations that supplied important raw materials for American industry. The mutual reductions of tariffs, however, did little to stimulate economic demand. Though perhaps useful as propaganda, reciprocity was, as Secretary of the Interior Harold Ickes quipped, "like hunting an elephant in the jungle with a fly swatter." Defense budgets sagged in order that more money could go into the recovery effort, and New Dealers naturally wanted other nations to cut back military spending as well. But by and large, the immensity of the Depression simply forced international matters into the background.

Recognizing the Soviet Union

Ever since Woodrow Wilson had refused to recognize the Communist regime in 1918, Americans had found many justifications for ignoring the Soviet Union. Wilson himself scarcely believed that a new government which made such radical pronouncements would survive in a country so wedded to a feudal past. Then, too, the Russians had angered the West in many ways. Lenin signed a separate peace with Imperial Germany early in 1918, panicking the Allies with fears of an onslaught against the western front. The Communists brooked no opposition to their plans for a proletarian paradise; police murdered thousands of potential subversives, including the Tsar and his family. The Soviets blithely defaulted on all their country's bonded debt and announced the start of a world revolution against capitalism. And so Wilson and his Republican successors, for reasons of diplomatic pique, personal distaste, genuine irritation and anger, and political expediency at home, never opened formal relations with the Soviet Union.

Time slowly mellowed American attitudes. The world revolution collapsed quickly after brief coups in Hungary and Germany; by the thirties, with Stalin committed to "building socialism in one country," it was depression, not Communism, that threatened the American way of life. Soviet financial sins seemed less offensive when France, and later almost all of America's debtors, defaulted on their public debts. Roosevelt himself thought it foolish to continue non-recognition of a regime that was clearly stable and secure; he also calculated that a Russian-American rapprochement might restrain Japan in the Far East. Many businessmen transferred old dreams about the China market into new dreams about the Russians: "If only they all bought just one pair of shoes," a boot manufacturer mused, "my industry would

march back to prosperity." Stalin had been dumping Soviet grain on world markets at absurdly low prices in a desperate effort to pay for expensive technological equipment; a trade agreement might boost sales for Yankee industry and keep Russian grain at home, benefiting both countries.

Roosevelt's first overtures to the Russians brought Stalin's Commissar for Foreign Affairs, Maxim Litvinov, to Washington for talks. On November 16, 1933, the President and Litvinov reached an accord that regularized relations between their two countries and reopened negotiations about the complex counterclaims each held against the other. (Wall Street bankers wanted payment on Russia's prewar bonds; the Soviets sought compensation for damages caused by American troops during Wilson's intervention in their civil war.) The Roosevelt-Litvinov accord also included a pledge by the Russians not to "spread Communist propaganda" in the United States, and guaranteed religious freedom and the right to a fair trial to Americans living in the Soviet Union. Roosevelt sent William Bullitt as America's first ambassador to the Soviet Union. Litvinov stayed on in Washington as the Soviet ambassador, but negotiations about claims collapsed, and Stalin ignored both the civil liberties of Americans (as he did those of Russians) and his promise to halt subversive activities in the United States. Bullitt unsuccessfully tried to interest the Russians in American culture; at one point he distributed baseball bats and gloves to the somewhat bewildered citizens of Moscow. Businessmen and farmers, too, were disappointed: Soviet-American trade actually declined after 1933, and the Russians continued to dump huge amounts of grain on world markets. Recognition of the Soviet Union had no significant impact on Roosevelt's war against the Depression.

The Good Neighbor

"In the field of world policy," Roosevelt had pledged during his inaugural address, "I would dedicate this nation to the policy of the good neighbor—the neighbor who respects the rights of others." Hoover already had shied away from the successive interventions in Caribbean affairs characteristic of Theodore Roosevelt, William

Howard Taft, and Woodrow Wilson. Testing whether or not the new President would take yet more liberal steps, leaders from Argentina and Mexico challenged him to renounce unilateral intervention in Latin America at the Seventh International Conference of American States, which met at Montevideo, Uruguay, during December

1933. Cordell Hull, chairman of the American delegation, was expected to do what his predecessors had always done in such situations: veto the agenda. But instead the Secretary of State proclaimed that "No state has the right to intervene in the internal or external affairs of another," and signed a formal convention condemning intervention, while retaining a loophole permitting the United States to move against "outlaw" regimes. Argentina, however, wanted a more foolproof disclaimer. So at the next inter-American meeting, in Buenos Aires in 1936, the twenty-one republics now proclaimed their "absolute juridical sovereignty." But Hull added a phrase to the resolution committing the signatories to "respect . . . the existence of a common democracy throughout America."

Washington in effect "pan-Americanized" the Monroe Doctrine. Alarmed by Hitler's rhetoric and by the rise of Fascism in Japan and Europe, Roosevelt concocted the practice of "consultation": whenever an outside force threatened "the peace and independence" of the Western Hemisphere, the nations of the New World would attempt to react in common. Most Latin states, already frightened by events elsewhere, welcomed the implied protection almost as much as they rejoiced in the ending of a unilateral Monroe Doctrine. Consultation worked smoothly during the tense years of World War II; on three occasions before 1942 the countries of the New World met together, the last time to declare war against the Axis powers. (The Argentines alone held to neutrally until early 1945, seeing in Fascism both a solution for their economic troubles and a possible opportunity for hemispheric leadership.)

Roosevelt's concern for national security made it hard for him to be a good neighbor to Cuba. This 700-mile-long-island commands the defense of America's southern coasts; instability there had always prompted intervention. A treaty of 1904 formally obligated the United States to maintain internal order. When President Gerardo Machado's dictatorial ways threatened an outbreak of civil war, Roosevelt sent diplomat Sumner Welles to calm the island. Machado was forced to resign, but this failed to restore order, and Roosevelt then sent warships into the area. The confident Welles made plans with local army officers, themselves trained by American advisers, to foist upon Cuba an "acceptable" President, while Roosevelt withheld recognition from more "threatening" candidates. More in the spirit of the good neighbor, the Senate in 1935 ratified a new treaty which abrogated American control over Cuban affairs, although the U.S. Navy retained its huge base at Guantanamo Bay.

Elsewhere in the Caribbean, where United States security concerns were less pressing, Washington's diplomats acted with more restraint. By late 1934 Roosevelt, following a plan laid down by Hoover, withdrew the last contingent of marines from Haiti, although a Yankee "fiscal representative" stayed behind to insure repayment of debts to American creditors. An American customs supervisor also controlled revenue in the Dominican Republic, as did a supervisor in Nicaragua. In Puerto Rico, Roosevelt's governors-general—especially former brains-truster Rexford Tugwell—diversified the island's economy and struggled against widespread illiteracy. A mini-New Deal, emphasizing public works, relieved some of the Depression gloom in the largest city, San Juan, but not until the postwar years would tourism, together with large-scale emigration to the mainland, invigorate the Puerto Rican economy.

Roosevelt's good-neighborliness survived its greatest interwar test which came in Mexico. In 1934 Mexican voters elected as President Lazaro Cardenas, who wanted to accelerate the mildly Socialist revolution begun in 1912. He nationalized most foreign-owned land suitable for farming, turning it over to local communities, and organized industrial workers into a single giant union. Then early in 1938, Cardenas confiscated most major oil lands in Mexico from their British and American owners. In theory, he was acting to force the companies to accept a new labor contract which, with some justification, they had rejected. But Cardenas almost at once offered to buy out the oilmen, offering about $25 million for all above-ground equipment. They, however, claimed compensation for below-ground oil reserves as well, some $260 million altogether. Although the companies conducted private negotiations with the government, Roosevelt (unlike leaders in England) refused to pressure the Mexicans. Eventually the President, as the approach of war in Europe stirred memories of the Zimmerman note, moved to resolve the issues clouding relations with Mexico. Just two weeks before Pearl Harbor, the two nations settled all outstanding differences: the United States promised to maintain its purchases of Mexican silver, to increase its humanitarian aid, and to conclude a reciprocal trade treaty. In return, the Mexicans paid $40 million to satisfy long-standing claims of American creditors. Each country appointed a commissioner to settle the oil dispute. They awarded the companies some $24 million for above-ground equipment.

The Good Neighbor policy, so richly praised since the early 1930's, was more than rhetoric, yet less than revolution. That sense of contentiousness, of Latin fear and Yankee bluster, did lessen. Roosevelt withdrew the remaining symbols of American dominance, those Marines stalking the streets of small Caribbean capitals, and resisted temptations in Mexico. In return, despite Argentina's opposition, the Latin Americans followed Washington's careful steps toward war in the early 1940's. The Monroe Doctrine now became a multilateral device for deflecting threats from the Old World. The Americas could live as good neighbors, though only as long as Washington felt its interests to be secure.

Neutrality

The World Economic Conference, the recognition of the Soviet Union, the Good Neighbor Policy—all these were merely adjustments to present realities rather than any sort of "new deal" in foreign affairs. Roosevelt instinctively shrank from adventures abroad that might jeopardize economic recovery or his new political coalition. In those days before the cold war with Russia, Presidents shared decision-making about foreign affairs with Congress, and legislators reflected the attitudes of their constituents. A majority of Americans during the thirties were steadfast isolationists who believed involvement overseas to be futile and dangerous.

Depression itself contributed to the widespread American cynicism about international relations during Roosevelt's first two terms in office. Most governments seemed inept in their failure to solve

Citizen Kane, *1941. The technical audacity of twenty-six-year-old Orson Welles in presenting the thinly disguised story of William Randolph Hearst made this the single most influential film since Birth of A Nation. By purposefully fictionalizing biography, Citizen Kane convincingly exposed the egomania, greed and finally sentimentality that were the well-springs of a supposedly great man's life.*

the riddle of capitalist breakdown; perhaps it had been such ineptitude, not German malevolence, that had "caused" the Great War. Besides, the Versailles settlement seemed geared toward expanding the British Empire. College students leavened their skepticism with whimsy: some joined a new organization, the Veterans of Future Wars (VFW). Set up in 1935 at Princeton University, the VFW wanted a bonus now, before they fought, so they could enjoy it while young and not yet injured. But as events overseas became more ominous, such jests faded away.

American involvement in World War I had become a subject for massive re-examination. George Norris, a progressive Republican from Nebraska, convinced his colleagues in the Senate to investigate the role of "those merchants of death," the munition's makers, in America's decision to enter World War I. Norris, like many progressives in both parties, believed that big businessmen started wars for their own profit. Then, too, he hoped—again like many of his colleagues—to foster congressional initiative in foreign affairs, all the more because of the President's rapidly growing economic powers under the New Deal. So Norris maneuvered the unknown, and therefore presumably neutral, Senator Gerald P. Nye of North Dakota into the chairmanship of a special committee named in 1934 to ferret out the truth.

After months of highly visible hearings, Nye and his colleagues proved the obvious: American businessmen had made millions selling arms during the war. J. P. Morgan, Jr., testified about the international banking practices that had facilitated such purchases, and rows and rows of accounting books, all grandiloquently subpoenaed into the public record, showed enormous profits. Secret documents demonstrated, at least to true believers, that Wilson and his Secretary of the Treasury eventually had caved in to pressure from New York City bankers, first to lend money to

Britain, then to enter the war to protect that investment and for still greater profit. It seemed far fetched to suggest that a great nation went to war solely to protect the investments of a few citizens, yet much of the American public accepted this interpretation, although the Nye committee itself never formally did. Revisionist historians like Charles A. Beard and Walter Millis added academic prestige—and the authority of footnotes—to a hysteria that seized the nation. The complex legalities of neutral rights, the novelty of submarine warfare, Wilson's own fierce moralism, America's national interests, all were forgotten by people now certain that businessmen had tricked America into the tragedy of a needless war.

Congress reacted predictably, and speedily, to this rising mood. No doubt happy at last to take the initiative in national affairs, the legislators passed a series of "neutrality acts." Each tried to plug loopholes through which, isolationists claimed, leaders in 1917 had maneuvered the United States into war "by the back door." As events in Europe became more threatening, each act further restricted presidential options. By the terms of the first Neutrality Act of 1935, whenever the President proclaimed that a state of war existed anywhere in the world, U. S. arms shipments to belligerents on both sides had to cease. No American ships could transport war material, and Americans might be warned against traveling on neutral ships. Roosevelt himself thought it would "drag us into war instead of keeping us out," but still he signed the bill rather than risk making the presidential election of 1936 a fight over isolation instead of a referendum on the New Deal. Congress quickly added a second neutrality act, extending all the provisions of the first and adding another: American bankers could not lend to belligerents.

In 1937 a third act forbade Americans to travel on belligerent ships, even at their own risk. Nations at war might purchase nonmilitary goods in the United States, but only on a "cash and carry" basis. That same year, however, Roosevelt officially ignored the outbreak of hostilities between China and Japan in order to ship munitions to the Chinese, America's traditional ally in the Far East. Aware of the country's isolationist spirit, already at loggerheads with Congress over his plans for reform of the Supreme Court, and worried about the sharp economic downturn that occurred during 1937-38, Roosevelt chose not to open other wounds.

The Descent into War, 1937-1941

A hopeful rhetoric of neutrality in the United States could not alter the growing thrust toward war elsewhere. Totalitarian regimes arose in Germany and Japan, glorifying war as man's greatest enterprise, oppressing the individual to advance the state, fostering racial hatreds and violence. Nearly four decades later, scholars and laymen quickly dismiss as unattainable Japan's plans for a "new order" in Asia and Hitler's dreams for a Third Reich modeled on the Roman Empire. But in the depressed thirties the lure of Fascism was seductive. Germany's prosperity mocked the persisting depression in England, France, and America. The future, many thought, lay with "ordered" regimes and not with "outdated" notions of personal liberty and self-regulating economies; Adolf Hitler, who became Chancellor of Germany only five weeks before Roosevelt became President of the United States, with his dictator allies—Benito Mussolini in Italy and Francisco Franco in Spain—would triumph amidst the decline of the West, ushering in a new, truly modern epoch.

Their temporary success owed much to the inaction of their rivals. Though possessing the greatest standing army in Europe, France feared war. Germany's demographic advantage—its greater population and birth rate— meant that a fresh conflict could well end in France's defeat, perhaps even in its disappearance as a nation. A vast empire, spread over a quarter of the globe on six continents, drained Britain's power away from Europe. Depression and popular sentiment distracted the United States from world affairs. Stalin sought mainly to stabilize the Soviet revolution with blood purges and massive coercion of their people. With potential opposition so fragmented and the world so disillusioned, the Fascists easily persuaded themselves that they could remold society. Hitler's monomaniacal schemes seemed almost plausible set against the failure of the West to project any alternate vision of the future.

Fascism appealed to those unhappy with the present and worried about the future. The Fascists would tear down old elites and install in their place

Confessions of a Nazi Spy, *1939. Based on an exposé of the German-American Bund and the Nazi spy organization in the United States, this film aroused protests from American First and other isolationist groups. It was only the forerunner of a number of anti-Nazi films that appeared before America entered the Second World War.*

dictators who expressed the spiritual will of the people. Democracy must yield to the imperative need of the state for territorial growth; individuals must sacrifice liberty so that their collective genius, their civilization, could endure and triumph. Only in war could a nation achieve its full greatness. In Italy, Mussolini boasted: "We have buried the putrid corpse of liberty." In Germany, Fascism was early coupled with an intense racism. Writing in *Mein Kampf*, a book that roughly sketched out his dreams and his hatreds, Hitler blamed "subhuman" Jews for defeat in World War I, an explanation that eased national guilt and humiliation while it aroused violent prejudice. In the utopian future as the Nazis envisioned it, "mongrel" races would serve their natural superiors, a master race of Germans who would rule a European empire for a thousand years. The nation must earn this magnificent destiny by obedience and sacrifice. Such melodramatic and irrational ideas inspired millions in Germany who had suffered so much from war and economic crisis.

Also driving the Fascists were fears of communism. Capitalist leaders in some western countries openly proclaimed their preference for Hitler over Stalin. The long-term success of the Bolshevik Revolution in Russia had alarmed Europe's propertied classes. Fascists played on these anxieties, accusing the Communists of destroying religious values and robbing the middle class of its modest wealth. The threat seemed believable in Germany, where radicals had staged several coups in Bavaria and Berlin just after the war. The example of Stalin's cruelty and his ruthless collectivization of rural lands created its own horror. Hitler promised to protect his people from "alien Marxism, a Jewish plot against Germany's destiny." Elsewhere, many people tolerated Fascist excesses, relieved that Germany and Italy were containing the "Red Menace." British prime ministers often argued that a strong central Europe would serve to prevent Soviet expansion. Paris conservatives chanted at rallies, "Better Hitler than Blum"—Blum being a moderate Socialist who became Premier of France in 1936. By offering an alternative to the Bolsheviks, Hitler and his counterparts in Italy and Spain and Japan gained support at home and distracted the western democracies throughout the 1930's.

Aggression bracketed the decade. In 1931 the Japanese attacked and rapidly conquered the Chinese province of Manchuria, the industrial center of the Far East. No one believed their pretext that the Chinese troops had struck legitimate Japanese positions along the Chinese Eastern Railway. But Russia—still desperately weak from war and revolution, and shunned in any case by the capitalist west—could do nothing. British leaders worried about the empire in East Asia and their country's overextended position in general. So Foreign Secretary John Simon quietly asked his counterpart in Washington, Henry Stimson, whether America would cooperate in a "forward policy." President Hoover said no, but he and Stimson suggested instead the idea of "nonrecognition." If all the powers officially refused to accept Japan's conquest, moral persuasion alone might dissuade future aggression. This feeble reaction convinced the British to bend rather than stand firm in Asia. The League of Nations found Japan guilty of aggression, but it voted no sanctions of any kind. In its first major test, collective security suffered a major defeat.

Adolf Hitler

A pattern of German challenge and weak democratic response continued through the thirties. Hitler, in many ways the most sophisticated German diplomat since Bismarck, steadily maneuvered his way toward imperial domination in Europe. Gradually he destroyed those parts of the

Versailles Treaty that cast Germany in a second-class role: he began to rearm on both land and sea; he meddled in Austrian affairs, bringing that country closer to Germany; then, in 1936, he marched his new, though still small, army into the Rhineland. This last act terrified the French, who wanted Britain to join them in military reprisals. But English diplomats demurred after Hitler promised not to embark upon a naval arms race. Hitler further isolated France in 1937 when he signed an alliance with Mussolini's Italy. Then the two Axis powers intervened in the Spanish civil war on behalf of Francisco Franco. In Spain, the dictators experimented with new techniques of war, especially air attacks designed to demoralize civilian populations. Airplanes had replaced ships at sea as the dominant military mode, a development that would work to Britain's disadvantage. Although the Soviet Union supplied the Spanish republicans, many of whom were Socialists, Britain and France again refused to act. The American Congress applied its neutrality legislation to civil as well as international wars, thereby depriving the United States of any role at all. By 1939 the Fascists had won the brutal conflict in Spain.

Certain that the western democracies would not block him, the Nazi Chancellor already had begun a war of nerves that netted him important territories. His approach, as always, was both novel and flexible. Hitler appealed for "fair play": just across German frontiers, he wailed, millions of Germans languished under oppressive regimes. Until they could "rejoin the fatherland," Europe could have no peace. Nazi agents sparked pro-German rallies in these areas, and many ethnic Germans responded enthusiastically. In Austria they saw union with Germany both as economic salvation and as a return to former imperial glory; Germans living in the Sudetenland, a part of Czechoslovakia bordering Germany, longed to escape what they perceived to be second-class citizenship in a second-class country; Germans in Poland protested that country's notorious treatment of its minorities. For eighteen dramatic months, Hitler exploited these discontents, achieving huge territorial gains for Germany and eventually bringing Europe into another war.

In early 1938 active Nazi sympathizers so bedeviled the regular government in Austria that its leaders called for a plebiscite. The people, they thought, would reject union with Germany. Hitler reacted quickly, sending an army into Austria before the voting in March. Stormtroopers marched through Vienna, reinforcing a martial image abroad as well as terrorizing the Austrian populace. The powers had not really recovered from this coup—which at one stroke made Germany the leading nation in Europe—when Hitler began to pressure the Czechs. He wanted the Sudeten Germans and the mountain areas where they lived. The minority Germans refused Czech offers of negotiation while Hitler's speeches became more and more hysterical and his armies gathered along the frontier. By early fall, war seemed inevitable: if Hitler attacked, the Czechs would fight back, and the French and Russians would have to come to their aid. No one thought much of the Red Army, however, and the French cowered behind the defensive wall of the Maginot Line. British ministers sought to mediate or, if that failed, to encourage war between Nazi Germany and Soviet Russia. Prime Minister Chamberlain flew several times to meet Hitler in Germany, where he finally secured an agreement at Munich in late October. Hitler immediately occupied the Sudetenland, but promised to settle all future disputes without war. Unfortunately, this much-heralded "peace in our time" collapsed. Four months later Hitler marched into the rest of Czechoslovakia and then, during the summer of 1939, took up a familiar refrain. "So long as Germans in Poland suffer grievously, so long as they are imprisoned away from the Fatherland," he said again and again, "Europe can have no peace."

Toward the United States Hitler displayed incredible arrogance. Roosevelt was a "pettifogging Jew" and "the completely Negroid appearance of his wife" showed she was a half-caste. When the President asked Hitler for assurances that weak nations would not be attacked, the Führer titillated the paunchy delegates in the Reichstag by solemnly promising not to invade the United States.

War in Europe and the Far East

Everyone realized now that Hitler was determined upon great conquests, not mere revisions of the status quo. But an odd twilight lingered over Europe; everyone, even the Germans, hesitated about taking the final steps toward war. Chamberlain's government issued a unilateral guarantee of

Polish independence. This maneuver, probably designed to reassure the Russians about British intentions, failed. By late August 1939 Stalin had signed a nonaggression pact with Hitler, thereby spurning Anglo-French offers for a formal alliance. Days later, on September 1, the Nazis attacked Poland with the new weapons of *blitzkrieg*, "lightning war." Airplanes strafed Polish troops and urban centers, while German motorized divisions sped across eastern Europe's wide plains; badly organized and poorly equipped, the Poles fell back on all fronts. Then the Russians invaded from the east, and within six weeks Stalin and Hitler divided the country between them. Britain and France had declared war a few days after the German invasion, but they could scarcely save Poland or, for that matter, take up an offensive. French generals, remembering the lessons of World War I, worshiped at the altar of defense. A hastily gathered British army did land in western Europe, but it numbered only about 300,000 soldiers.

Still hoping for a negotiated settlement and not yet ready for war in the west, both sides stalled for time. Then the *sitzkrieg*, or "sitting war," ended abruptly in 1940. Hitler attacked Denmark, then Norway. A new British prime minister, Winston Churchill, pledged to destroy the Nazis, not negotiate with them. The revered Maginot Line crumpled against a new *blitzkrieg*, and within six weeks Hitler had conquered France, trapping its armies in a great semicircular sweep through Belgium and driving the British off the Continent in an improvised evacuation at Dunkirk. Hitler was master of the Continent, and only England fought on against him.

A spreading danger in the Far East paralleled the European descent into war. Leaders in Japan, a militarist state where philosophers glorified war and businessmen hungered for colonies, dreamed of dominating all Asia. Raw materials from the European empires there and control over the huge China market could satisfy even the most ambitious imperialism. Soon after consolidating their control in Manchuria, the Japanese stepped up pressure against Chiang Kai-shek's Nationalist government in Nanking. But the Chinese rallied against this new threat of foreign invasion—the Communist leader Mao Tse-tung even called off his civil war—and leaders in Tokyo backed down. Both sides nonetheless prepared for war, which finally came in mid-1937. Western diplomats argued that an embargo would only force the Japanese into Indonesia and Indochina, bringing on the war it aimed to avoid. The future depended upon which of two factions came to dominate Japan's aristocratic government, the moderates who favored only economic expansion or the militarists who promoted war. For the moment, however, everyone was transfixed by Hitler's adventure in Europe.

From Neutrality to Undeclared War, 1937-41

These climactic events startled the American people, but only reinforced a desire to retreat. When the Japanese sank the U.S. gunboat *Panay* in December 1937, on the Yangtze River in China, the reaction of most Americans (over seventy percent) was that the United States should withdraw from the Far East. Roosevelt was personally convinced that his country eventually must join Britain and China in the fight against Fascism in Europe and Asia, but he faced a difficult situation. Most Americans, certain of their own security, believed that war could come only if they stumbled into it; aloofness seemed to guarantee peace, at least in the New World. In any case, the United States possessed only a tiny army, and its modest navy was spread over two oceans. Reflecting popular suspicions about presidential meddling overseas, Congress' neutrality laws limited executive action. Still, the country drifted toward war, nudged by Roosevelt's convictions, a reinvigorated interventionist movement, and the reality of the Fascist menace.

Roosevelt sounded warnings. On October 5, 1937, during a speech delivered in Chicago, he denounced Japan's war against China and likened the spread of violence to a disease that peace-loving nations must halt. His call to "quarantine the aggressors" jolted British diplomats into quick action. Seeking to protect Britain's empire in Asia, they rushed a resolution through the League of Nations calling on the signatories of the Nine-Power Treaty to consider countermeasures, presumably economic sanctions of some sort. But the quarantine speech prompted an even more vigorous reaction within the United States, nearly all of it adverse. Press and radio polls revealed hostility toward any kind of intervention. Two-thirds of the legislators on Capitol Hill opposed sanctions, most agreeing that economic retaliation was only "a back door to war." So Roosevelt explained during one of his fireside chats that the Nine-Power Conference at Brussels would consider only peaceful solutions to the Sino-Japanese war. This limitation, however, destroyed in advance any possibility of strong action by the nine powers.

However much isolationist sentiment encouraged the dictators and hobbled the President, Americans began to attend to military defense. Only three weeks after Hitler's invasion of Poland, representatives of all the republics in the Western Hemisphere gathered at Panama. Pledging joint action against any threat to their security, they issued the Declaration of Panama, which marked out a war free zone three hundred miles out to sea, surrounding the neutral Americas. Meanwhile, Roosevelt had succeeded in modifying some of the neutrality acts. He believed, before the summer of 1940, that England and France could defeat the Nazis if the United States supplied them generously. The Pittman Act, passed in November 1939, repealed the embargo on arms shipments abroad—a considerable gain for the Allies—although it still banned any trade in American ships: the "cash and carry" policy remained intact. Over the next six months, the British bought several billion dollars' worth of munitions.

Then the Nazi *blitzkrieg* of May 1940 shocked American politicians into action. Roosevelt asked for increases in the Army and Navy, and huge expenditures for military equipment—capped by a pledge to build 50,000 planes a year. Congress passed the necessary appropriations; but where were the soldiers and sailors? Widespread anti-militarist sentiment, the Army's reputation for harsh treatment, and new openings in private industry discouraged volunteers. Although most citizens favored conscription, congressmen thought that the pending selective service bill might anger just enough voters to defeat them at the next election.

Ardent demonstrations all over the country and raucous debate on Capitol Hill, punctuated with insults and even fistfights, could not, however, overcome clear military necessity. In early 1940 the United States Army had only 100,000 soldiers—making it nineteenth in size among world powers. A Selective Service Act became law on August 25, 1940, but was limited in effect to only one year. In the summer of 1941 the House extended the draft by only one vote. Nonetheless, about 1,600,000 men were conscripted during the

next year under the first peacetime draft in American history.

Against this backdrop of step-by-step rearmament, a great debate broke out all across the nation about America's proper world role. Isolationists geared up for a holy crusade against war. The fall of France in June 1940, however, convinced many moderate Americans that their country must do something to aid England, even at the risk of combat. Still, the isolationists remained a vital, though diverse force. Some of their leaders like Father Coughlin and Gerald L. K. Smith defended Fascism and believed Hitler would win the war. Socialists and Communists also were strong isolationists: Norman Thomas, for example, denounced the war as one more plot against the working class. Midwesterners seemed especially caught up in the tide of isolationism: old progressives, small-town businessmen, and many Protestant ministers in that region spoke vigorously against involvement. By September most of these diverse groups had come together in a loose coalition called the America First Committee. Millions agreed with its purpose: a vigorous defense of the United States, but noninvolvement in "Europe's War."

Many other Americans reacted differently to Hitler's conquests. Most New Deal liberals shared Roosevelt's instinctive revulsion against Fascism. Democrats in Congress, especially those from Eastern and Southern states, supported him. Many journalists and university professors who had once been isolationists now warned about the Nazis' aims and philosophy. Big industrialists and nearly all metropolitan newspapers popularized interventionist thinking: a German victory would threaten American security; the nation must rouse itself now, before it was too late. After the conquest of France, newspaper editor William Allen White organized the Committee to Defend America by Aiding the Allies. By the middle of that summer over 600 local chapters were cajoling citizens with their simple, forceful plea to stop Hitler's threatening advance.

The debate over the war became part of the presidential campaign of 1940. Meeting in Philadelphia only days after the French surrender, the Republicans nominated Wendell L. Willkie of Indiana, a progressive Midwestern businessman who turned his back on the strong isolationist bloc within the GOP. A former Democrat, Willkie himself supported most New Deal reforms and approved aid to England. Three weeks later, Roosevelt who wanted an unprecedented third term but was worried, with good reason, about being accused of excessive ambition maneuvered the Democratic convention into drafting him. Party regulars acquiesced in his renomination, but many urban bosses were clearly disgruntled with the too liberal, too independent, too cocksure squire from Hyde Park.

Roosevelt shunned active campaigning for two months. He stayed in the White House, directing a large-scale buildup of American defenses: expanding the armed services with more money and more men; arranging joint defense measures with Canada; securing a new pledge from the Latin American republics for common resistance to any attack in the Western Hemisphere. Then, shortly after Hitler launched a massive air attack against England, Churchill asked for U.S. destroyers. Roosevelt and most Americans were anxious to help, but a major legal obstacle stood in the way—isolationists had amended a naval appropriations bill to forbid any transfer of equipment unless the service chiefs certified that it was not needed for defense. So Roosevelt made a deal on September 2, 1940: fifty aged destroyers went to Britain in exchange for long-term American leases on military bases in Newfoundland, Bermuda, and the Caribbean. This trade vastly improved America's defense posture, outflanking the isolationists, and at the same time ended neutrality. Now neither at war nor at peace with Nazi Germany, the United States adopted a "nonbelligerent" status: all aid to England short of war.

At this point, Willkie shifted his campaign strategy against Roosevelt. The Republican had challenged the President not so much on his platform, most of which Willkie himself accepted, as on the issue of the third term. Yet in public opinion polls he lagged far behind the popular, dynamic FDR. Lacking an effective issue, he also lost his voice during much of the campaign. But now, in early October, Willkie charged that nonbelligerency "surely meant wooden crosses for sons and brothers and sweethearts." Suddenly Willkie's crowds grew more and more enthusiastic, and Democrats around the country worried about the rise in antiwar sentiment. But Roosevelt, who had shrewdly appointed two prominent Republicans to his cabinet, then toured the Northeast, reiterating the rationale for aid to England in New York City and finally, pledging in Boston, "I have said this before, but I shall say it again and again and again: Your boys are not going to be sent into any foreign wars." These dramatic words blunted Willkie's charges, although the President also said that a defense of the United States required the defense of England. Roosevelt won another term by another landslide, but Willkie did reduce his popular margin.

Just after his victory, Roosevelt faced a strategic situation of great complexity. Feisty English pilots and a new invention, radar, had denied Hitler that superiority in the air necessary for a cross-channel invasion. But victory in the "Battle of Britain" did not signal defeat for the Germans, now the masters of central and western Europe. Indeed, Hitler loosed "wolf packs," patrol after patrol of submarines, against Britain's merchant marine. Slow strangulation, he hoped, could achieve what the quick blow had not. The move was well timed, for strangulation loomed from still another source: the cash-and-carry provisions of America's Neutrality acts. English dollar resources had dwindled to about $2 billion. Churchill told Roosevelt privately that Britain could never take the offensive against Germany without extensive American credits for new military weapons and a firm undertaking to keep the North Atlantic sea lanes open.

Roosevelt reacted strongly and swiftly. Recalling the simple human duty to "lend a garden hose" to a neighbor whose house "had caught fire," the President declared that "We must be the great arsenal of democracy." America would supply the materiel, Britain the men, for the war against Fascism. By March 1941 Roosevelt's proposal for "Lend-Lease"— under which the United States was to lend Britain some $7 billion in goods—had passed Congress.

So began a period of challenge and response that eventually drew the United States into war. Hitler marked off a huge area of the North Atlantic between Iceland and Britain as a war zone, where submarines aided by aircraft "spotters" attacked merchant shipping headed for England. Almost 500,000 tons of ships a month disappeared beneath the waves, a lethal rate if it continued for long. Roosevelt extended the so-called American neutrality patrol almost to Iceland; within that huge area, United States naval vessels reported on Nazi maneuvers. When the Nazis sank an American freighter, the *Robin Moor*, on May 21, 1941, the President ordered the Navy to convoy American ships across the "neutral" area. This quasi-war continued for about four months, until the Germans attacked another destroyer, the *Greer*, in Icelandic waters. In September the President announced a policy of "active defense." The Navy now would guard the sea lanes all the way to Iceland for all ships, opening fire on sight at any German vessels or aircraft. When another destroyer was sunk in October with 100 lives lost, Woody Guthrie wrote a ballad about it: "What were their names, tell me, what were their names? Did you have a friend on the good *Reuben*

James?" Roosevelt then pushed through Congress a measure which armed U.S. merchant ships and permitted them to carry cargo directly to British ports. Despite howls from isolationists, most citizens now agreed with the President that America must aid Britain at all costs. That cost was indeed high: by the fall of 1941, the United States had abandoned its neutrality laws and joined in the Battle of the Atlantic. The "arsenal of democracy" already had entered a shooting war.

Japan

Violence and war were raging in another part of the globe as well. During 1938, and well into 1939, Japan and America had tried to ignore one another. Tokyo continued its military adventure in China, certain that the economic health of its empire required exclusive access to markets there; the United States still insisted upon the traditional Open Door policy. Events in Europe diverted attention from this deadlock for many months.

The outbreak of war in Europe forced Britain to cut back its commitments to Chiang Kai-shek. Almost at once, Roosevelt moved to take on a stronger role in Asia, a course that the State Department happily encouraged. Convinced that Japan's leaders would never dare fight the United States, he adopted a policy of firmness, pressuring them constantly to withdraw from China. For two years, from late 1939 until late 1941, America gradually severed its commercial and financial relations with Japan in a slowly escalating economic war. Embargoes on scrap iron and steel, industrial chemicals, and oil, aid to China's war effort, and the freezing of Japanese assets in the United States all reflected Roosevelt's grim determination. Apparently most of the leadership in Tokyo felt that they could not yet afford to go to war against the Americans, especially since the Soviet Union remained a potential danger on their flank.

Hitler's conquests in Europe, however, made the Japanese less cautious. The fall of France and the Netherlands bewitched most of Prime Minister Fumimaro Konoye's cabinet: raw materials from Indochina and the Dutch East Indies could replace those embargoed by the United States. Still, moderates in Japan and many naval leaders shrank from action that could provoke war. So when Roosevelt widened the embargo, Konoye temporarily backtracked and turned to diplomacy.

By April 1941 his foreign minister, the militant Yosuke Matsuoka, had negotiated a non-aggression pact with the Soviet Union as well as an alliance with Germany and Italy (the so-called Tripartite Pact of 1940). Shortly afterward, Hitler attacked Russia and thereby strengthened Japan's strategic security, while the Americans' increasing involvement in the Battle of the Atlantic made them seem less of a threat to Japan in the Pacific. By July, the Japanese had occupied all of Indochina. Roosevelt's reaction to this seizure, however, was one of outrage. He now imposed sweeping economic restrictions against Japan, almost snuffing out commerce between the two nations.

Without quite realizing it, the two Pacific antagonists had worked themselves into something of a trap. If the Japanese pushed forward to secure vital raw materials, the United States might well declare war; yet Roosevelt would not supply these goods peacefully unless Tokyo abandoned Southeast Asia and China. For six months moderates on both sides sought a way around this impasse, hoping to avoid war.

Konoye suggested a face-to-face meeting with Roosevelt, but the President refused unless, as Secretary Hull insisted, the issue of China were settled beforehand. This requirement amounting, in effect, to a demand that Japan retreat from all its conquests since 1937 toppled Konoye and brought to the premiership a militant expansionist, General Hideki Tojo. Like most of his fellow army officers, he sought war. A collision now seemed inevitable. Although last-minute negotiations during November held out the possibility of an agreement—resumption of trade in exchange for a Japanese withdrawal for Indochina and a compromise settlement in China —both Churchill and Chiang rejected the idea. Hull fell back upon America's unvarying prerequisite for peace: an Open Door in China.

After receiving this renewed demand, the Japanese Imperial Council voted for war on December 1. Most of those present knew how desperate this gamble was; but they worried even more about the nation's economy, and its honor, if they submitted to Roosevelt's terms. A huge fleet of aircraft carriers had left the Kurile Islands on November 25 for Pearl Harbor, and a massive army mobilized in southern Indochina for an attack on Malaya, the strategic key to Southeast Asia. American intelligence, both in the Pacific and in Washington, had predicted an attack on Singapore, while fog and the absence of radar camouflaged Japanese ships moving toward Hawaii. At the same time the U. S. naval commander there, Admiral Husband E. Kimmel, ordered all American aircraft carriers out to sea and grouped airplanes together on runways as a safeguard against sabotage. Then, a little before 8 a.m. local time on December 7—just as the Japanese ambassador was cutting off negotiations in Washington—hundreds of Japanese planes attacked America's greatest naval installation, destroyed most of the planes bunched on the ground, and then turned toward the fleet. One dive bomber intentionally crashed into a ship. A second wave of bombers appeared an hour later to continue the assault almost unopposed, so completely were the Americans surprised. The United States' eight battleships were disabled, the Oklahoma and Arizona sunk outright. More than 2,300 Americans died. Still, Kimmel had saved the aircraft carriers which would prove decisive in waging the Pacific war.

The next day President Roosevelt, appearing before the jointly assembled House and Senate, called the attack "a day which will live in infamy," and Congress declared war against the Empire of Japan. FDR reacted in the same way he had during the banking crisis of 1933. He started at once to do the things he had to do—and with perfect assurance that the country would be able to meet any situation whatever. Honoring the Tripartite Pact, Hitler and Mussolini declared war on the United States three days later. Now almost all Americans, including the isolationists, at once closed ranks behind the President; "the only thing to do now is to lick hell out of them," Senator Burton Wheeler wrote, catching the national mood. Some, it is true, persisted in believing that FDR had known of the Japanese attack, welcoming it as a means of uniting the country against Fascism. This was not true, or at least our intelligence experts refused to believe the warning signals that they did receive. "Noise," or conflicting signals, in the intelligence network had confused an antiquated reporting system divided among several Washington bureaus.

With the United States now fully committed to the struggle, the three major Allies—America, Britain, and the Soviet Union came together in the Grand Alliance. The Soviet Union had been Hitler's ally until June 1941, when Nazi Germany had suddenly launched a massive invasion of Russia, and the Russians were now bearing the full brunt of German power.

And So to War

War and the preparations for war revived to some extent a reformist impulse in American society, an impulse that had withered in the late 1930's. Global conflict not only honed the skills of government bureaucrats and academic intellectuals, making both more expert in social planning, but also changed radically the status of blacks and of women. The population shifted northward to industrial centers in Chicago, Cleveland, Pittsburgh, New York, and New Jersey, and westward to defense plants in Southern California. A new sense of noble purpose and community replaced the malaise of the Depression years. War saddened but also invigorated the nation. The times were badly out of joint, and Americans now went forward in a high crusading spirit to set them right.

In the first months of war, despite the chatty optimism pervading the country's newspapers, military planners in Washington had considerable cause for worry. Early in 1942 Hitler's troops were camped outside Moscow, almost in sight of the golden glint of the Kremlin's ancient churches. In North Africa the Nazi legions of General Rommel, the "Desert Fox," had by midsummer swept almost to the gates of Alexandria, Egypt, threatening to cut Britain's vital links with its empire. German submarines infested the Atlantic, their skilled commanders sinking ships far more rapidly —nearly 750,000 tons a month—than the Allies could replace them. In 1942 the Germans destroyed 1,664 ships. Elated by such success, Admiral Doenitz wanted to send every U-boat he had to the United States's eastern seaboard, where a mere dozen subs had sunk fifty-seven percent of America's tankers in a few weeks. But Hitler preferred to rely on his attacks of intuition —"Norway," he said emphatically, would be his

RECONQUEST OF EUROPE
World War II

Normandy Landings
June 6, 1944

Allied advances

German battle lines

MILES
0   200

Southern France
Landings
August 15, 1944

"zone of destiny." "Norway?" the Admiral asked incredulously. The Führer rolled his eyes towards the map.

Nonetheless, Germany had accomplished the amazing feat of waging war effectively on three fronts.

Meanwhile, the Japanese descended upon the British, Dutch, and American possessions in Asia. An army moving overland down the Malay Peninsula captured the key British naval base of Singapore. Now the Japanese roamed almost at will across East Asia, conquering Burma, most of the East Indies, and the Philippines. General Douglas MacArthur, commander of United States forces in the Pacific, directed a gallant but futile defense in America's colonies there. Last-ditch

battles on Bataan Peninsula and Corregidor, together with a rearguard naval action in the Java Sea, could do no more than slow the Japanese advance. By summer, both Australia and India lay open to attack. (A few Japanese fishing vessels even shelled Los Angeles in early 1942, but the Pacific's vast expanses of salt water protected America's west coast from any serious assault.) In these desperate circumstances, the Allies could only try somehow to hold on, hoping that the forces of Fascism had overextended themselves. The United States had now to gear up its industrial might for a war of attrition.

Mobilization proved a cumbersome task. The experiences gained in depression were no guide for the present: worries about too few workers replaced those about too many; inflation, not falling prices, bedeviled government economists. Congress again granted the President sweeping powers to organize the economy, and Roosevelt immediately set up a central agency, the War Production Board, to oversee all industry. WPB chief Donald Nelson faced a difficult problem: most businessmen did not want to make heavy investments in military plants which would probably be useless at war's end, yet any suggestion that the government itself manufacture war goods raised howls of protest. Nelson finally swung private industry toward conversion with the carrot of guaranteed profits and the stick of banning all nonessential production. Even then, bottlenecks appeared, so he organized a committee to allocate scarce raw materials. A scrap-rubber campaign aroused popular enthusiasm—a set of rubber galoshes appeared in the White House mail—but produced little usable rubber; not until 1943 did a massive expansion of synthetic rubber plants, together with wartime rationing, make it possible to meet industrial demands. A bittersweet shortage soon appeared: too few workers in defense plants. Avoiding any effort to regiment labor

Casablanca, *1942. Humphrey Bogart and Dooley Wilson inside "Rick's Cafe." Casablanca merged romance with contemporary history; anti-Nazism was not only morally necessary, it was glamorous. Americans found their twentieth century hero in the wary, grave face of Bogie. What Ernest Hemingway and later Norman Mailer defined as heroism, Bogart personified in this and most of his subsequent roles.*

directly, the administration wooed men with offers of high pay or with threats of the draft if they remained in more lucrative consumer production. Women entered the war industries in full force. Although the Democrats delayed stringent wartime controls until after the 1942 elections, they converted the national economy to wartime production in a reasonably effective, though piecemeal, fashion. Private business survived, even profited from mobilization, and workers looked forward to steady paychecks. The "arsenal of democracy" began to make its essential contribution to the Allied cause.

In all, nearly fourteen million American men and women went into uniform. Huge training camps transformed farmland outside cities and towns into miniature battle fronts or vast barracks for citizen-soldiers. Depression made physical training doubly difficult: poverty had condemned many to inadequate diets and so to weak bodies; and few doctors, nutritionists, or physical trainers were graduated from college during the 1930's. The only people accustomed to handling large numbers of young men, it turned out, were the nation's high school coaches. Thousands of them left local playing fields for basic training camps in the South and California, so many that for several years the traditional weekend football and basketball games disappeared in small towns. GIs—so called because everything they owned was government-issued—received four to six months of conditioning, good food, and patriotic propaganda.

Critics worried that this mass experience in military uniformity might weaken America's individuality and diversity. The citizen army, though, quickly dispelled such fears. Soldiers spoke of "SNAFU": "situation normal, all fouled up." Officers rounded up for service —"ninety-day wonders," hastily trained in special camps—did not glorify war. (Some commanders forgot this characteristic of their armies. George Patton, a dynamic general whose bold tank maneuvers destroyed the enemy in Africa and southern Italy, once struck and humiliated a young soldier suffering from combat fatigue. Public anger forced him from his command, and he later publicly apologized.) Military service, Americans assumed, was a temporary thing, a necessary duty to be abandoned once victory was won. They were fighting a war to preserve American liberties, not weaken them.

The Home Front

War pervaded the home front itself. Millions of Americans left familiar jobs or the unemployment lines to work in weapons factories or for wartime bureaucracies. All citizens paid swollen tax bills. The fighting itself, however, was far distant. In the Pacific, battles on oddly named atolls invisible on most maps erupted sporadically; in Europe, the Allies avoided any decisive move against Hitler's entrenched Fortress Europa until well into 1944. No bombs fell on American cities, no armies threatened invasion. War was work: the average adult held one full-time and one part-time job. War was also scarcity: a cornucopia of guns, ships, aircraft, bombs, and ammunition spilled into distant battle fronts, leaving few goods behind for ordinary consumers. Americans worked harder and longer and earned more than they had in years, but they found little to buy in department stores or groceries or car lots. To prevent black markets and runaway inflation, the federal government rationed shoes, meat, sugar, tires, gasoline, chocolate, and many other goods. Each citizen received a quota of special ration stamps; retail goods "cost" both dollars and stamps. Shortages sometimes had unexpected consequences. Disappearing supplies of cloth, for example, prompted government officials to order a reduction of yardage in women's clothes. One result: the skimpy two-piece bathing suit replaced the one-piece skirted model popular during the 1930's.

Although struggling to defeat racist regimes in Germany and Japan, Americans ironically extended their own bigotry into the war effort. Many defense contractors hired blacks only when whites were unavailable. New Deal bureaucrats pledged not to challenge "local social patterns." The armed forces segregated blacks into separate barracks and units, and excluded them from all but menial tasks, mostly jobs in mess halls. The Air Corps and Marines—self-styled elite forces —rejected blacks altogether. Urban blacks suffered unfamiliar harassments in small towns near training camps. One black soldier, Lloyd Brown, wrote of an incident in Salina, Kansas: he and several friends, all in uniform, entered a restaurant. "You boys know we don't serve colored here," the waiter told them. Brown remembers, "We just stood there, staring. For sitting at the counter having lunch were six German prisoners of war. The people of Salina would serve these enemy soldiers and turn away black American GIs."

Japanese-Americans living in California understood Brown's lament, for they and others of Asian origin there had long endured discrimination. Tokyo's attack on Pearl Harbor set off an unusually fierce hysteria against them as "subversives." Local army commanders ruthlessly rounded up some 100,000 Japanese and corralled them into "relocation centers" hundreds of miles inland. "A Jap's a Jap . . . whether he's an American citizen or not," General John DeWitt explained. Many lost all their property and their businesses, an injustice never remedied.

But the early 1940's were more than work and bigotry. Americans entertained themselves, inventing fads and emulating new heroes. Gasoline rationing limited most travel, so film and radio and newspaper brought the world home. Americans watched and listened. "Movie Tone" news clips preceded double features everywhere. Edward R. Murrow won overnight fame for his dramatic broadcasts which, as German bombs exploded eerily in the background, he would begin with the words, "This . . . is London." Hollywood film-makers lost much of their creativity, although they produced a record 982 movies in three years. No *Gone With the Wind* caught the spirit of the world war; instead, a wearying genre of patriotic films repeated a litany of American virtue, enemy perfidy, and the final triumph of a righteous people. Still, movies like *For Whom the Bell Tolls* and the great Humphrey Bogart—Ingrid Bergman classic *Casablanca* showed the human drama and poignancy inherent in war.

Even America's comic strips reflected a nation at war. *Superman* came prominently on the scene during the 1940's, a time when Americans needed to persuade themselves that they could defeat evil forces. Joe Palooka, formerly a boxer, enlisted in the army in 1941: "No, I ain't gonna be an officer," he told his girlfriend, Rosie, "just a buck private. I don't deserve t' be an' don't know enuff t' be." The next year, as Joe stood with a pal on dangerous anti-sniper duty, their dialogue summed up a nation's thoughts: "Yeah, Joe, I was an isolationist. I really believed I was right then." "A man's certainly entitled to 'is b'lifs, George." "But when the big test came I realized how wrong I was. . . ." In *Terry and the Pirates*, an older pilot, Colonel Flip Corkin (loosely based on an authentic Army air hero, Colonel Philip G. Cochran) lectures Terry in the strip of October 17, 1942: "You'll get angry as the devil at the army and its so-called red tape . . . but be patient.

. . . Somehow, the old eagle has managed to end up in possession of the ball in every war since 1776—so just humor it along . . . remember, there are a lot of good guys missing from mess tables in the South Pacific, Africa, Britain, Asia and back home who are sorta counting on you to take it from here. Good night, kid!'' (Terry salutes as Corkin waves.) And the leader of the "pirates" in the strip, the sinister sexpot known as the Dragon Lady, turns after years of crime to patriotism: "Follow me against the invader [Japan] who threatens to engulf China!" Her band replies, "We fight for Dragon Lady! We march with Dragon Lady against foreign armies!"

America's young people indulged themselves with fads: yo-yos, mismatched shoes, slumber parties, and bubblegum. Then Frank Sinatra introduced the country to another phenomenon —teeny-boppers and singing idols. On the night before New Year's Eve of 1942, Sinatra appeared at New York's Paramount Theater, where the audience, mostly young high school girls, alternately shrieked and "swooned" as "the Voice" crooned favorites like "Fools Rush In" and "Night and Day." Wherever he appeared, girlish screeching created pandemonium; souvenir hunters tore his clothes and preserved his footprints in mud; a concert in 1944 required some 400 police to control a crowd of 30,000. Parents and psychiatrists professed bewilderment: this puny kid with greased hair and flamboyant antics so completely contradicted the all-American image of helmeted, soft-spoken GIs. Well-publicized love affairs, hints of

deals with organized crime, a garish life-style in Southern California, all created a new kind of American celebrity, entertaining as much offstage as onstage.

Some attributed the wacky Sinatra craze to an anomaly of war: few young men remained at home. College women worried about their prospects for a "MRS. degree," then one of the major reasons many parents sent daughters to colleges. One coed at the University of Nebraska, for example, complained, "They're all either too old or too young or too sick." (Men not drafted for physical reasons, even if quite legitimate, often suffered unjust scorn as "4-F'ers.") Women did not use the opportunity of war for feminist reform. The image of "Rosie the Riveter," so cultivated by business leaders desperate for labor, always seemed to some degree unnatural. Most women yearned for "normal" times, when men would again take up their dominant status. Women's fashions aped the missing masculine presence: squared-off shoulders, buttoned tunics and straight lines adorned Fifth Avenue mannequins. Hasty trips to the altar produced a growing number of divorces, then a severe social stigma. The birth rate increased, however. War converted love-making into an urgent rite which, without widely available contraceptives, quite frequently produced "blessed events" nine months later. American women, then, continued to value most the traditional roles of wife and mother—a desire made more, not less, intense by war.

The War in Europe and the Pacific

As the United States geared up to supply the means for an eventual victory, the Allies weathered still more assaults by their enemies. Although the Pacific war vitally affected their interests, all three nations, the U. S., Britain, and the Soviet Union, agreed that they must postpone taking the initiative against Japan. Against their more dangerous opponent, Nazi Germany, the coalition was divided by conflicting purposes and divergent needs. In August 1941, when Churchill met with Roosevelt in Newfoundland, the two leaders issued a communique, soon dubbed the "Atlantic Charter." A blueprint of sorts for the postwar world, this document pledged self-determination for all people, freedom of the seas, equal

commercial opportunities (the Open Door), and disarmament. These high principles, however, masked a calculated swap. Churchill in effect promised to open the British empire to American trade; in turn, the British and Americans together would dominate the world. Self-determination presumably would limit Russian expansion in eastern Europe. With British and German troops only fifty miles from Moscow, Stalin was not about to argue. On New Year's Day 1942, the United States, Britain, and Russia, together with twenty-three other nations at war against the Axis powers, signed the Declaration of the United Nations. All committed themselves to uphold the Atlantic Charter and promised not to make a separate peace. The Allies, despite Stalin's badgering, refused to recognize large Soviet territorial gains in Poland and the Balkans.

Hitler launched a huge new offensive against Russia during early 1942: Leningrad was encircled, and the Sixth Corps under General Paulus ramrodded south into the Ukraine and beyond, toward the oil fields of central Asia. Stalin appealed urgently to his allies for some action to counter German strength in Russia, preferably an invasion of France across the English Channel. Lower-echelon military planners in the United States agreed, but their chiefs knew that the Anglo-Americans could at best secure a beachhead in France, not open a major front there. Some indirect evidence suggests, also, that they hoped Hitler would exhaust Germany's armies against Stalin, considerably easing their own task. Worried that an early assault with American supplies might well bog down, creating a stalemated front reminiscent of World War I, Churchill flatly rejected any scheme to invade France. His concern, instead, was to preserve the British empire and its lifeline in the Mediterranean.

Rather than risk decisive action on the continent, the British Eighth Army in Egypt, under General Bernard Montgomery, and a hastily trained American force, commanded by Dwight Eisenhower, attacked German positions in North Africa. The giant pincer movement of "Operation to RCH" began in late October, Montgomery moving west, Eisenhower landing in Morocco. General Rommel slowly retreated, conserving his forces to defend Tunisia—since Roman times, the strategic key to North Africa and the Mediterranean Sea. But Anglo-American tanks relentlessly closed around him, and his troops surrendered on May 12, 1943.

Elsewhere, too, during the fall and winter of 1942 to 1943, the Allies halted the Axis advance and took the initiative. In the most important theater of war, the Russian front, Hitler's legions had driven rapidly forward, reaching the Caucasus in the south and the Volga River in the east. But immensely long supply lines, a foolishly harsh occupation policy that used many soldiers for garrison duty, and a devastatingly cold winter slowed, then stopped, German armies. The turning point came at Stalingrad. General Paulus laid furious siege to the city throughout the fall, but the Russians staved them off in hand-to-hand, building-by-building fighting. Then, at the peak of winter, Stalin, buoyed by the arrival of American lend-lease from Iran, launched a surprise counterattack. The Russians encircled the Sixth Army, capturing or killing 600,000 German soldiers. The great victory came on February 2, 1943—now a national holiday in the Soviet Union —and marked the beginning of a Soviet offensive that ended in Berlin.

American victories in the Pacific paralleled those of the Russians in eastern Europe. Enraged by the attack on Pearl Harbor, Admiral Chester Nimitz regrouped a carrier task force and struck at the Japanese-held Marshall and Gilbert Islands in the central Pacific. Army Air Corps bomber squadrons, led by Jimmy Doolittle, raided Tokyo itself on April 18, 1942. Only a month later, aircraft from the *Lexington* and *Yorktown* thwarted an attack on Port Moresby, New Guinea, in the Battle of the Coral Sea. These reverses prompted navy leaders in Tokyo to send a huge armada into the central Pacific. The capture of Midway Island, they thought, would cut American communications with Asia. Nimitz met this force on June 3, and for three days a giant battle raged in the air (the fleets themselves were some 400 miles apart). American pilots sank four carriers and two heavy cruisers, and put four destroyers out of commission. Admiral King, the new commander in Hawaii, called the battle "the first decisive defeat suffered by the Japanese Navy in 350 years." Then a fierce struggle broke out for the Solomon Islands, southeast of the Dutch East Indies. From August 1942 until February 1943, soldiers, sailors, and pilots fought over Guadalcanal, the key to the area; but American persistence eventually won out. Now Americans in the Pacific—like the Russians in eastern Europe—began an offensive which would carry them steadily closer to the enemy's home territory.

Coalition Diplomacy, 1943-45

As the tide of victory flowed more and more in the Allies' favor, their leaders turned to the delicate and difficult question of postwar objectives. Early diplomacy among them, during the dark years of 1941 and 1942, had glossed over controversy with general statements of high moral purpose that, in effect, pointed toward Anglo-American world dominion (as, most notably, in the Atlantic Charter). At the same time Roosevelt, concerned lest quarrels over the spoils of war weaken the Grand Alliance, insisted upon "no predetermination." A postwar peace conference would settle things. Roosevelt and Churchill always worried that Stalin, if sufficiently disgruntled, might negotiate a separate peace with Hitler.

In early 1943 the British and American leaders met at Casablanca, and decided that Germany must surrender unconditionally. This promise probably reassured the Soviets, already suspicious that their allies planned to impose the chief burden of the fighting on them. Some commentators have argued that the prospect of total defeat encouraged the Germans to fight to the bitter end, so that the demand for unconditional surrender needlessly prolonged the war. Yet the alternative—a negotiated settlement with Hitler—was hardly either realistic or morally desirable.

As the Allies everywhere began their offensives during 1943, the realities of military occupation made postwar planning necesary. George Patton's Third Army and Montgomery's British troops swept across Sicily and part way up the Italian peninsula during the winter; both commanders received secret offers of surrender from King Victor Emmanuel. Ignoring Russian protests, Roosevelt and Churchill negotiated separately with these agents, finally accepting surrender terms which insured that moderate capitalists and their allies would dominate postwar Italy. Already suspicious of every Anglo-American move, Stalin was infuriated.

Arguments broke out even between the Americans and the British. Churchill insisted that the Western Allies should first invade "the soft underbelly of Europe"—that is, strike northward through the Balkans and Italy into Austria and Czechoslovakia. Army Chief of Staff George C. Marshall angrily replied that "No American is going to land in that god-damned [region]." In-

stead, the Americans argued, an invasion across France into the Rhineland would more quickly end the war, and would more surely keep the industrial heartland of western Europe out of Russian control. After several particularly strained meetings among Big Three planners and foreign ministers, Churchill, Roosevelt, and Stalin agreed to meet at Teheran. (Stalin did not want to travel too far from the front, where he was supreme commander.) On their way to the Iranian capital, Churchill and Roosevelt stopped at Cairo, where they conferred briefly with Chiang Kai-shek. The three leaders demanded unconditional surrender from the Japanese, vowing to deprive that country of all its empire: Manchuria and Formosa returned to China; the islands of the Pacific handed back to their former imperial masters, or given to the United States.

The Teheran Conference, held during the last days of November 1943, was the first face-to-face meeting of President, Prime Minister, and Generalissimo. Roosevelt, Churchill, and Stalin discussed both military strategy and postwar relations. The Americans outlined their campaign against Japan in the Pacific, and the Russians promised to join the war there after Germany's defeat. Stalin pressed the other leaders vigorously for an invasion of France, now code-named OVERLORD, but they dodged all commitments. Agreement came more easily on less immediate matters. The three men pledged to partition Germany, reducing it forever to a third-rank military power. To prevent future wars, a United Nations would oversee collective security. The Allies would jointly administer all liberated countries until representative institutions were set up. Roosevelt thought the Teheran Conference encouraged a spirit of frankness, openness, and cordiality: "We came here with hope and determination," he told reporters, "We leave here, friends in fact, in spirit, and in purpose."

1944: The Final Struggle

The Allies still faced formidable military tasks in Europe and the Pacific. The Anglo-Americans opened an immense three-pronged campaign against Hitler's western stronghold during 1944. Their air war, which had carried destruction to Germany itself as early as 1942, entered a new phase. Radar bombsights tripled the destructive

power of nighttime raids, and new long-range fighters permitted daytime sorties. Round-the-clock bombing, made possible by immense amounts of equipment and men from the United States, targeted German aircraft plants, communications systems, and chemical factories. Incessant bombing may have discouraged many Germans, already fatigued by years of warfare, although its strategic effectiveness remains questionable. (Hitler's minister of production, Albert Speer, claimed that the Allies' scattergun approach to bombing never seriously disrupted the output of war material. In contrast, a postwar survey by the American army claimed that the raids so upset the German economy that production eventually ceased altogether.) Certainly, Germany endured an immense amount of firepower: some attacks, like those against Dusseldorf and Dresden, nearly destroyed entire cities; a total of almost three million tons of bombs fell on Hitler's Reich from 1942 to 1945.

In those pre-atomic days, however, wars were still decided on the ground. The battle for western Europe began in earnest on January 22, 1944, when an Anglo-American army landed at Anzio behind the German front in Italy. But this effort soon bogged down. That spring a slow, hard advance began against the German divisions south of Rome. It linked up with the Anzio beachhead and then, on June 4, captured Rome itself. The Germans retreated to their so-called Gothic Line, some 150 miles north of the city, where the fighting stabilized.

On June 6, two days after the fall of Rome, the biggest amphibious landing in history, Operation OVERLORD, began. Supreme Commander Dwight Eisenhower had planned the attack well: air bombardments softened up beach defenses (Hitler's famous "westwall") and disrupted German communications; three airborne divisions landed the night before behind German lines, there to disrupt defense strategy; finally, at 7 a.m., some 125,000 soldiers scurried ashore in Normandy. The Allies had gone to great lengths to convince Hitler, successfully, that their principal landing site would instead be farther north, around the city of Calais, with the result that the main German force, Gen-

Dwight D. Eisenhower and President Roosevelt.

eral Rommel's Seventh Army, stayed away for several critical days. Despite enormous casualties, which sometimes reached a hundred percent at places like Omaha Beach, the Allies established their beachhead. Within five days, sixteen more divisions landed and occupied some eight miles of coastline.

Unlike the Italian campaign, the fighting in France quickly took on the character of a *blitzkrieg* in reverse. On July 18 the strategic village of St. Lo fell to the Allies after stubborn fighting. Then General Patton's Third Army raced into Brittany and down the Loire Valley, while another Allied force under Montgomery drove eastward to Paris. Under orders not to retreat, the Seventh Army counterattacked: a Canadian army cut off this advance, trapping the entire German force at Falaise. Now the road to Paris lay open, and on August 25 its citizens rebelled against the Nazis. British and Canadian troops streamed along the coast into Belgium and the Netherlands; American soldiers headed for Luxembourg. The Allied rush halted in early September at the Siegfried Line, a string of powerfully defended German forts in the Rhineland. Overextended lines of supply forced nearly three months of preparation for the final assault.

General Gerd von Rundstedt, Rommel's successor, decided not to wait: on December 16, 1944, his armies attacked along the thinly held front in the Ardennes Forest. Spearheaded by tanks, the offensive carried rapidly forward. Then a column of American troops blunted the advance and rescued the besieged city of Bastogne. This Battle of the Bulge was a very near thing for the Allies, although it proved to be Germany's last

major effort on the western front. The Germans tenaciously defended their Rhineland cities that winter, but on March 7, 1945, the Allies captured the strategic bridge at Remagen. Their armies flooded across the Rhine into Germany. The end was near.

Meanwhile, the Soviets had destroyed Hitler's main force on the plains of eastern Europe, where the Nazis had concentrated nearly eighty percent of their military strength. Despite huge losses at Stalingrad, Hitler launched still another offensive against Russia in July 1943. But increasingly scarce supplies and poor morale robbed his legions of their elusive victory. The eastern front became a vast war of attrition, trench warfare in motion. American equipment and Russian blood guaranteed Allied triumph. As his dreams faded, a monomaniacal Hitler threw every possible unit, every possible weapon, against the Soviet advance. Nothing availed. Russian soldiers pushed the Germans out of the Ukraine in March 1944 and then that summer drove into Poland. The people of Warsaw, like those in Paris, rebelled at the approach of their liberators. But Stalin halted his advance supposedly to regroup his scattered forces, while the Nazis viciously slaughtered the Polish patriots and had already wiped out the city's fiercely resisting Jewish ghetto. Stalin welcomed this outcome, for it killed many who might otherwise have battled a communist takeover of the country. That fall, the Red Army drove into the Balkans, routing German armies in Romania, Bulgaria, and Hungary. By late November, Soviet troops were marching through the streets of Vienna. All that remained was the final drive on Berlin.

Yalta and the Postwar World

Diplomacy acquired an urgency until now reserved for the battlefield. Despite preliminary agreements about unconditional surrender, the partition of Germany, and a joint occupation of liberated areas, troubles among the Allies intensified as their armies approached one another. The Western Allies worried about the principles of self-determination in Eastern Europe, where the Red Army installed puppet regimes controlled by the Kremlin. Since the British and Americans were sure to dominate the industrialized parts of Germany, the Soviets wanted reparations; yet reparations presumably must come principally from the

Rhineland and Bavaria, precisely the areas under Western control. United States military experts calculated that the war against Japan required Soviet help. Clearly, only another meeting of the Big Three could sort out these complicated and increasingly political postwar issues.

Churchill, Roosevelt, and Stalin came together once again, in February 1945, this time at the Black Sea resort of Yalta, for eight days of difficult talks about the future. Each wanted something from the others. Worried by military estimates that the Pacific war might require two more years and a million American casualties

Churchill, Roosevelt, and Stalin. (National Archives.)

—MacArthur predicted 50,000 casualties on the first day of the invasion of Japan—Roosevelt sought a helping hand from his Allies. Stalin was determined to erect pliant if not subservient governments along Soviet borders, especially in Eastern Europe, Iran, and China. Churchill looked forward to an enlarged British empire, presumably in the Middle East, and financial aid from America. Churchill and Stalin already had mapped out their respective spheres of influence in the Balkans, a plan that Roosevelt rejected. Nevertheless, a spirit of amity—signaled by the appearance of carafes of vodka at the breakfast table—prevailed. On broad declarations of principle, there was ready accord. All agreed about Germany: that nation would never again cause war. All agreed about the United Nations: a conference would meet in San Francisco on April 25, 1945, to work out institutional arrangements for a new collective security. All agreed on the liberated countries: they would have self-determination. The particulars, however, were thick with conflicting interests.

Many Americans at times since 1945 have blamed Roosevelt for dooming Eastern Europe to "communist slavery." Military and political realities, however, both the presence of the Red Army and Stalin's predictable demands for securi-

ty in that region, made unlikely there any regimes which the Soviet dictator considered unfriendly. The President understood, as most Westerners did not, that the area by and large contained two classes: crypto-feudal landowners, usually pro-Nazi or at least tainted with collaboration, and poor peasants. No middle-class, democratic, capitalist alternative existed in Poland, which became a test case of sorts, or anywhere else in Hungary, Romania, Bulgaria, and Yugoslavia. The three leaders issued a Declaration on Liberated Europe, which guaranteed free elections and self-determination. This solved a public-relations problem in England and America, but just as clearly opened the way for Stalin. Most people in Eastern Europe, now ready for radical reform, knew that it was not so much a question of choosing between socialism or capitalism as it was of avoiding outright Soviet domination. Cooperation with Stalin, they hoped, would permit some degree of national autonomy.

The conference's determinations on Germany and on the Pacific were both big with problems for the postwar era. His country desperately weak, Stalin greedily eyed Germany's industrial plants, those factories which lay almost exclusively in the western zones. He accepted an Anglo-American plan which divided the country into four sectors—three for Britain, the United States, and France in north-central, south and Rhineland areas, one for Russia in the pastoral east—on condition that Russia receive $10 billion in reparations "in kind," that is, goods not money. All four powers would garrison the capital, Berlin, although it lay deep within the Soviet sector, and would jointly decide Germany's future. Stalin promised Roosevelt that Russia would enter the war against Japan as soon as possible, but his price was high: virtually the return of that Russian dominance in northern China exercised by the tsars before 1905. The Yalta agreements—bargainings by victors distrustful of each other—did not work out as their planners had hoped. However reasonable and realistic they seemed at the time, without the cooperation among the powers induced by war, the compromises of Yalta would soon collapse into the conflicts of the cold war.

Within three months both the symbol of Allied unity, Roosevelt, and its common danger, Nazi Germany, were gone. During that early spring of 1945, Anglo-American and Russian troops closed in on Hitler's last strongholds. General Eisenhower vetoed Montgomery's plan to drive straight for Berlin. The Americans, always more interested in winning the war than in politicking about the future, considered this British plan likely to prolong the conflict if Nazi armies escaped to a southern redoubt in Bavaria. Instead, they wanted to surround and destroy German armies in the Rhineland, then push south of the capital toward the Elbe River. Churchill argued furiously with Eisenhower that "We should shake hands with the Russians as far to the east as possible." Roosevelt did not resolve the issue, for the exhausted President was now in Warm Springs resting for the coming United Nations Conference. Around noon on April 12, he complained of a terrible headache; that afternoon he lay dead of a cerebral hemorrhage. Eisenhower now followed his own plan. Russian and American troops met at the Elbe, some 200 miles south of Berlin, on April 27. That same day, Hitler committed suicide, and Russian soldiers raised the hammer-and-sickle flag over his command post. German armies in Italy, Austria, Holland, and Denmark, some one million men, stopped fighting during the next week; General Alfred Jodl, on behalf of the German high command, surrendered unconditionally on May 7, 1945. The war in Europe was over. "I moved amid cheering crowds," Churchill wrote later, "but with an aching heart and a mind oppressed by forebodings."

Suggested Readings

Robert Dallek's *Franklin D. Roosevelt and American Foreign Policy, 1932-1945* (1979) is a fine book. The second world war is the subject of William L. Langer and S. Everett Gleason, *The Challenge to Isolation, 1937-1940* (1952) and *The Undeclared War, 1940-1941* (1953), and Christopher Thorne, *Allies of a Kind: The United States, Britain, and the War Against Japan, 1941-1945* (1978). Richard Polenberg believes that the war made for great changes in American society, among them a further mechanization of agriculture, an increase in the membership of labor unions, a weakening of the ideology of racism, and a growth in government: *War and Society: The United States, 1941-1945* (1972). Roger Daniels gives a survey of the persecution of Japanese-Americans during the war in *Concentration Camps, USA* (1971); see also Jacobus ten Broek *et al.*, *Prejudice, War and the Constitution* (1954).

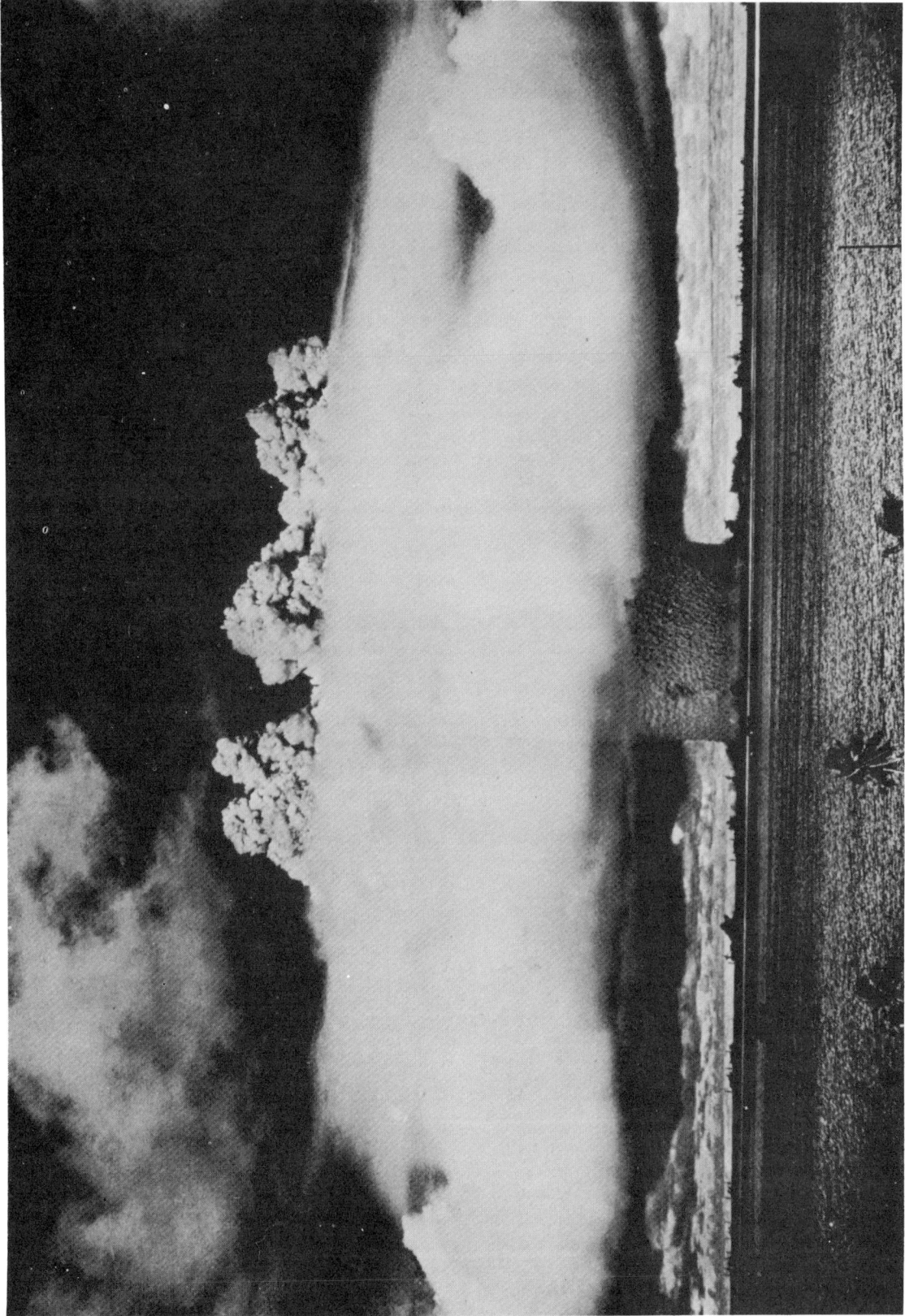

A postwar experimental atomic explosion.

Chapter XXVI
Truman

Hiroshima

Hiroshima—the name means "broad island"—had never suffered conventional bombing during the war. On the morning of August 6, 1945, a lone American bomber, the *Enola Gay* (its pilot ultimately became insane after returning to the United States) approached the city from the southeast. As the plane's bombardiers released the atomic bomb it carried, the sky above Hiroshima was blue and serene, the air flooded with glittering sunlight. Ironically, an all-clear air raid signal had just sounded, and the inhabitants were going about their daily business. Suddenly there came a great flash of light, "brighter than a thousand suns," followed by the lacerating heat of a giant fireball, then the sound of a blast bringing the force of hurricane winds, and finally, the now-familiar multicolored mushroom cloud rising high above the city.

The bomb, with a destructive force equivalent to twenty thousand tons of TNT, exploded at a height of 1,800 feet, near the center of the flat city, built mostly of wood. Within a radius of two miles of "ground zero," the destruction was total: metal and stone melted, and human beings were incinerated. Then fire spread everywhere. The city almost disappeared. Some 78,000 Japanese died at Hiroshima. Human suffering from burns was terrible. A devoutly religious domestic worker who survived wrote in her diary as though her world had collapsed: "There is no God, no Buddha."

Three days later, another atomic bomb was dropped on Nagasaki, Hiroshima's neglected historical sister. Mass open cremations followed, and 40,000 people died; life and death went out of cycle with one another.

Only gradually did the world come to realize that an even more wretched curse had been visited on the two cities in the form of a slow, painful, invisible contamination—radiation poisoning. The course of the disease consisted of vomiting; diarrhea with large clots of blood in the stool; fever; loss of hair; ulceration and purple spots on various part of the body from bleeding into the skin. Some deaths came from cancer years later. The Pandora's box of modern technological warfare had been fully opened.

Why had America's political and military leaders sanctioned using the atomic bomb on Japan? For President Harry Truman, the decision was plain: its use might save many thousands of American lives by shortening the war, and, after all, the Japanese had struck us at Pearl Harbor without warning. (Truman lied when he announced that Hiroshima was a military center without a significant civilian population.) Some advisers had suggested that we explode a demonstration bomb in an uninhabited area in the Pacific to convince the Japanese of the new weapon's terrible power. But government scientists feared that the bomb might prove a dud, and there existed a very limited number of bombs to detonate. Besides, failure might have evoked renewal of Japanese confidence. Even if the detonation were successful, it was felt, the fanatical Japanese militarists—who still harbored hopes for ultimate victory by luring the Americans into an invasion of the islands—might not have been sufficiently impressed by a mere demonstration of the bomb's destructive capacity.

The Japanese agreed to surrender on August 10, the day after Nagasaki was destroyed.

The use of the atomic bomb deprived America to some extent of the position of moral superiority it had held through most of the war. No longer did the total evil of the Axis contrast so sharply with the total righteousness of the Allies. The United States was the first and only country to commit such an act of monumental devastation. Critics have argued that the violence the world has accepted since World War II—such as the use of napalm in Vietnam and elsewhere—would not have been countenanced but for this earlier use of atomic bombs. "After Hiroshima," writes Howard Zinn, "the use of the atomic bomb was debatable, the extermination of villages and cities debatable, modern wars of annihilation debatable." Some have even suggested that the principal reason the United States used the bomb was its desire to demonstrate its military superiority to the Soviet Union; that it was thus the first act of the cold war as much as the last of the war against Japan. Put most crudely, this argument contends that we incinerated more than 100,000 Japanese to show the Soviets we were made of strong stuff.

One justification possibly deserves some measure of consideration: perhaps these actual demonstrations of the atomic bomb's awesome power served to instill a degree of caution in the world's leading powers. Nations ready to upset a normal balance of power have so far hesitated to tip the balance of nuclear terror atop which we survive. With the proliferation of atomic weapons, and the availability of nuclear raw materials, however, that restraint is increasingly unlikely to persist.

Harry S Truman

One of the President's closest aides, Steve Early, said only: "Harry, please come over to the White House right away."

Several hours before on that day, April 12, 1945, in Warm Springs, Georgia, President Franklin D. Roosevelt had died of a massive cerebral hemorrhage.

Almost a legend by 1945, Roosevelt, through his reassuring manner no less than his virtuoso leadership, had guided a nation through the anxieties of depression and the fears of global war. His leadership of the United Nations might perhaps have inspired a new spirit of friendship and confidence among the Allies then fast becoming adversaries. "We have learned to be citizens of the world," he had proclaimed during his fourth Inaugural address, "members of the human community." Now, when Vice President Harry Truman arrived at the White House, he was met by Eleanor Roosevelt, who said simply, "Harry, the President is dead." "I felt," Truman remarked a little later, "like the moon, the stars and all the planets had fallen on me."

Harry S Truman of Missouri considered himself a plain man, taking pride only in his honesty and self-reliance. His mother had inculcated a resolute spirit in this middle-class child: do your best and don't worry about it afterwards. Truman's early life was quite ordinary, except for unusually bad eyesight which forced him to wear thick glasses. The family farm prospered during the Progressive Era; he served creditably as an artillery captain in World War I; the postwar recession ruined a haberdashery venture in Kansas City. Out of work, Truman gratefully accepted an endorsement from the Pendergast machine to run for county judge. A reputation for integrity and a folksy campaign style won the election, and Truman settled into the comfortable life of presiding over a quiet court.

Some ten years later, in 1934, a dispute among Democratic bosses in Missouri gave Truman a chance to run for United States Senator. His political finesse and a workmanlike record carried him to Washington, where he vigorously supported Roosevelt and the New Deal. But by 1940 his future seemed bleak. Scandal had destroyed the Pendergast machine in Kansas City, and fresh party leaders wanted to replace him with someone more pliant. Yet the junior senator decided to fight for renomination in the primary. Truman's jalopy bounced all over the state, especially in the rural areas his opponents ignored, and he reminded voters of his strong Democratic record. Once again he won. Back in Washington, Senate leaders put Truman in charge of a watchdog committee on government contracts, a difficult job he performed with sober dispatch. But even though the Truman Committee saved millions of dollars for taxpayers, its chairman lacked charisma. No aura of destiny surrounded him, at least not before 1944.

In that year, however, a bitter squabble broke out in the Democratic party over the vice-presidential nomination. Liberal Democrats supported the incumbent, Henry A. Wallace, while Southerners preferred Senator James Byrnes of South Carolina. Many Midwesterners thought Wallace too quixotic, too "flighty." And some party leaders feared that Byrnes, who was an ex-Roman Catholic, would lose votes in the urban North. Busy with the war, and not wishing to offend, an increasingly ill Roosevelt allowed the bosses who controlled the 1944 Democratic convention to pick Truman, a good campaigner from an important border state. Labor leaders backed him enthusiastically, and everyone respected his reputation for honesty. The election that fall made Truman Vice President; Roosevelt's death five months later made him President.

A Quicksilver Peace: From Allies to Adversaries

The new chief executive faced giant problems. As Vice President he had been excluded from any role in policy and decision-making; and now, inexperienced in foreign affairs, and surrounded by advisers far more knowledgeable than he, Truman had somehow to gather the reins of government into his own hands. In Europe, Allied armies raced toward each other across the ruins of Hitler's empire. In the Pacific, the bloody but successful American landings at Iwo Jima foretold a

long and brutal struggle against the Japanese homeland. Roosevelt had fought for collective security, institutionalized in the United Nations but enforced by four "policemen"—England, China, Russia, and the United States. Others, even before his death, set out to chart a far different course: a *Pax Americana* rooted in monopoly control over that new weapon of weapons, the atomic bomb. Events tumbling over one another in the last months of the war and the first days of peace enabled Truman to establish his authority almost immediately.

"We may not get 100% of what we want in the postwar world," Truman told his advisers, "but I think we can get 85%." The United Nations Charter reflected the President's determination. At the Dumbarton Oaks Conference in 1944 and again at the Yalta Conference early the following year, the powers had pledged to replace the discredited League of Nations with a new, more effective instrument of collective security. But when they gathered in San Francisco during April 1945, negotiations proved unpredictable and difficult. Friction over Poland and disputes over procedure led Truman abruptly to inform Stalin that the United States would go ahead with the United Nations project with or without the Soviet Union. Stalin relented. The Charter allowed all member nations to discuss any question and vote in the General Assembly, but the Assembly's recommendations required approval from the Security Council. This super-cabinet, with five permanent members—the United States, Britain, France, the Soviet Union, and China—and six temporary members elected by the General Assembly, would meet to take acion in times of crisis. Each of the five great powers could veto any proposed UN action, a concession to the American Congress and British Parliament. A Secretariat administered dozens of economic, social, financial, and relief agencies, all to be headquartered with the rest of the UN in New York City and largely financed by the United States.

New rivalries quickly crushed hopes for world-wide cooperation. At a meeting in July 1946 of the "Big Three" at Potsdam, near Berlin, Truman, Stalin, and Clement Attlee (who replaced Churchill as British Prime Minister halfway through the conference) pondered the future of eastern Europe, the occupation of Germany, and the war against Japan. They demanded an unconditional surrender from the Japanese, and Stalin again promised to send Soviet troops against enemy armies in Manchuria and North China. In other areas, the problems proved intractable. Huge Soviet armies in the Balkans and eastern Europe added compelling force to Stalin's demand for "friendly regimes" there. This prospect horrified Truman, familiar with the feelings of America's immigrants from these regions. Churchill privately warned Attlee about Soviet imperialism. Unable to compromise, the three men simply postponed decisions about Poland, Hungary, Romania, Austria, Yugoslavia, Bulgaria, and Greece. The future of Germany proved an even more divisive issue. Stalin, already angered by Washington's refusal of a postwar loan to rebuild his war-shattered country, demanded a joint occupation of all Germany and immense reparations. The British and Americans succeeded in imposing a zonal occupation, coinciding roughly with the Allies' respective distribution of troops. Stalin satisfied himself with a promise from the other Allies to turn over fifteen percent of Western Germany's factories and movable equipment as reparations in kind.

Domestic Whirlwinds: Demobilization and Reform

Roosevelt's death and the end of the war threw American politics into prolonged uncertainty. Democrats argued heatedly among themselves over Negro rights, labor policy, and demobilization. Yet the Republicans, deeply divided over foreign policy and weakened by so many years of defeat, seemed unlikely to provide a strong, effective alternative. Some citizens wanted to dismantle what they called "the welfare state" and "government interference with business." Others looked forward to still more reform in health care, redistribution of income, and racial equality. Everyone feared the return of depression once the war ended, but no one knew quite how to prevent it. And everyone entertained the hope of a new era of peace, achievement, and growing affluence.

As soon as Japan surrendered, Americans demanded first and foremost a return to normal peacetime pursuits. Some twelve million soldiers wanted to come home as soon as possible. The army discharged men rapidly at first, but slowed the pace early in 1946 when international tensions revived. Within weeks, some riots broke out among troops stationed abroad, and angry protesters demonstrated at home. Demobilization continued.

This flood of veterans complicated the task of converting the nation's economy to peacetime production without returning to high prewar rates of unemployment. Congress soon passed the "GI Bill of Rights." Veterans took advantage of a wide range of benefits: hospital services and vocational training, favorable mortgage terms for houses and small businesses, payments for college attendance, weekly unemployment checks if necessary. Four out of five GIs went back to school, most to colleges which welcomed them gratefully after fifteen years of half-empty classrooms. For the first time in American history, many middle-class males now looked forward to a university education as a matter of course.

Reconversion of the larger economy proved far more complicated and controversial. President and Congress fought for nearly three years about inflation and union policy, while workers and employers struggled through months of protracted strikes. Wartime agencies had strictly regulated prices and profits and had rationed scarce commodities. After V-J Day, pent-up consumer demand soon broke through these restraints. One woman rushed into Bonwit Teller's department store in New York City and bought 57 pairs of nylons; she explained to the clerk that she was afraid there would be "hoarders." Black markets boomed: under-the-table payments to car dealers and appliance salesmen were widespread. Truman set up a Civilian Production Administration (CPA), presumably to enforce price controls. But the administration soon gave in, deregulating prices on many consumer goods and easing wartime rations. Prices of scarce consumer goods jumped upward since business had hardly begun to reconvert factories. Congress reduced taxes and subsidized investment for new plants, but this only reinforced demand. The government next auctioned off some $15 billion of its own manufacturing capacity, about one-fifth of the country's total. Although supply slowly caught up with demand, businessmen boosted prices to reap large profits. The rising cost of living, in turn, brought insistent demands for wage hikes from the nation's great unions. The country seemed trapped in a classic inflationary spiral. Even worse, unemployment had tripled during the summer of 1945, to some 3.5 million.

Labor-management relations deteriorated rapidly. Union members, worried about job security and declining purchasing power, demanded pay hikes. President Walter Reuther of the United Automobile Workers argued that if workers' real wages did not increase, they could not buy the increased output of American factories, and that high peacetime profits could finance higher pay without any boost in retail prices. Employers disputed both contentions, although firms like General Motors refused to open their accounting records. In November 1945 workers walked off their jobs in all GM plants. Electrical workers, meatpackers, and steel workers followed suit during January 1946. That

spring John L. Lewis ordered the United Mine Workers out, threatening to close down a wide range of satellite industries dependent upon soft coal. These strikes were settled, but in late May a strike shut down the country's railroads. Faced with the prospect of economic chaos, Truman reacted quickly. The President promised a nationwide radio audience that he would draft the strikers and order the army to run the trains unless they returned to work. Intimidated, the railway brotherhoods relented at once.

Most Americans, though distressed by soaring prices and inconvenienced by strikes, talked angrily of busybody bureaucrats mismanaging the economy. Eager to spend, yet finding goods scarce or overpriced, consumers came to believe that a market free of government controls would reduce prices by boosting output. Congressmen, responding to public agitation for rapid decontrol, revised the CPA, severely restricting its powers. Truman vetoed the bill, with the result that all controls expired. Prices skyrocketed. As Truman anticipated, Congress rushed through a second measure, which he signed, but it proved ineffective. When the CPA clamped down on the high price of meat, for example, livestock producers boycotted all markets. Complaints from consumers and farm state legislators soon forced the agency to backtrack. Late in the year, Truman abandoned the effort to control prices. Within fourteen months of the war's end, the nation had returned to a free market. The American public clearly preferred inflation to shortages of consumer goods.

Although economic troubles preoccupied most of the country, Truman quickly decided to extend "the humane principles of the New Deal." During his first major address in September 1945, he declared that "Government exists not for the benefit of a privileged few, but for the welfare of all the people." But Truman's sometimes abrasive style alienated many legislators, and his efforts on behalf of national health care, regional development projects, extended social security, and civil rights were sidetracked by a conservative coalition of Southern Democrats and Republicans. The public, too often distracted by the alarms of cold war with Russia or the inconveniences of reconversion, was largely indifferent to reform. Despite these hurdles, Truman did maneuver an important progressive measure through Congress during 1946, the Full Employment Act. Based on the theories of the British economist John Maynard Keynes, the bill in its original form directed the government to assure full employment by spending public funds whenever business recessions occurred. Conservatives objected vigorously, citing the arguments of an Austrian economist, Friedrich von

Hayek, that such government meddling ultimately destroyed individual liberty. But the wartime example of government planning, together with lingering fears of another depression, persuaded most Congressmen to vote for a compromise version. A Council of Economic Advisors would make recommendations to the President on how best to achieve full employment.

The future of progressive reform depended upon the future of the Democratic Party. Southerners worried about Truman's well-known Progressive record in race relations, an issue that FDR had always soft-pedaled. Unions fumed over his strike-breaking action against the railroad workers. Truman's public spats with two men closely identified with the New Deal, Secretary of the Interior Harold Ickes and Secretary of Commerce Henry Wallace, discouraged liberals. Wallace, for example, brusquely challenged the course of American foreign policy during a speech in New York City. "I deplore those architects of a tough stance," he charged, "who have replaced friendship and cooperation with the Soviet Union with a narrow, nationalist rivalry." Secretary of State James Byrnes promptly offered his resignation, and many others protested Wallace's readiness to make concessions to the Soviets. Truman finally fired his Secretary of Commerce, which further underscored the bickering within the government.

Even worse, the congressional election of 1946 strikingly rebuked those who wanted to maintain Roosevelt's legacy. The Republicans turned popular dissatisfaction into a stunning victory which gave them control of both the Senate and House of Representatives for the first time in sixteen years. The timing was perfect. Labor disputes and inflation frustrated many independents, who thought Truman's leadership too erratic and the Democratic Party too tied to special interests. And the New Deal's usual supporters—trade unionists, Southerners, and liberals—were all unhappy with the President, precisely because he had not catered to their needs. The Wallace affair and the meat boycott, occurring just before the election, pointed up Truman's apparent inability to run the government in orderly fashion or to solve the nation's postwar problems. For their part, the Republicans conducted a hard-hitting campaign. Fresh faces, like Richard Nixon of California and Gerald Ford of Michigan, added new energy and appeal. Conservatives and moderates within the party, traditionally at odds, came together at the prospect of victory. After the Republicans triumphed in November, everyone expected a difficult two years in domestic politics—with a progressive President now confronting conservative legislators. Nonetheless, Senator Robert Taft, the Republican leader, did promise advances in some areas. "You don't get decent housing from the free enterprise system," he observed, for instance. And in foreign affairs a bipartisan approach to policy-making soon produced a record of action and innovation.

Atomic Diplomacy

The American atomic monopoly reinforced the widespread assumption of total United States security while making Stalin even more insecure. More than ever he thought he needed compliant regimes in those nations that bordered the Soviet Union in eastern Europe, central Asia, and the Far East. Yet his maneuvers in these areas only strengthened America's determination not to yield. Truman and his new Secretary of State, James Byrnes, labored on proposed peace treaties to resurrect a unified but neutral Germany as a buffer state against Stalin. Given the experience of two world wars, however, Stalin understandably disrupted, postponed, and ignored these negotiations. By the middle of 1947, the two opposing sides had tacitly divided Europe: Italy and the heavily industrialized western portions of Germany in the United States's sphere of influence; eastern Europe and most of the Balkans in the Soviet sphere. In effect, Stalin brushed aside the apparently slim possibility of friendly relations with the United States in order to assure his country's security.

After peacemaking in Europe wound down to a division of spoils based upon military occupation, the United States offered a revolutionary proposal for disarmament. In June 1946, thirteen months after the Germans had surrendered, Bernard Baruch submitted a plan to the United Nations for the international control of atomic energy: an agency independent of any country would operate all uranium mines and production plants. This group would also oversee nuclear research, monitor all explosions, and administer the peaceful use of atomic energy. Composed of scientists from many lands, the new body would inspect unhampered all atomic installations everywhere, and punish violators. No veto could block its decisions.

Proponents of the Baruch Plan saw in it a precursor of world government: UN control of atomic power might force universal peace upon the nations. Stalin, however, rejected this idea. Aware that his own scientists would soon be exploding atom bombs, he preferred the more familiar—if more dangerous—path of rivalry. Any agreement to freeze the existing strategic situation would help to assure the United States its huge lead in industrial output and its dominion over the world's resources; Washington would not permit Moscow anything like equality of status. Stalin was convinced that the Americans were determined to exploit their economic power. Allies had now become adversaries.

During 1947 the climate of world politics changed dramatically. Secretary of War James V. Forrestal had already outlined plans for American naval bases scattered throughout the Mediterranean. During a visit to the United States the previous year, Winston Churchill had publicly warned of Soviet imperialism in eastern Europe, charging in a speech at Fulton, Missouri, that an "iron curtain" had descended across the continent "from the Baltic to the Adriatic." In Moscow, George F. Kennan, a counselor at the United States Embassy there, reported an ominous warning from Stalin: "The present capitalist world order makes peace impossible." Kennan drafted a long dispatch to the State Department, highlighting Russian paranoia about the outside world. "The Soviets," he concluded, "are committed fanatically to the belief that it is necessary to disrupt the internal harmony of our society

and to break the international authority of our state, if Soviet power is to be secure." The proper response—which Kennan anonymously proposed in a famous article of 1947 by Mr. "X" in the prestigious journal *Foreign Affairs*—was for the United States to "contain" Communist power by rebuilding American military might as a "counterweight" to Soviet "expansive tendencies."

Since early 1945, the Soviet Union had given moral support to local Communist guerrillas in Greece, while England had aided the embattled Greek monarchy with money and troops. But in 1947 the British ambassador told Truman that his country could no longer sustain the financial burden involved. At the same time, Stalin was leaning heavily on Turkey to gain control of the Bosporous Straits. The Soviets seemed likely to replace the British throughout the eastern Mediterranean. Thereupon, Truman boldly went to Congress for $400 million in military assistance for Greece and Turkey. "It must be the foreign policy of the United States," he explained, "to support free peoples who are resisting attempted subjugation by armed minorities or by outside pressures." The new Secretary of State, former Army Chief of Staff George Marshall, heartily approved this so-called "Truman Doctrine," despite its potentially global implications. Congress voted the money, Republican Senator Arthur Vandenberg of Michigan counseling the members of his party, "Politics must stop at the water's edge." Greece and Turkey survived, and became firm allies of the Western powers. With the Truman Doctrine, the United States was now fully engaged in a "cold war." Inexperienced, unprepared, but fully determined, the nation entangled itself in the affairs of Europe and, soon enough, in Asia as well.

Containment in Action: The Marshall Plan, NATO and Rearmament

Just a few days after the Republicans settled into the new Congress, Truman rushed aid to Britain in the eastern Mediterranean. Then he turned to the long-range problem of containing Russia's worldwide expansion. In western and central Europe, economic catastrophe and a growing sense of frustration seemed likely, many feared, to push the whole continent into Stalin's embrace. The war's destruction made recovery seem a remote dream, and the unusually harsh winter of 1946-47 edged the suffering populace towards despair. Already French and Italian Communists had

demonstrated impressive voting strength. "The choice," Secretary of State George Marshall told the new Republican leaders in Congress, "is between acting with energy or losing by default." Everyone in Washington knew that something more comprehensive, more permanent, had to replace stopgap responses to Communist pressure.

Acting quickly and forcefully, the administration within two months had radically altered American foreign policy. In a commencement address at Harvard University, Marshall set the stage for rescuing Europe's economic health in the world. "There can [otherwise] be no political stability and no assured peace," he declared. "Our policy is directed against . . . hunger, poverty, desperation and chaos." Instantly applauded throughout a troubled Europe, Marshall's project was breathtaking in its scope. Within three weeks, British, French, and Soviet leaders gathered in Paris to work out specifics for the European Recovery Program (ERP). But the Russians, angered by what they saw as a scheme to undermine their control over eastern Europe, quickly left the conference, denouncing the ERP, or Marshall Plan, as "an imperialist plan to subjugate independent nations."

Certainly Truman had many motives for this spectacular scheme: humanitarianism blended almost imperceptibly with hopes for American gain. A prosperous Europe would provide markets for Yankee manufacturers; a capitalist "showcase" would halt the drift toward Socialism there and dampen Communist appeal elsewhere in the world.

Still, the Marshall Plan encountered significant opposition from the new Congress. Determined to lower taxes and reduce the role of government in American life, Republicans wondered about the long-term result of massive aid to Europe. Some internationalists considered unilateral action a dangerous affront to the Russians; others, like Robert Taft, worried about "entangling alliances." Nonetheless, despite these hurdles, the Marshall Plan moved steadily through Congress.

In early 1948 sixteen western European nations submitted a comprehensive report, outlining their specific needs and asking for $20 billion during the next four years. Hearings began several months later before Senator Vandenberg's sympathetic Foreign Relations Committee. Suddenly, on February 25, 1948, the Soviet Union staged a successful *coup d'etat* in Czechoslovakia. The seizure of this industrialized country convinced Congress and many officials of Stalin's aggressive designs. Within six weeks, the legislators had voted $17 billion in Marshall aid. American money and materials flooded western Europe for the next four years, creating a recovery so fast and so complete that renewed confidence soon halted Communist gains. The Marshall Plan also ended any chance for reconciliation with the Soviet Union.

Western Europe became America's military ally as well as its economic protectorate. Even before Congress passed the Marshall Plan, the administration had toyed with ideas for a permanent, peacetime alliance. Speaking of the Brussels Pact—a defensive agreement among Britain, France, and the Benelux countries aimed against Soviet expansion—Truman praised "the deter-

mination of the free countries of Europe to protect themselves" and promised "an equal determination on our part to help them." Generals and admirals made tentative plans for an integrated European defense system. Once again, however, action by the Russians thrust the United States into another radical departure from its past diplomatic practice.

All during 1947 the Soviets had bickered with the Anglo-Americans over Germany's future. Stalin aimed for a weak, neutral Germany, forever unable to wage modern war, while the West stubbornly insisted upon a strong capitalist state. Russia advocated joint control over Germany's industrial areas, including the Ruhr Valley, not just a regional division into east and west. But as the Marshall Plan moved toward adoption, Britain, France, and the United States made plans to merge their three zones into a single political and economic unit. A furious Stalin then impeded Western ground access to Berlin, isolated some 110 miles inside the Soviet occupation zone; the Russians, however, abiding by the strict wording of a wartime agreement, did not limit air transport. In response the Western Allies speeded up plans for a single regime, announcing in June 1948 that a new *deutschmark* would replace the much-devalued war currency. Events tumbled over themselves during the next week: the Soviet Union introduced a new mark for its own zone, including East Berlin; the Americans and British extended the *deutschmark* into their sectors of the capital. Both acts violated the Potsdam Agreements.

The monetary issue masked a complex economic conflict. Backed by its huge financial resources, the West could insure the greater purchasing power of its mark, thereby ruining Soviet efforts to rebuild eastern Germany. The Red Army responded by blocking all ground access to Berlin on June 25. Soviet propaganda clarified Stalin's aims: to force the West either to give up its plan to unify Germany or risk losing its advanced position in Berlin.

The administration dramatically defended Berlin and created a vast new alliance system. For nearly a year, the Russians surrounded the former German capital. Realizing that a false step might precipitate a third world war, Truman responded with a sophisticated use of air power. Hundreds of British and American planes flew in all essential supplies to some two million people trapped behind the blockade. The technical skills of the pilots and flight crews, together with the great courage of the Berliners, matched Russian stamina.

Meanwhile, diplomats anxiously negotiated. At first, Stalin rejected all proposed solutions, including one put forward by neutral nations on the

Security Council. The commander of America's troops in Europe, Lucius D. Clay, vowed that the Russians "can't drive us out by any action short of war." Eleven months passed. Suddenly Stalin proposed a scheme which in effect masked his surrender, promising to respect Berlin's independence in return for the resumption of regular meetings of the largely ceremonial Council of Foreign Ministers.

The Berlin crisis of 1948-49 had a tremendous impact upon the United States. Just before the Soviets blockaded Berlin, the Senate had passed the Vandenberg Resolution, approving "collective armaments for mutual aid." The State Department quickly opened talks aimed at establishing a defensive alliance with Britain, France, Italy, the Netherlands, Denmark, Norway, Portugal, and Canada. Procedural details required almost a year of delicate diplomacy, largely to convince members of the British Parliament that England would not lose its historic freedom of action. And, despite the continuous prod of the Berlin blockade, opposition to a comprehensive alliance developed in the Senate. Taft opposed the idea because it violated the collective-security assumptions of the United Nations and "committed this country to the policy of a land war in Europe." Nonetheless, the North Atlantic Treaty Organization (NATO) passed in both the British and American legislatures, primarily because of the immediacy of the Soviet threat. The key element of the new compact, Article 5, provided that "an armed attack against one or more of the signatories . . . shall be considered an attack against them all." Truman spoke of NATO's new strategic dimension, that of deterrence: "If we can make it sufficiently clear in advance that any armed attack affecting our national security would be met with overwhelming force, the armed attack might never occur."

This formula made explicit the need for a standing American army. Truman pushed through a major reorganization of the military establishment. The National Security Act of 1947 unified all the armed forces under the administrative control of a new Department of Defense. James Forrestal became its first Secretary and began the long task of molding the rival services into a cooperative military enterprise. A Joint Chiefs of Staff, composed of top military leaders from the Army, Navy, Air Force, and Marines, worked under the Secretary, although at times they "leap-frogged" over him by appealing to sympathetic congressmen or directly to the public. To supply the President with information relating to international affairs, intelligence functions and personnel were brought together in the Central Intelligence Agency (CIA). The secretaries of State, Defense, and the Treasury became members—with a large number of experts and special assistants—of the newly formed National Security Council, which coordinated decision-making about pressing questions of military intervention. This streamlined apparatus acquired a hefty fleshing out in 1948 and again in 1949, when Congress passed successive acts reinstituting a selective draft. (Truman had asked for universal military training.) Except for a brief lull during 1949, America's new standing army grew rapidly. Rearmament, the Marshall Plan, and the NATO alliance revolutionized United States foreign policy. A nation that had never had a standing army of any substance in peacetime, and had not entered a formal military treaty alliance since the compact with the French during the Revolutionary War, now took on heavy overseas commitments, both economic and political, and boasted the muscle to defend those interests with force if necessary. In a faraway place few Americans cared about, that resolve would soon be tested.

Politics as Usual: The Eightieth Congress and Election of 1948

Although Congress and President together had fashioned precedent-shattering military and diplomatic policies, they continued to quarrel on domestic issues. Truman confronted an alliance of conservatives on Capitol Hill who not only blocked future reform but also aimed at undoing important parts of the New Deal. Its leader, Senator Robert Taft of Ohio, argued that "We have got to break with the corrupting idea that we

can legislate prosperity, equality and opportunity." Taft, and his followers in both parties, yearned for the days when the federal government did little meddling in the marketplace. Many legislators also believed that Congress had given too much power to the chief executive during the war years, and that the time had now come for a rebalancing. Southern Democrats, seriously alarmed by Truman's increasing commitment to civil rights, often joined with the Republicans. "The New Deal is kaput," gloated the conservative New York *Daily News*, like "the Thirty Years' War or the Black Plague or other disasters. . . . [Its demise] is like coming out of the darkness into sunlight. Like feeling clean again after a long time in the muck."

A stormy battle erupted early in 1947, almost as soon as the new Eightieth Congress convened, over the future of labor unions. Unions, many (especially conservatives) argued, abused their power and upset plans for achieving economic stability. Militant leaders like John L. Lewis, chief of the United Mine Workers, ordered strikes in defiance of court orders. Labor unrest at first baffled, then angered most Americans, who blamed both high prices and scarce goods upon the "greed" of big unions. This anti-labor mood of the postwar 1940's, combined with conservative control of Congress, produced the Taft-Hartley Act of 1947.

This complicated statute outlawed major union weapons: the closed shop, which required workers to join a union before applying for a particular job; the secondary boycott, in which a union picketed firms not directly involved in a labor dispute; and the checkoff, which directed employers to deduct union dues from paychecks. In addition, the act banned contributions to political campaigns and required workers to notify management of a strike in advance and to postpone any walkout for eighty days if it "affected an entire industry" or "imperiled the national health or safety." Taft-Hartley thus blunted labor's only really powerful weapon, the strike, and limited the control of union leaders over the rank and file. Truman vetoed the bill at once, arguing that it would "encourage distrust and suspicions and . . . threaten our democratic society." The next day, Congress overrode his veto. Republicans everywhere were elated: Taft-Hartley redeemed a major campaign promise, reversed the course of New Deal reform, and humiliated Truman. Labor unions, however, pledged a no-holds-barred struggle to repeal what they called "the slave labor law."

Congress and the President battled as well over inflation and tax policy. The GOP wanted to lower income taxes, so as to encourage consumers to spend and businessmen to invest. Twice during 1947 Congress passed bills reducing taxes by some twenty percent; Truman vetoed both of them. The President argued that a tax cut would aggravate inflation, not cure it. Although most economists agreed with him, political pressures during the election year of 1948 enabled Congress to override

Truman's veto of a third tax cut. The angry President forcefully noted that the reductions benefited the upper classes more than working people, and that Congress still had not acted on his wage-and-price-control proposals. These immediate economic issues were rapidly becoming the stuff of an exciting presidential election.

Few observers gave the embattled President—or any Democrat, for that matter—much of a chance in the 1948 election. Only eight percent of the electorate expected the next president to be of that party. The scent of victory lured numerous candidates into the contest for the Republican nomination. The primary battles, however, gradually narrowed the choice to two men: Senator Taft and Governor Thomas E. Dewey of New York, the nominee in 1944. Though at ease with Taft's more conservative philosophy, most Republicans worried that the stilted oratory and unyielding views of the "somber senator" might needlessly risk GOP defeat. Taft had, moreover, alienated some of his colleagues by promising to push the smartest senators forward, and the dumbest ones to the rear. In contrast, Dewey was a younger, more personable man who, in addition to a record as the successful governor of a large state, still carried a certain glamour from his earlier role as a "racket-busting" district attorney who had prosecuted "Murder, Incorporated," an organized gang of assassins for hire. Dewey campaigned effectively, stressing a moderation that essentially embraced the New Deal while suggesting that few new reforms should be initiated. Dewey's position appealed to middle-of-the-road Americans as well as to many delegates at the Philadelphia convention eager to unite behind a winner. Sophisticated politicking quickly isolated Taft, who withdrew on the third ballot, making Dewey's nomination unanimous. The convention then approved his choice for vice-president: another moderate governor, Earl Warren of California.

The GOP platform, influenced by the Berlin crisis which broke out during the convention, readily took up Vandenberg's bipartisan, internationalist foreign policy, lauding "collective security against aggression" and praising the Marshall Plan and the NATO alliance. The party routinely took credit for the Taft-Hartley Act as "a sensible reform of the labor law," and promised more tax reductions and stronger civil rights legislation. Surprisingly, the Republicans did not attack the New Deal, and even called for federally sponsored slum clearance and low-cost housing projects.

If the lure of victory unified Republicans on a strategy of moderation, the apparent certainty of defeat led Democrats into battles over ideology. While Henry Wallace vigorously pushed for conciliation with the Soviets, liberal Democrats who supported containment gathered round the Americans for Democratic Action (ADA). Its leaders, particularly the mayor of Minneapolis, Hubert H. Humphrey, struggled mightily to commit the party to civil rights. Southern Democrats protested this attack on local traditions and countered with a tough rejoinder: respect states' rights or risk destroying the party. A vicious battle over the platform broke out during the convention. In an impassioned speech, Humphrey called on Democrats to guarantee the "rights of full and equal political participation, equal opportunity for employment, and security of person." After a terrific struggle, the liberals won what would prove a historic victory: the platform pledged the party "to eradicate all racial, religious and economic discrimination." They also pushed through promises of federal aid to education, national health insurance, repeal of Taft-Hartley, and increases in the minimum wage and social-security coverage. The 1948 Democratic platform was an agenda for reform.

The convention nominated Truman unanimously, but the party did splinter. Angered by the anti-segregation platform, the Alabama and Mississippi delegations walked out of the convention and organized a States Rights Party at a meeting in Birmingham several days later. This mini-convention, attended primarily by reactionary elements long familiar to the South, nominated the governor of South Carolina, James Strom Thurmond, for President. A blunt platform attacked the federal government and all others who tried to interfere with local "social custom." Few in the South or elsewhere openly supported the bigoted aims of these "Dixiecrats," especially so soon after a world war fought in part against racism and its terrifying consequences. Nonetheless, Dixiecrat leaders controlled local election machinery in some states, and many citizens at least sympathized with their propaganda.

Meanwhile, Henry Wallace, running as the candidate of the newly formed Progressive Party, denounced containment and the Marshall Plan. "A peace program of abundance and security," the party platform argued, "must replace an imperialist agenda of scarcity and war." On most domestic matters it agreed with the Democrats. Some urban liberals in particular flocked to the Wallace banner, hoping—like the Dixiecrats—to set future policy for the regular Democratic Party after Truman's anticipated defeat. The Communist organization in the United States officially endorsed Wallace during August, and many Socialists joined his campaign. It was thought that a large turnout for Wallace in Manhattan, for example, might steal enough votes from Truman to give New York State's critical electoral votes to Dewey.

Few expected Truman to win, except the President himself and his intimate political advisers. The President, ever a fighter, called the Eightieth Congress back into session during late July, challenging the Republicans to enact their own platform. GOP congressmen at first vacillated and then blundered, when several senators spoke of reducing taxes, long a Republican theme, by ending farm price supports. Truman laced into the "party of privilege" and "old mossbacks in a do-nothing Congress" throughout his grueling thirty-thousand mile whistlestop campaign in those regions his planners shrewdly judged critical for his success, the normally Republican areas of the upper Middle West and Far West. Truman orchestrated a populist message in a plucky style: he reminded his audience, sometimes in earthy language, of his own hard-working background; appealing frankly to the working class and the farmers, he pounded home the message that only the Democrats cared about the "little guy." Oganized labor supported Truman vigorously, if only because of the Taft-Hartley veto, and farmers everywhere recalled the "Hoover" Depression. One of them, ninety-two-year-old Bill Moore of Nebraska, summed up rural sentiment: "The only time we've ever had prosperity on the farm," he told a newspaper reporter, "was when a Democrat was in the White House." Truman also appealed to Roman Catholics with his strong anti-Communist policies. He courted Jews and blacks by quickly recognizing Israel and by reducing segregation in the federal government.

Dewey badly underestimated both the sophistication of Truman's strategy and his appeal as an underdog. With four out of five newspapers supporting the New Yorker and Republicans outspending the Democrats three to one, polls predicted a huge landslide. Dewey, conducting the nation's first media campaign, muted controversy. Campaign workers canvassed door-to-door, telephoned voters, and conducted opinion surveys. And yet, for all its technical polish, Dewey's machine-like campaign aroused little enthusiasm even among Republicans. During the last three weeks of October, Dewey spent hours planning for his inaugural. Even worse, he ignored the issues that Truman had so effectively raised.

Early returns on election night seemed to confirm Dewey's anticipated victory. The New

Yorker won the Northeast, except the Democratic bastions of Massachusetts and Rhode Island. The Dixiecrat Thurmond would almost surely capture South Carolina, Alabama, Mississippi, and Louisiana. The headline of the conservative Chicago *Tribune's* late edition read, "Dewey Sweeps Nation." At home in Independence, Missouri, Truman simply told his family not to worry and went to bed. As the President slept, ballot-counters recorded a startling trend. Not only did Truman win all the border South and Texas, but also, in the early morning, the rural vote in Ohio, Illinois, and Iowa put their states into the Truman column. Now the candidates were running even. Still, Dewey seemed a sure winner, for the Far West traditionally supported the GOP. Yet every single Western state except Oregon went for Truman. This surprising sweep gave him the election, and the irresistible opportunity to needle the pollsters and editors who had unctuously predicted his defeat.

"It defies all common sense for the country to send that roughneck ward politician back to the White House," complained Taft when the result became clear. In retrospect, however, the outcome seems less amazing. Complacency had kept many Republicans away from the polls. Truman was helped by strong Democratic candidates for state and local office. The President's clever campaign in rural areas and his dynamic handling of the Berlin crisis appealed to the average American. The Dixiecrat rebellion highlighted Truman's own strong position in favor of civil rights, bringing many urban blacks to the polls in the industrial Middle West and border South. Truman's attacks on the Wallace campaign convinced many of the President's hardline anti-Communism, winning him an important margin of votes in the more conservative areas of Western states. Most important, though, the United States in 1948 was at peace and more prosperous than at any time in two decades. Truman represented that slow, progressive reform which had brought a measure of security and well-being to millions of Americans. Dewey, surrounded by those who talked of dismantling New Deal reforms, frightened voters who had benefited from them. The election of 1948 exalted a man close to the people, a man combative in foreign affairs and ready to press for new reforms at home.

The Fair Deal, 1949-1952

Now President in his own right, Truman left no one in doubt about his liberalism. His State of the Union message in January 1949 announced a sweeping agenda of domestic change: aid to education, national health insurance, a revised farm program, regional development projects, civil rights legislation, wider coverage for social security, repeal of Taft-Hartley, public housing, a reorganization of the federal bureaucracy. Truman dubbed this whopping list of social-welfare proposals the "Fair Deal." At the time prospects for its passage seemed good. A bubbling economy disposed many Americans to help those less fortunate. The prod of cold war added another dimension: in its contest with Communism, capitalism must demonstrate greater compassion. And the Democrats had recaptured control of both houses of Congress. Yet, even before the outbreak of war in Korea some eighteen months later, the Fair Deal stumbled. Truman, so skillful with voters, proved inept in his dealings with Capitol Hill, and special-interest groups sidetracked many specific reforms.

Misunderstanding the nature of national health insurance, the American Medical Association (AMA) fought a fanatical campaign against "socialized medicine." Federal aid to education succumbed to the fiscal worries of conservatives and the powerful protests of the nation's Roman Catholics, whose parochial schools were absent from the administration's bill. Truman and the trade unions overreached themselves in an ill-advised effort to repeal the Taft-Hartley Act.

The President's commitment to civil rights, together with his schemes for public works and welfare spending, revived the conservative coalition of Southern Democrats and Northern Republicans. Horse-trading with their considerable voting power in the Senate, the Southerners joined the GOP to block "creeping Socialism," while Republicans supported "local government," a euphemism for white supremacy. Truman asked Congress to guarantee every citizen "equal opportunities for jobs, for homes, for education, for health, for equal protection under the law." But anti-lynching and anti-poll-tax measures quickly lost out to Southern filibusters which GOP senators refused to help break. Similarly, administration plans to create hydroelectric complexes and develop natural resources along the Missouri, Colorado, and Columbia rivers all failed when Southern Democrats and Republicans joined together to vote against "government interference" and "wasteful, inefficient public works." The alliance, worried about government domination of the market, destroyed a new plan for subsidizing crops, worked out by Secretary of Agriculture Charles F. Brannan, that would have lowered food prices for the consumer and reduced government storage costs.

Despite these setbacks, Truman enjoyed success on issues where clear popular support overwhelmed his congressional opponents. New social security laws covered nearly eleven million more persons, and doubled benefits to offset postwar inflation. The administration pushed through an increase in the minimum wage from 40 cents to 75 cents per hour. Desperate shortages prompted Congress to pass the National Housing Act of 1949, which subsidized slum clearance projects and built almost one million new houses for low-income families. Legislators also granted Truman authority to streamline the federal bureaucracy. Following the recommendations of a commission headed by former President Herbert Hoover, Truman reduced the number of agencies and improved staff work.

In one area, the Chief Executive battled almost alone: civil rights. Stymied by congressional inaction, Truman used his powers as commander in chief to end segregation in the armed forces—despite vigorous opposition from most generals and admirals—and employed his office to open all levels of the federal civil service to people regardless of race. He welcomed blacks to White House functions. By threat of a government boycott, he forced Washington's hotels to end their Jim Crow policies. More than any other President since Lincoln, Truman acted courageously to end the shame of America's racial bigotry.

Overall, however, Truman's spotty record of achievement disappointed most liberals. While many applauded his courage and recognized that he had in fact moved the nation closer to economic security for its citizens, liberals generally attributed the meagerness of the results to the President's political ineptitude. Yet Truman's skill on the one hand or blundering on the other only partly accounts for the limited success of the Fair Deal. Americans had never enjoyed such affluence, a cornucopia of consumer goods, many available even to the poor. That urgency which feeds reforming zeal waned as poverty became less visible and novel foreign policy issues commanded more public attention than domestic problems. Moreover, after two decades of political excitement, many Americans simply demanded a rest. Liberalism would have to wait.

America at Mid-Century: Money and Mobility

By 1950, statistics told a story of prosperity: gross national product nearly doubled between 1940 and 1950, to some $350 billion; real personal income increased by half; unemployment rarely reached five percent of the work force. American society changed in less tangible ways, too. New wealth, and its apparent permanence, brought different ways of living and changed cultural values. The making of money preoccupied most citizens, giving society its distinctive flair and comforting a generation worried by cold war.

The pace of mobility and innovation, always so characteristic of American life, speeded up even more after the war. Steadily rising costs scissored farm income, driving millions off the land. Migrants crowded into already bursting cities; by 1950 nearly two thirds of the population lived in non-rural areas. New industries such as plastics

emerged across the Northeast, southern California, and along the Great Lakes. Giant chemical corporations, spurred by government contracts during the war, prospered even more as synthetics created a rush of new consumer goods: plastics often replaced wood and metal; detergents and insecticides eased housework; drugs cured illness. The appliance and electronics industries in particular galvanized the postwar economy. Always entranced by gadgets, Americans welcomed air-conditioners, electric blankets, gasoline-powered and electric lawn mowers, and automatic washing machines. Communications networks seemed ready to change American life in permanent, exciting ways: television sets, some three million by 1950, could unify the country instantly and at the same time convince viewers to buy the fruits of technology. An infant computer industry prom-

Beach Blanket Bingo. *Movies catering to the teenage audience were so lucrative that one production company, American Independent, became a great success by aiming exclusively at the teen market.*

ised a future of startling efficiency and frightening centralization. Rapid advances in aviation accelerated the break from localism.

That sense of place which had traditionally reassured Americans gave way to a pervasive restlessness, not just geographical but cultural as well. Together, mobility and affluence created the suburb, that mode of living so characteristic of the postwar era. As early as 1947, a Long Island builder erected ten thousand homes, all identical except for their front doors, some twenty miles outside New York City. Each house in "Levittown" sold for $7,500, including appliances and landscaping, well within the financial resources of most of the working middle class. Another Levittown rose near Philadelphia the next year, and by 1950 suburbs had exploded around all major cities. Population pressures expanded their growth: beginning at the war's end, a "baby boom" swept all sections of the country. During the 1930's economic conditions had mandated only two children per family, but now three, four, or even more seemed normal to many Americans. Since most cities prolonged wartime rent controls,

landlords refused to build new apartments. Federal tax benefits for homeowners and liberal mortgage terms for veterans soon turned meadowlands into suburbs.

The long rows of matchbox houses were more than shelters; they became a new way of life. Clustered together, Americans soon organized themselves into a bewildering variety of groups. Scout troops multiplied, and Little League baseball entertained children; local politics preoccupied many adults; church membership increased sharply; PTAs brought parents into school activities; small businessmen joined chambers of commerce; hobbyists gathered monthly, or even weekly; fraternal orders like the Elks and Masons spread rapidly. Leisure-time activities, particularly bowling and camping, occupied many others. Beautification societies landscaped parks and streets. Soon enough, "strip zoning" converted those highways which entwined the suburbs into massive corridors of storefronts, "drive-ins," and used-car lots. Critics belittled the intellectual sterility of the homogeneous suburbs and decried their frankly materialist pursuits. Norman Mailer called the 1950's one of the worst decades in the history of man. Yet the decade saw millions of workers rescued from city tenements, and improvement of educational standards, the re-creation for many of a sense of community, and provision of an unparalleled variety of entertainment. By mid-century, Americans hoped that the middle-class housing development might soon erase poverty altogether as new industries hired more and more workers to produce more and more consumer goods. In fact, many suburbanites forgot about that other America of urban blight, racial bigotry, organized crime, regional poverty. More aware of taxes and their own local interests, they shied away from progressive reforms and big government. Then, in successive shocks during the early 1950's, these new Americans felt their way of life threatened by unfamiliar kinds of war in Asia and anxieties about Communist subversion at home.

The United States and East Asia, 1945-1953

The Far East has always intrigued Americans with its mineral wealth, its vast populations, its singular culture. Neither Yankee trader nor Protestant missionary much affected the Orient. Then the upheaval of global war and the collapse of

Japanese power destroyed the regional balance of power there. Between 1937 and 1949, China moved from close ally and friend of the United States to bitter enemy, whereas Imperial Japan became a virtual American protectorate. A terrific struggle broke out for control of what had been the Japanese empire in Korea, Formosa, and Indochina. Such startling events stunned the American people, already preoccupied by unexpected developments in Europe. Yet the gains to be made in that legendary, largely unknown part of the world hypnotized leaders in Washington more and more. The ex-haberdasher from Kansas City first committed his Presidency, and then his nation's destiny, to the ideal of a Westernized Asia.

Denied raw materials and geared almost exclusively for military production, the Japanese economy collapsed in late 1945. Catastrophic defeat in war disgraced the governing clique of industrialists and soldiers who had long ruled the country. Americans moved swiftly, methodically, to crush the old elite. Democratic ideals and capitalist profits must replace feudal values and Japan's monopoly industry. Although authority after the surrender was nominally in the hands of a four-power commission, it was General Douglas MacArthur, commander of the only armed forces in the region, who made all decisions. Ruling almost without restraint for several years, MacArthur reformed the educational system, rewrote the Japanese constitution, broke up the great cartels, and encouraged trade unions and a two-party political system. The Japanese, realizing the totality of their defeat and ready to abandon the past, eagerly accepted these changes. Western styles swept the nation; businesses welcomed American methods and investment; and all citizens enjoyed civil liberties and social mobility, freedoms long denied in traditional Japan.

By 1947, Truman was ready to negotiate a peace treaty, presumably to anchor Japan in the America sea of economic influence. He ignored Soviet claims altogether and instructed John Foster Dulles, a prominent Republican lawyer, to arrange an end to the technical state of war. This task required many months, however, largely because of Australian and Filipino worries about a resurgent Japan. Finally, in 1951, forty-eight nations signed a "peace of reconciliation" in San Francisco. Japan lost all its prewar empire, and found itself restricted to its four home islands. The United States gained most of Japan's empire in the Pacific, which it admistered under a United Nations mandate. The treaty also allowed America to "restore order in case of disturbance caused by an outside power." Several days earlier, the United States had signed a bilateral defense treaty with the Philippines (independent since 1946). With the addition of the NATO-like ANZUS pact with Australia and New Zealand, the Pacific Ocean had become an American lake.

The "Fall" of China, 1945-1949

Control of the Pacific, the dream of American Presidents since James K. Polk, was only a preliminary to keeping China—that vast land where Yankee businessmen yearned for profits and Washington diplomats hoped for strategic security against Russia—in the American camp. But the Chinese spurned Yankee blandishments. Their revolution, begun in 1911 by intellectuals and urban leftists, entered its last stages after World War II. Disputes still raged over whether the Chinese masses, the peasants, workers, and small shopkeepers, should benefit most from reform, or whether China's traditional ruling classes, the mandarins and their warlord allies, should retain economic power. During the interwar period the traditionalists, led by Chiang Kai-shek, had maintained control over most of China, warding off the challenge they faced from the Communists, led by Mao Tse-tung. Although the two adversaries had largely suspended their struggle during the war against Japan, both braced for a final, climactic test of strength after 1945. Each side thought its victory certain: Chiang and his Nationalist regime relied upon military and financial aid from the United States, while the Communists took comfort in Marxist predictions of inevitable triumph.

Truman and most Asian experts in the State Department believed that civil war in China would postpone economic recovery and invite Soviet intervention. Even worse, Mao and his Communists probably would win any prolonged conflict. Chiang's ramshackle, corrupt regime alienated both peasants and urban workers. Persistent inflation convulsed the economy. Local warlords abused their troops and avoided decisive engagements. Mao's guerrilla armies, in contrast, rooted themselves deep in the village structure of rural China, where Communist promises of peace and land won many converts. The Russians had withdrawn from Manchuria—the industrial heartland of mainland East Asia—in such a way that Mao fell heir to Japanese positions there. With sophisticated propaganda and a dedicated, well-trained fighting force, the Communists slowly penetrated southward.

The United States, Truman decided, must mediate. In late 1946, he sent Army Chief of Staff George C. Marshall to China to secure a ceasefire. Promises of vast reconstruction aid, it was thought, could convince the two sides to join together in a coalition regime. Marshall arranged a truce that winter but in the spring, when military operations could resume, both sides broke the agreement. For eight months Marshall struggled with "reactionaries in the Nationalist Party" and "irreconcilable Communists." Discouraged, he returned to the United States in early 1947. Truman was by that time preoccupied by dramatic events in Europe, but several months later he sent another general, Albert C. Wedemeyer, to China. Wedemeyer's report underscored the American dilemma: only far-reaching administrative reforms could end the corruption that so alienated the Chinese people; yet Chiang and his cronies rejected all of Wedemeyer's suggestions. They could not transcend their mandarin mentality, and they assumed that the United States had no alternative but to support them. Like Marshall before him, Wedemeyer told Truman that only direct military intervention, perhaps millions of American soldiers, could rescue the Nationalist cause. Largely because of shrill propaganda by the "China Lobby"—a collection of anti-Communist conservatives in Congress and industry—Truman did continue to send money and equipment to Chiang; but after 1947 Washington concentrated upon containing the Soviets in Europe. No one was ready for a war in Asia, least of all the Joint Chiefs of Staff, who argued that American power could not cope with Communist moves in both Europe and the Far East at the same time.

Less than two years later, newspapers across America trumpeted the "fall" of China. Mao captured Peking in 1948 and crossed the Yangtze River early in 1949. Chiang's armies disintegrated, often surrendering without a fight or simply melting away into the countryside. Mao proclaimed the People's Republic of China (instantly nicknamed "Red China" by Americans). Chiang, protected by the United States Seventh Fleet, set up an exile regime on Taiwan, vowing to return someday to the mainland. The "fall" of China shocked Americans. Who was to blame? The China Lobby vitriolically denounced the President and called for "a holy crusade against godless communism in the Far East." Republicans like Senator William Knowland of California argued that the United States must give top priority to Asia, not Europe. Senator Taft even attacked some experts in the State Department as "pro-Communist." Dean Acheson, who had succeeded the ailing Marshall as Secretary of State in 1949, outraged such critics with his sensible suggestion that the United States recognize the new regime. "We are all on the same planet," he declared, "and must do business with each other." Congressional hearings correctly pinpointed Chiang's corruption and Mao's popular reforms as the basic reasons for the Communist victory. Nonetheless, many Americans, inexperienced in the complexities of foreign affairs, looked for scapegoats—a search which quickly degenerated into a quest for "subversives" within the United States.

Then, in early 1950, the Soviet Union announced its possession of operational atomic bombs and fears about America's safety escalated. The Truman administration struggled to redefine its foreign policy. Top officials finally put together a new blueprint for cold war strategy: National Security Council Paper No. 68's starting assumption was that the Communists were aiming at world domination. They were seeking to achieve their goal, the paper argued, by a process of gradual, step-by-step conquest (the so-called "domino theory"). It followed that United States national security could only be preserved through maintenance of the global status quo, and so the United States was now obliged to patrol the world. This new mission, in turn, required a huge buildup of military force. Rearmament must proceed regardless of cost, even if it consumed as much as a fifth of the nation's output.

The Democrats also realized that NSC 68 was good politics: its hard line offset Republican criticism, and the heavy defense it called for stimulated the economy. In response to the ending of its atomic monopoly and to the Communist victory in China, the United States took up a global role, determined to crush any future threats to the balance of power, wherever such threats appeared.

The Korean War, 1950-1953

In early January 1950, Secretary of State Acheson spoke of America's "defense perimeter," those areas the United States considered vital to its own security. Attacks against Alaska, Japan, the Ryukyu Islands, or the Philippines, he explained, would mean instant retaliation. The Secretary of State pointedly excluded from this umbrella of protection two former Japanese colonies on the Asian mainland, Korea and Indochina. Both countries seemed likely to follow China's example: populist coalitions, calling for Socialist reform and backed by outside Communist powers, were challenging local dictators financed and armed by the United States. French soldiers had already fought unavailingly for four years against a guerrilla rebellion in Indochina led by Ho Chi Minh. Korea, too, had disappointed leaders in Washington. After the war ended, Soviet troops occupied the northern half of the country, bordering Russia, while American GIs garrisoned the southern half, which protected the Japanese home islands. By late 1948 the United States was supporting a capitalist, pro-Western regime under a reactionary president, Syngman Rhee, while the Russians countered by establishing a Communist government in the north. Although both the Americans and the Soviets then withdrew their troops, skirmishes broke out constantly along the 38th parallel, the dividing line between the two Korean states. Both North and South dreamed of a reunited country, and civil war seemed likely at any time.

North Korea now boldly asked for Soviet aid in a war of liberation against the South. Stalin apparently calculated that America would not fight to rescue Rhee, so he encouraged the North Koreans, shipping them arms and food. Russian advisers trained a sophisticated ground force of ten divisions, one motorized. On June 25, 1950, these troops attacked along a broad front. Truman quickly implemented NSC 68, telling the American people that "to conquer independent nations, communism has now resorted to armed invasion and war." His response was indeed global: in the Pacific, the Seventh Fleet steamed toward Taiwan to protect it from possible Communist-Chinese attack; American money and military equipment flooded into Indochina to help the French preserve their colonial authority there; and in Korea itself, an American army mobilized to repulse the North Korean invaders. The United States then boosted its commitments of men and matériel to the European NATO alliance, now enlarged to include West Germany. Congress passed huge appropriations not only for the war in Korea but also for massive rearmament. This determined, wide-ranging response caught Stalin off guard: the Soviets were boycotting Security Council sessions when Truman pushed a resolution through the United Nations calling for joint action to punish "unprovoked aggression in Korea."

The military situation there at first looked bleak. The North Koreans rapidly pushed southward, overwhelming Rhee's ill-trained troops. Some evidence indicates that Rhee may have precipitated his army's retreat to force the Americans into rescuing his regime. Although GIs from Japan quickly joined in defense of the South, the North Koreans had conquered most of the peninsula by mid-August, trapping the United States Eighth Army in a 140-mile semicircle around Pusan. General Douglas MacArthur then launched a brilliant amphibious assault at Inchon, a port well behind enemy lines, on September 15. Meanwhile, the newly supplied Eighth Army, commanded by General Matthew Ridgway, punched its way out of the Pusan perimeter. By early October, American forces had cleared all South Korea of Communist troops.

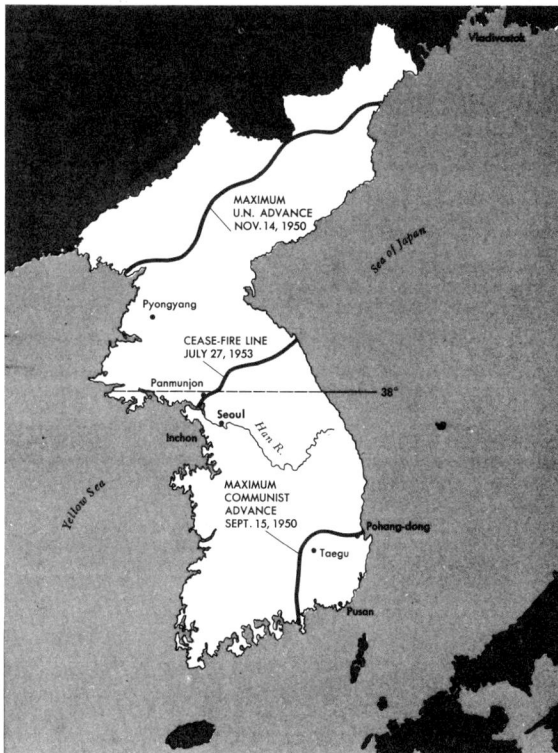

The Korean War, 1950-53

This rapid success elated Truman, who now, however, overreached himself. Once again turning to the United Nations, the President received its approval for "steps to insure stability throughout Korea"—that is, to destroy the North Korean regime altogether. American armies rushed northward. "All resistance," MacArthur told Truman at a meeting on Wake Island on October 14, "will end by Thanksgiving."

This time the General's calculation proved disastrous. North Korea bordered China's industrial heartland, Manchuria. For weeks Chinese Premier Chou En-lai had been warning the West that the People's Republic would not "supinely tolerate seeing their neighbors invaded by imperialists." Still the American troops drove forward. Then, on October 26, China's troops crossed the Yalu River and in November attacked MacArthur's widely scattered armies. The Communists skillfully retook much lost territory, until the Eighth Army finally stopped their advance at the 38th parallel in January 1951. Here the front stabilized and the war became a stalemate, although hard fighting continued for many months over the cold, rocky terrain.

The Truman-MacArthur Controversy

Humiliated by his miscalculation and driven to destroy what he called "an alien, despised communism," MacArthur wanted to bring all possible force to bear against Chinese troops in Korea: bombing the bridges across the Yalu, opening a second front with Nationalist troops from Taiwan— even, if necessary, using atomic weapons. If this brought war with China, so much the better. "Here in Asia," he wrote GOP Minority Leader Joseph W. Martin, Jr., "is where the communist conspirators have elected to make their play for global conquest. If we lose the war to communism in Asia, the fall of Europe is inevitable." Always ready with a pungent phrase, the General proclaimed to Martin that "There is no substitute for victory." Then he issued a battlefield pronouncement—against Truman's direct orders— that United Nations troops might "depart from their tolerant effort to contain the war in Korea." These startling statements confused America's allies, contradicted national policy, and squarely challenged the authority of the commander in chief.

One week later, on April 11, 1951, Truman relieved MacArthur of his command. The immediate issue was clear: "If I allowed him to defy the civil authority," Truman said, "I myself would be violating my oath to uphold and defend the Constitution." Most citizens, including generals in the Pentagon, agreed that MacArthur had overstepped, crossing that line which long had isolated the American military from politics. But some Republican politicians raised a larger issue; flattering the impressionable MacArthur, they used him as a foil to attack the whole notion of containment. Congressional hearings, televised across the nation, broadcast their aim: the destruction of Communism in the Far East.

The administration countered with strong arguments for maintaining the policy of containment. General Omar Bradley summed up the case succinctly: a wider conflict in Korea, he told a Senate committee, "would involve us in the wrong war, at the wrong place, at the wrong time, and with the wrong enemy." MacArthur enjoyed a hero's welcome at first, but his imperious manner soured all but his most devoted followers. A short-lived presidential campaign in 1952 revealed just how old-fashioned and authoritarian were his ideas about American society. Nonetheless, although the old soldier himself faded away, the larger issue raised by the Truman-MacArthur controversy remained; should America merely contain its adversaries or go further, to liberate those "captive nations," as Senator Taft melodramatically phrased it, "struggling under the yoke of Communist tyranny."

A Second Red Scare

After 1945 Americans never recaptured the sense of "normalcy" which had followed World War I. Jolting events overseas uncovered a new menace which soon replaced the fears about Fascism of a few years earlier. Strategic security evaporated in a nuclear age: oceans no longer isolated the New World from troubles in Asia and Europe. Mao's victory in China, the news of a

Russian atomic bomb, and the fustrations of limited war in Korea all provoked a sense of dread. Americans simply could not understand how a nation endowed in 1945 with a mighty army, navy, and air force and a fully operating industrial plant amidst a world in ruins could, in such a short space of time, find itself facing such threats and feeling so insecure. Surely something must be wrong; some sinister and mysterious force must have subverted the easy security that was an American birthright. Searching for an answer, citizens untutored in world affairs succumbed to the irresistible temptation to attribute these setbacks to "subversive plots." Nonconformists had undermined American strength; conspiracies within had opened the way for external enemies. Bureaucrats and busybodies now began to hound critics of American society, convincing many citizens that it was domestic Communists who were chiefly responsible for the country's postwar ills.

This second Red Scare began slowly. Early in 1947, Truman set up regional loyalty boards to unmask "radicals" within the sprawling federal bureaucracy. Over the next six years, however, only 384 "security risk" employees were dismissed, mainly homosexuals. The House Un-American Activities Committee (HUAC) grilled suspected Communists about their presumed efforts to infiltrate American society. Because of its dubious legal tactics and unlikely charges—that trade unions, colleges, and the Hollywood movie industry were all jammed with Communist-sympathizing "fellow travelers" ready to overthrow democracy—most Americans held HUAC in low repute.

Still, entertainment moguls blacklisted performers accused of holding unpopular opinions; anti-labor politicians called for tighter regulation of trade unions; academic freedom gave way to academic conformity. Partisan politics strengthened the chill wind which blew across the land. To defuse potential Republican charges in advance, Truman lambasted "subversives" during his 1948 presidential campaign. His Attorney General rashly exclaimed that Communists were "everywhere—in factories, offices, butcher stores, on street corners, in private businesses." *Marvel Comics* warned: "Beware, commies, spies, traitors, and foreign agents—Captain America is looking for you yellow scum." A gumball machine in Wheeling, West Virginia, was quickly impounded when it was found to dispense geography lessons under the hammer-and-sickle Soviet flag, reading: "U.S.S.R. population 211,000,000. Capital Moscow. Largest country in the world."

Such hysterics probably convinced few Americans, at least until a number of spy trials alarmed the country with evidence of a wide-ranging Soviet espionage network. Testifying before HUAC, Whittaker Chambers, a senior editor of *Time* magazine, admitted his membership in the Communist Party for some fourteen years before the war. He named seven persons still active in the Soviet underground. One of the accused men, Alger Hiss, then president of the prestigious Carnegie Institution for International Peace and a former official in the State Department, angrily denied the charge. While under oath, he told HUAC, "I have never been a member of the Communist party. . . . I have never laid eyes on Chambers." Hiss then sued Chambers for libel, but the former Communist produced evidence that lent credence to his charge that Hiss had given him copies of secret government documents during the 1930's. Chambers claimed to have hidden microfilms of these papers in a pumpkin on his farm in Maryland, and he dramatically revealed them to a startled court. This disclosure prompted a federal grand jury to indict Hiss for perjured testimony before HUAC. Two trials followed; the first ended in a hung jury, but on January 21, 1950, Hiss was convicted, and he went to jail. His defenders thought him illegally convicted with secret and doctored evidence, persecuted by vindictive congressmen—especially by a tenacious young Californian on HUAC, Richard Nixon, who first achieved national prominence through the Hiss case.

Before the eighteen-month furor about Hiss died down, British agents arrested Klaus Fuchs, a physicist who had evidently supplied the Soviets with information about Anglo-American atomic research during the war. Many blamed Fuch's treachery for the Soviet Union's unexpectedly rapid development of nuclear power. During his trial, he implicated several Americans, including Julius and Ethel Rosenberg, two members of the New York City Communist Party. Ethel's brother, David Greenglass, who had been an army sergeant at Los Alamos, had supposedly turned over detailed diagrams of America's first atomic bomb to the Rosenbergs, who in turn, Greenglass charged, had given them to the Soviet consul in New York City. The Rosenbergs made moving declarations of their innocence, but after a sensational trial both were sentenced to die for "a crime worse than murder." Still, whatever the actual degree of Soviet infiltration—and the various trials clearly indicated that at least some had occurred—the reactions of many people were greatly out of proportion. Wild accusations and strong fears swept the country. "How much more are we going to take?" screamed Homer Capehart, a conservative Republican senator. "Fuchs and Hiss and hydrogen bombs threatening outside and New Dealism eating away at the vitals of the nation. In the name of Heaven, is this the best America can do?"

Into this frenzied climate strode a bizarre figure from the Midwest: Senator Joseph McCarthy of Wisconsin. A crude bully, McCarthy had scored upset victories for local and national office with campaigns of innuendo against his opponents. Once in Washington, he compiled an opportunistic, negative record which angered many of his constituents; one poll of newspaper reporters ranked him the most ineffective member of the Senate. Anxious to refurbish his image, McCarthy decided to capitalize on the growing anti-Communist hysteria. His first opportunity came on February 8, 1950, when he addressed a meeting of the Republican Women's Club in Wheeling, West Virginia. Waving a piece of paper, he charged that some 279 subversives had "thoroughly infested" the State Department. "The reason we find ourselves in a position of impotency," he explained to his receptive audience, "is because of traitorous actions by those who have been treated so well by this nation." McCarthy expanded on this theme throughout the spring and summer of 1950, accusing both high officials and simple clerks of Communist sympathies, although he never produced proof for any of these "documented cases." Culling old, mostly outdated information about Soviet spy rings from often discredited sources, McCarthy relied mostly upon his gifts of rhetorical embellishment.

During the next four years, the junior senator from Wisconsin verbally abused thousands of people, including Presidents, the much-respected George C. Marshall, and many skilled experts in government service. His lack of respect for constitutional procedures and his guilt-by-association tactics prompted some protests. Richard Rovere, a reporter for *The New Yorker*, dismissed him as "a pool room politican grandly seized with an urge to glory." Many others, however, including intellectuals like Daniel Boorstin and politicians like Senator Robert Taft, endorsed McCarthy's efforts to purge America of subversives. GOP conservatives especially lauded his cause, and various Republican newcomers won major elections by lightly smearing opponents with charges of Communism. Richard Nixon destroyed the reputation of his opponent, Helen Gahagan Douglas, during the 1950 race for the Senate in California by permitting underlings to refer to "the pink lady." (Her lieutenants in turn labeled him a Fascist and an anti-Semite.) McCarthy himself so mercilessly attacked Senator Millard Tydings of Maryland, an early foe of red-baiting, that many credited him with wrecking Tydings' hopes for reelection. More and more, McCarthy's critics silenced themselves: this acquiescence only encouraged him into greater excesses.

Sensationalist newspapers played up the senator's cause; he was, after all, good copy, and publishers learned that publicity insured protection from his vitriolic temper. McCarthy condemned the Democrats for "twenty years of treason," and many Americans believed him. How else, they wondered, could Communism have triumphed in eastern Europe and China? In reality, however, McCarthy never commanded a mass following; his main supporters were conservative Republicans, and in 1954, after he claimed that the army "coddled" Communists he lost support and earned the censure of the Senate.

The Election of 1952

By 1952 the country seemed stagnated, mired in limited war in Korea and, many thought, betrayed by subversives at home. Then another cloud—political corruption—darkened the shadows of mistrust. A Senate subcommittee unearthed evidence that a presidential aide, Harry Vaughan, had influenced the awarding of government contracts, directing business to several friends. In gratitude, one of them sent him a freezer, then a glamorous new appliance, worth $500. Other bureaucrats, the Senate committee discovered, charged a flat five-percent fee for favorable action. Federal tax collectors in several big cities lowered tax bills in return for bribes. Truman, never personally involved in any of these scandals, vigorously prosecuted the wrongdoers, forcing many IRS agents to resign and even firing his Attorney General. Corruption also surfaced on the local level, where organized crime prospered under the official blindness of urban politicians. An investigating committee headed by Democratic Senator Estes Kefauver of Tennessee exposed widespread corruption, illegal gambling, and shake-down rackets. Television beamed the dramatic testimony of underworld figures like Frank Costello—who endlessly "took the Fifth" (Amendment) while nervously tapping his fingers —to a nation both fascinated and repelled by such real-life gangsters.

The issues of Korea, Communism, and corruption all afflicted the country. Truman's popularity rating plunged to less than thirty percent—the worst in history for an incumbent Chief Executive.

Many Midwesterners again vigorously supported the candidacy of the conservative Robert Taft. Republicans from urban states along the East Coast worried that Taft's outspoken hostility to New Deal reforms and his anti-labor reputation might alienate millions of voters. Senator Henry Cabot Lodge, Jr., of Massachusetts and Thomas Dewey of New York persuaded General Dwight D. Eisenhower to resign his command of NATO forces in Europe and enter the race.

Born in Texas and reared in the modest surroundings of Abilene, Kansas, Dwight D. Eisenhower was a product of the American frontier town. The young Eisenhower possessed the quick mind of one accustomed to making his own way. He secured entrance to West Point and, despite a mediocre academic record, distinguished himself in campus leadership. At Command and General Staff School in Fort Leavenworth, Kansas, he graduated first in his class after a year's study in 1925-26. As a soldier, Eisenhower did not affect the bluff arrogance and the disdain for civilian direction that can go with the military temperament; in 1932 he participated in the dispersal of the makeshift camp of unemployed veterans—the Bonus Marchers—on Anacostia Flats in Maryland. But he later faulted the haughty chief of staff, Douglas MacArthur, for disobeying President Hoover by marching on Anacostia with bayonets and destroying the shacks. Eisenhower's military and strategic skill was demonstrated during the Second World War by his conduct during the 1942 North African invasion and later as supreme commander of Allied forces in Europe. He owed thanks for his rapid promotions to Chief of Staff General George C. Marshall, who perceived in him both an excellent administrator and strategist.

After the war, Eisenhower served as Army Chief of Staff and then for two-and-one half years as president of Columbia University. There he instituted the American Assembly, a forum for discussion of major national problems, and, as he later recollected with some pride, an academic "Chair of Peace." Late in 1950 President Truman

appointed him military commander of NATO. The General at first resisted those who urged him to provide leadership at home; he believed that a military man was unsuited for national politics. Ultimately, Eisenhower's decision in 1952 to resign as NATO commander and seek the Presidency— so his *Memoirs* assert—came from a fear that the foreign policy commitments of Senator Robert A. Taft of Ohio might otherwise prevail. Taft denied that America had a duty to extend its institutions abroad; conscious of the limits of American power, he shied away from foreign commitments, asserting that America could sustain itself on its own domestic markets, which should be protected by high tariffs.

As matters turned out, the Republicans dared not risk going with the dour Taft (who probably better represented the personal views of the delegates); they nominated instead the easygoing and politically promising "Ike." Eisenhower's record equaled Taft's for high seriousness and more than matched it for drama; and Ike's personality was by far the more attractive. For Vice-President the Republicans chose Richard M. Nixon, whose success in prosecuting Alger Hiss had won him national fame.

The Democrats settled on a presidential candidate at least as cerebral as Taft: Governor Adlai E. Stevenson of Illinois. As governor he had increased funds for schools and roads, combatted downstate gambling operations, and modernized the state bureaucracy. Other candidates had presented themselves, most notably Senator Estes Kefauver of Tennessee, whose face had become familiar through daily television appearances as head of the Senate Crime Investigating Committee. But President Truman, in firm control of the convention, wanted Stevenson, even though the governor possessed an introspective manner that bordered on indecision. Stevenson never quite sought the nomination, describing himself as unfit for the Presidency, and indeed was not formally a candidate until the moment he was nominated on the third ballot in Chicago.

The 1952 campaign sparkled with Stevenson's cultivated, witty speeches that he wrote himself; but his manner and bearing were both an asset and a liability. To Republicans and many independents, the speeches conveyed an impression that he did not take seriously the charges against the Truman administration. Many Democrats, on the other hand, found him an exciting leader for a party demoralized and in retreat. "Volunteers for Stevenson" groups sprang up all over the country, stressing their candidate's humility, intelligence, and rectitude. But though the governor campaigned hard, he could not hope to overcome Eisenhower's popularity.

Stevenson actually had wanted Eisenhower to win the Republican nomination, fearing the effect of Taft's foreign policy ideas on the Western alliance. For Stevenson, like Eisenhower, represented an internationalist position that the Truman administration had itself sustained and that contrasted with Taft's beliefs. The language of this internationalism may sound belligerent today, for its proponents looked toward American leadership on a world-wide scene. Speaking standard foreign policy to a Kansas audience, for example, Stevenson explained that we were fighting in Korea "so we wouldn't have to fight in Wichita"; Korea was "a crucial test in the struggle between the free world and communism."

Eisenhower, meanwhile, worked to heal wounds in the Republican Party. He welcomed Taft to a breakfast at Morningside Heights, Columbia University, after which they agreed on the essentials of domestic policy. Easily projecting his folksy style across the land, the General spent more time campaigning in the South than had any previous Republican candidate. And he deleted from an important speech a remark criticizing the redhunters like Senator Joe McCarthy and William Jenner; Eisenhower did little to support his old boss, General Marshall, against their attacks. A storm broke when the *New York Post* charged Senator Nixon with accepting money from friendly businessmen for personal expenses. Nixon rebutted the claim—Stevenson had a similar fund to supplement the salaries of public officials—and also demonstrated a command of "television politics" in a highly sentimental and effective speech. Both major candidates seemed ready to accept the accomplishments of the New and Fair Deals, though neither was anxious to promote civil rights in the spirit of the 1948 Democratic convention.

The results on election day shocked no one. After October 24, when Eisenhower promised, in the event that he won, to "go to Korea," the polls showed his margin to be widening. On November 7 Eisenhower won fifty-five percent of the popular vote, and even carried the Southern states of Virginia, Florida, and Texas. He received a majority vote from all income groups and drew unexpected support from normally Democratic Roman Catholics. What Eisenhower offered in the 1952 campaign, and would achieve in the first term of his Presidency, was something the country needed rather desperately: an easing of tensions after the hectic recriminations of the Truman years.

The early fifties, the time of Joe McCarthy and the Korean War, had reflected political and social turmoil. The breakdown of the wartime Russian-American alliance, the "fall" of China to the Communists, the Russian nuclear threat, the fear of internal subversion, and the emerging tensions over race relations marked by a split in the Democratic Party—all contributed to the national malaise, a mood of irritation and sour discontent. Soon after the new President took office, the Eisenhower "decade" opened: the time of political calm began with the Korean armistice in midsummer 1953 and the Senate censure of McCarthy in January 1954.

Eisenhower continued most of the policies of economic regulation, social welfare, and internationalism associated with his Democratic predecessors. But by removing these policies from partisan debate, first in the campaign and then later in handling congressional Democrats (who often supported him more strongly than did his own party), Eisenhower shaped them into a national consensus that achieved its greatest appeal after the end of the Korean War. Unfortunately, the political tranquility of the Eisenhower era was short-lived, ending in October 1957 with the strange beeps from space of the Soviet earth satellite Sputnik, and ensuing criticisms of economic and cultural trends. Four years in which people feel a bit more placid hardly constitutes a dominant trend.

Suggested Readings

Alonzo Hamby gives a rather favorable interpretation of Truman's domestic policies in *Beyond the New Deal: Harry S Truman and American Liberalism* (1973). Maeva Marcus examines the events of Truman's seizure of the steel mills during the Korean War, and goes into the constitutional issue that the Supreme Court confronted in its invalidation of Truman's act: *Truman and the Steel Seizure Case: The Limits of Presidential Power* (1977). See also Robert J. Donovan, *Conflict and Crisis: The Presidency of Harry S Truman, 1945-1948* (1977). Allen Weinstein, in *Perjury: The Hiss-Chambers Case* (1979), goes over the evidence bearing on the guilt or innocence of Alger Hiss, convicted of perjury for having falsely denied to a congressional committee the charge made by Whittaker Chambers that Hiss had engaged in espionage for the communists. The author concludes that Hiss was probably guilty. The importance of the book for a general public lies not in the answer to that particular question but in its taking the reader back to that time, when feelings about the Hiss case were connected with more general public attitudes about the seriousness of communist subversion. Thomas G. Paterson presents an illuminating study of the problems and policies that led to the Cold War and the continuing antagonism between the United States and the Soviet Union: *Soviet-American Confrontation: Postwar Reconstruction and the Origins of the Cold War* (1973). Joyce and Gabriel Kolko, covering the same period, strongly condemn American policy: *The Limits of Power: The World and United States Foreign Policy, 1945-1954* (1972). Barton J. Bernstein studies a critical issue in *The Atomic Bomb* (1976), and John W. Spanier reviews *The Truman-MacArthur Controversy and the Korean War* (1959).

Chapter XXVII
FDR, the Great War, and the Cold War

I. Forrest McDonald: a) A Government that Hindered Business
                          b) Soviet Imperialism

During the 1930s the pace of history began to quicken, not only in America but in most other parts of the world as well. Outside the United States destruction became wholesale, and so did change; traditional ways of life, centuries in the developing, were radically disrupted, and whole peoples were virtually annihilated; men slaughtered one another on an unprecedented scale, often doing so in the name of liberation even as they spread tyranny. The United States itself, as always the most blessed of nations, was spared most of these horrors, at least in their worst forms. Indeed, even during the depths of the Great Depression most Americans had more material comforts and economic security than any but the richest had elsewhere; and though the New Deal, the War, and the Fair Deal brought profound changes and an enormous increase in the power of government, the United States remained, compared to most parts of the world, a model of political and social freedom and stability. Despite that relative immunity, however, alterations of accustomed norms in America took place faster and on a larger scale than most people could accommodate.

In these circumstances, the American people were forced to grow up too fast and to learn more, in a short span of time, than they had the capacity to learn. They learned false lessons and made commitments on the basis of them—lessons which they must unlearn and commitments they must undo if they are to survive.

Two of the false lessons, or misapprehensions of what happened, pertained to the New Deal. First, despite Franklin Roosevelt's antibusiness rhetoric ("Businessmen hate me," he declared in 1936, "and I welcome their hatred"), it became consensus, both among Washington policy-makers and among historians, that the central aim of the New Deal had been to reform capitalism to save it from its own failings. It is true that the New Deal rejected both the socialist and fascist alternative to democracy and capitalism—though it contained elements of each—and instead followed a pragmatic middle course. Yet to applaud the federal government and the Roosevelt administration for rescuing capitalism is rather like cheering a mugger for picking up the victim he has knocked down. What brought the economy to its knees in the first place was neither the workings of an abstract "business cycle" nor any weakness inherent in the free operations of a market system, but the bungling interference of governments and of the incompetent politicians who ran them. More such interference was unlikely to remedy the problems it had created.

The second misapprehension followed from the first: it is the notion that the New Deal did in fact revive the economy. The Roosevelt administration's economic measures had three broad designs, relief, reform, and recovery. The relief programs (such as the Civilian Conservation Corps and the Federal Emergency Relief Administration) were extremely useful in the emergency, but they contributed little to permanent recovery and had some unwholesome long-term implications. Specifically, they established the principle that workers have a *right* to jobs and government has the duty of fulfilling that right, and they politicized what had previously been the function of private charity. Both of these changes undermined traditional American values regarding freedom and responsibility and paved the way for the development of the welfare mentality and the welfare state. As for reform measures, some (such as those creating the Securities Exchange Commission and the Federal Deposit Insurance Corporation) were of positive benefit, others (such as the Tennessee Valley Authority) were rather in the order of boondoggles, and still others (such as the Holding Company Act and the Communications Act) established federal regulatory agencies that did as much harm as good. None contributed appreciably to economic recovery.

As for programs specifically aimed at making the economy function well again, it is difficult to imagine that anyone seriously believed they would work, since for every major policy the New Deal adopted it also embraced, with equal vigor, an opposite policy. The administration set out simultaneously to balance the federal budget and to begin large-scale deficit spending, to inflate (or "reflate") prices and to hold prices down, to establish a "planned economy" through centralization and consolidation and to return to a bygone small-business paradise by decentralizing and breaking up large units of production. These contradictory approaches, each pushed as the single avenue to recovery, cancelled one another, and recovery could proceed only by fits and starts. There was gradual but steady improvement for three years, irregular movement for another two, and then, thanks to inept federal fiscal activity, a sudden and deep plunge. Thus in the winter of 1938-39 unemployment was almost as severe as it had been during the winter of 1932-33. What actually brought the return of prosperity was military spending, which increased appreciably in 1939 and soared thereafter, and the removal of twelve million people from the civilian job market into military service during the next six years.

The impact of military spending, in combination with fuzzy thinking about the effectiveness of governmental "pump priming" and with an unrelated false lesson learned during the war—the idea that superior technology, and especially air power, is adequate to win a modern war—completed the economic miseducation of the United States. The war seemed to have borne out one of the cardinal tenets of the economic theories of John Maynard Keynes, namely that economic downturns can be prevented by what is called counter-cyclical government spending. That impression was reinforced during the Truman years. The GI Bill of Rights kept millions of returning veterans off the job market by putting them in college; and renewed defense spending, stimulated first by the emergence of the Cold War and then by the Korean War, created millions of new jobs. A perpetually high level of defense spending, American policy-makers came to believe, would serve the twin objectives of maintaining peace abroad and prosperity at home.

We shall return in a moment to the question whether military spending contributes to world peace. Meanwhile, let us consider its internal economics. Military production costs more than civilian production for the simple reason that the investment in plant and equipment necessary for producing, say, fighter planes becomes worthless as soon as the war is over or the planes become obsolete. Capital investment must therefore be added to the costs of production, whereas the capital investment in civilian production can, with minor additions and improvements, be made to last for many years. The costs of military procurement proved to be so high, in fact, that the United States government was unable to pay them out of tax revenues during the war and has rarely been able to do so since. To pay its bills, the government thus found it necessary to resort to deficit financing, which is to say it borrowed the money. It could borrow some of what it needed by selling bonds to ordinary citizens, but most had to come from banks. That created a dilemma. If the government had simply borrowed money which otherwise would have been lent to private producers and consumers, the effect would have been not to stimulate but greatly to depress the private sector of the economy; and though Americans willingly endured many shortages during the war, there were limits to what they would tolerate even then, and their tolerance would drop sharply when the war ended. The problem was temporarily alleviated in 1943, when the government stopped collecting income taxes at the end of each year and instead started withholding them from paychecks—which meant that in 1943 taxpayers paid both their 1942 and their 1943 taxes—but that was a one-time expedient. Then the government's fiscal managers stumbled across a technique which had been used sparingly in the past but now became normal operating procedure. The technique was, in effect, to print up money as it was needed, but to disguise the practice in the trappings of fiscal orthodoxy: the government borrowed from banks and allowed the Federal Reserve System to issue equivalent amounts of new currency.

At first it seemed that this practice might be continued endlessly without producing serious side-effects, and except for minor ups and downs the economy was in fact booming throughout Truman's presidency. But there were some built-in catches. The national debt steadily increased, and it was obvious that in due course the interest on the debt would become prohibitively expensive. In the face of that prospect, the temptation to avoid it by cheapening the currency through inflation became irresistible, and the means of inducing inflation were inherent in the mechanism. That is, though continuous expansion of the money supply was not inflationary if it did not exceed the rate of economic growth, all that was needed to make it inflationary was to expand the supply a bit faster; and that is what the government did.

But inflation, too, had a catch, quite in addition to the temptation it posed for non-military bureaucrats who wanted to use it to finance the expansion of their own activities. In an overall context of rising prices, the cost of military procurement (given its self-inflating internal economics) rose even faster: fighter planes, for example, which cost $54,000 apiece during World War II, were costing $298,000 apiece by the end of the Korean War. (By the late 1970s navy fighters would be costing $16.8 million apiece.) Moreover—and here was the real rub—costs could not be reduced by cutting back military spending, for a cutback in the quantity of military hardware being purchased produced a corresponding increase in the unit costs, since fewer units had to absorb a proportionately higher share of the capital costs. Yet the wizards in Washington had a solution for this problem, too. In 1948 and 1949 the Truman administration, for reasons having nothing to do with defense procurement costs, was adopting a policy of collective security to contain Soviet expansion (NATO came in 1949, other treaty organizations later). America's NATO allies needed arming, so American military suppliers furnished them with what they needed, which brought the unit costs of production back within reason. NATO procurement, in the main, was financed by the United States government through the same deficit means as were being employed in its own procurement.

Soon or late, the NATO market would be saturated, and as the fifties gave way to the sixties and seventies, it would become necessary to support the defense industries by selling arms to more and more countries. Meanwhile, the Soviet Union (which despite being "communist" was subject to the economic logic that beset the United States) was doing the same thing. Thus both the world's great powers ensnared themselves in an absurd trap: to defend themselves and supposedly preserve world peace they were placing arms in the hands of everyone, including the least experienced and the least responsible.

While all this was happening in domestic affairs, the United States was learning and acting upon equally false lessons in its relations with the rest of the world. Americans entered the war with a mixed bag of convictions, some sound and some unsound, about what had gone wrong with the peace settlements effected after World War I. Most were convinced that disarmament had been carried too far and too fast, which was doubtless true. Most believed, at least vaguely, that American participation in the League of Nations might have prevented the war, which was a half-baked notion. Most were certain that appeasement of totalitarian governments is fatal, which was true only under particular conditions. Most were amenable to the idea that it would have been in the interest of the United States to have financed the reconstruction of Europe after the First War, which was unreservedly true.

There was also another set of attitudes, shared by President Roosevelt and the liberal intellectual community, but which had to be taught to the American people against their intuitive better judgment. Roosevelt had, as Woodrow Wilson's Assistant Secretary of the Navy, witnesesed a painfully ugly side of American nationalism during World War I, the persecution of German-Americans and other "hyphenated" citizens. He had, as President, witnessed the rise of a monstrous perversion of nationalism in Nazi Germany, and of something which appeared to be kin to it in Japan. For these reasons he, along with most liberal intellectuals, surrendered to wishful thinking about the reality of nationalism and ethnicity: disregarding those powerful, primeval forces, the government of the United States took the position that peoples have no enduring characteristics, good or evil, but behaved one way or another only as their actions were determined by their political or economic systems. Socialism and democratic capitalism were benign systems in this scheme of reckoning, fascism was a malign one; and the war was being fought not between peoples but between systems. Americans should therefore not hate Germans, they should hate Nazism.*

That attitude bore bitter fruit. When it became generally known (what the Roosevelt administration knew about all along, but did not take even minimal steps to prevent) that the Nazis had murdered six million Jews, six million Poles, and large numbers of Gypsies, it was pathetically inadequate to attribute such horrors to a mere political system; and when it turned out that Stalin's Russia had murdered quite as many people and imprisoned even more than Hitler's Germany had, a merely political explanation was equally vile. To hold blameless a people which allows its government to commit such atrocities is to forfeit all claim to human decency: it is to deny the existence of evil, and to deny the existence of evil is to succumb to evil.

In less cosmic terms, the fruits of the attitude were poisonous enough. In the last year of the war and the first year of peace the Soviet Union's Red Army, ten million strong, swept over Eastern Europe and replaced German tyranny there with Russian tyranny. The Russians were impelled by greed, fear, and opportunism, not by ideology; they were, like any other ruthless nation-state, simply taking all they could get. When the Truman administration decided to stop Russian expansion, it did so out of concern for the national interests of the United States. But, given the commitment to the view that the only bona fide confrontations are between systems, not between nation-states, it was virtually inevitable that this confrontation, too, would be perceived in such terms. Thus was born the Cold War between the "free world" and the "worldwide Communist conspiracy."

That misperception would lock the United States into a policy straitjacket; it would prevent Americans from recognizing and acting in their own interests and blind them to the motives of other peoples. Americans would regard all Communist regimes as part of a single monolithic organization directed from Moscow, even when evidence to the contrary was overwhelming. They would attribute to that imaginary monolith demonic powers. They would perceive every stirring of national feeling among colonial peoples as Communist-inspired. Mistakenly believing that colonialism, poverty, and racism were breeding grounds for Communism, they would force their allies to abandon their colonial possessions, thereby contributing mightily to international instability; and in competing with the Soviet Union for influence in the "third world" thus created, they would set off a revolution in expectations that undermined stability even further. Worst of all, their fear of the bogey of the international Communist conspiracy obscured from them the real and potentially terrible danger of Soviet Russian imperialism.

This was the context of the Korean War, during which Americans learned one more lesson. The war succeeded in its limited aim of halting "Communist aggression" (in reality Soviet aggression), and its success convinced American policy-makers that limited warfare was a viable strategy. But that conviction rested on the assumption that the United States dared not attempt to win the war, lest it provoke retaliation from a unified Communist

---

*An exception was made for the Japanese, who were not just a different ethnic group but a different race. Some efforts were made to attribute their conduct to fascism, but the efforts proved futile and hatred of the Japanese became officially acceptable.

world. It also rested on the assumption that the American people, temperamentally, had the patience to engage in limited warfare. Both assumptions were wrong, and both portended disaster in the future.

There was a paradox in all this. In 1953, after twenty years of awesome ordeal and tribulation, the American people had emerged triumphant, rich, and powerful. And yet, instead of being filled with pride and confidence they were filled with doubts and fears; instead of facing the future boldly, as they had earned the right to do, they were obsessed with securing themselves against the hardships of the recent past. In a way, their mood was best expressed in the vow that returning veterans brought back with them from World War II. Those young men, in many respects the best and toughest generation the nation had ever produced, came home determined to marry, to have a lot of children, and to do whatever was necessary to ensure that their children would not have to go through what they had gone through.

That determination to protect their children from challenges and hardship—which had made them what they were—may have been the greatest mistake of all.

II. Eugene D. Genovese: a) A Government that Saved Business
b) Atomic Diplomacy

The 1930s brought the most destructive economic depression in the history of world capitalism, and almost fittingly they ended with the onset of the most destructive war in world history. No country or people wholly escaped the impact. National and international politics largely consisted of a series of desperate attempts to survive an unprecedented disaster, first economic, then military. The New Deal must be understood, at least in part, through comparison with other nations' reactions to the crisis.

The advanced capitalist countries faced three broad possibilities, each of which had numerous variants. They might abolish private property, nationalize basic industry and financial institutions, and initiate radical economic planning—that is, they might overthrow capitalism and install socialism. Or, they might preserve capitalist private property, strengthen big business, and institute a political dictatorship of the extreme right—that is, they might preserve the fundamentals of the capitalist system by means of fascism. Or, they might try to preserve capitalist private property under a traditional parliamentary state but charge it with feeding the hungry, creating jobs, and ending the slump. In no Western country did the working-class movements, socialist or communist, prove strong enough to effect a socialist solution. Only in the Soviet Union did socialism triumph and carry with it a remarkable industrial revolution and social transformation during the very decade in which the capitalist world was wallowing in misery. In the event, however, Stalin's great "revolution from above," which transformed the Soviet Union from a backward agrarian country to a formidable industrial one in barely ten years, came with a harsh dictatorship and at a high social cost, with political ramifications that have not yet run their course.

Germany, Italy, and Japan, as well as lesser states, turned fascist, whereas Britain, France, and the United States led the bourgeois democracies in a search for a third way. The fascist states did restore full employment and resume economic growth, but no more than the bourgeois-democratic countries could they simply annul the economic laws of the business cycle. Rather, they solved immediate problems by extensive militarization, paid for by a staggering rate of deficit spending. With millions of men in the army and millions more put to work to equip the war machine, a kind of prosperity returned, although the working class bore the brunt of the sacrifices while big business reaped enormous profits. The prosperity, in any case, rested on vast debts that could only be repaid by the acquisition of unprecedented spoils. In effect, Germany, the most virulent of the fascist states, prepared to repay its financiers and industrialists, and to keep its people employed, by conquering and enslaving the rest of Europe. Fascist economic policy and fascist military-political policy, therefore, complemented each other.

In Britain, despite the temporary pretense of a "national government," the conservatives held sway and tried to weather the crisis by selective interventions in the market; at that, they had to intervene much more than they theoretically preferred. It is amusing to recall that since the 1930s all conservative governments including those in the United States, have followed interventionist policies and scorned the free market; only in election speeches and in the writings of professors does the free market hold any attractions any longer. The primary difference between conservatives and liberals in this respect is that they tend to be connected with different sections of big business and therefore to intervene to support somewhat different corporate interests.

In France a turn to the left in 1936 brought to power a "Popular Front" of Socialists and Radicals (i.e., middle-class liberals) with Communist support. Its policies paralleled those of the New Deal in providing public works, social benefits, and deficit spending. That government only lasted a year and represented the most leftwing moment in France during the decade. Yet, again, its policies differed from those of the liberal and conservative governments that preceded and followed it not in being more interventionist—the others were also interventionist and only paid lip service to the free market—but in being willing to intervene on behalf of the working class and small business more readily than big business.

In the United States the New Deal was, at first, sharply attacked from the Left as well as by such conservatives as Herbert Hoover as proto-fascist. And indeed, the unabashed encouragement to big business and outright monopoly (e.g., the NRA) raised justifiable fears of an American "corporate state" patterned on Mussolini's. Yet, Roosevelt was ready to go in almost any direction and remained essentially pragmatic and committed only to steering a capitalist America through the crisis. In 1934, when conservative measures had failed and he needed labor support, he turned sharply to the left. The final shape of the New Deal was significantly influenced by the rising power of organized labor, which Roosevelt encouraged but sought to manipulate. The New Deal thus emerged as a political coalition of conservative southern Democrats, organized labor, liberals of all stripes, and minorities, but it always retained—despite all demagogy and rhetoric—significant big business support as well. For the New Deal did save capitalism and big business, and at least some of the corporate giants had the wit to acknowledge the facts, whereas others were benefiting directly and were in no position to argue.

Examples might be piled up to demonstrate the New Deal's basically big business orientation; let us settle for one that helps illuminate the role of the southern Democrats in the coalition. The government paid southern planters not to produce. That is, while people all over the world were in the throes of starvation we were paying people not to grow food. The government, in effect, was taxing the American people in order to make the richest section of southern agriculture a good deal richer. Although the program theoretically was supposed to aid the poor farmers as well, it soon enough became clear that the poorest, white and black but increasingly black, tenant farmers and share-croppers would pay dearly. With the curtailment of production and the receipt of large subsidies, the planters began to move toward mechanization of cotton production and to dispense with the laborers who had worked their land as tenants, croppers, or wage-workers. The mechanization was, to be sure, in the general interest of the national economy, but its overhead cost had been wholly shifted to the backs of the poorest people, while the richest were allowed—in fact, encouraged—to rack up unprecedented profits for doing less than ever. In the wake of such atrocities social miseries unfolded. The origin of many northern ghettoes and slums rests in the forced migration of blacks, and more southern whites than is generally appreciated. The poor drifted north in search of work. More often than not, they found poverty and degradation and had to go on the dole. They added to the costs of the general public in their adopted areas, while those who had driven them from their homes began to grumble loudly about "welfare cheats" and high taxes—and to vote Republican.

The basic conservative criticism of the New Deal, increasingly echoed in retrospect by the Left, nonetheless contained much validity, even if the conservative alternatives continue to look much worse. The New Deal did concentrate enormous power in the hands of a Federal government increasingly dominated by a swelling bureaucracy; and the resultant welfare state has, in fact, been less concerned with full employment and popular participation in a democratic society than in doles, pacifiers, and party politics. From then to now people's control over their daily lives has steadily eroded. And far from encouraging the growth of socialism, as radical supporters once hoped and conservative opponents feared, it has greatly strengthened the influence of big business over the government as well as the economy.

Each further bureaucratization of the economy has created processes that only larger businesses have been able to afford or manipulate. New Deal labor policy fostered oligopolies that could meet minimum wage standards, process the papers for workers' benefits, satisfy government regulations for contracts, negotiate effectively with unions, and amass sufficient political power to affect legislation. (I say nothing of being strong enough to command subsidies, bail-outs, favored treatment, and other forms of legal bribery.)

The New Deal did feed the hungry, take responsibility for creating jobs, and relieve the people of the worst of their direct misery—things its conservative critics were perfectly willing to leave to the mercies of a merciless marketplace. It did not end the depression. The year 1938 brought a renewed slump of grim proportions, and not until the outbreak of the European war did the economy start to recover. The conservatives may be right in arguing that deficit spending and government intervention only prolonged the depression, although they take a notoriously easy view of the intense suffering imposed upon workers, farmers, and lower middle-class people whenever the market is left to correct itself. That capitalism can cure its cyclical ills by violent contractions at the expense of millions of hardworking people needs no elaboration. But those hardworking people are no longer willing to pay the price and go like sheep to the shearing. Roosevelt and his New Deal saved American capitalism—in no small part from the greed and shortsightedness of the capitalists themselves. Whether it was worth saving is another matter.

The New Deal's foreign policy was not much more coherent than its economic policy. Like the bourgeois democracies of Western Europe, the United States long deluded itself that it could either appease Hitler or tempt him into a war with the Soviet Union—really, two expressions of the same policy. Repeatedly, the Soviets asked for a collective security pact against the Nazis; repeatedly, the western powers refused to sully themselves by a pact with the godless communists. Finally, the Western powers went to Munich, with Roosevelt's support, betrayed Czechoslovakia, gave Hitler what he wanted, and left the USSR isolated. The policy was not merely venal, it was stupid. For a variety of reasons the Poles, who hated the USSR but were not willing to make the concessions Hitler demanded, ruined the prospects for a Nazi-Soviet war in 1939. And more to the point, Stalin destroyed the policy with one blow by reversing his ground and signing his own pact with Hitler. To this day he is vilified in the West for having done what others were trying to do to him—and indeed virtually did do at Munich.

In the end, the collective security that might have prevented World War II and cut Hitler down early, emerged from the war itself in the form of the Grand Alliance compelled by the Nazi onslaught. In the aftermath, Europe, including the Soviet Union, was devastated by human casualties and economic destruction never before experienced. The United States came out virtually unscathed and determined to establish itself as the center of world politics. From the American point of view, the Soviets were behaving outrageously in attempting to establish a sphere of influence in Eastern Europe, which had twice in a quarter-century been used as a springboard for a massive invasion of Russia.

The United States did not consider outrageous its own establishment of bases, including atomic bases, all around the Soviet borders, its direct intervention in a number of countries, and its insistence that it had the right to serve as international arbiter. The United States, it seems, was doing these things to protect freedom. It was to protect freedom, therefore, that the United States effectively used economic pressure—and the threat of military intervention in Italy—to drive the communists out of the Western European governments to which they had been elected. And it was to protect freedom that George Kennan, among many American diplomats and political leaders, cooly advocated dismembering the USSR as a price for peace, while generals, statesmen, and philosophers (notably, Bertrand Russell) suggested that the USSR be A-bombed if it did not see reason and give up its interests in Eastern Europe. After all, the Soviet pressure on Eastern Europe proved conclusively that Stalin was seeking world domination.

Stalin was many things, including a butcher, but he was not a fool. The suggestion that he was plotting world revolution and Soviet expansion at a time when he was licking his wounds and digging in for a long and slow recovery is unworthy of discussion. But he made his share of mistakes, and his ruthlessness at home and abroad—if it can be counted a "mistake"—certainly made his detractors look a lot more plausible than they in fact were. I shall return to some of the problems of foreign policy in the next section, for they can better be evaluated within the context of a longer time span. But a couple of myths cannot be allowed to pass. The United States did exercise restraint in Europe when we had an A-bomb monopoly. But that was mainly a military decision. The A-bomb, unlike the H-bomb, was not a decisive weapon, merely a terribly destructive one. It could not have prevented the Soviets from overrunning Western Europe, especially since they had the support of well armed leftwing guerrillas behind the American lines. In any case, a renewed war, after so bloody and long a war, would have had little or no support from people anywhere. Each side could prepare for another war, but neither was in any position to force the issue until the early 1950s. And by that time, both sides had the H-bomb, and everyone began to get thoughtful.

When the "limited" wars did come, first in Korea and then in Vietnam, it is not true that we did not try to win. We tried and failed. It is true that we fought under constraints, but so did our enemies, perhaps under greater constraints than we did. For example, did the Chinese have a "privileged sanctuary" across the Yalu? Yes—but not so vulnerable a privileged sanctuary as we enjoyed in Japan. In the end, nuclear weapons and the threat of a general war has imposed severe constraints on both sides, and it is not at all clear that the United States has suffered more than others. To win such wars today means to win within the constraints. They did; we did not.

John F. Kennedy (National Archives)

Chapter XXVIII
New Frontiers

John F. Kennedy's Inaugural Address, January 20, 1961

John Kennedy set proud goals for his administration in 1961, promising that "a new generation of Americans" would march forth to do battle with "the common enemies of man: tyranny, poverty, disease and war itself." But the Kennedy administration was to be a brief one—two years and ten months from the "trumpet summons" of the inauguration to the muffled drums and caissons marching slowly up Pennsylvania Avenue in November 1963. This foreshortened story of beginnings and promises, then, is a hard one to interpret. Was there substance behind the glittering style? Was the New Frontier a beckoning horizon or an armed border? The answers remain "blowing in the wind"—a phrase from the Kennedy era.

Kennedy's inaugural address set the tone for his administration as few such addresses have ever done. The elevation, the magnetic tone of dedication and of hope come across in the way of words chiseled in granite. Thousands, perhaps millions, of Americans have read these words on Kennedy's tombstone in Arlington National Cemetery. Yet a close reading of this famous speech reveals subtle counterthemes that suggest possible answers to the questions that were raised after John F. Kennedy's death: about his place in American history. Ask yourself what the various publics listening to this speech would have understood by it. What would a civil rights worker have derived from it? A Pentagon policy planner? This Soviet foreign ministry? John F. Kennedy was never easy to evaluate, and his untimely death left a legacy of controversy and unanswered questions:

We observe today not a victory of party but a celebration of freedom—symbolizing an end as well as a beginning—signifying renewal as well as change. For I have sworn before you and Almighty God the same solemn oath our forebears prescribed nearly a century and three quarters ago.

The world is very different now. For man holds in his mortal hands the power to abolish all forms of human poverty and all forms of human life. And yet the same revolutionary beliefs for which our forebears fought are still at issue around the globe—the belief that the rights of man come not from the generosity of the state but from the hand of God.

We dare not forget today that we are the heirs of that first revolution. Let the word go forth from this time and place, to friend and foe alike, that the torch has been passed to a new generation of Americans—born in this century, tempered by war, disciplined by a hard and bitter peace, proud of our ancient heritage—and unwilling to witness or permit the slow undoing of those human rights to which this nation has always been committed, and to which we are committed today at home and around the world.

Let every nation know, whether it wishes us well or ill, that we shall pay any price, bear any burden, meet any hardship, support any friend, oppose any foe to assure the survival and the success of liberty.

This much we pledge—and more.

To those old allies whose cultural and spiritual origins we share, we pledge the loyalty of faithful friends. United, there is little we cannot do in a host of cooperative ventures. Divided, there is little we can do—for we dare not meet a powerful challenge at odds and split asunder.

To those new states whom we welcome to the ranks of the free, we pledge our word that one form of colonial control shall not have passed away merely to be replaced by a far more iron tyranny. We shall not always expect to find them supporting our view. But we shall always hope to find them strongly supporting their own freedom— and to remember that, in the past, those who foolishly sought power by riding the back of the tiger ended up inside.

To those peoples in the huts and villages of half the globe struggling to break the bonds of mass misery, we pledge our best efforts to help them help themselves, for whatever period is required—not because the communists may be doing it, not because we seek their votes, but because it is right. If a free society cannot help the many who are poor, it cannot save the few who are rich.

To our sister republics south of our border, we offer a special pledge—to convert our good words into good deeds—in a new alliance for progress—to assist free men and free government as casting off the chains of poverty. But this peaceful revolution of hope cannot become the prey of hostile powers. Let all our neighbors know that we shall join with them to oppose aggression or subversion anywhere in the Americas. And let every other power know that this Hemisphere intends to remain the master of its own house.

To that world assembly of sovereign states, the United Nations, our last best hope in an age where the instruments of war have far outpaced the instruments of peace, we renew our pledge of support—to prevent it from becoming merely a forum for invective—to strengthen its shield of the new and the weak—and to enlarge the area in which its writ may run.

Finally, to those nations who would make themselves our adversary, we offer not a pledge but a request: that both sides begin anew the quest for peace, before the dark powers of destruction unleashed by science engulf all humanity in planned or accidental self-destruction.

We dare not tempt them with weakness. For only when our arms are sufficient beyond doubt can we be certain beyond doubt that they will never be employed.

But neither can two great and powerful groups of nations take comfort from our present course—both sides overburdened by the cost of modern weapons, both rightly alarmed by the steady spread of the deadly atom, yet both racing to alter that uncertain balance of terror that stays the hand of mankind's final war.

So let us begin anew—remembering on both sides that civility is not a sign of weakness, and sincerity is always subject to proof. Let us never negotiate out of fear. But let us never fear to negotiate.

Let both sides explore what problems unite us instead of belaboring those problems which divide us.

Let both sides, for the first time, formulate serious and precise proposals for the inspection and control of arms—and bring the absolute power to destroy other nations under the absolute control of all nations.

Let both sides seek to invoke the wonders of science instead of its terrors. Together let us explore the stars, conquer the deserts, eradicate disease, tap the ocean depths and encourage the arts and commerce. . . .

And if a beach-head of cooperation may push back the jungle of suspicion, let both sides join in creating a new endeavor, not a new balance of power, but a new world of law, where the strong are just and the weak secure and the peace preserved.

All this will not be finished in the first one hundred days. Nor will it be finished in the first one thousand days, nor in the life of this Administration, nor even perhaps in our lifetime on this planet. But let us begin.

In your hands, my fellow citizens, more than mine, will rest the final success or failure of our course. Since this country was founded, each generation of Americans has been summoned to give testimony to its national loyalty. The graves of young Americans who answered the call to service surround the globe.

Now the trumpet summons us again—not as a call to bear arms, though arms we need—not as a call to battle, though embattled we are—but a call to bear the burden of a long twilight struggle, year in and year out, "rejoicing in hope, patient in tribulation"—a struggle against the common enemies of man: tyranny, poverty, disease and war itself.

Can we forge against these enemies a grand global alliance, North and South, East and West, that can assure a more fruitful life for all mankind? Will you join in that historic effort?

In the long history of the world, only a few generations have been granted the role of defending freedom in its hour of maximum danger. I do not shrink from this responsibility—I welcome it. I do not believe that any of us would exchange places with any other people or any other generation. The energy, the faith, the devotion which we bring to this endeavor will light our country and all who serve it—and the glow from that fire can truly light the world.

And so, my fellow Americans: ask not what your country can do for you—ask what you can do for your country.

My fellow citizens of the world: ask not what America will do for you, but what together we can do for the freedom of man. . . .

Eisenhower Diplomacy: I

Eisenhower's good fortune in foreign policy was more impressive than his work at home. A peace-loving man, Eisenhower quickly ended the Korean War and began the task of resolving the victors' clash over the spoils of World War II. At the same time, the Soviet Union moved toward improved relations with the West. Freed of Stalin's arbitrary cruelty by his death on March 5, 1953, and perhaps sobered by Truman's determined containment politics and the unexpected strength of decadent capitalism, Georgi Malenkov, Stalin's nominal successor, sought detente. He received support from Foreign Minister Vyacheslav Molotov, Defense Minister Nikolai A. Bulganin, and Nikita Khrushchev, first secretary of the Communist party. Although a three-year struggle for dominance ensued among Stalin's successors—a contest Khrushchev won largely because of timely support from Marshal Zhukov, a war hero who controlled the Red Army—the dispute nevertheless increased hopes for a more stable world order. So far did the so-called "thaw" go that Khrushchev later announced the doctrine of peaceful coexistence and economic competition, both direct repudiations of Marxist militancy. Old habits and problems did not magically disappear, but given an atomic standoff (in 1953 the Soviet Union exploded its first hydrogen bomb), the decline of McCarthyism in America, and new faces on both sides of the Iron Curtain, the world appeared headed toward a more peaceful future.

In Washington, a new tenor and even a new substance entered the making of foreign policy. The President's caution and his immense following prevented the public furor and congressional alarms that had plagued the Democrats. His word on military matters was definitive. And Dwight Eisenhower knew the horrors of war: in *Crusade in Europe* (1948) he recalled the harrowing experience of entering the Falaise Gap zone in Normandy in 1944. "It was literally possible," he wrote, "to walk for hundreds of yards at a time, stepping on nothing but dead and decayed flesh." Eisenhower turned the day-to-day control of foreign affairs over to John Foster Dulles, a somber, able man who espoused an unbending anticommunism. Soon famous for his willingness, at least rhetorically, to "go to the brink" of nuclear war in order to contain communism, the new secretary of state's caution occasioned less comment and recognition. Though "brinkmanship" implied militancy, perhaps it no less forcefully

evoked pacifism: to the brink, not into the abyss.

The most dramatic break with Democratic foreign policy concerned Korea. Although Ike's threat to use atomic weaponry there echoed Truman's belligerency, America's most successful recent general became the nation's first President in over a century to halt a war short of victory. Soon afterward Eisenhower managed to stabilize the postwar disputes that had long divided the European continent. Dulles negotiated the Paris Accords, which guaranteed French security and at the same time brought West Germany into the NATO alliance. Although this move provoked the Soviets into the Warsaw Pact, an alliance system in Eastern Europe, the continent seemed more stable when organized into two blocs.

The Republicans also fashioned a new approach to the Soviet Union. Both Eisenhower and Dulles relied heavily on the deterrent power of nuclear weapons as opposed to conventional forces. This strategy produced "more bang for the buck" in the colorful words of economy-minded Charles Wilson, the secretary of defense. Yet the nuclear approach generally restricted the United States either to doing nothing or to threatening catastrophe, and Russia's acquisition of nuclear weapons blunted the device. Dulles believed that the best way to maintain peace was for America to make known what it would do in a given situation; in this way we might have avoided Korea. Eisenhower himself probably never thought nuclear war to be an option. Surely his diplomatic initiatives—forging new alliances, holding summit meetings, supporting the United Nations, and offering the open skies disarmament proposal—were all calculated to avoid confrontation.

In the most dramatic departure from the techniques of the Truman and Acheson years, Eisenhower sought direct meetings with Soviet leaders—a diplomatic device unused since 1946. In the afterglow of the Korean settlement, Winston Churchill proposed a "summit meeting" to resolve outstanding European problems. But by the time the four heads of government reached Geneva, their goals had become less ambitious. Eisenhower; Bulganin and Khrushchev for the Soviets; the new British prime minister, Anthony Eden; and Premier Edgar Faure of France attempted only to list problems and outline procedures for their solution. Meeting in late July 1955, the statesmen discussed three principal topics: German unification and the closely allied issue of European security, disarmament, and increased communication between East and West. Although considered the least important at the time, the third objective alone achieved realization. Since 1955 a small but sustained series of mutual concessions has reduced the barriers to the exchange of "people, ideas, and goods" between the formerly almost isolated blocs.

When the foreign ministers met in the fall to work out concrete proposals for solving the remaining problems—a united Germany and disarmament—they failed to reach any agreement. The West's NATO and the East's Warsaw Pact had already divided the continent. Not just the Soviet Union, but every nation in Europe feared a revival of German militarism. Many West Germans, particularly in the Rhineland and Bavaria, questioned whether the prosperous West should bail out the depressed East. But though Germany remained divided, the greatest disappointment was the failure on disarmament. At Geneva Eisenhower had outlined his famous "open skies" proposal: mutual aerial surveillance and an exchange of military blueprints. The Russians politely scuttled the idea. Despite this setback, the first summit meeting had positive results: both moved away from the cold war rhetoric of accusation and threat; everyone understood that nuclear war would be, in Eisenhower's words, "race suicide." The Russians apparently accepted the President's protestations of America's peaceful intent. The summit launched the "spirit of Geneva": fundamental tensions remained, but peace—defined as the absence of war—seemed possible.

Eisenhower Diplomacy: II

Throughout 1956 and 1957 caution dominated American foreign policy as lightning changes left the administration bewildered. Both the Communist and the Western blocs suffered internal rebellions during the summer and fall of 1956. First, the Soviet empire in Eastern Europe nearly collapsed. Some 15,000 impoverished Polish factory workers revolted in Poznan on June 28. While the Kremlin hesitated, the Poles demanded that Wladyslaw Gomulka take over the government. A national Communist who opposed "hasty" collectivization, Gomulka refused to compromise with Soviet leaders clearly caught off guard. After a bewildering series of Byzantine maneuvers, he forced Moscow to accept a revisionist politburo under his leadership.

Gomulka's success triggered the much more devastating Hungarian rebellion of October and November, which sought political independence as well as economic reform. On October 23, a demonstration supporting Polish liberation quickly changed into a huge mob of workers, soldiers, and students who demanded the return of Imre Nagy, a former Communist minister. Nagy, who opposed Soviet economic methods and Moscow's political domination, formed a new government on the Polish model. But demonstrations turned into armed rebellion; the provinces almost immediately went over to the rebel cause and Budapest soon followed. Encouraged by signs of support from the West, the revolutionaries opted for complete independence. Although Moscow offered a remarkable and often overlooked compromise solution—Hungarian membership in a "commonwealth of socialist countries"—Nagy and his cabinet could no longer control events. When the Hungarians persisted in trying to escape its orbit, Moscow brought in a heavy military force to forestall piecemeal breakdown of the Warsaw bloc.

Worried about nuclear confrontation and tacitly recognizing Soviet dominance in Eastern Europe, the West never considered intervention. In any case, events elsewhere had dissolved Western unity into barely disguised animosity. On November 5 England, France, and Israel launched a joint attack on Egypt, ostensibly to reopen the Suez Canal which President Gamal Abdel Nasser had nationalized in July. But the canal issue was only a pretext. For the Israelis, the operation had all the trappings of preventive war. In Paris the moribund Fourth Republic hoped to recoup its prestige after frustrations in Vietnam and Algeria; Premier Guy Mollet belligerently overreacted to Nasser's act. Only Britain hesitated. If anxious to topple Nasser, whose action against British interests in the Suez created a dangerous example to other Arab states, London understood the enormous military risks. British officials misread Eisenhower's mild warnings—the election campaign was just peaking in the United States—and concluded that he would not object. Given Soviet preoccupations in Hungary, Washington's response determined the outcome of the tripartite maneuver; the United States, anxious to avoid identifying itself with European colonialism, abruptly condemned the attack. Eisenhower even threatened to bankrupt the British pound unless Eden withdrew British troops. Beset on all sides—the entire Arab world had broken off diplomatic relations—the prime minister accepted a Canadian-American proposal for a United Nations peacekeeping force in the Sinai peninsula. If this solved a diplomatic dilemma for the West, Egypt did not forget that troops were stationed only on its soil, not on Israel's.

The next jolt occurred outside the field of politics. On October 4, 1957, the first Sputnik beeped the beginning of the space age and seemed to tip the tactical balance in favor of the Soviet Union. Economies in the Defense Department, together with an exaggerated reliance upon manned bombers, had limited America's missile development program. Despite the quiver that ran through the Western world, the new earth satellite had little strategic significance; America's military technology and gross national product far surpassed those of the Russians. Yet in less than fourteen months, both the Communist and Western blocs had suffered severe internal divisions, the cold war had moved into the third world, and Soviet rocket engineers had given their government a strong propaganda weapon.

Eisenhower responded characteristically to these events: the former general decided to "wage peace." He envisioned a prudent defense against Soviet power, executed less belligerently and less myopically than under Dulles, who left office in 1959 and soon died of cancer. At the same time, Soviet policy became less aggressive. Khrushchev's colleagues rebuked him severely for the disastrous effects of Soviet intervention in Hungary, particularly the damage to Russian prestige in the third world. Yet with the decisive help of the army, the skillful Ukrainian solidified his control over the Soviet state. Growing Russian power and Western division tempted Khrushchev; memories of Hungary and the devastation of his homeland in World War II held him back. A balance of sorts developed unintentionally, creating a pushing and pulling, a minute-by-minute policy. Until John Kennedy raised the specter of a "missile gap" the two superpowers moved, if not toward reconciliation, at least toward a mutual determination to avoid nuclear war.

Despite his restrained reaction to potentially explosive situations, Eisenhower never believed in making a virtue of weakness. With his encouragement Secretary Dulles strengthened collective security in Europe by granting Germany a non-

nuclear role in NATO. In 1957 Dulles also enunciated the Eisenhower doctrine for the Middle East, offering not only economic assistance but also American soldiers, if requested, to governments protecting their territorial integrity against Communist advances. The new policy resulted from the rapid erosion of the West's position throughout the strategically significant Near East. Nasser's attempt to unify the region politically, together with general Arab confidence that their oil reserves would fend off reprisals and gain concessions, accelerated the trend toward nationalism. Prospects of an independent role outside the bipolar, Soviet-American world undercut the pro-West Baghdad Pact, a military alliance composed of Iraq, Turkey, Iran, Pakistan, and Great Britain. For many reasons, its viability depended primarily upon Iraq. But Nasserism had permeated the Iraqi army, and in July 1958 its leaders ousted Premier Nuri es-Said. The new regime immediately realigned Iraq's foreign policy with Nasser's increasingly successful drive for Arab unity.

In Lebanon during 1958, a confused, intricate civil war erupted between Christians and Arabs, pro-Nasser and anti-Nasser factions, and Western-oriented, urban Beirut against the native impulses of the hill areas. Shortly after the Iraqi coup, the pro-Western President of Lebanon asked the United States for military support to end the civil war. Eisenhower invoked his new doctrine and dispatched 3,500 marines, a force that eventually grew to 14,000. The intervention, so brief, bloodless, and well-executed, deserved commendation at least for its technical skill. But the larger purpose of the landing failed; the attempt to set up an alternative to Nasser in the Middle East collapsed around regional fears of renewed colonialism and the Arab countries' reluctance to combine with outside powers against one another.

Eisenhower deftly handled another crisis, potentially the most serious of the decade, when Russia sealed off East Berlin in the late summer of 1958 to thwart black market currency operations by West Berliners and to halt an embarrassing efflux from East Germany. His determination to stand firm without overreacting quickly diminished tension. As if to reiterate the common resolve to avoid war, Khrushchev paid a successful visit to the United States in 1959, and met a cordial Eisenhower at Camp David, Maryland. Observers spoke of the "spirit of Camp David," the dissipation of mistrust. The Eisenhower peace offensive was to culminate in a summit conference planned for Geneva on May 14, 1960. But on May 1, deep inside the Soviet Union, Russian artillery shot down an American U-2 spy plane; Khrushchev used the incident, following contradictory White House statements, as an occasion for jettisoning the conference.

If Eisenhower oversaw a sophisticated and for the most part successful relationship with the Soviet Union, his administration never satisfactorily solved another dilemma. As illustrated in the inconclusiveness of the Lebanon intervention, America seemed unable to deal with the challenge of the so-called underdeveloped world. Although the lack of urban-industrial areas, the existence of fragmented social structures, and native hostility to notions of materialistic progress seemed unpromising ground for Marxist ideas, the Republican administration, like its predecessor, seemed to equate neutralism with procommunism. The breakup of Europe's empires promoted political and economic revolution as nationalists sought to destroy the remnants of colonialism, particularly its class structure. Superimposed over this struggle was the necessity to restore economic balance after years of European "warping." Throughout Africa and much of Asia, imperial emphasis upon extractive wealth and protected colonial markets had inhibited native manufactures, weakened agriculture, and created parasitic cities that functioned principally as administrative capitals and pleasure domes. The struggle to break these colonial legacies, occurring within the context of cold war, guaranteed years of violent change and frustrating complexity. Eisenhower himself was so disillusioned that he frankly admitted to John Kennedy in 1961 that foreign affairs were "in a mess."

In 1959 a revolutionary leader, Fidel Castro, overthrew the heavyhanded Cuban dictator, Fulgencio Batista. At first the administration easily adapted to the change; only six days after Batista fled Cuba, Washington recognized his bearded, thirty-two-year-old successor. Worried about their large investments, several American corporations paid their Cuban taxes a year in advance, a transparent and ineffective attempt to change Castro's goals. In March the new premier declared 1959 the Year of Revolution; even more than executions in Cuba, Castro's propaganda appeals to American minorities shocked domestic public opinion. If Cuban-American relations faltered in 1959, in the next year—the so-called Year of the Agrarian Reform—they collapsed. After Castro nationalized one billion dollars of American property in Cuba and publicly consorted with Khrushchev at the 1960 United Nations General Assembly meeting, Eisenhower tried to isolate Cuba by cutting first its economic lifeline, the all-important sugar quotas, and then its political connections with the Organization of American States. That Castro subsequently turned to the Communist bloc surprised no one except a few Americans. Eisenhower himself had already authorized a possible attack on Cuba, which would ultimately materialize as the Bay of Pigs fiasco under Kennedy.

Economic and Social Policy in the 1950's

The domestic economy, like foreign policy, underwent a transition during the 1950's. Within the Republican party three major economic strategies contended for predominance: classical theory decrying government involvement and urging free competition existed almost wholly in rhetoric; a belief in the possibility of economic stability and steady growth by means of monetary policy, primarily developed by the federal reserve system; and a third position which few Republicans acknowledged but which actually prevailed—the academically orthodox Keynesian emphasis upon fiscal policy and carefully defined policies for government spending and taxing. Overt Keynesianism awaited the Kennedy-Johnson years. Yet under Eisenhower even Arthur F. Burns, the cautious chairman of the Council of Economic Advisers, remarked that "it is no longer a matter of serious controversy whether the Government should play a positive role in helping to maintain a high level of economic activity."

During the recession of 1953-54, Eisenhower used both fiscal and monetary policies to reinvigorate the economy; he remarked at this time that controls practically guaranteed no depression would occur. Especially from 1954 on, monetary policy gained popularity with the administration, notably manipulation of the rediscount rate and extensive open market operations. The problem was that the reserve policies came in response to various economic problems rather than in anticipation of them.

Levittown, Long Island, New York, 1949

Unemployment was the central economic issue of the decade. The three recessions of the 1950's, each one worse than the last, were puzzling phenomena. The end of the Korean War and a sharp cut in military expenditures brought on the first recession in 1953-54. An easy money policy adopted by both the Treasury and the Federal Reserve Board, combined with a tax cut and an increase in old age and unemployment payments, eventually managed to offset the economic decline resulting from postwar layoffs. But the administration, worried over inflation, reacted slowly to another recession in 1957-58; with unemployment rates remaining at 7 percent during the congressional elections, Republicans suffered disastrous consequences. Even in 1960, though a presidential campaign hung in the balance, inflation troubled Eisenhower more than unemployment or the slow rate of economic growth.

The President's advisers, though they prevented a weak economy from slipping into depression, were unable to avoid repeated economic declines and an unemployment rate of up to 7.7 percent. They failed to stem inflationary price increases even as the national economic growth rate remained below levels then prevailing in Western Europe and apparently in the Soviet Union. Russian annual growth averaged 7.1 percent between 1950 and 1958, nearly 50 percent above that of the United States. In America greater productivity per man hour required an economy expansive enough to supply new jobs; the postwar rise in the birth rate further increased the demand. Neglect of what John Kenneth Galbraith termed the public

sector of the economy, of needs in health, welfare, and education, also suggested a need for a more active economy yielding larger tax receipts.

The Eisenhower administration no doubt wanted to curb rising prices, but it could not do it with voluntary restraints, especially when the steel industry resisted. Large firms aimed not for competition at home and abroad, but for secure growth based on rising prices in a carefully planned market, or for an "administered price." The elites of organized labor pressed for higher wages, passing the resulting higher price on to the consumer. Even in agriculture ever higher payments to keep land out of production balanced lower farm support prices. In the 1950's business-oriented Republicans appeared fearful of stimulating more rapid economic growth, while at the end of the decade, Democrats, less frightened by inflation, made growth their major objective.

During the 1950's investments in new plants and equipment shrank far below any comparable European figures. As usual, the poor suffered most during the economic doldrums. Blacks, Indians, Mexican Americans, and growing numbers of the elderly were, in Michael Harrington's apt word, "invisible"—physically shut away and forgotten in slums, on reservations, in migrant workers' camps, and in filthy nursing homes as medical indigents. Mass-produced clothing masked their true economic condition. These same groups were also politically invisible, lacking a voice even in the Democratic party, which had its institutional base in the unions.

On social issues, much activity resulted in little action. Aid to public education was so popular, and the need for classrooms so great, that most people expected Eisenhower to implement his campaign pledge for direct federal aid as "the American answer." Yet he failed to do so. Perhaps the President had expressed his true sentiments in 1949 when he testified while president of Columbia University in opposition to a school-aid bill, calling it socialistic and paternalistic, even though Senator Taft sponsored it.

Congress did pass one important education measure, the National Defense Education Act of 1958. Yet both the act's provisions and Congress's motivation seemed far removed from concern over the quality of local education. During the near-hysterical period following the 1957 Russian launching of Sputnik I, the national government had quickly decided to improve college-level education, primarily in the applied sciences and engineering. Implementing this decision, NDEA provided loans, scholarships, and fellowships directly to students and a lesser amount in grants to the colleges themselves. Yet perhaps more important than these provisions of NDEA was its psychological impact: for better or for worse, education had become a concern of the federal government. For the remainder of Eisenhower's term, however, the President's inaction and congressional friction over race prevented further subsidies.

Caution also marked the concern over health care. Skyrocketing medical costs had troubled some congressmen since the 1930's when Congress first debated a program for universal health insurance under social security. Truman had revived the issue, but Eisenhower and the American Medical Association denounced such projects as "socialized medicine." (Secretary of Health Oveta Culp Hobby even opposed the free distribution of the Salk polio vaccine.) Although the AMA grudgingly advanced broad-based private health plans financed in part by government, Eisenhower kept silent and Congress ignored his requests for aid to hospitals. Yet the issue would not go away, despite presidential opposition.

By the mid-fifties, health care became linked with another issue, the plight of the elderly. Prodded by organized labor, Congress took up the Forand Bill, a modest proposal including limited hospital benefits for those over 65. The AFL-CIO and most Northern Democrats actively supported the legislation. Strident AMA protests suggested ulterior motives and its extensive propaganda campaign against the measure actually made people more aware of the problem. The Eisenhower administration initially opposed the Forand Bill, preferring voluntary health insurance plans. Most Republicans, the medical lobby, and the insurance industry opposed any government scheme, even one by the new HEW secretary, Arthur Flemming, for voluntary social security taxes. Together with Southern congressmen, the Republicans passed the Kerr-Mills Act, providing limited aid to the indigent. This returned the issue to where it had started—an attempt to prevent medical catastrophe from pauperizing the elderly; thereafter frustrated Democrats as well as several Republicans found ready allies among senior citizens for a more comprehensive program.

Eisenhower's determination not to expand federal patronage or the federal budget surfaced emphatically in the struggles over environmental bills. In 1960 the President vetoed a water pollution bill which would have established federal grants to build sewage treatment plants. He argued that pollution was "a uniquely local blight," and that responsibility rested with state and local governments. This theme pervaded his statements concerning natural resources and conservation. Half-convinced that the Tennessee Valley Authority represented "creeping socialism," he backed the Dixon-Yates utility proposal to sell private power in the area to the Atomic Energy Commission. This plan ended in scandal and failure, but the Submerged Lands Act of 1953 assigned lucrative offshore oil and natural gas interests to the coastal states. Although the few bills providing new programs for clean air, recreation areas, wilderness preservation, and highway beautification ran afoul of Eisenhower's states' rights philosophy and budgetary concerns, the President did not hesitate to improve areas already under federal jurisdiction. In 1956, he inaugurated a ten-year program to modernize facilities in the national parks; in contrast, he delayed efforts to purchase private seashore for public use.

If caution and philosophical objections guided Eisenhower's approach to social and ecological issues, the Republican President was curiously ambivalent about federal spending on "internal improvements." Public works projects that promoted the economic development of the country—what economists call the "capital infrastructure"—received quick, almost enthusiastic approval despite often costly drains on government funds. The Middle West welcomed plans for joint United States-Canadian construction of the Saint Lawrence Seaway, a dream of Herbert Hoover's brought to fruition in 1959, thirty years after he recommended it to Congress. Massive highway building programs, justified to a frugal Congress as an aid to "national defense," gained support from local businessmen and commuters, as well as construction companies and unions. But in 1959 Eisenhower rejected a bill providing for low-income housing as too inflationary. During his last term, Congress passed two area redevelopment bills that called for federally guaranteed loans to "depressed" or chronically poor areas, but Eisenhower vetoed both, primarily because they would "greatly diminish local responsibility."

Eisenhower's Second Term

Moderation in both major parties marked the 1956 campaign, which featured the same candidates as in 1952. Stevenson presented a vision of possible disengagement from the Cold War; he recommended a unilateral halt to nuclear testing and an end to the draft. At the same time, however, he implied that Eisenhower had sacrificed our national security in exchange for a balanced budget and had failed to answer Russian ideology with an articulate program and philosophy. Early in 1956 Stevenson told a Los Angeles audience that the use of federal troops to enforce school desegregation court orders would be "a fatal mistake." He explained: "That is exactly what brought on the Civil War. We must proceed gradually, not upsetting habits or traditions that are older than the Republic." Like his hero Abraham Lincoln, Stevenson put the issue of maintaining national unity before that of racial justice. Many Negro newspapers backed Eisenhower, who later ran well in black precincts. Senator Estes Kefauver of Tennessee, whom Stevenson defeated at the 1956 convention, had represented a reformist impulse of greater drive and tenacity, and might have provided a more distinctive program for the Democrats. Kefauver, for example, favored rapid conformity to the Supreme Court decisions on school desegregation, while Stevenson stuck to gradualism—and won an important early primary in Florida. The luster of Stevenson's reputation has been preserved as in amber, but he was a man far removed from the issues that would prevail in the mid-sixties and it is questionable whether he provided much of an alternative to the middle ground of Republican moderates.

In the 1956 election Eisenhower faced the political disadvantages of a serious heart attack suffered in 1955 and of a major operation performed in June 1956. Stevenson, in a moment of bad taste on the eve of the voting, reminded the electorate of the President's condition, commenting that an Eisenhower victory would make Nixon President within four years. But Eisenhower occupied an unassailable position. He had ended the war in Korea and avoided others in Vietnam or China. He also had the good fortune to run while the economy was healthy. Beyond that, Eisenhower stood for reducing tension; in a decade of rapid social change the gentleness and strength of the man—qualities he naturally projected—created an unbeatable appeal. In the last days of the campaign the Middle East crisis further strengthened Eisenhower. His margin of victory did not reach the fabled triumph of FDR twenty years before, but a tally of 457 to 73 electoral votes and a nine million popular vote margin gave the Republicans much reason for self-congratulation. It was a far more conclusive triumph than that of 1952. Even the Democratic Solid South crumbled; Stevenson lost Virginia, Florida, Louisiana, and Texas.

Had they read the congressional returns more carefully, however, the Republicans might have been somewhat less jubilant, for they had not built a lasting national majority. In 1956 Eisenhower ran 6.5 million votes ahead of the Republican congressional candidates. All through the fifties, in fact, the Democrats gradually regained congressional seats they had lost in 1952.

The congressional elections of 1958 produced a landslide for the Democrats and reflected national concerns. The 1957 recession suggested that perhaps only under the Democrats could a stable prosperity be sustained. The Republicans unwisely chose 1958 to push "right to work" or open shop laws through state referenda. The Eisenhower agricultural program favored large farms that employed the latest technology and indirectly forced more and more small farmers to sell their holdings and to become tenants or move into the cities. Here more than in any other area, the Republicans tried to reverse twenty years of Democratic rule, but they scarcely altered the agricultural structures erected by Roosevelt and Truman.

Ever new concerns in foreign policy hampered the Republicans. The Soviets had launched their two Sputniks in October 1957; the second one demonstrated that they had perfected the rocket fuel necessary for space exploration, and that the booster rocket could propel a nuclear weapon at high speed to a radius of 4,000 miles. These developments shocked those who presumed that under a military man, America would naturally hold its own in competition against the Russians. Questions about the administration had already appeared with the dismissal of Eisenhower's closest adviser, Sherman Adams, for accepting gifts. On a broader scale, sociological muckrakers like C. Wright Mills, and journalistic popularizers like Vance Packard, were exposing unsettling social problems. As public opinion polls indicated, attitudes were changing on the government's role in the economy and on a whole range of social issues.

The criticism by publicists probably had less influence on the 1958 election than it did on the Kennedy-Johnson programs of the 1960's. But even Eisenhower, upon leaving office in January 1961, warned of the "military-industrial complex" that Mills and others had described. Certainly the postwar era—the period defined by the problems World War II had created—was coming to an end. No one anticipated in the mid-fifties that the next decade would bring distinct generational shifts among the young. The sixties would also bring much progress, much discord, and much complexity. Even the horror of totalitarianism would lose its simple face. The trial in Israel of Adolf Eichmann revealed that Nazism was the product not only of a mad demagogue, but also of "sensible" bureaucrats. A society might evade madmen with luck, but there seemed no clear way to control the morality of those essential technocrats whose attitudes the culture had revered as a bar against the romantic, the irresponsible, and the sinister.

The Civil Rights Movement and the Warren Court

In spite of his cautious attitude on domestic issues, Eisenhower had appointed one of the most activist of Supreme Court chief justices. The Court under Earl Warren spanned the years 1953—1969, a time of increasingly militant confrontations over civil rights and race relations and of unprecedented dissent from American foreign policy. The Court majority headed by Warren repeatedly intervened in American social life with a series of dramatic decisions, prompting critics to claim that the Court was usurping legislative power and willfully imposing its own blueprints of reform. The energy displayed by the Warren Court was hardly unique: the great chief justices beginning with John Marshall gained renown not for the elegance of their constitutional arguments but for their involvement in social transformation. Surely the Court's enunciation of the doctrine of "separate but equal" in *Plessy* v. *Ferguson* (1896) savored as much of political motivation as the rejection of that position in *Brown* v. *Board of Education* (1954). The defenders and critics of the Warren Court divided ultimately not over the Court's methods but over the wisdom of its decisions.

The personnel of the Warren Court created the most intriguing puzzle. In all, sixteen associate justices served during the Warren years, but the central figures were only three: Warren himself, and Justices Black and Douglas. Warren came to the bench from the moderate wing of the Republican party after two terms as governor of California and an unsuccessful vice-presidential bid as Dewey's 1948 running mate. His appointment by President Eisenhower in 1953 was scarcely taken as a green light for social engineering. Hugo Black, a Democratic Senator from Alabama, had been an honorary Klansman when FDR appointed him to the Court in 1937, yet he staunchly and consistently defended civil liberties. William O. Douglas, the particular target of those who saw the Court as the embodiment of wickedness, worked as a young lawyer for a Wall Street firm and headed the Securities and Exchange Commission before his appointment; his nomination in 1939 aroused in Congress only the fear that he would be too subservient to corporate wealth. Yet these three men gave the Court its distinct cast much more than the appointees of Presidents Kennedy and Johnson.

The impact of the Warren Court's first major decision is still sharply evident; the furor over school desegregation mounted as the focus of compliance moved from South to North. The NAACP, through a team of lawyers headed by Thurgood Marshall, had been hammering away at school segregation for fifteen years before 1954, but the Supreme Court under Chief Justice Vinson responded only by tightening the equality promised under "separate but equal." Then the Warren Court, overturning the "separate but equal" doctrine of *Plessy* v. *Ferguson* (1896), unanimously held in *Brown* v. *Board of Education of Topeka* that "separate educational facilities are inherently unequal." In its unanimous decision the Court mentioned social and psychological factors. The basic constitutional issue, Chief Justice Earl Warren wrote, was whether segregation on the basis of race, even though all other factors were equal, deprived the minority group of equal educational opportunity. "We believe that it does," the nine judges asserted. Since the Fourteenth Amendment guaranteed the "equal protection of the laws," segregation was clearly unconstitutional. Aware that desegregation was not a simple matter, the Court further ordered that steps be taken to implement the decision "with all deliberate speed," a

MY DEAR FELLOW CLERGYMEN, While confined here in the Birmingham City Jail, I came across your recent statement calling our present activities "unwise and untimely." Seldom, if ever, do I pause to answer criticism of my work and ideas. If I sought to answer all of the criticisms that cross my desk, my secretaries would be engaged in little else in the course of the day and I would have no time for constructive work. But since I feel that you are men of genuine good will and your criticisms are sincerely set forth, I would like to answer your statement in what I hope will be patient and reasonable terms. . . .

You deplore the demonstrations that are presently taking place in Birmingham. But I am sorry that your statement did not express a similar concern for the conditions that brought the demonstrations into being. I am sure that each of you would want to go beyond the superficial social analyst who looks merely at effects, and does not grapple with underlying causes. I would not hesitate to say that it is unfortunate that so-called demonstrations are taking place in Birmingham at this time, but I would say in more emphatic terms that it is even more unfortunate that the white power structure of this city left the Negro community with no other alternative.

In any nonviolent campaign there are four basic steps: (1) collection of the facts to determine whether injustices are alive; (2) negotiation; (3) self-purification; and (4) direct action. We have gone through all of these steps in Birmingham. There can be no gainsaying of the fact that racial injustice engulfs this community. Birmingham is probably the most thoroughly segregatd city in the United States. Its ugly record of police brutality is known in every section of this country. Its unjust treatment of Negroes in the courts is a notorious reality. There have been more unsolved bombings of Negro homes and churches in Birmingham than any city in this nation. These are the hard, brutal, and unbelievable facts. On the basis of these conditions Negro leaders sought to negotiate with the city fathers. But the political leaders consistently refused to engage in good faith negotiation.

Then came the opportunity last September to talk with some of the leaders of the economic community. In these negotiating sessions certain promises were made by the merchants—such as the promise to remove the humiliating racial signs from the stores. On the basis of these promises Reverend [Fred] Shuttlesworth and the leaders of the Alabama Christian Movement for Human Rights agreed to call a moratorium on any type of demonstrations. As the weeks and months unfolded we realized that we were victims of a broken promise. The signs remained. As in so many experiences of the past, we were confronted with blasted hopes, and the dark shadow of a deep disappointment settled upon us. So we had no alternative except that of preparing for direct action, whereby we would present our very bodies as means of laying our case before the conscience of the local and national community. . . .

Letter from Birmingham City Jail by The Reverend Martin Luther King, Jr.

King's attack on white moderates who counseled patience is a literary classic; note the stress on non-violence.

loose phrase which allowed a further decade of inaction. Though surprising to laymen, the decision climaxed a long chain of Court action against discrimination. Although the Court did not invent the racial tensions that came to dominate American politics, the Brown decision served as a constant reference point and helped initiate the civil rights movement.

Eisenhower rarely put the moral prestige of his office clearly behind the Court's decision; he told a friend that it had set back progress in the South by at least fifteen years. He believed that the battle against intolerance had to be won in "the hearts of men," not in legislative chambers. Once again, the President resisted expansion of the powers or scope of federal government. A curious ambivalence marked Eisenhower's position on the rights of minorities. Soon after taking office he abolished most public segregation in the District of Columbia and completed desegregation in the armed forces. When violent resistance to school desegregation erupted in Little Rock, Arkansas, in 1957, Eisenhower did not hesitate to enforce federal supremacy. A state court had blocked an integration plan approved by the Little Rock School Board on grounds that violence would break out if it went into operation. When a federal court countermanded this decision and ordered integration, Governor Orville Faubus mobilized the Arkansas National Guard to bar entrance to black students. Eisenhower quickly backed up the authority and supremacy of the federal court. At a private meeting with Faubus, he forced the governor to replace soldiers with policemen and on September 23 blacks entered the school. A violent mob gathered and school authorities sent the black students home. The next day, when the crowd refused to leave, Eisenhower placed the National Guard under federal authority and also ordered paratroops from the United States Army into Little Rock. With bayonets fixed, the troops broke up the mob and stood guard while the integration plan went into effect. Throughout the crisis, the President approached the problem as a constitutional one, a conflict between state and federal authority. He never commented on the *Brown* case—believing a President should not discuss Court decisions—and he did not personally aid desegregation efforts. But in the Little Rock crisis he placed the faith and power of the national government fully, if temporarily, behind the civil rights movement.

In 1956 Attorney General Herbert Brownell transmitted arguments for a strong civil rights bill to Congress, although Eisenhower himself approved only two sections—one calling for an investigatory commission, the other reorganizing the civil rights unit in the Justice Department. Republicans hoping to gain a high Negro vote in the 1956 election convinced the President in October to give lukewarm endorsement to the rest of the proposed legislation, which extended the injunctive powers of the federal government in protecting civil and voting rights. But in July 1957, as the bill was receiving serious consideration in Congress, the President withdrew his support from the critical Part III; at a news conference he answered "no" on whether the attorney general should be allowed to bring about school desegregation suits if local authorities did not request such action. In spite of pleas from prominent blacks to veto a weakened measure and demand something better, the President signed it. Nevertheless, the Civil Rights Act of 1957 was the first federal civil rights legislation in more than eighty years.

Still, the party of emancipation did not take the lead in implementing Negro rights. During the last three years of Eisenhower's administration only forty-nine school districts desegregated—slowing down that must be attributed in part to the President's attitude. And the 1957 legislation added few southern blacks to the voting rolls by 1959. An attempt to pass Part III of the 1957 bill failed again in 1959 with the President flatly opposed. The Civil Rights Act of 1960 at last empowered federal courts to review state voting laws.

Despite the inactivity of the Eisenhower administration, black Americans were changing their perspective on their country more rapidly than any other group. World War II had cracked some of the old customs of segregation. The war economy and subsequent good times produced a new black middle class, more aggressive than its prewar predecessor and unequivocally committed to some type of integration. The Reverend Martin Luther King, Jr., became the foremost spokesman of the new civil rights movement. The bus boycott he directed in 1955 in Montgomery, Alabama, was its first great nonviolent triumph. The National Association for the Advancement of Colored People, founded in 1909, began to push with new force its goals of legal, political, and social equality—the classic aims of integration traditionally contrasted with the self-help methods of Booker T. Washington. Government and education, not business enterprise, would ease entry into the white world.

JFK

Millions of Americans remember the hope and energy that attended the presidency of John Kennedy. He possessed intelligence, good looks, a Harvard education, a war hero's record, and a beautiful wife. For all its overuse, the word "image" is inescapable in any discussion of the Kennedy years. Perhaps the clearest achievement of his administration was his communicating an image of dynamic youthfulness.

The Massachusetts senator of the 1950's gave clues to the later man. A political figure notable for his independence, Kennedy was neither a member of the Senate's inner club nor one of a group of consistent dissenters. In an obvious effort not to antagonize his Irish Catholic supporters, he kept silent on Joseph McCarthy in the early 1950's. When Eleanor Roosevelt asked him to go on record against the late senator at the end of the decade, Kennedy pointed out that doing it then would be hypocritical, though it would bring needed convention support. It was hard to comprehend an eager young senator who denounced the labor leader Jimmy Hoffa on grounds that he had "no discrimination or taste or style. . . . " In short, he was refreshing and unpredictable, commanding the resources of an immense fortune; yet because of his Roman Catholic religion he was a political underdog.

When he first entered national politics in 1956 as a candidate for the vice-presidency, Kennedy allowed his adviser Ted Sorenson to leak a memorandum arguing that a Catholic candidate would strengthen rather than harm a national ticket. Kennedy also let himself be cast as a Northerner friendly to the South and willing to let that section move slowly on the race issue. He thus lost in 1956 to Senator Estes Kefauver of Tennessee. In 1958 he won re-election in Massachusetts by 875,000 votes, the largest majority in the state's history. He apparently sensed the changed priority in the electorate in the later 1950's, for he dwelt on national preparedness and the need for "moving ahead" in all areas of national life.

Thanks to shrewd political methods and an able staff, by 1960 Kennedy held a commanding lead in the race for the Democratic presidential nomination. But party leaders worried about his religion and his youthfulness—he would have to prove himself in the primaries. The first major test came in early April against Minnesota's Senator Hubert Humphrey in Wisconsin. But the results were inconclusive, for although Kennedy won a majority of the votes, the state's large Catholic population made it untypical of the nation at large. He would have to prove his vote-getting ability again in West Virginia on May 10. Humphrey campaigned strenuously in that state on economic and social issues. Kennedy obviously responded to what he saw of poverty, and he strongly emphasized the need for a more active economy. He repeatedly drew attention to his religion, asserting that it posed no threat to other Americans. He believed the Protestant Democrats of West Virginia would not consider religion a leading issue, for the nation had changed in the years that separated Kennedy from Al Smith, the Catholic Democratic presidential candidate in 1928. Also, the average West Virginian sensed that he was being tested and that his state's vote would be seen by the country at large as a repudiation or an endorsement of religious bigotry. Accordingly, Kennedy won 61 percent of the primary vote.

After West Virginia it was plain that Kennedy would be the nominee. The tumultuous greeting given him in mid-July outside the Biltmore Hotel in Los Angeles showed he had garnered an enthusiastic convention following. Senator Eugene McCarthy of Minnesota eloquently nominated Adlai Stevenson, who was willing to be drafted: "Do not reject this man who made us all proud to be called Democrats . . . ." Stevenson replied with some characteristically self-deprecatory humor—he seemed, so said his detractors, to want to be appointed President. Kennedy, who easily defeated all his challengers, hoped for a united party despite the platform's strong civil rights section. Many Northern Democrats and labor leaders were chagrined at Kennedy's choice of Lyndon B. Johnson of Texas as his running mate, but they had nowhere to turn because the Republican party had nominated their old enemy, Vice-President Richard Nixon.

Nixon enjoyed a substantial lead in postconvention polls, but bad luck plagued him throughout the campaign. Nixon suffered an infected knee in August which postponed the beginning of his campaign for two weeks and left him fatigued and an easy prey to colds. Nixon's running mate, Henry Cabot Lodge, Jr., was a slow-paced campaigner. President Eisenhower's planned May summit meeting with Khrushchev collapsed after the Soviet Union shot down a U-2 reconnaissance plane deep in Russian territory. Later in the spring Ike canceled a visit to Japan because of anti-American sentiment. The President hardly helped Nixon by an offhand response to a reporter's question about what major administrative decisions Nixon had participated in: "If you give me a week I might think of one." And in the closing weeks of the campaign Nixon could not make use of Eisenhower, who was in fragile health. Finally, Norman Vincent Peale, Nixon's own pastor, condemned Kennedy on religious grounds, giving credence to the view that the Catholic candidate was indeed a victim of prejudice. Methodist leaders gave Kennedy a dramatic opportunity to prove to a skeptical audience of Houston ministers—by way of television to the nation at large—that they had no religious reasons to fear him. Here again Kennedy stood in sharp contrast to Al Smith. Smith had regarded as bigotry the mere questioning of his faith, while Kennedy welcomed queries and responded openly and at length.

In the course of the campaign Kennedy emerged as the more activist candidate, while Vice-President Nixon had to defend the Eisenhower administration. When Kennedy endlessly said it was time "to get moving again" he referred principally to the national economy. But economic expansion also had its foreign policy dimension. Kennedy repeatedly charged that the Russians held a lead over America in the development of missiles. He managed to link the issues of national prestige and economic growth, implying that Nixon, as a high official in the decent but ineffectual Eisenhower administration, could not solve these problems. Kennedy's charm and confident handling of the complexities of public problems cast him as a man with a more dashing and more effective response to the familiar problems of the 1950's. Nixon agreed to a series of television debates in which Kennedy appeared fresher and more vibrant, thus confirming in the minds of voters the contrast between him and the exhausted Republican candidate.

Still, the electorate expressed no clear preference for Kennedy over Nixon. Kennedy won the election with less than 51 percent of the two-party vote, and by 303 to 219 in the electoral college. The solid South, broken in the 1950's by Eisenhower, remained split in 1960: Nixon received almost half its vote. Anti-Catholicism weighed against Kennedy in the South, though his losses in that section were partially balanced by gains in im-

Various ethnic jokes were popular in the 1960's.

portant urban areas in evenly contested states. Many voters in 1960 clearly preferred the tension-reducing style of Nixon to the vigorous thrusts of Kennedy. The new President—the second youngest, at forty-three, in American history—seemed to sense that, for he immediately took steps to draw the nation together. He met with Nixon in Florida after the election. He retained such icons of government as J. Edgar Hoover of the FBI and Allen Dulles of the Central Intellegence Agency. This meant not only that he wanted continuity in government but also that he had patience with symbols of the past. In January he forced through a change in the size of the House Rules Committee, "packing" it with his supporters, but here the closeness of victory reinforced a cautious approach to the domestic scene.

A Darkening Plain: Kennedy Foreign Policy

It was in foreign affairs that Kennedy determined to leave his mark. Although remarkably bellicose, he foresaw the end of atomic confrontation and the coming of a new age of wars of na-

tional liberation. With problems like Cuba and Laos in mind, Kennedy joined Generals Maxwell Taylor and Matthew Ridgway in calling for a more mobile and technically skilled armed forces

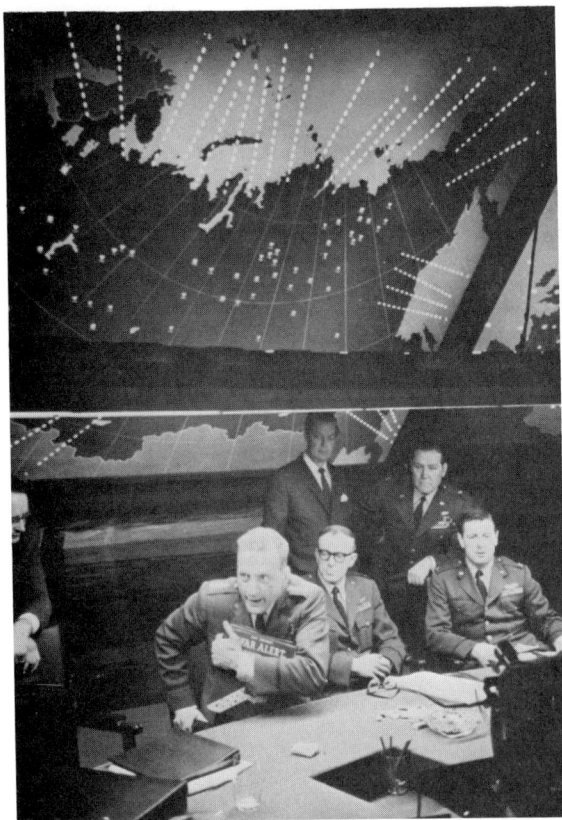

Dr. Strangelove, or, How I Stopped Worrying and Learned to Love the Atomic Bomb, 1964. *A bitter satire of American politics and the Cold War, Dr. Strangelove put the blame for atomic disaster on the fathomless idiocy of human beings.*

capable of fighting in limited wars. (Taylor, who had retired in 1959 protesting Eisenhower's policies, returned in 1961 as a prime adviser and in 1962 became chief of staff.) Kennedy's background made him especially receptive to the new brand of warfare: a naval hero, a reader of James Bond stories, the creator of the Green Berets, he combined a fascination for military technology with a sense of military dash and elitism. He welcomed the opportunity to build heroic new armed forces. Yet at the same time Kennedy seemed to believe that he could bring about an easing of international tension.

The main thrust of Kennedy's foreign policy was suggested by his cabinet selections. For secretary of state Kennedy turned to the State Department bureaucracy for Dean Rusk, a strong-willed man who favored cold war policy goals if not traditional techniques. Robert McNamara brought a degree of efficiency to the Defense Department, but rarely disagreed on policy with the joint chiefs of staff.

Some of the foreign policy attitudes Kennedy brought to office quickly took concrete form in the Bay of Pigs fiasco. Under the Eisenhower administration, the Central Intelligence Agency had prepared an invasion force to spark a general uprising against Fidel Castro in Cuba. More than a thousand Cuban refugee guerrillas awaited orders on a coffee plantation in a mountainous region of Guatemala. To cancel the planned invasion, Kennedy reasoned, would make the new administration look weak. So in April of 1961 he gave the signal. The CIA chose a well-fortified landing spot, which allowed the rebels no opportunity to retreat to the mountains. The motley force put large quantities of radio equipment and munitions in a single boat, which was blown up; air cover was wholly inadequate. Castro easily destroyed the invaders.

Kennedy apparently thought that the well-entrenched Castro could be overthrown without the cooperation of the United States air force, army, and navy. Perhaps the anti-Communist traditions of his family and church, and the memory of congressional resolutions calling for the "liberation" of Eastern Europe, had engendered in Kennedy such naivete. He may have entertained the fallacious premises that people who lived under any form of communism yearned for freedom and would revolt if given an opportunity, and that since communism was evil it could not succeed. Certainly the President braced himself for conflict. He believed that during his administration America would face the greatest crises of its history. His inaugural and state of the union addresses conveyed the need for austere self-discipline in order to prepare for an era of testing and danger.

One Kennedy response to the failure in Cuba was to press for an Alliance for Progress, a $10 billion, decade-long program of economic aid to Latin America. Also in 1961 the Development Loan Fund provided over a billion American dollars in aid to underdeveloped nations. The Bay of Pigs, which ironically lifted his standing in public opinion polls, made Kennedy more rather than less belligerent. He pushed harder for greater military spending, and in 1961 Congress responded with a 15 per cent increase. Kennedy discounted the argument that building up an arsenal of new weapons would provoke the Soviet Union into a like response. Nevertheless, the Russians did respond with a similar increase in their defense expenditures.

In June 1961 Kennedy and Khrushchev met in Vienna, where they accomplished little except an exchange of views. As Kennedy judged his rhetoric, Khrushchev seemed intransigently committed to disrupting world order, for he threatened to sign a peace treaty with East Germany. At worst this could lead to a ban on entering Berlin, at best force us to negotiate with a government we had not recognized. Kennedy hoped that future changes in the world would take place without upsetting this balance between West and East. For Khrushchev, any sort of global freeze would disrupt the revolutionary process itself. At Vienna the Soviets sought to counter Western economic expansionism with an assertion of the right to rebel against reactionary governments.

The encounter discouraged Kennedy. Upon returning home he increased draft quotas, called up the reserves, demanded a crash civil defense program that led to a popular frenzy of bomb shelters and asked for estimates on casualties in the event of a nuclear war. Dean Acheson urged a hard line on Berlin, calling it a "simple contest of wills." He recommended sending a division of American troops on the autobahn through East Germany to Berlin, and urged Kennedy to make it clear that we would fight a nuclear war if necessary. Since there was nothing to negotiate, a willingness to go to the conference table would be taken as a sign of weakness. When Khrushchev in August acceded to the construction of the Berlin Wall, sealing off East Berlin from the western sector, Kennedy remained distraught, remarking that there was one chance in five of a nuclear exchange. He sent 1,500 troops from West Germany to West Berlin, and Vice-President Johnson came to pledge American lives to the defense of the city. When it eventually became clear to Washington that the wall was only a defensive measure, some congressmen charged that the administration had overreacted on Berlin, that Kennedy had created a pseudo-crisis.

Apart from Berlin, world tension remained high. In September 1961 Russia began to detonate nuclear bombs of enormous power; America followed suit in the spring of 1962. The older Eisenhower-Dulles policy of massive retaliation now existed perilously alongside a new Kennedy policy of conventional arms and a willingness to use them in any part of the world. On every continent ambitious third powers threatened to upset the world balance and precipitate the ultimate conflict between the Soviet Union and the United States.

In distant Southeast Asia, the existing regimes in both Laos and South Vietnam were endangered by indigenous Communist forces. In Laos the President, remembering the Bay of Pigs, avoided

direct intervention. He also sensed that America, as he uncharacteristically expressed in a speech at the University of Washington in November 1961, "cannot impose [its] will upon the other 94 percent of mankind . . . . We cannot right every wrong or reverse each adversity. . . . There cannot be an American solution to every world problem." Kennedy eventually compromised by abandoning a right-wing faction in Laos and supporting a "neutral and independent" government. Here perhaps the President had made some headway with Khrushchev in Vienna: the Russians also exercised their influence in behalf of neutrality. Eventually the parties agreed on a "troika" coalition government in 1962, which at least succeeded in approving a genuine cease-fire.

In October 1962 the world came close to nuclear war. The previous winter the United States stopped altogether the importing of Cuban sugar. In response, Castro decided in the late spring to allow the Russians to place intermediate-range missiles in Cuba; never before had the Soviet Union placed missiles outside its own national boundaries. Our air surveillance first revealed the sites as their construction neared completion. Kennedy quickly decided that we could not tolerate interference in an area so patently within America's sphere of influence. Although quite congruent to international law, and no real military threat to the United States, the placing of missiles was a blatant challenge to the balance of power dictum Kennedy had outlined in Vienna. Khrushchev had evidently decided to test American intentions. His justification was the protection of a sovereign Cuba against a United States invasion—a possibility Kennedy's Bay of Pigs fiasco made not unreasonable even in the opinion of our allies.

Both the President's military consultants and Dean Acheson recommended an immediate air strike, which would wipe out Russian advisers along with the missiles. But Robert McNamara and Robert Kennedy disagreed; the attorney general argued that it was not in the American grain to launch an air attack against a small island unable to retaliate. America would be faithless to its past if it attacked Cuba much as the Japanese had attacked Pearl Harbor.

The President decided on a less drastic course; he instituted a naval blockade against Russian ships bringing additional missile equipment to Cuba. Kennedy set the barrier as close to the Caribbean as he dared, hoping that Khrushchev would decide not to risk an incident. The US permitted a harmless tanker to penetrate the quarantine area, but then, as millions waited breathlessly, the first ship carrying technical equipment turned back. Some critics blamed Kennedy for bringing the world close to the brink of nuclear war—unnecessarily because he could have brought about an exchange: the Soviet Union evidently would have given up the missile sites if the United States had relinquished some useless Turkish bases on its borders. Khrushchev, they said, displayed the greater maturity by refusing to risk war. But Kennedy, too, had exercised some restraint in the face of a Soviet provocation, and did promise not to attempt further aggression against Cuba. Before his countrymen Kennedy appeared a courageous and mature statesman. Since the crisis occurred just before the mid-term elections, it probably helped the Democrats to achieve an excellent performance for a party in power at off-year.

After the missile crisis, antagonism between Russia and the United States shifted to the third world. There confrontation would continue but with less immediate risk of world-shaking consequences. Direct relations between the two superpowers, in fact, underwent a kind of thaw. A "hot line" insured instantaneous telephone communication in emergencies. Kennedy, in a speech at American University in June 1963, heralded a new era of cooperation between the two countries. In that year, too, the Soviets rejected Chinese militance, insisting on an era of peaceful coexistence and the avoidance of nuclear war. Finally, the Test Ban Treaty of 1963 outlawed atmospheric testing of nuclear weapons. This became the only enduring accomplishment of Kennedy's foreign policy, even though two powers close to a nuclear capacity, France and Communist China, refused to sign.

Until the missile crisis Kennedy had to direct his abundant energies largely toward foreign policy. Congress in 1961 passed several administration measures: a higher minimum wage law; a Housing Act, which granted almost $5 billion for urban renewal projects; an Area Redevelopment Act, which provided funds for retraining in areas of high unemployment; and money for water pollution control. Although some of his cabinet appointees, like Stewart L. Udall of the Interior Department, promoted conservation programs, the President did not press Congress for new welfare or social legislation. Udall, after speaking to the President about conservation in the summer of 1961, remarked: "He's imprisoned by Berlin." In 1962 and 1963 few Kennedy laws passed Congress. The President himself lacked the time or patience necessary to work on details of legislation. Whenever Secretary of Health, Education and Welfare Anthony Celebrezze tried to engage him in discussion about proposed laws, the President cut him off, saying, "You were the mayor of a large city. You know how to handle these problems. Now handle them."

The Civil Rights Movement: II

On the major domestic issue of the era, that of civil rights, John Kennedy brought to the Presidency a record of compromise and expediency. He voted twice to weaken the 1957 Civil Rights Act: to return the bill to committee where Senator James Eastland of Mississippi might strip it to nothing; and in favor of a successful amendment guaranteeing jury trials in contempt cases (white Southern juries could be relied upon not to convict civil rights violators). But Title III of the act, which promised decisive action in school desegregation, received his support. In both Kennedy's Vice-Presidential campaigns he sought support from the most truculent segregationist governors. He seemed scarcely aware of the moderate civil rights movement that crystallized after the Supreme Court desegregation decision of 1954.

The first massive direct action in the civil rights movement came in Montgomery, Alabama. There, in 1955, under the leadership of Martin Luther King, Jr., blacks refused to patronize the city's public transportation system, which required that they sit in the rear of buses. After months of unrelenting economic boycott, the city fathers agreed to end the demeaning practice, in the first great victory of the movement. In February 1960 four black college students in Greensboro, North Carolina, sat down at the local Woolworth's segregated lunch counter. They asked for cups of coffee but were summarily refused. They remained seated. The next day sixteen fellow students joined their sit-in and the group attracted attention in the national media. On the third day, more than fifty students came, joined by a few white girls from the prestigious Women's College of North Carolina.

The effect was electric. The sit-ins spread, first to other stores in Greensboro and later to more than a hundred other towns and cities. The white-led Congress of Racial Equality assumed leadership, offering a generation of experience with nonviolent direct action techniques. The legal defense fund of the National Association for the Advancement of Colored People, founded in 1911, aided students imprisoned by local authorities. The membership of the Southern Christian Leadership Conference expanded, and the Student Non-Violent Coordinating Committee—the guiding force of the student movement in the South—was born. Even the staid Urban League, under its new leader Whitney Young, Jr., supported the campaigns of Martin Luther King.

President Kennedy did not seem to care deeply about the fleeting dream of the early civil rights movement, a community of brotherhood bound by love. In January he omitted civil rights from a list of the "real issues of 1960." Along with Richard Nixon, Kennedy made promises during the presidential campaign, but he translated few of them into concrete proposals after he took office. His telephone message of sympathy to Mrs. Martin Luther King while her husband sat in an Atlanta jail was a symbolic gesture of great political value, but it ironically summed up his detachment—it was a gesture that led to no lasting achievement.

Genuinely fearful of losing support for other programs, Kennedy sent no new civil rights legislation to Congress in 1961 and 1962. During the campaign he had castigated President Eisenhower for tolerating segregation in federally financed housing. It took Kennedy two years to make good on his promise to eliminate it with "a stroke of the presidential pen" (he received thousands of pens through the mail), and even then he acted deviously, burying the order among more striking acts so that the presidential deed earned him little credit or blame. He did appoint Vice-President Johnson to head a new Committee on Equal Employment Opportunity, and Johnson, with some success, used his powers of persuasion to insure that blacks would be employed under all types of federal contracts. In addresses at Gettysburg and Detroit in 1963, Johnson spoke sincerely and strongly for full civil rights—and with a southern accent. Kennedy also appointed the prominent Negro, Robert C. Weaver, to be federal housing administrator. yet the President generally followed the Eisenhower pattern and seemed not to realize the explosive potential of the race situation. Had he sensed it he would never have appointed his brother attorney general, for that office would bear the brunt of white resentments. Robert Kennedy, in fact, accomplished what little the government did for the Negro before 1963. He tried to enforce the weak laws of the fifties, especially those requiring the desegregation of transportation facilities, and he speeded voter registration of Southern blacks. The freedom rides of 1961, designed to desegregate bus station waiting rooms, required Robert Kennedy to send federal marshals into Alabama to protect the young people, although he had tried to discourage the project. But RFK's efforts were cancelled out when his brother appointed outspoken segregationists to lifetime positions on several Southern district courts.

The civil rights movement proceeded without Kennedy, eventually forcing him to act. Coverage by the media sustained the conviction of coming success with television in particular dramatically transmitting the new tactics: confrontation, the threat of violence from the opposition, the posing of moral issues in absolute terms. The forward momentum continued in 1961 with the freedom rides and in the fall of 1962 with James Meredith's attempted enrollment at the University of Mississippi. The next year federal troops came to the university to enroll Meredith, and Vivian Malone entered the University of Alabama under similar conditions in the spring of 1963. The most incendiary situation, however, developed in Birmingham, Alabama, during May 1963. The only strategy that could work for the oppressed blacks in that city was the forcing of masssive arrests. Vivid events transpired: police dogs, electric cattle prods, and fire hoses; rioting, bombing, and three small Negro children dead. And Kennedy, foreseeing the "fires of frustration and discord . . . burning in every city, North and South," responded. He asked Congress to pass a civil rights bill ending segregation in most public places. At last the national administration of the Democratic party drew its mantle about the civil rights movement.

In 1963 Kennedy, a majority of Congress, the churches, and much of the nation finally awakened to some of the inequities suffered by American blacks. The President requested a partial ban on discrimination in public places, asked for Justice Department powers to sue for school desegregation if requested to do so, and urged broader powers to withhold funds from federally assisted programs in which discrimination occurred. Congressional civil rights leaders pushed Kennedy further, persuading him to give the attorney general power to intervene in all civil rights cases. But Kennedy told a press conference that tax reform was more important than the rights bill; a stronger economy, he believed, would help blacks more than anything else. Before his death later that fall, he secured an agreement from congressional leaders that would probably have led to the passage of a civil rights act in 1964.

Martin Luther King complained in June 1963 that Kennedy might have done "a little more" for blacks than Eisenhower, but "the plight of the vast majority of Negroes remains the same." King himself was the hero of the early movement. When 250,000 people marched on Washington the next August to be counted for the proposed legislation, King addressed them: "I have a dream that one day on the red hills of Georgia the sons of former slaves and the sons of former slaveholders will be able to sit down together at the table of brotherhood. I have a dream that one day even the state of Mississippi, a desert state sweltering with the heat of injustice and oppression, will be transformed into an oasis of freedom and justice . . . I have a dream that one day the state of Alabama . . . will be transformed into a situation where little black boys and black girls will be able to join hands with little white boys and white girls and walk together as sisters and brothers." Despite Kennedy's failure to share King's vision, in few places did the President's assassination that November arouse such an outpouring of grief as in black communities. Efforts to pass legislation gained strength by construing it as a memorial to Kennedy; Congress easily approved the first law in 1964, and others followed in 1965 and 1966.

The early, nonviolent civil rights movement died with Kennedy or soon afterward. It had always been a fragile coalition. Dependent on keeping the race problem confined to the South and on the acquiescence of lower-class blacks not able to profit from its goals, the movement broke apart in the era of ghetto riots, Northern demonstrations, and growing black nationalism.

The New Frontier: Substance or Style?

Kennedy's most successful domestic accomplishment came belatedly in his handling of economic problems. In the 1960 campaign he had charged the Eisenhower administration with failing to maintain as high a national growth rate as that of Western Europe or the Soviet Union. Once in office, though, Kennedy acted cautiously. To cure the recession that Nixon later claimed had cost him the Presidency, Kennedy relied on piecemeal measures including the raising of social security payments and the minimum wage—techniques akin to those Eisenhower had employed. Increased military spending, too, helped alleviate unemployment. Until the third quarter of 1962 his prudent policies held the cost of living steady without causing either substantial new unemployment or inflation.

A severe drop in the stock market began in May 1962. It threatened the somewhat shaky prosperity and persuaded Kennedy to embark upon a venturesome new policy. Treasury Secretary Douglas Dillon, a Republican, had been convinced of the need for more federal action through the patient counsel of Kennedy's chief economic adviser, Walter Heller. For the first time during relatively prosperous times, an administration proposed a budget deficit through tax reduction, much more acceptable to business than new spending. The Senate concurred in a reversal of its earlier views. When Senator Paul Douglas had asked for a $6 billion tax cut in 1958 he was rebuffed by a vote of 65 to 23. Yet in 1964, 77 senators favored a tax cut of over $10 billion—and at a time when the economy merely lagged. The economy responded; the tax cuts helped spur a $30 billion yearly increase in stable dollars in the gross national product, and unemployment declined sharply.

Although businessmen profited enormously from the expansive economy, they never trusted John Kennedy. Kennedy signed tax credits and a generous depreciation allowance for business in 1962, and reduced corporate income taxes by 20 percent in 1963, gifts of unprecedented generosity. The Trade Expansion Act of 1962 won some business concessions from the European Common Market through a mutual reduction of tariffs. But in April 1962 Kennedy so confronted the steel industry that, for many businessmen, his name would join that of a despised Franklin Roosevelt.

On April 10, late in the afternoon, Roger Blough, chairman of United States Steel, appeared at the White House for an appointment with the President. He told Kennedy that even as they spoke press releases were announcing a steel price rise. The President was furious. Labor Secretary Arthur Goldberg had persuaded the unions to settle for a modest wage hike on the understanding that prices would remain steady. Blough seemed both to deceive and insult the President of the United States. Kennedy privately quoted his father's denunciation of businessmen as "sons of bitches" and launched an unprecedented government attack on the industry. The Defense Department threatened to shift steel contracts to the small companies that had not yet raised prices; the Justice Department and the Federal Trade Commission threatened antitrust action and the passage of new antitrust laws; the Treasury hinted at a tax investigation. Kennedy himself spoke on television: "In this serious hour in our nation's history, when we are confronted with grave crises in Berlin and Southeast Asia . . . , the American public will find it hard, as I do, to accept a situation in which a tiny handful of steel executives whose pursuit of private power and profit exceeds their sense of public responsibility can show such utter contempt of the interests of 185 million Americans." It was a spectacular display of presidential power (including an obscure role for the FBI) in the service of what he believed to be the public interest. Big steel, following the lead of some smaller companies, grudgingly rescinded the increase.

Belatedly successful in managing the economy, Kennedy gave promise later in 1963 of responding to more domestic needs in the next years of his administration. Then he went to Dallas. Riding unprotected in an open car, Kennedy was an easy target for an assassin's bullet. Lee Harvey Oswald, a refugee of the political Left, evidently killed Kennedy. The presidential plane promptly flew his body home to Washington where the next day, November 23, a Roman Catholic mass was held in the White House. Chief Justice Earl War-

ren directed a comprehensive but hurried report on the killing, which uncovered no evidence of conspiracy. Subsequent efforts to link Oswald with one or more additional marksmen or conspirators remain highly speculative.

The achievement of the Kennedy administration lay elsewhere than in a relatively meager legislative record. Kennedy occupied the office during a demanding time. His ultimate success with the economy and the fruitful negotiation of the Test Ban Treaty brightened only the end of his 1,000 days. But, as all Presidents, he gave something intangible to the country. The Kennedy style, whatever the vague word means, had its trivial side. Memory of him was colored by his youthful appearance and his vigor, by fashionable form more than by substance. Yet, Kennedy's name, quite apart from the President's acts or statements, rekindled hope. A people of growing affluence, still emerging from a restricting past, reacted in different ways to the inflated values the Kennedys represented. Most important was the President's effect on many of the young. By the end of his administration the life of business no longer held great appeal for college students; they increasingly desired something more personally rewarding and idealistic, such as the Peace Corps. He surely had some impact on their changing taste. Through the office of the attorney general, he gave some legitimacy to their new political involvements, and along with it to a more relaxed life-style, to passive nonviolence, and to the stirrings of a coming estrangement.

LBJ

President Kennedy once told an off-the-record press conference that he did not have much hope for solving America's problems. Kennedy's pessimistic vision of what was possible for mankind—a side of his intellectual sophistication not sufficiently appreciated—inevitably narrowed his perspective and his goals. In sharp contrast to Kennedy, Lyndon Johnson's strength—and his weakness— lay in a faith that in America government could accomplish almost anything. Johnson's pride, daring, and technical skill reached their greatest effectiveness in attacking stubborn domestic ills. During his years in office Congress passed more laws for civil rights, health, and education, the arts and science, the eradication of pover-

ty, and aid for the cities than in any earlier era.

Johnson's confidence originated in the New Deal of Franklin Roosevelt. Raised in the hill country of central Texas, Johnson himself knew at first hand the brutalizing effects of poverty. His calculating ambition was evident at Southwest Texas State Teachers College: he dominated the student body and managed to influence the administration as well. Afterward he taught briefly in a rural school and learned somthing of the needs of poor Mexican Americans. In 1931 he moved to Washington, D.C., where he served as secretary to a Texas congressman and soon aspired to Congress himself. Securing the friendship of President Roosevelt helped: an appointment as Texas director of the National Youth Administration gave Johnson a base from which he campaigned successfully for a congressional seat in 1937. Roosevelt's efforts to raise Johnson to the Senate came to naught, but under the President's tutelage Johnson grew to appreciate both New Deal welfare programs and the art of political manipulation.

After the war Texas politics became more cautious, and Johnson seemed to bend with the times. He became closely identified with some of the natural gas and oil interests and took special care of the burgeoning aircraft industry. In 1947 he voted with the majority of Congress to override President Truman's veto of the moderately antilabor Taft-Hartley Act. He judged well in taking such a course; it helped him to win an extremely close, contested election to the United States Senate in 1948. Though often an ally of Southern segregationists, he remained sufficiently independent to earn the trust and respect of many Northerners, including Senator Hubert Humphrey of Minnesota.

With the coming of the Eisenhower era Johnson moved to the political center; in 1955, by virtue of his impressive legislative skill and bland ideology he won the post of Senate majority leader. Willing to work with the President on foreign policy and economic matters during his first term in the White House, Johnson by 1957 had abandoned the Republican pleas for thrift and called for greater public spending to offset the recession and to fill defense needs. Everything Johnson did portrayed him as a masterful politician. Many Democrats were delighted when in 1959 he led them in a stereotyped crusade against the appointment of Admiral Lewis Strauss as secretary of commerce.

Given his personal temperament, Johnson probably thought of running for the presidency at an early date, but was deterred by a major heart attack in 1955. In 1960, however, he became a presidential candidate although he entered no primaries, preferring to stick to Senate business in Washington. Johnson's Southern origins hindered his efforts. While John Kennedy's Roman Catholicism was both a positive and a negative reference point in the nation at large, Johnson's presumed sectionalism, in a time when the civil rights movement was reaching its full strength, counted against him outside the South. After Johnson's candidacy failed, Kennedy thought it desirable to have the popular Southerner as a running mate. Analysts who wonder why Johnson was willing to "retire" to the Vice-Presidency perhaps fail to remember the obsessive fascination the highest office holds for inveterate politicians like Lyndon

Johnson; though an isolated position, the Vice-Presidency brought him closer to the White House than he had been in the Senate.

What made the new office lonely was the lack of power and status attached to it. Except for executive control over Texas patronage, Johnson had to search out positions of leadership. By 1961, if not before, he had become convinced of the civil rights movement's moral status and political appeal among many Northerners, and he gladly accepted an offer to head the President's Committee on Equal Employment. Here he learned the limits of persuasion as a means to accomplish fair employment practices. Johnson also became a spokesman for the exploration of space, heading up a committee for that end; he was always on hand for each new extraterrestrial encounter.

Johnson's best-known role as Vice-President was that of a traveling emissary of the United States. In Berlin, during a tense weekend in 1961, he magnificently reassured the people of the Western sector who were anguished over the erection of the Berlin Wall. Always a hard-liner on the Cold War, Johnson had contemptuously rejected efforts to conciliate the Soviet Union. In 1954, anxious to secure a strong position against Joe McCarthy, he had said that Red China should never be admitted to the United Nations; in that year he also helped Hubert Humphrey pass a bill outlawing the American Communist party. In 1956 he disdained Adlai Stevenson's suggestions to end nuclear testing or to abolish the draft. Johnson's views seemed unchanged during his Vice-Presidency. In 1961 he visited Premier Diem of South Vietnam and called him the "Churchill of Asia," and recommended greater United States involvement in Southeast Asia. Throughout the Kennedy years he supported the growing commitment in Vietnam.

In the days following the assassination of Kennedy, Johnson behaved with skill and tact. He publicly dedicated himself to fulfilling the Kennedy program and reassured the nation by persuading Chief Justice Earl Warren and other notable figures to serve on a panel to investigate the killing. He persuaded all of Kennedy's advisers to stay on, at least for a time, and gave Jacqueline Kennedy ample time to leave the White House. There is good reason to suppose that Kennedy would have expanded his social programs into something like Johnson's Great Society; before his death his executive staff was working on antipoverty proposals that became law in 1964 and 1965. The tax cut, already assured in October 1963, created an expansive economy in which his reelection would have been likely. But Johnson's aggressive mastery carried such programs to a greater intensity. He gathered into his policy much of what had latently existed for a decade, and he completed and presided over a loose coalition that had its origins in the elections of 1958.

Such coalitions as Johnson's are familiar in American history, accomplishing in a few years of intense activity what reformers had wanted for many years. The Johnson coalition, or convergence of interest groups, originated in the spring of 1963, drawing energy from the new economic and civil rights proposals of Kennedy, whose death gave it added force.

To Republican party leaders the nomination of Barry Goldwater for President in 1964 was a calculated risk. A year so bleak for the Republicans could put to the test an old proposition that there was a large potential electorate made up of nonvoters and working-class Democrats that would awaken and come to the polls for the right candidate. Goldwater accepted the nomination in the spirit that would dominate his campaign: "Anyone who joins us in all sincerity we welcome. Those who do not care for our cause, we don't expect to enter our ranks . . . . Extremism in the defense of liberty is no vice . . . . Moderation in the pursuit of justice is no virtue."

During the course of the campaign Goldwater retreated from some of his extreme positions expressed earlier in his books, *Why Not Victory?* and *The Conscience of a Conservative.* Although signed by Goldwater, ghost writers had composed them. In the campaign he still revealed a knack for making a handicap of honesty. In Appalachia he insisted on attacking the poverty program; in Knoxville, Tennessee, he declared in favor of selling part of the Tennessee Valley Authority; in St. Petersburg, Florida, a city filled with retired people, he criticized social security; in North Dakota he told farmers that a decline in price supports would be good for them. Vice-Presidential candidate Miller on Labor Day criticized liberal immigration policies before an audience composed chiefly of first-and second-generation immigrants.

Many Republicans deserted Goldwater. The Democrats seized the opportunity to portray Goldwater as extreme and unpredictable: one television commercial showed a social security card being ripped in two; another vicious one (repudiated by Johnson) pictured a little girl counting petals plucked from a daisy until a mushroom cloud appeared, while a voice urged the prudent to vote for Johnson. One magazine had the audacity to poll psychiatrists by mail in an attempt to demonstrate Goldwater's psychic shortcomings; it was no credit to the profession

that hundreds offered highly speculative responses.

Goldwater was a patriot; at his Arizona ranch an electronic gadget raised the American flag at dawn and lowered it at sunset. But Johnson's use of two minor incidents in the Gulf of Tonkin to justify retaliatory bombing of North Vietnam made it impossible for him to be cast as an appeaser. Most of Johnson's attention went, in Richard Rovere's words, "to evangelistic and almost utopian views of the future." Bold and all-encompassing, the Johnson program remained in the tradition of the New Deal, and by the 1960's this was a moderate position. On the other hand, many voters perceived the Goldwater alternative as a dangerous departure from the status quo. Crop subsidies and social security were preferable to some ill-defined and risky adventure against international communism.

All the pollsters agreed that November 4 would be a cold day for Goldwater. The election turned on the question of whether Goldwater should be President; the answer was a resounding no. He carried only his home state, plus Mississippi (where he won 87 percent of the vote), Louisiana, Alabama, South Carolina, and Georgia. The Democrats maintained their two-to-one Senate margin and picked up thirty-eight more seats in the House, enhancing prospects for Great Society legislation. Such were the results of the Republican candidate's "Southern strategy." In part its employment was simply premature; the candidacy may have marshaled opposition to bureaucratic reform with a substantial future impact. The race issue had not yet ripened to cause a backlash against the Democrats among whites in the North.

The first landmark of the Great Society was the tax reduction bill of 1964, which had been in the works for some time. By reducing income tax rates a total of $11 billion, individuals and corporations would have increased spending power. This resulting increase in demand would then spur production, slacken unemployment, and ultimately swell federal revenues. Some economists who endorsed the idea doubted whether $11 billion was enough to produce the desired effect, while the prospect of bigger federal deficits alarmed fiscal conservatives. To pacify those who charged fiscal irresponsibility, Johnson promised to cut spending by $4 billion, beginning with the symbolic gesture of turning off the White House lights at night. But Congress defeated attempts to couple tax reduction to tax reform by closing some long-standing loopholes. The final bill cut personal income taxes by $9 billion and corporate taxes by $2 billion, with impressive results. Unemployment fell in 1965 to the lowest level in eight years, and federal revenues actually rose. On the other hand, the tax cut, along with other incentives to activate business and the pressures of massive spending for the war in Indochina, probably contributed to the inflationary economy of the late 1960's and 1970's.

President Johnson had seen much of poverty during his youth; its abolition became his next major goal. In the Eisenhower era urban renewal had simply aggravated the social conditions its advocates sought to improve. As with tax reform, Kennedy realized the potential political dividends and had prepared the way. His poverty programs included the retraining and rehabilitation of the unemployed, area redevelopment, the eradication of illiteracy, youth employment, and accelerated public works in poverty regions. By 1963 coordinated efforts were underway in several large cities. Johnson brought these programs and others together early in 1964 by declaring a "war on poverty"—a theme he found irresistible considering the impending presidential campaign. After hearing from the Council of Economic Advisers that 20 percent of all American families were "poor," Congress passed the Economic Opportunity Act of 1964, appropriating $800 million for the first year. Programs under OEO differed from past efforts in design as well as in size. Three hundred million dollars supported local community action agencies, the central innovation of the program. In each community, advisory boards, comprised of local business and political interests and representatives of the poor themselves, administered the funds. Another major emphasis of OEO programs was on the young. The Job Corps, an urban version of the New Deal's Civilian Conservation Corps, established remedial vocational and educational training facilities for young slumdwellers. The Neighborhood Youth Corps provided summer jobs paying $50 a week for high school students, with an eye toward pacifying ghetto youth during the "long, hot summers." A work-study program assisted many college students. One of the most controversial programs, the Volunteers in Service to America (VISTA), a domestic equivalent of Kennedy's Peace Corps, sent teams of idealistic young people into communities across the country to assist in federal and local programs.

Following the 1964 election came an ingenious manipulation of Congress by the President, who continued to capitalize on the memory of Kennedy as well as on his own long-standing legislative skills. Johnson showered Congress with Great Society proposals. Aid to public education was the first on Johnson's list of priorities. Eisenhower had managed to secure passage in 1958 of the National Defense Education Act, which aided the nation's universities especially in science and engineering. Kennedy signed an important bill for vocational education, and increased loans and fellowships to college students came into being during his administration. But large-scale aid to elementary and secondary schools had not been realized. Johnson effectively steered the legislation through Congress between the threats of race and religion: antisegregation amendments had marked the downfall of good bills in the past, and loss of support from Roman Catholic congressmen had killed others. But now civil rights legislation had removed the need to attach racial provisos to school bills, and the President included just enough parochial school aid to satisfy the Catholics without alarming the Protestants. Private schools received funds for "special services" like transportation and medical care but not for pedagogy in standard fields. No one, moreover, wanted a religious squabble while the memory remained fresh of John Kennedy, who had done so much to quiet the objections of purists on the separation of church and state.

For the first time Congress passed $1 billion in aid for elementary and secondary schools, concentrating on districts with pupils from low-income families. Johnson flew to the small Texas schoolhouse where he had once taught to provide a dramatic context for signing the bill. Another of Johnson's major legislative goals was Medicare, health care for the elderly funded through social security. Despite continued opposition from the AMA, the legislation passed rather easily. The basic plan provided hospitalization, rest home, and home care benefits for people over sixty-five; a supplemental voluntary plan permitted individuals to enroll for coverage of doctors' bills and laboratory fees. Within two years, 17 million Americans had taken advantage of this opportunity. Legislation in 1965 and 1966 extended federal medical care to other large categories of needy people—dependent children, the blind and disabled, and many low-income families—under the Medicaid program. Although Medicare and Medicaid laws set maximum amounts of coverage and required patients to assume responsibility for a deductible amount, they still constituted a major victory for the administration.

Not satisfied with the Water Quality Act of 1965, which provided demonstration grants for sewage control, Johnson demanded $6 billion for a six-year national program with the federal government ultimately imposing water purifying standards. The Clean Water Restoration Act of 1966 authorized $3.5 billion to be spent over five years, but Presidents Johnson and Nixon used less than one-third of these funds. Under Johnson legislation set standards for exhaust emission on combustion engines, but left the enforcement date to government discretion. Here was an example of cooperation between business and government: the deadline for nearly fume-free combustion engines was later advanced to the 1980's.

Black Americans and LBJ

Negro rights was a main goal of Johnson. In 1963 great peaceful demonstrations had a favorable effect on some legislators, and the violence in Birmingham during May frightened others. More important, the churches—a force behind the successful enactment of prohibition a generation before—influenced church-oriented senators in the direction of social justice. Churchmen, along with many Republicans and the President himself, besieged Senator Everett Dirksen, a key figure in his post as minority leader. Success came on a vote to end the Southern filibuster, 71-29, in June 1964; it was the first time Congress invoked cloture on civil rights. Then a new civil rights law passed by an even wider margin. Only five Republicans from outside the South, including Barry Goldwater, and even fewer nonsouthern Democrats opposed the bill.

The new law covered a wide range of subjects, generally promising more than it could deliver. Title I of the act barred unequal application of voter registration requirements, but did not abolish literacy tests, a traditional device for disenfranchising both poor blacks and poor whites. The most controversial portion, Title II, outlawed discrimination in hotels, motels, restaurants, theaters, and all other public accommodations engaged in interstate commerce; this section exempted "private clubs" without defining "private," making evasion of the law fairly simple. Title III encouraged the desegregation of public schools and authorized the attorney general to file suits to compel desegregation, but explicitly stated that it did not authorize busing to overcome *de facto* residential segregation. Title IV authorized but did not require the withdrawal of federal funds from projects and programs which practiced discrimination. Title VII outlawed discrimination in employment in all businesses exceeding twenty-five people; it also created an Equal Employment Opportunity Commission with broad powers to investigate and review complaints but with little power to enforce compliance. In fact, a lack of power to enforce the various provisions weakened the entire act; the maximum penalty for violations was a $1,000 fine and six months in prison. Furthermore, the law placed responsibility for enforcement on aggrieved individuals, who were required to pursue costly and time-consuming legal action in order to gain satisfaction.

In spite of major weaknesses, the Civil Rights Act represented a signal victory for the activists and friends of the civil rights movement. The public accommodations provisions were generally obeyed. Those for equal employment worked no radical change on the composition of the labor force but did facilitate opportunities for skilled blacks. The legal commitment to racial equality embodied in the act provided another weapon for organizations like the NAACP which could now argue simply for enforcement of the law. With the elimination of legal inequality, both the civil rights movement and the Johnson administration shifted their attention to the problems of social and economic inequality.

In 1965 Congress strengthened the guarantee of voting rights which the 1964 Civil Rights Act had promised. The Voting Rights Act empowered the attorney general to appoint federal examiners to supervise voter registration in states and counties that had used such devices as literacy tests to maintain a low number of registered voters. By the end of 1965, examiners had been appointed in thirty-five counties, and within five months Negro registration in Deep South states increased 40 percent. The Voting Rights Act worked in tandem with the Twenty-fourth Amendment, ratified in 1964, which eliminated poll taxes in federal elections. Together they provided a base of voters in many areas for the election of the first black officials since Reconstruction.

Johnson made his most controversial civil rights request in January 1966. He wanted laws prohibiting discrimination in the sale or rental of all housing and punishing interference with the rights of Americans in education, employment, jury service, and travel. Congress responded with legislation in these areas, although some whites had begun to resist such demands. When Martin Luther King led a group of followers into a white suburb of Chicago, a mob met them filled with a rage King claimed never to have encountered before, even in Mississippi or Alabama. The popular image of the civil rights movement had changed from nonviolence to militant demands for black power. By 1966 Johnson's support in domestic and foreign affairs was waning. Ghetto rebellions, most notably those in Los Angeles (1965) and Detroit (1967), frightened even those voters who lived far from black neighborhoods.

The black revolution of the 1960's inevitably directed judicial attention toward the system of law enforcement, and some of the most controversial decisions of the Warren Court concerned criminal procedure and the rights of the accused. In *Gideon* v. *Wainwright* (1963) the Court guaranteed the right to legal counsel in all felony cases. Clarence Earl Gideon, a white Southerner with a long criminal record, had been convicted of breaking and entering a Florida poolroom at a trial in which insolvency forced him to carry on his own defense. His handwritten appeal to the Supreme Court combined a moving personal history with imperfect legal terminology; the actual argumentation in the case before the Court was handled by Abe Fortas, a prestigious Democratic lawyer in Washington who later became an associate justice until he resigned over a conflict of interest. The guarantee in *Gideon* of courtroom counsel regardless of capacity to pay expanded to cover the police station three years later in *Miranda* v. *Arizona,* wherein the Court affirmed a prisoner's right to see an attorney before answering questions.

Concern for individual rights also shaped other decisions. With one notable exception the Court consistently refused to uphold obscenity convictions, protecting the sales of such cultural gems as the novel *Lustpool.* Only in *Ginzburg* v. *United States* did the Court depart from its norm to sustain Ralph Ginzburg's conviction for publishing some rather pretentious, high-art erotica. Even more shocking to conventional sensibilities than permissiveness toward pornography, a series of decisions in 1962-1963 outlawed compulsory bible reading and similar religious practices in public schools. The Court rejected not only an apparent abridgment of the separation of church and state, but also the enforcement, however symbolic, of a particular morality on the individual student. The Warren Court's most notable dictum on political life also had an individualist ring: the principle of "one man, one vote." In a series of legislative apportionment cases beginning with *Baker* v. *Carr* (1965), the court required that both houses of the legislature in each state reflect the actual distribution of population in that state. This ruling ended some of the more extreme cases of rural areas dominating big cities.

A political stalemate characterized the final two years of the Johnson administration. Appropriations for the war on poverty remained fairly constant, but no new programs were initiated. Congress slashed the administration's foreign aid requests. To decrease the deficits caused by Vietnam War spending, the President asked for a 10 percent tax surcharge in 1967, claiming that the surcharge was necessary if the federal government was to provide both guns and butter. Congress grudgingly passed the measure in 1968, but also forced budget reductions that began to cut into the butter. Symbolic of the new congressional mood was the defeat of an appropriation for a ghetto rat-control program; the debate centered not on the amount of money, a relatively small $100 million, but on the extent of the federal government's interest in social welfare. In 1968 Congress enacted the Omnibus Crime Bill, allocating funds to upgrade local police forces, broadening the wire-tapping authority of law enforcement agencies, and attempting to restrict some of the Supreme Court's guarantees of the rights of the accused.

The most important political event in the mid-1960's took place not at home but in Vietnam. For too many years both cabinet members and the President had been promising that the war, which began full-scale in 1965, would soon begin to wane. The antiwar movement, initially a product of young activists, began to attract all elements of society.

Suggested Readings

Recent studies of Eisenhower emphasize his caution and cooperation in domestic programs, his restraint in the use of presidential powers, and the absence in his foreign policy of dangerously large involvements. See, for example, Charles C. Alexander, *Holding the Line: The Eisenhower Era, 1952-1961* (1975) and Elmo Richardson, *The Presidency of*

Dwight D. Eisenhower (1979). One of many good recent books on John Kennedy is Lewis J. Paper, *The Promise and the Performance: The Leadership of John F. Kennedy* (1975); an up-to-date look at *The Kennedy Dynasty* (1980) has been published by David Burner and Thomas R. West. Arthur Schlesinger, Jr., describes John and Robert Kennedy as expressing the best ideas and possibilities of their times: *A Thousand Days* (1965) and *Robert F. Kennedy and His Times* (1978). In disagreement with the work cited above by Lewis Paper, Carl Brauer holds that Kennedy supported the civil rights activists strongly and effectively and within the limits imposed by politics and the legal system: *John F. Kennedy and the Second Reconstruction* (1977). Another controversial topic of the Kennedy presidency is covered by Robert A. Divine, ed., *The Cuban Missile Crisis* (1971).

Kent State University, May 4, 1970

VIETNAM AND AFTER

Chapter XXIX
Vietnam and After

The Kent State Massacre

Kent State University in Northeastern Ohio could have stood as a symbol of the growth of higher education in the 1960's even before it became the focus of national attention on May 4, 1970. Although it was common for public universities to grow rapidly in this era of expansion, few had mushroomed like Kent State. During the 1960's, enrollment tripled to over twenty thousand students. Rapidly erected new buildings could not keep pace with the influx of new students, as enrollment jumped by as much as fifteen percent in a single year. Dormitories and classrooms were overcrowded and as more and more students moved off-campus, friction increased between "town and gown." Students would confront the street kids from Kent and young people from the surrounding dry counties in the bars along North Water Street. If fights started, a call from the University's President or from the Mayor would settle things down: the bars would give free beer for an hour or so until the local police got things cooled off. On campus, students began to complain of alienation: size, the pace of growth, the high attrition rates typical of open access state institutions, and the conflicts its first-generation college students often felt between their workingclass backgrounds and their middle class aspirations gradually eroded the comfortable collegiate atmosphere the school had once had. The annual mudfight on the first warm spring night was still a tradition; the football team was important. But even Kent State, a middle-American school that had been silent when Harvard and Columbia were erupting in the spring of 1968, became politicized toward the end of the decade. When Mark Rudd, a leader of the Columbia uprising visited the campus in 1968, the school newspaper printed his picture and detailed his remarks on page three of an edition devoted largely to pictures of homecoming parade floats and candidates for homecoming queen. But radical groups soon appeared on the campus: Black United Students and a chapter of Students for a Democratic Society among the white students. And three students were arrested in the dormitories for possession of LSD. Hair began to grow profusely on boys rapidly moving from early Beatle to full Rolling Stones regalia. The youth culture had arrived: observers estimated that a sizable minority of the student body had joined the counterculture.

Serious radical activity began at Kent State in November 1968 when the Black United Students and SDS sat in to protest the presence on campus of recruiters from the Oakland, California police. (Warfare between the Oakland police and the Black Panthers was a major story at the time.) Then, in April 1969, SDS members attacked the administration building demanding abolition of ROTC. A week later, their suspension hearing turned into a fistfight between fraternity men and SDS'ers leading to the entrance of the Ohio Highway Patrol onto the campus and the arrest of fifty-eight students. Several SDS leaders went to jail for six months and the organization was banned from the campus. Somewhat late, 1960's campus politics had arrived at Kent State.

Still, the campus was scarcely aflame. Protests against cafeteria food brought out more demonstrators than a lightly attended anti-war march in April 1970. Anti-war demonstrations at the University of Akron, at Ohio University, and at Ohio State University in the winter of 1969-70 produced no reasonance at Kent State. Then President Richard M. Nixon went on national television on the evening of April 30 to announce that as part of our withdrawal from the war in Vietnam, we had invaded neighboring Cambodia. "All the kids were around TV sets in the dorm," the student government president recalled. "They had horrified stares on their faces."

The first response was tame. A small radical group, predominantly graduate history students, created an instant protest organization: World Historians Opposed to Racism and Exploitation (WHORE) whose sole activity was burying, with appropriate ceremony, a copy of the United States Constitution, which they had torn from a United States history text-book. Then, that evening, a seductively warm spring night, students and non-students in the bars announced a "street festival," which turned to vandalism. The local police chief, nervous because the SDS leaders from the previous year had just been released from jail, persuaded the mayor to alert the National Guard. By the next day, officials were convinced that radical "Weathermen" were on campus and that plans were afoot to burn the town. Town officials slapped a curfew on the town and called in the National Guard. Ohio Governor James Rhodes, who had expended more for National Guard service in the past two years than the *total* of the other forty-nine states, readily complied as he had about three other campus disturbances in the previous six months. By the time the Guard arrived, already exhausted from six days service at a truckers' strike, radical students had actually given them an occasion to be there: on the night of May 2, a group of students burned the rickety old wooden ROTC building.

The campus mood was ugly. Communication among local officials, the Guard, and the university were awkward at best. Students were quick to anger and the Guardsmen nervous and testy. When a group of students tried to begin a dialogue with a Guard commander on Saturday, the Guard was ordered to march on the peaceable students with leveled bayonets. Only the intervention of a sheriff's deputy, who interposed himself between the advancing Guards and the students, pressed against a dormitory wall, prevented a potential tragedy. On Sunday, with unconfirmed rumors circulating of snipers in the library, danger mounted. Neither the Guards nor the students had control of their emotions, and the Guards were ill equipped for their duty, essentially crowd control. First, they had received no training and might not remain steady under provocation. Second, their weapons were absurdly, tragically disproportionate to the job. Well trained, well directed guard units in other states were equipped with bird shot and buckshot and were forbidden to carry loaded weapons until directly ordered to do so by their commanders. In Ohio, the Guards keep their guns in "locked, loaded, and ready" position. Any tired, nervous young guard could—litererally—trigger catastrophe. Moreover, their weapon was the M-1, the bullets of which could pass through an eighteen-inch tree trunk at close range or could travel for two miles. The odds on killing bystanders in an altercation was high. And these young men, eager to get home after harrowing duty amidst violent teamsters taking pot shots at any who dared to move trucks during the strike, were exhausted, confused, and ill-led.

On Monday, tragedy came. Students had conflicting information about what might happen: all assemblies on campus were forbidden, they heard. Yet classes were still scheduled and so was a rally called for noontime. Or was it? Sometime after 11 a.m. someone began tolling a bell and students began to gather for the possible rally. Some fifteen hundred students gathered: "There was a lot of kids there who had just come back from the weekend and didn't know what was coming off," one student recalled. "You had super-straight Joe Fraternity and ultra-radical Joe Freak out there," said another. Soon the Guard tried to disperse the crowd, which responded first with obscene chants and then, here and there, with flying stones. Wind and noise drowned out any clear commands. A reporter, standing with some Guardsmen heard an officer call: "Fix bayonets, gas masks, load [rifles]." "I could not believe it," recalled the reporter. "What were these guys going to do, mount a charge against a bunch of kids who weren't harming anything or anybody?" With the students about one hundred yards away from this small contingent of troops, the gas canisters began to plop. The wind was blowing back toward the troops and students could easily pick up the canisters and lob them back. No weapons were left except bayonets and the awesome M-1s. The crowd started to disperse. But they were perhaps not so panicky as the soldiers who chased students even as they fled. Then the troops marched into a football practice field practically devoid of students and found themselves virtually trapped against a fence. Students now began to gather around them heaving small stones from perhaps eighty to one hundred twenty-five feet away to no effect. Suddenly, some of the troops dropped to a kneeling position and pointed their rifles at the crowd. Then they began what the students interpreted as a withdrawal up Blanket Hill, so named because students were traditionally supposed to gain their first sexual experiences there. Some students ran up the hill behind them, coming closer than before to throw their rocks—perhaps now to somewhat more effect. At the top of the hill the Guardsmen stopped, turned, and in the next thirteen seconds, fired sixty-one shots, killing four students and wounding nine.

Initial reaction was one of disbelief. A ritual that everyone had seen countless times on the evening news had no place in it for real bullets and real blood. Many assumed the Guardsmen had fired blanks. One reporter said that the radicals' use of animal blood to give the impression of injury was in terrible taste. A freshman thought it was fingerpaint. A veteran of the war in Vietnam seeing the corps helicopter above and the bloodshed imagined himself back in Vietnam: "I didn't realize the guys were shooting at the kids," one Guardsman reported, "until I saw this kid's chest break into blood." The alert commanding general gave orders—rather late—that the men should not fire again unless an officer "tapped him on the shoulder and told him to fire." But at the same time he called for re-enforcements and prepared a fresh sweep through the crowd. Glenn Frank, voted the outstanding professor in the university the previous year, begged for a chance to calm the crowd. The general reluctantly gave him five minutes. Crying, desperate, Frank addressed the crowd. "We're going to get slaughtered . . . People died here, but please, because of their martyrdom, let's not have any more martyrs. I beg you, let's move." And move they did. By the narrowest of margins, there was no more bloodshed at Kent State. By 5:00 p.m. the campus was empty. Dangling from a dormitory window near Blanket Hill were several bedsheets tied together to form the backdrop for a large sign scrawled in red paint with the word WHY? Why indeed? One can point to the inappropriateness of using the National Guard; to Nixon's speech and his unfortunate reference the following day to student dissidents as "bums"; to the hysteria of local officials who called in the Guard; to the governor of Ohio's overuse of them; to the sour mood of 1970 as the nation unhappily faced the prospect of final defeat in Indo-China (four days after the Kent State killings, a group of construction workers on Wall Street in New York attacked a group of peaceful student anti-war demonstrators, badly injuring fifty of them). Yet the question remains: in genuine tragedy there is never any answer. One radical slogan of the time was to "Bring the war home." The victims' war. "All I know is that my daughter is dead!" the distraught father of Allison Krause exclaimed. "I'm not on anybody's side. We were so glad we had two daughters so they could stay out of Vietnam. Now she's dead. What a waste. What a horrible waste."

Vietnam: To 1960

Since the middle of the nineteenth century, Southeast Asia's vast deposits of raw materials and its relative accessibility have attracted rival empires and ideologies. In Indochina (Vietnam, Laos, and Cambodia) France established itself in two spurts, first during the 1850's and later in the 1870's. Local Frenchmen in Vietnam almost immediately seized control of the new colony and, together with native mandarins, ruled Indochina largely for private gain. The two groups set up a Grand Council which taxed the Vietnamese, protected monopolies, and enclosed vast estates —mostly for the benefit of a few hundred Frenchmen. This oligarchy thwarted reforms proposed by a few capable governors.

Economic exploitation and Vietnamese fears about French cultural aggression prompted resistance almost from the beginning. When Paris vetoed moderate reforms during the early 1920's, nationalists adopted more militant tactics. In 1925 leftists set up the Thanh Nien, which Ho Chi Minh —who had earlier studied Marxism in France —reorganized in 1930 as the Communist party. Ho called for immediate land reforms and a mass uprising against French rule; as a result, the Grand Council viciously suppressed the fledgling Communist movement in its first years. For the remainder of the decade, native religious sects channeled discontent into more other-worldly outlets. During the Japanese occupation of Indochina from 1940 to 1945, however, internal bickering plagued these sects, and they could not counter Ho's skillful building of the Vietminh, a united front of anticolonialists. And when Japan's power disintegrated during early 1945, Vietminh guerrilla forces seized northern border provinces and a genuine popular revolution swept the colony. The only tightly organized party uncorrupted by collaboration either with the French or with the Japanese, the Vietminh formed a government on September 2, 1945, when Ho Chi Minh declared Vietnam's independence.

Although President Franklin Roosevelt tended to favor an end to colonial rule, Britain had fought World War II in part to protect its empire, not free it, and the new French Republic under General Charles de Gaulle demanded a return of all French possessions. Accordingly, Anglo-French occupation troops forcibly installed a colonial government in Saigon late in 1945; the Vietminh immediately launched a guerrilla counteroffensive against what rapidly became a French war of reconquest. Dreams of imperial glory and a be-lief in its military superiority led the Fourth Republic to repudiate a compromise agreement worked out with Ho in early 1946.

The First Indochina War developed in two markedly different stages. From 1947-50 the French demonstrated great military pressure throughout all of Indochina, but still could not break Vietminh dominance in the countryside or growing Communist control over the nationalist movement. Attempts to reestablish the Vietnamese monarchy under Emperor Bao Dai failed because of his obvious domination by the French. Then, from 1950 until 1954 the entire complexion of the war changed: Vietminh military strength flourished and desperate French generals took increasingly ill-advised risks in an effort to defeat the guerrillas. At the same time, Paris began to justify the war not as one of colonial reconquest, but as an anti-Communist effort in support of the legitimate Bao Dai government. French bureaucrat also developed the idea of "association"—a unified Vietnam would exercise semiautonomous powers internally while still associated with the French Union in affairs monetary, diplomatic, and cultural. The refusal to grant political independence or significant economic reform undermined the French military effort as well as the emperor's credibility. In fact, association actually forced nationalists into the Vietminh camp as the only alternative to collaboration.

During this second period events elsewhere lifted the war onto the international stage. Late in 1949 Mao Tse-tung defeated Chiang Kai-shek and established the People's Republic of China. Almost immediately American policy toward Indochina shifted from an apathetic disinterest to a determined effort at blocking further Communist expansion in Asia. When President Truman extended massive military aid to the French in 1950, the National Security Council justified the new policy largely in "domino" terms: if Indochina were "lost," Thailand would be next; this would upset the balance of power in Southeast Asia, and communism might then reach out for either India or the rich islands of Indonesia. Modeled on the fall of Austria, Czechoslovakia, and other European countries to Hitler after 1938, the simple domino theory substituted communism for facism and Asia for Europe.

Communist control of the nationalist movement left the United States in a curious dilemma: the best way to defeat the Vietminh would be to replace the French with a non-Communist, nationalist regime, but America's diplomatic needs in Europe required French support, so aid to the French war effort became the only alternative. The French had superior firepower and were well trained in the mode of orderly European combat, but Ho's native forces knew the land and fought an effective guerrilla war of attrition. The French army could not control the countryside—or even move very far from the main roads, for that matter—nor could France oust the Vietminh from their stronghold in the Northern provinces outside of Hanoi and Haiphong.

Then, late in 1953, General Vo Nguyen Giap moved the bulk of his Vietminh forces toward Laos in an attempt to win territory and to lure French armies under General Henri Navarre away from their coastal strongholds. Navarre, to prevent future attacks against Laos, converted a small frontier outpost at Dien Bien Phu into a major fortress. By March 1954 when the battle began that would bring the first Indochina War to a stalemate, France had concentrated there nearly 25,000 of its best troops, built an airstrip to supply the fort, and set up massive artillery ranges. Navarre was confident that at last he could wipe out the Communists' main force. Yet Giap's forces not only outnumbered the French two-to-one, but, with the aid of China and thousands of Vietnamese who back-packed ammunition into the remote area, he had assembled superior firepower around the hills of Dien Bien Phu. Though the French retained control of the air, bombing strikes could not destroy the well-hidden Communist embankments which soon knocked out the French airstrip and covered repeated infantry attacks. Then Giap encircled the post; the garrison fell to the Vietminh army. The French military effort to reassert colonial control had collapsed.

While most diplomats moved toward ending the war, Secretary of State John Foster Dulles took the first steps toward prolonging and Americanizing it. The Eisenhower administration seriously considered active military intervention, not only to save the outpost at Dien Bien Phu but also to bolster the entire French effort, which it believed to be an anti-Communist campaign. Washington abandoned ideas of direct interference only after the French govermnent itself refused to continue the war and the military situation in northern Vietnam became hopeless. If the United States were to launch an anti-Communist crusade in Southeast Asia, it would have to find a vehicle other than French colonialism.

Only one day before the fall of Dien Bien Phu, the nations involved in Indochina—France, Britain, Russia, China, the United States, and repre-

sentatives of Ho Chi Minh's Hanoi-based government and the French puppet regime under Bao Dai—convened in Geneva, Switzerland, to settle the Indochina War. Negotiations were complex. After six weeks the representatives reached agreement, largely because Russia and China forced Ho Chi Minh to accept Western terms. The Geneva accords granted independence to the three Indochinese states of Laos, Cambodia, and Vietnam. To facilitate military disengagement, Vietnam was temporarily divided at the 17th parallel; nationwide elections within two years would determine the country's permanent political future. None of the new states was to permit foreign troops or bases on its soil or to join an outside alliance. This outcome satisfied neither Dulles nor Eisenhower. Rather than a compromise, Washington wanted to guarantee the existence of a non-Communist alternative. Thus, the State Department announced that the United States, which had not signed the Geneva accords, would adhere to its terms, but would treat North and South Vietnam as separate entities. Then, in September of 1954, Dulles negotiated the Southeast Asia Treaty Organization (SEATO,) a milder version of the NATO alliance, pledging assistance "in accord with constitutional process." The original signatories—France, Great Britain, the United States, Australia, New Zealand, the Philippines, Pakistan, and Thailand—later extended the pact's protection to include Cambodia, Laos, and South Vietnam. Convinced that his only other option was disengagement and the gradual fall of all Southeast Asia to communism, Eisenhower pledged vast economic aid to the native but increasingly elitist South Vietnamese premier, Ngo Dinh Diem. In 1956 the United States supported Diem's open break with the Geneva settlement, and acting on Dulles' explicit approval, the premier called off elections, which the nationalist Communists would probably have won. By this series of actions, Washington committed itself to the creation and then to the defense of a non-Communist government in South Vietnam.

Supporting Diem eventually backfired, for he took American money and built a personalist regime. At first, however, the new leadership seemed altogether viable. Between 1954-57, generously supported by American financial aid, the country made substantial economic growth and even achieved some land reform. The government suppressed gangsters in Saigon and brought under control the religious sects, many of whose leaders had set up independent fiefdoms in the countryside. But Diem never gained broad popular support, and because the rural areas remained in the hands of opponents, he adopted increasingly repressive tactics. When the United States protested, the mandarin pointed out that, without his regime, the country would succumb to the Communist insurgency which had broken out in 1957.

According to an analyst in the Department of Defense, Diem's "increasingly oppressive and corrupt regime" had provoked the new revolt, and a united front of anti-Diem factions—nearly all native to South Vietnam—called for genuine land redistribution, representative government, and a decentralized administration. Not until 1959 did the rebellion seriously threaten the Saigon government. Then widespread frustration with Diem, together with surreptitious North Vietnamese support for the rebels, gradually weakened the premier's control over the country. Only American financial aid and military hardware main-

tained the government in Saigon. As American aid to Diem skyrocketed, so too did Hanoi's support for the insurgents, primarily through training southerners. With its industrial development program accelerated, however, North Vietnam could also send more and more materials to the rebels in the South.

By the end of the decade the Republican administration had dispatched some 685 American "advisory" personnel to Vietnam; but the non-military alternative, land reform and economic growth, collapsed because of Diem's opposition. Ironically, while Eisenhower "could conceive of no greater tragedy than for the United States to become involved in an all out land war in Asia," his secretary of state announced that "the free world would intervene in Indochina rather than let the situation deteriorate."

Vietnam: Kennedy and Johnson

The Diem government approached chaos in the early sixties. All social and economic reform halted, and even retrogressed, as Diem concentrated on maintaining his power and eliminating all opposition. In response, thousands of Southern insurrectionists joined the newly organized National Liberation Front (NLF), and many took the trek north for military training. Support from the new Kennedy administration, which eventually sent 16,000 American advisers along with artillery and fighterbombers to Vietnam, kept the Diem regime alive. Washington also expanded the elaborate clandestine war against North Vietnam, which it first began in 1955. Kennedy now ordered secret agents to sabotage lines of communication throughout the North and American advisers directed military raids across Hanoi's frontiers and into Laos. At first these tactics appeared successful: during 1962 the NLF lost some of its earlier territorial gains. Although some of Kennedy's apologists later insisted that he would have avoided full-scale conflict, his decisions had enlarged American goals in Vietnam without assuring the achievement of these goals. By 1963 this discrepancy could no longer be ignored. Chief of Staff Maxwell Taylor's hopes for counterinsurgency warfare required popular support and extensive reforms in Vietnam. Yet under Kennedy Washington skirted social and economic problems and concentrated instead upon military victory.

Kennedy escalated the war gradually, perhaps aware that his decisions slowly committed the United States to a military victory. He observed that sending troops to Vietnam was a little like having a drink: the effect wears off and you have to have another. Once the principles of American aid and troop support were well established, the size or character of the military effort could scarcely be held in check. Then, too, American soldiers began to die in Vietnam—sixty by 1963. Advocates of further escalation could employ the effective argument of redemption: for what had these men died? In 1956 Kennedy had declared: "Vietnam represents the cornerstone of the free world in Southeast Asia, the keystone to the arch, the finger in the dike." But Kennedy certainly did have doubts about taking further steps in Vietnam. By September 1963 he said: "In the final analysis it is their war." Yet he still believed that a United States withdrawal could mean the collapse of Southeast Asia.

The Diem government's persecution of Buddhists sickened the entire world. The ruling family persuaded the legislature to pass laws requiring Buddhists to obey Catholic moral laws, and Diem's Roman Catholic sister-in-law, Madame Nhu, gained notoriety for her cynical dismissal of Buddhist "barbecues" —self-immolation as a form of political protest. Beginning in May 1963, the Buddhists organized strong demonstrations against the Saigon regime; in an attempt to squash

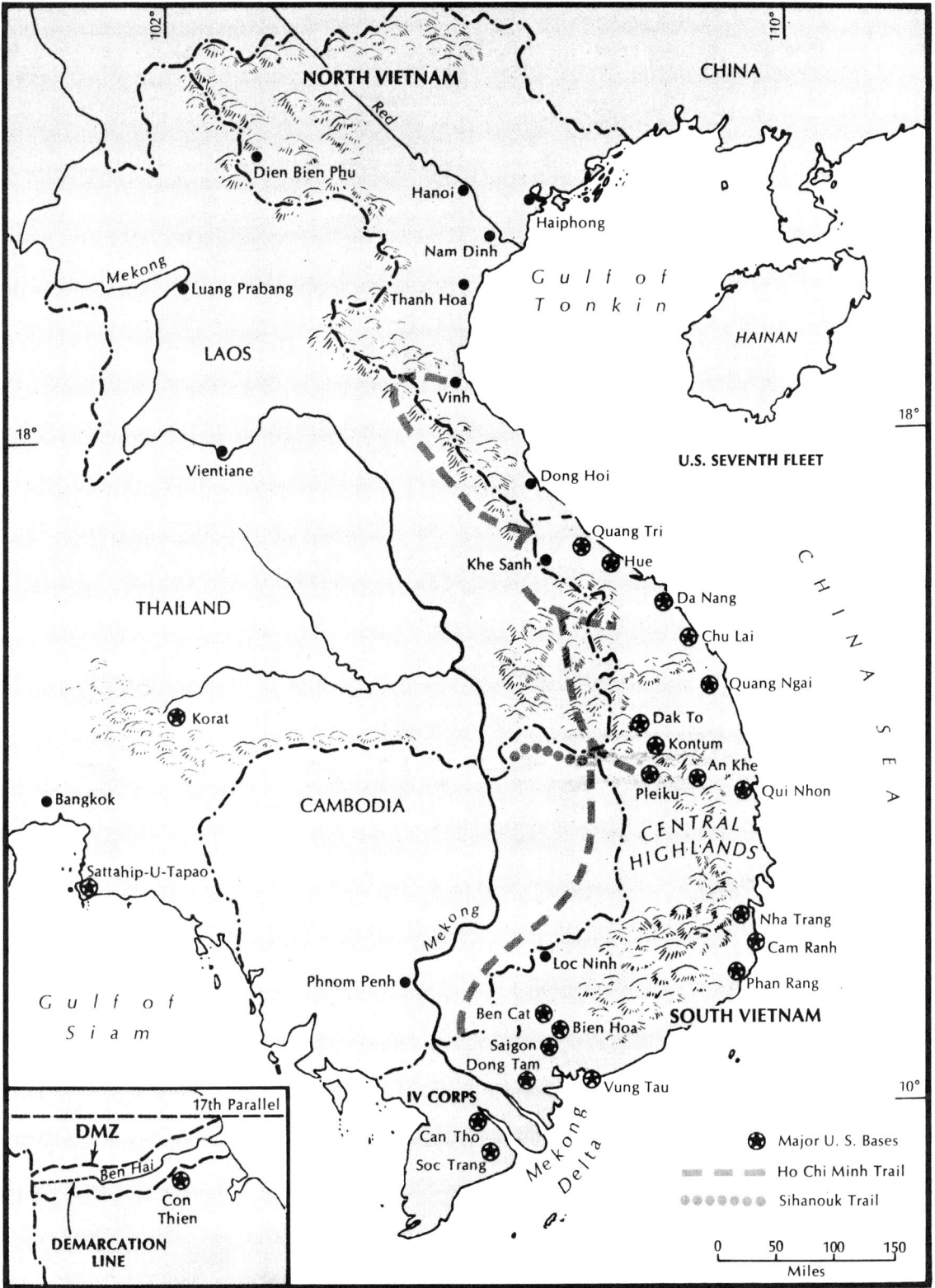

Vietnam

this threat, Diem's brother attacked Buddhist temples and pagodas throughout South Vietnam in August. When it became clear that the Diem army raids had alienated the urban middle class, most religious sects, and intellectuals everywhere, the United States abandoned its support of the premier, while Ambassador Henry Cabot Lodge actively collaborated with a cabal of generals. On November 2, 1963, the group assassinated Diem and set up a new government under Major General Nguyen Khanh. The United States acquiesced in and abetted the military coup against Diem not so much because of the regime's corruption but because of its ineffectiveness.

The United States might have used the Diem crisis as a convenient reason for withdrawing from the war. Robert Kennedy urged a course of disengagement during a cabinet meeting, and *Time's* editors suggested the possibility of neutralizing all of Southeast Asia. But McNamara and Taylor visited Vietnam in September and on October 2 reported that most American tasks there would be accomplished in fifteen months, with perhaps a thousand troops returning home by the end of 1963. No wonder pursuing the war seemed the practical course—one that prudently weighed cost against advanage.

By the time President Johnson took office in November 1963 he had few political alternatives. He inherited not only the war itself but also Kennedy's principal advisers on foreign affairs; the United States had many troops in the country and South Vietnam's new government was completely dependent on American economic and military aid. In any event, Johnson had long since decided that the "broad lines" of Kennedy's policy were correct. The new President approached Vietnam on the basis of his knowledge of World War II and Korea, quickly identifying the problem as one of halting aggression.

Diem's legacy of unresolved social and economic problems, together with his elimination of political opponents, had created a political vacuum in South Vietnam. During 1964 a musical chairs of military juntas in Saigon undermined the anti-Communist effort; the Vietcong made rapid, large-scale gains. As Vietcong strength spread, the American administration became more and more interested in bombing the North as a substitute prosecution of the counterinsurgency campaign in the South. As a result of these pressures, 1964 marked the beginning of the Second Indochina War: Johnson would commit vast resources and wage war throughout the former French colony in order to reach American's goal, a non-Communist South Vietnam.

A pretext to attack North Vietnam—the so-called Gulf of Tonkin crisis—occurred during early August 1964. The navy had helped South Vietnam to conduct extensive operations against shore installations in North Vietnam. The spy ship *Maddox*, loaded with electronic equipment, had supported these raids, often cruising inside the twelve-mile limit by Hanoi. After one such incursion, manned by South Vietnamese but supported by Americans, Hanoi sent several PT boats into the Gulf of Tonkin. The *Maddox*, now over twenty miles from the coast, apparently fired first upon the approaching North Vietnamese ships, which then returned the fire. Two days later, on August 4, as the *Maddox* and another destroyer, the *C. Turner Joy*, cruised in the same general area, they reported a second attack by North Vietnamese boats. Because of intense darkness and malfunctioning sonar and radar equipment, overanxious naval captains may have imagined this second "attack." Although Hanoi may have planned another strike, no material evidence has surfaced that it actually occurred.

But in Washington, Johnson publicly denounced "unprovoked aggression" and used the temporary feeling of crisis to extract congressional approval for a project the administration had contemplated for several months. To insure his freedom of action and demonstrate American unity in an election year, Johnson secured a sweeping authorization "to take all necessary measures . . . to prevent further aggression." Although aware of the 34-A raids, a nearly unanimous Senate adopted the de facto declaration of war, 88-2. Only a few isolated senators, Wayne Morse of Oregon in particular, questioned its ultimate purpose or the advisability of open-ended commitments.

During the next four months the administration moved quickly toward full-scale war. Policy debates in late 1964 revolved around the question of whether to bomb North Vietnam on a regular basis. Initially, the administration announced a "reprisal policy": the United States would attack North Vietnam only after a specific incident of aggression. What amounted to the first reprisal came in August when the air force bombed PT boat bases in North Vietnam in response to the Gulf of Tonkin "incidents." Then, as the political and military situation in the South worsened, Washington made its first major miscalculation: that systematic air attacks against the North would either end Hanoi's support of the southern insurgency or lead to a formal settlement.

By January 1965 the policies and attitudes had crystallized which would, for the next three years, sustain America's escalation of the war, including the use of more and more United States ground combat troops, all-out air attacks upon North Vietnam, and consistent rejection of serious peace talks with the enemy. On one level, the administration anticipated that escalation would improve morale in South Vietnam and bring military victory there. On another level, President Johnson hoped that the conflict would "contain" China and prevent an Indonesia-North Vietnam-North Korea bloc that might squeeze the United States out of East Asia. Johnson saw the war in South Vietnam as a "demonstration" to convince Communists everywhere of America's resolve to deter "aggression." The United States must at all costs avoid defeat, not only because of the supposed domino consequences for Southeast Asia, but also because a withdrawal would produce psychological tremors throughout East Asia and perhaps even Africa and Europe. The Vietnamese war would show America's ability to defend its vision of world order and its international credibility.

Largely because of these considerations, Johnson decided to fight the war tactically somewhere between the extremes of "unmanly withdrawal" and the quick, massive attacks against North Vietnam and the Vietcong advocated by the joint chiefs of staff. He believed that a calculated, steady increase in force would convince his opponents that they could not win. Sustained bombing of North Vietnam began in March 1965. He sent hundreds of thousands of combat troops into South Vietnam to protect American outposts and to aid Vietnamese units threatened by Vietcong attack. Finally, Johnson authorized independent action by American soldiers; the first "search and destroy" mission involving large numbers of American men took place several miles north-west of Saigon in late June.

Washington military planners soon tripped over more misconceptions. Guerrilla methods often confused generals trained for wars of maneuver; increasing aid did not automatically overwhelm the rebellion. Only a few men, such as Undersecretary of State McGeorge Bundy and some on-the-spot CIA agents, foresaw what the troop needs in Vietnam would be or cautioned that the insurgency might spread as United States support increased. Experts in guerrilla warfare estimated that United States forces would have to outnumber Vietcong-North Vietnamese troops about ten to one. And every time Washington added more soldiers, so too did Saigon's opponents. By early 1968, for example, Hanoi had fielded roughly 135,000 men in the South, the United States about 550,000; double that number would be required just to offset Hanoi's troops.

Initially, optimistic reports from his political and military advisers pressed Johnson toward an ever-widening war. This elusive hope for victory was only one consideration that prevented a compromise settlement; the President's determination to "negotiate from strength" and North Vietnam's own determined militancy scuttled early opportunities to meet at a conference table. As early as July 1964, for example, U Thant, secretary-general of the United Nations, suggested reactivating the Geneva Conference. The French, under the shrewd leadership of DeGaulle, quickly agreed, and so did the Soviet Union, North Vietnam, and even China. But Johnson, fearing that a conference might restrict his maneuverability, answered: "We do not believe in conferences called to ratify terror." A scant nine months later, however, during a speech at the Johns Hopkins University, the President offered to attend a peace conference at any time, and he outlined plans for an Asian Development Bank to rebuild Southeast Asia. Sincere in his hope for peace, Johnson would have negotiated, but he would not jeopardize the war's "demonstration effect," and the demand for a non-Communist regime in Saigon was to the North Vietnamese and Vietcong tantamount to a capitulation. When the Communists not unexpectedly rejected Johnson's terms, he interpreted each rejection as further "proof" of aggression, and could then in good conscience further escalate the war.

Illusory hopes eventually gave way to near cynicism. To check domestic critics and create an aura of peaceful intent, Johnson ordered a halt to the air war, a dramatic thirty-seven-day bombing pause against North Vietnam from December 1965 to January 1966. The President's closest advisers realized that his "terms" were those of victory, not of compromise, and that he undertook the effort largely to justify renewed escalation. But ironically the pause also spread a growing realization that the Rolling Thunder bombing operations against the North had not materially damaged Hanoi's willingness to fight. When bombing resumed in February 1966—because, it was said, Ho Chi Minh refused to negotiate—the case was altered: no longer would the United States attempt to force North Vietnam out of the war; instead, the air force would concentrate on cutting Hanoi's supplies to the Vietcong.

Stymied by the inefficiency of Rolling Thunder and by Hanoi's refusal to cave in at an American bargaining table, Johnson massively escalated the ground war in Vietnam during the spring of 1966. For nearly twenty-four months, the world witnessed America's military attempt to pursue a will-o'-the-wisp victory and to insure a non-Communist South Vietnam. Still, two obstacles remained: the unstable, often arbitrary government in Saigon and a swelling tide of discontent within the United States. In South Vietnam disagreements over military tactics and economic reforms plagued the junta that had replaced Diem. Even after two generals, Nguyen Van Thieu and Nguyen Cao Ky, emerged on top, Saigon could not heal the split between countryside and city which fueled the insurgency, partly because the rebels held much rural territory, partly because the United States command focused on military victory. But at a meeting in Honolulu during February 1966 with President Thieu and Vice-President Ky, Johnson extracted promises that the junta would permit an elected government and begin large-scale land redistribution. It was a delicate diplomatic maneuver, for while Johnson threatened to cut off American aid to force compliance, the two Vietnamese leaders knew that they were the President's only option. American insistence upon the appearance, if not the reality, of democracy, together with the temporary eclipse of Communist progress during the massive United States buildup of 1966, finally brought about nationwide elections for a Constituent Assembly. Unfortunately, this "constitutional convention" was rigged: no Communist delegates attended; the regime blocked neutralist candidates; and the generals quickly reasserted their personal control over the new government apparatus.

If Johnson fashioned events in South Vietnam, his own countrymen proved less malleable. After a brief rather positive reaction to their latest military crusade against communism, many Americans increasingly went sour. The inconclusiveness of the struggle was immensely frustrating. The more the United States bombed North Vietnam, for example, the more Ho scattered his factories, infiltrated the South, and whipped up war fever in the North. Indeed, because the country was not heavily industrialized, American bombers quickly discovered that they lacked advantageous targets, and fears about reactions in the Soviet Union and China prevented an assault against the major port of Haiphong. In addition, the air force could not interdict supplies flowing south along the Ho Chi Minh Trail, for it was a jungle path, not an interstate highway; its location, and even at times its existence, was problematical. The bulk of war material moved at night in small vehicles or on human backs: American "damage" could be easily repaired or simply avoided.

Meanwhile, the ground war in South Vietnam remained locked in a stalemate despite repeated

reinforcements. Over half a million American troops guarded major cities and many rural outposts by 1968, but the Communists dominated much of the countryside. When combat units embarked upon "search and destroy" missions, North Vietnamese regulars shunned combat and Vietcong guerrillas hid among the population. Despite vastly improved "kill ratios," American military forces could not keep up with Communist recruitment and North Vietnamese infiltration.

Johnson's program to "win the hearts and minds of the Vietnamese people" was similarly indecisive. To "pacify" the countryside, Washington launched the strategic hamlet program. American troops would move into a village, secure it with a series of fortifications, and leave a garrison of soldiers. Although the tactic protected the village from Vietcong attack, the spectacle of peasants living under American guns in barbed-wire enclosures provoked memories of concentration camps. It seemed possible that both political and military victory could prove elusive.

If inconclusiveness soured public support for Johnson's policy, a growing antiwar movement within the United States questioned its very purpose. By 1967 Senator J. William Fulbright, who earlier had guided the Gulf of Tonkin resolution through the Senate, now attacked the administration's "arrogance of power." "Power," observed Fulbright, "tends to confuse itself with virtue." He believed that its history of victory, prosperity, and power gave the United States a dangerous sense of omnipotence and self-righteousness, which, at its worst, could distort reality—as in Vietnam. According to the Senator, American "world-saving" in Asia started out by assuming that Western institutions and political methods could establish themselves in an alien culture. While Fulbright and other critics worried about misplaced motives, a mushrooming antiwar coalition directly questioned the war's morality. In October 1967, a rally of 200,000 students, leftists, and "ordinary" Americans demonstrated in a march through the nation's capital. An important portion of the Democratic party had rejected Johnson's leadership.

During 1968 the realities of Vietnam and of domestic disillusionment forced Johnson to shift his tactics, though not his objective. It was plain to most congressional and military leaders that the United States would not be able to win the war in Vietnam for many years, if ever. Despite our bombing, possibly because of it, North Vietnam appeared to be the most stable government in Southeast Asia. In the South the mightiest nation in the world could not, short of nuclear weapons, defeat an army of willful peasants operating without an air force or heavy artillery. To most Americans, it seemed even clearer that the United States was in serious trouble after the Tet offensive of late January-February 1968. On the night of January 29, the American embassy and all the major cities of South Vietnam came under attack. Saigon nearly fell to the enemy and most of the northern city of Hue came under Vietcong control for several days. Only a brutal counteroffensive restored the cities to allied control, though the Vietcong still dominated the rural areas. Their mission had been accomplished in secrecy and dedication; President Thieu's forces appeared inept in contrast.

General Westmoreland immediately flew to the United States and asked for 200,000 more reinforcements, a request that coincided with a major review of war policy in Washington. At this point, Johnson's decision was relatively straightforward: he could not send more men to South Vietnam without endangering America's commitments elsewhere and producing severe strains on the inflated American economy; in addition, the President would have had to mobilize the reserves and increase taxes, but both steps required congressional approval, and he doubted whether Congress or the general public would acquiesce. By this time, Johnson also seemed to have realized the futility of escalation. When Westmoreland explained that he could not guarantee victory even with the additional troops, the President replied: "Then where will it all end?" Dismayed and disillusioned, he entrusted the search for an alternative to a study group chaired by a personal friend, Clark Clifford. Since military victory was not in sight, the Clifford committee turned to "the lesser of evils," diplomacy as a solution for the war.

The decision to reorient American policy was not unexpected. For well over a year, Secretary of Defense Robert McNamara had advocated a negotiated settlement in South Vietnam based upon a coalition government. Former Secretary of State Dean Acheson added his voice of skepticism. Growing disintegration of support for the war at home and a spreading malaise among United States military forces in Vietnam intensified the pressure for negotiation. The disaster of Tet triggered in many military men a hysteria for revenge and a sense of frustration that led to a breakdown in discipline: widespread drug use and even occasional mutinies threatened to destroy morale. Since "body count," not territory, defined the terms of victory in Vietnam, the step was a short one to mass murders of Viet civilians by American soldiers at My Lai and Song My. At these places and elsewhere, company commanders and their troops lost all sense of restraint and committed atrocities not revealed to the American public until 1970 and 1971.

Meanwhile, domestic events further restricted options. When, in March 1968, Senator Eugene McCarthy received nearly 40 percent of the vote in the New Hampshire Democratic primary, voters were rebuking the incumbent President. Soon it appeared that a majority in the party apparently favored someone other than the man who had led the Democrats to a landslide victory only four years earlier. Students throughout the nation, as well as many journalists, teachers, and groups interested in domestic change, more and more protested the course of the war. A desire to unify his party and the country largely motivated the President in his decision to reverse the course of the war.

In a dramatic television appearance on March 31, 1968, Johnson officially announced the results of the Clifford policy review: the United States would halt bombing north of the 19th parallel in an effort to bring about serious peace negotiations; Westmoreland was to receive only a tenth of his troop request. In addition, South Vietnam would take over active prosecution of the war gradually, an approach President Nixon later expanded into "Vietnamization." Yet Johnson's desire for even partial victory imperiled his search for peace; the administration wanted to negotiate, but did not want to compromise along the collaborationist lines suggested by McNamara. Instead, Johnson believed that the Tet offensive had severely weakened Communist ground forces and that a new spirit, a new effectiveness in South Vietnam, would enable the Saigon regime to defeat the Vietcong. The limit on American troops, the bombing restriction, and the beginning of Vietnamization—Thieu promised to raise 135,000 additional troops—were genuine moves toward peace, but still an American peace with American objectives: a non-Communist South Vietnam.

To insure the bombing halt and probably to see what sort of deal the United States contemplated, Hanoi replied favorably to Johnson's offer for talks. For several weeks the two powers debated an appropriate site for the negotiations, each advocating a city sympathetic to its own position. Hanoi finally suggested Paris, presumably to take advantage of DeGaulle's growing anti-Americanism; Johnson could not refuse. On May 10, the peace talks opened at the Majestic Hotel; Xuan Thuy represented Hanoi, Averell Harriman, former ambassador to Moscow, was the chief United States negotiator. Almost immediately, the talks stalled. For five months, the diplomats deadlocked over a question of timing. North Vietnam insisted that meaningful talks could begin only after the United States pledged to stop bombing. Johnson countered that he must continue raids across the Demilitarized Zone (DMZ) to protect American troops; the question of permanent cessation, he argued, should be included in the peace talks, not decided beforehand. The United States position was one of "reciprocity" from Hanoi: a mutual winding down of the war and the participation of both the Saigon regime and the National Liberation Front in any political settlement. By mid-October 1968 the President had accepted an arrangement worked out between Harriman and Thuy whereby the United States would halt all bombing if Hanoi "by its silence" agreed to negotiate with South Vietnam, not increase its aid to the Vietcong, and permit American reconnaissance flights.

1968

Senator Eugene McCarthy of Minnesota, a handsome gray-haired man of fifty-one, seemed a study in political detachment and nonchalance. But when Attorney General Nicholas Katzenbach told the Senate Foreign Relations Committee in August 1967 that a President could no longer lose time by consulting the Congress on whether to involve the country in war, McCarthy lost his customary composure. Angrily he told Katzenbach that such extensive executive authority deprived the Senate of any decision-making role in foreign policy. In the thinking of McCarthy, who had written a book on the American political process, the Katzenbach interpretation was unconstitutional.

Late in November McCarthy decided to oppose the President in the coming spring primaries. The first contest came in New Hampshire on March 21 when snow still covered the ground. An energetic band of young students carried the antiwar message across the state. The Democratic governor and senator mismanaged the Johnson campaign, employing heavy-handed tactics such as a signed postcard pledge to support the President. Gene McCarthy exerted a positive appeal on New Englanders; he was, in his dry and self-contained manner, almost a New Englander himself. His arguments against the war were low key and highly factual. Beyond that, however, he stood for an end to conflict between generations and a renewing of traditional political institutions. In the vote itself, McCarthy's Roman Catholicism must have counted, for about two-thirds of the state's Democrats shared his faith. The Senator won 42 percent of the two-party vote, almost as much as Johnson's write-in total of 49 percent. It was unprecedented to come so close to winning against an incumbent President during a war.

Three days later, in what appeared to some the quintessence of opportunism, Senator Robert Kennedy of New York announced that he, too, would oppose the President in those primaries he could still enter. The timing of the entry reflected his political practicality: only a Kennedy, so he believed, could unseat Johnson. Yet Kennedy's campaign lost its initial momentum when Lyndon Johnson delivered a television speech on March 31, just two days before the Wisconsin primary. The President declared that the time had come to deescalate the war. He would cut back bombing of the North and would turn down army requests for more troops. Then in a surprising coda he remarked that since he wanted to devote full time to the search for peace, he would not seek reelection in November.

Deprived of their most effective campaign issue —the President himself—Kennedy and McCarthy then had to campaign, to a great extent, against each other. Because they were thoroughly different in temperament, the rivalry between the two men became highly personal. In the process of their bickering the peace movement fragmented. McCarthy, never an admirer of the Kennedy clan, found offensive RFK's fascination with power. Kennedy thought McCarthy lazy, snobbish, and politically ineffectual. The two competed for the support of the young, who could be of assistance in the remaining primaries. McCarthy, after winning decisively against Johnson in Wisconsin, lost to Kennedy in Indiana and Nebraska. Then McCarthy made an unexpected comeback by winning easily in Oregon. One final primary would in large part determine the winner; Kennedy promised to drop out of the race should McCarthy defeat him in California on June 4. Kennedy won by a few percentage points, but on the very night of the election he was shot down by a Jordanian immigrant, Sirhan Bishara Sirhan. Six weeks before, on April 24, a criminal had shot and killed Martin Luther King, Jr., an event that sparked riots in the nation's capital and other major cities.

Curiously, McCarthy scarcely attempted to unite the antiwar forces after California. He ran very well in the mid-June New York primary, but instead of building support for the convention, he set aside part of each day to write poetry and finally withdrew for a period to a Benedictine retreat. When polls showed him to be only slightly ahead of Vice-President Hubert Humphrey, McCarthy appeared uninterested in politics. His virtual neglect of the Soviet injuries to Czechoslovakia during the summer called his judgment seriously into question.

But if the McCarthy candidacy petered out in the weeks before the convention, the peace movement itself was still strong. The Humphrey forces had no wish to alienate the peace Democrats and quietly agreed to sweeping reforms in the Democratic party. In Chicago, a broad democratization of delegate selection through the primaries was instituted for 1972. In retrospect it appears that McCarthy never believed he would win the nomination. Though his wit, intellect, and uncompromising virtue had its attraction for college campuses, he willfully resisted using pat formulas for political success.

On at least one occasion McCarthy recognized political practicality. At the Chicago convention Richard Daley encouraged an effort to draft the surviving Kennedy brother, Edward, a Massachusetts senator, and McCarthy offered to withdraw in his favor. It was the last hope of the amorphous peace movement. Edward Kennedy might well have denied the nomination to Vice-President Humphrey, who was so closely identified with an unpopular Johnson. Thousands of young people demonstrating outdoors reminded the delegates of their passionate dislike for the administration and for its policy in Vietnam. Several large states would have supported Kennedy, and in the psychology of a national convention enthusiasm for him as a potential winner might have put him across. But Kennedy refused to run.

The peace forces broke into anarchic fragments at the convention. A platform provision calling for a halt to all bombing in Vietnam failed by a 3 to 2 vote. Outside the convention hall in Grant Park the Chicago police battled with the young, engaging in what a government report later termed a "police riot." Inside, Senator Abraham Ribicoff of Connecticut told the delegates about the outside skirmishes and lashed out at the "Gestapo tactics of the police." After the riots Humphrey's nomination by a 2 to 1 margin over McCarthy and another peace candidate, Senator George McGovern of South Dakota, seemed anticlimactic. The drama of the convention centered on the confrontation between police and students, which included both harassment of young people by the police and the goading of authorities by the youths. Late in the evening the police invaded hotel suites used by McCarthy supporters, who had showered the police with assorted debris. The violence was an enduring monument to the nation's temper in 1968. And the events in Chicago cast a pall over the coming Democratic campaign.

Vice-President Hubert Humphrey was a particularly enigmatic figure. Just two decades before he had forced a split in the Democratic party on the issue of civil rights. He had also symbolized support for various welfare programs. But when asked as Vice-President what happened to the program he once had battled for, he answered simply and correctly: "We passed it." The voluble Humphrey welcomed opportunities to explain our intervention in Vietnam. He informed University of Pittsburgh students about Vietcong atrocities. Before an AFL-CIO convention he associated the critics of the war with appeasers of Hitler. He compared the corruption of South Vietnam's government with that of American cities. The Chinese Communists, he said, prolonged the war.

Understandably, the Humphrey presidential candidacy dismayed anti-war Democrats. Any skillful Republican candidate could hope to draw their support in the November election. The first Republican candidate was Governor George Romney of Michigan, a strong civil rights advocate. But Romney's casual and contradictory remarks on the Vietnam War worried the voters, and his reference to a "brainwashing" given him by briefing officers proved a catastrophe. After poor showings in early national polls he withdrew from the race. At the end of April Governor Nelson Rockefeller of New York, who favored the war, declared his candidacy. But even a $5 million media campaign did not compensate for his late start. Governor Ronald Reagan of California, the only rightwing candidate, stayed publicly out of the race, but he was privately available and friends paid for a low-pressure television campaign. The strongest contestant was the vintage Republican, former Vice-President Richard Nixon. He hewed to the political center and won victories in the spring primaries. Reagan tried to whittle away Nixon's southern support. Rockefeller hoped that preconvention polls would show him as the strongest candidate. But neither strategy succeeded. Nixon needed only 667 votes to win—and on the first ballot he received 691.

Richard Nixon was real Americana: Protestant, Anglo-Saxon, clean-cut, ambitious. As a boy he had cranked homemade ice cream at parties, played the piano at church, and led his high school debating team. While serving in the navy in the South Pacific, he set up a hamburger stand. He worked his way through Whittier College and Duke University Law School. Legal training, as well as skills in debate and card playing, constituted good preparation for a career in politics.

Nixon conducted the public investigation of Alger Hiss, accused of having been a Communist agent in the 1930's. But he was quite scrupulous about procedural rights, as some other members of the House Committee on Un-American Activities were not. Of course, he won votes by portraying his congressional opponent in 1946, Jerry Voorhis, as indifferent to communism, and he also pursued the theme in 1950. But the successful Senate campaign of that year against Helen Gahagan Douglas was a crude spectacle on both sides; the incumbent's lieutenants charged Nixon with both anti-Semitism and fascism—and he tried to link Douglas with radical congressmen who voted similarly. Nixon's voting record in the House and Senate is hard to characterize. In 1952 he certainly found no difficulty in supporting President Dwight Eisenhower over Robert Taft, whom he regarded as the weaker candidate politically. Nixon's fame in the Hiss case, his prestige as a California senator and influence with the state's convention delegates, his service and uncontroversial voting record in both houses of Congress all cast him as a strong vice-presidential candidate.

Nixon went on to become an active Vice-President. The President's Quaker running mate outdistanced him on the issue of civil rights. A member of the NAACP after 1950, Nixon received Eleanor Roosevelt's approval for his work promoting nondiscriminatory hiring as chairman of the Committee on Government Contracts. The Vice-President's trip to Russia in 1959, and his famous debate there in the kitchen of a model house, was but one of a long series of world journeys as emissary of the United States. After losing to Kennedy in 1960, Nixon moved to California and two years later failed in his bid for the governorship. During the 1964 presidential campaign he supported Barry Goldwater and thereby survived the year with political currency among party regulars. In mid-decade he practiced law in New York City, defending the right to privacy in *Time Inc.* v. *Hill* (1966). The case, however, followed by a year Nixon's intemperate denunciation of a then Rutgers University assistant professor (a co-author of this book) who had said he would welcome an enemy victory in Vietnam. Nixon thereafter avoided a clear position on Vietnam. By 1968 he seemed more relaxed and confidently in command of himself and his career than ever before. In the presidential campaign Nixon spoke in generalities, intent on keeping his large lead over Humphrey in the public opinion polls.

The Humphrey campaign, inaugurated so dismally in Chicago, got off to an unpromising start. Repeatedly the candidate misspent his energies in answering antiwar hecklers, who may have had some impact on forcing him to reconsider his position on Vietnam. For some months Humphrey had had growing doubts about the war, but the President was so hypersenitive and Dean Rusk so dogged about it that the candidate dared not speak his own thoughts. When Humphrey did promise an early end to the war, Rusk said that no one could predict when it might let up. Not until a nationwide television speech on September 30 did Humphrey dissociate himself from Johnson, calling for an immediate and unconditional halt to all bombing of North Vietnam. At once the gap in the polls between him and Nixon began to narrow.

A special dimension to the 1968 campaign was added by the candidacy of Alabama's Governor George Wallace, whose American Independent supporters listed him on the ballot in all fifty states and launched the most ambitious third party candidacy since Robert La Follette's in 1924. Wallace had become the candidate of the South on the strength of a single slogan: "Segregation now—Segregation tomorrow—Segregation forever." But now he reached out for a broader and more generalized campaign theme and insisted he was no racist. He blasted "bearded bureaucrats," "pointy-headed professors," and "poor-folks haters"—his campaign resembled a class movement, fueled by the divisions in taste, style, values, and education that have eclipsed wealth as social differentia. The Wallace campaign employed the slogan "law and order," which took on a menacing tone in the context. Above all, Wallace took as his target the Supreme Court under Chief Justice Earl Warren. Wallace denounced a long series of decisions, beginning with the school desegregation case of 1954 but also including those that outlawed school prayers, protected the rights of accused criminals, and strengthened the civil rights of minorities.

As late as the second half of September the Gallup poll credited Wallace with about 20 percent of the vote, most of it formerly Democratic. But labor unions used scare tactics, portraying Alabama as a low-wage, open-shop state. In California, long-haired boys and girls confused the candidate's audiences by pretending to be on his side, sometimes shouting "Sieg Heil, y'all!" Wallace's vice-presidential candidate, General Curtis LeMay, proved a liability. In a moment worthy of Barry Goldwater he said: "We seem to have a phobia about nuclear weapons . . . . I don't believe the world would end if we exploded a nuclear weapon."

Wallace's presence in the campaign permitted Nixon to portray himself as a middle-of-the-road candidate, even though he pursued a "Southern strategy" on civil rights and civil disorder. Spiro Agnew's addition to the Republican ticket was a gesture to the South. In the course of the campaign, Agnew made numerous blunders. Vernacular gibes about "Polacks" and "that fat Jap," while not delivered in an intentionally mean spirit, made no friends. He charged Humphrey with being "soft on communism" and then retracted the phrase, pleading unfamiliarity with its "political history." Democrats bought a television ad that showed his face and played the sound of a beating heart, suggesting the possibility of President Agnew. The running mate on the Democratic ticket, Senator Edmund Muskie of Maine, conducted an effective campaign, quietly gaining the loyalty of traditionally Democratic supporters among labor and the foreign born.

Nixon almost lost the 1968 election. At the end of October peace talks began in Paris and the bombing of North Vietnam ceased; had these signs of the war's diminution come a bit sooner, Humphrey might have won. As it was, Nixon won by almost as close a margin as he lost eight years before. Humphrey took some 88 percent of the black vote and even more of the Mexican American. Not one large city went Republican, and that party gained only four House seats along with five in the Senate. The Democratic coalition had held together remarkably well under the pressures of Vietnam.

Vietnam: Nixon's Policies

During the 1968 campaign, Nixon claimed to have a plan to end the war in Vietnam, which he preferred to withhold lest he upset any progress Johnson might make in the negotiations. After taking office Nixon appointed Henry Cabot Lodge chief American negotiator in Paris. Almost at the outset Lodge insisted on separating the military and political issues in face of North Vietnamese and Vietcong insistence on their inseparability. In May 1969 the Vietcong offered a ten-point proposal which included American withdrawal, free elections, and a coalition government. In reply, Nixon submitted a phased mutual withdrawal over a twelve-month period, including adding a Communist retreat from Cambodia and Laos. Neither side waivered from these proposals, but Nixon decided to move unilaterally toward disengagement. Scarcely a month later, Secretary of State Rogers remarked that the United States was not wedded to the Saigon regime, thereby raising the possibility of a coalition government. Nixon announced that he would reduce the 540,000 troops in Vietnam by 25,000 at the end of August, after which he would make further cuts.

In April 1970, the United States and South Vietnamese troops began a large-scale troop operation in Cambodia, designed to destroy enemy supplies and sanctuaries. As with earlier offensive actions, the administration defended this tactic on the grounds that it would speed American withdrawal. Such reasoning infuriated war critics: protests and strikes spread throughout the nation, especially on college campuses. In a demonstration against ROTC at Kent State University on May 4, National Guardsmen, called out in response to the burning of an ROTC building the night before, shot and killed four students. National Guard claims of sniper fire (never substantiated) could not suppress the outrage felt across the country; three days later eighty colleges had closed down and hundreds of others undertook various forms of protest, while construction workers attacked a group of war protesters in New York City. To cool the atmosphere, Nixon promised to end his criticism of students. (Only a few days earlier he had referred to campus radicals as "bums" in comparison with American soldiers who were "the greatest.")

One of the most sensitive issues in the peace negotiations was the fate of prisoners of war. Many American pilots shot down over North Vietnam had been POWs for four or five years. As their relatives began to insist on concessions to win their release, both pro and antiwar advocates embraced the POW issue for their own ends. On November 23, 1970, the administration authorized massive air strikes on North Vietnam and sent a rescue team to a suspected POW camp. When the news seeped out that no POWs had been rescued, the antiwar people sharpened their criticism, insisting on full withdrawal to win the POWs rapid release. In Paris the Vietcong and North Vietnamese made firm offers to release POWs in return for a definite date on complete American withdrawal from Indochina.

The Nixon administration would not set a date for a final pullout; indeed, in February 1971 the United States and the South Vietnamese launched an offensive in Laos. Although providing air support for South Vietnamese combat forces, the American command insisted that no American combat soldiers aided in the operation. Again Nixon explained the invasion as a means of carrying out Vietnamization and assuring the return home of soldiers by destroying enemy sanctuaries and supply depots. Even though the South Vietnamese soon abandoned the Laos invasion, the administration insisted upon its success. On April 7, 1971, President Nixon announced a further withdrawal of 100,000 troops by December 1971.

Although criticism of the Laos operation did not match the strident denunciation of the invasion in Cambodia a year before, protesters asserted that such a move, along with increased bombing missions, brought neither soldiers nor POWs home. By April demonstrators in Washington and San Francisco called for a specific date for withdrawal from Southeast Asia. Leading Democratic presidential contenders echoed the sentiment, and a special contingent of Vietnam veterans gathered in the Capitol to discard their medals. Yet Nixon promised to maintain a United States residual force in Vietnam until all POWs were released and until the South Vietnamese could defend themselves. In July the administration rejected a seven-point peace plan that assured the safety of withdrawing troops and promised the release of all prisoners if the United States would pull out by the end of 1971. A few days later, Le Duc Tho, one of the highest ranking North Vietnamese, announced a significant concession: withdrawal and POWs could be negotiated separately. Despite this marked departure from the position that political and military issues were inseparable, Nixon refused the offer.

The Long Road Toward Peace

Nixon continued to withdraw troops from Vietnam at a rate of 13,000 per month (the average since July 1969). On November 12, 1971, he announced a slightly accelerated withdrawal of 45,000 more in the months of December and January. This left 139,000 in Vietnam.

Scarcely two months later, beginning on December seventeenth, the United States launched against North Vietnam the heaviest bombing campaign yet. For two weeks, with a thirty-six-hour break for Christmas, American planes night after night bombed targets closer to urban populations and to the Chinese border than ever before. Huge B-52's carried on "carpet bombing"—the dropping of bombs by several planes simultaneously in an area over a mile long. This damaged many buildings in Hanoi not themselves targets including foreign embassies and a major hospital. World opinion reacted with shock. Yet Hanoi's reaction to the holocaust seemed restrained, as did that of Peking and Moscow. Renewed signs of North Vietnam's desire to negotiate, reinforced by the high costs of the bombing in American men and planes, produced an end to the attacks and a reopening of talks in early January.

This time the see-saw rose faster and higher than ever before and stayed up. A peace agreement, signed on January 23, 1973, made possible the separation of military and political questions, a compromise accepted by both sides only within the year. Finally, on March 29, with the release of the last prisoners of war and the departure of the last American troop units from Vietnam, the United States apparently ended its direct military role in Vietnam.

Relief but little celebration characterized the American response to the armistice. President Nixon, in his message announcing the peace, did not once use the word "victory," although he continuously reiterated his favorite phrase of "peace with honor." Few would have believed him if he had. The war that was ending had produced, in the words of one journalist, "no famous victories, no national heroes and no stirring patriotic songs."

In the months between the spring of 1972 and 1973, public expectations concerning Vietnam rode a see-saw that alternately raised fervent hopes of coming peace and deflated those hopes by dropping back toward seemingly endless fighting. The fruitless negotiations of early 1972

UNITED STATES MILITARY FORCES IN SOUTH VIETNAM, 1965-1972

Year	Number
1965	184,300
1966	385,300
1967	485,600
1968	536,100
1969	475,200
1970	334,600
1971	157,800
1972	95,500

Source: United States Department of Defense, Office of the Secretary, *Selected Manpower Statistics,* annual and unpublished data.

gave way to one of the war's most bitter battles. On April 1, after three days of intense bombardment, North Vietnamese regulars crossed the DMZ to attack South Vietnam with great force. A few days of unsuccessful resistance demonstrated that the South Vietnamese needed help. And on April 6, United States planes began making systematic strikes against North Vietnamese targets, although not bombing above the 20th parallel (about seventy miles south of Hanoi). But nine days later the United States began the first night attacks on the Hanoi-Haiphong area since March 1968 and the first use of B-52's in this region. On May 8 President Nixon announced that the United States would mine North Vietnamese ports and systematically attack all supply lines.

Yet, just as a see-saw at its lowest point can only go up, the May 8 speech included new possibilities for negotiation even as the mines were being planted. President Nixon stated two basic conditions for peace: the return of American prisoners of war and an internationally supervised cease-fire. For the first time, the American position mentioned no political requirements for United States withdrawal, at last separating the military and political problems in Vietnam. It soon became clear that the presidential trip to Russia would not be cancelled. Nixon conferred with Soviet leaders, exchanged gifts, addressed the Russian people, and played the tourist; in newspaper headlines ballet replaced battle. Yet the visit was not irrelevant to Vietnam; Russian influence on Hanoi during the next few months, though hard to gauge, was almost certainly significant in pushing for peace.

Even as the war continued, negotiations were clearly underway again. By mid-July presidential adviser Henry Kissinger began slipping out of Washington about every two weeks for secret Paris meetings with North Vietnamese representative Le Duc Tho. Something was happening though few knew precisely what. Kissinger himself described the climate accurately in commenting that "Those who talk don't know, and those who know don't talk."

A flurry of pronouncements near the end of October revealed the progress in Paris. On the twenty-fourth, administration sources stated that bombing north of the 20th parallel had been temporarily halted. The next day North Vietnam announced an agreement that could be signed immediately. Forced by this statement to offer some explanation, Kissinger declared on October 26, "Peace is at hand," and suggested that one more negotiating session should wrap up the cease-fire. But at least one party to the war had not yet agreed to anything. President Thieu of South Vietnam quickly emerged as a major obstacle to immediate accord by demanding the withdrawal of all North Vietnamese troops from the South before any cease-fire. Moreover, it rapidly became clear that Hanoi and Washington did not share the same understanding of several points necessary to the peace. More talks produced only a deterioration in relations. Kissinger charged the North Vietnamese with reopening settled questions and with being obstructive; further meetings were suspended. The see-saw which had risen so buoyantly turned downward once more.

Suggested Readings

A good introduction to the Vietnam War is Frances Fitzgerald, *Fire in the Lake: The Vietnamese and the Americans in Vietnam* (1972). She tells of the disruption of traditional Vietnamese society as a result of the war and the American presence. Michael Herr, a journalist in Vietnam, writes of the effect of the war on particular American soldiers: *Dispatches* (1977). David Halberstam, *The Best and the Brightest* (1972) contains a mountain of information based on extensive personal interviews. H. Y. Schandler, *The Unmaking of a President: Lyndon Johnson and Vietnam* (1977), explains why Johnson decided in March 1968 not to press the war harder; Schandler argues that the failure of the war came because of an effort to solve by military means a problem that was fundamentally political.

Three Mile Island Nuclear Power Plant. Harrisburgh, Pennsylvania

Chapter XXX
New Boundaries

Three Mile Island

Nuclear power plants like Three Mile Island, near Harrisburg, Pennsylvania, contain an abundance of protective devices. The uranium fuel pellets are held in steel fuel rods, which trap and hold radioactive materials. The bundles of fuel rods are encased in a steel reactor vessel with walls over eight inches thick. This giant steel tank is, in turn, enshrouded in a set of two steel and concrete shields over nine feet thick. Hugging this entire apparatus is a containment building with four-foot concrete walls. Within this fortress are redundant systems to control the nuclear reaction and to maintain appropriate temperatures. The failure of any one system automatically shuts off the reaction and triggers a back-up system to cool the rods. And a nuclear explosion is impossible: unlike the breeder reactors—now in development—which can become, for all intents and purposes, nuclear bombs, fundamental laws of physics make it impossible for these light water fission reactors to explode. Their main danger (although one which both the nuclear power industry and the industry's federal watchdog, the Nuclear Regulatory Commission—NRC—deemed too incredible to take seriously) was known as the "China Syndrome." If, incredibly, the hundred tons of uranium in a reactor were somehow to be left without proper cooling, the core would—theoretically at least—heat to the point where it would melt through the reactor vessel, through the containment building and, perhaps, on down into the ground "to China." (Actually, it would eventually be quenched by groundwater, producing a murderous flume of radioactive steam with unknown but presumably formidable capacity to damage human beings and other animals. "What melts in the ground and not in your mouth?" asked a riddle popular in early April 1979. The answer, a nearby town, Hershey, Pennsylvania.

Three Mile Island Unit Two had received its operating license from the NRC in February 1978. In late March, the plant, still in the testing stage, had its first startup. In one day, a blown fuse forced a shutdown. When a relief valve stuck open, threatening a loss of coolant, the backup system, called the Emergency Core Cooling System (ECCS), jumped in to keep the core covered with water. This event, so similar to the episode that riveted national attention a year later, was the first of many problems. Several losses of coolant and resulting shutdowns occurred in the next months. In fact, during the remainder of 1978, the plant was down for repairs for over two-thirds of the period. However, the Metropolitan Edison Company, whose plant it was, brought Unit Two on line for commercial generation on December 30, 1978. By generating power commercially before the close of 1978, the company gained somewhere between $45 and $60 million in tax credits and depreciation writeoffs.

In the early morning hours of Wednesday, March 28, 1979, Unit Two came within an ace of that supposed impossibility—a core meltdown. When a pump supplying water to the reactor's steam turbine stopped functioning at thirty-six seconds after 4:00 a.m., the steam turbine shut down within two seconds, as it was supposed to do. When there was no longer steam to carry away heat from the pressurized water that circulated through the nuclear core, a valve opened to release the pressure—as it was supposed to do. Within eight seconds, the control rods that absorb neutrons and halt the reaction had dropped into place—right on schedule. Heat from ongoing fission reaction ceased. All that remained was for emergency pumps to provide water to absorb the residual heat from the rods. An operator checked: the emergency pumps were running. What he did not know was that a valve was closed, preventing the water from entering. One light, which would have indicated this, was covered by a maintenance tag and another—for reasons unknown—was missing. This was the first of several technical problems in which reading the control board misinformed the operators. One problem piled upon another: soon a hundred alarms were ringing, making it nearly impossible to connect what one saw on the board with what was occurring within the reactor. "I would have liked to have thrown away the alarm panel," one operator recalled. "It wasn't giving us any useful information." The operators missed several serious signals. One indicator that the reactor temperature had reached 2300 degrees was dismissed as unbelievable. Another pipe temperature which might have indicated the most critical problem—an open valve that prevented the water from staying in the reactor and covering the rods—was ignored because the gauge always read high owing to a perennial problem. "I had been living with a leaky relief valve for quite some time," testified one operator. For over two hours, the operators and other TMI officials notified by the crew labored over their problems. Finally at 6:22 a.m. someone—apparently a shift foreman reporting for work and therefore not yet confused by the surplus of signals—shut the correct valve. A report commissioned by the Nuclear Regulatory Commission, the so-called Rogovin Report, stated that:

If that valve had remained open, our projections show that within 30 to 60 minutes a substantial amount of reactor fuel would have begun to meltdown—requiring at least the precautionary evacuation of thousands of people living near the plant, and potentially serious public health and safety consequences for the immediate area.

By now, radiation levels within the plant were dangerously high. Supervisors declared a "site emergency" and began notifying various officials. "And I said to myself, 'This is the biggie, ' " recalled one of the first Pennsylvania officials to be informed.

A biggie it was. While more and more operators and supervisors struggled to get the plant under control, a bewildering variety of personnel—from Met Ed, from various Pennsylvania agencies and municipalities, from the NRC—tried to make sense of the story for a nervous public. None of these groups fared very well. Within the plant, remedial efforts produced a further uncovering of the core. Outside, some Met Ed spokesmen reassured the public while others conceded that radioactive materials had been vented. A sudden "thud" in the control room puzzled everyone: a day later the scientists would realize that it had been a small explosion of hydrogen released in the reactor.

The biggest danger had ended at 6:22 with the avoidance of a meltdown, but no one was sure of this until much later. People controlled their jitters through Thursday, but as scientists began worrying about a bubble of hydrogen in the reactor and evidence accumulated of radiation releases (although there was a world of uncertainty about their extent and danger), on Friday the governor of Pennsylvania recommended the evacuation of pregnant women and children under the age of two years from a five-mile radius about the plant. In the next days, as scientists studied the bubble—which eventually dispersed without or despite their activities—and President Carter arrived to inspect the plant, the nation's attention fixed not only on Three Mile Island, but on the entire nuclear power industry. Many who had scarcely noticed the existence of seventy-two operating reactors in the United States and ninety-one more under construction began to wonder about their safety and whether their development should continue. By Monday, April 2, the public knew that TMI would not explode. But the nuclear power issue would.

In a sense, the Three Mile Island incident was far from over. Cleanup—itself a potentially hazardous process—would take years and cost hundreds of millions of dollars. Within months, the NRC would find cleanup workers who had received doses of radiation in excess of nationally-set health standards. Contractors estimated that the cleanup would require 2,000 workers who would go through 200,000 cloth coveralls, 1,000,000 paper coveralls, 1,000,000 plastic coveralls, 100,000 raincoats, 1,000,000 pairs of plastic booties, 100,000 pairs of rubber boots, 1,000,000 pairs of rubber gloves, 100,000 surgical caps, 1,000 hard hats, 10,000 sponge mops, and 1,000,000 square feet of plastic sheeting. Millions of cubic feet of contaminated air and water would have to be chemically cleaned as well. Nuclear power sharply posed the conflict between the need for energy and the compelling concern to protect the health and safety of the public. And the mystery and uncertainty of it all troubled the nation. Pennsylvania governor Richard Thornburgh sensitively portrayed the episode as "an event that people are not able to see, to hear, to taste, to smell. . . ." Indeed, it will be years before what happened within the core at Unit Two can be fully assessed. The ultimate statement was on a briefly popular T-shirt—the usual spot for ultimate statements: "I survived Three Mile Island—I think."

With a boost from continued high government defense spending and consumer outlays on goods unavailable under war rationing, the gross national product jumped from $200 billion in the five years after World War II. By the end of the 1960's, economic activity reached the dazzling figure of one trillion dollars—aided somewhat by growing inflation. Both profits and wages rose steadily through most of the two postwar decades, although difficulties began to appear in the economy late in the 1960's.

Advanced industrial nations have an increasingly large number of workers who provide consumer services, and postwar affluence of the United States originated in part with unparalleled growth in this area. The percentage of the labor force engaged in sales and service occupations—retailing, hotels and motels, restaurants, health spas, movie theaters—leapt sharply upward. Consumers in the 1950's and 1960's were barraged with every sales technique Madison Avenue could devise. Advertising costs in 1970 measured eight times those of 1940. To some, consumerism demonstrated the superiority of American life relative to those societies—especially the Soviet Union—where people still struggled to obtain basic necessities. Yet critics like the popular sociologist Vance Packard perceived a strong element of mindless accumulation.

The growth of the American economy encouraged the unprecedented expansion of social services, and government spending on social programs, especially education, increased steadily after World War II. In addition to its political effect, this spending contributed to the swelling professional, technical, and clerical occupations in public education and government bureaucracies. As their numbers increased and the institutions employing them became more stratified and bureaucratized, some public employees turned to unions, with the American Federation of Teachers the prominent example. Additional needs for white-collar workers enlarged a "new middle class," a dynamic element that fueled political movements, influenced cultural styles and tastes, and provided the themes for countless novels and movies from *The Man in the Gray Flannel Suit* to *The Graduate*. C. Wright Mills, an academic sociologist, published in 1951 the first systematic treatment of the "new middle class" and its implications in *White Collar*.

The Social Spectrum

Women—married and single—entered the labor force in record numbers during the postwar era. During World War II, many women held factory jobs, filling vacancies created by the manpower needs of the armed forces. Pushed out of these jobs by returning soldiers, women found that the good times meant widespread opportunities in clerical work, teaching, and nursing—the traditional female fields. But their concentration in low-paying jobs was hardly satisfying; women continued to comprise nearly one-third of unskilled workers, especially in textiles and other light industries. Few business and professional women held the better positions, and in general they received less for their work. At the same time, women were having more and more babies. The birth rate per 1,000 population reached a high 24.1 in 1950 and peaked at 25.0 in 1955 before declining steadily. This postwar "baby boom" led to a number of important social developments. The bumper crop of children necessitated building programs in the public schools; overcrowded classrooms brought about school financing crises and a national furor over "why Johnny can't read."

These postwar children, in elementary school when the Soviet Union launched its Sputnik satellite in 1957, became the target of elaborate programs of curriculum reform with particular emphasis on mathematics and the sciences. More babies also would furnish an immense audience for television and create a record market for rock and roll music, automobiles, surfboards, clothes, skin creams, magazines, movies, and innumerable other commodities. By the mid-1960's, greater opportunities in public higher education tripled enrollments in publicly controlled institutions, as state colleges and community junior colleges multiplied. Finally, the postwar generation created the base for student movements and much of the cultural experimentation of the 1960's.

Mobility continued to characterize Americans. Long-term movements from farms to cities and from parts of the South to the rest of the nation continued, especially into California, which passed New York in the late 1960's to become the nation's most populous state. Black and Spanish-speaking people crowded into decaying inner cities while large numbers of whites fled to the suburbs.

Neither slums nor suburbia was a new phenomenon, but the pace of movement quickened rapidly. Gary, Indiana; Cleveland; and Newark, New Jersey elected black mayors for the first time. Income as well as race caused the polarization between city and suburbs; some affluent blacks made inroads into suburbia and many working-class whites remained in the urban enclaves. The "urban crisis" continued unabated despite a succession of renewal programs and President Nixon's announcement in early 1973 that it had been solved.

In another cultural area the upsurge of science fiction during the fifties, both in books and on film, bore a definite if indirect relation to political concerns. A best-selling writer of the period, Robert Heinlein, typically featured a masculine superhero who wiped out the forces of evil with a combination of brute strength and advanced engineering while delivering soliloquies about the effeminacy of the democratic process in time of crisis. Heinlein's fiction embodied the political philosophy of Ayn Rand, an Eastern European refugee whose books, widely read among a segment of college students, stressed an ultra-individualist ethic as a counterpoise to socialist but not corporate collectivism. Many science fiction movie plots centered around a threat posed to society (usually American) by an alien force whose characteristics—unemotionalism, lack of individuality, militarism, expansionism—matched those popularly attributed to the Soviet bloc.

All through the postwar period academic social scientists moved in and out of government, notably in the area of foreign policy: the Harvard professor Samuel Huntington essentially wrote the South Vietnamese Constitution, and Henry Kissinger, also a Harvard government professor, progressed from writing European diplomatic history to orchestrating the Vietnam settlement and the detente with China. Other university social scientists turned their attention to the problems raised by the cold war by producing study after study on Soviet and Eastern European affairs. Many of the prominent scholars in this field, themselves political refugees from Communist countries, gave their work distinctive vehemence. Drawing on the apparent similarities of communism and fascism—centralized authority, neglect of civil liberties and formal democratic procedures, glorification of mass action—these social theorists grasped the idea of a "totalitarian" society as a menace to "free" society.

Unlike totalitarian societies, America, with its advanced electronic weaponry, had its complement in sophisticated gadgetry for industry and home—copiers, credit card billing, eight-track and cassette tape recorders, direct distance dialing, TV dinners, drive-in banking—a seemingly endless list. Such mechanical innovations had implications reaching far beyond their immediate impact: the copying machine and the cassette recorder, for example, threatened the copyright laws, making it easy for individuals to reproduce materials without paying the original producers, authors, and performers. Inexpensive, high-fidelity recordings of all kinds of music became available, along with improved phonographic equipment. Paperback books, bringing to mass audiences not only a variety of cheap leisure reading but also ready access to serious and scholarly work, vastly improved high school and college curriculums and contributed to what some labeled a knowledge explosion. Factories and stores introduced piped-in Muzak, soothing and cushioning workers and shoppers from the rough edges of everyday life. Air travel for affluent Americans became commonplace, while special fares for young people accustomed them to a convenience that had been a mere fantasy for their parents. Heavy consumer goods reached a far greater market than ever before: by 1970, 99 percent of American households owned at least one television set. But the new technology had a double edge: it meant greater comfort, faster service, and increased leisure for those who could afford it; at the same time, mass-production of comforts and culture brought standardization and homogenization.

Critics reacted strongly to the emerging mass culture symbolized by television's situation comedies and popular music's banal lyrics. Newton Minow, chairman of the Federal Communications Commission under President Kennedy, aptly called television a "vast wasteland." Writers for television defended themselves, complaining that sponsor censorship, strict network guidelines on "controversial" subjects, and the difficulties of fitting dramatic action to the precise time segments between commercial breaks restricted originality. The ability of record companies to create rock and roll stars out of adolescents with no musical talent—the most notorious case involving a performer named simply Fabian—unnerved those who placed value on tradition. Some suggested that mass culture might be the harbinger of a dangerous social and political stupor. The sociologist David Riesman called contemporary Americans *The Lonely Crowd,* members of a mass society in which individuals were "other-directed," lacking in personal autonomy, conformist in a thorough-going way. He contrasted this with a picture of an earlier society in which individuals had been "inner-directed," self-motivated, individualistic. Riesman's book contained more loose description than scientific analysis, but it captured one important strain of social criticism.

In 1960 the sociologist Daniel Bell proclaimed the "end of ideology." An advanced industrial society eliminated class conflict, the traditional engine of change, and this, he said, led to "the exhaustion of political ideas in the fifties." Daniel Boorstin, Louis Hartz, and a school of "consensus" historians projected this image back on the American past, finding uniqueness in stability and in the absence of conflict that had characterized European history. These historians provided a useful corrective to more romantic earlier interpretations, but they also seemed to ignore or even denigrate those groups and forces that had fought sharply for change, and they often applied rather tortuous explanations to such obvious conflicts as the Civil War. Such versions of the American past and present came under attack in the 1960's when undeniable social turbulence made judgments of inevitable consensus look somewhat hasty.

In 1967 a series of revelations unveiled the participation of the Central Intelligence Agency in subsidizing and channeling cultural and intellectual life. The CIA and other federal agencies, through an elaborate network of dummy foundations, for years paid the bills for a number of unlikely (and sometimes unwitting) people and groups—Socialist party chairman Norman Thomas, the liberal National Student Association, the literary intellectuals in America and Britain associated with *Encounter* magazine, and the Congress for Cultural Freedom. What the CIA received for its money could not be precisely specified, but the intellectual and academic community had apparently learned a lesson, one which widespread disillusionment with United States policy in Indochina reinforced. Intellectuals grew suspicious of the comfortable and noncritical stance toward government they and their predecessors had adopted in the fifties.

American Subcultures

Beyond the confines of both traditional "high" culture and the spreading, popular "mass" culture, a distinctive body of writing originated during the 1950's. The aftermath of World War II, like that of World War I, produced a "lost generation" of disillusioned young adults: the F. Scott Fitzgeralds and the Jazz Age found a counterpart in the beats of North Beach, San Francisco, and Greenwich Village, New York City. The popular press used "beat," short for beatnik, a spin-off from Sputnik; a few "beats" explained it as short for "beatific," indicating a state of tranquil disengagement from the rat-race America with which they could not identify. Never so self-conscious and organized as the groups of the 1960's, their work did not assume the same commercial importance of some later movements. Yet the beats, their numbers tiny, initiated a literary and cultural flowering. Jack Kerouac gained the largest reputation as a beat spokesman with *On the Road* (1956) and a series of other novels; his effortless, stark prose chronicled beat culture semiautobiographically, detailing the simple pleasures and pains of cross-country hitchhiking, evading the police, appreciating "cool" black jazz, discovering marijuana, dabbling with Zen Buddhism, and generally avoiding the incomprehensible larger society. A revival of Kerouac's novels in the late sixties evidenced a newer generation of alienated youth searching for models and insights. Although Kerouac's novels had the widest audience, the voice of the beat generation spoke in poetry. Allen Ginsberg, coming from a radical middle-class family in Paterson, New Jersey, bummed his way around the world several times before composing the central statement of beat culture, "Howl!" in 1956. Its opening lines clearly expressed the beats' view of oppressive America:

I saw the best minds of my generation   destroyed
by madness,
    starving hysterical naked,
dragging themselves through the negro streets
  at dawn looking for
    an angry fix

Ginsberg and another poet, Gary Snyder, also popularized Indian and Oriental religion and philosophy among avant-garde groups; they approached Eastern religion with seriousness and a discipline not matched by the casual borrowings of the Beatles and others in later years. Ginsberg, possibly because of his radical background, maintained a more distinctly political stance than most beats; he became a fixture at antiwar demonstrations in the sixties, chanting rhythmic Indian mantras in an attempt to immobilize the police. With novelist Ken Kesey and satirist Paul Krassner, Ginsberg represented a direct link between the beats and the experimenters of the sixties. Lawrence Ferlinghetti, another beat poet, ran City Lights bookstore and its small publishing company in San Francisco, providing the beat community with publisher, seller, and general meeting place.

Beat culture, outwardly all exuberance and irreverence, ultimately posed serious questions unnoticed by the majority of apparently frivolous young Americans. By the late fifties, a distinct adolescent subculture emerged, nurtured by a degree of affluence and swelled by the postwar baby boom. Teen-age life revolved around two technological wonders of advanced industrial society—the automobile and the 45 rpm record. The automobile, of course, had been busily reweaving the pattern of American life since Henry Ford introduced the Model T, but only in the fifties could significant numbers of adolescents afford to buy their own cars and modify them in accord with current hot rod styles. Access to automobiles expanded unsupervised dating among adolescents; cars became essential to social success for many high school males and an integral part of masculine identity. James Dean's classic role in the movie *Rebel Without a Cause*—the rebellious, hard-drinking, drag-racing high school stud who defies his middle-class parents and the police in resolving his identity crisis—terrified parents and excited their children.

The adolescent subculture provided a ready market for the musical explosion of rock and roll. Early rock and roll relied on two musical strains with long traditions and independent audiences. The primary appropriation, black "rhythm and blues," gave the drive, the beat, and the solid, earthy feeling of the music. Rhythm and blues in turn had its roots in black jazz, gospel, and blues music, all representing an autonomous market for recorded music until the advent of rock and roll. Some rhythm and blues performers—Little Richard, Fats Domino, the Coaster—successfully moved to the newer and larger white audience, but much of black rhythm and blues was simply picked up and bleached by white performers and recording studios without payment or acknowledgement. White country music, the other musical source of rock and roll, contributed some vocal patterns, the distinctive lead guitar sound, and many of the most important performers. The Everly Brothers and Buddy Holly came directly from the country tradition, and Elvis Presley, the dominating figure of early rock, worked as a

Blackboard Jungle, *1955. Juvenile delinquency and rebellious youth furnished themes for many films in the 1950s and after. This movie, centering on the experiences of an urban slum school teacher, paid tribute also to the developing youth culture. It was the first major film to have a rock'n'roll musical score. The definitive statement of hostility to established norms was uttered by Marlon Brando in* The Wild One *(1953.) Asked what he is rebelling against, the chieftain of the "Black Rebels Motorcycle Club" replies, "Whaddaya got?"*

string bass player on the Grand Ole Opry in Nashville. Before his first major recording contract in 1956 and the release of "Heartbreak Hotel"—a hit with country, popular, and rhythm and blues audiences—Presley had been an acclaimed country performer. Unsophisticated music, rock and roll nonetheless possessed a vitality with which a new generation readily identified.

The adolescent devotees of the rock culture and the hot rod consciously circumscribed themselves by their purposeful separation from the adult world. Most Americans preferred an entirely different range of experience. Neither knowing nor caring about Allen Ginsberg, they read *Reader's Digest,* with a monthly circulation of about ten million copies. The most popular books of the fifties were not Kerouac's novels, but the *Reader's Digest Condensed Books,* abridgments of milder best-sellers, which consistently sold millions of copies. Similarly, the biggest box-office attractions of the fifties were not James Dean films but romantic comedies starring Rock Hudson and Doris Day, and such spectacular movies as *Ben-Hur* and *The Ten Commandments.* Among adult Americans not Elvis but Lawrence Welk ruled, serving waltzlike, romantically light "Champagne Music" over prime-time national television in the late 1950's and 1960's. Instead of drag racing, tens of millions of Americans sat and watched, in a stadium or on television, baseball, football, and horse racing. Most Americans felt reasonably secure in a relatively tranquil society; consequently they responded to passive forms of entertainment, not to the more jarring chords of the teen-agers and beats.

By far the largest commercial culture empire of the fifties was Walt Disney Productions, Inc. In the 1940's Disney achieved success by producing highly innovative animated cartoons and feature movies. By the fifties, he had left the drawing board to oversee a colossal business enterprise, producing cartoons, comic books, a weekly television series, and a host of other projects. "Davy Crockett," a Disney three-part television series, later made into a feature film, ultimately released the largest preteen-age merchandising fad ever seen in America. In 1955 Disney fulfilled his lifelong dream by opening "Disneyland" in Anaheim, California, incontestably the world's greatest amusement park. Drawing on themes and characters from every cartoon and movie Disney had produced, Disneyland created a fantasy world comprehensive enough to appeal to almost everyone. Soviet Premier Nikita Khrushchev was miffed when security problems made it impossible for him to visit Disneyland during his trip to America in 1959—but more than five million Americans did show up annually. The pleasures of Disneyland perhaps evoked a widely shared mood of the fifties—safe, tranquil, vaguely unreal, more than a trifle sugary. But just as Disneyland itself would later be invaded by thousands of antiwar demonstrators, the calm surfaces of mainstream culture would be disrupted by the political tensions of the mid-1960's.

Another comforting fact of the fifties was the steady rise in church membership, increasing more rapidly than the total population. Between 1950 and 1956, Roman Catholics added five million members, Protestants eight million. Actual church attendance also grew, although precise measures of this are difficult to reconstruct. Bishop Fulton J. Sheen conducted a weekly, half-hour television program for several years blending Catholic doctrine with common sense, wit, and even what might have seemed irreverence—"angels" erased the blackboard he used to illustrate his talks. A central figure in evangelical Protestantism, the Reverend Billy Graham crusaded across America and throughout the world. Although Graham's origins were orthodox, he presented a nonsectarian image and served as an unofficial "spiritual adviser" to a number of Presidents. Graham functioned as a popularizer of Christianity rather than as a theologian; by the mid-1960's he was appropriating the language of the youth culture, letting his own hair grow a bit, and appearing on late-night television talk shows. While organized religion remained a powerful institution, Protestant membership leveled off in the mid-sixties and declined thereafter; the Roman Catholic Church suffered in 1971, for the first time in its history, a small absolute decline in its American membership.

Civil Rights and Student Movement

The rise of the civil rights movement in the later fifties foreshadowed an America of greater conflict. In their struggle for justice, black Americans received early sympathy from many whites, but the campaign inevitably exposed deep-seated inequalities and prejudices that could not be conquered simply by goodwill. Civil rights in particular helped to uncover the problem of poverty in America. The poor had long faced daily poverty, but that fact did not receive national attention at least until the publication in 1962 of Michael Harrington's *The Other America*. Harrington and others demonstrated that more than one-fourth of the population remained underfed and ill-housed, trapped in urban slums or depressed rural areas with no political or economic leverage to improve their situation. As the civil rights movement shifted its focus from formal legal and political demands to challenges for economic equality, resistance stiffened.

At the same time, black intellectuals and artists stressed the cultural separation between blacks and whites. James Baldwin wrote moveingly of the black experience in books aptly titled *Another Country* and *Nobody Knows My Name*. Black jazz musicians, for years the leading edge of black culture, began to experiment with new musical forms. The restraint and symmetry in the music of Count Basie and Duke Ellington, or even of Miles Davis and Thelonius Monk, was replaced by the free-form emotional expression of John Coltrane and Ornette Coleman—powerful, discordant expressions of black sensibility; bassist Charles Mingus titled one of his compositions "Fables of Faubus" in scornful memory of the governor of Arkansas. The stirrings of black intellectuals and

We are people of this generation, bred in at least modest comfort, housed now in universities, looking uncomfortably to the world we inherit.

When we were kids the United States was the wealthiest and strongest country in the world; the only one with the atom bomb, the least scarred by modern war, an initiator of the United Nations that we thought would distribute Western influence throughout the world. Freedom and equality for each individual, government of, by, and for the people—these American values we found good, principles by which we could live as men. Many of us began maturing in complacency.

As we grew, however, our comfort was penetrated by events too troubling to dismiss. First, the permeating and victimizing fact of human degradation, symbolized by the Southern struggle against racial bigotry, compelled most of us from silence to activism. Second, the enclosing fact of the Cold War, symbolized by the presence of the Bomb, brought awareness that we ourselves, and our friends, and millions of abstract "others" we knew more directly because of our common peril, might die at any time. We might deliberately ignore, or avoid, or fail to feel all other human problems, but not these two, for these were too immediate and crushing in their impact, too challenging in the demand that we as individuals take the responsibility for encounter and resolution.

While these and other problems either directly oppressed us or rankled our consciences and became our own subjective concerns, we began to see complicated and disturbing paradoxes in our surrounding America. The declaration "all men are created equal . . ." rang hollow before the facts of Negro life in the South and the big cities of the North. The proclaimed peaceful intentions of the United States contradicted its economic and military investments in the Cold War status quo.

The Port Huron Statement
by Students for a Democratic Society

SDS met in Port Huron, Michigan, in 1962, and wrote an agenda for reform. Tom Hayden was one of its authors.

---

artists toward a separate cultural identity played a prelude to the strain of political separatism prominent a few years later.

An awareness of racial and economic injustice impelled thousands of white college students to go south in "Freedom Summer," to work for blacks' civil rights, particularly in Mississippi. They met injustice face to face and learned the skills of practical politics. The civil rights movement formed the crucible for several student movements, as politically involved students brought back their experiences and applied them to their universities and to society in general. The civil rights work provided a trained leadership that mobilized campuses around the country during the next few years in massive opposition to the escalating war in Indochina.

The early student movement emerged between the 1962 founding convention of the Students for a Democratic Society (SDS) and the 1964 Free Speech Movement (FSM) at the University of California at Berkeley. The SDS convention convened in Port Huron, Michigan, and developed the "Port Huron Statement" reflecting a mixture of support for American ideals and desire for major changes. SDS called for social reform, not social revolution; the platform coupled its opposition to America's role in the cold war with explicit opposition to communism, a demand for educational reform with a strong belief in the university as a vehicle for social change, and a systematic critique of American society with an insistence on nonviolence. The slogan of SDS during the 1964 presidential campaign, "half the way with LBJ," revealed the group's ambivalence. The Free Speech Movement at Berkeley, though ostensibly for specific political rights such as bringing in speakers and distributing political literature on university property, presented in embryo a challenge to the concept Chancellor Clark Kerr called "The Multiversity." While servicing large numbers of students, Kerr's modern university remained closely tied to business and government, performing the research and analysis tasks that supported defense industries, domestic social policies, and corporate product development. Labeling this orientation a highly sophisticated prop of the status quo, FSM counterpoised the somewhat vague and idealistic notion of "a free university in a free society."

Student movements came at a receptive time. In the early 1960's students enrolled in colleges and universities in greater numbers than ever before. Some states advanced an unprecedented one-half of all high school students to some form of college study. California and New York led the nation in the expansion of their universities, state colleges, and two-year junior colleges. Their numbers and a degree of common experience gave some college students a sense of collective identity and potential power. At Berkeley the FSM coalition covered all shades of political opinion; even Young Republicans and Young Americans for Freedom joined in demanding an end to campus restrictions. Surface similarities in dress, hair, and musical taste on some campuses further contributed to an underestimation of the student diversity that splintered college movements a few years later.

SDS in its early years aimed for the creation of "participatory democracy" in America. This vision of a decentralized and debureaucratized community in which everyone affected by any social policy would have a voice in its determination suggested community control of schools, increased student power in universities, citizen control of police forces, and even worker determination of working conditions. SDS helped organize the first major antiwar demonstration in Washington in April 1965, and surprised everyone by drawing 25,000 people. Campus SDS chapters began campaigns against research sponsored by the Department of Defense, against recruiting by the Dow Chemical Company, which manufactured napalm, and most important, against ROTC. The training of military officers seemed to many a direct link between the university and American foreign policy; and there were objections to the special status of ROTC courses and staff members. Campus after campus exploded in protest. The shootings at Kent State in 1970 came in the wake of a prolonged struggle over ROTC. On a few leading campuses, successful campaigns produced a denial of academic credit or university facilities to ROTC, which in effect eliminated these programs altogether.

The increased size and militance of student protests coupled with their more sweeping demands produced serious confrontations with college administrators. When small groups resorted to the occupation of buildings and were met with tear gas and police squadrons, broader revolt ensued in 1968 at Columbia, Harvard, and San Francisco State College. The size of antiwar demonstrations in major cities escalated immensely. These levels of protest created internal divisions within student movements over the nature of civil rights and antiwar activities, and a proliferation of groups and organizations with differing strategies followed. SDS split into several factions at a stormy convention in 1969.

But in the middle years of the 1960's, the student movement had supported the creation of a self-conscious and many-faceted youth culture. Students and nonstudents worked to reshape themselves, their environment, and ultimately the larger society. The demand for relevant and unprescribed education led to the establishment on some campuses of "free universities"—educational experiments including open registration and courses ranging from traditional academic offerings or political study groups to auto mechanics, transcendental meditation, and macrobiotic cooking. "Underground" newspapers, made possible by technical progress in inexpensive offset printing, appeared in every major city. The Berkeley *Barb,* the Los Angeles *Free Press,* the East Village *Other,* and the Atlanta *Great Speckled Bird* carried a mixed assortment: political analysis and polemics, music reviews, discussions of experimental life-styles, more or less inventive graphic art work, and excursions into mysticism, Oriental religion, and the effects of "mind-expanding" drugs.

A vocal minority of students found marijuana and eventually other drugs useful tools in their search for spontaneity. Estimates of the number of college students who at least tried marijuana reached by the late seventies as high as one-half. The stronger drugs which found more limited use—LSD, hashish, mescaline, and amphetamines—were stimulants and "psychedelics" unlike the still popular depressant drugs. Psychologist Timothy Leary involuntarily left his post at Harvard to preach the necessity to "turn on, tune in, drop out"; novelist Ken Kesey and his band of Merry Pranksters spiked the punch at rock concerts with the dangerous but not yet illegal LSD.

Rock music remained a major component of the youth culture in the sixties. With the infusion of fresh musical ideas from England via the Beatles and the Rolling Stones, and with the introduction of highly sophisticated electronic equipment for recordings and performances, rock blossomed into a powerful form and a major industry. The beats and the earlier activists who had discovered the strengths of American folk music provided some of the audience for the "urban folk revival" of the late fifties and early sixties which popularized authentic performers like Doc Watson, Mississippi John Hurt, and Jean Ritchie. The revival also produced a number of young, topical folksingers—notably Phil Ochs, Joan Baez, and Bob Dylan—who combined their musical talent with political commentary. Though this resurgence established a permanent audience among college students for folk and country music, its importance increased in 1964-65 as louder and more commercial rock music became dominant. Bob Dylan was booed off the stage during the 1965 Newport Rock Festival for using electric instruments in his back-up band, but the disapproval of purists hardly slowed his career.

The association of rock with drugs produced innumerable lyrics and a style known as "acid" or "psychedelic" rock—the special province of San Francisco-based groups such as the Grateful Dead, the Jefferson Airplane, and Big Brother and the Holding Company. San Francisco's Haight-Ashbury district became the center of 1967's "summer of love" as thousands of young people swarmed in from across the country. The Grateful Dead gave free concerts in the park; food was distributed by the Diggers, named after a seventeenth-century British sect advocating the abolition of private property. Others pitched in to establish free medical clinics and a host of other services. The "summer of love" also occasioned a minor business boom as hundreds of small entrepreneurs profited from the provision of drug-culture paraphernalia—black-light posters, water pipes, and chrome-plated roach clips. The "head shops" merchandising such items merely foreshadowed a systematic commercialization of youth movements, culminating perhaps in the advertising campaign to "hear the revolution on Columbia Records."

Theodore Roszak's *The Making of a Counter-Culture* (1969) offered a label for what was happening and tried to elevate youthful dissent into a profound social dynamic, suggesting that modern society's technological abundance had spawned an inevitable revolt by its own younger generation. Yale professor Charles Reich, in a popular but conceptually slippery book, predicted that the emerging culture would lead to *The Greening of America* (1970), a new consciousness transcending the older mentalities of the frontier and of business enterprise.

According to many observers, American society and particularly the young experienced a "sexual revolution" in the postwar years. The Kinsey reports (1948 and 1953), the first major attempt at a systematic investigation of actual sexual practice, based on thousands of interviews, had already presented results that challenged the comfortable presumption of widespread, happy monogamy. The Kinsey methodology was less than airtight, but the report documented an undeniable prevalence of homosexuality, infidelity, pre- and extra-marital sexuality, and practices conventionally labeled "abnormal." Later, increased availability of contraceptive information and devices, most notably birth control pills for women, allegedly accelerated sexual permissiveness. Masters and Johnson's *Human Sexual Response* (1966) and *Human Sexual Inadequacy* (1970) became best-sellers though concerned with the dry, clinical presentation of basic sexual physiology. *Human Sexual Response* shattered a number of unexamined myths and helped to legitimize further serious study of the subject. The sixties also saw greater acceptance of male and female homosexuality. Homosexuals, or "gays," became more visible, forming gay power groups to fight against various forms of discrimination.

In the late sixties and seventies a particularly distinctive revolution occurred in the way most educated, younger Americans perceived male and female homosexuals. "Gays," undoubtedly the major casualty in Senator Joseph R. McCarthy's redbaiting crusade against security risks, have always lived in jeopardy of their employment. Whether in private industry, government, or teaching, thousands of gay people have been mercilessly dismissed upon discovery of their sexual orientation. Worse still is the social stereotype that has stamped homosexuals as emotionally ill. Hollywood films, for example, have almost invariably portrayed them as sick, vicious, or insipid. Two results of such stereotypes are intolerance among the impressionable young and a tendency of the homosexual to accept the beliefs espoused by the culture. Using the civil rights movement as a model, gays have fought these stereotypes and have achieved notable acceptance. In San Francisco, openly homosexual police and city council members now go about their daily routines like any other American citizens.

The Women's Movement

Women had been granted the vote in 1920 and for a time actively participated in politics and social reform movements. But after this relatively brief period the women's movement became dormant, not to resurface until the 1960's.

Yet important changes greatly affected women during the interim decades. Some of the most significant occurred in the work force. During the Depression working women were blamed for taking jobs from men, but the actual proportion of working women had not changed, and they earned fifty to sixty-five percent less than men. World War II changed the image of the working woman. More than one out of every three worked and almost half who did were married. For the first time the composite female workers was middle-aged, married, and a mother. In addition, educated, white middle-class women were entering the work force in large numbers. Eleanor Roosevelt, by her active political involvement and extensive travels, was an outstanding example of a woman assuming new responsibilities. The symbol of "Rosie the Riveter" was that of a woman who assumed a traditionally male job.

The years after World War II saw an abrupt shift in attitudes. Woman was idealized as wife and mother, told to use newly acquired managerial skills to organize the household, arrange the car-pools, and run the PTA. A post-war "baby boom" finally peaked in 1955, but maintaining their family's mental and physical wellbeing became a full-time commitment for many women; they adopted the identity of "supermom," a concept Betty Friedan termed "the feminine mystique."

The number of working women was still higher than before the war, and continued to rise steadily. They were mainly working in occupations defined as female—clerical, domestic service, teaching; many other occupations, especially the professions, were increasingly restricted to women. And despite an increase in the total number of students attending college after World War II, women were acquiring a smaller proportion of degrees than they had forty years before. Still, by 1960 the number of working women was almost equal to that of men, and by the end of the decade almost nine out of every ten women, regardless of economic or social background, would be a part of the work force at some time in their lives.

The revival of the women's movement in the 1960's was closely related to the other reform movements of that period. The prosperity of the United States in the 1950's had meant that the average American enjoyed a standard of living higher than anywhere else in the world. This also served to point out many social and economic inequities. Black Americans were the first group actively to protest against discrimination and deprivation, but activism soon spread to other groups. Women were involved in all of the reform movements of the sixties. But they soon realized, as they had a century earlier while participating in the abolitionist movement, that their needs were different from those of other groups and it would be necessary to organize an independent movement to deal with the specific problems of women.

The first major recognition of the women's movement came when President Kennedy set up the President's Commission on the Status of Women in 1961. Its purpose was to investigate institutional discrimination against women and to provide concrete recommendations for change. The report confirmed that there was widespread discrimination, both in the public and private sectors, and it urged the passage of new legislative and administrative laws. Title VII of the 1964 Civil Rights Act prohibited job discrimination because of race, color, religion, sex or national origin; it is still the most powerful legal tool women possess when fighting work-related inequalities.

In addition to the awareness women gained from the protest movements, several other influences helped to make them think of themselves as a distinct minority group. In 1953 Simone de Beauvoir's *The Second Sex* tracing the subordination of women throughout history, was published in the United States. In 1963 Betty Friedan wrote *The Feminine Mystique.* She examined the contemporary middle class and questioned the value and satisfaction to be had from devoting one's life to being a mother and housewife. This book, along with Kate Millett's *Sexual Politics* (1970) and Germaine Greer's *The Female Eunuch* (1971), had enormous impact on women. Also influential was an anthology of shorter writings by less prominent women entitled *Sisterhood is Powerful,* which presented important articles on housework, the psychology of women, marriage, minority group women, and a broad range of other topics.

Women formed their own groups to press for an end to discrimination. The National Organization of Women (NOW) was founded in 1966 with Friedan as its first president; it quickly became the largest and most influential women's group. From the beginning the local chapters were completely autonomous. NOW concentrated on legal challenges and non-partisan political activity, allowed men to join, and functioned as an umbrella covering many disparate tendencies. Primarily NOW was concerned with two fundamental issues: passage of the Equal Rights Amendment and obtaining the right of every women to have an abortion if she wanted one.

In 1963 the Women's Equity Action League was formed to lobby for legislation concerning women's work and education. Women's groups initiated national education campaigns to inform women of their rights and to explain the procedures used in fighting discrimination. Feminists have also been able to increase significantly their role in determining political party policies and goals. One of their most effective groups has been the national Women's Political Caucus, a nonpartisan group formed in 1971 to lobby for specific issues or candidates.

Women also carried the fight into state and federal courts, challenging statutes and practices that used sex as a legal classification. Three states now allow a husband to be prosecuted for raping his wife. Attention to these issues, along with others like battered wives and child care services, have helped the movement reach women on all levels of society. Many activists avoided permanent organizations, forming groups and caucuses to battle within universities, social welfare agencies, neighborhoods, hospitals, and places of employment. In 1973 both houses of Congress approved the Equal Rights Amendment, but in 1979 an extension of the ratification date was granted. Passage by three more states was necessary before ERA could become part of the Constitution.

One of the most important legal gains came in 1973 when the Supreme Court handed down two decisions severely restricting the rights of states to prohibit abortion. Although "prochoice" groups applauded the decisions and regarded them as a victory, abortion remains a controversial issue. Roman Catholics particularly oppose it, and federal legislation now permits medicaid funding for abortion only when a woman's life is in danger. Abortion has emerged as a powerful and emotional issue.

A less structured movement composed of younger, unmarried women developed parallel with the older, more established feminist groups; these single feminists stressed the oppression of women by men and showed how childhood socialization results in stereotyped sex roles. The Redstockings issued a manifesto in 1969 in which they declared male supremacy to be "the oldest,

most basic form of domination"; we "do not need to change ourselves, but to change men." From within these unstructured, deliberately leaderless groups came the technique of "consciousness raising"—small, non-directed discussions in which women shared experiences and feelings concerning men, other women, children, jobs, and housework. Many consciousness-raising groups contained activist women, but they generally sought strength and education, not the confrontation of larger political issues. Women were encouraged to share personal experiences in order to gain a sense of sisterhood and unity.

Women in the movement wanted changes far beyond the political and economic sectors. They worked to eliminate the traditional stereotype of feminine behavior, challenging sex role identity that went from the pink blanket in the hospital bassinet to the female senior citizen who received less social security benefits than her male counterpart. The increased sexual permissiveness of the 1960's seemed a mixed blessing for many American women. The work of Masters and Johnson and later researchers contributed to a more accurate understanding of women's sexuality, exploding repressive stereotypes inherited from the nineteenth century. Contraception provided security against unwanted pregnancy and so allowed freer sexual expression. At the same time, some women found their sex dehumanized, used to entertain men at topless bars, presented halfclad in multimillion dollar advertising campaigns to sell everything from automobiles to shaving cream. Popular music, and especially masculine rock lyrics—witness the Rolling Stones' "Stupid Girl" and "Under My Thumb"—celebrated primarily women's sexuality, never their intelligence, courage, or character. Though the birth control pill was an effective contraceptive, some medical reports began to appear linking it with possibly dangerous side effects; many women in any case resented the assumption that contraception was solely a woman's responsibility. Even within radical political groups, women found themselves treated as typists and lovers; the comment by Stokely Carmichael, militant black leader, that "the only position for women in the movement is prone," aroused understandable outrage. Women repudiated the sexual double standard and openly explored the whole question of female sexuality.

They questioned assumptions implicit in marriage, the family, the church, and called for openminded biological and psychological research on the nature of heterosexual relationships. Within consciousness raising groups questions about female sexuality led to discussions about homosexuality, and the fight began against restrictive and discriminatory laws concerning sexual orientation. Feminist lesbians sought legal changes and protection of their civil rights; they also wanted to change attitudes toward lesbianism. Radical lesbians argued that existing heterosexual relationships exploited women and only homosexuality could free women from this oppression. NOW was at first divided on homosexuality; many members felt the issue too controversial and destructive to the movement. But in 1973 NOW adopted a resolution on sexuality fully supporting "civil rights legislation designed to end discrimination based on sexual orientation."

By the 1970's the separate movements could be subsumed under the all-encompassing rubric, the women's movement, a combination of many diverse organizations with a consensus on changes necessary to achieve equality. In addition to agreement on the necessity of the ERA, women seek to insure enforcement of the equal opportunity laws and affirmative action programs and explore new areas like sexual harassment on the job.

Many prominent female leaders have endorsed the aims of the movement: former Congress-women Bella S. Abzug and Shirley Chisholm, actresses Jane Fonda and Lily Tomlin, and writers Gloria Steinem and Nora Ephron have fought for female equality. Ms. Gloria Steinem's *MS.* magazine is principally devoted to issues of interest to the contemporary working woman.

Femininism today is essentially a continuation of the earlier movement that first captured national attention at the Seneca Falls convention in 1848 and then resurfaced in the struggle for the vote. Feminist advances traditionally come during periods of social disorganization, but the contemporary movement differs somewhat because the social goals sought fit into the prevailing trends of our society. Female work patterns had already begun changing during World War II; even before rapid advances in contraceptive knowledge, the birth rate had already begun to fall; and changing attitudes toward human sexuality—the so-called sexual revolution, embodying changes not always necessarily beneficial to women—encompassed concepts that coincided with the feminist viewpoint.

Nixon: Years of Triumph

In 1969 Richard M. Nixon came to the presidency after eight years of Democratic rule; but his narrow victory hardly represented the landslide he would have liked. Yet a victory of any kind seemed a remarkable feat for a man who could not win the governorship of California six years before. The new President's political views differed markedly from those of his immediate predecessor, Lyndon Johnson. Richard Nixon decried a deeper involvement of the federal government in social problems, racial discrimination, or poverty. Instead, Nixon directed his appeals toward a "silent majority" of middle-class people who had tired of paying taxes to support welfarism. Capitalizing on their discomfort and fear over student and black protest on the one hand and a rising crime rate on the other, Nixon followed Alabama Governor George Wallace in appealing for "law and order." For many people he represented a rejection of government activity in social matters, of liberal federal spending, of creeping moral degeneration, and of student and black activism. A problem aggravated by Vietnam challenged Nixon at home: inflation threatened to get completely out of hand.

If the President did not act decisively to curb rising prices, he could lose the "silent majority" as quickly as he had gained their approval.

In his inaugural address, Nixon asked that everyone "go forward together." He asserted that the government could not solve all problems and appealed to the young to lower their voices. But his new executive appointments reflected only a narrow segment of American society. The President stocked the White House with long-time followers of homogenous background whose essential qualification was loyalty to Richard Nixon. The cabinet assembled to heal division and turmoil in the nation contained no blacks, Jews, women, or Democrats. William P. Rogers, one of Nixon's closest friends, took office as secretary of state, and Professor Henry Kissinger of Harvard University succeeded Walter Rostow as head of the National Security Council. Only Walter J. Hickel, designated secretary of the interior, encountered senatorial opposition; his background with Alaskan oil companies suggested to some senators that he might favor corporate over environmental goals. Ironically, Hickel later voiced disagreements with the President and eventually resigned, a victim of the White House penchant for loyalty.

Nixon began to fulfill his promise of aggressive action in foreign policy soon after the inaugural speech in which he observed: "After a period of confrontation, we are entering an era of negotiation." Accordingly, only a month afterward the President flew to Europe to meet with the leaders of friendly nations and to reassert United States commitments. In particular, he attempted to improve relations with Charles deGaulle, whose resistance to American leadership in Europe had prompted French withdrawal from NATO's military forces and seriously divided the nations of Western Europe.

The first elaboration of the President's foreign policy, the Nixon Doctrine of 1969, stated that the United States was reducing its military role in Asia but would continue to respect its world obligations. A more comprehensive explanation came in his first "State of the World" message in 1970. Again he asserted his readiness to negotiate with friend and foe, continuing the major American role but asking our allies to shoulder more of the burden. Concrete applications took the form of troop reductions in Korea, an agreement to return Okinawa to the Japanese, and the apparent goal of disengagement in Vietnam.

But the question that required immediate attention in 1969 was strategic arms limitation talks with the Soviet Union. After the Russian invasion of Czechoslovakia in 1968, the United States had postponed these discussions until tensions eased. Nixon himself preferred to engage in negotiations from a position of strength, and so proposed in March 1969 a modified antiballistic missile plan at a cost of $2.5 billion instead of the $5.5 billion budgeted by Lyndon Johnson. To convince Congress of the need for such a plan, Secretary of Defense Melvin Laird warned repeatedly of Soviet capabilities, pointing to the advanced construction of ABMs around Moscow and the deployment of missiles with 25-megaton warheads. Democratic senators objected to the cost and questioned the effectiveness of the program, but the Senate passed ABM by a single vote, 51 to 50 (the tie was broken by Vice-President Agnew). Some who voted in favor believed that Nixon would hold off deployment for fear of jeopardizing talks with the Soviet Union. And the veiled threat of an ABM system seemed to work: in October the Russians did begin SALT talks in Helsinki, Finland; in May 1971 they finally agreed to concentrate on limiting ABMs. America had wanted a more comprehensive agreement covering both defensive and offensive weapons.

The major powers also reached important agreements on Berlin early in 1971, owing in part to the rising prominence of the Social Democrats and Chancellor Willy Brandt in West Germany. Brandt himself began talks with Russia, East Germany, and other Eastern European nations; he softened Germany's stance toward Poland. An overall agreement on Berlin allowed "unimpeded" access to West Berlin with provisions for two million West Berliners to visit relatives periodically and to transact business in East Germany. The final draft included additional clauses making West Germany the sole representative for West Berlin in international affairs, yet limiting its political activity there.

Closer to home, Latin Americans increasingly demanded economic and political independence from the United States. The government of Peru had seized the American-owned International Petroleum Company in 1968, prompting the administration to enforce laws which cut off aid in the event of insufficient compensation. But Peru nationalized other companies, while Ecuador seized American fishing vessels, claiming they had violated their territorial rights, and Chile elected an ill-fated Marxist President, Salvador Allende, who fell to a CIA-military coup. These events strongly indicated a lessening of United States influence in Latin America. Burdened by commitments in Asia, the Nixon administration could not provide significant economic assistance, especially when Congress consistently reduced the foreign aid budget.

In Africa, Nixon maintained a neutral stance in the Nigerian civil war, but when it ended he tried to provide aid to both sides to ease the suffering and starvation, particularly severe among the Ibos of rebellious Biafra. The Middle East gave Nixon even more problems. The Arab states demanded that the Israelis withdraw from territories occupied in the six-day war of 1967 before any peace settlement. Israel refused to acquiesce without assurance of future security and in turn insisted on face to face negotiations. Some Israelis wanted to hold permanently such key areas as Jerusalem and the west bank of the Jordan. In January 1969 sporadic attacks by Israelis and Arabs occurred almost daily despite a cease-fire. And at times both engaged in large-scale operations—assaults on oil refineries, missile sites, pipelines, and troop emplacements.

President Nasser of Egypt offered a plan that called for Israeli withdrawal and a declaration of nonbelligerency, the territorial integrity of all countries in the Mideast including Israel, freedom of navigation on international waterways, and a just solution to the Palestine problem. On the same day President Nixon accepted a French offer to hold Big Four talks on the Mideast at the United Nations. Israel, however, rejected the Nasser proposal and resisted American pressures to ease its stance on withdrawal. Both sides accepted a cease-fire. This only shifted the focus to Palestinian Arab guerrillas and almost continuous acts of terrorism, including several spectacular airplane hijackings. These led to studied, deadly effective Israeli retaliation. The Israeli-Arab cold war was the most explosive situation in a world otherwise moving slowly toward peace.

In his most surprising reversal of foreign policy goals, Nixon again opened the door to China. In his State of the World message on February 26, 1971, he cited the "People's Republic of China" by name and proposed more trade and the beginning of a "serious dialogue." In early April 1971 the People's Republic invited an American table tennis team and three newsmen to visit Peking. Shortly afterward, Chou En-lai, the Chinese prime minister, stated that more American newsmen would be admitted; at the same time President Nixon announced an easing of the China trade embargo and the removal of American export restrictions on several nonstrategic items. In Nixon's view this was a significant way to "remove needless obstacles" to more contact between the American and Chinese peoples. The contacts with China continued during a brief, embittered war between India and Pakistan in the summer of 1971. Both China and the United States gave their official support to Pakistan, although to no avail. The eastern or Bengali portion of Pakistan seceded and, backed by Indian arms, became the new nation of Bangladesh.

The magnitude of the new thaw became obvious when Nixon announced in a short television address that Henry Kissinger had met with Chou En-lai in Peking from July 9 to 11. The meeting had been in secret, newsmen having received a bulletin that Kissinger was in bed in Pakistan with a stomach ailment. More dramatic still, Nixon announced a planned visit to Peking to "seek the normalization of relations between the two countries and also to exchange views on questions of concern to the two sides." He stressed that the visit would not be at the expense of old friends, meaning the Nationalists on Formosa. Yet Chiang Kai-shek was displeased. When Nixon suggested

that the Nationalist Chinese accept a "dual" formula for the China seat in the UN, both Taipei and Peking rejected it. Subsequently, despite half-hearted American opposition, the General Assembly voted to seat the People's Republic of China and to expel the Nationalist Chinese.

Before his trip to Peking in February 1972, Nixon ordered an end to all spy flights over China, presumably to avoid any incident such as the U-2 that sabotaged the Eisenhower-Khrushchev meeting and contributed to Nixon's presidential defeat in 1960. After months of preparation, the President finally landed in Peking on Monday, February 20, 1972, where he was greeted by Chou En-lai. During Nixon's five-day visit, Henry Kissinger, Nixon's master diplomat, accompanied him in all meetings with Chou and on an early visit to Mao Tse-tung; Secretary of State Rogers apparently was never present at the secret sessions but met instead with other Chinese officials. At the end of the week Nixon and Chou En-lai issued a joint communique pledging peaceful coexistence and recognizing Taiwan as an "internal" Chinese problem. In effect, Nixon had granted the fact of a single China; he even promised eventual withdrawal of American forces from Taiwan.

The historic trip to China ruffled many feathers. Japanese-American relations, already strained because of economic conflict, steadily worsened. The Soviet Union, aligned against both China and the United States on the India-Pakistani conflict, sensed possible isolation. Moscow had supported Peking's entry into the UN, but this did little to relieve the intense distrust between the two major Communist powers. Yet the Soviet Union and the United States moved toward greater understanding in several areas—the SALT talks, a treaty to ban nuclear weapons from the sea bed, increased cooperation in space, and modernization of the hot line through satellite communications. To cap his new offensive for peace, Nixon announced that he would visit Moscow in May 1972 in order to discuss all major issues that divided the two countries. The trip to Moscow took place as planned, and with considerable fanfare. In the midst of the grave domestic crisis created by the Watergate affair in 1973, Premier Brezhnev made a return visit to the United States.

Nixon: The Home Front

In contrast to his confident handling of foreign affairs, Nixon faced endless frustration in dealing with domestic problems. His first major concern had to be an economy threatened by inflation and by increasing deficits in the balance of payments. Nixon appointed Paul McCracken chairman of the Council of Economic Advisers; Arthur F. Burns became his closest economic consultant and head of the Federal Reserve Board. Nixon pared the budget with a $1.1 billion reduction in defense and $2.9 in domestic items. His basic policy included the continuation of "tight money" through higher reserve bank rediscount rates, a reduction in Medicaid, in housing, in space programs, and in federal aid for impacted school districts. Congress, however, was not about to accept reduced spending. While most Democrats approved of cuts in defense appropriations, they objected to domestic cutbacks, and stalemate ensued.

The President soon asked for striking programs of welfare reform and revenue sharing. His welfare proposal guaranteed $1,600 annually for a family of four regardless of state contributions. Families could earn an additional $720 a year with no loss in benefits, but beyond this assistance would decrease $.50 on the dollar until wages reached $3,920. The program, to be administered by the Social Security Administration, would have required recipients to register at the nearest unemployment office and to accept suitable jobs or undergo training; no more food stamps would be issued. Not all proponents of welfare reform liked the program. Many, favoring the establishment of a larger guaranteed annual income, objected to Nixon's assertion that such assistance "would undermine the incentive to work." Nixon's plan for revenue sharing involved turning tax dollars back to state and local governments, many of which were in serious financial difficulty. The mayors of large cities were particularly interested, for the flight of the middle class and businesses to the suburbs had eroded their tax base.

Like Lyndon Johnson, President Nixon could not easily accept criticism. He evidently placed Vice-President Agnew in the political foreground to make scathing remarks about the national news media and campus radicals. In a November 1969 speech the Vice-President claimed that the three major television networks distorted the news, especially CBS and NBC. While disclaiming any wish for censorship, Agnew challenged the power of a "small and unelected elite" to control public opinion and warned against allowing such a monopoly in communications.

Agnew was to continue his often colorful attacks during the 1970 campaign, singling out particular senators who had voted against Clement Haynsworth and Harrold G. Carswell—both Nixon nominees who had failed to win confirmation in the Senate to fill vacant Supreme Court seats. Nixon's first appointee to the Court, Chief Justice Warren E. Burger, faced little opposition as the successor to Earl Warren. Despite Democratic requests for a qualified southern nominee, Nixon angrily contended that the Senate was not interested in "righting" the balance of the Court; he then nominated Harry Blackmun of Minnesota, who won approval 94 to 0. In 1971 the Senate did approve a Southerner, Lewis Powell of Virginia, along with William Rehnquist, an assistant attorney general in the Justice Department and a former Goldwater supporter.

The "new" Supreme Court refused to back down from strong civil rights decisions handed down after 1954. It ruled unanimously that school districts must end segregation "at once" and operate integrated school systems "now and hereafter." In other important decisions, the Court negated residency requirements for welfare recipients, applied a statute of limitations of five years on failure to register for the draft, decided that states had to help the poor pay divorce costs, and held that ethical as well as religious reasons were a sufficient basis for conscientious objection.

When the Court voted against delays in desegregation, Nixon promised to execute the ruling faithfully. Nevertheless, the United States Commission on Civil Rights, lawyers in HEW, and blacks who had been appointed to high government positions were sharply critical of Nixon's reluctance to push civil rights. The other side also sniped at the President. Senator Strom Thurmond of South Carolina repeatedly contended that Nixon had failed to live up to his campaign promises of greater consideration toward the South, and George Wallace held out the threat of running again in 1972 if Nixon continued to force integration. Wallace made particular use of the issue of school busing, forcing Nixon closer to his own position. On April 20, 1971, however, the Court ruled 9 to 0 that school busing was a proper means to achieve school integration. Nixon wanted no more busing than the minimum required by law, and the issue was a major one in the 1972 primaries and campaign. As late as 1973 there was simply no concerted attempt to roll back the decisions of the Warren Court. In its first major decision the Court early that year held that states could not deny a woman's right to legal abortion; the vote was a lopsided 7 to 2, with three of Nixon's four appointees in the majority. A later case in 1973 gave localities more power to restrict pornography, but the Court still pursued no clear juristic path.

Other legal issues made headline news. The nation witnessed theatrical courtroom outbursts in the cases of the "Chicago 8," indicted for conspiring to incite riot at the 1968 Democratic Convention in Chicago, and of the "Panther 21," a group charged with conspiracy to blow up buildings in New York City. The trial of the Panthers, postponed for over two months, resumed only when the defendants promised to restrain themselves. In Chicago Bobby Seale, the chairman of the Black Panther party, so infuriated Judge Julius Hoffman that he declared a mistrial and cited Seale for contempt of court. The other seven and their lawyers, although acquitted of the major charge of conspiracy, were convicted on a lesser charge; all received jail sentences on multiple counts of contempt of court, but secured a reversal of these through appeal.

Across the country the Black Panthers were a particular target of arrest and trial, owing in part to fears of a conspiracy to kill policemen. In some large cities gun battles took place between Panthers and police: in December 1969 Chicago police broke into an apartment and killed Fred Hampton, chairman of the Illinois Black Panthers, and Mark Clark, a Panther leader from Peoria. Although an interracial jury declared the killing justifiable, the government eventually dropped felony charges against the surviving Panthers and in August 1972 a grand jury indicted Illinois state attorney Edward V. Hanrahan along with thirteen others (including policemen) for conspiring to block the prosecution of police officers responsible for the raid on Hampton's apartment. In fact, in almost every trial of Black Panthers from 1969 to January 1972 the juries failed to return convictions either through direct acquittal or, as in the celebrated case of Seale, by a mistrial.

Although there had been scattered outbreaks of prison violence and related demands for reform, none drew as much attention as that at Attica, New York. On September 9, 1971, one thousand inmates—mostly minority group members—revolted and seized thirty-three guards as hostages. New York's Corrections Commissioner Russell Oswald negotiated with the prisoners for four days and ac-

ceded to twenty-eight demands but refused the key request for amnesty. Then, on September 13, with the consent of Governor Rockefeller, who had refused to meet with the prisoners, over a thousand state troopers and deputy sheriffs stormed the prison after helicopters dropped tear gas. Nine hostages and twenty-nine prisoners died. When it was disclosed that gunshot wounds and not slashed throats killed the hostages, a national furor arose over the incident. Although Governor Rockefeller and President Nixon defended the action, many prison officials around the country criticized the way the revolt was handled.

The 1970 election returns seemed to indicate that the economy had been a more effective issue than law and order. Democrats gained important new Senate seats; in the House they made significant inroads in California, Florida, Ohio, Illinois, and New Jersey. Democrats also showed surprising strength in gubernatorial elections, gaining ten additional state houses.

Despite the concern with the economy which swayed election returns in 1970, the excitement surrounding the first live moon landing in July 1969 momentarily obliterated worries. As early as December 1968 Apollo 8 had orbited the moon, and the flights of Apollo 9 and 10 followed soon after, testing the lunar module that was to make the landing. On July 16, 1969, Apollo 11 lifted off for the moon with astronauts John Young, Neil Armstrong, and Nelson Aldrin aboard. Five days later Armstrong and Aldrin landed on the moon, and six hours later millions watched on television as Armstrong stepped onto the surface. As John Kennedy had promised, Americans had landed on the moon before the end of the decade. When they returned to earth on July 24, Nixon greeted them on his way to the Far East, but they had to spend eighteen days in quarantine before being cheered and lauded from the White House and across the country. While on the moon, Armstrong and Aldrin set up a seismometer to measure moonquakes, a solar wind screen, and an American flag; they brought home samples of rock showing the moon to be billions of years old. Subsequent flights provided more scientific information. Astronauts Allen Bean and Peter Conrad of the Apollo 12 mission set up a scientific station and inspected an old Surveyor 3 spacecraft. Apollo 13, which was supposed to land in the lunar highlands, ran into trouble when an oxygen tank exploded and a resulting shortage briefly imperiled the lives of the astronauts aboard. But Apollos 14 and 15 made additional successful trips.

Despite the excitement over the conquest of space, many Americans voiced a preference for the application of resources to domestic problems such as poverty and pollution. Public pressure mounted quickest for programs against water and air pollution. Oil spills in the Santa Barbara channel in February 1969 offered an immediate opportunity to take strong action against companies responsible for pollution. Environmentalists, at first upset with Walter Hickel's appointment as interior secretary, were pleased by his call for stiffer laws governing off-shore drilling. In his 1970 State of the Union message Nixon committed himself to improving the "quality of life" by preserving the environment. He first proposed a $10 billion program to clean up the nation's waterways. The federal government would provide $4 billion and the states would contribute the other $6 billion. Nixon also responded to concern over air pollution. Conceding that the proposals were greater than any made before, most Democrats argued that they were still inadequate.

In contrast to his environmental program, the President's urban and educational programs looked toward a reduced role for the federal government. Nixon had backed away from Johnson's war on poverty although certain popular programs such as Head Start continued under different auspices. He favored returning power to the states and localities and suggested a national population balance to let rural areas survive and hold back the movement toward the suburbs and cities. His education message of March 1970 emphasized his doubts that federal aid could be as effective as improved social and economic circumstances. Probably this was the basis for his veto, in the summer of 1970, of a $4.4 billion education bill—a veto that Congress promptly overrode.

Nixon also faced stiff opposition on defense spending. In addition to those who wished to end the draft, many wanted cutbacks in general troop strength and the closing of unneeded facilties. Nixon responded to many of these demands. He ·approved the first draft lottery, held December 1, 1970, a basic demand of those who opposed the student exemptions; he closed down numerous 'military bases; he declared an end to American germ warfare research and turned the army facility at Fort Dietrich, Maryland, over to cancer research. Many of these measures he announced in the course of the debate over ABM.

The results of cutbacks in defense were soon reflected in the economy, which began to cool down as defense contractors who had tooled up for the war or the exploration of space no longer needed so many employees. The Boeing Corporation of Seattle was already in trouble when the debate on a supersonic transport arose. The French had lately begun to test their Concorde and the Russians had a quite different SST, while America had spent over $1 billion and did not yet have even a prototype. Scientists and environmentalists alike were beginning to have grave doubts about the potential effects of the plane on the environment. They warned of eliminating ozone from significant areas in the upper atmosphere, and reiterated that steady waves of sonic booms would accompany the plane in flight. In spite of Nixon's contention that the defeat of additional appropriations could lead to the end of United States leadership in the aircraft industry, loss of business to the French and Russians, and widening unemployment, the Senate voted 51 to 46 to end the program.

Finally, on August 15, 1971, Nixon took drastic action by instituting a wage-price freeze for ninety days. He proposed new tax cuts plus programs to add new jobs. In order to right the balance of payments, the President suspended the convertibility of dollars into gold until proper adjustments were made by other nations. (That is, he was refusing to devalue the dollar unless there was some sort of reciprocal change.) In hopes of stemming American spending abroad Nixon proposed a 10 percent import surcharge on existing duties with certain products exempted.

Although the stock market leapt ahead, labor leaders were not pleased. George Meany called the freeze discriminatory against his AFL-CIO workers, whose wages were frozen while industry received tax benefits and unlimited profits. But labor leaders eventually supported the plan even though they insisted that they wanted all pay increases called for in existing contracts. They bridled at Nixon's October 7 proposal of Pay, Price, and Rent Boards, but went along with these, too. No limits were to be set on profits, but the Price Board could seek reductions in the event of "windfall profits." The President also sought authority to impose mandatory controls on interest rates, and asked that lending institutions restrain dividend and interest increases. The freeze slowed but did not stop the pace of inflation.

The economic measures seemed to be most successful abroad. The Japanese agreed to remove their own quotas on certain agricultural products and lowered tariffs on thirty industrial items. But Nixon was looking for more than trade concessions. The yen had been valued at 360 to the dollar before the suspension of gold payments and the Japanese had consistently refused to revalue. In December a ten-nation monetary agreement devalued the dollar by 8.57 percent. The yen and the mark were revalued upward in relation to the dollar. As other nations also revalued upward, Nixon removed the import surcharge.

The balance of payments problem eased for the moment but a sluggish economy still plagued the administration. Nixon's 1972 budget had forecast a deficit of only $11.6 billion; it was actually $38.8 billion. His 1973 budget called for expenditures totalling $246.3 billion with receipts of only $220.8 billion. Nixon's first three budgets would have a total deficit of $87 billion. This was a turn-about for a man who in 1969 insisted on a budget surplus and who contended that he could meet all needs, cut inflation, and reduce unemployment.

In 1972, an election year, many new Nixon proposals sounded unmistakably political. Taking note of high property taxes, he promised a search for alternative methods of financing public schools. He proposed a "joint partnership" between government and industry to encourage new jobs. He announced lower draft calls, more federal aid to black colleges, greater purchases of farm surpluses, and new authority for the Civil Rights Commission to eliminate discrimination against women.

Aspiring Democratic candidates attacked Nixon for neglecting domestic problems and prolonging the war, even as they began the long, costly primary tour that could lead to a nomination in July. Few voters and even fewer politicians took George McGovern seriously when he began his campaign for the presidency a year and a half before the nominating convention. McGovern, a first-term senator from South Dakota, was not well known; and his main issue, the Vietnam War, seemed nearly exhausted by long exposure. Yet the long-time Democratic front-runner, Senator Edmund Muskie of Maine, made a poor showing in the first primary, in New Hampshire, and went downhill from there. Another presidential contender, Governor George Wallace of Alabama, campaigned vigorously in several states until May 15 when he was shot down and paralyzed by a would-be assassin's bullets. Hubert Humphrey posed a threat until defeated by McGovern and his devoted precinct workers in the June 6 California primary.

George McGovern received the presidential nomination from a convention which, in part as a result of his leadership, gave greater representation to women, minorities, and youth. The candidate's long struggle read like *Cinderella,* but sometime during the convention the clock struck midnight, for the magic of the primary campaign suddenly disappeared. By directing his appeal to the most cohesive and energetic factions within the Demo-cratic party—youth, peace activists, blacks —McGovern won key primaries and the nomination but at the same time gained a vaguely visionary or radical image that almost insured his defeat in November. His unbelievably inept handling of the vice-presidential selection further prejudiced his campaign. Without careful background investigations, McGovern selected Senator Thomas Eagleton of Missouri as his running mate. Ten days later Eagleton, prodded by newspaper rumors, admitted earlier hospitalization and shock therapy for severe depression. The Presidency was one of the few jobs in America for which prior serious mental illness should be a disqualification. After first backing Eagleton by "one thousand percent," McGovern eventually forced a crushed Eagleton to withdraw as a candidate. After an embarrassing search for a willing replacement, he finally turned to R. Sargeant Shriver, a Kennedy kinsman and an energetic speaker. This whole fiasco reinforced earlier and exaggerated charges that McGovern was indecisive and weak, even as it seemed to his more idealistic supporters an all too cynical capitulation to political pressure.

Richard Nixon remained calm, his "back-porch" campaign all the more effective because the porch was attached to the White House. No element of suspense invested his renomination on August 23. Some early jockeying over the vice-presidential slot gave way to the matter-of-course choice of Spiro Agnew, who retooled his style for 1972—more poised, restrained, and independent. After the Republican convention, President Nixon cooly sent forth his staff and cabinet members to do battle while protecting and nourishing his image as statesman. He coasted toward November.

One of the most spectacular political incidents in several decades occurred during the summer of the campaign, but although repeatedly brought up by McGovern it aroused little voter reaction. On June 17 five men were captured inside Democratic National Headquarters in Washington while involved in a bugging and spying attempt. Investigators quickly established definite connections between the five and President Nixon's reelection committee, but little more was learned before election day.

Much as the pollsters predicted, Americans on November 7 gave Richard Nixon 60.8 percent of the popular vote and 521 of 538 electoral votes; only Massachusetts and the District of Columbia went to George McGovern. President Nixon interpreted the overwhelming victory as a great personal mandate, as a prelude to a triumphant second term.

Watergate

Sometime during the middle of Nixon's first term, some members of the White House staff began to use their power to pursue partisan, even personal, vendettas. They pointed to the "lawlessness" of their opponents: antiwar demonstrators had pledged "to stop the business of government"; radicals had bombed the Capitol building; Daniel Ellsberg stole secret documents, the Pentagon Papers. Believing that the mass media often romanticized such actions, Nixon and his assistants rationalized that their predecessors had used equally sharp practices. Mostly young lawyers and former advertising men lacking political experience, they ignored the traditional rules of Washington politics. By 1972 many of the President's men claimed that the national interest required Nixon's re-election, justifying crimes as necessary for national security. The Committee to Re-Elect the President (CREEP) organized a burglary of Democratic Party offices at the Watergate Building early in June 1972. A White House official, G. Gordon Liddy, and a man working for him, E. Howard Hunt, recruited a group of anti-Castro Cubans; and CREEP's director of security, James McCord, led this small band of seven people on two raids. Acting perhaps under orders from Nixon himself, the burglars planted microphones and took pictures of files in the Democratic National Committee. During the second one, a night watchman discovered their entry and called police. Moments later the President's burglars were under arrest. Evidence at the scene quickly connected them to Liddy and to CREEP.

Despite repeated protestations of presidential and White House innocence, some newspapers reporters continued to investigate. Amid media speculation, Nixon ordered a staff inquiry and told the public on August 29, 1972, that "what really hurts is if you try to cover up" a crime. In September a federal grand jury indicted James McCord and his accomplices, plus Liddy and Hunt. All pleaded guilty, and thus no trial or legal reckoning could be made. But Judge John Sirica, like many others, doubted that these brief judicial proceedings had solved the Watergate case. Then in mid-March 1973 McCord wrote to Sirica, charging the White House had pressured the defendants into silence with offers of executive clemency and hush money. Government officials approved the Watergate burglary, McCord claimed, and had conspired also to cover up their own involvement. McCord's letter prompted the Watergate grand jury and the Senate's special

Watergate committee, chaired by Sam Ervin of North Carolina, to probe further these mysterious White House activities.

Nixon loyalists could not contain the scandal. One of them, John Dean, thought that the President might blame the whole affair on him, and began to bargain with federal prosecutors from the grand jury. At about the same time, early April, the former deputy chairman of CREEP, Jeb Stuart Magruder, admitted that he had lied in his appearances before the jury: now, he admitted, the bugging of Democratic headquarters was not "a wild scheme concocted by Hunt" but a much-discussed plan, which Attorney General John Mitchell had approved directly. Just at this point, another scandal broke. Two years before, a group of White House operatives authorized to plug security leaks (the "plumbers") had burglarized the office of a Los Angeles psychiatrist treating Daniel Ellsberg. On April 27, 1973, at Ellsberg's trial for theft of government property, the prosecution admitted the illegal entry by the plumbers. The judge declared this a violation of Ellsberg's civil rights and ordered a mistrial.

Shaken by the sudden reversals, Nixon jettisoned three of his top advisers and tried once more to seal off the Oval Office from the spreading ooze of Watergate. He told a national television audience on April 30, 1973, that he accepted the responsibility—but not the blame—for the actions of "overzealous subordinates." Absorbed in the business of running the country, he explained, he had failed to monitor their campaigning. He also announced the resignations of Ehrlichman and Haldeman, "two of the finest public servants it had been my privilege to know." Dean also left the staff. Under pressure from Congress and even close friends, Nixon appointed a special prosecutor, Harvard law professor Archibald Cox, and promised him "complete independence" to investigate the Watergate affair. These moves provided only temporary surcease for the embattled President.

In the Senate Watergate hearings, Senator Sam Ervin—with his stock of white hair, and trembling jowls—became a national symbol of honor and rectitude. The star witnesses, Jeb Magruder and John Dean, told their stories. Magruder suggested presidential involvement in the cover-up, and Dean linked Nixon directly with illegal activities. Speaking carefully and displaying a remarkable memory, Dean quoted the President as saying that it would be "no problem" to raise a $1 million hush-fund and that payments should be made through E. Howard Hunt. Dean implicated Ehrlichman, swearing that he had instructed him to "deep-six" evidence in the Potomac River. Throughout his lengthy testimony, the young lawyer revealed a White House staff and a President as petty, vindictive, and unconcerned with legalities. Other witnesses testified about Watergate and other misdeeds, a string of bizarre activities that Mitchell called "the White House horrors."

Richard Nixon had his defenders. Mitchell attempted to refute the charges leveled against him and the President. Nixon, Mitchell assured the committee, had known nothing about the break-in or the cover-up. Ehrlichman and Haldeman claimed that neither they nor the President had done anything wrong. A combative, arrogant Ehrlichman defended the Ellsberg break-in on grounds of national security. Crew-cut Bob Haldeman, once the second most powerful man in Washington, softly denied everything. Such give-and-take—Dean's word against Ehrlichman's, Magruder's against Haldeman's—might finally have bored the public; certainly by late summer the Senate committee was running out of energy and new information.

During the hearings, however, the committee staff stumbled upon a crucial discovery. A former White House aid, Alexander Butterfield, reluctantly testified on July 16 that sophisticated recording equipment had taped the majority of presidential conversations for the last two years. Presumably these reels could determine, once and for all, the extent of Nixon's role in the Watergate affair. The Senate committee, as well as Special Prosecutor Cox and the Watergate grand jury, requested segments of the tapes; but the President argued that their disclosure would violate the confidentiality of the Presidency and erode the separation of powers. A complicated legal battle ensued. Frustrated, Cox finally told a televised press conference that he would ask Judge Sirica to declare the President "in violation of a court ruling" for his delay in turning over a set of tapes. When Nixon fired Cox, the top two officials in the Justice Department quit in protest. This "Saturday Night Massacre" produced an outpouring of popular protest appearing as it did that Nixon was trying to get Cox before Cox got Nixon.

Continuing scandal seemed to envelope Nixon. Just ten days before the Saturday Night Massacre, Spiro Agnew had resigned the vice presidency to escape a jail term for evading income taxes on bribes from Maryland building contractors. His blatant plea-bargaining—Agnew threatened a constitutional crisis unless promised leniency—clashed with his long-standing alliterative protests against judges "soft on criminals." The smooth working of the Twenty-Fifth Amendment soon installed Agnew's successor, House Minority Leader Gerald Ford. Popular with his fellow congressmen, Ford also enjoyed the reputation, perhaps undeserved, of an intellectual lightweight.

Almost daily revelations now plagued Nixon. When the White House finally handed over a few tapes, prosecutors discovered that recordings of some conversations "had never existed" and that others contained sizable gaps, erasures that technical experts later judged intentional. During the winter of 1973, newspapers had reported that the President had become a millionaire while in the White House, partly because he had paid miniscule income taxes. Now Nixon accepted the judgment of a congressional committee and a ruling of the Internal Revenue Service that he owed nearly $450,000 in back taxes. Congressional investigators began probing federal expenditures for extensive remodeling of his estates at Key Biscayne, Florida, and San Clemente, California. The Watergate grand jury, now directed by a new special prosecutor, Texas attorney Leon Jaworski, indicted forty-one people for obstruction of justice and other crimes during the 1972 campaign. Convinced of Nixon's involvement, yet unwilling to confront constitutional issues, the jurors listed Nixon as an "unindicted co-conspirator."

Pressed by public skepticism and a growing pile of subpoenas and court orders for more and more tapes, in late April 1974 Nixon released edited transcripts—not the actual recordings—of meetings concerning Watergate. Even Nixon's version—he had deleted a number of items that damaged the President's claims of innocence—showed a dubious morality. The new evidence implicated him in the cover-up and openly told of schemes for political revenge against "enemies."

Already at work on articles of impeachment was a Judiciary Committee of the House of Representatives, twenty-four Democrats and fourteen Republicans. Nixon made a last, double-edged counterattack. His lawyer, James St. Clair, fought to prevent release of further tapes. Nixon himself spoke to carefully selected audiences, often in the deep South, hoping for a show of public support. But his statement, "Your president is not a crook," shocked more than it soothed. And when he argued that only criminal acts would justify impeachment, many thought it a tacit admission of serious wrongdoing.

During late July and early August 1974, a tangle of events closed in, finally ending any doubts about the President's fate. The Judiciary Committee heard both its Democratic and Republican counsels urge impeachment. Nixon had, they concluded, obstructed justice in the Watergate cover-up and abused government power in attempts to compromise federal agencies. On July 24 the Supreme Court ordered the White House to turn over 64 additional tapes. That same day the Judiciary Committee began its televised debate on impeachment.

Contrary to fears that Nixon's impeachment would "tear the country apart," people seemed strangely calm, relieved that constitutional process would soon end months of uncertainty. Serious, fair-minded discussion among committee members reinforced this mood. Most of the President's accusers appeared more saddened than vindictive. Though no "smoking pistol" of irrefutable presidential involvement in Watergate had yet surfaced, most Democrats and a few Republicans argued that a pattern of presidential behavior and a mountain of indirect proof implicated Nixon in obstruction of justice. He had interfered repeatedly in the FBI's investigations of Watergate and, so John Dean claimed, ordered payment of hush-money. William Cohen, a Republican from Maine, compared the President's guilt to snow falling in the night: no one saw it happen, but the next morning it was there.

In compliance with the Supreme Court order, Nixon released additional tapes on Monday, August 5. Though they "might damage my case," he still maintained that he had done nothing to justify his removal from office. But almost no one in Washington believed him any more. Among other things, the new transcripts revealed that Nixon had been deceiving his own attorney. After see-ing the new evidence, the President's chief of staff, Alexander Haig, began preparations for the accession of Gerald Ford. The tape of a conversation on June 23, 1972—Nixon's first day back in Washington after the Watergate break-in—showed the President and Haldeman planning to cloak White House involvement in the crime. Here, after eighteen months of protestations of innocence, was the "smoking pistol." Nixon's defenders on the Judiciary Committee belatedly switched their votes, and leading Republican senators visited the White House, telling the President that his removal was a certainty. On August 8 Richard Nixon told the nation that he would resign, but he still confessed only "wrong judgment," not impeachable offenses. His calm, dignified speech dwelled on his hopes for world peace and his accomplishments in foreign affairs.

But the private man, Richard Nixon himself, did not leave until the next morning, when he said goodby to the White House staff. During a speech filled with self-pity, Nixon rambled through a variety of disconnected topics. He tearfully recalled his mother and his father. He told his staff and friends, "Never hate those who oppose you, for you will end by destroying yourself," advice he apparently ruefully wished he had heeded. As he left for his seaside estate in California, many thought Richard Nixon a lonely, driven man, somehow overwhelmed by the temptations of his office or betrayed by flaws in his character. Others disagreed, insisting that Nixon and his aides had started the nation toward tyranny. His successor, Gerald Ford, spoke more kindly. "May the man who brought peace to millions find peace within himself."

The Appointed President: Gerald Ford

As a presidential jet carried Nixon into seclusion, Ford took the oath of office, the nation's first appointed President. "I am acutely aware," he said at his hastily improvised inauguration, "that I have received the votes of none of you." Still, the new chief executive drew upon the nation's yearning for normalcy. He found trust, even respect, from a country eager "to put Watergate behind." He and his staff intentionally downplayed the imperialist trappings of the Nixon years. "I'm a Ford, not a Lincoln," he quipped to White House reporters. Bemused Americans watched the President fix his own muffins for breakfast; the first family celebrated a fireside Christmas at a Colorado ski resort. Ford liked people, the folksy politician sometimes shaking hands with surprised tourists waiting in long lines to visit the White House. He experimented with low-key talks on television to explain complicated economic issues and held as many press conferences and delivered as many speeches in eighteen months as Nixon had in five years. The President, a former college football star at the University of Michigan, smiled a lot, mispronounced a few words, and soon charmed the nation.

However much this open affability contrasted with Nixon's isolated moodiness, Ford could not escape his predecessor's legacy. Kissinger stayed on as Secretary of State, his immense reputation for diplomatic skill now one of the administration's chief assets. Yet even his wizardry did not slow the final collapse of South Vietnam. The ceasefire there so laboriously worked out had never really functioned. Viet Cong cadres infiltrated areas reserved to Saigon, and North Vietnam stepped up its propaganda campaign against Thieu and his "American stooges." Thieu fought back. Intermittent war returned again to most of South Vietnam. Nyugen Giap, Hanoi's legendary general, planned a giant assault by both Viet Cong and North Vietnamese soldiers for the spring of 1975. Growing chaos in the South facilitated his scheme: Thieu arrested opponents indiscriminately, banned political parties, closed down newspapers and television stations. Rumors spread that the ruling clique had squirreled vast amounts of money into secret bank accounts. As dictatorship settled over the country, Thieu's regime alienated all but those who profited from it.

The end came suddenly, "not with a bang but a whimper." Hard-pressed by enemy attacks, Thieu retreated from the three northernmost provinces of South Vietnam. This maneuver consolidated his deteriorating military position and, he calculated, might frighten the Americans into sending more hardware. But Giap's troops turned retreat into rout. Lacking American air support and demoralized by corrupt leaders, Thieu's armies flocked southward, pillaging their own villages rather than protecting them. Hundreds of thousands of civilian refugees clogged the roads. South Vietnamese generals did manage an improvised defense of Xuan Loc, a key provincial capital some thirty miles north of Saigon; Giap's crack troops captured the city in a few days. They overran the capital a week later, on May 1, 1975, renaming it Ho Chi Minh City. The last images of this televised war showed American officials escaping aboard helicopters, while helpless Vietnamese grabbed for a handhold on the departing machines.

Most Americans had anticipated something like this. Yet Ford and Kissinger, anxious to recoup Yankee prestige overseas and repair confidence at home, "toughed out" a new, more aggressive foreign policy. Just three weeks after the communist victory in South Vietnam, a pro-Hanoi Khmer Rouge regime triumphed in neighboring Cambodia. During the confusion, overzealous local commanders seized an American merchant vessel, the *Mayaguez*, and jailed its crew for smuggling countraband. Ford sent a naval task force and nearly two thousand Marines to rescue the

thirty-one Americans involved. Later he startled a press conference with talk that the United States "did not rule out a first strike with nuclear weapons," a feisty warning to the North Koreans to drop any plans for "liberating" their countrymen further south. Kissinger traveled quietly in western Europe, reassuring NATO allies that the United States would never yield to neo-isolationists. The White House blocked all congressional efforts to cut military spending or reduce the number of American troops stationed overseas.

And Ford enthusiastically took up Kissinger's formulas for stability in the Middle East. Opportunities there abounded while Giap's armies overran Vietnam. Leaders in the Arab world, particularly Egypt's Anwar Sadat, attributed their defeat in the 1973 Arab-Israeli war to backsliding by fainthearted Russians. Kissinger thought peace possible once the Arabs realized that only Washington, not Moscow, could prod Israel into returning occupied Arab lands. He delicately negotiated the wide space of ancient hatreds separating Jew and Arab into a narrow band of agreement. By the fall of 1975, after more rounds of shuttle diplomacy, he secured a ceasefire. Sadat dropped old Egyptian dreams for uniting the Muslim world and rejected demands by Arab militants for Israel's destruction. In return for this long-sought "right to exist," the Israeli Knesset promised to restore Egypt's lost territories in the Sinai peninsula. The United States underwrote the arrangement, pledging still more military aid to the Israelis and technological aid for the Egyptians.

Years of tug-and-pull diplomacy remained. Both the Shah of Iran and Saudi kings worried about future Soviet adventures, so they sold vast amounts of crude oil to the United States in return for military weapons and modern, western industry. Republican foreign policy had ousted the Soviet Union from the Arab world and replaced the Russian presence with an American one.

Flashy achievements abroad, though, did little to soothe the lesions in American society at home. "Economics bores me," Nixon had once told Haldeman, but double-digit inflation forced President Ford into at least an appearance of action. An economic summit gathered together businessmen, labor leaders, and professors. Its sessions provided no clear prescription for "stagflation," that paradox of increasing unemployment and higher prices. Ford decided to "Whip Inflation Now"—WIN—with a lackluster plan centered upon income tax surcharges, investment incentives, and consumer conservation. The economy then skidded into the worst depression since the 1930's. Huge drops in automobile sales triggered large layoffs elsewhere. Housing starts declined so much that the total number of dwellings in the United States actually decreased. Joblessness rose to 13 percent. Frightened by this sharp recession, Ford reversed course, now focusing on unemployment. He asked Congress to cut taxes, and the budget office forecast a federal deficit of some $60 billion. But Congressional politicking slowed the introduction of these expansionary schemes. The legislators finally agreed to rebate some taxes paid in 1974, reduce the withholding rate on personal incomes, and provide credits for new home buyers. All together, these countermeasures prompted a modest revival

during the summer of 1975. But inflation, too, returned.

Within weeks after his inauguration, President Ford had pardoned Nixon for "any and all crimes." Many wondered whether compassion for a sick man or an earlier deal had motivated the act. Polls showed over three-fourths of the voters critical of both President and Congress. The November 1974 elections returned strong Democratic majorities in 1975, and the deadlock between the two branches of government so characteristic of the Nixon years also plagued Ford's administration.

The Carter Years

The presidential election of 1976 was the first in twelve years not dominated by the conflict in Vietnam. An unknown Southern governor, Jimmy Carter, blitzed state primaries and captured the Democratic nomination. Even more surprising, Ronald Reagan challenged his party's incumbent in the White House, Gerald Ford, and almost won. Both insurgent candidates had run "against Washington." They were outsiders, not part of Watergate corruption or bureaucratic fossilization. Deeply distrustful of government, voters apparently longed for fresh leaders they could trust. Carter swept early primaries—and established a front-runner momentum—by promising, "I'll never lie to the American people." Reagan emphasized his undiluted commitment to conservative goals, frequently scoring Ford for his practical politics. The spread of presidential primaries and federal financing eased access to the White House. Alone of all Democrats, Carter adjusted to this new terrain, looking for convention votes in all states, projecting a homespun, honest image, and charting a centrist course that eased past most issues. He handily won the nomination on the first ballot at the New York City convention.

Carter argued for full employment, achieved if necessary by the government acting as "an employer of last resort" for those unable to find work in the private sector. Most Democrats took little issue with Kissinger's balance-of-power maneuverings, and Carter offered no changes, except a promise to "avoid future Vietnams." Both candidates "waffled," avoiding specific commitments. Ford bumbled during a public debate with Carter, telling a rather stunned American audience that the Soviet Union "does not dominate

eastern Europe." Carter shocked many when he explained to *Playboy* magazine that he had "lusted after other women in his heart." If some people worried that Ford was not bright enough to handle the presidency, others were uneasy about

President Jimmy Carter

Carter's fundamentalist religious faith. This un-focused campaign bored many voters; only half went to the polls, an historical low. Carter won the election by rekindling Franklin Roosevelt's coalition of urban East-upper Midwest with Southern gulf and border states. Democrats swept Congressional races, establishing a two-thirds majority in the House and a 62-38 margin in the Senate. The political hassling between White House and Capitol Hill so characteristic of the Nixon-Ford years seemed likely to end. Americans looked forward to watching their anti-establishment President deal with the grandest of establishment jobs.

The decade of the 1970's—already encompassing an oil boycott, a disgraced President, and a stumbled retreat from war overseas—continued to surprise the American people. The economy fretted between recession and inflation. Fiscal crises plagued giant cities, amidst calls for less taxation. Crime worsened, especially in suburbs and rural areas unused to violence. Periodic shortages of gasoline threatened the nation's half-century reliance on the automobile. Oil companies wrested maximum short-term profits from the energy crisis. An institutional arthritis weakened American society: the nation was buffeted by change, yet its people could not act collectively. Then, as the new decade of the eighties began, America faced a Soviet military takeover in Afghanistan and a nationalist revolution in Iran.

Carter promised an open presidency, a frugal and efficient White House staff, a chief executive in touch with the people. He had begun his presidency with symbols reminiscent of Andrew Jackson. Dispensing with traditional limousines, he and his family walked down Pennsylvania Avenue after the inauguration. He still called himself "Jimmy." *Sequoia*, the presidential yacht so favored by Nixon, went on the auction block. The new chief executive held press conferences twice a month, traveled to town meetings across the country, and—in an attempt to manipulate "images"—occasionally telephoned "ordinary" people. No White House chief of staff funneled reports to an isolated president; instead, all Carter's top aides spoke with him directly. He banished platoons of expensive lawyers from the administration. He wore a cardigan sweater when he addressed a television audience in February 1977. During this "fireside chat," the President promised to reduce government spending, shrink the bureaucracy, and limit regulation. Carter was dismantling the "imperial presidency."

But the former Georgia governor, an outsider, soon ran into trouble with Washington's insider politics. Federal bureaucrats, long the butt of his jibes, remained aloof, advising the President correctly but avoiding initiatives. As a result, Carter relied more and more upon his own staff, mostly young people from his home state with little national experience. Relations with Capitol Hill quickly deteriorated, too. Unfamiliar with the niceties of Congressional politics, Carter inadvertently angered legislators with clumsy efforts at persuasion or by quixotically changing his mind. Before the year ended, federal investigators charged Bert Lance, head of the budget office, with shady, perhaps illegal practices in his banking business. As the case played itself out in courtrooms and the press, opinion polls recorded Carter's skid in public esteem; many citizens thought him a decent, kind man, but quite lost in the complexity of national affairs.

The President's attempts to deal with the nation's queasy economy and its growing energy crisis speeded his decline as a leader. Carter did attempt to close loopholes in income taxes which favored the rich, deriding deductions like "the three martini business lunch." But lobbyists eventually killed most of his reform measures. A spurt in consumer spending boosted the inflation rate even higher, to thirteen percent by 1978 and 1979, scaring Carter away from expensive projects. The Federal Reserve Board tightened credit sharply. Interest rates rose to record levels in late 1979; even the most reliable borrowers paid over fifteen percent. Yet the expected slowdown did not materialize. The credit crunch did ruin the automobile industry and slowed housing starts, but retail sales and personal income pushed ahead while unemployment dropped under six percent. Carter unsuccessfully tried to "jawbone" inflation with voluntary guidelines that limited wage and price increases to seven percent a year. Treasury officials quietly sold gold and foreign currencies to support the dollar internationally. This effort, too, proved disappointing. The dollar slowly declined on world money markets, making suppliers less willing to take paper currency in payment for their raw materials.

Energy, not economics or reform, preoccupied the President. New welfare proposals withered; national health insurance languished. Shunning these traditional Democratic goals, Carter tried to focus on America's future energy needs. The United States gulped some sixteen million barrels of oil per day in the late 1970's, mostly gasoline to fuel private cars and crude oil to run electricity plants. Half of this amount was imported, principally from friendly Saudi Arabia. Optimists predicted that world reserves might last another

Saudi Arabian Oil Minister Ahmed Zaki Yamani (middle of first row), at OPEC Conference, December 1978.

eighty years; pessimists thought the end only twenty years away. The "energy crisis," then, combined dependence on uncertain sources of supply and depletion of resources.

Carter proposed a two-track solution. To discourage wasteful uses of energy, selective taxes could discourage gas guzzling cars and promote home insulation. Lowered thermostats, more carpooling, government aid to mass transit, all could conserve scarce fuel. To provide more assured sources of energy supplies, federal programs would speed conversion of existing oil-fired electrical plants to coal, a resource in good supply within the United States. An extensive chain of nuclear power stations would further reduce dependence on fossil fuels. Most of these proposals succumbed to lobbying, the President's own lackluster style, and—above all—public apathy and arrogance. Automobile manufacturers gutted the gas guzzler tax. The accident at the Three Mile Island nuclear plant galvanized protests against atomic power, already much delayed by bureaucratic regulation. Environmentalists blocked conversion to coal, a far greater pollutant than oil. Solar power advocates denounced Carter for virtually ignoring the earth's only renewable

source, sunlight. Conservatives in the Senate challenged presidential plans for an active government role; they preferred the free market mechanism of higher prices to reduce consumption and encourage exploration for new oil and natural gas. Yet the oil companies often used swollen profits to diversify into other industries rather than to reinvest in their own. For four years the interest groups debated, largely canceling each other out. Cosmetic conservation substituted poorly for what Carter once had called "the moral equivalent of war."

Presidents traditionally salvage sagging reputations at home with an energetic course overseas, an arena uncluttered by political infighting. Carter was no exception. Certainly the Democratic President embraced detente with the Russians, an American peace for the Middle East, and closer cooperation with old European allies. But Carter added two elements of his own. From the beginning, he spoke eloquently of "human rights," defending freedom fighters in countries where tyrannical regimes oppressed individual liberty. And the style of crisis management changed, Carter adopting tactics of gradual escalation in contrast to Kissinger's method of full, immediate response to provocation.

Carter and his national security adviser, Zbigniew Brzezinski, were both anxious to control strategic nuclear weapons. The first SALT treaty had not cut into either super-power's stockpile; it only limited production in the future. Its major contribution was to stop proliferation of expensive, potentially destabilizing ABM rockets. (In the wonderland of nuclear strategy, no one power can permit an opponent any technological breakthrough that might temporarily create superiority.) The next logical step was balancing existing weaponry into a rough equilibrium, thus ending the costly arms race and further insuring a nuclear standoff. Three years of negotiating followed. Despite footdragging by the military services on both sides, a second SALT treaty was in place by early 1979. It permitted the Soviets to increase their single-warhead guided missiles to match the total number of America's multiple-warhead rockets (MIRVs). The agreement provided only for indirect off-site inspection and did not cover airplanes at all. Since Carter already had axed plans for a super-bomber, the B-1, critics called the SALT II agreement a needless giveaway. The Soviets could build more ICBMs than the United States, though America's MIRVs guaranteed equality in the number of nuclear weapons. Distrust of Russia slowed SALT II progress in the Senate; then Brezhnev's adventures in the Middle East stalled the ratification procedure altogether early in 1980.

The apparent demise of a nuclear arms agreement illustrated the dilemma of Soviet-American relations: the range of potential cooperation was excruciatingly narrow. Brezhnev denounced Carter's "meddling in Russia's domestic affairs." If the rhetoric of cold war gradually returned, so too did its substance. Cuban troops, financed by Moscow, roamed across Angola and Ethiopia. The United States countered with a call for local, black majority rule throughout the continent. Communist rebels in Yemen threatened the rear flanks of Saudi Arabia, now armed more and more heavily with American weapons. Carter justified the early return of the Panama Canal to Panama primarily to counter Yankeephobia elsewhere in Latin America. (The United States retained its rights to defend the strategic waterway.) All points of contact between the two great powers resulted in more rivalry, not more agreement.

Nowhere was this growing animosity more worrisome or more apparent than in the Middle East. Carter continued Kissinger's plans for an American presence there. He pressured Israel for concessions to convince Arab moderates, like Egypt's Anwar Sadat, that the United States—not the Soviet Union—could best insure return of their occupied lands. Runaway inflation in Israel and a nightmarishly backward economy in Egypt further encouraged the two enemies toward com-

promise. Sadat and his counterpart, Menachim Begin, finally signed a peace treaty in 1978 at a ceremony at the White House. Egypt formally recognized Israel's right to exist; in turn, the Israelis restored Sinai to the Egyptians. (Other thorny issues, like the future status of Jerusalem and the Palestinian refugees, remained unresolved.) But hopes for stability in the Middle East, a region vital to United States security and energy needs, quickly evaporated.

The United States long had supported the Shah of Iran in his efforts to modernize that country; huge amounts of Iranian crude oil were exchanged for sophisticated technological apparatus and also military weapons. But religious fundamentalists among the country's Muslims, together with rebels angry at the Shah's cruel dictatorial rule, combined to overthrow the monarchy early in 1979. Their leader, the Ayatollah Khomeini, turned his back on everything western, cutting oil exports by one-third, reviving Islamic social customs, halting the drive toward modernization. Then, in a dramatic move to consolidate his personal power, Khomeini unleashed a torrent of anti-American propaganda. "Students" stormed the American embassy in Teheran and took hostage some fifty Americans still working there. The militants demanded that the United States extradite the Shah, then at a hospital in New York City, to stand trial for crimes against the Iranian people. Until he returned, the Americans would remain hostage. Carter, publicly at least, refused to negotiate with the "outlaws" and slowly increased pressure against the Iranians, securing United Nations condemnation of the act and squeezing the country with economic sanctions. Brezhnev, meanwhile, calculated that the Iranian crisis might divert attention from a daring Russian adventure in the Middle East.

The Soviets attacked neighboring Afghanistan on December 27, 1979, invading the country with an army of up to 200,000 soldiers. This poor nation, filled with mountains and barren plateaus, was of great strategic value, and was blessed with considerable oil reserves. A Marxist regime had come to power there some years earlier, but the same Islamic backlash that had seized Iran now operated against the pro-Russian rulers in Kabul. When tribal resistance almost toppled the new regime, its leaders appealed to Moscow for help. Just weeks before the invasion, Carter had sought reassurance from Brezhnev, who promised no military action. "He just plain lied to me," the President later admitted. The Red Army quickly overran the backward country. Russian puppets replaced old Marxists in the government; the Russian ruble served as Afghanistan's new currency; more and more Russian troops flooded into the country which resisted fiercely. Caught off guard and preoccupied by the lingering hostage crisis, the Carter administration exhibited its strongest quality, that of patience, until April 1980 when he approved a reckless rescue operation that ended with failure and eight American lives lost. Soviet vetoes blocked action in the United Nations. Red Army divisions took up positions along Iran's border, just eighty miles from the oil fields of the Persian Gulf. Renewed war scares filtered around the world. The White House cut grain shipments to the Soviet Union, threatened to boycott the 1980 Moscow Olympics, and finally decided to furnish the Pakistani dictatorship, a staunch American ally, with military weapons. Nothing budged the Russians from the Afghani conquest. Nixon's detente, like the "thaw" of the 1960's, was itself an impermanent peace.

The Election of 1980

In 1980 Ronald Wilson Reagan, the former Republican governor of California, defeated Jimmy Carter for the presidency by an unexpectedly wide margin. An open, friendly man, Reagan offered a clear alternative to a presidential administration that had lost its political bases. Though in the course of the campaign he had presented himself as interested in a better administration of the government's social programs, Reagan represents a conservatism that has little taste for large expenditures on health, education, welfare, and the environment. He promised to spend more on defense and to restore America's pre-eminence in the world. He also espoused, on issues such as the ERA, a cultural conservatism that drew much support from normally Democratic Catholic and evangelistic Protestant voters.

In contrast to Reagan's positive positions, Carter seemed a study in irresolution in face of the Iranian hostage crisis. The OPEC oil price increases, moreover, crippled the national economy with inflation, and the failure of Carter to maintain economic controls at a critical early juncture had aggravated the situation. The independent candidacy of the Illinois congressman John Anderson —and the President's studied arrogance toward it— also harmed Carter's campaign, as did Senator Edward Kennedy's harsh words for the President in the Democratic primaries.

Was Reagan's election an important turn to the conservatism evoked in these pages by Professor Forrest McDonald, who supported the Republican candidate in the campaign? Certainly the Congress, for the first time in a generation, came into the hands of a coalition of conservatives after the defeat of many prominent liberals. But Reagan, who will be approaching his mid-seventies in 1984, is likely to be a one-term President like Carter himself. Continuity of presidential leadership had already been shattered in the preceding generation; Dwight Eisenhower was the last President to serve out two terms. But there is little assurance that an aging President can win to a right-wing ideology a country of independent voters by his likeable personality and the absence of real alternatives. Reagan faces myriad problems: nuclear proliferation, continuing inflation, demands by interest groups of every stripe. Perhaps the overriding question—as the liberal-moderate American might phrase it—is simply whether the conservatives who exert some control in every branch of government will concentrate on invigorating the economic system for the benefit of all Americans, as they have promised to do, or simply try to build into a weakening economy an institutionalized selfishness benefiting established interests.

Suggested Readings

Garry Wills has recently revised his perceptive *Nixon Agonistes: The Crisis of the Self-Made Man* (rev. 1979); see also Richard M. Nixon, *RN: The Memoirs of Richard Nixon* (1978). Carl Bernstein and Bob Woodward's *All the President's Men* (1974) is a partisan effort to be read critically. Philip B. Kurland, *Watergate and the Constitution* (1978) and John R. Labovitz, *Presidential Impeachment* (1978) are important works. Henry Kissinger's own memoirs, *The White House Years* (1979), should be supplemented by *Uncertain Greatness: Henry Kissinger and American Foreign Policy* (1977). Another important book on foreign affairs is William B. Quandt, *Decade of Decisions: American Policy Toward the Arab-Israeli Conflict, 1967-1976* (1977); a related early study of energy questions is Anthony Sampson, *The Seven Sisters: The Great Oil Companies and the World They Made* (1975). Christopher Lasch, *The Culture of Narcissism: American Life in an Age of Diminishing Expectations* (1978), freely employs Freudian terms to comment on the condition of American civilization, or that part of it that can be evoked as "narcissistic." Lasch distinguishes narcissism from simple selfishness: the Narcissist, not having been provided with the interior restraints that would make it possible to direct the passions and desires, lacks an identity and searches self-indulgently for images of himself. Norman O. Brown, in *Love Against Death* (1958), celebrates a "polymorphous perversity" that is more in agreement with the lifestyles of the late 1960's. Another important book is Robert Heilbroner, *An Inquiry into the Human Prospect* (1974).

Epilogue
America in Retreat?

I. Forrest McDonald: The Excesses of Liberal Moralism

For its first century and three-quarters as a nation, the United States had faith in itself—in its basic goodness and its ability to do what it must no matter how hard the trials. And then, in a single generation, it ceased to believe. It lost its nerve and lost its wits into the bargain.

Quickly as the transformation came about, however, it was not an event but a process, one that took a succession of forms. In the 1950s there was panic. Having failed to "win" the war in Korea, the United States confronted "world communism"—which, at the time, it vastly outmatched militarily, technologically, and economically—by fleeing to the shaky sanctuary of regional defense pacts. In the early sixties there was arrogance. Having faced down the Soviet Union in the Cuban missile crisis, the Kennedy and Johnson administrations took upon themselves the role of liberator and Lord Protector to the Third World—of which they were ignorant and in which they were unwelcome. In the late sixties and early seventies there was guilt. Having less to be ashamed of than any nation on earth, the American people nonetheless responded to the accusing finger—pointed first by blacks with legitimate grievances and then by mobs of spoiled young whites who had never been required to behave themselves—by crying mea culpa, I am guilty, and wallowing in humiliation. As the seventies turned into the eighties, there was a pathetic urge to be loved. Having become convinced that the war in Vietnam was a dreadful sin—which in fact it was, but only because the United States first blundered into it and then, once in, betrayed its fighting men by refusing to let them win—the government now tried to atone by yielding to the demands of anyone at home or abroad who claimed to have been "victimized" by American sins in the past. As one foreign minister complained, "the trouble with having the United States as an ally is that you never know when it is going to stab itself in the back."

The malady that plagued the republic was a grave one, but it needed not prove fatal, for the affliction was curable if it were accurately diagnosed. The trouble arose not from abroad, as many Americans thought—not from the Soviet Union, though that country posed a real and present danger; nor from the OPEC nations, though those banditti held the survival of industrial civilization in their greedy hands; nor from Communism, though that godless religion was deadly poison to all who partook of its sacraments. Rather, the basic cause of the American malaise was a home-grown ideology, a form of statism which for a half century had passed under the deceptive label of liberalism.

Liberalism was a perversion of qualities deeply rooted in American history. First and foremost it had derived from what was worst in the character of old Puritan Yankees, at the expense of what was best in that character. (The worst, which became fundamental to liberalism, was a compulsion to run people's lives "for their own good," a refusal to recognize that there are evils and imperfections beyond human control, and an inability simply to let things happen. The best, which liberalism rejected, had to do with the work ethic and with such virtues as piety, thrift, perserverance, and self-reliance.) Secondly, liberalism had derived from what—apart from racism—was the worst in the Southern tradition, again at the expense of what was best. (The bad, ardently embraced by liberalism, was the Bolingbroke-Jefferson-Jackson legacy of suspicion, envy, and hostility toward profit-making; the best, rejected with equal ardour, had to do with valuing the quality of life above the possession of things and with such virtues as courage, honor, family loyalty, and an ability to tolerate eccentricity without sanctioning it.) Over the years, liberals had built a powerful following by creating vested interests in their policies—among many businessmen and almost all bureaucrats no less than among labor leaders, self-appointed spokemen for minorities, and recipients of handouts. These interests were, of course, only short-range interests, for in the long range liberalism was to no one's advantage. And as the 1980s began, the gap between long and short range had closed almost to the vanishing point.

It is instructive to observe the ways that liberals arrived at their policies. First the liberal became conscious of a "problem," usually as reported (or invented) by television newscasters, the *Washington Post*, and/or the *New York Times*. Engaging the cliché or set of conditioned reflexes that served him as a substitute for a brain, the liberal politician automatically set out to solve the problem by a) voting for a large appropriation of the taxpayers' money and b) establishing a regulatory agency. When it turned out, as it almost invariably did, that the solution created a rash of new problems and worsened the old, the liberal conducted an investigation (either through a congressional committee or through an agency of the federal bureaucracy), probing for information from the affected segments of what he called the "private sector" of society. Representatives of those segments, seeking to protect their own interests, lied to him and misled him, and self-appointed spokesmen for "the public interest" lied to him and misled him further, whereupon he a) voted another large appropriation and b) established another regulatory agency. The process was endlessly repeated, and appropriations and government agencies expanded at a geometric ratio. So did confusion and misinformation. Ultimately only three groups—the congressional committees, the bureaucratic functionaries, and the private individuals or organizations directly concerned—had any comprehension of the original problem, for it had become a problem in a vacuum.

Lest it be thought that this a parody, let us consider a case history, that of the policies which created the energy crisis. For a number of years the tangled network of regulations and tax laws governing the oil and natural gas industries had been such as to make profitable operations dependent upon them—not upon skill or luck or efficiency, not upon the capacity to find, develop, produce, and market oil and gas at a reasonable price and profit, but upon government regulations and the tax laws. Even so, the major companies and the independent operators (though often working at cross-purposes) had regularly found and marketed the oil and gas; and a cheap and steadily cheaper energy supply fueled America's spectacular economic growth. Then, in the 1960s, liberals discovered the problems of pollution and the upsetting of the ecological balance, and a host of new regulations and new tax laws were forthcoming. It became impossible for oil and gas companies to operate profitably in the United States. Accordingly, they looked for, found, developed, and came to depend upon fields in other countries. They also stopped building refineries at home—environmental protection legislation and regulations made it almost impossible to build them in the United States—and started building them abroad, too.

In 1973, when the federal government discovered the energy problem that government policies had created, there were already seventy-four different federal agencies regulating the energy supply, not to mention countless state and local agencies and twenty federal bureaus which regulated water power. In addition, to solve the problem of the destruction of the environment, the government had passed laws and regulations effectively preventing the development of an alternate energy source which the United States had cheaply and abundantly available, namely coal. Every year thereafter, billions of dollars were appropriated, new regulations were established, new agencies were created; and with each passing year the problem became more acute. Then someone discovered that the real problem was over-regulation, and the President of the United States came up with an "energy package" that would solve that problem by appropriating more money and creating new agencies. Part of the package was a "windfall profits tax," aimed at preventing the oil and gas industry from keeping the profits it might earn after "deregulation."

The energy crisis was severe, it was real, and it was almost certain to get worse. And yet there was in the continental United States in 1980 enough immediately recoverable coal to supply all the country's energy needs for 800 years, enough natural gas to supply those needs for at least fifty years, and enough oil for at least ten to twenty years. But the endowments of nature are not "resources" unless they can be used profitably, in the broad sense of that term. Earlier, being able to do so profitably, American business enterprise had created natural resources. Now government had destroyed natural resources, just as surely as if it had removed them with a magic wand.

Nor was the energy crisis an isolated phenomenon. Consider education. After billions of dollars in appropriations and millions of pages of studies, reports, recommendations, and regulations, the system was a shambles. By every reasonable standard of measurement, the level of student performance (reflecting teacher performance) had declined precipitously, while grades had risen sharply. Consider the blacks. Though liberals stoutly claimed to be the champions of blacks, they actually believed blacks inferior to whites, as was attested by liberal programs (and appropriations and regulations and court orders) which regularly set lower standards for blacks. Consider the poor. By government count, there were in the United States in 1975 some 25 million poor people. During the previous decade the amount spent annually on social welfare programs had increased by $209 billion. Had the increase (not the total, just the increase) been simply given to the poor, every one of them would have received $8,000 a year, or $32,000 tax-free for a family of four—which would have made every poor person in America a relatively rich person. Instead, the bulk of the money was paid to bureaucrats for counseling the poor, studying the problems of the inner cities, and recommending new appropriations and programs. Consider the elderly. Social Security and medicare and related programs ostensibly provided for them; but the Social Security system was bankrupt, having nearly five trillion dollars in unfunded liabilities; and elderly beneficiaries of the other programs were stripped of their dignity by requirements that they take a veritable pauper's oath before qualifying. Consider the ordinary white American of good health, working age, and middling status. Taxes consumed no less than 40 percent of the gross national income, and were steadily rising. It has been reckoned that the "exploitation rate" of medieval serfs—that is, the percentage of their labor which was taken from them—was only about 33 percent.

Thus it came to pass that government in the United States had all but ceased to function by 1980, and instead had become a metastisized cancer, infesting and devouring one part of American society after another. And in the summer of 1979, in a nationwide television address, the President of the United States (a devout liberal) solemnly declared that the nation was suffering from a crisis of confidence, and scolded the American people for lack of faith in their leaders.

Men are not angels, and they therefore need government to protect them in their lives, their liberty, and their property, and they need government to provide for the common defense and promote the general welfare. Liberalism had destroyed the capacity of government to perform its legitimate and necessary functions. When the Federal Register required 60,000 pages of small print just to list the new federal regulations promulgated in a single year; when the Department of Health, Education, and Welfare spent a third of a trillion dollars annually and in the doing hastened the decline of the nation's health, education, and welfare; when the Interstate Commerce Commission issued its trillionth separate regulation; when federal judges ordered that black children be integrated with white children by busing them 100 miles a day to attend schools that whites had long since abandoned; then any resemblance to government, good or bad, theoretical or historical, had ceased to exist.

At this point—upon the collapse of government and its replacement by an inept but all-pervasive something so lacking in precedent that it had no name—the paths of radicalism and conservatism intersected. "Conservative" derives from the Latin word *conservare*, meaning to keep, guard, protect, preserve. "Radical" derives from the Latin word *radix*, meaning roots; to be radical means to get at the roots, to get down to fundamentals. In the 1980s the time had come for Americans to take radical measures, while there was still a chance that radical measures might succeed. Otherwise, there would be nothing left to keep or guard, nothing left that was worth protecting and preserving.

II.   Eugene D. Genovese: The Necessity for a Radical's Morality

In the late 1960s and early 1970s the American people learned that they too are mortal.

In the wake of the war in Vietnam, the Watergate scandals, and the collapse of the illusion of permanent economic growth, Americans discovered that their national morals were not superior to those of others—or at least that others had good reason to express doubts; that their country's motives, not to mention its performance, in international affairs could be despicable; that in assuming the United States to be a much beloved country throughout the world, they may have been assuming the opposite of the truth; that their vaunted political system was in fact amenable to gross manipulation of the popular will; that their vaunted economic system may well have seen the last of sustained economic growth; that the long-hidden problems of racial and class injustice could no longer be hidden and, worse, might prove insoluble without fundamental changes in the social order; and that their hallowed if childish myth of the invincibility of American arms had been laid to rest by a third-rate power, and a non-white one at that. (Actually, the myth was not only hallowed and childish, it was a lie. The British, by any reasonable standard, humiliated us in the War of 1812; our victory in the Seminole War was less than clear cut; and we at best got a draw against China during the Korean War, at a time when the Chinese were exhausted from decades of civil war and had not had time to create a modern army. These and other unpleasant details could be swept under the rug by public relations men and academic hucksters. There was no sweeping away Vietnam.)

It has become fashionable to denigrate the popular upsurge that rocked the campuses and the country generally during the 1960s and to confuse the causes of our national disorder with the attempts to cure it. The "Movement," as it came to be known, had its seamy side: There was considerable incoherence, misdirected violence, nihilistic excesses, and, yes, even that much lamented outpouring of pointless guilt feelings and silly breast-beating. No vibrant historical period, no brave and militant social upsurge, comes pure and sweet and gentle. The rebels of the 1960s preferred struggle to complacency; they fought the Establishment wherever they could, including in the streets. In the course of those struggles millions of Americans protested against a disgraceful and unjust war and against a ferocious and entrenched racism and thereby saved the honor of their country and made it a better place to live.

It is certainly true that the peace movement imposed restraints on the government, as Nixon and Kissinger have never stopped reiterating. In so doing, the peace movement established itself as the most successful mass movement of its kind in history, even if it could not end the war by its own efforts. In effect it prevented the government from using nuclear weapons, destroying the North Vietnamese dikes and thereby slaughtering a few million civilians, invading North Vietnam, and escalating the violence in various other ways; and it applied incessant and eventually effective pressure for troop withdrawals. There is no doubt that many of the measures not taken would have provoked China's entry into the war. The government had, in effect, been restrained from suicidal adventures in a disreputable cause that was earning us the enmity of much of the world.

America's excuse for being in Vietnam was that a communist victory in what was civil war—the division of the country had been imposed from without as a temporary expedient—would represent Chinese expansion and disrupt the balance of power in Asia. The excuse was eventually exposed as a clumsy fabrication. All American intervention accomplished was to force the intensely nationalistic Vietnamese into a tighter alliance with the Soviet Union as a counterweight to the hostility of the United States and—would you believe?—our new ally, communist China. American intervention never made sense as national policy; it was a brazen attempt to reestablish the worldwide dominion we briefly held after World War II.

The United States came out of World War II the big winner. Our losses had been trivial relative to the losses of the other big participants. The Soviet Union had suffered an estimated 20,000,000 dead—about 10% of its population—and the destruction of much of its economy. The rest of Europe was prostrate. China had suffered more than Japan, which had gone down to defeat and had had its cities A-bombed. The United States was in a position to dictate terms to the world. Or so it seemed.

The origin and course of the Cold War—the degree of responsibility that falls to each side—cannot be explored here, but one aspect of the problem requires comment. The United States simply took it for granted that it would determine the shape of the postwar world. The Soviet Union was in no condition to mount a direct challenge, and just about every other country was depending on our economic support. And we had a monopoly of atomic weapons. The United Nations in those halcyon days was overwhelmingly a club of American satellites. It is enough to recall that our repeated interventions in other countries in flagrant disregard of the UN Charter—e.g., in Guatemala and Iran in the early 1950s—never drew so much as a slap on the wrist from the UN. The United States even threatened to use force in Italy if the communists won a free election in 1948; it made expulsion of the communists and leftwing socialists from the governments of Western European countries the price for economic aid; it built military bases all around the Soviet Union; and it acted as if its atomic monopoly and command of the world economy would never end.

The end came as early as 1949, although few recognized it. After decades of bloody civil war against Chiang Kai-shek and a protracted war against Japan, the communist armies entered Peking and rolled south in a lightning conquest of the mainland. The world's most populous nation—one destined by the qualities of its people, its natural resources, and its centuries-old civilization to become a superpower—had shifted from the capitalist to the socialist camp. With Eastern Europe and North Korea now communist, the strategy of isolating the Soviet Union, which had failed disastrously after World War I, had failed once more.

By the late 1950s the western colonial empires had crumbled. The wiser imperialists cut their losses and tried to maintain economic control of the newly independent African and Asian nations; the less prudent were compelled to learn the hard way during subsequent decades, when revolutions broke their power in Egypt, Iraq, Algeria, Angola, Mozambique, and elsewhere. In short, a "Third World" emerged, some of it socialist, much of it radical, and most of it determined to avoid recolonization in any form.

By the late 1950s the Stalinist dictatorship over the communist movement had also crumbled, and in the wake came many communisms, some of which were at sword's point with others, and more of which were asserting their autonomy. The simple days of a Cold War between two blocs gave way to an extraordinarily complex world of shifting coalitions and intricate power politics. The United States picked this very era to intervene in Vietnam, which it insisted on seeing—or pretending to see—as a simple case of monolithic communist expansionism. In the end we found ourselves in alliance with China against a victorious Vietnam and in support of one communist faction against another in Cambodia. The peace movement, not the government, spoke for sanity and realism, not to mention decency, when it threw its efforts into ending that stupid and vicious war.

The South had remained racially segregated during the 1950s. It may seem hard to believe, but until about twenty years ago black southerners could not attend school with whites, could not eat at the same lunch counters or restaurants, could not drink from the same fountain, could not sit in the front of buses or trains. Lynching, although less frequent than it had been before World War II, still occurred for offenses real and imagined, serious or trivial, or for the simple "impertinence" of a black's trying to exercise his right to vote or do what any white might do. Blacks could not vote in most of the places where their ballots would have gained them needed power and protection. They were for the most part still confined to the poorest paying jobs, with a large percentage kept in abject proverty, and with no way to change their condition. No ostensibly civilized country in the world, except South Africa, flaunted so disgraceful a system of legal and institutionalized racism—at least not after the demise of the Third Reich.

Two observations. First, the Federal government made an indispensable contribution to the ending of these outrages. Its motives certainly were not pure: It needed to court favor with the emerging African nations and to remove a powerful Soviet propaganda weapon. But if the conservatives had had their way and had blocked Federal "interference," blacks would still be riding in the backs of those buses or, alternatively, would have had to shoot their way up front.

Second, the black liberation movement was supported actively by thousands of whites and passively by millions more, but it was led and staffed primarily by blacks. The movement, like the peace movement which Dr. Martin Luther King and many other black leaders participated in, did not always behave politely. It was often loud, discourteous, shrill, and sometimes even violent. It had to be. Until it applied mass pressure, which can never be tidy, no one would listen. In the end it won a great if incomplete victory and smashed legal segregation and at least the most overt and degrading forms of racial oppression. It thereby removed a centuries-long stain from our country, much as the abolitionist movement had done a century earlier. Perhaps it will be enough to observe that while conservatives continue to dwell on the movement's shortcomings and excesses, they have yet to tell us just what they were doing to end racism, discrimination, and the daily humiliation of black Americans. The question would seem fair enough since the states in which legal segregation and its attendant horrors were taking place were under the leadership of conservative politicians.

The 1970s brought defeat in Vietnam, Soviet military parity, the national shame of Watergate, foreign policy reversals in Africa and elsewhere, and considerable political disarray. And during this grim and spiritless decade the economic bubble burst. It has become fashionable to blame "Third World bandits," who have outraged Americans by insisting, after decades and indeed centuries of being brutally exploited by the West, that they, not we, own their natural resources. Apparently, the apologists for capitalism really believed that we could go on forever buying oil ridiculously cheap by first buying off corrupt politicians in semi-colonies and then selling industrial commodities at prices rigged to our convenience, that is, the convenience of big business. In any event, the OPEC squeeze merely brought to the surface the deeper structural deformity of a crumbling world capitalist system.

The United States has the resources to solve its problems; it has the technology and experience to support the world economy as a whole. New sources of energy could be developed; present sources allocated more rationally; old sources revitalized. But to do these things in any combination and simultaneously to provide needed and worthwhile protection for the environment, as well as a fair distribution of sacrifices, duties, responsibilities, and benefits, will require the kind of careful planning that no capitalist regime has ever been able to provide. The question is not whether we can satisfy everyone but whether we can arrive at the most equitable solution—and that will require a full employment policy that even apologists for capitalism no longer pretend to be able to sustain. Women, blacks, minorities can no longer be thrown or kept out of work to make room for entrenched white males. But their reasonable demands for elementary opportunities cannot be met unless there is plenty of work to go around. Thus, the ERA, for example, does not provide equal access to the Ladies Room; it provides equal pay for equal work. And it will take much more than a constitutional amendment to do justice to women. It will take a comprehensive social policy and national economic planning that are incompatible with an economy run for private profit.

Once again we are hearing, in the best tradition of the 1920s, that lower taxes—in effect, greater subsidies—for business will cure everything. Business will of course reinvest the profits in such a way as to maximize social advantages for all. There is not a shred of evidence for this fairy tale. Time and again, the plowback has proven grossly inadequate, and in particular it has done little to correct the staggering inequities that always plagued the poor, the female, and the black, and that increasingly plague the white working and "new middle class" as well. There is, however, another "solution" open to capitalist politicians: They can rekindle the Cold War and step up armaments production. For a variety of reasons even the brighter reactionaries know that those measures can no longer work as they once did; and after Vietnam it is not clear that the American people will allow themselves to be panicked into pointless and bloody wars that cannot be justified and, increasingly, cannot be won.

The case for a socialist solution will have to await a more appropriate time and place. For the moment it will have to suffice to suggest that all is not lost. A long quiet labor movement can no longer bear the burden of inflation, unemployment, and declining power. Middle-class reformers concerned with the environment and quality of life can no longer deceive themselves that they can prevail if the economy remains in the doldrums. Nor can blacks, women, and minorities who are desperately fighting to be able to earn a decent living. These groups and many others—farmers who cannot stand up against the spread of agribusiness, any citizens determined to keep the world from a nuclear holocaust—have often been at cross-purposes in the past. It will not be easy for them to come to terms now on a program of radically restructuring the American economy. Many internal disagreements and conflicting interests will have to be compromised if a unified political program is to be hammered out. But a solution to our problems that is worthy of the best in our national history depends on such a prospective political coalition. And that coalition will have one great advantage: agreement that mass participation in a democratic politics alone can do the job.

Appendix A

The Authors of . . .
THE AMERICAN PEOPLE

DAVID BURNER, a native of Cornwall, New York, earned his A.B. at Hamilton College and his Ph.D. at Columbia University. Burner has studied both the Democratic and Republican Parties: he has published *The Politics of Provincialism: The Democratic Party in Transition, 1918-1932* (1968); *Herbert Hoover* (1979); and *The Kennedy Dynasty* (1980). A Guggenheim Fellow, Burner is now writing a study of the environmental movement. He is Professor of History at the State University of New York at Stony Brook.

EUGENE D. GENOVESE, son of a dockworker, earned his B.A. at Brooklyn College and his Ph.D. at Columbia University. A distinguished radical historian, he is editor of *Marxist Perspectives* and was President of the Organization of American Historians in 1979. His studies of slavery include *The Political Economy of Slavery* (1965), *The World the Slaveholders Made* (1969), *Roll, Jordon, Roll* (1974). Genovese, a Rockefeller Fellow, teaches at the University of Rochester. His stand against the Vietnam War won him a vituperative attack from Richard Nixon in 1965.

FORREST McDONALD earned his Ph.D. at the University of Texas and is now Distinguished Senior Fellow at the University of Alabama Center for the Study of Southern History and Culture. A Guggenheim Fellow, McDonald has published major works on the founding of the nation and in recent American history, among them *We the People: The Economic Origins of the Constitution* (1958); *Insull* (1962); and *Alexander Hamilton* (1979). A brilliant, prolific, and controversial historian, McDonald served as northeast co-chairman of Citizens for Goldwater in 1964.

Appendix B

Part I

Eugene D. Genovese
Point of View

There are today many Marxisms, as anyone who reads a newspaper should be able to tell. There always have been many, but during the quarter-century or so of Stalin's rule in a largely unified communist movement only his brand of Marxism got much of a hearing. It is not true that Marxists have a party line. The only point at which their politics converges is a commitment to socialism, much as the politics of conservatives converges on a commitment to capitalism. And at that, Marxists do not by any means agree on what they mean by socialism or, more precisely, on what kind of socialism they want. For socialism, like capitalism, is compatible with democracy or dictatorship, freedom or tyranny. Those who want an introduction to the range of Marxisms might well start by reading the issues of the quarterly journal *Marxist Perspectives*, which is open to all tendencies and which also publishes critiques by liberals and conservatives.

The differences between socialist Marxists and communist Marxists are, moreover, not the only or even the greatest differences. Even the once monolithic communist movement now has a dizzying array of viewpoints, not to mention of bitter political and military rivalries.

Marxists do, however, share some controlling assumptions about historical process. They also share a political commitment to equality and the abolition of class exploitation—as well as to the abolition of all forms of racism and sexism—although like other people they do not always live up to their highest ideals. For our immediate purposes let us settle for a few general points on which Marxists agree, even if they diverge in their elaborations.

Marxism is not an economic determinism, and it does not advance the view that human beings are what the mode of production makes of them—that they are therefore not responsible for their actions. Indeed, some Marxists, myself included, flatter themselves that they need no lectures from conservatives on the problem of evil—on the "sinfulness" in man's nature and the impossibility of creating a utopia or of "perfecting" human nature.

Marxism does assert that the motor force of great historical changes and of essential social progress has been class struggles for the social surplus—i.e., struggles between those who own the means of production and live off the labor of others and those who are exploited and produce the surplus off which the rulers live. Marxism also insists that the great ideas, ideals, and values—however good and worthy in themselves—arise from the material conditions of social life and not from some God-given spirit.

I doubt that these or other assertions could be explained or defended to your satisfaction or mine in any brief account. In my short interventions in this book I try only to raise some questions and suggest that an alternative viewpoint does exist; naturally, I hope that students will make an effort to learn much more about it. After all, Marxism, notwithstanding its many variations, has been the most dynamic and successful political and ideological movement of our century; it now guides perhaps half the world and exercises considerable influence in the other half. It compares in this respect with Christianity and Islam in their golden ages; indeed, not since the great wave of Islamic conquests more than a thousand years ago has the world seen anything like it. Accordingly, you might ask if your university offers rigorous courses in Marxism, taught by friend and foe alike—and if not, why not?

One caveat about my contributions to this book: They emphasize the negative. They have to, for my job here is to press criticism of the ideological position of the text and of Professor McDonald's response to it. (Yes, I regret to say that even Professor McDonald has an ideology, whatever he may wish to call it.) Still, I do not think that Professor Burner, Professor McDonald, and I are far apart in one vital respect: our appreciation of the greatness of the United States, not merely in the military-political sense but in the moral-political. They are quite right to emphasize, each in his own way, that our country has been the world's leader in attempting to reconcile freedom, democracy, equality, and social justice, and that, whatever its crimes and blemishes, its performance has, on the whole, been admirable. I suspect that, if pushed, I would agree with Professor McDonald's flat assertion that the United States has less to feel guilty about than any other great nation. Still, it has enough, and nothing could be worse than a national failure to correct evils and mistakes. We disagree on the nature of the historical experience: on who should get the credit for our national greatness, on who should be held accountable for our national crimes and mistakes, and above all on what kind of a social system America needs now.

Part II

Forrest McDonald
Point of View

Though I have been counted as a "conservative" throughout my career, I find it no simple matter to define what is meant by the term.

It is easy enough to say what conservatism is not: it is not an ideology. There is no party line among conservatives, no position that automatically qualifies one for expulsion from the ranks of the faithful. By contrast, there are convenient touchstones for adherents of most other isms. I believe, for instance, that I could write a series of interpretive essays about American history which would pass as Communist, fascist, socialist, or liberal. In other words, I think I can anticipate what they would say on most subjects; but no one, neither they nor even other conservatives, can devise an easy formula for anticipating what I may say. Conservatives disagree with one another, and conservatives who teach from this book will disagree with me in many particulars; and yet they will somehow recognize in me a kindred soul.

Because conservatives do disagree, particularly in regard to matters of current political concern, it may be useful to the reader to know where I stand in the contemporary political spectrum. I am neither a libertarian nor an authoritarian in any absolute sense, for it seems obvious to me that government is as necessary as freedom is desirable. The proper functions of government, in my view, are two—to protect the citizens in their lives, liberty, and property, and to provide legal and institutional machinery conducive to the realization, through voluntary efforts, of the legitimate aspirations which they value as a society. Regarding the first, almost all conservatives would agree; regarding the second, they are in considerable disagreement. Let us consider a specific historical example. One legitimate aspiration of Americans throughout most of their history (though not one that all peoples have shared) has been to attain for themselves and their families an improved material standard of living. Toward that end, the accumulation of liquid capital is extremely useful. Most conservatives would agree with me that government policies which discourage the accumulation of capital are pernicious, as are policies which impose handicaps on those who, by some socially approved means, earn their way, and policies which reward those who do not. But many conservatives would argue that the creation and manipulation of fiscal machinery to facilitate the accumulation of private capital is not a proper function of government. I not only disagree, but also maintain that government activity was historically more efficacious in the accumulation of liquid capital than were work, savings, or the reinvestment of profits. (Contrary to what leftists prefer to believe, such capital was in no way stolen from anybody; nor did the labor of slaves contribute much to the accumulation, for almost all the fruits of their toil were either consumed or reinvested in the expansion of plantation slavery.)

But the attitudes which identify conservatives and distinguish them from liberals and leftists are of considerably broader moment than mere questions of politics. Conservatism is a set of principles, values, and premises from which to view and respond to the ongoing human drama; it is a complex of articles of faith about what is moral, what is possible, what is desirable, and what is prudent.

What is moral? The very use of the word is old-fashioned. In an age to which terrorism, murder, extortion, and every known perversion are not only commonplace, but are defended as valid forms of political expression or as rights of oppressed minorities, to use the word may seem positively quaint. Morality does, however, have a meaning, or rather two meanings, and unless the present generation has received a special dispensation, both forms of morality remain necessary to human survival. In its first and narrower sense, "moral" derives from an ancient Latin word which meant customary, normal, habitual, or conventional. To behave morally, in this sense, is merely to do what is expected, to do more or less what everyone else does—but it is not to be taken lightly for that reason, for knowing what to expect of people is a prerequisite to sanity. Nor is this form of conventional morality to be belittled because it is often attended by a goodly measure of hypocrisy. Hypocrisy is pretending to be what we are not—and to the extent that we successfully pretend to be civilized and rational creatures than barbarians and animals, to that extent do we become civilized and rational creatures.

In its second and broader sense moral also derives from the ancient world, but this time from the Greeks and from the Roman philosopher Cicero, who taught that every human being is endowed with the capacity to know right from wrong, good from evil. In the Western world, Europe and America, the Ciceronian view became central to the Judeo-Christian religious tradition: what was good or right emanated from Jehovah, what was evil or wrong emanated from Satan. To many students, western religious tradition may seem to have no relevance to the problems of living in the world today, but it is precisely there that it is especially relevant. In the framework of the

Judeo-Christian cosmology, Satan's most artful device is to convince people that he (or evil) does not exist: if people behave badly, it is because of their circumstances (or, in the Marxist superstition, because individual behavior is a product of the "forces of production"). The conservative holds, on the contrary, that you are personally responsible for what you do. You cannot blame society, fate, your parents, the economic system, or any other person or thing for the way you act. You alone are to be held accountable—both to society and to God. That is the meaning of justice: you know what is expected of you, and you will be judged accordingly. (Perhaps that is why conservatism has rarely been popular. Thomas Jefferson once said that he cried for his country when he contemplated the notion that there was a "just" God. It was much less painful to believe that God was more merciful than just.)

What is possible? The limits are of two general descriptions. The first is historical and cultural: history is cumulative, which means that individuals and societies can build only on what has gone before, and that efforts to effect sudden and total changes in accustomed norms of behavior are futile if not self-destructive. The second is biological: it is not possible to employ the organized power of the state to effect any fundamental changes in the nature of man. Man is a social animal, which means that without organized society he cannot subsist, and that such social institutions as marriage, families, rituals attending "rites of passage" from one generation or status to another, and the very idea of status itself are programmed into the human genes. To attempt to transcend these limits—to try to force humans to behave in extrahuman ways—is to open the door to mass murder.

What is desirable? What is desirable is to let other human beings behave in ways that are acceptable to them, as long as in doing so they do not force others to behave in ways that contradict either God's law or their own social laws.

And what is prudent? To a conservative, to be prudent is to know what can be changed and what ought to be changed, what can be preserved and what ought to be preserved. It is to perceive that rights and responsibilities are inseparable, that neither can be expanded without a compensating expansion of the other. Above all, it is to recognize that there are no easy paths to knowledge, understanding, or wisdom, and that no one has a monopoly on truth. Anyone who tells you otherwise is either a fool or someone seeking to make you his fool.

Appendix C

The Declaration of Independence

When in the Course of human events, it becomes necessary for one people to dissolve the political bands which have connected them with another, and to assume among the Powers of the earth, the separate and equal station to which the Laws of Nature and of Nature's God entitle them, a decent respect to the opinions of mankind requires that they should declare the causes which impel them to the separation.

We hold these truths to be self-evident, that all men are created equal, that they are endowed by their Creator with certain unalienable Rights, that among these are Life, Liberty and the pursuit of Happiness. That to secure these rights, Governments are instituted among Men, deriving their just powers from the consent of the governed, That whenever any Form of Government becomes destructive of these ends, it is the Right of the People to alter or to abolish it, and to institute new Government, laying its foundation on such principles and organizing its powers in such form, as to them shall seem most likely to effect their Safety and Happiness. Prudence, indeed, will dictate that Governments long established should not be changed for light and transient causes; and accordingly all experience hath shown, that mankind are more disposed to suffer, while evils are sufferable, than to right themselves by abolishing the forms to which they are accustomed. When a long train of abuses and usurpations, pursuing invariably the same Object evinces a design to reduce them under absolute Despotism, it is their right, it is their duty, to throw off such Government, and to provide new Guards for their future security.—Such has been the patient sufferance of these Colonies; and such is now the necessity which constrains them to alter their former Systems of Government. The history of the present King of Great Britain is a history of repeated injuries and usurpations, all having in direct object the establishment of an absolute Tyranny over these States. To prove this, let Facts be submitted to a candid world.

He has refused his Assent to Laws, the most wholesome and necessary for the public good.

He has forbidden his Governors to pass Laws of immediate and pressing importance, unless suspended in their operation till his Assent should be obtained; and when so suspended, he has utterly neglected to attend to them.

He has refused to pass other Laws for the accommodation of large districts of people, unless those people would relinquish the right of Representation in the Legislature, a right inestimable to them and formidable to tyrants only.

He has dissolved Representative Houses repeatedly, for opposing with manly firmness his invasions on the rights of the people.

He has refused for a long time, after such dissolutions, to cause others to be elected; whereby the Legislative Powers, incapable of Annihilation, have returned to the People at large for their exercise; the State remaining in the mean time exposed to all the dangers of invasion from without, and convulsions within.

He has endeavoured to prevent the population of these States; for that purpose obstructing the Laws of Naturalization of Foreigners; refusing to pass others to encourage their migration hither, and raising the conditions of new Appropriations of Lands.

He has obstructed the Administration of Justice, by refusing his Assent to Laws for establishing Judiciary Powers.

He has made Judges dependent on his Will alone, for the tenure of their offices, and the amount and payment of their salaries.

He has erected a multitude of New Offices, and sent hither swarms of Officers to harass our People, and eat out their substance.

He has kept among us, in times of peace, Standing Armies without the Consent of our legislature.

He has affected to render the Military independent of and superior to the Civil Power.

He has combined with others to subject us to a jurisdiction foreign to our constitution, and unacknowledged by our laws; giving his Assent to their acts of pretended legislation:

For quartering large bodies of armed troops among us:

For protecting them, by a mock Trial, from Punishment for any Murders which they should commit on the Inhabitants of these States:

For cutting off our Trade with all parts of the world:

For imposing taxes on us without our Consent:

For depriving us in many cases, of the benefits of Trial by Jury:

For transporting us beyond Seas to be tried for

pretended offences:

For abolishing the free System of English Laws in a neighbouring Province, establishing therein an Arbitrary government, and enlarging its Boundaries so as to render it at once an example and fit instrument for introducing the same absolute rule into these Colonies:

For taking away our Charters, abolishing our most valuable Laws, and altering fundamentally the Forms of our Governments:

For suspending our own Legislature, and declaring themselves invested with Power to legislate for us in all cases whatsoever.

He has abdicated Government here, by declaring us out of his Protection and waging War against us.

He has plundered our seas, ravaged our Coasts, burnt our towns, and destroyed the lives of our people.

He is at this time transporting large armies of foreign mercenaries to compleat the works of death, desolation and tyranny, already begun with circumstances of Cruelty & perfidy scarcely paralleled in the most barbarous ages, and totally unworthy the Head of a civilized nation.

He has constrained our fellow Citizens taken Captive on the high Seas to bear Arms against their Country, to become the executioners of their friends and Brethren, or to fall themselves by their Hands.

He has excited domestic insurrections amongst us, and has endeavoured to bring on the inhabitants of our frontiers, the merciless Indian Savages, whose known rule of warfare, is an undistinguished destruction of all ages, sexes and conditions.

In every stage of these Oppressions We have Petitioned for Redress in the most humble terms: Our repeated Petitions have been answered only by repeated injury. A Prince, whose character is thus marked by every act which may define a Tyrant, is unfit to be the ruler of a free People.

Nor have We been wanting in attention to our British brethren. We have warned them from time to time of attempts by their legislature to extend an unwarrantable jurisdiction over us. We have reminded them of the circumstances of our emigration and settlement here. We have appealed to their native justice and magnanimity, and we have conjured them by the ties of our common kindred to disavow these usurpations, which, would inevitably interrupt our connections and correspondence. They too have been deaf to the voice of justice and of consanguinity. We must, therefore, acquiesce in the necessity, which denounces our Separation, and hold them, as we hold the rest of mankind, Enemies in War, in Peace Friends.

We, therefore, the Representatives of the United States of America, in General Congress, Assembled, appealing to the Supreme Judge of the world for the rectitude of our intentions, do, in the Name, and by Authority of the good People of these Colonies, solemnly publish and declare, That these United Colonies are, and of Right ought to be Free and Independent States; that they are Absolved from all Allegiance to the British Crown, and that all political connection between them and the State of Great Britain, is and ought to be totally dissolved; and that as Free and Independent States, they have full Power to levy War, conclude Peace, contract Alliances, establish Commerce, and to do all other Acts and Things which Independent States may of right do. And for the support of this Declaration, with a firm reliance on the Protection of Divine Providence, we mutually pledge to each other our Lives, our Fortunes and our sacred Honor.

Appendix D

The Constitution of the United States

We the people of the United States, in Order to form a more perfect Union, establish Justice, insure domestic Tranquility, provide for the common defense, promote the general Welfare, and secure the Blessings of Liberty to ourselves and our Posterity, do ordain and establish this CONSTITUTION for the United States of America.

ARTICLE 1

Section 1. All legislative Powers herein granted shall be vested in a Congress of the United States which shall consist of a Senate and House of Representatives.

Section 2. The House of Representatives shall be composed of Members chosen every second Year by the People of the several States, and the Electors in each State shall have the Qualifications requisite for Electors of the most numerous Branch of the State Legislature.

No Person shall be a Representative who shall not have attained to the Age of twenty-five Years, and been seven Years a Citizen of the United States, and who shall not, when elected, be an inhabitant of that State in which he shall be chosen.

Representatives and direct Taxes shall be apportioned among the several States which may be included within this Union, according to their respective Numbers, which shall be determined by adding to the whole Number of free Persons, including those bound to Service for a Term of Years and excluding Indians not taxed, three fifths of all other Persons. The actual Enumeration shall be made within three Years after the first Meeting of the Congress of the United States, and within every subsequent Term of ten Years, in such Manner as they shall be Law direct. The Number of Representatives shall not exceed one for every thirty Thousand, but each State shall have at Least one Representative; and until such enumeration shall be made, the State of New Hampshire shall be entitled to chuse three, Massachusetts eight, Rhode-Island and Providence Plantations one, Connecticut five, New-York six, New Jersey four, Pennsylvania eight, Delaware one, Maryland six, Virginia ten, North Carolina five, South Carolina five, and Georgia three.

When vacancies happen in the Representation from any State, the Executive Authority thereof shall issue Writs of Election to fill such Vacancies.

The House of Representatives shall chuse their Speaker and other Officers; and shall have the sole Power of Impeachment.

Section 3. The Senate of the United States shall be composed of two Senators from each State, chosen by the Legislature thereof, for six Years; and each Senator shall have one Vote.

Immediately after they shall be assembled in Consequence of the first Election, they shall be divided as equally as may be into three Classes. The Seats of the Senators of the first Class shall be vacated at the Expiration of the second Year, of the second Class at the Expiration of the fourth Year, and of the third Class at the Expiration of the sixth Year, so that one-third may be chosen every second Year; and if Vacancies happen by Resignation, or otherwise, during the Recess of the Legislature of any State, the Executive thereof may make temporary Appointments until the next Meeting of the Legislature, which shall then fill such Vacancies.

No Person shall be a Senator who shall not have attained to the Age of thirty Years, and been nine Years a Citizen of the United States, and who shall not, when elected, be an Inhabitant of that State in which he shall be chosen.

The Vice President of the United States shall be President of the Senate, but shall have no vote, unless they be equally divided.

The Senate shall chuse their other Officers, and also a President pro tempore, in the absence of the Vice President, or when he shall exercise the Office of the President of the United States.

The Senate shall have the sole Power to try all Impeachments. When sitting for that purpose, they shall be on Oath or Affirmation. When the President of the United States is tried, the Chief Justice shall preside: And no person shall be convicted without the Concurrence of two thirds of the Members present.

Judgement in Cases of Impeachment shall not extend further than to removal from Office, and disqualification to hold and enjoy an Office of honor, Trust, or Profit under the United States: but the Party convicted shall nevertheless be liable and subject to Indictment, Trial, Judgment, and Punishment, according to Law.

Section 4. The Times, Places and Manner of holding Elections for Senators and Representatives, shall be prescribed in each state by the Legislature thereof; but the Congress may at any time by Law make or alter such Regulations, except as to the Places of Chusing Senators.

The Congress shall assemble at least once in every Year, and such Meeting shall be on the first Monday in December, unless they shall by Law appoint a different Day.

Section 5. Each House shall be the Judge of the Elections, Returns and Qualifications of its own Members, and a Majority of each shall constitute a Quorum to do Business from day to day, and may be authorized to compel the Attendance of absent Members, in such Manner, and under such Penalties, as each House may provide.

Each House may determine the Rules of its Proceedings, punish its Members for disorderly Behavior, and, with the Concurrence of two thirds, expel a Member.

Each House shall keep a Journal of its Proceedings, and from time to time publish the same, excepting such Parts as may in their Judgment require Secrecy; and the Yeas and Nays of the Members of either House on any question shall, at the Desire of one fifth of those Present, be entered on the Journal.

Neither House, during the Session of Congress, shall, without the Consent of the other, adjourn for more than three days, nor to any other Place than that in which the two Houses shall be sitting.

Section 6. The Senators and Representatives shall

receive a Compensation for their Services, to be ascertained by Law, and paid out of the Treasury of the United States. They shall in all Cases, except Treason, Felony, and Breach of the Peace, be privileged from Arrest during their Attendance at the Session of their respective Houses, and in going to and returning from the same; and for any Speech or Debate in either House, they shall not be questioned in any other Place.

No Senator or Representative shall, during the Time for which he was elected, be appointed to any civil Office under the Authority of the United States, which shall have been created, or the Emoluments whereof shall have been increased, during such time; and no Person holding any Office under the United States shall be a Member of either House during his continuance in Office.

Section 7. All Bills for raising Revenue shall originate in the House of Representatives; but the Senate may propose or concur with Amendments as on other bills.

Every Bill which shall have passed the House of Representatives and the Senate, shall, before it become a Law, be presented to the President of the United States. If he approve he shall sign it, but if not he shall return it, with his Objections, to that House in which it shall have originated, who shall enter the Objections at large on their Journal, and proceed to reconsider it. If after such Reconsideration two thirds of that House shall agree to pass the bill, it shall be sent, together with the objections, to the other House, by which it shall likewise be reconsidered, and if approved by two thirds of that House, it shall become a Law. But in all such Cases the Votes of both Houses shall be determined by Yeas and Nays, and the Names of the Persons voting for and against the Bill shall be entered on the Journal of each House respectively. If any Bill shall not be returned by the President within ten Days (Sundays excepted) after it shall have been presented to him, the Same shall be a Law, in like Manner as if he had signed it, unless the Congress by their Adjournment prevent its Return, in which Case it shall not be a Law.

Every Order, Resolution, or Vote to which the Concurrence of the Senate and House of Representatives may be necessary (except on a question of Adjournment) shall be presented to the President of the United States; and before the Same shall take Effect, shall be approved by him, or being disapproved by him, shall be repassed by two thirds of the Senate and House of Representatives, according to the Rules and Limitations prescribed in the Case of a Bill.

Section 8. The Congress shall have Power To lay and collect Taxes, Duties, Imposts and Excises, to pay the Debts and provide for the common Defence and general Welfare of the United States; but all Duties, Imposts and Excises shall be uniform throughout the United States;

To borrow money on the credit of the United States;

To regulate Commerce with foreign Nations, and among the several States, and with the Indian Tribes;

To establish an uniform Rule of Naturalization, and uniform Laws on the subject of Bankruptcies throughout the United States;

To coin Money, regulate the Value thereof, and of foreign Coin, and fix the Standard of Weights and Measures;

To provide for the Punishment of counterfeiting the Securities and current Coin of the United States;

To establish Post Offices and post Roads;

To promote the Progress of Science and useful Arts, by securing for limited Times to Authors and Inventors the exclusive Right to their respective Writings and Discoveries;

To constitute Tribunals inferior to the Supreme Court;

To define and punish Piracies and Felonies committed on the high Seas, and Offences against the Law of Nations;

To declare War, grant Letters of Marque and Reprisal, and make Rules concerning Captures on Land and Water;

To raise and support Armies, but no Appropriation of Money to that Use shall be for a longer Term than two Years;

To provide and maintain a Navy;

To make Rules for the Government and Regulation of the land and naval forces;

To provide for calling forth the Militia to execute the Laws of the Union, suppress Insurrections and repel Invasions;

To provide for organizing, arming, and disciplining the Militia, and for governing such Part of them as may be employed in the Service of the United States, reserving to the States respectively, the Appointment of the Officers, and the Authority of training the Militia according to the discipline prescribed by Congress;

To exercise exclusive Legislation in all Cases whatsoever, over such District (not exceeding ten Miles square) as may, by Cession of particular States, and the acceptance of Congress, become the Seat of Government of the United States, and to exercise like Authority over all Places purchased by the Consent of the Legislature of the States in which the Same shall be, for the Erection of Forts, Magazines, Arsenals, dock-Yards, and other needful Buildings;—And

To make all Laws which shall be necessary and proper for carrying into Execution the foregoing Powers, and all other Powers vested by this Constitution in the Government of the United States, or in any Department or Officer thereof.

Section 9. The Migration or Importation of such Persons as any of the States now existing shall think proper to admit, shall not be prohibited by the Congress prior to the Year one thousand eight hundred and eight, but a tax or duty may be imposed on such Importation, not exceeding ten dollars for each Person.

The privilege of the Writ of Habeas Corpus shall not be suspended, unless when in Cases of Rebellion or Invasion the public Safety may require it.

No Bill of Attainder or ex post facto Law shall be passed.

No capitation, or other direct, Tax shall be laid unless in Proportion to the Census or Enumeration herein before directed to be taken.

No Tax or Duty shall be laid on Articles exported from any State.

No Preference shall be given by any Regulation of Revenue to the Ports of one State over those of another: nor shall Vessels bound to, or from, one State, be obliged to enter, clear, or pay Duties in another.

No Money shall be drawn from the Treasury, but in Consequence of Appropriations made by Law; and a regular Statement and Account of the Receipts and Expenditures of all public Money shall be published from time to time.

No Title of Nobility shall be granted by the United States: And no Person holding any Office of Profit or Trust under them, shall, without the Consent of the Congress, accept of any present, Emolument, Office, or Title, of any kind whatever, from any King, Prince, or foreign State.

Section 10. No State shall enter any Treaty, alliance, or Confederation; grant Letters of Marque and Reprisal; coin Money; emit Bills of Credit; make any Thing but gold and silver Coin a Tender in Payment of Debts; pass any Bill of Attainder, ex post facto Law, or Law impairing the Obligation of Contracts, or grant any Title of Nobility.

No State shall, without the Consent of the Congress, lay any Imposts or Duties on Imports or Exports, except what may be absolutely necessary for executing its inspection Laws: and the net Produce of all Duties and Imposts, laid by any State on Imports or Exports, shall be for the Use of the Treasury of the United States; and all such Laws shall be subject to the Revision and Control of the Congress.

No State shall, without the Consent of Congress, lay any duty of Tonnage, keep Troops, or Ships of War in time of Peace, enter into any Agreement or Compact with another State, or with a foreign Power, or engage in War, unless actually invaded, or in such imminent Danger as will not admit of delay.

ARTICLE II
Section 1. The executive Power shall be vested in a President of the United States of America. He shall hold his Office during the Term of four years, and, together with the Vice-President, chosen for the same Term, be elected, as follows:

Each State shall appoint, in such Manner as the Legislature thereof may direct, a Number of Electors, equal to the whole Number of Senators and Representatives to which the State may be entitled in the Congress; but no Senator or Representative, or Person holding an Office of Trust or Profit under the United States, shall be appointed an Elector.

The Electors shall meet in their respective States, and vote by Ballot for two persons, of whom one at least shall not be an Inhabitant of the same State with themselves. And they shall make a List of all the Persons voted for, and of the Number of Votes for each; which List they shall sign and certify, and transmit sealed to the Seat of the Government of the United States, directed to the President of the Senate. The President of the Senate shall, in the Presence of the Senate and House of Representatives, open all the Certificates, and the Votes shall then be counted. The Person having the greatest Number of Votes shall be the President, if such Number be a Majority of the whole Number of Electors appointed; and if there be more than one who have such Majority, and have an equal Number of Votes, then the House of Representatives shall immediately chuse by Ballot one of them for President; and if no Person have a Majority, then from the five highest on the List the said House shall in like Manner chuse the President. But in chusing the President, the Votes shall be taken by States, the Representation from each State having one Vote; a quorum for this Purpose shall consist of a Member or Members from two-thirds of the States, and a Majority of all the States shall be necessary to a Choice. In every Case, after the Choice of the President, the Person having the greatest Number of Votes of the Electors shall be the Vice President. But if there should remain two or more who have equal votes, the Senate shall chuse from them by Ballot the Vice-President.

The Congress may determine the Time of chusing the Electors, and the Day on which they shall give their Votes; which Day shall be the same throughout the United States.

No person except a natural-born Citizen, or a Citizen of the United States, at the time of the Adoption of this Constitution, shall be eligible to the Office of President; neither shall any Person be eligible to that Office who shall not have attained to the Age of thirty-five years, and been fourteen Years a Resident within the United States.

In Case of the Removal of the President from Office, or of his Death, Resignation, or Inability to discharge the Powers and Duties of the said Office, the same shall devolve on the Vice-President, and the Congress may by Law provide for the Case of Removal, Death, Resignation, or Inability, both of the President and Vice-President, declaring what Officer shall then act as President, and such Officer shall act accordingly, until the disability be removed, or a President shall be elected.

The President shall, at stated Times, receive for his Services a Compensation, which shall neither be increased nor diminished during the Period for which he shall have been elected, and he shall not receive within that Period any other Emolument from the United States, or any of them.

Before he enter on the execution of his Office, he shall take the following Oath or Affirmation:—"I do solemnly swear (or affirm) that I will faithfully execute the Office of President of the United States, and will, to the best of my Ability, preserve, protect, and defend the Constitution of the United States."

Section 2. The President shall be Commander in Chief of the Army and Navy of the United States, and of the Militia of the several States, when called into the actual Service of the United States; he may require the Opinion, in writing, of the principal Officer in each of the executive Departments, upon any subject relating to the Duties of their respective Offices, and he shall have Power to Grant Reprieves and Pardons for Offences against the United States, except in Cases of Impeachment.

He shall have Power, by and with the Advice and Consent of the Senate, to make Treaties, provided two thirds of the Senators present concur; and he shall nominate, and by and with the Advice and Consent of the Senate, shall appoint Ambassadors, other public Ministers and Counsuls, Judges of the supreme Court, and all other Officers of the United States, whose Appointments are herein otherwise provided for, and which shall be established by Law: but the Congress may by Law vest the Appointments of such inferior Officers, as they think proper, in the President alone, in the Courts of Law, or in the Heads of Departments.

The President shall have Power to fill up all Vacancies that may happen during the Recess of the Senate, by granting Commissions which shall expire at the End of their next Session.

Section 3. He shall from time to time give to the Congress Information of the State of the Union, and recommend to their Consideration such Measures as he shall judge necessary and expedient; he may, on extraordinary occasions, convene both Houses, or either of them, and in Case of Disagreement between them, with respect to the Time of Adjournment, he may adjourn them to such Time as he shall think proper; he shall receive Ambassadors and other public Ministers; he shall take Care that the Laws be faithfully executed, and shall Commission all the Officers of the United States

Section 4. The President, Vice President and all civil Officers of the United States, shall be removed from Office on Impeachement for, and Conviction of, Treason, Bribery, or other high Crimes and Misdemeanors.

ARTICLE III

Section 1. The judicial Power of the United States, shall be vested in one supreme Court, and in such inferior Courts as the Congress may from time to time ordain and establish. The Judges, both of the supreme and inferior Courts, shall hold their Offices during good Behaviour, and shall, at stated Times, receive for their Services, a compensation, which shall not be diminished during their Continuance in Office.

Section 2. The judicial Power shall extend to all Cases, in Law and Equity, arising under this constitution, the Laws of the United States, and treaties made, or which shall be made, under their Authority;—to all Cases affecting ambassadors, other public ministers and consuls;—to all cases of admiralty and maritime Jurisdiction;—to Controversies to which the United States shall be a Party;—to Controversies between two or more States;—between a State and Citizens of another State;—between Citizens of different States,—between Citizens of the same State claiming Lands under Grants of different States, and between a State, or the Citizens thereof, and foreign States, Citizens or Subjects.

In all Cases affecting Ambassadors, other public Ministers and Consuls, and those in which a State shall be Party, the supreme Court shall have original Jurisdiction. In all the other Cases before mentioned, the supreme Court shall have appellate Jurisdiction, both as to Law and Fact, with such Exception, and under such Regulations as the Congress shall make.

The trial of all Crimes, except in Cases of Im-

peachment, shall be by Jury; and such Trial shall be held in the State where the said Crimes shall have been committed; but when not committed within any State, the Trial shall be at such Place or Places as the Congress may by Law have directed.
Section 3. Treason against the United States, shall consist only in levying War against them, or in adhering to their Enemies, giving them Aid and Comfort. No Person shall be convicted of Treason unless on the Testimony of two Witnesses to the same overt Act, or on Confession in open Court.

The Congress shall have power to declare the Punishment of Treason, but no Attainder of Treason shall work Corruption of Blood, or Forfeiture except during the Life of the Person attainted.

ARTICLE IV
Section 1. Full Faith and Credit shall be given in each State to the public Acts, Records, and judicial Proceedings of every other State. And the Congress may by general prescribe the Manner in which such Acts, Records and Proceedings shall be proved, and the Effect thereof.
Section 2. The Citizens of each State shall be entitled to all Privileges and Immunities of Citizens in the several States.

A Person charged in any State with Treason, Felony, or other Crime, who shall flee from Justice, and be found in another State, shall on demand of the executive Authority of the State from which he fled, be delivered up, to be removed to the State having Jurisdiction of the crime.

No Person held to Service or Labour in one State, under the Laws thereof, escaping into another, shall, in Consequence of any Law or Regulation therein, be discharged from such Service or Labour, but shall be delivered up on Claim of the Party to whom such Service or Labour may be due.
Section 3. New States may be admitted by the Congress into this Union; but no new State shall be formed or erected within the Jurisdiction of any other State; nor any State be formed by the Junction of two or more States, or parts of States, without the Consent of the Legislatures of the States concerned as well as of the Congress.

The Congress shall have Power to dispose of and make all needful Rules and Regulations respecting the Territory or other Property belonging to the United States; and nothing in this constitution shall be so construed as to Prejudice any Claims of the United States, or of any particular State.
Section 4. The United States shall guarantee to every State in this Union a Republican Form of Government, and shall protect each of them

against Invasion; and on Application of the Legislature, or the Executive (when the Legislature cannot be convened) against domestic Violence.

ARTICLE V
The Congress, whenever two-thirds of both Houses shall deem it necessary, shall propose Amendments to this Constitution, or, on the Application of the Legislatures of two-thirds of the several States, shall call a Convention for proposing Amendments, which, in either Case, shall be valid to all Intents and Purposes, as part of this Constitution, when ratified by the Legislatures of three-fourths of the several States, or by Conventions in three-fourths thereof, as the one or the other Mode of Ratification may be proposed by the Congress; Provided that no Amendment which may be made prior to the Year One thousand eight hundred and eight shall in any Manner affect the first and fourth Clauses in the Ninth Section of the first Article; and that no State, without its Consent, shall be deprived of its equal Suffrage in the Senate.

ARTICLE VI
All Debts contracted and Engagements entered into, before the Adoption of this Constitution, shall be as valid against the United States under this Constitution, as under the Confederation.

This Constitution, and the Laws of the United States which shall be made in Pursuance thereof; and the Treaties made, or which shall be made, under the Authority of the United States, shall be the supreme Law of the Land; and the Judges in every State shall be bound thereby, any Thing in the Constitution of Laws of any State to the Contrary notwithstanding.

The Senators and Representatives before mentioned, and the Members of the several State Legislatures, and all executive and judicial Officers, both of the United States and of the several States, shall be bound by Oath or Affirmation to support this Constitution; but no religious Test shall ever be required as a qualification to any Office or public Trust under the United States.

ARTICLE VII
The Ratification of the Conventions of nine States shall be sufficient for the Establishment of this Constitution between the States so ratifying the same.

Done in Convention by the Unanimous Consent of the States present the Seventeenth Day of September in the Year of our Lord one thousand seven hundred and Eighty seven, and of the Independence of the United States of America the

Twelfth. In Witness whereof We have hereunto subscribed our names.

Articles in Addition to, and Amendment of, the Constitution of the United States of America. Proposed by Congress, and Ratified by the Legislatures of the Several States, Pursuant to the Fifth Article of the Original Constitution.

AMENDMENT I [1791]

Congress shall make no law respecting an establishment of religion, or prohibiting the free exercise thereof; or abridging the freedom of speech, or of the press; or the right of the people peaceably to assemble, and to petition the Government for a redress of grievances.

AMENDMENT II [1791]

A well regulated Militia, being necessary to the security of a free State, the right of the people to keep and bear Arms shall not be infringed.

AMENDMENT III [1791]

No Soldier shall, in time of peace, be quartered in any house, without the consent of the Owner, nor in time of war, but in a manner to be prescribed by law.

AMENDMENT IV [1791]

The right of the people to be secure in their persons, houses, papers, and effects, against unreasonable searches and seizures, shall not be violated, and no Warrants shall issue, but upon probable cause, supported by Oath or affirmation, and particularly describing the place to be searched, and the persons or things to be seized.

AMENDMENT V [1791]

No person shall be held to answer for a capital or otherwise infamous crime, unless on a presentment or indictment of a Grand Jury, except in cases arising in the land or naval forces, or in the Militia, when in actual service in time of war or public danger; nor shall any person be subject for the same offence to be twice put in jeopardy of life or limb; nor shall be compelled in any criminal case to be a witness against himself, nor be deprived of life, liberty, or property, without due process of law; nor shall private property be taken for public use, without just compensation.

AMENDMENT VI [1791]

In all criminal prosecutions, the accused shall enjoy the right to a speedy and public trial, by an impartial jury of the State and district wherein the crime shall have been committed, which district shall have been previously ascertained by law, and to be informed of the nature and cause of the accusation; to be confronted with the witnesses against him; to have compulsory process for obtaining witnesses in his favor, and to have the Assistance of Counsel for his defence.

AMENDMENT VII [1791]

In suits at common law, where the value in controversy shall exceed twenty dollars, the right of trial by jury shall be preserved, and no fact tried by a jury, shall be otherwise reexamined in any Court of the United States, than according to the rules of the common law.

AMENDMENT VIII [1791]

Excessive bail shall not be required, nor excessive fines imposed, nor cruel and unusual punishments inflicted.

AMENDMENT IX [1791]

The enumeration in the Constitution, of certain rights, shall not be construed to deny or disparage others retained by the people.

AMENDMENT X [1791

The powers not delegated to the United States by the Constitution, nor prohibited by it to the States, are reserved to the States respectively, or to the people.

AMENDMENT XI [1798]

The Judicial power of the United States shall not be construed to extend to any suit in law or equity, commenced or prosecuted against one of the United States by Citizens of another State, or by Citizens or Subjects of any Foreign State.

AMENDMENT XII [1804]

The Electors shall meet in their respective States and vote by ballot for President and Vice-President, one of whom, at least, shall not be an inhabitant of the same State with themselves; they shall name in their ballots the person voted for as President, and in distinct ballots the person voted for as Vice-President, and they shall make distinct lists of all persons voted for as President, and of all persons voted for as Vice-President, and of the number of votes for each, which lists they shall sign and certify, and transmit sealed to the seat of the government of the United States, directed to the President of the Senate;—The President of the Senate shall, in the presence of the Senate and House of Representatives, open all the certificates and the votes shall then be counted;—The person having the greatest number of votes for President, shall be the President, if such number by a majority of the whole number of Electors appointed; and if no person have such majority, then from the persons having the highest numbers not exceeding three on the list of those voted for as President, the House of Representatives shall choose immediately, by ballot, the President. But in choosing the President, the votes shall be taken by states, the representation from each state having one vote; a quorum for this purpose shall consist of a member or members from two-thirds of the states, and a majority of all the states shall be necessary to a choice. And if the House of Representatives shall not choose a President whenever the right of choice shall devolve upon them, before the fourth day of March next following, then the Vice-President shall act as President, as in the case of the death or other constitutional disability of the President.—The person having the greatest number of votes as Vice-President, shall be the Vice-President, if such number be a majority of the whole number of Electors appointed, and if no person have a majority, then from the two highest numbers on the list, the Senate shall choose the Vice-President; a quorum for the purpose shall consist of two-thirds of the whole number of Senators, and a majority of the whole number shall be necessary to a choice. But no person constitutionally ineligible to the office of President shall be eligible to that of Vice-President of the United States.

AMENDMENT XIII [1865]

Section 1. Neither slavery nor involuntary servitude, except as a punishment for crime whereof the party shall have been duly convicted, shall exist within the United States, or any place subject to their jurisdiction.

Section 2. Congress shall have power to enforce this article by appropriate legislation.

AMENDMENT XIV [1868]

Section 1. All persons born or naturalized in the United States, and subject to the jurisdiction thereof, are citizens of the United States and of the State wherein they reside. No State shall make or enforce any law which shall abridge the privileges or immunities of citizens of the United States; nor shall any State deprive any person of life, liberty, or property, without due process of law; nor deny to any person within its jurisdiction the equal protection of the laws.

Section 2. Representatives shall be apportioned among the several States according to their respective numbers, counting the whole number of persons in each State, excluding Indians not taxed. But when the right to vote at any election for the choice of electors for President and Vice-President of the United States, Representatives in Congress, the Executive and Judicial officers of a State, or the members of the Legislature thereof, is denied to any of the male inhabitants of such State, being twenty-one years of age, and citizens of the United States, or in any way abridged, except for participation in rebellion, or other crime, the basis of representation therein shall be reduced in the proportion which the number of such male citizens shall bear to the whole number of male citizens twenty-one years of age in such State.

Section 3. No person shall be a Senator or Representative in Congress, or elector of President and Vice-President, or hold any office, civil or military, under the United States, or under any State, who, having previously taken an oath, as a member of Congress, or as an officer of the United States, or as a member of any State legislature, or as an executive or judicial officer of any State, to support the Constitution of the United States, shall have engaged in insurrection or rebellion against the same, or given aid or comfort to the enemies thereof. But Congress may by a vote of two-thirds of each House, remove such disability.

Section 4. The validity of the public debt of the United States, authorized by law, including debts incurred for payment of pensions and bounties for services in suppressing insurrection or rebellion, shall not be questioned. But neither the United States nor any State shall assume or pay any debt or obligation incurred in aid of insurrection or rebellion against the United States or any claim for the loss or emancipation of any slave; but all such debts, obligations, and claims shall be held illegal and void.

Section 5. The Congress shall have the power to enforce, by appropriate legislation, the provisions of this article.

AMENDMENT XV [1870]

Section 1. The right of citizens of the United States to vote shall not be denied or abridged by the United States or by any State on account of race, color, or previous condition of servitude—

Section 2. The Congress shall have power to enforce this article by appropriate legislation.

AMENDMENT XVI [1913]

The Congress shall have power to lay and collect taxes on incomes, from whatever source derived, without apportionment among the several States, and without regard to any census or enumeration.

AMENDMENT XVII [1913]

The Senate of the United States shall be composed of two Senators from each State, elected by the people thereof, for six years; and each Senator shall have one vote. The electors in each State shall have the qualifications requisite for electors of the most numerous branch of the State legislatures.

When vacancies happen in the representation of any State in the Senate, the executive authority of such State shall issue writs of election to fill such vacancies: *Provided,* That the legislature of any State may empower the executive thereof to make temporary appointments until the people fill the vacancies by election as the legislature may direct.

This amendment shall not be so construed as to affect the election or term of any Senator chosen before it becomes valid as part of the Constitution.

AMENDMENT XVIII [1919]
Section 1. After one year from the ratification of this article the manufacture, sale, or transportation of intoxicating liquors within, the importation thereof into, or the exportation thereof from the United States and all territory subject to the jurisdiction thereof for beverage purposes is hereby prohibited.
Section 2. The Congress and the several States shall have concurrent power to enforce this article by appropriate legislation.
Section 3. This article shall be inoperative unless it shall have been ratified as an amendment to the Constitution by the legislatures of the several States, as provided in the Constitution, within seven years from the date of the submission hereof to the States by the Congress.

AMENDMENT XIX [1920]
The right of citizens of the United States to vote shall not be denied or abridged by the United States or by any State on account of sex.

Congress shall have power to enforce this article by appropriate legislation.

AMENDMENT XX [1933]
Section 1. The terms of the President and Vice-President shall end at noon on the 20th day of January, and the terms of Senators and Representatives at noon on the 3d day of January, of the years in which such terms would have ended if this article had not been ratified; and the terms of their successors shall then begin.
Section 2. The Congress shall assemble at least once in every year, and such meeting shall begin at noon on the 3d day of January, unless they shall by law appoint a different day.
Section 3. If, at the time fixed for the beginning of the term of the President, the President elect shall have died, the Vice-President elect shall become President. If a President shall not have been chosen before the time fixed for the beginning of his term, or if the President elect shall have failed

to qualify, then the Vice-President until a President shall have qualified; and the Congress may by law provide for the case wherein neither a President elect nor a Vice-President elect shall have qualified, declaring who shall then act as President, or the manner in which one who is to act shall be selected, and such person shall act accordingly until a President or Vice-President shall have qualified.
Section 4. The Congress may by law provide for the case of the death of any of the persons from whom the House of Representatives may choose a President whenever the right of choice shall have devolved upon them, and for the case of the death of any of the persons from whom the Senate may choose a Vice-President whenever the right of choice shall have devolved upon them.
Section 5. Sections 1 and 2 shall take effect on the 15th day of October following the ratification of this article.
Section 6. This article shall be inoperative unless it shall have been ratified as an amendment to the Constitution by the legislatures of three-fourths of the several States within seven years from the date of its submission.

AMENDMENT XXI [1933]
Section 1. The eithteenth article of amendment to the Constitution of the United States is hereby repealed.
Section 2. The transportation or importation into any State, Territory, or possesion of the United States for delivery or use therein of intoxicating liquors, in violation of the laws thereof, is hereby prohibited.
Section 3. This article shall be inoperative unless it shall have been ratified as an amendment to the Constitution by conventions in the several States, as provided in the Constitution, within seven years from the date of the submission hereof to the States by the Congress.

AMENDMENT XXII [1951]
No person shall be elected to the office of the President more than twice, and no person who has held the office of President, or acted as President, for more than two years of a term to which some other person was elected President shall be elected to the office of the President more than once.

But this Article shall not apply to any person holding the office of President when this Article was proposed by the Congress, and shall not prevent any person who may be holding the office of President, or acting as President, during the term within which this Article becomes operative from holding the office of President or acting as President during the remainder of such term.

AMENDMENT XXIII [1961]

Section 1. The District constituting the seat of Government of the United States shall appoint in such manner as the Congress may direct:

A number of electors of President and Vice President equal to the whole number of Senators and Representatives in Congress to which the District would be entitled if it were a State, but in no event more than the least populous State; they shall be in addition to those appointed by the States, but they shall be considered, for the purposes of the election of President and Vice President, to be electors appointed by a State; and they shall meet in the District and perform such duties as provided by the twelfth article of amendment.

Section 2. The Congress shall have power to enforce this article by appropriate legislation.

AMENDMENT XXIV [1964]

Section 1. The right of citizens of the United States to vote in any primary or other election for President or Vice President, for electors for President or Vice President, or for Senator or Representative in Congress, shall not be denied or abridged by the United States or any State by reason of failure to pay any poll tax or other tax.

Section 2. The Congress shall have the power to enforce this article by appropriate legislation.

AMENDMENT XXV [1967]

Section 1. In case of the removal of the President from office or his death or resignation, the Vice President shall become President.

Section 2. Whenever there is a vacancy in the office of the Vice President, the President shall nominate a Vice President who shall take the office upon confirmation by a majority vote of both houses of Congress.

Section 3. Whenever the President transmits to the President pro tempore of the Senate and the Speaker of the House of Representatives his written declaration that he is unable to discharge the powers and duties of his office, and until he transmits to them a written declaration to the contrary, such powers and duties shall be discharged by the Vice President as Acting President.

Section 4. Whenever the Vice President and a majority of either the principal officers of the executive departments, or of such other body as Congress may by law provide, transmit to the President pro tempore of the Senate and the Speaker of the House of Representatives their written declaration that the President is unable to discharge the powers and duties of his office, the Vice President shall immediately assume the powers and duties of the office as Acting President.

Thereafter, when the President transmits to the President pro tempore of the Senate and the Speaker of the House of Representatives his written declaration that no inability exists, he shall resume the powers and duties of his office unless the Vice President and a majority of either the principal officers of the executive departments, or of such other body as Congress may by law provide, transmit within four days to the President pro tempore of the Senate and the Speaker of the House of Representatives their written declaration that the President is unable to discharge the powers and duties of his office. Thereupon Congress shall decide the issue, assembling within 48 hours for that purpose if not in session. If the Congress, within 21 days after receipt of the latter written declaration, or, if Congress is not in session, within 21 days after Congress is required to assemble, determines by two-thirds vote of both houses that the President is unable to discharge the powers and duties of his office, the Vice President shall continue to discharge the same as Acting President; otherwise, the President shall resume the powers and duties of his office.

Appendix E
Admission of States to the Union

1	Delaware	Dec. 7, 1787	26	Michigan	Jan. 26, 1837
2	Pennsylvania	Dec. 12, 1787	27	Florida	Mar. 3, 1845
3	New Jersey	Dec. 18, 1787	28	Texas	Dec. 29, 1845
4	Georgia	Jan. 2, 1788	29	Iowa	Dec. 28, 1846
5	Connecticut	Jan. 9, 1788	30	Wisconsin	May 29, 1848
6	Massachusetts	Feb. 6, 1788	31	California	Sept. 9, 1850
7	Maryland	Apr. 28, 1788	32	Minnesota	May 11, 1858
8	South Carolina	May 23, 1788	33	Oregon	Feb. 14, 1859
9	New Hampshire	June 21, 1788	34	Kansas	Jan. 29, 1861
10	Virginia	June 25, 1788	35	West Virginia	June 19, 1863
11	New York	July 26, 1788	36	Nevada	Oct. 31, 1864
12	North Carolina	Nov. 21, 1789	37	Nebraska	Mar. 1, 1867
13	Rhode Island	May 29, 1790	38	Colorado	Aug. 1, 1876
14	Vermont	March. 4, 1791	39	North Dakota	Nov. 2, 1889
15	Kentucky	June 1, 1792	40	South Dakota	Nov. 2, 1889
16	Tennessee	June 1, 1796	41	Montana	Nov. 8, 1889
17	Ohio	Mar. 1, 1803	42	Washington	Nov. 11, 1889
18	Louisiana	Apr. 30, 1812	43	Idaho	July 3, 1890
19	Indiana	Dec. 11, 1816	44	Wyoming	July 10, 1890
20	Mississippi	Dec. 10, 1817	45	Utah	Jan. 4, 1896
21	Illinois	Dec. 3, 1818	46	Oklahoma	Nov. 16, 1907
22	Alabama	Dec. 14, 1819	47	New Mexico	Jan. 6, 1912
23	Maine	Mar. 15, 1820	48	Arizona	Feb. 14, 1912
24	Missouri	Aug. 10, 1821	49	Alaska	Jan. 3, 1959
25	Arkansas	June 15, 1836	50	Hawaii	Aug. 21, 1959

Appendix F
Population of the United States, 1790—1980

1790	3,929	1838	16,264	1886	57,938	1934	126,374
1791	4,056	1839	16,684	1887	59,217	1935	127,250
1792	4,194	1840	17,120	1888	60,496	1936	128,053
1793	4,332	1841	17,733	1889	61,775	1937	128,825
1794	4,469	1842	18,345	1890	63,056	1938	129,825
1795	4,607	1843	18,957	1891	64,361	1939	130,880
1796	4,745	1844	19,569	1892	65,666	1940	131,669
1797	4,883	1845	20,182	1893	66,970	1941	133,894
1798	5,021	1846	20,794	1894	68,275	1942	135,361
1799	5,159	1847	21,406	1895	69,580	1943	137,250
1800	5,297	1848	22,018	1896	70,885	1944	138,916
1801	5,486	1849	22,631	1897	72,189	1945	140,468
1802	5,679	1850	23,261	1898	73,494	1946	141,936
1803	5,872	1851	24,086	1899	74,799	1947	144,698
1804	5,065	1852	24,911	1900	76,094	1948	147,208
1805	6,258	1853	25,736	1901	77,585	1949	149,767
1806	6,451	1854	26,561	1902	79,160	1950	150,697
1807	6,644	1855	27,386	1903	80,632	1951	154,878
1808	6,838	1856	28,212	1904	82,165	1952	157,553

Year	Value	Year	Value	Year	Value	Year	Value
1809	7,031	1857	29,037	1905	83,820	1953	160,184
1810	7,224	1858	29,862	1906	85,437	1954	163,026
1811	7,460	1859	30,687	1907	87,000	1955	165,931
1812	7,700	1860	31,513	1908	88,709	1956	168,903
1813	7,939	1861	32,351	1909	90,492	1957	171,984
1814	8,179	1862	33,188	1910	92,407	1958	174,882
1815	8,419	1863	34,026	1911	93,868	1959	177,830
1816	8,659	1864	34,863	1912	95,331	1960	178,464
1817	8,899	1865	35,701	1913	97,227	1961	183,672
1818	9,139	1866	36,538	1914	99,118	1962	186,504
1819	9,379	1867	37,376	1915	100,549	1963	189,197
1820	9,618	1868	38,213	1916	101,966	1964	191,833
1821	9,939	1869	39,051	1917	103,414	1965	194,237
1822	10,268	1870	39,905	1918	104,550	1966	196,485
1823	10,596	1871	40,938	1919	105,063	1967	198,629
1824	10,924	1872	41,972	1920	106,466	1968	200,619
1825	11,252	1873	43,006	1921	108,541	1969	202,599
1826	11,580	1874	44,040	1922	110,055	1970	203,875
1827	11,909	1875	45,073	1923	111,950	1971	207,045
1828	12,237	1876	46,107	1924	114,113	1972	208,842
1829	12,565	1877	47,141	1925	115,832	1973	210,396
1830	12,901	1878	48,174	1926	117,399	1974	211,894
1831	13,321	1879	49,208	1927	119,038	1975	213,631
1832	13,742	1880	50,262	1928	120,501	1976	215,142
1833	14,162	1881	51,542	1929	121,770	1978	218,931
1834	14,582	1882	52,821	1930	122,775		
1835	15,003	1883	54,100	1931	124,040		
1836	15,423	1884	55,379	1932	124,840		
1837	15,843	1885	56,658	1933	125,579		

Appendix G

Presidential Elections, 1789—1976

Year	Candidates	Party	Popular Vote	Electoral Vote
1789	**George Washington**			69
	John Adams			34
	Others			35
1792	**George Washington**			132
	John Adams			77
	George Clinton			50
	Others			5
1796	**John Adams**	Federalist		71
	Thomas Jefferson	Democratic-Republican		68
	Thomas Pinckney	Federalist		59
	Aaron Burr	Democratic-Republican		30
	Others			48

1800	**Thomas Jefferson**	Democratic-Republican		73
	Aaron Burr	Democratic-Republican		73
	John Adams	Federalist		65
	Charles C. Pinckney	Federalist		64
1804	**Thomas Jefferson**	Democratic-Republican		162
	Charles C. Pinckney	Federalist		14
1808	**James Madison**	Democratic-Republican		122
	Charles C. Pinckney	Federalist		47
	George Clinton	Independent-Republican		6
1812	**James Madison**	Democratic-Republican		128
	DeWitt Clinton	Federalist		89
1816	**James Monroe**	Democratic-Republican		183
	Rufus King	Federalist		34
1820	**James Monroe**	Democratic-Republican		231
	John Quincy Adams	Independent-Republican		1
1824	**John Quincy Adams**	Democratic-Republican	113,122 (30.9%)	84
	Andrew Jackson	Democratic-Republican	151,271 (41.3%)	99
	Henry Clay	Democratic-Republican	47,531 (12.9%)	37
	William H. Crawford	Democratic-Republican	40,856 (11.1%)	41
1828	**Andrew Jackson**	Democratic	642,553 (55.9%)	178
	John Quincy Adams	National Republican	500,897 (43.6%)	83
1832	**Andrew Jackson**	Democratic	701,780 (54.2%)	219
	Henry Clay	National Republican	484,205 (37.4%)	49
	William Wirt	Anti-Masonic	100,715 (7.7%)	7
1836	**Martin Van Buren**	Democratic	763,176 (50.8%)	170
	William H. Harrison	Whig	550,816 (36.6%)	73
	Hugh L. White	Whig	146,107 (9.7%)	26
	Daniel Webster	Whig	41,201 (2.7%)	14
1840	**William H. Harrison** **(John Tyler, 1841)**	Whig	1,275,390 (52.8%)	234
	Martin Van Buren	Democratic	1,128,854 (46.8%)	60
1844	**James K. Polk**	Democratic	1,339,494 (49.5%)	170
	Henry Clay	Whig	1,300,004 (48.0%)	105
	James G. Birney	Liberty	62,103 (2.3%)	
1848	**Zachary Taylor** **(Millard Fillmore, 1850)**	Whig	1,361,393 (47.2%)	163
	Lewis Cass	Democratic	1,223,460 (42.4%)	127
	Martin Van Buren	Free Soil	291,501 (10.1%)	
1852	**Franklin Pierce**	Democratic	1,607,510 (50.8%)	254
	Winfield Scott	Whig	1,386,942 (43.8%)	42
1856	**James Buchanan**	Democratic	1,836,072 (45.2%)	174
	John C. Frémont	Republican	1,342,345 (33.1%)	114
	Millard Fillmore	American	873,053 (21.5%)	8
1860	**Abraham Lincoln**	Republican	1,865,908 (39.8%)	180
	Stephen A. Douglas	Democratic	1,382,202 (29.4%)	12
	John C. Breckinridge	Democratic	848,019 (18.0%)	72
	John Bell	Constitutional Union	591,901 (12.6%)	39

1864	**Abraham Lincoln** (**Andrew Johnson**, 1865)	Republican	2,218,388 (55.0%)	212
	George B. McClellan	Democratic	1,812,807 (44.9%)	21
1868	**Ulysses S. Grant**	Republican	3,01͟,650 (52.6%)	214
	Horatio Seymour	Democratic	2,708,744 (47.3%)	80
1872	**Ulysses S. Grant**	Republican	3,598,235 (55.6%)	286
	Horace Greeley	Democratic	2,834,761 (43.8%)	66
1876	**Rutherford B. Hayes**	Republican	4,034,311 (47.9%)	185
	Samuel J. Tilden	Democratic	4,288,546 (50.9%)	184
1880	**James A. Garfield** (**Chester A. Arthur**, 1881)	Republican	4,446,158 (48.2%)	214
	Winfield S. Hancock	Democratic	4,444,260 (48.2%)	155
	James B. Weaver	Greenback-Labor	305,997 (3.3%)	
1884	**Grover Cleveland**	Democratic	4,874,621 (48.5%)	219
	James G. Blaine	Republican	4,848,936 (48.2%)	182
	Benjamin F. Butler	Greenback-Labor	175,096 (1.7%)	
1888	**Benjamin Harrison**	Republican	5,443,892 (47.8%)	233
	Grover Cleveland	Democratic	5,534,488 (48.6%)	168
1892	**Grover Cleveland**	Democratic	5,551,883 (46.0%)	277
	Benjamin Harrison	Republican	5,179,244 (42.9%)	145
	James B. Weaver	People's	1,024,280 (8.5%)	22
1896	**William McKinley**	Republican	7,108,480 (51.0%)	271
	William J. Bryan	Democratic; Populist	6,511,495 (46.7%)	176
1900	**William McKinley** (**Theodore Roosevelt**,1901)	Republican	7,218,039 (51.6%)	292
	William J. Bryan	Democratic; Populist	6,358,345 (45.5%)	155
1904	**Theodore Roosevelt**	Republican	7,626,593 (56.4%)	336
	Alton B. Parker	Democratic	5,082,898 (37.6%)	140
	Eugene V. Debs	Socialist	402,489 (2.9%)	
1908	**William H. Taft**	Republican	7,676,258 (51.5%)	321
	William J. Bryan	Democratic	6,406,801 (43.0%)	162
	Eugene V. Debs	Socialist	420,380 (2.8%)	
1912	**Woodrow Wilson**	Democratic	6,293,152 (41.8%)	435
	Theodore Roosevelt	Progressive	4,119,207 (27.3%)	88
	William H. Taft	Republican	3,486,383 (23.1%)	8
	Eugene V. Debs	Socialist	900,369 (5.9%)	
1916	**Woodrow Wilson**	Democratic	9,126,300 (49.2%)	277
	Charles E. Hughes	Republican	8,546,789 (46.1%)	254
1920	**Warren G. Harding** (**Calvin Coolidge**, 1923)	Republican	16,133,314 60.3%)	404
	James M. Cox	Democratic	9,140,884 (34.1%)	127
	Eugene V. Debs	Socialist	913,664 (3.4%)	
1924	**Calvin Coolidge**	Republican	15,717,553 54.0%)	382
	John W. Davis	Democratic	8,386,169 (28.8%)	136
	Robert M. La Follette	Progressive	4,814,050 (16.5%)	13

1928	**Herbert C. Hoover**	Republican	21,411,991 (58.2%)	444
	Alfred E. Smith	Democratic	15,000,185 (40.7%)	87
1932	**Franklin D. Roosevelt**	Democratic	22,825,016 (57.4%)	472
	Herbert C. Hoover	Republican	15,758,397 (39.6%)	59
	Norman Thomas	Socialist	883,990 (2.2%)	
1936	**Franklin D. Roosevelt**	Democratic	27,747,636 (60.7%)	523
	Alfred M. Landon	Republican	16,679,543 (36.5%)	8
	William Lemke	Union	892,492 (1.9%)	
1940	**Franklin D. Roosevelt**	Democratic	27,263,448 (54.7%)	449
	Wendell L. Wilkie	Republican	22,336,260 (44.8%)	82
1944	**Franklin D. Roosevelt**	Democratic	25,611,936 (53.3%)	432
	(Harry S. Truman, 1945)			
	Thomas E. Dewey	Republican	22,013,372 (45.8%)	99
1948	**Harry S. Truman**	Democratic	24,105,587 (49.5%)	303
	Thomas E. Dewey	Republican	21,970,017 (45.1%)	189
	J. Strom Thurmond	States' Rights	1,169,134 (2.4%)	39
	Henry A. Wallace	Progressive	1,157,057 (2.3%)	
1952	**Dwight D. Eisenhower**	Republican	33,936,137 (55.1%)	442
	Adlai E. Stevenson	Democratic	27,314,649 (44.3%)	89
1956	**Dwight D. Eisenhower**	Republican	35,585,245 (57.3%)	457
	Adlai E. Stevenson	Democratic	26,030,172 (41.9%)	73
1960	**John F. Kennedy**	Democratic	34,221,344 (49.7%)	303
	(Lyndon B. Johnson,1963)			
	Richard M. Nixon	Republican	34,106,671 (49.5%)	219
1964	**Lyndon B. Johnson**	Democratic	43,126,584 (61.0%)	486
	Barry M. Goldwater	Republican	27,177,838 (38.4%)	52
1968	**Richard M. Nixon**	Republican	31,783,148 (43.4%)	301
	Hubert H. Humphrey	Democratic	31,274,503 (42.7%)	191
	George C. Wallace	Amer. Independent	9,901,151 (13.5%)	46
1972	**Richard M. Nixon**	Republican	47,170,179 (60.6%)	520
	George S. McGovern	Democratic	29,171,791 (37.5%)	17
1974	**Gerald R. Ford**	Republican	Appointed on August 9, 1974, as President after the resignation of Richard M. Nixon.	
1976	**Jimmy Carter**	Democrat	40,828,587 (50.1%)	297
	Gerald R. Ford	Republican	39,147,613 (48.0%)	240

Year	**Candidates**	**Party**	**Popular Vote**	**Electoral Vote**
Year	**Candidates**	**Party**	**Popular Vote**	**Electoral Vote**
Year	**Candidates**	**Party**	**Popular Vote**	**Electoral Vote**

Appendix H

The Cabinet 1789-1980
and the Vice Presidents

SECRETARY OF STATE
(1789—   )

Thomas Jefferson	1789
Edmund Randolph	1794
Timothy Pickering	1795
John Marshall	1800
James Madison	1801
Robert Smith	1809
James Monroe	1811
John Q. Adams	1817
Henry Clay	1825
Martin Van Buren	1829
Edward Livingston	1831
Louis McLane	1833
John Forsyth	1834
Daniel Webster	1841
Hugh S. Legaré	1843
Abel P. Upshur	1843
John C. Calhoun	1844
James Buchanan	1845
John M. Clayton	1849
Daniel Webster	1850
Edward Everett	1852
William L. Marcy	1853
Lewis Cass	1857
Jeremiah S. Black	1860
William H. Seward	1861
E. B. Washburne	1869
Hamilton Fish	1869
William M. Evarts	1877
James G. Blaine	1881
F. T. Frelinghuysen	1881
Thomas F. Bayard	1885
James G. Blaine	1889
John W. Foster	1892
Walter Q. Gresham	1893
Richard Olney	1895
John Sherman	1897
William R. Day	1897
John Hay	1898
Elihu Root	1905
Robert Bacon	1909
Philander C. Knox	1909
William J. Bryan	1913
Robert Lansing	1915
Bainbridge Colby	1920
Charles E. Hughes	1921
Frank B. Kellogg	1925
Henry L. Stimson	1929

Cordell Hull	1933
E. R. Stettinius, Jr.	1944
James F. Byrnes	1945
George C. Marshall	1947
Dean Acheson	1949
John Foster Dulles	1953
Christian A. Herter	1959
Dean Rusk	1961
William P. Rogers	1969
Henry A. Kissinger	1973
Cyrus Vance	1977

SECRETARY OF THE
TREASURY (1789—   )

Alexander Hamilton	1789
Oliver Wolcott	1795
Samuel Dexter	1801
Albert Gallatin	1801
G. W. Campbell	1814
A. J. Dallas	1814
William H. Crawford	1816
Richard Rush	1825
Samuel D. Ingham	1829
Louis McLane	1831
William J. Duane	1833
Roger B. Taney	1833
Levi Woodbury	1834
Thomas Ewing	1841
Walter Forward	1841
John C. Spencer	1843
George M. Bibb	1844
Robert J. Walker	1845
William M. Meredith	1849
Thomas Corwin	1850
James Guthrie	1853
Howell Cobb	1857
Philip F. Thomas	1860
John A. Dix	1861
Salmon P. Chase	1861
Wm. P. Fessenden	1864
Hugh McCulloch	1865
George S. Boutwell	1869
William A. Richardson	1873
Benjamin H. Bristow	1874
Lot M. Morrill	1876
John Sherman	1877
William Windom	1881
Charles J. Folger	1881
Walter Q. Gresham	1884

Hugh McCulloch	1884
Daniel Manning	1885
Charles S. Fairchild	1887
William Windom	1889
Charles Foster	1891
John G. Carlisle	1893
Lyman J. Gage	1897
Leslie M. Shaw	1902
George B. Cortelyou	1907
Franklin MacVeagh	1909
William G. McAdoo	1913
Carter Glass	1919
David F. Houston	1919
Andrew W. Mellon	1921
Ogden L. Mills	1932
William H. Woodin	1933
Henry Morgenthau, Jr.	1934
Fred M. Vinson	1945
John W. Snyder	1946
George M. Humphrey	1953
Robert B. Anderson	1957
C. Douglas Dillon	1961
Henry H. Fowler	1965
David M. Kennedy	1969
John B. Connally	1970
George P. Shultz	1972
William E. Simon	1974
Michael W. Blumenthal	1977
G. William Miller	1979

SECRETARY OF WAR
(1789—1947)

Henry Knox	1789
Timothy Pickering	1795
James McHenry	1796
John Marshall	1800
Samuel Dexter	1800
Roger Griswold	1801
Henry Dearborn	1801
William Eustis	1809
John Armstrong	1813
James Monroe	1814
William H. Crawford	1815
Isaac Shelby	1817
George Graham	1817
John C. Calhoun	1817
James Barbour	1825
Peter B. Porter	1828
John H. Eaton	1829

Lewis Cass	1831	S. L. Southard	1823	Donald Rumsfield	1974
Benjamin F. Butler	1837	John Branch	1829	Harold Brown	1977
Joel R. Poinsett	1837	Levi Woodbury	1831		
John Bell	1841	Mahlon Dickerson	1834	**POSTMASTER GENERAL**	
John McLean	1841	James K. Paulding	1838	**(1789—1970)**	
John C. Spencer	1841	George E. Badger	1841	Samuel Osgood	1789
James M. Porter	1843	Abel P. Upshur	1841	Timothy Pickering	1791
William Wilkins	1844	David Henshaw	1843	Joseph Habersham	1795
William L. Marcy	1845	Thomas W. Gilmer	1844	Gideon Granger	1801
George W. Crawford	1849	John Y. Mason	1844	Return J. Meigs, Jr.	1814
Charles M. Conrad	1850	George Bancroft	1845	John McLean	1823
Jefferson Davis	1853	John Y. Mason	1846	William T. Barry	1829
John B. Floyd	1857	William B. Preston	1849	Amos Kendall	1835
Joseph Holt	1861	William A. Graham	1850	John M. Niles	1840
Simon Cameron	1861	John P. Kennedy	1852	Francis Granger	1841
Edwin M. Stanton	1862	James C. Dobbin	1853	Charles A. Wickliffe	1841
Ulysses S. Grant	1867	Isaac Toucey	1857	Cave Johnson	1845
Lorenzo Thomas	1868	Gideon Welles	1861	Jacob Collamer	1849
John M. Schofield	1868	Adolph E. Borie	1869	Nathan K. Hall	1850
John A. Rawlins	1869	George M. Robeson	1869	Samuel D. Hubbard	1852
William T. Sherman	1869	R. W. Thompson	1877	James Campbell	1853
William W. Belknap	1869	Nathan Goff, Jr.	1881	Aaron V. Brown	1857
Alphonso Taft	1876	William H. Hunt	1881	Joseph Holt	1859
James D. Cameron	1876	William E. Chandler	1881	Horatio King	1861
George W. McCrary	1877	William C. Whitney	1885	Montgomery Blair	1861
Alexander Ramsey	1879	Benjamin F. Tracy	1889	William Dennison	1864
Robert T. Lincoln	1881	Hilary A. Herbert	1893	Alexander W. Randall	1866
William C. Endicott	1865	John D. Long	1897	John A. J. Creswell	1869
Redfield Proctor	1889	William H. Moody	1902	James W. Marshall	1874
Stephen B. Elkins	1891	Paul Morton	1904	Marshall Jewell	1874
Daniel S. Lamont	1893	Charles J. Bonaparte	1905	James N. Tyner	1876
Russell A. Alger	1897	Victor H. Metcalf	1907	David M. Key	1877
Elihu Root	1899	T. H. Newberry	1908	Horace Maynard	1880
William H. Taft	1904	George von L. Meyer	1909	Thomas L. James	1881
Luke E. Wright	1908	Josephus Daniels	1913	Timothy O. Howe	1881
J. M. Dickinson	1909	Edwin Denby	1921	Walter Q. Gresham	1883
Henry L. Stimson	1911	Curtis D. Wilbur	1924	Frank Hatton	1884
L. M. Garrison	1913	Charles F. Adams	1929	William F. Vilas	1885
Newton D. Baker	1916	Claude A. Swanson	1933	Don M. Dickinson	1888
John W. Weeks	1921	Charles Edison	1940	John Wanamaker	1889
Dwight F. Davis	1925	Frank Knox	1940	Wilson S. Bissel	1893
James W. Good	1929	James V. Forrestal	1945	William L. Wilson	1895
Patrick J. Hurley	1929			James A. Gary	1897
George H. Dern	1933	**SECRETARY OF DEFENSE**		Charles E. Smith	1898
H. A. Woodring	1936	**(1947—)**		Henry C. Payne	1902
Henry L. Stimson	1940	James V. Forrestal	1947	Robert J. Wynne	1904
Robert P. Patterson	1945	Louis A. Johnson	1949	George B. Cortelyou	1905
Kenneth C. Royall	1947	George C. Marshall	1950	George von L. Meyer	1907
		Robert A. Lovett	1951	F. H. Hitchcock	1909
SECRETARY OF THE NAVY		Charles E. Wilson	1953	Albert S. Burleson	1913
(1798—1947)		Neil H. McElroy	1957	Will H. Hays	1921
Benjamin Stoddert	1798	Thomas S. Gates, Jr.	1959	Hubert Work	1922
Robert Smith	1801	Robert S. McNamara	1961	Harry S. New	1923
Paul Hamilton	1809	Clark M. Clifford	1968	Walter F. Brown	1929
William Jones	1813	Melvin R. Laird	1969	James A. Farley	1933
B. W. Crowninshield	1814	Elliot L. Richardson	1973	Frank C. Walker	1940
Smith Thompson	1818	James R. Schlesinger	1973	Robert E. Hannegan	1945

J. M. Donaldson	1947
A. E. Summerfield	1953
J. Edward Day	1961
John A. Gronouski	1963
Lawrence F. O'Brien	1965
W. Marvin Watson	1968
Winton M. Blount	1969

ATTORNEY GENERAL
(1789—)

Edmund Randolph	1789
William Bradford	1794
Charles Lee	1795
Theophilus Parsons	1801
Levi Lincoln	1801
Robert Smith	1805
John Breckinridge	1805
Caesar A. Rodney	1807
William Pinkney	1811
Richard Rush	1814
William Wirt	1817
John M. Berrien	1829
Roger B. Taney	1831
Benjamin F. Butler	1833
Felix Grundy	1838
Henry D. Gilpin	1840
John J. Crittenden	1841
Hugh S. Legare	1841
John Nelson	1843
John Y. Mason	1845
Nathan Clifford	1846
Isaac Toucey	1848
Reverdy Johnson	1849
John J. Crittenden	1850
Caleb Cushing	1853
Jeremiah S. Black	1857
Edwin M. Stanton	1860
Edward Bates	1861
Titian J. Coffey	1863
James Speed	1864
Henry Stanbery	1866
William M. Evarts	1868
Ebenezer R. Hoar	1869
Amos T. Ackerman	1870
George H. Williams	1871
Edward Pierrepont	1875
Alphonso Taft	1876
Charles Devens	1877
Wayne MacVeagh	1881
Benjamin H. Brewster	1881
A. H. Garland	1885
William H. H. Miller	1889
Richard Olney	1893
Judson Harmon	1895
Joseph McKenna	1897
John W. Griggs	1897
Philander C. Knox	1901

William H. Moody	1904
Charles J. Bonaparte	1907
G. W. Wickersham	1909
J. C. McReynolds	1913
Thomas W. Gregory	1914
A. Mitchell Palmer	1919
H. M. Daugherty	1921
Harlan F. Stone	1924
John G. Sargent	1925
William D. Mitchell	1929
H. S. Cummings	1933
Frank Murphy	1939
Robert H. Jackson	1940
Francis Biddle	1941
Tom C. Clark	1945
J. H. McGrath	1949
J. P. McGranery	1952
H. Brownell, Jr.	1953
William P. Rogers	1957
Robert F. Kennedy	1961
Nicholas Katzenbach	1964
Ramsey Clark	1967
John N. Mitchell	1969
Richard G. Kleindienst	1972
Elliot L. Richardson	1973
William Saxbe	1974
Edward H. Levi	1974
Griffin B. Bell	1977
Benjamin R. Civiletti	1979

SECRETARY OF THE
INTERIOR (1849—

Thomas Ewing	1849
T. M. T. McKennan	1850
Alexander H. H. Stuart	1850
Robert McClelland	1853
Jacob Thompson	1857
Caleb B. Smith	1861
John P. Usher	1863
James Harlan	1865
O. H. Browning	1866
Jacob D. Cox	1869
Columbus Delano	1870
Zachariah Chandler	1875
Carl Schurz	1877
Samuel J. Kirkwood	1881
Henry M. Teller	1881
L. Q. C. Lamar	1885
William F. Vilas	1888
John W. Noble	1889
Hoke Smith	1893
David R. Francis	1896
Cornelius N. Bliss	1897
E. A. Hitchcock	1899
James R. Garfield	1907
R. A. Ballinger	1909
Walter L. Fisher	1911

Franklin K. Lane	1913
John B. Payne	1920
Albert B. Fall	1921
Hubert Work	1923
Roy O. West	1928
Ray L. Wilbur	1929
Harold L. Ickes	1933
Julius A. Krug	1946
Oscar L. Chapman	1949
Douglas McKay	1953
Fred A. Seaton	1956
Steward L. Udall	1961
Walter J. Hickel	1969
Rogers C. B. Morton	1971
Thomas S. Kleppe	1975
Cecil D. Andrus	1977

SECRETARY OF
AGRICULTURE
(1889—)

Norman J. Colman	1889
Jeremiah M. Rusk	1889
J. Sterling Morton	1893
James Wilson	1897
David F. Houston	1913
Edward T. Meredith	1920
Henry C. Wallace	1921
Howard M. Gore	1924
William M. Jardine	1925
Arthur M. Hyde	1929
Henry A. Wallace	1933
Claude R. Wickard	1940
Clinton P. Anderson	1945
Charles F. Brannan	1948
Ezra Taft Benson	1953
Orville L. Freeman	1961
Clifford M. Hardin	1969
Earl L. Butz	1971
John A. Knebel	1976
Bob Bergland	1977

SECRETARY OF COMMERCE
AND LABOR (1903—1913)

George B. Cortelyou	1903
Victor H. Metcalf	1904
Oscar S. Straus	1906
Charles Nagel	1909

SECRETARY OF COMMERCE
(1913—)

William C. Redfield	1913
Joshua W. Alexander	1919
Herbert Hoover	1921
William F. Whiting	1928
Robert P. Lamont	1929
Roy D. Chapin	1932
Daniel C. Roper	1933

Harry L. Hopkins	1939
Jesse Jones	1940
Henry A. Wallace	1945
W. A. Harriman	1946
Charles Sawyer	1948
Sinclair Weeks	1953
Lewis L. Strauss	1958
F. H. Mueller	1959
Luther Hodges	1961
John T. Connor	1965
A. B. Trowbridge	1967
C. R. Smith	1968
Maurice H. Stans	1969
Peter G. Peterson	1972
Frederick B. Dent	1973
Elliot L. Richardson	1974
Juanita M. Kreps	1977
Philip M. Klutznick	1979

SECRETARY OF LABOR
(1913—   )

William B. Wilson	1913
James J. Davis	1921
William N. Doak	1930
Frances Perkins	1933
L. B. Schwellenbach	1945
Maurice J. Tobin	1948
Martin P. Durkin	1953
James P. Mitchell	1953
Arthur J. Goldberg	1961
W. Willard Wirtz	1962
George P. Shultz	1969
James D. Hodgson	1970
Peter J. Brennan	1973
W. J. Usery, Jr.	1974
Ray Marshall	1977

SECRETARY OF HEALTH, EDUCATION, AND WELFARE
(1953—   )

Oveta Culp Hobby	1953
Marion B. Folsom	1955
Arthur S. Flemming	1958
Abraham A. Ribicoff	1961
Anthony J. Celebrezze	1962
John W. Gardner	1965
Wilbur J. Cohen	1968
Robert H. Finch	1969
Elliot L. Richardson	1970
Caspar W. Weinberger	1973
David Matthews	1974
Joseph A. Califano, Jr.	1977
Patricia R. Harris	1979

SECRETARY OF HOUSING AND URBAN DEVELOPMENT
(1966—   )

Robert C. Weaver	1966
George W. Romney	1969
James T. Lynn	1973
Carla Anderson Hills	1974
Patricia Harris	1977
Moon Landrieu	1979

SECRETARY OF TRANSPORTATION
(1967—   )

Alan S. Boyd	1967
John A. Volpe	1969
Claude S. Brinegar	1973
William T. Coleman	1974
Brock Adams	1977
Neil E. Goldschmidt	1979

SECRETARY OF ENERGY
(1977—   )

James R. Schlesinger	1977
Charles W. Duncan, Jr.	1979

SECRETARY OF EDUCATION
(1979—   )

Shirley M. Hufstedter	1979

VICE PRESIDENT

John Adams	1789-97
Thomas Jefferson	1797-1801
Aaron Burr	1801-05
George Clinton	1805-13
Elbridge Gerry	1813-17
Daniel D. Tompkins	1817-25
John C. Calhoun	1825-33
Martin Van Buren	1833-37
Richard M. Johnson	1837-41
John Tyler	1841
George M. Dallas	1845-49
Millard Fillmore	1849-50
William R. King	1853-57
John C. Breckinridge	1857-61
Hannibal Hamlin	1861-65
Andrew Johnson	1865
Schuyler Colfax	1869-73
Henry Wilson	1873-77
William A. Wheeler	1877-81
Chester A. Arthur	1881
Thomas A. Hendricks	1885-89
Levi P. Morton	1889-93
Adlai E. Stevenson	1893-97

Garret A. Hobart	1897-1901
Theodore Roosevelt	1901
Charles W. Fairbanks	1905-09
James S. Sherman	1909-13
Thomas R. Marshall	1913-21
Calvin Coolidge	1921-23
Charles G. Dawes	1925-29
Charles Curtis	1929-33
John Nance Garner	1933-41
Henry A. Wallace	1941-45
Harry S. Truman	1945
Alben W. Barkley	1949-53
Richard M. Nixon	1953-61
Lyndon B. Johnson	1961-63
Hubert H. Humphrey	1965-69
Spiro T. Agnew	1969-73
Gerld R. Ford	1973-74
Nelson W. Rockefeller	1974-76
Walter F. Mondale	1977-81
George Bush	1981-

Appendix I

WRITING YOUR FAMILY HISTORY

Family history projects have become very popular recently. Part of the reason is the rebirth of ethnic and racial consciousness in the late 1960's and early 1970's. Alex Haley's *Roots* dramatically proved that one person's family history could increase the awareness and pride of an entire group. Another reason is that historians have begun to pay more attention to the day-to-day lives of ordinary Americans. No longer are we satisfied to write the history of the rich and powerful alone. We want to reconstruct how the vast majority, who were neither rich nor powerful, organized their lives. And family history is especially powerful as a research tool because the family was usually at the center of people's lives. Finally there is the not inconsequential consideration that family histories are interesting both to research and to read. Thus students and instructors can unite in looking forward to them.

If you decide to do a family history, you should get in touch with as many family members as you can as soon as you can. You should explain your project to them, and ask if they would be willing to cooperate with you on it. In making this request you should impress upon them the limits of the time you have to complete the project. You need to get across the message that you can not afford to wait too long for information. You need their help, and SOON.

Once you have enlisted your family's cooperation, you should draw up a preliminary inventory of source materials. Are there any scrapbooks, old diaries, photo albums, or family Bibles floating around somewhere? There may very well be, and you should make every effort to find them. In addition, it may turn out that some valuable documents—like your grandfather's naturalization papers, for example—have been locked away years ago and forgotten. So do not just ask if there are any old family papers lying around. Ask instead about specific kinds of records, such as deeds, diplomas, and marriage and birth certificates. The more specifically you ask the question the more likely you are to jog your relatives' memories.

You may discover that someone has had the family's genealogy traced; if so, a great deal of work has already been done for you. If not, then you will have to reconstruct the family tree yourself. In most cases this is easy enough for the first three or four generations. Family members usually keep this information in their memories. And, usually, you will not need to go back more than three or four generations to write your essay.

Reconstructing your family tree will serve to introduce you to your family's oral tradition. Virtually all families have such a tradition. Stories are passed from generation to generation (often assuming mythical dimensions in the process). You have likely heard many a tale about the "good old days." When you start on your family history project, you are going to have to master this tradition in a systematic and careful fashion. You will have to treat these stories and the memories they contain as you would any historical source. This means checking, wherever possible, what you are told against other sources. This is one reason why it is so important to locate family records. People, including you and your relatives, remember selectively, so the stories are usually true, but true after a fashion. Details may be exaggerated, or forgotten altogether.

Yet this oral tradition is immensely valuable. It preserves what most other historical records omit, the emotions of the past. From it you can learn what it felt like to live in another time. It is one thing to read in a textbook about the Great Depression; it is quite another to talk with someone who has lived through its terrors. This oral tradition preserves the living, breathing reality of the past, and so your relatives' memories are an invaluable historical resource.

Most of your relatives will probably be happy to help in whatever way they can, but some may hesitate about having non-family members (such as your instructor) find out everything about the family. You should make it clear that you will not use anything without permission; on the other hand, your own approach to them may encourage them to leave in your hands the matter of discretion.

You can decide for yourself how structured your interviews with your relatives ought to be. There is a kind of trade off involved. The less formal the interview, the more relaxed the participant, the more enjoyable the experience, and the more likely you are to get unguarded responses to your questions. On the other hand, the more likely the interview is to wander away from the questions you are really interested in. Probably you will not want to stick to a set order of questions, but you will want to have some sort of list of questions you can refer to. Your role is to move the conversation back to the main subjects without disrupting the natural flow of talk. It is a good trick. But you already know these people, and you probably know how to talk to them.

In the same way, you have to decide whether to use a tape recorder. The advantages are obvious. The disadvantages vary. Some people become very self-conscious when confronted with a machine: they hesitate, become embarrassed by slips of the tongue, and—in extreme cases—freeze altogether. Others quickly forget the machine is even there. Since you already know your subjects, you can probably guess how they will respond to the presence of a recorder.

Once you have your relatives talking, your job becomes finding the right questions to ask. The right questions are those which elicit information about the experiences of *your* family. And since families differ, it is not possible to prepare a single master list of questions which would fit them all. The following list, therefore, is intended only as a model. It is designed to elicit information about the experiences of European immigrants and their descendants, and the questions may or may not prove relevant to your project. But, even if there were no immigrants in your family, you still may find it useful to look them over. They may suggest better questions to you.

Family History Assignment

"Old World" Conditions: Place of origin (village/town, province, country); Occupation; Education; Religion. Other information which might be helpful would include memories of social, political, and economic conditions in the old country; motives for emigration; geographical mobility before emigration; occupational mobility before emigration; immigrant's rank order in family (father, oldest son, second daughter, etc.). Had other family members preceded immigrants to the U.S.? If so, had they settled in the same destination? Had others from the same village or town settled in this destination earlier? Did the immigrant subsequently send for other members of the family?

The Journey: Trace as exactly as possible the immigrant's route. Had he or she previously moved about in the old world (For example from a village to a city, or from one country to another?) How long did the journey take? What were the travelling accommodations like?

Arrival: What was the port of arrival? What was the ultimate destination? If the two were different, how did the immigrant get to final destination? What were his or her initial experiences in America? Include here whatever information you could find about contacts with American immigration officials.

The First Generation: List the immigrant's first occupation and places of residence. When did he or she marry? How many children were there? Did the immigrant become a citizen? If so, how long did it take after arrival? Did he or she learn English? Attend school here? Join any ethnic associations? Read the foreign language press? Join a union? Become active in politics? Become active in a church or synagogue?

The Second Generation: How much education did these children receive? Did they attend public or parochial schools? What was the first and last job of each? Did they move from place to place in this country? How many married within the ethnic group? How many married within the religious group? Were any bilingual? Did any join ethnic associations? Read the ethnic press? Become active in politics? Become active in any church? And if they did, was it an ethnic church?

The Third Generation: Same questions as above.

Few students would be so lucky as to find out all the information itemized here. As a general rule, however, most should be able to get reasonably full information for at least three generations. Getting the information is just a first step. The real task is to use it to illuminate the immigrant's experience. Thus one can use the information to see how long it took the family to establish itself economically. Who had the first white-collar or skilled blue-collar job? Who in the family was the first to own a house or a business? Who was the first to attend college or business or professional school?

Similarly, one can use the information to see how long the family retains its ethnic identity. Who is the first family member to marry outside of the group? Who is the first to marry outside of the religion? How long did the family preserve the old country language? How long did it observe national holidays? Or participate in ethnic associations? One can also observe the process of assimilation. Does intermarriage seem to correlate with economic conditions? Or education? Or attendance at public or parochial schools? Does it involve a generational battle?

Beyond all of this tracing of patterns is the human dimensions. What did it feel like to leave your home, arrive at Ellis Island, and make a life for yourself in a new country?

An excellent guide is David B. Kyvig and Myron A. Marty, *Your Family History: A Handbook For Research and Writing* (KHM Publishing Corp., 1978).

INDEX

Sheffield, Lord: 88
Shepherd, William Gunn: 431
Sherman, Roger: 72
Sherman, William T.: 298, 300
Sherman Antitrust Act (1890): 338, 462, 471; under President Taft, 477
Sherman Silver Purchase Act (1890): 332, 376, 382
Shirley, Governor William: 48
Shunpikes: 208
Sibley, Henry: 397
Siegfried Line: 598
Sierra Nevada: 390-91
Simkhovich, Mary: 450
Simon, Sir John: 531
Sinatra, Frank: 594
Sinclair, Upton: 462-64, 475, 563
Sinners in the Hands of an Angry God: 35
Sioux Indians: 397-400
Sirhan Bishara Sirhan: 673
Sirica, John: 702
Sitting Bull: 398-99
Sitzkrieg: 585
Slaughterhouse Cases: 337
Slave codes: 242
Slave life: 218-21
Slave revolts: 43, 167, 220, 239, 241
Slavery: 103, 203; and Civil War and Reconstruction, 296-315 (see antislavery); in colonial times, 40-41; outlawed in Old Northwest, 82; 288 (see John Brown); revival of, 163ff.; and cotton crop, 218-21; in the territories, 244-45; and *Uncle Tom's Cabin*, 258-49; in Kansas and Nebraska, 260-65; Lincoln's views, 268-70; interpretations, 279-86; in new guise, 314
Slavery as It Is (1839): 241
Slaves: in 1800, 139
Slidell, John: 247
Smith, Adam: 190, 20, 335
Smith, Alfred E.: 431, 500-01, 503, 563, 647
Smith, Erminnie: 360
Smith, Gerald L. K.: 563, 566, 586
Smith, Hoke: 468
Smith, John: 14-15
Smith, Joseph: 223
Smith-Lever Act (1914): 490
Smith, Margaret: 176ff.
Smith, Seba: 233
Smith, William: 57
Snyder, Gary: 687
Social Darwinism: 335, 407
Social Democratic Party: 367
Social Feminism: 448-50
Social Security Act (1935): 566
Socialism (see Eugene V. Debs; Daniel DeLeon; Victor Berger; Morris Hillquit; Socialist Party): 368-69, 439-41
Socialist Labor Party: 368
Socialist Party: 562; after World War I, 494
Soil exhaustion: and tobacco, 163
Song My: 672
Sons of Liberty: 57-58, 62
Sorensen, Ted: 647
Soulé, Pierre: 250
The Souls of Black Folk (1903): 484
Sousa, John Philip: 432
South, The (see Civil War; Slavery): antislavery, 239-41, 242-43; proslavery movement, 241-42; see individual states
South Carolina: 41, 43; and Nullification Crisis, 184-85; and secession, 291-96; and Fort Sumter, 294-96
South Carolina Declaration: 291
Southeast Asia Treaty Organization (SEATO): 666
Southern economy: antebellum, 218-21
Southworth, Mrs.: 231
Soviet Union: and Japan, 527; recognition of, 579; and Hitler, 583; and Sputnik, 641-3; and Kennedy, 649-51; and Nixon (detente), 695-97
Spain: exploration in America, 7, 9; relations within 1780's, 87-88
Spanish-American War: 412-18, 425
Spanish Armada: 12
Specie Circular 1836: 189, 193
Specie payments: 186ff.
Spencer, Herbert: 335
The Spirit of St. Louis: 509
Spirituals: 221

Spooner, John C.: 470
Sports: early development of, 348-49
Sputnik: 641-43, 685
Stalin, Josef: 595-96; non-aggression pact with Hitler, 585; at Yalta, 598-600; in Cold War, 608-9
Stalingrad: 598
Stamp Act: 55-57, 63
Stanford, Leland: 391
Stanton, Edwin: 312
Staple Act (1663): 19
The Star Spangled Banner: 152
Starr, Ellen Gates: 448
States (see ratification of Constitution; Confederation): in progressive era, 462-68
Statue of Liberty: 317-20
Statute for Religious Liberty in Virginia: 83
Steel making: 327-28
Steffens, Lincoln: 342, 446-47, 466
Steinem, Gloria: 695
Stephens, Alexander H.: 291, 297
Stevens, John L.: 411
Stevens, Thaddeus: 313-15, 428
Stevenson, Adlai: 655; election of 1952, 621-23, on civil rights, 643; election of 1956, 643; election of 1960, 647
Stewart, A.T.: 331
Stiles, Ezra: 35
Stimson, Henry L.: 528, 583
Stock Market Crash (1929): 502-05
Stone, Lucy: 229
Story, William: 57
Stowe, Calvin: 258
Stowe, Harriet Beecher: 258-59
Strasser, Adolph: 367
Strauss, Lewis: 655
"Stream of consciousness": 445
Streetcars: 341
Strikes (see also Labor; Labor Unions): Homestead, 334, 354-56; Pullman, 366; Coal (of 1902); of 1919, 493-94; of 1930's; 499
Strong, Josiah: 409
Student movement: 689-92
Student riots: at Kent State, 662-64; at Columbia University, 662, 691; at Harvard University, 662, 691
Students for a Democratic Society (SDS): 662-64, 690-91
Submarine: warfare in World War I, 516-17; warfare in World War II, 585ff.
Submerged Lands Act: 642
Suburbs: after World War II, 613-14; in 1950's, 640-45; flight from cities, 670
Subways: 341
Sudetenland: 584
Suffolk Resolves: 64
Sugar: 43
Sugar Act of 1733: 32
"Summit" meetings: 637,
Sumner, Charles: 265-66, 406; and Reconstruction, 313-15
Sumter, Fort: 294-96
Sunday, Billy: 501, 516
Superman: 593
Supreme Court (see individual cases): 446; creation of, 113; see Marshall, John; Taney, Roger; Holmer, Oliver Wendell; Warren, Earl; Burger, Warren 611-12; Roosevelt's plan to expand membership, 568-69ff.
Sussex: 516

Taft, Robert A.: 577, 606, 641, 675; Senate Republican leader, 609-12; on Marshall Plan, 608; candidate for President, 610-11, 620-21
Taft, William Howard: 535; and Philippines, 418; in Philippines, 476-77; in election of 1912, 479-81; and "dollar diplomacy," 513-15
Taft-Hartley Act: 610; attempts to repeal, 655
Taft-Katsure Agreement (1905): 510
Talleyrand: 128, 168
Tallmadge, James: 164-65
Tallmadge Amendment: 164-65
Tammany Hall: 452
Tampico Incident: 515
Taney, Roger B.: 189, 190, 267
Tappan, Arthur: 241, 242
Tappan, C.: 242
Tappan, Lewis: 241

Tariff: 159
Tariff of 1816: 162
Tariff of Abominations (1828): 162, 184
Tariff of 1833: 186
Taylor, Frederick: 437
Taylor, John: death of, 255
Taylor, John W.: 165
Taylor, Maxwell: 648; and Vietnam, 677-73
Taylor, Zachary: 247-49, 252
Tea Act of 1773: 63, 66
Teapot Dome Scandal: 496-97
Tecumseh: 146, 150, 194
Telephone (see Alexander Graham Bell): 434
Teller Amendment: 415
Teller, Henry: 384
Temperance: 227
Tenant farmers: 314
Tenements: 442-44
Tennessee Coal and Iron Co.: 476. 479
Tennessee Valley Authority: 556, 642, 656
Terry and the Pirates: 593-94
Tertium Quids: 145
Test Ban Treaty (1963): 654
Tet offensive: 672
Texas (see Battle of the Alamo; Mexican War): 236-38; and Mexican War, 245-51
Theatre: 349-50
Thieu (see Nguyen Van Thieu)
Third Internationale: 494
Thomas, Jesse B.: 165
Thomas, Norman: 562, 566, 586
Thompson, David: 135
Thompson, Jacob: 293
Thomson, Charles: 64
Thoreau, Henry David: 249-50
Three-Fifths Compromise: 113
Three-Mile Island: 682-84
Thurmond, J. Strom: 611, 698
Tilden, Samuel J.: 315
Tillman, Benjamin: 384, 477
Timberlake, John: 181
Time Inc. v. Hill (1966): 675
Tippecanoe and Tyler, Too: 194-96
Tippecanoe, Battle of: 191
Tobacco: 25, 41-44
Tocqueville, Alexis de: 179, 228, 239
Tojo, Hideki: 588
Tonnage Act: 117
Tories: end of Revolution, 55
Toussaint l'Overture: 142
Townsend, Francis: 563-64
Townshend, Charles: 57ff., 59
Townshend Duties: 59-60, 63
Trade Expansion Act (1962):
Trail of Death (Trail of Tears): 184
Transportation (see Esch-Cummins Act): in 1800, 139ff.; problems, 159; twentieth century, 434-37
Transportation Revolution: 208-11
Travis, William Barret: 237
Treaty of Greenville: 124
Treaty of 1778: 129
Treaty of Ghent (1814): 152
Treaty of 1818 (Canadian boundary): 169
Treaty of Guadalupe-Hidalgo: 249, 261, 487
Treaty of Fort Laramie: 397
Treaty of Paris (1763): 54
Treaty of Paris (1783): 81, 86, 93-94
Treaty of Portsmouth (1905): 510
Treaty of Versailles: 524-27
Trenton, Battle of: 78
Triangle Shirtwaist Factory Fire: 430-31
Trist, Nicholas P.: 249
Trolleys: 341
Trollope, Mrs.: 207
Trotter, William Monroe: 483
Troup, Governor George: 173
Truman Doctrine: 607
Truman, Harry S: becomes president, 603; and Cold War, 606-9; and domestic affairs, 604-6; and Congress, 609-13 ; and labor, 605-6; and Germany, 608-9; reelection as president, 611-12; second term as president, 612-13; and Vietnam, 665-66
Trumbull, Jonathan (Governor): 61, 70
Trustbusting: 534
Trusts (see Theodore Roosevelt's presidency; Franklin Roosevelt's presidency; William McKinley's presidency)
Truth, Sojourner: 251

Tubman, Harriet: 251
Tugwell, Rexford: 556
Turner, Frederick Jackson: 405, 407
Turner, Nat: 185, 220, 241
Turner, Joy, C.: 669
Turnpikes: 208
Tuskegee Institute: 481
Twain, Mark: 263-64
Tweed, William Marcy: 342, 344
Tydings, Millard: 620
Tydings-McDuffie Act: 418
Tyler, John: 245-46, 294
Types of Mankind (1854): 242

U-2, Flight: 647
Udall, Stewart L.:
Uncle Tom's Cabin (1852): 258-59
Underground Railroad: 243
Underwood Tariff (1913): 490
Unemployment: see Depressions; in 1950's, 641
Union: life in the, 302
Union Pacific Railroad: 324, 390
Union Party: 564
Unions: in New Deal, 557-58, 564-65, 569
United Automobile Workers: 605
United Fruit Company: 513
United Mine Workers: 605, 610
United Nations: founding of, 599-600; during
    Truman administration, 606-9
United States Employment Office: 492
United States Steel: 334, 476, 479; and John
    Kennedy, 653-54
United States v. Butler (1936): 568
United States v. E.C. Knight (1895): 338, 471
U.S.S. Constitution: 149
Universal Negro Improvement Association:
    486-87
Universities: 346-47
Up From Slavery (1901): 481
Upshur, Abel P.: 246
Urban renewal: 651
Urbanization: before Civil War, 215-16; late
    nineteenth century, 339-44; Progressive Era,
    465-67

Valentino, Rudolph: 458
Vallandigham, Clement: 305
Valley Forge: 78
Van Buren, Martin: 178, 246-47, 252; vs. John
    C. Calhoun, 181-82; defeat of, 196
Vandenberg, Arthur: 609
Van Devanter, Willis: 569
Vanzetti, Bartolomeo: 495
Vaudreil, Marquis de: 52-53
Venezuela: boundary and debt disputes, 411-12
Venezuela Affair (1902-03): 511
Veracruz: marines occupy, 514-15
Vergennes, Comte de: 71, 81
Versailles: 79
Versailles Treaty: 524-28
Vesey Conspiracy: 167
Vesey, Denmark: 167
Vespucci, Amerigo: 7
Veterans: 494, 604-5
Veterans' Bureau: 497
Veterans of Future Wars: 581
Veto, presidential: origins of, 115
Vicksburg, Battle of: 298
Vienna Summit: 649-50
Vietcong: 665-79 *passim*
Vietminh: 665ff.
Vietnam: 665-79; French involvement, 665-6;
    Truman's policies, 665-67; Eisenhower's
    policies, 666-67; Kennedy's policies, 667-79;
    Johnson's policies, 679-73; Nixon's policies,
    676-78; map, 668; Ford's policies, 704
Vietnamization: 672
Villa, Pancho: 514-15
Villard, Oswald Garrison: 484
Virginia: 22, 41-44; settlement of, 13-15; vs.
    New England, 18-19
Virginia Plan: 113
Virginia Resolution: 129
Vom Rath, Ernst: 576
von Rundstedt, Gerd: 598
Voting Rights Act: 658

Wabash v. Illinois: 338
Wade-Davis Bill (1864): 310

Wages (see Labor): 423
Wagner Act: 564-65, 569
Wagner, Richard: 318
Wagner, Robert F., Sr.: 431, 557, 577
Wagner-Rogers Bill: 577
Wagner-Steagall National Housing Act: 570
Waite, Morrison: 337
Wald, Lillian: 484
Walker, David: 243
Walker, Patrick: 61
Wallace, George: presidential candidacy,
    675-76, 695, 701
Wallace, Henry A.: 556, 603, 606; runs for
    President in 1948, 611-12
Wallace, Henry C.: 495
Walsh, Thomas J.: 497
Wanamaker, John: 329
War Debts: after era of World War I, 529-31
War Finance Corporation: 503
War Hawks: 146
War of 1812: preliminaries, 144-47, 147-54
War Production Board: 536, 591
War Revenue Acts (World War I): 517
Ward, Aaron Montgomery: 331
Ward, Artemas: 68
Warhouse Act: 492
Warren Court (see *Gideon v. Wainwright;
    Miranda v. Arizona; Brown v. Board of
    Education; Baker v. Carr):* and civil rights,
    644-46; and rights of accused, 659
Warren, Earl: 644, 675; as Chief Justice,
    644-46, 659; report on Kennedy assassina-
    tion, 654
Warren, Robert Penn: 288
Warsaw Pact: 637, 638
Washington, Booker T.: 471, 481-82
Washington, George: in French and Indian
    War, 46, 48, 55; in Revolutionary War,
    66-84 *passim*; at Constitutional Convention,
    110-16; as President, 117-22, 127; and
    whiskey rebellion, 107-09; supports
    Hamilton, 122
Washington, burning of (1814): 151
Washington, Martha: 125
Washington Naval Conference: 527-28
Water power (see Muscle Shoals; Tennessee
    Valley Authority; Water Power Act): 557
Water Power Act (1920): 492
Water Quality Act (1965): 657
Watergate: 701-4
Watson, Thomas: 385
Wayne, General "Mad" Anthony: 124
Wealth of Nation (1776): 190
Wealth Tax Act: 566
Weaver, James B.: 381, 387
Weaver, Robert C.: 652
Webb, James Watson: 191
Webster-Ashburton Treaty: 245
Webster, Daniel: 182, 187, 255, 390; and Dart-
    mouth College Case, 161; as secretary of
    state, 245; Seventh of March Speech, 255
Webster, Noah: 228
Wedemeyer, Albert C.: 616
Weems, Mason: 233
Weld, Theodore Dwight: 227, 241-42, 258
Welk, Lawrence: 688
Welles, Sumner: 580
Wesley, John: 34, 225
West Indies: 19, 32, 43, 55, 88, 90, 123, 149
West, Mae: 459
Western settlement: 55, 95-96, 103
Westward expansion: 155-57, 216-18; (see
    Louisiana Purchase); Lewis and Clark Ex-
    pedition, 132-35
Westmoreland, William: 672
Weyler, General Valeriano: 413
Whig Party: 189-92
Whigs: 245, 266; nominate Harrison, 194-96;
    "conscience," 266
Whiskey Rebellion (see also Whiskey Tax):
    107-09, 121
Whiskey Tax: 121
White Collar: 685
White, Hugh Lawson: 191
White, William A.: 586
Whitefield, George: 34
Whitlock, Brand: 525
Whitney, Eli: 138, 164, 213-14
Whitman, Walt: 231-33
Whittier, John Greenleaf: 318

Why Europe Leaves Home: 452-54
Wickersham, George W.: 477
Wilderness, Battle of: 300
Wiley, Harrey W.: 475
Wilkinson, James: 143, 150
Willard, Frances: 347
William and Mary: 24, 36
Williams, Roger: 17
Willkie, Wendell L.: 586
Wilmot, David: 262
Wilmot Proviso: 251-52
Wilson, Charles: 637
Wilson, William B.: 493
Wilson, Woodrow (Thomas Woodrow Wilson):
    446, 468, 535 (see also Federal Reserve Act);
    and high cost of living, 441; as governor of
    New Jersey, 478, 480; in election of 1912,
    479-81; and "New Freedom," 480; first
    term, 490-92; second term, 492; Latin
    American policies, 513-15; the Fourteen
    Points, 524; and League of Nations, 524-27
Winthrop, John: 15
Winthrop, John, IV: 35
Wirt, William: 183-84, 191
Witchcraft, in Salem: 27-30
Wolfe, General James: 48-49, 52-54
Woolworth, F.W.: 432
Women: in the West, 156-57; in Confederacy,
    301-02; at Centennial Exhibition, 320; and
    sports in late nineteenth century, 349;
    workers in late nineteenth century, 358-61;
    in progressive era, 448-50; in films, 459; in
    1950's, 685, 693; in 1960's, 685, 693-95; in
    1970's, 693-95
Women's Movement: 229, in progressive era,
    537
Women's Trade Union League: 431, 450
Woodford, Stewart: 414
Wool, John: 151
Woolworth's: 331
Worcester v. Georgia (1832): 184
Workers (see Labor)
Works Progress Administration: 564, 572
World Antislavery Convention (1840): 242-43
World Court: 528
World Economic Conference: 578
World War I: U.S. neutrality, 515-17; at home,
    517-18; U.S. entry, 518-24
World War II: in Europe before 1941, 584-85;
    home front, 593-94; battles of, 594-98
World's Fair (1939): 573
Wright Brothers: 434
Wright, Chauncey: 445
Wright, Frances: 221

Xuan Thuy: 672
"X, Y, and Z" Affair: 228

Yale College: 36
Yalta: 598-600
Yancey, William: 271
Yates, Robert: 111
Yellow journalism: 413ff.
York: 134
Yorktown, Virginia: 81
Young, Brigham: 223-24
Young, John: 699
Young, Owen D.: 529
Young Plan: 529

Zenger, John Peter: 36
Zenith: 457
Ziegfeld, Florence: 350
Zimmerman note: 580
Zinn, Howard: 601-02